Twentieth-Century Literary Criticism

Guide to Gale Literary Criticism Series

When you need to review criticism of literary works, these are the Gale series to use:

If the author's death date is:	You should turn to:

After Dec. 31, 1959
(or author is still living)

CONTEMPORARY LITERARY CRITICISM

for example: Jorge Luis Borges, Anthony Burgess,
William Faulkner, Mary Gordon,
Ernest Hemingway, Iris Murdoch

1900 through 1959

TWENTIETH-CENTURY LITERARY CRITICISM

for example: Willa Cather, F. Scott Fitzgerald,
Henry James, Mark Twain, Virginia Woolf

1800 through 1899

NINETEENTH-CENTURY LITERATURE CRITICISM

for example: Fedor Dostoevski, Nathaniel Hawthorne,
George Sand, William Wordsworth

1400 through 1799

LITERATURE CRITICISM FROM 1400 TO 1800
(excluding Shakespeare)

for example: Anne Bradstreet, Daniel Defoe,
Alexander Pope, François Rabelais,
Jonathan Swift, Phillis Wheatley

SHAKESPEAREAN CRITICISM

Shakespeare's plays and poetry

Antiquity through 1399

CLASSICAL AND MEDIEVAL LITERATURE CRITICISM

for example: Dante, Homer, Plato, Sophocles, Vergil,
the Beowulf Poet

Gale also publishes related criticism series:

CHILDREN'S LITERATURE REVIEW

This series covers authors of all eras who have written for the preschool through high school audience.

SHORT STORY CRITICISM

This series covers the major short fiction writers of all nationalities and periods of literary history.

ISSN 0276-8178

Volume 33

Twentieth-Century Literary Criticism

**Excerpts from Criticism of the
Works of Novelists, Poets, Playwrights,
Short Story Writers, and Other Creative Writers
Who Died between 1900 and 1960,
from the First Published Critical Appraisals
to Current Evaluations**

Paula Kepos
Editor

Marie Lazzari
Thomas Ligotti
Joann Prosyniuk
Laurie Sherman
Associate Editors

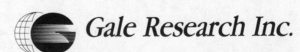 *Gale Research Inc.*

Detroit, New York, Fort Lauderdale, London
Toll-free Telephone Number: 1-800-347-GALE

STAFF

Paula Kepos, *Editor*

Marie Lazzari, Thomas Ligotti, Joann Prosyniuk, Laurie Sherman, *Associate Editors*

Susan Windisch Brown, Susan Miller Harig, Sandra Liddell, Michelle L. McClellan,
Assistant Editors

Jeanne A. Gough, *Permissions & Production Manager*
Linda M. Pugliese, *Production Supervisor*
Jennifer E. Gale, Suzanne Powers, Maureen A. Puhl, Lee Ann Welsh, *Editorial Associates*
Donna Craft, Christine A. Galbraith, David G. Oblender, Linda M. Ross, *Editorial Assistants*

Victoria B. Cariappa, *Research Supervisor*
Karen D. Kaus, Eric Priehs, Maureen R. Richards, Mary D. Wise, *Editorial Associates*
Rogene M. Fisher, Kevin B. Hillstrom, Filomena Sgambati, *Editorial Assistants*

Sandra C. Davis, *Permissions Supervisor (Text)*
H. Diane Cooper, Kathy Grell, Josephine M. Keene, Kimberly F. Smilay, *Permissions Associates*
Maria L. Franklin, Lisa M. Lantz, Camille P. Robinson, Shalice Shah, Denise M. Singleton,
Permissions Assistants

Patricia A. Seefelt, *Permissions Supervisor (Pictures)*
Margaret A. Chamberlain, *Permissions Associate*
Pamela A. Hayes, Lillian Quickley, *Permissions Assistants*

Mary Beth Trimper, *Production Manager*
Marilyn Jackman, *External Production Assistant*

Arthur Chartow, *Art Director*
C. J. Jonik, *External Production Assistant*

Laura Bryant, *Production Supervisor*
Louise Gagné, *Internal Production Associate*
Shelly Andrews, Sharana Wier, *Internal Production Assistants*

Copyright © 1989
Gale Research Inc.
835 Penobscot Building
Detroit, MI 48226-4094

Library of Congress Catalog Card Number 76-46132
ISBN 0-8103-2415-6
ISSN 0276-8178

Printed in the United States of America

Contents

Preface

Since its inception more than ten years ago, *Twentieth-Century Literary Criticism* has been purchased and used by nearly 10,000 school, public, and college or university libraries. With this edition—volume 33 in the series—*TCLC* has covered over 500 authors, representing 56 nationalities, and more than 25,000 titles. No other reference source has surveyed the critical response to twentieth-century authors and literature as thoroughly as *TCLC*. In the words of one reviewer, "there is nothing comparable available." *TCLC* "is a goldmine of information—dates, pseudonyms, biographical information, and criticism from books and periodicals—which many libraries would have difficulty assembling on their own."

Scope of the Series

TCLC is designed to serve as an introduction for students and advanced readers to authors who died between 1900 and 1960, and to the most significant interpretations of these authors' works. The great poets, novelists, short story writers, playwrights, and philosophers of this period are frequently studied in high school and college literature courses. In organizing and excerpting the vast amount of critical material written on these authors, *TCLC* helps students develop valuable insight into literary history, promotes a better understanding of the texts, and sparks ideas for papers and assignments. Each entry in *TCLC* presents a comprehensive survey of an author's career or an individual work of literature and provides the user a multiplicity of interpretations and assessments. Such variety allows students to pursue their own interests; furthermore, it fosters an awareness that literature is dynamic and responsive to many different opinions.

TCLC is designed as a companion series to Gale's *Contemporary Literary Criticism,* which reprints commentary on current writing. Because of the different periods under consideration (*CLC* considers authors who were still living after 1959), there is no duplication of material between *CLC* and *TCLC*. For additional information about *CLC* and Gale's other criticism titles, users should consult the Guide to Gale Literary Criticism Series preceding the title page in this volume.

Coverage

Each volume of *TCLC* is carefully compiled to present:

- criticism of authors who represent a variety of genres and nationalities
- both major and lesser-known writers of the period (such as non-Western authors increasingly read by today's students)
- 14-16 authors per volume
- individual entries that survey the critical response to each author's works, including early criticism to reflect initial reactions; later criticism to represent any rise or decline in the author's reputation; and current retrospective analyses. The entries also indicate an author's importance to the period (for example, the length of each author entry reflects the amount of critical attention he or she has received from critics writing in English, and from foreign criticism in translation)

An author may appear more than once in the series because of continuing critical and academic interest, or because of a resurgence of criticism generated by such events as a centennial or anniversary, the republication or posthumous publication of a work, or the publication of a new translation. Several entries in each volume of *TCLC* are devoted to criticism of individual works that are considered among the most important in twentieth-century literature and are thus frequently read and studied in high school and college English classes. For example, this volume includes entries devoted to D. H. Lawrence's *Women in Love* and Marcel Proust's *A la recherche du temps perdu (Remembrance of Things Past)*.

Organization of the Book

An author entry consists of the following elements: author heading, biographical and critical introduction, list of principal works, excerpts of criticism (each preceded by explanatory notes and followed by a bibliographic citation), and a bibliography of additional reading.

- The *author heading* consists of the author's full name, followed by birth and death dates. The unbracketed portion of the name denotes the form under which the author most commonly wrote. If an author wrote consistently under a pseudonym, the pseudonym will be listed in the author heading and the real name given in parentheses on the first line of the biographical and critical introduction. Also located at the beginning of the introduction to the author entry are any name variations under which an author wrote, including transliterated forms for authors whose languages use nonroman alphabets.

- The *biographical and critical introduction* outlines the author's life and career, as well as the critical debate surrounding his or her work. References are provided to past volumes of *TCLC* and to other biographical and critical reference series published by Gale, including *Short Story Criticism, Children's Literature Review, Contemporary Authors, Dictionary of Literary Biography,* and *Something about the Author.*

- Most *TCLC* entries include *portraits* of the author. Many entries also contain reproductions of materials pertinent to an author's career, including manuscript pages, title pages, dust jackets, letters, and drawings, as well as photographs of important people, places, and events in an author's life.

- The *list of principal works* is chronological by date of first book publication and identifies the genre of each work. In the case of foreign authors with both foreign-language publications and English translations, the title and date of the first English-language edition are given in brackets. Unless otherwise indicated, dramas are dated by first performance, not first publication.

- *Criticism* is arranged chronologically in each author entry to provide a perspective on changes in critical evaluation over the years. All titles of works by the author featured in the entry are printed in boldface type to enable the user to easily locate discussion of particular works. Also for purposes of easier identification, the critic's name and the publication date of the essay are given at the beginning of each piece of criticism. Unsigned criticism is preceded by the title of the journal in which it appeared. Many of the excerpts in *TCLC* also contain translated material. Unless otherwise noted, translations in brackets are by the editors; translations in parentheses or continuous with the text are by the critic. Publication information (such as publisher names and book prices) and parenthetical numerical references (such as footnotes or page and line references to specific editions of works) have been deleted at the editors' discretion to provide smoother reading of the text.

- Critical excerpts are prefaced by *explanatory notes* providing the reader with information about both the critic and the criticism that follows. Included are the critic's reputation, individual approach to literary criticism, and particular expertise in an author's works. Also noted are the relative importance of a work of criticism, the scope of the excerpt, and the growth of critical controversy or changes in critical trends regarding an author. In some cases, these notes cross-reference excerpts by critics who discuss each other's commentary.

- A complete *bibliographic citation* designed to facilitate location of the original essay or book follows each piece of criticism.

- The *additional bibliography* appearing at the end of each author entry suggests further reading on the author. In some cases it includes essays for which the editors could not obtain reprint rights.

Cumulative Indexes

Each volume of *TCLC* includes a cumulative index listing all the authors who have appeared in *Contemporary Literary Criticism, Twentieth-Century Literary Criticism, Nineteenth-Century Literature Criticism, Literature Criticism from 1400 to 1800, Classical and Medieval Literature Criticism,* and *Short Story Criticism,* along with cross-references to the Gale series *Children's Literature Review, Authors in the News, Contemporary Authors, Contemporary Authors Autobiography Series, Dictionary of Literary Biography, Concise Dictionary of American Literary Biography, Something about the Author, Something about the Author Autobiography Series,* and *Yesterday's Authors of Books for Children.* Useful for locating an author within the various series, this index is particularly valuable for those authors who are identified with a certain period but who, because of their death dates, are placed in another, or for those authors whose careers span two periods. For example, F. Scott Fitzgerald is found in *TCLC,* yet a writer often associated with him, Ernest Hemingway, is found in *CLC.*

Each volume of *TCLC* also includes a cumulative nationality index, in which authors' names are arranged alphabetically under their respective nationalities.

Title Index

TCLC also includes an index listing the titles of all literary works discussed in the series since its inception. Foreign language titles that have been translated are followed by the titles of the translations—for example, *Voina i mir (War and*

Peace). Page numbers following these translated titles refer to all pages on which any form of the titles, either foreign language or translated, appears. Titles of novels, dramas, nonfiction books, and poetry, short story, or essay collections are printed in italics, while all individual poems, short stories, and essays are printed in roman type within quotation marks. In cases where the same title is used by different authors, the author's surname is given in parentheses after the title, for example, *Collected Poems* (Housman) and *Collected Poems* (Yeats).

Suggestions Are Welcome

In response to suggestions, several features have been added to *TCLC* since the series began, including explanatory notes to excerpted criticism, a cumulative index to authors in all Gale literary criticism series, entries devoted to a single work by a major author, more extensive illustrations, and a title index listing all literary works discussed in the series since its inception.

Readers who wish to suggest authors to appear in future volumes, or who have other suggestions, are cordially invited to write the editors or call our toll-free number: 1-800-347-GALE.

Acknowledgments

The editors wish to thank the copyright holders of the excerpted criticism included in this volume, the permissions managers of many book and magazine publishing companies for assisting us in securing reprint rights, and Anthony Bogucki for assistance with copyright research. We are also grateful to the staffs of the Detroit Public Library, the Library of Congress, the University of Detroit Library, the University of Michigan Library, and the Wayne State University Library for making their resources available to us. Following is a list of the copyright holders who have granted us permission to reprint material in this volume of *TCLC*. Every effort has been made to trace copyright, but if omissions have been made, please let us know.

COPYRIGHTED EXCERPTS IN *TCLC,* VOLUME 33, WERE REPRINTED FROM THE FOLLOWING PERIODICALS:

ADAM International Review, n. 319-21, 1967. © *ADAM International Review* 1967. Reprinted by permission of the publisher.—*The American Slavic and East European Review,* v. IV, August, 1945. Copyright 1945, renewed 1973 by American Association for the Advancement of Slavic Studies Inc. Reprinted by permission of the publisher.—*Australian Journal of French Studies,* v. II, January-April, 1965 for "C. F. Ramuz and the Alps" by R. T. Sussex. Copyright © 1965 by Australian Journal of French Studies. Reprinted by permission of the publisher and the author.—*Books Abroad,* v. 42, Autumn, 1968. Copyright 1968 by the University of Oklahoma Press. Reprinted by permission of the publisher.—*Carnegie Series in English,* A Modern Miscellany, v. XI, 1970. Copyright © 1970 by the Department of English. Reprinted by permission of Carnegie-Mellon University Press.—*Commentary,* v. 49, March, 1966 for "The Other Singer" by Irving Howe. Copyright © 1966 by the American Jewish Committee. All rights reserved. Reprinted by permission of the publisher and the author.—*Comparative Literature Studies,* v. VI, June, 1969. Copyright © 1969 by The Pennsylvania State University Press, University Park, PA. Reprinted by permission of the publisher.—*Critical Quarterly,* v. 25, Winter, 1983. © Manchester University Press 1983. Reprinted by permission of Manchester University Press.—*Dutch Studies,* v. I, 1974. © 1974 by Martinus Nijhoff, The Hague, The Netherlands. All rights reserved. Reprinted by permission of the publisher.—*Encounter,* v. LII, February, 1979. © 1979 by Encounter Ltd. Reprinted by permission of the publisher.—*English Literature in Transition: 1880-1920,* v. 31, 1988. Copyright © 1988 *English Literature in Transition: 1880-1920.* Reprinted by permission of the publisher.—*L'Esprit Créateur,* v. XXIV, Summer, 1984. Copyright © 1984 by L'Esprit Créateur. Reprinted by permission of the publisher.—*Essays in Criticism,* v. XVII, April, 1967 for " 'Women in Love' " by F. H. Langman; v. XXXIV, April, 1984 for "Gurney's 'Hobby' " by Geoffrey Hill. Both reprinted by permission of the Editors of *Essays in Criticism* and the respective authors.—*The German Quarterly,* v. LIV, January, 1981. Copyright © 1981 by the American Association of Teachers of German. Reprinted by permission of the publisher.—*Grand Street,* v. 1, Autumn, 1981 for "Translating Proust" by Terence Kilmartin. Copyright © 1981 by Grand Street Publications, Inc. All rights reserved. Reprinted by permission of the publisher and the author.—*Italian Studies,* v. XXIII, 1968. Reprinted by permission of the publisher.—*Journal of the American Academy of Religion,* v. LII, March, 1984. © 1984 American Academy of Religion. Reprinted by permission of the publisher.—*The Journal of the Hellenic Diaspora,* v. X, Winter, 1983. Copyright © 1983 by Pella Publishing Company. Reprinted by permission of the publisher.—*London Review of Books,* v. 5, February 3-16, 1983 for "Gurney's Flood" by Donald Davie. Appears here by permission of the *London Review of Books* and the author./ v. 9, March 5, 1987. Appears here by permission of the *London Review of Books.*—*Monatshefte,* v. LIII, March, 1961. Copyright © 1961 by the Board of Regents of the University of Wisconsin System. Reprinted by permission of The University of Wisconsin Press.—*The New Hungarian Quarterly,* v. XXI, Spring, 1980 for "How Modern Was Zsigmond Móricz?" by Péter Nagy. © *The New Hungarian Quarterly,* 1980. Reprinted by permission of the author.—*New Statesman.* v. 113, May 22, 1987. © 1987 The Statesman & Nation Publishing Co. Ltd. Reprinted by permission of the publisher.—*The New York Review of Books,* v. 9, August 24, 1967. Copyright © 1967 Nyrev, Inc. Reprinted with permission from *The New York Review of Books.*—*The New York Times Book Review,* December 3, 1922; May 24, 1931; March 6, 1932; March 12, 1933; September 13, 1936; November 22, 1953. Copyright 1922, 1931, 1932, 1933, 1936, 1953 by The New York Times Company. All reprinted by permission of the publisher./ November 3, 1974. Copyright © 1974 by The New York Times Company. Reprinted by permission of the publisher.—*Northwest Review,* v. VI, Winter, 1963. Copyright © 1963 by *Northwest Review.* Reprinted by permission of the publisher.—*Pacific Coast Philology,* v. VI, April, 1971. Reprinted by permission of the publisher.—*Poetry,* v. CIV, June, 1964. © 1964 by the Modern Poetry Association. Reprinted by permission of the Editor of *Poetry.*—*A Review of English Literature,* v. 3, April, 1962 for "The Poetry of Ivor Gurney" by E. D. Mackerness; v. 8, April, 1967 for "The Language of 'Women in Love' " by Derek Bickerton. © Longmans, Green

COPYRIGHTED EXCERPTS IN *TCLC,* VOLUME 33, WERE REPRINTED FROM THE FOLLOWING BOOKS:

Philip. From " 'The Radetzky March': Joseph Roth and the Habsburg Myth," in *The Viennese Enlightenment*. Edited by Mark Francis. Croom Helm, 1985. © 1985 Mark Francis. Reprinted by permission of the publisher.—Mathew, Celine. From *Ambivalence and Irony in the Works of Joseph Roth*. Lang, 1984. © Verlag Peter Lang GmbH, Frankfurt am Main 1984. All rights reserved. Reprinted by permission of the publisher.—May, Derwent. From *Proust*. Oxford University Press, Oxford, 1983. © Derwent May, 1983. All rights reserved. Reprinted by permission of Oxford University Press.—Momaday, N. Scott. From "To Save a Great Vision," in *A Sender of Words: Essays in Memory of John G. Neihardt*. Edited by Vine Deloria, Jr. Howe Brothers, 1984. Copyright © 1984 by John G. Neihardt Foundation, Inc. All rights reserved. Reprinted by permission of the publisher.—Moynahan, Julian. From *The Deed of Life: The Novels and Tales of D. H. Lawrence*. Princeton University Press, 1963. Copyright © 1963 by Princeton University Press. All rights reserved. Reprinted with permission of the publisher.—Murray, Jack. From *The Proustian Comedy*. French Literature Publications Company, 1980. Copyright 1980 French Literature Publications Company. Reprinted by permission of Summa Publications, P. O. Box 20725, Birmingham, AL 35216.—Nagy, Péter. From an introduction to *Be Faithful unto Death*. By Zsigmond Móricz, translated by Susan Kőrösi László. Corvina Press, 1962. © Corvina, Budapest, 1962. Reprinted by permission of Péter Nagy.—Neihardt, John. From *Black Elk Speaks: Being the Life Story of a Holy Man of the Oglala Sioux*. By John G. Neihardt. University of Nebraska Press, 1988. Copyright © 1960, 1979, 1988 by the John G. Neihardt Trust. Reprinted by permission of The John G. Neihardt Trust.—Onís, Federico de. From "Foreword: Alfonso Reyes," in *The Position of America and Other Essays*. By Alfonso Reyes, edited and translated by Harriet de Onis. Knopf, 1950. Copyright 1950, renewed 1977 by Alfred A. Knopf, Inc. All rights reserved. Reprinted by permission of the publisher.—Pacifici, Sergio. From *A Guide to Contemporary Italian Literature: From Futurism to Neorealism*. World Publishing Company, 1962. Copyright © 1962 by The World Publishing Company. All rights reserved. Reprinted by permission of the author.—Paz, Octavio. From "The Rider of the Air," translated by Lysander Kemp, in *The Siren & the Seashell and Other Essays on Poets and Poetry*. By Octavio Paz, translated by Lysander Kemp and Margaret Sayers Peden. University of Texas Press, 1976. Translation copyright © 1976 by Octavio Paz. All rights reserved. Reprinted by permission of the publisher and Lysander Kemp.—Phelps, William Lyon. From an introduction to *The Way of All Flesh*. By Samuel Butler. Dutton, 1916. Copyright, 1916, by E. P. Dutton, Inc. Renewed 1944 by John J. McKeon. Reprinted by permission of J. M. Dent and Everyman's Library.—Poggioli, Renato. From "A Correspondence from Opposite Corners," in *Perspectives of Criticism*. By Walter Jackson Bate and others, edited by Harry Levin. Cambridge, Mass.: Harvard University Press, 1950. Copyright 1950 by the President and Fellows of Harvard College. Renewed 1977 by Harry Tuchman Levin and Walter Jackson Bate. Excerpted by permission of the publishers.—Poggioli, Renato. From *The Poets of Russia: 1890-1930*. Cambridge, Mass.: Harvard University Press, 1960. Copyright © 1960 by the President and Fellows of Harvard College. Renewed © 1988 by Sylvia Poggioli. Excerpted by permission of the publishers.—Rogers, B. G. From "Proust and the Nineteenth Century," in *Marcel Proust, 1871- 1922: A Centennial Volume*. Edited by Peter Quennell. Weidenfeld and Nicolson, 1971. Copyright © 1971 by George Weidenfeld and Nicolson Limited. All rights reserved. Reprinted by permission of the publisher.—Sanger, Curt. From "The Experience of Exile in Joseph Roth's Novels," in *Exile: The Writer's Experience*. Edited by John M. Spalek and Robert F. Bell. University of North Carolina Press, 1982. © 1982 The University of North Carolina Press. All rights reserved. Reprinted by permission of the publisher and the author.—Schulz, Max F. From "The Family Chronicle as Paradigm of History: 'The Brothers Ashkenazi' and 'The Family Moskat'," in *The Achievement of Isaac Bashevis Singer*. Edited by Marcia Allentuck. Southern Illinois University Press, 1969. Copyright © 1969, by Southern Illinois University Press. All rights reserved. Reprinted by permission of the publisher.—Silkin, Jon. From *Out of Battle: The Poetry of the Great War*. Oxford University Press, London, 1972, Ark Paperbacks, 1987. © Jon Silkin 1987. Reprinted by permission of Ark Paperbacks.—Sinclair, Clive. From *The Brothers Singer*. Allison & Busby, 1983. Copyright © 1983 by Clive Sinclair. All rights reserved. Reprinted by permission of the author.—Slonim, Marc. From *Modern Russian Literature: From Chekhov to the Present*. Oxford University Press, 1953. Copyright 1953 by Oxford University Press, Inc. Renewed 1981 by Tatiana Slonim. Reprinted by permission of the publisher.—Stabb, Martin S. From *In Quest of Identity: Patterns in the Spanish American Essay of Ideas, 1890-1960*. University of North Carolina Press, 1967. Copyright © 1967 by The University of North Carolina Press. Reprinted by permission of the publisher and the author.—Strietman, Elsa. From " 'Occupied City': Ostaijen's Antwerp and the Impact of the First World War," in *Unreal City: Urban Experience in Modern European Literature and Art*. Edited by Edward Timms and David Kelley. St. Martin's Press, 1985. Copyright © Manchester University Press 1985. All rights reserved. Used with permission of St. Martin's Press, Inc.—Sussman, Herbert L. From *Victorians and the Machine: The Literary Response to Technology*. Cambridge, Mass.: Harvard University Press, 1968. Copyright © 1968 by the President and Fellows of Harvard College. All rights reserved. Excerpted by permission of the publishers.—Tamás, Attila. From "Zsigmond Móricz," in *A History of Hungarian Literature*. By István Nemeskürty and others, edited by Tibor Klaniczay, translated by István Farkas and others. Corvina Kiadó, 1982. © Tibor Klaniczay 1982. Reprinted by permission of Attila Tamás.—Taylor, Samuel S. B. From "The Emergence of a Distinctive Suisse-Romande Literary Culture, 1900-1945," in *Modern Swiss Literature: Unity and Diversity*. Edited by John L. Flood. St. Martin's Press, 1985. © 1985 Oswald Wolff (Publishers) Ltd., London. All rights reserved. Used with permission of St. Martin's Press, Inc.—Torres-Rioseco, Arturo. From "Diogenes of Anáhuac," in *Mexico in a Nutshell and Other Essays*. By Alfonso Reyes, translated by Charles Ramsdell. University of California Press, 1964. Copyright © 1964 by The Regents of the University of California. Reprinted by permission of the publisher.—Vivas, Eliseo. From *D. H. Lawrence: The Failure and the Triumph of Art*. Northwestern University Press, 1960. Copyright ©, 1960, by Northwestern University Press. Reprinted by permission of the publisher.—West, James. From *Russian Symbolism: A Study of Vyacheslav Ivanov and the Russian Symbolist Aesthetic*. Methuen & Co. Ltd., 1970. © 1970 by James West. Reprinted by permission of the publisher.—Willey, Basil. From *Darwin and Butler: Two*

Versions of Evolution. Chatto & Windus, 1960. © The Hibbert Trust 1960. Reprinted by permission of the author and Chatto & Windus.—Williams, C. E. From *The Broken Eagle: The Politics of Austrian Literature from Empire to Anschluss.* Barnes & Noble, 1974. Copyright © 1974 C. E. Williams. All rights reserved. Reprinted by permission of the publisher.—Zabel, Morton Dauwen. From *Craft and Character: Texts, Method, and Vocation in Modern Fiction.* The Viking Press, 1957. Copyright © 1957 by Morton Dauwen Zabel. Renewed 1985 by Viking Penguin Inc. Reprinted by permission of Viking Penguin Inc.—Ziolkowski, Theodore. From *Fictional Transfigurations of Jesus.* Princeton University Press, 1972. Copyright © 1972 by Princeton University Press. All rights reserved. Reprinted with permission of the publisher.

Authors to Be Featured in Forthcoming Volumes

Sholom Aleichem (Ukrainian-born Yiddish short story writer) Sholom Aleichem was one of the founders and most important writers of Yiddish literature, noted for his humorous, often poignant portrayals of Jewish life in rural Russia.

Bertolt Brecht (German dramatist)—Ranked among the most influential modern playwrights, Brecht is recognized in particular for his creation of the "epic" dramatic style, in which elements such as plot and characterization are subordinated to intellectual concerns. *TCLC* will devote an entry to his play *Mutter Courage und ihre Kinder (Mother Courage and Her Children),* which is regarded as one of Brecht's most effective expositions of his concern for the fate of the virtuous individual in a corrupt society.

Benedetto Croce (Italian philosopher and critic)—Considered the most influential literary critic of the twentieth century, Croce developed aesthetic theories that became central tenets of modern arts criticism while establishing important critical approaches to the works of such authors as William Shakespeare, Johann Wolfgang von Goethe, and Pierre Corneille.

Theodore Dreiser (American novelist)—A prominent American exponent of literary Naturalism and one of America's foremost novelists, Dreiser was the author of works commended for their powerful characterizations and strong ideological convictions.

John Gould Fletcher (American poet)—Fletcher was an innovative poet and major contributor to the development of Imagism, an influential early twentieth-century movement dedicated to replacing traditional poetics with freer rhythms and a more concise use of language.

André Gide (French novelist and critic)—Although credited with introducing the techniques of Modernism to the French novel, Gide is more highly esteemed for the autobiographical honesty and perspicacity of his work, which depicts the moral development of a modern intellectual. *TCLC* will devote an entry to *Les faux monnayeurs (The Counterfeiters),* Gide's most ambitious and stylistically sophisticated novel.

James Joyce (Irish novelist and short story writer)—The most prominent writer of the first half of the twentieth century, Joyce was the author of virtuoso experiments in prose which redefined both the limits of language and the form of the modern novel. *TCLC* will devote an entry to his only short story collection, *Dubliners,* which is regarded as a landmark in the development of the genre.

Sinclair Lewis (American novelist)—One of the foremost American novelists of the 1920s and 30s, Lewis wrote some of the most effective satires in American literature. *TCLC* will devote an entry to his novel *Babbitt,* a scathing portrait of vulgar materialism and spiritual bankruptcy in American business.

Desmond MacCarthy (English critic and novelist)—A member of the influential Bloomsbury circle, MacCarthy was among the most prominent literary and dramatic critics of his time, praised for the great erudition and objectivity of his evaluations.

Thomas Mann (German novelist)—Mann is credited with reclaiming for the German novel an international stature it had not enjoyed since the time of the Romantics. *TCLC* will devote an entry to his novel *Buddenbrooks,* a masterpiece of Realism which depicts the rise and fall of a wealthy Hanseatic family.

Stanislaw Przybyszewski (Polish dramatist and novelist)— Enormously popular during his lifetime, Przybyszewski remains well known for his romantic, often mystical, dramas and for his frank autobiographical writings.

Italo Svevo (Italian novelist)—Svevo's novels, which demonstrate the influence of the psychoanalytic theories of Sigmund Freud, earned him a reputation as one of the most original and influential authors in modern Italian literature.

Algernon Swinburne (English poet)—Controversial during his lifetime for his powerfully sensual verse, Swinburne is today recognized as one of the most talented lyric poets of the late-Victorian period.

Marina Tsvetaeva (Russian poet)—Tsvetaeva's Modernist experiments with poetic rhythms and syntax are considered a unique and important contribution to Russian literature.

Mark Twain (American novelist)—Considered the father of modern American literature, Twain combined moral and social satire, adventure, and humor to create such perennially popular works as *The Adventures of Tom Sawyer* and *The Adventures of Huckleberry Finn. TCLC* will devote an entry to the novel *A Connecticut Yankee in King Arthur's Court,* in which Twain satirized romantic idealizations of medieval life such as those presented in Sir Thomas Malory's *Morte d'Arthur.*

Emile Zola (French novelist)—Zola was the founder and principal theorist of Naturalism, one of the most influential literary movements in modern literature. His twenty-volume series *Les Rougon-Macquart* is a monument of Naturalist fiction and served as a model for late nineteenth-century novelists seeking a more candid and accurate representation of human life.

Black Elk

1863-1950

Native American autobiographer and cultural historian.

Black Elk Speaks, the life story of Black Elk, is considered the most authentic literary account of the experience of the Plains Indians during the nineteenth century. In addition to garnering praise for presenting native American religion and culture in a way that non-Indians can understand, *Black Elk Speaks* has been called the "bible" of younger generations of native Americans seeking to learn more about their heritage. Along with *The Sacred Pipe,* which recounts the seven sacred rituals of the Sioux, *Black Elk Speaks* has played a crucial role in preserving native American traditions and in encouraging the expression of a native American heritage and consciousness.

Black Elk, whose father and grandfather were both medicine men, was born along the Little Powder River, probably in the region that is now the state of Wyoming. While his people, the Oglala Lakota branch of the Sioux nation, were able to maintain their traditional way of life during Black Elk's earliest years, the westward migration of settlers soon made that impossible. During the 1870s and 1880s, the Sioux engaged in a series of battles with the United States Army for control of their tribal lands. These included the Battle of the Little Big Horn, in which Black Elk participated when he was thirteen. After Chief Crazy Horse, Black Elk's cousin, was assassinated by United States soldiers in 1877, Black Elk's tribe fled to Canada, where they remained until 1880.

After his tribe returned to the United States, Black Elk acted on a vision he had experienced when he was nine. In Sioux religious tradition such experiences are often used as guides to determine the course to be taken by individuals and entire tribes. In the vision Black Elk foresaw the destruction of a "sacred hoop" representing the unity of his people, and was instructed in the manner in which he might one day use a sacred herb to destroy his nation's enemies and restore unity. Following an enactment of the vision by his tribe, in accord with Sioux custom, Black Elk began a career as a medicine man. Compelled to take on an even larger role, Black Elk accepted an offer to join Buffalo Bill's Wild West Show in 1886, explaining, "I thought I ought to go, because I might learn some secret of the Wasichu [whites] that would help my people somehow." After spending three years touring with the show through Great Britain and Europe, featuring a performance at Queen Victoria's Golden Jubilee, he returned to the United States in 1889. While he had learned about European cultures and traditions, he felt that he had lost the power of his vision while he was away.

Upon returning to his tribe, which was now living on Pine Ridge reservation in South Dakota, Black Elk found famine, disease, and despair among the Sioux and learned that a millenarian religious movement called the Dance of the Ghosts was spreading across the reservations. Black Elk joined the Ghost Dance when he perceived significant similarities between its prophecy of a new world for native Americans and the image of the restoration of the sacred hoop in his own vision. The incessant and frenzied dancing associated with the

movement greatly alarmed officials on the reservations, who called in the United States Army to preserve order; tension between the native Americans and soldiers finally erupted on December 29, 1890, when soldiers massacred approximately three hundred unarmed men, women, and children camped along Wounded Knee Creek on Pine Ridge reservation.

The massacre at Wounded Knee marked the end of the native Americans' hope for preserving their land and their autonomy. Black Elk remained on the Pine Ridge reservation after the massacre, continuing to act as a medicine man despite the expressed disapproval of Jesuit priests who had founded a mission there. In 1904, Black Elk joined the Catholic church; it is not known why he converted after years of maintaining traditional religious practices. Whatever his motivation, attempting to reconcile the two religions would be a continuing process for Black Elk. He became a respected leader in the local Catholic community, serving as a Catholic catechist and traveling to other reservations in that capacity.

In 1930, Black Elk was approached by John G. Neihardt, an author seeking information about the Ghost Dance and the Wounded Knee massacre for an epic poem depicting the history of the American West. While Neihardt's interest was at first restricted to Sioux history, Black Elk announced that he felt a spiritual kinship with Neihardt and wanted to share his vision with him in order to preserve it. Neihardt decided that he could create a book based on Black Elk's life rather than simply incorporating the material into his poem, and he returned to Pine Ridge for a series of extensive interviews. The resulting narrative, *Black Elk Speaks,* was published in 1932. With the publication of the book, Black Elk was again in conflict with the Jesuits, who were appalled that one of their most reliable catechists had apparently re-embraced his ancestral religion. The publicity surrounding *Black Elk Speaks* also brought additional writers and scholars to Pine Ridge to interview Black Elk. Joseph Epes Brown, an anthropology student, lived with Black Elk for several months during the winter of 1947-48 and recorded his account of Sioux religious rituals, publishing the information as *The Sacred Pipe* in 1953, three years after Black Elk's death. While *The Sacred Pipe* is considered a valuable resource in the preservation of Sioux cultural history, it is judged inferior to *Black Elk Speaks* as a literary work and has received little critical attention.

Black Elk Speaks tells the story of Black Elk from his early childhood to the Wounded Knee massacre in 1890. Widely praised for vividly portraying both the personality of Black Elk and the native American way of life, the book has been variously examined as autobiography, ethnology, psychology, and philosophy. At the same time, critics agree that *Black Elk Speaks* is preeminently a work of literature, not scholarship, praising in particular the book's simple and forceful prose style. While some critics contend that Neihardt's success at representing qualities of the Lakota language in English is proof of his faithfulness to Black Elk's words, others argue that the highly literary nature of the prose is evidence that the words are Neihardt's and not Black Elk's. This dispute raises larger questions regarding Neihardt's role in the creation of *Black Elk Speaks* which are the focus of much of the commentary on the work.

Neither Black Elk nor Neihardt could speak, read, or write the other's language, and the interview procedure was complex. Black Elk's spoken Lakota was translated into English by his son Ben Black Elk, restated by Neihardt, translated back to Black Elk for further clarification when necessary, and recorded in shorthand by Neihardt's daughter Enid, who later arranged her notes in chronological order and typed them. Neihardt then wrote the text of *Black Elk Speaks* from Enid's typewritten transcripts; he told Black Elk's story in the first person but also included descriptions of events and battles that Black Elk did not experience or was too young to remember, which were provided by other Sioux who were present during some of the interviews.

Critics have questioned Neihardt's chosen focus for the book, noting that by ending *Black Elk Speaks* with the massacre at Wounded Knee in 1890, Neihardt omitted a forty-year period in Black Elk's life and ignored his conversion to Catholicism. Some commentators suggest that these decisions reflect Neihardt's desire to portray Black Elk's life as a symbol for the demise of the Sioux nation, the theme he was exploring in his own work. Critics have also questioned Neihardt's depiction of Black Elk's vision, noting that he eliminated some of the violent aspects of Black Elk's description, including the destructive herb. While Raymond J. DeMallie argues that Neihardt was justified in this decision because Black Elk himself rejected violence by becoming a Christian, others maintain that he unjustifiably misrepresented Black Elk's story in order to emphasize its universal aspects and to avoid alienating white readers. Commentators have also criticized Nei-

hardt for portraying Black Elk as a tragic and pathetic figure, maintaining that the transcripts of the Black Elk interviews belie this portrait.

While *Black Elk Speaks* received positive reviews, it was not popular among readers, and suffered several decades of neglect. In the 1950s, Carl Jung and other European psychologists and anthropologists rediscovered the book and studied Black Elk's vision as an example of the importance of cultural symbols, and their examination sparked renewed interest in the work in the United States. During the 1960s and 1970s, concern for the status of ethnic minorities and the environment focused attention on native Americans, and *Black Elk Speaks,* considered the preeminent account of the native American experience, became increasingly popular. While debate regarding Neihardt's editorial role continues, the importance of *Black Elk Speaks* as both a work of literature and a source for the understanding of native American culture has been widely acknowledged.

(For a discussion of John G. Neihardt's life and career, see *Contemporary Literary Criticism,* Vol. 32.)

PRINCIPAL WORKS

Black Elk Speaks: Being the Life Story of a Holy Man of the Oglala Sioux as Told to John G. Neihardt (Flaming Rainbow) (autobiography) 1932
The Sacred Pipe: Black Elk's Account of the Seven Rites of the Oglala Sioux [recorded and edited by Joseph Epes Brown] (cultural history) 1953
The Sixth Grandfather: Black Elk's Teachings Given to John G. Neihardt [edited by Raymond J. DeMallie] (interviews) 1984

JOHN CHAMBERLAIN   (essay date 1932)

[*Chamberlain is an American essayist and critic who has edited several popular American magazines, including* Harper's Magazine *and* Life, *and is noted for his writings on social and economic subjects. In the following excerpt, he favorably reviews* Black Elk Speaks, *praising the work's narrative artistry and philosophical perspective.*]

Mr. Neihardt was anxious to get Black Elk's story because this holy man of the Oglala Sioux was related to the great Chief Crazy Horse, who had whipped General Crook ("Three Stars," to the Indians) in 1876, after gold had been discovered in the Black Hills and the Americans had broken the treaty of 1868, a treaty that had guaranteed the mountain fastnesses to the red men "as long as grass should grow and water flow." Mr. Neihardt felt that here was a matchless chance to talk to one who had "seen Shelley plain," not once but many times. His sanguine attitude is fully justified in the event, for the story of Black Elk—with its memories of Crazy Horse, of the "rubbing out of Long Hair" (General Custer) on the Little Big Horn, in 1876, and of travel with the early Buffalo Bill show—is one of the saddest and noblest that has ever been told.

What will immediately strike the reader is the obvious, but nonetheless terribly poignant, anti-climax of Black Elk's life. Save for the postscript of Mr. Neihardt, the story comes down only to 1890—to the massacre at Wounded Knee, in South Dakota, which ended the last dim glimmerings of the Indian power in the United States. That was two generations ago—and the succeeding years are a blank in the chronicle of Black Elk. These years of attrition have sharpened the memory of the ancient Sioux; brooding has greatly magnified his evocative powers. From long mulling over, no doubt, the events of the twenty years from 1870 to 1890 have taken on a clarity and an order that have resulted in excellent straight-forward narrative. It is only when this Indian holy man comes to describe his "visions" that the white-skinned reader is at a loss. Then one wonders what an Ernest Renan would have made of Black Elk's "conversion."

Black Elk's memories, as translated by Mr. Neihardt, are purely poetic. Abstraction has not laid its desiccating blight upon the Ogalala holy man. To him the months are not so many metrical units; they are straight out of nature. April is "the Moon of the Red Grass Appearing." January is "the Moon of Frost in the Tepee." March is "the Moon of the Snowblind," and May, "the Moon When the Ponies Shed." Battle accounts are not in terms of ammunition used nor of numbers slain; they are, rather, in terms of very human and tragic miscellany. For example, when Black Elk is recalling the massacre at Wounded Knee (which is one of the many sins for which Manifest Destiny has to answer), he remarks, "I saw a little baby trying to suck its mother, but she was bloody and dead." For such scarifying detail, at once pathetic and horrifying, one will have to go to Tolstoy's *War and Peace* to find its equal.

Black Elk's memories begin before the "iron road" (the Union Pacific) had split the vast aboriginal bison herd, which meant life to the plains Indian, into two smaller herds. The next years were good, for the Wasichus (the whites) "had made their iron road along the Platte and traveled there." The buffalo that remained north of the Platte were sufficient unto the needs of the Sioux, the Cheyenne, the Arapahoe and the Crows, for "they were more than could be counted." As a boy, Black Elk led the life his forebears had led since time immemorial—or at least since the wild horse, escaping from the Spaniards to the South, had appeared on the plains to give the Indians a mount and the fierceness incidental to added speed. The young Black Elk practiced endurance:

> Our adviser [he told Mr. Neihardt] would put dry
> sunflower seeds on our wrists. These were lit at the
> top, and we had to let them burn clear down to the
> skin. They hurt and made sores, but if we knocked
> them off or cried Owh!, we would be called women.

He played war games with other little boys of the tribe, after the buffalo hunt when the women were busy cutting the bison meat into strips and hanging it to dry:

> When it got dark [our adviser] would order us to
> go and steal some dried meat from the big people.
> He would hold a stick up to us and we had to bite
> off a piece of it. If we bit a big piece we had to get
> a big piece of meat, and if we bit a little piece we
> did not have to get so much. Then we started for
> the big people's village, crawling on our bellies, and
> when we got back without getting caught, we
> would have a big feast and a dance and make kill
> talks, telling of our brave deeds like warriors.

Thus were the young Ogalala "conditioned" for the neolithic huntsman's life, complicated by the introduction of the rifle and six-shooter, that they had to lead. An account of an Indi-

an wooing is interspersed among more serious things; this is pure comedy, almost in the manner of Booth Tarkington's "Seventeen." The story of the young Black Elk's "vision" is amorphous and vague, but possibly the ritual of the Catholic or the high Episcopal church would be just as nebulous to the Indian intelligence, so we can hardly blame Black Elk and Mr. Neihardt on that score. And then, passing out of his childhood, Black Elk brings his story down to the breaking of the treaty made by the whites with Red Cloud in 1868. The whites had discovered some of the "yellow metal" that "makes them mad," and the Black Hills were being overrun with prospectors and soldiers. The Hang-around-the-forts, a type of Indian for whom Black Elk's scorn is very real, were willing that the treaty be broken; but not so Crazy Horse. The young Black Elk's admiration for Crazy Horse is very plain; he boasts that the Wasichus could not kill him in battle, and had to resort to duplicity to "rub him out." Black Elk's father also admired Crazy Horse, and the family left the Soldier's Town to join the great man and fight, "because there was no other way to keep our country." And because of this decision Black Elk saw the fight with Crook, and the massacre of Custer's men. Black Elk's account of this celebrated battle is fully as bloody as that old chromo that was the standard adornment of bar room windows before Mr. Volstead inspired a song writer to offer to give a dry America back to the Indians.

"You can see that I am only a pitiful old man after all," Black Elk remarks to Mr. Neihardt, but this "pitiful old man" is a philosopher with a serenity to be envied. He reveals himself as a sort of Indian Platonist: "Crazy Horse dreamed and went into the world where there is nothing but the spirits of all things. That is the real world that is behind this one, and everything we see here is something like a shadow from that world." And the Indian Platonist is also a critic of greed: "I could see that the Wasichus did not care for each other the way our people did before the nation's hoop was broken. They would take everything from each other if they could, and so there were some who had more of everything than they could use, while crowds of people had nothing at all and maybe were starving." (This observation was provoked by Black Elk's trip with the Buffalo Bill show to Victorian England, where he performed before the Queen herself. Victoria told him that if he were a Canadian Indian she would not permit him to be used as entertainment.) The Indian criticism of gold fever has been mentioned; the buffalo meant far more to Black Elk than any "yellow metal"—and perhaps the nations that are breaking their necks for a favorable balance of trade in terms of this metal will on the advent of Utopia agree with him. (pp. 4, 14)

*John Chamberlain, "A Sioux Indian Tells a Tragic
Story," in* The New York Times Book Review,
March 6, 1932, pp. 4, 14.

MARQUIS W. CHILDS (essay date 1932)

[*Childs is an American journalist, novelist, and author of books
on political and economic subjects. In the following review of*
Black Elk Speaks, *he praises the compelling narrative and powerful depiction of Black Elk's vision.*]

Within the past twenty or thirty years the Indian has been reduced, possibly by way of easing the American conscience, to a pretty picturesqueness; he is made a noble player in a banal legend, the province of the art calendar and Hollywood. Indian culture has for the most part been so obliterated and distorted that it is difficult to get intelligent interest in anything Indian. One hears, "But the Indians are so dull"; and perhaps in the abject state in which they are forced to live this is quite true.

To those who have thought the Indians "dull" this book will come as a shock. It is curiously modern in tone. The description of the fight with Custer might almost have been written by Ernest Hemingway, and that is a great tribute indeed to Mr. Hemingway. In all the battle passages there is a bleak, stark grandeur. The Sioux were not fighting in the name of rhetorical patriotism, manufactured in a bureau of propaganda. One sees plainly throughout the narrative those deep sources of primitive being which have been so glossed over by modern life.

A frenzy possesses the great camp when the criers announce the coming of the soldiers. There is the wildest disorder everywhere. But beneath this the battle fury flows in a strong stream. A father says to his son, "Do not fear. Only the earth lasts." Naked on horseback, the Sioux rush out to meet Custer and Reno, crying, "It is a good day to die, it is a good day to die." Black Elk and the friends who occasionally supplement his narrative are undeterred by Christian remorse; they tell in plain, simple sentences of the scalping and the other bloody acts that followed the victory.

But the power and beauty of Black Elk's "Great Vision" are so compelling as to overshadow even the heroic proportions of the narrative, with its inevitably tragic conclusion. It was this vision, as he glimpsed it in his first chance conversation with Black Elk, that undoubtedly led Mr. Neihardt to set down the book. The vision is so complex and so rich in symbolism that it is difficult to discern all its meaning. In its essentials, however, as it was given to Black Elk when he was nine years old, it was a prophecy of the destruction of the primitive unity of his people, their oneness. The sacred hoop is destroyed, the flowering staff withers and dies. On the third ascent, where his ultimate failure as a life-giver is made clear to him, he sees his people in confusion, running about, each with his "own little vision." "I think we are very near that place now," Black Elk remarked, "and I am afraid that something very bad is going to happen all over the world." In a footnote Mr. Neihardt points out that Black Elk is an illiterate and knows nothing of world affairs.

This could stand as a type vision. It might well have troubled the sleep of the Papuans and the Samoans, the Aztecs and the Zulus. The conflict between the "civilized" white and primitive man has been the great world drama of the past four hundred years. In that vast drama, so often disguised by rhetoric or neglected altogether, this book must have an important place. Throughout, it is apparent that Mr. Neihardt has set his sensitive poet's mind the task of recording faithfully and without intrusion Black Elk's words. He has been a keen and scrupulous editor.

Marquis W. Childs, "Morituri," in The New Republic, Vol. LXXI, No. 916, June 22, 1932, p. 161.

OLIVER LA FARGE (essay date 1953)

[*La Farge was an American anthropologist and fiction writer whose interest in native American culture is evident in both his scholarly and creative works. His novel* Laughing Boy (1929), *the story of a Navaho boy, won the Pulitzer Prize. In the following review of* The Sacred Pipe, *he questions the accuracy of Epes Brown's editorial practices yet asserts the literary and anthropological value of the book.*]

To report that a book deals with the mystic side of Sioux religion, as expounded by the oldest surviving Sioux priest, is to risk frightening away readers. Many believe that American Indian religion is unworthy of serious consideration. Nowhere, however, is that idea more effectively refuted than in *The Sacred Pipe.*

All interested in comparative religion, and all curious to know how high the thought of primitive man can reach will find this book worthy. It is not, properly speaking, an anthropological work, although it makes a contribution to that science. With a minimum of footnoting and documentation, it records the loftier aspects of Sioux religion as conceived by a single, highly qualified individual—Black Elk, already well known through John Neihardt's writings.

It is a noble and often a beautiful document. The method of the exposition is to recite the procedures of the seven major rituals as, according to the myths, they were originally established, and explain the higher significance of the various acts and articles. Inevitably this leads to many repetitions, as does the description of ritual in any religion. Some of these repetitions have a force of their own; others, one skips. Aside from such passages, the book is all real literature.

The Sioux religion according to Black Elk is monotheistic. God—*Wakan Tanka*—is conceived in lofty terms. Union and communion with *Wakan Tanka* lead in this life to having prayers answered and keeping the world in order; in the next life the devotee is absorbed within Him. There are various intermediaries, but these are not so much gods or demi-gods in their own rights as conceptually materialized aspects of *Wakan Tanka.* The approach to God is through mysticism supported by the practice of a saintly asceticism.

Joseph Epes Brown is no scientist. He states frankly that he set out to learn what the old Indian priests might know in order to verify a preconception he had formed. He chose to concentrate on the Plains Indians because of another, quite arbitrary preconception—that "the nations of the prairies were, in a sense, the aristocrats among the other nations." His preface does not state what editing or rewording he may have done, or abstained from doing. As a result, the reader is inclined to suspect that some of the lofty concepts and expressions are in reality the product of the common human tendency to find what, in advance, one expects to find.

Fortunately, he quotes various passages from statements of other Sioux religious leaders, taken down by unsentimental, dry-minded scientists, which show that the concepts were common to many of these Indians. There still remains a suspicion that what Black Elk said has been improved to match the meanings Mr. Brown had set out to verify. Readers who have thought of the Sioux as an egotistical, touchy, rather disagreeable people will be astonished by the aspects that *The Sacred Pipe* reveals.

Yet, no matter what discount one may make for the editor's contribution, this account leaves no doubt of the priceless spiritual values that we, in the arrogance of our material culture, have been so industriously destroying.

Oliver La Farge, "Wakan Tanka and the Seven Rituals of the Sioux," in The New York Times Book Review, November 22, 1953, p. 6.

JOHN NEIHARDT   (essay date 1972)

[*Neihardt was a poet, fiction writer, critic, biographer, and autobiographer whose most significant work was* A Cycle of the West *(1915-1941), a five-part epic poem that blends classical literary techniques with historically accurate details and regional folklore. Neihardt has lived among native Americans, and much of his work, including* A Cycle of the West, *is concerned with the effect of the westward expansion of white settlers on the native Americans and on the whites themselves. The following excerpt is taken from Neihardt's introduction to* Black Elk Speaks. *Written in 1960 and originally published in the 1961 Bison Books edition, the introduction has since been revised for inclusion in subsequent publications. In this excerpt, Neihardt recounts his initial meeting and collaboration with Black Elk and describes the obligation he feels to share Black Elk's message.*]

It was during August, 1930, that I first met Black Elk. I was then working on *The Song of the Messiah,* which now stands as the fifth and final narrative poem in my *Cycle of the West.* This *song* is concerned with what white men have called the "Messiah craze"—the great Messianic dream that came to the desperate Indians in the middle 80's of the 19th century and ended with the massacre at Wounded Knee, South Dakota, on December 29, 1890.

With my son, Sigrud, I had gone to Pine Ridge Reservation for the purpose of finding some old medicine man who had been active in the Messiah Movement and who might somehow be induced to talk to me about the deeper spiritual significance of the matter. (p. 227)

Through the Field Agent-in-Charge at Pine Ridge Agency I learned of an old Sioux by the name of Black Elk, who lived among the barren hills some twenty miles east of the Agency near Manderson post office. Black Elk was a "kind of preacher," I was told—that is to say, a *wichasha wakon* (holy man, priest)—and he had been of some importance in the Messiah affair. Also, he was second cousin to Crazy Horse, the principal hero of my *Song of the Indian Wars,* and had known the great chieftain well.

So my son and I drove over to Manderson to try our luck with the old man. Flying Hawk, an interpreter with whom I was slightly acquainted, was living there, and he was willing to go with us to see Black Elk at his home about two miles west of Manderson. It was a dead-end road that led through the treeless, yellow hills to Black Elk's home—a one-room log cabin with weeds growing out of the dirt roof.

When we arrived, Black Elk was standing outside a shade made of pine boughs. It was noon. When we left, after sunset, Flying Hawk said, "That was kind of funny, the way the old man seemed to know you were coming!" My son remarked that he had the same impression; and when I had known the great old man for some years I was quite prepared to believe that he did know, for he certainly had supernormal powers.

Shaking hands with Black Elk, I told him that I was well acquainted with the Omaha Indians and with many of the Sioux; that I had come to get acquainted with him and have a little talk about old times. "Ah-h-h!" he said, indicating that my suggestion was satisfactory.

For some time, Black Elk, with his near-blind stare fixed on the ground, seemed to have forgotten us. I was about to break the silence by way of getting something started, when the old man looked up to Flying Hawk, the interpreter, and said (speaking Sioux, for he knew no English); "As I sit here, I can feel in this man beside me a strong desire to know the things of the Other World. He has been sent to learn what I know, and I will teach him."

Finally, the old man began talking about a vision that had come to him in his youth. It was his power-vision, as I learned later, and his fragmentary references to it were evidently intended only to arouse my curiosity, for he could not speak freely about a matter so sacred before the assembled company. It was like half seeing, half sensing a strange and beautiful landscape by brief flashes of sheet lightning.

Often I broke the old man's prolonged silences by referring to the old times before the evil days began and the white men possessed the land. I recalled great battles, high moments in Sioux history, and he would respond politely; but it was increasingly clear that his real interest was in "the things of the Other World."

The sun was near to setting when Black Elk said: "There is so much to teach you. What I know was given to me for men and it is true and it is beautiful. Soon I shall be under the grass and it will be lost. You were sent to save it, and you must come back so that I can teach you." And I said: "I will come back, Black Elk. When do you want me?" He replied, "In the spring when the grass is so high" (indicating the breadth of a hand).

That winter I corresponded with Black Elk through his son, Ben, who had attended Carlisle for a year or two, and thus arrangements were made for an extended visit the following spring.

During early May, 1931, in company with my eldest daughter, Enid, who had been my secretary for several years, and my second daughter, Hilda, I returned to Black Elk's home that he might relate his life-story to me in fulfillment of a duty that he felt incumbent upon him. His chief purpose was to "save his Great Vision for men."

It was my function to translate the old man's story, not only in the factual sense—for it was not the facts that mattered most—but rather to recreate in English the mood and manner of the old man's narrative. This was often a grueling and difficult task requiring much patient effort and careful questioning of the interpreter.

Always I felt it a sacred obligation to be true to the old man's meaning and manner of expression. I am convinced there were times when we had more than the ordinary means of communication.

For the last forty years it has been my purpose to bring Black Elk's message to the white world as he wished me to do. (pp. 227-29)

Black Elk Speaks is spreading all over the United States and also over Europe, having been translated into eight languages. In 1972 it will go into mass publication.

The old prophet's wish that I bring his message to the world is actually being fulfilled.

Those who are acquainted with *Black Elk Speaks* will remember the old man's prayer on Harney Peak when he wept in the drizzling rain and cried out in desperation to the Grandfathers of the Universe: "A pitiful old man you see me here, and I have fallen away and have done nothing."

Perhaps with his message spreading across the world he has not failed. (pp. 229-30)

John Neihardt, "The Book That Would Not Die," in Western American Literature, *Vol. VI, No. 4, February, 1972, pp. 227-30.*

SALLY McCLUSKEY (essay date 1972)

[*In the following excerpt, McCluskey affirms the importance of Neihardt's role in the creation of* Black Elk Speaks, *offering as evidence comparisons of* Black Elk Speaks *and* The Sacred Pipe.]

Black Elk Speaks has been many things to many people, and has been studied at various times as anthropology, as sociology, as psychology, and as history. It has been cited as evidence of a religious revival and used as an ecological handbook. But no one, as far as I know, has written about **Black Elk Speaks** as literature, and while its protagonist, Black Elk, has become a sort of culture hero and underground prophet, the man who wrote Black Elk's story, John G. Neihardt, has received surprisingly little credit for the artistry with which the book is written. Neihardt's very faithfulness to Black Elk's spirit and his skill in expressing that spirit have, ironically, eclipsed the effort he spent in writing the book, and often Neihardt has been ignored by press and scholars as if he were merely the instrument Black Elk used to tell his story, and not the shaping intelligence and lyric voice of the book. (p. 231)

There are difficulties in discussing the book as literature, for it had a peculiar genesis and belongs to no clear-cut genre unless one accepts Robert Sayre's term "Indian autobiography": an Indian's life story written down by a white interviewer, editor or translator. **Black Elk Speaks** is not really an autobiography, for Black Elk could neither read nor write; indeed, because he could not speak English, he told his story to Neihardt through his son, Ben Black Elk, who acted as interpreter. Neihardt's daughter Enid took stenographic notes, and Neihardt used the transcript of these notes to write the book. The content is partly biography, partly history, partly anthropology, partly anecdote, but all told through Black Elk. Robert Sayre, who examined parts of Enid Neihardt's original transcript and compared them to the finished book, concluded that Neihardt was faithful to what he had heard [see Sayre entry in Additional Bibliography]. Dee Brown pronounced it the finest book in existence on the American Indian, and Oliver La Farge lauded it. Paul Engle wrote that it "seems as close as we can ever get to the authentic mind and life of the plains tribes."

But the book's power is in the persona of Black Elk and in the texture of the prose itself. His story progresses in seemingly artless fashion and at a leisurely pace, but on closer examination we can see that Neihardt, as editor, was careful to catch the details that made Black Elk human. One can pick up any "as told to" autobiography recounting the life of some celebrity and encounter literary personality and prose style flatter than the pages that contain them. But Black Elk emerges fully rounded, and so does the world he lived in. He is a human being, a boy who cries all night when his cousin is killed by whites; a young man who went with Buffalo Bill to England and thought Queen Victoria fat, but nice; and an old man, who forty years after Wounded Knee still wept and prayed, "O make my people live!" He is not a saint, for he recounts quite calmly how he cut off a white man's finger to get the ring, how he scalped a corpse at Little Big Horn, and laughed as squaws stabbed to death a wounded soldier. His faith, his fears, his rage, and his humanity unite, making him a complex human being who walked real roads, saw real clouds, smelled real winds, and tasted real meat.

Neihardt's use of the first person, he said, was a literary device, for he had to fashion Black Elk's story from many days of talk, many reminiscences recalled not necessarily in order. That Neihardt's conversations with Black Elk contained a good deal more information than Neihardt included in **Black Elk Speaks** is indicated by the novel *When the Tree Flowered*, published some twenty years later, and showing a great knowledge of Sioux rite and ritual, much more rite and ritual than is included in **Black Elk Speaks.** It is my guess that he edited such information from **Black Elk Speaks** so that he could include more detail about Black Elk's life. (pp. 231-33)

It is not that Neihardt neglected religion in the book: Black Elk's faith is presented, but in clean outlines. Scientific accounts of Indian religion tend to pile rite on rite, folk tale on folk tale, and to compound the confusion with rising tides of footnotes pointing out analogues, sources, and parallel practices noted in the Fiji Islands. Religion becomes a jumble of disparate details united only by the compiler's belief in the ubiquity of Corn Gods. Black Elk was a holy man, and one haunted by the religious vision he had early in his life. But his religion emerges neither as incomprehensible dogma nor quaint superstition. His pantheism permeates the book, and his frequent spiritual insights illuminate it, but he appears here as a priest second, a man first.

Neihardt captures the spirit of Black Elk's faith, rather than exploring the intricacies of its letter; and the book shows Sioux religion as it was lived and felt; it is the spiritual truth and not the sociological corpse that is given to us. The rites presented are actual rites, with real men taking the parts and real children on the sidelines.

Similarly, the history the book recounts is told dramatically. The dust and myth blow away when Black Elk tells it:

> They told Crazy Horse they would not harm him if he would go to the Soldiers' Town and have a talk with the Wasichu chief there. But they lied. They did not take him to the chief for a talk. They took him to the little prison with iron bars on the windows, for they had planned to get rid of him. And when he saw what they were doing, he turned around and took a knife out of his robe and started out against all those soldiers. Then Little Big Man, who had been [his] friend . . . , took hold of Crazy Horse from behind and tried to get the knife away. And while they were struggling, a soldier ran a bayonet into Crazy Horse from one side at the back and he fell down and began to die.

There is also plenty of action, as in Black Elk's account of the Battle of Little Big Horn, and humor as in the "High Horse's Courting" episode. And there is pathos, as when, after having fled to Canada, Black Elk and a few other braves go out into the bitter cold on a hunting party. Black Elk's hands freeze to his gun, and in tearing them loose he finds them so hurt and frozen he cannot use them. It takes his father and another man all day to skin the frozen buffaloes they have shot, and at night they camp under the shelter of the raw robes:

> The wind went down and it grew very cold, so we had to keep the fire going all night. During the

night I heard a whimpering outside the shelter, and
when I looked, there was a party of porcupines
huddled up as close as they thought they dared to
be, and they were crying because they were so cold.
We did not chase them away, because we felt sorry
for them.

This vignette of the cold exiles sharing their heat with "a
party of porcupines" is an example of what divorces the book
from most accounts of Indian life. The humanity that shines
through this simple incident, though not important to scholar
or scientist, is very important in making real the suffering of
Black Elk and his people.

It is this emotional range and the lyrical quality of the prose
that gives *Black Elk Speaks* its power, for it has no plot to
speak of, and no suspense—we all know who won the Indian
wars. It does not follow the standard form of an autobiography, for other old Indians speak in it besides Black Elk.
Standing Bear, Iron Hawk, and Iron Thunder occasionally
break into the narrative to tell what they saw. It does not even
recount the whole life of Black Elk, but only the first twenty-
seven years, and one eighth of the narrative is taken up by
Black Elk's first power vision. It is a loose, free recollection,
held together by the powerful persona of Black Elk, and the
increasing conviction on the reader's part that it presents, in
the story of one man, the tragedy of two nations, red and
white.

It is the personality of Black Elk that dominates the book,
and while his story is that of a mystic, and therefore strange,
and of dramatic times, and therefore interesting, it is ultimately the *way* the story is told that endows it with greatness,
and Black Elk's language which creates the power of *Black
Elk Speaks.* Of all the things that have been said or written
about *Black Elk Speaks,* little mention has been made that
it reads like poetry, and was, indeed, "written through" a
poet. "Written through" is how Neihardt asked it to be set
down on the title page of the book, and his name, given to
him by Black Elk, indicates his function in the book's creation. He was renamed "Flaming Rainbow" by Black Elk,
for the flaming rainbow in the first power vision, the rainbow
that was the entrance to the teepee of the six Grandfathers,
the Powers of the World. One had to pass through this rainbow to see the powers of the world, and it leaped and flick-
ered as they spoke.

Neihardt was, for Black Elk, a portal through which his vision could pass to the world, the means by which men would
learn about a vision Black Elk felt was great and holy. The
relationship between the poet and the Holy Man was unique;
as Robert Sayre notes, Black Elk couldn't have been "more
different from the 'informant' sought out, solicited and paid
by many anthropologists. In Neihardt's account of these relations, it is clear that Black Elk, on the contrary, had chosen
Neihardt, in so far as he could. Neihardt was not a prying
scientist . . . while Black Elk was a . . . holy man . . . with
a Vision to pass on. The purposes were separate, yet mutually
supportive, clearly defined and yet compatible." (pp. 233-35)

Black Elk felt he could entrust his vision to Neihardt, and an
unexpected book was born. Neihardt did his work well, so
well that many people seemed to forget he had a part in it at
all. (p. 236)

Dee Brown, historian of the Indian wars, said if he could save
but one book on the American Indian, that book would be
Black Elk Speaks. In *Bury My Heart at Wounded Knee* he

quotes it several times, and he ends it with a moving passage
from *Black Elk. The Wall Street Journal,* reviewing Brown's
book, quoted the passage again:

I did not know then how much was ended. When
I look back now from this high hill of my old age,
I can still see the butchered women and children
lying heaped and scattered all along the crooked
gulch as plain as when I saw them with eyes still
young. And I can see that something else died there
in the bloody mud, and was buried in the blizzard.
A people's dream died there. It was a beautiful
dream . . . the nation's hoop is broken and scattered. There is no center any longer, and the sacred
tree is dead.

It is a beautiful and a fitting end to Black Elk's book, and to
Dee Brown's book and to the *Wall Street Journal's* review—
but Black Elk never said it. For all its ring of authenticity,
it is Neihardt's.

The book's opening is also his, and as the ending fooled the
educated ear of Dee Brown, the beginning was taken by Robert Sayre to be Black Elk's and only Black Elk's:

My friend, I am going to tell you the story of my
life, as you wish; and if it were only the story of my
life, I think I would not tell it; for what is one man
that he should make much of his winters even when
they bend him like a heavy snow? So many other
men have lived and shall live that story, to be grass
upon the hills. It is the story of all life that is holy
and it is good to tell, and of us two-leggeds sharing
in it with the four-leggeds and the wings of the air
and all green things; for these are children of one
mother and their father is one spirit.

Sayre commented that this passage shows Black Elk emphasizing the communal or tribal nature of what is about to be
said, and that "Black Elk's sense of what he is doing . . .
shows a . . . higher appreciation of books and of leaving a
distinct, permanent record of his life than most readers will
have."

But it is Neihardt, speaking for Black Elk, who knows what
he is doing; and these two experts' mistaken identification of
what is Neihardt's as Black Elk's is a sort of tribute to Neihardt, who, when the occasion demanded, assumed a negative capability and became an Indian. He said that there were
certain things Black Elk was not capable of saying, things he
would have said if he could; and Neihardt, both as poet and
spiritual son, said for him, pulling the parts of the book together into an artistic whole. I do not mean to imply that Neihardt fabricated *any* part of Black Elk's story, *or* toyed with
the facts told him, only that as an artist he forged them into
an organic whole, unified in tone, and as structured as far as
it was possible to structure without falsification.

When I visited Neihardt in April of 1971, I happened to follow hot in the footsteps of two other men, one who had come
to talk about *Black Elk* as religion, the other as sociology.
Both, apparently, had believed that Neihardt had "recorded"
the book, and Neihardt remarked to me that he had "set
them straight," but there had been a good deal of difficulty
about his part in writing *Black Elk.* With a sigh, he remarked, "Why don't I just give you a statement, so it gets
down for once and for all." Here is that statement:

Black Elk Speaks is a work of art with two collaborators, the chief one being Black Elk. My function
was both creative and editorial. I think he knew the

kind of person I was when I came to see him—I am referring to the mystical strain in me and all my work. He said, "You have been sent so that I may teach you and you receive what I know. It was given to me for men and it is true and it is beautiful and soon I will be under the grass." And I think he knew I was the tool—no, the medium—he needed for what he wanted to get said. And my attitude toward what he has said to me is one of religious obligation.

But it is absurd to suppose that the use of the first person singular is not a literary device, by which I mean that Black Elk did not sit and tell me his story in chronological order. At times considerable editing was necessary, but it was always worth the editing. The beginning and the ending are mine; they are what he would have said if he had been able. At times I changed a word, a sentence, sometimes created a paragraph. And the translation—or rather the *transformation*—of what was given me was expressed so that it could be understood by the white world.

The organization, he said, was his, and he purposely ended Black Elk's story with the Battle of Wounded Knee, knowing it was the most dramatic point. His word "transformation" is most apt; for his editing, his careful interpolations, his prose style give **Black Elk** its form as well as its peculiar luminosity. (pp. 237-39)

Epes Brown used the same first person techniques [in **The Sacred Pipe**] that Neihardt did in **Black Elk Speaks,** and his first chapter is essentially the same as Neihardt's, recounting

Black Elk and Neihardt in 1947.

the legend of the gift of the sacred pipe to the Sioux; **The Sacred Pipe** owes a great deal both to Neihardt and to the book Neihardt wrote. . . . We have the same narrator, Black Elk, and the same translator, Ben Black Elk; and in the first chapters, we have the same story, the appearance of White Buffalo Woman, who bestowed upon the Sioux their sacred pipe. In both books the account is essentially the same, but the manner of telling is different, and in the slight differences we can see how Neihardt's rendition "transformed" the facts into something closer to poetry. Here is Epes Brown's version:

> Early one morning, very many winters ago, two Lakota were out hunting with their bows and arrows, and as they were standing on a hill looking for game, they saw in the distance something coming towards them in a very strange and wonderful manner. When this mysterious thing came nearer to them, they saw that it was a very beautiful woman, dressed in white buckskin, and bearing a bundle on her back. Now this woman was so good to look at that one of the Lakota had bad intentions and told his friend of his desire, but this good man said that he must not have such thoughts, for surely this is a *waken* woman. The mysterious person was now very close to the men, and then putting down her bundle, she asked the one with bad intentions to come over to her. As the young man approached the mysterious woman, they were both covered by a great cloud, and soon when it lifted the sacred woman was standing there, and at her feet was the man with bad thoughts who was now nothing but bones, and terrible snakes were eating him.

Here is Neihardt's version:

> A very long time ago, they say, two scouts were out looking for bison; and when they came to the top of a high hill and looked north, they saw something coming a long way off, and when it came closer they cried out, "It is a woman—" and it was. Then one of the scouts, being foolish, had bad thoughts and spoke them, but the other said: "that is a sacred woman; throw all bad thoughts away." When she came still closer, they saw that she wore a fine white buckskin dress, that her hair was very long and that she was young and very beautiful. And she knew their thoughts and said in a voice that was like singing: "You do not know me, but if you want to do as you think, you may come." And the foolish one went; but just as he stood before her, there was a white cloud that came and covered them. And the beautiful woman came out of the cloud, and when it blew away the foolish man was a skeleton covered with worms.

Neihardt's account is more rhythmic, more dramatic, and more concrete. His syntax is simpler, and his sentences more climactic than Epes Brown's. Neihardt confines himself to simpler and shorter words and phrases than Brown does, and later in **The Sacred Pipe** Epes Brown used such words as "establish," "relationship," "participating," "originators," "regarded," "represent," "responsibility," "obligations," "circumstance," "influence," "observe," "customary," "demonstrate," and "constructing." Epes Brown uses the passive voice a good deal, and his sentences seldom vary in length or structure. (pp. 239-41)

Neihardt, throughout the book, used parallelism and other means to insure the rhythm of his prose, and he often began sentences with "And," a device that often makes the prose echo the King James version of the Bible.

> And while I stood there I saw more than I can tell and I understood more than I saw; for I was seeing in a sacred manner the shapes of all things in the spirit, and the shape of all shapes as they must live together like one being. And I saw that the sacred hoop of my people was one of many hoops that made one circle, wide as daylight and as starlight, and in the center grew one mighty flowering tree to shelter all the children of one mother and one father. And I saw that it was holy.

Neihardt said that, of course; his training as a poet made a difference in his writing the book, and such passages as this show how the peculiar collaboration that is *Black Elk Speaks* reads not only as the voice of a holy man, but of a poet as well. Neihardt listened to Black Elk's story with a poet's ear, and he retold it with a poet's gifts. Black Elk speaks, and Neihardt, under "religious obligation," gave that speech to the white world; but his own voice, giving form and beauty to that utterance, is softly audible behind every word.

If the book touches a generation that never saw a buffalo, never saw an eagle flying free, and never knew anything of Indian life except what it saw on the screen, it is because John Neihardt was the kind of man he was, and a writer of sensitivity and discipline. (pp. 241-42)

Black Elk said to him, "What I know was given to me for men and it is true and it is beautiful." He also said, "You were sent to save it." Neihardt did save it, by seeing in an illiterate and nearly blind old man who thought of himself as "a prisoner of war" a human being, and a man who was an instance of the tragedy of the West: the destruction inherent in progress; and of the tragedy of man: the eternal abyss between the vision and the reality. *Black Elk Speaks* is not just autobiography, or history, or anthropology, or philosophy, but literature, which incorporates all these things—and beauty besides. (p. 242)

> *Sally McCluskey, " 'Black Elk Speaks': And So Does John Neihardt," in* Western American Literature, *Vol. VI, No. 4, February, 1972, pp. 231-42.*

MICHAEL CASTRO   (essay date 1983)

[*Michael Castro is the author of* Interpreting the Indian: Twentieth-Century Poets and the Native American. *In the following excerpt from that work, he compares sections in the transcripts of the Black Elk–Neihardt interviews with the corresponding passages in the text of* Black Elk Speaks *to elucidate Neihardt's editorial contributions to the book.*]

The vision itself can be said to be the real subject of [*Black Elk Speaks*]. For Black Elk, it is all that gives his life importance. The vision does not compel him to renounce a real world; in his vision the spiritual and material worlds are inseparable. Black Elk's vision prophetically projects the world events that follow it, flashing onto the page the story of Sioux cultural unity and strength declining gradually into disunity and weakness. In his vision Black Elk is given special powers, in the form of gifts from the six grandfathers, with the implied responsibility for using these to stave off the impending tragedy he is shown, and the implied hope that somehow he will be able to restore "the broken hoop" and "flowering tree." Black Elk's struggle to understand this spiritual obligation parallels and intertwines with his people's struggle to walk the dark road from the Little Big Horn to Wounded Knee.

Despite the apocalyptic grandeur of this sacred vision, despite speaking for the holy man at the center of this book's events, Neihardt's triumphant achievement lies in keeping *Black Elk Speaks* on a movingly human level. We get to know Black Elk initially through what seem convincingly to be his own words. Neihardt did, in fact, follow closely the English translation of Black Elk's narrative, as recorded in a transcript prepared from the original interviews by his daughter Enid. Interestingly, however, a textual analysis by Sally McCluskey [see excerpt dated 1972] that compares the story of White Buffalo Woman as told by Black Elk in *Black Elk Speaks* and in *The Sacred Pipe* (1953), Joseph Epes Brown's narrative also drawn from conversations with Black Elk, finds the sentences in Neihardt's book to be more rhythmic, more dramatic, more concrete, simpler in syntax, and yet more apt to be so constructed as to rise to a climax. If nothing else, this stylistic heightening represents a further tribute to Neihardt's ear for Indian idiom, even if it meant that, for the most part, he had the good sense to leave well enough alone.

We further sense Black Elk's full humanity in *Black Elk Speaks* by following him from childhood to manhood to old age, through periods of laughter and tears, joy and despair, anguish and anger, confusion and power. We see the shaman and healer as a complex individual, sharing our own feelings and weaknesses, overwhelmed and bewildered at times by the special burdens imposed by his power in the midst of historical and spiritual forces that are beyond him. *Black Elk Speaks,* a book of prose, is, ironically, Neihardt's greatest poetic achievement. It may prove to be, equally ironically, Black Elk's greatest healing ceremony. As literature, it is tragedy in the greatest sense—a moving human story of declining fortune and ultimate fall from power, but one with a transcendent vision that inspires and uplifts all those who read it with understanding.

The story of how Neihardt managed to write this book is interesting and instructive, for no white writer before or since has so effectively managed to reveal Native American consciousness and spirituality in such a moving and human way. Neihardt's previous experience with the Omaha, his writings, his historical research, his spiritual attitudes and experiences all prepared him to write *Black Elk Speaks.* Similarly, the spiritual affinity quickly established between the two men helped in the book's making, as did Black Elk's active and enthusiastic guidance and collaboration. But it was the nature of his collaboration—his being so clearly the holy man and teacher fitted to the task of teaching the vision imposed—that had the most immediate and profound effect.

The transcript of the interviews on which *Black Elk Speaks* is based reveals that the book is not, as is often assumed, simply a literal recording of Black Elk's story. Much is, apparently, drawn verbatim from the original translation of Black Elk's account, but Neihardt exercised important editorial choices in shaping the final book. As he related in a 1971 interview with Sally McCluskey:

> *Black Elk Speaks* is a work of art with two collaborators, the chief one being Black Elk. My function was both creative and editorial. I think he knew the kind of person I was when I came to see him—I am referring to the mystical strain in me and all my work. He said, "You have been sent so that I may

teach you, and you receive what I know. It was given to me for men and it is true and it is beautiful and soon I will be under the grass." And I think he knew I was the tool—no, the medium—he needed for what he wanted to get said. And my attitude toward what he has said to me is one of religious obligation.

But it is absurd to suppose that the use of the first person singular is not a literary device, by which I mean that Black Elk did not sit and tell me his story in chronological order. At times considerable editing was necessary. . . . The beginning and the ending are mine; they are what he would have said if he had been able. At times I changed a word, a sentence, sometimes created a paragraph. And the translation—or rather the *transformation*—of what was given me was expressed so that it could be understood by the whole world.

Effectively to transform what Black Elk related "so that it could be understood by the whole world" required that Neihardt himself have a clear sense of what precisely needed to be understood—what, essentially, Black Elk's message actually was. As Neihardt wrote, "it was not the facts that mattered most"; rather, it was the transcendent teaching to be found in those facts of Black Elk's life, in the complex sequence of images that made up his vision, in "the mood and manner of the old man's narrative," and in the verbal and nonverbal ways in which Black Elk related to Neihardt and his two daughters during the spring of 1931 when the interviews were conducted. (pp. 85-7)

Black Elk's mood, manner, ceremonies, and remarks all underscored for Neihardt that the central message implicit in his story was "the brotherhood of man and the unity and holiness of all life."

The editorial decisions that Neihardt made were primarily intended, in a spirit of "religious obligation," to reinforce that main theme. Neihardt created several key passages and deleted several powerful but distracting sections of the vision to focus better this teaching of what Black Elk called "the great circle of relatedness which is the power of the world." The most significant of Neihardt's created additions is found in the "Great Vision" chapter and represents one of the most frequently quoted passages in the book. It occurs toward the end of the visionary sequence, after the fourth and final ascent in which Black Elk sees himself restoring his fractured and fragmented nation to health with the aid of a sacred healing herb of power. Following this vision, Black Elk flies on horseback to the top of a great mountain:

> I looked ahead and saw the mountains there with rocks and forests on them, and from the mountains flashed all colors upward to the heavens. Then I was on the highest mountain of them all, and round about beneath me was the whole hoop of the world. And while I stood there I saw more than I can tell and understood more than I saw; for I was seeing in a sacred manner the shapes of all things in the spirit, and the shapes of all shapes as they must live together as one being. And I saw that the sacred hoop of my people was one of many hoops that made one circle, wide as daylight and as starlight, and in the center grew one mighty flowering tree to shelter all the children of one mother and one father. And I saw that it was holy.

Prior to this point in the Great Vision account, Neihardt had followed Black Elk's original description, as recorded by

Enid, almost verbatim. But the transcribed speech that corresponds to this passage is much more prosaic:

> As [I] looked [I] could see the great mountains with rocks and forests on them. I could see all colors of light flashing out of the mountains toward the four quarters. Then [the grandfathers] took me on top of a high mountain where I could see all over the earth.

Neihardt evidently created this vision of "one of many hoops that made one circle" himself. Probably he did so for both poetic and thematic reasons. Neihardt chose this climactic moment in the account of the Great Vision to expand and develop Black Elk's recurrent imagery of the sacred hoop or circle in order to crystalize for the reader the universal significance of the book's central teaching.

Literarily, this creation by Neihardt proves a brilliant stroke, but Neihardt did not exactly pluck this vision out of the air. Black Elk had looked "all over the earth," and in an aside during the initial interviews he had told Neihardt, "the sacred hoop means the continents of the world and the people shall stand as one." The passage illustrates the kind of poetic license that Neihardt occasionally employed. When he made changes, Neihardt almost always used or developed Black Elk's imagery or thought rather than creating something totally new. The beginning and ending passages that Neihardt added, for instance, largely serve the literary need for an overview, and these likewise depend on the pervasive tree-and-hoop imagery and on comments attributed to Black Elk elsewhere in the transcript. Unlike most other poets who took liberties in translating Indian materials, Neihardt's changes tend to read like extensions of his informant's consciousness, reflecting less the white writer's independent and impressionistic judgment than a hard-earned mutual understanding and trust. Often, Neihardt relates, reaching this understanding proved "a grueling and difficult task requiring much patient effort and careful questioning of the interpreter." The degree of mutual commitment to the project and the spiritual affinity that quickly developed between the two men appear to be the main sources of the unique personal rapport that determined the ultimate success of the translation.

Just as he created, Neihardt likewise deleted several powerful sequences of Black Elk's vision. These omissions from *Black Elk Speaks,* never before discussed in the literary, anthropological, or psychological literature touching on the book, change the overall pattern and tone of the vision significantly—a fact that may shock religious, anthropological, or ethical purists. They are justifiable, however, if we accept the premise that is supported, I believe, in comments quoted earlier and attributed to both Neihardt and Black Elk in the transcript, that the book's purpose was to reveal not the original vision but the teaching of the Black Elk of 1930. Essentially, Neihardt's deletions tone down the militaristic and violent content of the vision, thereby enhancing the pacific message of unity.

The first change is small but significant. Neihardt described thus the fifth grandfather encountered by Black Elk during his Great Vision:

> He stretched his arms and turned into a spotted eagle hovering. "Behold," he said, "all the wings of the air shall come to you, and they and the wind and the stars shall be like relatives. You shall go across the earth with my power." Then the eagle soared above my head and fluttered there; and sud-

denly the sky was full of friendly wings, all coming toward me.

The implication left here is that the power of this grandfather is associated with the unity between man and the beings of the sky, and in Black Elk's original account, he does say in less ornate style that "things in the sky shall be like relatives." The original description continued, however, defining this grandfather's power quite differently:

> They shall take you across the earth with my power. Your grandfather shall attack an enemy and be unable to destroy him, but you will have the power to destroy. You shall go with courage. That is all.

In Black Elk's original account the vision of unity, which Neihardt used, is linked with the warlike power to destroy, which he omits.

The second deletion is even more important, for it occurs during the fourth ascent, prior to another vision of the unity and holiness of life included by Neihardt. In Neihardt's version, Black Elk is shown his entire nation starving and suffering and fighting continually. He is given a song of power and a sacred herb that he uses to heal his scrawny, starving horse. A vision of horses follows and then a vision of four virgins. The virgins, carrying the sacred gifts of the wooden cup of water, the white wing, the pipe, and the sacred hoop dance amid beautiful, healthy horses:

> The virgins danced, and all the circled horses. The leaves on the tree, the grasses on the hills and in the valleys, the waters in the creeks and in the rivers, and the lakes, the four-legged and the two-legged and the wings of the air—all danced together to the music of the stallion's song.

A more concise version of this vision of the unity and holiness of living things is found in Black Elk's original account. It is preceded there, however, by a long description of a vision that Black Elk has of himself attacking and defeating an enemy:

> The horse's tail was lightning and the flames were coming out of his horse's nose. As I went I could see nothing but I could only hear the thunder and lightning and of course I could see the flames. All the rest of the troops went around this enemy. A spirit said: "Eagle Wing Stretches, take courage, your turn has come." We got ready and started down on the cloud on our bay horses. One Side and I were coming down together. I could see the lightning coming off my arrows as I descended. Just as we were about to hit the earth, I struck something. I could hear thunder rolling and everyone cheered for me, saying: "Unhee!" (Kill!). . . . I made a swoop again on the west side of the enemy, whatever it was, and when I killed it, I looked at it and it was a dog, which had a very funny color. One side of him was white and the other side was black. Each one of them struck the dog (couped), meaning all had a hand in killing it. (This meant that when you go to war you should kill your enemy like a dog.)

As in the account of the fifth grandfather, Neihardt retained the vision of unity and holiness while dropping the militaristic vision linked to it.

The third and most striking omission occurs after the fourth ascent and the mountaintop vision that climaxes the "Great Vision" chapter. Neihardt's account follows Black Elk from the mountaintop to "the center of the world" where the grandfathers give him the daybreak-star herb, symbolic of his power to heal as a medicine man. In Black Elk's original account, however, he describes being given not one, but two gifts: the healing daybreak-star and a terrifying, destructive, "war herb":

> I looked down upon the earth and saw a flame which looked to be a man and I couldn't make it out quite. I heard all around voices of moaning and woe. It was sad on earth. I felt uneasy and I trembled. We went on the north side of this flaming man. I saw that the flame really was a man now. They showed me the bad in the form of a man who was all in black and lightning flashes going all over his body when he moved. He had horns. All around the animals and everything were dying and they were all crying. . . . They said: "Behold him. Someday you shall depend upon him. There will be a dispute all over the universe." As they said this the man transformed into a gopher and it stood up on its hind legs and turned around. Then this gopher transformed into a herb. This was the most powerful herb of all that I had gotten. It could be used in war and could destroy a nation.

The grandfathers give this "most powerful herb of all" to Black Elk, prophesying that "there will come a time of dispute of nations when you will defend your nation with this herb." The devastating destructive power of this war herb terrifies Black Elk. He does not want the awesome responsibility of having to use it, going on at some length in his original account to Neihardt about the power of this herb and his fear of it. Even in 1931, the memory of this herb seems vivid to him, its terror immediate. It reminds the modern reader of a nuclear weapon, so awesome does it seem to Black Elk. To Black Elk, the "soldier weed" is an ever-present force of evil for which he feels somehow responsible:

> If you touch this herb it will kill you at once. Nothing grows near it because it is killed immediately if it does. . . . This herb is in the Black Hills. Every animal that is near it dies. Around where it grows there are many skeletons always. This medicine belongs only to me—no one else knows what this herb looks like—and it looks like a little tree with crinkly leaves, reddish in color.

At one place in his original account Black Elk says that he was not old enough when the time came to use this herb. Later, he seems to contradict himself, saying that he was intended to use it when he was thirty-seven years old, but that he worried so much over the harm it would do to innocent women and children that he forsook ever using it and instead joined the Catholic church. Neihardt, unfortunately, apparently never sought a clarification. In any case, the war herb is the only part of the vision that Black Elk himself seems to reject. "It was too terrible to use," he tells Neihardt, "and I am glad I did not use it." Later he indicates that he is at peace with himself about this decision: "Perhaps I would have been a chief if I had obeyed [and used the herb], but I am satisfied that I didn't become a chief."

The deletion of the war-herb passage underscores the fact that Neihardt was more interested in the teachings of the man, Black Elk, who had had a Great Vision than in the literal content of the vision itself. He did not approach the writing of *Black Elk Speaks* with an anthropologist's absolute dedication to factual accuracy. Instead, he approached the collaboration as a poet, interested in images and in essences. He succeeded in telling, through the development of memorable imagery true to its original source, a moving human story that remains essentially Black Elk's. Neihardt's editorial decisions tended to reduce ambiguity and enhance the clarity and power of what he interpreted as Black Elk's essential teaching: "the brotherhood of man and the unity and holiness of all life."

Any controversy surrounding the poetic license employed by Neihardt in *Black Elk Speaks* is best put into perspective by these comments of the contemporary Sioux essayist Vine Deloria:

> Present debates center on the question of Neihardt's literary intrusions into Black Elk's system of beliefs and some scholars have said that the book reflects more of Neihardt than it does of Black Elk. It is, admittedly, difficult to discover if we are talking with Black Elk or John Neihardt, whether the vision is to be interpreted differently, and whether or not the positive emphasis which the book projects is not the optimism of two poets lost in the modern world and transforming drabness into an idealized world. Can it matter? The very nature of great religious teachings is that they encompass everyone who understands them and personalities become indistinguishable from the transcendent truth that is expressed. So let it be with *Black Elk Speaks.* That it speaks to us with simple and compelling language about an aspect of human experience and encourages us to emphasize the best that dwells within us is significant. Black Elk and John Neihardt would probably nod affirmatively to that statement and continue their conversation. It is good. It is enough [see Deloria, 1979, in Additional Bibliography].

The transcendent truth that Deloria speaks of is attested by the national and international popularity of *Black Elk Speaks.* Significantly, the book is highly regarded by contemporary Native Americans, including the Sioux. (pp. 89-95)

Black Elk Speaks paints a movingly human picture of Indian consciousness. It goes far toward pinning down the Native American's holistic awareness that is implied and suggested by other American poets. Black Elk's humane values are posed implicitly by Neihardt as a challenging alternative to whites. In the book we see Black Elk's magnanimity and sense of unity opposed to the selfish and competitive individualism he encounters in his associations with whites. We see underscored, through Black Elk's eyes, how the white society confines—confining the individual within himself, misfits in jails, Indians on reservations. Black Elk on the other hand, embodies the more open gesture of giving—the giving of food to the needy within the tribe, the giving of personal power to the people through ceremonialism and healing, the giving of the vision and its teaching to the world through *Black Elk Speaks.* (pp. 95-6)

> Michael Castro, "Translating Indian Consciousness: Lew Sarett and John G. Neihardt," in his Interpreting the Indian: Twentieth-Century Poets and the Native American, *University of New Mexico Press, 1983, pp. 71-97.*

CLYDE HOLLER (essay date 1984)

[*Holler is an American educator and critic. In the following*

discussion of Black Elk Speaks, *he demonstrates ways in which Neihardt misrepresented Black Elk's theology in transforming his narrative into a work of literature.*]

John G. Neihardt's *Black Elk Speaks: Being the Life Story of a Holy Man of the Oglala Sioux* (1932) is a literary work with considerable significance for the study of native American religion and culture. . . . [Black Elk] was a Lakota holy man (*wicaša wakan*) who matured in the twilight of the plains Indian culture, witnessed the events leading to the denouement of the Indian Wars at Wounded Knee in December 1890, and participated in the Ghost Dance, the great revitalization movement that swept the plains tribes in the last decade of the century. The historical and religious significance of *Black Elk Speaks* is thus considerable, for Black Elk provided Neihardt with a full account of his power vision and with firsthand information on Lakota religion and culture during an important period in Lakota history.

Yet major difficulties attend the appropriation of Neihardt's narrative for scholarly purposes. Neihardt was a literary artist, not an ethnologist or comparative religionist, and *Black Elk Speaks* is not a work of scholarship. The work's artistic virtues and its scholarly shortcomings are opposite sides of the same coin; each is a necessary function of the other. On the one hand, Neihardt created a genuine literary work of art that has had much wider circulation than any work of ethnography or religious scholarship and has done much to increase understanding and appreciation of traditional Lakota religion and culture. As a literary artist, Neihardt was able to present Black Elk's story in the context of a sympathetic and gripping portrait of Black Elk himself and the traditional culture that nurtured him. This artful combination of authentic information, deep human interest, and literary quality has made the work a widely used classic in courses in literature, anthropology, and religion.

On the other hand, Neihardt's literary reshaping of the Black Elk interviews raises important questions. In order to create a work of literature from the materials of the interviews, Neihardt necessarily sacrificed strict fidelity to the chronology and actual wording of the interviews. But Neihardt made more substantial changes as well. A comparison of the transcript of the interviews with the finished work reveals that Neihardt omitted certain aspects of Black Elk's vision that concerned military conquest and destruction. This sort of change is no longer merely stylistic in nature and clearly reveals the problematic dimension of *Black Elk Speaks.* In this particular case, Neihardt's omission of an important element of Black Elk's power vision affects not only our understanding of Black Elk, but also our understanding of the role of the *wicaša wakan* in Lakota religion. And Neihardt's creative and editorial changes are more extensive than previous studies suggest. This paper will show that Neihardt sacrificed strict reporting of Black Elk's theological convictions in order to express his own. There is thus a significant difference between the theology of Black Elk and the theology attributed to him in *Black Elk Speaks.* The ultimate message of the book, not merely its details, is Neihardt's, not Black Elk's. (pp. 19-20)

The significant cross-cultural aspects of the collaboration between Neihardt and Black Elk that produced *Black Elk Speaks* are immediately evident in Neihardt's accounts of his initial meeting with Black Elk [see excerpt dated 1972]. To begin with, Black Elk impressed his visitors by appearing to be expecting them. This and similar experiences convinced

Neihardt that Black Elk had "supernormal powers." Neihardt was conversant enough with Sioux culture to have brought cigarettes, and the group smoked together, thus establishing the appropriate context for the meeting. According to Neihardt, Black Elk announced that he could feel in Neihardt a strong will to know the things of the other world and that a spirit standing behind Neihardt had compelled him to come so that Black Elk could teach him. Since Neihardt had thus been sent by the spirits, Black Elk was willing to instruct him despite the traditional taboo. Black Elk then presented Neihardt with a representation of the morning star, the symbol of the wisdom and sacred knowledge of the Lakotas: "Here you see the Morning Star. Who sees the Morning Star shall see more, for he shall be wise." After explaining the symbolism of this sacred ornament, which he had worn while officiating at the Sun Dance, Black Elk began to speak of his power vision, deflecting Neihardt's questions about the original subject of his visit, Sioux history. Finally Black Elk announced that Neihardt had been sent to save his sacred knowledge for men, and asked Neihardt to return in the spring, which was the appropriate time to receive his instruction.

Black Elk's words and actions seem so odd from the point of view of European culture that one scholar [David H. Brumble] has suggested that Neihardt simply invented the account of his initial meeting with Black Elk in order to serve his own literary ends. But it is important to realize that Neihardt's visit to Black Elk set in motion a ritual process that must be interpreted with due sensitivity to Lakota cultural conventions. Neihardt approached Black Elk for help in the traditional way a Lakota holy man is approached, with the offer of tobacco (*opagi*). By smoking with Neihardt, Black Elk accepted the commission Neihardt brought him. Within this ritual context, Black Elk's style of speaking is natural and appropriate, for, in the context of Lakota culture, Black Elk's words and actions convey specific ritual messages. **William K. Powers's** ethnographic narrative, *Yuwipi,* gives an account of the dialogue between Plenty Wolf, a modern Lakota holy man, and Wayne Runs Again, a person seeking Plenty Wolf's services for the healing ritual called *Yuwipi.* Powers makes it clear that Plenty Wolf does not know Wayne Runs Again is coming, and, because of failing eyesight, even has to ask his wife who is at the gate. Yet, in a striking parallel to Neihardt's account, when Wayne greets Plenty Wolf with a ritual greeting (*Hau Tunkašila,* Hau Grandfather) instead of the conventional one (*Hau kola,* Hau friend), Plenty Wolf too acts as if he knew Wayne was coming, and speaks of spirit presences:

> Wayne came closer so he could be recognized, and the old man greeted him with "*Hau Takoja,*" Hau Grandson, the appropriate ritual response. "They said you would come," he said in Lakota, and this astonished Wayne. "The spirits," Plenty Wolf added in English, and laughed a "he-he-he" not in keeping with the dignity of his vocation. . . . Wayne was flustered because the old man had expected him, and he tried to explain his reason in Lakota but faltered. . . . Plenty Wolf was patient. He said, "Smoke first. *Cannunpa.*" . . . After they had smoked Plenty Wolf asked the boy what was troubling him.

It is important to realize that Plenty Wolf is not necessarily claiming literal precognition, but is instead continuing the traditional dialogue initiated by the proper ritual greetings. The intention of this dialogue, and indeed the intention of the

entire *Yuwipi* ritual, is to relate the client's actions to the traditional values of Lakota religion. This ritual dialogue thus serves both to establish and to confirm the proper relationship of the holy man to the person seeking his services and to the powers of the other world. As Harold H. Oliver's studies in the hermeneutic of myth have shown, the intention of mythical speech is "relational," not "referential." Thus understood, Plenty Wolf's speech does not mean "there exist spirits who informed me of your arrival" (referential), but rather "your coming is appropriate" (relational). Since right relationship is perhaps the central principle of native American, and especially Sioux, religion, it is not surprising that the Lakota holy man speaks in such a way as to place his transaction with his client, the person seeking his aid or instruction, in a relational (sacred) context, by relating their actions to the other world of the spirits. (pp. 21-3)

The interviews, like the initial meeting, . . . took place in a traditional ritual context. Black Elk's instruction of Neihardt was a matter of public concern to the tribe, and the feast served to set the interviews in the context of the community, with the active presence and support of distinguished elders, some of whom (Fire Thunder, Standing Bear, Iron Hawk) assisted Black Elk in providing additional information during the interviews. It is important to realize that this indicates that while Neihardt was acting as a private individual, Black Elk acted as the representative of his tribe in instructing Neihardt in Lakota sacred knowledge. This is the key to understanding the collaboration from Black Elk's perspective. Black Elk hoped that his people as a whole would benefit from Neihardt's book, which would increase understanding of traditional Lakota religion and lifeways, symbolized by the flowering tree in the center of the Sun Dance circle. By instructing Neihardt, Black Elk understands himself to be carrying on his vision-given role as the intercessor for his people, whose responsibility it is to make the tree flower for the people. (p. 26)

[The] rituals, in addition to expressing Black Elk's hope that his teaching would help the Lakotas and whites walk the Good Road of peace together, express the great responsibility now devolving on Neihardt. Black Elk hoped that by giving his power vision to Neihardt, the traditional religion and lifeways of the Lakotas would be respected by all people, and the sacred tree would thus flower in the new context of the world in which both Lakotas and whites must live together. These rituals thus reflect the way in which traditional societies control the use of sacred knowledge, by restricting its use to responsible parties bound by ties of kinship, discipleship, and religious obligation. In addition to the information he had come to gain, Neihardt had new ties of kinship to the Oglalas, of discipleship to Black Elk, and of religious obligation to the Grandfathers, all binding him to a sensitive and appropriate use of Lakota sacred materials.

But what was the proper use of this material in the very different cultural context of English literature? Black Elk could tell Neihardt of his hopes for the book, but he could not tell him how to realize them in the different context of literate expression. Enid Neihardt had taken extensive shorthand notes of the interviews, and she quickly provided Neihardt with a typescript. Neihardt thus had an accurate record of Black Elk's words, as translated by Ben Black Elk. The major decision Neihardt had to make was how to shape this material most effectively. Neihardt could have published the transcript more or less verbatim, in the manner of ethnographic interviews, but as a literary man, Neihardt was not sympathetic with ethnography. So his first decision was tacit: *Black Elk Speaks* would be literature, not ethnography. Neihardt could have chosen to cast the work in the form of either biography or autobiography, since he wished to set Black Elk's life story in the context of the Indian Wars. Neihardt's decision to write in the first person, to tell Black Elk's life story as autobiography, is responsible for much of the power of the book. But this decision also introduced another cross-cultural factor, since autobiography, unlike biography, clearly implies that the point of view on the life being told is that of the speaker (Black Elk), not the collaborator. The reader of *Black Elk Speaks* is thus dependent on Neihardt's integrity and cross-cultural sensitivity, for Black Elk was not in a position to read and correct the manuscript before publication, as is usual in "as told to" autobiography. Neihardt was aware of these problems, but he was clearly confident that he understood Black Elk's intentions and faithfully mediated them to the white reader, despite the creative function he necessarily performed in the collaboration. . . . Neihardt also expressed this confidence in a striking way by changing, in 1961, the author's credit from "as told to John G. Neihardt" to "as told through John G. Neihardt."

The extent to which Neihardt's confidence in his transformation of Black Elk's words from their Lakota context to the context of English literature is justified can be judged by comparison of *Black Elk Speaks* to Enid Neihardt's transcript of the actual interviews, which now exists in two versions. The first point to emerge from examination of the transcripts is that Black Elk's words have at this point already begun to be divorced from their ritual context, which can be reconstructed only partially from Enid Neihardt's diary, occasional indications in the transcripts, various letters, and Neihardt's fragmentary statements about the collaboration. The severing of Black Elk's words from their ritual context is the first giant step away from the Lakota world in which Black Elk's instruction took place. The loss of the full ritual context of the interviews is the greatest loss attributable to Neihardt's lack of anthropological training. It evidently did not occur to him that ritual description was relevant, and his cross-cultural sensitivity seems to fail him to a certain extent with respect to ritual. . . . To the extent that Black Elk's words are divorced in the transcript from their communal ritual context, Black Elk has already become the subject of a modern autobiography, a (European) "I."

As far as Neihardt's actual editing of the words preserved in the transcripts is concerned, it is worth noting that Neihardt utilized most of the material in the transcript, though he did omit certain portions likely to interfere with the favorable reception of the book by its intended audience. Thus he omits the part of Black Elk's account of the giving of the sacred pipe to the Lakotas that describes the birth of an old woman from a buffalo, some of the kill talks, a story of a priest who died soon after interfering with a traditional ritual, a portion of Black Elk's account of his vision dealing with a "soldier weed" to be used to wipe out the whites, and Black Elk's mention of his Catholicism. The chronological organization of the transcript, as judged by comparison of the 1980 to the 1931 transcript (which is in the order used in *Black Elk Speaks*) reveals that Neihardt reorganized the transcript for greatest chronological coherence and dramatic effect. The diction of the transcript is rough in places, . . . and Neihardt exercised his literary art in order to create a graceful and dignified English idiom for Black Elk, which, according to Mc-

Cluskey [see excerpt dated 1972], echoes the King James Version of the Bible. These editorial and stylistic changes account for much of the beauty and power of the book and are enough to establish that *Black Elk Speaks* is a literary work and not merely a record of Black Elk's words. But Neihardt's account of Black Elk's involvement in the Ghost Dance reveals that his transformation of the Black Elk interviews into a work of literature had an interpretive dimension as well, so that the ultimate message and theology of *Black Elk Speaks*—and not merely the chronology and diction—are Neihardt's, not Black Elk's.

The theology of *Black Elk Speaks* emerges clearly from Neihardt's interpretation of the Ghost Dance, the great revitalization movement that emanated from a vision of the Paiute Messiah, Wovoka, in 1889 and spread to most of the Western Indian tribes in a remarkably short time. . . . As a new religion, the Ghost Dance emerged in the context of the crushing domination of the Indian by the white man and the consequent loss of Indian autonomy and devaluation of traditional values. The Ghost Dance was nativistic, and its doctrine united many tribes that had previously been hostile or indifferent to one another in a common rite that expressed deep yearning for the traditional lifeways of the Indians. The central doctrine of the Ghost Dance, as reported by its official investigator, was "that the time will come when the whole Indian race, living and dead, will be reunited upon a regenerated earth, to live a life of aboriginal happiness, forever free from death, disease, and misery." This was to be hastened by, or at least anticipated in, the Ghost Dance itself, in which the dancers entered a trance and had visions of their relations already living on the regenerated earth. (pp. 28-32)

The eventual appearance of troops called out to control the disturbances [resulting from the Ghost Dance] led some 3,000 Lakotas from Pine Ridge and Rosebud reservations, including Black Elk, to break out and flee to the Badlands. The attempted arrest of Sitting Bull, which led to his being killed while resisting arrest, increased panic among the Sioux. The outbreak was nearly under control, with the Indians who had fled to the Badlands encamped near the Pine Ridge agency, when the attempt to disarm Big Foot's band resulted in the massacre at Wounded Knee that is bitterly remembered by the Sioux today. (p. 32)

In the light of Neihardt's interpretation of the Ghost Dance . . . as the tragic mistake of the Sioux people, it is understandable that in *Black Elk Speaks,* Black Elk seems clearly to repudiate the Messiah and the Ghost Dance:

> We danced [the Ghost Dance] there, and another vision came to me. I saw a Flaming Rainbow, like the one I had seen in my first great vision. Below the rainbow was a tepee made of cloud. Over me there was a spotted eagle soaring, and he said to me: "Remember this." That was all I saw and heard.
>
> I have thought much about this since, and I have thought that this was where I made my great mistake. I had had a very great vision, and I should have depended only upon that to guide me to the good. But I followed the lesser visions that had come to me while dancing on Wounded Knee Creek. The vision of the Flaming Rainbow was to warn me, maybe; and I did not understand. I did not depend upon the great vision as I should have done; I depended upon the two sticks that I had seen in the lesser vision. It is hard to follow one great vision in this world of darkness and of many

changing shadows. Among those shadows men get lost.

This is Neihardt's own interpretation of Black Elk's great and tragic mistake as his participation in the Ghost Dance outbreak that led to Wounded Knee. What Black Elk really said was quite different:

> The last vision I had was in a ghost dance again. I was back here again. The only thing I saw was towards the west I saw a flaming rainbow that I had seen in the first vision. On either side of this rainbow was a cloud and right above me there was an eagle soaring, and he said to me: "Behold them, the thunderbeing nation, you are relative-like to them. Hence, remember this." During the war I was supposed to use this rainbow and the thunderbeings but I did not do it. I only depended on the two sticks that I had gotten from the vision. I used the red stick.

> It seems to me on thinking it over that I have seen the son of the Great Spirit himself. All through this I depended on my Messiah vision whereas perhaps I should have depended on my first great vision which had more power and this might have been where I made my great mistake.

Neihardt's Black Elk regrets joining the Ghost Dance; the real Black Elk regrets not using a more powerful vision against the whites. Neihardt's omission of the phrase "I have seen the son of the Great Spirit himself" (the Messiah) is consistent with Neihardt's omission of Black Elk's explicit claim to have invented the ghost shirt ("So I started the ghost shirt") and to have been the chief ghost dancer. It is, of course, unlikely that Black Elk would have mentioned or invented these details if he had in fact repudiated the Messiah, and Black Elk nowhere indicates that he is ashamed of the militant role that he actually played in the Ghost Dance disturbances. Neihardt is able to imply that Black Elk was unfaithful to the original vision by converting to the Ghost Dance only because he has already omitted the warlike and destructive aspects of the great vision itself, with its "soldier weed" that Black Elk was to use to wipe out the whites. The great vision was, if anything, more militant than the Messiah vision. In both these instances, Neihardt omits or alters statements that indicate that Black Elk was affected by the blindness Neihardt discerns in traditional Lakota religion.

The literary strategy of *Black Elk Speaks* becomes clear when considered in the light of Neihardt's belief that the militant perversion of the Ghost Dance was the tragic mistake of the Sioux people. . . . [It was Neihardt's] intention to use the Black Elk interviews to tell the story of the Sioux people, and *Black Elk Speaks* thus takes Black Elk's life to be symbolic of the life of the entire Sioux nation. The literary means to this end was Neihardt's creation of a beginning and ending for the book setting Black Elk's life in the larger context of Sioux history, thus establishing the symbolic interpretation of Black Elk's life as the life of the Sioux. In the beginning of the book, Black Elk is made to say, "My friend, I am going to tell you the story of my life, as you wish; and if it were only the story of my life I think I would not tell it; for what is one man that he should make much of his winters, even when they bend him like a heavy snow?" The ending Neihardt devised for *Black Elk Speaks* carries this theme further, by tying together Black Elk's personal life, the Ghost Dance,

and the final death of the old Sioux religion at Wounded Knee:

> And so it was all over.

> I did not know then how much was ended. When I look back now from this high hill of my old age, I can still see the butchered women and children lying heaped and scattered all along the crooked gulch as plain as when I saw them with eyes still young. And I can see that something else died there in the bloody mud, and was buried in the blizzard. A people's dream died there. It was a beautiful dream.

> And I, to whom so great a vision was given in my youth,—you see me now a pitiful old man who has done nothing, for the nation's hoop is broken and scattered. There is no center any longer, and the sacred tree is dead.

These are the most quoted words in *Black Elk Speaks,* although most commentators have not been aware that Black Elk never spoke them. This ending to Black Elk's life story shows that the book has as much affinity with the genre of tragedy as it does with autobiography. "As literature, it is tragedy in the greatest sense—a moving human story of declining fortune and ultimate fall from power, but one with a transcendent vision which inspires and uplifts all those who read it with understanding" [Michael Castro; see excerpt dated 1983]. The extent of this tragedy is expressed in Neihardt's decision to end Black Elk's life story at Wounded Knee, despite the fact that Black Elk was only twenty-seven in 1890 and had lived another forty years when Neihardt interviewed him in 1931. It is as if Black Elk died at Wounded Knee, and in the literary structure of *Black Elk Speaks,* Wounded Knee is the entire Sioux culture's symbolic death. Not only is Neihardt's Black Elk a pitiful old man who has done nothing, but his people's dream is dead, "the nation's hoop is broken"; "there is no center . . . and the sacred tree is dead."

Black Elk Speaks is thus a literary work that interprets Black Elk's life as a tragedy that symbolizes the larger tragedy of the American Indian. The autobiographical form of Neihardt's tragedy implies that Black Elk himself shared Neihardt's interpretation of the Ghost Dance and of his own life, and Neihardt explicitly claims this when he says that the final three paragraphs are what Black Elk "would have said if he had been able." But as the foregoing has shown, there are significant discrepancies between Black Elk's actual statements and Neihardt's interpretation of them in *Black Elk Speaks.* For Neihardt, the essential theological point is that the traditional Lakota religion and culture are dead. But as we have seen, it is precisely Black Elk's intention in collaborating with Neihardt to revive the traditional wisdom and values of the Lakotas, to "make the tree flower" even in the hostile context of the white world. (pp. 34-7)

The comparison of the transcript of the Black Elk interviews with the final text shows that the theology of *Black Elk Speaks* is Neihardt's, not Black Elk's. It remains to consider the significance of this conclusion for the study of native American religion. Vine Deloria, Jr., [in an introduction to *Black Elk Speaks;* see Additional Bibliography] argues that "Neihardt's literary intrusions into Black Elk's system of beliefs" do not matter because "the very nature of great religious teachings is that they encompass everyone who understands them and personalities become indistinguishable from the transcendent truth that is expressed." This irenic view is tempered by Deloria's belief that Black Elk's works will become the canon or the core of a North American Indian theological canon that will eventually challenge both the Eastern and Western traditions. Deloria's remarks call to mind the analogy between *Black Elk Speaks* and the synoptic Gospels. John Neihardt, like John Mark, transformed the oral teachings of a great religious master into a narrative work of literature that preserved those teachings for a dominant culture based on literature, not on story and parable. And, as Deloria implies, scholarly research in both cases leads to the conclusion that the theology of the master and the theology of the disciple are not necessarily identical. But Deloria urges scholars and native American theologians not to make an effort parallel to that of New Testament scholars to distinguish the theology of the master from that of the evangelists: "That [*Black Elk Speaks*] speaks to us with simple and compelling language about an aspect of human experience and encourages us to emphasize the best that dwells within us is sufficient."

There is no doubt that this is sufficient to ensure that *Black Elk Speaks* will retain a permanent place in the canon of American literature. But there is good reason to doubt that it is sufficient to satisfy the demands of a pan-Indian theological canon. It is not only that Neihardt disagrees with Black Elk on the interpretation of the Ghost Dance or on the viability of the traditional Lakota lifeways, for Neihardt's negative judgment on these aspects of Black Elk's faith may well be shared by future native American theologians. The deeper discontinuity between Neihardt and Black Elk is expressed in their disparate attitudes toward ritual. As this paper has shown, Black Elk's theology is expressed in ritual, while Neihardt's is expressed in the medium of literary symbolism and narrative. Neihardt found it possible to accept that Black Elk possessed supernormal power, but he found it impossible to accept that Black Elk's rituals had power, for the relational meaning of ritual, and its transforming power, was largely lost on Neihardt. The intention of Black Elk's ritual giving of his vision to Neihardt was to "make the tree flower." The message of *Black Elk Speaks,* on the other hand, is that the tree is dead. The deepest and most essential changes Neihardt made in the editing of the transcript express this conviction and suppress Black Elk's continued faith in the efficacy of Lakota ritual. This fact reveals the essential difference between the Gospels and *Black Elk Speaks* that renders the parallel between them invalid. The Gospels express the conviction of the Christian community that though the master is dead, his teaching and real presence are alive in the ritual process of the community of faith. In *Black Elk Speaks,* the master lives on, but the ritual process is dead. Neihardt is thus not Black Elk's evangelist, but his tragic poet, and the tragic poet of Indian religion and culture. (pp. 40-1)

Clyde Holler, "Lakota Religion and Tragedy: The Theology of 'Black Elk Speaks'," in Journal of the American Academy of Religion, *Vol. LII, No. 1, March, 1984, pp. 19-45.*

N. SCOTT MOMADAY (essay date 1984)

[*Momaday is a native American novelist, memoirist, and poet whose works have been praised for their imaginative interweaving of native American myth, history, and contemporary experience. He was awarded a Pulitzer Prize in 1969 for his novel* House Made of Dawn, *the story of a contemporary native*

Black Elk presents a rosary to a youthful catechumen.

American. In the following excerpt, Momaday discusses Black Elk Speaks *as an example of the native American oral tradition.*]

John Gneisenau Neihardt must . . . have had the sense that he had entered into the realm of the sacred when he visited Black Elk in May 1931 on the Pine Ridge Indian Reservation in South Dakota. Earlier, on the occasion of their first meeting, Black Elk had said to him:

> There is so much to teach you. What I know was given to me for men and it is true and it is beautiful. Soon I shall be under the grass and it will be lost. You were sent to save it, and you must come back so that I can teach you [see Neihardt excerpt dated 1972].

If this statement surprised the Nebraska poet he did not acknowledge it. Neihardt accepted this trust more than willingly. If the old Sioux holy man's chief purpose in seeing Neihardt was, as he said, "to save his Great Vision for men," Neihardt would be the instrument of preservation devoting his considerable talents to the task. Here is one of the truly fortunate collaborations in our American heritage, bridging times, places, and cultures.

It is through the intercession of John Neihardt, then, that we have access to a principal world view of one of the major tribes of American Indians. *Black Elk Speaks* is now deservedly recognized as a classic in literature by teachers in our high schools and universities. We know this without knowing what the book is, exactly, without knowing precisely where to place it in our traditional categories of learning. Such rubrics as Literature, Anthropology, Folklore, and Religious Studies, not to mention American Studies, and Native American Studies, seem equally appropriate frames of reference, immediate contexts in which the book exerts its prominence. Indeed, the book bears importantly upon all of these categories and more.

But we need not concern ourselves with labels here, any more than we need concern ourselves with the question of authorship or the quality of translation or transcription. It is sufficient that *Black Elk Speaks* is an extraordinarily human document—and beyond that the record of a profoundly spiritual journey, the pilgrimage of a people towards their historical fulfillment and culmination, towards the accomplishment of a worthy destiny. That the pilgrimage was in a tragic sense abruptly ended at Wounded Knee in 1890, that Black Elk's words at last take a tragic turn—"There is no center any longer, and the sacred tree is dead"—is of little consequence in the long run, I believe. For in that sudden and absolute investment in the tragic, in the whole assumption of a tragic sense, there is immeasurable vindication, the achievement of a profound and permanent dignity, an irreducible impression on the records of human history.

I have stated above that I believe *Black Elk Speaks* is preeminently a human document. By this I mean not that this account tells us of the Oglala Sioux, or even that it reveals to us the extraordinary man Black Elk (or, indeed, that other extraordinary man, John Neihardt), but that it tells us of ourselves and of all humankind. I am interested in the universal elements of the narrative, first as an example of oral tradition, then as literature.

Black Elk's account, of course, is centered in the oral tradition. What does this mean, exactly? It means that the storyteller is illiterate and that his understanding and his use of language are determined by considerations of which we, who function within the written tradition, are only vaguely aware at best. If we are to understand the basic, human elements of Black Elk's account, we must first understand what those considerations are.

Black Elk is first and foremost a storyteller. I use that term advisedly. In the oral tradition the storyteller is he who takes it upon himself to speak formally, as Black Elk does in this case. He assumes responsibility for his words, for what is created at the level of his human voice. He runs the risk of language, and language is full of risks—that it might be miscarried, that it might be abused in one or more of a thousand ways. His function is essentially creative, inasmuch as language is essentially creative. He creates himself, and his listeners, through the power of his perception, his imagination, his expression, his devotion to important detail. He realizes the power and beauty of language; he believes in the efficacy of words and is careful to use them with precision remembering their efficacy. He is a holy man; his function is sacred. He is the living bridge between the human and the divine.

Perhaps we can better examine these matters if we look at a specific passage. Early on in Black Elk's story he recounts the following incident:

It was when I was five years old that my Grandfa-

ther made me a bow and some arrows. The grass was young and I was on horseback. A thunder storm was coming from where the sun goes down, and just as I was riding into the woods along a creek, there was a kingbird sitting on a limb. This was not a dream, it happened. And I was going to shoot at the kingbird with the bow my grandfather made, when the bird spoke and said: "The clouds all over are one-sided." Perhaps it meant that all the clouds were looking at me. And then it said: "Listen! A voice is calling you!" Then I looked up at the clouds, and two men were coming there, headfirst like arrows slanting down; and as they came, they sang a sacred song and the thunder was like drumming. I will sing it for you. The song and the drumming were like this:

"Behold, a sacred voice is calling you; All over the sky a sacred voice is calling."

I sat there gazing at them, and they were coming from the place where the giant lives (north). But when they were very close to me, they wheeled about toward where the sun goes down, and suddenly they were geese. Then they were gone, and the rain came with a big wind and a roaring.

I did not tell this vision to any one. I liked to think about it, but I was afraid to tell it.

It seems to me that such a passage as this one reflects very closely the nature and character of oral tradition, especially the American Indian oral tradition. Taken as a whole, this account appears to be more or less like other vision stories in the same tradition. Let us consider, for the sake of comparison, this somewhat similar Kiowa story.

Long ago there were bad times. The Kiowas were hungry and there was no food. There was a man who heard his children cry from hunger, and he went out to look for food. He walked four days and became very weak. On the fourth day he came to a great canyon. Suddenly there was thunder and lightning. A voice spoke to him and said: "Why are you following me. What do you want?" The man was afraid. The thing standing before him was covered with feathers. The man answered that the Kiowas were hungry. "Take me with you," the voice said, "and I will give you whatever you want." From that day Tai-me has belonged to the Kiowas.

Both narratives proceed from a cosmology inherent in the Plains culture, a cosmology at the center of which is the Sun Dance. Both narratives proceed then from a vested interest in the so-called Vision Quest—proceed from, perpetuate, and celebrate that ideal. In both narratives the vision (and with it the invisible voice; we must not lose the force of the oral, audible element) is paramount. In both, that which is seen is strange and unaccountable. And both stories are extremely portentous. Both of these accounts are revelations, but what is revealed is suspended in doubt. The meaning of these stories is not to be discovered at once. The quest extends not only to the vision but most importantly beyond it to the central meaning itself. Finally, both questers after visions are afraid, the one of what he sees, the other to tell of what he has seen. This detail of being afraid underscores the supernatural center of the vision and of its relation in language as well.

The vision *and* the story in which it is conveyed are intrinsically powerful.

The Kiowa story is self-contained. Black Elk's account is, of course, the fragment of a much larger whole. Notwithstanding, there is a perceptible integrity even in the fragment and little if any extraneous matter. The implications and consequent meanings of the passage are important. That the gift of a bow and arrows should come from a grandfather, that the arrows should prefigure the two men in the vision, that the sacred voice "all over the sky" which informs the sacred song should anticipate a rain storm complete with "a big wind and a roaring"—these things are entirely in keeping with both the structure and character of oral tradition.

The attitude of the storyteller towards his story is in the oral tradition appropriately formal. Black Elk stands apart from his story in a sense. He is careful not to intrude upon it. It is not a personal story, not autobiographical essentially; essentially it is a testament. The telling of the story is a spiritual act, and the story-teller has a profound conviction of the religious dimension in which the act is accomplished. Everything comes together in the telling of the story, forming a fabric of whole cloth yet distinguishing elements in their particularity. A passage from *Black Elk Speaks* vividly illustrates the complex interweaving of elements which form this seamless religious garment:

> You have noticed that everything an Indian does is in a circle, and that is because the Power of the World always works in circles, and everything tries to be round. In the old days when we were a strong and happy people, all our power came to us from the sacred hoop of the nation, and so long as the hoop was unbroken, the people flourished.
>
> The flowering tree was the living center of the hoop, and the circle of the four quarters nourished it. The east gave peace and light, the south gave warmth, the west gave rain, and the north with its cold and mighty wind gave strength and endurance. This knowledge came to us from the outer world with our religion.
>
> Everything the Power of the World does is done in a circle. The sky is round, and I have heard that the earth is round like a ball, and so are all the stars. The wind, in its great power, whirls. Birds made their nests in circles, for theirs is the same religion as ours. The sun comes forth and goes down again in a circle. The moon does the same, and both are round. Even the seasons form a great circle in their changing, and always come back again to where they were.
>
> The life of a man is a circle from childhood to childhood, and so it is in everything where power moves. Our tepees were round like the nests of birds, and these were always set in a circle, the nation's hoop, a nest of many nests, where the Great Spirit meant for us to hatch our children.

I point to this passage in particular, not only because it is an eloquent explication of the Lakota world view at its center with the synthesis of everything gathered together in its unity, but also because it describes the shape of the story itself. Implicit in this passage is the acknowledgement that language, too, is circular. Words follow one upon another, and in the formulation of meaning they return upon themselves. *Black Elk Speaks* is a remarkable example of this principle. It is the circumference of itself; it begins and ends at the same

point. It is to Neihardt's credit that he intuitively perceived the underlying structure of the oral tradition and instead of delving into it to discern historical or philosophical truth, merely helped to assist the story to achieve its final polished form.

So the story begins with a reflective mood in which the old man establishes the basic shape of the narration:

> . . . These things I shall remember by the way, and often they may seem to be the very tale itself, as when I was living them in happiness and sorrow. But now that I can see it all as from a lonely hilltop, I know it was the story of a mighty vision given to a man too weak to use it; of a holy tree that should have flourished in a people's heart with flowers and singing birds, and now is withered; and of a people's dream that died in bloody snow.

And so the story is begun. And in the end it comes round to this:

> I did not know then how much was ended. When I look back now from this high hill of my old age, I can still see the butchered women and children lying heaped and scattered all along the crooked gulch as plain as when I saw them with eyes still young. And I can see that something else died there in the bloody mud, and was buried in the blizzard. A people's dream died there. It was a beautiful dream.

Thus there is a consistent symmetry in Black Elk's account. He is at every moment aware of the aesthetic foundation of the storyteller's function. He orders his words. He fashions his language according to ancient conceptions of proportions, design, and perspective. The aesthetic realization of his story is not immediately of his own invention. Rather he fits his narrative into the universal scheme which ensures that it will complete itself of its own accord. The motion of his voice is the motion of the earth itself. Everything returns to its origin and in becoming circular establishes its own unity and integrity.

To the extent that Black Elk re-creates his vision in words, he re-creates himself and in so doing re-affirms himself. He also affirms that he has existence in the element of language, and this affirmation is preeminently creative. He declares, in effect: *Behold, I give you my vision in these terms, and in the process I give you myself.* In the ultimate achievement of the storyteller's purpose, he projects his spirit into language and therefore beyond the limits of his time and place. It is an act of sheer transcendence. Spiritually he will survive as long as his words survive. He inhabits his vision, and in the telling his vision becomes timeless. The storyteller and the story told are one.

John Neihardt was a man of letters; indeed he was a poet and he was an epic poet. His poet's sensibility must have made him peculiarly receptive to Black Elk's recitation and the measured cadence of Black Elk's words must certainly have informed him that here was a substance unique in its own kind. Even though he could not understand the language that Black Elk spoke, we cannot doubt, I think, that he discerned quite readily the rhythms, the inflections and alliterations of the holy man's speech. And this discernment was worth a great deal. Without it the book would have lapsed into mere biography of an Indian. With the rhythms and pacing well reproduced, we have a masterpiece of transformation of the oral tradition from one language and culture into another without the loss of the essential spirit of the original narration. Consider the rhythm of this paragraph:

> Late in the Moon of the Dark Red Calf or early in the Moon of the Snowblind, Spotted Tail, the Brule, with some others, came to us. His sister was Crazy Horse's mother. He was a great chief and a great warrior before he went over to the Wasichus. I saw him and I did not like him. He was fat with Wasichu food and we were lean with famine.

The quality of writing here is essentially poetic. Consider the sustained hissing of the "s" sounds throughout, or the alliteration in the final sentence. But I mean not only the immediate quality which informs the translation, but also that fundamental quality which inheres in the substance and integrity of the statement itself. The lyrical names, the precise ordering of detail, the evocation of the great warrior ideal, these constitute a kind of common denominator whose fundamental nature is affirmed by the mere arrangement of them in the speech. These things constitute a kind of common denominator which establishes a bridge between the poem and the song, between literature and legend, between the written tradition and the oral tradition. The transformation of speech into writing (and particularly *this* speech into *this* writing) is a matter of great importance, I believe. And Neihardt believed it also. He brought extraordinary care, sympathy and dedication to his task of faithfully reproducing the essence of the speech. (pp. 30-7)

John Neihardt was committed to a written tradition, and his commitment was greater than most people similarly engaged. He made much good of it in his lifetime. In *Black Elk Speaks,* he exceeds his tradition for a moment and makes that moment live forever thereafter. He is made the gift of another man's voice, and he allows us to hear it distinctly, in the full realization of its meaning.

My day, I have made it holy.

Like the sun of this song, which sanctifies the day in its light, Black Elk makes holy his story in the telling. The sacred vision is preserved "for men." For this task, successfully completed, among other things, we owe to the poet John Neihardt our best thanks. (p. 38)

> N. Scott Momaday, *"To Save a Great Vision,"* in A Sender of Words: Essays in Memory of John G. Neihardt, *edited by Vine Deloria, Jr., Howe Brothers, 1984, pp. 30-8.*

GRETCHEN M. BATAILLE (essay date 1984)

[*An American educator and critic, Bataille is the author of several books on native Americans. Much of her writing is devoted to correcting stereotypes and distortions in the way native Americans are presented in textbooks and the media. In the following excerpt, she examines* Black Elk Speaks *as an example of "prophetic autobiography" and notes parallels between native American religious ceremonies depicted in the book and classical drama.*]

Although [*Black Elk Speaks*] is usually classified and discussed as an autobiography, a life story told by the writer, John Neihardt makes no such claim. In the 1961 reissue of the book Neihardt requested that the title page read "told through" John G. Neihardt. To determine its authenticity as autobiography critics have compared the book to field notes taken by Neihardt's daughters during the conversations held

in 1930 and to ethnological studies of the Sioux. But autobiography is always problematical, and categorization is never neat. Autobiography melds history and literature, combines objective facts and subjective interpretations. Life narratives are *told through, recorded by, edited by,* and *corrected by* editors. Working with a sixty-seven year old Oglala Sioux who did not speak English, Neihardt cannot be faulted for whatever editorial intrusions he might have made to tell the story of Black Elk. His additions at the beginning and in the conclusion conveyed the spirit of Black Elk, if not always the exact words.

Critical discussion on the authenticity of the words and sequence of stories often overlook the point of the book and certainly miss the value to be gained by reading the story of a life within a community, the way Black Elk perceived his relationship to the Sioux community of which he was an integral part. By its very nature any autobiography is elusive; it is a personal self-examination which results in self-creation and self-regeneration. The person who appears in print is not ever the same flesh and blood person who told or wrote the story. Neihardt recognized this truth and in the introduction to the Pocket Books edition of *Black Elk Speaks* [see excerpt dated 1972] he wrote,

> It was my function to translate the old man's story, not only in the factual sense—for it was not the facts that mattered most—but rather to recreate in English the mood and manner of the old man's narrative.

It is this *recreation* which is significant in the analysis of the book and the character of Black Elk.

The story, the narrative, is more important than the recounting of a single life history. The story of Black Elk is the story of a prophet, a man who interpreted the present in terms of the past and on the basis of both predicted the future. Neihardt described him as "kind of a preacher." Black Elk was a man who believed in prophecy, who saw pictographs on a rock bluff which had predicted the defeat of Custer and who believed that they had been put there long ago. He saw himself as a representative of and for his people, not as a savior who would redeem them, but an ordinary mortal endowed with special gifts which would provide him with the spiritual strength to endure when others faltered or perished. Yet he was plagued with a constant gnawing doubt that he had either understood his vision improperly or not acted in proper response to it. As a prophet Black Elk can be favorably compared to other prophets of history, men and women whose place in their societies paralleled that of Black Elk in his tribe.

G. Thomas Couser describes in his study [*American Autobiography: The Prophetic Mode*] the impulse of autobiographers to assume the role of prophet. His theories are appropriate to describe the story of the life of Black Elk. Black Elk in the role of prophet was no doubt on Neihardt's mind, for it was his desire to learn more about the Ghost Dance and Wovoka, the prophet of the "new religion," which took him to South Dakota to collect information for *The Song of The Messiah.* Couser writes that autobiographers tend to reflect times of crisis—religious, moral, political or philosophical. Black Elk in his story responds to his memories of the crisis of Wounded Knee and to the realities of the crises posed by twentieth-century encroachments on American Indian values and lifestyles. His story is told to avert the continuing crises and to alter history in such a way as to improve the life of the Sioux people, his people, and of all people.

Couser says that the prophetic autobiography flourishes in times of crisis, when change threatens communal values or when historical development demands new modes of interpretation. All of these circumstances were present at the time Black Elk told his story to Neihardt. As autobiographer Black Elk was a representative of his Oglala Sioux community, an interpreter of the past and the present, and a shaper of the history of his people. As a shaper, he functioned as a prophet. In his vision Black Elk saw himself as the sixth Grandfather, the Spirit of the Earth, and he knew his work was to be done on earth, that his power was to be used in his community and for the Sioux people. In his vision historical time ceased to exist and was replaced by mythical time of a dream world, but it was a visionary world which had implications for reality because to Black Elk it was more real than the world in which he lived: "That is the real world that is behind this one, and everything we see here is something like a shadow from the world." Later he says: "I knew the real was yonder and the darkened dream of it was here."

Couser recognizes the importance of vision to a prophet:

> . . . for the anthropologist the prophet's function is to offer society a vision or a visionary experience which revises the culture's traditional mythology in such a way as to resolve communal crises. . . . If his vision gains credence . . . it may . . . create an illusion of change and thus bring relief by easing psychological tensions.

The vision of Wovoka which initiated the Ghost Dance, the vision of Ghost Shirts to protect the wearers, and the visions recounted by Black Elk all served to ease the psychological tensions introduced by the influx of the wasichus and provided hope for the future. It is this function which Black Elk served in the recitation of his life story. In the narrative he offered his vision to the world beyond the Sioux reservation; he offered a hope for a better future for the greater community. The rain which fell on Neihardt and Black Elk on the top of Harney Peak confirmed the vision and offered hope for the next ascent.

In *Black Elk Speaks* the reader learns to appreciate Indian ceremony as drama. The initial setting for the telling of the life story is like that of Greek drama, with Black Elk as the main actor and his friends Standing Bear, Fire Thunder, and Iron Hawk acting as a chorus, reiterating the significance of certain events, explaining the context, or providing asides that Black Elk would not feel free to share. The storyteller's pauses to nap were brief intermissions, no doubt designed to give the major performer time to rest, but also to allow what had been presented to the audience time to be absorbed and understood. The most obvious presentation of drama, however, comes during the ceremonies themselves.

Neihardt provides a hint that he saw the elements of classical drama re-enacted on the South Dakota plains. He writes, "Truth comes into this world with two faces. One is sad with suffering, and the other laughs; but it is the same face, laughing or weeping." He is describing the two masks of reality, life acted out as it is in ceremony and ritual, the raw material of drama. Black Elk tells of the *heyoka* ceremonies and the reader can easily identify the dramatic principles at work. The ceremony is acted out in a theatre of the round with an audience who at times become a chorus, commenting and re-acting to the performance. The performers are costumed and acting out a ritual which is familiar, yet it is created anew each time it is performed. The pageantry is enhanced by special props, color and animals. When the end of the ceremony comes, the people are renewed. Black Elk describes the audience: "They were better able now to see the greenness of the world, the wideness of the sacred day, the colors of the earth, and to set these in their minds." The dramatic re-enactment of the vision provided a catharsis and in the imitation of nature art was created, a dramatic production which portrayed the traditional symbols of Sioux culture in a new way. The horses, the four directions, the lightning, and the sacred bows were all familiar Sioux symbols, but they were given new meaning in Black Elk's vision and in the ceremonies which recreated that vision.

The continuation of the vision and of the prophet's message was ensured by the dramatic presentation during Black Elk's youth, by its retelling in 1931, and by the publication of Neihardt's book. In 1972 Neihardt wrote, "The old prophet's wish that I bring his message to the world is actually being fulfilled." (pp. 138-41)

In his vision Black Elk gave his people life. In his later years he felt that he had failed, but perhaps Black Elk has misinterpreted the prophecy for his own life. By keeping their traditions alive, the people continue to live. Through the telling of his life story, Black Elk fulfilled his vision. He had performed the ceremonies and he had recreated them now in words which would immortalize them. John Neihardt was the amanuensis who made it possible. (p. 142)

Gretchen M. Bataille, "Black Elk—New World Prophet," in A Sender of Words: Essays in Memory of John G. Neihardt, *edited by Vine Deloria, Jr., Howe Brothers, 1984, pp. 135-42.*

RAYMOND J. DeMALLIE (essay date 1984)

[*DeMallie is an American anthropologist who has studied native Americans, especially the Lakota Sioux. He is the editor of* The Sixth Grandfather, *the published transcript of the Black Elk–Neihardt interviews. In the following excerpt from his introduction to that work, he examines the results of the collaboration between Black Elk and Neihardt, discussing the effects of Neihardt's editorial priorities on his shaping of Black Elk's narrative.*]

Neihardt wrote *Black Elk Speaks* in longhand, on oversize sheets, working primarily from Enid's transcript. For historical data on battles, and for some of the information on Crazy Horse and other chiefs, he referred to the source material he had amassed during his work on *The Song of the Indian Wars*. Neihardt was an extraordinarily faithful spokesman for Black Elk; what he wrote was an interpretation of Black Elk's life, but not one that was embellished in any way. Instead, he tried to write what he thought the old man himself would have expressed. The book is Black Elk's story as he gave it to Neihardt, but the literary quality and the tone of the work are Neihardt's. Much later Neihardt commented in an interview [see McCluskey excerpt dated 1972]: "*Black Elk Speaks* is a work of art with two collaborators, the chief one being Black Elk. My function was both creative and editorial. . . . The beginning and the ending [of the book] are mine; they are what he would have said if he had been able. . . . And the translation—or rather the *transforma-*

tion—of what was given me was expressed so that it could be understood by the white world."

In line with his assertion that this was to be "the first absolutely Indian book," Neihardt minimized everything that reflected Black Elk's knowledge and experience in the white man's world previous to his travels with the wild west shows. The book retains the intensely personal quality of the interviews; Black Elk becomes both the spokesman for and the symbol of the Indian people as his life experiences reflect their gradual defeat by the inevitable force of white civilization. The book is written in deceptively simple language. Neihardt told Black Elk at the outset that he would "use as much of your language in it as possible." Lucile F. Aly, Neihardt's literary biographer, notes that the simplicity of the style reflects our expectation of Indian speech patterns. The use of Indian expressions like "yellow metal" for gold and "four-leggeds" for horses reinforces the illusion of Indian speech. But she also notes that the simple, concrete style frequently reflects underlying abstraction. Similarly, Neihardt's dependence in the book on "flattened" adjectives like "good" and "bad" again reinforces the impression of Indian style and simultaneously suggests Indian stoicism. Only a literary master like Neihardt could use these techniques with such precision as to prevent them from degenerating into stereotypical "Indian talk" of the Hollywood movie variety. And Neihardt succeeded brilliantly. (pp. 51-2)

It was Black Elk's great vision that must have presented Neihardt the greatest challenge as a writer. This was, after all, the core of what Black Elk had wanted to tell Neihardt in order to record it for posterity. The historical events and autobiographical anecdotes were all incidental to Black Elk's purpose: to save his vision for mankind. But from a literary perspective the problem was what should be saved, the details of the vision or its meaning? Black Elk never stated succinctly what he considered the meaning to be; he left this for Neihardt to interpret. In one sense the meaning is that the powers of the Lakota universe exist and have the ability to aid mankind in all endeavors, to protect people from disease and from their enemies and to bring joy and contentment. These powers were not simply replaced by the Christian God whom Black Elk came to accept; instead, they represented an alternate approach to the unknowable, another path to the "other world." Therefore the vision was good and true and important to save for mankind, as a lesson and perhaps as a plan— to make the "tree blossom," bringing Indians and non-Indians together in the harmony of a common circle. It is this universalistic message that Neihardt chose to emphasize, generalizing the vision as a means to understanding humanity writ large. Thus he presented the vision as an integral whole, of and for itself, drawing no parallels to other religious systems, and letting the vision's very uniqueness speak for its universal value.

To that end, Neihardt presented the vision in his narrative at the chronological moment in Black Elk's life when it occurred, developing the theme of the vision as a pattern for Black Elk's life. Neihardt resisted the publisher's attempt to relegate the vision to an appendix. Although it was long and involved, and posed the danger of boring or losing the reader, it was essential for understanding the mission and purpose of Black Elk's life. It was necessary to abridge the vision so that it would be appreciated by a non-Indian reader, however, cutting it down to essentials so that it would fit into a manageable chapter. Cultural details were not so important to Nei-

hardt as were the mood and the message. Accordingly, he decided to minimize the imagery of warfare and killing—the power to destroy that complemented the power to make live. By so doing, Neihardt set off Black Elk's vision from other published Lakota vision accounts, most of them centered on the bestowal of power for success in warfare. Though warfare was integral to traditional Lakota culture, it was not the aspect of that culture to emphasize in order to develop the universalistic message of the vision. So Neihardt cut and edited, focusing the published story of the vision on the powers to heal that Black Elk used later in life to help his people. Black Elk himself had rejected the power to destroy when he turned his back on the vision and embraced Catholicism, and this alone gave Neihardt justification for accentuating those aspects of the vision that were most important for understanding Black Elk as a healer.

One other important decision colored Neihardt's presentation of the great vision. This was a Thunder-being vision—a vision of the powers of the west, the vision of a *heyoka*. Although in it Black Elk was presented with powers from all six directions (the four quarters—north, east, south, and west—as well as earth and sky), the first grandfather's house to which he was taken was the cloud tipi of the Thunder-beings, a conventional Lakota vision symbol for the west. But later in his life, when Black Elk went on a vision quest at the age of eighteen, he had a second Thunder-being vision (which Neihardt called "the dog vision"), after which he at long last performed the *heyoka* ceremony. To have emphasized the extent to which the first vision was a Thunder-being vision would have forced either cutting the later vision or presenting repetitious material. Because the reader's patience was likely to be taxed by these vision accounts, Neihardt chose to minimize the Thunder-being powers of the great vision. This was doubly appropriate because the west presented Black Elk with destructive powers. Minimizing the association of the great vision with Thunder-beings simultaneously minimized the warlike symbolism and heightened the emphasis on the vision's curative, life-giving powers.

Neihardt's interpretation of Black Elk's vision is valid and consistent. It hews closely to the way Black Elk himself interpreted his vision later in life. It seems likely that for Black Elk, minimization of warlike themes in the vision resulted from his Christian perspective. Neihardt's motives for minimizing them, on the other hand, stemmed more from humanitarian than dogmatic concerns. Although motivated differently, both men developed the same meaning out of the vision. While working on the book, Neihardt expressed his intentions in a letter to Black Elk: "We are going to do something real with this book about "The Tree That Never Bloomed" [the working title for ***Black Elk Speaks***] and I am sure that you are going to be a good deal happier because of this book. Keep a good heart and be patient until next spring when the book appears. I have to work hard on the book and be patient too, and I can do both with a strong heart because I know that the book is wise and good and that thousands of people will find good in it."

Black Elk's great vision forms the heart of ***Black Elk Speaks*** just as it formed the core of the teachings Black Elk gave to Neihardt. From the idyllic union of man with the cosmic forces of the universe that is represented by the vision, all develops in a downward spiral as human life fails to match supernatural expectation. In the vision Black Elk saw the troubled times ahead, but he was also given powers that were to protect his people from danger. *Black Elk Speaks* emphasizes Black Elk's sense of failure, his inability to use the spiritual powers given to him, and his sense of personal responsibility for the downfall of his people. Lest the reader miss the tragedy of the destruction of the Lakotas' way of life that is mirrored in Black Elk's own failure, Neihardt concluded the work with this now-famous passage:

> I did not know then how much was ended. When I look back now from this high hill of my old age, I can still see the butchered women and children lying heaped and scattered all along the crooked gulch as plain as when I saw them with eyes still young. And I can see that something else died there in the bloody mud, and was buried in the blizzard. A people's dream died there. It was a beautiful dream.
>
> And I, to whom so great a vision was given in my youth,—you see me now a pitiful old man who has done nothing, for the nation's hoop is broken and scattered. There is no center any longer, and the sacred tree is dead.

The author's postscript relating the ceremony on Harney Peak does little to buoy hope. There the old man prayed that the sacred tree might bloom again and the people find their way back to the sacred hoop and the good red road. He cried out, "O make my people live!"—and in reply a low rumble of thunder sounded, and a drizzle of rain fell from a sky that shortly before had been cloudless. Whether this sign was a hopeful one or, more likely, a tragic recognition of the power that Black Elk had been given but failed to use is one of the dynamic issues that makes the book a literary success. *Black Elk Speaks* can be best characterized as an elegy, the commemoration of a man who has failed in his life's work, as well as of a people whose way of life has passed.

There is no doubt that Black Elk expressed the sense of despair that Neihardt attributes to him in *Black Elk Speaks.* When the time came in his life to implement the power to destroy that had been given him in the vision, he chose to turn his back on it and joined the Catholic Church instead. He rejected the traditional Lakota value of warfare for the Christian virtue of charity. True to his new religion, he did no longer practice his native healing rituals. But Black Elk's attitude toward his people's future held more hope than thoughts of doom. The sense of irreversible tragedy that pervades *Black Elk Speaks* reflects Neihardt's interpretation. Lakota culture does not emphasize the irreversible, but rather the opposite: what once was is likely to be again. This was the hope that Black Elk voiced again and again in talking to Neihardt, that together they could "make the tree bloom." With its unrelenting sense of defeat, *Black Elk Speaks* became an eloquent literary restatement of the theme of the vanishing American.

Did Neihardt misunderstand Black Elk? On the one hand, it seems likely that Neihardt did not fully appreciate the Lakota attitude of prayer. Sorrow and despair were outward expressions of traditional Lakota prayer, for the efficacy of prayer depended upon making oneself humble and pitiable before the powers of the universe. But this was a ritual attitude, not an expression of hopelessness. On the other hand, Neihardt perceived Black Elk through the lens of his own lifework, *A Cycle of the West.* The purpose of this epic poem, Neihardt had written, was "to preserve the great race-mood of courage that was developed west of the Missouri River in the 19th

century." The corollary to the triumph of the "westering white men" was the inevitable defeat of the Plains Indians. It is not that Neihardt misunderstood Black Elk, but that he perceived his life as embodying the whole tragic history of defeat whose emotional tone he was trying to convey in verse in *A Cycle.*

Because it was written in the first person, *Black Elk Speaks* opens Black Elk's innermost life for public inspection, although it does so with a pervasive sense of dignity. The book's success is due in large part to Neihardt's empathy with Black Elk's "otherworldliness"—a spirituality that set him apart. The mystic in Neihardt and the mystic in Black Elk were kindred souls. At times in the book, Black Elk's "other world" becomes the "outer world" of Neihardt's poetic imagination. Black Elk in the book is left poised, seemingly helplessly, on the brink of civilization; the pitiful old man at the end of *Black Elk Speaks,* sorrowing over the destruction of his people, is a powerful literary figure. And in one sense this is an accurate reflection of Black Elk's sense of failure to use his vision powers as he was directed. Yet this image is far removed from Black Elk's daily life as patriarch, rancher, catechist, and community elder—one of the most successful old-time, uneducated Indians in adapting to the exigencies of life on the Pine Ridge Reservation. In a practical sense, far from failing, he had made a successful life for himself and his family.

The extent to which Neihardt succeeded in making mysticism the central theme of Black Elk's entire life intensified the degree to which the old holy man came to be interpreted as saintly, as a person far removed from life's normal cares. Again, this is an effective literary device, a powerful one for generalizing Black Elk into the very symbol of his people, but it leads away from understanding Black Elk as a person and toward the creation of Black Elk as a myth.

Literature and biography are very different genres, however; as Neihardt said, *Black Elk Speaks* was intended as a work of art, transcending the ordinary to make a larger statement about humanity. In the process the book becomes an interpretation of the whole of Lakota culture, for Neihardt had an intuitive appreciation and understanding of other modes of thought, and he had a gift for translating between cultures. Neihardt was satisfied that the book preserved "the finest things" in Black Elk's life. And to Ben Black Elk, Neihardt wrote: "There seems to be good reason to believe that a great many people are going to know about your father within the next two years, and I think this book is going to make him a happier man." (pp. 52-7)

Raymond J. DeMallie, "Nicholas Black Elk and John G. Neihardt: An Introduction," in The Sixth Grandfather: Black Elk's Teachings Given to John G. Neihardt, *edited by Raymond J. DeMallie, University of Nebraska Press, 1984, pp. 1-74.*

ADDITIONAL BIBLIOGRAPHY

Almqvist, Kurt, with Lambert, Stephen. "The Three Circles of Existence." *Studies in Comparative Religion* 17, Nos. 1-2 (1985): 24-9.

Explores the symbolic value of the circle or hoop in Black Elk's vision and native American tradition.

Berner, Robert L. "Trying to Be Round: Three American Indian Novels." *World Literature Today* 58, No. 3 (Summer 1984): 341-44.
Relates the structure of novels by N. Scott Momaday, James Welch, and Leslie Marmon Silko to the "basic American Indian perception of the symbolic significance of the directions and the seasons" as presented in *Black Elk Speaks.*

Brumble, H. David, III. "Anthropologists, Novelists, and Indian Sacred Material." *The Canadian Review of American Studies* 11, No. 1 (Spring 1980): 31-48.
Discusses anthropologists' attitudes toward the recording and publication of native American sacred material. Brumble compares types of collaborations between writers and their native American subjects, including that of Neihardt and Black Elk, in order to "piece together a coherent account of the development of American Indian literature in the twentieth century."

Copeland, Marion W. "*Black Elk Speaks* and Leslie Silko's *Ceremony:* Two Visions of Horses." *Critique* 24, No. 3 (Spring 1983): 158-72.
Demonstrates similarities between the visions and experiences of Black Elk and Tayo, the protagonist of the novel *Ceremony.*

Deloria, Vine, Jr. Introduction to *Black Elk Speaks: Being the Life Story of a Holy Man of the Oglala Sioux as Told through John G. Neihardt (Flaming Rainbow),* pp. xi-xiv. Lincoln: University of Nebraska Press, 1979.
Recounts the critical history of *Black Elk Speaks.* Deloria maintains that the debate regarding Neihardt's role as editor is irrelevant to the central message of the book.

————, ed. *A Sender of Words: Essays in Memory of John G. Neihardt.* Salt Lake City, Utah: Howe Brothers, 1984, 177 p.
Commentaries and tributes by well-known western writers commemorating the centennial of Neihardt's birth. In addition to the essays by N. Scott Momaday and Gretchen M. Bataille excerpted above, the volume includes an essay by Frank Waters which compares Black Elk's vision with other religious traditions, especially other native American systems of belief; an examination by Roger Dunsmore of the ways in which Black Elk's vision affected his entire life; and an essay in which Carl J. Starkloff explores the possibilities for synthesis of native American religions and Christianity and analyzes the role of the missionary.

Holler, Clyde. "Black Elk's Relationship to Christianity." *The American Indian Quarterly* 8, No. 1 (Winter 1984): 37-49.
Studies the ways in which Black Elk integrated elements of native American religion and Christianity and how his synthesis was interpreted by other native Americans and by whites.

Holly, Carol T. "*Black Elk Speaks* and the Making of Indian Autobiography." *Genre* 12, No. 1 (Spring 1979): 117-36.
Compares *Black Elk Speaks* with other autobiographies, including *The Autobiography of Malcolm X, The Autobiography of Benjamin Franklin,* and St. Augustine's *Confessions,* to examine the format and conventions of the genre. Holly also discusses the editorial contributions by Neihardt that "made *Black Elk Speaks* such a unique blend of western literary form and native American consciousness."

Lincoln, Kenneth. "Word Senders: Black Elk and N. Scott Moma-day." In his *Native American Renaissance,* pp. 82-121. Berkeley and Los Angeles: University of California Press, 1983.
Discusses *Black Elk Speaks* and the writings of the Kiowa poet and novelist N. Scott Momaday, demonstrating that despite their different tribes and eras, "Momaday's influence from Black Elk recovers an impressionist reverence for the land, the elders, the traditions, and the spirits alive in all these."

Olson, Paul A. "*Black Elk Speaks* as Epic and Ritual Attempt to Reverse History." In *Vision and Refuge: Essays on the Literature of the Great Plains,* edited by Virginia Faulkner with Frederick C. Luebke, pp. 3-27. Lincoln: University of Nebraska Press, 1982.
Suggests that in sharing his vision with Neihardt, "Black Elk, as a religious thinker and master of ritual speech, acted at that moment in the life of the Sioux nation when epic as the meaningful combination of allegory and history was possible and had a function in assisting the culture to survive."

Rice, Julian. "*Akicita* of the Thunder: Horses in Black Elk's Vision." *Melus* 12, No. 1 (Spring 1985): 5-23.
Provides a detailed account of Lakota religious symbolism, without which, Rice asserts, the symbolic associations of Black Elk's vision cannot be properly understood.

Sayre, Robert F. "Vision and Experience in *Black Elk Speaks.*" *College English* 32, No. 5 (February 1971): 509-35.
Summarizes Black Elk's vision and explores the ways in which it affected his emotional life and his relationships with other members of his tribe. Sayre examines Black Elk's experience as an example of the function of visions, symbols, and rituals in a society.

Spresser, James Clarence. "Fantasy Theme Analysis as Applied to the Oglala Sioux Indian Text *Black Elk Speaks.*" *Journal of American Culture* 8, No. 3 (Fall 1985) 75-8.
Uses an analytical technique developed by scholars of rhetoric to explain how Black Elk's vision and the communal ritual performance of the vision helped the Oglala Sioux comprehend the expansion of white settlers into lands held by native Americans.

Stone, Albert E. "Collaboration in Contemporary American Autobiography." *Revue français d'études américaines* 7, No. 14 (May 1982): 151-65.
Investigates the presentation of a single personality through the creative participation of two people, using as examples *Black Elk Speaks, The Autobiography of Malcolm X,* and *All God's Dangers: The Life of Nate Shaw.* Stone maintains that Black Elk's story is recounted successfully through his collaboration with Neihardt.

Swann, Brian, ed. *Smoothing the Ground: Essays on Native American Oral Literature.* Berkeley and Los Angeles: University of California Press, 1983, 364 p.
Writings exploring native American literature as a link to the American past. The essays address such topics as critical approaches to oral literature, traditional native American stories and myths, and the relationship between native American culture and the dominant American culture. In an essay on Black Elk, William Nichols uses Erik Erikson's concepts of identity and generativity to compare elements of the lives and philosophies of Mohandas Gandhi and Black Elk.

Samuel Butler

1835-1902

English novelist, essayist, biographer, and poet.

For further discussion of Butler's works, see *TCLC,* Volume 1.

Butler is one of the most renowned English authors of the late-Victorian period. A notorious iconoclast, he presented a scathing portrait of Victorian family life in the autobiographical novel *The Way of All Flesh,* created pungent satires of English society in his *Erewhon; or, Over the Range* and *Erewhon Revisited Twenty Years Later,* and opposed dominant literary, religious, and scientific ideas of his day in numerous essays. Butler's perceptive criticisms of Victorian England, influential during his lifetime, exerted even greater impact on subsequent generations of writers and thinkers. As a result, he is often cited as one of the primary progenitors of the early twentieth-century reaction against Victorian attitudes.

Butler was born in a small village in Nottinghamshire, the son of an Anglican clergyman and the grandson of a bishop. Educated first at a boarding school near his home, he later attended the prestigious Shrewsbury School, where the curriculum emphasized classical studies. Butler continued his classical studies at Cambridge, and, after graduating in 1858, he followed family tradition by preparing to enter the clergy. However, during his clerical training he developed grave theological doubts, and in 1859 he announced to his father that he did not wish to be ordained. After much debate, during which alternate careers in medicine, art, and diplomacy were proposed by both sides, it was decided that Butler would be allowed to emigrate to New Zealand with a small endowment and there attempt to establish himself as a rancher. He left England soon afterward, arriving in the Canterbury region of New Zealand in January of 1860.

Butler remained in New Zealand for nearly five years, establishing a highly successful sheep ranch and eventually doubling the value of his original investment. As owner of the ranch, his duties were light, and he was able to read a great deal during this period. Sometime in 1861, Butler read Charles Darwin's *Origin of Species* (1859), a book that strongly influenced him; he later commented that, for him, the theory of evolution had replaced Christianity. Beginning in 1862, he submitted a series of articles to the *Canterbury Press* defending and extrapolating from Darwin's theory. Butler's writings attracted much attention throughout New Zealand, and in 1863 Darwin himself wrote to the *Press,* praising Butler's clear comprehension of his work. That same year, Butler's father compiled a collection of his son's letters and had them published as *A First Year in Canterbury Settlement, with Other Essays.* Soon afterward, Butler sold his ranch to become a full-time contributor to the *Canterbury Press.*

Returning to England late in 1864, Butler settled in London, and, having long aspired to a career as a painter, enrolled at Heatherley's School of Art. However, after several years of determined effort, he came to feel that his artistic talents were limited at best, and in 1870 he began writing his first major

satire, *Erewhon.* Published anonymously in 1872, *Erewhon* was an immediate success; when Butler let it be known that he was the author, he was thrust into the limelight. His renown was soon augmented by the publication of *The Fair Haven,* a satirical denunciation of Christian doctrines which, to Butler's great amusement, was misinterpreted by some clergymen as a brilliant defense of those beliefs. Butler next began work on the novel *The Way of All Flesh,* but soon realized that its intensely negative portrait of his family would gravely offend those members still living, and in 1878 he set the uncompleted work aside.

For the next decade Butler pursued a course he had established early in 1878 with the publication of *Life and Habit,* in which he addressed the issue of biological evolution. After long consideration of Darwin's theory, Butler had come to believe that Darwin had failed to accurately identify the mechanism by which evolutionary adaptations were passed from one generation to the next. Adopting a teleological approach, Butler developed in *Life and Habit* and in three subsequent volumes the theory that biological traits are inherited through an unconscious memory of adaptations made by an organism's progenitors in response to some specific need or desire, suggesting that this memory was incorporated into the physical structure of an embryo at the time of conception.

Butler's concern with Darwin's work led to a celebrated conflict between the two men, produced not by the differences in their theories, but by a misunderstanding. In 1879, Darwin wrote a preface for the English translation of Dr. Ernst Krause's essay on Darwin's grandfather, who had also written about evolution. For the translation of his essay, Krause added negative remarks concerning Butler's theory, and Butler, who had read the original German version, erroneously attributed these revisions to Darwin. Embittered by what he considered unfair and unprofessional attacks on his ideas, Butler harbored resentment toward Darwin for the rest of his life, and his subsequent volumes of scientific writings contain numerous acerbic references to Darwin's work.

During the last two decades of his life, Butler continued to oppose dominant ideas of his time by publishing two controversial philological essays, contending in one that the *Odyssey* had been written by a woman and in the other that Shakespeare had written his sonnets for a homosexual lover, who, although socially inferior to the playwright, had treated him in a cavalier fashion. He also wrote a sequel to *Erewhon,* published English translations of the *Iliad* and the *Odyssey,* collaborated with his friend Henry Festing Jones on a number of musical compositions, and intermittently returned to the manuscript of *The Way of All Flesh.* Before his death in 1902, Butler left instructions that this last work should not be published until after the deaths of his two sisters, but his literary executor, R. A. Streatfeild, ignored those instructions and published *The Way of All Flesh* in 1903.

Critics regard *The Way of All Flesh* as Butler's most important work, significant both as a perceptive autobiography and as a brilliant criticism of Victorian attitudes and institutions. Through the central character of the novel, Ernest Pontifex, Butler portrayed his own childhood in a pious household, his early attempts to transcend his intellectually stifling social milieu, and his ultimate rejection of the ideals and mores of his family. The plot of the second half of the novel diverges drastically from the facts of Butler's life, with Pontifex spending time in prison for attempting to solicit the sexual favors of a woman he mistakes for a prostitute, marrying a servant, and receiving a large inheritance. The primary foci of Butler's animosity in *The Way of All Flesh* are the fiercely patriarchal Victorian family and the Christian church. Remembering his own feelings of frustration at his father's absolutism and frequent use of corporal punishment, Butler portrayed Ernest Pontifex's childhood as a period of emotional and physical agony. As a clergyman, Pontifex's father, Theobald, also embodies Butler's view of the Anglican church as not only ossified and morally impotent but actually perverse in its stubborn adherence to practices antithetical to such true Christian ideals as charity and tolerance. While critics praise the satiric wit and keen intelligence displayed in these criticisms, many suggest that Butler's bitterness led him to subordinate fictional elements such as plot and characterization to invective, resulting in a powerful but nevertheless flawed work of literature. Others, however, have defended the depth and subtlety of Butler's characterizations and note with surprise that the only unsuccessful character in the novel is Ernest Pontifex, who appears to have been imbued with Butler's great intelligence but with limited emotional depth.

Butler satirized Victorian England in a different fashion in *Erewhon* and *Erewhon Revisited.* In the former, Butler created a fictional nation, Erewhon (suggestive of "Nowhere" reversed), by skewing and in some cases reversing features of his own society. Thus, the Anglican church is represented in *Erewhon* by "Musical Banks," which dispense currency that is monetarily worthless yet important as a mark of status, while the courts treat crime as an illness and doctors treat illness as a crime. Butler also incorporated elements of his evolutionary theories into the futuristic society depicted in *Erewhon,* most notably in the section entitled "The Book of the Machines," wherein he suggested that machines represent humanity's attempt to transcend its physical limitations and are therefore another step in human evolution. Butler added a further element of satire in *Erewhon Revisited* by having the unnamed narrator of *Erewhon,* now identified as Mr. Higgs, return to Erewhon after an absence of twenty years to find that his departure in a hot air balloon inspired a new religion called Sunchildism, whose adherents are engaged in a fierce sectarian dispute with the leaders of Erewhon's established religion, Ygrundism (a name parodying that of the fictional character who exemplified Victorian intolerance, Mrs. Grundy).

Aside from his two philological studies, *The Authoress of the "Odyssey"* and *Shakespeare's Sonnets Reconsidered,* the bulk of Butler's discursive writings deal with his theory of evolution. Of these, critics regard *Life and Habit* as by far the best, suggesting that *Evolution, Old and New* is essentially a restatement of the ideas set forth in the earlier book, while later essays appear to have been inspired largely by Butler's resentment of Darwin. In addition, Butler wrote a number of essays describing his annual trips to Italy, and some critics contend that these writings are among Butler's best, displaying humor and eloquence while avoiding the acrimonious didacticism that occasionally mars his other works.

During his lifetime, Butler's critical reputation was based on the success of *Erewhon.* His scientific writings were viewed with interest but were generally dismissed as inferior to those of Darwin, who seemed more qualified to discuss questions of biological evolution. Nevertheless, a number of commentators have noted that Darwin himself failed to adequately describe the mechanisms of natural selection and maintain that Butler's approach was, although incorrect, a well-wrought extrapolation of the teleological evolutionary theories of eighteenth-century scholars Georges-Louis Buffon, Jean-Baptiste Lamarck, and William Paley. After 1903, the widely read and much-discussed *Way of All Flesh* overshadowed all of Butler's previous writings; appearing during one of the first waves of anti-Victorian reaction, the novel was hailed by critics as a brilliant exposé and praised for its satiric wit. *The Way of All Flesh* was admired in particular by Bloomsbury critics Virginia and Leonard Woolf, Desmond MacCarthy and E. M. Forster, who, while admitting that the novel was flawed, nevertheless found in it the embodiment of their own ideals. During the 1920s and 1930s, however, Butler's reputation suffered a decline, with many politically and socially radical critics viewing his iconoclasm as limited and entirely conventional. In a renowned, caustic biography of Butler, Malcolm Muggeridge suggested that despite his outward posture of dissent Butler in fact failed to free himself from the most essential preconceptions of Victorian society, concluding that he was "not so much the anti-Victorian, as the ultimate Victorian." Stuart P. Sherman dubbed him "the unregarded Diogenes of the Victorians," implying that Butler's opposition to entrenched ideas served no purpose and had little effect.

Several recent studies have focused on these charges and others pertaining to elements of Victorianism in Butler's thought; most contemporary critics suggest that while his radicalism was limited, his criticisms of Victorian society were deeply felt, intellectually profound, and undeniably influential in formulating modern attitudes toward that era. His writings and ideas have been cited as a primary source of inspiration for a number of major twentieth-century authors, including Forster, Virginia Woolf, Bernard Shaw, and James Joyce. In addition, two of Butler's works, *The Way of All Flesh* and *Erewhon,* are acknowledged as literary classics in their own right.

(See also *Contemporary Authors,* Vol. 104 and *Dictionary of Literary Biography,* Vols. 18 and 57.)

PRINCIPAL WORKS

A First Year in Canterbury Settlement, with Other Essays (essays) 1863

The Evidence for the Resurrection of Jesus Christ (essay) 1865

Erewhon; or, Over the Range (novel) 1872

The Fair Haven (satire) 1873

Life and Habit (essay) 1878

Evolution, Old and New (essay) 1879

God the Known and God the Unknown (essay) 1879

Unconscious Memory (essay) 1880

Alps and Sanctuaries of Piedmont and the Canton Ticino (essays) 1882

Luck, or Cunning, as the Main Means of Organic Modification? (essay) 1887

The Life and Letters of Dr. Samuel Butler (biography) 1896

The Authoress of the "Odyssey" (essay) 1897

Shakespeare's Sonnets Reconsidered (essay) 1899

Erewhon Revisited Twenty Years Later (novel) 1901

The Way of All Flesh (novel) 1903; also published as *Ernest Pontifex; or, The Way of All Flesh,* 1964

Essays on Life, Art, and Science (essays) 1904

Seven Sonnets and "A Psalm of Montreal" (poetry) 1904

The Note-Books of Samuel Butler. 2 vols. (notebooks) 1907-12

The Shrewsbury Edition of the Works of Samuel Butler. 20 vols. (essays, novels, satires, notebooks, and letters) 1923-26

Further Extracts from the Note-Books of Samuel Butler (notebooks) 1934

Letters between Samuel Butler and Miss E. M. A. Savage (letters) 1935

The Correspondence of Samuel Butler with His Sister May (letters) 1962

THE TIMES LITERARY SUPPLEMENT (essay date 1903)

[*The following is a review of* The Way of All Flesh.]

It is very unlikely that [***The Way of All Flesh***] by the late Mr. Samuel Butler will command the immediate reputation achieved by his ***Erewhon*** thirty years ago; but we think it likely enough that this, more than the former, work will preserve his memory. Fresh and novel speculation, brightly and forcibly delivered, will, with luck, delight an author's contemporaries; but by the time that "posterity" has arrived the specu-

lation is apt to have become a little stale. But posterity will not tire of vivid and informed accounts of life in previous ages. It is more interesting now to read Fielding than Locke—not that Mr. Butler, with all his various and considerable gifts, is to be compared to the one or the other. ***The Way of All Flesh*** is, of course, full of theory and argument, for theory and argument were the breath of Mr. Butler's nostrils. The main theme of the book, however, inspired though it is by a theory, is the life of a man, written in detail, and plainly with a strong personal emotion. That fact, we think, will say something to posterity. Unfortunately for its present popularity, however, the human interest of the book falls between two stools; it has for average readers neither the piquancy and importance of the present nor the curiosity of the fairly remote past. The book is concerned chiefly with the years 1835 to 1867—a period which for average readers is obsolete without being strange—and, having in it a strong militant purpose, seems to be fighting a battle already lost and won. From those, however, for whom the humanity of the last or preceding generation can be as interesting, in its material customs and spiritual conflicts, as that of other generations, and who have intellect enough themselves to enjoy the working of an intellect both powerful and nimble, the work is sure of a ready and attentive acceptance.

To come to details. Internally the writing, as well as the subject, is plainly "dated," as they say of plays; but we are furthermore furnished with a note by the editor, Mr. R. A. Streatfeild, which tells us that Mr. Butler began to write ***The Way of All Flesh*** in 1872 and finished it in 1884. But there is more significance in the chronology than that indicates. The hero, whom Mr. Butler takes in detail from his birth to his thirty-third year, was born in 1835. Now that is the year of Mr. Butler's own birth; and, when the reader observes the bitterness with which the hero's early years are described, he cannot help the suspicion (though the writer is supposed to be the hero's godfather and not the hero himself) that there may be something of personal recollection—so far as concerns boyhood and childhood, for later on there can be no correspondence. Knowing nothing of the matter, we are content sincerely to hope that this is not the case, and even that some one who does know may set the suspicion at rest; for anything more lamentable than this childhood and boyhood can hardly be imagined. Mr. Butler sets out with the theory that the bringing up of children was thoroughly bad, that they were constantly sacrificed to the ignorance, selfishness, and vanity of their parents, and that this was especially the case with the children of clergymen. Clearly he meant his hero's case to be typical. We cannot believe it; we are convinced he exaggerates. The Rev. Theobald Pontifex (the father) is represented as a vindictive, malevolent, cruel bully, but also as a man who persuaded himself that he meant well and was doing his duty. Now could such a one beat a child of seven for saying "tum" instead of "come"? All this part of the book is painful to the last degree, and fills an ordinarily kind-hearted reader with maddening wrath. Exaggerated or not, it has little or no application to the present day. We treat children very differently; and the Rev. Theobald and his wife would hear of the S.P.C.C.

When the boy escapes to school the cloud lifts a little, and the portraits, still sketched with the bitter irony of which Mr. Butler was a master, are relieved with more humour. Our author is still, of course, in opposition. Witness his treatment of Dr. Skinner, who is given as the popular ideal of the earnest schoolmaster—one's imagination fears to suggest which incarnation of that ideal may be intended. "Whatever else a Roughborough man might be, he was sure to make any one feel that he was a God-fearing, earnest Christian, and a Liberal, if not a Radical, in politics. Some boys, of course, were incapable of appreciating the beauty and loftiness of Dr. Skinner's nature. . . . They not only disliked him, but they hated all that he more especially embodied, and throughout their lives disliked all that reminded them of him." Then follows a delightfully wicked account of a supper at Dr. Skinner's. We have no space to pursue the story; it is enough to say that the hero's evil up-bringing has its evil results, and that his nature ultimately triumphs over them, and that these matters are presented with a wealth of observed detail. The book is at times perhaps too full—as when an essay and a sermon are given at length; but the careful student of developments will welcome them also. We do not attach great importance to Mr. Streatfield's statement that the work is a practical illustration of the theory of heredity embodied in *Life and Habit.* The hero seems to throw back to his great-grandfather, and we are reminded that we are largely the creatures of our ancestry, and that is about all. The author is really concerned to denounce evil systems of training, false ideas of respectability, and what he believed to be bad conventions generally, and to illustrate the benefits which may be got by defying them. Many readers, perhaps most, will disagree with a great deal of what he says. But none who have humour or appreciation of effective writing can fail to admire the ironical presentment of character and the pithy, caustic phrases in which the book abounds. "The successful man will see just so much more than his neighbours as they will be able to see too when it is shown them, but not enough to puzzle them." "They would have been equally horrified at hearing the Christian religion doubted and at seeing it practised." "Those virtues which make the poor respectable and the rich respected." Such flashes are on every page.

As for the philosophy, it appears to us to be wholly negative. The dogmas of religion are put aside, but so are the dogmas of science. "The spirit behind the Church is true, though her letter—true once—is now true no longer. The spirit behind the high priests of science is as lying as its letter." Professedly the teaching is that the only criterion of virtue is worldly success and comfort. That, we perceive, is ironical; but the author recurs to this irony again and again; and when once the irony is removed the philosophy is one of despair. And we cannot help thinking that he is often very near this despair. That, or something very like it, is the impression the book finally leaves on us. It is the work of a man who saw the contrasts, the futilities, and the hypocrisies of life very clearly, and who could exhibit them very wittily—but who felt them bitterly and almost hopelessly. We admire Mr. Butler almost more in this book than in anything else he did; but we liked him better when he was using his intellect and knowledge to prove that the *Odyssey* was written by a woman.

"A Bitter Legacy," in The Times Literary Supplement, *No. 71, May 22, 1903, p. 158.*

THE TIMES LITERARY SUPPLEMENT (essay date 1908)

[*In the following excerpt from an overview of his works, the critic praises Butler's satirical wit.*]

A clever man, with a reckless tongue and an impatience of formulas and stereotyped expressions, always exposes himself to the heavy-handed judgment which declares that he has no settled principles. A brilliant man, people say, but betrayed by his own cleverness and love of paradox, and therefore not to be taken in earnest. Butler was not likely to be an exception to this rule. It is easy to enjoy his brilliance and to chuckle over his thousand strokes of wit and malice; but it is easier to overlook the fact that every one of his restless flights had its origin in a fixed principle, which he held with all his strength from his first book to his last. If he appeared to have none, or none that he was not at any moment ready to throw over, it only meant that his fundamental convictions were sound enough to be left alone in the certainty that they would not crumble away while his fancy was disporting itself above. His ultimate principle was intellectual honesty, the importance of seeing things as they really are, and this was so securely his that he felt free to talk of it as lightly as he chose. He paid to the full the penalty of misunderstanding and misrepresentation which such frivolity entailed. Sometimes, indeed, he seemed to go out of his way to court it. In the introduction to *Luck, or Cunning,* for example, he declared that he believed his theories to be "as nearly important as any theories can be which do not directly involve money or bodily convenience." To introduce a serious book with such an admission as this was obviously to ask for trouble. People were ready enough as it was to call him an irresponsible jester, and among his exiguous public there would be ten who would call his candour a piece of bare-faced cynicism for one who would stop to consider how wide, in practical life, is the gulf between the importance of things which directly bear upon personal comfort and of things which do not. It was only Butler's irony which was taken seriously.

How far autobiography is to be read into Butler's one novel, *The Way of All Flesh,* we do not know. The external history of its hero, Ernest Pontifex, may be purely fictitious, though it cannot be denied that much of it rings very like fact. The agitated development of Ernest's mind, however, is a different matter. Here the evidence is unmistakable, for it is not merely a question of internal indications; it is supported by everything else that Butler wrote. Ernest, it will be remembered, was gifted by nature with a candid and ingenuous mind, which in his early years fell an easy victim to the different varieties of priggishness with which he was thrown in contact. He implicitly believed that everyone else was just as good and wise and intellectual as they gave him to understand they were. He was appalled to find how easy virtue and wisdom seemed to be to other people and how difficult to himself. He tried to copy their manners and their opinions, in the hope that he might attain to their inner spirit. By successive disasters he gradually discovered that he had been basing his life upon an unwarranted assumption—the assumption that people did in fact believe what they professed to believe and like what they wished him to think they liked. His honest mind, which had first led him to make this assumption, now lost no time in clearing it away. He began to think fast and furiously for himself. Something like this must have been the history of Butler's own mind. There is a rancour in the way in which he speaks of prigs—a word of wide meaning as he used it, covering all who practise self-deception—which seems to tell of old wrongs, hard to be forgiven, that had hampered his own progress in the art of seeing clearly. Once free from entanglements, his only object was to see things as they are. What chiefly struck him, as he shifted his penetrating gaze to and fro, was not so much that people's actions differed from their professions, as that they seemed for the most part to be genuinely unaware of the discrepancy. "They would have been equally horrified," he says of the congregation to which Theobald Pontifex ministered, "at hearing the Christian religion doubted, and at seeing it practised." The same confusion of mind seemed to be the rule in all departments of life. Nobody appeared able to give intelligible reasons for their conduct. Reasons of a kind they were ready enough to give, but they were reasons for a different sort of conduct altogether. The human mind evidently had an inexhaustible power of cheating itself. It could make men act with a view to their own enjoyment and sincerely believe they were acting upon some altruistic principle. At this point the honest onlooker, whose integrity forbids him to lie to himself, must choose which alternative he is going to adopt for his own guidance. Is he to take over the principles which he hears professed and follow them out in the scheme of conduct which they demand? Or is he to accept other people's practice and to work back from it to a new set of logical principles? Butler definitely rejects the first alternative. The principles which men praise so glibly may have their beauty and value—he is not concerned to deny that—but, as a matter of fact, they are too hard and fast to be practicable in the world with which we have to deal. What, then, is to be the motive substituted, the motive which, keeping tight hold of reality, we may discern in the background of life as it is lived? Why, what but the purest, simplest, most far-reaching hedonism? People act as they do in order to get what they want. It is no use abusing it as a low motive if it is the only one effective or possible. Besides, people do not necessarily want ignoble things; they may want all manner of virtuous and exalted pleasures; only let them recognize that they desire them because they like them, because they are pleasures in fact, not because they conform to some standard imposed on them from outside, without reference to their likes and dislikes. For instance, a man may deny himself comforts in order to give money in charity; but if he does so it is because it is more disagreeable to him to feel ungenerous. It matters very little what you want, so long as it is not something which it is inconvenient to others to let you have. Lie to others if you must—indeed, in this makeshift world it will often be necessary—but in no circumstances whatever lie to yourself. That is Butler's final injunction; it underlies all his work and is insisted upon with all the wit and eloquence and irony at his command.

Such, then, was Butler's principle, and in his most fantastic moods he never betrayed it. He argued with his eyes firmly fixed on life as he found it. He saw that nothing is in fact either perfectly good or perfectly bad, moral or immoral, true or false; and that humanity unconsciously recognizes this by acting in any given case upon some kind of compromise. Thus, his incessant preaching of compromise as the only reasonable guide of life was due to no surrender of principle. It was the direct result of his perception that life cannot get on without it. The one sin against principle, in his view, would be the refusal to admit the presence of facts. This, he was fully aware, is a danger that especially besets any one who tries to construct a theory of life, even a theory so purely empirical as his own. The one safeguard against becoming a doctrinaire he held to be a sense of humour. Only if you possess the faculty of rounding on yourself, of treating your own argument lightly, of seeing that there is no reason for being solemn about it, are you safe to avoid the academic outlook which forces facts to suit its theory. Hence his vehement denunciations of what he called "earnestness," the state of mind which gets so much absorbed in its argument that it forgets to be perpetually correcting it by facts. He wished to be consistent, but not too consistent. Compromise again! A slave to his theories he certainly was not. His personal idiosyncrasies break

out freely in all his books. He never made the smallest attempt to sink his own preferences. His violent literary and artistic prejudices are seldom far out of sight; and, whatever the subject in hand may be, methods of evolution or Homer or Alpine Sanctuaries, any turn of the page may find him pausing to slap Raphael or Dickens, or to extol Handel at the expense of all other musicians, with a serene assumption that there can be no disagreement on the matter among sensible men. This constant irrepressibility keeps his books bubbling with life, challenging the attention and the intelligence of the reader with their sharply individual savour. An infusion of prejudice did not defeat the object which was always before him—the perception of reality. On the contrary, it gave just the seasoning necessary to counteract a tendency towards over-logical precision. In the Butler language, logic should always be crossed with a certain amount of inconsistency to arrive at a result which is true to life.

Whether this extraordinarily fresh and sharp-sighted mind really left out nothing essential in its summing up of human nature, or whether for all his candour Butler was constitutionally unable to give all sides of life their due, there can be no question of the refreshing effect upon any matter that he chose to handle. His part was to trouble stagnant waters. He had the rare gift of putting old things in new lights, of revealing unsuspected properties in objects so familiar that most people take them for granted without a glance, like the pictures and wall-papers of their own rooms. The shock of pleasure, or at any rate of interest, which is started by such revelations, shows how unusual they are and how hard it is to look at the world with fresh eyes. The interest of *Erewhon* is mainly this. A critic has called the book "a shrewd and biting satire on modern life and thought," and so indeed it is; but for the most part the satire consists in simply inverting certain ordinary beliefs and customs. If you wish to make sure that your umbrella will not be inadvertently carried off by some one else, a good plan is to put it in the stand upside down. You thus call attention to it and force people to notice that it is not theirs. Similarly when we find that the Erewhonians punish disease and cure crime, our own treatment of crime and disease is pushed into prominence. Its illogicalities do not need to be pointed out; they betray themselves the moment our method is set in a position so peculiar that special notice is attracted to it. The device is, of course, a great deal older than Erewhon, but Butler made it particularly his own. As a piece of literary construction *Erewhon* has no great merit. It is badly laid out, the characterization is very slight, the fabulous country fails to seem actual. The topsiturviness, in part so well contrived, is not carried far enough. Most of the time the Erewhonians are indicated as living in an elaborate civilization, comparable to our own—as indeed the point demands; but occasionally they appear as simple primitive folk of another epoch altogether. In other words, the contrast between them and ourselves is made at times to depend upon a different kind, and at times upon a different stage, of civilization; and the confusion destroys the verisimilitude. From this aspect the sequel, *Erewhon Revisited,* which appeared thirty years later, is a far better book. It is more compact, and more use is made of character. But in neither are the purely literary qualities the point. The point is for Butler to throw his cool, unmerciful light upon certain of our ideas and institutions, and this he does in both to admiration.

It is clear, indeed, that the view of writing as an art had small interest for Butler. He was even not above trouncing it as academic and priggish, forgetting that art is of necessity present whenever a writer succeeds in making a concise and intelligible sentence. Such a book as *The Fair Haven,* an ironic defence of the miraculous element in Christianity, is of course art of a very ambitious kind. It is a studied argument, strictly sustained "in character," the character being a fictitious divine who is gravely introduced to the public in a prefatory memoir. But the fact that on its first appearance it was in some quarters taken seriously is not a tribute to its artistic merit. Irony ought not to defeat itself by being kept so fine as all this, and *The Fair Haven* is reasonably open to the charge of dulness, the only one of Butler's books of which this could be said. The three books in which he attacked Darwin's treatment of the theory of evolution, *Life and Habit, Evolution, Old and New,* and *Luck, or Cunning,* are in his most characteristic manner. We must not venture to pronounce on their scientific value, though their vigorous statement of difficulties must have been at least of indirect use. But there can be no two opinions of their exhilarating torrent of wit and sarcasm, their profusion of ingenious illustrations, their shrewd flashes of insight. Much the same may be said of that queer book, *The Authoress of the Odyssey,* in which the acutely argued theory, though meant to be taken quite literally, moves in an atmosphere of high spirits which seem continually hanging on the verge of a burst of laughter. *Alps and Sanctuaries* and *Ex Voto* are concerned with the mountain shrines of Piedmont and the Ticino, a country which Butler returned to again and again and knew intimately. They are far more than a description of exquisite places and little-known monuments of a fine local art. They brim over with the author's swift mocking laughter, as well as with his innumerable fads and fancies. Any one who wishes to make Butler's acquaintance should begin with the first of these two books. In no other did he write with a freer, fuller, more felicitous self-abandonment.

Finally, we have *The Way of All Flesh,* the novel at which he worked intermittently for many years, without ever satisfying himself that it was ready for publication. It was not issued till the year after his death. Butler had designed to rewrite it, and it is certainly true that nothing less was needed to correct its shapelessness, its top-heavy diffuseness, its awkward chronology. But it may be doubted whether he had the power to make it faultless in these respects, and its searching biting truthfulness needed no revision. With all its obvious flaws it is an extraordinary book. Butler was in no way disposed to conceal the bitter animus which he felt against the side of middle-class life with which it deals, and from the first page to the last pours out hatred and scorn upon very nearly all the characters it contains. Yet it is not really one-sided. It is not the work of a soured or jaundiced mind, but of a mind goaded with a passion for truth and honesty. The ferocious sarcasm of such a portrait as that of old Mr. Pontifex, Ernest's grandfather, is strictly just, for the author never suggests that the cowardly, bullying, lying old humbug is to be blamed, in any simple sense. He cannot help being a humbug. It is the clear-sighted Ernests of the world who are to be blamed if they put up with humbug and pomposity, even in their parents and grandfathers—that is the moral of the story. To sting them to revolt Butler pours out all the plentiful phials of his wrath on the soul-destroying stupidity which deliberately teaches that truth should not be looked in the face. Not till we are certain that the Pontifex family have completely died out can his denunciations seem shrill or exaggerated. It may be felt that truth had best assert itself in other ways than by revolt—that is another question altogether. But whatever may be thought of the moral, Butler's steel-pointed wit remains a pure delight. The most stimulating quality a book can possess is the sense that behind it there is a critical intelligence which is always on the watch, piercing through and through its material, never taking things for granted, never allowing itself to be drugged by picturesque phrases or unreal sentiment. There are not so many such that Samuel Butler's high integrity, his hatred of insincerity and mystification, his fearlessness, his splendid power of satire, can be overlooked or lightly valued. (pp. 329-30)

"Samuel Butler," in The Times Literary Supplement, *No. 352, October 8, 1908, pp. 329-30.*

FRANCIS HACKETT   (essay date 1910)

[*Hackett was a respected Irish-American biographer, novelist, and literary critic who wrote during the first half of the twentieth century. His reviews appeared in the* New Republic, the Saturday Review of Literature, *and other prominent American periodicals. In the following excerpt from an essay originally published in 1910, Hackett commends the iconoclastic spirit manifested in* The Way of All Flesh.]

[In] Samuel Butler there is little of the conventional rococo which endears Winston Churchill, poor man, to his enormous and quite uncritical audience. But the astonishing and delightful thing about Samuel Butler is that he does not write *The Way of All Flesh* to satisfy the lovers of pure and plain principle and clap them on the back. He does not seek to justify the select few to their estimable selves, at the expense of the purveyors of conventional fodder. No, indeed. Samuel Butler's sword is not only Castilian but double-edged. With one edge he undoubtedly attacks the uncritical, but with the other, and the keener, he cuts into the supercilious prig. It would be a mistake to say that his novel shows indifference to idealism. It is limited in its appeal precisely because it can interest only those who have endured introspection and the tortures of conscience and the agonies of self-criticism. But the small company that has an intellectual sense (usually a proud intellectual sense) of affinity with Hamlet need not suppose that Samuel Butler is going to do for them what the Russian novelists have done. On the contrary, the whole burden of his novel is the follies of Hamletry. If his book is merciless to the ordinary religious father and mother in England, it is equally relentless toward their mollycoddle son. But there is this difference: Samuel Butler understands the mollycoddle to the core and loves him: and he exhibits his evolution because he knows that the follies which he detects could not exist except in a soul that is to be valued.

Ernest Pontifex, Samuel Butler's hero, suffers horribly from idealism. When at last he begins to see the idiocy of trying to be absolutely perfect, it is only to discover that the huge majority of the men have never been troubled by any such idiocy, but have quite naturally adopted the Eleventh Commandment, "Thou Shalt Not Be Found Out." It stands to reason that those who have never worried morbidly about their imperfection will take a thoroughly Rooseveltian attitude toward Ernest, call him a mollycoddle, and have done with it. The curious thing is that Butler himself seems to agree with Roosevelt. He singles out one Towneley as the graceful, lovable, well bred, "red-blooded" type—an empiric man who would generally echo John Mitchel's dictum that a certain nation of mollycoddles "would have been saved long ago if it wasn't for their damned souls." Ernest Pontifex adores Towneley and he sums up the difference between that eupeptic gentleman and his confused self in these words: "I see it all now. The people like Towneley are the only ones who know anything that is worth knowing, and like that of course I can never be. But to make Towneleys possible there must be hewers of wood and drawers of water—men, in fact, through whom conscious knowledge must pass before it can reach those who can apply it gracefully and instinctively as the Towneleys can. I am a hewer of wood, but if I accept the position frankly and do not set up to be a Towneley, it does not matter."

This attitude of Butler's is summed up in the phrase, "The result depends upon the thing done and the motive goes for nothing." But there is a difference, after all, between this scorn for fine-spun and high-flown theories that don't work out in practice and the ordinary scorn of the rationalist. Ultimately Butler is not a red-blood. Ultimately he has "confidence that it is righter and better to believe what is true than what is untrue, even though belief in the untruth may seem at first most expedient." But he is sick of the writers who do nothing except prate about idealism. He is sick of the idealistic pimple that is priggishness. He is sick of the people, unconventional or conventional, whose ideals are heard but not seen.

The hatred of rules is no small part of Samuel Butler's nature, especially the rules of parents and schoolmasters. The only rules he regards as worth knowing are not the fixed rules of institutions, but the rules of thumb by which human beings are living. Over and over again he parallels that philosophy which says that an actress who remains chaste is a prig. "Extremes are alone logical, and they are always absurd, the mean is alone practicable and it is always illogical. . . . Sensible people will get through life by rule of thumb as they may interpret it most conveniently without asking too many questions for conscience's sake." This lesson, of course, would be wasted on the Average Man, who is seldom even aware of his illogicality. It would be wasted on the ordinary American, who would be bored even at hearing it discussed. But it will not be wasted on those who, like Samuel Butler himself, want primarily to live a life as honest as is compatible with happiness, and who are feeling like Judge Grosscup, the deplorable "need for honesty" in others. *The Way of All Flesh* is, in the clever phrase of H. G. Wells, a Dreadnaught. It is of about the same length as *Tono-Bungay* and little shorter than *The Old Wives' Tale,* or *It Never Can Happen Again.* To my mind it is a wiser book than any of these, which is saying a good deal. It has less brilliance than *Tono-Bungay* and less suggestiveness. It has less background and less social idiom than Bennett's great book. It is less whimsical and less ingratiating than De Morgan's. But it knows more about the old Adam than any of the three, and can give them fifty yards in a hundred for critical intelligence. Occasionally in novels you read of a Great Writer whose work is so stupendous that the novelist doesn't dare to quote from it (unless he be as foolhardy as May Sinclair). Well, Samuel Butler would be an ideal figure for that Great Writer. In *The Way of All Flesh* there is not (me judice) one meretricious line. The same might be said of *The Old Wives' Tale,* but the difference between a successful novel of ideas and successful novel of manners is like the difference between exploding dynamite and discharging a rifle.

Butler admits you into an easy and humorous free masonry, if you happen to be his sort. Not with a wink, but quietly and serenely. He tells you what you've always privately known,

but never admitted, and he also clears up many things you thought you knew, but didn't. He is not above a certain perversity about the idealist, but he makes no easy jokes and works off nobody else's wisdom or sentiment. What he has is his own, and it is very astonishing and shrewd of its kind. (pp. 85-9)

Francis Hackett, " 'The Way of All Flesh', " in his Horizons: A Book of Criticism, *B. W. Huebsch, 1918, pp. 83-91.*

WILLIAM LYON PHELPS (essay date 1916)

[An American critic and educator, Phelps was for over forty years a lecturer on English literature at Yale. His early study The Beginnings of the English Romantic Movement *(1893) is still considered an important work, and his* Essays on Russian Novelists *(1911) was one of the first influential studies of the Russian Realists written in English. In the following excerpt from his introduction to* The Way of All Flesh, *Phelps characterizes Butler's work as "diabolical" but nevertheless finds value in his caustic criticisms.*]

[Bernard Shaw] informed us that he learned more from Butler than from any other writer; a statement easier to believe than some of his affirmations. Unfortunately the disciple is so much above his lord in popular estimation that we have all been withholding honour where honour is due. After one has read Butler, one sees where many of Shaw's perversities and ironies came from. The foundation of Butler's style is the paradox; moral dynamics are reversed; the unpardonable sin is conventionality. His masterpiece answers no questions; solves no problems; chases away no perplexities. Every reader becomes an interrogation point. Butler rubs our thoughts the wrong way. As axiom after axiom is ruthlessly attacked, we pick over our minds for some missile to throw at him. It is a good thing for every man and woman whose brain happens to be in activity to read this amazingly clever, original, brilliant, diabolical novel. And for those whose brains are in captivity it may smash some fetters. Every one who understands what he reads will take an inventory of his own religious and moral stock.

Butler delighted in the rôle of Advocatus Diaboli. In his *Note-Books* he has the following apology for the Devil: "It must be remembered that we have heard only one side of the case. God has written all the books." Well, He certainly did not write this one; He permitted the Devil to have his hour. The worst misfortune that can happen to any person, says Butler, is to lose his money; the second is to lose his health; and the loss of reputation is a bad third. He seems to have regarded the death of his father as the most fortunate event in his own life; for it made him financially independent. He never quite forgave the old man for hanging on till he was eighty years old. He ridiculed the Bishop of Carlisle for saying that we long to meet our parents in the next world. "Speaking for myself, I have no wish to see my father again, and I think it likely that the Bishop of Carlisle would not be more eager to see his than I mine." Melchisedec "was a really happy man. He was without father, without mother, and without descent. He was an incarnate bachelor. He was a born orphan."

One reason why *The Way of All Flesh* is becoming every year more widely known is because it happens to be exactly in the literary form most fashionable in fiction at this moment. It is a "life" novel—it is a biography, which, of course, means that it is very largely an autobiography. Three generations of the hero's family are portrayed with much detail; the plot of the story is simply chronological; the only agreeable woman in the book was a personal friend of the author. Not only are hundreds of facts in the novelist's own life minutely recorded, it is a spiritual autobiography as well. It was his habit to carry a notebook in his pocket; whenever a thought or fancy occurred to him, immediately to write it down. An immense number of these fatherless ideas are now inwoven in this novel. The result is that the reader literally finds something interesting and often something valuable on every page. The style is so closely packed with thought that it produces constant intellectual delight. This is well; for I can recall no delight of any other kind. (pp. vi-viii)

[Butler] has released all the repugnance, the rebellion, the impotent rage of childhood. He had an excellent memory, and seems to have forgiven nothing and forgotten nothing that happened to him in the dependent years of his life. It is an awkward thing to play with souls, and Butler represents the souls of boys treated by their parents and by their schoolteachers with astonishing stupidity and blundering brutality. It is a wonderful treatise on the art of how *not* to bring up children; and I should think that every mother, father, and teacher would feel some sense of shame and some sense of fear. For a good many years children are in the power of their elders, who so greatly excel them in physical strength and in cunning; but every child, no matter how dutifully he may kiss the rod, becomes in after years the Judge of his parents and of his teachers. Butler's sympathy with children, whose little bodies and little minds are often in absolute bondage to parents both dull and cruel, is a salient quality in his work. One is appalled when one remembers how often the sensitive soul of a little boy is tortured at home, simply by coarse handling. This championship of children places Butler with Dickens, though I suppose such a remark would have been regarded by Butler as an insult.

I think that the terrific attack on "professing Christians" made in this novel will be of real service to Christianity. Just as men of strong political opinions have largely abandoned the old habit of reading the party paper, and now give their fiercest opponents a hearing, so I think good Christian people will derive much benefit from an attentive perusal of this work. The religion that Butler attacks is the religion of the Scribes and Pharisees, and unless our religion exceeds that, none of us is going to enter the Kingdom of Heaven. The Church needs clever, active antagonists to keep her up to the mark; the principle of Good is toughened by constant contact with the principle of Evil; every minister ought to have in his audience a number of brilliant, determined opponents, who have made up their minds they will believe nothing he says; I have no doubt that God needs the Devil.

Thus, although I firmly believe this is a diabolical novel, I think it will prove to be of service to Christianity. I know it has done me good. I cannot forget Butler's remark about all those church-goers who would be equally shocked if anyone doubted Christianity or if anyone practised it. (pp. viii-ix)

William Lyon Phelps, in an introduction to The Way of All Flesh *by Samuel Butler, E. P. Dutton & Company, 1916, pp. v-x.*

[V. WOOLF]   (essay date 1919)

[*Woolf is one of the most prominent figures of twentieth-century English literature. Like her contemporary James Joyce, with whom she is often compared, Woolf is remembered as one of the most innovative of the stream-of-consciousness novelists. Concerned primarily with depicting the life of the mind, she revolted against traditional narrative techniques and developed her own highly individualized style. Woolf's works, noted for their subjective explorations of characters' inner lives and their delicate poetic quality, have had a lasting effect on the art of the novel. A discerning and influential critic and essayist as well as a novelist, Woolf began writing reviews for the* Times Literary Supplement *at an early age. Her critical essays, which cover almost the entire range of English literature, contain some of her finest prose and are praised for their insight. In the following review of* The Way of All Flesh, *she contends that the chief strength of the novel lies in its intellectual honesty.*]

" . . . like most of those who come to think for themselves, he was a slow grower," says Samuel Butler of Ernest, the hero of *The Way of All Flesh.* The book itself has had the same sort of history, and for much the same reason. For seven years after the first publication in 1903, it sold very slowly. It was reprinted, "widely reviewed and highly praised," but still hung fire. Then, in 1910, the flames caught; twice in that year it was reprinted, and the impression before us is the eleventh of the second edition. A wise author might choose that fate rather than one of more immediate splendour. No reading public is going to be rushed into buying an author who thinks for himself; its instinct of self-preservation protects it from that folly; first it must go through all the processes of inspection and suspicion. But the public is fundamentally sagacious. It makes up its mind after seven years or so as to what is good for it, and when it has made up its mind it sticks to it with dogged fidelity. Therefore, one is not surprised to find that in the year 1915 "Butler's writings had a larger total sale than in any previous year since their publication."

Satisfactory as this record is, it is also much in keeping with the character of *The Way of All Flesh.* The book was written very slowly. Butler worked at it intermittently during twelve years. It is thus like a thing that has grown almost imperceptibly, a cactus or a stalactite, becoming a little shapeless, but more and more solid and sturdy year by year. One can imagine that he had grown too fond of it to part with it. Such a work is too uncompromising to make many friends when it first appears. It bears in every part of it the mark of being a home-made hobby, rather than the product of high professional skill. All his convictions and prejudices have been found room for; he has never had the public in his mind's eye. So, just as Butler himself would have appeared in a crowd of fashionable people, *The Way of All Flesh* appeared among the season's novels, awkward, opinionated, angular, perverse. Nor, upon re-reading, does it appear that time has softened these qualities, and, to speak the truth, they are not qualities that are admirable in a novel. The note-book which, according to Butler, every one should carry in his waistcoat pocket, has left that secret post of observation and thrust itself forward. Shrewd, didactic passages taken from its pages constantly block the course of the story, or intrude between us and the characters, or insist that Ernest shall deliver them as if they were his own. For this reason Ernest himself remains a sheaf of papers, written all over with the acute and caustic observations of his maker, rather than an independent young man. Such is the penalty that a writer pays for indulging his hobby too far, even though the hobby be, as it was with Butler, the hobby of using his brain. The scene when Ernest attempts the seduction of Miss Maitland is a proof that when Butler's young men and women stepped beyond the circle illuminated by his keen intelligence they found themselves as thin and faltering as the creations of a tenth-rate hack. They must at once be removed to the more congenial atmosphere of the Law Courts. There are certain scenes, it appears, which must be written a great deal too quickly to allow of the deliberate inspection of a note-book, and viewed with a passion impossible to the disillusioned eyes of the elderly. There is a sense, after all, in which it is a limitation to be an amateur; and Butler, it seems to us, failed to be a great novelist because his novel writing was his hobby.

In every other respect his gifts were such as to produce a novel which differs from most professional novels by being more original, more interesting, and more alive. The elderly and disillusioned mind has this advantage—that it cares nothing what people think of it. Further, its weight of experience makes up for its lack of enthusiasm. Endowed with these formidable qualities and a profound originality which wrought them to the sharpest point, Butler sauntered on unconcernedly until he found a position where he could take up his pitch and deliver his verdict upon life at his ease. *The Way of All Flesh,* which is the result, is thus much more than a story. It is an attempt to impart all that Butler thought not only about the Pontifexes, but about religion, the family system, heredity, philanthropy, education, duty, happiness, sex. The character of Christina Pontifex is rich and solid, because all the clergymen's wives whom Butler had ever known were put into her stew. In the same way Dr. Skinner has the juice of innumerable headmasters in his veins, and Theobald is compounded of the dust of thousands of middle-class Englishmen. They are representative, but they are, thanks to Butler's vigorous powers of delineation, distinctly themselves. Christina's habit of day-dreaming belongs to her individually, and is a stroke of genius—if Butler did not promptly remind us that it is a little silly to talk about strokes of genius. We should not like to say how often in the course of reading *The Way of All Flesh* we found ourselves thus pulled up. Sometimes we had committed the sin of taking things, like genius, on trust. Then, again, we had fancied that some idea or other was of our own breeding. But here, on the next page, was Butler's original version, from which our seed had blown. If you want to come up afresh in thousands of minds and books long after you are dead, no doubt the way to do it is to start thinking for yourself. The novels that have been fertilized by *The Way of All Flesh* must by this time constitute a large library, with well-known names upon their backs.

[V. Woolf], "The Way of All Flesh," in The Times Literary Supplement, *No. 910, June 26, 1919, p. 347.*

J. MIDDLETON MURRY (essay date 1919)

[*Murry is recognized as one of the most significant English critics of the twentieth century, noted for his studies of major authors and for his contributions to modern critical theory. Perceiving an integral relationship between literature and religion, Murry believed that the literary critic must be concerned with the moral as well as the aesthetic dimensions of a given work. In addition, he considered the critic's primary duties to be the differentiation between greater and lesser artists and the creation of a hierarchical delineation of those worthy of further study. Anticipating later scholarly opinion, Murry championed the writings of Marcel Proust, James Joyce, Paul Valéry, and*

D. H. Lawrence in numerous books and essays, and while his critical approach led some commentators to question his ability to render objective assessments of the authors he discussed, his essays are highly valued for their originality and insight. In the following excerpt, Murry objects to the basic assumptions of The Way of All Flesh *while praising some of its characterizations.*]

Like all unique works of authors who stand, even to the most obvious apprehension, aside from the general path, [*The Way of All Flesh*] has been overwhelmed with superlatives. The case is familiar enough and the explanation is simple and brutal. It is hardly worth while to give it. The truth is that although there is no inherent reason why the isolated novel of an author who devotes himself to other forms should not be "one of the great novels of the world," the probabilities tell heavily against it. On the other hand, an isolated novel makes a good stick to beat the age. It is fairly certain to have something sufficiently unique about it to be useful for the purpose. Even its blemishes have a knack of being *sui generis.* To elevate it is, therefore, bound to imply the diminution of its contemporaries.

Yet, apart from the general argument, there are particular reasons why the praise of *The Way of All Flesh* should be circumspect. Samuel Butler knew extraordinarily well what he was about. His novel was written intermittently between 1872 and 1884 when he abandoned it. In the twenty remaining years of his life he did nothing to it, and we have Mr. Streatfeild's word for it that "he professed himself dissatisfied with it as a whole, and always intended to rewrite, or at any rate, to revise it." We could have deduced as much from his refusal to publish the book. The certainty of commercial failure never deterred Butler from publication; he was in the happy situation of being able to publish at his own expense a book of whose merit he was himself satisfied. His only reason for abandoning *The Way of All Flesh* was his own dissatisfaction with it. His instruction that it should be published in its present form after his death proves nothing against his own estimate. Butler knew, at least as well as we, that the good things in his book were legion. He did not wish the world or his own reputation to lose the benefit of them.

But there are differences between a novel which contains innumerable good things and a great novel. The most important is that a great novel does not contain innumerable good things. You may not pick out the plums, because the pudding falls to pieces if you do. In *The Way of All Flesh,* however, a *compère* is always present whose business it is to say good things. His perpetual flow of asides is pleasant because the asides are piquant and, in their way, to the point. Butler's mind, being a good mind, had a predilection for the object, and his detestation of the rotunder platitudes of a Greek chorus, if nothing else, had taught him that a corner-man should have something to say on the subject in hand. His arguments are designed to assist his narrative; moreover, they are sympathetic to the modern mind. An enlightened hedonism is about all that is left to us, and Butler's hatred of humbug is, though a little more placid, like our own. We share his ethical likes and dislikes. As an audience we are ready to laugh at his asides, and, on the first night at least, to laugh at them even when they interrupt the play.

But our liking for the theses cannot alter the fact that *The Way of All Flesh* is a *roman à thèses* ["thesis novel"]. Not that there is anything wrong with the *roman à thèses,* if the theses emerge from the narrative without its having to be obviously doctored. Nor does it matter very much that a *compère* should be present all the while, provided that he does not take upon himself to replace the demonstration the narrative must afford, by arguments outside it. But what happens in *The Way of All Flesh?* We may leave aside the minor thesis of heredity, for it emerges, gently enough, from the story; besides, we are not quite sure what it is. We have no doubt, on the other hand, about the major thesis; it is blazoned on the title page, with its sub-malicious quotation from St. Paul to the Romans, "We know that all things work together for good to them that love God." The necessary gloss on this text is given in Chapter LXVIII, where Ernest, after his arrest, is thus described:—

> He had nothing more to lose; money, friends, character, all were gone for a very long time, if not for ever; but there was something else also that had taken its flight along with these. I mean the fear of that which man could do unto him. *Cantabit vacuus* ["A penniless man has nothing to lose"]. Who could hurt him more than he had been hurt already? Let him but be able to earn his bread, and he knew of nothing which he dared not venture if it would make the world a happier place for those who were young and lovable. Herein he found so much comfort that he almost wished he had lost his reputation even more completely—for he saw that it was like a man's life which may be found of them that lose it and lost of them that would find it. He should not have had the courage to give up all for Christ's sake, but now Christ had mercifully taken all, and lo! it seemed as though all were found.
>
> As the days went slowly by he came to see that Christianity after all met as much as any other extremes do; it was a fight about names—not about things; practically the Church of Rome, the Church of England, and the free thinker have the same ideal standard and meet in the gentleman; for he is the most perfect saint who is the most perfect gentleman. . . .

With this help the text and the thesis can be translated: "All experience does a gentleman good." It is the kind of thing we should like very much to believe; as an article of faith it was held with passion and vehemence by Dostoevsky, though the connotation of the word "gentleman" was for him very different from the connotation it had for Butler. (Butler's gentleman, it should be said in passing, was very much the ideal of a period, and not at all *quod semper, quod ubique* ["that which is always and everywhere"]; a very Victorian anti-Victorianism.) Dostoevsky worked his thesis out with a ruthless devotion to realistic probability. He emptied the cornucopia of misery upon his heroes and drove them to suicide one after another; and then had the audacity to challenge the world to say that they were not better, more human, and more lovable for the disaster in which they were inevitably overwhelmed. And, though it is hard to say "Yes" to his challenge, it is harder still to say "No."

In the case of Ernest Pontifex, however, we do not care to respond to the challenge at all. The experiment is faked and proves nothing. It is mere humbug to declare that a man has been thrown into the waters of life to sink or swim, when there is an anxious but cool-headed friend on the bank with a £70,000 life-belt to throw after him the moment his head goes under. That is neither danger nor experience. Even if Ernest Pontifex knew nothing of the future awaiting him (as we are assured he did not) it makes no difference. *We* know he

cannot sink; he is a lay figure with a pneumatic body. Whether he became a lay figure for Butler also we cannot say; we can merely register the fact that the book breaks down after Ernest's misadventure with Miss Maitland, a deplorably unsubstantial episode to be the crisis of a piece of writing so firm in texture and solid in values as the preceding chapters. Ernest as a man has an intense non-existence.

After all, as far as the positive side of *The Way of All Flesh* is concerned, Butler's eggs are all in one basket. If the adult Ernest does not materialise, the book hangs in empty air. Whatever it may be instead it is not a great novel, nor even a good one. So much established, we may begin to collect the good things. Christina is the best of them. She is, by any standard, a remarkable creation. Butler was "all around" Christina. Both by analysis and synthesis she is wholly his. He can produce her in either way. She lives as flesh and blood and has not a little of our affection; she is also constructed by definition, "If it were not too awful a thing to say of anybody, she meant well"—the whole phrase gives exactly Christina's stature. Alethea Pontifex is really a bluff; but the bluff succeeds, largely because, having experience of Christina, we dare not call it. Mrs. Jupp is triumphantly complete; there are even moments when she seems as great as Mrs. Quickly. The novels that contain three such women (or two if we reckon the uncertain Alethea, who is really only a vehicle for Butler's very best sayings, as cancelled by the nonexistent Ellen) can be counted, we suppose, on our ten fingers.

Of the men, Theobald is well worked out (in both senses of the word). But we know little of what went on inside him. We can fill out Christina with her inimitable day-dreams; Theobald remains something of a skeleton, whereas we have no difficulty at all with Dr. Skinner, of Roughborough. We have a sense of him in retirement steadily filling the shelves with volumes of Skinner, and we know how it was done. When he reappears we assume the continuity of his existence without demur. The glimpse of George Pontifex is also satisfying; after the christening party we know him for a solid reality. Pryer was half-created when his name was chosen. Butler did the rest in a single paragraph which contains a perfect delineation of "the Oxford manner" twenty years before it had become a disease known to ordinary diagnosis. The curious may find this towards the beginning of Chapter LI. But Ernest, upon whom so much depends, is a phantom—a dream-child waiting the incarnation which Butler refused him for twenty years. Was it laziness, was it a felt incapacity? We do not know; but in the case of a novelist it is our duty to believe the worst. (pp. 107-13)

> *J. Middleton Murry, "Samuel Butler," in his* Aspects of Literature, *W. Collins Sons & Co. Ltd., 1920, pp. 107-20.*

PAUL ELMER MORE   (essay date 1921)

[More was an American critic who, along with Irving Babbitt, formulated the doctrines of New Humanism in early twentieth-century American thought. The New Humanists were strict moralists who adhered to traditional conservative values in reaction to an age of scientific and artistic self-expression. In regard to literature, they believed a work's implicit reflection of support for the classic ethical norms to be of as much importance as its aesthetic qualities. More was particularly opposed to Naturalism, which he believed accentuated the animal nature of humans, and to any literature, such as Romanticism, that broke with established classical tradition. His importance

as a critic derives from the rigid coherence of his ideology, which polarized American critics into hostile opponents (Van Wyck Brooks, Edmund Wilson, H. L. Mencken) or devoted supporters (Norman Foerster, Stuart Sherman, and, to a lesser degree, T. S. Eliot). He is especially esteemed for the philosophical and literary erudition of his multivolume Shelburne Essays *(1904-21). In the following excerpt, More discusses Butler's iconoclastic approach to science and literature.*]

In a moment of candour [Butler declared] that he had "never written on any subject unless [he] believed that the authorities on it were hopelessly wrong"; and the authorities happen to have included the philologians entrenched in the universities, the most eminent names in science, and in religion both the orthodox theologians of the Church and the sceptics of the higher criticism. It is not wonderful that he should have exclaimed with a sad pride: "In that I write at all I am among the damned."

His bout with the philologians took place in the lists of Homeric and Shakespearian criticism. To supplant the "nightmares of Homeric extravagance," as he calls them, rightly enough, "which German professors have evolved out of their inner consciousness," he evolved for his part a delicious fancy that the *Odyssey* was composed by a young woman, and that the palace of Odysseus was set by her in her own home in the Sicilian Trapani. I have never met a Greek scholar who would confess that he had even read Butler's work on *The Authoress of the Odyssey;* they prefer the Butlerian canon of condemning without reading. Well, I have perused the book, but I shall neither accept nor condemn. It is uncommonly clever, and the part at least which deals with the question of authorship is amusingly plausible; but the argument, of course, is all based on inference, and does not amount to much more than a *jeu d'esprit.* His other contention in philology, in which he rearranges the order of Shakespeare's Sonnets and builds up a new story of the events underlying them, should, I feel, be taken rather more seriously. I would not say that, in my judgment, he has made out his case; for here again the evidence is too inferential, too evasive, to be thoroughly conclusive. But I do think that he has demolished the flimsy theories of Sidney Lee and certain other so-called authorities, and that his own constructive criticism is worthy of attention.

But these tilts with the entrenched philology of the universities were mere skirmishes, so to speak; the real battle was with the authorities in science and theology. These were the gentlemen, "hopelessly wrong," whom Butler undertook to set right by the genial art of "heaving bricks." In science the great enemy was none other than Darwin himself, with all those who swore by the name of Darwin. The dispute did not touch the fact of evolution itself, for Butler to the end was a staunch evolutionist; nor did it concern the Darwinian theory of the survival of the fit, for here again Butler was thoroughly orthodox. The question at issue was the cause of those variations out of which the more fit were selected for survival—and this, I take it, is still the *casus belli* ["cause for war"] which renders the resounding warfare of the biologists so amusing a spectacle to one who has set his feet in the serene temples of scepticism. . . . (pp. 182-84)

On the one side stood in array the host of Darwinians—or ultra-Darwinians, for Darwin himself was provokingly muddled and inconsistent in his statements—who held that the *via vitae* was a path of incalculable hazard, to whom life was pure mechanism and evolution meant a transference to biology of the mathematical law of probability. On the other side,

Self-portrait painted by Butler when he was twenty-nine years old.

in which for some time Butler was almost the sole champion in England, stood those who believed that the significant variations arose from the purposeful striving of individual creatures to adapt themselves to their surroundings, and that the selective power of fitness was part of a grand design working itself out consciously in the evolution of life.

Now it is not my business to pronounce judgment in so learned a dispute; the non-scientific critic who should presume to come between such quarrelsome kinsfolk would probably fare like the proverbial peacemaker between man and wife. I can only say that to Butler the dignity of science and the very issues of life seemed to be involved in the debate: "To state this doctrine [of the Darwinians]," he declares, "is to arouse instinctive loathing; it is my fortunate task to maintain that such a nightmare of waste and death is as baseless as it is repulsive." Butler's particular contribution to the Lamarckian side was what he called "unconscious memory," the theory, that is, that the acquired experience of the parent was passed on to the embryo and carried by the offspring into life as an instinctive propensity. Later he learned that the same theory had been propounded by an Austrian biologist named Hering, and thereafter he was careful to ascribe full credit to his predecessor. (pp. 184-86)

But I hasten to descend from the aërial heights of pure science to a region where the critic of letters may feel that he is walking with his feet on the ground. The notable fact is that

Butler's whole literary career took its start from his interest, at first merely amateurish, in the Darwinian theory of evolution. Readers of *Erewhon* will remember the three chapters of that Utopian romance entitled "The Book of the Machines." These chapters stand out as the most brilliant section of the romance; they are furthermore the germ out of which the whole narrative grew, and in a way strike the keynote of much of his later writing. No one, I think, can read this "Book of the Machines" without feeling that it is the work of a powerful and original intellect, but one is likely also to lay it down with a sense of bewilderment. There is insight here, the insight of a mind brooding on the course of human history and speaking with apparent sincerity of a terrible danger to be avoided. Yet there is withal a note of biting irony; and what precisely the object of this irony may be, or how this irony is to be reconciled with the tone of sincerity, the book itself gives one no clue to determine.

Nor do the author's direct allusions to his purpose give us much ease. In a letter to Darwin accompanying a present of the first edition of *Erewhon,* in 1872, Butler disclaims any intention of being "disrespectful" to the *Origin of Species,* and avows that the chapters on Machines, written primarily as a bit of pure fun, were rewritten and inserted in *Erewhon* as a satire on the pseudoscientific method of Bishop Butler's *Analogy.* Again, in the preface to the second edition of the book published a few months after the first, he expresses his "regret that reviewers have in some cases been inclined to treat the chapters on Machines as an attempt to reduce Mr. Darwin's theory to an absurdity." He is surprised that the specious misuse of analogy really aimed at should not have occurred to any reviewer. Evidently he is alluding again to Bishop Butler, yet if one turns to page 84 of the narrative itself, one sees that Paley's famous analogy of the watch, and not Bishop Butler at all, was in the author's mind when he wrote the book. This is already a little confusing, but confusion is worse confounded by the statement in a letter written shortly before our Erewhonian's death. Now, looking back at the matter through the bitterness engendered by what he regarded as a long persecution, he says: "With *Erewhon* Charles Darwin smelt danger from afar. I knew him personally; he was one of my grandfather's pupils. He knew very well that the machine chapters in *Erewhon* would not end there, and the Darwin circle was then the most important literary power in England."

Here is a beautiful case for genetic criticism—if the word "genetic" has any meaning outside of the dictionary and the laboratory—and by following the development of Butler's ideas one may learn perhaps how the baffling mixture of irony and sincerity got into the famous chapters on Machines and became a kind of fixed habit with him. Darwin's *Origin of Species* reached Butler in New Zealand soon after its publication, and evidently quite carried him off his feet. Under the first spell of admiration he composed a little essay on **"Darwin among the Machines,"** which was printed in the *Press* of Canterbury, New Zealand, in 1863. Years later, commenting in one of his scientific books on this article, he admits that he had taken Darwin at his face value without much reflection; "there was one evolution" for him then, and "Darwin was its prophet." And the article itself fully bears out this statement. Caught by the plausible simplicity of evolution as an extension of purely inorganic law into the organic world, Butler carried the mechanical analogy a step further and undertook to show what would happen when machines had progressed to the stage of independent racial existence and had surpassed man, just as the animal kingdom had been evolved out of the vegetable, and the vegetable from the mineral. His conclusion is "that war to the death should be instantly proclaimed against them. Every machine of every sort should be destroyed by the well-wisher of his species. . . . Let us at once go back to the primeval condition of the race."

It must be remembered that Butler wrote this essay while living in the free primitive uplands of New Zealand, during the happiest period of his life, and that the note of primitivism in his peroration is probably in large measure sincere. At the same time there is a word in his later comment which points to another trait in his intellectual make-up which was active from the beginning. He started, he says, with the hypothesis of man as a mechanism, because that was the easiest strand to pick up, and because "there was plenty of amusement" to be got out of it. Now one may amuse one's self with a theory which one holds in all sincerity; but fun of that sort has a way of running into irony or sarcasm, and so one may detect in this first essay the germ of Butler's later manner. He was ever prone to make fun, and sometimes a very strange sort of fun, when he was most in earnest.

It is clear that Butler was both attracted and teased by Darwin's great work, and that he did not rest with his first impression. Two years later, having meanwhile returned to England, he sent another letter to the Canterbury *Press,* which he entitled **"Lucubratio Ebria"** and signed with a different name. "It is a mistake, then," he says in this second letter, "to take the view adopted by a previous correspondent of this paper." His thesis now is that machines are really an extension, so to speak, of a man's limbs, of the tools, that is to say, which the mind invents in its progress towards a higher organization; as such the development of machinery is the measure of an inner growth and need not be feared.

As yet, apparently, the fun of the thing was still uppermost in Butler's mind. He put the two essays together as "The Book of the Machines" and wrote his Utopian romance about them without feeling any serious discordance in the points of view, and could even send the volume to Darwin with an assurance of his loyalty. But the rift was already there. As he continued to reflect on the matter, the significance of the second point of view took on more importance and he began to see its scientific implications. Out of these reflections grew his book on *Life and Habit,* in which he first, frankly and definitely, announced himself as a champion of the teleological theory of evolution against the mechanistic principles of the ultra-Darwinians.

But our concern now is with the fact that in the latest, revised edition of *Erewhon* the two essays on machines, though much enriched and enlarged in the process of revision, still lie side by side, with no word to tell the reader which of the two represents the author's real views. The result is piquant to say the least. In one chapter the dread of machines, as they have been developed to a state of almost independent consciousness, is expressed with a depth of conviction that can leave no doubt of the author's sincerity. Here he speaks as a Darwinian *à outrance* ["to the bitter end"], but as a Darwinian filled with loathing for the spectres conjured up by his own science. Yet turn a few pages, and you will find machines glorified "as a part of man's own physical nature," the instruments by which alone he advances in "all those habits of mind which most elevate [him] above the lower animals":

Thus civilization and mechanical progress advanced hand in hand, each developing and being developed by the other, the earliest accidental use of the stick having set the ball rolling, and the prospect of advantage keeping it in motion. In fact, machines ought to be regarded as the mode of development by which human organism is now especially advancing, every past invention being an addition to the resources of the human body.

What is one to make of this flagrant contradiction? I might answer by asking what one is to make of the contradictions of life. It is true that the progress of civilization seems to be coincident with mechanical invention. We believe that; and yet can any one look at the state of the world today, at the monotony of lives that have been enslaved to machinery, at the distaste for work and the unrest of the worker that have arisen partly as a consequence of this subservience, can any one seriously contemplate the growing materialism of modern life, its dependence for pleasure on the whirl of wheels and the dance of images, with its physical distraction and its lessening care for the quiet and ideal delights of the intellect—can any one see these things and not feel a stirring of something like terror in the soul at the tyranny of the creatures we have evoked from the soulless forces of nature? Life is a dilemma, and only the fool thinks it is simple. In "The Book of the Machines" one of its enigmas is presented with a keenness of observation and a cogency of style that must give the author a high place among the philosophical writers of the age.

However Butler may have been disposed towards the evolution of machines, the Erewhonians themselves chose to see in them a menace to humanity, and decreed that they should be ruthlessly destroyed. *Erewhon* is thus the story of a people who are living backwards, so to speak, of a country seen through the looking-glass and conceived in the spirit of irony. There is no doubt of this intention, you will feel it on every page of the romance; only, and this is the tantalizing spell of the book, it is not always easy to guess against whom the irony is directed. We know from Butler's statement elsewhere, not from the book itself, that the account of the Erewhonian treatment of crime as a disease to be cured in hospitals and of disease as a crime to be punished in prisons was meant to be taken *au pied de la lettre* ["literally"] and that the law of *Erewhon* was commended by way of satirizing the law of England. But no sooner has the reader adjusted his mind to this form of attack than he finds himself engaged in that terrible arraignment of the Church as working through the so-called Musical Banks, where the Erewhonians themselves become the object of irony. And so the satire sways this way and that from chapter to chapter. It is all good fun, but it is mighty bewildering unless one comes to the book with a knowledge of Butler's ideas derived from other sources; and even then one does not always know on which side of the mouth to laugh—though of the laughter there is never any doubt. The fact is that irony had become a habit with Butler, and of its application he little recked. He could even believe he was ironical when in truth he was perfectly sincere; which is still more delightfully puzzling than his ambiguous application of irony.

This trait comes out in his treatment of Christianity. He had early become interested in the problem of the Resurrection of Christ as the corner-stone of the whole dogmatic edifice, his own sober conclusion apparently being that Christ did not die on the Cross, but was buried while in a trance, and afterwards appeared actually in the flesh to the disciples. His first

thoughts on the question were published in a pamphlet, now quite forgotten; and late in life he wrote his *Erewhon Revisited,* which is nothing less than an elaborate and vicious satire, in rather bad taste, on the miraculous birth and the Ascension. But between these two publications comes *The Fair Haven,* as enigmatical a work as ever was penned. Here the problem of the Resurrection is discussed by a priest, who, having fallen into scepticism, finds for himself at last a haven of peace in the solution of every doubt. Now, for all that one can learn from Butler's life, the solution offered by his fictitious hero was intended to be taken ironically, and the whole treatise should be regarded as a diatribe against Christian dogma. To his friend, Miss Savage, it is "sanglant satire," and so apparently it appeared to Mr. Jones. Very well; but what really happened? The book was reviewed in several of the Evangelical periodicals of the day as perfectly orthodox, and so alert a critic as Canon Ainger sent it to a friend whom he wished to convert. And to-day a candid reader, even with full knowledge of Butler's avowed intention, is likely to close the book with an impression that, despite a note of irony that breaks through the language here and there, the argument as a whole forms a singularly powerful and convincing plea for Christianity. The hallucination theory of the Resurrection propounded by Strauss is analysed and refuted with remorseless logic. Even the trance theory, which Butler himself was inclined to accept, is answered, briefly indeed, but plausibly. On the other side Dean Alford's half-hearted attempt to reconcile the discordant Gospel narratives of the Resurrection undergoes the same deadly analysis. But the truth of the Resurrection, Butler then argues, is dependent on no such reconciliation of the records; in fact a divine revelation, he maintains, designed for the needs of all sorts and conditions of men, ought, in the nature of the case, to present the truth in a variety of manners. Here at last one begins to feel that the satire of Christianity itself is coming out into the open, and in [Henry Festing Jones's *Samuel Butler*] a bit of conversation is recorded which would seem to confirm such a view. Butler is talking with the Rev. Edwin A. Abbott:

> He said to me: "And did you really mean none of that part seriously?"
> I said: "Certainly not; I intended it as an example of the kind of rubbish which would go down with the *Spectator.*"
> Abbott said: "Well, I can only say you would have found a great many to sympathize with you, if you had meant it seriously."
> I said, rather drily: "That, I think, is exceedingly probable," meaning that there was no lack of silly insincere gushers.

That has a categorical ring; yet in an article published in the *Universal Review* four years after the date of this conversation, where there can be no possible suspicion of irony, Butler is repeating as his own this same argument for the adaptability of revelation and of the Christ-Ideal.

What can we make of all this? The key to the difficulty may be found, I think, in a sentence of his preface to *The Fair Haven:* "I was justified," he says, "in calling the book a defence—both as against impugners and defenders," i.e., of Christianity. Butler held it his mission to "heave bricks" at two groups of eminent men: he was himself deeply immersed in science, but he nursed a magnificent grudge against the professional scientists of his day both for their bigotry and for personal reasons; and in like manner he was interested in religion and indeed always called himself a churchman of a sort, but he hated any one else who assumed that name. And so in *The Fair Haven* he was having his fun—and powerful good fun it is—with Strauss and the scientific impugners on the one side, and with Dean Alford and his tribe of puzzled defenders on the other; he enjoyed the sport so much that he persuaded his friend and almost made himself believe that he was having fun also with the object impugned and defended by them. But besides the faculty of irony Butler possessed in equal measure the faculty of hard logic. And so it happened that when he came to present the case in support of Christianity any lurking intention of irony was soon swallowed up in the pure delight of building up a constructive argument such as the professional champions of the Church, in his opinion, had quite failed to offer. He was helped in this by his firm belief that of the two the professors of science were a more bigoted and dangerous class than the professors of religion.

In this union of logic with irony Butler belongs with Huxley and Matthew Arnold, as he is their peer in the mastery of a superbly clear and idiomatic English style. He differs from them in that he possessed also a certain gnome-like impudence of fancy which led him into strange ambiguities and throws a veil of seeming irresponsibility over much, not all, of his writing. Readers who are not made uneasy by this remarkable combination of qualities, and who have no fear for their own heads where brickbats are flying, will find in him one of the most fascinating authors of the Victorian age. Only, perhaps, a word of caution should be uttered in regard to Butler's one regular novel, *The Way of All Flesh.* There is no irony here, but the bludgeoning of a direct and brutal sarcasm; he is no longer our Victorian Swift of *A Tale of a Tub* or of *Laputa,* but a voyager to the land of the Yahoos. It is a powerful book, even a great book in a way; but it is bitter, malignant, base, dishonourable, and dishonest. Unfortunately, to the smudged and smeared minds of a Bernard Shaw and a Gilbert Cannan [see Additional Bibliography] it appeals as Butler's masterpiece, and much of his fame, so far as he is known to the general public, derives from Shaw's eulogy of this one work. That is a pity, in my judgment; for the true Butler, perhaps I should say the finer Butler, is not there, but in the books where irony plays waywardly backwards and forwards through a network of subtle logic. (pp. 187-99)

Paul Elmer More, "Samuel Butler of Erewhon," in his A New England Group and Others: Shelburne Essays, eleventh series, *1921. Reprint by Phaeton Press, 1967, pp. 167-200.*

C. E. M. JOAD (essay date 1924)

[*Joad was a minor English philosopher and the author of numerous volumes, most of which address questions of ethics, religion, and human nature. He became popular and widely known in England during World War II through his participation in the B.B.C. panel-show "Brains Trust." Through the radio program and his written works, Joad espoused his own philosophy based on rationalism, pacifism, and distrust of much of modern science for its role in industrializing and standardizing society. In the following excerpt, he discusses humor in Butler's writings.*]

Butler was a much more irresponsible man than Shaw; less serious, less earnest, less grown up. He felt what he felt strongly, but he could always forget it on occasions and take a mental holiday. He was not always grinding the axe of creative evolution; he was not always girding at the professionals; more often than not he was playing with ideas as a boy

plays with a ball and, incidentally, shocking the pundits for the sheer fun of the thing. This boyish irresponsibility is the source of most of Butler's wit. His intellectual fortune was spent in buying penny crackers to put beneath the pedestals of the great. Yes! But they were not always the great. Any one would do at a pinch, if none of the great were within earshot.

Butler had an inordinate love of mischief. He loved to shock and to startle. He is like a schoolboy sticking pins into the master's chair; when the master jumps nobody is more delighted than Butler. Hence his wit is much less frequently than Shaw's the pointed expression of a serious conviction. When he tells us that God did not allow tobacco to be discovered earlier, because he knew that, if he had, St. Paul would certainly have forbidden its use, he is having a sly dig at St. Paul because it annoys him to see people taking St. Paul so seriously. St. Paul is a favourite subject with Butler. "Paul," Ernest reflects, "had fought with wild beasts at Ephesus— that must indeed have been awful—but perhaps they were not very wild beasts; a rabbit and a canary are wild beasts; but, formidable or not as wild beasts go, they would nevertheless stand no chance against St. Paul, for he was inspired; the miracle would have been if the wild beasts escaped, not that St. Paul should have done so."

An excessive reputation for piety or moral eminence is too much for Butler's equanimity. It is like a china ornament on a shelf to a boy with a tennis ball, a standing temptation to be knocked over. It is not that the boy has any special grudge against the ornament as an ornament, but he dislikes the "don't touch me air" with which the veneration of his elders has surrounded it. Any one whom Butler considers smug and priggish like the ornament, as for example, Mendelssohn, Tennyson, or St. Anthony, is gently taken down. St. Anthony, Butler thinks, must have liked the devils that tempted him better than other devils for old acquaintance sake, and showed them as much indulgence as was compatible with decorum. "Besides . . . St. Anthony tempted the devils quite as much as they tempted him; for his peculiar sanctity was a greater temptation to tempt him than they could stand. Strictly speaking, it was the devils who were the more to be pitied, for they were led up to St. Anthony to be tempted and fell, whereas St. Anthony did not fall."

Butler is like a schoolboy, too, in his sexlessness. A bachelor himself, he achieves all his literary effects without women. There is a shrill treble in his accents which bids them take warning that his interests lie elsewhere; he is interested in ideas, not in women, just as a boy of fourteen is interested in steam engines and not in girls, and this comparative freedom from the pre-occupation of most adults enables him, while maintaining a philosophic aloofness from the more emotional aspects of life, to concentrate the more keenly on those intellectual problems which were the only stimulus he acknowledged. While robbing his work of warmth and colour, it enhances its intellectual force and clarity; while diminishing him as a man, it enlarges him as a thinker. It helps us, moreover, to understand his irreverence and his brilliance. He is irreverent like a school boy and brilliant like a clever schoolboy. When he tells us that it is better to have loved and lost than never to have lost at all, he is making a fool of Tennyson, as a fifth form boy can on occasion make a fool of his teacher. The joke has no intellectual content; it expresses no real conviction about the importance of losing one's wife; it does not even prevent Butler from expressing exactly the reverse sentiment on the next page. He says it for the sheer love of saying a clever thing. And it is no doubt very clever, so clever that, like many of his remarks, it dazzles us into thinking that it really means something, besides its cleverness. Now much of Butler's work has this dazzling yet deceptive quality. It is iridescent as a bubble when it catches the light, but there is nothing inside it; it is brilliant with the surface brilliance of a well soaped bald head, but there is nothing beneath it.

This mental frivolity expresses itself in many different ways, and of these two, at least, are sufficiently important to demand separate treatment, since they have led critics to include Butler's *jeux d'esprit* among his real convictions. The first is in his love of topsy-turvydom, the second in his predilection for bluffing.

An early and famous cartoon represents Shaw standing on his head and gesticulating with his legs. It would have been apter as a cartoon of Butler. He loves to startle people by disturbing their conventional beliefs, and his favourite way of doing this is to take a conventional belief and turn it inside out.

His experiments in Erewhonian morality are perhaps the best example of this tendency. The Erewhonians turn our moral ideas upside down; they observe the same code as ourselves, but it is inverted and, on each of the two occasions on which Higgs visits them, differently inverted. On his first visit he finds that they regard moral deficiency as an accident, lying entirely outside the control of the individual, demanding sympathy and condolence, and, in certain cases, treatment at the hands of the family straightener, but meriting neither shame nor punishment. Bodily illness on the other hand is regarded with all the feelings of conscientious repugnance which we reserve for moral wrong doing. The person who is taken ill is treated as a criminal, punished not infrequently by death, and driven accordingly to make his illness worse by depriving himself of all those remedies which the necessity of concealing it from his friends and acquaintances places out of his reach.

But illness is only treated in this way because it is a special case of misfortune. All misfortune is culpable; but undeserved misfortune is doubly so, since the victim, knowing that he has done nothing to merit his sufferings, suffers the more keenly. His suffering makes him doubly disagreeable to his friends; being miserable himself he is a cause of worry to others, while the necessity for sympathy which his misfortune calls forth only makes those the more uncomfortable who feel that they have none to give.

Erewhon contains the account of a trial in which a youth is charged with the misfortune of having been defrauded of his estate. The judge delivers a lengthy speech, in which all the strictures which we pass upon moral guilt are applied to undeserved misfortune. The judge concludes by pointing out that the youth has been either truly or falsely accused. In the first case the charge is a just one and he must suffer accordingly; in the second case he is guilty of the misfortune of being the victim of a false accusation, and must again suffer accordingly. "There are two classes of people in this world," says Butler in *The Way of All Flesh,* "those who sin, and those who are sinned against; if a man must belong to either, he had better belong to the first than to the second."

On Higgs' second visit to Erewhon he finds that these principles have been largely abandoned, and that, as a result of what is understood to have been his teaching on his former visit, wickedness is now encouraged and virtue penalised; this at least is the case in the establishments known as Moral Deformatories, in which instruction in imperfection is given to the young. Higgs finds that the Moral Deformatories teach precisely the reverse of the precepts instilled in European schools. Youths are here taught consistently to aim at imperfection on the ground that it may well be attainable within a reasonable time, whereas perfection can never be realised. The master rings the bell on a half-holiday in order to provoke the boys to disobey the summons to return to school, as a means of stimulating their refractory systems. Insincerity is encouraged on the ground that the greatest happiness of the greatest number must be promoted, and that most people dislike sincerity in others. Classes are held in gambling and book-making, and boys are caned for telling the truth or saying what they think. On the same visit Higgs is present when a girl is arraigned before the Mayor for being deficient in childish vices. The only fault that her father can find with her is that of occasionally breaking things. The Mayor reproves him for having omitted to punish her for this fault and so providing her with a motive for deception. "How can you," he says, "expect your child to learn those petty arts of deception without which she must fall an easy prey to any one who wishes to deceive her? How can she detect lying in other people unless she has had some experience of it in her own practice?" The importance of teaching children to lie early by punishing them when found out is then impressed on the parent, and George Washington's words, "I cannot tell a lie," interpreted "in their most natural sense, as being his expression of regret at the way in which his education had been neglected."

It is difficult to believe that Butler means all this very seriously. In *Erewhon Revisited* he takes no trouble to apply his inversion of morality consistently, and frequently forgets all about it, while many of his examples are perilously near the borderline of farce. Butler is simply trying to persuade his readers of his own conviction that morality is relative and not absolute. In his view morality is a biological growth, designed to safeguard the particular stage of advancement that society happens to have reached. Morality changes, and changes rapidly. There is no virtue to-day which has not at some time or other been thought a vice, and there is scarcely any offence for which people are now put in prison that has not been regarded, not only as a virtue, but even as a sacred and religious duty, by some nation of antiquity. In order to illustrate this truth Butler resorts to his favourite device of topsy-turvydom. He wants to show that what we do is no more within our control than what we feel, that there is no real distinction between the animating mind and the animated body, and that, accordingly, it is just as logical to praise and blame people for what they feel in their bodies as for the actions which they falsely believe they initiate, through what they are pleased to call their free wills.

Butler possessed a natural contradictoriness of temperament, which made him more anxious to compel people to think than to tell them what to think. He, therefore, takes a current belief which men have obtained ready made from the social shop just as they obtain their boots and their clothes, turns it upside down, shows that there is almost if not quite as good a case to be made out for its contrary as for itself, and then leaves the reader to his thoughts.

Partly with this object, partly from sheer devilment, Butler is never so happy as when he is taking a current *cliché,* as often as not a text, and by the alteration of sometimes no more than a word or two, entirely reversing its meaning. The following are a few examples of this process taken at random from his works.

Butler soliloquising on Ernest's mistake in taking the honest girl for the prostitute: "If the better part of valour is discretion, how much more is discretion the better part of vice"; inscription on the Moral Deformatory in **Erewhon Revisited:** " 'When the righteous man turneth away from the righteousness that he hath committed, and doeth that which is a little naughty and wrong, he will generally be found to have gained in amiability what he has lost in righteousness.'—Sunchild Sayings, Chap. XXII., v. 15"; Professor Panky in **Erewhon Revisited** substituting "and forgive us our trespasses, but do not forgive them that trespass against us," for the current version of the Sunchild's prayer, on the ground that nobody would be such an ass as deliberately to insist that the forgiveness of his own sins should be made dependent upon his forgiveness of other people's. "Resist good, and it will fly from you," "Jesus with all thy faults I love thee still," are other sayings of Butler's in the same vein.

The above are jokes pure and simple, jokes which conceal an idea but do not express a conviction. There is no seriousness of intention in their utterance, no sting in their tail, and in this respect they are sharply to be distinguished from the epigrams of Swift or even of Shaw, whose wit is the normal vehicle for the expression of their bitterness and indignation. Only very occasionally are Butler's shafts barbed, as when he says of the farmers who composed Theobald's congregation that "they would have been equally horrified at hearing the Christian religion doubted or seeing it practised."

Butler has a habit of constructing careful and elaborate theories which he does not hold. His object in doing so is conjectural. It may be simply his desire to make people think at any price; it is more probable, however, that these carefully elaborated hypotheses are simply the expressions of his natural mischievousness. They are, in short, gigantic bluffs. The most famous of them is contained in the chapter entitled, "The Book of the Machines," in **Erewhon.** This chapter contains extracts from the treatise of an extinct Erewhonian professor, who endeavoured to show that machines represent the next level of evolutionary achievement, and that, just as man had supplanted the Mesozoic reptiles, so would machines supplant man. The following is a brief summary of the Professor's arguments, which are very ingenuous.

The first stage of the argument consists in showing that there is no real difference in kind between men and machines. The thesis here falls into two parts. First, machines are alive just as much and just in so far as men are alive; secondly, men are pieces of mechanism just as much and just in so far as machines are pieces of mechanism.

Taking the first point first, we notice that machines have evolved biologically just as men have, growing ever more complex and highly developed in the process. It is true that evolution proceeds by means of the struggle for survival, and that machines cannot struggle; but then they have induced man to do their struggling for them. As long as he fulfils this function all goes well with him, but "the moment he fails to do his best for the advancement of machinery by encouraging the good and destroying the bad, he is left behind in the race of competitors; and this means that he will be made uncomfortable in a variety of ways and perhaps die." In the process of evolution machines have developed digestive and reproductive organs. The early machines, such as ploughs and carts, ate through man's stomach, the fuel which set them going having first to be burnt in the furnace of a man or a horse, whence it was transferred into the energy of the ploughman or carthorse. But whereas animals were formerly the only stomachs of machines, many have now developed stomachs of their own and consume their own food. The stoker is as much a cook for his engine as our own cooks are for ourselves. Colliers, pitmen, coal merchants, coal trains, and the men who drive them, are all employed in tending the material wants of machines.

As for reproductive systems, it is obvious that machines produce other machines. Man, it is true, causes them to do so; but do not insects effect the fertilisation of many plants, would not the plants die out unless they could get agents utterly foreign to themselves to do their own fertilisation for them, and is that any reason for saying that plants do not reproduce themselves? Machines, then, are alive; their order of life is admittedly different from that of men, but it is not less real on that account.

But if machines are like men in respect of their aliveness, still more are men like machines in respect of their automatism. What is a man after all but the mechanical resultant of a number of different forces? Some of these forces act upon him before birth and are comprised under the term heredity; others act upon him after birth under the names of environment and education. A man's nature, therefore, is entirely determined by external agencies; he is what he is because of the various influences to which he has been subject, and what he does is the direct result of his being what he is. His actions are, in fact, just as much the result of past and present external stimuli, as are those of a machine; they are as regular and as automatic. Admittedly man believes that he possesses free-will; but this belief is a delusion, born of his ignorance of the forces that act upon him. Recognising only some part of these forces, we are led to suppose that the actions for which we can see no antecedent cause are spontaneous, or are due to luck, to chance or to fortune; but these are only words invented to flatter human conceit, whereby we may escape the admission of our own ignorance. The future depends on the present, the present on the past, and the past is unalterable; from which it follows that the future is the same both for men and for machines.

Hence there is no essential difference in point of freedom between men and machines. They are, in fact, of like nature, a circumstance which might be expected from the fact that the former have made the latter. Machines are, in short, human extensions; they are the limbs which man has made outside himself. A hen makes an egg-shell and a nest; the former she makes inside herself, the latter outside; but that does not alter the fact that each is biologically speaking an extension of the hen. Similarly, eyes are the organs which man has made within himself to enable him to see; telescopes and microscopes are extensions of the same organs, which man has found it more convenient to make outside. But if we once begin to regard machines as organisms which we have created outside ourselves for our own use, does not the testimony of evolution require us to suppose that these organisms will gradually supplant those who made them? Each form of life known to biology, beginning as a development of a lower form, has gradually superseded that from which it arose. Man himself began in this way, as an unimportant development of the ape, yet gradually made himself master of the planet, consigning his simian ancestors to a position of comparative insignificance. Nor should this surprise us. It is the way in which evolution proceeds; life can make nothing out of nothing; it is only by working on the forms already achieved that it can generate new ones. Each new species represents a higher level of development than the one that preceded it, and, rising to power on the shoulders of its predecessors, continues pre-eminent until it in its turn is superseded.

The next chapter in the history of evolution will be the supersession of men by machines. Even now the machines are gradually acquiring a mastery. Created to serve us, they will only serve on condition of being served, "and that, too, upon their own terms; the moment their terms are not complied with, they jib, and either smash themselves and all whom they can reach, or turn churlish and refuse to work at all. How many men at this hour are living in a state of bondage to the machines? How many spend their whole lives, from the cradle to the grave, in tending them night and day?" Already there are more men engaged in tending machines than in tending men. And, since the number of those who are bound to the machines as slaves and of those who spend their lives in seeking machine advancement is increasing; must we not suppose that the machines are daily gaining ground on us?

The professor concludes by exhorting the Erewhonians to destroy the machines while there is still time, which advice, after long and disastrous wars between the machinists and the anti-machinists, they carry out so thoroughly that not a machine is left in the land.

I have given at some length the theories of the Erewhonian professor with regard to the dominance of machines, not only because of the intrinsic interest of the argument, which is highly ingenious and very characteristic of Butler, but also because it conveys in a very significant way his premonition of what was to come.

This is not the place for a dissertation on the growing mechanisation of civilisation, and the sacrifice of spiritual values to mechanical efficiency. It is, indeed, needless to point out how accurately Butler seems to have foreseen the admitted evils of our age. America and all it stands for, big business and large scale production, the cult of efficiency for its own sake and the tendency to value achievement in terms of material success, above all the growing complexity of life with the consequent loss of leisure and tranquility, are all of them phenomena which arise directly from the increasing part played by machinery in human existence. In delegating to machines an ever larger share of human functions, man has increasingly cut himself off from those sources of instinctive happiness which are bound up with the performance of natural actions. Living in towns and conveyed hither and thither in tubes, he has banished himself from Nature and condemned himself to spiritual wretchedness for want of her; reduced from the status of a craftsman to the *rôle* of a mere feeder and tender of machines, he has robbed his work of joy and choked the natural expression of his creative impulse.

Nor is Butler's attribution of intelligence to machines so fantastic as it might seem at first sight; at least, subsequent developments have made it less so. A typewriter capable of writing, and of translating as it writes into Irish, Gaelic, Russian, Greek or Persian, capable also of transcribing the higher mathematics, is one of the mechanical monsters of our age. Beside the efficiency of such a marvel, our poor human acquirements, so painfully won, so quickly lost and so liable to

go astray, seem such a clumsy and makeshift device that one is tempted to wonder how it is that Nature delays so long to make her next evolutionary move, and supersede us entirely by machines. Meanwhile, however, we become increasingly subordinated to and dependent upon them. We cannot live without them, and we devote most of our lives to making theirs more tolerable. Nobody who has read Karel Capek's play *R. U. R.*, and grasped its searching criticism of the mechanism of our times, will be disposed to laugh Butler's "Book of the Machines" too lightly out of court. Treat it as allegory or as prophecy, and it stands out as one of the most remarkable pieces of insight of the last century.

But for all this it would be a mistake to place too serious an interpretation on the "Book of the Machines." From most points of view it is little more than a piece of mischief on a large scale, written to amuse Butler and to startle his readers. It contains, for example, several doctrines which are the exact antithesis of his most profoundly held convictions. Machines, like men, evolve in the course of the struggle for survival; the weaker go to the wall and are superseded by those who are fitter to survive. What is this but sheer Darwinism? Butler did not believe that the struggle for survival was the cause of evolution. Why survival, he would have asked? What is the point of surviving unless one survives for a definite end, and in pursuance of a definite purpose? The survival of the fittest, if it means anything, means the survival of those who are fit only to survive. It is an expression of that mechanistic view of evolution to which Butler was so violently opposed.

And what of the doctrine of thorough-going determinism which is invoked to prove man's likeness to machines? Is it not attacked root and branch in all Butler's books on biology? He did not hold that man is a product of antecedent circumstances, and that his actions are the mechanical resultants of conflicting forces. On the contrary, he contended for man's innate creativeness, regarding him as the expression of an immanent vital principle, which moulds and directs what is material in the pursuit of a goal for which it unconsciously strives. Man for Butler is free just because perpetual change is the very essence of his being; he can make his own future just because there is no future until life, acting in and through man, brings it into being.

There is a passage in *Unconscious Memory* in which Butler comments upon the "Book of the Machines," and tells us how he came to write it. Although for the most part it expresses views which he had never held, or had long abandoned, it prepares the way for his own distinctive standpoint. From regarding machines as limbs which we had made outside ourselves, it was but a step to the conception of limbs as machines which we had made within ourselves. But the assertion of man's ability to make for himself in his own organism whatever he finds useful for the purposes of evolution, is the essence of the doctrine of Creative Evolution. Man is what he is, and has evolved as he has because he has wanted to in the past, just as his desire in the present provides the motive power for further evolutionary advances in the future.

This, as we have said, is Butler's real view. For the rest the "Book of the Machines" was written, as Butler himself admits, mainly for the purposes of amusement. "I soon felt that though there was plenty of amusement to be got out of this line, it was one that I should have to leave sooner or later."

Still it was certainly amusing, even though Butler did not believe a word of it. Why not, then, run it for fifty pages or so, and make the professors sit up? (pp. 167-84)

C. E. M. Joad, in his Samuel Butler (1835-1902), *Leonard Parsons, 1924, 195 p.*

LEONARD WOOLF (essay date 1927)

[*Woolf is best known as one of the leaders of the Bloomsbury group of artists and thinkers, and as the husband of novelist Virginia Woolf, with whom he founded the Hogarth Press. The Bloomsbury Group, which was named after the section of London where the members lived and met, also included Clive and Vanessa Bell, John Maynard Keynes, Lytton Strachey, Desmond MacCarthy, and several others. The group's weekly meetings were occasions for lively discussions of philosophy, literature, art, economics, politics, and life in general. Although the group observed no formal manifesto, Woolf and the others generally held to the tenets of philosopher G. E. Moore's* Principia Ethica *(1903), the essence of which is, in Moore's words, that "one's prime objects in life were love, the creation and enjoyment of aesthetic experience, and the pursuit of knowledge." Deeply interested in promoting the growth of experimental, modern literature, the Woolfs founded the Hogarth Press in 1917 "as a hobby," and through the years their efforts enabled the works of many new, nontraditional writers, such as T. S. Eliot and Robert Graves, to appear in print for the first time. A Fabian socialist during the World War I era, Woolf became a regular contributor to the socialist* New Statesman *and later served as literary editor of the* Nation *and the* Athenaeum, *in which much of his literary criticism is found. Throughout most of his life, Woolf also contributed essays on economics and politics to Britain's leading journals and acted as an advisor to the Labour Party. In the following excerpt, he assesses Butler's importance as a writer and thinker.*]

Butler is not, nor will he ever become, a popular writer. When time has had the last word with him and has given him his final and fossilized place in the strata of literature, he will be less popular and in a lower stratum than he is to-day. This judgement is not the result of prejudice or of some lack of sympathy with Butler. In my own private hierarchy of letters he occupies an extremely high place. His peculiar humour, his dialectic, his precise eccentricities, a certain dryness of mind which seems able to convert so many things to a pinch of fine dust—all these qualities happen to appeal very strongly to me personally. But the critic ought sometimes to allow his mind to work undisturbed by his personal likes and dislikes.

To read through Butler's early miscellaneous writings . . . , and then to go on from them to his later and latest works, gives one a solid basis for criticism. At first sight, it is extraordinary how little of the characteristic Butler of *Erewhon, The Way of All Flesh,* and *The Note-Books* there appears to be in the early writings. Only very rarely does one catch a glimpse of the original and satirical mind which later made its temporary home in Clifford's Inn and the British Museum. And yet closer inspection reveals the fact that the foundation upon which the later books were built had already been laid in the Cambridge essays and *Canterbury Settlement.* Here is a mind which thinks, not other people's thoughts, but its own—honest, clear, argumentative, singularly unemotional; and here is a style which never sinks below or attempts to rise above a certain level. In *Erewhon,* Butler found both a subject and himself. The elaborate satire on English life and society in the nineteenth century gives scope for the qualities mentioned above, and also for his eccentricities,

originalities, and humour. Yet it remains in many ways the queerest satire that has ever been written. It is extraordinarily unemotional. With Swift or Cyrano de Bergerac or any other of the writers who have created these inverted Utopias somewhere on the other side of the moon or the mountains, one always feels that they are animated by some human emotion towards the customs or institutions which they are satirizing. They feel anger or indignation or pity or mere amusement at the antics of mankind which they show us through the telescope or microscope of satire. But when Butler describes the Musical Banks or the attitude of the Erewhonians towards disease, it is impossible to detect the least flicker of emotion either towards us and our ways or the Erewhonians and their ways. This makes *Erewhon* a very queer book, for what can be more strange and disquieting than a humorist who is apparently never amused? It appeals to me personally, I repeat; I happen to have a particular liking for cranks, and the explanation of much which is puzzling in Butler should be looked for in crankiness. But this kind of queerness, crankiness, and unemotional frigidity is bound to narrow the circle of an author's readers. I will not enter upon the question whether it also precludes the book from greatness, whether, in fact, a great book, as some of our modern critics declare, must have something in it capable of appealing to all men. I rather suspect these vague generalizations about greatness and goodness. But in Butler's case, I think, the qualities which prevent him from being widely popular also prevent him from being a great writer. *Erewhon* and *The Way of All Flesh,* despite their originality of thought and humour, are not great books, and the reason is that the thought is always twisted a little, and kept from soaring by a twinge of crankiness, while thought, humour, satire, and language, owing to the absence of emotion, lack the warmth or glow which seems inseparable from great literature.

Erewhon, The Way of All Flesh, and the *Note-Books* contain the best things which Butler wrote, but *The Fair Haven* in some ways reveals more nakedly than any of Butler's other works the peculiar way in which his mind operated. It is an attack upon Christianity, and it is designed to show that the evidence for the Resurrection which we find in the New Testament cannot be accepted. The form of the book is elaborately ironical. It is supposed to be written by an imaginary person, the late John Pickard Owen, whose imaginary brother, William Bickersteth Owen, writes a prefatory memoir. The imaginary author is represented as having lost and then recovered his faith in Christianity, and the object of his posthumous book is to put his own experiences at the service of the infidel and the atheist, and so to convert them. His theory is that the kernel of Christianity is to be found in the story of the Resurrection, and that, while much of the New Testament must be rejected as unhistorical, if the central fact of the Resurrection can be established, everything else which really matters will remain. On the surface, the book professes to prove conclusively that Christ died on the cross, was buried, and rose again on the third day.

Butler's irony consists in making John Pickard Owen unconsciously disprove the very thing which he thinks that he is proving. So far there is nothing extraordinary in the scheme and form of the book; there are many precedents, particularly in English literature, for this kind of irony, which solemnly and elaborately disproves what on the surface you are solemnly and elaborately professing to prove. But the great ironists have never left the reader in any doubt as to what the real meaning is behind the façade of irony. One would have to be a very stupid person to misunderstand Swift when, in *A Modest Proposal to the Publick,* he writes:

> I have been assured by a very knowing *American* of my acquaintance in *London,* that a young healthy child, well nursed, is at a year old a most delicious, nourishing, and wholesome food, whether *stewed, roasted, baked,* or *boiled;* and I make no doubt that it will equally serve in a *fricassé,* or a *ragoust.* I do therefore humbly offer it to the *publick consideration,* that of the hundred and twenty thousand children already computed, twenty thousand may be reserved for breed, whereof only one-fourth part to be males. . . . That the remaining hundred thousand may, at a year old, be offered in sale to the persons of *quality* and *fortune* through the kingdom; always advising the mother to let them suck plentifully in the last month, so as to render them plump, and fat for a good table. A child will make two dishes at an entertainment for friends; and when the family dines alone, the fore or hind quarter will make a reasonable dish, and seasoned with a little pepper or salt, will be very good boiled on the fourth day, especially in *winter.*

All Butler's paraphernalia is in this passage of Swift's; the extraordinarily detailed, reasonable, quiet, serious argument which the reader is not intended to "take seriously." The remarkable thing about Butler is that nearly all his readers did take him seriously. The façade of irony is so delicate, the argument is so detailed and intricate, the real meaning below the surface so elusory, that, even though his book appeared in 1873, when the Resurrection was still a burning question of controversy, very few people saw what was its real meaning. Most reviewers and religious papers accepted Owen as a real person and the book as a defence of Christianity and orthodoxy, and Canon Ainger "sent it to a friend whom he wished to convert." So wide was the misunderstanding that Butler decided to bring out a second edition immediately, under his own name and with a preface in which he made it clear that the book was intended to be ironical.

I read *The Fair Haven* for the first time over twenty years ago, and I remember being astonished that its real meaning had not been understood. On re-reading it more carefully I am inclined to revise that original judgement. Of course, if one reads the book knowing its history, knowing that it is by Samuel Butler, the author of *Erewhon,* it is easy enough to detect the irony, though I believe that a large number of people who profess to understand the book would not be able to state clearly the exact way in which Butler makes Owen's proof of the Resurrection disprove it. But I am convinced that in 1873 it would have been the easiest thing in the world to fail in detecting that the book was ironical. There is nothing obviously ridiculous anywhere in the book. The irony is most marked in the prefatory memoir, in the incident of the lady saying her prayers, and in a sentence such as: "He therefore, to my mother's inexpressible grief, joined the Baptists, and was immersed in a pond near Dorking." The argument of the book and the hinge of irony upon which it turns are so elaborately contrived that, as I have said, very few even of those readers who know that the book is an attack on Christianity could explain exactly how the hinge is supposed to work. If I ever had to set an examination paper in English Literature for advanced students, one of the questions would be: "Summarize as briefly as possible John Pickard Owen's defence of the Resurrection in *The Fair Haven.*"

Whether it has to be reckoned as a failure on the part of the satirist and ironist if, for some reason, the vast majority of his readers mistake his meaning and intentions is an interesting question. In the case of Butler the failure was not due to any bungling or want of skill on his part, but to the very odd, individual conformation of his mind. His squib misfired, not because it was badly made, but because it was made to go on fizzling, fizzling, fizzling ironically, and never to explode. It is not everyone who can appreciate a squib which does not go off, or a rocket which never bursts into coloured stars. But for those who do, for those who can acquire a taste for caviare, or for the products of queer and "cranky" minds, *The Fair Haven* is a fascinating book. None of Butler's other books are more characteristic of his method of approaching and handling a subject or of his curious sense of humour. It has, however, upon me a strange psychological effect which I cannot explain, but which, to a much less degree, some of his other books also have: I enjoy reading it immensely; the elaborate argument and irony give me great intellectual pleasure; I am never at all bored by it; and yet from time to time I put the book down and say to myself: "Really, it is almost inconceivable that any human being ever had the patience to *write* this book."

The Fair Haven will always remain a literary curiosity, and Butler's fame will probably always rest on *Erewhon, The Way of All Flesh,* and *The Note-Books.* In some ways, however, he is at his best in *Alps and Sanctuaries,* a charming book which is the model of all modern books of ruminating, philosophical, cultured travellers. Those who knew Butler say that you can hear him talking in it, and what higher praise could there be than that? It flows on easily like good talk, giving infinite opportunities for that curious humour, irony, and gently twisted thought of its author. It is not a great book, though an extremely good one, and I can see in it no trace of a little man's mind. But if you turn to Butler's scientific works on evolution you see him at his worst, for he shows unexpectedly an exasperating littleness of mind. There can be no question of the cleverness and ability displayed in them. And though much of the controversy is dead, one can still read them with interest and with pleasure. No books on scientific subjects have ever been better written, and the flicker of Butler's irony gives them a strange, twinkling light of their own which is very attractive. And yet there is a littleness of mind displayed in them which is extremely irritating. It comes out partly in the personal hostility of Butler towards those with whom he disagrees. No doubt, Butler had much to complain about in his treatment by the scientists. They looked upon him with the jealous eye which professionalism and trade unionism always turn upon the amateur interloper. In fact, they ignored him. This may explain, but, to my mind, it does not excuse, Butler's tone of personal rancour and pique. It is the tone of a small-minded man nursing a grudge and unable to give his undivided attention to anything because he must always stop to see how he may "get his own back" on someone. Butler's charges against Darwin in *Unconscious Memory* are certainly not substantiated, and Darwin was quite justified in refusing to be drawn into a long, personal, acrimonious, and useless controversy. The continual girding at Darwin, which had already begun in *Evolution, Old and New,* becomes in the two later books intolerably irritating. And when exactly the same note begins to be struck in *Luck, or Cunning?* against Herbert Spencer, Romanes, Huxley, and when one notices that in most cases the point about which Butler is arguing is his own claim to be this or to have done that, the gusts of one's irritation become more violent and more prolonged.

It is becoming fashionable to make exaggerated claims for Butler as a scientific thinker. Thus, in a little book by Mr. Joad, the whole point of which is that it should be informative, if not educative, one is told that Butler made "an original contribution to the theory of Creative Evolution on the biological side, the inspired audacity of which places him second to none, not even to Darwin himself, among the pioneers of the nineteenth century." The statement is absurd. Butler was a man of great cleverness and intelligence, with a mind of considerable, but curiously limited, originality. When, in his prime, he applied his mind to the problem of evolution—at the moment when Darwinism was carrying all before it—he achieved two things. He subjected the Darwinian theory, particularly with regard to natural selection, to a very salutary criticism. He struck out for himself a highly ingenious theory that the offspring is one in personality with its parents, that instinctive and habitual actions are performed through unconscious memory of what we did in past generations when we were in the persons of our ancestors, and that evolution is due to variations which have been caused by the wants and endeavours of the living forms in which they appear. Both these achievements were of considerable interest, but it is fantastic to apply Mr. Joad's words to them. In both cases Butler stopped short long before he had produced anything of first-class importance. He stopped his constructive criticism to go off into interminable sterile personal controversy as to whether Darwin had committed a scientific felony or Herbert Spencer given him (Butler) the credit due to him. He left his own theory in the air, one of those clever improvisations which obviously contain much which is not true, but which may contain a vague adumbration of subsequently discovered truths. That may be inspired audacity, but it does not entitle Butler to the first place among scientific pioneers of the nineteenth century.

Butler's place in literature is really not very different from his place in science. *The Way of All Flesh* is the nearest he came to writing a great book, but it misses greatness. Its cleverness and originality are very great; the drabness of its irony is tremendous; it is solid and its characters are solid. It ought to have been either one of the great satires or of the great novels, but it is neither; it falls in between, into the place reserved for the "queer" books which one can always re-read and which always slightly disappoint one. The kink of crankiness in Butler's mind gives a kink to the book which only passion could have straightened out. But Butler was without passion. The temperature of his writing is, in fact, too low; it is cold to the touch, like something that is dead or nearly dead. Or to put it in another way, the atmosphere of his writing is like the atmosphere of the reading-room in the British Museum.

Though Butler cannot be numbered among the greatest writers, his books will probably be read by a small number of people long after many greater names are only remembered in histories of literature. In the history of English society he himself ought to have an honoured place. For he was a great iconoclast. The end of the nineteenth century was a time of breaking up, the breaking up of images and bonds and creeds and superstitions. In that salutary process of destruction Samuel Butler was one of the earliest and most efficient of the pioneers. (pp. 46-56)

Leonard Woolf, "Samuel Butler," in his Essays on

Butler's desk at Clifford's Inn.

Literature, History, Politics, Etc., *L. and Virginia Woolf, 1927, pp. 44-56.*

CLARA G. STILLMAN   (essay date 1932)

[*In the following excerpt, Stillman discusses Butler's influence on early twentieth-century authors and his anticipation of later intellectual trends.*]

Butler's influence on the writers of the past twenty-five years, especially the writers of fiction, has been immense. *The Way of All Flesh,* begun in 1870 and not touched after 1885, was so modern when it was published in 1903, that it may be said to have started a new school. One has only to compare it with the best-known novels that appeared between the dates of its beginning and its publication, and with those that came after, to see how profoundly it affected the period that followed. No one wrote in that vein before and a whole generation has tried to write in it since. According to M. Abel Chevalley, "a portion of the philosophy and literature in contemporary England, and even elsewhere, should be labelled 'After Butler'," and M. Valery Larbaud, whose translations and articles have made Butler known in France, is of the opinion that even as France was Voltairian at the end of the eighteenth century, so by 1910 intellectual England had become Butlerian. This was not due exclusively to Butler but partly also to the rapid penetration of twentieth-century fiction by psychoanalytical modes of thought, which his treatment of Ernest Pontifex foreshadows, and by the development of many of the social views he had anticipated in *Erewhon.*

It is not surprising that Butler's appeal should be so great in our day and that it was so negligible in his. His temper fits with extraordinary prevision into our own, into all that most sharply differentiates it from that of the latter half of the nineteenth century, in which he wrote. He was rebellious not with the manner and perceptions of his day, but of ours, and this distinguishes him from even the most rebellious of his contemporaries and has made him the one Victorian writer whose works are increasingly read, whose reputation is in the ascendant, who is in fact still and increasingly "news." Ruskin and Carlyle, Dickens, Thackerary, George Eliot, Charlotte Brontë, and even Meredith, whose feminism endeared him to a portion of posterity even if his style did not—however admirable they remain—have already a quaintness, a period quality which marks them as of the past. We must doubtless except from this list Mill and Hardy, who from something more basic and universal in their work are, within the range of their different fields and manners, more close to us in idiom and point of view; but these others have become so soon somewhat strange in their outmoded literary styles or faded dogmas, or their outgrown notions of morals, character or destiny. They are classics, a part of literary and social history, but Butler, who was their contemporary, though in some cases he did not begin writing until they had ceased, is our contemporary as well. He was alone among English writers in thoroughly transcending the current philosophic and psychological assumptions of his period, and he is alive today because many of his ideas have become the current assumptions of ours and because many are still controversial. "His merest platitudes," says a writer in the *Athenaeum,* "are the epigrams of Bernard Shaw and H. G. Wells." He foresaw the role of the machine with a terrifying vividness and completeness. He thought that disease was a crime and crime a disease, that education should consist largely of learning by doing, that poverty and wealth have a profound spiritual significance, that the process of growth to maturity consists largely of freeing oneself from one's parents, that the basis of all human activity is unconscious. His criticism of the natural selection hypothesis was one of the most brilliant of his day and has been reinforced by many critics since. He evolved a theory of heredity based on Lamarck which orthodox biology has never accepted, though some of its more important aspects have been carried forward by a thin but continuous line of biological thinkers, sometimes with recognition of Butler, sometimes without. He had moreover a far wider range than any other writer of his time, and in each of the many fields in which he wrought, he distinguished himself by some unique insight or discovery, which commends itself more easily, if not to our acceptance, at least to the larger scale of our curiosity and tolerance. For time has placed us above most of the battles in which he fought. A generation or two has enabled us to catch up with him. And we have the immense advantage of having *The Way of All Flesh* and the other books which give us the facts of his life, so intimately related to his work, and of having that work in its entirety.

But in spite of the revolution that has been operating in Butler's favour for more than a quarter of a century and is still going on, he is still incompletely known. His reputation rests only upon a fragment of what he did, and since all his more important writings are closely related to his personal development and to each other, the full significance even of the fragment escapes the reader who has no knowledge of the forces that moulded Butler's thought and no knowledge of his philosophic works. For lack of this knowledge many who have been vociferous in praise of *The Way of All Flesh* or of *Erewhon* have failed to grasp all the meanings these books contain.

Butler's books on evolution, hardly known even now except to a comparatively small number of students, are the key to all the others. Unless one has read *Life and Habit* and *Evolution, Old and New* one can have no realization of the unifying conception that underlies all his thought on psychology, sociology, art and literary criticism. Satirist, novelist, artist and critic that he was, he was primarily a philosopher, and it is from the biological foundation that we must ascend to the wide reaches of his philosophic outlook. He had an intuitive conception of the unconscious forces of our natures that in *Life and Habit* he sought to place on a scientific foundation. His biology was a bridge to a philosophy of life which sought a scientific basis for religion and endowed a naturalistically conceived universe with a soul. It was also, by its treatment of unconscious habit, a bridge to psychoanalysis about which Butler knew a good deal even though neither he nor anyone else had yet heard of it. Although he was a forerunner in this field to a remarkable degree, it is quite likely that, with his tendency to dislike those who were doing in some way other than his own the work of spiritual liberation, he would have recoiled with dismay from such an imputation. Nevertheless he understood pretty well the significance of his own insights. It is because his interest in biology was primarily philosophic that his books on evolution are often referred to as his philosophic works.

The artist and satirist persisted in the philosophic writer. The close-knit argument of *Life and Habit* is clothed in beauty and wit, and in the last chapter he wrote, "I have been trying to paint a picture," which naturally scandalized the scientists whose views he was combating, although they too were trying to paint a picture without knowing it. Darwin was painting a picture of evolution in the *Origin of Species,* in which natural selection was the dominant value. His subject is the same as Butler's but the conception, the point of view, the colour, the emphasis are different. There is plenty of impressionism in Darwin as later critics have shown. It was inevitable that it should be so with a subject so vast and new, so simple in outline, so baffling in detail, so subversive, intricate, and elusive. Since Darwin the picture of evolution has been variously repainted, its values undergoing changes both subtle and striking in various directions.

The most advanced of modern physicists, too, have discovered the value of the pictorial method which Butler applied to biology. It is prominent in the writings of Jeans, Whitehead and Eddington. "The artist desires to convey significances which cannot be told by microscopic detail," says Eddington, "and accordingly he resorts to impressionistic painting. Strangely enough the physicist has found the same necessity; but his impressionist scheme is just as much exact science and even more practical in its application than his microscopic scheme. . . . Through a picture we gain the insight necessary to deduce the various observable consequences." It is in this spirit that Butler tried to paint a picture in *Life and Habit.*

His complex nature contained many apparent contradictions. A pioneer and a conservative, a seeker for freedom and a hater of people with "causes," a ranger of many fields, with limited sympathies in each, profound, superficial, aggressive, shy, caustic and tender, devoted and egotistic, trustful, suspicious, eccentric and sane, the soul of courtesy, the pink of rudeness, charming, infuriating, he was full of generosity, envy, dislike, irritation and love. It is little wonder that he has puzzled not only the unsympathetic but many who have had a sense of his greatness and were capable of understanding it.

The explanation lies in the lasting damage done to Butler's affectional nature in his childhood and in his life-long effort to compensate himself in the multiple and complicated ways his subtle, indomitable spirit could devise. The root is one but the branches are many, and some of them bear strange fruit. His contradictory opinions, his excessive or insufficient emotions, his whimsical dislikes, his oddities of behaviour, his sensitiveness, his self-protective way of life were the tentative, unconscious efforts at adjustment of a soul that had not received its full birthright of initiation in human relations. But his most brilliant and profound conceptions had a similar origin. Butler's mind was so acute and powerful, so vivid and subtle, that whatever his life, he would probably have used it in some creative way, but the fact remains that his peculiar misfortunes were the very things that sharpened and stimulated his natural faculties and determined the material they should work on. "Man," says Anatole France, "has created everything out of his sorrow, even his genius." This is conspicuously true of Butler, who would perhaps have been a genius under any conditions, but who became the kind of genius he was through the defeats and victories of his own spirit. His predicament is a common one, but his response to it and his understanding of it were unique and brilliant. Though he reacted in bitter pride and energy against the crushing of his will so zealously pursued by his parents, he had an instinctive recognition that he had been injured not merely as an individual, but in some basic and mysterious way in the very core of physical and spiritual harmony. Some secret equation between the race and the individual had failed of solution, some essential rhythm between conservation and change, between matter and spirit had been broken. By his father's action he had been cast out from his rightful place in the scheme of things. The mainspring of his life was the determination of a thwarted and diminished ego to fulfil itself, to set itself on high, to triumph in complete liberty and power over the forces that threatened to crush it. But his mind was at once too intuitive and too speculative to permit the struggle to remain a merely personal one. What concerned him was to establish his nature, his aspirations and their fulfilment upon a philosophic basis, to identify them with the nature, the aspirations, the fulfilment of all humanity—and more than that—with the fulfilments of the universe. Only so could he be safe and mankind be safe. He and all humanity stood or fell together. His struggle became generalized, symbolic, tremendous. His theories are all rooted in his personal struggle, and in his ardent and brilliant attacks on entrenched and fossilized authority, on pedantry, bigotry and humbug wherever he detected them, he was revenging himself magnificently for the wrong they had done him in the person of his father.

All philosophies are subjective and all contain truth, but none are true, and their proportion of objective value and applicability varies greatly. There was a fundamental sanity and vigour in Butler, a strong sense of reality, a keen analytical faculty and a power of turning accepted ideas upside down and inside out in order to get a fresh view of them, which amounted to an innovation in method and resulted in some of his most "future-piercing" conceptions. This method had its genesis in the vigourous protest of his own spirit against the tradi-

tional implications that threatened to stifle it. His thought, nourished by the complex subjectivity of an unusually brilliant, versatile and realistic nature, is so rich in objective values that it has more truth for us today than it had for his contemporaries. He was far more sensitive both to what had been thought and to what would be thought than to what was being thought. The present was the least congenial of periods to him; he had far more affinities with the past and the future. For the present irritated him constantly but the evolutionary process fascinated him, and as he saw the future unrolling itself out of the past, strongly bound to it, yet ever differing from it, he evolved an explanation of that unity and that difference which reconciles for us his most divergent opinions and his most conflicting emotions. It is this unique interplay and balance of the centripetal and centrifugal forces of a nature at once so sensitive and so constructive as Butler's, as well as his importance as a pioneer in many of the most significant tendencies of present-day thought, that makes the study of his life and thought an adventurous and rewarding pursuit. (pp. 6-13)

> *Clara G. Stillman, in her* Samuel Butler: A Mid-Victorian Modern, *The Viking Press, 1932, 319 p.*

THEODORE DREISER   (essay date 1936)

[*Considered among America's foremost novelists, Dreiser was one of the principal American exponents of literary Naturalism. He is known primarily for his novels* Sister Carrie *(1901),* An American Tragedy *(1926), and the Frank Cowperwood trilogy (1912-47), in each of which the author combined his vision of life as a meaningless series of chemical reactions and animal impulses with a sense of sentimentality and pity for humanity's lot. Deeply concerned with the human condition but contemptuous of traditional social, political, and religious remedies, Dreiser associated for many years with the American socialist and communist movements, an interest reflected in much of his writing after 1925. In the following excerpt, he suggests that the flaws in* The Way of All Flesh *are offset by Butler's intellectual acuity.*]

[*The Way of All Flesh* is] the product and reflection of a very special and, in the main, friendly and agreeable English temperament, informed, studious, witty, honest and yet critical as well as satirical, as who would not be in such a mysterious and puzzling world as this.

But while it is as good as this, it is also a puzzling book, since in the main it departs, and almost astonishingly, from so many of the customs and commonplaces of novel writing. It has no plot, and also no stirring action to speak of. Far from being a piece of fiction, it is little more than the thinly fictionized life of Butler himself, and most meticulously set down at that. Yet a novel it is, by reason of the care and charm with which Butler has pieced his own and his parents' lives together. On the other hand, it is really as much a book of philosophy as a novel or autobiography, since in the main, and fully enough, it sets forth the philosophic concepts of Butler, which are those of an agnostic, convinced of the truth of the Darwinian theory of evolution, but by no means satisfied, as he elsewhere shows (*The Fair Haven*) that it is all a process of natural selection, or, as Spencer phrased it, "the survival of the fittest." Rather, as he sees it, it is one of cellular or, even better, protoplasmic memory of various past states, compulsions, environments, necessities, and of the guides they offer to further protoplasmic or cellular adaptability, and by reason of that, development. And with this notion, the mechanists of today are certainly in full accord.

Not only that, but Butler had a free and original mind; one of the best and, like that of Nietzsche, it was beyond good and evil. For he seems never to have been able to make up his mind finally and fatally about anything. A thing might be evil, and again it might be good, like faith, like tradition, like social acceptances, taboos, rules. Indeed, this whole work, apart from its qualities as novel and autobiography, may well be termed a volume on agnostic thought, achieved through a series of personal and most disillusioning experiences.

For throughout his youth, if we can (and I think we can) safely accept this volume as a study as well as a report of his own life, his was by no means a strong or even a healthy temperament. He was too nebulous, shy, sensitive, and too uncertain of the significance or import of things he saw going on about him to reach any conclusion, even under instruction, as to what was his true relationship, let alone his duty to life and people. And, worse, or perhaps better for him, and for us, since this book is a product of what may best be described as his mental ambivalence, he was blessed or cursed by a father and mother who were anything but intellectually or philosophically equipped to deal with such a character. They were of a lesser mental content and worse, stupid, humdrum, in at least their outward adherence to most of the duties and taboos of the doctrinaire, religious and educational world of which they were a part. Of course, it is Butler who is telling the story, and it is his lacerated temperament which is responsible for his at times acid presentation of the world he shows. None the less, because of the excellence of his mind and its reactions as compared with theirs, one cannot help sympathizing with him intensely. In short, it is the glitter as well as the color of his mind, with all its aesthetic selectiveness as well as its crotchets, that cause this book to remain sharp and perhaps ineradicable in the consciousness of those who read it. At any rate, to this hour, its fame is growing, not waning. (pp. vi-viii)

Theodore Dreiser, in an introduction to The Way of All Flesh by Samuel Butler, The Heritage Press, 1936, pp. v-xxx.

MALCOLM MUGGERIDGE   (essay date 1936)

[*An English man of letters, Muggeridge has long had a reputation as an iconoclast. A socialist and outspoken atheist during the 1930s, he later eschewed socialism and embraced Christianity during the 1960s. His conversion, however, did nothing to mitigate his stinging satire. Organized religion, public education, and egalitarianism have all been the objects of his wrath. Muggeridge was the author of a highly acerbic biography of Butler, written to counter what he considered unwarranted adulation of an essentially shallow thinker. In the following excerpt from that work, he contends that Butler's revolt against Victorian society was circumscribed and entirely conventional.*]

It is more as a portent than for anything he wrote or thought that Samuel Butler must be regarded as one of the most significant figures of the latter part of the last century. His own generation ignored him. His fame was almost wholly posthumous. In so far as he was known at all in the flesh it was as an oddity, an eccentric with a number of queer bees in his bonnet, as that the Odyssey was written by a woman, that the credit for formulating the Theory of Evolution must go rather to Erasmus Darwin, Buffon and Lamarck than to Charles Darwin, and that habit, not chance, was the chief factor in producing variations. His painting, to which he devoted a great deal of time, was with one exception—his picture "Family Prayers"—too mediocre to merit serious attention; his musical compositions, to which he also devoted much time, were scarcely even mediocre; his books, apart from **Erewhon,** which he published anonymously, were ignored or slated, more often ignored, and each was in smaller demand than the last. His death in 1902 attracted as little notice as his life.

Yet a few years later his reputation had swollen to immense proportions. His autobiographical novel, **The Way of All Flesh,** published in 1903, was hailed as a masterpiece; his friend Festing Jones wrote a two-volume *Life,* in which his smallest doings and sayings were meticulously recorded; his **Note-Books,** in which he had jotted down his thoughts from day to day over a large number of years, were published and appreciatively received, and even his scientific works were reissued and shared in the general revival of interest in him. He was presented by his many admirers as the first great exploder of Victorian hypocrisy, the pioneer rebel and inveigher against cant, as one who successfully and courageously undermined the most cherished contemporary institutions, and who, in drawing a satirical, yet authentic, picture of the family life of a country clergyman, had exposed the appalling insincerity of family life as such. In their opinion he was a wholesome wind blowing away the stuffiness of a hypocritical age, clean thought invading the dreary habitations of tepid superstition and self-interested humbug, the voice of one crying in the wilderness: "Make straight the way for Bernard Shaw!"

This view of him still persists. "It was Samuel Butler," Mr. Joad writes, "who first laughed at the gods of Victorian England; it was Samuel Butler who thawed that first tiny hole in the icy crust of Victorian morality, through which were soon to pour the floods of Shavian invective; it was Samuel Butler who first took the portentous lay figure of Victorian complacency by the throat and shook it until the stuffing came out. . . . He pricked the bubbles, the reputations popped, and the mischievous laughter of the schoolboy was heard in the background." Others, however, have grown skeptical about this process of shaking the stuffing out of the portentous lay figure of Victorian complacency. A conviction has grown on them that the floods of Shavian invective are fountain-like, ornamentally sprinkling the source whence they came, and that the only stuffing Butler and his like shook out was their own.

The revolt against Victorianism, in fact, has come to seem only the crowning unreality of that unreal time; the final elaboration, the final fantasy that brought the whole structure tumbling down, to lie now rotting on the ground. This necessitates a revaluation of Butler. Did he draw aside the curtains of his father's rectory, letting in daylight; or hang still thicker ones, plush curtains, making even more extravagant shadows than the others, a chillier twilight that bred more fabulous dreams? Was he, not so much the Anti-Victorian, as the Ultimate Victorian, fleeing more frenziedly and further afield even than his contemporaries did; where they buried their appetites under deep layers of sentimentality, trying to abolish his altogether; outdoing their pattern of domestic felicity with another of solitary felicity; stuffing ideas, instead of conventions, into the mouth of passion to silence it; laying up treasure not even of gold, but of paper money.

Like his fellow-Victorians, the deepest need of his nature was to escape from the reality of his own existence; only he escaped by means of ideas, and they by means of emotions. He was a pioneer idealogue. His mind was his refuge; and he lived secure amongst its shadows and fantasies. Where for instance Dickens shaped his turbulent appetites into creatures of darkness and light, making a melodrama of them, Butler shaped his into thought and made a utopia of them. His utopia was Erewhon, Nowhere, a quiet twilit place where banks were churches, doctors priests, and disease alone evil. It has very largely come to pass. Waiting at a bank-counter faces are reverent; and angels glow with health, not holiness—airmen or potent gamekeepers; and the psychoanalyst, or, as Butler called him, Straightener, ministers to all who travail and are heavy-laden; and virtue is assessed in public health statistics.

He created his Nowhere like any god—Let there be this, let there be that! The trick has caught on—Let there be peace, let there be progress. Whatever horrified, why, pluck it out! If his soul offended, pluck that out; if his appetites, pluck them out, too. A fellow-reader in the British Museum Reading Room, Karl Marx, adopted a similar technique. He, too, god-like, created and abolished, and his Nowhere has also come to pass. It is a strange fact that at a time when so many prophetic voices were being noisily raised, the future should have lain with these bearded, morose two, so that today they have their capitals, Moscow and Geneva, with the world almost divided between them.

Having created his Nowhere Butler had to give it a Law. A Promised Land filled in the space he had cleared between himself and the horizon; but the tablets of stone were still unwritten on, the Covenant had still to be drawn up and ratified. Darwinism met his need. Oh, the joy that came to him when he laid down *The Origin of Species* after his first reading of it! What had seemed incomprehensible became comprehensible, what had terrified was now unformidable; chaos a pattern, and that pattern securely in his mind. He rolled up his sleeves. He got to work, not indeed in a laboratory, or even in the fields, but in the British Museum Reading Room. There he mastered the subject, first whimsically abolishing the superstitious débris of the past, then laying firm foundations for the future; thought placed on thought, orderly, impregnable. He soon left Darwin as far behind as the Thirty-Nine Articles. Darwin believed in chance, and chance was outside the Law. Chance had been abolished along with Heaven and Hell. It was as fiendish as speculation. Fixed-interest-bearing securities, trustee stock, for him. From amoeba to *homo sapiens,* yes; but not just as the gentle wind doth blow, inevitably like compound interest; and not stopping at *homo sapiens,* on and on and on and on, and up and up and up and up, until *homo supersapiens,* supermen.

Men of science were resentful. Who was this amateur to come breaking in on their preserve? Why, he had never so much as been inside a laboratory, never handled a specimen or peered down a microscope or warmed up a test-tube, never studied fauna and flora. They forgot that the matter in hand had nothing to do with anything that ever was on sea or land. It was abstract, Erewhonian, as unconnected with life as an oil share with oil. To complain that Butler had never been in a laboratory was as unreasonable as complaining that a theologian had never been in a church. Brilliantly, ingeniously, he elaborated his theory, that habit and not chance produced

variations, and that the spur thereto was an innate urge to progress, like the innate urge of office-boys to become managing-directors, back-bench Members of Parliament Cabinet Ministers, private soldiers, generals, down-at-heel scribblers, oracular men-of-letters, all mankind healthy, wealthy and wise. The *Zeitgeist* worked in him; and, expounding it, he laid about him with a heavy hand, confident that, though scorned and rejected while alive, recognition would sometime come. His confidence was justified. In the brave new world that the *Zeitgeist* produced he was acknowledged a prophet.

However much he might reduce the pressure of living, his own personal life went on. He did not manage to evolve himself creatively into an idea. A residue of unidealized living remained. Not much of a residue—

> I get up about seven and immediately, in my nightshirt, go into my sitting-room and light my fire. I put the kettle on and set some dry sticks under it so that it soon heats enough to give me warm water for my bath. At eight I make my tea and cook my breakfast—eggs and bacon, sausages, a chop, a bit of fish or whatever it may be, and by 8:30 I have done my breakfast and cleared it away. Then I read *The Times* newspaper which takes me about 40-45 minutes. At 9:15 I do whatever little bits of work I can till Alfred comes at 9:30 and tells me all about the babies and whatever else interests him. We arrange what he is to do for the morning and I get away to the British Museum as quickly as I can; I am there about 10:15-10:30, according as I have any marketing to do or no. I work at the Museum till one. . . . Then I go out and dine either at home or at a restaurant, but I never have more than one plate of meat or vegetables and no soup or sweets. I find the less I eat the better for me. Alfred and I generally waste half an hour or so till about 2:30 or three, settling this, that or the other. From three till five or 5:30 I write letters or work at home while Alfred typewrites for me . . . and at four we always have a cup of tea together. At 5:30 I have my real tea, which consists generally of a bit of fish and bread and butter, and after that I may smoke. I may smoke after four if any one comes or if I have to go calling anywhere, but never otherwise. From six till eight I am alone and quiet. . . . At eight I almost always go to Jones, unless he comes to me . . . At 9:30 I leave him, come home, have some bread and milk, play two games of patience, smoke a cigarette and go to bed about eleven.

Even so, this residue, such as it was, remained.

It was not quite as bare as it looked. Hate enlivened it; a grudge worked on it, engendering *The Way of All Flesh.* As Butler imposed his own pattern on the outside world so he imposed a pattern on the life within him. He hated his father, and therefore fatherhood was hateful. It was the Law that sons should hate fathers and fathers sons. Theobald and Christina, his father and mother in *The Way of All Flesh,* were fatherhood and motherhood, and Ernest, himself, new life painfully shaking itself free of the old, struggling to achieve a better and separate existence. This, too, was the *Zeitgeist.* How joyously resentful sons seized on the doctrine! They might hate their fathers with impunity; more, it was their nature, their duty, so to do. The great Youth bubble began to blow itself up; the great idea that not the meek but the young inherit the earth, to start on its triumphant course. And why stop at father and son? What of husband and wife? Was not that an irksome relationship? The same doctrine applied to matrimony. If Ernest rightly gave up Theobald and Christina for Truth's sake, so might Theobald give up Christina or Christina Theobald. It might even be right to become, if not eunuchs, at least homosexual for the sake of the Kingdom of Truth. *The Way of All Flesh* has borne a rare progeny of young men and women living their own lives in their own way in their own rooms and in front of their own gasfires; of earnest promiscuity—he matters to her, she matters to him, may matter, once mattered, matters no longer, mattering and not mattering and perhaps mattering; of poets in colored shirts who love one another, and are Communists, and sing of the worker in his factory, the miner in his mine; of quiet, kindly, solitary persons who take each other's arms, and smile meekly as the kettle boils for tea, and go for country walks discussing the League of Nations on their way; of other novels—how many other novels! which empty out the insides of their authors as Butler, in *The Way of All Flesh,* emptied out his inside, dissecting relationships, streaming consciousness.

In the end Nowhere became Everywhere. Erewhon, revisited, was just like Clifford's Inn, in the same way that Overton in *The Way of All Flesh,* living his complacent, orderly life, with his pattern for living, buying milk rather than keeping a cow, was just like Butler. Erewhonian railways were started; the Bank of England became a Musical Bank, and men supermen. The ideal and the real coalesced, became one, so that Butler, looking at a row of books he had written, could glow with fatherhood, and grow food to eat by compound interest, letting his capital sprout it. He lived quietly and amiably enough in this twilight formed by the merging of the ideal and the real, constantly sharpening the one faculty he exercised—thought; ideas vivacious shadows along his path, and in his heart the certainty that as surely as lower organisms, wanting to become him, had become him, so would he, wanting to become what he admired—"big and very handsome . . . impossible to imagine a more agreeable and lively countenance . . . good at cricket and boating, very good natured, singularly free from conceit, not clever but very sensible . . . father and mother drowned when he was only two years old . . . heir to one of the finest estates in the South of England—" would become what he admired.

This superman vein has turned out to be rich indeed, richer even than he anticipated. And how zealously has it been worked! Two paths led Butler to it. His sense of personal inferiority made him transfigure into supermen all who possessed the qualities he felt he lacked; and his horror at having put down God made him enthrone Man in God's seat. He looked wistfully at whoever was unlike himself, seemingly unafraid of what terrified him, movements and manners easy, clothes well cut, knowing without the boredom of laborious study, sinning as unself–consciously as breathing, secreting money as effortlessly as glands their fluids, and saw in him a higher form of life; Darwinism, amended to become creative evolution, held out a promise that this higher form of life was within the reach even of such as he, in the same way that Samuel Smiles's *Self-Help* held out a promise that wealth was within the reach even of the poor. (pp. ix-xviii)

[Butler's] hand is in nursery school classes being taught the facts of life, no "mysteries where nature had made none" and therefore no "ambush of young days"; in birth-control clinics ladling out the sterility he loved; in the blithe companionship of comradely loves. His spirit dwells in clergymen with nicknames drowning unbelief in earnestness—

> Does any man of science believe that the present orthodox faith can descend many generations longer without modifications? Do I—does any freethinker who has the ordinary feelings of an Englishman—doubt that the main idea underlying and running through the ordinary faith is essentially sound? . . . Tell me that Jesus Christ died upon the Cross, and I find not one title of evidence worthy to support the assertion. Tell me that therefore we are to pull down the Church and turn every one to his own way, and I reject this as fully as I reject the other. I want the Church as much as I want free–thought. . . .

His authentic voice speaks still, bidding the tide of human folly and bestiality and ecstasy to hold back because mind has conceived a quieter and more orderly pattern; his Promised Land has many mansions now wherein are "troops of young men and maidens crowned with flowers and singing of love and youth and wine."

One great change has, however, taken place. The Promised Land, as he envisaged it, had a single absolute—money. All else was changing; gods came and went; fecundity became no more than a handclasp; life climbed upwards to aerial regions where it was as impalpable as thought; but still there was money. He blew, and lo! mountains of misguided faith melted like snow, an eternity of chaos formed comprehensible order, the seven humbugs of Christendom stood revealed, the veil of the Temple was rent and its foundations shaken; but compound interest endured. He felt secure in the shadow of compound interest, indifferent alike to Heaven and Hell and his own fleshly being as long as accounts kept by double-entry were valid.

Now his absolute has taken on the same changeful quality as the rest. His Kingdom's single prop has collapsed. Money, too, like living organisms, has begun to go up and up and up. There have been super-currencies as well as supermen, and doubts have arisen about compound interest as earnest as Butler's about the Thirty-nine Articles. It alters the whole significance of his life—all shadow-fighting until the climax, the longed-for moment when his father died, and he laid hands on an inheritance in which he had implicit trust. What would he have felt if his inheritance had been brushed aside as lightly as he brushed aside the bond between parent and child, man and woman, present and past, time and eternity? How strange if the same uncertainty had gnawed at him about it as about the existence of a God! What havoc then!

This havoc has come to pass. Butler, living amidst desolate and desecrated temples of an abolished faith, insistence of abolished appetites, shrieks of souls tormented in an abolished Hell and demanding an abolished Heaven, clung to money. Now money too has been abolished, and his Promised Land become a wilderness, with, for content, only the fitful play of mind, cold light reflecting hate's heat—that's nothing. We are sprung from Butler's loins, and watching him is watching our begetting. (pp. xx-xxii)

Malcolm Muggeridge, in his A Study of Samuel Butler: The Earnest Atheist, *G. P. Putnam's Sons, 1937, 260 p.*

H. V. ROUTH   (essay date 1937)

[*In the following excerpt, Routh discusses Butler's works in the context of his vitalist evolutionary philosophy.*]

Butler would probably have remained an amateur of art and music, if he had not also been quite consciously a moralist, anxious to know how industrial civilisation (including the investment of capital) could be adjusted to our spiritual needs. Having discarded theology and cultivated science he realised that he must first form some idea of the universal principle of life. Otherwise he would not understand what human existence involves, nor our chances of fitting into the scheme of creation.

To judge by *Darwin on the Origin of Species,* "Darwin among the Machines," "Lucubratio Ebria," *Erewhon; or, Over the Range,* his first important work, and *The Fair Haven,* he had already formulated his philosophy of life by the time he was thirty-six years old.

This philosophy consisted in completing and readjusting Darwinism. The biologists had more or less disproved the older idea of divine supervision and had left man to find his own way through life on this earth, thus revealing our immense responsibility to ourselves. Thereby, they had also left a glimpse of what the superman might become. If we had evolved all the way from apes, in fact from the embryonic cell, we could and must evolve incredibly further still. Nay more, we had already evolved with the help of machines; we had created a new physical and mechanical environment. It remained to improve these yet further and also to create an intellectual, moral, and spiritual environment, in adaptation to which we could far outstrip the present generation. Having formed a scientific and unprejudiced conception of man's nature, we must redirect culture and civilisation with a view to his potentialities. Such was Butler's moral philosophy.

Butler's problem was to adopt or invent an artistic medium, such as would give true effect to these convictions. He was not successful. One might almost say that he missed his proper place through weakness in authorship. As he wrote only when ideas clamoured for expression, he lacked the first quality of a great writer: the determination at all costs to be read. Butler missed this urge which is the first salvation, not "the last infirmity," of genius. He could not or would not learn how to persuade or surprise others into thinking his thoughts. *Erewhon,* his first sustained effort, was the most successful. It took the form of an imaginary state and he very cleverly exposed the falsities and inconsistencies of British civilisation as it is—all that in his day thwarted the progress of man. As a satire the fantasy is not profound, for after all he only ridicules what every enlightened contemporary knew to be wrong. Yet the book exercises a fascination because of its irony and insinuations which make the reader co-operate with the author, and substantiate the accusations. We enjoy the illusion of being ourselves the satirist. Thanks to this quality *Erewhon* attracted attention. It was translated into Dutch in 1873 and into German in 1879, and despite the posthumous appearance of *The Way of All Flesh,* the author's name is still associated with the earlier work. Yet this parable, in the highest sense, is a failure because there is too much of Moropolis and too little of Utopia in *Erewhon.* Butler did not give full effect to the original and creative ideas with which it abounds. He resorted to the Platonic myth. But whereas Plato rises into an allegory only as the consummation or supplement of his argument, Butler introduces it without any such preparation. As we see from the *Note-Books,* he was fond of pushing his theories to the logical extreme, to the last and most paradoxical combination of consequences. But in *Erewhon* he starts with his whimsical conclusions and leaves the reader to work backwards to the theory. For instance, his fable of the "World of the Unborn," has been admired as a fantasy and compared to Lamb's "Dream Children," but really implies his whole vitalistic doctrine, and furthermore his theory of our reactions between luck and cunning. The reader must indeed be a student of unusual insight and imagination if he can grasp the full implication from the hint. Most of Butler's admirers closed the volume with full recognition of its author's provocative and stimulating genius, and hoped that his following books would answer their questions and mature the ideas which he had planted in germ. At any rate Butler had created his opportunity.

But he did not know how to follow up his success. In fact seven years later his publisher, Trübner, was still speaking of him as a "one-book man" though his aims had become more constructive. He was now intending to expound what he had so far only prefigured, to extricate from Darwinism the neglected Nietzschean element of the *superman:* that power of self-determination which must be immanent in all life, and which we human beings should tend, cultivate and worship as God, if we must worship something. Darwin, as has been noted, had not disproved this neoteleology, he had merely diverted attention to the influence of environment. His principle worked so well that scientists lost interest in the other aspects. They thought more of natural selection than of human self-determination. Butler, though not of their fraternity, was original enough to appreciate what they ignored—the latent energy and purposiveness without which the surviving species would not have mastered their destinies. He realised that Darwinism held the secret of life, and he might have produced a really great work if he had a great writer's sense of other people's minds. But there was too much aggressiveness and solipsism mixed with his intellect and generosity. While casting about for a suitable approach, he found to his surprise that the teleological principle had already been propounded by the pre-Darwinian evolutionists, and he jumped to the conclusion that they, the holders of truth, were now being superseded in order that their successors might enjoy more than their due. The temptation was too great. Not having yet given shape to his thoughts, he turned them into a protest. Thus, instead of spiritualising evolution and opening its vistas till they illuminated morality, he weakened his purpose by lapsing into controversy.

Even a hurried glance at his scientific polemics will show what we have lost. *Life and Habit,* the first and best, peers into the mysterious sources whence we derive our power of resisting death, and the author finds that each member of each species shares its vitality with all its predecessors, nay, with the one primal and universal energy, a sort of racial purpose created out of the immemorial desire to survive; a continuous hereditary memory of all the difficulties each species has overcome since its origin, of all the needs which it has supplied. Thus we live in our remotest ancestors and in our most distant descendants, participating in one composite, surviving personality which underlies the transitory thoughts and impulses by which we think that we recognise ourselves.

Evolution, Old and New is an effort to return thanks for this illumination where they are due. As in private duty bound he must first dispose of the older pre-scientific teleologists, especially Paley and his watch found on Robinson Crusoe's is-land; and then, having refuted what is now termed "interventional teleology," he passes on to the natural philosophers who taught that the species are not manufactured but grow. Again he touches on the same profound idea, though in a different aspect. If an animal feels any given want it will gradually develop the structure to meet that want. Consequently, evolution must imply design as necessarily and more intelligibly than the theological view of creation; but the designers are ourselves or rather the vital urge of which we are the momentary expression. Would that his readers had been told more of this myriad-handed and myriad-lived artisan who labours at constructing himself, till at last his own plan develops into thought and an omnipresent instinct becomes omnipresence of mind. But Butler devotes most of his space to a brilliant exposition of Buffon, Erasmus Darwin and Lamarck, at the expense of Charles Darwin.

He made amends in the papers which he contributed in 1879 to *The Examiner,* from May to July, and published in book-form as *God the Known and God the Unknown.* In this slim volume he discusses the spirit which creates, governs and upholds all living things, what we might call the parent from which all species have sprung, a comprehensive but incomprehensible essence; as it were many animals infinitely varied, yet parts of one and the same animal, which comprises them as a tree comprises all its buds. This infinity in unity, this polytypism leading to monotypism, is our only true God. "If man is a microcosm then kosmos is a megalanthrope and that is how we come to anthropomorphise the deity," he afterwards wrote. Whereas man is only a few end-links in an endless chain and God can be conceived only as the continuity which vitalises it. We worship God as often as we love the beauty of animals, birds and insects, or love our own normal healthy bodies, or rejoice to serve the Creative Power which flashes into each being a ray from its heat. Nor does Butler ignore the mystery which encompasses our self-knowledge. This million-bodied deity (God the Known) is only quasi-omnipotent, being finite in space and time, and must itself be the product of a yet vaster and more composite personality (God the Unknown). So if we have eyes to study the visible expressions of the World Spirit we shall penetrate to the boundary beyond which human sympathies are lost in metaphysical speculation.

In one sense this theory is not new, in fact it gains in significance because it is old; because this man's intellect, all compact of modern art and scientific knowledge, nevertheless reverts to it. On the other hand, the theory is new in the sense that it is tested by new standards. Pantheism is being reinterpreted as panzoism. Such an interpretation, however, must be founded on imagination, intuition, and intellectual instinct—something similar to Newman's *illative sense*—not only on the mastery of facts, and Butler could not rise to the height of his argument. He hints at what his religion ought to mean for others, but instead of simplifying our motives and straightening our actions, he relapses into controversy for which he was not equipped and the old gladiatorialism of assaulting reputations. Nor did he yet lay down his arms. In 1880 he published *Unconscious Memory* to corroborate his theory by quotations from Von Hartmann and especially from Ewald Hering, though he confesses in his *Note-Books* that "I forced my view on him, as it were, by taking hold of a sentence or two in his lecture." In 1887 he produced *Luck, or Cunning, as the Main Means of Organic Modification* to

assert once more that the differentiation of species was caused by the organism's intelligent striving.

Thus Butler, like so many others then and since, fell a victim to the spirit of debate which John Mill did so much to enthrone. The author of *On Liberty* was at heart a simple soul and believed that when all men were free to advocate all opinions our culture would acquire the inventiveness, vision, and sympathy that we find mirrored in Plato's leisurely and creative dialogues. He probably did not realise that in protesting so effectively against the restrictions of public opinion and in releasing the powers of research and speculation, he also released other and less amiable energies. Unfettered discussion (however salutary) led to the establishment of one's own opinions at the expense of other people's; it became almost a habit to create by means of demolition; and though much rubbish has thereby been cleared away, the edifice reared in its place is inhospitable, built with destructive tools. It is easier to discredit a fallacy than to vitalise a truth. Such is the price we pay for the progress that he exemplifies and in one sense inaugurated. Butler, not having found his special vein of creativeness, fell an easy victim to the mode.

This consequence was all the more deplorable, because our author had been drawing valuable conclusions from his principles. As will readily be granted, he was not a materialist. He believed in an unseen world; he notes how things come up from it into the visible world and then go down again into the invisible. He is convinced that this abstraction is utterly beyond our comprehension, and that we nevertheless move and think in its energy every day of our lives. We feel its influence whenever the cells of our body listen to the memoried instincts of all previous generations and carry on the work of adaptation. Our destiny is to follow its promptings, to merge our petty intellectualised will in the universal natural will; to convert purposiveness into purpose. Nor was Butler really an iconoclast. He broke only idols of clay. This panzoist distrusts indoctrination and ideology simply because the springs of our nature lie deeper than thought. The subconscious self directs the conscious self, and so our progress must be experimental and individualistic, each human being solving his own problem. Preaching and teaching are sure to imply a priggish assumption of more than human wisdom. That is the only reason why he disliked Virgil, Dante and Pope so intensely and confessed that as far as he was an author he was one of the damned. But that is also why he valued so intensely Homer, Holbein, Bellini, Shakespeare, Rembrandt and Handel—"those who do actually live in us, and move us to higher achievements though they be long dead, whose life thrusts out our own and overrides it." Again, he seems to be an iconoclast because he cut across social classifications even more thoroughly than did Hardy, and instanced the Italian peasant, or the Breton, Norman and English fisherman as about the best types of men that nature could produce. Such preferences appear in their proper light when we remember that Butler valued human beings according to their adjustments. In fact he had much to say for the grace, gentleness and health which were, or could be, cultivated by the "swells." Nor need we complain that he protested against the tyranny of nineteenth-century culture. Since the truth lies hidden in the vital urge transmitted through our tissues, only known to us as the effort to make the best of our circumstances, it is dangerous to seek for spiritual certainty and guidance among man-made theories. Even words fail us when we use them as accurate instruments of thought, for ideas "are like shadows—substantial enough till we try to grasp them." So he held that common sense and good feeling were our safest guides, and moreover insisted that the more we could preserve of tradition and continuity the less we should suffer from friction in our daily work of readaptation. New ideas should be grafted onto old forms. As he wrote in **Alps and Sanctuaries:** "The power of adaptation is mainly dependent on the power of mistaking the new for the old."

Butler had certainly himself accomplished a delicate adjustment of ideas and he believed that his contributions to scientific thought would eventually ensure his immortality. But one cannot be surprised that his apotheosis was long delayed and never completed. As his years multiplied, his reputation dwindled and he became more whimsical, petulant and aggressive, wasting time and temper on digressions into the bibliography of *The Sonnets* and the authorship of the *Odyssey*. Apart from these intellectual dissipations, he wrote on his love of travel and music and late in life he returned to his idea of **Erewhon** and revisited that land of dreams, in which British eccentricity ran riot. Once again, his bitterness confines his imagination. He is too oppressed by his own caricatures of our national hypocrisy and disingenuousness to create more than a sketch of the perfect man of the future, his own and Arowhena's son, whom the father loves, admires and would feign imitate. There were immense possibilities in the meeting of those two.

This failure need not have mattered. Since the 'seventies Butler had been engaged on a work which should explain the ethics of panzoism and trace "the way of all flesh" among the morals and manners which the humanist could observe for himself. That book should have been the consummation of Butler's career, for it looked as if he had at last created the outline which would give full effect to his idea. He visualised a family with strong hereditary characteristics—moral, artistic and acquisitive—which had found free play in the artisan class of the late eighteenth century and gradually rose in the social scale till the now black-coated descendants of old Edward Pontifex found their natural aptitudes entangled among the money values, sectarianism and pseudo-culture of the educated Victorians; the three generations slowly and successively emerging out of business into the Church, and out of the Church into the free air of creativeness and self-determinism. The difficulties and readjustments involved in this progress were to be the true theme of the book. It was a most felicitous idea and **The Way of All Flesh** ought to have joined *Euphues* and *Wilhelm Meister* (not without a touch of *Tom Jones*), one of those rare studies in self-education, a new stage in the history of the modern individual seeking his proper place in the scheme of things. Butler seems to have realised his opportunity; he kept the book by him for more than a quarter of a century; he died before he was satisfied to publish it.

He might well be dissatisfied; even at the age of sixty he had not learnt to develop his ideas without developing his resentments, and the more he drew on his personal experiences and observations to give life to his theory, the more he gave life to his personal grievances. So this brilliant attempt at a philosophico-scientific novel was narrowed into a satire on Victorian domesticity, education and worship, in which Anglicanism has become a congenial refuge to vulgar or servile natures, the Rev. Theobald Pontifex grows into a monster of unctuous inhumanity, Christina becomes a figure of fun, and Overton and Ernest join characters to represent the author's

idea of himself. So Butler's name must be added to the long list of Victorian failures.

Yet he is a post-Victorian success. He awoke after death to a career which is not yet ended. His posthumous influence is, in the first place, due to the very qualities which hindered his progress when alive—restlessness, resentment and irony. His impatience with philistinism and stupidity was a sure passport to the next generation, and no sooner were his younger readers in sympathy with his mood than they found themselves in sympathy with his theories. They met him half-way, forgave his pedestrian manner, let him make up their minds for them and then discovered that he was already in possession of their favourite ideas. They were particularly interested to find him explaining that the human mind is not a clean wax tablet waiting for the selected inscription, but a palimpsest on which layers of impressions had been superimposed since the dawn of the animal creation; that our only chance of self-fulfillment and consequently of happiness depends on fusing these layers and adjusting the fusion to an ever-changing environment; that the more we study each his own nature, instead of poetic sentiments, the deeper we shall penetrate to an unexpected and fundamental self and the less we shall talk about righteousness and evil as two conflicting powers within the breast of man. (pp. 347-55)

> *H. V. Routh, "Chapter XXIII," in his* Towards the Twentieth Century: Essays in the Spiritual History of the Nineteenth, *The Macmillan Company, 1937, pp. 346-66.*

MORTON DAUWEN ZABEL   (essay date 1956)

[*Zabel was an American poet, critic, and prominent scholar. From 1928 to 1937 he was associate editor, then editor, of Harriet Monroe's magazine* Poetry, *which was the only journal at that time devoted solely to contemporary poetry. Throughout this period he wrote extensively on English and American poetry. Later in his career, Zabel was influential in increasing the study of North American literature in South America. During the mid-1940s he held the only official professorship on North American literature in Latin America, and wrote two widely used American literary studies in Portuguese and Spanish. In the following excerpt, Zabel discusses Butler's importance in the development of English literature.*]

The Way of All Flesh is one of the milestones in the history of the English novel. The fact was recognized almost as soon as the book was published in 1903, but it is a fact that could have astonished no one more than its author. He was not a professional novelist. He wrote only one novel and never published it during his lifetime. To find it claiming a rank with the other books that set the dates and mark the progress of English fiction—*Robinson Crusoe, Pamela, Tom Jones, Tristram Shandy, Pride and Prejudice, Waverley, Pickwick, Vanity Fair, Adam Bede, Richard Feverel*, and their peers—could hardly have entered the calculations of his ironic mind. Yet this book, first issued two years after the death of Victoria, a year after Samuel Butler's own death, and about twenty after its completion, is not only the work by which Butler chiefly survives in literature but a book that marks as distinctly as any the point of division between the Victorian age and the Twentieth Century. (p. 97)

In **The Way of All Flesh** Butler says that

> accidents which happen to a man before he is born,
> in the persons of his ancestors, will, if he remem-

bers them at all, leave an indelible impression on him; they will have moulded his character so that, do what he will, it is hardly possible for him to escape their consequences. If a man is to enter into the Kingdom of Heaven, he must do so, not only as a little child, but as a little embryo, or rather as a little zoosperm—and not only this, but as one that has come of zoosperms which have entered into the Kingdom of Heaven before him for many generations. Accidents which occur for the first time, and belong to the period since a man's last birth, are not, as a general rule, so permanent in their effects, though of course they may sometimes be so.

The determinism he repudiated so violently in scientific theory claimed him in his personal fate. But against this belief his sense of justice enabled him to see also the plight of parents: that, as Edmund Wilson has pointed out, "parents have not chosen their children any more than their children have chosen them and that the plight in which the situation places us may be equally cruel for both"—thus the chapter called "The World of the Unborn" in *Erewhon.* This double burden of hurt and guilt never eased its weight in Butler. It came as close as it ever has among modern talents to inhibiting his gifts and canceling the liberty and birthright he won for himself through his harsh ordeal.

He has been accused by some critics—by Malcolm Muggeridge for one, in the most scathing of the indictments drawn against him [see excerpt dated 1936]—of being a character essentially deformed who read his personal liabilities back into the age and conditions that produced him, of owning a nature dominated by defeatism and an egocentricity that could only hate. A share of this indictment is true: Butler never carried his resentment into a full intellectual or creative maturity like the greatest of the Victorian rebels. His books deny more effectively than they affirm. The worm of rancor and frustration gnaws their roots. Except in flashes he never won the vision of human suffering that animates the greatest satirists, from Aristophanes and Juvenal to Swift and Voltaire. The hurt he suffered was so much a part of himself that he could never disown it, never disengage himself from its injuries. He prized his wound and nursed his grievance; held the world at arm's length because he feared it; and protected himself with that world's own weapons—money, self-conceit, a protective suspicion of life. He knew himself a failure in compassion as much as in love, and he knew too much of great art—of Homer, Shakespeare, Handel, Bellini—to believe he had realized himself fully as an artist. He remained a Victorian—rebel and victim, agonist and apologist, radical and reactionary—to the end.

So much is evident. Butler does not stand in the highest rank of English or Victorian genius. He belongs to a radically limited order of English talent—it appears in such contemporaries as Beddoes, Lewis Carroll, Walter Pater, and Housman—that shows an ingrowth of imagination and spirit and that produces an art curtailed by doubt, self-indulgence, or eccentricity. His notebooks, with their flat cynicism, staled vituperation, and facile cheapness in deflationary witticism or crude raillery, show the sterility of emotion and moral insight that is betrayed when the mask of imagination is dropped. But such a talent can make its mark by a strategy of its own. It often appears on the scene of history at opportune moments to seize what more vigorous men may miss—the canker at the heart of human nature or society that inhibits the flowering of life. Its own defects become a clue to a prevalent malady of the human spirit. By recognizing that malady in

itself, it sometimes gains its own definition of honor and justice. That, in the face of the endemic cant and confusion of his age, is what Butler won for himself, for the contemporaries who gave him a hearing, and for the followers who took and assessed the cue he gave them. He used those least popular of keys, common sense, imagination, and justice, to unlock certain important secrets of moral energy and to make them available to the thought and art of a new century.

The Way of All Flesh maintains its importance, if for no other reason, because it records the ordeal necessary to such liberation in himself and his generation. *Life and Habit* is probably, as Clara G. Stillman argues in her excellent book on Butler, his "most important book from the point of view of his contribution to scientific and philosophic thought," and for what it and its sequels, *Evolution, Old and New* and *Luck, or Cunning?,* gave to Shaw, Bergson, and a new age of moral and ethical values. *Erewhon* is his most original work and his real title to a place in the satirical tradition. His poetic gifts and aesthetic capacities are best seen in *Alps and Sanctuaries.* But *The Way of All Flesh* gives his conflict of spirit its substance of fact and human actuality, of a tonic quality of wit and disillusioned insight that will remain Butler's distinctive achievement in the art of words. This gives it its rank among modern examples of the novel of initiation and education in life, the *Bildungsroman,* where its companions, to name only English examples, are *Pendennis, Great Expectations, Feverel, Adam Bede, Jude the Obscure,* Forster's *The Longest Journey,* Wells's *Tono-Bungay,* Bennett's *Clayhanger,* Lawrence's *Sons and Lovers,* and Joyce's *Portrait of the Artist as a Young Man.* Among these it is and will remain a landmark.

Reading it today we are able to see it as something more than the pure polemic or indictment verging on caricature that its reputation for iconoclasm and irreverence once made it appear. Butler's failure to publish it in his lifetime is far from meaning that he did not write it with all the seriousness in his power. He wrote it slowly, revised it conscientiously . . . , and kept it in his desk as a kind of investment or insurance against the impermanence he felt his other books might suffer. He seems also to have felt the difficulties under which a book that issued so intimately from his own history labored. These are quite visible in its pages. By dividing himself into two men—the callow victim and prig Ernest, and the seasoned and disillusioned narrator Overton—he distanced his ordeal but he also inhibited the imaginative reality of his hero. Ernest is unfortunately the weakest part of the story. Compare him with Dickens' Pip, with Forster's Rickie Elliott, with Lawrence's Paul Morel or Joyce's Dedalus, all of them drawn with equal intimacy from their authors' selves, and his blankness as a character is apparent. The agony of the boy is continuously attenuated by Overton's mature wisdom. He lives too much after the fact to live convincingly within the fact, and thus becomes one of the least impressive heroes of his kind. For Ernest, says Mr. Pritchett, "one cares very little. Unlike Butler he does not act; because of the necessities of the book he is acted upon. His indiscretions are passive. He has no sins; he has merely follies." But Pritchett's further argument that "the characters are dwarfed and burned dry by Butler's argument," that he "chose them for their mediocrity and then cursed them for it," and that he did not sufficiently listen to Miss Savage when "she pointed out the dangers of his special pleading," is not so convincing. A close reading of the book shows that this special pleading yielded to a sound imaginative instinct in the best parts of it and permitted Butler to create certain characters that are triumphs of their sort.

These are old Mr. Pontifex of Paleham and his wife, Butler's tribute to the soundness in the older stock of his breed that came to suffer so sorry a decline in later generations; the grandfather of Ernest, George Pontifex, a portrait of canting hypocrisy that competes with Dickens' Pecksniff; Ernest's Aunt Alethea, briefly drawn but convincing as Butler's portrayal of the life-giving sympathy and generous instincts from which he felt genuine goodness to derive; and of course Ernest's parents, Theobald and Christina. Here Butler's sense of justice was put to its severest test. He knew them in all their meanness, self-conceit, and fatuity, their jealous smallness and niggardly complacency; he had not lost his sense of their enmity to him and the kind of life he valued; but some instinct—perhaps the very link of family attachment and tribal identity he never succeeded in breaking—kept him in sufficient sympathy with their misguided natures to permit a wholeness and complexity in the portraiture. He makes palpable their smugness, their selfish stratagems, the insinuating craftiness of their cruelty, but he shows where, in parental influence and social deceit, these originated, and before he has finished with them he makes us pity them as much as we blame them.

If, as Shaw said, Butler "actually endeared himself by parricide and matricide long drawn out," it is as much because he drew his dissection of these two characters out to its inevitable conclusion of pathos and tragedy as because he avenged himself and his generation for the blight they had suffered at the hands of Victorian parenthood. By the time we see Christina dying or Theobald in his comfortless old age we know how just but also how pitiful Christina's torturings of Ernest on the inquisitorial sofa or Theobald's fear of marriage on his ludicrous honeymoon make these scenes of their final despair. The lesser characters in the book—Ernest's sisters, the Cambridge evangelists, the Dickensian Mrs. Jupp, the sinister Pryer, even the ill-fated, vigorously drawn Ellen—show the lively realism of people taken directly from their moment in time. Here Butler's task was easier, though he met it with remarkable accuracy in comic invention. It was his more complex relations with his parents and grandfather that made his dealings with them difficult, and that saved him from facile caricature when he brought them to the bar of comic justice. That he did not shirk these difficulties is shown in the fact that he succeeded in lifting them to a level which makes possible not only a sound moral realism but the elements of tragedy.

By the time the book ends Ernest is saved. He is honest at last, a man of humanity and humor, a redeemed prig, a sane creature won over from the powers of ignorance to the side of life. He is not, however, oppressively or heroically edifying. He is happy to be well off, feels no scruples in leaving his children to be raised as wards of a Thames bargee, and means to live a life of modest effort and intelligent selfishness. His will has never recovered, will never fully recover, from its almost fatal testing. He will not impose or oppress, but he is unlikely ever to command and create. He mirrors, in this, his inventor. Both he and Butler have known too well what it means to be edifying in the wrong way to risk the dangers of becoming edifying in the right way. The book ends on a sigh of relief, a note of caution, an audible shudder of relaxation. The will

has at last been cured of mania and excess. A soul has been saved and claimed its birthright.

Butler succeeded in putting the whole of himself into the novel. His shrewd if amateur scientific feeling is there; his sense of the conflict between conscious and unconscious forces in the human psyche is everywhere implicit; his hatred of mechanistic doctrine and the moral heartlessness it breeds is argued; his love of music and art is voiced by Overton's taste and Ernest's devotion to the organ; his contempt of the duplicity and inverted ethic of bourgeois morality suffuses the book, bringing the fantasy of *Erewhon* to terms with the realistic claims of fictional art. Overton's commentary, however intrusive and damaging to the imaginative freedom of the tale, nevertheless sums up the wisdom that Butler wrested from his personal history, and this is what makes the book, however short in the ultimate passion and vision of moral genius, a point of definition in the experience of its century. Osbert Sitwell has said that "the indictment against the Victorian age is not that it was not comfortable, or, in spite of its many cruelties, kindly; but that it left its debts, mental, moral, and physical, to be paid by a later generation." Butler, who missed in his age the greater vision and capacity for idealism that even critics as merciless and scathing, and as different, as Dickens and Baudelaire, Ibsen and Rimbaud, defined for it, was yet one man who determined to do his share in preventing that insolvency. It is for this reason—sufficient for his representative importance in modern experience and conflict—that the Twentieth Century has been grateful to him, has called *The Way of All Flesh* a classic among records of the human spirit in its struggle toward liberty and truth, and has granted him his honorable place among its benefactors. (pp. 107-13)

> *Morton Dauwen Zabel, "Samuel Butler: The Victorian Insolvency," in his* Craft and Character: Texts, Method, and Vocation in Modern Fiction, *The Viking Press, 1957, pp. 97-113.*

BASIL WILLEY (lecture date 1959)

[*Willey is an English critic and the author of numerous studies of English literature. In the following excerpt, he discusses Butler's attitude toward religion.*]

I want to consider Butler's attitude to religion . . . , and I will take as my text his description of God in *Luck, or Cunning?* as "the ineffable contradiction in terms whose presence none can either enter, or ever escape."

All through his life Butler was vexed by this contradiction; he wanted to escape from God—at least from the God of his father—but he also wanted to enter into God's presence. The dilemma was foreshadowed in that early Darwinian dialogue, when he had said "I believe in Christianity and I believe in Darwin." And as Mr. Malcolm Muggeridge has said, the reason why "a haphazard bringing about of variations did not really suit him," was that "it left out God; and though he wanted God left out in a certain sense, he also wanted Him included."

There are some well-known aphorisms in Butler's *Note-Books* which are often taken (by those who consider them at all) to embody the very essence of Butlerism. I mean such things as these:

> To love God is to have good health, good looks,

good sense, experience, a kindly nature and a fair balance of cash in hand.

> The good swell is the creature towards which all nature has been groaning and travailing until now. He shows what may be done in the way of good breeding, health, looks, temper and fortune. . . . He preaches the gospel of grace. . . .

These and many more of Butler's proverbs of hell were exciting when they first appeared, and what gave them added piquancy was that the devil's disciple was citing Scripture to his purpose—that is, inverting it. The identification of love of God with worldly success, of the gospel of grace with physical grace and good fortune, and the preference given to amiability over righteousness—these pleasantly Satanic reversals sent an agreeable *frisson* down the spine. The generation that discovered Butler, which was a generation in revolt against what it called "Victorianism," found in his oracles precisely the right tone; it found plain-speaking, insight, emancipation from humbug, mockery which was somehow earnest, and blasphemy which was somehow reverent. What a very clever and original man Mr. Butler must have been, to be able to prophesy while standing on his head! How witty and courageous of him to say, for instance, "An honest God's the noblest work of man!" or of Miss Savage, asking Butler to forgive her for not replying to a letter, to say "As you are not a Christian perhaps you will."

This trick of turning phrases and notions upside-down is related to another of Butler's characteristic habits: that of turning things inside-out—or shall we say, expecting insides to correspond to outsides, and feeling cheated when they don't. Of course, he was continually being let down in this way, and that was what made him a satirist and a debunker. The shock of finding that things are not what they seem began for him in boyhood, when, as we read in the Memoir of "John Pickard Owen" (a largely autobiographical sketch prefacing *The Fair Haven*), he first saw a fowl being trussed, and discovered "that fowls were not all solid flesh, but that their insides— and these formed, as it appeared to him, an enormous percentage of the bird—were perfectly useless. He was now," he goes on, "beginning to understand that sheep and cows were also hollow as far as good meat was concerned. . . . What right had they, or anything else, to assert themselves as so big, and prove so empty? . . . The world itself was hollow, made up of shams and delusions, full of sound and fury signifying nothing." Here is the germ of a satirist's indignation, and one remembers Swift's "last week I saw a woman flayed, and you will hardly believe how much it altered her person for the worse." From fowls and sheep the unmasking proceeded to family relations, moral codes, scientific theories, reputations, and at last to Christianity itself. He was puzzled, quite early in life, by the repetition of the General Confession in Church every week: could it be really necessary for good and pious folk to declare, so regularly and so everlastingly, that they were miserable offenders and that there was no health in them? If this were indeed so, what good was their religion doing them? Later, when he was conducting a Sunday class for young people in a London slum, he discovered to his great surprise that one of his favourite pupils had never been baptized. . . . (pp. 87-90)

It is not surprising—it is only what we should have expected—that Butler, having discovered the hollowness of fowls and sheep, of compulsory family affection, and of baptismal regeneration, should turn his quizzical and prosaic eye upon

the Christian faith itself. In *The Way of All Flesh,* Ernest Pontifex, during his brief parsonical phase, visits the sceptical thinker Mr. Shaw with a view to converting him. Mr. Shaw confounds him by asking him to summarize the Resurrection story as given in St. John's Gospel. This Ernest cannot do; he mixes up "the four accounts in a deplorable manner," and Shaw advises him to go home and read these accounts carefully, with attention to the differences between them. Butler himself began a similar comparative study of the Gospels while he was at Cambridge, and went on with it in New Zealand. The effect of this study upon him was the same as that produced upon Ernest Pontifex: "his belief in the stories concerning the Death, Resurrection and Ascension of Jesus Christ, and hence his faith in all the other Christian miracles . . . , dropped off him once and for ever." The just, he still believed, shall live by faith; faith, not reason, is the *ultima ratio.* But by what faith shall a just man live in the nineteenth century? "At any rate not by faith in the supernatural element of the Christian religion." Having discovered that he had been humbugged once again, this time in a matter of such great concern, his first thought was to disabuse his fellow-countrymen. And to Ernest Pontifex it seemed best to start with the Archbishop of Canterbury:

> If he could only manage to sprinkle a pinch of salt, as it were, on the Archbishop's tail, he might convert the whole Church of England to free thought by a *coup de main.* There must be an amount of cogency which even an Archbishop . . . would not be able to withstand. When brought face to face with the facts, as he, Ernest, could arrange them, his Grace would have no resource but to admit them; being an honourable man he would at once resign his Archbishopric, and Christianity would become extinct in England within a few months' time.

Butler is here being ironical at his own expense; he knew, by the time he wrote this passage, that stating "truths" is not the same thing as winning acceptance for them. But it took him most of his life to learn this. (pp. 91-2)

In the account of the Musical Banks [in *Erewhon*] the ambivalence of Butler's attitude to the Church comes out distinctly; he laughs at it and thinks it a fraud, yet he respects it and hankers after it. The Musical Bank currency was treated in *Erewhon* as *the* true currency, and "all who wished to be considered respectable, kept a larger or smaller balance at these banks." Yet this currency had no commercial value in the outside world. Even one of the black-gowned bank-attendants (vergers), when offered a tip in the bank currency, "became so angry that I had to give him a piece of the other kind of money to pacify him." The Banks, though spoken of everywhere as "the most precious of all institutions," were generally almost empty, and seemed to be doing very little business. The cashiers and managers (clergy) had an unpleasant appearance and expression; they lacked "the true Erewhonian frankness"; the look in their faces was not, like that of the High Ydgrunites (gentlemen, men of the world), one to be emulated and diffused. They were indeed mostly good, well-meaning men, and very poorly paid,

> but they had had the misfortune to have been betrayed into a false position at an age for the most part when their judgment was not matured, and after having been kept in studied ignorance of the real difficulties of the system.

The practical neglect of the Banks by the very people who professed to rate them most highly was deplored by the

Caricature of Butler.

and is powerful"; and of the unseen power to which man "gives the name of God."

> The Erewhonian Musical Banks, and perhaps the religious systems of all countries, are now more or less of an attempt to uphold the unfathomable and unconscious instinctive wisdom of millions of past generations, against the comparatively shallow, consciously reasoning, and ephemeral conclusions drawn from that of the last thirty or forty.

This passage, in spite of its Burkean tone, is to be thought of in relation not to Burke (whom, it is tolerably certain, Butler had not read) but to Butler's notions about unconscious memory in *Life and Habit.* The things we do best of all, such as breathing, are the things of which we are least conscious, because we have done them longest. And similarly with belief in God: this belief is only perfect when held unquestioningly, unconsciously and as a matter of instinctive hereditary wisdom; it withers under rational "demonstration." The things we know best are those that we know without knowing that we know them. In this context, Butler characteristically adopts for his own purposes the Christian distinction between Grace and Law: unconscious knowers and believers are under Grace, conscious knowers under Law. The carefree natural man who has "good health, good looks, good temper, common sense, and energy"—that is, who loves God—is under Grace; he is master of a better science than the earnest scientific discoverers, the professors and the theologians, who are under Law. (pp. 93-5)

The showing-up of orthodox Christian theology was only an incidental motif in *Erewhon,* but it remained Butler's central preoccupation until about 1877, when it began to be superseded by the showing-up of Darwin. His first imperative need was to extricate himself from the bogus religion of Langar Rectory; he must first (in the sense and with the reservations I have tried to indicate) learn to do without God before he could slang Darwin for doing the same. It is not surprising, then, that after publishing *Erewhon* he should write *The Fair Haven,* his most elaborate and sustained attack upon Christianity.

The Fair Haven is an ironical defence of Christianity—specifically of the Resurrection story—which, under the guise of orthodox zeal, undermines its miraculous foundation. Like *Erewhon,* it was first published anonymously, but in *The Fair Haven* Butler carries the mystification a degree further by ascribing the work to "the late John Pickard Owen" and adding a memoir of the author by his brother "William Bickersteth Owen." According to R. A. Streatfeild, the book was not a deliberate hoax; perhaps, however, it would be nearer the truth to say that it was not a hoax and nothing more. Butler seriously hoped to make people study and compare the gospel narratives (as Shaw made Ernest Pontifex do); he hoped to sow, in the minds of many who would never have read an avowedly unorthodox book, doubts about their historical accuracy. But it is also certain that Butler enjoyed the fun of taking in those who were too dense to see through the irony. Why should anyone ever write ironically instead of stating his case in plain terms? Why did Swift write *A Modest Proposal* and *An Argument Against Abolishing Christianity?* Surely for sheer intellectual pleasure, the joy of creation; and because the oblique method, being a more subtle and controlled form of rhetoric, is far more persuasive than undisguised anger or zeal. In the Preface to the second edition (in which he acknowledged his authorship), Butler,

Erewhonians, and one of the Bank Managers explained to the narrator that something was being done about it. For instance, new stained glass had been put into all the Bank windows; the organs had been enlarged; and the presidents "had taken to riding in omnibuses and talking nicely to the people in the streets and to remembering the ages of the children, and giving them things when they were naughty. . . ." But as for doing anything to give the currency real value and meaning, this was considered "not in the least necessary."

The other side of Butler's attitude, the side that hankered after the Church and hated the new pseudo-religion of science, comes out first in his description of the Bank architecture: it was "an epic in stone and marble": it "carried both imagination and judgment by storm"; he was "charmed and melted"; he felt humbled, made aware of a remote past and of his own insignificance; and reflected that "the people whose sense of the fitness of things was equal to the upraising of so serene a handiwork, were hardly likely to be wrong in the conclusions they might come to upon any subject." And then, in one of those passages where Butler drops the allegory and gives us his own opinion in plain terms, he goes on to explain the true *raison d'être* of the Banks: they are a standing witness, he says, to the reality of "a Kingdom that is not of this world," of which we know nothing "save that it exists

still enjoying himself hugely, gives a further turn to the screw by alleging, as his reason for anonymity, that if *The Fair Haven* had been at once known to proceed from the author of *Erewhon* it might have been suspected of being satirical.

The ostensible plan is to show how John Pickard Owen, after passing through every stage of sceptical doubt, and after considering every possible argument of infidelity, at last reached safe anchorage in the fair haven of orthodox faith. In reality, a very large portion of the book is devoted to stating, with great cogency and detail, the negative side; and although Mr. Owen continually assures us that he is only letting the infidels have their say in order to triumph over them at the end, the triumph, when it comes, is as perfunctory as Gulliver's over the King of Brobdingnag—that is to say, it only gives away the case still more completely. It would be tedious, and would nowadays serve no useful purpose, to rehearse the many "Difficulties felt by our Opponents," or to summarize Butler's reasons for holding that Jesus never actually died upon the Cross, and consequently did not rise from the dead or ascend into heaven. Behind all the analysis of discrepancies in the gospel texts lies the determining presupposition, common in the 1870's (when, besides *The Fair Haven, Ecce Homo* and *Literature and Dogma* also appeared) that miracles do not happen. The chapters (V-VIII) in which the infidel case is set forth, represent Butler's own view quite directly; they were . . . worked up from his early pamphlet on the evidence for the Resurrection. It may seem extraordinary that any of his first readers should have taken the book seriously as a defence of orthodoxy, yet this did happen. Canon Ainger was completely taken in, and sent a copy of *The Fair Haven* to a friend of Miss Savage "whom he wished to convert." *The Rock* newspaper said that "the work contains many beautiful passages on the discomfort of unbelief, and the holy pleasure of a settled faith, which cannot fail to benefit the reader." Butler himself thought that his real drift should have been obvious to all but the very stupid; he had even included, in the Memoir of John Pickard Owen, the statement that the late lamented author had gone out of his mind after writing the book.

But even though we may be warier than Canon Ainger or *The Rock,* we may still be puzzled by certain parts of *The Fair Haven.* There are passages, for instance, where Butler seems to be a serious apologist, not indeed for traditional Christianity, but for modernist Christianity; he also appears zealous for a concordat between religion and science. He uses the method of apologetics-by-concession, now favoured by some theologians: that is to say, you concede to the rationalists that many of the old beliefs (formerly thought essential) are untenable, and you expect them in return to abate something of their self-confidence and arrogance. Owen is said to have tried in this way to explain the contending parties to each other; he must show, says the Memoir, that "Rationalists are right in demurring to the historical accuracy of much that has been too obstinately defended by so-called orthodox writers." This is exactly what the demythologizers do today, and we feel that Butler ought to have meant it seriously himself. But did he? One's confidence that he did is shaken by finding that another part of Owen's task is to prove that Christians are right, on rationalist principles, in clinging to the traditional view of the Resurrection—and this we know to be ironical. He is serious when he says that Christians must not be disingenuous like Dean Alford; we must not pretend that the gospels could be "harmonized" if we only knew *all* the facts; we must not

pretend to be "sure" of things in the way that science alone can be "sure." But what of the following passage:

> . . . where, upon the Christian side, was the attempt to grapple with the real difficulties now felt by unbelievers? Simply nowhere. . . . Modern Christianity seemed to shrink from grappling with modern Rationalism, and displayed a timidity which could not be accounted for except by the supposition of a secret misgiving that certain things were being defended which could not be defended fairly. This was quite intolerable; a misgiving was a warning voice from God, which should be attended to as a man valued his soul. On the other hand, the conviction reasonably entertained by unbelievers that they were right on many not inconsiderable details of the dispute, and that so-called orthodox Christians in their hearts knew it but would not own it—or that if they did not know it they were only in ignorance because it suited their purpose to be so—this conviction gave an overweening self-confidence to infidels, as though they must be right in the whole because they were so in part; they therefore blinded themselves to all the more fundamental arguments in support of Christianity because certain shallow ones had been put forward in the front rank, and been far too obstinately defended.

How familiarly this reads! It might easily occur in a twentieth-century course of Gifford or Hibbert Lectures, or in a history of the Victorian science-and-religion controversy by a sensible and impartial modern Christian. Ought not Butler to have meant every word of this? Can he really be scoffing at the very idea of reconciliation, and satirizing the notion that when all is conceded that the rationalists could legitimately desire, the "fundamentals" of Christianity still remain? Everything depends, of course on what the "fundamentals" are taken to be. The modernist apologetic-by-concession, from Jowett to the present time, has always presupposed that *something* fundamental remains undamaged, whether it be the mystery of the Incarnation, the example of Christ's life and teaching, the existence and vitality of the Church, the facts of spiritual experience, the Christian character and ethic, or a combination of such elements. Butler, we may agree, is satirizing this very method in so far as the fundamental to be presupposed is the Resurrection, or indeed any of the Christian miracles. His irony glances sharply upon the trick of making concessive gestures without really making any important concession at all. . . . (pp. 97-102)

Butler professed to believe that all things work together for good to them that love God, and he believed that he himself loved God in some sense—and perhaps not merely in the sense indicated by the extract quoted at the beginning of this lecture. He believed, like Ernest Pontifex, in "something as yet but darkly known which makes right right and wrong wrong." But his explicit theology, as set forth in the book *God the Known and God the Unknown* is hardly more satisfactory than Comte's. Instead of deifying Humanity, he deifies all living creatures, all Life, the Life Force. There is no meaning, he says, in the idea of a God who is not a living person; "an impersonal God is as much a contradiction in terms as an impersonal person." Where are we to find this person? There is no harm in using the word "God" to mean the personification of "our own highest ideal of power, wisdom and duration," but a personification (as Arowhena had pointed out) is not a person. "God is," he concludes, "the animal and vegetable world, and the animal and vegetable world is God," a vast leviathan, composed of all living creatures as the body is composed of cells. What then of the mineral Kingdom—is this no part of the Kingdom of God? This very question afterwards occurred to Butler, and he realized that he could not logically deny "life" to every material particle in the universe. He meant to rewrite the articles on this new assumption, but never did so. If all life is God, the whole universe is the living God, and mind is omnipresent. The Life Everlasting is life in this God—the life still being lived now, for instance, by Bellini or Handel.

This, then, is "God the Known." But Butler goes on to ask, what can this "panzoism" tell us of the origin of matter, or of the primordial life-cell? The world was made and prepared to receive life; hence there must have been a "designer," "some far vaster Person who looms out behind our God." If so "we are members indeed of the God of this world, but we are not his children; we are children of the Unknown and Vaster God who called him into existence." Butler's God, then, is not only composed of material units, but is himself a unit in an unknown and vaster personality who is composed of Gods. This is "God the Unknown." It is remarkable that Butler, having reduced God to "all life considered as a whole," goes on to bring in—almost as an afterthought—this super-God who really is transcendent, and who has designed the world and the World-Gods. To which is our worship and reverence due? He says in one place that his World-God, being living and visible, can be believed in, loved, and devotedly served; it is presumably to him, then, that we are in duty bound. But this God lacks the numinous quality of the Super-God; he has no power to inspire reverence or demand service. In Butler there is, as far as I can discover, little or no sense of the holy, and (in spite of his praise of I Corinthians xiii) very little love.

Not long after writing *Erewhon*—and we may safely suppose it to have been while writing *The Fair Haven*—it occurred to Butler to wonder what effect would have been produced upon the Erewhonians by the apparently miraculous escape of Higgs at the end of the story: his ascent into heaven in a balloon with an earthly bride. He decided that to a people like the Erewhonians, who were losing grip on their own official faith, such an event would appear to be an authentic miracle, and would serve as the nucleus of a new religion. What an opportunity he had thus unwittingly given himself to satirize Christianity again! It was too good to miss, but he knew that he must wait for at least twenty years to give the new religion time to take shape. Actually it was nearly thirty years before Butler published *Erewhon Revisited.*

It will be remembered that when Higgs revisits Erewhon he finds that he has been deified as the "Sunchild," and that Sunchildism, the new cult based upon his ascension, has become the established religion of the country, complete with churches, scriptures (his own sayings and doings, garbled, glossed and swollen with accretions), priesthood and theological professors. The balloon has become a horse-drawn chariot, and there is even a sacred relic (dung alleged to have fallen from the horses). Higgs's moral problem is whether to risk his own life, and risk destroying Sunchildism, by publicly declaring his identity. It is, I think, unnecessary to analyse this book in any detail. The allusion to the rise of any supernatural religion, Christianity included, is obvious. "If," says Butler "there be a single great, and apparently well-authenticated miracle, others will accrete round it; then, in all religions that have so originated, there will follow temples, priests, rites,

sincere believers and unscrupulous exploiters of public credulity."

The prosaic, eighteenth-century, Gibbonian part of Butler, still active in his last years, greatly relished exposing the natural growth of a myth, and perhaps even more the hanky-panky of the theologians in darkening counsel and sophisticating the evidence. But Butler went out of his way to explain that he did not mean to poke fun at Christianity, and still less to suggest any allusion to its Founder; he only meant, he said, to suggest a parallelism "between the circumstances that would almost inexorably follow such a supposed miracle as the escape of the Sunchild, and those which all who think as I do believe to have accreted round the supposed miracle, not of the Ascension, but of the Resurrection." The satire is great fun, but the most interesting point in *Erewhon Revisited* is that, after showing up all the imposture, Butler still wants to preserve institutional Sunchildism. This reflects his hankering, which grew upon him with advancing years, for reconciliation with the Church. In the Preface to *Erewhon Revisited* he declares, rather surprisingly to some readers, that he has never ceased to profess himself "a member of the more advanced wing of the English Broad Church." "What those who belong to this wing believe, I believe. What they reject, I reject." And he endorses, as acceptable to such people, the advice given by Higgs to the Erewhonians after the secret is out. Assuming, as I do, that this passage represents Butler's mature view of what should be done with the Church now that its miracles have been exploded, I will conclude with a short account of it.

At the Mayor's dinner-party, after the dénouement, Dr. Downie (Broad Church) says: "And now Mr. Higgs, tell us, as a man of the world, what are we to do about Sunchildism?" The counsel of perfection, Higgs replies, would be make a clean breast of the whole affair, declare publicly who and what he is, and admit the whole vast mistake. But this would never do, says Dr. Downie; things have gone too far. What would the leaders of the English Church do if they found themselves in the same plight as the Musical Bank managers? This is Higgs's answer:

> Our religion sets before us an ideal which we all cordially accept, but it also tells us of marvels like your chariot and horses, which we most of us reject. Our best teachers insist on the ideal, and keep the marvels in the background. . . . Roughly, then, if you cannot abolish me altogether, make me a peg on which to hang all your own best ethical and spiritual conceptions.

They must, he says, get rid of that wretched relic and other crudities, "let the cock-and-bull stories" tacitly drop, and invent no new ones. If they will do this, "I really cannot see why I should not do for you as well as any one else."

> Your Musical Bank people [he goes on] bear witness to the fact that beyond the Kingdoms of this world there is another, within which the writs of this world's Kingdoms do not run. This is the great service which our Church does for us in England, and hence many of us uphold it, though we have no sympathy with the party now dominant within it. "Better," we think, "a corrupt church than none at all." Moreover, those who in my country would step into the church's shoes are as corrupt as the church, and more exacting.

"Then," says Higgs's son George, "you would have us up-hold Sunchildism, knowing it to be untrue?" Higgs replies:

> Do what you will, you will not get perfect truth. And if you will follow the lead which I believe Dr. Downie will give you, that is to say, get rid of cock-and-bull stories, idealise my unworthy self, and . . . make me a peg on which to hang your own best thoughts—Sunchildism will be as near truth as anything you are likely to get. But if Hankyism triumphs [this means, Butler has explained, everything that we understand by Jesuitry], come what may you must get rid of it, for he and his school will tamper with the one sure and everlasting word of God revealed to us by human experience. He who plays fast and loose with this is as one who would forge God's signature to a cheque drawn on God's own Bank. (pp. 107-13)

Basil Willey, "Butler and Religion," in his Darwin and Butler: Two Versions of Evolution, *Chatto & Windus, 1960, pp. 87-113.*

G. D. H. COLE (essay date 1961)

[*Cole, an English economist and novelist, wrote widely on socialism and Marxism in a manner accessible to the common reader and was a prolific author of detective fiction. In the following excerpt, he discusses Butler's major themes and assesses his achievements.*]

While Butler lived, *Erewhon* was by far his best-known book. Indeed, no other had reached at all a wide public. Even *Erewhon* was never a "best-seller," and brought its author little enough in money. For the rest, Butler paid for the printing and publication of his own books, and usually lost on them. He was incapable of writing anything that he did not really want to write, apart from getting money by it; and the books he wanted to publish were not such, apart from *Erewhon,* as any large numbers of his contemporaries wanted to read. But with *Erewhon*—and of course posthumously with *The Way of All Flesh*—he did catch the taste of a substantial public. *Erewhon Revisited,* written nearly thirty years later, had no corresponding success, although it is in a number of respects a better book than its predecessor. It has some attempt at characterization—whereas *Erewhon* has none; it is much more of a story, and much better constructed; and its satire is not less pointed or effective. To some extent these very merits tell against it. Satire does not go well with delineation of character, especially of characters the author likes. The story does not allow the digressions which make up some of the best of *Erewhon.* The satire is more concentrated on a single theme, and that theme—the growth of the Sun-Child legend—is of a sort to antagonize a good many readers. But the thing that matters most is that *Erewhon Revisited,* as a sequel, could not possibly make its impact with the same freshness and surprise as *Erewhon.* The reader knew what manner of satire to expect, though not the direction in which it would be launched; and that took some of the gilding off the gingerbread.

In *Erewhon,* from title to subject-matter and from matter to style of writing, Butler first showed his remarkable talent for turning familiar things the wrong way round. Nothing pleased him . . . better than to invert a proverb or a quotation in such a way as to present a startling thought—a verbal paradox that was much more than a play on words. His *Note-Books,* and his correspondence with Miss Savage, are full of

such inversions; and he loved, having made one, to keep on juggling with it for his own—and posthumously for his readers'—delight. In *Erewhon* he juggled in public, but not so much with phrases as with observances and familiar habits which most people had taken for granted. One example is the Erewhonian treatment, not merely of crime as illness, but of illness as crime—a most pleasant conceit, with enough of underlying truth in it to enable the paradox to bear a large burden of elaboration. Another example, no less evocative, is that of the "Musical Banks," which proceeds from the paradox of a currency of high moral prestige that lacks all purchasing power to the still more entertaining notion of the Church as a Bank for laying up treasure in heaven by fair pretensions. This is excellent satire on the worldly church-goer, who was much more in the social ascendant then than now. Admirable fun, too, is the goddess Ydgrun (Mrs. Grundy the wrong way round), to whom the Erewhonian ladies gave their real worship. Moreover, "The Book of the Machines" was finely pointed paradox at a time when Darwinism was new, and the controversy between mechanistic and spiritual interpretations of the world raging in every articulate section of society, under the first full impact of science on the popular mind. *Erewhon* was too shocking to become a best-seller, and also too intellectual to be read except by intellectuals. But among intellectuals it was read quite widely, with a sense of novelty and of a number of caps fitted very neatly to the correct heads.

Erewhon had its serious side. Butler meant what he said about the Musical Banks. But for the most part it was a putting out of the tongue at his contemporaries, with no attempt at persuading them. In *Erewhon Revisited,* on the other hand, Butler presented his readers, in the form of a tale, with a development of his theory about the Resurrection, which he had expounded previously in his early pamphlet, and, in a different satirical form, in *The Fair Haven.* The ascent of the Sun-Child into heaven and the subsequent growth of the legend of his divinity are an open and direct satire on the entire supernatural element in the Christian religion, an attempt to show, logically, how the beliefs embodied in it could have developed without any real foundation, and how vested interests could have grown up round them, committed to uphold their influence by all means. This, however well done, could not be quite such fun as the sheer irresponsibility of the paradoxes of the earlier book; and it was bound, being more open, to give even greater offence in many quarters. Last but not least, by the time *Erewhon Revisited* appeared, the Higher Criticism had come to be regarded as *vieux jeu* ["old-fashioned"] by many of the intellectuals who were Butler's public. God, and Anti-God, were both rather out of fashion in 1901: indeed, Butler's *Note-Books* make it plain that he thought so himself. "God," he informed an imaginary lexicographer, "is simply the word that comes next to 'go-cart,' and nothing more."

Nevertheless, Butler could not stop thinking about God, and making notes about him. God had been so dinned into him in childhood, and so closely identified with Canon Butler, that the son could never get either of them out of his mind. Towards both, when he had escaped from them, he achieved a degree of tolerance in retrospect; but essentially he continued to dislike them both, as wielders of irrational and repressive power. This comes out in many passages in the *Note-Books;* and *Erewhon Revisited* shows that, even if he had become milder about God, he had not changed his attitude to clergymen or to Churches.

The second main theme developed in *Erewhon Revisited* is largely a repetition of the chapters in *Erewhon* about the "Colleges of Unreason." Professors Hanky and Panky and Professor Gargoyle are legitimate successors to Mr. Thims and the Professor of Worldly Wisdom. What is new in the later book is the attempt to paint—say, rather, the success in painting—portraits of pleasant people, such as Mrs. Humdrum and the Sun-Child's son by Yram, George.

George, in *Erewhon Revisited,* Towneley, in *The Way of All Flesh,* these are the people Butler most admired, and would most have wished to be like. They are happy, healthy, good-looking, and well-to-do. They understand the world, not from having learnt about it, but by instinct. They have no money troubles, no uncertainties about themselves. They are amiable without cost, because nothing thwarts them. They get what they want without meanness and without trampling upon others. They are kind, because they are kindly by nature; but they do not vex themselves about other people's troubles unless they are obtruded upon them. They do good works when the doing comes their way; but "good works," done of set moral purpose, they have no use for. Take this, from the *Note-Books,* as an epitome. "To love God is to have good health, good looks, good sense, experience, a kindly nature and a fair balance of cash in hand." Or this, from the same source: "Heaven is the work of the best and kindest men and women. Hell is the work of prigs, pedants, and professional truth-tellers. The world is an attempt to make the best of both."

I know a number of people who do not like Butler's *Note-Books.* They find his paradoxical inversions irritating, and many of his preoccupations out of date. It is quite possible to be as allergic to Butlerisms as some people are to puns, and to dismiss his wisecracks as no more than verbal displays. For my part, I enjoy his verbal juggling and the uses he puts it to. I too have lived in Arcadia—or near enough to it to have a lively sense of the absurdities and crampings of that Victorian world. I have encountered, though not in my own upbringing, the Victorian father and his wife: I have come across will-shaking disinheritors, and the shams of pseudo-religious respectability. I have dined, cheek by jowl, with Professors of Unreason: I have met plenty of aggravating dogmatists of science, as well as of religion. These enemies of the spirit of man are fewer than they were, and have to walk more warily; and now devils a great deal worse have arisen in their place. But, though it would be better to be off with the old devils before we are on with the new, that is not how these things happen. There are enough of the old still left to give Butler's satire continuing point. Its point is, nevertheless, I agree, less penetrating than it was; and the new devils are well-armoured against it. *The Way of All Flesh,* much more than *Erewhon,* is becoming a period-piece, because the changes in family life have gone further than those in many other fields. The growth of democracy and of the Welfare State has eclipsed the patriarchal father and taxed away the Towneley's incomes so that they can no longer lord it as they could. "Three per cents, paid quarterly" are no longer what they were, after two wars and the inflations they have brought with them. "Good works" have given place to social justice, and "social workers" have lost their awfulness in the process. It is now possible to be both possessed of a social

conscience, and reasonably human and sinful to a moderate degree.

These changes would have perplexed Butler, who was fully as much a child as a critic of his own time. Intellectually, he made daring sallies against his contemporaries; but he remained tied on a string to many of their conventions. He envied the Towneleys, who could be gentlemen without effort and could carry all before them with hardly a thought; but he knew that such a way of living was not for him. He was too timid in action, except with a pen; too much a worrier; and too self-conscious. He wanted to be respectable, as well as a prodigal: a gentleman, as well as a *gamin.* Above all, once bit by speculation, he wanted to be secure, and at the same time to go his own way, flouting the world's opinion, and yet deferring to it. (pp. 38-42)

His achievement as a writer I know not how to sum up. I regard *The Way of All Flesh* as a great novel, despite its falling off in its later chapters—of which Miss Savage was well aware. I regard both *Erewhon* and *Erewhon Revisited* as excellent satires, and the John Pickard Owen memoir in *The Fair Haven* as a little masterpiece in the same genre. I believe Butler had something real and important to say about evolution, especially human evolution, though I do not think he said it quite right, largely because he could never disentangle his doctrine of unconscious memory from his quarrel with the Darwinians about Natural Selection. I delight in *Alps and Sanctuaries,* enjoy his Homeric translations, and feel sure he was mainly in the right about Shakespeare's *Sonnets.* I can always quarry happily in the *Note-Books:* I like declaiming *A Psalm of Montreal;* and I am astonished at the excellence of two or three of his few sonnets. But I do not believe that a young woman composed *The Odyssey,* and I doubt if it was composed in Sicily. I am quite unconvinced that either the scientists or the literary critics were in a conspiracy to befoul Butler's name; and I am not prepared to accept his version of his father's character as more than three-parts of the truth, or quite to forgive him some of the ungenerous things he wrote about Miss Savage when his bad mood was on him. In short, I have a strong, but not an uncritical, liking for his books, but, at bottom, no great liking for the man who wrote them. That, however, from the standpoint of his artistic achievement, is neither here nor there. Butler has what he asked for, and rather more—a narrow, but not precarious, niche in the temple of literary fame. (pp. 43-4)

G. D. H. Cole, in his Samuel Butler, *revised edition, Longmans, Green & Co., 1961, 52 p.*

DANIEL F. HOWARD   (essay date 1964)

[*Howard is an American critic and a prominent Butler scholar. In the following excerpt, he suggests that Butler's evolutionary concept of social change accounts for the relative moderation of his revolt against Victorian society, contrasting Butler's position with that of Bernard Shaw.*]

Have you read Samuel Butler's posthumous *Way of All Flesh?* If not, get it instantly. It is one of the great books of the world. You will throw Shelley, Thomson, Meredith & all the rest out of the window and take Butler to your heart forever. I do not exaggerate: it is enormous.

George Bernard Shaw wrote this in 1903, just after the novel was published. As a young reviewer twenty-five years before, Shaw had been one of the few to praise Butler's studies on evolution, and in the interim had increasingly come to see him as a precursor of his own iconoclastic modernism. Shaw had also tried to make Butler his friend; he had introduced him to his circle in London and urged Grant Richards to publish *Erewhon Revisited.* But for his part, Butler wanted none of Shaw; while acknowledging Shaw's "confiscating power," he wrote in 1897: "I have long been repelled by him."

Butler had too many crotchets of his own to have patience with Shaw's devotion to Wagner, Ibsen, and Goethe, but his disagreement with Shaw, his most effective *claqueur,* was more than personal: they differed fundamentally in their understanding of Butler's literary and social role, and though over the years Shaw has brought Butler countless readers, his insistence upon him as a social prophet has unfortunately encouraged many of them to read this novel as a Shavian document, anarchistic and revolutionary.

Butler considered himself merely an intelligent individual, aware of the corruption and stupidity of social institutions—indignant, but indifferent to active reform. Through agonies like those of Ernest, he had come to private terms with the world as it was, and he did not want his balance upset by any general change. He therefore sought an audience different from the potentially revolutionary public Shaw wrote for (and in part created); he sought the solitary, intelligent reader who stood apart from Victorian society or who would exist only in some dimly seen posterity. Where Shaw urged his audience to action, Butler encouraged individual adjustment, like that of Higgs in *Erewhon:* a knowledgeable adaptation to the world, however fantastic and illogical it might be. Butler drew an analogy from his study of evolution: a man should no more expend his energy to change the world around him than the prehistoric sea lizard who found its ocean turned to land should have exhausted its strength trying to swim; no organism can change its environment, and the successful one develops legs to walk on the world as it really exists.

To Butler it seemed naive to expect one's personal discovery of society's irrationality to produce any general effect. When Ernest discovers inconsistencies in the Gospels he boyishly imagines that the Archbishop of Canterbury will instantly admit that they destroy the foundation of belief, and, being an honest man, will resign his archbishopric at once, thereby effectively destroying Christianity in England. Butler smiles affectionately, for he knows—and Ernest will learn—that the knowledge of the unreasonableness of any institution is private knowledge which neither can nor should be translated into social action. Therefore at the end of the novel, though Ernest is more aware than ever of the shams around him, he wisely addresses himself to isolated readers and no longer seeks to topple archbishops.

To express his evolutionary (not revolutionary) view of the individual and society, Butler arranged the events of his novel in a plot that differs from the traditional social plot which served Shaw. Shaw's typical hero first appears as a brash, commanding fellow who moves inexorably toward a union with the forces of life—toward the formation of a new society. But *Ernest Pontifex; or, The Way of All Flesh* begins with no hero at all, and sixteen chapters, twenty-eight years, and two generations pass before the main character even appears—and then he is a helpless infant. As a child Ernest is obviously too weak to change his world even if he wants to; the best he can do is try to understand it and accommodate himself to it. But when he tries to do so he finds that his natu-

ral impulses put him in conflict with the adults around him: his affection for his mother leads him to confess secrets for which his father punishes him; his faith in Pryer leads to the loss of his money. And if his impulses are poor guides to the world as it is, the instructions of his parents and schoolmasters are even poorer: he is taught to be charitable to the unfortunate, but his charity to Ellen at Battersby brings only suspicion and censure; he is taught to tell the truth, but his truthfulness about his friends' small secrets at Roughborough disgraces him at the school.

For the honest, literal-minded Ernest there is no way to reconcile himself with society, and consequently the book does not proceed, like a more traditional novel dealing with a young man's life, toward a final harmony of the main character and the world around him; it proceeds from minor and comic to increasingly serious manifestations of an inevitable, hopeless conflict. As Ernest grows older his blunders become more and more disastrous, for the scene of his actions expands from home, to school, to Cambridge, finally to London—and the consequences of his actions become irreversible. At last, after ludicrously trying to apply his training to the real world of London, he imagines that he has discovered that a sophisticated young man is expected to make improper advances to a girl whose name is Snow but whose character is not white. But in trying to make himself see white as black, Ernest is too flatly literal: lacking Towneley's intuitive sense of reality, he perceives no difference between Miss Maitland and Miss Snow, and his mistake results in his arrest and imprisonment. Then with Ernest an exile, the novel begins to move more directly toward its logical conclusion—not, as in a Shaw play, toward a marriage, unifying the individual and his world, but toward a total isolation, expressed first by the prison and later by a bachelor flat in the Temple. The middle class in which Ernest was raised renounces him, and to save himself he renounces it: he refuses to see his parents, and casts off the clothes that symbolize his position in the clergy, as well as his education, which was directed toward the church. Now at last Ernest catches a glimpse of a private, as yet dimly understood destiny apart from the world he has known:

> Monstrous as such a faith [in his personal salvation] may seem in one who was qualifying himself for a high mission by a term of imprisonment, he could no more help it than he could help breathing; it was innate in him. . . . Achievement of any kind would be impossible for him unless he was free from those who would be forever dragging him back into the conventional. The conventional had been tried already and had been found wanting.

After a long, more-than-physical sickness in the prison hospital, Ernest tries to enter the lower classes by becoming a tailor and a shopkeeper. But it is impossible for a man trained as he has been to work as a lower-class man. "If he had begun at fourteen," Overton's tailor says,

> it might have done, but no man of twenty-four could stand being turned to work into a workshop full of tailors; he would not get on with the men. . . . A man must have sunk low through drink or natural taste for low company before he could get on with those who have had such different training from his own.

Ernest finds temporary success buying and selling used clothes, but he is not a natural shopkeeper either, and it is only Ellen and the money Overton supplies that let him imagine he has found his true vocation. He is still at this point the over-literal young man who lacks an instinctive understanding of other people, and he confuses commerce with love. Convinced that Ellen is his salvation, he marries her. The marriage is hopeless from the start: literally confined to the shop which is its only reason for being, it fails as the shop fails, and proves at last to have been even legally void, Ellen having been already married. When it is clear that Ernest cannot become part of the lower classes, cannot even understand their ways, he suffers a second symbolic sickness of alienation, like the one he suffered in prison after being turned out by the middle class. "He had been saved from the church—so as by fire, but still saved—but what could now save him from his marriage? He had made the same mistake that he had made in wedding himself to the church, but with a hundred times worse result."

Ernest recovers from his attempt to become a lower-class man and from his false marriage under the nursing of Overton, a rich, essentially classless man who comments on the world in stage burlesques—a bachelor who is fortunate enough to have seen the only woman he might have married die before the mistake was made. Overton's medicine for Ernest proves to be gold, a nostrum so dangerous as well as efficacious that he has had to withhold it until his patient's case is most critical. Then large doses cure Ernest, for with money he too can be classless—part of no profession or trade: not a clergyman or a tailor or a shopkeeper; not of the natural aristocracy of Towneley, the middle class of his family, or the lower class of Ellen. With money, Ernest finds himself in the same position of economic power as a long line of characters in the English novel, from Moll Flanders to Becky Sharp and Pip and Bulstrode; but unlike these characters he does not try to use his money to buy into the fashionable world, to establish himself within an already existing social structure. Money in this novel is not the means for realizing social dreams—a plantation in Virginia, a fashionable life in London, a respected name in Middlemarch; rather it is an absolution from the necessity of seeking any place at all within society.

The plot of ***Ernest Pontifex; or, The Way of All Flesh*** leads its hero to his gilded isolation through a series of experiences that are conventionally supposed to unite a young man with his society: christening, public school, the university, ordination, and marriage. Unlike the ordinary young man, however, Ernest's participation in the ceremonies connected with these experiences is always ironic: beginning with his christening, their real effect is to isolate him and bring him closer and closer to the anti-social life for which he is destined. At his christening, for example, which would usually signify his entrance into a traditional order of spiritual grace, it is not the religious ritual, the literal making of a Christian, that matters for Ernest; nor is it the painful family celebration; it is the practical fact that on this occasion his grandfather changes his will in his favor, and that Alethaea, who will give him only non-institutional and secular means of salvation, becomes his "godmother." At his confirmation Ernest senses "one of the great turning points of his life," but the "apparition" of the bishop who lays his hands on the boy as he kneels in the school chapel actually fixes an image in his mind not of confirmation but of fear and repudiation. The ironic confirmation takes place on Guy Fawkes Day, and in the afternoon Ernest unconsciously celebrates the real meaning of the day's

business by half-guiltily helping his classmates burn his father in effigy.

The contrast between the traditional meaning of events and their meaning for Ernest is again marked when he is ordained, for in nominally accepting a vocation in the church he moves as far as he can go in the opposite direction from his true vocation as a solitary author. His marriage to Ellen, the birth of his children, and the death of his mother are similarly ironic and definitive, but the key event is his sentencing for the attack upon Miss Maitland. Ordinarily a sentence to prison is a social catastrophe (Theobald, the spokesman for the conventional, sees it as such), but the inverted pattern of Ernest's life makes it a triumph: exiled from the middle classes in which he cannot live and isolated in prison, he catches the first glimpse of his ultimate destiny and begins to discover the way of life of his greatgrandfather Old Pontifex—a sign of which is his reawakened interest in playing the organ in the prison chapel. Ernest emerges from society's prison as from a personal House of Holiness, purged of some of his illusions about himself and set on a truer course in life. The judge who sentences him reveals the irony of Ernest's life up to this point: he reviews what he apparently regards as Ernest's advantages in life—a sheltered childhood, the guidance of religious parents, a privileged education at Roughborough and Cambridge—and marvels that someone so trained could go so wrong, while the reader perceives by contrast how pernicious every stage of Ernest's training has been.

Shaw considered Butler's representation of the middle-class and lower-class society from which Ernest is at last freed so graphic and painful that readers would cry out for reform. Historically Shaw was right: the effect of the novel on the public was great; but if we read the novel on its own terms and not as Shaw's anti-Victorian manifesto, we see that paradoxically enough Ernest's final isolation is defined only in terms of middle-class institutions, and therefore that if there were reforms in the family, in education, and in the church Ernest would cease to exist. Indeed, when Ernest at last succeeds in isolating himself it is the brilliantly drawn conventional world which the reader misses most; for it is the particulars of this world—the other characters, the inverted education-of-a-young-man plot, the mocking language of prigs and hypocrites which sounded so clearly in the earlier chapters—that have made the character Ernest, and thus at the end he appears only as a sad shadow of his former self. At this point even a journey back to Battersby cannot revive him, for the fine clothes that symbolize his prosperity effectively insulate him from the old world, and the tyrant Theobald is now old and weak, and Christina is dying. Thus even in the setting of his tortured childhood Ernest finds almost nothing that affects him at all, and his final triumph over Battersby (and Roughborough and Cambridge)—toward which the novel has moved with skill and energy equal to that moving a Shavian play to its culminating marriage—turns out to be artistically empty. Indeed, the reader may come to dislike Ernest, because as the novel fails to maintain its values dramatically, the reader begins to apply his own and to see Ernest as a self-satisfied prig. Even Henry Festing Jones felt he had to apologize for the drabness of the end: "Had Butler rewritten the book," he tried to explain, "he might have thought it worth while to emphasize Ernest's final success and happiness which, it may be, is presented in a form that may strike some readers as not unlike failure."

Butler's artistic difficulty in presenting Ernest's final state as the apotheosis of individual—as opposed to social—life proceeded from the absence of traditional narrative forms for expressing it. He had created a new kind of hero in a situation that was to become common in the twentieth-century novel, and he had succeeded up to the very end, until Ernest's non-tragic disengagement from and involvement with his society could no longer be expressed by an ironic plot, and yet the alternatives, the violence and death of the romantic hero, or the marriage and new life of the social hero, were inappropriate.

Butler's attempt to give narrative form to his curiously modern view of the individual and society was to fascinate James Joyce, who read *The Way of All Flesh* just after it was published and while trying to give form to his own complicated involvement with his family, church, and nation. First in *A Portrait of the Artist as a Young Man,* which he was just beginning, and later in *Ulysses,* Joyce expressed the uniqueness of his hero through a complex, ironic relation of the young Stephen Dedalus to a variety of religious, social, and personal ceremonies. But since Joyce did not believe in the final triumph that Butler so devoutly wished but could not achieve for Ernest, the similar forces which act upon Stephen find only a series of momentary narative resolutions. Butler wanted something more permanent, a resolution older and more satisfying, and when at the end of his novel he found he could not present it, he asserted it. But he was too fine an artist to be fooled; he refused to publish *Ernest Pontifex* and set it aside for eighteen years, hoping that somehow he might solve one of the great problems with which the twentieth-century novel has had to deal. (pp. xv-xxi)

> *Daniel F. Howard, in an introduction to* Ernest Pontifex; or, The Way of All Flesh *by Samuel Butler, edited by Daniel F. Howard, 1964. Reprint by Methuen & Co. Ltd., 1965, pp. v-xxi.*

F. W. DUPEE (essay date 1967)

[*Dupee was an American editor, educator, and critic. An ardent Marxist, he served as editor of the left-wing journal* Partisan Review *from 1937 to 1941 and remained politically active throughout his subsequent teaching career. In the following excerpt, he provides a reassessment of* The Way of All Flesh.]

There are in [*The Way of All Flesh*] no pockets of ambiguity or symbolism inviting exploration by the curious critic. Its virtues, too, are as obvious as its faults, and the faults are many. *The Way of All Flesh* is not for those "lovers of perfection alone" to whom Ezra Pound directed his poems and James Joyce his novels. Nor is it for the lovers of, or apologists for, *im*perfection—those who are inclined to see in faulty workmanship an assertion of the primacy of "life" over "art." In *The Way of All Flesh* there is a lot of "life" but no more than is to be found in Pound's best poems or the novels of Joyce, Conrad, James, and so on back to the chief founder of the novel-as-art line, Flaubert. True, present-day readers have been mainly nurtured on the works in that line and on the criticism arising from it. Faced with *The Way of All Flesh,* those readers may have to make certain concessions to its unmannerly conduct—unless they happen to be wearied by the excesses of the modernist novel in its present state of intermittent decadence and therefore turn to Butler's novel with uncritical relief.

As social history the book is certainly not the bombshell it originally was. Our war with the Victorian age was long ago

won. That quarrel has died down in proportion as our quarrel with ourselves has grown more bitter. Profound changes have occurred in the nature of family relationships. The present situation, with children tyrannizing over their parents rather than the reverse (as parents may see it!) could have been invented by Butler himself, since his irony thrived on the literal inversion of existing values. What guarantees the book's continuing interest is, partly, the truth and the vivacity of the formula underlying his picture of Victorian manners. In satirizing them he is satirizing the very phenomenon of manners. Manners, he shows, are forms of behavior in which the members of a given class participate more or less unconsciously in whatever period of history. Manners therefore exemplify an element of automatism that remains constant in human behavior. "Stay—I may presently take a glass of cold water and a small piece of bread and butter." The first part of Dr. Skinner's little speech is Victorian gentility at its most precious; it sounds like Matthew Arnold's prose at *its* most precious. The second part is the giveaway: Dr. Skinner is moved by simple animal hunger. The hunger and the impulse to broach it elegantly, as if tipping his hat to a lady he coveted, are both forms of automatism in an individual who, as a headmaster and a distinguished intellectual, has every reason to think himself superior to mere habit or animal appetite. For Butler, manners, when observed from the outside or in retrospect, are seen to be necessary, yet in their extreme forms laughable. For Butler as for Proust, the more superior a person thinks he is, the more striking and funny are the manifestations in him of the automaton.

In the rigor of his formula and the relentless irony it gives rise to, *The Way of All Flesh* was in its time exceptional among novels in English. I say "English" because in certain other ways, and ignorant or contemptuous as Butler was of English fiction, it is very much in the English vein. It tempers the severity of its social psychology with overt idealism. The novel begins and ends with what are really Utopian parables: the picture of Old Pontifex's world and the picture of the world of the mature Ernest Pontifex. The former is made believable by a great deal of affectionate detail. The latter is pure didactic allegory. In both, however, the Butlerian irony is largely in abeyance. A natural harmony reigns in Old Pontifex's life, so far as he is concerned. His drawings ("always of local subjects") are remembered by Overton as "hanging up framed and glazed in the study at the Rectory, and tinted, as all else in the room was tinted, with the green reflected from the fringe of ivy leaves that grew around the windows." Similarly with Old Pontifex as a man of property. For him his possessions extend beyond his house, his workshops, and his grounds to include the distant greenwood and the setting sun. Once this natural harmony is shattered, the troubles begin and the irony sets in with a vengeance. Nature, ignored or perverted, avenges itself on most of the Pontifexes, subjecting them to the tyranny of social and biological necessity. George Pontifex, of the second generation, is an agent rather than a victim of this tyranny. Theobald and Cristina, of the third generation, are wholly victims and are therefore enveloped by a certain pathos. Their marriage is the result of a union of pure chance (the card game at which she wins from her sisters the right to woo Theobald) and of virtual necessity (the pressures of family, profession, money, etc.). The marriage remains loveless, static, sterile. Cristina and Theobald cooperate in preserving domestic order. Each is otherwise locked up in the private world of his own preoccupations, Theobald in his concern with maintaining his position in the world and his authority in the family; Cristina in her daydreams of glories beyond such immediate realities. Thus encased, neither of them can do any lasting harm to themselves or others. In the end their actions meet, not with large successes or disastrous failures, but simply with rebuffs.

As applied to Ernest's parents, Butler's irony is thus of a subtle kind. It is not unique with Butler but it is one of his specialties. It distinguishes himself from his English predecessors, Dickens, and to a considerable extent George Eliot, for both of whom decisive acts must have their decisive consequences. The evaporating of this irony is largely fatal to the concluding chapters of the novel. Ernest is exempted from it when he comes into money and embarks on his planned existence. Without underrating the benefits of money in reasonable amounts and to reasonable people, we can't help noting that Ernest has endured much only to learn what his father and grandfather might have told him: that money, especially inherited money, is absolutely vital to the good life. Butler's psychological determinism here vanishes with his irony. Ernest's treatment of his children is notorious among readers of the book. He gives his children into the care of a bargeman's family living on the lower Thames. Butler presents this transaction as a straight-faced parable of the good life, an "experiment in family living." Psychologically interpreted its different meaning is unmistakable. Ernest has simply inverted the family pattern, abandoning his children rather than, like the older Pontifexes, smothering them with self-serving care and righteousness. *The Way of All Flesh* ends up by being as loveless as it is—except slyly—sexless. Butler evidently lacked the artistic means or the courage to represent sex and love in the intense degree that he had known them himself. But at least he had the sense not to try to attempt what he couldn't do and what, if he *had* attempted it, would probably have come out mawkish and unreal, wrecking the cold but not frigid irony that gives *The Way of All Flesh* its peculiar distinction.

As narrative art, *The Way of All Flesh* requires further concessions, although these may again be made by some readers quite willingly. The story bumbles along agreeably while defying many of the novelistic refinements that were in force as far back as 1873, when he commenced work on the book. His inexperience in novel-writing may be blamed for some of its faults: after all, *The Way of All Flesh* was Butler's "first novel" as well as his only one. But there may also be a certain element of deliberation in his defiance of sophisticated novelistic procedures. His known opinions on art encourage this assumption. He preferred Giotto's simple solidity to the work of later painters equipped with the sciences of perspective and chiaroscuro. He preferred Handel's open musical forms to the grandiose syntheses of Wagner. And when we look in *The Way of All Flesh* for the "artist" who looms in most novels of adolescence, we don't find him in the ultimate products of family history, the Little Hannos or Stephen Dedaluses or Marcels, but in Old Pontifex, the family's founder and, as we have seen, "natural" exponent of artistic creation.

Whether Butler had a theory about "the novel" or was simply following his instincts is immaterial. What he did in *The Way of All Flesh* was to disintegrate the novel form into what had originally been its constituent elements: the narrative of romance or allegory, the stage play, and the essay or aphorism. What other novelists had labored to fuse he more or less broke up, or at least let fall more or less apart of their own volition. Thus *The Way of All Flesh* has a far-off resemblance to old chronicles of national or local history—episodic, anec-

dotal, full of documents, real and invented. The documents, such as Cristina's death letter and Theobald's bill of particulars regarding the misconduct of the pupils at Roughborough School, are striking in themselves and an innovation on Butler's part. It was taken up by Joyce, say in the "Hell Fire Sermon" of the *Portrait,* and so passed on into modernist fiction and poetry. In this case instant modernization of Butler *is* possible.

Elsewhere it is not. Butler's use of Overton as narrator looks sophisticated. It promises to put needed distance between the author's personality, which we know was insistent, and the materials of the novel, which were largely autobiographical. But Butler's use of his narrator is capricious. Overton's credentials, including his mysterious affair with Alethea Pontifex, are transparent fabrications. He fades in and out, useful only as a mouthpiece for Butler's wisdom and as a fairy godfather to the plot. The narrative, too, is shaky, tending to lapse into single episodes or sequences of eipsodes or into impromptu performances of virtuosity on the author's part. He was a wonderful mimic, a wonderful miniaturist in the representation of character and action. These relatively isolated passages are among the best things in the novel.

There is in *The Way of All Flesh,* despite the general grimness of it, a great deal of simple but exquisite "fun," as when Theobald's tendency to think of himself as a martyr to responsibility culminates in his being actually burned—in effigy—by Theobald's schoolmates. And Butler's performances in the art of mimicry are expert, even when they become ends in themselves, interrupting the narrative. Having hit upon the idea of reproducing George Pontifex's recorded travel impressions, he develops them into a full-scale burlesque of the mawkish impressions of all sentimental travelers in that Byronic age. True, George's sensibility is peculiarly at odds with his real nature, which is severely practical. So his effusions are correspondingly ghastly. George visits the Great St. Bernard in the Alps, one of the standard stops on the nineteenth-century Grand Tour. There he writes, among other things: "The thought that I was sleeping in a convent and occupied the bed of no less a person than Napoleon, that I was in the highest inhabited spot in the old world and in a place celebrated in every part of it, kept me awake some time."

George also composes some verses for the visitor's book of the Great St. Bernard. Butler manages shrewdly the shift in tone from George's labored poetic solemnity—

> These are thy works, and while on
> them I gaze
> I hear a silent tongue that speaks
> thy praise—

to the rude prose of Butler's own ensuing comment: "Some poets always begin to get groggy about the knees after running for seven or eight lines," etc. This might be Huckleberry Finn remarking on the posthumous works of Emmeline Grangerford; and in fact Butler has more affinities, fortunate and unfortunate, with Mark Twain than with any of his English contemporaries. But *The Way of All Flesh* is no such unintentional masterpiece as *Huckleberry Finn* is. The artistic insouciance that Mark Twain shared with Butler seems to have submitted, in Mark Twain, to the control of some angel of relevance who presided over Huck's mental and physical wanderings and kept them firmly in the picture. It was not in Butler's character to invite, or submit to, dictations from above or, for that matter, from below: the "Unconscious" is recognized and called by name in *The Way of All Flesh* but only as an Idea, one of Butler's many Ideas. It didn't supply the author with any subliminal and unifying passion comparable to the passion excited by the realities of Death in the Mark Twain of *Huckleberry Finn.*

Butler adds to George's travel impressions some actual outpourings of Mendelssohn's in the Uffizi. These are prodigiously funny in their self-congratulatory spirit. But they have stalled the narrative, forcing from Butler—or Overton—as he resumes the story one of his jolting and, here, grammarless transitions: "Returning to Mr. Pontifex, whether he liked it or not what he believed to be the masterpieces," etc.

Butler's transitional vehicles often sag ominously, as if the whole narrative were about to break down. At one point he briefly describes Mr. Allaby's relief at finally getting Cristina married to Theobald and the bridal couple off on their wedding journey. Then Butler writes: "And what were the feelings of Theobald and Cristina when the village was passed and they were rolling quietly by the fir plantation? It is at this point that stoutest heart must fail," etc. He couldn't have done it better if he had been deliberately parodying the labored locutions of inept novelists. What follows is, nevertheless, one of the great passages in the novel: the long wearisome ride in the carriage, the muted contest of will between the two occupants, poor Theobald's too easy triumph over poor Cristina, and the celebration of this triumph by way of the cheery little supper at the inn. The episode might be something out of the artful Flaubert or Maupassant, except that in Butler there is no denouement in the bedroom. (pp. 29-31)

F. W. Dupee, "Butler's Way," in The New York Review of Books, *Vol. 9, No. 3, August 24, 1967, pp. 26-31.*

HERBERT L. SUSSMAN (essay date 1968)

[*Sussman is an American critic and the author of* Victorians and the Machine: The Literary Response to Technology. *In the following excerpt from that work, he suggests that Butler had not yet formulated his modifications to Darwin's theory of evolution when he wrote* Erewhon, *and that it would therefore be incorrect to view "The Book of the Machines" section of that work as a satire on the mechanistic view of evolution. For a response to Sussman's arguments, see the excerpt by Govind Narain Sharma below.*]

In the preface to *Erewhon* in 1872, Butler warns his readers that the "Book of the Machines" has been incorrectly read as a refutation of Darwin and suggests that his real satirical target is the "specious misuse of analogy" in another book, probably Joseph Butler's popular religious work, *The Analogy of Religion.* As usual, the statement is itself ambiguous, but it provides an important indication as to the meaning of the "Book of the Machines" in mentioning the "specious misuse of analogy" as the external object of ridicule. If it is an exceedingly indirect attack on the use of analogy in religion, it is more explicitly concerned with the use of the machine analogy in describing organic life. But the satire of the 1872 version of *Erewhon* is unresolved on the question of biological mechanism—only in the last year of his life did he revise the work to make it a defense of vitalism. Similarly, the first version is equally ambivalent in its attitude toward industrial mechanization, but in revising the work for the final version

of 1901, Butler added material which turns the work into a satire of Victorian antimachine criticism.

In *Life and Habit,* his first scientific treatise on biological vitalism, he says that once the biologist accepts the machine as a conceptual model for organic life, once he assumes that any animal, even man, is "such and such a machine, of which if you touch such and such a spring, you will get a corresponding action . . . he will find, so far as I can see, no escape from a position very similar to the one which I put into the mouth of the first of the two professors who dealt with the question of machinery in my earlier work, *Erewhon.*"

The account of the first professor, which makes up the bulk of the "Book of the Machines," can indeed be read as a satire in which the external object of ridicule is biological mechanism, and the method a *reduction ad absurdum* refutation of the machine analogy. The first professor, a scientist at the Colleges of Unreason, traces out the philosophical implications of biological mechanism with a logical rigor worthy of Thomas Henry Huxley. But without any authorial comment, the reader can only evaluate the professor's account by shifts in diction. The professor often begins with restrained scientific language that appears straight out of Huxley but moves to rephrasings that are palpably absurd. For example:

> If it be urged that the action of the potato is chemical and mechanical only, and that it is due to the chemical and mechanical effects of light and heat, the answer would seem to lie in an inquiry whether every sensation is not chemical and mechanical in its operation? . . . Whether strictly speaking we should not ask what kind of levers a man is made of rather than what is his temperament?

The final chapter of the "Book of the Machines" continues to explore the machine analogy but moves from biological theory to the more general implication of psychological determinism. Here again Butler tests the mechanistic hypothesis by having the first professor carry it to its logical extreme; here again the testing turns into a refutation of mechanism by showing the absurdity of the deterministic implications. The professor answers the objection that the machine cannot displace man because it lacks volition by using the machine analogy to show that man himself has as little, or as much, volition as a complex modern machine. Butler's philosophical point here, as in the early essays, is that the mechanistic hypothesis necessarily implies a complete philosophical determination. Again the rhetorical signals for the satire of the first professor and his theory are provided by the shifts of tone, from the scientific statement of the premise, "a man is the resultant and exponent of all the forces that have been brought to bear upon him, whether before his birth or afterwards . . . As he is by nature, and as he has been acted on, and is now acted on from without, so will he do, as certainly and regularly as though he were a machine," to the whimsical description of the logical conclusion:

> At first sight it would indeed appear that a vapour-engine cannot help going when set upon a line of rails with the steam up and machinery in full play; whereas the man whose business it is to drive it can help doing so at any moment that he pleases. . . . The driver is obedient to his masters, because he gets food and warmth from them, and if these are withheld or given in insufficient quantities he will cease to drive; in like manner the engine will cease to work if it is insufficiently fed.

It would be tempting in the light of Butler's later conversion to vitalism to read the "Book of the Machines" in its original context as Butler himself did in his later career, as a spoof of the mechanistic hypothesis. But it is clear that the work as it stands in the 1872 edition is totally ambivalent; if Butler was dissatisfied with the implications of a mechanistic Darwinism, he was equally unsure about the vitalistic alternative. There are no rhetorical signs to indicate that the assertions of biological vitalism are to be taken with any more seriousness than those of biological mechanism. For example, after taking the mechanistic hypothesis to the seemingly untenable conclusion that chemistry could predict temperament from a single hair, he immediately mentions, but only in passing, the central principle of his later vitalistic theory. He says in serious scientific prose that "a great deal of action that has been called purely mechanical and unconscious must be admitted to contain more elements of consciousness than has been allowed hitherto." And yet the examples that follow from this premise are given with the same whimsical tone that is used to show the absurdity in the implications of mechanism: "Even a potato in a dark cellar has a certain low cunning about him which serves him in excellent stead. . . . What deliberation he may exercise in the matter of his roots when he is planted in the earth is a thing unknown to us, but we can imagine him saying, 'I will have a tuber here and a tuber there, and I will suck whatsoever advantage I can from all my surroundings'."

And yet, it is this very ambivalence, this lack of rhetorical certainty, that makes the "Book of the Machines" such an engaging work. For its only statement is a paradox—man's actions are as predictable as those of a machine, and yet to compare man to a machine, to equate the locomotive with its engineer, is palpably absurd. The attractiveness of the work lies in Butler's skill in using modern technology to express this paradox. Or, to generalize, the delight lies in his ability to play with the modern machine as philosophical metaphor for the central paradox of Western philosophy, the conflict between the deterministic implications of science and the inward apprehension of volitional freedom.

The appeal of the "Book of the Machines" to the modern reader is also in Butler's uncanny ability inadvertently to describe the twentieth century. The Erewhonian "straighteners," for example, meant as a satire of the Anglican clergy, appear as perfect types of the modern psychoanalyst. So, too, with Butler's conscious machines. The vision of two vapor engines sitting outside their shed and watching their offspring frolic is not meant in its context as a prediction of technological development, but as part of his questioning of the mechanistic hypothesis. In an ironic sense that Butler might himself appreciate, the public fears of the twentieth century have caught up with his satire. For the logic of his satire depends on the implicit agreement of the reader that any theory that can show a machine to have the same degree of intellect and consciousness as man must be untrue. But if the nineteenth century feared that the machine would replace man first as laborer, then as artisan, the twentieth fears that it will replace man as thinker. In our time, the public debate over the man-machine analogy concentrates less on the question of physiology, which has been resolved in favor of the mechanists, than on the question of whether thought, and even consciousness, is uniquely human. And so, the "Book of the Machines" can be read in two ways, as an engaging account of the twentieth-century fears of the machine as thinker and, in its historical context, as a spoof of philosophical mechanism.

The "Book of the Machines" considers industrial mechanization with the same ambivalence shown in the treatment of philosophical mechanism. Butler rehearses the argument of **"Darwin among the Machines,"** that the machine will supersede and enslave mankind, and, with increased skill in using evolutionary metaphors, extrapolates the effects of mechanization into a future where men have become "affectionate, machine-tickling aphids." But the opposing, pro-machine viewpoint is also given with no rhetorical signals enabling the reader to choose. In the final chapter, a second professor is quoted as having answered the Erewhonian attack on machinery. He suggests the notion introduced in **"Lucubratio Ebria"** and turned into evolutionary theory in the scientific works, the idea that men extend their ability by creating new and more efficient limbs through technological progress. "Its author said that machines were to be regarded as a part of man's own physical nature, being really nothing but extracorporeal limbs. Man, he said, was a machinate mammal." As in **"Lucubratio Ebria"** and the scientific writing, this idea is associated with a more purposive, less mechanistic form of evolution:

> Machines are to be regarded as the mode of development by which human organism is now especially advancing, every past invention being an addition to the resources of the human body. Even community of limbs is thus rendered possible to those who have so much community of soul as to own money enough to pay a railway fare; for a train is only a seven-leagued foot that five hundred may own at once.

If, then, the "Book of the Machines" suggests contradictory views about mechanization as it does about biological mechanism, so too it uses the *reductio* technique to test the criticism of the machine. Butler takes the premise of so much nineteenth-century writing, that the machine is enslaving man, and through the narrative carries it to its logical conclusion, that all machinery must be destroyed. The critical question, then, is whether this method is used here to criticize industrial mechanization or, in a manner similar to that of the philosophical sections, to refute Victorian antimachine critics. I would suggest that the "Book of the Machines" as first written is as ambivalent in its treatment of technological progress as it is in its exploration of biological mechanism. But even the most cursory consideration of Butler's character indicates that he would have increasingly less sympathy with the critics of technological progress. Like Dickens, he was too solid a member of the middle class ever to consider restraining the profit motive as a means of restraining the machine. He considered it his duty to remain, if not rich, at least extremely comfortable, and if prosperity depends on technological progress, so be it. When he returned from New Zealand he invested his capital in companies that manufactured machinery and that used machinery in production. Just as in later life he looked back to see the "Book of the Machines" as a satire on mechanistic biology, so, too, he saw the same ambivalent piece as a satire of antimachine literature. And he added the chapters on "The Views of an Erewhonian Prophet Concerning the Rights of Animals" and "The Views of an Erewhonian Philosopher Concerning the Rights of Vegetables" in the final version not only to establish his vitalistic theory as the norm against which the philosophical discussion is to be judged but also to set up the common bourgeois virtues of comfort and prosperity as the norm against which antimachine arguments are to be compared.

The chapter on the "Views of an Erewhonian Prophet Concerning the Rights of Animals" opens with an unusually direct evaluation of the Erewhonians by the narrator.

> It will be seen from the foregoing chapters that the Erewhonians are a meek and long-suffering people, easily led by the nose, and quick to offer up common sense at the shrine of logic, when a philosopher arises among them, who carries them away through his reputation for especial learning, or by convincing them that their existing institutions are not based on the strictest principles of morality.

The Erewhonians are, of course, the English, and the "philosopher" bears a strong resemblance to Ruskin. Here, as throughout these added chapters, the destruction of the machines is judged against the norm of what Butler calls "common sense," by which he means an instinctive mode of judgment, rather than purely rationalistic argument. The very form of the work is an attack on reason, showing that just as sophistic logic can lead men, as the narrator says, "to cut their throats in the matter of machinery," so, too, rationality combined with an overdeveloped moral sense can lead them to give up even the natural process of eating. The added chapters, then, satirize antimachine criticism by showing that an argument which asks men to suppress their natural instinct for pleasure for the sake of an abstract ideal can, when taken to a logical extreme, persuade men to starve themselves to death, again for the sake of moral principle. The suggestion that the philosopher is arguing for the rights of vegetables as an indirect means of attacking prohibitions on meat accurately applies to Butler's own indirect method in arguing for vegetarianism as a means of satirizing the opponents of technological progress: "Many think that this philosopher did not believe his own teaching, and, being in secret a great meat-eater, had no other end in view than reducing the prohibition against eating animal food to an absurdity, greater even than an Erewhonian Puritan would be able to stand."

And yet, even with the additional material, the work as a whole remains ambivalent because it is conceived within the conventions of nineteenth-century antimachine literature. With its fruitful land, its clear skies, its healthy people, the land over the range is the pastoral utopia of the machine age. In typical Victorian fashion, its primitivism is even expressed in terms of the medieval ideal: "They were about as far advanced as Europeans of the twelfth or thirteenth century; certainly not more so." For Butler writing in 1872, as for Morris writing almost twenty years later, the medieval pastoral utopia becomes the metaphor for their belief that physical grace and sensual fulfillment could exist only outside the mechanized world. And so, in its treatment of mechanization, *Erewhon,* for all its wit, dramatizes only the Victorian ambivalence to the machine. It is in part an evocation of the "natural" life that could be regenerated in a world freed from the pattern of the machine, and in part a satire of the dreamy unreality of those writers who envisioned such a utopia.

In using the hypothesis of a conscious locomotive to test biological mechanism, as later in using the development of the steam engine to illustrate creative evolution, Butler is following a typical nineteenth-century rhetorical pattern, exemplified earlier in the century by Carlyle, of using modern technology as a figure for philosophical mechanism. But for all Butler's philosophical wit, his literary use of the machine is neither as rich nor as effective as that of Carlyle, Dickens, or Ruskin. When Carlyle rejects the idea of the universe as a "huge, dead, immeasurable Steam-engine," the machine becomes a complex symbol relating his philosophical rejection of an indifferent universe to his moral outrage at the application of this same mechanistic thought to an industrial society. But Butler never linked his intellectual objection to mechanistic thought with social or moral criticism. In *Erewhon,* the "Book of the Machines" is a separate text set off from the main narrative; Butler in no way dramatizes the relation between the absence of machinery and the quality of Erewhonian life. Nor, in *Erewhon Revisited,* is the reintroduction of machinery linked to the social and religious transformations the narrator describes. In discussing mechanization, an Erewhonian refers to "the consequences that are already beginning to appear, and which, if I mistake not, will assume far more serious proportions in the future," but these consequences are nowhere elaborated. This consistent separation in his works between the discussion of intellectual mechanism and industrial mechanization, this failure to turn the machine from an intellectual analogy into a complex symbol indicates Butler's own persistent refusal to recognize the social and psychological implications of the mechanistic philosophy he so intensely distrusted. (pp. 151-61)

> Herbert L. Sussman, *"Evolution and the Machine: Samuel Butler,"* in his Victorians and the Machine: The Literary Response to Technology, *Cambridge, Mass.: Harvard University Press, 1968, pp. 135-61.*

GOVIND NARAIN SHARMA   (essay date 1980)

[*Sharma is an Indian-born Canadian critic and scholar. In the following excerpt, he responds to Herbert L. Sussman's suggestion (above) that Butler had not yet formulated his vitalist modifications to Darwin's theories when he wrote* Erewhon.]

"In his youthful essays on evolution and the machine, as well as in the first (1872) edition of *Erewhon,*" says Herbert Sussman, "Butler approaches mechanistic biology with nearly perfect intellectual ambivalence, with an ironic detachment that only seeks to play with the paradoxes of philosophical mechanism rather than resolve them. Only after *Erewhon* did Butler change from satirist to scientist as he sought to develop a vitalistic theory that could supplant the mechanistic system of Darwin." And he concludes his discussion of Butler with the statement: "Butler never linked his intellectual objection to mechanistic thought with social or moral criticism. In *Erewhon,* the "Book of Machines" is a separate text set off from the main narrative; Butler in no way dramatizes the relation between the absence of machinery and the quality of Erewhonian life." It will be my contention in this essay that though Butler had not made up his mind on the Darwinian theory when he published the first edition of *Erewhon,* the direction of his thought was distinctly towards a teleological view, the position being the same as with *Life and Habit* in which, though he was not aware of it at the time of writing it, "the spirit of the book was throughout teleological." Also the "Book of Machines," far from being "a separate text," is central to the artistic and moral economy of *Erewhon,* to the projection of Butler's satiric as well as his utopian vision.

There has been a great deal of controversy about Butler's purpose in writing the machine chapters and his own contribution has been to increase rather than diminish the confusion. In the preface to the second edition he repudiated the sugges-

Butler (seated) with his friend and collaborator Henry Festing Jones.

tion that they were an attempt to reduce Darwin's theory to an absurdity and wrote to Darwin himself disavowing any such intention. But he has also said that he wrote the preface to "stroke him [Darwin] down," suspecting that the machine chapters were the "peccant matter" offending him. Whichever of these statements we accept, they leave little doubt that Butler did see a connection between his view of the machines and the Darwinian theory of evolution, the reflections on machines being a direct consequence of his acquaintance with the theory of evolution as set forth by Charles Darwin. Commenting on the latter's observation in the preface to his last edition of the *Origin of Species* that Lamarck was partly led to his conclusions by the analogy of domestic productions, Butler says in *Life and Habit:* ". . . If they imply that Lamarck drew inspirations from the gradual development of the mechanical inventions of man, and from the progress of man's ideas, I would say that of all sources this would seem to be the safest and most fertile from which to draw. Plants and animals under domestication are indeed a suggestive field for study, but machines are the manner in which man is varying at this moment."

Thus the study of machines has a direct bearing on the study of human evolution and hence of all organic life. Since the latter study is for Butler never confined to the biological aspect alone, it is reasonable to assume that his reflections on machines have relevance to man's social and moral problems.

But what exactly is the nature of this relevance, the link between Butler's objection to mechanistic thought as represented by the Darwinian view of evolution and his social and moral outlook? Dwight Culler is one of the few critics who have tried to explore this link in a most forthright way by examining Darwin's influence on *Erewhon.* The influence, according to him, "lies somewhere not in the substance but in the total feeling and structure of the book," more particularly in Butler's satiric technique, in the embodiment of the upside-down view of England through a device which he calls the Darwinian reversal. *Erewhon,* however, appears to be Darwinian even more in substance than in form. Erewhonian morality seems to be "natural," evolution being the basis of the ethics: "a physical excellence is considered in Erewhon as a set-off against any other disqualification," and disease is regarded as a crime. "Moreover, they [the Erewhonians] hold their deities to be quite regardless of motives. With them it is the thing done which is everything, and the motive goes for nothing." There is the example of the air-god who will kill a man if he stays without air for more than a few minutes, whatever be his motives. In their social norms too Darwinism is a powerful determinant. They respect wealth and success, and in their eyes earning money is synonymous with "doing good" to society, the true philanthropy. "So strongly are the Erewhonians impressed with this, that if a man has made a fortune of over £ 20,000 a year they exempt him from all taxation, considering him as a work of art, and too precious to be meddled with; . . . so magnificent an *organization* over-awes them; they regard it as a thing dropped from heaven." This attitude of the Erewhonians may appear irreverent to those who would prize moral virtue more highly than worldly success, but it is not so; it is based on a "spirit of the most utter reverence for those things . . . which are, which mould us and fashion us, be they what they may; for our masters therefore." Obviously, for the Erewhonians there is no distinction between "is" and "ought": the "is" dictates the "ought."

The Erewhonian attitude to machines is also Darwinian. In a ruthless struggle for survival a living being's first duty is to look after his own survival. The machines, evolving at a terrific pace and acquiring a greater degree of sophistication every day, hold the possibility of supplanting man and reducing him to a state of servitude. Evidently, if he is to ensure his own survival, he has to stop the proliferation and development of machines. But this very way of looking at things, of looking at the machine as a competitor and an adversary, betrays a deeper concern than could be explained in terms of "mere fun" or "gigantic bluffs," and the writer's attitude could scarcely be described as that of "perfect intellectual ambivalence."

I would suggest that the machine is the key symbol in *Erewhon,* embodying the antithesis between mechanism and life, which, according to Basil Willey, is the central problem of Butler's thought. This antithesis forms the basis of his utopian and satiric vision and projects itself into the leading ideas which are worked out in *Erewhon:* for example, on crime and disease, Hebraism and Hellenism, reason and faith, logic and common sense, duty and pleasure. It helps us in understanding the relationship between man and his laws, customs and institutions. The latter, like machines, are good friends and allies but bad masters. Insofar as they contribute to human development and happiness, they are good; when they stand in the way of these they are undesirable. When the machine tends to become machinery in Arnold's sense of the word, and when it leads men to erect impressive and elaborate structures of thought in the realm of religion, morals, philosophy or science, it becomes positively dangerous. It is then a symbol of rigidity and dogmatism, whereas it is moderation, flexibility and compromise which are man's prime needs in life. But men cannot do without the machine entirely: he needs the prop of customs, laws and institutions to function till he reaches "the true millennium," "the unconscious state of equilibrium which we observe in the structures and instincts of bees and ants, and an approach to which may be found among some savage nations." If these customs, laws and institutions are flexible, can move with the spirit of the times, they can be of immense value to man. In fact, to mould them in this manner, to modify and perfect them to suit his needs, is a challenge to him. His success in doing so would be a mark of his intelligence and cunning, just as the invention of superior machines has been, and would ensure the victory of life over mechanism.

The antithesis can first be seen in the projection of the author's satiric outlook. It is characteristic of what Northrop Frye calls "the second or quixotic phase of satire." The central theme in this phase of satire is the setting of ideas and generalizations and theories and dogmas over against the life they are supposed to explain. Butler's preferences are clear.

He emphasizes the superiority of life over ideas—of faith and instinct over reason, of the unconscious over the conscious. It is an important feature of Butler's philosophical strategy in *Erewhon* to bring out the dichotomy between the Erewhonians' unconscious and conscious life, the essential rightness of the former and the intriguing hypocrisy of the latter. It is mainly the latter which finds expression in their articulated doctrines and beliefs—their banishment of machinery, their penal code, double coinage and Birth Formulae; and in the institutions which are supposed to uphold them—the Colleges of Unreason, the law courts, the Musical Banks. Whenever they try to be logical and consistent—in other words, set ideas above life—they end up in absurdities and self-deceiving clichés. But this should not tempt us to laugh them out of court; they have a native common sense, an instinctive mother-wit which guides them and in their practical conduct makes them steer clear of a slavish subservience to their dogmas and theories. They recognize the supreme value of the principle of compromise and make it the lodestar of their lives. In the instinctive recognition of this value lies the superiority of the high Ydgrunites, who exemplify best the maxim that "perfect ignorance and perfect knowledge are alike unselfconscious." They are "nice, sensible, unintrospective people" in whom right living has become an instinct which "does not betray signs of self-consciousness as to its own knowledge. It has dismissed reference to first principles, and is no longer under the law but under the grace of a settled conviction." The rest of the Erewhonians have not attained to this perfection of unconscious knowledge; they are still dominated by machinery in the form of the abstract systems which advocate prescribed modes of thought and behaviour like beliefs in the objective personalities of hope, justice and love, ritualistic worship at the Musical Banks and assiduous pursuit of the hypothetical language. They can be imposed upon by any prophet who can make a show of learning and wisdom, thus sacrificing common sense at the shrine of logic. The high Ydgrunites, on the contrary, though they are faithful believers in "conformity until absolutely intolerable," the law of Ydgrun ("Grundy" in the first edition), and would never run counter to her dictates, yet when there is ample reason for doing so and necessity arises, they are capable of overriding her with due self-reliance without being punished by the goddess, "for they are brave, and Ydgrun is not." Thus "they have no real belief in the objective existence of beings [like justice, love and hope] which so readily explain themselves as abstractions, and whose personality demands a quasi-materialism which it baffles the imagination to realise." They have no sense of a hereafter, and their only religion is that of self-respect and consideration for other people. Though they have studied the hypothetical language, it did not have much hand in making them what they are; rather the fact of their being generally possessed of its rudiments is one reason for the reverence paid to the hypothetical language itself.

Butler's chief device to put forward his own point of view is his invention of the naive hero, later in *Erewhon Revisited* given the name Higgs. Higgs is in some respects Butler himself, or what he would have liked to be—a handsome, personable young man with blue eyes and light hair, having much to glory in the flesh. These attractions appear, however, to be partly marred by his priggish Anglicanism and his religious zeal which makes him continually harp on his favourite tune of earning religious merit by converting to Christianity the Erewhonians whom he takes to be the descendants of the lost ten tribes of Israel. But in actual fact, these obsessions do not put us off very much: the angularity of his character turns out to be a comic trait which proves endearing, like the patriotism of Gulliver or the optimism of Candide. Like the hero of the low mimetic mode, of most comedy and realistic fiction, he is superior neither to other men nor to his environment but one of us, and we respond to a sense of his common humanity. He has also some of the characteristics of the hero of the ironic mode, the awkwardness of his personality giving us a sense of superiority to him and thus flattering our vanity and sustaining our interest in his thoughts and deeds. But he is not as simple as he appears. Far from being silly, obtuse and self-deceived, he has the *eiron's* sense of his own shortcomings, occasionally deprecates himself, as opposed to the *alazon,* who pretends or tries to be something more than he is. There can be no doubt of his shrewd intellegence, even his essential decency and good sense. This, according to A.E. Dyson [see Additional Bibliography], is a trump-card that Butler keeps up his sleeve in case readers become overconfident. His decency is strong enough to keep him in the right direction, even when his reasoning seems to be going wildly astray. As in the case of the Erewhonians, his instincts and settled convictions—the promptings of his unconscious—are sound; his doctrines and theories—the dictates of his conscious—are defective.

His very first encounter while entering Erewhon is significant. The Ten Statues creating a frightful cacophony scare him, but these represent nothing else than the decrees of his conscious self, his superego, the injunctions of the Mosaic code which have been a part of his moral drill since childhood. If he wishes to enter Erewhon he must free himself of this "thou-shalt-not" morality. Those like Chowbok (Kahabuka) who are unable to do so shall not enter the utopian land of Erewhon. It is clear that the Erewhonians reject the morality of the categorical imperative. The moral point of view according to them is not that of impartial legislators like Moses, as Kant supposed, but rather the point of view of the man with certain interests, specifically in human happiness and welfare. Such a man will believe in compromise and moderation. Unlike many other utopians, Butler's utopian outlook is free from any doctrinaire bias, and the symbol of the machine is highly relevant here. His conception of society is rather functional than ideological, the principle of function being the secret of the good community. Happiness would be achieved not by creating new customs, laws and institutions but by trying to observe and work the existing ones in the proper spirit. Erewhon, though not an ideal world, is certainly an attractive one in which people live more "naturally" and happily than in our own. If their lives are more "natural" it is not because they follow the evolutionary morality based on Darwinism, either in the personal or social sphere, for instance, by treating disease as a crime and giving the greatest respect to the most successful men. The "naturalness" of their lives lies in their disregard of reason and logic and in the instinctive adherence to modes of behaviour whose soundness has been demonstrated through long usage. They are happy and "ideal" not because they have freed themselves from the anomalies and hypocrisies which riddle our world but because they have accepted their existence. In his role of a literal-minded Evangelical the narrator finds them "really a very difficult people to understand" because

> the most glaring anomalies seemed to afford them no intellectual inconvenience; neither, provided they did not actually see the money dropping out of their pockets, nor suffer immediate physical

> pain, would they listen to any arguments as to the waste of money and happiness which their folly caused them.

The narrator is, however, shrewd enough to note the desirable consequences of this inconsistency and evasiveness;

> But this had an effect of which I have little reason to complain, for I was allowed almost to call them life-long self-deceivers to their faces, and they said it was quite true, but that it did not matter.

What Butler seeks to emphasize is that the happiness of the Erewhonians has been purchased at the price of an unlimited number of compromises, from permitting the use of machinery which was more than 271 years old to acceptance of the Musical Bank coinage as the more valuable one in theory. The Erewhonian Birth Formulae, for instance, require every child to sign a confession that he had been a free agent in coming into the world. This the Erewhonians make him do at an age when "neither they nor the law will for many a year allow any one else to bind him to the smallest obligation." Professors generally are not a very pleasant breed, being doctrinaire, rigid and dogmatic, and the Erewhonian ones were no different from their peers elsewhere in this respect. But the Professor with whom Higgs talked was a delightful person and his defense of this practice was most disarming: the world is full of compromises and there is hardly any affirmation which would bear being interpreted literally; the boy would have to begin compromising sooner or later, and this was part of his education in the art. In simple words, the sooner he learnt to disregard the constraints imposed by machinery the better it would be for his health and happiness in life.

Erewhon has been called a utopia and is undoubtedly so in many respects. But if the utopian impulse can be identified as idealistic and visionary, dominated by reason and logic and in love with order and perfection, then ***Erewhon*** is as much of a satire on utopias as a utopia. Paradoxical as it may appear—nothing unusual in the case of a writer like Butler—the Erewhonian world is utopian only insofar as it repudiates the utopian impulse and embraces the spirit of realism and compromise, accepting the validity of experience in preference to theory, of unreason in preference to reason, of unconscious instinctive wisdom in preference to the conscious. Where it sets out to be consciously utopian, it betrays life and becomes a slave to the machine. (pp. 3-10)

> *Govind Narain Sharma, "Butler's 'Erewhon': The Machine as Object and Symbol," in* The Samuel Butler Newsletter, *Vol. III, No. 1, Summer, 1980, pp. 3-12.*

JAN JEDRZEJEWSKI   (essay date 1988)

[*In the following excerpt, Jedrzejewski discusses the evolution of Butler's religious attitudes as they are manifested in* Erewhon *and* Erewhon Revisited.]

Wide-rangingly amateurish as Samuel Butler's interests were—from Italian culture to biology, from classical studies to biography—it is possible to point to two areas which seem to have been closest to his mind and which found fullest expression in his writings. The first is the theory of evolution, seen basically in its non-Darwinian version following the theories of Buffon and Lamarck; the second is the wide range of problems concerning the Christian religion, particularly the question of the source and role of the miraculous, which constitutes such an important part of the doctrine and teaching of the Church. Both issues were dealt with in different ways throughout Butler's career as a writer, not only in the form of directly expository books and essays but also more indirectly under the guise of fiction, in turn so various and distinct as, on the one hand, the allegory of *Erewhon* or, on the other, the approximation of the typical nineteenth-century realist convention in *The Way of All Flesh.* Thus, for example, the question of the resurrection of Christ constitutes the main problem of works so different and so distant in time as the pamphlet on *The Evidence for the Resurrection of Jesus Christ* (1865) and *Erewhon Revisited* (1901). Necessarily, this temporal and formal diversity is parallelled by considerable modification of the ideas presented in the books, which reflects the author's development as a thinker. Possibly the best example of this is provided by Butler's decision to introduce substantial changes into the 1901 edition of *Erewhon.* The process seems to be of particular interest when comparing *Erewhon* and *Erewhon Revisited,* written at a distance of almost thirty years from each other. Because of the essential similarity of their subject-matter, they clearly exemplify the directions in which Samuel Butler's views as well as his literary technique developed. (pp. 415-16)

First published in 1872, *Erewhon* occupies a special position among Butler's writings, both as his first major book and as the only one, apart from the posthumously published *The Way of All Flesh,* to achieve lasting popularity. Although not the first work of the then 36-year-old author to appear in print, *Erewhon* was in a sense Butler's real literary debut, the book in which he gave for the first time full expression to his views on many of the subjects that were later to become the major topics of his numerous books and essays. *Erewhon* thus turns out to be a kind of *summa* of the ideas Butler held in the 1860s and at the beginning of the 1870s; characteristically, writing of *Erewhon* in his *Note-Books* several years later, he made the following remark: "I had written all I had to say; indeed if I had had another page of matter in me it would have gone into *Erewhon.*"

As is clear from Butler's own Preface to the revised edition published in 1901, the germs of many of the chapters of *Erewhon* are to be found in articles written and partly published during Butler's stay in New Zealand in the early 1860s; similarly, a great deal of the descriptive detail so abundant in the first chapters of the book derives, as has often been shown, from Butler's own depiction of New Zealand in *A First Year in Canterbury Settlement.* Those diverse earlier elements are linked together by the main line of the story, written between the autumn of 1870 and the spring of 1871, and describing, in a manner somewhat reminiscent of Swift's *Gulliver's Travels,* the expedition which the narrator, an anonymous English settler living in an unidentified far-off colony clearly modelled on New Zealand, undertakes in order to visit the mysterious country lying "over the range"—farther than any other European had previously been able to penetrate.

The land that unfolds before the eyes of the narrator—and the reader—turns out to be a place both similar to and different from Europe, inhabited by people, though somewhat different from Europeans, still closely resembling them in their appearance, behaviour, and customs. The narrator's continuous stress on these similarities seems to function, alongside the very convention in which the story is presented, as a kind

of signpost alerting the reader to the fact that everything that happens in the country over the range is actually a replica—somewhat distorted, sometimes reversed, but always clearly recognizable—of what is typical of Europe, or more particularly, of nineteenth-century England. Butler's comments on Erewhon, direct or merely implied, can therefore be read as his comments on the England of his time, on the contemporary society, on the system of justice, on education, and, last but not least, on the Christian religion, basically as understood and practised by the Church of England.

It is not, however, only through the existence of these numerous parallels that *Erewhon* becomes a comment on the life and ideas of the Victorians. Another, structurally most important, link is provided by the fact that the traveller-narrator of *Erewhon* is by no means an objective witness, telling his story in a detached and "transparent" way. On the contrary, he is obviously definable as a personality shaped by his family background, his education, his religion—by the whole system of values in which he was born and brought up. It is not insignificant that from the beginning of the book the narrator carefully avoids introducing himself by name: "If the reader will excuse me, I will say nothing of my antecedents, nor of the circumstances which led me to leave my native country; the narrative would be tedious to him and painful to myself." Even though he gradually discloses more and more details about himself, he retains his somewhat ambiguous anonymity, which seems to indicate that he is a kind of Everyman (or Every-Englishman, or Every-Victorian) rather than a clearly individualized character. Therefore, before considering the implications of the vision of the Christian religion inherent in the very shape of the world of Erewhon, we must analyze the comments that Butler makes on Christianity through the presentation and construction of the character of his narrator.

The most characteristic feature of the narrator's attitude towards religion, as well as of his mind in general, is his rather nonchalant sense of self-satisfaction, his "comfortable belief that in the midst of his own confusion of sense and nonsense he remains a conventional Church-of-England Christian." Indeed, from the very beginning of the book, the reader feels the presence, in a way behind the narrator's voice, of a solid social background, permitting him to speak in a very assertive and opinionated way even when he obviously lacks the knowledge and experience necessary to pronounce the authoritative opinions that he holds about the world around him. A typical example is found in the passage describing the narrator's attempts to convert Chowbok to Christianity. He betrays not only his sense of his cultural and racial superiority over Chowbok, but also his own intellectual and religious self-assurance, resulting from his having grown up in a particular kind of family background, but not necessarily supported by good education or deeper reflection. It seems in this context quite characteristic that for all his claims to theological knowledge the narrator does not seem to know his Bible very well. In fact, at the beginning of the very next chapter he mixes up his biblical references, mistaking Mount Nebo for Mount Sinai: "It was such an expanse as was revealed to Moses when he stood upon the summit of Mount Sinai, and beheld that promised land which it was not to be his to enter."

The shallowness of the narrator's beliefs is disclosed again later in the book, in the passage describing his dispute with Arowhena over the question of the Erewhonian religion. He does not seem to realize that the traditional arguments he uses in his attempts to defend Christianity against Arowhena's doubts, and with which he is apparently completely satisfied, are in fact outdated, empty, and meaningless, even to the point of becoming illogical and, from a rational point of view, absurd, as in the reference to the hand laid over a prophet's face. The narrator is unable to see the analogies that Arowhena draws between the polytheism of Erewhon and the Christian religion as he understands and describes it. (The conversation takes place before they are married and settled in England, so Arowhena's only experience of Christianity is through the accounts given her by her future husband). Even if his complacency is for a moment disturbed ("I did wince a little"), he immediately hides behind the comfortable bulwarks of his unquestioningly accepted beliefs and decides to limit his apostolic zeal to persuading his wife to be baptized into the Church of England, apparently without much conviction on her part. In this way the satirical treatment of the narrator's unsuccessful missionary efforts results in an unexpected comic effect. The scene exemplifies an interesting reversal of the conventional Victorian social roles and patterns of behaviour, which tended to associate religious doubt with men rather than women, and which sometimes involved an obligation to conceal, in courtship or marriage, unorthodox (rather than orthodox) views.

Both of these passages point to still another important feature of the narrator's religious standpoint—his practicality and business-mindedness, leading him to perceive religion as a kind of business enterprise and as a result to evaluate his faith and the importance of his religious practices largely in terms of loss and gain. If he wants to convert Chowbok, he acts on St. James's promise that "Brethren, if any of you do err from the truth, and one convert him/ Let him know, that he which converteth the sinner from the error of his way, shall save a soul from death, and shall hide a multitude of sins." If he later imagines himself preaching Christianity to the Erewhonians, he immediately thinks of the glory that would afterwards await him:

> To restore the lost ten tribes of Israel to a knowledge of the only truth; here would be indeed an immortal crown of glory! My heart beat fast and furious as I entertained the thought. What a position would it not ensure me in the next world; or perhaps even in this! What folly it would be to throw such a chance away!

Indeed, as has been observed by A. E. Dyson [see Additional Bibliography], the narrator of *Erewhon* "is good-natured rather than the reverse, but his good nature is always at the mercy of his religion; and this in turn is far more at the mercy of concealed self-interest than he ever begins to perceive." This kind of attitude, to be discerned throughout the story, finds its fullest expression (even if it is far-fetched to the point of being grotesque) in the narrator's final project of a scheme designed "for the conversion of Erewhon." What is supposed to be missionary work turns in the narrator's mind into plain slave-trade, and the spirit of Christian charity is transformed into that of economic exploitation, all apparently without any misgivings or doubts on his part:

> I can see no hitch nor difficulty about the matter, and trust that this book will sufficiently advertise the scheme to insure the subscription of the necessary capital; as soon as this is forthcoming I will guarantee that I convert the Erewhonians not only

into good Christians but into a source of considerable profit to the shareholders.

Absurd as the idea may be, it nevertheless shows very clearly the way in which Butler, through his manipulation of the often unconscious self-characterization of the narrator, pronounces his view on the real influence that Christianity exerts on the life and attitudes of an average man. The thoughtless and basically indifferent assimilation of meaningless dogmas, the groundless sense of superiority over others, the narrow-mindedness and lack of the power of critical reasoning—all these seem to have been caused, in the case of the traveller to Erewhon, by his having grown up under the influence of the Church of England. If, for all his self-confidence and naïveté, he remains capable of more altruistic feelings, it is because of his natural rather than his cultural instincts. He can be good only in spite of his religion rather than because of it; if "he is, essentially, a man of goodwill[,] there can be no question of religion having made him a better man than he otherwise would have been. His inherited values are so obviously less good than those he would have arrived at unaided."

Samuel Butler's ironic treatment of Christianity inherent in his presentation of the character of his narrator is not only very important in the overall construction of his book, but also, in contrast to the implications of his picture of Erewhon itself, remains relatively clear, consistent, and unified. Indeed, the institutions, customs, and ways of thinking that obtain in the country over the range, though clearly shaped after those of Victorian England, are by no means unambiguous, largely because of Butler's constant shifting from one fictional mode to another: from the realism of the opening to the transparent parody and satire of the chapters on the Colleges of the Unreason, from the utopian vision of the narrator's first arrival in Erewhon to the dystopia of the scene of the trial. As a result, the diversity of possible associations and conclusions that can be drawn on the basis of the often inconsistent details of Erewhonian life leads to interpretations of the book ranging from appraisals of its multidirectional satire as "the element of insoluble dilemma which gives substance to *Erewhon* and makes it deeply disturbing" [Ellen Douglas Leyburn, *Satiric Allegory: Mirror of Man*] to condemnations of the book as meaningless "because no serious criticism or consistent view can be found in it "[A. O. J. Cockshut, *The Unbelievers*]. Overstated as both of those viewpoints appear to be, however, it seems possible to find in the world of Erewhon numerous elements that can clearly be read as declarations of the author's opinion about Christianity in general and the Church of England in particular.

In this respect the most important section of the book is of course the chapter on "The Musical Banks," in which Butler, using the rather transparent disguise of the Church as a place of business rather than worship, attacks Victorian religion for its artificiality, lack of deeper involvement on the part of the laity as well as the clergy, separation from real, everyday problems of contemporary life, and claims to moral and spiritual authority. The satirical effect, resulting from the substitution of the idea of money for that of faith, with all consequent changes and readjustments, is in its main framework fairly consistent.

The emptiness and meaninglessness of the religious practices of the "respectable" Victorians and the irrelevance of their avowed religious beliefs to their everyday lives are, for example, hinted at in the metaphor of the two Erewhonian currencies, representing very clearly two different moral systems, two hierarchies of value existing side by side in Victorian England. The Christian morality, formally universally adhered to, but practically often misunderstood or disregarded, is thus contrasted with the modern areligious ethic of materialism, competition, and gain. (pp. 416-20)

The symbolic function of money in *Erewhon* is not, however, limited to suggesting Butler's criticism of the religious hypocrisy of his contemporaries. Indeed, the description of the official musical bank currency provides some very straightforward insight into Butler's opinions on the real meaning and value of the teaching of the Church and its relevance to the problems man faces in everyday life:

> On reviewing the whole matter, I can be certain of this much only, that the money given out at the musical banks is not the current coin of the realm. It is not the money with which the people do as a general rule buy their bread, meat, and clothing. It is like it; some coins very like it; and it is not counterfeit. It is not, take it all round, a spurious article made of base metal in imitation of the money which is in daily use; but it is a distinct coinage which, though I do not suppose it ever actually superseded the ordinary gold, silver, and copper, was probably issued by authority, and was intended to supplant those metals. Some of the pieces were really of exquisite beauty; and some were, I do verily believe, nothing but the ordinary currency, only that there was another head and name in place of that of the commonwealth. . . . Some of the coins were plainly bad; of these last were not many; still there were enough for them not to be uncommon. These seemed to be entirely composed of alloy; they would bend easily, would melt away to nothing with a little heat, and were quite unsuited for a currency. Yet there were few of the wealthier classes who did not maintain that even these coins were genuine good money, though they were chary of taking them. Every one knew this, so they were seldom offered; but all thought it incumbent upon them to retain a good many in their possession, and to let them be seen from time to time in their hands and purses.

Christianity is not, therefore, seen as completely false per se; it is regarded as a system composed of elements widely different in meaning and value, some of them essentially right and true (one might possibly think here of at least some of the Ten Commandments), some obviously false and artificial, easily disproved, but still outwardly upheld by the majority of believers. The conformist acceptance of those beliefs, and in consequence of double existential standards, is of course nothing but intellectual dishonesty and hypocrisy. . . . (pp. 421-22)

Apart from the chapter on "The Musical Banks," Butler makes comments on Christianity also through his presentation of the two systems of religion practised in Erewhon—on the one hand, the officially upheld polytheistic belief in gods personifying different human qualities (justice, strength, love) and natural forces (air, time, space), and, on the other hand, Ydgrun, the goddess of conformity, "held to be both omnipresent and omnipotent," but at the same time publicly criticized and abused. Here again, as in the case of the musical bank section, the criticism of Christianity is twofold, directed against the very essence of the Christian faith as well as against its practical implications within the very institution of the Church and among its adherents.

Thus, for example, the passage describing Arowhena's theological dispute with the narrator of the story functions, apart from providing some very important insight into the character of the narrator and the quality of his religious beliefs, also as an important statement of a possible line of criticism of religion, according to which the anthropomorphic God is "but man's way of expressing his sense of the Divine," "the expression which embrace[s] all goodness and all good power." In the context of the whole chapter, in which the sincerity and goodness of Arowhena (however strongly her portrait may be idealized) is contrasted with the self-betraying shallowness and rather crude naïveté of the narrator, her views seem to receive Butler's sanction and can, in consequence, be treated as his important comment on the essence of Christianity. (pp. 423-24)

In the light of these observations, *Erewhon* turns out to be, as a statement of Butler's views on Christianity, a very outspoken and radical book, criticizing, though relatively mildly, both what might be called the contents of the Christian religion, and, much more fully and directly, its form—the way in which religion functions in real social life, in the institutionalized hierarchy of the Church, among the clergy as well as the laity. As A. E. Dyson points out, "Butler's true indignation is not that of a Christian who sees his beliefs betrayed by its other adherents. It is the still deeper indignation of a Non-Christian who sees Christians betraying the one belief of any value they are supposed to uphold." Indeed, it was not until the revised edition of 1901 that Butler decided to add to the chapter on "The Musical Banks" a passage recognizing the role of religion and the Church as at least the embodiments of mankind's inherited, shared knowledge of the unseen aspects of the world:

> Some Erewhonian opinions concerning the intelligence of the unborn embryo, that I regret my space will not permit me to lay before the reader, have led me to conclude that the Erewhonian Musical Banks, and perhaps the religious systems of all countries, are now more or less of an attempt to uphold the unfathomable and unconscious instinctive wisdom of millions of past generations, against the comparatively shallow, consciously reasoning, and ephemeral conclusions drawn from that of the last thirty or forty.

Somewhat inconsistent with the rest of the book as the passage is, it nevertheless demonstrates very clearly the kind of structural difficulty in which Butler often finds himself in his attempts to incorporate into a work of fiction (which *Erewhon* certainly is) elements of a magazine article or an expository satirical essay. Just as in the passage in question, the conscious shaping of the story as told by its subjective, individualized narrator-protagonist sometimes gives way to Butler's own eloquence and turns the narrator, even if formally still speaking in the first person, into a mere mouthpiece of the author; sometimes, again as above, details from different chapters are mixed up and lead to illogicalities and inconsistencies. In the original version, the analogy between the musical banks and the Church, however obvious, is never stated directly and as a consequence has to be established by the reader; when mentioned directly in the 1901 revision, it becomes rather trivial and loses a good deal of its ironical effect. Still, for all its imperfections, *Erewhon* remains a significant document of Butler's early social, philosophical, and religious views, as well as an important step in his artistic evolution as a writer of fiction.

Written towards the end of Butler's life and published, together with the revised edition of *Erewhon,* in 1901, the last of the author's major works to appear in print in his lifetime, *Erewhon Revisited* occupies a very important though often underestimated place among Butler's writings. Overshadowed in popularity as well as in critical acclaim by its 1872 predecessor and by the posthumously published *The Way of All Flesh,* the book is not only Butler's last work of fiction, but also his last literary statement of his views on society, particularly as regards the nature of its religious beliefs. The two stories of Erewhon in this way form a kind of framework within which one can observe the changes that took place in Butler's attitudes during the twenty-nine years separating the publication of the books, certainly at least in part as a consequence of the changed intellectual atmosphere of the time. Just as *Erewhon* is an expression of the views held by Butler in his youth, its sequel can be described [in the words of W. G. Bekker (see Additional Bibliography)] as "an aftermath of Butlerian opinions." No longer the enthusiastic reader of Darwin's *The Origin of Species* and presumably also *Essays and Reviews,* himself engaged in critical studies of the Bible and drawing from them radical conclusions about the doctrine of the Church, the Butler of 1901 appears to have been, for all his eccentricity and unconventionality, a much more open-minded and tolerant man. He recognizes, possibly under the influence of the writings of Matthew Arnold as well as the late nineteenth-century Broad Church trends in English Christianity, the need of reconciling, on the one hand, the rational vision of the world resulting from the achievements of modern science, and, on the other hand, the larger moral and philosophical issues such as the problem of the existence and definition of God. At the same time, the two Erewhon books provide some very direct evidence of the development of Butler's literary technique. Because of his handling of the plot, characterization, and imagery, the structure of the story in *Erewhon Revisited* becomes relatively closely integrated, making the book, interesting as it is for the ideas that it conveys, also a significant artistic achievement.

The story of *Erewhon Revisited* is that of the journey to the country over the range undertaken by Higgs (the narrator of the first book, now no longer anonymous) twenty years after his escape with Arowhena from Erewhon back to the ordinary world of European civilization. His attempted return to his wife's native land turns out, however, to be far from successful. As Higgs gradually comes to realize, in the twenty years that have elapsed since his first visit to Erewhon, the whole story of his coming and his eventual escape has been turned into an idealized, miraculous legend on the basis of which the Erewhonians have developed a new religion, Sunchildism, with himself as the central figure and the object of worship. Moreover, his continued presence in Erewhon and the possibility of his speaking out about the events of twenty years before constitute a direct threat to the newly-developed status quo and, as such, have to be prevented by all possible means. After various complications, Higgs finally manages to leave Erewhon; he returns to England, though, a broken man and dies soon afterwards, having only managed to relate the story to John, his English-born son, who is the main narrator of the book.

As can be inferred even from this very brief summary, unlike in *Erewhon,* the structure of *Erewhon Revisited* is organized much more along lines characteristic of a traditional novel, rather than of a memoir or a travelogue. Indeed, in the earlier book the central place is occupied clearly by the main narrator, controlling, more or less successfully, all the events of the story and bringing together elements so diverse as paraphilosophical speculations, easily attributable to Butler himself, and subjective descriptions of Erewhonian life from the point of view of a somewhat narrow-minded and often bewildered visitor from the outside world. *Erewhon Revisited,* on the other hand, has at its centre a well-developed plot, to which all other elements, such as characterization and setting, are clearly subordinated. This stress on the plot results inevitably in a change in the function of the narrator. John Higgs, remaining for most of the book outside the events presented and providing little or virtually no commentary on them of his own, is not much more than a technical device, and certainly not a character in his own right. His function is primarily that of presenting in a relatively detached and transparent way the experience and reflections of his father, now, in contrast to *Erewhon,* not only twenty years older and more mature, but also rather more intelligent, more sensitive, and in a way more intellectual. Higgs is "no longer a hybrid, a puppet, but a man who knows what his principles are, and who is able to expound them clearly and succinctly." In fact, he is a mouthpiece for the author himself. The change in Higgs is characteristically noticed by his son, who at the beginning of his account observes:

> He had hardly left, before I read his book from end to end, and, on having done so, not only appreciated the risks that he would have to run, but was struck with the wide difference between his character as he had himself portrayed it, and the estimate I had formed of it from personal knowledge. When, on his return, he detailed to me his adventures, the account he gave of what he had said and done corresponded with my own ideas concerning him; but I doubt not the reader will see that the twenty years between his first and second visit had modified him even more than so long an interval might be expected to do.

Higgs sets out for Erewhon in search of consolation after the death of his wife; as his son says, "his unrest . . . assumed the form of a burning desire to revisit the country in which he and my mother had been happier together than perhaps they ever again were." The Erewhon he encounters is, however, no longer the country he knew twenty years earlier. From his very first meeting with Hanky and Panky onwards, he is confronted with a new reality, full of new situations, ideas, and even words, which are to him at first a strange mixture of completely unintelligible phrases, but which later gradually begin to form, out of mere allusions and scraps of conversations, a meaningful pattern—that of the country's new religious and social system, a new Erewhonian equivalent of Christianity: Sunchildism.

The analogies between the two, first suggested by the idea of the new Erewhon calendar, become as the book progresses more and more numerous and direct; indeed, for all that Butler may say in his preface to the contrary, it seems impossible not to admit that "the parallels between Sunchildism and Christianity are too close to be anything other than intended." This is inevitable, not only because no book on religion written in the cultural and intellectual context of modern Europe can ignore Christianity, but also for reasons internal to the story of Erewhon itself. Sunchildism is, at least in some aspects of its teaching and ritual, a conscious, though at the same time consciously corrupted, imitation of Christianity, the religion first brought to the country over the range by Higgs the Sunchild himself. . . . Moreover, the incorporation of Sunchildism into the musical bank system, clearly identifiable with the Anglican Church, stresses the directness of the reference and leaves the reader no room for doubt. Sunchildism *is* Christianity; everything that Butler says about it in his book can safely be interpreted as pertaining to the religion of nineteenth-century England.

Many of the allusions to Christianity in *Erewhon Revisited* are not very different from those that are to be found in the earlier book; this is true, for example, of the description of the musical bank service, inserted in the chapter on Higgs's first meeting with Hanky and Panky:

> "Altar-piece! Altar-piece!" again groaned my father inwardly.
>
> He need not have groaned, for when he came to see the so-called altar-piece he found that the table above which it was placed had nothing in common with the altar in a Christian church. It was a mere table, on which were placed two bowls full of Musical Bank coins; two cashiers, who sat on either side of it, dispensed a few of these to all comers, while there was a box in front of it wherein people deposited coin of the realm according to their will or ability. The idea of sacrifice was not contemplated, and the position of the table, as well as the name given to it, was an instance of the way in which the Erewhonians had caught names and practices from my father, without understanding what they either were or meant. So, again, when Professor Hanky had spoken of canonries, he had none but the vaguest idea of what a canonry is.

The picture is obviously that of a Christian Eucharist, with the characteristic Erewhonian inversion of material and spiritual values. Additionally, the sense of continuity with the earlier volume is here stressed by the method used to introduce the analogy. Like the musical bank section of *Erewhon,* the scene is presented not dynamically but by means of a relatively static description, with a strong emphasis on the importance of the narrator in his capacity as the observer, even if not very clearly as the speaker.

Butler's most important comments on Christianity in *Erewhon Revisited* are, however, conveyed in a less direct way, which nevertheless makes a more sophisticated use of the opportunities provided by the novel form which the book approximates much more closely than *Erewhon.* In the earlier work, individual scenes, though incorporated into some larger patterns unified by the controlling voice of the narrator, retain a considerable degree of independence; they function as a series of vignettes illustrating various aspects of Erewhonian life. On the contrary, in *Erewhon Revisited* the main meaning is concentrated in and expressed by the organization of the plot and the characterization of the protagonists, individual scenes being significant mainly insofar as they are part of the larger structures through which the main ideas of the book are communicated.

This is true, of course, of the main plot of the novel, centred around the figure of Higgs and his role as the founder of Erewhon's new religion; he becomes the Erewhonian equivalent of Jesus Christ. The analogies are straightforward and numerous: Higgs becomes Sunchild, just as Christ is the Son of God; his supposed teaching is written down in the book

of Sunchild's Sayings, just as the words of Christ are collected in the Gospels. Most importantly, Higgs's escape from Erewhon in a balloon is interpreted as his miraculous ascent to Heaven, just as the miraculous character of the whole story of the Resurrection is recognized and accepted as the crucial element of the faith preached by the Christian Church. The parallels, then, are there. The essential meaning of the book lies, though, in the fact that, for all the similarities, Higgs is *not* really the Son of God, but an ordinary man, owing his elevation to the position of a deity to little more than mere chance—a series of favourable coincidences, involving in the first place his having found himself in a particular place at a particular moment of time. It is not insignificant in this respect that Higgs should in *Erewhon Revisited* no longer be the anonymous "I" that he was throughout *Erewhon.* The individualization that results from the loss of anonymity strengthens the image of Higgs as an essentially average Englishman, a man of flesh and blood, possibly somewhat more experienced and therefore more mature than an average man in the street, but by no means unique. Butler seems to suggest that the same is true of Christ and Christianity. Just as there is nothing divine about Higgs, there is no reason to believe that there was anything divine about Christ. Though both have become recognized and accepted as belonging to a world essentially different from that of men, this does not necessarily mean that such acceptance does not depend on ignorance, misunderstanding, or conscious misrepresentation.

Of these three sources of what might be called "religious fallacy," the first two, ignorance (typical of the credulous, uneducated masses) and misunderstanding (represented in the book by the naïve, if well-meaning Mr. Balmy), are criticized relatively mildly. In fact, they result only from human weakness and as such, though wrong, may be pardonable.

Butler's real criticism is directed clearly against people like the two Professors of Worldly and Unworldly Wisdom, Panky and, primarily, Hanky—hypocritical opportunists, who use religion to manipulate others into accepting views and beliefs which they themselves know to be false, but which at the same time are for them necessary tools without which they would not be able to fulfill their personal ambitions and to achieve their different individual goals:

> It will be enough to say that in further floods of talk Mr. Balmy confirmed what George had said about the Banks having lost hold upon the masses. That hold was weak even in the time of my father's first visit; but when the people saw the hostility of the Banks to a movement which far the greater number of them accepted, it seemed as though both Bridgeford and the Banks were doomed, for Bridgeford was heart and soul with the Banks. Hanky, it appeared, though under thirty, and not yet a Professor, grasped the situation, and saw that Bridgeford must either move with the times or go. He consulted some of the most sagacious Heads of Houses and Professors, with the result that a committee of inquiry was appointed, which in due course reported that the evidence for the Sunchild's having been the only child of the sun was conclusive. It was about this time—that is to say some three years after his ascent—that "Higgsism," as it had been hitherto called, became "Sunchildism," and "Higgs" the "Sunchild."

Characteristically, Hanky and Panky are presented, from their very first appearance in the book, as liars and intriguers, ready to accept any form of deception or even violence that might help them to achieve the goals they have chosen:

> "Perhaps," said Panky, "but we should never have talked the King over if we had not humoured him on this point. Yram nearly wrecked us by her obstinacy. If we had not frightened her, and if your study, Hanky, had not happened to have been burned . . ."

> "Come, come, Panky, no more of that."

> "Of course I do not doubt that it was an accident; nevertheless, if your study had not been accidentally burned, on the very night the clothes were entrusted to you for earnest, patient, careful, scientific investigation—and Yram very nearly burned, too—we should never have carried it through. See what work we had to get the King to allow the way in which the clothes were worn to be a matter of opinion, not dogma. What a pity it is that the clothes were not burned before the King's tailor had copied them."

The irony of the Professors' position is that when they are faced with the danger of Higgs's undermining the very foundations of the system they have developed, the only thing they can do to remain in power is discredit and afterwards physically get rid of their opponent, whom they know to be essentially right. The whole conflict constitutes the core of the plot of **Erewhon Revisited;** in this way, the criticism of the methods by which human credulity and naïveté can be exploited by promoters of "revealed religions" becomes closely integrated with the story presented in the book and expressed in fictional rather than abstract essayistic terms.

Towards the end of the story, however, Higgs is finally allowed to express his—and Butler's—views on Hanky and Panky directly, thus pinpointing the target of the book's satire:

> "And how about Hanky?"

> "He will brazen it out, relic, chariot, and all: and he will welcome more relics and more cock-and-bull stories; his single eye will be upon his own aggrandizement and that of his order. Plausible, unscrupulous, heartless scoundrel that he is, he will play for the queen and the women of the court, as Dr. Downie will play for the king and the men. He and his party will sleep neither night nor day, but they will have one redeeming feature—whoever they may deceive, they not deceive themselves. They believe every one else to be as bad as they are, and see no reason why they should not push their own wares in the way of business. Hanky is everything that we in England rightly or wrongly believe a typical Jesuit to be."

> "And Panky—what about him?"

> "Panky must persuade himself of his own lies, before he is quite comfortable about telling them to other people. Hanky keeps Hanky well out of it; Panky must have a base of operations in Panky. Hanky will lead him by the nose, bit by bit, for his is the master spirit. In England Panky would be what we call an extreme ritualist."

Fortunately, it is not with people like Hanky and Panky that the whole power and future of Sunchildism rests. The views of the two Professors, and in particular those held by Hanky, are contrasted with the attitudes of Dr. Downie, a man of honest compromise, accepting the positive values of the existing system, but refraining from committing himself openly on any doubtful or controversial points:

> Dr. Downie had a jumping cat before his mental vision. He spoke quietly and sensibly, dwelling chiefly on the benefits that had already accrued to the kingdom through the abolition of the edicts against machinery, and the great developments which he foresaw as probable in the near future. He held up the Sunchild's example, and his ethical teaching, to the imitation and admiration of his hearers, but he said nothing about the miraculous element in my father's career, on which he declared that his friend Professor Hanky had already so eloquently enlarged as to make further allusion to it superfluous."

Even if originally satirized for the vagueness of his views "There was Dr. Downie, Professor of Logomachy, and perhaps the most subtle dialectician in Erewhon. He could say nothing in more words than any man of his generation. His text-book on the *Art of Obscuring Issues* had passed through ten or twelve editions, and was in the hands of all aspirants for academic distinction. He had earned a high reputation for sobriety of judgment by resolutely refusing to have definite views on any subject; so safe a man was he considered, that while still quite young he had been appointed to the lucrative post of Thinker in Ordinary to the Royal Family." Dr. Downie becomes in the course of the book not only an ally of Higgs's, taking an active part in helping him out of Erewhon, but also, in a way, a personification of the traditional values of continuity, tolerance, and stability, embodied in his understanding of Sunchildism, equivalent to that represented in England by the Broad Church:

> I think Dr. Downie will do much as I said. He will not throw the whole thing over, through fear of schism, loyalty to a party from which he cannot well detach himself, and because he does not think that the public is quite tired enough of its toy. He will neither preach nor write against it, but he will live lukewarmly against it, and this is what the Hankys hate. They can stand either hot or cold, but they are afraid of lukewarm. In England Dr. Downie would be a Broad Churchman. . . . And if you can follow the lead which I believe Dr. Downie will give you, that is to say, get rid of cock-and-bull stories, idealize my unworthy self, and, as I said last night, make me a peg on which to hang your own best thoughts—Sunchildism will be as near truth as anything you are likely to get."

Higgs's acceptance of the direction taken in his interpretation of Sunchildism by Dr. Downie is symptomatic also of a more general aspect of the views on Christianity that **Erewhon Revisited** implies—namely, of the general support that Butler clearly gives to the idea, first suggested in the 1901 version of **Erewhon,** that the Church as the institution not only protects the traditional values against the dangers of the destructive modernity of the contemporary world, but also preserves the idea of the existence, outside man's material world, of another reality, one unseen but equally important and true:

> Still, you Musical Bank people bear witness to the fact that beyond the kingdoms of this world there is another, within which the writs of this world's kingdoms do not run. This is the great service which our Church does for us in England, and hence many of us uphold it, though we have no

sympathy with the party now dominant within it. "Better," we think, "a corrupt Church than none at all." Moreover, those who in my country would step into the church's shoes are as corrupt as the church, and more exacting. They are also more dangerous, for the masses distrust the church, and are on their guard against aggression, whereas they do not suspect the doctrinaires and faddists, who, if they could, would interfere in every concern of our lives."

In the world of *Erewhon Revisited* Christianity is no longer, as in the earlier book, just a false system of beliefs based on false premises and producing harmful or at best nonsensical effects in actual social life; on the contrary, the overall message of Butler's last book is the quiet acceptance of the spirit of Christianity, even if its letter is nothing but a myth or a legend. As was observed by W. G. Bekker, in *Erewhon Revisited* "the satire is directed against the *miraculous element* in religion, and though it is unsparing in its grave severity, it serves but to illuminate the central truth of religion with a purer radiance." In this way, the atheism of *Erewhon* is in its sequel transformed into a variant of the typical Victorian agnosticism, best described by Butler himself in a letter written during the later period of his life:

That there is an unseen life and unseen kingdom which is not of this world, and that the wisdom of this world is foolishness with God; that the life we live here is much but, at the same time, small as compared with another larger life in which we all share though, while here, we can know little if anything about it; that there is an omnipresent Being into whose presence none can enter and from whose presence none can escape—an ineffable contradiction in terms . . . ; that the best are still unprofitable servants and that the wisest are still children—who that is in his senses can doubt these things? And surely they are more the essence of Christianity than a belief that Jesus Christ died, rose from the dead, and ascended visibly into heaven.

Technically and according to the letter of course they are not. According to the spirit I firmly believe they are. Tell me that Jesus Christ died upon the Cross, and I find not one tittle of evidence worthy of the name to support the assertion. Tell me that therefore we are to pull down the Church and turn everyone to his own way, and I reject this as fully as I reject the other. I want the Church as much as I want free thought; but I want the Church to pull her letter more up to date or else to avow more frankly that her letter is a letter only. If she would do this I, for one, would not quarrel with her. Unfortunately, things do not seem moving in the direction in which I would gladly see them go and do all in my power to help them go.

(pp. 425-34)

Jan Jedrzejewski, "Samuel Butler's Treatment of Christianity in 'Erewhon' and 'Erewhon Revisited'," in English Literature in Transition: 1880-1920, Vol. 31, No. 4, 1988, pp. 415-36.

ADDITIONAL BIBLIOGRAPHY

Bekker, W. G. *An Historical and Critical Review of Samuel Butler's Literary Works.* New York: Russell and Russell, 1925, 258 p.
  An early critical study of Butler's writings.

Bissell, Claude T. "A Study of *The Way of All Flesh.*" In *Nineteenth Century Studies,* edited by Herbert Davis, William C. DeVane, and R. C. Bald, pp. 277-303. Ithaca, N. Y.: Cornell University Press, 1940.
  Discusses *The Way of All Flesh* as a demonstration of Butler's vitalist philosophy.

Booth, Alison. "The Author of *The Authoress of the Odyssey:* Samuel Butler as a Paterian Critic." *Studies in English Literature, 1500-1900* 25, No. 4 (Autumn 1985): 865-83.
  Draws parallels between "[Walter] Pater's evocations of the artist in his milieu and Butler's personification of a primary source of Western civilization."

Breuer, Hans-Peter. "Samuel Butler's 'The Book of the Machines' and the Argument from Design." *Modern Philology* 72, No. 4 (May 1975): 365-83.
  Suggests that, for Butler, the conflict between Darwinian and neo-Lamarckian theories of evolution was not a matter of biological mechanism versus strict vitalism, but a question of whether the development of living forms can be described in a nonpurposive manner.

————. "Samuel Butler's *Note-Books:* The Outlook of a Victorian Black Sheep." *English Literature in Transition: 1880-1920* 22, No. 1 (1979): 17-37.
  Discusses Butler's alienation from Victorian society.

Buckley, Jerome Hamilton. "The Way of Samuel Butler." In his *Season of Youth: The Bildungsroman from Dickens to Golding,* pp. 116-39. Cambridge: Harvard University Press, 1974.
  Views the *The Way of All Flesh* in the context of Butler's own intellectual development.

Cannan, Gilbert. *Samuel Butler: A Critical Study.* London: Martin Secker, 1915, 194 p.
  Early, highly sympathetic critical study.

Cohen, Philip. "Stamped on His Works: The Decline of Samuel Butler's Literary Reputation." *Journal of the Midwest Modern Language Association* 18, No. 1 (Spring 1985): 64-81.
  Contends that the exposure of biographical details in Henry Festing Jones's 1919 memoir of Butler [see entry below] aided in the decline of Butler's reputation during the 1920s and 1930s.

Coveney, Peter. "The End of the Victorian Child." In his *The Image of Childhood: The Individual and Society, A Study of the Theme in English Literature,* pp. 280-302. Baltimore: Penguin, 1967.
  Discusses *The Way of All Flesh* as an accurate portrait of Victorian attitudes toward children.

Cunliffe, John W. "Mid-Victorian Novelists." In his *Leaders of the Victorian Revolution,* pp. 188-227. New York: D. Appleton-Century, 1934.
  Views Butler as a principal instigator of the revolt against Victorian society.

DeLange, Petronella Jacoba. *Samuel Butler: Critic and Philosopher.* Amsterdam: W. J. Thieme, 1925, 174 p.
  Traces the evolution of Butler's philosophical viewpoint.

Dyson, A. E. "Samuel Butler: The Honest Sceptic." In his *The Crazy Fabric: Essays in Irony,* pp. 112-37. London: Macmillan, 1965.
  Discusses the element of irony in *The Way of All Flesh, Erewhon,* and *Erewhon Revisited.*

Fleishman, Avrom. "*The Way of All Flesh:* Disfiguring the Figures."

In his *Figures of Autobiography,* pp. 257-74. Berkeley and Los Angeles: University of California Press, 1983.
> Structuralist analysis of *The Way of All Flesh* as autobiography.

Furbank, P. N. *Samuel Butler (1835-1902).* Second edition. Hamden, Conn.: Archon, 1971, 124 p.
> Study of critical reaction to Butler's works.

Ganz, Margaret. "Samuel Butler: Ironic Abdication and the Way to the Unconscious." *English Literature in Transition: 1880-1920* 28, No. 4 (1985): 366-94.
> Examines ironic humor in Butler's writings as a foreshadowing of the "modern perception of uncertainty and contradiction at the heart of experience."

Garnett, Mrs. R. S. *Samuel Butler and His Family Relations.* London: J. M. Dent and Sons, 1926, 228 p.
> Biographical study written "as a defence of the family circle held up to ridicule in *The Way of All Flesh.*"

Gosse, Edmund. "Samuel Butler." In his *Aspects and Impressions,* pp. 55-76. London: Cassell, 1922.
> Biographical essay.

———. "Samuel Butler's Essays." In his *Leaves and Fruit,* pp. 293-301. London: William Heinemann, 1927.
> Review of *Essays on Life, Art, and Science* in which Gosse concludes: "The most durable part of Butler's writing . . . will probably prove to be its humour. . . . No one ever approached the citadel of tradition waving a merrier pickaxe, or flung himself upon the task of demolition in higher spirits."

Gounelas, R. M. "Samuel Butler's Late Works: The Motives and Methods of a Controversialist." *English Miscellany* 28-29 (1979-1980): 293-320.
> Examines Butler's strong identification with the subjects of his later works.

Harris, John F. *Samuel Butler, Author of Erewhon: The Man and His Work.* London: Grant Richards, 1916, 303 p.
> Sympathetic study of Butler's works.

Henderson, Philip. *Samuel Butler: The Incarnate Bachelor.* London: Cohen and West, 1953, 242 p.
> Biography.

Henkin, Leo J. "Evolution and the Idea of Progress." In his *Darwinism in the English Novel, 1860-1910: The Impact of Evolution on Victorian Fiction,* pp. 197-220. New York: Russell and Russell, 1963.
> Examines elements of evolutionary thought in *The Way of All Flesh.*

Henkle, Roger B. "Meredith and Butler: Comedy as Lyric, High Culture, and Bourgeois Trap." In his *Comedy and Culture: England 1820-1900,* pp. 238-95. Princeton, N. J.: Princeton University Press, 1980.
> Study of *The Way of All Flesh* in which Henkle suggests that in that novel "the Puritan model of serious self-examination and spiritual conversion is blown inside out. The novel describes a spiritual struggle and a conversion experience, all right, but it is a struggle against religion and its supports and a conversion to self-regarding pleasure."

Hicks, Granville. "Samuel Butler, Cautious Rebel." In his *Figures of Transition: A Study of British Literature at the End of the Nineteenth Century,* pp. 145-76. New York: Macmillan, 1939.
> Biographical and critical essay.

Hoggart, Richard. "Samuel Butler and *The Way of All Flesh.*" In his *Speaking to Each Other,* vol. 2, pp. 144-68. London: Chatto and Windus, 1970.
> Discusses *The Way of All Flesh* as a synthesis of autobiographical elements and scientific and philosophical discourse.

Holt, Lee E. *Samuel Butler.* New York: Twayne, 1964, 183 p.
> Study of Butler's works from a developmental point of view.

Jeffers, Thomas L. *Samuel Butler Revalued.* University Park: Pennsylvania State University Press, 1981, 146 p.
> Study of Butler's ideas. Jeffers notes in his introduction that Butler has erroneously been viewed as "a lonely seer, a studious eccentric who exhumed and galvanized the ideas of forgotten theorists," when in fact his ideas clearly continue "the pre-Victorian tradition of libertarianism in education, hedonism in ethics, and a sort of reverent agnosticism in natural theology."

Jones, Henry Festing. *Samuel Butler: Author of Erewhon.* 2 vols. London: Macmillan, 1919.
> Sympathetic biography written by a friend and collaborator.

Knoepflmacher, U. C. "Samuel Butler: The Search for a Religious Crossing" and "Reality and Utopia in *The Way of All Flesh.*" In his *Religious Humanism and the Victorian Novel: George Eliot, Walter Pater, and Samuel Butler,* pp. 224-96. Princeton, N. J.: Princeton University Press, 1965.
> Analysis of the development of Butler's vitalism and a discussion of *The Way of All Flesh* as "a private exercise, written and rewritten to test out Butler's theories about heredity, theories which were themselves an attempt to free himself from his personal doubts."

———. "The End of Compromise: *Jude the Obscure* and *The Way of All Flesh.*" In his *Laughter and Despair: Readings in Ten Novels of the Victorian Era,* pp. 202-39. Berkeley and Los Angeles: University of California Press, 1971.
> Compares Thomas Hardy's *Jude the Obscure* and *The Way of All Flesh,* concluding: "In *Jude the Obscure* Hardy wrote a tragedy that is not a tragedy; in *The Way of All Flesh* Butler wrote a comedy that fails to be comical in its affirmation. . . . The English novel demanded a new form that would once again combine these opposites, that would, like the Victorian masterpieces of the past, again mingle denial with hope."

Lovett, Robert Morss. "*The Way of All Flesh.*" In his *Preface to Fiction: A Discussion of Great Modern Novels,* pp. 68-80. Chicago: Thomas S. Rockwell, 1931.
> Discusses *The Way of All Flesh* in the context of the development of the modern English novel.

Lucas, F. L. "The Importance of Being Earnest." In his *Authors Dead and Living,* pp. 131-39. New York: Macmillan, 1926.
> Asserts that *The Authoress of the "Odyssey"* is persuasively argued and praises Butler's translation of the *Iliad.*

MacCarthy, Desmond. "Samuel Butler." In his *Criticism,* pp. 1-16. London: Putnam, 1932.
> Biographical essay. MacCarthy was acquainted with Butler and spent much time in the author's company during childhood and adolescence.

Mais, S. P. B. "Samuel Butler." In his *From Shakespeare to O. Henry: Studies in Literature,* pp. 179-220. London: Grant Richards, 1923.
> Survey of Butler's works.

Marshall, William H. "The End of the Quest." In his *The World of the Victorian Novel,* pp. 381-450. South Brunswick, N.J.: A. S. Barnes, 1967.
> Views *The Way of All Flesh* as a record of "the protagonist's . . . struggle to sustain the sense of his own identity and emotional affirmation in the face of continual social repudiation and ultimate religious disbelief."

O'Connor, William Van. "Samuel Butler and Bloomsbury." In *From Jane Austen to Joseph Conrad: Essays Collected in Memory of James T. Hillhouse,* edited by Robert C. Rathburn and Martin Steinmann, Jr., pp. 257-73. Minneapolis: University of Minnesota Press, 1958.
> Discusses the reaction of Bloomsbury critics, most notably Vir-

ginia and Leonard Woolf and Desmond MacCarthy, to Butler's works.

O'Neill, H. C. "Samuel Butler, 1835-1902." In *The Great Victorians*, edited by H. J. Massingham and Hugh Massingham, pp. 97-107. Garden City, N. Y.: Doubleday, Doran and Co., 1932.
    Assesses Butler's importance as a writer.

Philmus, Robert M. "Darwin and the Utopian Nightmare: Science and Metaphysics." In his *Into the Unknown: The Evolution of Science Fiction from Francis Godwin to H. G. Wells*, pp. 108-26. Berkeley and Los Angeles: University of California Press, 1970.
    Analyzes Butler's amendments to Darwin's theories and discusses their relation to Butler's "Book of the Machines."

Rattray, R. F. *Samuel Butler: A Chronicle and an Introduction*. London: Duckworth, 1935, 216 p.
    Biographical and critical study.

Remington, Thomas J. " 'The Mirror up to Nature': Reflections of Victorianism in Samuel Butler's *Erewhon*." In *No Place Else: Explorations in Utopian and Dystopian Fiction*, edited by Eric S. Rabkin, Martin H. Greenberg, and Joseph D. Olander, pp. 33-55. Carbondale: Southern Illinois University Press, 1983.
    Argues that "*Erewhon* is not an idealized picture of Victorian society at its best or its worst; rather it is a work which holds a mirror up to that society, presenting it recognizably as it is, but in a strangely reversed perspective."

Robinson, Roger. "Samuel Butler: Exploration and Imagination." *Samuel Butler Newsletter* 3, No. 2 (December 1980): 33-50.
    Discusses the importance of Butler's experiences in New Zealand for the subsequent creation of *Erewhon*.

Roppen, Georg. "Butler's More Living Faith." In his *Evolution and Poetic Belief*, pp. 317-43. Oslo: Oslo University Press, 1956.
    Analysis of Butler's writings on evolution.

Rosenman, John B. "Evangelicalism in *The Way of All Flesh*." *CLA Journal* 26, No. 1 (September 1982): 76-97.
    Contends that *The Way of All Flesh* "should be seen as a socio-historical document of [Evangelicalism] during the nineteenth century and of the beliefs and attitudes it engendered."

Rubenstein, Jill. " 'Business Is Business': The Money Ethic of Samuel Butler." *English Literature in Transition: 1880-1920* 19, No. 4 (1976): 237-47.
    Discusses Butler's ambivalence toward wealth.

Salter, W. H. "Samuel Butler." In his *Essays on Two Moderns: Euripides, Samuel Butler*, pp. 69-93. London: Sidgwick and Jackson, 1911.
    Survey of Butler's works. Salter praises both Butler's intellect and his writings.

Shaw, Bernard. "Samuel Butler: The New Life Reviewed." In his *Pen Portraits and Reviews*, pp. 52-64. London: Constable, 1932.
    Review of Henry Festing Jones's memoir of Butler [see entry above]. According to Shaw: "*The Way of All Flesh* is one of the summits of human achievement in that kind."

Sherman, Stuart P. "Samuel Butler: Diogenes of the Victorians." In his *Points of View*, pp. 269-90. New York: Charles Scribner's Sons, 1924.
    Review of Henry Festing Jones's memoir in which Sherman expresses an extremely negative opinion of Butler, finding him vindictive and conventional.

Sieminski, Greg. "Suited for Satire: Butler's Re-Tailoring of *Sartor Resartus* in *The Way of All Flesh*." *English Literature in Transition: 1880-1920* 31, No. 1 (1988): 29-37.
    Contends that the similarities between Thomas Carlyle's *Sartor Resartus* (1833-34) and *The Way of All Flesh* "are the result of a deliberate effort by Butler to mimic *Sartor Resartus* for his own satiric purposes."

Simpson, George Gaylord. "Three Nineteenth-Century Approaches to Evolution." In his *This View of Life: The World of an Evolutionist*, pp. 42-62. New York: Harcourt, Brace, and World, 1947.
    Brief account of the Darwin-Butler feud, sympathizing with Darwin.

Willcocks, M. P. "Samuel Butler." In her *Between the Old World and the New*, pp. 277-93. New York: Frederick A. Stokes, 1925.
    Sympathetic biographical essay.

Williams, Orlo. "*The Way of All Flesh*." In his *Some Great English Novels: Studies in the Art of Fiction*, pp. 205-34. London: Macmillan, 1926.
    General discussion of *The Way of All Flesh*.

Yeats, John Butler. "Recollections of Samuel Butler." *Essays Irish and American*, pp. 9-21. 1919. Reprint. Freeport, N. Y.: Books for Libraries, 1969.
    Reminiscences.

Ivor (Bertie) Gurney

1890-1937

English poet and composer.

Gurney is considered one of the most talented English poets of the First World War. In the collections *Severn and Somme* and *War's Embers, and Other Verses,* he described his experiences as a private on the Western Front during 1916 and 1917, focusing on seemingly inconsequential and unheroic moments in the lives of common soldiers rather than on the greater questions of the nature of war and its effects on humanity. In this way Gurney presented a balanced view—neither blindly patriotic nor bitterly remonstrative—of the life of the English private during World War I. According to P. J. Kavanagh, Gurney's "is the poetry of a particularized, not a generalized humanity, of the flesh and nerves rather than of the intellect." His works also reflect his considerable musical talent and deep appreciation of natural beauty, especially that of his native Gloucestershire, while many disclose the mental illness that plagued him during the latter half of his life.

Gurney was the second of four children born to a tailor and his wife in Gloucester. In 1899 he was accepted into the local church choir. Showing exceptional interest and adequate ability in music, Gurney later won a place in Gloucester's Cathedral Choir, a position that enabled him to transfer from the state school he had been attending to the cathedral school, where lessons in music theory, composition, and performance were mandatory; by age seventeen he was writing songs that displayed a marked degree of accomplishment and a developing individual style. He often found inspiration for his compositions while reading poetry or while hiking in the Gloucestershire countryside. In 1911 Gurney won a scholarship to the Royal College of Music and moved to London. At the college he was nicknamed "Schubert" after examiners noted similarities between his musical style and that of the great Austrian composer, and he gained a reputation as an authentic but virtually unteachable genius. His most noted musical achievements of this period are the "Elizas," a song-cycle comprising settings of five Elizabethan lyrics, completed in 1912.

When England went to war in the summer of 1914, Gurney volunteered for service and was inducted into the army the following February. He served in Flanders with the 2nd/5th Gloucester Regiment, taking part in the Somme Offensive of 1916 and in the Third Battle of Ypres (Ieper), among other battles. Under the limitations imposed by trench life, poetry afforded a more practical creative outlet than music, and Gurney accordingly shifted his artistic focus to verse. He composed works during idle moments at the Front and mailed them to friends in England, who subsequently arranged for their publication. Wounded in April 1917 and reinstated to active duty six weeks later, Gurney was gassed in September of that year and sent to Edinburgh to recuperate. While convalescing in an army hospital, he read the proofs of his first collection, *Severn and Somme.* The lingering physical and emotional effects of his gassing curtailed his active service, and he was treated for depression and delayed shell-

shock before being discharged from the army in October 1918. Returning to the Royal College of Music in 1919 to complete his scholarship, Gurney ultimately failed the final examination. His psychological condition deteriorated significantly in the postwar years: he became severely depressed and suffered from the delusion that unseen persecutors were torturing him with electrical shocks. He sought work in Gloucester, where he was staying with relatives, but was unable to maintain a job. During this time he wrote prolifically, and spent many nights wandering the countryside rather than sleeping. He continued to write after being admitted to Barnwood House, a mental hospital in Gloucester, in 1922. He was transferred to the City of London Mental Hospital in Dartwood, Kent, later that year and remained there until his death from tuberculosis in December 1937.

According to critics, Gurney's literary career may be divided into three distinct periods: the war years, an early, developmental period during which he experimented with his new medium; the pre-asylum years, marked by achievement of an individual lyric style; and the asylum years, a time of uneven accomplishment characterized by flashes of brilliant originality in the midst of progressive mental deterioration. However, Gurney's subjects and themes remained fairly constant throughout his life, reflecting the influences of his wartime experiences and the Gloucestershire landscape, as well as his engrossment with music and poetry.

The two collections of Gurney's poetry published during his lifetime contain, for the most part, conventional works modeled on the pastoral verses of the popular Georgian movement, which, in reaction against both fin-de-siècle decadence and literary realism, romanticized nature and rural life while overlooking unpleasant aspects of modern society. In their war poetry, Georgian soldier-poets often embraced traditional English responses to battle based on patriotic acceptance of duty and adherence to a code of honor. Critics consider Gurney's response to the war singularly balanced, revealing an unassuming patriotism disinterested in politics. Unlike poets of the officer class—including Wilfred Owen, Siegfried Sassoon, and Edmund Blunden—Gurney felt no anger, remorse, or responsibility for the horrors in which he took part. Instead, his poems of the Front commemorate the unaffected courage and vitality of his fellow infantrymen and celebrate the natural beauty he discovered even in war-torn Belgium. As Gurney's technical ability developed he abandoned Georgian conventions in favor of a more personal style of expression distinguished by tortured syntax, energetic rhythms, and irregular line lengths. Critics generally consider Gurney's postwar period the one in which his finest works were composed, and most concur with Andrew Waterman's contention that Gurney's postwar poetry "shows a startling transformation of minor talent into adventurous creative genius; a poet who indeed 'modernised himself all on his own,' in imaginative perspectives, method, and language." The modernism of Gurney's later style continues to impress critics, yet some consider his achievement uneven and his potential as a poet largely unfulfilled. Many have expressed surprise that Gurney rarely used his poems to comment on his confinement or illness, and they consider his few autobiographical poems highly significant—not for the mental collapse they expose, but rather for their unexpected sanity and poignancy. Andrew Motion has suggested that these works represent an original and courageous response to the desperate conditions of Gurney's life as well as twentieth-century society in general. Some of his late verses express anger at England's financial and emotional abandonment of the war veterans who had sacrificed for its benefit, while others reveal Gurney's fascination with American subjects. Notable are his poetic "portraits" of Walt Whitman, Henry David Thoreau, and Washington Irving, which are among the finest of his later works.

During his lifetime and for several decades afterward, Gurney's musical compositions were considered his primary artistic achievement, but his literary works have received greater attention in recent years as new collections of his poetry have been issued. According to Motion: "Although his madness meant that he was effectively locked out of England for much of his life, he was one of the very few, and one of the very best, poets of his time to adapt the jaded literary traditions he grew up with, and allow them to accommodate the anxieties and preoccupations of the post-war years."

PRINCIPAL WORKS

Severn and Somme (poetry) 1917
War's Embers, and Other Verses (poetry) 1919
Poems by Ivor Gurney (poetry) 1954
Poems of Ivor Gurney: 1890-1937 (poetry) 1973

Collected Poems of Ivor Gurney (poetry) 1982
Ivor Gurney: War Letters (letters) 1983
Stars in a Dark Night (letters) 1986

THE TIMES LITERARY SUPPLEMENT (essay date 1919)

[*The following is a review of* War's Embers, and Other Verses.]

Mr. Gurney—in the thick of [the war], whether "out there" or at home—gives us [in *War's Embers, and Other Verses*] one more of those ever fascinating, ever disturbing revelations of what the young men who did the dreadful work thought and felt in the doing of it. Some of Mr. Gurney's metrical practices will not find favour with pedants. He begins a sonnet with the line "Wakened by birds and sun, laughter of the wind"; and ends it with the line "Might sit to receive homage, from the whole earth"; and we can imagine many interesting columns of letters to the Editor disputing about how to cut them up correctly into feet. The "general" reader will nearly always recognize Mr. Gurney's purpose in scrambling or dancing, instead of marching; and that, too, in cases more difficult than the fairly obvious one of the beautiful first line we have quoted. When we come to **"On Rest"** we are challenged anew by the doubt whether this now fairly common flinging down of impressions in rhyme is worth the doing. For the present, no doubt, that is the only way in which a jumble of insistent impressions of war can be noted. But this kind of pointillism has not, in most cases, the proper effect of pointillism: the points do not merge into vibrating but unified colour.

> Porridge and bacon! Tea out of a real cup
> (Borrowed). First day on Rest, a Festival
> Of mirth, laughter in safety, a still air.
> "No whizzbangs," "crumps" to fear, nothing to
>   mind,
> Danger and the thick brown mud behind.
> An end to wiring, digging, end to care.

Mr. Gurney, after "throwing it at us" in that style for a good many lines, tries hard to unify the medley at the close of his poem. The end is gentle and wistful. But by that time it is too late. **"On Rest"** is good journalism. It is not poetry.

Of poetry, nevertheless, there is a great deal in Mr. Gurney's little volume. It is the poetry for the most part of conflict. His love of beauty is constantly outraged by the facts of war, and the outrage shocks him into expression. He is not, as we see him, one of those who were "made poets" by the war; but doubtless the poetry that was bound to bloom out of his sensitive and passionate mind in time was forced into early bloom by the fires of war. And thus it is that his love of his county, of music, of quiet, of all beauty is continually being pierced by flashes of hell-fire.

> He's gone, and all our plans
>   Are useless indeed.
> We'll walk no more on Cotswold
>   Where the sheep feed
>   Quietly and take no heed.
>
> His body that was so quick
>   Is not as you
> Knew it, on Severn river

Under the blue
Driving our small boat through.

You would not know him now . . .
   But still he died
Nobly, so cover him over
   With violets of pride
   Purple from Severn side.

Cover him, cover him soon!
   And with thick-set
Masses of memoried flowers—
   Hide that red wet
   Thing I must somehow forget.

Yet his poetry is not all concerned with this incessant conflict. He reveals now and then the inner vision which unifies; in **"The Volunteers,"** for instance, which is the first poem in this volume, and in a very striking poem on the ancient camps in France the glory and grief of soldiering find poignant expression:—

            War's just-bright embers
That Earth still keeps and treasures for the pride
In sacrifice there shown; with love remembers
   The beauty and quick strength of men that died.

Who died as we may die, for Freedom, beauty
   Of common living, calmly led in peace,
Yet took the flinty road and hard of duty,
   Whose end was life abundant and increase.

But—when Heaven's gate wide opening receives us
   Victors and full of song, forgetting scars;
Shall we see to stir old memories, to grieve us,
   Heaven's never-yet-healed sores of Michael's
      wars?

    "Outer and Inner," in The Times Literary Supplement, *No. 916, August 7, 1919, p. 421.*

WALTER DE LA MARE   (essay date 1938)

[*An English poet, novelist, short story writer, dramatist, and critic, de la Mare is considered one of modern literature's chief exemplars of the romantic imagination. His complete works form a sustained treatment of romantic themes: dreams, death, rare states of mind and emotion, fantasy worlds of childhood, and the pursuit of the transcendent. Best remembered as a poet and writer of children's verse, de la Mare is also recognized for his novel* Memoirs of a Midget *(1921), a study of the social and spiritual outsider, a concern central to de la Mare's work. In the following excerpt, he offers an appreciative overview of the subjects of Gurney's poetry.*]

To many lovers of English poetry, Ivor Gurney's must still be a name unfamiliar, if not unknown. His first poems, *Severn and Somme* were published in 1917, *War's Embers* two years afterwards; and although both these volumes are still in print, many more poems than are contained in them remain in manuscript. Certain recent anthologies of verse have included his **"Song of Pain and Beauty,"** but he is absent, I think, from those devoted solely or chiefly to twentieth-century verse.

Fashion, even in poetry, may change—for a while; the war and its immediate consequences was a devouring fire; but it is nevertheless difficult to account for this comparative neglect. No living writer, in spirit, temperament and imagination, is more English than he—English, that is, with Clare, Hardy, Edward Thomas, with Skelton, even; and, more remotely, with Ben Jonson and A. E. Housman. And just as the heart beats its continuous refrain in a certain place in one's body, so *his* heart's affection is centred in what is perhaps the loveliest of all the English counties.

In a brief preface to *Severn and Somme*—a dangerous venture for a poet, but in this case one as happy and characteristic as the flight of a bird to a tree before it begins to sing—he says: "Most of the book" (and nearly all of it was "written in France and in sound of the guns") "is concerned with a person named Myself, and the rest with my county, Gloucester, that whether I live or die stays always with me"; but "I never was famous, and a Common Private makes but little show." There, simple and direct, is the keynote to all his work.

This, however, is only a fraction of the truth. "Myself," as is the usual way with poets, is certainly everywhere present in his work—free, ardent, generous, intensely aware. . . . But it is a self seldom introspective, and far more intent on the world around it, its life and beauty and humanity—laughing, loving, suffering, daring, enduring; and it brims over with a passion for friendship and a faithful all-welcoming love for objects, common or rare, that have won his devotion.

Although, too, Gloucester, with its men and its unrivalled towns and villages, its hills and woods and meadows, predominates in his poems, London also, and particularly its east and liveliest end—Southwark, Aldgate—hardly less entrances him. He explores it again and again with a darting and engrossed delight. Fresh and impetuous, opaque at times with mountain silt, often brawling a little harshly and hoarsely over obstructive stones (he has himself referred to his own "roughness" in technique), but forcing their way towards his goal, his poems recall a wild and lovely river; a river glassing in its quiet waters not only his own intent eyes but everything on its green and sun-bright banks; and, in particular, all that goes with Spring. And when, with hardly less avidity, he returns to the metropolis, then his verses resemble this river, a Thames always surmounted by his beloved dome of St. Paul's. Only Dunbar indeed among the poets could sing a descant to his fervent solos on "the floure of Cities all." Above all, he delights in the people of every kind and kin who throng its streets. If only, he pleads for them in his love and compassion, he could share with them his own Gloucester!

Occasionally he may fail as craftsman or artist, for want of patience, because words are rebellious, and because he has so much to tell of, and therefore must assiduously condense the telling—"to say it all out in one word," was his own poetic ideal;—but never because the well has gone dry; never because the fire of his feeling has died down beneath his thoughts; never because, although bereft for the moment of the requisite skill, his affectionate and sympathetic heart has failed him.

Lyrical poets are seldom ranked according to the range of their subject-matter; a few even among the finest are in this respect curiously restricted. But if they were, Ivor Gurney would be peering out from well towards the top of the green and golden tree. He has written, for mere example, and not counting **"Solace of Men,"** three poems at least hymning tobacco. If he were a painter as well as a poet, he would be a master of skies and clouds. Flower, bird, tree—he not only knows his chosen among them by heart but rejoices to name them. Nor are his flowers solely beautiful or lesson-conscious or merely floral. They may, being nature's too, have crooked stalks and stained and bitten leaves, just as a black cat may have a tuft of white in its tail. He delights in an endearing particularity, refuses abstractions. Every season of the year has been closely, tenderly, reiteratedly lived with, lived into. Music, above all, continually haunts his verse. So too he always names his villages; rejoices in racy and well-seasoned words; and can at need be content with "nothing-doing," "deadest still," "hush-awe," and "queer tube" (for a clarinet)—and all these in a few stanzas.

When he speaks of God, he speaks—not as do so many writers, in easy derision of other men's gods—but of his own. And he has his own clear ideal of the poetic impulse:

> Is wonder gone
> The common marvelling at air and sun,
> The taking in to being of Being's essence?
> Or is the skill of words lapsed deep, too deep?
> The elemental wonder never lessens,
> Whether with Autumn frost
> Or the Spring's light rain-ghost
> The Summer's passionate or Winter's sullen
> Raining and down-weeping, on the fallen
> Or light showered hanging fantasies of leaves. . . .

With that impulse, he is as intent and imaginative an observer as he is wide-ranging not only in observation but in knowledge; and not only of nature and mankind but—and no less—of books. Such a poem, for example, as **"The Lock Keeper"**—a full-length portrait for which that of the same title in **War's Embers** was a sketch—and over four pages long—is pressed down and running over with the best of all human knowledge—that of things at first hand, of natural and living things, *and* of the man himself. Occasionally his poems may be difficult, because the link between thought and thought appears to be missing; but that is the reason; not indolence, or indifference to his own intelligence or his reader's. There are songs that only he himself could put to their appointed music. And last—but these are few—there are poems tragic and desperate. But how infinitely less unreasonably so by comparison with the lamentations common in our own day!

> What evil coil of Fate has fastened me
> Who cannot move to sight, whose bread is sight,
> And in nothing has more bare delight
> Than dawn or the violet or the winter tree?
> Stuck in the mud—Blinkered-up, roped for the
>   Fair.
> What use to vessel breath that lengthens pain?
> O but the empty joys of wasted air
> That blow on Crickley and whimper wanting me!

The paramount effect on the mind after reading these new poems is a sense of supreme abundance. One has ascended to the top, as it were, of some old Gloucestershire church tower, and surveyed in a wide circuit all that lies beneath it. And then, as with the reader of *The Dynasts,* one sinks unjarred to earth again; and all that is now close and precise reveals why the distant seemed so lively, so lovely, and brim-full of grace. (pp. 8-10)

> *Walter de la Mare, in an excerpt in* Music and Letters *Vol. XIX, No. 1, January, 1938, pp. 8-10.*

EDMUND BLUNDEN   (essay date 1954)

[*Blunden was associated with the Georgians, an early twentieth-century group of English poets who reacted against the prevalent contemporary mood of disillusionment and the rise of artistic Modernism by seeking to return to the pastoral, nineteenth-century poetic traditions associated with William Wordsworth. In this regard, much of Blunden's poetry reflects his love of the sights, sounds, and ways of rural England. Blunden is also considered one of his generation's war poets—he was badly gassed while serving in World War I and the horror of war is a major theme in his work. As a literary critic and essayist, he often wrote of the lesser-known figures of the Romantic era as well as the pleasures of English country life. In the following excerpt from his introduction to the 1954 collection* Poems by Ivor Gurney, *Blunden discusses prominent characteristics of Gurney's later poetry.*]

In the current edition of Grove's great *Dictionary of Music and Musicians* and in other works of reference the name of Ivor Gurney, 1890-1937, is not overlooked. He is given his place because of his distinction as a songwriter, and the already extensive list of his published music together with the appreciations of some of his fellow composers at once illustrates the rightness of the inclusion. The catalogue of all Ivor Gurney's publications, however, discloses that this remarkable song-writer was also the author of two collections of poems, which in fact at one time drew plenty of intelligent attention to his literary personality and promise. The two small volumes were **Severn and Somme,** 1917, and **War's Embers,** 1919. By way of these books and the occasional appearance of poems by him in the *London Mercury* and other journals, Gurney became known and has never been completely forgotten as one of the young poets brought to light in the First World War. It may even be true that his name has signified something through his verse to some who were unaware of his musical capabilities.

It is rarer than might be thought to find in a man the twofold gift of Ivor Gurney. We may instance among Englishmen the Elizabethan doctor Thomas Campion, the eighteenth-century entertainer Charles Dibdin, and, a little hopefully, the experimental Gerard Manley Hopkins. William Blake, we read, sang his lyrics to his own melodies, but could not record those melodies. The words of Sir John Squire nevertheless remain apt: "I have known composers with a fine literary sense and poets who loved music but could neither compose nor play. I have known no man save Gurney who had the double creative gift that Rossetti had in *his* two arts." The time was when Gurney could exercise his faculties for literary and musical composition more or less together; at other periods the practical difficulties of his daily life reduced his chances of writing songs and other music, and when things stood thus he turned with full devotion and adventure to his poetical vocation. In the end, his writings in verse amounted to a varied collection, of which the two published volumes had given only a small part. . . . (p. 15)

Gurney's confinement on the ground of insanity [in 1922] meant in general his banishment from public attention and his modestly won reputation, although his musical compositions were now and then brought out, and his setting of A. E. Housman was acclaimed. Old friends, Dr. Vaughan Williams, Dr. Herbert Howells, Miss Marion Scott, paid him visits. In many letters to all sorts of people—but the letters were not posted—he appealed for "rescue"; some bore American addresses; and in these queerly phrased petitions there was no mistaking the derangement which kept him where he was. He was smouldering with anger which had for him the dreadful and undeniable cause that he, a lover of England if ever one existed, had been flung into a trap by England the beloved. "The earth had opened," a worse crater than any in Flanders and Picardy, for this defender.

In this dejection he had recourse to his music, but that was not at all easy; it was in poetry that in the ordinary way he found the going better, and he wrote a multitude of poems, planning new volumes capably enough, yet never attaining coherence quite long enough. This was an old characteristic now unfortunately emphasized. But there was meaning flashing within his faltering schemes. For a time—it is difficult to date his papers precisely—Gurney gave himself up in particular to the full and circumstantial account of his war experiences, into which of course his remembered Gloucestershire occupations and pastimes were for ever inwoven. He saw himself as "the first war poet," and as one who had been shamelessly and cruelly treated; the obsession needs little comment except that, so far as his reading went, and in the notion that he was a complete writer, Gurney might fairly claim to be writing in verse of the soldier on the Western Front with a solitary originality. He described the life of the infantryman . . . in a subtle series of reminiscence, catching many details and tones which had combined in the quality of seasons and moments, anguish and relief never again to occur. The poems may be still defective, most of them may swerve into ultimate confusion with themes not quite assimilated, but to this day they express part of the Western Front secret of fifty years ago with distinctive, intimate, and imaginative quickness.

It is not a serious disadvantage, surely, that these poems here and there contain a place-name or a war-term which is now unfamiliar or obsolete, nor even that other wars have been and other soldiers have brilliantly observed their pictures and paradoxes. The manner of Gurney's writing is already that of one perceiving a local and limited experience as sharing in the mystery of "never again," *nous n'irons plus,* and giving to the names of some Flanders farm or cluster of cottages the value of a legend. There is no need, we may decide, for his reader to look up the map of North-East France in order to find exactly where La Gorgue is, or to consult military authorities concerning Dead End or Crucifix Corner. Such places, if we at length visit them, are not the places Gurney knew once "like a passion" and always had in mind; those exist only in his poems as "part of the music he heard," as fragments of the dream of life which seemed to his forlorn self to pause, through the magic contrast, long enough to simulate the eternal.

Much else which Gurney wrote in the approaches of his mental illness, and after its manifest arrival, was striking in the display of his ever-springing response to life physical and intellectual. Had he been able to keep a quiet mind, at the point when the business of meeting the demands of society, plain necessity, and prosaic citizenship had to be stubbornly faced, his prospects as a poet of the universal sort, with much more to give than Gloucestershire alone or the 2nd-5th Gloucesters taught and inspired, were good. But the crisis defeated the soldier from the wars. His subsequent efforts to defy his adversities exhausted what power he retained; his clearness lost its edge, and his once shrewd, even if it might be harsh, decision of language slackened into murmuring. Gurney's later manuscripts themselves, it is readily seen, betray the inability of a mind, somewhat conscious of intended form and content as a whole, to deliver any more than a loose and blurred shad-

ow of these. The decline of his power of writing lyrics, once so intense and never facile, was physically inevitable.

Yet this poet was incapable of not writing his own especial nature into whatever verse even the last years produced. He saw and reflected for himself, and had shaped for himself a diction and a metrical action which the inferior piece or the scrap left unfinished share with the best; the ancient and the modern were curiously mixed in him, for he had lived as a wanderer in both ages. (pp. 19-21)

It now remains to speak of his manuscript poems. . . . Some of these pieces of the years of seclusion were grouped by the author for publication volume by volume. "Rewards of Wonder: Poems of Cotswold, France, London" is a title too good to lose. "Poems to the States," "Six Poems Of the States," "Memories of Honour; Infantry Poems of the State of New York," belong to a mood in which Gurney tries to be another Whitman or "a son of Walt." The poem on New York begins,

> To all I know lies there, farm land, plough or green
> I cry, to the kindness of faces I have not seen,
> I, war poet, maker of verse and infinite song,
> Who by the right of comradeship gathered knowl-
> edge
> And by comradeship had knowledge earned and
> known.

"Poems in Praise of Poets, Poems of States" were intended as another collection. Besides all these there are numerous verses which apparently never were assembled with any design of forming distinct volumes. The whole is a profusion of poetry, through which the selector moves with the usual difficulty that its allusions and interests are often iterated and paralleled, that the subject with which Gurney began many a poem winds into another, and possibly yet more, according to his favourite sequence of retrospects or thoughts.

Many of these unpublished poems, then, interesting and stirring as they might be if they stood by themselves, are in a sense variants of the same foundational poem; but to decide which of them are the prototypes or at any rate the strongest and most communicative of the essentials in his outlook is a puzzle. There is in turn little to choose between one and another, and the solution of the editorial puzzle appears to be to take examples in which the principal topic survives least entangled with one or two of the others always crowding upon Gurney's memory. The constant regret which attends on the reading of these later poems is that the author's poetical resources and idea of poetry are felt to be decidedly greater than those he had in the days of his published volumes, but all is slowed down by an afflicting incoherence; we must accept the confusion continuing between imaginative purpose and the solace of merely enumerating as much as possible what had happened to the writer in times of comparative liberty. To resort to every gleam of remembrance for some humble comfort was natural to one in Gurney's situation and is observable in other ill-starred poets, in Christopher Smart and in John Clare, too; their best things when they were incarcerated necessarily took their rise from things past; but Gurney in his turn is even more strongly drawn away from the actual than those geniuses by his passion for what once was. His poems from his "prison" too rarely reveal the new observation and fascination which brightened some of those written by Clare, when he was a mental patient at Epping and afterwards at Northampton. (pp. 22-3)

However that may be, it may not be fruitless to give a short description of one of his manuscript volumes—and I take for the sake of example a solid exercise book which he has filled up quite systematically. The title-page at once reveals, if anything can, the opposition between sense and delusion (if that is the right word) in his mind: it stands thus,

"First Poem"

O what will you turn out, book, to be?
Who are not my joy, but my escape from the worst
And most accurst of my woe? Shall you be poetry,
Or tell truth, or be of past things the tale rehearsed?

"The book of Five makings"

Feb. 1925
(in torture)

Ivor Gurney

On the end page he writes a self-examination.

There is nothing for my Poetry, who was the child
    of joy,
But to work out in verse crazes of my untold pain;
In verse which shall recall the rightness of a former
    day.

And of Beauty, that has command of many gods;
    in vain
Have I written, imploring your help, you have let
    destroy
A servant of yours, by evil men birth better at once
    had slain.

And for my Country, God knows my heart, and
    men to me
Were dear there, I was friend also of every look of
    sun or rain;
It has betrayed as evil women wantonly a man their
    toy.

Soldier's praise I had earned having suffered sol-
    dier's pain
And the great honour of song in the battle's first
    gray show—
Honour was bound to me save—mine most dread-
    fully slain.

Rapt heart, once, hills I wandered alone; joy was
    comrade there though
Little of what I needed, was in my power; again—
    again
Hours I recall, dazed with pain like a still weight
    set to my woe.

Blood, birth, long remembrance, my County all
    these have saven
Little of my being from dreadfullest hurt, the old
    gods have no
Pity—or long ago I should have not good, they
    would have battled my high right plain.
                                                        I.B.G.

Between the preliminary and final verses the poet writes with retrospection as his haunting mood, and it takes him alike to Gloucestershire and to the provincial France he had seen in war; it recurs occasionally to the London of his broken hopes. If he gets free from these soliloquies about his experiences, he tries a straightforward poem on a general subject, the Elizabethans it may be, or the palm willow, or (again the broad comparison with John Clare is obvious) a dead child. . . . Sometimes he revises with firmness, but as the collection grows he appears to lose the artistic detachment and concen-

tration implied in such care. The lyrical outflash is rarer now; the inclination is meditative, conversational, and so the versification itself goes, sometimes grows clogged almost completely. But the poet's eagerness will take its turn, as in the discussion of "the lost things" of Elizabethan dramatic poetry:

What! not to outdo "Cataline"—not write "Ham-
    let" more fine?
Is Webster alone to surprise with beauty the soul
    of the eyes?
All honour to master, must we always serve George
    Chapman?
Or follow with love the nobility of John Marston?

It is remembered that even in his better situation Gurney was passionately moved by the new discoveries (surely Dr. Hotson's) on Marlowe's cruel death. Everywhere the pages of the MS. book described gleam with the personal force of their writer, but the confident light is intermittent, and in the end the chief effect is that of fits and starts of autobiography in need of excision and governed relationship.

From considerations like these it can be concluded that Gurney's abundant poetical remains offer plenty of possible selections, and that any one of those will create after all practically the same impression and bring the same report of the whole tantalizing legacy:

The splendid fragments of a mind immortal
With rubbish mixed, and glittering in the dust.

It is a mind of many faculties, adventurous and to some extent scholarly, observant and visionary, terse but desultory too, musical away from music itself, pictorial in expanses and in minuteness. (pp. 23-5)

Not much will be said here on the history of Gurney's poetics, or what is called technique, and on the influences which may have been important in it. He is often enough telling us of the authors in whom he delighted, and no doubt the indebtedness of this poet to Campion and to Carlyle, to A. E. Housman and to Edward Thomas, to American literature and to French will be investigated in course of time. The main truth concerning his way of writing is that he possessed from early days a peculiar unconventionality, not a quality hostile to traditions, but a view and a hearing of his own; and in poetics the masters of remote date or recent did not supply him with what he had not got, but energized his calls upon innate and personal strength. Gurney's "gnarled" style was not that of Hopkins or of Bridges (who did not always write translucencies), but when he found such poets achieving their victories over the flying moment with strenuous remodellings of language, he was reassured and newly animated in his own search for the shrewdly different in phrasing and in metring. Probably much of his style is consonant with the first stages of his quick sensibility awakening among ancient buildings, especially country churches; he grew up with the instances of old craftmanship in carved work, stone or wood, ever in view and in reach. His poetry has its sweetness but it has sharpness and severity, or what he calls "patterns like earth-sense strong"—something of the high-poised gargoyle against the flying cloud. It may have derived some of its uncommon melody from the wild tune of nature in the woods and waves, and some from the elder church music in which Gurney was proficient even as a boy. Whatever was attractive and poetically moving to the generation of writers called Georgians was so to him also, and he was content to be of that generation; but neither pussy-cat sentiment nor an indifferent "eye on the object" can be imputed to him, nor yet trivial languor nor studied homeliness of expression. He perished, one may say, war and consumption apart, from the merciless intensity of his spirit both in watching the forms of things moving apace in the stream of change and in hammering out poetic forms that should remain as their just representation and acclamation. (pp. 25-6)

> *Edmund Blunden, in an introduction to* Poems of Ivor Gurney: 1890-1937, *Chatto & Windus, 1973, pp. 15-26.*

E. D. MACKERNESS   (essay date 1962)

[*In the following excerpt, Mackerness traces prominent themes and subjects in Gurney's wartime poems and compares them to those of his later works.*]

Ivor Gurney's artistic reputation is based not on his poems but on a small number of exquisite musical compositions. The songs by which he is now chiefly remembered are settings of words by Nashe, Campion, Shakespeare, Fletcher, Bridges, Yeats, Edward Thomas and others. But the fact that Gurney did not often make use of the verses he had written himself has obscured his own considerable talent as a lyricist. Admittedly, his two early published volumes—*Severn and Somme* and *War's Embers*—contain nothing which has the anthology value of, say, Brooke's "The Soldier" and Owen's "Exposure." All the same, Ivor Gurney has his place among the trench poets of the First World War: and a consideration of his work must obviously start with some account of the pieces he wrote when serving, as the title-page of his first publication tells us, as "Private, of the Gloucesters."

In Gurney's wartime poetry we shall look in vain for startling or *recherché* qualities. *Severn and Somme* and *War's Embers* are more notable for their reaffirmations of simple pieties and common loyalties than for striking emanations of the *zeitgeist*. There is no wildly "nationalistic" sentiment behind Gurney's verse, no bellicose attempts to force the claims of his country right or wrong. Instead, we find an over-riding concern to place on record that sense of *belonging* to England which has thrust itself upon the consciousness of so many poets when on active service abroad. For instance, in "**Strange Service**" he recalls his native Gloucestershire in the following terms:

> Your hills not only hills, but friends of mine and
>   kindly,
> Your tiny knolls and orchards hidden beside the
>   river
> Muddy and strongly-flowing, with shy and tiny
>   streamlets
> Safe in its bosom.

And there are many other such reminiscences in these two volumes. Gurney's patriotism was a simple, trusting one and it was undisturbed by anything in the nature of political doubt, for the poet never questions the terms upon which he is being asked to fight. Yet for all his attestations of fidelity, there is nothing facile or maudlin in this strain of Gurney's feeling: it is informed by a profound respect for

> The old faith, the old pride
> Wherein our fathers died. . . .

And the west-country musings which make up so much of

Gurney's poetry—his evocation of the "grey-stone cottage colours" of Gloucestershire, the Malvern cloudscapes and so on—are not merely the out-pourings of a homesick patriot. They proceed naturally from the poet's intimacy with a texture of living which, as he knew, is specifically English and lies, as he puts it in "**The Tower**," "Permanent, past the reach of Time and Change."

Gurney's inclination to pay appropriate homage to the local deities of Ludlow and Teme reminds us of similar aspirations on the part of other Georgian writers. He was not the only war poet who strove to render in verse the fantastic difference between the quietude of the English countryside and those "dreadful evidences of Man's ill-doing" which had converted so many parts of France and Flanders into unsightly ruins. Yet Gurney knew better than to allow his verse to develop into an extended malediction on the war-mongers. The present was no time in which to be indulging in self-pity and dismal complaint: far better to try and define the image of a reality one knew than to conjure up deceptive fantasies. In this connection it is interesting to observe that Gurney seldom discusses the prospects of peace: he hardly ever dwells on the promise of a time when there will be no more fighting. There is, indeed, one instance which is an exception to this rule. It occurs in "**De Profundis**":

> Some day we'll fill in trenches, level the land and
>   turn
> Once more joyful faces to the country where trees
> Bear thickly for good drink, where strong sunsets
>   burn
> Huge bonfires of glory. . . .

But the notion of a return to "our old inheritance," the Paradise left behind, does not induce Gurney to resort to easily-released sentiments. He is aware that "comradeship in arms" has a curiously strengthening effect upon men's relationships with one another; and there are several poems, such as "**Recompense**" and "**The Day of Victory**," in which Gurney's thankfulness that he too has participated in the struggle makes itself plainly felt. Furthermore, he senses, in "**Camps**" for example, that the peculiar hazards of modern war can alter a man's ways of perceiving the shapes and colours of the world around him.

For Gurney, though anything but an Aesthete, frequently writes of Beauty and The Beautiful. The War, it seems, intensified his awareness of the enmity which exists between beauty and those two old calumniators Time and Change. Some of his best poetry comes to rest on the conception that Beauty manages to outlast Mutability; and he is anxious to make articulate his conviction that our intercourse with beauty gives us a kind of mastery over experience itself. As he writes in "**Eternal Treasure**":

> Take comfort then, and dare the dangerous thing,
> Death flouting with his impotence of wrath;
> For Beauty arms us 'gainst his envious sting . . .

The sort of confidence we have here is present in other poems from the two wartime volumes. Yet there can be no denying that occasionally the poet's faith in permanent values deserts him: and so he falls back on the incipient fatalism of "**Acquiescence**." In this poem Gurney, the serving soldier, argues that since he cannot revoke his destiny either by bribes, or prayers, or "any earthly force," it behoves him to adopt an attitude of stoical endurance:

I must gather together the whole strength of me,
My senses make the willing servitors;
Cherish and feed the better, starve the worse;
Turn all my pride to proud humility . . .

But this fatalism, it should be pointed out, is not an essentially cynical one, as is borne out by the delicacy with which in **"Hail and Farewell"** Gurney contemplates the irony of the situation in which "the fool at arms, Musician, poet to boot" (himself, no doubt) conceives of his own death as likely to occur at the hands of some "destined bullet."

Behind what has just been referred to as Gurney's fatalism stood the inescapable conviction that the President of the Immortals had washed his hands of human affairs. The poet's disgust at what he takes to be God's indifference to sublunary wretchedness comes out in a large number of these poems. There may be a "meaning" in the suffering which he and his companions have to endure; but what are we to make of a state of affairs when with

Men broken, shrieking, even to hear a gun—
Till pain grind down or lethargy numbs
The amazed heart cries out angrily on God?

Two pieces in particular from *War's Embers* examine this crucial dilemma; they are **"The Volunteers"** and **"The Target."** In the first of them Gurney represents his volunteer as going out to "test God's purposes": he is curious to discover what lies in store for him because "God is very secret" and will not make the disclosures all men crave for. **"The Target"** is slightly reminiscent of Wilfred Owen's "Strange Meeting," for in it the poet recalls an enemy he has been constrained to kill in self-defence: but since his own continued existence as a fighting man causes sleepless nights for his family back home, he wonders whether it would not have been better if *his* life had been taken. He seeks assurance one way or the other, only to find that

God keeps still and does not say
A word of guidance any way.

His only consolation rests in the possibility that after death he may have the opportunity of meeting the man he has slaughtered, and may then be able to make amends for this involuntary action. "All's a tangle," Gurney writes in **"The Target."** Throughout his poetry he makes no attempt to satisfy himself about the moral position in which orthodox believers had now placed themselves. The religion of the churches apparently meant very little to him. Yet although his "amazed heart" cries out vainly on God, Gurney is not openly disrespectful to the Deity. Indeed, several of his poems are passionate magnificats. But as we see from such pieces as **"Communion"** and **"Time and the Soldier,"** his main object of reverence is not a beneficent Creator so much as the beauty of the earth and the spacious firmament. "I cannot live with Beauty out of mind," he writes in **"Winter Beauty"**; and he concludes **"The Tower"** by remarking that he would prefer to put up with the dangers of a soldier's life rather than let

Beauty be broken
That is God's token,
And sign of Him . . .

Yet it is clear from this and other poems that Gurney contemplates the token itself with greater enthusiasm than he does the divine Original of which it is the symbol. Gurney's preoccupation with Beauty, however, did not inhibit him from depicting the crudities and makeshifts of day-to-day existence

up at the front. In this connection he does not go out of his way to assault the susceptibilities of his readers; indeed, one notices the coolness with which he passes over unpleasant details in **"Strafe"**:

The "crumps" are falling twenty to a minute,
We crouch, and wait the end of it—or us . . .

This does not, perhaps, have the ironic *bite* of Sassoon at his best; but it does reveal a certain easily achieved detachment. Gurney seems to have no particular desire to shock his readers by dwelling on the devastation brought about by high explosives; instead, he prefers to try and make available to us, in **"The Strong Thing"** for instance, the imagined experience of what it is like to have been through such horrors and to have still retained a sense of proportion. It was a rare strength of character which enabled Gurney temporarily to disengage himself from the agonies of battle and to fix his thoughts on durable realities more precious to him than the luxury of mere relaxation.

When reading *Severn and Somme* and *War's Embers* one is more impressed by Gurney's naïve honesty of feeling than by his technical skill in versification. The *Poems by Ivor Gurney* which were edited by Edmund Blunden from mainly unpublished manuscripts reveal—though on a slightly different scale—that combination of acute sensitivity and occasional waywardness which characterises the wartime poems. As Professor Blunden puts it [see excerpt dated 1954]:

The constant regret which attends on the reading of these later poems is that the author's poetical resources and idea of poetry are felt to be decidedly greater than those he had in the days of his published volumes, but all is spoiled by an incoherence and the confusion between imaginative purpose and the solace of merely enumerating as much as possible what had happened to the writer in times of comparative liberty.

There is, of course, nothing to be gained by a dogged analysis of verse that is acknowledged to be inferior. Many of the *Poems by Ivor Gurney* are, admittedly, conceptions which do not quite arrive at the stage of full realisation. This is not true, however, of the collection as a whole. There is enough good verse in the *Poems by Ivor Gurney* to arouse our admiration for a somewhat unusual phenomenon—that of a war poet who survived the conflict but who could not escape the psychological effects of its aftermath. (pp. 68-73)

The poems which Gurney produced after 1919 are the work of a wounded mind, embarrassingly aware of its awkward affliction. As he writes in **"From the Meadows"**:

I have forgotten joy
And know only sufficient black urge of pain . . .

Gurney now strove "to work out in verse crazes of my untold pain"; and in one place after another he stresses his consciousness that he is no longer able to enjoy the gratification of normal living. Not all these poems, however, represent a mood of despondency: some are lively evocations of recollected wartime experiences, as in **"Robecq Again," "Crucifix Corner"** and **"Behind the Line."** War-weariness is the subject of several pieces in the two early volumes; in the *Poems by Ivor Gurney* this is replaced by a more sharply defined disillusionment. After the war, naturally enough, Gurney became infuriated when he had to realise that it was possible for the efforts of himself and his comrades in arms to be passed over in silence. In **"What's in Time,"** for example, he complains bitterly about the inadequate response shown to his own war poetry. And in **"Strange Hells"** he calls to mind the subsequent fate of his fighting colleagues:

> Where are they now on State-doles, or showing
>   shop patterns
> Or walking town to town sore in borrowed tatterns
> Or begged Some civic routine one never learns.
> The heart burns—but has to keep out of face how
>   heart burns.

"War Books" is an extended rebuke of those who have expected more from these haggard warriors than it was in their power to give.

But the tone of prolonged castigation was foreign to Gurney's real nature. He was not a demonstrative individual; and the best pieces in the *Poems by Ivor Gurney* are possibly those in which he labours to free himself from the debility which was circumscribing his existence. He longs to partake in "clean action," to enjoy those "Adventurous things that salt the life of man." The pristine vigour such as is recalled in **"March"** ("My boat moves and I with her delighting . . .") is now lost once and for all; there remains the possibility of enjoying it vicariously by celebrating its existence in the prowess and exuberance of other men. The quality of *insouciance* which Gurney professed to find in certain Elizabethan poets is given implicit appraisal in **"The Bohemians"**: **"Tobacco"** and **"The Pedlar's Song"** are manifestations of Gurney's delight in an easily achieved spontaneity of feeling.

Despite the high calibre of his musicianship Gurney's poems on music itself (**"The Anger of Samson," "Schubert," "Beethoven"**) are not particularly convincing. He is much more lively when trying to make present to us the "spirit of place," especially if it concerns the west of England. He is not the only poet of his generation for whom local attachments have stood in lieu of what might broadly be called "faith": and these attempts of his to render in verse "What is best of England . . ." **"Tewkesbury"** are minor acts of piety which deserve serious recognition. But such poems as **"Cotswold Ways," "Kilns"** and **"By Severn"** are of less general significance than **"The Lock Keeper,"** an ambitious composition which shows Gurney's peculiar power with unusual aptness. And **"The Lock Keeper"** is of special interest here because it enables us to make a revealing connection between *War's Embers* and the *Poems by Ivor Gurney*. For a poem under this title (dedicated to Edward Thomas) had been included in the 1919 volume; and with this the later **"Lock Keeper"** invites close comparison. The earlier poem is an itemisation—in somewhat ungraceful couplets—of the qualities which have given the lock-keeper a place in the poet's memory:

> Handy with timber, nothing came amiss
> To his quick skill; and the mysteries
> Of sail-making, net-making, boat-building were
>   his . . .

The main point of the poem is that the lock-keeper, with his wise saws and unpolished speech puts the poet to shame, since he has developed capabilities and interests which make book-learning and sophistication in general seem relatively commonplace. On the whole this poem is pleasing enough; but its counterpart in the *Poems by Ivor Gurney* is a far more subtle and impressive performance.

The second **"Lock Keeper"** begins with a memorable opening passage:

> Men delight to praise men; and to edge
> A little off from death the memory
> Of any noted or bright personality
> Is still a luck and poet's privilege.

This serves to introduce a delineation which is far more intricate than the sketch given in the *War's Embers* poem. Not only does Gurney detail the great number of skills which the lock-keeper has had to acquire in his day-to-day work over the years.

> The nights in winter netting birds in hedges,
> The stalking wild-duck by down-river sedges.
> The tricks of sailing, the ways of salmon-netting;
> The cunning practice, the finding, the doing, the
>   getting . . .

He also suggests the manner in which this continual intercourse with nature and with the basic processes of existence has brought about a certain richness of living unknown to those who are remote from such simplicities:

> Man and element and animal comprehending
> And all-paralleling one. His knowledge transcend-
>   ing
> Books, from long vain searches of dull fact,
> Conviction needing instant change to fact . . .

Significantly, it is the lock-keeper's racy *talk* which most excites Gurney's admiration:

> There was a width about the chimney corner,
> A dignity and largeness which should make grave
> Each word of cadence uttered . . .

His personality has a wholeness and compelling vitality which seem to express themselves completely in the nervous rhythm and unconventional syntax of Gurney's verse:

> So the man flowed behind his talk, to endure,
> To perceive, to manage, to be skilled, to excel; to
>   understand
> A net of craft of eye, heart, kenning and hand,
> Thousand threaded tentaculous intellect . . .

To *excel* is the faculty which transforms the lock-keeper into a "worthy" and makes him a symbol of impulsive racial energies ("Norse, Phoenician, Norse, British? immemorial use"). So that what we have in this second lock-keeper poem is something more than a simple portrait of a country-dweller; his kind of wisdom, derived from long intimacy with a certain type of environment, stands in sharp contrast to the slender and slightly precious attainments of the poet:

> Clouded with smoke, wrapped round with cloak of
>   thought
> He gave more of desert to me, more than I ought—
> Who was so used to books, so little to life.

Before the poem comes to an end the poet is, as it were, exposed by the very strength of his own enthusiasms; he is forced into a position where all that remains for him to do is admit the extent of his humiliation—he is belittled by the lock-keeper's *savoir faire* and general mastery of life.

This second **"Lock Keeper"** is perhaps Gurney's finest essay in poetry. Despite its obvious affinities with poems by several of his contemporaries, it is a success from start to finish. A cursory glance through it might suggest that this is simply another rumination on country life and the appeal of rural quaintness. Yet further examination shows it to be something much more distinguished—a carefully descriptive poem which is adequately informed by a generous critical attitude towards the subject in hand. What makes it especially effective is the absence of the gawky and inharmonious phraseology which mars so many of Gurney's less felicitous pieces. The movement of the verse, too, is strangely apposite; instead of the persistent end-stopping of the first **"Lock Keeper"** we now have a rhythmical scheme which approximates to blank verse but yet does not discard rhyme altogether. The result is an ease of motion which, among other things, leaves one with the conviction that Gurney is thoroughly *engaged* by the topics he introduces into his poem; the element of whimsicality is entirely excluded from this poem, and by the side of it the first **"Lock Keeper"** is seen to be merely a feeble *simulacrum* of poetry proper.

Had Gurney often written as well as he does in the second of these two poems, there would be no question as to his real status among the poets of his time. Unhappily he was fated to carry no further the gifts which are so vividly displayed in this rewarding poem. A title-page dated February, 1925 records that Gurney wrote "in torture"; and the style of such later pieces as **"Like Hebredian"** and **"Of Cruelty"** would seem to imply the presence in Gurney's mind of tensions which verse-making alone could not resolve. But whatever we may think of his other poetical compositions, the second **"Lock Keeper"** does not appear to have been produced under such extreme conditions. If we cannot speak so confidently of all the seventy-six *Poems by Ivor Gurney* we must attribute this to the ironies of circumstance rather than to any deliberate eccentricities on the part of the poet himself. (pp. 73-7)

E. D. Mackerness, "The Poetry of Ivor Gurney," in A Review of English Literature, *Vol. 3, No. 2, April, 1962, pp. 68-77.*

JON SILKIN   (essay date 1972)

[*Silkin, an English poet and critic, edits the poetry review* Stand, *which he founded in the 1950s. In the following excerpt from his* Out of Battle, *a study of the English poets of the First World War, he discusses conflicting attitudes toward war in Gurney's poetry.*]

Gurney's first two books contain few poems that wholly, and from the then current and official viewpoint, tell the truth about war. The poems themselves differ, and there are even conflicting attitudes within the one poem. For example, in **"To His Love,"** one of three poems by Gurney included in Ian Parsons's anthology *Men Who March Away* (1965), a noticeable hesitation between contradicting attitudes occurs:

> You would not know him now . . .
>   But still he died
> Nobly, so cover him over
>   With violets of pride
>   Purple from Severn side.

The first line suggests that had you known the man, you would hardly, because of his mutilations, recognize him. It also suggests that hardly anyone else would recognize him, for the same reasons, as human. The line derives its force not merely from these ideas but by contrasting them with the conventional expressions of sorrow that those related to the man would feel, either as their own expressions of grief, or

else as those which they had been taught to feel. They would naturally feel sorrow, but the conventional idea consists in their feeling an inextricable pride also. The tone undermines this idea as doing no justice to the man's suffering, yet the stanza as a whole is ambivalent in that it also hesitates between acceptance and rejection of the pride. Enormous social forces would quite naturally cause such hesitations. Gurney is, of course, sympathizing with the bereaved, but he had to hold in relation to it the idea that the sentimental consolations of pride not only "harmed" the man's sacrifice, but perpetuated the sacrificing of others. Thus, he here seems to be saying: "Your grief would be all the more terrible in that you would be shocked to see the state he is in, but you do not see him, and therefore do not comprehend the nature of his death. I am glad that you cannot be so shocked, but I am sorry, for all the other soldiers' sakes, that you do not know the facts of warfare." Other hesitations accumulate. What right has he to oppose what is a time-honoured consolation of pride in the sacrifice? "Nobly" covers a number of related difficulties; and Gurney sees the problems, as [Edmund] Blunden also did (in part) in "A.G.A.V." "Nobly" is not merely the individual soldier's attribute; it is the propagandistic aura that the state awards the dead in an effort to persuade the living to continue their efforts.

After hesitating between these conflicting attitudes, Gurney, disappointingly, moves the stanza in the aureate direction by forcing an anthropomorphic change on his native Gloucestershire. Patriotic tradition and local pastoral were, after all, what he began with. Thus, Gloucestershire mourns one of its sons and sheds its blood in sympathy (having already shed it in the death of the man)—in sympathy, but also in pride. The resulting sentimentality is the product both of the anthropomorphism and the abstractions thus entailed. The poem, however, ends on a different note:

> Cover him, cover him soon!
>   And with thick-set
> Masses of memoried flowers—
>   Hide that red wet
>   Thing I must somehow forget.

"Red wet" expresses with raw precision the response of horror and nausea that shed blood elicits, and by ending the line on the adjective "wet" he transforms it momentarily into a noun, which reinforces the rawness. The man is no longer a person but a "wet thing." This is what Gurney must—and because must, cannot—forget. The "Masses of memoried flowers" is also complex—the flowers suggesting the conventional symbol of grief and respect, but the "Masses" suggesting by how much the corpse needs to be buried from sight, and memory.

"The Silent One" presents its problem with a more overall precision because, partly, it is less sensuous and requires therefore less complex attention. But Gurney has now more clarified objectives and to express them a greater linguistic precision.

> Who died on the wires, and hung there, . . .
> Yet faced unbroken wires; stepped over, and went
> A noble fool, faithful to his stripes—and ended.

Although this was apparently written in the period of madness, it shares an experience of reality, which is lucid in the interrelation of its parts, and acceptable in the version of reality it offers. "Noble" in this poem is carefully qualified and the two representative judgements on this man, and many others, are made in such a way as to qualify each other. By letting the man's courage into the poem, we are made to feel compassion, but this comes through because the courage and the foolishness hold each other in check. The victim's vitality is uncannily expressed in

> . . . had chattered through
> Infinite lovely chatter of Bucks accent. . . .

Gurney uses similar devices to express the absurdity and waste of combat. The politeness of the upper-class voice is made to sound absurd by making it articulate fearful demands, and by placing alongside these a parallel and polite refusal by the man to obey his officer's lethal demands:

> Till the politest voice—a finicking accent, said:
> "Do you think you might crawl through, there: there's a hole"
> Darkness, shot at: I smiled, as politely replied—
> "I'm afraid not, Sir." There was no hole no way to be seen
> Nothing but chance of death. . . .

The "finicking" accent of the controlling class is contrasted with the "lovely chatter of Bucks accent." Anger is certainly somewhere present in this poem, but it is explicit in **"What's in Time"**:

> God curse for cowards; take honour and all damn
> For bastards out of good blood, last leaving of diseases,
> The rulers of England, lost in corruptions and increases
> All mean, foul things they lap up like (powderless) jam—
> While the cheated dead cry, unknowing, "Eadem Semper."

Resentment is as explicit—and more coherent—in the poem Blunden cites in his introduction [to *Poems by Ivor Gurney* (see excerpt dated 1954)]:

> . . . who have let destroy
> A servant of yours, by evil men birth better at once had slain.
>
> And for my Country, God knows my heart, and men to me
> Were dear there, I was friend also of every look of sun or rain;
> It has betrayed as evil women wantonly a man their toy.

Had Gurney not become intermittently mad, would anybody have thought to say that this was the expression of someone deranged? Blunden writes:

> even in these queerly phrased petitions (for "rescue") there was no mistaking the derangement which kept him where he was. He was aflame with anger which had for him the clear and undeniable cause that he, a lover of England if ever one existed, had been flung into a trap by England the beloved. "The earth opened."

From the syntax it is not clear if the additional evidence of derangement is the accusation made against England; but if it is, I can only disagree with Blunden's contention that this is a sign of madness. Gurney's accusation may be unreasonable in that England did not deliberately sacrifice him in the way a woman may play with a man; but that he felt betrayed by his love for his country, casually betrayed as millions, he

would have felt, were, is hardly madness. Gurney was struggling to articulate a real grievance in which he felt men were unnecessarily sacrificed through their attachment, and he had to filter this through what was intermittently a deranged mind. But does this invalidate the grievance? Gurney wrote, in the same poem:

> Soldier's praise I had earned having suffered soldier's pain,
> And the great honour of song in the battle's first gray show—
> Honour was bound to me save—mine most dreadfully slain.

"Honour" is especially hard to paraphrase: does it mean "privilege of being a poet + due recognition"? Gurney seems to be saying that, as a soldier, he had earned the right to speak of his suffering in poetry, and that this poetry alone could save him from the effects of the war on his mind; but at the same time the war had mutilated his capacity to write. It is perhaps the most bitter and personal accusation he could make, but it seems to have substance to it.

Indignation of a similar kind, but explicitly on behalf of those who suffered, is at the heart of **"Mist on Meadows"**:

> Dreadful green light baring the ruined trees,
> Stakes, pools, lostness, better hidden dreadful in dark
> And not ever reminding of these other fields. . . .
>
> But they honour not—and salute not those boys who saw a terror
> Of waste, endured horror, and were not fearer, . . .
> But could not guess, but could not guess, alas!
> How England should take as common their vast endurance
> And let them be but boys having served time Overseas.

That "take as common" is surely the ubiquitous complaint of Sassoon and Owen, and may, in Gurney's instance, help to counterbalance the personal resentment so frequent in his poetry:

> But the body hurt, spirit is hindered and slow,
> And evil hurts me past my maker's right.

This, from **"The Bronze Sounding,"** is of course an expression of self-pity, but I have never fully understood the stoic form of objection to it. If it is that the self-pitier is withholding pity from others by focusing on his own pain, there is a double objection to this criticism. One is that the self-pitier is as valid an object of compassion as anyone else, and the other is that those who condemn are themselves withholding the very pity the man may need. Gurney, in any case, is not selfishly withholding his compassion for others, but complaining of his own suffering as one among many. There is nothing solipsistic in it.

"War Books" takes the complaint a stage further:

> What did they expect of our toil and extreme
> Hunger—the perfect drawing of a heart's dream?
> Did they look for a book of wrought art's perfection,
> Who promised no reading, nor praise, nor publication?
> Out of the heart's sickness the spirit wrote
> For delight, or to escape hunger, or of war's worst anger. . . .

Gurney's objections are to a philistine community unprepared to pay (in every sense of this word) for the kind of art that would emerge from war's experience. What was wanted, it seemed, was a perfectly "wrought" art impossible under the circumstances and inappropriate to the experience. He objects to an involuted "art for art's sake" style divorced from substance, the falsely decorative which Pound locates in "*E.P. Ode pour l'election de son sepulchre*":

> The "age demanded" chiefly a mould in
>   plaster, . . .
>   not, not assuredly, alabaster
> Or the "sculpture" of rhyme.

Gurney also seems to be implying that what the public wanted was not an honest response to the war but a distortion implicit in those "tales" from which they might obtain a vicarious sense of excitement. Thus Owen in "Dulce et Decorum Est":

>   you would not tell with such high zest
> To children ardent for some desperate glory,
> The old Lie. . . .

Nature, for Gurney, remained part of another era and another poetic, a refuge and a touchstone. It could not be handled with developing delicacy and understanding, because to disturb the relationship between himself and nature, as he understood it, would have meant destroying those springs with which he was intermittently but surely in touch. If Gurney was mad, his incompleteness has nevertheless some completely sane limitations, and it is this that makes him a tragic figure ("mine most dreadfully slain") as much as his madness. If the madness in some way helped him to discard his earlier conventional poeticisms (and he may have done this in perfect sanity), it also prevented him from merging the newly wrought components of his art as deliberately as he might have done, and from merging them with his apprehensions of nature in such a way as to transform these. Blunden deliberately chose the traditional order and has maintained a conscious relationship with it, but we do not know if the word "deliberately" is applicable to Gurney.

In the Introduction to his edition of *Poems of John Clare's Madness*, Geoffrey Grigson has written:

> [Clare's] biographers have suggested that, at times, he was actually sane. "To be sane, even for short periods, while confined within a madhouse, is perhaps one of the most exquisite horrors which can be imagined for any man; and Clare, in the years to come, must have endured this often." That is a dangerous attitude. It belongs more perhaps to the romanticism of the eighteen-thirties than to a justifiable estimate of Clare's case. One must guard oneself against such a romantic view. . . .

Equally, one must guard oneself against counter-reaction; for, if I understand Grigson correctly, he is suggesting that the insane do not suffer during their sane periods from a lucid realization of where they are, and why they are so confined. If one cannot say that Gurney was *definitely* tormented by a knowledge that at times he was mad, he was undoubtedly tormented by his confinement, and it would be correct to hear what he writes of this:

> Why have you made life so intolerable
> And set me between four walls, where I am able

> Not to escape meals without prayer, for that is possible
> Only by annoying an attendant. And tonight a sensual
> Hell has been put upon me, so that all has deserted
>   me
> And I am merely crying and trembling in heart
> For death, and cannot get it, and gone out is part
> Of sanity. And there is dreadful hell within me
> And nothing helps, forced meals there have been
>   and electricity
> And weakening of sanity by influence
> That's dreadful to endure, and there is orders
> And I'm praying for death, death, death
> And dreadful is the indrawing and out-drawing of
>   breath
> Because of the intolerable insults put on my whole
>   soul
> Of the soul loathed, loathed, loathed of the sun.

Gurney endured this until his death on 26 December 1937. In a letter of 3 June 1964 [William] Curtis-Hayward wrote to me:

> Although I am in favour of any attempts to get Gurney into print, I think it will be doing him a disservice if he is presented as a good minor poet who happened to be mad. I believe that what we have is the ruins of a major poet, and that his madness is of the essence of the fragments of really original poetry he left.

I am unsure of even this assessment and only feel certain that he is a considerable poet, fragmented by the war as well as by his own disabilities. (pp. 122-29)

> *Jon Silkin, "Edmund Blunden and Ivor Gurney,"*
> *in his* Out of Battle: The Poetry of the Great War,
> *1972. Reprint by Ark Paperbacks, 1987, pp. 102-29.*

ANDREW MOTION   (essay date 1982)

> [*Motion is an English poet, critic, and biographer whose works have been compared to those of Edward Thomas and Philip Larkin for their understated tone and precise use of conventional poetic forms. In the following excerpt, he discusses Gurney as a Modernist who adapted literary conventions to express a unique view of war, eschewing both heroic depiction of war and remonstrative commentary on war.*]

The last fifteen years of [Ivor Gurney's] life were spent in Stone House mental hospital in Kent. The poems he wrote there continue the celebrations of the English countryside and its history, and the ruminations about the war, that had dominated the two collections with which he had first made his name as a poet: *Severn and Somme* and *War's Embers*. But while the themes are consistent, the treatment is fascinatingly different. Predominantly Georgian qualities are consistently pressed out of shape by a mind which—for personal as well as literary reasons—can no longer trust the stabilities they represent. Gurney never departs from orthodoxy altogether, but challenges and buckles and reinvents it. The effect is not one of watching a thorough-going modernist such as Eliot emerge from a Georgian cocoon, but of seeing a simultaneously tormented and enlightened Georgian develop characteristics he would not have known to call "modernist," but which we can now see as being just that. . . .

[Gurney's] achievement can be compared to that of the contemporary who has also had to wait for more than half a century for recognition: Edward Thomas.

Having said that, it is important to insist on the differences between the two poets. . . .

Gurney was more strongly influenced by Thomas than by any other writer, and he borrows phrases, cadences and situations from him, as well as emulating his subtle playing of sentence against line and line against line-break. But his work nevertheless expresses a quite distinct poetic personality. This is partly a matter of landscape: where Thomas is involved with the south of England and its (usually) specifically British past, Gurney turns again and again to Gloucestershire, and sees the landscape as a palimpsest in which traces of the Romans mingle with indigenous relics. (The more disturbed Gurney's mind became, the more frequently he referred to the Romans—because of the order associated with them, and because as an invading force they allowed him to refract his recollections of the war.) In **"Cotswold Ways,"** for example, some of the "strangest things" he "comes across" walking are:

> Stream-sources happened upon in unlikely
>   places,
> And Roman-looking hills of small degree
> And the surprise of dignity of poplars
> At a road end, or the white Cotswold scars,
> Or sheets spread white against the hazel tree.
> Strange the large difference of up-Cotswold
>   ways;
> Birdlip climbs bold and treeless to a bend,
> Portway to dim wood-lengths without end,
> And Crickley goes to cliffs are the crown of
>   days.

This poem, typically, takes a greater risk with its syntax than one usually finds in Thomas—the elliptical last line—and that helps to produce a completely independent-sounding manner. Where Thomas is ruminative, scrupulous and fine-grained, Gurney is impetuous, occasionally naive, and enthusiastic. The pace of Thomas's thoughts, as suggested by his poems' rhythms, is slower than Gurney's—who looks and speaks with what he calls (speaking of Chapman) a "football rush." And where Thomas's mind can relax and spread into narratives ("As the Team's Head-Brass") and also compose itself sufficiently to produce finished meditations ("Old Man"), Gurney often seems hurried and driven, seeking less for a coherent resolution than for a means of matching the integrity of his mood with a sense of immediacy in its expression. For all his sufferings in the world, his tone of voice seems less worldly-wise than Thomas's.

The breathless, breathtaking rush that Gurney manages so well was initiated by his experiences in France, but only fully developed during his subsequent deliberations. Like Thomas, he avoided giving candid responses to well-known aspects of the war. His remark that "Great poets, great creators are not much influenced by immediate events: those must sink in to the very foundations and be absorbed" comes close to rephrasing Thomas's judgment that "by becoming ripe for poetry the poet's thoughts may recede far from their original resemblance to all the world's, and may seem to have little to do with daily events." Since Gurney spent a good deal longer than Thomas at the Front, he had many more of its "daily events" to accommodate—and at least one of the strategies he evolved to deal with them makes him unlike almost all his contemporaries. Partly by temperament, and partly because

A portrait from Gurney's asylum period.

he was not an officer, he eschewed the two most familiar accents of war poetry: he neither described obvious heroics, nor did he warn or remonstrate as did, say, Wilfred Owen. Instead, he adopted a tone of voice which mixes humour with incredulity and horror. The effect is to create simultaneously an impression of things being beyond his control, and a suggestion that events are so extremely pressing and demanding that the sweeping considerations one might expect—such as general estimations of suffering and pity—would misrepresent his overriding concerns at the time: which are to avoid getting hurt, or better still, to get the hell out of it and back to Blighty. Paradoxically, in other words, he contains the influence of his immediate surroundings by concentrating on their minute particulars, and by registering the lack of opportunity and inclination to consider the large moral issues that they raise. Many of his best war poems are intensely vivid accounts of a private soldier simply trying to survive—being shot at, being ordered about, resenting "this brass-cleaning life," enjoying the company of his friends, complaining about the weight of his pack and wanting a cup of tea. In **"Varennes,"** for example, while "the infantry drilled frozen":

> to the canteen went I,
> Got there by high favour, having run, finished
>   third,

In a mile race from Varennes to the next village
  end.
Canteen assistant, with a special care for B
  Company—
And biscuits hidden for favour in a manner
  forbidden.
Lying about chocolate to C Company hammering
  the gate.

Given the circumstances, Gurney managed to produce an extraordinarily large number of rounded, taut lyrics during the war. "The sound of the guns," he wrote to a friend, "should be reason enough to excuse any roughness in the technique." But **"Varennes"** (actually written in the asylum) illustrates the free, expressive diary form that he used increasingly often. These diary-like poems are best read in bulk—their cumulative effect is very impressive indeed—and their range is increased by a second and more familiar response to the demands of dealing with "daily events." From the very first, Gurney's extraordinarily deep love for England had led him to create a similar kind of ironical structure in his poems to that which frequently appears in the work of Owen, Blunden and others. As the title of his first book, *Severn and Somme,* indicates, landscapes of the present and the war are constantly being placed in his mind's eye beside those of the past and of peace. Like the details of the south country in Thomas's poetry, the towns, villages, rivers and hills of Gurney's Gloucestershire are the embodiment of unwavering patriotism which, because it takes this form, is absolutely without any trace of tub-thumping jingoism. But when the war ended, Gurney's attitude to England became more complicated. To start with, he was afflicted by a strong but reasonably straightforward feeling that his country did not sufficiently appreciate the sacrifice he had made. Work was inadequate or not to be had, there was no chance to exercise the "courage" he had known in France, there was no regularity to life, and—worst of all—there was no hope of recovering the comradeliness he had found in the trenches. "As for rest or true ease, when is it or what is it?" he asks in one poem. "With criss-cross purposes and spoilt threads of life, / Perverse pathways, the savour of life is gone." In another, **"Strange Hells,"** he beautifully imagines the waste of spirit in humdrum living which his former companions now suffer:

Where are they now, on state-doles, or showing
  shop-patterns
Or walking town to town sore in borrowed
  tatterns
Or begged. Some civic routine one never learns.
The heart burns—but has to keep out of face
  how heart burns.

For all its unpleasantnesses, the army checked Gurney's instability by imposing some order on his life. Without it, his old characteristics returned and were stimulated by the memories of what he had lost. In spite of making various efforts to pick up the threads of his former life—he returned to the Royal College of Music (where he had been given a scholarship in 1911), wrote, and visited friends—he could settle to nothing. And although tramping round England could still rekindle his feelings for its landscape, even these had a new, disturbing dimension. The act of walking, and the hardships he imposed on himself when undertaking a long journey, were almost a parody of his "moving and shifting about" in France, and therefore filled him with thoughts of the war. When he was confined, it was because he could only envisage one way out of his unhappiness:

Death is not here, save mercy grant it. When
Was cruelty such known last among like-and-like
  men?
An Interview? It is cried for—and not known—
Not found. Death absent what thing is truly
  man's own?
Beaten down continually, continually beaten clean
  down.

Until the end of his writing life, the war and Gloucestershire remain interlocked and dominant in his imagination. So much so, in fact, that almost all his late poems avoid mentioning the facts of his confined existence altogether. But evidence of his plight is evident everywhere. His original Georgian poetic addresses ("O blow here, you dusk-airs . . .") are transformed into tormented appeals to God, Death and even the police for deliverance. The early, strict and lucid lyric forms are twisted and packed to contain the bulging, irrepressible shape of his distress, and are frequently interrupted by comments which both welcome the idea of formal order and recognize that he cannot obey its requirements entirely:

             I musician have wrestled with the
  stuff in making,
And wrought a square thing out of my stubborn
  mind—
And gathered a huge surge of spirit as the great barriers bind
The whole Atlantic at them by Devon or west Ireland.

Even the stable sanctities of the English landscape can no longer provide the comfort that they once did. Since he can no longer actually visit Gloucestershire, it becomes a kind of hallucination; minutely and lovingly recalled, but a country of the mind; brilliantly lit by memory, but never to be enjoyed in the present except as a thought. He writes about it, as he does about the war, as if he were a ghost. He is almost as much out of life, the poems imply, as if he had been killed in France—but instead of being actually dead, or "happy alive," he is condemned to a "liberty" in which he can only envy death and yearn for the past:

Madness my enemy, cunning extreme my friend,
Prayer my safeguard. (Ashes my reward at end.)
Secrecy fervid my honour, soldier-courage my aid.
(Promise and evil threatening my soul ever-
  afraid.)
Now, with the work long done, to the witchcraft I
  bend
And crouch—that knows nothing good. Hell un-
  caring
Hell undismayed.

Criticism is disabled by poetry of such urgency and pain. . . . Even so, it is hard not to suspect that Gurney sometimes wrote too entirely to "keep madness and black torture away/A little" for the good of his poems. If this is the price one pays for his achievement, the achievement itself is never in doubt. Although his madness meant that he was effectively locked out of England for much of his life, he was one of the very few, and one of the very best, poets of his time to adapt the jaded literary traditions he grew up with, and allow them to accommodate the anxieties and preoccupations of the postwar years. The result is a large body of work which is extremely powerful in its own right, and is also a significant landmark in literary history. Gurney—like Thomas—secured and sustained a poetic line which was specifically English but nevertheless flexible and inclusive, at precisely the moment when the radical, cosmopolitan techniques of Pound and Eliot seemed to overwhelm it. For a long time we have been told that the modernists were a race completely apart, and the only people to face up to the modern period. Now we are beginning to know better.

Andrew Motion, "Beaten Down Continually," in The Times Literary Supplement, No. 4150, October 15, 1982, p. 1121.

P. J. KAVANAGH (essay date 1982)

[*Kavanagh is an English poet and critic. In the following excerpt from his introduction to the* Collected Poems of Ivor Gurney, *Kavanagh examines Gurney's unconventional view of the war as expressed in his poetry.*]

The first selection of Ivor Gurney's poems was published in 1954, long enough ago for those who know his work to have decided what it is like. But nearly a quarter of a century later he was still being described, when a plaque to him was unveiled in Gloucester Cathedral, as a "local" poet. It was well-meant—he was a local boy—but in the limiting sense of Edward Thomas's definition of poets "whom we can connect with a district of England and often cannot sunder from it without harm," Gurney was not a local poet at all.

"Yesterday Lost"

What things I have missed today, I know very well,
But the seeing of them each new time is miracle.
Nothing between Bredon and Dursley has
Any day yesterday's precise unpraisèd grace.
The changed light, or curve changed mistily,
Coppice, now bold cut, yesterday's mystery.
A sense of mornings, once seen, forever gone,
Its own for ever: alive, dead, and my possession.

You do not have to know Bredon or Dursley to see what he is driving at. His Gloucestershire is real, of course, but it is also a region of the mind, The Good Place. He is sparing of topography and more interested in the seasons (especially autumn) and in sky-effects—clouds, dawn-lights, sunsets, even "Novembery" lightlessness (he likes that too). If he is to be given a locality, he could with more justice be called a sky-poet.

But, like most poets, he is dependent on the particular and on being able to name it. After the war, when he could give the names of the places in France where he had served, his war poetry gains in immediacy. He had found wartime censorship more than usually cramping: "forbidden names or dates without which the poets / are done for. . . ." His details—the Machonachie pickle, the shared fag, the noise of the cleaning-out of dixies—and his awareness that everything is happening in one place rather than another, at a certain hour, under a never-to-be-repeated pattern of sky, are what give these poems distinctiveness. Whereas the other war poets (Owen, Sassoon, and so on) reacted against the war rhetoric of their elders with indignation and tell us truths we ought to have guessed, Gurney gives us pictures we would not have imagined: the gentleness of his first reception in the front line (in two poems, both called **"First Time In"**), the effect of a clarinet played in the trenches (**"New Year's Eve"** and **"Crucifix Corner"**). It is the poetry of a particularized, not a generalized humanity, of the flesh and nerves rather than of the intellect. His precisions can be journalistic but he almost invariably looks up to notice the behaviour of the

French sky. This widening of view after such narrowness of observation can be startling, putting the war itself in its place.

The avoidance of predictable anger and the fastening upon the unexpected detail make Gurney himself present in his war poems, even when he is talking about someone else. For example, in **"The Silent One,"** which begins:

Who died on the wires, and hung there, one of
two—
Who for his hours of life had chattered through
Infinite lovely chatter of Bucks accent. . . .

There is no mythologizing of the dead boy on the wires—surely the most appalling and demoralizing sight the troops on the Western Front had to endure—nor any attempt to shock. What is missed is his "chatter": not loss of promise, ending of beauty and youth—grander conceptions which may come later—but the sudden cessation of the small inconsequences of life. That the chatter had the stamp of Buckinghamshire on it would have been as significant to the dead soldier as Gurney's Gloucestershire background was to him.

Then the poem, in a domestic fashion, goes on to describe how Gurney disobeyed an order, on the grounds of common sense, and apparently got away with it:

Till the politest voice—a finicking accent, said:
"Do you think you might crawl through there:
there's a hole."
Darkness, shot at: I smiled, as politely replied—
"I'm afraid not, Sir." . . .

"Finicking" is precise, and the exchange of politenesses comic. Already, quickly moving, impressionistic, this is not quite like any war poem one has read. But there is more surprise to come. Gurney tells us he kept flat under the bullets:

And thought of music—and swore deep heart's
deep oaths
(Polite to God). . . .

That parenthesis could only have been written either by a man with no sense of the absurd (which we know from the previous lines, and from his letters, was certainly not the case with Gurney) or by a man who had risen above the absurd, who had lost all fear of being laughed at, had now no wish to appear sophisticated or knowing (although he was capable of appearing so) and who was in unembarrassed touch with the most childlike part of his nature.

So, at all events, I felt when I first read this poem, with its queer diction that matches the queer but precise content, an unpompous formality that controls shifts of tone and mood. Then, reading on among his other war poems and his agonized personal pieces, his exultations, praises, desperations, I found among his lyrics (which do sing) **"The High Hills"**:

The high hills have a bitterness
Now they are not known
And memory is poor enough consolation
For the soul hopeless gone.
Up in the air there beech tangles wildly in the
wind—
That I can imagine
But the speed, the swiftness, walking into clarity,
Like last year's bryony are gone.

The tune matches the sense, is a part of the meaning, and that is rare. I began to wonder why I had not come across his work before. True, among the knowledgeable his name was sometimes mentioned; W. H. Auden had printed **"The High Hills"** in his Commonplace book *A Certain World;* but where were the learned articles, biographies, generous selections in anthologies?

Then, as I learned more about Gurney, I began to suspect that, apart from his own disinclination to compete, or pretend, several other things were working against him.

First, he was acknowledged to be a musician, a composer of songs, of genius—and we always doubt whether a man can be good at two things. Second, he was mentally unbalanced: from about 1912, when he was twenty-two, he had been subject to mental breakdowns and in 1922 he was put in an asylum (where he wrote some of his best poems) for the last fifteen years of his life. So, Gurney was not only "primarily" a musician (and a "local" poet and an odd sort of war poet) he was a "mad" poet too, and the combination of all these things had caused him to be shunted off into a siding.

But at least seventy out of every hundred poems included [in the *Collected Poems of Ivor Gurney*] show no sign of mental disturbance at all—unless to be a poet is to be in such a condition, which is possible, and certainly Gurney showed himself unsuited to the routines of "ordinary" life. Also, where there are signs of unbalance, they are obvious; too many of his preoccupations crowd in at once and fall over each other: his sense of having been betrayed, his memories of his comrades in France, of Gloucestershire, of walks at night. The result, though seldom completely incoherent, is confused and painful. But these are also the themes of his best work and, right up to the end of his working life, he is capable of sudden, pictorial, simplicities.

Because there are so many interesting distractions on the way to a reading of Gurney's verse, my dearest wish would be for the reader to approach him first with no knowledge at all of his medical history. With a fate so dramatic and terrible this is hardly possible. But, so far as his poetry goes, by far the most extraordinary thing is that, apart from the occasional, terrible, shouts of indignation to God, there is hardly an event, certainly no fellow inmate, or attendant, from those last confined years, despite continuous writing, that is mentioned. It is as though, so far as the sources of his poetry are concerned, he simply ignores his situation. This surely should be a hint to the reader, at least at first, to do the same. (pp. 1-4)

Apart from shouts of indignation (**"To God"**) and the "Appeals for Release" addressed to the Prime Minister, the Metropolitan Police, and so on, [Gurney] writes on the whole as if he were free. That he kept on writing, and reading, is remarkable enough, but to do so with such disdain for his fate is heroic. "But my blood, in its colour even, is known fighter":

> They have left me little indeed, how shall I best keep
> Memory from sliding content down to drugged sleep?
> But my blood, in its colour even, is known fighter.
> If I were hero for such things here would I make wars
> As love for dead things trodden under January's stars,
>
> Or the gold trefoil itself spending in careless places
> Tiny graces like music's for its past exquisitenesses.

> Why war for huge domains of the planet's heights or plains?
> (Little they leave me.) It is a dream. Hardly my heart dares
> Tremble for glad leaf-drifts thundering under January's stars.
>
> (**"Memory"**)
> (p. 10)

"Memory" shows the way Gurney's poems developed after his first two books. It is still traditional in shape, and Gurney always loved rhyme, but it is more direct. In a sense he consciously attempts to abjure literature—"He desiring books and I truth rather than the / Writing continual" as he said of Southey (**"To Gloucestershire"**). Whereas the early poems seem addressed to an audience, trying to impress (as was natural in a young writer), the later Gurney is talking to himself, to the air, and his relationship with the reader becomes easier and more private. But there are plenty of indications of the later Gurney in the first books. In *Severn and Somme* **"Pain"** shows that he was already better at indignation than self-pity and **"Only the Wanderer"** is almost pure music.

War's Embers did not mark a great advance. It contains humour (**"Companion—North-East Dug-Out"**) and touches a theme that recurs (**"Old Martinmas Eve"**): the hope for music to come to him, "some most quiet tune," so that he can catch and express the moment; then his regret, verbally musical, at its non-arrival. This poem is more than usually reminiscent of Edward Thomas, whose prose Gurney loved. If he had seen any poems of Thomas by this time, which seems likely, he shows himself quicker, and readier for his influence, than any of his English contemporaries. Also, in this second book, Gurney attempts transcriptions of the ordinary speech and slang of army life—dixies, whizzbangs, "revally" and the like—very jaunty, leading at least one reviewer to rebuke him for being too colloquial. On the other hand, it also caused Edmund Blunden to say of his war poems, [see excerpt dated 1954], "to this day they express part of the Western Front secret of fifty years ago with distinctive, intimate and imaginative quickness." However, it was perhaps not the kind of war poetry that the public wanted. His third collection, titled in manuscript *Rewards of Wonder,* was rejected.

This is understandable because Gurney begins to sound original, pressing music out of ordinary speech. With signs of the pressure too, queer contortions and omissions which became a part of his manner. They are intentional, as changes in his notebooks show, and are part of his homage to his beloved Elizabethans, especially Shakespeare: phrases like "nerves soothed were so sore shaken" (the "that" omitted) have an Elizabethan ring about them. He also goes in for outrageous rhymes:

> . . . fill full
> Those rolling tanks with chlorinated clay mixture
> And curse the mud with vain veritable vexture.
> (**"Crucifix Corner"**)

Later he would carry the combination of slang and a sudden wider perspective as far as it could be carried—maybe further—but the risk he takes is exhilarating:

> True, the size of the rum ration was still a shocker
> But at last over Aubers the majesty of the dawn's veil swept.
>
> (**"Serenade"**)

He served as a Private in the 2nd/5th Gloucestershire Regiment and his war is very much that of the private soldier: a cleaner business, humanly speaking, than that of someone with more responsibility. A conscripted Private's job in war is, rightly, to obey orders and stay alive, meanwhile making himself as comfortable as possible. In other words, to remain (unlike the Officer candidates in **"The Bohemians"**) triumphantly a civilian. Thus Gurney's account of his war contains stories of the scrounging of soft jobs (and guilt at this, for he was not, after all, an "ordinary" Private), descriptions of the pleasure of having clean straw to lie on, a candle-stub to write letters by. He permits himself few large statements about the war, indeed it is possible that he barely took it seriously, and in this he would surely have been at one with his fellow Privates. This is not to say that Gurney's war was "funny"—any more than the Douanier Rousseau's picture of War as a grinning child on a horse crossing a landscape of severed limbs is funny. But Gurney can be allowed to describe his war for himself. (The nearest thing to his version, uncannily so, is in prose, in the opening pages of Ford Madox Ford's *No More Parades,* which is set in Gurney's part of the Front.)

Behind his lyric poetry the drive is a determination to celebrate the sacredness of the moment, to share sudden accesses of joy, and also to deplore its absence. The intricacies of human relations are not his subject: he attempts very little love-poetry, and when there are people in his poems (**"The Lock Keeper"**) they are seen with a rather abstract, lonely, passion of respect. He is concerned with personal epiphanies, the sense of enlargement suddenly granted, say, by the silhouettes of certain trees in certain lights; and with the idea of history, present, all around him. In a sense, therefore, his subject is himself, as he said in his delightful preface to *Severn and Somme:* "I fear that those who buy the book (or even borrow), to get information about the Gloucesters, will be disappointed. Most of the book is concerned with a person named Myself, and the rest with my county, Gloucester, that whether I die or live stays always with me—being itself so beautiful, so full of memories; whose people are so good to be friends with, so easy-going and so frank."

In some ways he is a consciously "unpoetical" poet, refusing to enthuse about nightingales ("Three I heard once . . ."), preferring cabbages to "that ink-proud lady the rose" (**"The Garden"**). In **"The Escape"** he comes near to announcing a poetic:

> I believe in the increasing of life: whatever
> Leads to the seeing of small trifles,
> Real, beautiful, is good; and an act never
> Is worthier than in freeing spirit that stifles
> Under ingratitude's weight, nor is anything done
> Wiselier than the moving or breaking to sight
> Of a thing hidden under by custom—revealed,
> Fulfilled, used (sound-fashioned) any way out to
>   delight:
> Trefoil—hedge sparrow—the stars on the edge at
>   night.

"Wiselier" is typical Gurney. Such usages are not, I think, affectations. His occasional bathetic contrasts—the rum ration followed immediately by the majesty of the dawn in the extract from **"Serenade"** already quoted—are also intentional and a representation of the mind's movement. The risks that he takes with his rhymes hold the poems together, and he usually carries the meaning on and through them, avoiding the jog-trot. He is always musical, sometimes unforgettably so, but his tunes are his own, and you never feel that he

has allowed them to shape his thought. His faithfulness to his meaning is allowed to yield its own music.

He is the master of first lines. To go through his first lines in the archive . . . is like reading one huge mysterious poem. No poet could live up to so many splendid beginnings: grandiloquent ones such as "Darkness has cheating swiftness," "What evil coil of fate has fastened me," "Smudgy dawn scarfed with military colours"; and interestingly conversational ones, like "One comes across the strangest things in walks." (That is probably the single most important thing to say about Gurney: he is almost always interesting.) He is also capable of magnificent, poem-saving, last lines.

In between, there are sometimes flaws which are obvious: flat phrases, quirky ones, confusing syntax. These are often unfortunate later additions, but not always. He is a poet, on the whole, who should not be read line by line. His poems are more like jets of energy that hurry to their end. The bubbles, the hollow places, do not diminish the force of the jet if you allow yourself to be carried along with it. Even at his most contorted, his general meaning usually comes clear if we persist, not stopping, to the end; and individual obscurities clarify themselves when we go back. Gurney did however write some perfect poems (like **"The Songs I Had"**)—he is good at the short sprint, the poem expressed in two or three breaths.

But perfection of that kind is not what he was interested in. He is not a Georgian poet who "broke down" but one who consciously though unprogrammatically broke away, and was, as far as he knew, on his own, fortified by his beloved Whitman. His subjects are conventional, but the intensity with which he sees and expresses them is not. He knew this, and one can sense his impatience with his more popular contemporaries because their matter—hedgerows, skies and so on—he considered peculiarly his own. So, "free of useless fashions," he tries to go behind their verse, behind the verse of preceding centuries, back to his "masters," the Elizabethans and Jacobeans, in much the same way as the Lake poets went back to the Ballads. The impatience is in his language, as though he wished to be as free as the Elizabethans in fashioning a new one. He wants a poetry composed on the nerves, "a book that brings the clear / Spirit of him that wrote" (**"To Long Island First"**), and he hurls himself headlong, so that we feel "The football rush of him," as he says in admiration of George Chapman. The result is, although Gurney tells us surprisingly little about himself, that we feel he has entirely opened his heart; there is nothing withheld, or prudent.

In fact the imprudence is so obvious that any fool could have warned him that it would end in tears. The tragedy is that it did. A tragedy for us as well as for him because it seems to imply what we must not believe: that it is not possible to live—sanely—with such intensity. Whereas his advice (**"The New Poet"**) is entirely sane:

> Let him say all men's thought nor sleep until
> Some great thing he has fashioned of love inevita-
>   ble.
> For the rest, may he follow his happiness' true will.

(pp. 10-15)

Perhaps Gurney's time has now come. If we are, as we think we are, an age that admires honesty, it must be clear that there is seldom any striving for effect, any "putting it on," in Gurney; none at all after 1920. He wrung the neck of his early elegance ("no swank"). What may have seemed naive and unpolished to his contemporaries has for us the stamp of sincerity. He says of his own poems (**"As They Draw to a Close"**):

> When you were launched there was small rough-
>   ness in the touch of words,
> A woman's weapon, a boy's chatter, a thing for bar-
>   ter and loss:

And he goes on to claim, with justice, adopting the persona of Walt Whitman but surely talking about himself:

> But I have roughed the soul American or Yankee
>   at least to truth and instinct,
> And compacted the loose-drifting faiths and ques-
>   tions of men in a few words.

Like Whitman, he was concerned with finding and touching the core of innocence in his own nature and he addressed himself to ours. (p. 22)

> *P. J. Kavanagh, in an introduction to* Collected
> Poems of Ivor Gurney, *edited by P. J. Kavanagh,*
> *Oxford University Press, Oxford, 1982, pp. 1-22.*

DONALD DAVIE   (essay date 1983)

[*An English poet, critic, educator, and translator, Davie is respected for both his creative and critical contributions to literature. During the 1950s Davie was associated with The Movement, a group of poets, including Philip Larkin, Kingsley Amis, and Thom Gunn, who emphasized restrained language, traditional syntax, and the moral and social implications of art. In the following excerpt, Davie discusses* Collected Poems of Ivor Gurney *and* Ivor Gurney: War Letters.]

Some episodes in the history of Gurney's poems are enough to put most of us out of countenance: in particular, the indifference that greeted Blunden's selection in 1954, published by Hutchinson, and also Leonard Clark's Chatto selection of 1973, for which Clark himself put up some of the money. It's true that Blunden, thinking his own poems didn't fit the fashions of the early Fifties, tried to second-guess the reviewers by making an eccentric selection from Gurney; and both he and Clark handled only what are now seen to be inaccurate typescripts. All the same, there should have been someone, on both occasions, able to stand back from the rivalries with his contemporaries for long enough to see virtue in this poet who had died in an asylum in 1937. Certainly I blush to recall that it was the Russian poet Joseph Brodsky, a year ago in Nashville, Tennessee, who asked me if Gurney didn't excite me, and I wasn't able to answer.

It is hard to find excuses. Both Blunden and Clark printed, for instance, **"Townshend"**—a poem that honours a man who was patron to Ben Jonson:

> Knowing Jonson labouring like the great son he
>   was
> Of Solway and of Westminster—O, maker, maker,
> Given of all the gods to anything but grace.
> And kind as all the apprentices knew and scholars;
> A talker with battle honours till dawn whitened
>   the curtains,
> With many honourers, and many many enemies,
>   and followers.

The third line here conveys what Leavis would call "a limiting judgment"; and this had been anticipated in a poem to Beethoven that appeared in Blunden's selection, and Clark's (and also in *Music and Letters* in 1927):

> You have our great Ben's mastery and a freer
> Carriage of method, spice of the open air . . .
> Which he, our greatest builder, had not so:
> Not as his own at least but acquired to.

The judgment on Jonson limits him indeed, but only in the sense that it defines and characterises his excellence: not in any way to devalue "our great Ben," "our greatest builder," "labouring like the great son he was." And nothing more clearly marks off Gurney in his generation. Many of that generation vowed themselves, as Gurney did, to the great Elizabethans and Jacobeans, but no one else gave pride of place to the most *laborious* of those masters. Gurney sets no store at all by "spontaneity," except as an effect, an illusion achieved by great labour. And even the effect, precisely because he had himself achieved it in his beautifully mellifluous early work—see **"Only the Wanderer"** from *Severn and Somme,* or **"To His Love"** from *War's Embers*—ceased to be anything that he aimed for at all often. Labour, hard study and relentless practice, making, *building*—the emphasis is constant. Moreover, from P. J. Kavanagh's warm and judicious Introduction [to *Collected Poems of Ivor Gurney* (see excerpt dated 1982)], but also from the poems themselves, we get the clear impression that Gurney in the years after demobilisation went without sleep, went without food, quite simply overworked himself into his mental breakdown—which certainly wasn't any direct consequence of his trench-experiences. So far from being a nature-poet, Gurney is a poet of, and ultimately a martyr to, Art. He knows, and repeatedly asserts, that all the beauties of his beloved Gloucestershire are fugitive and therefore unconsoling unless someone like himself—and there *is* no one else, as he knows exultantly—can catch and seal them in the art of music or the art of poetry, or in the two arts married.

The strenuousness of this conception is not only asserted in the poems, it is enacted there, as in the wrenched compactness of "Given of all the gods to anything but grace," or (the same point rephrased) "Not as his own at least but acquired-to." Both phrases are perfectly clear, yet each is as far as possible from what the insufferable Robert Nye commends in the diction of [Geoffrey] Grigson: "how close that idiom comes to living speech." Much virtue in that "living"! For Gurney, the life that there is in English speech has been injected into it by lonely, learned and masterfully artificial speakers like Ben Jonson; our conviction that life in our speech is found on the contrary in what is casually spoken, and as casually overheard, in a corner of the saloon bar—this is the most likely, at all events the most respectable, reason why the poet Ivor Gurney has never yet got from us what, as he knew, he deserved. "A freer/Carriage of method"—this too has never been heard in any saloon-bar but how much more of the history of our tongue, how much more resonance, how much more *life* it has, than anything that might be heard there!

Gurney's third collection, *Rewards of Wonder,* was rejected and never published. (Nor was any other in his lifetime.) The publishers were right to reject it, and Gurney was right to be undeterred. . . . *Rewards of Wonder* seems to represent a violent mutilation by this lyrical poet of his lyric voice. There is one exercise after another in headlong mostly couplet rhyme, much of the time intolerably strained and grotesque, looping up extremely heterogeneous matter into six-foot or even seven-foot accentual lines. One such poem is called

The opening of Gurney's setting of John Masefield's poem "By a Bierside."

"What I Will Pay" (he means, for artistic mastery) and what Gurney will pay is unceasing work, and emulation of "Beethoven, Bach, Jonson," all so that he may "write fair on strict thought-pages." The harvest of this violence, the reward for which this price was paid, would come later.

It came soon, in the more than a hundred poems [included in *Collected Poems of Ivor Gurney*] that P. J. Kavanagh dates between May 1919 and September 1922, when Gurney was committed to a private asylum, Barnwood House, Gloucester. These are the poems that tell us we are in the presence of a great poet. Not many of them are consummated masterpieces. We shall be told that Gurney was too big a poet to bother about perfection. But this is, to take a leaf out of Grigson, piffle. All poets worth their salt, and Gurney among them certainly, aim at perfection: but when poems are coming at the rate of one or more a week over a period of two years, there just isn't time for perfecting. Accordingly, this work is rich in magnificent torsoes, passages of breathtaking mastery following starts that are merely and hastily roughed in. My fingers itch to copy them out. What strikes first is Gurney's unfailing touch with what Barbara Herrnstein Smith has taught us to call "closures." Even in *Rewards of Wonder* this had been evident, when brutally rhymed pieces would abandon rhyme so as to end on a heartbreaking cadence. Similarly here many a rough-and-ready piece is all but redeemed at the last moment by a closing line that is much more than a summing-up or a sweet coming-round: "And his man's friendliness so good to have, and lost so soon," or "And beauty brief in action as first dew." What is even more

to the point, because it is new, is Gurney's mastery of decorum. He now has at his command any number of distinct styles, and he chooses one or another according as the occasion requires: the ceremonious stateliness of **"Sonnet to J. S. Bach's Memory"** can be let down to turn a graceful compliment on the bicentenary of a local paper (**"On a Two-Hundredth Birthday"**). The lyric voice, so savagely extirpated from *Rewards of Wonder,* can now be re-admitted because the poet has a sure sense of when it is appropriate, when not. The influences—Hopkins in **"George Chapman—The Iliad,"** Edward Thomas in **"On Foscombe Hill"** and **"Up There"** and possibly **"Imitation,"** Jonson in **"We Who Praise Poets,"** Whitman and possibly D. H. Lawrence in **"Felling a Tree"**— are discernible but never for certain, because so thoroughly assimilated and turned to purposes that the originals would not have contemplated. **"Felling a Tree"** draws on the Romanticism of Whitman and/or Lawrence to enforce a thoroughly classical, because Roman-imperialist, sentiment. (Gurney is keenly aware of the Roman presence in his Gloucestershire.) And similarly **"We Who Praise Poets"** is not Jonsonian pastiche, because its Jonsonian diction is carried on a more than Jonsonian restiveness and barely controlled turbulence in the metre. Of the ten or so poems in this section that *are* perfected, Blunden or Clark or both picked up several: **"The Sea Borders"** (very Whitmanesque), **"Andromeda over Tewkesbury," "Clay," "The Bare Line of the Hill," "The Cloud," "From the Meadows—The Abbey," "The Not-Returning," "Looking There"** and **"Sonnet—September 1922."** They missed **"We Who Praise Poets,"** and also **"The Valley Farm"**:

> Ages ago the waters covered here
> And took delight of dayspring as a mirror;
> Hundreds of tiny spikes and threads of light.
> But now the spikes are hawthorn, and the hedges
> Are foamed like ocean's crests, and peace waits
>   here
>
> Deeper than middle South Sea, or the Fortunate
> Or Fabled Islands. And blue wood-smoke rising
> Foretells smooth weather and the airs of peace.
>
> Even the woodchopper swinging bright
> His lithe and noble weapon in the sun
> Moves with such grace peace works an act through
>   him;
>
> Those echoes thud and leave a deeper peace.
> If war should come here only then might one
> Regret water receding, and earth left
> To bear man's grain and use his mind of order,
> Working to frame such squares and lights as these.

The runover, "Fortunate/Or Fabled," is magisterial, and so is the audacious handling of the pentameter three lines from the end. Moreover, Gurney is in earnest: so far is the Severn valley from being a constant standard by which history's vacillations are judged, it is itself, and rightly, a symptom or register of man's history—let it be inundated afresh, and removed from man's dominion, if that dominion eventuates in what Gurney had seen in France. . . . [Far] more than Isaac Rosenberg's war, Gurney's is the war of the private infantryman, as against the subalterns' war of Owen or Grenfell, Sassoon or Blunden or Graves. Because he is not of the officer class, he feels no responsibility for the horror, hence no guilt about it, and so his revulsion from it is manageable. He is nearer to David Jones; one "soldiers on." His revulsion and protest come later, when post-war England makes light of its soldiers' sacrifices: "How England should take as common their vast endurance/ And let them be but boys having served time overseas." As Jeremy Hooker has noted, the crucial word is "honour": England refuses to honour the draft that Gurney, as soldier, musician and poet, has drawn upon her. And so in the poems of this period we detect increasingly a note that may be called confessional or indignant or both; as in **"Quiet Fireshine," "Kettle Song," "The Bronze Sounding," "Strange Hells"**; mounting in Mr. Kavanagh's arrangement to a crescendo of accusation in **"The Not-Returning," "Looking There"** and **"Sonnet—September 1922,"** all three of them consummated statements. (pp. 6-7)

The next poems, written in asylums, reveal immediately a development least to be expected by anyone who has followed Gurney's career to this point: his style becomes plain.

> Why have you made life so intolerable
> And set me between four walls, where I am able
> Not to escape meals without prayer, for that is
>   possible
> Only by annoying an attendant. And tonight a
>   sensual
> Hell has been put on me, so that all has deserted
>   me
> And I am merely crying and trembling in heart
> For death, and cannot get it. And gone out is
>   part
> Of sanity. And there is dreadful hell within me.

That is addressed **"To God,"** and though it is the cry of a soul in torment, it is also poetry. Nor does the plain diction come only with anguished themes: we find it in **"Cut Flowers,"** or in **"The Mangel-Bury,"** which starts out with the astonishing plainness of "It was after war; Edward Thomas had fallen at Arras. . . ."

By this stage we are no longer reading for pleasure, in any ordinary sense. If there is gratification (as there is), it is of the unearthly and inhuman sort that has to do with the indomitable spirit of Man, or suchlike unmanageable notions. And in any case Gurney is by now deranged. After the appalling plainness of a poem called **"An Appeal for Death,"** there come 30 poems which are, with only one or two exceptions and marginal cases, unhinged, incoherent. Blunden and Clark are to blame for printing many of these, and even Mr. Kavanagh, who says finely, "It is a period from which an editor would like to rescue him," seems to think some of these pieces can be salvaged. We have all heard about "the lunatic, the lover and the poet": but not Shakespeare nor anyone else can excuse us for being light-minded and unfeeling about the madnesses of mad poets. There are those who positively welcome such disorder, as if it authenticated a poet's vocation. But great poetry is greatly sane, greatly lucid; and insanity is as much a calamity for poets and for poetry as for other human beings and other sorts of human business.

Much more surprising and admirable is a group of half a dozen poems on American themes, which both Blunden and Clark significantly passed over. They are entirely sane, because judicious: on Whitman, on Thoreau, on Washington Irving, on George Washington's America (**"Portraits"**— perhaps the finest reflection on American history by an Englishman), Gurney passes firmly a commonsensical and limiting but in no way deflating judgment, just such as he had pronounced on Jonson. **"The New Poet"** and **"To Long Island First"** ought to derail in advance the attempt that will doubtless be made to enrol Gurney in the service of a supposedly native alternative to "modernism." Apparently there is a

great deal more Whitmanesque writing yet to see the light: for Mr. Kavanagh's exemplary edition is, it should be noted, a "Collected" not a "Complete," and there is some hint of the riches yet to be uncovered in, for instance, the splendid and not at all Whitmanesque **"Motetts of William Byrd,"** dated January 1925, which is relegated to an Appendix.

Astonishingly, the piteous story had still not run its course. There was, it seems, around September 1926, one more spurt of poetic energy; and it produced, along with more of that painful incoherence to which we are too ready to accord "rough power," work of a quite unprecedented kind which Mr. Kavanagh calls "timeless classical utterance." "Classical," I think, can be given a quite precise meaning. For in one of several poems where Gurney tries with some success to reconcile himself to what he sees as England's ingratitude, he adjures swallows to abandon England in favour of "the shelves / Of Apennine . . . or famed Venetian border"; and in a series of short but exquisite pieces that might even be called "imagist" Gurney evokes with plangent severity Graeco-Roman or Mediterranean emblems like Pan or "a cup of red clay/ Sparkling with bright water." The failure of this manoeuvre is also recorded—in a piece called (the title tells its own tale) **"Here, If Forlorn."** Mr. Kavanagh says of these poems that "though sometimes good, they seem bloodless compared to the previous work"—and the sentiment is understandable, though it will not be shared by readers who set less store by "blood" than by a pure diction. The last poem in the volume, **"As They Draw to a Close,"** is Whitmanesque and magnificent.

To most people, I daresay, and in most ways, Gurney the letter-writer will seem more engaging than Gurney the poet. It is from the letters, naturally enough, that we get the most vivid impression of Gurney's courage, his cheerfulness, his deprecating humorous tact, his anxiety under the most adverse circumstances to entertain, to have and provide *fun*. And yet the Gurney of the letters is, by and large, the author only of the less consequential poems. Partly this is because R. K. R. Thornton, working on a limited budget, chose reasonably enough to represent [in his volume of Gurney's letters] only the soldier, the Gurney who was yet to write the poems by which he has a claim on us. In fact, the Gurney who writes from the trenches still thinks of himself as musician first, poet a long way second; who accordingly measures his fellow musicians against a far more exacting standard than his fellow poets. Hence his extraordinary response to a magazine sent to him in France by his devoted correspondent, Marion Scott: "just what England needed—a magazine devoted to the interests of weak but sincere verse. Local poetry, local poetry is Salvation, and the more written the better." This is the same letter in which he harshly judges the musician Granville Bantock as "diffuse and ineffectual, and needs a great deal of material to make any effect." For Gurney in 1917 poetry was not a fine art, as music was, and so he can quite blithely accept that his poems do not meet the standards of Robert Bridges, or of Milton behind Bridges. Yeats's *Responsibilities* did force him reluctantly to acknowledge that poetry, too, exacts a discipline, that spontaneous imperfection and "sincerity" and local loyalties won't suffice for: "You will find that when I come to work again, I also shall show much greater scrupulousness than before. . . ." That was a perception, however, that Gurney at that point couldn't hold on to. And his free-wheeling or lighthearted oscillation about past masters like Milton or Wordsworth, or about near-contemporaries like Rupert Brooke and Sassoon, reinforces the testimony of teachers at the Royal College of Music before the war—that Gurney was unteachable. For all his charming self-deprecations, Gurney was, before and during the war and after it, wilful, headstrong. And this, though it just may have been the precondition of his achieving what he did, seems to have prolonged his apprenticeship to the point where the strain of it broke a personality diagnosed and self-diagnosed as "neurasthenic." And incidentally, does "neurasthenia" have a different or firmer meaning now than it had in 1912 or 1917? Uninstructed about this, we are quite at a loss before Gurney's aborted suicide attempt in 1918.

Gurney in 1915 approached poetry through the mish-mash of ignorant and sentimental prejudices that we call, as Gurney did himself, "Georgian." Though within a few years his trench experience, on the one hand, and, on the other, his readings in Whitman and Tolstoy, had shown him how the Georgian frame of reference would not hold up, we have no evidence, from the documents so far put before us, that he radically rethought his originally Georgian position. And if he didn't, the consequent gulf between theory and practice must have been one more disruptive tension inside a personality that always was, and knew itself to be, precariously balanced. How inadequate the Georgian vocabulary was for explaining to him where he had got to, and what he must do next, appeared from his verdict on his own *Severn and Somme:* "I have made a book about Beauty because I have paid the price which five years ago had not been paid. Some day perhaps the True, the real, the undeniable will be shown by me and I forgive all this." If we translate the Keatsian or sub-Keatsian vocabulary, we can see that this was a just and unsparing assessment of himself at this stage: but how obfuscating is this opposition of undefined Beauty to undefined Truth! And how incapable Gurney was of probing beneath such lax formulations may be seen from his sole comment on Imagism: "As for the Imagists—I hate all attempts at exact definition of beauty, which is a half-caught thing, a glimpse." What survives him, not dated at all but a persistent claim upon us, is "I have paid the price." He had indeed: and in these letters we see him paying it.

This Gurney was a prodigious poet; beside his achievement, Wilfred Owen's and Edward Thomas's seem slender at best. And Eliot? And Pound? Why yes, take them too in, say, 1925, and Gurney had outdistanced them—in the range of first-hand experience he could wrestle into verse, and even in the range of past masters in English whom he could coerce and emulate so as to digest that experience. The strain of the achievement was intolerable, and it broke him. Just why or how, it's impossible to say: though it seems that he soon set his face against irony, and irony, which we have overvalued for so long, is often—as we have learned to our cost—self-defensive. (p. 7)

Donald Davie, "Gurney's Flood," in London Review of Books, *Vol. 5, No. 2, February 3-16, 1983, pp. 6-7.*

ANDREW WATERMAN (essay date 1983)

[*Waterman is an English poet best known for his collection* Out for the Elements *(1981). In the following excerpt, he examines Gurney's evolution from a minor soldier-poet to an artist whose works are highly original in style and theme.*]

Gurney's poetry of his years between wartime army service and incarceration in the asylum in 1922, augmented less consistently by his writing during at least the first four years of the confinement which ended with his death from tuberculosis in 1937, shows a startling transformation of minor talent into adventurous creative genius; a poet who indeed "modernised himself all on his own," in imaginative perspectives, method, and language.

> The high hills have a bitterness
> Now they are not known
> And memory is poor enough consolation
> For the soul hopeless gone.
>
> Up in the air there beech tangles wildly in the
>   wind—
> That I can imagine
> But the speed, the swiftness, walking into clarity,
> Like last year's bryony is gone.

"The High Hills" shows how for Gurney knowledge meant experience, something lived not merely visualisable; and he lived at a rare pitch not only of intensity but of avidity. His slide towards madness seems not to have been primarily consequent upon his war service, although Gurney was wounded, gassed, and eventually discharged in October 1918 with "deferred shell-shock." The effects of such experience are of course incalculable, and its "embers" indeed glowed long in Gurney's imagination. But among war poetry Gurney's direct accounts of trench life, far from being cries of horrified protest, are uniquely balanced, amused where possible, unportentous. But his passionate need to preserve, in music or poems, life as it stirred him, rendered its hollows of routine orderliness and dutiful tasks, once he escaped military regimentation, unmanageable trivialities. **"Moments"** utters a sheer pain that "high autumn goes beyond my pen / And snow lies inexprest in the deep lane." The obverse of such avidity could be a hopeless unrest at its inevitable frustration, leaving Gurney craving the foreclosure of death equally in earnest. "Will there be one regret left" he asks in **"When I Am Covered,"**

> One sentimental fib of light and day—
> A grief for hillside and the beaten trees?
> Better to leave them, utterly to go away.

But **"The Escape"** expresses his happier, and creative, credo:

> I believe in the increasing of life: Whatever
> Leads to the seeing of small trifles,
> Real, beautiful, is good; and an act never
> Is worthier than in freeing spirit that stifles
> Under ingratitude's weight, nor is anything done
> Wiselier than the moving or breaking to sight
> Of a thing hidden under by custom—revealed,
> Fulfilled, used (sound-fashioned) any way out to
>   delight:
> Trefoil—hedge sparrow—the stars on the edge at
>   night.

His poem **"The Lock Keeper"** is a sustained celebration of the textures and minutiae of its protagonist's physical and mental being; while **"The Dearness of Common Things"** embraces

> Beech wood, tea, plate shelves,
> And the whole family of crockery,
> Woodaxes, blades, helves.
> Ivory milk, earth's coffee,
> The white face of books
> And the touch, feel, smell of paper.
> Latin's lovely looks.

Gurney's moments of epiphany were occasioned not only by the Gloucestershire landscape which so watermarked his spirit, but by small domestic things, architectural forms, the past poetry and music he knew so passionately; and his recurrent frissons of historical awareness in a county whose contemporary landscape had Roman undertones, so that when "A coin was ploughed up, heating thought till it sudden grew ruddy and glowed" the poet yearns towards "the Roman that lost this small penny-thing" (**"The Coin"**). For him, army life in Northern France reiterated surprisingly much of such experience:

> Riez Bailleul in blue tea-time
> Called back the Severn lanes, the roads
> Where the small ash leaves lie, and floods
> Of hawthorn leaves turned with the night's rime.

It added not only the utterly contrasting dimension of violent battle—"But the trench thoughts will not go" he must soon in **"Riez Bailleul"** allow—but also resonances rare in Gurney's poems with English settings, of human comradeship: "Tea finished; the dixies dried of the wet. / Some walk, some write, and the cards begin."

Of such things is Gurney's poetry made. Outside the communal context of army life, where affinities and interchange flicker, it includes little of interpersonal human emotions; but reading Gurney one may conclude that even without intense relationships life was all too much for him. Certainly his creativity functioned as a therapy, richly though so many of its products transcend the category. By the age of thirty-six, when in the asylum his creativity petered out, he had written about nine hundred poems and two hundred and sixty-five songs, as well as instrumental music. The bulk and best of his achievement in both forms occurred from 1919 to 1922. (pp. 4-7)

His continual writing of the earlier asylum years includes "appeals" "for Death," for "chance to work," often addressed to the Prime Minister or the English Police. Pervasive is a hurt that England had subsequently rejected her wartime soldiers. "There are strange hells within the minds war made," he begins a poem written shortly before his committal. Characteristically these turn out to be not those "one would have expected"—and **"Strange Hells"** vividly evokes the Gloucesters quelling their first bombardment by singing "That tin and stretched-wire tinkle, that blither of tune: / "Après la guerre fini," till all hell had come down"—but their later shame "on state-doles or showing shop-patterns."

But much of Gurney's asylum poetry is astonishingly untainted by the obsessions, incoherences, least of all the physical immediacies, of his insanity. In 1915 he had commented: "Rupert Brooke would not have improved with age, would not have broadened; his manner had become a mannerism, both in rhyme and diction. I do not like it. . . . Great poets, great creators are not much influenced by immediate events: these must sink in to the very foundations and be absorbed." His trenchant perception of Brooke's Georgian parameters implies Gurney's early understanding that his own poetry must live by evolving; the concluding generalisation unwittingly anticipates a test he would surmount heroically when the asylum confronted him with its extremes. The poetry Gurney wrote in confinement scarcely ever adverts to his present surroundings. **"To God"** provides a rare annotation of "life so intolerable" set "between four walls, where I am able / Not to escape meals without prayer, for that is possible

/ Only by annoying an attendant. . . ." Later in the same poem, "Gone out every bright thing from my mind" is poignantly of a piece with the pain other poems occasionally cry out without circumstantial documentation. But mostly Gurney's poetry of this time is not only sane, but uninfluenced by "immediate events" occupies itself with the "foundations" of his being: the Gloucestershire he would never again see, the war and its comradeship, literary and musical loves, other memories. Many poems show meticulous shapings of rhythm and teasings out of thought and image, which testify to Gurney's sustained absorption in his creative craft despite his predicament. **"The Incense Bearers"** illustrates all this:

> Toward the sun the drenched May hedges lift
> White rounded masses like still ocean-drift
> And day fills with the heavy scent of that gift.
>
> There is no escaping that full current of thick
> Incense; one walks, suddenly one comes quick
> Into a flood of odour there, aromatic,
>
> Not English; for cleaner, sweeter, is the hot scent
>   that
> Is given from hedges, solitary flowers, not
> In mass, but lonely odours that scarcely float.
>
> But the incense bearers, soakers of sun's full
> Powerfulness, give out floods unchecked, wonder-
>   ful
> Utterance almost, which makes no poet grateful,
>
> Since his love is for single things rarely found,
> Or hardly: violets blooming in remote ground,
> One colour, one fragrance, like one unaccompanied
>   sound
>
> Struck upon silence, nothing looked-for. Hung
> As from gold wires this May incense is swung,
> Heavy of odour, the drenched meadows among.

We exactly apprehend Gurney's sensibility there through the consummate artistry with which he articulates its response to a specific experience. The poet is fully in command of his expression, its thought, imagery, and rhythms. The precision with which cadence enacts feeling shows, as do Edward Thomas's poems, how fully an original imagination could utter itself by variation within, rather than wholesale rejection of, given metrical forms lesser versifiers padded out mechanically.

Imprisoning his person, Gurney's predicament did not constrain his artistic freedom. This included freedom to objectify his own plight, which becomes a tacit, assimilated charge in his feelings about **"Cut Flowers"**:

> These wild things cruelly tamed—
> Taken from the blowing day
> Exiled, uprooted, hurt, lamed,
> That the hedgerows miss and the copse.
> O if flowers must be cut
> To spoil an earth plot's hopes
> Take them with eyes shut. . . .

One detours into writing of Gurney's sad life not gratuitously for the sake of biographical curiosity, but because Gurney's was a tragedy of intensity, and the intensity was the heart of what his talent shaped to poetry. The uncomfortable truth that what made him a poet destroyed him as a person confronts criticism with its bleak paradox. It should be said, however, that even when pain distorts or mars his work's literary validities, anything Gurney writes remains not only "almost always interesting," which [P. J.] Kavanagh rightly insists is "probably the single most important thing to say about Gurney" [see excerpt dated 1982], but infused with a delicate integrity and yearning for beauty that throughout all endured intact.

Gurney's literary claims rest on about two hundred of his poems. Among these, many show his invariable attentive authenticity of feeling achieving quite masterful expression. His double gift for music and poetry was itself of course astonishing. The musician Michael Hurd, whose 1978 biography *The Ordeal of Ivor Gurney* [see Additional Bibliography] provides one's information about its subject's life, judges: "He must be admitted to the galaxy of great British song composers." Gurney's wartime letters show him strongly aware of his creative potential, indeed formidably ambitious, but making music his priority:

> If only once I can get to the stage of being able to think high and sustainedly for only two pages, as Prelude I Book II (the 48)! Then all the world shall have grace to know of the beauty of my County, of stars, and moving water, of friendship and the companionable solace of tobacco; all in little black dots of notes and fiddle sounds and the harshest touches of the piano, but not in words, for towards Literature I feel slightly contemptuous. "All art strives constantly to the precondition of music."

Music retained this loyalty, not least as his fullest emotional expression. Hurd quotes an unpublished essay written in the 1920s where Gurney describes Wordsworth's *Prelude* as "but the shadow and faint far-off indication of what Music might do—the chief use of poetry seeming to be . . . to stir the spirit to the height of music, the maker to create, the listener worthily receive or remember." Hurd adds: "later, commenting on his own creativity, he wrote that 'the bright visions brought music; the fainter verse or mere pleasurable emotion'."

But that this fidelity to music's purer intensities did not leave Gurney a dilettante in the denotative art of verse is demonstrated not only by the meticulous working of his imaginative apprehensions into individual poems, but by the pressures of his sustained development away from Georgian routines of theme and form. He had foreseen the need in his 1915 comments on Brooke; but with the letter containing them he enclosed a sonnet, **"To the Poet before Battle,"** which Brooke might have contrived on an off-day:

> Now, youth, the hour of thy dread passion comes;
> Thy lovely things must all be laid away;
> And thou, as others, must face the riven day
> Unstirred by rattle of the rolling drums. . . .

But Gurney immediately abandoned such platform-address to audience. In **"Strange Service,"** another early *Severn and Somme* poem, the voice is already intimate, the home thoughts from abroad nakedly accessible to a corresponding innocence in the reader:

> I was a dreamer ever, and bound to your dear service,
> Meditating deep, I thought on your secret beauty,
> As through a child's face one may see the clear spirit
> Miraculously shining.

> Your hills not only hills, but friends of mine and kindly,
> Your tiny knolls and orchards hidden behind the river
> Muddy and strongly-flowing, with shy and tiny streamlets
> Safe in its bosom.

Conventional enough in subject and some trappings—Georgian writing was all too fond of diminutive adjectives—this is wholly personal to Gurney in its sensibility, and cadences. Some of the *Severn and Somme* poems aspire indeed to the condition of music, and virtually achieve it, for example **"Song"**:

> Only the wanderer
>   Knows England's graces,
> Or can anew see clear
>   Familiar faces.
>
> And who loves joy as he
>   That dwells in shadows?
> Do not forget me quite,
>   O Severn meadows.

Others annotate army life, its lulls where imagination blossoms as well as its fears and horrors, naturalistically enough.

Gurney was well read in contemporary verse, where the Georgians were the dominant presence. Although sharply discriminating among them, in 1918 he found the poets in Marsh's third Georgian anthology overall "very interesting, very much in earnest, and very gifted; out of them a great poet should come." His early letters also confirm the conventional aspiration his poem **"Time and the Soldier"** formulates, "Beauty's my master." This is all understandable. Gurney evidently turned to writing verse when, in war circumstances, insufficient access to a piano inhibited musical composition. It was naturally from Georgianism he first took his bearings. After the war, the dynamic of his compulsive, and attentive, creativity carried Gurney far beyond Georgian routines of content and expression. Discovering through writing what Eliot would later define as "the essential advantage for a poet . . . to be able to see beneath both beauty and ugliness; to see the boredom, and the horror, and the glory," Gurney flexed language and rhythms to encompass the abundance he felt. **"The Sea Borders"** offers analogy for the containing effort of musical composition:

> I musician have wrestled with the stuff in making
> And wrought a square thing out of my stubborn mind—
> And gathered a huge surge of spirit as the great barriers bind
> The whole Atlantic at them by Devon or West Ireland.

This holds for his poetic labour too. It was not Gurney's nature to bite off less than he could chew. While never, as poems already quoted show, abandoning his gift for haunting lyric verse, he evolved new strategies to accommodate disparate materials and tones, elisions of sequence or syntax to create telling juxtapositions.

The war had of course supplied experience requiring such response. Like Rosenberg and David Jones, but unlike most who wrote creatively about the war, Gurney served as a private, and has the appropriate perspective on events. Owen's poetry can slip into a sentimentalised officer's-eye-view of war's victims as undifferentiated "boys" from rural "sad shires." Gurney was one of those boys. As a private soldier his was not to reason why, but only to do as he was told, and to try not to die; occasionally to hanker for a "Blighty" wound, and meanwhile to enjoy comradeship and wangle as much incidental solace as circumstances allowed. His poetry vivifies this unidealising conspectus as does no other except David Jones's *In Parenthesis,* which was not published until the year of Gurney's death. **"To the Poet before Battle,"** written while Gurney was training in England, aspired "to make / The name of poet terrible in just war, / And like a crown of honour upon the fight." After the event, he wrote in quite different vein, not omitting war's pain and horror, but often enacting in verse its relaxed interstices; moments of "tea-talk," thoughts of Bach, a stroll to see "Tangled in twigs, the silver crescent clear" (**"After-Glow"**); in **"La Gorgue,"** "a Making-delay" is celebrated, a French house above a canal to which "privates as wasps to sugar" repair for coffee and hospitality. A retrospective asylum poem, **"The Bohemians,"** characteristic in being at once moving and entertaining, combines mature human discrimination with elegy:

> Certain people would not clean their buttons,
> Nor polish buckles after latest fashions,
> Preferred their hair long, putties comfortable,
> Barely escaped hanging, indeed hardly able;
> In Bridge and smoking without army cautions
> Spending hours that sped like evil for quickness,
> (While others burnished brasses, earned promotions).
> These were the ones who jested in the trench,
> While others argued of army ways, and wrenched
> What little soul they had still further from shape,
>
> And died off one by one, or became officers.
> Without the first of dream, the ghost of notions
> Of ever becoming soldiers, or smart and neat,
> Surprised as ever to find the army capable
> Of sounding "Lights Out" to break a game of
>   Bridge,
> As to fear candles would set a barn alight:
> In Artois or Picardy they lie—free of useless fashions.

Gurney's ranging attentiveness to the actual texture of experience, and capacity for unusual connections, show when in **"First Time In"** he sardonically disposes of preconceptions that the front is where " 'The stuff of tales is woven' " by this annotation of reaching it:

>   one took us courteously
> Where a sheet lifted, and gold light cautiously
> Streams from an oilsheet slitted vertical into
> Half-light of May. We entered, took stranger-view
> Of life as lived in the line, the line of war and daily
> Papers, despatches, brave-soldier talks, the really,
>   really
> Truly line, and these the heroes of the story.
>
> Never were quieter folk in teaparty history.
> Never in "Cranford," Trollope even. And as it
>   were, home
> Closed round us. They told us lore, how and when
>   did come
> Minnewerfers and grenades from over there east;
> The pleasant and unpleasant habits of the beast
> That crafted and tore Europe. What line-mending
>   was
> When guns centred and dug-outs rocked in a haze

> And hearing was difficult—(wires cut)—all necessary
> Common-sense workmanlike cautions of salutary
> Wisdom—the mechanic day-lore of modern war-
>   making,
> Calm thought discovered in mind and body shaking.

Then talk "turned personal." And so,

>   disputeless the romantic evening was
> The night, the midnight; next day Fritz strafed at
>   us,
> And I lay belly upward to wonder: when—but useless.

Such almost affectionate naturalism, combining colloquial language and wide perspectives, was not the sort of war poetry, either of glorification or protest, England expected in 1919 when Sidgwick & Jackson rejected Gurney's third collection *Rewards of Wonder.* He was far from insensitive to war's horrific waste. Writing to Marion Scott, in 1917, an account of bombardment, Gurney adds:

> Does it sound interesting? May God forgive me if I ever come to cheat myself into thinking that it was, and lie later to younger men of the Great Days. It was damnable. . . . We have been lucky, but it is not fit for men to be here—in this tormented dry-fevered marsh, where men die and are left to rot because of snipers and the callousness that War breeds. "It might be tomorrow. Who cares? Yet still, hang on for a Blighty."

And yet, the men who "contemplate such things . . . do not lose laughter nor the common kindliness that makes life sweet—And yet seem such boys—Yet what consolation can be given me as I look on and endure it?"

In **"The Silent One"** Gurney's various awarenesses resolve to a superb poem, showing the power he developed, after the transitional *Rewards of Wonder* writing where aspirations to heterogeneity could stretch him to bumpy couplets, to combine and unify disparate tones and material:

> Who died on the wires, and hung there, one of
>   two—
> Who for his hours of life had chattered through
> Infinite lovely chatter of Bucks accent:
> Yet faced unbroken wires; stepped over, and went
> A noble fool, faithful to his stripes—and ended.
> But I weak, hungry, and willing only for the chance
> Of line—to fight in the line, lay down under unbroken
> Wires, and saw the flashes and kept unshaken,
> Till the politest voice—a finicking accent, said:
> "Do you think you might crawl through there:
>   there's a hole."
> Darkness, shot at: I smiled, as politely replied—
> "I'm afraid not, Sir." There was no hole no way to
>   be seen
> Nothing but chance of death, after tearing of
>   clothes.
> Kept flat, and watched the darkness, hearing bullets whizzing—
> And thought of music—and swore deep heart's
>   deep oaths
> (Polite to God) and retreated and came on again,
> Again retreated—and a second time faced the
>   screen.

The dead soldier is no casual peg for sentiment but a mourned individual evoked in his "chatter of Bucks accent." Contrasting with his extinguished vitality is the "finicking voice" of the officer; and with an effect of widely diverse levels of apprehension converging, the guarded politeness of the helpless exchange of dialogue and Gurney's impassioned private oaths, his juxtaposed awarenesses of death and music, and sardonic annotation of tragic futility within the huge grinding repetitions of battle. The poem does not need to comment on the material it has composed to such telling pattern.

But the terrain most nourishing Gurney's poetry, whether he was physically there or inhabiting it imaginatively from the trenches and later the asylum, was Gloucestershire, the city and its environs, the Severn, the Cotswolds, the villages of Framilode, Maisemore, Hartpury, his poems cherish. Gurney's poetry transcribes rural detail with the prodigal fluent evocativeness of his admired Elizabethans: "White Cotswold, wine scarlet woods and leaf wreckage wet" (**"Old Thought"**); "Cowslips, celandine, buglewort and daisies / That trinket out the green swerves like a child's game" (**"Larches"**). The city's architecture, with its ancient towers, sanctioned Gurney's conception of form in the arts he practiced, his recurring analogue of framed squareness and the like for musical and poetic composition. And always in his poetry is the infinitely varying sky. He celebrates a native landscape that had for him the preternatural gleam of an Eden one can only lose, that the fields around Helpstone had for John Clare a century earlier. Thus both poets' local worlds, however particularised, indeed by virtue of their cherished details, have universal resonances, achieving their purest expression in lyrics such as **"The Songs I Had"** and **"The High Hills."** Personal Edens are precarious estates, betrayed not only by one's own aberrations but by the world's. Only incidentally a social critic, Gurney regrets such **"Changes"** as, where once "Peasants and willow pattern went together," now "Villas are set up where the sheepfolds were, / And plate glass impudent stares at the sun."

His valuing of each particular "thing hidden under by custom" as its irreplaceable self was intense. In that poem **"The Escape,"** as elsewhere, his idiom, terms like "wiselier" or the characteristic bracketed "(sound-fashioned)," and springing rhythms, as well as the sensibility, suggest an admiration for Hopkins. Gurney's first, 1916 encounter with the newly-discovered Victorian poet elicited only a complaint about "Hopkins or what's his names of the crazy precious diction." Here, as in other respects, Gurney lived and learned. However, although **"Felling a Tree"** salutes its victim's tragic fall, "Like Trafalgar's own sails imperiously moving to defeat," Gurney's sense of each thing's vulnerable uniqueness, unlike Hopkins's horror at the felling of his "Binsey Poplars," is tempered by pragmatic reflection that this, after all, is "the common fate of trees," and his "noble" ash has its future human use as "fuel for the bright kitchen—for brown tea, against cold night." And where Hopkins's poem is anguished at landscape's dislocation, as "Strokes of havoc unselve / The sweet especial scene," Gurney's thoughts have characteristically dwelt upon continuities, "Rome's hidden mild yoke / Still on the Gloucester heart strong after love's fill of centuries."

Walt Whitman, "Bought of me just a hesitator in old Gloucester" as an asylum poem given the American's name recalls, was a poet Gurney consciously took as exemplar. One sees how Whitman encouraged Gurney to risk in poetry elasticities of style serving an omnivorous imaginative appetite.

These songs of the earth and art, war's romances
   and stern . . .
The seaboard air encompasses me and draws my
   mind to sing nobly of ships . . .
Or the look of the April day draws anthems as of
   masters from me—
(O, it is not that I have been careless of the fashioned formal songs!)
For rough nature, for gracious reminder, I have
   sought all my days
For men and women of the two-fold asking, for democracy and courtesy wherever it showed.

Thus, in the asylum, Gurney writing **"As They Draw to a Close"** ventriloquises through Whitman his own imaginative affirmations. Whether or not admiration had deviated into mental confusion, this is not a voice English poetry had any use for in 1926. Yet at that time also, in the final outpouring of his poetry, Gurney's "fashioned formal songs" flowered also, as his lifelong immersion in Elizabethan lyrics gave rise to lucid classical verses of his own. **"Traffic in Sheets"** exquisitely laments his personal lost Eden:

> I could have sung, but knew no fitting tunes
> (For all my lore) of the spread
> Of coloured sheets of the flood that ensure all
>   June's
> Dark fan-grasses of the pretty head.

But Gurney's closest poetic affinities are with Edward Thomas. In 1917, sending Marion Scott Thomas's poems from hospital, Gurney commented: "But he had the same sickness of mind I have—the impossibility of serenity for any but the shortest space." Thomas, that other compulsive walker and depressive victim of an unstructured life, was constrained at least by deadlines for his literary hackwork and by family responsibilities, which Gurney never had as aids to practical functioning. His romance with a nurse, around the time of this comment, came to nothing. Both men seem to have found emotional relief in the involuntary regimentation of army life. Gurney had long admired his elder contemporary's prose writings on nature and people, which like the poems of his late fulfilment intimately realise the responding sensibility of their author. Later, Gurney set many of Thomas's poems to music. His own early poem **"Old Martinmas Eve"** recalls Thomas's paradoxical enactments, as in his similarly moonlit "Liberty," of an expansion of spirit registering chiefly through its frustration, around a still moment:

> If some most quiet tune had spoken then;
> Some silver thread of sound; a core within
> That sea-deep silentness, I had not known
> Ever such joy in peace, but sound was none—
> Nor should be till birds roused to find the dawn.

But Gurney's resemblances of perception and feeling are numerous, as his imagination is activated by "small trifles," contacts with nature, incidental toil, chance encounters as in **"The Mangel-Bury"** where a musing upon the war and Thomas's death is no accidental opening to a poem that has Gurney soon "heaving at those great rounded / Ruddy or orange things" to load the cart of a passing farmer. And, as Thomas can cherish "the dust on nettles" as readily as "the bloom on any flower," Gurney in **"The Garden"** is better pleased by "curly and plain cabbages" than "that ink-proud lady, the rose." But Gurney is more varied than Thomas, and of course more uneven, both within and among poems. Thomas's artistic triumph is to figure imagination resolving life's turbulence to steadiness, in poems achieving what Frost called "a momentary stay against confusion." Gurney's equally sincere temperament retained, as his shorter songs or a poem such as **"The Incense Bearers"** show, capacity for such poise, but was commonly willing to put it at risk in order to encompass life whole. In Gurney's asylum poems the disintegrations resulting from this impulse, which can have their own singular imaginative logic, cannot always be neatly disentangled from the incoherences of derangement. T. S. Eliot's notorious separation of "the man who suffers and the mind which creates" has of course its salutary application as pointer to what Gurney's poetry exemplifies, that in his own terms "creators are not much influenced by immediate events"; but at the level of what is absorbed "at the very foundations," the inextricable texture of Gurney's life and art are its refutation.

When his urge to wrestle "a square thing out of my stubborn mind" matches his Whitmanesque appetite, poems such as **"The Valley Farm"** result:

> Ages ago the waters covered here
> And took delight of dayspring as a mirror;
> Hundreds of tiny spikes and threads of light.
> But now the spikes are hawthorn, and the hedges
> Are foamed like ocean's crests, and peace waits
>   here
> Deeper than middle South Sea, or the Fortunate
> Or Fabled Islands. And blue wood-smoke rising
> Foretells smooth weather and the airs of peace.
>
> Even the woodchopper swinging bright
> His lithe and noble weapon in the sun
> Moves with such grace peace works an act through
>   him;
> Those echoes thud and leave a deeper peace.
> If war should come here only then might one
> Regret water receding, and earth left
> To bear man's grain and use his mind of order,
> Working to frame such squares and lights as these.

The shaping, of the whole and its vibrant details, is as remarkable as the poem's scope. Apropos the wholly characteristic stress placed within that scope Donald Davie, a late advocate of Gurney's merits, has pertinently observed: "so far is the Severn valley from being a constant standard by which history's vacillations are judged, it is itself, and rightly, a symptom or register of man's history," forfeit against extension of "what Gurney had seen in France" [see excerpt by Davie dated 1983].

Gurney's capacity to gather the most intense personal emotions to shaped forms, to art in which the emotion lives in the poem and not because one knows of the suffering beyond the poem, is demonstrated in two sonnets written directly prior to his committal. **"The Not-Returning"** refines to stark enactment the desperation of loss, a stripping of every joy and peace and spiritual expansion to leave "Only the restless searching, the bitter labour, / The going out to watch stars, stumbling blind through the difficult door." That placing of "difficult" shows artistic judgment mastering its painful material. The bare statement of this poem is complemented by the rich original figurative concepts in **"Sonnet—September 1922"**:

> Fierce indignation is best understood by those
> Who have time or no fear, or a hope in its real good.
> One loses it with a filed soul or in sentimental
>   mood.
> Anger is gone with sunset, or flows as flows
> The water in easy mill-runs; the earth that ploughs

> Forgets protestation in its turning, the rood
> Prepares, considers, fulfils; and the poppy's blood
> Makes old the old changing of the headland's
>   brows.
>
> But the toad under the harrow toadiness
> Is known to forget, and even the butterfly
> Has doubts of wisdom when that clanking thing
>   goes by
> And's not distressed. A twisted thing keeps still—
> And that easier twisted than a grocer's bill—
> And no history of November keeps the guy.

Such confident range of reference and modulation of rhythm and idiom show how thoroughly Gurney had "modernised" his poetic sensibility and ingredients. The basis and manner of this achievement were quite distinct from Eliot's or Pound's. He does not share their symbolist lust to strip image of discourse, but achieves strange harmonies between figurative and expository expression. Nor is relation to the past "tradition" for him an issue, or matter for conspicuous display. The poets and composers of the past with whom Gurney was deeply familiar were, as much as the Cotswolds or the trenches, presences in his imagination, apt to quicken it, and naturally alluded to. Yet he writes himself as a poet wholly unhampered by literary precedents, freely discovering his own imperatives of content and utterance. In 1909 Edward Thomas had written: "In slow course of years we acquire a way of expression gradually as fitted to the mind as an old walking stick to the hand that has worn and been worn by it." In fact, this is a rare achievement, which Thomas managed in prose before he began poetry. In Gurney's poetry one follows a remarkable apprenticeship, carrying him beyond the Georgian concepts which pervade his wartime letters and circumscribe his verse in the two volumes he published, through the rejected collection in which he prided himself there was "no swank," to his postwar creative maturity, poems such as **"The Silent One"** or **"Sonnet—September 1922"** where his impulse to authentic expression of necessary material cares nothing for conventional expectations. Gurney's radical poetic self-revolutionising, assimilating such diversities of theme and form, feeling and language, had his writing been known at the time could have demonstrated an integrative way forward for English verse. Remarkably, his achievement was as solitary as it was original, unsupported by allies, or theories, as intuition and practice and his immense imaginative avidity carried Gurney far beyond the notions of poetry with which he began. The unprogrammatic directness and scope his poetry attained required of him, as Gurney well understood, the persevering intricacy of artistic toil for which one poem, **"Hedger,"** written in the asylum, finds image and sanction in a recollection of rural craftsmanship:

>   I saw one weave
> Wonderful patterns of bright green, never clearer
> Of April; whose hand nothing at all did deceive
> Of laying right
> The stakes of bright
> Green lopped-off spear-shaped, and stuck notched,
>   crooked-up. . . .

(pp. 8-19)

Andrew Waterman, "The Poetic Achievement of Ivor Gurney," in Critical Quarterly, *Vol. 25, No. 4, Winter, 1983, pp. 3-19.*

GEOFFREY HILL　(lecture date 1984)

[*Hill is considered one of the most important English poets of the post–World War II era. While working within traditional poetic forms, he has experimented with meter, rhyme, and language, producing poetry that ranges from simple to opulent. His frequent use of paradox, irony, pun, and allusion contributes to the various layers of meaning in his verse. Hill's work is informed by a mythic and religious sensibility, through which he explores such themes as the relationships between sacrifice and salvation, ritual and violence, doubt and faith, and the discrepancies between artifice and experience. In the following excerpt, he examines Gurney's changing perception of poetry, noting the influence of Hillaire Belloc, Rupert Brooke, G. K. Chesterton, and Walt Whitman on his work and ideas.*]

From an Edinburgh hospital in October 1917, awaiting the reviews of his first book *Severn and Somme,* Gurney wrote to his friend Marion Scott: "they will not say much to affect me, for the sight of the whole thing in proof convinced me that humility should be my proper mood, and gratitude for a hobby found when one was needed." It is hard to accept that a poet who had already written **"Strange Service," "Pain,"** and **"Servitude"** could, at the heart of his intelligence, suppose that what he practised was "pursued merely for the amusement or interest that it affords," or with a devotion "out of proportion to its real importance."

A brusque but reasonable retort would be that "hobby" is the *mot juste* and that when Gurney, later in the same letter, writes of having a "larger and finer string to my bow" he preempts one's objection. As a musician he trained to professional standards though not, in the end, to the satisfaction of his examiners, at the Royal College of Music. As early as 1912 he had composed "Sleep," a setting of words by John Fletcher, which some musicians regard as one of the finest English songs of the twentieth century. As a poet, however, he had to get by without formal instruction and his letters are a record of predilections and prejudices, discoveries and disenchantments. As his autodidact's rage of discovery turned into a discovery of rage, he drew sustenance and example from the political philosophy of Belloc and the poetry of Whitman. In a letter to Miss Scott, on New Year's Day, 1916, he wrote that he had ordered a copy of Belloc's *The Servile State,* clearly approving its anti-Socialist, anti-Collectivist, thesis. Whitman's poetry, he wrote, had taken him "like a flood." Among his late asylum poems there is verse not only "in the manner of . . . Whitman" but also possessed by, or purporting to be possessed by, the spirit of the American poet who is credited, gnomically, with co-authorship: "Walt Whitman./(Ivor Gurney here./probably all-altering/F. W. Harvey's *Ironical* work)."

The editor of the **Collected Poems of Ivor Gurney** [P. J. Kavanagh] advises us to take due note of *"Ironical."* He warns that Gurney "detested irony." If that is true then this is a way of confusing "them," the daemonic Ironies that interfere with mortal destinies, or the human persecutors, the enemy, those who engineered and directed the "electrical influences" which were tormenting him. There is some evidence to suggest that Gurney had a depressive's gift for clowning. He, like others, relished the collocations of subsistence-level English and French ("Compree no grub?") and improved on the donné: "Bide a wee, s'il vous plait." He cherished daft puns, nicknames, and flat-footed witticisms. Herbert Howells, addressed as "My dear Howler" or as "Erbert Owls," was provided with a curriculum vitae and list of publications including "the great (Sanscrit) Te Deum, for the opening of the new lavatory in the Dead Language Section of the British Museum," a Mrs. Chapman unwittingly became La Comptesse Tilda, a revered poetic invocation was made to face about: "Dear houses, the very God does seem asleep."

On 3 November 1917 he wrote: "There's a bit of luck; owing to slight indigestion (presumably due to gas; wink, wink!) I am to go to Command Depot for two months. . . ." He had endured over a year's front-line existence with patient courage and had already been wounded; nevertheless he seems overscrupulously to have felt some remorse at having escaped the trenches. Expecting "no more than a week's sick," he found that he had got "Blighty" and "wink, wink!" hints at doctored evidence, mimes a skiver's self-congratulation. Miss Scott is made both confidante and spectator of a comic turn, a send-up of confessions and self-betrayal which is nonetheless a genuine attempt to appease the Accuser, who, as Blake said, is the God of this World. It is the uneasy jauntiness of the cornered man. Donald Davie has praised Gurney's "mastery of decorum," his command, in the poems, of "any number of distinct styles" [see excerpt dated 1983]. I do not question this knack but believe it may be less important than Gurney's other decorous mastery, his grasp of the way words and tones sit within our lives and the way they situate the life of one man in relation, or disrelation, to his comrades and his superiors. P. J. Kavanagh considers that "the intricacies of human relations are not his subject" [see excerpt dated 1982]. It is true that he is not a story-teller, as Browning and Frost are; but "wink, wink!" is no less aware of "intricacies" and contingencies than are "My Last Duchess" or "Snow." One's "subject" may be one's theme; but it can equally be the substance that we subject to our disinterested possessive contemplation—the texture of the material in which we work. "Texture" is a word that Gurney weaves into his theories and ideals: Schubert's C Major Quintet "looks to have / Very good texture," there is a "true / Texture of rare living / Azure." "The Artist respects his materials, loves their peculiarities of texture and management, and deals with them gently as with his own flesh and blood." He anticipates by several years Brophy's and Partridge's published work on the songs and slang of the British soldier, "little bits of jargon," "grub, Fritz, and Blighty," "poor bare jests . . . 'On the wire, at Loos' . . . 'Gassed at Mons' . . . 'my numbers up.' . . ." He notes abrupt thoughts and sayings that have the "intricacies of human relations" still clinging to them: "When on a sudden, 'Crickley' he said. How I started/At that old darling name of home!" Or:

> I saw a scrawl on a barn door a few days ago. It will
> 　　interest you, I think.
> 　　"Where is my wandering Boy tonight?
> 　　　　　　Neuve Chapelle" (and date.)
> That's all, and pretty grim at that.

His hearing of these snatched and shaken things is not random, though it may sound so. He plainly intended his five "Sonnets 1917" as a riposte to Brooke's "1914" sonnets which, he said, "were written before the grind of the war and by an officer (or one who would have been an officer)." This "protest," the assertion of "the accumulative weight of small facts against the one large," reminds us of his admiration for Belloc and Chesterton. Belloc argued that the Socialist, or Collectivist, reformer is "disturbed by multitudinous things"; "all that human and organic complexity which is the colour of any vital society offends him by its infinite differentiation." Those details in Gurney to which Kavanagh and Davie justly attend, "the silhouettes of certain trees in certain lights," "all the beauties of his beloved Gloucestershire," are not degraded by the political collocation. "Infinite," "infinitely," like all words that make gestures towards the "exalted spiritual," is to be used with caution. Belloc's "infinite differentiation" compounds it with the quotidian, the intricacies of human relations; and Gurney, who on occasion uses the word as convention prescribes ("And infinitely far that star Capella"), more often rams it against the human and organic, as in his poem about Canadian troops returning from the trenches, "Faces infinitely grimed in." The first two words anticipate a commonplace of long-suffering, or a long-suffering commonplace (". . . infinitely patient, cheerful, resourceful, weary . . ."), the third and fourth repel the truism, though without wholly annulling it or the decent traditional sentiments that go with it. "Infinitely," having been situated within the technology of the line, doesn't know where to put itself, though Gurney, who has here embarrassed it, is elsewhere considerate enough in the duties he places on it ("Infinite lovely chatter of Bucks accent"; "Everyday things the mind/Infinitely delighted"; "one of my infinite dead generations of brothers"). Kavanagh claims that Gurney's "occasional bathetic contrasts . . . are . . . intentional." I would question whether "bathos" is precisely the right word; I see the contrast as being deliberately, even aggressively, oxymoronic: "nothing/But loathing and fine beauty," "England, terrible/And dear taskmistress."

That invocation is from the final poem in *Severn and Somme,* proofs of which, recently read, had triggered his remark about poetry being a "hobby."

> The unnoticed nations praise us, but we turn
> Firstly, only to thee—"Have we done well?
> Say, are you pleased?"

The sense of formal petition in these lines, intensely conscious of twin consecrations, patriotism and poetic vocation, sits as oddly with his self-humbling "gratitude for a hobby found" as does a friend's recollection of his "astonishing creative pride." From the opening pages of *Severn and Somme* to the asylum poem, **"Chance to Work,"** with its prefix "For the English Police / For Scotland Yard," he insistently pleads "the great honour of song," the seriousness, the high significance of the poet's duty to his craft and to England, the distinction of the craft, the recognition that is its due.

"Hobby" does not do justice, then, to Gurney's dedication or to his position. Brooding on the word may nevertheless help us to appreciate what that position was and to see that justice is done. "A favourite occupation or topic, pursued merely for the amusement or interest that it affords, . . . an individual pursuit to which a person is devoted (in the speaker's opinion) out of proportion to its real importance." Once we allow the OED's caveat "in the speaker's opinion" we find that we are dealing with a shifty status-word. A "hobby" may be pursued in the intervals of employment; it lacks public utility, status, or prestige. The word can parody and dwarf the value of human activity, and is ready to hand for complicitous bouts of self-deprecation or self-therapy. It is also susceptible to mystical enfranchisement and elevation. A hobby may be whatever is not "competitive" or "bureaucratic toil." It may even take on the aura of "universal duty": "Woman . . . should have not one trade but twenty hobbies." In context, Chesterton's observation is less patronising than it sounds. He is urging, so he says, "The Emancipation of Domesticity," an emancipation envisaged in accordance with his Catholic

sociology, stressing the central importance of family life and private property in the creation and preservation of democracy. He is obliged to contend with an already-prejudiced usage, seeking to show that these so-called "hobbies" are in fact true professions, untainted by commodity. "Hobby," a word in which solipsism and public bias are compacted, is, in effect, itself oxymoronic: eccentric yet central, peripheral but focal, an "amusement" attended by devotion and sacrifice. Of amateur status it may be pursued with a degree of emotional and technical concentration more intense than that bestowed upon day-labour or a salaried profession.

As one might expect, given the various contingencies, we find Gurney, in his poems and letters, vacillating between two notions. On the one hand poetry is a spontaneous though imperative way of relieving the feelings ("Out of the heart's sickness the spirit wrote / For delight, or to escape hunger, or of war's worst anger"). On the other it is a craft, a discipline to be acquired with difficulty and by way of laborious trial and error. "Do as you please," "punctuate as you please," he writes to his amanuensis Marion Scott in late 1916 and early 1917. "The grammar of my book is, technically speaking, often shaky. Never poetically. I say what I want to say." "Poetically" here signifies an essence, independent of, uninhibited by, "shaky" grammar, uncertain punctuation. This is a dangerously volatile notion. For a young man in Gurney's circumstances—and he is always insistent that particular circumstances are acknowledged—the necessity to make something of oneself, to proclaim one's identity by expressing oneself, strongly felt by any artist, is experienced with particular intensity: "There is no time to revise here [in the trenches], and if the first impulse will not carry the thing through, then what is written gets destroyed." "Neither he [F. W. Harvey] nor I have lived in the proper atmosphere to write much yet—the company of men who are trying for the same end and prize of a modern technique." These observations, eight months apart, place a common stress on circumstance, but the first speaks of "impulse," the second of "technique." It would be wrong, however, to see an irreversible process of definition in Gurney's thinking at this period. It remained, during the war years, intermittently self-contradictory, expressing a perplexity not wholly of his own making. In the midst of his recurrent references to what he calls "craft," "method," "scrupulousness," "care," "respect . . .[for] . . . materials," he will appear abruptly to go against the grain of this growing concern. "It seems to me," he remarks on 3 August 1917, "a work of Art never should be greatly praised for its perfection; for that should set off its beauty, and its beauty or truth should be the chief impression on the mind. To praise a thing for its faultlessness is to damn it with faint praise." This, however, is less a contradiction than a synthesis. It is not that technical mastery precludes creative mystery; it is that the greatest craft is one which is transfigured into the most telling simplicity: "I say, I would like to get hold of some of Verhaeren. He seems to have hold of an artistic dogma that is my foundation stone, and perpetual starting point—that simplicity is most powerful and to be desired above all things whatsoever."

"Foundation-stone" is a four-square civic word with which to commemorate a private sense of dedication. Gurney is not unique in finding that he has encountered an oxymoronic circumstance in which a derisory hobby is nonetheless born of common experience and speaks not only to our common humanity but also to the "corporate life and mutual obligations." The uniqueness is always a matter of texture. "Common" is one of his value-words, as it is for Belloc, who writes of England's vanquished "common life which once nourished [the] social sense." Gurney has "the dearness of common things," "beauty / Of common living," "the common goodness of those soldiers shown day after day," "the day's / Common wonder." But against this wondrous and dear commonness we have to set those other occurrences in his poetry, where "common" is as common parlance would have it, a word that imposes extrinsic "standards" upon the intrinsic qualities of the thing described: "the commonness of the tale," "To be signallers and to be relieved two hours / Before the common infantry," "Casual and common is the wonder grown," "a Common Private makes but little show," "How England should take as common their vast endurance." What is the precise difference, we may fairly ask, between "the day's / Common wonder" and the "wonder" that has grown "common"? The attempt to answer one's own question is a slow and perplexing business but through it we may reach to the crux of Gurney's perplexity and achievement. A reader of Belloc's *The Servile State* is soundly instructed in that distinction between "inertia and custom" and "instinct" and "tradition" which lies at the heart of the "Distributist" philosophy. Gurney endures a process of self-discovery and self-loss where that distinction, though still applicable, is for a time far less clear. It is not so much that there is an impassable gulf between the precious "common wonder" and the indifferent curiosity of the world. It is rather that our truths of first inscription, the objects of our love and fealty, are at the same time slighted, marginal to the world's mart and focus of interest, and further, that we have no privilege of remaining aloof from the crassest misjudgement, the cruellest slight.

When Gurney arranges the title-page of his first book: "*Severn and Somme*/by/Ivor Gurney/Private, of the Gloucesters" he briefly holds in balance what Trilling would later call "the reality of self" and "the reality of circumstance." "Private" is at once bluntly descriptive and elliptically challenging. The five "Sonnets 1917" which end the volume, were, we recall, "intended to be a sort of counterblast against" Brooke's "1914" yet they are dedicated "To the Memory of Rupert Brooke." Does this rebut Kavanagh's assertion that Gurney "detested irony," or does it show not only a readiness to compromise with public sentiment but also an eagerness to be seen as Brooke's rightful heir? Gurney was not alone in criticizing Brooke's sequence. Rosenberg, who dismissed those "begloried sonnets" gives the impression of quietly pushing them aside as items of no concern or challenge to his own search for a poetry that is complex yet "as simple as ordinary talk." *Severn and Somme,* published by Sidgwick and Jackson, Brooke's publishers, is much more "after the English manner," as consecrated by Brooke, Binyon, and the general consensus. The "radiant shining" of "**Requiem**" recollects the largesse of Brooke's "The Dead": "a gathered radiance, / A width, a shining peace, under the night." However, Gurney's book also makes a determined bid to wrest the "English manner" from the hands of the officer class and to bestow it upon comrades in "heavy servitude," "The boys who laughed and jested with me but yesterday,/So fit for kings to speak to. . . ."

"Mind you take care of him. His loss would be a national loss." General Sir Ian Hamilton's instructions to Brooke's commanding officer, on the eve of departure for the Aegean and the Dardanelles, define by stark antithesis the national status of Gurney's "hobby," of his "great honour of song," devoted to "England's royal grace and dignity." "These sonnets are personal—never were sonnets more personal since Sidney died—and yet the very blood and youth of England seem to find expression in them." That encomium which appeared on March 11, 1915, more than a month before Brooke's death, anticipates the tone of Churchill's myth-making *Times* obituary of April 26th. It cannot be claimed that Gurney's "Preface" to *Severn and Somme,* dated "Spring, 1917," intentionally echoes the tone of that 1915 press notice, but neither does it positively exclude such resonances: "Most of the book is concerned with a person named Myself, and the rest with my county, Gloucester, that whether I die or live stays always with me. . . ." Gurney's tone here is both derivative and uncertain: ". . . I never was famous, and a Common Private makes but little show" tries for a plain man's self-reliant jocularity but, like one or two other phrases in the "Preface," sounds merely gauche. There can be little doubt that with *Severn and Somme* Gurney aimed to set to rights certain matters of social prerogative and privilege. A "Common Private" would be seen to have made a considerable showing and would therefore be accorded his rightful place in the English pantheon. The book was amiably received and after twelve months went into a second impression. By 1917, however, Harvey's *A Gloucestershire Lad* had reached its fourth impression, Brooke's *1914 and Other Poems* its twenty-first. Gurney's second volume, *War's Embers,* was less successful than *Severn and Somme* and a third collection, *Rewards of Wonder,* was rejected in the same year. I see no reason to dispute Blunden's claim that, as the evidence of rejection accumulated, Gurney was "aflame with anger" or Hurd's suggestion [in *The Ordeal of Ivor Gurney;* see Additional Bibliography] that "he began to feel that he had been betrayed by the country he loved and whose cause his art and his life had served." Statements from the later poems confirm these opinions: "(I was a war poet, England bound to honour by Her blood)"; "Who, first war poet, am under three Hells and lie/(Sinned against desperately by all English high-sworn to Duty)." It may be thought that I have misconstrued Gurney's intention in these phrases and that the indignation is less wounded literary *amour-propre* than exemplary rage on behalf of "boys bemocked at." I do not say that the disinterested indignation is excluded. Even so, an acute personal disappointment is subsumed. Gurney, at once ambitious and innocent, remained unreconciled to the discovery that acclaim is not commensurate with achievement.

Jon Silkin, in an eloquent and just appreciation of Gurney [see excerpt dated 1972], argues that the minute particulars of word-choice may be ultimately traceable to "enormous social forces." Turning for substantiation to some lines from *War's Embers* ("But still he died / Nobly, so cover him over / With violets of pride . . ."), he observes that " 'Nobly' is not merely the individual soldier's attribute; it is the propagandistic aura that the state awards the dead. . . . After hesitating between these conflicting attitudes, Gurney, disappointingly, moves the stanza in the aureate direction." "Aureate" is ponderable in the circumstances. In one of his last letters, to Abercrombie (Edward Marsh quotes it in his "Memoir"), Brooke remarked "I've been collecting . . . one or two of the golden phrases that a certain wind blows from (will the Censor let me say?) Olympus, across these purple seas." Marsh consecrates the self-consciousness more solemnly than Brooke perhaps intends. "Of the 'golden phrases' only the merest fragments remain."

In such circumstances the cliché may briefly appear to be vivified by "reality of self." Rosenberg, Gurney, and Sorley were all privately sceptical of Brooke's publicly acclaimed qualities. Rosenberg referred scathingly to his "second hand phrases 'lambent fires' etc." It is one's recognition of the hiatus between private intelligence and public sentiment that vindicates Silkin's reference to enormous social forces. It was Gurney's own recognition of this hiatus which concentrated his creative insight as it drained his psychic resilience. Brooke, with his "red-gold waves of hair" and his "golden phrases," was, and for some evidently remains, an "*embodiment* of poetry." How is it possible, one asks, for superficial verbal glister to be accepted as the outward sign of "some inner, spiritual, reality"? The *Collected Poems* of 1918 is lavishly "aureate": "golden hours," "misty gold," "golden glory," "Golden Stair," "golden dream," "golden height," "golden sea," "gold air," "golden space," "Golden forever, eagles, crying flames."

W. W. Gibson's slim volume *Friends* (1916), dedicated "To the Memory of Rupert Brooke," was described by Gurney in the preface to **Severn and Somme** as "a great little book." Its language attempts to embody that original "simple act of presence and of direct communication" to which Brooke's admirers paid homage, but succeeds merely in reduplicating cliché: "golden sky," "golden head," "golden words," "golden rhyme," "pure gold," "gold casket," "terrible golden fury," "golden height," "golden glow," "golden peace," "golden light," "burnished gold," "gold wings," "gold glow." Whether such inane repetitiousness is to be characterized as ineptitude or as a self-restricting minor aptitude may seem to be a question defying analysis. Judgment in these matters should not, however, depend on the toss of a half-sovereign. One seeks a word. The word is perhaps "absorption." Gibson has successfully absorbed Brooke's influence; he is in that sense an opportunist and a *pasticheur;* yet, at the same time, he is sincerely absorbed in his zealous homage to the "inner, spiritual, reality" of Brooke's "presence" and "direct communication." He is sufficiently doting to overlook the kind of cynical frisson which Brooke sometimes favours, as in "Menelaus and Helen": ". . . her golden voice / Got shrill as he grew deafer." As F. W. Bateson acutely perceived, Brooke occasionally "carried off" the artificiality of his Pre-Raphaelite diction "by half-laughing at it."

There is also a strong "aureate" vein in Gurney, however; a "golden room" bard immured in his isolation: "Bask in the warm, dream poetry of the gold flame," "Let me but have a room/Of golden night quiet," "homely songs of gold," "O warmth! O golden light!," "lamp shadows/Golden and black on gold," ". . . lit with gold firelight thrown/Lovely about the room," "dark with firelight's gold power." It is the complicity between received opinion and personal expectation that is rebuffed by his spasmodically bitter and violent conjunctions: "Golden firelight or racked frost hurt me to the nerve." Belloc had written, in *The Servile State,* of "every form of touting and cozening which competitive Capitalism carries with it." Gurney's painful discovery is that this "touting and cozening" involves and compromises not only the most highly valued poetic idiom of the day but also his own ambition which had rejoiced in the sincerest emulation. When he writes of post-war "disappointed men/Who looked for the golden Age to come friendly again," it is the particular quality of his imagination to seize on that word of Georgian largesse and to place it in all its cozening power. At the same time it is as though he takes the bankrupted stock into the re-

ceivership of his own idiom; in more than one sense he is going to make it pay:

> O for some force to swing us back there to some
> Natural moving towards life's love, or that glow
> In the word to be glow in the State, that golden age
>   come
> Again, men working freely as nature might show,
> And a people honouring stage-scenes lit bright with
>   fine sound
> On a free soil, England happy, honoured and joy-
>   crowned.

The "men working freely," "England happy," are with difficulty enfranchised from a syntax that is far from free. "That glow/In the word to be glow in the State" is at once over-deliberate and under-defined. The ungainly thrust of the word "glow" athwart the slowed-down gabble of the metre is an effort to wrest activity from inertia, a concept from a cliché; to affirm what the "golden age come/Again," the unity of poetic and political vision, might be in England if it could only be brought into being. This is one of those instances, however, where the raw etymology of a word contains more energy than is released in the poetic context by which it is constrained. Such verbal bafflement is at the root of Gurney's undeniable failings and failures but also of his incontestable grandeur. According to *The Servile State* the "moral strain . . . arising from the divergence between what our laws and moral phrases pretend, and what our society actually is, makes of that society an utterly unstable thing." There is, nonetheless, a condition of equilibrium, or suspension, where craft and expediency meet and where minor talents are well able to secure themselves. Gurney's "curious originality," his "peculiar unconventionality . . . not hostile to traditions," is, in large part, a refusal to adjust craft-logic to reasons of expediency. He, like other poets, draws upon the common dole, the distributed received opinions, but increasingly in his work these take on the weight of the circumstantial, the contingent. This capacity to comprehend that words exist by some other law than that of one's own fancy, even while subjecting them to the discipline of imagination, increasingly distinguishes Gurney's poetry from that of the more successful Georgians whom he admired. The jolt of his phrases, at times disabling, at others releasing, is a recognition not only that goodness and sincerity may be other names for humiliation and bewilderment, but also that simplicity is most powerful and to be desired above all things whatsoever, and that "We shall enter unsurprised into our own."

"The Homelessness of Jones." In the eleventh chapter of *What's Wrong with the World* (1910) Chesterton envisages a man who "has always desired the divinely ordinary things," who "has chosen or built a small house that fits like a coat. . . . And just as he is moving in, something goes wrong. Some tyranny, personal or political, suddenly debars him from the home." Gurney observed in a letter to Miss Scott that she had "a great house in London, but I doubt whether it can be to you what a tiny house may be, even if . . . the piano leaves little room for free movement." Hurd notes that "at one point, in May 1920," Gurney believed "that he had found the cottage he had dreamed of in the trenches . . . though [it] proved an impossibility." In the asylum poem **"Chance to Work"** he is perhaps reliving that period of concentrated hope and disappointment: "Many songs . . . then a good farm / Took me. . . . Yet it is difficult / In a house not one's own to work." This "work" was not the farmwork, which he enjoyed ("Hedging, plough-

helping, stone shifting, Labour was good"); it was merely what he was supremely gifted to do ("Working in strict discipline, music or strict rhyme"), his "hobby" in other words. One's hobby is not necessarily what one chooses, it may be one's lot; that which is by tacit decree one's hobby since it cannot be seen to be work. "Did they look for a book of wrought art's perfection, / Who promised no reading, nor praise, nor publication?" Or:

> The pages fill with blank notes, the paper-bill goes
> Up and up, till the musician is left staring
> At a String Quartett nobody in the world will
>   do . . .
> Now, had it been a joke, or some wordy, windy
>   poem
> About Destiny or Fatal-Way or Weltmüth or Sar-
>   sparilla,
> London would have hugged to it like a glad
>   gorilla . . .

This churlish lampooning of poetry as a metropolitan raree-show compounds a dislike of modernism with a reminder that poetry has sometimes been a profitable commodity; had, indeed, proved recently to be so, under the auspices of Edward Marsh. Frank Swinnerton has described how "this remarkable character was apparently destined by Nature to be Private Secretary to innumerable Cabinet Ministers, and in his spare time to be one of the greatest encouragers of young poets that the world had seen." The ludicrous disproportion of the last phrase should not cause us to underestimate the real power of social cachet, of the semi-official stamp of approval, or to overlook the professional zeal with which Marsh conducted his hobby of literary patronage. Statements such as Swinnerton's are in fact a form of floatation; they procure a ready assent by simply taking for granted that it will not be withheld. General Hamilton's absolute confidence in Brooke as a major national asset has a similar aplomb, and Gibson's *Friends* easily buys into the same serious and thoughtful complacency. In his *Commonplace Book* for January 8th, 1914, R. H. Tawney wrote that "the economic conditions of the unprivileged classes are determined not by consent, but by *force majeure*." It may seem perverse to claim that the gentle overabundance of Gibson's "Rupert Brooke" is itself a manifestation of *"force majeure"* but the perversity, like the pressure, is already there, in what Whitman called "words of routine" as in that nexus of expectation and accolade which Owen came to recognize and condemn as "Poetry": "Above all I am not concerned with Poetry," "(That's for your poetry book)." It would be unjust to deny Marsh's several acts of generosity to both Rosenberg and Gurney; it would be sentimental to claim that he valued them as he valued Brooke, or even Gibson, or Abercrombie. Tawney added that "in modern society the individual is not face to face with nature. Between him and nature stands a human superior." In much Georgian verse the "human superior" is Marsh, or Hamilton, or Gosse "like a king . . . with favourites, his chosen heirs, young men and women of promise," or the "red-gold" apparition of Brooke himself. Poetry, in this ambience, is hardly to be distinguished from Patrimony. The significance of Gurney and Rosenberg is not that they were "unprivileged" men, nor even that they were unprivileged men of genius, but that their poetic intelligences proved able to take that strain arising from the divergence between what phrases pretend and what society actually is. To say this is not to underrate the severity of the strain or, in Gurney's case, the denseness of the perplexity. It is, after all, a perplex-

ing matter to receive an inheritance that is at the same time an imposition, an ancient right that is also a deprivation.

Gurney found himself possessed of a dual heritage, a double burden, a twofold deprivation: *Patria* and Patrimony. In the earlier poems the two are spiritually, as well as etymologically, entwined: "Ere he has scorned his Father's patrimony." In the later work the patrimony becomes more and more the question of an unhonoured draft, and the unfailing love of the *patria* (Gloucestershire and England) becomes a separate thing from the hatred of a ruling caste, "the Prussians of England":

> We'll have a word there too, and forge a knife,
> Will cut the cancer threatens England's life.

Belloc had seen the growth of the servile state exemplified "in Prussia and in England." Though Lord Milner had "sincerely attempted to introduce German efficiency" to this country, Chesterton did not commend his efforts. Gurney acknowledged the patrimony of his political thought: "My dear lady your eagle eye will detect Belloc here; and why not?" Reading between the lines of his letters it is evident that he had been brave, in atrocious conditions, in the way he most admired, with "that half cynical nobility and clearness of eye that forbid men to complain much," that "stoical fatalism" which Hardy regarded as characteristically English. Such qualities Gurney saw epitomized, simply and profoundly, in the comrades of his own regiment, the 2nd/5th Gloucesters, of whom he spoke in the "Preface" to *Severn and Somme,* and to whom he dedicated three poems in *War's Embers.*

But Gurney was not a simple man; and for a complex mind and spirit, I would guess, even to be comradely is not a simple act. Its own form of consciousness, even self-consciousness, is a palimpsest: knowing one's worth while knowing that one is expected to know one's place. Hurd quotes a letter from Gurney to Edward Marsh, *c.*1922, in which he said, of his "5 Songs of Rupert Brooke," "I do not think very much [of them] but they are probably better than those of most folk." Hurd says that "Marsh did not reply. Nor did he return the manuscript." Gurney's tone, at once incisive and unsure, self-affirming and fatalistic, recurs in the letters and poems: "Some men have to form themselves, to control their every tiniest movement of spirit, and indeed to create their own world." "This dumbness would not matter, only that it makes distrust in oneself." Or:

> . . . the politest voice—a finicking accent, said:
> "Do you think you might crawl through there:
>   there's a hole."
> Darkness, shot at: I smiled, as politely replied—
> "I'm afraid not, Sir." There was no hole, no way
>   to be seen . . .

This, while sounding unpremeditated, is exquisitely balanced ("exquisitely" keeps its distance from "finicking," I hope). "As politely" both matches and counters "the politest" and "There was no hole, no way to be seen" puts the kibosh on "there's a hole." The perfect good manners of the episode are simultaneously a tone-poem of the class-system, and a parody of what it is that brings two men, through the exercise of traditional discipline and reason, into a situation of unpremeditated terror and absurdity. It may be that on this subject Gurney is not quite the equal of C. H. Sorley at his best. He does not match the cogency and economy of Sorley's perception that the loud, public acclaim for Brooke's "1914" sonnets is consonant with the poetry's eloquent, innocent complicity in "conduct demanded by the turn of circumstances, where non-compliance with this demand would have made life intolerable." It is necessary to add, therefore, that the strength and finesse of Sorley's intelligence, so manifest in the letters, is sacrificed in the poems to a noble but constricting patrimony. It is not that Sorley's phrases lack stoical or even sceptical irony ("So be merry, so be dead"; "And the blind fight the blind"; "Who sent us forth? Who brings us home again?"; "It is easy to be dead") but that the pitch and rhythm of the voice are subject to a predetermined rule of measurement and value that is stronger than the solitary dissentient intelligence. W. R. Sorley dedicated *Moral Values and the Idea of God* (1918) to his son's memory and the memory of "many thousands who gave their lives freely in a great cause." The volume also carries a two-page advertisement for *Marlborough and Other Poems,* quoting extracts from sixteen press-notices. Those words and that gesture publicly immolate the personal pride and grief. Quiet grief and dignity themselves draw upon a patrimony in which national identity and Idealism are compounded. W. R. Sorley cites the poets in his treatise, Goethe, Keats, and Donne among them, but though he recognizes what Gurney calls "texture" he evades its implications, here preferring "higher vision" and there rebuking "the licence of a poet." The charge that in the last stanza of "Ode on a Grecian Urn" there is "a confusion of values" might be sustainable if Keats were simply taking a "message" or reading a "lesson," as Sorley supposes. It was presumably he who re-grouped his son's poems in the "definitive" edition of 1919, titling the four sections "Of the Downs," "Of School," "Of Life and Thought," "Of War and Death." The most generous sentiment does not equal the justice attained by accuracy of thought, since sentiment is already entailed and accuracy of thought starts afresh with each new context and texture.

That which at times stands between Gurney and his own nature is something more overt, more violently remarked on. The "finicking accent" is the voice that calls the tune (". . . as politely replied . . ."). The Marsh-Gurney episode is instructive. To speak out, in certain ways, is a solecism to be rebuked by silence. And "silence" itself is both active and passive: either punitively imposed or self-inflicted. "Dumb" recurs in Gurney like the negation of "the beauty/Of common living," and like the substantiation of "a Common Private makes but little show." "And having arrived were to accept the thing in dumb / Acquiescence"; "Men I have known fine, are dead in France, in exile, / One my friend is dumb, other friends dead also . . ."; "Leave dumb the love that filled me." "Patriotic tradition and local pastoral were . . . what he began with," as Silkin says; and from that he pushed forward, not only into a realization of the *patria*'s sanctions and restrictions but also into a finely judged equivalent of what Army regulations categorized as "dumb insolence." *Severn and Somme* embodies the process. There had to be the finding of some negotiable ground between the ephemeral bravura of "make/The name of poet terrible in just war" and the enduring witness of "the silent dead . . . fallen in such a war," "the noblest cause." **"Spring: Rouen, May 1917"** is a vision of the coinherence of *patria* and rightful patrimony: "Living and dead, we shall come home at last / To her sweet breast, / England's; by one touch be paid in full. . . ." In that time Gurney asks, rhetorically, even out of his own "dumb[ness]" "what music shall not come?" This poem both affirms a conviction and presages a disenchantment. A number of finer later poems, notably **"It Is near Toussaints,"** are haunted by it. In **"Spring . . ."** itself, of course, the affirmation is made in the form of a question which sets out to be an "aureate" rhetorical question but turns into a real one, even as it is uttered. The answers to that real question are forthcoming, not only in the direct accusation that England has neglected those whom she should have cherished and cheated those whom she should have paid in full, but also in the awkward factual insistences on just and unjust price, on "pittance" and the "unpaid hand," on "the hours, the wage hours" and "the vulgar / Infantry—so dull and dirty and so underpaid."

Belloc wrote, in *The Servile State,* "It is difficult indeed to dispossess the possessors. It is by no means so difficult . . . to modify the factor of freedom." Gurney's "hobby" is at once a transformation of this ambiguous "factor of freedom" and a recognition that you cannot dispossess the possessors by staking the claims of native genius. It is both creating one's own world and dumbly acquiescing in the fact that it is unlikely ever to be anything but one's own world. The estate of poetry is akin to the condition of those whom Belloc calls "dispossessed free men."

Hilaire Belloc, who "was all our master," is the author (unnamed) of four lines of verse which Gurney quotes in a letter and evidently esteems:

> Of Courtesy, it is much less
> Than Courage of Heart or Holiness,
> Yet in my Walks it seems to me
> That the Grace of God is in Courtesy.

As Gurney says, "that's true and memorable enough"; but it also shows why, at the same time, Belloc was not good enough and why others whom Gurney admired, Chesterton and Gibson, were not good enough either. With Belloc, as with Sorley, the prosaic insight fails to penetrate the lyric sensibility. Or, rather, the lyric metre and diction rebuff the rhythms and inflexions of the otherwise independent mind. The verse is very lively but it is not alive with sensuous intelligence. (pp. 97-115)

Both Blunden and Kavanagh have pointed out that the poet who was clearly moved and delighted by the great church-edifices of Gloucester and Tewkesbury came increasingly to associate the "square shaped" creations of men's minds and hands with "a sense of rightness and order." When he writes of the "square shaping" of Byrd's "Motetts" (he had bought a volume of them for a shilling in the Faringdon Road), it is possible that he is linking typography, the square breves and semi-breves, the spade-headed minims, of Tudor church music with Byrd's rectitude, his dual fidelity as recusant and craftsman. Recusancy in a general sense appealed to Gurney (though he himself was brought up an Anglican). He saw himself as having "wrought a square thing out of my stubborn mind," though the stubbornness here is awkwardly ambiguous. Is the mind "stubborn" because it will not yield, or because it will not yield? Belloc and Chesterton, laureates of intractability, were hugely forthcoming and Gibson's *Collected Poems 1905-1925* is a volume of nearly 800 pages. Gurney began with Belloc-like lyric notions: "At present I am writing a ballad of the Cotswolds, after Belloc's 'South Country.'. . . I find ballad writing very grateful and comforting to the mind. . . . Someday maybe I'll write music with not less facility." Some seventeen months later, in February 1917, he writes: "You see, most of my (always slow) mind is taken up with trying not to resist Things, which means a passive unrhythmical mind and music." The hobbyist has found his vocation. While metre and rhythm in such poems as **"Tewkesbury"** and **"It Is near Toussaints"** seem to hover between standard pentameter and alexandrine, with abrupt stress-clusters making each line a law to itself, the "slow spirit" of the sense goes straight on, taking enjambement in its stride, taking the measure of the "passive unrhythmical mind and music," the "trying not to resist Things," those massive determinisms which he sensed in the energies, inertias and attritions of the war and the post-war years.

The reaction of the creative spirit when it first discovers that it has been taken in, has taken, or mistaken, album trillings for "wrought art's perfection," is one of rage; and it may take some time to discover that there is a wrought art's perfection quite over and above the deft management of aureate cliché. Gurney does discover that; but he prefers for some time to realize in musical terms his awareness of verbal power. He quotes three lines of Whitman and immediately relates them to a "chord on trumpets" which he scribbles on a treble stave. . . . He calls "this chord on trumpets" "my mind-picture of triumph and restrained gloriously-trembling exultation." This is from a letter of late September 1915. Just over two years later, 23 October 1917, he writes from the trenches that he "illicitly walked under the stars, watching Orion and hearing his huge sustained chord . . . through the night." Again he scribbles out a patch of stave . . . and, immediately afterwards, quotes some verse; four lines of Belloc, seven of Yeats's "The Folly of Being Comforted," adding: "The great test of Art—the Arts of Music, Writing, Painting anyway is to be able to see the eyes kindly and full of calm wisdom that would say these things behind the page." What he says is less than what he does. "The eyes kindly and full of calm wisdom" is a literary autodidact's philosophizing. What he conceives and embodies in his scribbled chords is something other than his own fondness for synaesthetic imagery ("the song Orion sings," "Music of light," "Some silver thread of sound," "music's gold") and something more than the device, employed by Belloc in *The Path to Rome* and *The Four Men,* of inserting song melodies and snatches of tune. I am convinced that it is in these two pages where Gurney strikes his chord that we get close to his creative being. For that which "strikes a chord" in him, he finds that he can strike a chord. It is like Whitman's "clef of the universes." Gurney's chord is a figure or emblem of technique as "exultation," linking the cosmic architecture of the stars in the night sky to the minute particulars with which man expresses his "cunning and masterful mind." "The attitude towards Bach," he writes around New Year 1916, "can hardly be called by so cold a word as admiration, it is an enormous and partly incredulous love; a wonder at such a wealth of wonderfulness and such a control." This "partly incredulous love" is the positive of which "The amazed heart cries angrily out on God" is the negative. Gurney's emblem is of control at such a pitch that technical perfection is itself the chord of the "calm wisdom," that "foundation stone" of belief in "simplicity . . . most powerful" which is "to be desired above all things whatsoever." As we read Gurney's simple phrases our minds move from that which upholds us ("foundation stone") to that which we look up to ("to be desired above all things whatsoever"):

> What is best of England, going quick from beauty,
> Is manifest, the slow spirit going straight on,
> The dark intention corrected by eyes that see,
> The somehow getting there, the last conception

> Bettered, and something of one's own spirit outshown;
> Grown as oaks grow, done as hard things are done.

These lines are from **"Tewkesbury,"** belonging to the 1919-1922 period, just prior to the poet's committal to Barnwood House asylum, Gloucester. Gurney here returns upon the stubbornness and stumbling of his own autodidacticism, transfiguring the innocent self-absorption of the "hobby," the good intentions of the barrack-room debating club. "Somehow," "something," those mere space-filling words, are realized, as a musician "realizes" a figured bass; "outshown" is almost "outshone"—you have to blink your eyes to make sure that it is not "outshone"; plain speech is wrought from impediment, from inept repetitiousness. **"Tewkesbury,"** to Gurney, is first and foremost the tower of the noble abbey-church, just as "Gloucester" is above all the great cathedral and its massive yet delicate tower. These "fair-fashioned" shapes of "Square stone," appearing to rise so effortlessly yet slowly and painfully constructed "by the laboured thought," unite the centuries-old huddle of common life with the great cosmic architecture visible in the night sky in hard-won exultant contrast and commingling:

> Square tower, carved upward by the laboured thought,
> The imagined bare concept, how must that soften
> Now to the ivory glow and pride unsought—
> Queenly Andromeda not so exalted often.

Gurney's achievement, seen in this light, is to have composed an architecture of rhythm and phrasing that is at once "laboured" and "bare" and "exalted":

> It is near Toussaints, the living and dead will say:
> "Have they ended it? What has happened to Gurney?"
> And along the leaf-strewed roads of France many brown shades
> Will go, recalling singing, and a comrade for whom also they
> Had hoped well. His honour them had happier made.
> Curse all that hates good. When I spoke of my breaking
> (Not understood) in London, they imagined of the taking
> Vengeance, and seeing things were different in future.
> (A musician was a cheap, honourable and nice creature.)
> Kept sympathetic silence; heard their packs creaking
> And burst into song—Hilaire Belloc was all our master.
> On the night of all the dead, they will remember me,
> Pray Michael, Nicholas, Maries lost in Novembery
> River-mist in the old City of our dear love, and batter
> At doors about the farms crying "Our war poet is lost.
> *Madame—no bon!*"—and cry his two names, warningly, sombrely.

This, it could be argued, is the work of a man simultaneously unable to leave things well alone and too obsessed to attend well to details that need tending. It is made up of hoarded bits and pieces, "little bits of jargon," "poor bare jests." In certain details of syntax and rhyme it seems "amateurish," it has the "faults or deficiencies" sometimes found in the work of "one who cultivates anything as a pastime": "remember me: Novembery"; "his honour them had happier made." It sounds like a beginner's work, though by this time he is far from that; the verse carries a heavy burden of echo and obsessed recollection. **"It Is near Toussaints"** recalls *War's Embers:* "It was the day of all the dead—/Toussaints." Belloc had set the last part of *The Four Men* on "The Second of November 1902," the inspiration of the "Duncton Hill" song. Gurney has conflated "La Toussaint," November 1st, and La Fête des Morts, November 2nd, but in this, one gathers, he may simply be following French custom. In a poem of 1919-1922 he goes back over the ground of that first **"Toussaints."** "Merville" is named in both, but of the "tolling summons" and "other land memories" he now writes "These were of All Souls' Day indeed." Before even *Severn and Somme* appeared, he had said "I want badly to write an 'All-Hallows Day' and 'A Salute,' but cannot get time to think, and am not big enough for what I want to say." In the years that followed he wrote himself into what he wanted to say and attempted also to write himself out of the anger and suffering, in the process of writing it out through an intermittent but reiterative series of Hallow-tide poems. We first hear the theme in any strength in **"Spring: Rouen, May 1917"** of *Severn and Somme:* "We shall come home, / We shall come home again, / Living and dead, one huge victorious host—." In the **"Toussaints"** of *War's Embers,* the "lines of khaki without end . . .," common yet ominous, march living into a landscape of the dead; unvanquished rather than victorious. In **"It Is near Toussaints,"** "along the leaf-strewed roads of France many brown shades/Will go, recalling singing . . ." and it is the same scene, but they are revenants. It is Hallowe'en, "the night set apart for a universal walking abroad of spirits," "the night," as Gurney says, "of all the dead." The poem uneasily involves the unearthly and the familial, the threatening presences and the decent pieties. It is the mood of **"To the Prussians of England"** accosting a remembrance of *patria* and patrimony, the "beauty / Of common living," "the old City of our dear love," the "house of steadfastness and quiet pride."

Walt Whitman, who celebrated "spontaneous songs," "ecstatic songs," was a dedicated reviser and reworker of his texts, "returning," as he said, upon his poems, "considering, lingering long." Gurney, his disciple in craft as in thought, was also a reviser in that original sense of the word: he looked again or repeatedly at; he looked back or meditated on; he went through again what he had once been through. A quatrain from one of the *War's Embers* poems: "Where's Gurney now, I wonder,/That smoked a pipe all day;/Sometimes that talked like blazes,/Sometimes had naught to say?," is recalled and retuned: "Have they ended it? What has happened to Gurney?" That which may strike us as awkwardness is in fact both intensification and opening out, a release from harmless metrical prattle into a "new rhythmus" as Whitman had called it. The falling trochaic cadences of ". . . ended . . . happened . . . Gurney . . ." caught in the rising inflection of the two-fold question remind us of Whitman's "recitative," as in "This Compost," a poem which Gurney particularly admired: "Where have you disposed of their carcasses?/Those drunkards and gluttons of so many generations?"

In **"It Is near Toussaints"** formal homage is still paid to Belloc, which is fitting. There are things in the poem that chime with a sentence from *The Path to Rome:*

The mind released itself and was in touch with

whatever survives of conquered but immortal Spirits.

As I have tried to show, Belloc could invoke, with some grace and panache, the idea of "release" from various forms of collectivist secularist constraint. He could not release himself, or those who were constrained by his eloquence, from the limitations of an agreeable fluency. Nevertheless his paradox "conquered but immortal," like Chesterton's "adamantine tendernesses," points us towards the centre of Gurney's argument, his indignant vision of "The rulers of England, lost in corruptions and increases/. . . While the cheated dead cry, unknowing, 'Eadem Semper'." This is like Owen's "old Lie"; it is also like Belloc's "divergence" between "moral phrases" and "touting and cozening." *"Madame—no bon!"* is Gurney's retort to "unknowing" and knowing one's place, and pretty grim at that. Brophy and Partridge have described the typical war-time *estaminet* and its proprietress who "must have no objection to tobacco smoke and ribald choruses in English and pidgin French." It is here that Gurney sets the scene of several poems, **"The Estaminet," "Toasts and Memories," "On Rest," "Le Coq Français," "Laventie," "Robecq Again," "It Is Winter."** "No bon," like "Tray bong" and "Na pooh fini," is a bit of the pidgin French that Gurney enjoyed. *"Madame—no bon!"* is, however, something more than the sum-total of these memories. The impassive matriarch of the *estaminet,* gathering to herself Gurney's regal amanuensis, "La Comptesse Tilda," and the "Unknown Lady" of *Severn and Somme,* is even so the intolerant *patria,* "England the Mother," "darling Mother and stern," now sternly rebuked, sombrely warned, in the "two names" of the poet and in the name of the "cheated dead," those "conquered but immortal Spirits." Love and "fierce indignation" may be perilously balanced here, but the balance is held; and the indignation, like the love, is wholly accounted for, not only by the evidence of the "life" but also, and more importantly, within the perplexed yet open measures of the work. But there would be little point and even less justice in claiming so much for Gurney's indignant vision if one did not believe that, in **"It Is near Toussaints"** and others of his finest poems, he had worked his own release from what Gibson cheerily termed "the manifold/Delights a little net of words may hold" and had discovered, within the texture of diction, syntax and rhythm, the exact, and exacting, sense of "stumbling blind through the difficult door," the matching of "lines and reality."

The assertion that Gurney "detested irony" is allowable if we take "irony" to mean "sarcasm," "ridicule," "dissimulation," "pretence," any of those thoughts, words or gestures which he, like Whitman, would deem a betrayal of comradeship. I further concede that he thought Hardy's *The Return of the Native* "perverse" in its exploitation of "all those feelings that make one lump the world's experiences." I could not agree that he rejected a more magnanimous ironic awareness, a sense of the "contradictory outcome of events as if in mockery of the promise and fitness of things." The constant witness of his poems and letters attests not only to his angry bewilderment but also to his stubborn grasp of the promise and fitness of things. "Lump" is demotic; it is also magisterial. Our capacity to endure is both judge and thrall of the mere necessity to endure. It is a form of assent that squares with the adamantine tenderness of Whitman's "And often to me they are alive after what custom has served them, but nothing more." For such poets as Whitman and Gurney there are always two tunes: the tune that is called and what they make of it. And that, in a double sense, is their calling (or their hobby). (pp. 117-25)

Geoffrey Hill, "Gurney's 'Hobby'," in Essays in Criticism, *Vol. XXXIV, No. 2, April, 1984, pp. 97-128.*

ADDITIONAL BIBLIOGRAPHY

Bergonzi, Bernard. "Poets II: Graves, Blunden, Read, and Others." In his *Heroes' Twilight: A Study of the Literature of the Great War,* second ed., pp. 60-91. London: Macmillan Press, 1980.

Discusses Gurney's career in the context of World War I poetry, seeing his wartime works as "conventional but accomplished." Of Gurney's later poetry Bergonzi concludes: "It is not difficult to see in these poems, crude and fragmentary as so many of them are, evidence of their author's mental disorder, but there is a strength about them which is, on the whole, lacking in Gurney's early work."

Enright, D. J. "Sanity of a Sorely Tried Mind." *Observer Review* (London) (3 October 1982): 32.

Praises the authenticity and artistic control of Gurney's poetry. According to Enright: "There is more sanity at every stage than can be found in most verse, and the later work . . . shows no obvious deterioration, certainly no anaesthesia; the late 'To Clare' is one of his most moving poems, powerful by virtue of its reasonableness."

Fuller, John. "The Mound and the Hole." *The Listener* 91, No. 2,345 (7 March 1974): 310-11.

Includes a review of *Poems of Ivor Gurney.* According to Fuller: "The first dozen pages [of the collection] are worthless, and then he simply collapses into pastiche of Hopkins. Nothing seems to go right. He has Blakean obsessions without vision, and a weakness for rhetoric, gush, and doggerel. But after 1922 . . . Gurney's work begins to gell. . . . There are excellent poems on darkness, Schubert, water, and finding coins. None are without flaws of some kind, but they arrest and please."

Fussell, Paul. *The Great War and Modern Memory.* New York and London: Oxford University Press, 1975, 363 p.

Discusses Gurney's "To His Love" and "Ballad of the Three Spectres" in a study of English literature of the Western Front from 1914 to 1918.

Grigson, Geoffrey. "Bright Tracks." *New Statesman* 86, No. 2,217 (14 September 1973): 355-56.

Reviews *Poems of Ivor Gurney,* noting deficiencies in the selection, editing, and indexing of the book. According to Grigson, Gurney was not typical of Georgian poets as Blunden maintained [see excerpt dated 1954]: "What distinguishes the type of Georgian utterance . . . is a time-serving timidity and thinness of diction of the kind Ivor Gurney was rejecting."

Hurd, Michael. *The Ordeal of Ivor Gurney.* Oxford: Oxford University Press, 1978, 230 p.

Biography.

Kavanagh, P. J. "Focus." *The Spectator* 250, No. 8,066 (12 February 1983): 22-3.

Reviews *Ivor Gurney: War Letters.* According to Kavanagh: "His letters show that from the outset he was fascinated by technique in an original way; his conscious aim was for an immediacy of expression at the expense, if necessary, of 'perfection,' which anyway he despised even though he was capable of it."

Lucas, John. "Poetry and Pity." In his *Modern English Poetry from Hardy to Hughes: A Critical Survey,* pp. 70-102. London: B. T. Batsford, 1986.

Examines the influence on Gurney's poetry of the Gloucestershire landscape, war, and the poetry of Walt Whitman, as well as the works of Elizabethan, Jacobean, and Georgian writers. According to Lucas: "More than any other poet of his generation Gurney seems to me to have had the sense that the continuities he evoked or wished to take for granted were under immediate threat, or had been wiped out."

Poole, Michael. "Bright Tracks." *The Listener* 109, No. 2,800 (24 February 1983): 27-8.

Praises evocation of place, attention to detail, and concreteness in Gurney's poetry. According to Poole: "Gurney was a compulsive walker and the fields and hedgerows he tramped became a kind of shorthand for every conceivable state of mind. This expansive quality, somewhere between Gerard Manley Hopkins's 'inscape' and the modernist epiphany, is what distinguishes Gurney's interest in landscape from the fashionable ruralism of the Georgian poets."

Stanford, Derek. Review of *Collected Poems of Ivor Gurney,* edited by P. J. Kavanagh. *Books and Bookmen,* No. 328 (January 1983): 33.

Focuses on the works originally intended for Gurney's third volume of war verse, *Rewards of Wonder,* which was rejected by his publishers in 1919.

Review of *Severn and Somme,* by Ivor Gurney. *The Times Literary Supplement,* No. 827 (22 November 1917): 571.

Praises the collection, noting that "a burning love for Gloucester, Severn, and Cotswold shines through almost every poem of Mr. Gurney's, and it is expressed with the force and simplicity natural to so genuine a passion."

"Hero Betrayed." *The Times Literary Supplement,* No. 3,730 (31 August 1973): 996.

Favorable review of *Poems of Ivor Gurney.* According to the critic: "Gurney's patriotism was undeniable; and it may well have been the powerful presence of this which militated against his wide acceptance by the pacifistically-inclined generations, readers of Siegfried Sassoon and Wilfred Owen, in the 1930s and following the Second World War."

Tomlinson, Charles. "Ivor Gurney's 'Best Poems'." *The Times Literary Supplement,* No. 4,318 (3 January 1986): 12.

Discusses a manuscript compiled by Gurney in about 1925 of the poems he considered to be his best, including "Felling a Tree," "Of the Sea," "Song—Past My Window," and others.

Trethowan, W. H. "Ivor Gurney's Mental Illness." *Music and Letters* 62, Nos. 3 and 4 (July-October 1981): 300-09.

Describes Gurney's mental deterioration and its effect on his career.

Vyacheslav (Ivanovich) Ivanov

1866-1949

Russian poet, philosopher, critic, essayist, dramatist, and novelist.

Ivanov was one of the most prominent members of the Russian Symbolist movement, the dominant literary movement in Russia during the first decades of the twentieth century. Inspired by the French Symbolist movement of the 1880s and 1890s, Russian Symbolism was similarly based on the concept that esoteric parallels exist between the material and the spiritual worlds and that insight into the latter can be attained by means of symbolic art and literature. While its earliest adherents considered Russian Symbolism a purely aesthetic doctrine, a "second generation" of writers, led by Ivanov, Andrey Bely, and Aleksandr Blok, regarded Symbolism as a religious worldview, utilizing Symbolist techniques to explore metaphysical concerns, propounding a view of the artist as visionary and possessor of higher knowledge, and ultimately seeking to synthesize art and religion. Ivanov was one of the movement's principal theorists and poets, and his works reflect his Symbolist aesthetic principles as well as his strong religious faith, humanist values, and fascination with classical culture. Renato Poggioli has written, "Ivanov cultivated the theoretical and artistic heritage of the [Symbolist] school, integrating it with the metaphysical traditions of the past, thus acting as the only religious humanist of his sect."

Born in Moscow, Ivanov was the son of a land surveyor and his wife. With the death of his father when Ivanov was five, his mother became the dominant influence on his development. A devoutly religious woman who claimed to have prophetic dreams and visions, she guided his religious education, which included a thorough knowledge of the Eastern Orthodox liturgy. Later in life he remarked, "I inherited elements of my mother's spiritual nature." A precocious and self-motivated youth, Ivanov began writing poetry at the age of nine and studying Greek at the age of twelve; in these and other intellectual pursuits, he was encouraged by his mother, who wanted her son to achieve academic excellence.

Graduating with honors from the classical gymnasium in Moscow, Ivanov then attended Moscow University, where he studied with the historical-philological faculty. He demonstrated significant promise as a classical scholar, and in 1886 received a scholarship to study with the renowned German historian Theodore Mommsen at the University of Berlin. In Berlin, Ivanov continued to pursue his interest in classical philology and wrote his thesis on the Roman fiscal system. While researching his thesis in Rome in 1893, he met Lydia Zinovieva-Annibal, whom he eventually married. Their relationship had a profound influence on Ivanov: according to some commentators, it was she who first made Ivanov aware of his potential as a poet. As a result of his outstanding academic performance at the University of Berlin, Ivanov was offered opportunities to continue his scholarship and to teach, but he declined, choosing instead to devote himself to poetry. He later wrote of this decision, "To everyone's surprise, I veered off in an entirely different direction; I immersed myself in poetry and my whole life has followed a different course." Freed from the academic structure and rou-

Portrait of Ivanov by K. A. Somov.

tine of his university days, Ivanov became engaged in a thorough study of Dionysian worship and the works of Friedrich Nietzsche, intellectual interests that would have a lifelong influence on his thought and writing. For the next decade, he wrote poems while traveling with Lydia in western Europe, Greece, Palestine, and Egypt. In Russia, a mutual friend showed one of Ivanov's poems to the philosopher and poet Vladimir Solovyev, who praised its "absolute originality." On subsequent trips to Russia, Ivanov met and developed a close friendship with Solovyev, who became an important influence on his spiritual and intellectual development.

Ivanov's first collection of poems, *Kormchie zvyozdy,* was published in St. Petersburg in 1903. Marked by complex diction, ornate style, formal precision, and metaphysical themes, these poems were highly praised by Symbolist writers, and Ivanov was immediately recognized as one of the leading poets of the movement. During the next year, he published another volume of poems, a drama, a treatise on Dionysus, and several philosophical essays. By the time he and his wife returned to Russia to live in 1905, Ivanov was well known in Russian literary circles. Their apartment in St. Petersburg, known as the "Tower," became the gathering place for Sym-

114

bolist writers and artists, who congregated for informal weekly meetings known as "Wednesdays."

Ivanov was devastated by the unexpected death of his wife in 1907. For the next five years, he remained in St. Petersburg and continued to publish poetry, including *Cor Ardens,* a two-volume series of sonnets dedicated to his wife's memory. After a brief return to Rome in the winter of 1912-13 to research the origins of the cult of Dionysus, he settled in Moscow with his new wife, Vera, Lydia's daughter from a previous marriage. Unlike many Russian intellectuals, he assumed no conspicuous political position regarding the Bolshevik Revolution, though he occasionally defended religion in public debates and published a short volume of poetry, *Pesni smutnogo vremeni,* which criticized militant atheism and the Red Terror. Despite the hardships of the Civil War, during 1919 and 1920 Ivanov published *Zimnie sonety* and *De profundis amavi,* collections of sonnets considered among his finest work. Vera died in 1920, and Ivanov was treated for illness and exhaustion at the Sanitorium for Scientific and Literary Workers near Moscow. There he met the philologist and philosopher Mikhail Gershenson, with whom he engaged in an epistolary debate on the importance of culture which was later published as *Perepiska iz dvukh uglov* (*Correspondence between Two Corners of a Room*). Later that year, he accepted the chairmanship of the department of classical philology at the University of Baku, Azerbaijan, and moved there with his son and daughter. After numerous requests, he and his children were allowed to visit Italy in 1924, and they did not return to Russia. Soon after his arrival in Rome, he joined the Catholic Church, an act he did not consider a traditional conversion but rather a natural extension of his belief in ecumenicity. He served as a professor of Russian literature at the University of Pavia from 1926 until 1934, when he was offered a position as professor of Slavic literature at the University of Florence. Because he was not a member of the Fascist Party, however, the Italian government refused to confirm the appointment, and Ivanov returned to Rome, where he remained active as a poet and scholar until his death in 1949. While his poetic output decreased in the decades after he left Russia, he did publish the highly acclaimed *Rimskie sonety* and *Rimsky dnevnik.*

Ivanov's worldview was based on what he saw as the collective and universal nature of all aspects of human culture, and throughout his writings he sought to reconcile and synthesize diverse disciplines, ideologies, and artistic styles. In his religious philosophy, for example, Ivanov incorporated elements from various systems of belief, in particular attempting to reconcile Christian doctrine with the Dionysian worship practiced in classical Greece. Viewing Dionysianism as a forerunner of Christianity in its emphasis on suffering and sacrifice, Ivanov suggested a symbolic and mystical identification between Dionysus and Christ. He regarded poetry, and art in general, as both an expression of human striving for the divine and a means of religious revelation. Embracing the Symbolist view of objects in the material world as symbols of higher realities, Ivanov considered the artist a possessor of mystical insight who plays a critical role in uncovering the meaning of symbols.

Victor Terras has noted that Ivanov's thought is "perfectly mirrored" in his poetry. Many of his poems are concerned with metaphysical questions and contain frequent allusions to classical thought and mythology. Maurice Bowra maintains that Ivanov's formal traditionalism, especially his frequent choice of the sonnet form and use of classical meters, reflects his belief that poetry is a mystical activity and should have the same dignity and decorum as a religious ritual. While Ivanov used traditional forms almost exclusively, his inventive use of language, often incorporating ecclesiastical Russian, Greek idioms, and archaisms, has been praised by many critics. Much of his early poetry, which is highly ornate and rich in scholarly allusions, was considered esoteric and difficult; however, critics generally agree that in his later poetry he developed a more personal lyric voice, and that these works are simpler and less obscure. In the words of Herbert Steiner, "He developed from a masterly refined and erudite style to one of masterly simplicity."

Ivanov's works in other genres also reflect his philosophical ideas and intellectual interests. His tragedies *Tantal* and *Prometei* demonstrate his concern with exploring the relationship between symbolism and mythology. In *Correspondence between Two Corners of a Room,* described by Poggioli as "one of the greatest and noblest documents of the time," Ivanov defended traditional religious and cultural values against his correspondent Gershenson, who argued that a true social revolution would serve to free humanity from the burden of oppressive conventions and traditions. Ivanov regarded *Povest o Svetomire tsareviche: Skazanie startsa inoka,* though unfinished at his death, as one of his major works; in a style echoing medieval romance, this novel combines religious allegory, elements of Russian history, and description of his own spiritual development. Ivanov was also a highly regarded literary critic who examined the works of Pindar, Homer, Petrarch, Johann Wolfgang von Goethe, Aleksandr Pushkin, and Nikolai Gogol. His most respected critical writings, a series of essays on Fyodor Dostoevsky, have been called unusual because of the emphasis they place on mythical aspects of Dostoevsky's writings.

In the early part of the twentieth century, Ivanov was well known and highly regarded as a poet and philosopher. As one of the leaders of the Russian Symbolists, he was quite influential in literary and intellectual circles through personal contact with fellow artists. Among most readers, however, his works were considered obscure and pedantic; Marc Slonim maintains that even among his peers Ivanov was "more admired and talked about than read." In the West, Ivanov's work has attracted increasing attention. He is currently regarded as one of the most original and influential poets and thinkers of the Russian Symbolist school.

(See also *Contemporary Authors,* Vol. 122)

PRINCIPAL WORKS

Kormchie zvyozdy (poetry) 1903
Prozrachnost (poetry) 1904
Tantal (drama) 1905
Eros (poetry) 1907
Po zvyozdam (criticism) 1909
Cor Ardens. 2 vols. (poetry) 1911
Nezhnaya taina (poetry) 1912
Borozdy i mezhi (criticism) 1916
Rodnoe i vselenskoe (essays) 1917
Mladenchestvo (poem) 1918
Prometei (drama) 1919
De profundis amavi (poetry) 1920
Perepiska iz dvukh uglov [with Mikhail Gershenson] (philosophy) 1921

[*Correspondence between Two Corners of a Room,* published in journal *Mesa,* 1947; also published as *Correspondence across a Room,* 1984]
Dionis i pradionisiistvo (treatise) 1923
Dostojewskij: Tragödie-Mythos-Mystik (criticism) 1932
[*Freedom and the Tragic Life: A Study in Dostoevsky,* 1952]
Chelovek (poetry) 1939
Rimsky dnevnik (poetry) 1944
†*Svet vecherny* (poetry) 1962
‡*Sobranie sochineny.* 3 vols. (poetry, novel, essays, criticism, and letters) 1971-79

*This work was originally published in German.

†This work contains *Zimnie sonety* (written in 1919 and 1920) and *Rimskie sonety* (written in 1924).

‡This work includes the novel *Povest o Svetomire tsareviche: Skazanie startsa inoka.*

Translated selections of Ivanov's poetry have been published in *Russian Poetry: The Modern Period,* edited by John Glad and Daniel Weissbort; *Modern Russian Poetry,* edited by Babette Deutsch and Avrahm Yarmolinski; *Russian Poetry,* edited by Babette Deutsch and Avrahm Yarmolinski; and *A Treasury of Russian Verse,* edited by Avrahm Yarmolinski.

VALERY BRYUSOV (essay date 1910)

[*One of the originators and leading theoreticians of Russian Symbolism, Bryusov edited and published the first collections of Russian Symbolist writings and promoted the development of the movement both as editor of the Symbolist journal* Vesy *and as a founder of the Skorpion publishing house. He was also the author of a large body of poetry and fiction, which is considered to exemplify many of the principal themes and techniques of the movement and is praised for its technical brilliance. One of the primary proponents of Symbolism as a purely aesthetic doctrine, Bryusov opposed the efforts of Ivanov and others to establish Symbolism as a worldview. In the following excerpt, he responds to essays by Ivanov and Aleksandr Blok published in the journal* Apollon, *disputing their assertions that Symbolist literature should constitute "something higher" than art.*]

For me, like the majority of people, it seems useful for each object to serve a definite purpose. A hammer is used for driving nails, not for painting pictures. It's better to shoot with a gun than to drink liqueur from it. A cookbook should teach the preparation of various foods. A book of poetry. . . . What should a book of poetry give us?

Grandpa Krylov warns us against those singers whose chief merit is that they "never touch spirits." Together with Krylov, I also demand that singers most of all be good. Their attitude toward alcoholic drinks is, it's true, a matter of secondary importance. Similarly, I expect poets to be most of all poets.

Mr. Vyacheslav Ivanov and Mr. Aleksandr Blok, in their mutually complimentary articles printed in the eighth issue of *Apollon,* evidently do not share my (I must confess, rather "banal") views. Both of them strive to demonstrate that a poet should not be a poet, and a book of poetry not a book of poetry. They say, it's true: "a book, not of poetry, but of something higher than poetry," and "not a poet, but some-

thing greater than a poet." But Krylov's hero, who had such a praiseworthy aversion to intoxicants, was probably certain that his singers were "higher" than simple singers.

Summarizing his article, Vyacheslav Ivanov writes: "From every line of what has been posited above it follows that Symbolism did not want to be and could not be only art." A. Blok, calling himself V. Ivanov's Baedeker, develops this thought in a repentant article, in which he confesses his sin, that he, A. Blok, was a "prophet" and lowered himself to the point where he became a "poet." This, in the stern language of A. Blok's teacher, Vl. Solovyov, seems to mean: "He replaced the soul's delight with a circumspect deception, the living language of the gods with servile speech, and the muses' shrine with a noisy puppet show."

I very much doubt that the verses of Vl. Solovyov quoted in the article had exactly the same sense that A. Blok wants to give them. It would be amazing if Vl. Solovyov, given his well-known attitude toward poetry, the language of "poets," i.e., the language of poetry, would have called it "servile speech." But for A. Blok (and for V. Ivanov?) this is so. Poetry is "servile speech," a "deception," a "puppet show." Whence the conclusion: don't be a poet, be something higher than a poet, or as the "Baedeker," A. Blok, says: "be a theurgist."

I think that after reading these statements, very many people, together with me, will decisively stand up in defense of poetry, although V. Ivanov and A. Blok have declared it to be "servile speech." To be a theurgist, of course, is not a bad thing at all. But why does it follow from this that to be a poet is something to be ashamed of? In my opinion, for example, it is honorable to be an astronomer. But will I really abuse some historian with these words: "Deceiver, slave, puppeteer, aren't you ashamed to study history and not astronomy?"

It's true that both V. Ivanov and A. Blok are not talking about poetry in general, but exclusively about Symbolist poetry, about Symbolism. How do they understand this appellation, however?

Do they understand the word "Symbolism" in a broad sense, in accordance with the notion that Aeschylus and Goethe can and should be called Symbolists (for Symbolism is the natural language of any art)? But then the concept "Symbolist poetry" coincides with the concept of poetry in general. Or do V. Ivanov and A. Blok have in mind just the artistic movement of the last decades? Evidently, the last supposition is the fairest, since V. Ivanov speaks of Tyutchev as the first Russian Symbolist, speaks of the "common, international character of this phenomenon," about the "essence of Western influence on the most recent Russian poets," etc. Then. . . . Well, then one must reckon somewhat with history.

No matter how much I respect V. Ivanov's artistic gifts and energy of thought, I still cannot agree that whatever he likes should be called "Symbolism." "Symbolism," like "Romanticism," is a defined historical phenomenon, connected with definite dates and names. The "Symbolist" movement arose as a literary school in France (not without some influence from England) at the end of the nineteenth century and found followers in all the literatures of Europe, impregnated other arts with its ideas, and could not help reflecting on the epoch's world view. But it always developed exclusively in the field of art. V. Ivanov can point to whichever future goals of Symbolism he likes, and his Baedeker—the paths to these goals, but they have neither the right nor the power to change the past. No matter how disappointing this is for them, "Symbolism" *wanted to be* and always *was only art*.

The "Symbolists'" books, thank God, still haven't perished because of some elemental catastrophe; you can obtain them in any library. Many "Symbolists," leaders of the movement, are still among us. Ask Verhaeren and Vielé-Griffin, George and Hofmannsthal, and here, Balmont, and I'm certain that they will all say, unanimously, that they wanted one thing: to serve art. They saw (and see) their greatest pride and highest honor in the name "artist," and "poet." How could they suddenly announce: "Symbolism did not want to be and could not be only art?" With such an attitude toward historical facts, who will stop V. Ivanov from announcing tomorrow that: "Romanticism always was and could only be an original geological theory!"

Symbolism is a *method* of art, realized in that school which got the name "Symbolist." By this method, art is distinguished from rationalistic cognition of the world in science, and from attempts at non-rational penetration into its secrets in mysticism. Art is autonomous; it has its method and its own purposes. When will it be possible not to repeat this truth, which long ago should have been considered a truism? Really, after it was forced to serve science and society, now they compel it to serve religion! Give it some freedom finally!

There are, of course, no reasons for limiting a person's field of activities. Goethe is twice as dear to us because he was not only the greatest poet of the nineteenth century but also a powerful scientific mind in his time. In Dante Gabriel Rossetti, the harmonic combination of a poet's gifts and an artist's colors enchants us. Why can't a poet also be a chemist or a politician, or if he prefers, a theurgist? But to insist that all poets necessarily be theurgists is as absurd as insisting that they all be members of the State Duma. And to demand that poets stop being poets in order to become theurgists is even more absurd.

As Blok, at the end of his article, asks: "Is what happened with us correctable or not?" In other words: "is it possible to stop being a 'poet' and again become a 'theurgist'?" It seems already sufficiently clear that this question does not relate to Symbolism in general. Not wishing at all to condemn this path of spiritual development, which, in easily interpreted allegories, A. Blok depicted in his article, it is in no way possible to accept this path as typical for the contemporary poet. Those sins, which A. Blok confesses, "Symbolism" does not accept as its own, and there is nothing that needs to be "corrected." Symbolists will remain poets, as they always have been.

But, in so far as we are talking about V. Ivanov and A. Blok, their aspiration to "correct" something, and with the most radical means, this can lead us into some apprehension. And what if these corrections turned out to be like those of many Russian municipal councils, who often find it necessary to raze this or that building because it is "not pretty," and then because of a lack of funds, leave a vacant lot in its place? V. Ivanov and A. Blok are wonderful poets; they have shown us that. But whether they will make simply "good," and I don't even say great, theurgists, is a matter of completely permissible doubt. For some reason, I have a hard time believing in their theurgical calling.

I am calmed by the consideration that V. Ivanov's and A. Blok's theories have not yet prevented them from becoming true artists. And A. Blok slanders himself when he says that his most recent verses are "servile speeches." Fortunately for us, and everyone for whom art is dear, this is genuine and, at times, wonderful poetry. In regard to V. Ivanov's call, and that of his interpreter, which leads the whole development of contemporary Symbolism to a new road, i.e., shifts poetry from the path it has followed for not less than ten millenia, this is less a cause for apprehension, I think. Alexander the Great had sufficient strength to pull the Pythian, against her will, onto the tripod; but I don't see Alexander's strength here, only a much more difficult undertaking! (pp. 166-69)

> *Valery Bryusov, "About 'Servile Speech', in Defense of Poetry," in* The Russian Symbolists: An Anthology of Critical and Theoretical Writings, *edited and translated by Ronald E. Peterson, Ardis, 1986, pp. 166-69.*

D. S. MIRSKY   (essay date 1926)

[*Mirsky was a Russian prince who fled his country after the Bolshevik Revolution and settled in London. While in England, he wrote two important histories of Russian literature,* Contemporary Russian Literature *(1926) and* A History of Russian Literature *(1927). In 1932, having reconciled himself to the Soviet regime, Mirsky returned to the USSR. He continued to write literary criticism, but his work eventually ran afoul of Soviet censors and he was exiled to Siberia. He disappeared in 1937. In the following excerpt from* Contemporary Russian Literature, *Mirsky provides a brief overview of the styles and subjects of Ivanov's poetry and prose.*]

[Lev] Shestov, who is a master of pointed epigram, has given Ivanov the nickname of Vyacheslav the Magnificent, and "magnificent" is the best definition one can think of for his style. In his first book [**Pilot Stars**] there was still a certain primitivism, a "ruggedness," which gave it a certain freshness that is absent from his mature work. But **Cor Ardens** is the high-water mark of the ornate style in Russian poetry. His verse is saturated with beauty and expressiveness; it is all aglow with jewels and precious metals, it is like a rich Byzantine garment. "Byzantine" and "Alexandrian" are two very suitable epithets for his poetry, for it is all full of the product of past ages, very scholarly, conscious, and quite unspontaneous. Ivanov is the nearest approach in Russian poetry to the conscious and studied splendours of Milton. In his verse every image, every word, every sound, every cadence are part of one admirably planned whole. Everything is carefully weighed and used with elaborate discrimination to the best effect. His language is archaic, and he likes to introduce Greek idioms. This is in the great tradition of ecclesiastic Russian and adds powerfully to the majesty of his numbers. Most of his poems are metaphysical; he has also written many love lyrics and political poems, but love and politics are always treated *sub specie aeternitatis*. His poetry is of course difficult, and hardly accessible to the man in the street, but, for those who can move in his sphere of ideas, there is in his heady and spiced wine an attractively troubling flavour. In his magnificence and his scholarship is hidden the sting of a refined and ecstatic sensuality—the sting of Astarte—rather than that of Dionysos. His poetry may be exclusive, Alexandrian, derivative (in so far as our culture is derivative), but that it is genuine, perhaps great poetry, there can be no doubt. The only objection that can be advanced against it is that it is too much of a good thing. Somewhat apart from the rest of his work stand **The Winter Sonnets** (1920); they are simpler, more human, less metaphysical. Their subject is the survival of the undying intellectual flame in the presence of elemental enemies—cold and starvation. Like so many Symbolists, Ivanov was also a translator, and his versions of Pindar, Sappho, Alcaeus, Novalis, and especially the unpublished version of *Agamemnon*, are among the greatest achievements of Russian translated verse.

Ivanov's prose is as magnificent as his verse—it is the most elaborate and majestic ornate prose in the language. His earlier essays are contained in two volumes—***By the Stars*** (1909) and ***Furrows and Boundaries*** (1916). In them he develops the same ideas as in his poetry. He believed that our times were capable of reviving the mythological creation of religious ages. He discovered in Dostoevsky a great creator of myths, and he believed that the modern theatre might become religious and choric like the Dionysian theatre of Athens. His most remarkable prose work is the dialogue of letters which he carried on with Gershenzon, when the two philosophers lay convalescent in two corners of the same hospital ward in the worst days of Bolshevik destruction (*A Correspondence between Two Corners,* 1920). In it Gershenzon aspires, Rousseau-like, after a new and complete liberty, after a naked man on a new earth, free from the yoke of centuries of culture. Ivanov takes up the defence of cultural values, and speaks with pointed force and noble enthusiasm for the great past of human achievement against his nihilistic opponent. The six letters which form his part of the dialogue are a noble and proud defence of culture, all the more impressive from the circumstances in which they were written. (pp. 207-09)

Prince D. S. Mirsky, "Vyacheslav Ivanov," in his
Contemporary Russian Literature: 1881-1925, *Alfred A. Knopf, 1926, pp. 205-09.*

RENATO POGGIOLI (essay date 1947)

[*Poggioli was an Italian-born American critic and translator. Much of his critical writing is concerned with Russian literature, including* The Poets of Russia: 1893-1930 *(1960), which is one of the most important examinations of this literary era. In the following excerpt, Poggioli analyzes in detail the philosophical arguments presented by Ivanov and Gershenson in* Correspondence between Two Corners of a Room.]

This investigation will begin by a detailed analysis of the ***Correspondence,*** by means of a logical rather than a critical résumé, and by making use, in the words of their authors, of the passages which seem the highlights of this lofty dialogue. The very first sentence of Ivanov's opening letter must have made a strong impression on his friend. "I know," says Ivanov to Herschensohn, "that you are overtaken by doubts about man's immortality and the person of God," and he proceeds by affirming the presence within man's soul of a "luminous guest" who is like the promise of our future rebirth, a guarantee given by God the Father to all his sons (I). In his reply Herschensohn, after accepting the principle of personality as the supreme value, as the only reality, confesses candidly his temperamental dislike of metaphysics; and he adds that, in the present human and historical condition, his instinctive and fundamental distrust involves something more solid and substantial than metaphysics alone, that is, culture itself. Under the impact of present experience, culture seems to him not merely useless, but harmful:

> For some time I have been finding oppressive, like an excessive load, or too heavy clothes, all the intellectual conquests of mankind, the entire treasure of notions and knowledge, of values collected and

crystallized by the centuries. . . . Such a feeling began to trouble my soul a long time ago, but it has now become customary with me. It must be a great happiness, I think, to dive into the river Lethe, cleansing one's soul within its waters, clearing away the remembrances of all religious and philosophical systems, of all wisdom and doctrine, of poetry and the arts, and land again naked on the shore, naked as the first man, light and merry, freely stretching and raising one's naked arms, remembering of the past but one thing, how one felt burdened by those clothes, and how one now feels easy and free without them. . . . Our elegant clothing did not weigh upon us as long as it remained unsoiled and unspoiled, but since during these years it has been torn and now hangs in rags from our shoulders, we would like to take it off our body and throw it away (II).

In his answer, Ivanov does not defend reason, the usual object of hatred on the part of instinct, and one which seems to him deserving of hatred, although on other grounds; he rather defends the spirit, not culture alone, but that ultimate and primordial kind of culture which cannot be conceived outside religion, because it rests on religion and is nourished by it. Herschensohn is reproached by his friend for thinking of culture in the usual modern terms; it is for this reason that culture is, to him, slavery to the letter instead of being freedom of the spirit:

> That state of mind now dominating and greatly torturing you, that excruciating feeling of the intolerable load of the cultural inheritance weighing on your soul, is essentially due to the fact that you experience culture not as a living treasure of gifts, but as a system of the subtlest restrictions. No wonder, since culture has aimed at being no more than that. But for me it is the stairs of Eros and a hierarchy of venerations (III).

Herschensohn replies by referring to Ivanov's "work in progress" (a translation of Dante's *Purgatorio*), and by expressing a feeling of nostalgia for the "harmonic" civilization of the Middle Ages, but turns immediately back to the present, asking a rhetorical question:

> How, in such circumstances, can we trust our reason, when we realize that reason itself has derived from culture and, naturally enough, bows before it, like a slave to the master who has raised him? . . . I am not judging culture, I merely witness that I suffocate within it. Like Rousseau, I see in my dreams a condition of bliss, of perfect freedom, where the unburdened soul lives in an Edenic thoughtlessness. I know too many things, and this load tortures me.

Herschensohn's criticism of culture, as well as of the body of knowledge it implies, seems here dictated by the desire to escape from history, by the wish to live in the individual passions of the moment: "As for that knowledge, I have no use for it when I am in love or in sorrow." An attack follows on philosophical idealism, which Herschensohn accuses of having destroyed the immediate sense of reality and of having reduced the experience of life to a ghost: "That century-long illusion has passed away, but how many awful traces it has left behind!" After the attack on modern culture, there follows the attack on modern civilization and its technology, on the *embarras de richesses* of modern industry, which in itself is merely a consequence of that "cultural inheritance weighing on our personality with the pressure of sixty atmospheres" (IV).

Ivanov's reply is still inspired by his belief in the syncretism of religion and culture, by his definition of religion as a kind of transcendental culture:

> It seems to me that you are unable to conceive of the permanence of culture without one's substantial fusion with it, without one's merging within it. As for myself, I believe that our consciousness must at least partly transcend culture itself. . . . The man believing in God would not consent at any price to consider his faith as a part of culture: this is what I believe, although I am convinced that every great historical culture springs forth from a primordial religious fact. A man enslaved by culture (such is the conception of modern thought) will instead consider his faith as a manifestation of culture, whatever his definition of faith might be. . . . Only through faith is man able to transcend the "temptation" of culture. . . . The dream of Rousseau sprang forth from his disbelief (V).

The dream of the *tabula rasa,* says Ivanov, is not the dream of a new culture, or of a life liberated from it: it is the dream of a new morality, or of the destruction of traditional morality, even of morality itself—in other words, an attempt to erase from the soul of man the traces of original sin. Herschensohn replies by denying the possibility of a coexistence of culture and faith: "But it is not of this that I wish to speak. . . . I do not know or wish to know what man will find beyond the wall of the jail he is going to leave, and openly acknowledge my indifference toward 'the work of preparing freedom's roads.' . . . I merely *feel* . . . an urgent need of liberty for my spirit and conscience" (VI). Herschensohn ends by comparing himself to a Greek of the sixth century, oppressed by the complexity of his pantheon of gods, and to an Australian aborigine, tired under the weight of his totems and taboos.

In the following letter we find the first discreet hint, on the part of Ivanov, that his friend's viewpoint is due to Herschensohn's desire to share in the cave of his soul the collective and historical experience now taking place outside its walls: "Perhaps the last of Faust's temptations ought to become for you the first: the enchanted dream of the canals and the new world, the illusion of a free land for a free people." It is the revolutionary illusion that leads Herschensohn, in Ivanov's judgment, to think that culture is an abandoned temple, a ruined city, or simply an empty shell. Ivanov sees that Herschensohn's denial of culture had been dictated by his wish to merge, morbidly, unconsciously, and passively, into the stream of historical contingency. It is the convulsive force of contemporary events, Ivanov tells his friend, that makes him feel that culture is a static weight, though it really is a dynamic power: "not only a monument, but also an instrument of spiritual initiation" (VII).

But Herschensohn has no use for that monument or instrument: "The revelations of truth which descended on our forefathers have changed into mummies"; modern man is tyrannized by objectivized and abstract values, which may be classified into "fetish-values," that is, the traditional taboos of morality and religion, and into "vampire-values," that is, the bloodless totems of metaphysical and philosophical abstractions. "It may be that the last war has been but a hecatomb never witnessed before, forced upon Europe by a few intelligible values allied to each other through their priests." It is to real, personal, immediate, everlasting, and metacultural values that man must return. "When around a simple prayer one has built an immense structure of theology, religion, and church," Herschensohn says, we need a religious revolution, such as the Reformation; and when similar structures have been built also in the field of social life, we need a political revolution, such as happened in France in 1789. A similar house cleaning or clearing of the air is taking place at the present time: "Now a new storm is shaking the world: the individual right to work and property forces us to go out, into the open, into the free air, from century-long complications, from the monstrous complexities of abstract social ideas" (VIII).

Ivanov's answer is an argument *ad hominem:* "Yesterday's values are now shaken from their roots, and you are one of those who feel joy in this earthquake"; but it is also a keen criticism of his friend's presuppositions about the acultural or anticultural essence of the Russian revolution. Ivanov sees in it not merely a mystical, popular outburst, but the plan of a new civilization, of a new culture to be built: "The anarchistic current does not seem to predominate within it" (IX). Herschensohn feels that he has been touched on a sore spot and reacts by accusing Ivanov of treating him as a physician treats a sick man, unaware that his diagnosis is wrong. He too finds a weak spot in the armor of his friend, whose great learning, in spite of his transcendental religious beliefs, leads him to historicism; that is, to an attitude which implies a justification rather than a judgment of culture. And he takes upon himself again the task of the judge: culture was created by man as an instrument to make it possible for him to live better in his environment, but now the instrument is so complicated and heavy that it has become harmful. "The deer developed horns as a means of frightening his enemies and defending himself, but in some species they have reached such dimensions as to prevent him from running through the woods, and the species is dying. Is it not the same thing with your culture? Are not your values those horns?" (X). Perhaps the proletariat will destroy those horns; perhaps it will adapt them to changed conditions; perhaps it will create better organs for the new men.

In his answer, Ivanov recognizes that the controversy has reached a dead end, that from now on it will be only a repetition of opposite statements. He sees that there is no meeting ground for his "humanism and mysticism," and for the "anarchic utopianism and cultural nihilism" of his friend (XI). Herschensohn, discovering signs of bad humor and even of bad temper in their dialogue, concludes it with an apparent compromise, postulating a new culture, different from the old one, which is only "a daily habit . . . not an intellectual nourishment" (XII). The correspondence can go no further; and Herschensohn, defining himself as a stranger and a pilgrim searching for the promised land, while Ivanov feels at home on the native soil of history and culture, ends by saying that their brotherly souls will find, in the house of the Father, a common abode.

It is difficult to conceive of a loftier discussion, of an exchange of ideas on a higher plane, of a polemic about history more detached from the superficial passions aroused by current events, and at the same time more concerned with the absolute and essential reality underlying the facts that take place before one's eyes, within the relativity of time and of human things. The war and the revolution, Russia and Bolshevism, are hardly mentioned, or referred to only a few times; still, their presence is deeply and constantly felt, and the sense of this presence has a direct bearing on what each of these two speakers says, thinks, or feels. The *Correspondence,* however, needs not to be praised, but to be appraised. What one must try to achieve is a critical interpretation of this text, and to extract from it useful lessons for all, valid conclusions for the present manifestations of the same crisis, still torturing the West and the world.

The position of Herschensohn is easier to deal with, and even to find fault with, and this task of faultfinding is expertly performed by Ivanov himself. Ivanov is right when he maintains that Herschensohn's viewpoint is not new: that a similar palingenesis, beyond culture or without it, with identical intellectual and ethical implications (the longing for a simplification of life, for the regained paradise of primitivism, for an escape from any tie and any bond) had already fascinated Leo Tolstoy, who, as Ivanov tells his friend, "must naturally attract you" (XI). Even before, the same dream had possessed the soul and mind of Rousseau, in whom Ivanov recognizes a decadent *avant la lettre* ["before the word was coined"] (V). In this, too, it is easy to agree with him, since Rousseau's ethical, political, and social ideal is nothing but the projection into the future of a retrospective utopia, of an Eldorado dimly seen in a distant time, discovered by looking backwards into the darkness of the past. Ivanov is equally right when he implies that a "transvaluation of all values" succeeds only in achieving the destruction, or at least the dethronement, of the values of the past, but that it always fails to transform them into new values, or to create values of its own. Any transvaluation of this kind is another symptom of decadence of the nihilistic or cynical type, and Ivanov is again in the right when, after the names of Tolstoy and Rousseau, he brings in, to explain or rather to judge the viewpoint of his friend, a far more dangerous and suggestive name—the name of Friedrich Nietzsche. "At bottom, the problem of Nietzsche is your own: culture, personality, values, decadence, and health—above everything, health" (IX). We could add that, while Nietzsche aims at being the "physician of culture," at becoming its regenerator and healer, Herschensohn would rather be the priest performing the burial rites of culture, singing over its body a requiem for the peace of its soul. For, in spite of the fact that he says, "Let the dead bury their dead," we know that he, too, is one of the living dead.

Herschensohn is rather perplexed at this kind of criticism. His reactions are varied: now he denies, now he accepts, now he modifies or qualifies Ivanov's strictures. For instance, he answers the reference to Rousseau in a rather conciliatory way: "It seems to me that even Rousseau, who shook Europe with his dream, did not contemplate a *tabula rasa*" (VIII). It is easy to accuse Herschensohn of many such inconsistencies and perplexities, or to admit that his dreamed-of palingenesis points at a cultural renaissance of its own. On the other hand, credit must be given to him for candidly recognizing, more than once, the absurdity of a denial of culture based on culture itself. Yet, when all this is said, there is no doubt that the idea of the *tabula rasa* coincides with his utopia or promised land, with his ideal aim, with the object of his dreams.

To agree with Ivanov's criticism of Herschensohn's position, to accept the *pars destruens* of his argument, does not mean an approval of his positive viewpoint, an acceptance of the *pars construens* of his system. After all, the dream of the *tabula rasa* is dialectically the cultural equivalent of the socialist ideal, as Dostoevski was able to demonstrate and anticipate in his *Possessed.* On the other hand, provided that that ideal be realized without becoming totalitarian, one must admit that it springs forth (and it is only on such soil that it may flourish and live) from the human need for a terrestrial and historical justice: a need, to be sure, not easily satisfied by theological and metaphysical justice, the only kinds offered to us by religion and by historicism. It is only in this sense that, against the cultural and religious consciousness of Ivanov, against what he calls the "vertical line," in a given epoch of crisis, in a given historical experience, man's conscience may have its good reasons for preferring the solutions of intuition and sentiment, Herschensohn's "horizontal line." This means that the controversy is not merely a philosophical one, as Ivanov seems to think, and as he felt it necessary to restate, many years later, by defining the *Correspondence* as "a peculiar re-evocation of the everlasting and protean dispute between *realism* and *nominalism.*"

That medieval dispute was a scholastic replica of the Platonic-Aristotelian alternative: were ideas, that is, the names of things, the only real essences, the only authentic values contained in those appearances, in those non-values that are the concrete objects? Or were those ideas only names, *flatus vocis,* mere conventional or practical labels, deprived of any existence of their own, while reality belongs to solid objects and to concrete things? The realist considered as true the first hypothesis; the nominalist, the second one. In such a sense, there is no doubt that Ivanov is the realist, and Herschensohn the nominalist, for the former considers culture, which is a collection of ideas, of name-things, as the human equivalent of the Logos, which, as in religion, is made flesh; while, for the latter, culture is the dead letter and life the living spirit. Ivanov is of course nearer than his friend to Goethe, whom he often quotes or refers to, but here Herschensohn restates as his own the poetic truth of Goethe that "the tree of knowledge is gray, and the tree of life is green." And, like Goethe, Herschensohn does not care too much either for the eternal archetypes or for the *Ding an Sich* ["thing-in-itself"].

Yet, if Herschensohn were merely a nominalist, he would not take issue with culture, exactly because he would consider it only a collection of labels, a dictionary of names and nouns, a heap of dead or at least lifeless words. In such a case, he would not feel it necessary or worth while to make such a sweep of all the cultural traditions of the past, since human reality would remain outside them: one does not fight phantoms or kill ghosts. But Herschensohn is a modern man, and he knows, or thinks, that names, labels, ideas may not only be different from human realities, but possess a validity, solidity, and vitality of their own, and be filled with such an explosive energy as to act and react upon life, converting or perverting it. Herschensohn would agree with such different thinkers as Burckhardt, Benda, and Ortega y Gasset, for whom modern history and modern politics have been and still are a politics and a history of ideas, and of bad and harmful ideas at that. Herschensohn states as much when he says that the First World War had perhaps been a hecatomb forced upon mankind by ideas, that is, by the intellectual dogmas and the ethical creeds of the past.

In spite of the fact that Herschensohn's moral position and sentimental attitude differ very much from Sorel's and Marx's, to those ideas which he calls "fetish-values" one could easily give the Sorelian name of myths; and to those ideas which he calls "vampire-values," one could with equal justice give the Marxist name of ideologies. Sorel approves of social myths because of his Machiavellian sympathy for political activism; Marx, who naïvely expected that his so-called scientific socialism would not have any use or need for them, condemns ideologies as the intellectual weapons of the classes or of the social system he attacks. Unlike Sorel, we fear myths and hate ideologies, either of the Right or of the Left—for very different reasons from Marx's, and also because in this case we know better than he. One should agree therefore with Herschensohn's condemnation of myths and ideologies while differing from him in the awareness that the revolution in which he saw the dawn of a reborn human innocence is as guilty as any established society, or even more so, of creating or perpetuating "fetish-values" or "vampire-values," which enslave the soul and destroy the dignity of man.

Ivanov stands on solid ground when he tells Herschensohn that Bolshevism is also culture, even if it is a culture of its own, and that those anarchistic tendencies of which Herschensohn is so fond are absent from the revolution and seem alien to it. One could add that technology, the very technology which he condemns as harshly as he condemns culture itself, will be the most important economic and political business of the society of iron and blood that the revolution, in which he sees only "sweetness and light," will finally build. At any rate, as Ivanov rightly maintains, iconoclasm does not lead anywhere, not even to the city of Utopia, to that Erewhon which is a Nowhere.

On the other hand, Ivanov commits the opposite sin, the sin of spiritual and cultural idolatry. His idolatry of religion and historicism leads to an essential indifference to the tragedy of history, to the social condition of man. Yet one must accept the principle inherent in his position, that it is not through the iconoclasm of culture and history that man will be able to build a better house or a better life for himself. On the stage where the tragedy of history is performed, man rejects the intervention of a *deus ex machina,* which is Ivanov's theatrical trick; but he refuses also that too easy catharsis which Herschensohn naïvely offers in his belief that it will compensate for the catastrophe, for that unhappy ending which always involves grief, death, and bloodshed. One feels rather skeptical and doubtful of those who wish, like Herschensohn, to merge themselves mystically and morbidly into an elementary and telluric force, merely because it may clear the air in the old, dusty, and unhealthy dwellings of man. One must equally dislike the purely symbolical interpretation of Ivanov, and the too literal acceptance by Herschensohn, of the truth contained in Goethe's *Stirb und werde* ["die and become"], which after all is a command for man to act and to live.

On one side, Ivanov's defense of culture and religion, within and without history, *pro et contra,* for or above man, and, on the other side, Herschensohn's desire to throw away culture in order to be better able to embrace mankind (suffering—who knows?—either the pangs of childbirth or the agony of death), prove that the real issue at stake in this text is a question of vital importance not so much for the intelligentsia as for the intelligence of the West. The real theme of the **Correspondence** is not the antinomy of realism and nominalism, but the antithesis of two ideals: the humanistic and the humanitarian. It matters very little that Ivanov is a religious humanist, since, despite his affirmation of the supremacy of religion, he certainly yields to the temptation of culture, even though he condemns it. Thus his judgment against the hu-

manist, already quoted, applies to the judge himself: "A man enslaved by culture . . . will consider . . . his faith as a manifestation of culture, whatever his definition of faith might be" (V).

As for Ivanov's attempt at a conciliation of the humanistic and religious traditions, it is nothing new. Heine, Nietzsche, and Renan had already praised the Catholic Church for having achieved that conciliation during the Renaissance, and condemned the Reformation for having broken that ideal relationship. From Marsilio Ficino and Pico della Mirandola up to Cardinal Bessarion, the European mind had often tried, as Ivanov tries, to create a synthesis of the two antiquities, the classical and the biblical, to harmonize paganism and Christianity, Plato and Jesus, Hebraism and Hellenism, the civilization of Rome and the West and the culture of Byzantium and the East. Such a synthesis is still essentially humanistic in character, and therefore unable to change the essence of humanism, the ideal of which had been already perfectly stated by a pagan writer of the third century, Aulus Gellius, in a famous passage of his *Attic Nights* still worth quoting: "Those who created the Latin tongue and spoke it well never gave *humanitas* the notion inherent in the Greek word *philanthropia.* They gave that word the meaning of what the Greeks call *paideia,* i.e., knowledge of the fine arts."

But the humanitarian, Christian or not, radical or mystic, follower of Tolstoy or of Gandhi, is interested in philanthropy, both the word and the thing. Sometimes he is interested also in the humanities, but only when he thinks that there is no conflict between them and humanity. In a few short periods of Western history, in the eighteenth and in part of the nineteenth centuries, the two ideals coincided, the former being considered as the cultural instrument and the intellectual counterpart of the latter. But this coincidence between the humanistic and the humanitarian ideal broke down during the second half of the nineteenth century, when a few spirits, in their reaction against rationalism, historicism, scientism, and positivism, forced the humanitarian ideal to cope with the problem of personality and to find other foundations for its faith.

The mission of modern culture has been to react against four historical kinds of reason: *Verstand,* or the *raison raisonnante,* that is, "mathematical" reason; *Vernunft,* or "critical" or "idealistic" reason; and, derived respectively from the former and the latter, "scientific" and "historic" reason. In other words, modern culture has reacted against Descartes, Comte, and Taine, and against Kant, Schelling, and Hegel. Such a reaction had been anticipated by Rousseau, and was to culminate in the work of Dostoevski: two men who were dear to the heart of Herschensohn, a humanitarian basing his faith upon sentiment, intuition, and instinct. Such is the meaning of his attack on philosophical idealism, on historic and ideal reason; after all, Dostoevski had already aimed his telling blows at mathematical and scientific reason, in the first part of the *Notes from Underground.* If it is superfluous to note that Ivanov had no use for mathematical and scientific reason, it is perhaps worth while to remark that many words and ideas have, in Herschensohn's attack against philosophical idealism, a Bergsonian ring.

The humanitarian of the rationalistic, practical, utilitarian kind (as Dostoevski had already noted, in the novel mentioned above) is active and positive, at least in thought; while the humanitarian of the sentimental, intuitive, and instinctive type, *à la* Herschensohn, is negative and passive in character:

feminine and pacifistic, so to say. As a natural consequence, he is destined to be disappointed by that revolution he falls in love with, and which he greets, as Herschensohn does, in the name of personal freedom and the dignity of man—or, as he says, in the name of "the individual right to work and property" (VIII), as a liberation of all human faculties, as an opportunity for the self-development and self-expression of Everyman. He was dreaming of a Crystal Palace where there could be room also for the dissident and the heretic, for private life and individual idiosyncrasies, not only for the will, but even for the whims of man. If he had understood the dialectic of Dostoevski, the ironical inventor of that myth, he would have seen that in the Crystal Palace there is no room for this. The humanitarian must find out this truth by himself. The mystical humanitarian awakens only when he survives his dream, and then he is not only disappointed but crushed, because, unlike his more logical rivals or mathematical colleagues, he is unable to rationalize the cruel reality now oppressing him and his fellow men. Herschensohn was perhaps fortunate in being spared by death from witnessing the awful metamorphosis of the figure of his dream into a new Leviathan.

Exactly because of the blindness of his irrational hopes about the kind of future which the present will bring forth, Herschensohn's iconoclasm becomes a new idolatry, and Ivanov is right in condemning it. On the other hand, as already hinted, there is an idolatry in Ivanov too, the idolatry of the eternal, which is very often only the apotheosis of what is merely old. The iconoclast, as Ivanov rightly implies, is a decadent; yet the idolater is a decadent, too. The cultural idolatry of Ivanov and the cultural iconoclasm of Herschensohn have the same origin: both come from Nietzsche, who is the common spiritual master of their generation and of both men, even if both disciples later discarded him. Nietzsche condemned decadence, although he was a decadent himself, and this is what both Ivanov and Herschensohn do. This point is proved merely by quoting and using the beautiful definition of decadence given in this text by Ivanov himself: "What is decadence? The awareness of one's subtlest organic bonds with the lofty cultural tradition of the past, but an awareness tied up with the feeling, both *oppressive* and *exalting,* of being the last of the series" (VIII). It is that oppressiveness which leads the decadent Herschensohn to the blind and mystical acceptance of a new series, the series of a resurgent barbarism, replacing the traditions and beliefs of a tired and dying civilization; it is that exaltation which impels the proud Ivanov to keep faith with the cultural values and the spiritual creeds of the old series, and later to accept as his own the creed of the most dogmatic and canonical, ancient and permanent church of the West, Roman Catholicism, the most compact system of revelations ever devised by man.

Thus, in spite of the fact that both Ivanov and Herschensohn are, as the former accuses the latter of being, two "monologists" (IX), in spite of the fact that they stand, as Herschensohn says, "at the opposite ends of a diagonal not only in our room, but also in the spiritual world" (II), a dialogue between them is, up to a certain point, still natural and possible, owing to their common decadent background. It is decadent to believe that the only choice left to man lies between cultural traditionalism and religious conservatism on one hand, and revolutionary messianism on the other. It is a symptom of decadent psychology to feel that man's fate at this stage in history offers no alternative but being, as Herschensohn and Ivanov equally are, prisoners in a kind of Platonic cave, which resembles more than they think the corners of those squalid St. Petersburg flats where Dostoevski's heroes—or better, victims—live, suffer, and die. Both in their room and in their minds, like Dostoevski's "underground man," Ivanov and Herschensohn are cornered, as were their younger brothers of the lost generation after the First World War, as are we, too, members of another lost generation, unstable and unsafe survivors of so many social and political floods. Their discarded master, Nietzsche, was more right than they when he prophesied the advent, in a not too distant future, of what he cynically calls "war's classical age." We are even more oppressed and cornered than they are, because we feel more remorse for the past and more fears for the future of man.

This is why we have no right to dismiss either one of them with a curt *medice cura te ipse* ["physician, heal thyself"]. And yet we cannot afford to share the traditional faith, the metaphysical beliefs, the pre-established harmony of Ivanov; nor are we able to indulge in Herschensohn's desire to merge with the present, with those physical bodies which are called parties or masses, or even less, with that mystical body which is called revolution, or what you will. The Western reader is likely to prefer Ivanov's position, or at least to be won over by the greater consistency of his stand. Ivanov has the more powerful intellect of the two, and also the more virile and logical mind, able to avoid the contradictions, paradoxes, and anticlimaxes of the position of Herschensohn—which is that of a man of culture who, by denying it, hopes to save his soul. And if I think that Herschensohn's testimonial is the more important and poignant of the two, it is merely because his illusion is candid and fresh, and also because we have been lucky or unlucky enough to see it shattered before our own eyes. Only because we were young enough to become such eyewitnesses are we able to recognize that the obscure dialectics of Herschensohn's ideal involves not merely the "great betrayal" of culture, or even a betrayal of the revolution in Trotski's sense, but man's treason to man.

On the other hand, we are equally dissatisfied with any brand of ecclesiastical culture or of cultural religion, with intellectual mysticism, which is always fated to become an intellectual superstition, and like all superstitions, to end unconsciously in a kind of worldly and universal skepticism. The utopian and anarchistic messianism of Herschensohn is, of course, a religion, too, but not in the literal and positive sense of a sect or a church; and at bottom one should sympathize with his unconcern, or even disdain, not for the religious or the divine, but for theological and metaphysical problems, for the golden chains of revelations and dogmas, canons and myths. For this we are ready to forgive his confession of a medievalistic nostalgia, and even the final, eucharistic appeal to his friend. The important fact is that we agree with him that Jacob's ladder, the vertical line of transcendence, even if it may become the stairway of individual ascensions, is, like contemplation and prayer, unable to save us. We think that the only way to save our souls is to save our world. This is exactly what Herschensohn is asking for, but his horizontal line is different from ours.

We want a horizontal line able to take into account the irregularities of history, the accidents of geography, the idiosyncrasies of psychology, the peculiarities of life, and the absurdities of man; we reject his *tabula rasa,* that *tabula rasa* which, through that very culture, those very values he wanted to destroy, may be created only by the steam roller of revolution, by the juggernaut of the totalitarian state, or by the most radical and nihilistic leveler ever invented by man, the atomic bomb. Even in this case, we owe our attitude not to insight, but to hindsight, and therefore we feel as if we had no right to reproach Herschensohn for having failed to foresee what we have seen. But the vertical line of Ivanov may also be the one along which both the Ivory Tower and the Tower of Babel are built; in a certain sense, it is also the line along which the atomic bomb may fall. Idolatry of culture implies also the idolatry of science and, in the long run, of technology; and transcendental, not less than immanent, historicism is only a metaphysical justification of all of history's acts and deeds, and therefore also of the atomic bomb. At all events, not everyone is able, like Ivanov, to find a shelter in the Vatican, which was at least spared by aerial bombs.

What we are looking for is a conciliation, a synthesis, of the vertical and horizontal lines, between respect for what is transcendental in man and respect for what is immanent in society, in history, in the world. It is our duty to remember that the vertical line of humanism is a good corrective for the horizontal line of humanitarianism. While the humanist may care only for the happy few, the humanitarian may very well love mankind only in the general and in the abstract; sometimes, by looking at the masses, at the forest of men, he loses sight of the tree, of that suffering and thinking reed which is man. Only too often, as Dostoevski says in *A Raw Youth,* " 'Love for humanity' is to be understood as love for that humanity which you have yourself created in your soul." In other words, almost as easily as the humanist, the humanitarian may become the Narcissus of his own idea. If humanism is too easily satisfied with being merely humane, humanitarianism may frequently become inhuman, antihuman, too. Even more than the modern humanist, the modern humanitarian is too easily inclined to be a mere anthropologist.

Man's life must be built in extension and depth, on the cornerstones of the Others and of the Self; only in such a shelter, temporary or not, will man no longer feel that his back is against the wall. We want a house where we shall never feel cornered; we refuse to be overwhelmed either by the waves of the future or by the waves of the past. This means that we are not ready to discard, as Herschensohn advises us to do, the theoretical, practical, and ethical wisdom of our Western and Christian past; and on the other hand, we are not resigned, as Ivanov is, merely to conserving that tradition. We want to respect both values and life, or, in political terms, to enjoy the fruits of those ideals of spiritual freedom which are the legacy left to us by Ivanov and his peers; but we also feel a longing for that ideal of justice which, in spite of so many deviations and errors, is still the truthful message carried by Herschensohn to us. Liberty and justice are but different names for the vertical and the horizontal lines, which we want to see united again into a symbol of redemption, into the sign with which we shall conquer. In this year of our Lord, the son of man, either *homo sapiens* or *homo faber,* does not want to be crucified on any other cross. (pp. 214-27)

> Renato Poggioli, *"A Correspondence from Opposite Corners," in his* The Phoenix and the Spider: A Book of Essays about Some Russian Writers and Their View of the Self, *Cambridge, Mass.: Harvard University Press, 1957, pp. 208-28.*

MARC SLONIM (essay date 1953)

[*Slonim was a Russian-born American critic who wrote exten-*

sively on Russian literature. In the following excerpt, he discusses Ivanov's philosophic themes and poetic style.]

It is almost impossible to dissociate Ivanov's poetry from his philosophic writings, particularly from his ***Hellenic Religion of the Suffering God.*** Parting company with the doctrines of *The Birth of Tragedy* by Nietzsche, with whom he had so many points in common, Ivanov stressed the tragic fate of Dionysus. He interpreted the dismemberment and resurrection of God as "the keys to the mysteries of life." They represented supreme realities, eternal absolutes, which Greek mythology revealed under the guise of poetic symbols. Ivanov was not satisfied with the statement of Briussov: "In secret dreams I created a world of ideal nature, next to which all these steppes, rocks, and waters are mere dust." For Ivanov steppes, rocks, and waters reveal the splendor of the Lord's creation. The whole universe is a system of signs pointing to hidden truth. Ivanov's own fairly complicated mythology establishes a scale of concepts: Female and Male, I and Thou, Unity and Multiplicity, Nature and Man, and, finally, Dionysus and Apollo correspond respectively to the Earth and the Sun. Apollo symbolizes the power of contemplative vision in memory, as well as the principle of individualization, while Dionysus embodies the orgiastic exaltation of being. Dionysus is the tragic aspect of reality; he symbolizes pain, sacrifice, and horror, the sense of the tragic—oblivion—as opposed to memory. But he is also Resurrection, and therefore the religion of Dionysus is basically the religion of Christ.

From these premises Ivanov concluded that true culture was essentially religious; it had to include the sense of the tragic as well as the hope of resurrection, the ecstasy of ruin and the joy of renewal. Taking up Solovyov's idea of solidarity and community, he insisted on the collective and universal character of culture and identified the social with the religious. Art, too, was for him of a religious nature. It created myths with deep universal meanings, and the poet was bound to be the bearer of a spiritual message; he voiced the collective soul of the people, and in his theurgic activity was, like the priest, a bridge between Man and Divinity. The highest artistic achievements were collective—the epic, tragedy, popular songs, and mystery plays—and derived from the same source as that of myth and religion. This represented a complete break with the aesthetes and Parnassians, who spoke of "purposeless beauty."

Ivanov, like Solovyov, defined his own era as one of change and upheaval. Cultures had to die before new life could rise from the tomb, and he hailed the work of destruction in the cycle of eternal renewal. In his widely known poem, **"The Nomads of Beauty,"** he acclaimed the barbarian invasion that brings new blood, and compared poets with the Nomads:

> Hurl from your flooding numbers
> Your hordes in hurricanes,
> Where the low valley slumbers
> And slaves are proud of chains.
> Trample their paradises,
> Attila! Waste anew!
> And where your bright star raises,
> The steppe will bud for you.

(pp. 187-88)

The poetry of this scholar and master of versification offered a curious mixture of erudition and subtlety and, at times, of spiritual elation. His best collections of poems, *Eros* (1907) and *Cor Ardens* (1911), were ponderous, solemn, full of symbols, quotations, mythological names, and scholarly allu-

Ivanov in 1948.

sions. He used Church Slavonic expressions and terms from the Greek Orthodox liturgy side by side with neologisms of Latin and foreign origin, and achieved surprising linguistic effects. Anticipating Ezra Pound and T. S. Eliot, he delighted in intellectual acrostics, but the fabric of his long-winded or obscure ballads remained impeccably classical. As the Master, the High Priest of Apollo, he could not afford the liberty of a loose line or a defective rhyme. His stanzas either have the sculpturesque solidity of Grecian statues or resemble the chants of ancient religions, old rituals, and magic incantations. Critics compared the richness of their texture with the lavishly brocaded robes of the Byzantine clergy. This majestic poetry, constructed on several planes and reminding one of Derzhavin's sonorous declamatory style, never reached a large audience. Even among the elite, Ivanov was much more admired and talked about than read. A few initiates studied and commented on every line he wrote, as if each one were a kind of divine revelation. (pp. 188-89)

> Marc Slonim, "Blok and the Symbolists," in his Modern Russian Literature: From Chekhov to the Present, *Oxford University Press, 1953, pp. 184-210.*

O. DESCHARTES (essay date 1954)

[*Deschartes was Ivanov's close friend, editor, and biographer.*

In accordance with his wishes she completed his novel Povest o Svetomire tsareviche: Skazanie startsa inoka *after his death, and also collaborated with his son Dmitri in editing Ivanov's collected works. About her, Ivanov declared, "Only O. Deschartes can write about the real me, and she knows my life and writings as no one else does." In the following excerpt, Deschartes details the originality and the importance of Ivanov's theory of Symbolism. Translations in brackets are by Henri Peyre.*]

In literary history Ivanov is known as the founder and leader of religious, "realistic" symbolism in Russia. Together with Alexander Blok and Andrey Bely, he formed a triumvirate who advanced their new doctrine of realistic symbolism in opposition to the "decorative" symbolism of Bal'mont, Bryusov, and Sologub. Lack of understanding was a powerful enemy to the three pioneers: "No one was able either to hear our message or to understand what we said," Blok complained. But in the end victory was theirs.

At every stage in the history of art, Ivanov wrote, two inner forces, two trends, inherent in the very nature of art, have decided its direction and conditioned its development. These two equal and conflicting principles of artistic activity are, on the one hand, the principle of *signification*—the principle of the discovery and transfiguring of an object—and, on the other, the principle of *transformation*—the principle of the alteration and invention of an object. In the first case, something which has being is affirmed and revealed; in the second, through an effort of the will, something is seen to be worthy of being. The first tends towards objective truth, the second towards subjective imagination. Ivanov neatly and precisely characterizes various artists and historical epochs to show how these two fundamental principles can be seen in eternal conflict throughout the ages.

Having reached his own day, Ivanov dwells on the subject of Baudelaire's sonnet "Correspondances," which was accepted as the "fundamental teaching and, as it were, the profession of faith of the new school of poetry," and evaluates the two principles in it. In the first two quatrains the poet likens Nature to a temple:

> La Nature est un temple où de vivants piliers
> Laissent parfois sortir de confuses paroles;
> L'homme y passe à travers des forêts de symboles
> Qui l'observent avec des regards familiers.
>
> Comme de longs échos qui de loin se confondent
> Dans une ténébreuse et profonde unité,
> Vaste comme la nuit et comme la clarté,
> Les parfums, les couleurs et les sons se répondent.
>
> [Nature is a temple where living columns
> Sometimes murmur indistinct words;
> There man passes through forests of symbols
> That watch him with familiar glances.
>
> Like prolonged echoes that mingle in the distance,
> In a shadowy and profound unity,
> Vast as night and as the light of day,
> Perfumes, colors, and sounds respond to one another.]

According to Ivanov the symbols here are far from being a mere human device or a convention. They reveal the real mystery of nature, which is living and is based entirely upon esoteric correspondences, upon relations and harmonies in that which appears to our mortal ignorance to be disparate and inharmonious. The poem is a mystical investigation of the esoteric truth about things, a revelation of things that are more "real" than the things themselves (*realiora in rebus* ["reality in things"]).

But in the second part of the sonnet Ivanov considers that Baudelaire is unfaithful to himself:

> Il est des parfums frais comme des chairs d'enfants,
> Doux comme les hautbois, verts comme les prairies,
> —Et d'autres, corrompus, riches et triomphants,
>
> Ayant l'expansion des choses infinies,
> Comme l'ambre, le musc, le benjoin et l'encens,
> Qui chantent les transports de l'esprit et des sens.
>
> [There are perfumes, fresh as the flesh of children,
> Sweet as oboe music, green as meadows,
> —Others corrupt, rich, and triumphant,
>
> Having the expansion of things infinite,
> Like amber, musk, benzoin, and frankincense,
> Which sing the raptures of spirit and of sense.]

Here the poet no longer attempts to penetrate the hidden life of the essence of objects. He is content to make us experience in recollection a series of fragrances and to combine them by means of striking associations with a number of visual or auditory perceptions; this enriches our perceptive self. We have become sophisticated; we have made a psychological experiment, but the very conception of such an experiment is one of artificial experiencing. The mystery of the thing itself (*res*) is almost forgotten. This predilection for the artificial rather than for the essential in the new symbólism sprang from the Parnassian tradition; decadence has here extended Parnassian precept to its ultimate limits; it is merely a sham revolt against the canons of idealistic, pseudoclassical art.

Where then are we to seek the criterion for discriminating between the two elements? It lies in the very concept of "symbols." A symbol is a sign or a signification: it does not stand for or express any single definite idea. Otherwise it would be merely a hieroglyph, and a combination of several symbols would be "graphic allegory," a communication in code which needs to be read with the help of a key. In different spheres of consciousness the same symbol has different meanings. Like a ray of light a symbol travels through all the levels of being and all the spheres of consciousness; on each level it signifies different entities and in each sphere it fulfils a new function. The symbol, like a descending ray, appears at each point of intersection with each sphere of consciousness as a sign whose meaning is figuratively yet completely revealed by a corresponding myth. Thus, the snake has a symbolic relation both to the earth and to incarnation, to sex and to death, to sight and to knowledge, to temptation and to illumination. It represents different entities in different myths. Yet the whole body of snake-symbolism and every one of its different meanings are linked together by the great cosmogonic myth, in which each aspect of the snake-symbol has its place in a hierarchy of the planes of the divine all-pervading unity. A myth is the objective truth about entity, it is the key to the imaginative cognition of extrasensory entities. A true myth is far from being fiction or allegory; it is the hypostasis of a certain entity or "energy." In remote ages when myths were genuinely created, they answered the questions posed by experimental reason in that they represented *realia in rebus* ("realities in things"). (Not all myths, however, are collective in origin; some derive from a mystical vision, and have become popularized.) By disclosing symbols, i.e. signs of another reality in the reality of surrounding objects, art makes our reality significant.

Realistic symbolism presupposes that the poet possesses a mystical insight and demands a similar insight in his reader. Here the symbol is a principle linking disparate consciousnesses, which unites them through the common mystical contemplation of that objective reality which all can perceive. . . .

> Are signs seen by the poet in visions? Or is the
>   sign—the poet?
> I know only this: there can be no new song for the
>   world save a prophetic one.

"Idealistic" symbolism, on the other hand, is directed towards man's sensory perceptions. Its symbols are a poetic device designed to induce a single subjective experience in a number of readers. Its pathos lies in the creation of illusion; its illusion is coercive and imposes its will upon the surface of things.

But if the artist consciously strives to become a vessel for the creative powers of the World Soul, "for the earnest expectation of the creature waiteth for the manifestation of the sons of God" (Rom. viii. 19), then he will become the artist-theurgist and not the artist-tyrant; he will become him of whom it was said: "A bruised reed shall he not break, and the smoking flax shall he not quench" (Isa. xlii. 3; Matt. xii. 20). His ear will be attuned and the language of things will be revealed to him; his eyes will grow keen and he will learn to know the meaning of forms and to perceive the sense of phenomena. He will strive to interpret and proclaim the hidden purpose of entities. It is only through such spiritual receptiveness that the artist can become the bearer of the divine revelation.

But when Ivanov brilliantly characterizes representatives of "significatory" symbolism—of symbolism which is "realistic" in the highest sense—for example, Phidias, Aeschylus, Dante, Cimabue, Raphael, Michelangelo, Calderón, Shakespeare, Goethe, Dickens, and Dostoevsky, he passes beyond the limits of symbolism as a literary movement and trenches upon general questions of the psychology of creativeness, of the defining and elaboration of aesthetic principles, and of the establishing of the limits of art.

A great thinker, and especially an artist, cannot be contained within the limits of any one school. Ivanov established the nature of symbolism with exemplary clarity, and in so doing transcended it. And at St. Petersburg in January 1914, during a public debate on contemporary literature, the leader of Russian realistic symbolism made a speech in which he definitely claimed that he had done so:

> . . . Dante was thus a symbolist. What is the significance of this for our characterization of the Russian symbolist school? It means that we dissolve ourselves as a school. We do this not because we wish to repudiate anything or because we intend moving in a new direction; on the contrary, we remain absolutely true to ourselves and to the direction our work has taken from the start. But we have no use for sects; our creed is a universal one. The true symbolist is, of course, not concerned with the fortunes of what is ordinarily understood by a school or a trend, as defined by historical landmarks and the names of artists; he is concerned to establish firmly a certain single general principle. And this principle is the symbolism of all true art; even though time may show that we who have affirmed it were at the same time its least worthy exponents.

Thirty years after his first article on symbolism, Ivanov recalled its sources in Baudelaire and pronounced his verdict:

> Even in the embryonic stage of modern symbolism, one can distinguish two currents: the one a purely Latin idea of it as a latter-day form of art—the art of the *epigoni*—with a purely Alexandrian conception of the beauty inherent in decadence, of the seductive luxuriance of flowering decay; the other a presentiment of a new revelation, in which the mystery of the inward life of the world and its meaning shall be made plain. Both currents pulse in the veins of symbolism and make it seem hybrid and dual. And as a result of this original sin, the school which boasted of its honourable though now empty title of "symbolism," is now everywhere quite dead. Yet symbolism possessed an immortal soul, and since the great problems it posed have found no answers within its framework, we must await the appearance of other forms and more perfect expressions of "eternal symbolism" in the more or less distant future.

(pp. 49-52)

O. Deschartes, "Vyacheslav Ivanov," in Oxford Slavonic Papers, *Vol. V, 1954, pp. 41-58.*

RENATO POGGIOLI   (essay date 1960)

[*In the following excerpt from* The Poets of Russia: 1893-1930, *Poggioli examines technical and thematic aspects of Ivanov's poetry, stressing the syncretism of his thought and writings.*]

Ivanov's threefold concern with the tragic, the mythic, and the mystical suggests his conception of poetry. Poetry is for him essentially a religious search, and he views the poet as, if not a priest, at least an initiate. Ivanov himself, however, was not only a poet, but also a scholar: a seeker of knowledge, as well as of wisdom. This means that he was as attracted by the quaintness and complexity of his own lore as by the truth hidden within it. Thus, like every connoisseur or specialist, he often became a pedant, flaunting his learning and showing off his erudition. He did so by supplying his poems with exegetical notes and bibliographical references, a critical apparatus better suited for a philological paper, as if he were afraid that the complexity of his allusions would escape not only the understanding, but even the attention, of his reader.

Poetry of this kind naturally requires a special idiom. Ivanov's verse may be rightly considered the highest and most extreme manifestation in the history of Russian poetry of both "poetic diction" and "grand style." The very fact that Ivanov is the most typical Russian representative of a type of poetic language which in other literatures is mainly a Renaissance or post-Renaissance phenomenon is a proof of the uniqueness of the development of Russian poetry. Maurice Baring, limiting his consideration to the nineteenth century, and focusing his attention on Pushkin, compared Russian to Greek lyrical poetry, failing to realize that at least in part such eighteenth-century poets as Lomonosov and Derzhavin had indulged in neoclassical fashions and pseudoclassical mannerisms. Yet it is true that, in its main tradition, Russian poetry follows the Wordsworthian ideal of "common speech"; and it is equally true that only such a modern poet as Ivanov fulfills there the task accomplished in other traditions by such figures as Malherbe or Milton. Despite the fact that he was a Greek scholar by trade, Ivanov represents within the poetry of Russia the same tendency that in English literature is often defined by such epithets as "Latinate" and "Italianate." It is not merely coincidental that Lev Shestov gave Ivanov (not without irony) an appellative which was originally given to a great figure of the Italian Renaissance, and called him "Vjacheslav the Magnificent."

It is in the spirit of the Italian Renaissance that Ivanov spiritualized pagan themes and paganized Christian ones; and it matters very little that the hieratic pomp of his lines is achieved through the use of both Grecianisms and archaisms, the latter taken chiefly from Church Slavonic, in a manner which suggests an attempted reconciliation of Byzantine and classical taste. Such an art demands the almost exclusive practice of closed forms, primarily ancient or medieval in origin, which the poet treats with flawless perfection, controlling rigorously not only rhyme and rhythm, but also diction and syntax. With Pushkin, Ivanov was one of the few Russian practitioners of the Italian sonnet, and he handled that medium with such skill that he was once able, by solving with the mastery of a virtuoso the difficulty involved in repeated *en-*

jambements, to compose a sonnet made of a single sentence. In medieval fashion, he often treated the same verse form, which is normally limited to a single, self-sufficient poem, as if it were a stanza, one of the many flowers woven into what in ancient Italian poetry was termed a "crown" or "garland" of sonnets: and it was into such a "garland" that he shaped one of his masterpieces.

All this tends to prove that Ivanov's poetry leans all too deliberately toward an abstract compositional symmetry, that too many of his lyrics are written after a premeditated design. This is particularly true of the cycle *Man,* which is divided into two complicated, polimetric parts. The components of both sections are wrought in an identical series of different metrical molds, which in each case follow each other in reverse order. Since the poet fashioned each half after the scheme of the Pindaric ode, one may say with his own words that the first part proceeds from strophe to antistrophe, and the second, from antistrophe to strophe. To help the reader recognize this pattern of inversion and parallelism, the poet marked with the same letters the pieces occupying corresponding points on the twin criss-cross lines forming the geometry of his plan.

The inspiration of *Man* is Christian, and although its formal repertory contains two sapphic odes, most of its meters (such as the sonnet and the *ottava*) are taken from the literary tradition of the Catholic West, from the poetic storehouse of medieval Italy. Yet it is noteworthy that the poet chose to order that cycle according to one of the most elaborate Greek metrical structures. This may well indicate that even when treating Christian themes and Latinate forms, he still viewed the poetry of Greece as the supreme aesthetic ideal. Yet even within Greek poetry what he admires most is not the simple melos of monodic verse, but the complex choral music of the ode, the hymn, or the dithyramb. In his Hellenism the Dionysian urge overwhelms all Apollonian restraint; his muse always behaves like a Bacchante (see the poem **"The Maenad"**), even when she assumes the pose of a Sybil. The orgiastic temper of his poetry is not affected even by shifts of outlook, taste, or technique; and the poet often introduces a morbid aura of decadent Christianity even into the poems dealing with the most classical subjects. At once a pagan and a mystic, he seems to worship both Astarte and the Madonna. Speaking in the terms of ancient mythology, one could say that he sacrifices impartially to Venus Urania and to earthly Aphrodite; or, if we prefer a Christian metaphor, that he is all too often ready to impose the ritual garments of Sacred Love over the nude body of Eros.

It was perhaps this aspect of Ivanov's thought and work that led Prince Mirskij to label him a splendid sophist. Yet his philosophical and aesthetic conceptions are better understood through such terms as eclecticism and syncretism. In religion, he tried to join together dogma and myth, to reconcile the canonic tradition and the apocryphal one, to marry the holy with the unholy, or at least with profane cults. In culture, he sought a synthesis of knowledge and faith, and dreamed of an alliance between Christianity and humanism. In poetry, he attempted to merge the modern and the archaic, the classical and the primitive. Yet both as a poet and a thinker he looks more like an Alexandrian or a Byzantine than like a Hellene.

It is not for me to judge whether Ivanov purified his religious sophisms through his conversion to Roman Catholicism, toward which he had moved even before the Revolution, and which he had almost foreshadowed in his poem **"The Road to Emmaus."** Nor is this the place to discuss whether in his debate with Gershenzon he really succeeded in the attempt to bring together art and faith, Hebraism and Hellenism. All too often this master acted like a pompous hierophant or a ponderous mystagogue. Yet the man who was finally forced to avow, for himself and his brethren, "none of us is a true Symbolist," was able once in a while to express his view of life and the world in visions and transfigurations of his own.

This is certainly the case with one of the poems of *Man:* a poem which must be understood as an allegory of the spirit's liberation from the shackles of the self. The poem's theme is a death scene: a passer-by glimpses through an open door a priest keeping vigil over a dead old woman. To express the epiphany of death, the poet speaks to the reader in the three voices of the passer-by, the priest, and the deceased. The same visionary power triumphs in Ivanov's masterpiece, in those *Winter Sonnets* which convey the tragedy of the Revolution through the clear and simple images of an archaic, universal experience, still haunting the memory of the race. . . . [The] poems of that sequence symbolize the trials and the hardships of the present ordeal in man's ancestral struggle for physical and moral survival against the horrors and terrors of the primordial way of life. It is with a sense of both piety and awe that the author of that cycle reflects history's nightmare within the nightmare of prehistory, touching the heart and the mind of the reader by an immediacy of vision and a simplicity of statement all too rare in his poetry. (pp. 166-70)

Renato Poggioli, "Symbolists and Others," in his
The Poets of Russia: 1890-1930, *Cambridge, Mass.:*
Harvard University Press, 1960, pp. 153-78.

JAMES WEST (essay date 1970)

[*West is the author of* Russian Symbolism: A Study of Vyacheslav Ivanov and the Russian Symbolist Aesthetic. *In the following excerpt from that work, he presents the ideas put forth in "Two Elements in Contemporary Symbolism," analyzing Ivanov's aesthetic theories as presented in the essay and relating them to other aspects of his thought.*]

"Two Elements in Contemporary Symbolism" [was] first published in the periodical *The Golden Fleece* in April and May 1908, and republished in 1909 in the collection *By the Stars.* The "two elements" in question are "realism" and "idealism," viewed as two contrasting patterns in the mental processes involved in artistic self-expression. The essay is, in effect, a short statement of a psychology of creativity.

Ivanov begins the essay with the assertion that symbols do not designate single, particular ideas; they may be hieroglyphs, but they are polyvalent. "Like a ray of the sun, the symbol penetrates all levels of being and all spheres of consciousness, and represents different entities at each level, performs a different function in every sphere." The snake, for example, is linked symbolically with the ideas of earth, incarnation, sex, death, sight, and knowledge, temptation and enlightenment, but all these possible meanings of the snake-symbol are drawn together into "a great cosmogonic myth, in which every aspect of the snake-symbol finds its place in the hierarchy of levels of the divine unity." The assumption implicit in this statement, that symbolic representation is organically linked with religious experience, is made clear as the essay proceeds:

Revealing in the objects of everyday reality symbols, that is, signs of another reality, [symbolic art] presents reality as significative. In other words, it enables us to become aware of the interrelationship and the meaning of what exists not only in the sphere of earthly, empirical consciousness, but in other spheres too. Thus true symbolic art approximates to religion, in so far as religion is first and foremost an awareness of the interconnection of everything that exists and the meaning of every kind of life.

Moreover, Ivanov declares, the religious artist of the future will not be content to remain the passive vehicle of the religious idea. As Vladimir Solov'yov has prophesied, he will wield it actively and consciously. . . . (pp. 50-1)

How is the new religious artist to wreak a transformation upon the universe? He will not do it by filling the universe with his own creations, much less by becoming the artist-tyrant of whom Nietzsche dreamed. The artist is called not to impose his will on the external form of things, but to reveal the will that resides in them:

> As a midwife eases the process of birth, so should [the artist] help things to reveal their beauty. . . . The very clay itself will take on in his fingers the form which it had been awaiting, and words will form themselves into harmonies predetermined in the element of language.

This, Ivanov continues, is why realist art is preferable in the religious context to idealist art. He defines "realism" as "the principle of faithfulness to things as they are both in appearance and in essence," and "idealism" as "faithfulness not to things, but to the postulates of an individual, aesthetic mode of perception." At the conclusion of the opening section of **"Two Elements"** Ivanov combines Solov'yov's notion of the "reincarnation" of heavenly values on earth with a realist standpoint in the philosophical sense:

> . . . we hope to demonstrate that a realist viewpoint, as a psychological basis for the creative process and as the prime impulse to creativity, alone assures the religious value of the work of art: in order to "consciously direct the earthly embodiments of the religious idea" [these are Solov'yov's words, quoted earlier in the essay] one must first believe in the reality of what is being embodied.

In the next section of the essay, Ivanov takes up more explicitly the psychology of creativity he has already hinted at. Throughout the ages, he says, the form of art has been governed by two inherent tendencies. Man's mimetic urge to reproduce what he observes and experiences has always provided a passive "material substratum" to his artistic activities, but the active, "dynamic" side of his psychological make-up has caused this substratum to be overlaid by two equally fundamental forms of conscious striving. On the one hand, man feels the need to "celebrate" things as he reproduces them, and on the other, to transform them. The two strivings correspond to "realism" and "idealism," and also to the eternal antithesis of female and male: realism is the female, receptive type, idealism involves a masculine initiative. The history of art has seen a progression from a naive "symbolic realism," in which the artist remained receptive to whatever intimations of divine values his surroundings might reveal to him, to an idealism in which the artist endeavours to convey his own ideal, not revealed to him but conceived by him. Such an artist's ideal is of a beauty "which perhaps really exists

neither here nor in a higher world, but is none the less dear to him as a bird that has strayed from fabled lands. . . ." The most significant point to emerge from this distinction is that, for Ivanov, the *creative* contribution of the artist to the process of representation belongs only to that tendency which he calls idealist. Realism, by this token, may be interpretative, but is not creative; the artist has been described as a midwife, one who merely helps to bring about an inevitable happening, a revealer, not a maker. Ivanov distinguishes two processes within artistic "idealism":

> . . . the idealist artist either gives things back in a different state to that in which he received them, having re-wrought them not only negatively, by abstraction, but also positively by linking with them new features prompted by the associations of ideas that have arisen in the process of creation,—or, he produces compositions that are not justified by observation, but are the offspring of his despotic and wayward fantasy.

> (pp. 51-2)

After a brief digression to trace the history of the two principles in art, Ivanov applies his analysis to contemporary symbolist art, in three sections devoted respectively to realistic symbolism, idealistic symbolism and the criteria for distinguishing one from the other.

Baudelaire, says Ivanov, heralded the appearance of modern symbolism with a work of pure "celebratory" art, that is, art of the first of the two types distinguished. In the first two stanzas of his sonnet "Correspondances," Baudelaire laid bare the secret of nature—that nothing is random, and that nature is not dumb, rather we are deaf; that "for those who can hear it, there sounds in nature the myriad-voiced eternal word." Baudelaire's attempt to express symbolically this objective truth identifies him as a realistic symbolist. Ivanov traces the idea expressed in "Correspondances" back to Balzac's "mystical-romantic" tales *Louis Lambert* and *Séraphita*—back, that is, to a writer who in his view combined the realist and the romantic casts of mind. He takes care to point out that his "realistic symbolism" is linked both with the realist movement in literature, and with those features of the romantic movement exemplified by Novalis. He stresses a particular link with Goethe's symbolism, in which he discerns echoes of both Schiller and Dante. The conclusion of the section devoted to realistic symbolism is worth quoting at length:

> To bring about a direct understanding of the life that lies hidden in reality, by means of a portrayal which unshrouds the manifest mystery of this life— such is the task that only the realistic symbolist sets himself, for he sees the profound and true reality of things, *realia in rebus*, and does not deny the relative reality of the phenomenal world, in so far as it contains and stands for the more real reality. "Alles Vergängliche ist nur ein Gleichnis" ["That which is transitory is merely symbolic"]. . . . Goethe approaches idealist art with the only legitimate demand, the demand which is equally acceptable and sacred for realism (remember that Plato's ideas are *res*)—the insistent demand to discover and assert the general type in the changing and inconsistent variety of phenomena. . . .

Ivanov's "realistic symbolism" is clearly a much more complex conception than the form of Russian realism founded by Belinsky, and involves a (psychologically speaking) more far-reaching aesthetic, but it can still find expression in terms of the theory of type, the assumption that the artist conveys the general truth that lies hidden in the bewildering multiplicity of the particular.

The continuation of Baudelaire's sonnet, on the other hand, illustrates the reverse of realistic symbolism. The "parfums frais comme des chairs d'enfants" ["perfumes fresh as children's flesh"] seem to Ivanov to betray the idea of a divine unity to which all phenomena are linked; they are "correspondances" only on the sensual level, an enjoyment of associations between perceptions of the different senses, having nothing to contribute to the deepening of our understanding; they are a lapse into idealism, since they are on the level of "an individual aesthetic mode of perception."

Ivanov's next step is to establish a criterion by which to distinguish the contrasting strands that make up contemporary symbolism:

> The criterion by which one may make the distinction is given in the very concept of the symbol. . . . For realistic symbolism—the symbol is the goal of the revelatory process in art: any object, inasmuch as it is a hidden reality, is already a symbol, and the more directly and immediately the object partakes of absolute reality, the profounder it will be, and the harder it will be to fathom its ultimate meaning. For idealistic symbolism, the symbol, being only a means of artistic representation, is no more than a signal, designed to establish a community between the consciousness of disunited individuals. In realistic symbolism, the symbol is also, of course, the principle which links separate conscious beings, but their communion is attained by common mystical contemplation of the one essential, objective reality which is identical for all. In idealistic symbolism the symbol is a conventional sign by which individualists conspire to deceive one another, a secret sign, expressing a solidarity in their individual self-awareness, their subjective self-determination.

Ivanov has here classed symbols according to the form of communication they represent. Idealistic symbols, by his definition, suffer from the limitations of verbal communication; they are conventional signs, of a relative value only, owing what common meaning they have to a community of interests on a level that Ivanov finds trivial. They scarcely break the bounds of subjectivity. Realistic symbols, on the other hand, put men into communication with each other by enabling all to attain to a sphere of absolute awareness in which eternal values are to be found that do not depend on the self-interest of individuals, and so are objective. He is claiming that true symbols transcend the limitations of their medium—a claim which we may hope he will try to justify in more detail, particularly as regards the nature of, and the means of access to, that common sphere which is the resort of all realistic symbolists and (presumably) their public.

In concluding his essay, Ivanov treats this question more deeply. To state his thesis at its simplest: the common sphere is universal truth, made known through a universally accepted symbolic construction which is myth. Realistic symbolism creates new myths, where idealistic symbolism can only deal in old myths, distorting them as it does so. The function of myth in the process of artistic communication is stated as follows:

> For myth is a representation of realities, and to interpret genuine myth in any other way is to distort

it. A new myth is a new revelation of the same realities; and just as any private realization of an unconditional truth must necessarily become general as soon as it is proclaimed even to a few others, so any adequate signification of an objective truth about things, revealed to one person's cognitive faculty, will of necessity be accepted by all as important, true and inescapable, and will become a genuine myth in the sense of a generally accepted form of aesthetic and mystical perception of this new truth.

All symbols which genuinely reflect the eternal truth that resides in the realities for which they stand (Ivanov is saying) are, by virtue of this quality, in some sense inherently public; and when the realistic symbolist refers to a conglomeration of symbols as a myth, he is asserting their unconditional public validity. The force of truth is compelling, and all who once become aware of the vehicles of truth will accept them as such without demur.

However, for all that it has been made a term of the aesthetic process, myth has here lost none of its religious connotation. The symbolist artist's attainment, through myth, of eternal truth is described quite explicitly as an act of faith:

> Thus the poet believes, thus does he know by intuition. To create myth is to create belief. The mythmaker's task is indeed "the revelation of things unseen." And realistic symbolism is the laying bare of what the artist sees, as reality, in the crystal of a lower reality.

We are also constantly reminded that the "eternal truth" is a religious truth, the truth of the divine unity of the created world. Ivanov preaches a return to religious art, in the sense in which ancient Greek art was religious, and he claims to recognize in, for example, the works of Tyutchev and Vladimir Solov'yov, and in the interest shown by contemporary poets in mythology, signs that the soul of man is rediscovering its roots in myth. "It is not the folklore themes that are of value," he writes, "but the return of the soul and its new contact, however timid and haphazard, with the dark roots of being."

The final section of "**Two Elements in Contemporary Symbolism**" is concerned with the implications on a slightly more practical level of the "mythological" theory of art. The form of expression appropriate to symbolic myth in the age of classical tragedy (the golden age of religious art) was the chorus, which cannot be dissociated from the idea of myth. "The chorus is a postulate of our aesthetic and religious credo . . ." —a formulation which indicates more plainly than ever how closely his aesthetic and his religious beliefs are knit together. However, he eschews nostalgia, and is swift to add that there is no excuse for an attempt to artificially resurrect the chorus of classical drama on the modern stage, which is enslaved by the illusionism inherent in contemporary concepts of drama, and could only distort myth. For a reappearance of the chorus which is uniquely expressive of myth, we must await some future time "when science will have to take account of certain truths which are already clear to investigators of myth and symbol. . . ." The principal of these truths is that myth has come down through the ages as something at least potentially absolute and "common to all men." . . . "Popular" myth has survived the ever-present tendency of man to form esoteric groups of one kind or another in order to preserve the mysteries of a particular form of religion. This tendency bears the same relation to popular myth as idealistic symbolism bears to its realistic counterpart. Ivanov's conclusion follows naturally from the rôles he has assigned to myth and symbol in artistic creativity: the preoccupations of contemporary art are linked, through the realistic symbolism he advocates, with the wider issue of religion in an unpropitious age. Here is how the threads are pulled together:

> Religion is the bond uniting all that is real, and is knowledge of realities. Art, drawn into the sphere of religion by the magic of the symbol, inevitably runs the risk of becoming masked in the hieratic forms of non-religious reality, unless it adopts the slogan of realistic symbolism and myth: *a realibus ad realiora.*

The risk indicated here is that of lapsing from popular myth into an esoteric cult, of failure to rise above the "lower," the "non-religious" level of reality and attain a true, "higher," "more real" reality.

"Two Elements in Contemporary Symbolism" gives us scope for three generalizations which will be useful at the outset.

Ivanov sees the work of art as a representation of the phenomenal world, and insists that it should have its roots there, and nowhere else; but he envisages a representation which, without distorting the appearance of things, reveals their essential nature and their place in the divine scheme. Furthermore, he views this revelation (through art) of the hidden nature of the world as a force acting on reality, working upon it a "transformation" or "transfiguration" in terms of Solov'yov's notions of "theurgic art."

Secondly, when considering art under another of its aspects, as communication, Ivanov is never far away from this concept of representation-involving-revelation; the revelation of true reality has itself a value as communication, in that it gives common access to the truth.

Lastly, Ivanov stresses that art is knowledge, not simply a vehicle of knowledge but a mode of knowing, which stands in the same relation to some "higher," "more real," religious truth as our normal ways of knowing do to the concrete, visible world. Religion, he has said, is knowledge of reality. (pp. 53-7)

That art is a means of knowing is a fundamental assumption of Ivanov's aesthetic, expressed in its most categorical and cryptic form in one of his aphorisms:

> Poetry is perfect knowledge of man, and knowledge of the world through man's cognitive faculty.

In the essay **"The Testament of Symbolism"** (1910) Ivanov looks back to the age of ancient Greek civilization when— "The task of poetry was the incantatory magic of rhythmic speech, mediating between man and the world of divine beings." Symbolism, he then claims, represents a return to this heritage, of which one characteristic is "the conception of poetry as the source of intuitive knowledge, and of symbols as the means of realizing this knowledge." Ivanov acknowledges that the "knowledge" which poetry may impart consists not in rational ideas but in imaginative insight. We read in another aphorism:

> Characteristic of the lyric style are sudden transitions from one mental image to another, lightning leaps of the imagination. The multiplicity of the images evoked is made one by a single mood which can be called the lyric idea.

Implied in this statement are two assumptions which are widely familiar in our own day; that poetry deals in insights which have an immediacy and a fluidity denied to rational thoughts; and that the imagination has the power to synthesize what the reasoning mind cannot. It is on this latter quality of poetic knowledge, its power to bring order and wholeness, that Ivanov lays most stress:

> The task and purpose of lyric poetry is to be an organizing force, to proclaim and command order.

His view of the purpose of poetry goes beyond the simple recognition of intuitive knowledge; it has the ring of a psychologically-based aesthetic in which art is seen to order experience. It also has an obvious relevance to Solov'yov's conception of art as a "transfiguration" or transformation of the phenomenal world, for this too is an ordering activity. Moreover, as in the case of Solov'yov, epistemological considerations clearly lie at the centre of Ivanov's aesthetic, and this aspect of his thought must be examined in order for a meaningful analysis of his philosophy of art to be possible at all. . . . [For] Ivanov's consideration of the problem of knowledge transposes at every turn into the cognate problem of communication, thus emphasizing its close bearing on questions of aesthetics in the narrower sense.

In an essay on Vladimir Solov'yov, in which he suggests that Solov'yov strove for a form of knowledge in whose light all relative, historical truths will be seen to partake of the one divine principle, Ivanov describes what he regards as the crisis of contemporary theories of knowledge:

> Contemporary philosophy, from a desire to be strict and scientific, tries to confine itself to the sphere of theories of knowledge. . . . As a result of the investigations of the Neo-Kantians, the cognitive subject which the individual has become, sees itself trapped in a closed circle. Everything that lies within the magic circle is relative; everything outside it is an indeterminate datum. But woe betide the individual when the vicious circle is arbitrarily broken: a relativistic theory of knowledge, carried over into life, results in non-existence. . . .
>
> It is impossible to live in accordance with such a theory of knowledge; the circle of the particular consciousness can only be broken by the action of our collective will.

He is also rebelling against the Kantian tradition of the relativity of human knowledge, on the grounds that the relativistic epistemology constitutes a barrier confining the individual within himself, and that it obstructs communication. The obvious corollary at once suggests itself: that knowledge of the absolute furthers communication and liberates the individual from isolation. Indeed, this was hinted at in the passage quoted earlier from **"Two Elements in Contemporary Symbolism"** asserting the inherently public nature of unconditional truth.

The idea is taken a stage further in another essay, **"Lev Tolstoy and Culture."** Ivanov "places" Tolstoy as the Socrates of the nineteenth century, and draws a parallel between Socrates' Greece and Tolstoy's Europe. Both ages were characterized by "a general critical reappraisal of spiritual values," and by rootlessness and relativism in philosophy. Once relativism became established at the expense of man's communion with the "infinite being," then:

> . . . thought took fright in the labyrinth of its freedom, in which everything had become arbitrary,

deceptive and bound by appearances. . . . It was necessary to rebel against instinct and to save knowledge for living, at the expense of knowledge of the essence of things. If there was not a more real god to be found outside the natural creative instinct of life . . . then the divinity had to be sought in the normative value of rational consciousness, the capacity for logic had to be deified, and objective moral criteria had to be derived from human self-determination. Morality had to be used to exorcise the chaos of an existence deserted by the gods. It was hunger for real knowledge that made men moralists.

By ". . . save knowledge for living at the expense of knowledge of the essence of things," Ivanov is pointing to the danger inherent in an investigation of the world which provides man with more and more verifiable knowledge at the expense of his sense of non-material values. Man, who for Ivanov is a religious animal, has always reacted to this danger by deifying the mental processes that provide relative scientific knowledge; he has spuriously satisfied his hunger for spiritual values by worshipping his rational consciousness, and has wrung his moral values from the same source. However, in Ivanov's view, man has ultimately never been able to accept a world bounded by the canons of verifiable knowledge:

> If man were a "positivist" at root, he would never have broken out of the vicious circle of the world of phenomena, and it would never have occurred to him to discount any of his data.

Ivanov advocates, as the way of escape from the dilemma he has described, a form of knowing which restores mankind to an awareness of "the absolute," conceived in religious terms as the divine principle uniting all creation. The only correct attitude to human culture is one which seeks to make of it "a coordinated symbolic system of spiritual values, corresponding to the hierarchies of the divine world, and to justify the relativistic creations of man by their symbolic relation to the absolute," Ivanov finds in this apprehension of divine unity "a new degree of rational consciousness"; the attempt to claim for intuition the respectability of rational thought is very much in the spirit of Solov'yov.

In the *Correspondence from Two Corners,* Ivanov set awareness of the absolute even more clearly at the opposite pole to the confinement of men within themselves that had resulted from Kantian relativism. Mikhail Gershenzon, his correspondent, had spoken regretfully of the aftermath of Kantianism in European thought. Ivanov, who in this correspondence is arguing from the standpoint of Christian belief, replied that the believer has an immediate bond with the absolute, a bond that is not culturally conditioned, and so he declared:

> Thus, on the fact of our belief in the absolute, which is something other than culture, depends our interior freedom,—and this is life itself,—or our inward bondage to a culture that has long been godless in principle, for it has confined man (as Kant proclaimed once and for all) within himself.

There was a suggestion in "**Two Elements in Contemporary Symbolism**" that the knowledge gained through myth is ultimately knowledge of being. In the essay *Freedom and the Tragic Life,* written in emigration, Ivanov's preoccupation with the polarity of relative and absolute knowledge finds expression in a slightly different form with more emphasis on the question of knowledge of being.

In *Freedom and the Tragic Life* Ivanov argues that man always tries to think of his values and judgements as absolute; when he is forced to regard them as relative, his natural desire for unconditional knowledge is thwarted, and he is left "imprisoned in a subjectivist solitude," in which he either despairs, or imagines defiantly but vainly that he is dependent on nothing outside his subjective state. Dostoyevsky, in Ivanov's view, saw this dilemma clearly, and explored it in the vision of the convalescent Raskol'nikov in *Crime and Punishment.* It is the age-old problem of how we are to conceive of reality and share our experience of it if our conception and our experience are purely subjective and conditional. Dostoyevsky put forward as a solution, says Ivanov, the idea of a "higher" reality, the object not of theoretical cognition, with its antithesis of subject and object, but of an act of will and belief equivalent to Saint Augustine's *transcende te ipsum,* . . . an intuitive "penetration" of reality. Ivanov describes the "lower" reality that must be transcended as "of lesser ontological value," and knowledge of the "higher" reality as the key to the riddle of existence. Knowledge of reality of the type he envisages is "ontological" to the extent that the knower not only knows things outside himself, but is able to affirm his own existence from his "objective intuition" of other existences. This theory is expounded in detail in *Freedom and the Tragic Life,* and in two essays of the strictly symbolist period, "**Thou Art**" and "**The Religious Work of Vladimir Solov'yov**"; it has a vital bearing on Ivanov's aesthetic. The "act of will and belief" by which, in Ivanov's view, Dostoyevsky transcends the subjective, is akin to the religious experience of love; in terms of knowledge, it is acceptance of the existence of the object to the point of renouncing one's own existence as subject. "Thou art" ceases to be "thou art recognized by me as existing" and becomes "I experience thy existence as my own and in thy existence I again find myself existing." In other words, Ivanov puts forward a theory of knowledge based on mystical identification of the self with the object known, or, as Mr. Norman Cameron's translation of *Freedom and the Tragic Life* runs: "self-transposition into the other-Ego." Scriptural support is found for the idea in St. John's Gospel (xvii, 21-3), the text to which Tolstoy appeals in support of his characterization of the "religious consciousness" from which art derives its values: "I in them and thou in me, that they may be made perfect in one. . . ." Ivanov coined or adopted Latin formulae for all the pivotal concepts of his philosophy, and the appropriate tag in this case is *Es ergo sum.*

The value of such an ontology, Ivanov insists, is entirely dependent on belief. For the disbeliever, "thou art, therefore I am" can mean only "we both float equally pointlessly in the void," and the love of the "other-Ego" cannot be genuine. It is impossible to underestimate the importance of belief for Vyacheslav Ivanov; belief in God is inseparable from even the most widely valid parts of his aesthetic, and failure to give this fact due credit, however disturbing it may be to find logical investigation mingled with statements of belief, will only make nonsense of his theories. For, as he concludes for the case of Dostoyevsky, to believe or not to believe is quite simply to be or not to be.

In "**The Religious Work of Vladimir Solov'yov**," having observed that the individual is a prisoner of his own relativism and redeemable only by an act of collective will, Ivanov continues thus:

> In practical life this act [of collective will] is performed whenever my love addresses itself to another with the words: "thou art," dissolving my own being in the being of this other. The act of love, and love alone, postulates the other person not as an object but as a second subject, is an act of believing and willing, an act of life. . . . Only at this point does there awake in us another, higher consciousness, in comparison with which my former consciousness, confined by my lesser Ego, begins to seem a bad, false dream.

The idea is substantially the same in *Freedom and the Tragic Life,* except that in its earlier form it is linked more closely and significantly with the wider problem of knowledge. The problem is, for Ivanov, that if we lose our link with the absolute, knowledge becomes self-defeating and destroys our very conviction of our own existence. When we "believe in" an object outside ourselves, however, we know it absolutely, and in so doing reaffirm our own existence.

The essay "**Thou Art**" opens with a lament for the *cogito ergo sum* of our pre-Kantian ancestors, which comfortable formula, according to Ivanov, has been invalidated for us even down to its separate parts—neither *cogito* nor *sum* will do any longer. With the formula has gone the "whole individual" whose philosophical mainstay it was. The spiritual scene, however, is not totally desolate: it is rather "a ploughed field of individual consciousness," waiting to bear a fresh growth of religious creativity. Religious consciousness awakes in us in the moment of perceiving the differentiation of our Ego into an "I" and a "thou." There follows a characterization, in images of Dionysian myth, of the "frenzy" in which the bounds of individual consciousness can be broken. Next, the quest of the soul for God is presented in a variety of religious imageries, western and oriental. The soul is always seeking the Absolute, which in Christian mysticism is God the Father in Heaven; but it can only know the Father through the Son, with whom it can enter into a mystic union that enables it to realize itself, a union which is "ecstatic" in Dionysian terms. The Son of God of the Christian myth is equated with the Eros of the Dionysian myth. The psyche involves a male and a female principle; the female side draws it towards the ecstatic union in which it loses itself in becoming something greater than itself, while the male principle is the conscious self, able to exercise its will and choose between resisting or following the impulse for union with the divine, "between finite resistance to God and self-realization in the Son of God, between desire to transcend the individual and individual isolation. . . ."

There follows a detailed analysis of the Lord's Prayer in the light of the above, prefaced by this generalization:

> The "right" prayer which Christ taught, begins with an act of the will, directing our individual consciousness to realms higher than the individual,— with the assertion of the principle of Christ within us: "Our Father" is—"Thou art in us.". . .
>
> Heaven resides in man, and is revealed in his consciousness by an inward stirring of the will. . . .

The significance of the Lord's Prayer, Ivanov concludes, is that the future re-growth of religion will spring from within the individual, from the "microcosm," although history shows the majority of religions to have had their roots outside the individual in the "macro-cosmic" idea. The reason is that the soul will realize the macro-cosmic idea within itself:

> When the soul of present-day man finds anew the "Thou" in its "I," just as the soul of the ancients found it in the cradle of all religions, then it will understand that the macrocosm and the microcosm are identical,—that the external world is given to man only so that he may learn the name "Thou" both in his inaccessible neighbour and in his inaccessible God,—that the world is the revelation of his microcosm.

(pp. 58-64)

James West, in his Russian Symbolism: A Study of Vyacheslav Ivanov and the Russian Symbolist Aesthetic, *Methuen & Co. Ltd., 1970, 250 p.*

ALBERT LEONG   (essay date 1971)

[*In the following excerpt, Leong analyzes themes and techniques in the sonnet cycle* Zimnie sonety.]

The lyric cycle which we know as the *Zimnie sonety* (*Winter Sonnets*) was composed by Ivanov during the winter of 1919, when he used to travel in an open sleigh to visit his wife and children at a hospital six miles outside of Moscow, while the poet himself was half-starving and physically exhausted. The lyrical intensity, directness, and relative simplicity of these poems set them apart from the rest of Ivanov's verse. Unencumbered by the ornamental verbal encrustations and magnificently esoteric imagery which mark his earlier works, the *Zimnie sonety* therefore reveal more clearly the inner structure of his lyric poetry and its relationship to his complex metaphysical system.

The twelve poems of the *Winter Sonnets* form a unified cycle with common compositional and stylistic elements. Each poem is a meticulous realization of Italian sonnet form—a form which especially appealed to Ivanov due to the authority of its long history, allegedly dating back to thirteenth-century Sicily. In each poem, Ivanov superimposes a flexible rhythm which tends to omit the stress in the fourth foot. Ivanov does not exploit euphony for its own sake, but subtly integrates it into the poetic texture, where it redundantly underscores semantic shifts and emotional peaks. Besides assonance, alliteration, and onomatopoeia, Ivanov creates special phonic effects through his diction, which juxtaposes sharply-marked stylistic layers. Reflecting his predilection for "concrete-universals," Ivanov's poetry is a poetry of nouns. Where adjectives are found, their function is largely ornamental and redundant, as in fixed epithets, where their attributive function is attenuated. Comparative adjectives, however, play an important part by grammatically reinforcing key metaphors. Ivanov's verbs are usually static—intransitive, reflexive, or in passive participle form. Ivanov makes special use of present and preterite gerunds to express symbolic parallelisms or sequential moments in symbolic transformations. Conjunctions, as in Axmatova's verse, bear unusual semantic weight by effecting sudden transitions or shifts in direction. Consonant with his bookish, archaic diction, Ivanov's syntax emphasizes stylistic devices prominent in old Russian literature: the rhetorical question, the apostrophe, the fixed epithet, logical parallelisms and antitheses.

Emotionally and thematically, the sonnet cycle traces a progression from the nadir of despair to an impassioned declaration of faith through episodes of hope, indecisiveness, defiance, and affirmation. The **Winter Sonnets** describe a journey, a mythic quest made by a solitary traveler who encounters temptations, passes through the Purgatory of elemental chaos, and tastes of despair and self-doubt. He is at once Adam flung from Paradise and Odysseus homeward bound.

The hierarchy of images and symbols further binds the cycle into a unified whole. Both poles of reality—the world of appearances on the level of signification and the immutable world of true reality on the level of transformation—correspond to two sets of imagery in dialectical opposition: death / life; winter / spring; dreams / reality; night / day; cold / warmth; shadow / light; earth / heaven; descent / ascent; flesh / spirit; slavery / freedom; obscurity / clarity; heaviness / lightness; "here" / "there"; unconsciousness / consciousness; violence / tranquillity; the double / the true self; out / in; ice / fire; destruction / creation; isolation / union; depth / height; oblivion / recollection; inertia / vitality; Dionysus / Christ. (pp. 43-4)

> *Albert Leong, "The 'Zimnie Sonety' of Vjacheslav Ivanov," in* Pacific Coast Philology, *Vol. VI, April, 1971, pp. 43-9.*

VYACHESLAV IVANOV (essay date 1972)

[*The essay from which this excerpt was taken originally appeared in the journal* Trudy i dni *in 1912. An expanded version was included in the collection* Borozdy i mezhi, *published in 1916. This translation, which appeared in* Russian Literature Triquarterly *in 1972, was drawn from both sources. In the following excerpt, Ivanov offers his definition of Symbolism.*]

I met a shepherd mid deserted mountains
Who trumpeted upon an Alpine horn.
His song was pleasing; but his sonorous horn
Was only used to rouse a hidden echo in the mountains.
Each time the shepherd waited for its coming,

Manuscript page of Svet vecherny.

Having rung out his own brief melody,
Such harmony then came amid the gorges,
Such indescribable sweetness, that it seemed
An unseen chorus of spirits,
On instruments not of this world,
Was translating the language of earth
Into the language of heaven.
And I thought: "O genius! like this horn
You sing earth's song to rouse in hearts
Another song. Blessed is he who hears!"
From beyond the mountains a voice responded:
"Nature is a symbol like this horn,
It sounds for the echo—the echo is god!
Blessed is he who hears both song and echo!"

If, as a poet, I know how to paint with the word (poetry is similar to painting—*"Ut pictura poesis"*—classical poetics stated in the imitation of Simonides according to Horace), to paint so that the imagination of the listener produces what I depict with the clear visual quality of what is seen, and things which I name present themselves to his soul prominent in their tangibility and graphic in their picturesqueness, darkened or illuminated, moving or motionless, according to the nature of their perceived manifestation;

if, as a poet, I know how to sing with a magical power (for "it is not sufficient that verses be beautiful: let them also be melodious and willfully draw the soul of the listener wherever they so desire," "—*non satis est pulchra esse poemata, dulcia sunto et quocumque volent animum auditor is agunto"*—as classical poetry stated in the words of Horace, concerning this tender seductiveness), if I know how to sing so sweetly and so powerfully that the soul, entranced by the sounds, follows submissively after my pipes, longs with my desires, grieves with my grief, is enflamed with my ecstasy, and the listener replies with a harmonious beating of his heart to all the tremblings of the musical wave bearing the melodious poem;

if, as a poet and wiseman, I possess the knowledge of things, and gladdening the heart of the listener, I edify his mind and educate his will;

but, if, crowned with the triple crown of melodious power, I, as a poet, do not know how, through all this threefold enchantment, to force the very soul of the listener to sing together with me in another voice than mine, not in unison with its psychological superficiality, but in the counterpoint of its hidden depth—to sing about that which is deeper than the depths revealed by me, and higher than the heights unclouded by me—if my listener is only a mirror, only an echo, only one who receives, only one who absorbs—if the ray of my word does not betroth my silence to his silence through the rainbow of a mysterious covenant:

then I am not a Symbolist poet.

If art is in fact one of the mightiest forces for human union, one could say of Symbolist art that the principle of its activity is above all union, union in the most direct and most profound sense of this word. In truth, not only does it unite, it also combines. The two are combined by the third and highest. The symbol, this third, resembles a rainbow that has burst into flames between the ray of the word and the moisture of the soul which reflected the ray. . . . And in every work of genuinely symbolic art is the beginning of Jacob's ladder.

Symbolism combines states of consciousness in such a way

that they give birth "in beauty." The purpose of love, according to Plato, is the "birth in beauty." Plato's depiction of the paths of love is a definition of Symbolism. From enamorment of the beautiful body, the soul, growing forth, aspires to the love of God. When the esthetic is experienced erotically, artistic creation becomes symbol. The enjoyment of beauty is similar to the enamorment of beautiful flesh, and proves to be the initial step in erotic elevation. The meaning of artistic creation as that which has been experienced is itself inexhaustible. The symbol is the creative principle of love. Eros the leader. Between the two lives—that one incarnated in creation and that one creatively joined to it (creatively because Symbolism is the art which transforms whoever accepts it into a co-participant in creation)—is achieved what is spoken of in the ancient naive profundity of the Italian ballad where two lovers arrange a rendezvous on the condition that a third person will also appear together with them at the appointed hour—the god of love himself:

> *Pur che il terzo sia presente,*
> *E quel terzo sia L'Amor.*

"L'Amor/che muove il Sole/e l'altre stelle"—"The love that moves the Sun and other Stars. . . ." In this concluding verse of Dante's *Paradiso* images are composed into myth and music gains wisdom.

Let us examine the musical structure of this melodic line of verse. In it there are three rhythmic rests produced by the caesuras and underlining the words: *Amor, Sole, Stelle*—for on them rests the *ictus.* The radiant images of the god of Love, the Sun and the Stars seem blinding as a consequence of this word arrangement. They are separated by depressions in the rhythm, the obscure and undefined *"muove"* (moves) and *"altre"* (others). In the intervals between the radiant outlines of those three ideas is the gaping night. Music is embodied in a visual manifestation: the Apollonian vision emerges above the gloom of the Dionysian frenzy: indivisible and yet divided is the Pythian dyad. Thus, the starry firmament is imprinted, boundlessly and overwhelmingly, in the soul. But the soul, as the beholder of the mysteries, is not abandoned without some instructive direction clarifying that which is beheld by consciousness. Some hierophant standing over it intones: "Wisdom! Thou seest the movement of the radiant and heavenly vault, thou hearest its harmony: know then that it is Love. Love moves the Sun and other Stars." This sacred word of the hierophant (*ieros logos*) is the word as logos. Thus Dante is crowned by that triune wreath of melodious power. But this is not yet all that he achieves. The shaken soul not only accepts, not only echoes the omniscient word: it discovers within itself and out of the mysterious depths painlessly gives birth to its consummating inner word. The mighty magnet has magnetized it: it too becomes a magnet. Within itself is revealed the universe. What it espies in the heights above is unravelled in it here below. And within it is Love; for after all it already loves. *"Amor"* . . . at this sound which affirms the magnetism of the living universe its molecules arrange themselves magnetically. And within it are the sun and the stars and the harmonious tumult of the spheres moved by the might of the divine Mover. It sings in harmony with the cosmos that self-same melody of love that it sang in the soul of the poet when he prophesied his cosmic words—Beatrice's melody. The line of verse under discussion (which is examined not merely as the object of pure esthetics, but in realtion to the subject, as the perpetrator of the soul's emotion and inner experience) proves to be not simply filled

with an external musical sweetness and an inner musical energy, but is polyphonic as well, the consequence of the consummating musical vibrations summoned forth by it and the awakening of overtones clearly perceived by us. This is why it is not only an artistically perfect verse, but a symbolic verse as well. This is why it is divinely poetic. Being composed, moreover, of symbolic elements insofar as its separate words are pronounced so powerfully in the given connection and the given combinations that they appear as symbols in themselves, it represents in itself a synthetic pronouncement in which for the subjective symbol (Love) the poet's myth-creating intuition finds the effective word (moves the Sun and the Stars). And, thus, before us is the myth-creating climax of Symbolism. For the myth is the synthetic pronouncement where the predicative verb is joined to the subjective symbol. The sacred word, *ieros logos,* is transformed into the word as *mythos.*

If we had dared to give an evaluation of the afore-described effect of the concluding words of the *Divine Comedy* from the point of view of the hierarchy of values of a religio-metaphysical order, we would have had to recognize this effect as being theurgic. And with this example we might have tested the already frequently pronounced identification of a genuine and exalted Symbolism (in the above-designated category of examination, by no means, incidentally, unnecessary for the aesthetics of a Symbolist art)—with theurgy.

And thus I am not a Symbolist if I do not arouse in the heart of the listener with intangible nuance or influence those incommunicable sensations which resemble at times some primeval remembrance (and "for a long time on earth the soul languished, filled with a wondrous desire," "and the monotonous songs of earth could not replace for it the heavenly sounds"), at times a distant, vague premonition, at times a trembling at someone's familiar and long-desired approach—whereby this remembrance and this premonition or presence we experience as the incomprehensible expansion of our individual personality and empirically restricted self-awareness.

I am not a Symbolist if my words do not summon forth in the listener feelings of the connection between that which is his "ego" and that which he calls his "non-ego,"—the connection of things which are empirically separated; if my words do not convince him immediately of the existence of a hidden life where his mind had not suspected life; if my words do not move in him the energy of love towards that which he was previously unable to love because his love did not know of the many abodes it possessed.

I am not a Symbolist if my words are not equal to themselves, if they are not the echo of other sounds about which you know nothing, as though of the Spirit, whence they come and wither they depart—and if they do not arouse this in the labyrinths of souls.

I am not a Symbolist, then, for my listener. For Symbolism designates a relationship, and the Symbolist work in itself, as an object removed from the subject, cannot exist.

Abstract aesthetic theory and formal poetics examine an artistic work for itself; in this regard they have no knowledge of Symbolism. About Symbolism one can speak only by studying the work in its relationship to the perceiving subject and to the creating subject as to undivided personalities. Hence the following conclusions: (1) Symbolism lies outside all aesthetic categories; (2) Every artistic work is subordinated to appraisal from the point of Symbolism; (3) Symbolism is connected with the wholeness of both the individual as the author himself, as well as the one who experiences the artistic revelation.

Obviously the Symbolist-artisan is inconceivable; just as inconceivable is the Symbolist-esthete. Symbolism deals with man. Thus it resurrects the word "poet" in the old meaning—of the poet as a person (*poetae nascuntur*)—in contrast to the colloquial use of the word in our time which strives to lower the value of this elevated name to the meaning of "a recognized artist—versifier talented and refined in his technical area."

Is the symbolic element required in the organic composition of contemporary creativity? Must a work of art be symbolically effective in order that we consider it complete?

The demand of symbolic effectiveness is just as non-requisite as the demands of *"ut pictura"* or *"dulcia sunto. . . ."* What formal characteristic is at all unconditional in order that a work be considered artistic? Since this characteristic has not been named even in our day, there is no formal esthetic even in our time.

To make up for it there are schools. And the one is distinguished from the other by those particular seemingly superrequisite demands which it voluntarily imposes upon itself, as the rules and vows of its artistic order. And thus the Symbolist school demands of itself more than the others.

It is clear that those very same demands can be realized unconsciously outside of all rules and vows. Each work of art can be tested from the point of view of Symbolism.

Since Symbolism designates the relationship of the artistic object to the two-fold subject, creating and receiving, then upon our reception essentially depends whether the given work appears to be symbolic for us or not. We can, for instance, accept in a symbolic sense the words of Lermontov: "From beneath the mysterious, cold demi-mask I heard your voice. . . ." Although in all probability for the author of these verses the foregoing words were equivalent to themselves in their logical extent and content and he had in mind simply an encounter at a masquerade.

On the other hand, examining the relationship of the work to the integral personality of its creator we can, independently of the actual reception itself, reconstruct the symbolic character of the work. Of this sort we find in any case Lermontov's confession: "You will not meet the answer/Amid the noise of this world./Out of flame and flight/Is the word born."

Manifest is the effort of the poet to express in the external word the inner word and his despairing of the accessibility of this latter word to the reception of the listeners which nonetheless is necessary in order that the flaming word, the radiant word not be enveloped by darkness.

Symbolism is magnetism. The magnet attracts only iron. The normal state of molecules of iron is non-magnetic. And that which is attracted by the magnet becomes magnetized. . . .

And thus we Symbolists do not exist if there are no Symbolist-listeners. For Symbolism is not merely the creative act alone, but the creative reciprocal action, not merely the artistic objectivisation of the creative subject, but also the creative subjectivisation of the artistic object.

"Has Symbolism perished?"—reply others. Better were it for them to know whether Symbolism has perished for them. But we who have perished, bear witness, whispering in the ears of those celebrating at our funeral that there is no death.

But if Symbolism has not died, then how it has grown! It is not the might of its bannermen that has waxed strong and grown—I wish to say,—but the sacred branch of the laurel in their hands, the gift of the Muses of Helikon that bade Hesiod to prophesy only the truth—their living banner.

Not long ago many took Symbolism as the level of poetic depictiveness, related to Impressionism, formally capable of being carried over into the category of stylistics concerning tropes and figures. After the definition of the metaphor (it seems to me that I am reading some entirely modish textbook on the theory of philology that is quite in the process of being realized and yet not realized)—under the paragraph concerning the metaphor I envisage an example for grammar school pupils: "If the metaphor consists not of a single part of speech but is developed into an entire poem, then it is acceptable to call such a poem symbolic."

We have diverged significantly from the Symbolism of the poetic rebuses, of literary device (again merely device!) that consisted in art of summoning forth a series of conceptions capable of arousing associations, the coincidence of which forces one to guess at and, with special power, to perceive the subject or experience, purposely obscured, not as being expressed in their direct meaning, but having to be deciphered. This fashion, beloved in the period after Baudelaire by the French Symbolists (with whom we have neither an historical nor an ideological reason for joining forces) does not belong in the circle of Symbolism as outlined by us. Not only because this is merely device; the reason lies deeper. The goal of the poet becomes in this case—to afford the lyrical idea an illusion of greater compass, in order, little by little, to encompass the greater extent, to materialize and condense its content. We are becoming disillusioned concerning *"dentelle"* ["lace"] and *"jeu supreme"* ["supreme game"] and so on,—but Mallarme wants only that our thought, having described wide circles, alight on a single point designated by him. For us Symbolism is, on the contrary, energy, liberating itself out of the bounds of the present, lending the soul movement like a revolving spiral.

We wish, in opposition to those who call themselves "Symbolists," to be true to the purpose of an art that is modest in its presentation, yet is mighty in its creation, and not vice versa. For such is the humility of an art that loves modesty. It is more characteristic for genuine Symbolism to depict the earthly than the heavenly: the power of the sound is not important to it, but rather the might of the echo. *A realibus ad realiora. Per realia ad realiora* ["From physical things to Reality. Through physical things to Reality"]. Genuine Symbolism does not tear itself away from the earth; it desires to combine roots and stars and spring forth as the starry tower out of the native roots at hand. It does not replace things, and speaking of the sea, means the earthly sea, and by snowy heights ("And what age gleams whitely there, on the snowy heights but the dawn, the today the light of fresh roses is upon them,"—Tyutchev), is understood the peaks of earthly mountains. As art it strives towards one thing: the elasticity of the image, its capacity for inner life and vastness in the soul whither it falls like a seed which must give rise to the seed-pod. Symbolism in this sense is the affirmation of the vast energy of the word and of art. This vast energy does not avoid intersection with spheres that are heteronomous to art, for example with religious systems. Symbolism, as we expound it, does not fear a Babylonian Captivity in any of these spheres; it alone realizes the truly genuine freedom of art; it alone believes in its genuine might.

Those who have called themselves Symbolists, but did not know (as at one time Goethe, the distant father of our Symbolism, knew) that Symbolism speaks of the universal and the collective—they led us by the path of symbols through the radiant valleys in order to return to our prison, to the cramped cell of the insignificant "ego." Illusionists, they did not effect a return to that divine and broad expanse and knew only the broad expanse of fantasy and the enchantment of slumberous daydream out of which we awoke to find ourselves in a prison. Genuine Symbolism poses a completely different task for itself: the liberation of the soul (*katharsis*) as a development of inner experience. . . .

From the time of Goethe, the striving for the symbolic basis of art was definitely noted in the history of the artistic consciousness. With particular intensity and distinctness this striving was manifested in modern Russian philology. I shall restrict myself to the mention of Tyutchev in the sphere of verse, of Dostoevsky in the area of prose. I speak of their victories when I speak of the triumph of Symbolism and not of my contemporaries. I do not defend either our school, or our practices and canons, but I believe that in praising Symbolism I proclaim the dogma of the orthodoxy of art. And by expressing myself in this manner I hope that I shall not be accused of disrespect for that source from which I draw my comparison; for art is in truth a sacred thing and collectivity [*sobornost'*].

The protests directed against dogma will consequently be called heresy. There are various forms of esthetic heresy: alive until our day for example—however wondrous such longevity may be—is the heresy of social utilitarianism which found its final champion in Russia I believe in the person of D. S. Merezhkovsky. But he is too much a self-deluding person for one to easily believe in the wholesome sincerity of his demagogic outbursts on the similarity of Tyutchevism and Oblomovism and other similar comparisons and considerations. It is not the content of this preaching that is interesting, but rather its psychology; how is the phenomenon itself of Merezhkovsky, the Symbolist, seeking to awaken suspicions against Symbolism psychologically possible? The answer to this question adds a characteristic feature to the portrait of Symbolism in general—the feature of a positive knowledge in spite of all the lifeless monstrosity of its manifestation in the given individual instance. Characteristic of Symbolism is the desire to go beyond its actual boundaries. The form and likeness of higher realities, imprinted on the symbol, make up its living soul and moving energy; the symbol is not a dead copy or idol of this reality but semi-inspired bearer and participant. However, it is only half-inspired and would be completely so; it seeks to be united completely with the reality which is itself expressed by it. The symbol is the word which is in the process of becoming flesh, but is incapable of becoming it; if it did, it would then no longer be a symbol but theurgic reality itself. Thus, this *eros* of Symbolism for effectiveness is holy, but the cause for which Symbolism hungers is not mortal and human, it is immortal and divine. Merezhkovsky, however, seeks to pour the wine of his religious pathos, which he has newly pressed out, into the antique skins of the ancient irreligious radicalism of the times of Belinsky and the 1860s.

Another and more widespread esthetic heresy is the thoughtlessness of "art for art's sake." This opinion on the ultimate separation of art from the roots of life and its profound heart presents itself in an age of decline, in an age of superficial estheticism, and is founded essentially on misunderstanding. I shall express my relation to this heresy briefly.

The single task, the single object of all art is Man. Not man's benefit, but his mystery. In other words—man taken in the vertical, in his free growth into the depths and heights. The name of Man written with a capital letter defines in itself the content of all art; it has no other content. This is why religion always finds its place in great and genuine art; for God is in the verticalness of Man. The supine benefit of everyday life has no place in it, but only in the horizontalness of man, and the physical longing for utilitarianism immediately curtails all artistic activity. The more intently we peer into the nature of heresies, the more obvious the truth of true esthetic will become. (pp. 151-58)

Vyacheslav Ivanov, "Thoughts on Symbolism," translated by Samuel D. Cioran, in Russian Literature Triquarterly, *No. 4, Fall, 1972, pp. 151-58.*

ALEKSIS RANNIT   (essay date 1972)

[*Rannit was an Estonian-born American art historian and poet. In the following excerpt, he analyzes the style, structure, and themes of the poems in* Vespertine Light, *often comparing the poems with other forms of artistic expression such as architecture, sculpture, and music.*]

Vespertine Light consists of 142 poems and is, most probably, the best book written by Ivanov since his collections ***Subtle Secret*** (1912) and ***Childhood*** (1918). The cycles ***Winter Sonnets,*** consisting of twelve pieces, and ***Roman Sonnets,*** consisting of nine, are without a doubt not only the essence and affirmation of this collection, but also some of the most significant poems written in Russian.

Georgy Adamovich comments that Ivanov's poems make one "drowsy" at times, that perhaps they do elevate the spirit and direct it toward noble and important meditations, but that in them all the immediately "humane" is "eluded" and forgotten. A question, of course, arises as to what is meant by "humane": should it refer to qualities of the sentiment or the spirit? I think that man reveals himself by his highly *intellectual* receptivity to phenomena (and the refined "geometric" poetry of Adamovich himself correctly reflects his discord with the purely emotional and realizes the victory of the intellect). Ants Oras, who appreciates the poetry of Ivanov greatly, comments on creative intellectual power in general in the following words: "The sense of profundity contains more than an esthetic attraction. To many of us it appears as the arsenal of our spiritual existence, of the humane within us, and of the intellectual power which directs the living cosmos."

The "spiritual" man is incarnate in the poetry of Ivanov (especially in the ***Winter Sonnets***) with such strength that it can be sensed easily. Let us take, for example, his third sonnet:

Winter of the soul. With her oblique
Rays from far-off the living sun gives heat.

She of course freezes in the deaf-mute blizzards,
And the snowstorms sing for her their grief.

Heap an armful of kindling near the hearth;
Cook your millet: your hour is victory.
Then fall asleep—how all grows numb and hard!
O deep sepulchre of Eternity!

The tap of life-giving water is frozen over;
Stiff as ice, the fountain of liquid fire.
Do not look for me under that shroud!

My double drags his coffin, humble slave,
I, at least, am real, though changed to flesh.
Far-off, I build me a church no hand can shape.

Concerning the man "of soul" (i.e., the possibility of his artistic "assumption to heaven" including all his weaknesses and passions), Ivanov himself gives an answer in his article **"Thoughts on Poetry."**

> Why are we willing to ignore so many poets who annoy us with their self-revelation, using the icelike words of Lermontov: "What does it matter to us whether you suffer or not,/ Why should we know about your emotions,/ Your foolish hopes of the first years of your life,/ About the wicked regrets of your reason?" In the first case the psychological fact (reality) as such discloses itself prematurely and the existence of it is experienced before it is transformed into a distant, in itself defined, visionary and different existence. In the second case, however, the / which experiences the effect stands as if in a mirror reflection, which means that it is estranged from the creative / which is already free from the observed and depicted effect.

As early as 1912 Ivanov confessed that in poetry he "unlearned to distinguish the limits of the sacred" (foreword to **Subtle Secret**) "because poetry is our manysided life as experienced by the poet in the form of another existence" (**"Thoughts on Poetry"**). He defines the criterion of the poetical in poetry as the quality of the form. He presents the problem of form in a new way and gives it an original definition. He asserts that "the concept of artistic form is two-sided, that there must be a distinction between the creating form—*forma formans*—and the form which is being created—*forma formata*. The latter is the work of art itself, the thing—*res*—in the world of things; the former exists before the thing itself does, as form *ante rem,* as the active prototype of the creation in the thoughts of the creator." *Forma formans* is the "intelligent" capacity which forces itself upon the soul of the artist "unmistakenly knowing its ways and prescribing to matter its own laws of indispensable incarnation." According to Ivanov, "Poetry is the communication of the creating form to the one to be created. It is a true communion because the first, being an act of motion, not only creates the second, but it also evokes in someone else's soul an analogical creative motion" (**"Thoughts on Poetry"**).

Ivanov, the "magician of the word" as Zielinski called him, was intimately familiar with various Greek, Roman and Oriental meters; as used by him they all sound fluent and natural in Russian. He was the first to introduce the iambic trimeter into the language. We can find among his verses Alcaic and Sapphic strophes, shlokas, elegaic distichs, ghazals, and terza rima; he was especially fond of the Petrarchan sonnet. With striking poetic justice this characteristically Italian pattern became a central receptacle for the poet's experience of Mediterranean form, and this is as true of the early poetry in **Pilot**

Stars (1903) as it is of the second Italian period (1924 and after). He wrote more than two hundred sonnets, including two *crowns*. Virtuosity of external form was never his aim; rather, it remained a means to express the inner form, a way to communicate the complete creative force. In strict mode he delivers the experience of the spirit: a passing smile and pensive melancholy. In the poem **"The Holm Oak"** sincerity is expressed by the use of a traditional but vivid elegaic distich. Shaken by the distressing events in his homeland, the poet was silent for a long time. In 1924 he found himself in Rome, amidst the "ancient altars" which awoke in him the "intelligent force" and once more "verses started to flow freely." He rejoices and is sad at the same time:

"The Holm Oak"

Gloomy old Trappist, again I mutter my verses in
  secret:
  Even the holm oak will ring with its foliage of
  May.
Drowsing in bronze-chased mail under stormy Boreas in winter,
  Spring with its fresh green shows through on
  darkening slopes.
Go, look close at the black twigs: under the metal
  of parched leaves
  Tender and childlike the sprout laughs at its
  rust-eaten jail.

The lyrical confessions of Ivanov, of course, are far from the sentimental directness of Esenin or the emotional hypnosis of Blok, which excites one even when Blok speaks about his patriotic experiences, as for example in the poem "Again as in the golden years . . ." ("Opiat' kak v gody zolotye").

Ivanov has tasted the apple from the "ancient tree," he has been pierced by the "blue flame of cognition" which Voloshin wrote about in one of his poems. There is no return for him to the paradise of naive primitiveness. Fyodor Stepun, in his forceful article on Ivanov, writes: "A man of sharp senses, with a soul of many voices like an organ, Vyacheslav Ivanov could not, of course, become an innocent and artless poet-singer, a human nightingale, which many people still see as the prototype of a true poet. . . . Certainly God created Vyacheslav Ivnaov as a true poet—but he created him in one of his deeply meditative philosophical moments." . . . The simplicity of Ivanov is the edge of refinement—it is the manifestation of the balance between the elements of the natural and the spiritual, between the heavenly and the earthly:

We must survey the higher realm
Before measuring the depths of earth.
They say thinking and faith
Are for the soul one and the same.
That the cave of Bethlehem
Is the rock grave's very own mouth.

In one of the last poems of **Vespertine Light** the poet repeats his idea that art takes us into "the vicinity of another existence" at the moment when it "mirrors the visage of the earth," when the commonplace, the well-known, strikes us as a new revelation:

And we may well wonder, all alone,
Why we have not noticed until now
How the breeze caresses the plain,
How green is spruce under the snow.

In the hard and hungry year of 1919 Ivanov, overworked and exhausted, was sent to a rest home in the "Silver Forest."

There he wrote ten songs, dedicating them to the "green paradise." Here is the second poem in this group:

"Vesper"

The woods: growing down in the river.
Vesper emerged in a night
Skiff—and a diamond caught fire
Somewhere in the fathomless river.

I saw not once in my life,
In this hour of vespertine light,
Vesper comes up, to expire
Again on the sleepy river.
Then why should an old grief remembered
Start tears to stream from my eyes?

It's as if my far loved one's face
Had surfaced for me in a dream.
As if on my hand the ring
Had sought the ring that kept faith.

Gleb Struve, in his *Russian Literature in Exile* (1956), rightly separates this poem from Ivanov's later work, indicating that it reminds us more of the best poems of Fyodor Sologub than of the early work of Ivanov. As for the other qualities, it suggests Pushkin, Tyutchev, and Baratysnky.

"Farewell," "Night Calls," "Grave," "At the Threshold," "Peace," "Psalm," "Homeland," "The Third of February," "The Twelfth of February," "The Fifth of May," "The Sixth of August," "The Fourth of November," "The Fifth of December" should also be included among the best "simple" poems in *Vespertine Light.*

Theoretically, Ivanov asserts the indivisibility of spiritual growth and artistic perfection. This was *his* creative development; he changed from the solemn, splendid "Alexandrian" (so critics have styled it), brilliantly learned poems in *Cor Ardens* to the serene songs of *Vespertine Light.* With a smile, he confesses in his **"Roman Diary of 1944"**:

At the threshold of the neophytes
I was known as a mystagogue:
Now I am bringing the fruit of penitence
Speaking in a common tongue.

In his sonnet **"The Obvious Secret"** he tells us how "after wandering through the entire labyrinth of my soul" he started to sing "as simply and purely as a child."

The structure of Ivanov's poetry may be classified as an expression of the Corinthian Order—the most ornate of all Greek architectural styles. It is noteworthy that this style attained its widest and fullest development in ancient Rome. Just as in the Corinthian style, so in poetic reality Roman and Greek genius meet in the work of Ivanov. The Corinthian Order—the synthesis of wealth, fullness, abundance, sometimes even of extravagance—is widely represented in the architecture of Rome and its archetype, the Roman Pantheon, which Ivanov praised in his magnificent early distichs called **"Laeta"** (1903). But the poetry of Ivanov, in my opinion, is particularly close to the Corinthian Temple of Zeus in Athens, which is perhaps the most sublime architectural creation in this style. The temple's height and splendor, its rich play of light and shade, and its complicated rhythm of alternating rows of columns, are striking. In the poetry of Ivanov there is plenty of decor, both metonymic and metaphoric, reminding one of Corinthian columns adorned with complicated cornice-like capitals of stylized acanthus and volute leaves. But in spite of ornamental abundance, a strict harmony and clarity of rhythm predominate. The tall shaft of the column in the Temple of Zeus is, very possibly, the intellectual idea of Ivanov's poems, of the harmony of his composition, of the strength of the tectonic forms of his meter. The adornments—images, capitals, cornices, sculptural bas-reliefs—do not disturb the organic consolidation of his poetry. The synthesis of the decorative and powerful wording and the esthetic conception of "crystallized nature" is especially persuasive in the poet's *Roman Sonnets.* Here Ivanov is primarily an artist. The first of the sonnets, "Anew, the true pilgrim of the ancient arches," is cited frequently in articles about Ivanov, probably in part because of the analogy between Troy and old Russia, both reduced to ashes. Next to this, one of my favorite sonnets is the fifth, an example of a rare "light" mastery of the Corinthian beauty of movement, of the joy of life and happiness. Ivanov handles the "marble" from which the sonnet is made as though it were "wax," extracting from it painterly and sculptured effects. The poem is supple and expressive, due to its modulative, daring movement and the chromatism of its euphony:

"Fifth Roman Sonnet"

This dolphin-tangle brought out on their tails
An open bivalve. In it the Triton grows.
He plays on a snail trumpet; no rough tones.
The jet pierces the blue air with sunrays.

Amid hot stones thirsting for clouds of pines,
How the moss green makes a chiton on the creature!
The chisel's age-old dream resembles nature
In its primeval fantasy of lines.

Bernini—ours again!—I always will
Relish your play, going from the Four Fountains
To Pincio up this memorial hill,

Where Ivanov came to Gogol's cell-like room,
Where Piranesi with his fiery needle
Sang Titan architects and grieving Rome.

"Bernini [is] ours again" sings the **"Fifth Roman Sonnet."** The intensity of form, the dynamics of the artist's emotional intention, the inclination to the grandiose—all these cause Ivanov to love the baroque, the younger "brother" of the Corinthian style. I do not know whether Ivanov agreed with Spengler, who considered the baroque "the greatest style of Europe," but most likely he was ready to admit that Spengler's opinion might be correct, at least to a considerable degree. The central idea of the baroque in art—restless beauty—is interpreted as an ideal category rising above nature. Another important concept of the esthetics of the baroque is a heavy grace. And, finally, the third normative requirement is *decorum.* Giovanni Battista Marino wrote, "To evoke astonishment is the task of the poet on earth; he who cannot startle would do better to become a stable-boy." This attraction to the rare and extraordinary, the desire to create a dazzling spectacle, obviously captivated Ivanov, especially at the beginning of his creative period. In the baroque style multicolored marble and stucco, gilt bronze, murals and painted statues, strongly protruding cornices, frontons, pilasters, half-columns and niches have an exaggerated plastic elaboration; and the space demanded by them (dependent on them) is saturated with movement. Was it not this same movement which constantly reminded Ivanov of his first devotion—Dionysianism?

And when we come to accept the baroque, then we may also

admire one of its principal masters—Lorenzo Bernini. Bernini, as did Ivanov later, longed to produce majestic images which he saturated with pathos and passion. Ivanov fell in love with Bernini's "Apollo and Daphne" at first sight. He was amazed by the demonstrative metamorphosis of the maiden's body into the divine laurel. Bernini realizes this in marble with mastery and grace by applying the painterly texture which was, for his time, a revolutionary device. The sculpture forces us to forget about the ponderous material of the marble. In just this way we forget the weight of the sonnet's form in Ivanov's poems (not only in his own, but also in his remarkable translations of Petrarch), which he changes into a creative flight and a musical victory over strict structure. (pp. 268-75)

Strangely enough, Bernini as an architect in his old age created the most inspired works, but Bernini as a sculptor in his later years became too realistic and too carnal; his works on religious subjects, especially his exhausted St. Teresa, lose any possible connection with the work of the metaphysical poet Ivanov. The great force of Bernini as a sculptor is his "Naturstimme" ["natural voice"]; but Ivanov's voice, although he occasionally does have folklike elements, is a cultivated voice, the academic *bel canto*. Bernini's deviations from the classic style sometimes threaten that anarchy will find its way even into carefree baroque art. But Ivanov has discriminating taste which does not permit him to overflow the vessel of decorative art. Bernini, despite his vehemence, is in part a talent of a Balmont-like limitlessness. Ivanov, even in his exalted ornateness, even in his most expansive poem-murals, remains a masculine talent, synthesizing, self-restrained, and committed to a considerable discipline of thinking and to a demanding traditional form of versification.

But it is possible that in the creative gesture of Bernini and in the forceful movement of Ivanov's metaphors there is a common motion (among Russian Symbolist poets none except Ivanov achieved such powerful poetic tropes). One could cite some turns of speech from *Vespertine Light:* "And in the sunny camp-fire/ Of the days blinded by their brightness"; "The cries of the first birds . . . splashed gold through the cloud of sadness"; "Divided in itself/ Like the holy schism"; "Sky-blue salt sprinkled the stone"; "Where the heavenly intoxication became the vinegar of exile"; "The river flows through the meadow of immortality/ Toward its beginning, where the spring originates"; "I fled, and now at the foothills of Thebes/ I am eating the wild honey of silence"; "The ripe sweetness of the wordy grapes"; "Save yourself . . ./ Dark life, from the starry lances of the cold"; "And the flame of heaven, after having melted vault/ Plunged like golden faceless torrents." With many other poets I could name such dynamics of poeticism would give the impression of artificial showiness. But with Ivanov, in the frame of his creative thought and as a proper characteristic of his expressiveness, elevated to the category of a liturgical absolute, it is a great and persuasive style. (Some critics who accuse Ivanov of a "floridness of manner" do not understand that he represents the purity of *his* style in *this* way). (pp. 276-77)

"Ivanov and the fine arts"—what an appealing theme for an inspired art historian like Henri Focillon. "Ivanov and music"—what a fruitful theme for a musicologist-versologist like Frasibulos Georgiades. "Scriabin and Ivanov"—another provocative subject for controversial analytic parallels.

Scriabin and Ivanov both expanded the circle of images in Russian arts, and each enriched the expressive media of rhythm and texture in his respective field. Both the musical language of Scriabin and the poetic language of Ivanov are characterized by the art of rhetorical delivery and imperative intonations; their harmonies are sharp and saturated. Scriabin's musical images are of an abstract nature, as Ivanov's iconic metaphors often are; they are conditional symbols. Scriabin's Poem of Ecstasy and his mystery Prometheus express his faith in the transformation of the world through the magical power of art. This idea is similar to Ivanov's point of view. Under the influence of the Lithuanian painter M. K. Chiurlionis, to whose work Ivanov introduced Scriabin (as the poet himself told me), Scriabin hoped to achieve a "synthesis of arts" and introduce the "symphony of lights" in his Prometheus. The dramatic intensity, rejoicing, and mystic symbolism of Scriabin and Ivanov are, to a certain degree, analogous. But the nervous vehemence of Scriabin's modernistic rhythms and his dissonant intonation are traits which are definitely alien even to the dramatically decorative Ivanov. It is interesting to note that the best poem that Ivanov dedicated to Scriabin is written in such a tender tone that it seems that the poet is addressing instead a composer like Gluck or Schubert. In the sonnet **"Novodevichy Monastery"** Ivanov says: "And behind the nunnery, within the limits of the outer walls,/ as a raised altar, Scriabin's grave/ prayer for peace with heaven."

Here we have serenity and tenderness instead of Scriabin's tempest. Only in the two sonnets dedicated "to the memory of Scriabin" does the true Scriabin, the creator of "the lightning of the spirit" with the "sanctity of Prometheus," and with the flesh "turning the tongue of heaven into flame," rise before him. These sonnets are, nonetheless, what the Germans call a "Fehlschlag des grossen Meisters" ["wrong stroke of the great master"]. The rhetorical elements in them are much stronger than the esthetic ones; and therefore the result is nothing but mere "literature" in the Verlainean sense. In *Vespertine Light* the poet also mentions the names of Beethoven and Bach:

"Psalm"

To my daughter Lydia

Love does not know fear,
And our God is the God of living

In harmonies dear to our hearts
of Beethoven and Bach

Catch the echoes
of other worlds.

(pp. 278-80)

Bach is much closer to Ivanov [than is Beethoven], if only because of the spiritually philosophical content of his works, especially the cantatas, which represent almost a fourth of his production. Like Ivanov, Bach's gift is vocal and dramatic. The dual climax of Bach's vocal-dramatic music is the *St. Matthew Passion* and the *B Minor Mass*. The chorus "Et resurrexit" in this mass is in the style of an orchestral concert and may, in this regard, remind us especially of Ivanov's *Cor Ardens.* Interestingly enough, both in Bach's work and in Ivanov's, the dramatic qualities and the choral splendor correspond with the harmony of the structure (here, the baroque form-creating situation is somewhat similar to the synthesis of Ivanov's poems with the Corinthian style). Bach's musical language is distinguished by its perfected exuberance, as is the poetic language of Ivanov. The complex interplay of polyphonic and harmonic thinking, the abundance of color and deep logic, the contrapuntal and tonal development, the clear exposition of detail, and the strict balance of the large-scale with the minute all are esthetic antitheses which both Bach and Ivanov employed persuasively. The complicated polyphonic texture of Bach is uninterrupted throughout the composition, which requires of the audience (just as from the readers of Ivanov) a high degree of concentrated attention. But Ivanov does not follow the contrapuntal form exclusively. Starting his poem as a polyphony, the poet very skillfully interlaces the "voices" (the voices of sound metric as such) but then shifts, chiefly in his sonnets but also in many of the poems in the *Roman Diary,* to harmonic combinations of sounds. He does this to avoid exhausting the reader with his elaborations by keeping him in a constant state of tension. (pp. 280-82)

The themes of recollection are very strong in *Vespertine Light.* In one of his extremely non-orthodox poems (I do admire Ivanov's non-dogmatic dogmatism) the poet refuses to philosophize:

> The poet, too, teaches us something
> But not through his wisdom:
> With that he most likely would
> Only confuse or bore us.

Memory conditions our knowledge about the world and ourselves. Memory is the "crown of knowledge"—it is the "Mother of the Muses." Memory is the source of individual creative work and the prophetic gift: "A poet being the instrument of the folk consciousness is at the same time the medium of national remembrance. Through him the people recall their ancient soul and reestablish the possibilities dormant for ages." Ivanov combines the soul-remembrance of ideas (about which Plato speaks in the *Meno*) and the memory-imagination in his "Memory-River" using imagery unusual for its originality:

> That soars towards the springs of the past
> The returning river of time. . . .
>
> (It is not given to them to remember, but to flow.
> It means they have to live in the bed of the river),
>   to run
> To the spring of the [first] days. . . .
>
> The course of the returning current
> Towards the native springs. . . .
>
> And there the river flows through the meadow of
>   immortality
> Towards its beginnings, where the spring was
>   born. . . .
>
> This is the river of Memory. Render worship to the
>   waters—
> And you will see your own living twins. . . .

(pp. 283-84)

Ivanov believes that he is such a twin for himself, namely, a Hellene. *Vespertine Light* is full of poetic declarations of that kind. But the ancient Greek and Christian elements never collide, nor do they contradict one another in Ivanov's thought elsewhere. In his studies of the Dionysian cult he comes to the conclusion that "the Hellenic religion of the suffering God" was a religion of mysticism and "was the first to define the water-slope in terms of its direction and thus from that time on irrepressibly urge all religious creativity toward the ultimate conclusion—Christianity." Of course it never entered Ivanov's mind to identify Dionysius and Christ—a comparison of which he has been accused by some reviewers (and, quite possibly, tempted at one time or another by the example of the poet Holderlin). But Ivanov asserted that "the Church's Christology basically was alien to Hellenic wisdom; the stumbling-block was the person of the 'Galilean' (which, according to legend, Julian named Jesus Christ), that "Christianity lived and conquered the whole world just believing in *His* person and *His* unique significance." According to Ivanov, the cult of Dionysius "is the Bible of the pagans." In one of the poems in *Vespertine Light* he brings together both "bibles" as if they were two different tongues which speak with two voices about the same fears and expectations:

> [You,] for whom the Hellenic oration is not understandable,
> You must hear in the biblical symbols
> That message which has been instilled by the Muse
> To the meditation of the Pythagorean strings.

The Hellenic and Christian elements are intertwined and form a solid, harmonious "pattern." And the harmony is broken only once by an unexpected and sonorous, as well as esthetically persuasive, dissonance:

"Palinoidia"

> And did it really glut me: your honey from Hymettus?
> Who carted off your idol from the grove of myrtles?
> Or did *I* smash what oracles had taught me to eschew?
> Have I, in fact, Hellas, left off loving you?
> No: poor in heart, I never ever came to know your love,
> I came to dread the masks of soul that would not move,
> As light from lordly forms and the frame of Euclid's thought.
> But when with broken tune the subterranean flutes
> Revived the eyes of the hollow mask—the hour was ripe,
> Filled with mutinous anguish of an unruly night,
> As in old days—then, I heard a voice from heaven:
> "Depart, my servant, from this fluted temple of demons."
> Depart I did, and now, under the Theban foothills
> I eat the wild honey of silence, and raw locusts.

"Palinoidia" belongs to the period of Ivanov's creative work when, far away from his homeland, he recalled all that he had lived through and reevaluated his own spiritual property. With endearment he scrutinized the long road of the "race of Christians." Then like St. Hieronymus, he also renounces the intellectual luxury of the ancient world (from this source comes the image of the desert and expressions in the New Testament, "Wild honey. . ."). But the renunciation does not last. "All that was truthful, beautiful in Antiquity lives in Christianity": he remembers the words of the second century martyr, St. Justin. Thus Ivanov accepts humanism in a new way—as a religion.

In the heroic verses of **"Palinoidia,"** which may have the ring of Racine, passionate and sincere negations and renunciations resound, just as passionate and selfless as the love for Hellas. Everything is, nevertheless, authentic here: thought, feeling, and the very strain of the muscle of the word. These severe lines remind me of the simultaneously penetrating and estranged cosmic strophes of Mandelstam, who was a disciple of Ivanov:

> Then joyfully take my strange gift,
> Uncomely dry necklace
> Made of dead bees, who have transformed the
>   honey into the sun.
>
> (pp. 285-86)

In *Vespertine Light* the unity is formed of severe thought and of passionate impulse, of refinements of metrical schemes and of sober simplicity of speech, of Hellenistic and Christian pathos, of a decorative dithyrambic hymn and a lucidly quiet song. Paul Valery, another Hellene of the twentieth century, said that the perfect poetic work must be a *feast* of the intellect. *Vespertine Light* is such a feast. (p. 287)

> *Aleksis Rannit, "Vyacheslav Ivanov and His 'Vespertine Light': Notes from My Critical Diary of 1966," in* Russian Literature Triquarterly, *1972, pp. 265-88.*

ADDITIONAL BIBLIOGRAPHY

Banerjee, Maria. "The Narrator and His Masks in Viacheslav Ivanov's *Tale of Tsarevich Svetomir." Canadian-American Slavic Studies* 12, No. 2 (Summer 1978): 274-82.

> Examines the themes, plot, and structure of *Tale of Tsarevich Svetomir,* emphasizing the relationship between the way in which the story was constructed, with Olga Deschartes finishing the work after Ivanov's death, and the narrative technique employed.

Bowra, Maurice. Introduction to *Svet vecherny,* by Vyacheslav Ivanov, pp. xiii-xxiii. Oxford: Oxford at the Clarendon Press, 1962. Biographical and critical sketch.

Davidson, Pamela. "Vyacheslav Ivanov's Translations of Dante." *Oxford Slavonic Papers* 15 (1982): 103-31.

> Argues that Ivanov's translations distort Dante's works in order to reflect Ivanov's own philosophical orientation, particularly his concern with synthesizing elements of classical paganism and Christianity. As a result, Ivanov's versions present Dante as "an obscure, complex poet who anticipates in his verse the fundamental features of Symbolist aesthetics."

Donchin, Georgette. *The Influence of French Symbolism on Russian Poetry.* The Hague: Mouton and Co., 1958, 239 p.

> Traces the influence of French Symbolism on the development of the Symbolist movement in Russia, including a discussion of themes in Symbolist poetry, Symbolist aesthetics and technique, and the Symbolist press. Contains numerous references to Ivanov.

Jackson, Robert Louis, and Nelson, Lowry, Jr., eds. *Vyacheslav Ivanov: Poet, Critic, and Philosopher.* New Haven: Yale Center for International and Area Studies, 1986, 474 p.

> A collection of papers from an international symposium on the poetry, criticism, philosophy, translations, and life of Ivanov. The essays, contributed by such critics as James West, Victor Terras, Aleksis Rannit, Vladimir Markov, and René Wellek, examine a variety of topics, including analysis of specific works, Ivanov's role in the development of the Symbolist movement, the influence of Friedrich Nietzsche on Ivanov's thought and writing, and Ivanov's classical scholarship. The volume also in-

cludes an essay on recurrent motifs in Ivanov's works written by his son Dmitri Ivanov and personal reminiscences written by his daughter Lydia Ivanova.

Peterson, Ronald E., ed. and trans. *The Russian Symbolists: An Anthology of Critical and Theoretical Writings.* Ann Arbor, Mich.: Ardis, 1986, 223 p.

> A collection of essays by Russian Symbolists, including Konstantin Balmont, Andrey Bely, Valery Bryusov, Ivanov, Dmitry Merezhkovsky, Fyodor Sologrub, and Vladimir Solovyov. The book includes the editorial statements of four Symbolist journals and a general introduction by Peterson, as well as a bibliography listing works on Symbolism and on individual Symbolist authors.

Putnam, George F. "Viacheslav Ivanov on the Historical Role of the Symbolist Poet." *The Southern Review* n.s. 3, No. 1 (Winter 1967): 85-95.

> Presents ideas held by Ivanov and other Symbolists on the proper role of the artist in society and relates them to their historical and cultural context.

Rosenthal, Bernice Glatzer. "The Transmutation of the Symbolist Ethos: Mystical Anarchism and the Revolution of 1905." *Slavic Review* 36, No. 4 (December 1977): 608-27.

> Outlines the development and basic tenets of the doctrine of mystical anarchism, an ideology formulated primarily by Ivanov and Georgii Chulkov in the aftermath of the 1905 Revolution as the Symbolists sought to end their isolation from society. Rosenthal argues that while mystical anarchism was particularly popular among Symbolists, it also influenced other artists and intellectuals.

Seabrook, John. "The Odd Couple." *The Nation* 240, No. 13 (6 April 1985): 405-06.

> Favorable review of the first English translation of *Correspondence across a Room* published in book form.

Stammler, Heinrich A. "Vjačeslav Ivanov's Image of Man." *Wiener Slavistisches Jahrbuch* 14 (1967-68): 128-42.

> Examines selected works of Ivanov in poetry and prose to elucidate his philosophy of Christian humanism.

———. "Belyj's Conflict with Vjačeslav Ivanov over War and Revolution." *Slavic and East European Journal* 18, No. 3 (Fall 1974): 259-70.

> An account of political and ideological disagreements between Ivanov and Bely, which were characteristic of intellectual debate in Russia during the revolutionary period. According to Stammler, the dialogue "reveals some strength, but also weakness and error in the ideas of both men."

Terras, Victor. "The Aesthetic Categories of *Ascent* and *Descent* in the Poetry of Vjačeslav Ivanov." In *Russian Poetics: Proceedings of the International Colloquium at UCLA, September 22-26, 1975,* pp. 393-408. UCLA Slavic Studies, edited by Thomas Eckman and Dean S. Worth, vol. 4. Columbus, Ohio: Slavica Publishers, 1983.

> Analyzes imagery in Ivanov's poetry, particularly the poems collected in *Vespertine Light.* Terras asserts that Ivanov used images of movement along a vertical axis as expressions of spiritual development.

Venclova, Tomas. "On Russian Mythological Tragedy: Vjačeslav Ivanov and Marina Cvetaeva." In *Myth in Literature,* edited by Andrej Kodjak, Krystyna Pomorska, and Stephen Rudy, pp. 89-109. Columbus, Ohio: Slavica Publishers, 1985.

> Discusses Ivanov's and Tsvetaeva's dramatic adaptations of Greek myths, demonstrating that the plots, themes, and symbolism of these adaptations reflect their authors' interpretations of classical mythology.

Nikos Kazantzakis

1883-1957

(Also transliterated as Kazantzakēs; also wrote under the pseudonym Karma Nirvami) Greek novelist, poet, dramatist, essayist, and translator.

For further discussion of Kazantzakis's life and career, see *TCLC,* Volumes 2 and 5.

Kazantzakis is best remembered as the author of *Bios kai politeia tou Alexe Zormpa* (*Zorba the Greek*), *Ho teleutaios peirasmos* (*The Last Temptation of Christ*), and other philosophical novels in which he explored the spiritual and intellectual anguish of modern humanity. Throughout his life, he espoused and rejected many beliefs, and he ultimately developed a syncretic personal philosophy that drew heavily from the ideas of Henri Bergson and Friedrich Nietzsche, viewing existence as a constant struggle of opposing forces while affirming the progressive nature of human development. Kazantzakis's philosophy also included elements of Christianity tempered in later years by the skepticism characteristic of modern thought, and his unorthodox treatment of religious subjects and themes has often evoked censure from representatives of established religions.

Born in Iráklion, a port city on the northern coast of Crete, Kazantzakis grew up during a particularly turbulent period in Cretan history, when nationalist rebels were struggling to overthrow their Turkish rulers and return the island to Greek control. In 1897, rebel insurrections led to open warfare between Greece and Turkey, forcing the Kazantzakis family to seek refuge on Naxos, a small Greek island which was unaffected by the fighting. Kazantzakis returned to Crete in 1899; after completing his secondary education in Iráklion, he enrolled in the school of law at the University of Athens. He began to write fiction and dramas during this period, and he published his first work, the romantic novella *Ophis kai krinos* (*Serpent and Lily*), shortly after receiving his law degree in 1906.

The following year, Kazantzakis went to Paris to study law at the Sorbonne and to work on his doctoral thesis, in which he examined the influence of Nietzsche on the philosophy of law. While in Paris, he attended Bergson's lectures at the Collège de France; greatly impressed with the French philosopher's ideas, he thereafter considered himself a disciple of Bergson. Returning to Greece in 1909, Kazantzakis began to write verse dramas and to translate works by Bergson, Nietzsche, William James, and Charles Darwin, among others. Three years later, he was appointed to the cabinet of the future King George II of Greece, and he subsequently served the Greek government in a variety of official and semi-official capacities. However, he spent most of the next three decades traveling in Europe, Asia, and Africa and writing articles about his excursions.

During a 1922 sojourn in Berlin, Kazantzakis became interested in the political philosophy of Karl Marx and participated in leftist discussion groups. Soon afterward, he began promoting Marxism in his travels throughout Europe, chronicling his activities in the autobiographical novel *Toda Raba*. In 1925, he visited the Soviet Union to witness firsthand the benefits of Marxism, and two years later he returned to Moscow to participate in the celebration marking the tenth anniversary of the October Revolution. However, he became disenchanted with Marxism, and in fact with all existing ideological systems, in light of the worsening political and economic situation of Europe in the 1930s, and as the decade progressed he began to concentrate his energies on the completion of his most ambitious work, the massive verse epic *Odyseia* (*The Odyssey: A Modern Sequel*). Having created the first version of the poem between 1924 and 1927, he completely rewrote it four times in the next eleven years, altering the content to reflect his own disillusionment with political solutions as well as his increasing concern for the spiritual well-being of modern humanity.

The Odyssey drew little attention upon its publication in 1938, and it was not until the final decade of his life that Kazantzakis published the novels for which he is remembered today. Already well-known as a political activist, cultural ambassador, and translator, Kazantzakis gained popular success as a novelist with the publication of *Zorba the Greek* in 1946. The controversy regarding his heterodox Christianity began with the publication of his next novel, *Ho Christos xanastauronetai* (*The Greek Passion*), in which the modern Christian church is depicted as an ossified institution that has ceased to embody the teachings of Christ, and climaxed with *The Last Temptation of Christ,* a psychological study of Jesus. Despite harsh criticism of his theological viewpoint, Kazantzakis enjoyed popular and critical acclaim throughout this latter portion of his career, and in 1957, the year of his death from the complications of lymphoma, he was nominated for the Nobel Prize in literature.

Critics generally divide Kazantzakis's literary career into three phases, suggesting that each corresponds roughly to a stage in the author's philosophical development. During the initial, formative phase, which began with the publication of *Serpent and Lily* and ended with his 1922 conversion to activist Marxism, the young author struggled to reconcile the philosophies of his two principal mentors, Bergson and Nietzsche. Kazantzakis was particularly impressed with Nietzsche's delineation of the Apollonian-Dionysian dichotomy, which defines the opposition of humankind's physical (Dionysian) drives and its spiritual or intellectual (Apollonian) aspirations as the essential dynamic of life. Kazantzakis expanded this concept to describe a more profound conflict between matter and the *élan vital* (a term used by Bergson to designate a creative force inherent in the universe), believing that the *élan vital* informs and animates matter but seeks always to be free of the constraints imposed by the laws that control matter. He also drew from Bergson a belief in the progressive nature of this struggle, viewing every form of life as a step in the evolutionary process toward a more perfect being which would transcend the limitations of corporeal existence and become one with the *élan vital.* Kazantzakis associated Bergson's *élan vital* with the Christian god, and in *Salvatores Dei: Askētikē* (*The Saviors of God: Spiritual Exercises*), his most thorough exposition of his early philosophical views, he argued that it is the responsibility of each individual to assist in the process of "freeing" the divine spark within humanity by seeking spiritual communion with the universe. This conviction led Kazantzakis to espouse Eastern mysticism, particularly the renunciation of the physical world recommended by Buddha, and is reflected in the verse tragedies he created during this period, many of which focus on historical figures who sacrificed themselves for their transcendent ideals.

During the second, Marxist, phase of his career, Kazantzakis produced few finished works, concentrating instead on the dissemination of Marxist ideas and the furthering of worldwide political change. His *Odyssey,* begun during this period, is viewed as a transitional work, reflecting in both its philosophical viewpoint and its autobiographical content the author's spiritual journey from mysticism to political activism to Christian eclecticism. In Kazantzakis's sequel to Homer's *Odyssey,* Odysseus returns to Ithaca after his years of wandering, but soon becomes bored with ruling a kingdom at peace. He therefore gathers his warriors again and sets off for Sparta, where Helen is reportedly languishing in the company of the decrepit Menelaus. After abducting Helen, Odysseus and his men journey throughout the Mediterranean region, witnessing much political and social unrest; they eventually found a new city-state, which is subsequently destroyed by a volcanic eruption. Odysseus, essentially a soldier, is at first stimulated by violence, but he gradually overcomes his warrior nature and becomes a Christian. He is, however, perplexed by the questions that have traditionally challenged Christian orthodoxy, including the existence of evil and the conflict between humanity's inherently sensual nature and Christian asceticism, and he ultimately rejects all existing systems of belief. The ending of *The Odyssey* is considered philosophically ambiguous: Odysseus journeys to the South Pole, where he dies dreaming of Helen. While basing this narrative on his own experiences, Kazantzakis intended the work as a comprehensive exposition of the spiritual, intellectual, and political conflicts facing modern humanity. Although he offers no definitive solutions to the issues raised, critics suggest that the work ultimately asserts humanity's need for political and intellectual freedom. According to James F. Lea: "The positive value [of *The Odyssey*] lies in the dynamic example of one who rejects every false hope; who will not succumb to the void awaiting; who will not abdicate his freedom; who will not exchange his liberty for any Grand Inquisitor's mastery, mystery, and miracle."

During the final phase of his career, Kazantzakis continued to explore the spiritual plight of mankind, focusing in particular on the anguish that results from the Apollonian-Dionysian dichotomy. This concern is most explicitly manifested in *Zorba the Greek* and *The Last Temptation of Christ.* In the former, Kazantzakis presented two characters who exemplify the poles of the conflict, Zorba representing a sensual, Dionysian figure, while the man known as "the boss" embodies Apollonian traits. In *The Last Temptation of Christ,* the conflict is portrayed as the essential dilemma of Christ, who is torn between his wish to serve God and his physical appetites. Characteristically, Kazantzakis does not attempt to present a resolution to the Apollonian-Dionysian conflict in these novels: Zorba and his boss learn from their exchange of ideas but part essentially unchanged, while Christ, even as he is sacrificing himself on the cross, dreams of leading the sensually satisfying life of an ordinary man.

Although Kazantzakis regarded *The Odyssey* as his masterpiece, critics generally consider Kazantzakis's later novels more significant as illustrations of both his literary aims and his philosophy, praising the profound understanding of the human condition displayed in these works and commending Kazantzakis's affirmations of the value of human existence. In addition, many suggest that Kazantzakis's use of modern demotic Greek, rather than the accepted literary language, represents a significant advancement in the development of Greek literature. Long popular in his native country, his novels have been widely translated, and three of them—*Zorba the Greek, The Greek Passion,* and *The Last Temptation of Christ*—have served as the basis for films. As a result, Kazantzakis remains an important and much-discussed figure in world literature, reflecting the traditional culture of his native Crete while exemplifying the philosophical concerns of the modern European intellectual community.

(See also *Contemporary Authors,* Vol. 105)

PRINCIPAL WORKS

Ophis kai krinos   (novella)   1906
  [*Serpent and Lily,* 1980]
Salvatores Dei: Askētikē   (essay)   1927
  [*The Saviors of God: Spiritual Exercises,* 1960]
Toda Raba   (novel)   1931
  [*Toda Raba,* 1964]
Le jardin des rochers   (novel)   1936
  [*The Rock Garden,* 1963]
Ho morias   (essays)   1937
  [*Journey to the Morea,* 1965; also published as *Travels in Greece,* 1966]
Iaponia-Kina   (essays)   1938
  [*Japan-China,* 1963; also published as *Travels in China and Japan,* 1964]
Odyseia   (poetry)   1938
  [*The Odyssey: A Modern Sequel,* 1958]
Anglia   (essays)   1941
  [*England,* 1965]
Bios kai politeia tou Alexe Zormpa   (novel)   1946
  [*Zorba the Greek,* 1952]
Ho Christos xanastauronetai   (novel)   1951
  [*The Greek Passion,* 1953; also published as *Christ Recrucified,* 1954]
Ho kapetan Michales   (novel)   1954
  [*Freedom or Death,* 1956; also published as *Freedom and Death,* 1956]
Ho teleutaios peirasmos   (novel)   1955
  [*The Last Temptation of Christ,* 1960; also published as *The Last Temptation,* 1960]
Theatro: Tragōdies. 3 vols.   (dramas)   1955-56
Ho phtochoules tou Theou   (novel)   1956
  [*St. Francis,* 1962; also published as *God's Pauper: St. Francis of Assisi,* 1962]
Ispania   (essays)   1957
  [*Spain,* 1963]
Anaphora ston Gkreko   (autobiography)   1961
  [*Report to Greco,* 1965]
Hoi aderophades   (novel)   1963
  [*The Fratricides,* 1964]
Three Plays: "Christopher Colombus," "Melissa," "Kouros"   (dramas)   1969

Megas Alexandros (novel) 1979
　[*Alexander the Great*, 1982]
The Suffering God (letters) 1979
*Two Plays: "Sodom and Gomorrah" and "Comedy: A Trage-
　dy in One Act"* (dramas) 1982

TOM DOULIS (essay date 1963)

[*Doulis is an American novelist, translator, biographer and
critic, whose works reflect his interest in modern Greek culture.
In the following excerpt, he discusses Kazantzakis's synthesis
of Eastern and Western philosophies as exemplified in his view
of the value of suffering.*]

Since Greece, geographically, in the modern and ancient
world, has occupied a position between the East and the
West, the two philosophical and temperamental poles of
human thought and conduct, she has had to fight, trade, live
with, and understand both approaches to the human situation. And within herself, within her history, Greece has experienced actual and temperamental conquests by one or the
other. She, in other words, has been the disputed border territory of the two great and conflicting concepts of humanity.
Briefly and perhaps inadequately summarized, the values
which are considered Eastern are the superiority of the State,
the mass of the people, or the idea over the individual; self-
immolation before a dispassionate God; passivity before the
Omnipotence of the Creator; and the calm, unquestioning acceptance of suffering in human affairs without the satisfaction
of thinking that it has a justifiably intellectual place in the
world. The Western values are, on the other hand, the sacred
importance of the individual over the state, the mass and the
idea; pride in the qualities of man and his resistance to God
in Whom he sees his own image; the active search for truth
shown metaphorically in the highest symbols of the Western
man: Prometheus, Odysseus and Faust; and finally, the questioning of the unanswerable, the inability to accept calmly as
his part in life suffering injustice, "inhumanity," and ignorance.

These two concepts have always met in Greece and have always fought in that land because she is in modern times
bounded on one hand by Turkey and the Orient, and on the
other by Italy and Europe, and in the ancient world by the
sturdy, rude barbarian tribes of the West, and the over-
civilized and corrupt Persians of the East.

The Westerner, the creator and product of the West, is usually (again I am over-simplifying) realistic, pragmatic, certain
that life is real, actual and worthy, while the Easterner considers with alarming insistence that life is a dream and that
actual experiences have happened and shall happen again in
the same way. For the Westerner each moment and action
is unique; for the Easterner each action and time-space is insignificant, because if life is cyclical and dream-like, then Fate
does not admit any separable quality or essence to any particular event.

A perfect example, according to Kazantzakis, of the perme-
ation of a Western people by Eastern ideas can be found in
the personality of the Spaniard as it has been modified by the
Moorish invasion and occupation of the Iberian Peninsula.
After quoting the very significant lines of Calderon's drama,
La vida es sueño (*Life Is a Dream*), he goes on to define the

Spanish outlook in the way that most of his fictional personages are characterized when they are meant to exemplify the
Oriental mode of thinking.

　And there is another virtue of the Spaniard which
　emanates from his idea that all reality is a dream:
　his stoicism. The spectacle of the vanity of life, the
　surmise that all is a dream, gives him an heroic en-
　durance, an easy smile, and a proud and silent
　perseverance. . . .

　In harmony with the soul of the Spaniard is his
　thought. The Spaniard gazes fixedly at life, the ex-
　ternal and internal, and waits for the idea to uncov-
　er itself. His perceptions, but not his critical facul-
　ties, are extremely acute. He can make a synthesis,
　and he makes it joyfully, as if it were his only tal-
　ent—but with great difficulty and impatience does
　he undertake a critical analysis. The spiritual idio-
　syncrasy of the Spaniard is extraordinarily selec-
　tive; but he lacks the method, the technique, the pa-
　tience, the day by day labor.

It is the conflict between the dream world of the East and the
actual world of the West (i.e. between withdrawal and commitment) which Kazantzakis uses as the foundation of his
new synthesis.

In preparation for this task, Kazantzakis, his race's destiny
seriously in mind, has studied the Eastern philosophies and
religions, learning the original languages, reading deeply in
Mohammedanism, Buddhism, Confucianism, and Taoism, as
well as the Modern Western philosophers Aquinas, Kant,
Hegel, Marx, Nietzsche and Bergson. He has used the Ancients, the root of Greek thought, as a basis for his own and
his nation's philosophical synthesis. In essence, Kazantzakis'
collected work represents the final justification of the Western man's active search for truth as distinguished from the
Easterner's passivity before truth. It must be mentioned,
however, that in the final analysis Kazantzakis doubts the
saving power of the intellect of man, though he reaffirms the
Western idea that it is necessary to have an educated and sensitive mind in order to comprehend its final inadequacy.

In Kazantzakian fiction there are two worlds: the world of
peace, luxury, and security, and the world of rebellion, struggle, and suffering. Both are real. One, however, the world of
pleasure and security, is more conducive to the belief that life
is a dream because it is uninterruptedly comfortable. The life
of suffering, on the other hand, gives the sufferer the constant
assurance that life is real because his agonies are real; their
truth cannot be suspected.

With **Zorba the Greek,** Kazantzakis approaches the main
problem, the main preoccupation of his fiction; constructed
as it is, the novel is a debate between two men, one a scholar-
ascetic who "if offered a choice between falling in love and
reading a book about love would have chosen the book," and
Alexis Zorba, the symbol of the Greek *élan vital,* the naive,
trusting, yet biologically sophisticated representative of the
living Mediterranean man. The conflict which is faced by the
scholar-narrator of the myth-history is the traditional one between "body" and "mind-soul"; but in the center, the ful-
crum of the two poles, is the yawning Buddhist Nothing
which acts as the central force of the entire work.

The Boss, carrying his two beloved books, a Dante and a
Buddha, makes no human contacts on the island of Crete
where he had gone to try to participate in the active life; sig-

nificantly, he conducts correspondence with two former students, men with whom he could not get along in the university. Both are involved in the active life; one is in Russia on a patriotic mission; the other, in the heart of Africa, works as a nihilistic capitalist, using as his motivating force the power of hatred. It is Zorba, then, who opens up the world, the real world, to the ascetic. At first the Boss feels only a compassion "not only for men but for all life which struggles, cries, weeps, hopes and does not perceive that everything is a phantasmagoria of nothingness"; but later, after seeing Zorba's thrilling dance, the attempt of the human spirit to overcome its matter, after involving himself in a human enterprise, he makes the great attack on Nothingness (Nirvana) which, paradoxically, is the motivating force of his entire life. After spending some time with Zorba, he tries to reread a book of Mallarmé's poems and finds that they are "pale-blue, hollow words in a vacuum."

> In religions which have lost their creative spark, the gods eventually become no more than poetic motifs or ornaments for decorating human solitude and walls. Something similar had happened to this poetry. The ardent aspirations of the heart, laden with earth and seed, had become a flawless intellectual game, a clever, aerial and intricate architecture. . . .
>
> All these things which had formerly so fascinated me appeared this morning to be no more than cerebral acrobatics and refined charlatanism! That is how it always is at the decline of a civilization. That is how man's anguish ends—in masterly conjuring tricks: pure poetry, pure music, pure thought. The last man—who has freed himself from all belief, from all illusions and has nothing more to expect or to fear—sees the clay of which he is made reduced to spirit, and this spirit has no soil left for its roots from which draw its sap. The last man has emptied himself; no more seed, no more excrement, no more blood. Everything having turned into words, every set of words into musical jugglery, the last man goes even further: he sits in his utter solitude and decomposes the music into mute, mathematical equations.
>
> I started. "Buddha is that last man!" I cried. That is his secret and terrible significance. Buddha is the pure soul which has emptied itself; in him is the void, he is the Void. "Empty your body, empty your spirit, empty your heart!" he cries. Wherever he sets foot, water no longer flows, no grass can grow. . . .

At a less intellectual level, with uneducated men like the Agha of Lycovrissi and his little boy Youssoufaki in *The Greek Passion,* this Oriental nothingness, this suspicion of the reality of life is shown in their favorite *amané,* their favorite melancholy song. "World and dream are but one, *aman, aman,*" sings little Youssoufaki, and the Agha, bloated by food, raki, good living and security, is never more convinced that "world" and "dream" are synonymous. Captain Greenhorn Fortunas, the easy-going, pleasant Greek pagan, when he is ready to die, thinks that "he must surely have fallen asleep and dreamed that he was a captain and had plied between the ports of the White and Black Sea . . . and that now, so it appeared, he was passing away." But he thinks, "no, he wasn't dying, he was waking up, the dream was over, day was breaking."

Likewise, the young Indian prince in *The Last Temptation,*

coming to Magdala with the caravans, goes to visit the prostitute Mary Magdalene and seeing that he must wait in line for her, sits down and converses with an old man.

> "My young Indian prince, what does your God say about all these things? Does he allow them?"
>
> The youth opened his eyes. "About all what?" he asked.
>
> "This, men, women, crabs, love . . ."
>
> "He says that all is a dream, my brother."
>
> "Then you must be careful, my good youth," said the old man with the white beard, "be careful that you don't wake up."

And the incident completes itself when the Indian, after waiting for a long time, gets up and walks out without seeing the Magdalene; having satisfied himself with her in his dreams, in the phantasies, he is surfeited and awakens.

Only the man who does not distrust the reality of the world, who is committed to the struggle with the real and unjust forces of the waking-world, can ask the elemental and naive questions which beset living mankind at all times. The man who believes that there is no real world, that all phenomena are illusory, the man who, because he lacks the adequate analytical perceptions and vocabulary, and as a result, is confused as to the meaning of his sense impressions, does not bother himself unduly about an individual interpretation of value and meaning. He has an adequate and effective way of dealing with these questions: he can say that they do not exist, that he has dreamed them. It is only the Zorbatic man (the man who is convinced that his senses report impressions to him honestly) who is vexed by the eternal questions because the search for truth and certitude is, in a way, ultimately, a naive preoccupation. (pp. 35-9)

Once man accepts the fact that the world he sees is real, he is met with the problem of whether it is good or evil. The dream-believer does not worry about value and significance because to him everything external is "false" and illusory. Only occasionally does he wonder about this convenient escape, and that is, significantly, during moments of struggle and suffering. When the real, the external world, breaks into the false, hermetically sealed world of the escapist "oriental," he realizes that he has been fooling himself all his life. In *The Greek Passion,* the Agha's world crumbles when he finds his beloved Youssoufaki butchered.

> At this mild hour of the day's ending, the Agha's habit was to sit cross-legged on his balcony; at his side Youssoufaki would pour out his drink and light his chibouk. This evening doors and windows remained closed, the balcony was deserted, the Agha was moaning; how bitter and untrue it was— the song he loved: "World and dream are but one . . ." He held in his arms the small, lifeless body. "It isn't a dream, this," he said to himself; "no, it isn't a dream," and he burst out sobbing.

This intense and agonizing vision of reality, however, lasts only as long as the Agha is confused by the suffering. The Actor-Christ, taking his role in the Passion Play seriously, decides to take the guilt of the crime upon himself and thus save the village from the wholesale hangings. When Manolios, therefore, enters to confess to the murder, the Agha who unwittingly takes the role of Pontius Pilate in the

Passion Play thinks: " 'It was written' . . . He threw the sin of men upon God and was appeased . . . 'All that happens, happens by Thy will . . . Bow the head and be silent . . . All is written'." The Agha has had a dream, however, which told him that Manolios did not kill Youssoufaki, and here we must not confuse the nocturnal dream of the uncensored subconscious with the highly evolved idea that all life is a dream. The Agha asks Manolios to confess and Manolios says that the Devil urged him to commit the crime. "The Agha leaned against the wall and closed his eyes. 'Allah, Allah,' he murmured, 'the world is a dream'."

Thus suffering may break into the escape-world of the Oriental and force him to contemplate the confusing reality he has succeeded in evading, but once the suffering passes, the years of habit allow the Agha to revert to his dream-world by the comforting phrases of "it is written" or "it is willed." Suffering, in order to be finally and completely effective, must be fairly constant; it must also be experienced by people who are adventurous enough to require the vision of reality. The Agha, for example, knows that Manolios did not kill Youssoufaki, yet because of his spiritual and intellectual sloth, he decides to accept the Actor-Christ's false confession. This, of course, parallels Pontius Pilate's question: "What is Truth?" and his weakness when he turned Jesus over to the crucifiers, "washing his hands of the affair," even though he knew the Nazarene was guiltless.

Moreover, in all five novels, dreams, which are experienced by both Orientals and Westerners, play a vital role; if the real world and the dream world then are so inextricably bound, how is the poor, struggling Kazantzakian man to distinguish between the true and the untrue? Since Freud and the relatively new school of psychology, the West is aware that dreams are caused by the latent, suppressed ideas which the conscious mind forces into the deep well of the unconscious. At night, in dreams, these unwanted ideas, because of the relaxation of the censor, the conscious intellect, express themselves either as undisguised, disturbing images and scenes, or as harmless and baffling symbols which evade the censor and exhibit themselves to the unsuspecting dreamer. (pp. 40-1)

Since this is the case, there is only one way in which the Kazantzakian man can be certain that his dream, which he fully believes comes from either God or the Devil, is meant for his good. If it is pleasant, if it at all corresponds to his basest and least admirable nature, then he can be sure that it comes from the Tempter. If, on the other hand, it conflicts with what his baser nature, his comfort-loving flesh, tells him is good, then it most certainly comes as a dictate from God. (p. 41)

What may seem to be simply a philosophical and temperamental distinction between the people of the East and the West proves to be an individual interpretation of the most vexing problem mankind has ever confronted; the main search in Kazantzakis' fiction is for the value and meaning of human suffering. The Easterner is not concerned with these transient and illusory worries; he is certain, when life is stable of course, that the world is a lie, a dream, and that death awaits him with a final certainty which makes the individual and racial anguish at extinction not worthy of thought or wonder. And it is wonder that has made the Western man the traveler and searcher for truth that he is. In the East, at any rate before the people had contact with Western adventurers, the individual did not worry about himself and his universe as does his brother in the West. Originality is not considered the virtue in the Orient that it is in the Occident,

and originality and wonder are attributes of the naive Western heroes from Prometheus to Odysseus to Faust. Every new generation in the Western world must find its own answer to the eternal questions; it must make its own adjustments to the common fate of man. That same question: what is the meaning, the lesson of suffering? was answered for himself and for his time by Sophocles who said that "through suffering comes patience." In fact, the entire Greek drama seems to sum up the meaning of tragedy and suffering by saying that wisdom is the end-product of human agony. This answer, however, is inadequate for the modern man because he may very well ask: what is the value of wisdom since it can only cause added suffering to the wise man who sees ignorance triumph and innocence corrupted? In *The Brothers Karamazov,* Mitya, after the evidence of the witnesses and before being carried away, has a dream in which he sees a mother and her child crying; he asks: "Why are they crying? Why are its little arms bare? . . . Why are people poor? Why is the steppe barren? . . . Why don't they sing songs of joy? Why are they so dark from black misery?" and Dostoyevsky goes on to relate that "though his questions were unreasonable and senseless," he wanted to ask them just that way. "And he felt that a passion of pity such as he had never known before was rising in his heart"; for the Christian Dostoyevsky, then, suffering brings the passion of pity, the questioning of the unanswerable, the unreasonable: suffering brings pity and love. (p. 44)

We have seen up to now the two ways of life: the Eastern and its belief that world and dream are one, and the Western which does not doubt the reality of the world. In *Zorba the Greek,* Kazantzakis throws the creative, fecund flesh into direct conflict with the violent, ascetic soul; after this dualistic struggle which presumably settles the problem by showing the *élan vital's* weakness for the intellect, and vice versa, each half of man's nature withdraws and maintains its own integrity. After this partial commitment, Kazantzakis finds himself grappling with the greatest question man has ever considered: in the dream-world the problem does not exist except where suffering and tragedy break through the dream; in the real world, however, it is ever-present. The dilemma for the Western man is clear-cut: should he commit himself to life in the real world, or ignore the struggle between good and evil? If he succeeds in defeating the notion that life is a dream, and makes his commitment to the actual world in which good and evil battle, he is led directly to the tragic myth of betrayal, death, and salvation.

Kazantzakis was led to heroic tragedy in *Freedom or Death,* and divine tragedy presented symbolically in *The Greek Passion,* and actually in *The Last Temptation.* With the confrontation of the tragic view, of course, Kazantzakis is again forced to define the value and significance of suffering, but this time from a more withdrawn position, from an almost mythical remove. With *The Last Temptation,* it is interesting to note, he changes his approach to "reality." For the Agha of *The Greek Passion* the "reality" he may have evaded was a pragmatic reality; but in *The Last Temptation* the "true reality" becomes the *myth,* while the *fact,* which may on a lower level be true, in Divine perspective may be false.

Before attempting to supply Kazantzakis' answer to the value of suffering, we must cite the difficulties surrounding the problem for him. He must, first of all, reaffirm the Western man's desire to question, to understand, and to communicate the tragic experience a free, ideologically unfettered individual feels when he confronts the universe. The Easterner has his convenient dream-escape, but the Western man must make his own terms with a cosmos which gives him birth, confuses him, and, at a certain time in the future, takes away his life. In all these situations Kazantzakis has stressed the value of the confrontation of reality rather than the escape into the dream world, and he has exhibited the invincibility of man beset by suffering and struggle with what can be called grandeur.

In the final analysis, however, he distrusts the strength of man's rational mind to comprehend the almost irrational value and significance of suffering. Every one of Kazantzakis' heroes is an emotional malcontent who cannot adequately articulate the *rationale* of his existence. Every protagonist is speechless when he confronts the incomprehensible facts of man's life on earth. The reason for this cannot be stated simply by saying that Kazantzakis deals mainly with the unlettered and the ignorant. The Boss in *Zorba,* Priest Fotis in *The Greek Passion,* Kosmas in *Freedom or Death,* the many rabbis and abbots in *The Last Temptation,* and Francis in *The Poor Man of God,* are learned men. Although they are educated people, however, they place more value on the verbally incommunicable than they do on what can be expressed in words. When Christ expounds His idea to the old monk Abakoom in *The Last Temptation,* He states: "Words are the black bars of imprisonment wherein the spirit struggles and shouts. Between the letters and the lines, and around the blank paper, the liberated spirit circulates"; and thus, according to Jesus, the spirit of the law always transcends the letter, the *myth* is always truer than the *fact.* And this is analogous to what Christ does when He goes above His individual existence and participates in the Myth, which although using particular and concrete instances or stories, transcends itself and becomes the eternal and constantly reiterated Plot.

The clearest indication of man surmounting his concrete existence and participating in the Myth is in *The Last Temptation,* wherein Kazantzakis, through Matthew, recopies what the Archangel tells the Evangelist about the Life of Jesus. When, however, Jesus asks the Disciple to see the Gospel, He is horrified and throws it down on the floor.

> "What are these?" he shouted. "Lies, lies, lies! The Messiah has no need of miracles, He is the miracle, He doesn't need others. I was born in Nazareth, not in Bethlehem; I have never set foot in Bethlehem; I don't remember any Wise Men; I have never been in Egypt, and that which you write about the Dove at my baptism: 'This is my beloved Son,' who told you of it? I can't remember what it said, and you, who were not there, how do you know of it?"

But when Matthew tells Him of the Angel, Jesus stops in wonder. What if that which man considers falsehood is truth to God? He gathers the Gospel which He has thrown down in His anger, and gives it back to Matthew, saying that he is to write anything the Angel tells him. In His dream, while on the Cross, when Saul of Tarsus appears to Him and tells Him of his life as an Apostle, Jesus in agony, again repeats the statement that all these things, His birth in Bethlehem, the Three Wise Men, and the Dove, are lies. Saul tells Him that he is not interested in what men say about truth and falsehood; he is interested only in "what gives wings to man, in what gives birth to great deeds and great spirits and lifts us in stature above the earth; a lie is that which snips off the wings of man. . . . I don't care about 'truth' and 'falsehood,' whether I saw it or didn't see it, whether He was crucified or

not crucified. With madness, with joy, and with faith, I will create the truth. . . . I fix truth higher than man's stature and thus force greatness upon him by making him struggle to reach it."

And, as the reader of *The Last Temptation* knows, Jesus in His very person has incorporated all the inadequate myths of His time. In a chapter of magnificent irony, Kazantzakis discusses the many gods and creeds that Imperial Rome has accepted so that she would be able to take in all the wealth she desires. After mentioning Mazda, Mithras, Isis, Osiris, Adonis, Ati, Astarti, and the Olympians (in fact all the gods and goddesses who, by having themselves worshipped in Rome, have enriched the Imperial City), Kazantzakis asks: for whom did Rome win lands, legislate, become wealthy, enlarge herself over the earth, for whom?

> For the barefooted one who was at that time walking on the deserted road from Nazareth to Cana and was followed by a group of wretched raggedmen.

Always, at the basis of every inhuman, super-human, heroic or altruistic act is the irrational, the incomprehensible; Kazantzakis, however, so defines and exhibits the irrational in action and dialogue that it becomes clear and definable. The irrational is that which changes the comfortable, the secure, the sensually pleasing (and in the Kazantzakian context these are obstacles to the heroic man's salvation) to the insecure, the painful, and the tragic. The irrational, the new "madness," and their attendant suffering, become the cocoon which takes the ugly caterpillar and makes it a butterfly, which takes that which crawls on the pragmatic earth and gives it wings, which purges the weaknesses of the flesh, and which reassures the confused mind that what it experiences is real and not a dream. In ridding the spirit of its doubts, its fears, and its weaknesses, the irrational helps the soul of man attain immortality.

It is the obstacle of suffering which, I believe, saves Kazantzakis' fiction from the valid attack which could be made against him, namely, that he believes in a Manichean universe, that is, in a dualistic conflict between two active principles, God and the Devil, the two masks, which, according to the heresy, are equal in strength. The Devil in these novels, however—using in real life the temptations of ease, comfort and pleasure, and when these are inadequate, his last temptation, the idea that the world is a dream—acts only as a subordinate of God, and helps Him select the less virile, the less adventurous, the less "maddened" souls, and deflects them from their highest duty which according to Kazantzakis is "the transubstantiation into spirit of the matter given man by God in trust . . . [this duty is] higher even than ethics, and truth, and beauty" (Preface to *The Poor Man of God*).

Whereas for the ancient tragedians suffering meant wisdom, and for Dostoyevsky it meant pity and love, for Kazantzakis suffering means certitude in being chosen for salvation by the love of a compassionate and interested Creator. It exhibits to man the strength and resiliency of his nature by showing him how little he needs comfort and security. Within the irrational moment of suffering and tragedy he learns that he needs nothing, that he can be happy and joyous even with despair. In moments of the greatest agony man realizes that he experiences an indefinable exaltation which can best be approximated by the term "joy." He learns that he can carry, not how much he is capable of supporting, but as much as God cares to load him with; through tragedy man learns that his strength is limitless and that every temptation, every cause of human suffering, is just an obstacle put in man's way by the Father-God Who wants to test His son's spirit. Because of this love, a love which is mutual between God and His children, there is the necessity to submit to crush the will which enabled him to ascend to his Father; he must willingly lose his personality into that of God.

This submission is well shown in a parable Francis tells the thick-witted Leone.

> An ascetic struggled all his life to attain perfection; he shared all his wealth with the poor, withdrew into the desert and prayed to God day and night. He died, rose, and knocked on the door of Paradise.
>
> "Who is it?" a voice was heard behind the door.
>
> "Ego," the ascetic answered.
>
> "Two egos cannot fit here," the voice said. "Leave."
>
> The ascetic returned to earth and began his usual struggle: poverty, hunger, unending prayers, and tears. His day came again and he died. He again knocked on the door to Paradise.
>
> "Who is it?" asked the same voice.
>
> "Ego."
>
> "Two egos cannot fit here. Leave."
>
> The ascetic, in despair, tumbled again to the earth and began, more madly this time, the struggle to achieve salvation. An old man, a centenarian, he died. He knocked on the door of Paradise again.
>
> "Who is it?" asked the voice.
>
> "You, O Lord, You!"
>
> And immediately the door to Paradise opened and he entered (*The Poor Man of God*).

The eternal Kazantzakian hero, wearing different masks, is preoccupied with one central problem: he struggles and rebels against a stable, comfortable world for reasons he may not understand himself, purges himself of his weaknesses and errors through suffering and war (either a conflict between man's heroic soul and his material flesh, or an actual external conflict against someone other than himself), and through this struggle and rebellion, this purgation of matter which comes about through suffering, he fulfills the highest debt man owes to God his Creator: he transcends his nature, makes it spirit, and like the butterfly after breaking its cocoon, flies up and effects a union with God. (pp. 53-7)

> Tom Doulis, *"Kazantzakis and the Meaning of Suffering,"* in Northwest Review, *Vol. VI, No. 1, Winter, 1963, pp. 33-57.*

LEWIS A. RICHARDS   (essay date 1967)

[*Richards is a Greek-born American editor and critic. In the following excerpt, he examines Kazantzakis's highly personalized religious and philosophical principles.*]

Very little has been done with Kazantzakis' work in the field of literary criticism in the United States. Although his novel,

Zorba the Greek, was quite successful, and despite the fact that other of his novels, along with his long epic poem, *Odyssey,* have been published in English translations, Kazantzakis has remained relatively an unknown author. The American public, which unfailingly wakes critics into action, seems to care little for Kazantzakis. Three reasons for such lack of interest are quite possible: 1) Kazantzakis' Nietzschean philosophy, especially the strong belief in the concept of the superman; 2) his quite comprehensive nihilistic philosophy; 3) his strong anti-church pronouncements. These philosophical concepts expressed by Kazantzakis in his novels may well explain why, with the exception of *Zorba the Greek,* these novels have not been well received in this country. But I do not intend to examine the various reasons for the critical apathy or disregard of Kazantzakis' works in the United States. However, it would be of interest to add that even in his native country, Greece, Kazantzakis has fared little better than he has elsewhere. Today, he is little read and much less liked. Two of his best novels, *The Last Temptation* and *Freedom or Death,* have been proscribed by the Greek Orthodox and Catholic churches. Kazantzakis' philosophy, delineated mainly in his *Ascetic,* as well as in his many tragedies, is considered "deleterious." For a combination of reasons, many Greek critics have written passionately against Kazantzakis, the author and the man.

If in America we have ignored Kazantzakis, in Greece they have, for the most part, either misunderstood or misinterpreted him. To be sure, the most important aspects of Kazantzakian philosophy are neither constructive nor attractive to the public. To read only *Zorba the Greek* and attempt to judge Kazantzakis by that novel alone would be a grave error.

What Kazantzakis wants to do in his other novels is to point out and expose the corruption of the primitive qualities of Christianity by the organized church. In this respect he follows in the footsteps of Dostoevsky, France, Unamuno and Baroja. His messianic heroes, Manolios, St. Francis, and Father Fotis, are much more feared than loved. Kazantzakis' concept—which he followed relentlessly throughout his life—to translate matter into spirit, is not for general consumption; nor is his ascetic life a rosy path for imitation. After all, philosophic pessimism and nihilism are against the best interests of the organized western state and the church.

Yet despite his pessimistic outlook, obvious nihilism, and anti-church position, Kazantzakis has much constructive criticism to offer. One must be free from the narrow nationalistic and religious confines before he can see this constructivism in its proper perspective; as a consequence, the Greeks, who are strongly nationalistic and religious, have refused to approach him with open minds, and have misunderstood him much and abused him even more. Regardless of critical attitudes and opinions, here are three main keys necessary to unlock Kazantzakis' philosophy for anyone who is seriously interested in it.

The Greek Orthodox Church exercises a most powerful influence upon the people of Greece, and it is small wonder that when the church officially proscribed Kazantzakis' novels and publicly ostracized the author, the state followed suit.

At Kazantzakis' death, it was the church which refused to allow the author to be given an honorary burial in Athens, and the Greek state succumbed and yielded.

The next "key" in understanding Kazantzakis' work is to be found in the structure of the Cretan intra-family relations. In

Cretan society, the honor of the family is still defended by the might of arms. Crete, like Corsica, has the reputation of an island where the personal vendetta thrives, and where mixed marriages are scarcely tolerated. The birth of the first son is the greatest event in the family calendar—in any family where distinction is made between "sons" and "children," and where tradition is more sacred than logic. In Kazantzakis' time, the Cretans grew long beards and pointed mustaches—many still do today. They smoked heavily, swore easily, and beat their wives. They still wear wide, long trousers, knee-high black or yellow boots, and carry vests replete with knives and pistols. The girls dress in long gowns, almost ankle-long, and wear multicolored heavy vests. They wrap their heads in attractive, large scarfs. Up to a few years ago, they were not allowed either to speak to, or to be addressed by men. In *Freedom or Death,* Captain Mechales has not seen his own daughter for years, even though they both live at home. He either does not raise his eyes to look at her, or she stays out of view while he is at home. Thus, when he notices a beautiful young girl at a gathering, he asks his wife about her and discovers that the girl is his own daughter.

It is against such domineering church and autocratic parental authority that Kazantzakis has revolted. Tradition—public and private—exercised by patriarchal and inflexible people, along with his own nature (the third "key" in understanding Kazantzakis' works) moulded Kazantzakis' character and led him to asceticism. The author's mind, brilliant as it was, became excited, challenged, and alienated by the deleterious influence of dogmatism and brutal force. His nature became warped under stagnant and restrictive circumstances, to the extent that he had only to acquiesce to the friendly call of asceticim in order to refuse the pleasures which the flesh offered. It is thus that Kazantzakis turned to asceticism, and quite early in his life, 1922, became a Buddhist—an honest and conscientious Buddhist at that.

Perhaps the most striking concept pursued by Kazantzakis in his work in general and novels in particular is his differentiation between the institutional church and primitive Christianity; his conclusion is that the latter has been corrupted by the former. In this respect, Kazantzakis' most learned and enlightened Greek critic, Mr. P. Prevelakis, has noted: "in order to fill the gap, Kazantzakis wishes, from the very beginning, the resurrection of Evangelical Christ, free from ecclesiastical dogmas." Both Kazantzakis' major novels, *The Greek Passion* and *The Last Temptation,* have this "corruption" as their pivotal point. In *The Greek Passion,* Kazantzakis shows how the Utopian socialism of primitive Christianity regarding the community of property is opposed and destroyed by the organized church. The poor peasant, Manolios, who follows in Christ's footsteps, loses in his struggle for power with Father Gregory, who is the representative of the institutional church, much as Christ lost out in his own struggle with the Pharisees and the scribes. In *The Last Temptation,* Kazantzakis brings back to life the Evangelical Christ under the disguise of a poor cross-maker, and describes his social behavior, which leads to a second crucifixion. This novel, by the way, reminds one of Faulkner's novel, *A Fable.* In *God's Poor Man,* Kazantzakis recreates the life of St. Francis and shows this saint's love for asceticism; he also points out the basically different philosophies on life of a godly person, the ascetic St. Francis, and of a representative of the organized church, an unnamed Bishop.

In the above named novels, Kazantzakis is putting forth a concentrated effort to re-discover and re-assert the important Christian qualities of primitive Christianity such as love, brotherhood, humility, and self-renunciation. In doing so, he points out that these qualities are missing from today's church and is disappointed at his discovery. See for example, the conversation between the two prelates, Father Fotis and the Bishop; it is most illuminating. When the Bishop refuses to do justice to the suffering Christians, Father Fotis murmurs to himself:

> "Is this Christ's representative? Is this who preaches justice and love to people? . . ."

> The Bishop raised his arm.

> "Next time," he said, "when you come to the Bishop's, you should wear shoes."

> "I have none," answered Father Fotis; "I had; I haven't any longer; sympathize with me; even Christ walked barefoot, my Bishop."

> The Bishop frowned.

> "Father Gregory has talked to me about you," he said shaking his head threateningly; "you pretend, he says, to be Christ; you want to bring equality and justice to the world; . . . Aren't you ashamed? So there will not be any wealthy or any poor, nor, of course, Bishops . . . rebel! . . ."

> The Bishop now became infuriated.

> "Father Gregory is right; you are a bolshevik! . . ."

> "Yes, if He is too!" answered the priest and pointed again to the Crucified (*The Greek Passion*).

Kazantzakis is saying then that the institutional church has so much deviated in practice from the actual teachings of Christ that it is no longer Christ's church. St. Francis's message to the world, "poverty, peace, love," which St. Francis lived in actual life, contrasts with the apparent wealth, exhibitionism, and lack of true love—or inability to love—shown by the institutional church.

The very choice of the subject matter in *God's Poor Man* shows Kazantzakis' intense interest in asceticism and primitive Christian ethics. Throughout the novel, Kazantzakis compares and contrasts the primitive church with the institutional and finds the latter wanting in many worthwhile and important qualities. Specifically, St. Francis's life was a continuous struggle to elevate the spirit above the flesh, to subdue all demands of the flesh, and to live in absolute poverty. St. Francis's refusal to marry, his reluctance to satisfy his hunger, as well as his deliberate and savage punishment of the flesh are in direct contrast to the life of any church official, bishop, or priest in the organized church today. For this is in essence what St. Francis tells the Bishop in his significant final conversation with him:

> "The devil is pleased when he sees people who are afraid of poverty; to have nothing, nothing, this is the way to reach God; there is no other way."
> The Bishop now was infuriated; he pounded his fist on the Bible:
> "The devil is pleased when he sees you, Francis, disobey me; don't speak any more, go; . . . you are sick" (*God's Poor Man*).

It is as a consequence of such thinking that Kazantzakis'

Kazantzakis (second from right) on the Dnieper River with Panaït Istrati (center).

priests are either wholly evil or wholly good, from the unchristian Bishop, the villainous Father Gregory, the immoral monk, Demetrius, the warlike muezzin, and the deceitful unnamed monk in **Brothereaters,** to the Christ-like Fathers Fotis and Giannaros.

The philosophy in the novels of Kazantzakis differs considerably from that of his many tragedies and that of his earlier, more philosophical works like **Salvatores Dei** or **The Rockgarden.** In these earlier works, Kazantzakis is nihilistic, negativistic, and pessimistic. **Salvatores Dei,** influenced strongly by Nietzschean philosophy and style, is Kazantzakis' credo in the Nietzschean superman. **The Rockgarden** develops along the same line of nihilism-negativism. The underlying philosophy in both books is all too clear. The hero of the **The Rockgarden** gives up action in order to devote his life to the Buddhist philosophy. Here Kazantzakis realizes one of his most cherished philosophical ideals: to transmute the flesh into spirit. He writes: "the whole body of Buddha realized its highest aspiration: it became spirit, it evaporated into Zero." This is the ideal for Kazantzakis himself, as well as for his heroes.

Similarly, Kazantzakis' God depends on man for his existence and is to be sought within man; therefore, the way to save God is through the transmutation of our matter into spirit. "God will not save us; we will save God by fighting, creating, transmuting matter into spirit" (**The Rockgarden**). This, of course, is a different way of putting the concept of the death of the gods—and the longing for a superman. Yet not even when this transmutation takes place is there anything left besides man. For the "oneness" of God and man, as the "thrice blessed" know, is not a reality.

Such explanation and renunciation of God is, necessarily, also pessimistic for the future of man. Yet there is a rather original kind of optimism in Kazantzakis' thought. The author has formulated and often repeated the phrase: "To hope nothing, to fear nothing, that's what freedom means." "To win over hope," Kazantzakis explains, "to realize, after all, that there is no Salvation, and to extract from this discovery an indomitable pleasure—there you have the highest achievement which any man can long for" (**The Rockgarden**). Such belief is, in a sense, optimistic. It will have to be conceded, however, that this is the optimism not of our western culture but of a new one yet to be born.

Although nihilism and pessimism are clearly evident in these early semi-philosophical works, they have indeed receded considerably in his novels (which were written toward the end of Kazantzakis' life), despite outward appearances. For although Mechales, the hero in **Freedom or Death,** has inherited a good deal of Kazantzakis' abstract philosophy, he ends his life fighting a desperate pitched battle against the Turks when he knows that "we can't be saved, long live Crete." Mechales' last moments were heroic: "He raised high his broken head, opened his mouth, and shouted: 'Freedom or . . .'." Mechales falls dead before he can finish his motto. Similarly, Father Giannaros is shot because he refuses to compromise his beliefs—to let the communists usurp his freedom and human dignity. Thus positive, constructive, and glorious is the end of most Kazantzakian heroes. Heroism demands a transcendence of our commonplace human thought and behavior. Kazantzakis' heroes are not human but superhuman, yet they are not nihilistic. They possess most of the qualities of positive humanism. They are selfless, visionary, altruistic, humane, and good. St. Francis, Manolios, Father Giannaros, Father Fotis, and Captain Mechales are all positive heroes: they end up sacrificing themselves for the betterment of humanity.

The accomplishment of the highest aims of these heroes is achieved through a continuous and idealistic struggle. According to Kazantzakis, struggle is the marrow of man's existence. The essence of God is struggle. Man's purpose is struggle. Furthermore, this struggle cannot be understood by man because he is human and the struggle is superhuman. Man can only think in human terms, yet he must struggle for struggle's sake; otherwise, life has no real purpose. As a consequence of this philosophy, the highest achievement of man is not that he may be free, but that he may be engaged in the fight for freedom. Thus Kazantzakis creates an international faith from a national religion. (pp. 49-55)

> *Lewis A. Richards, "Christianity in the Novels of Kazantzakis," in* Western Humanities Review, *Vol. XXI, No. 1, Winter, 1967, pp. 49-55.*

ANDREAS K. POULAKIDAS (essay date 1969)

[*A Greek-born American critic and scholar, Poulakidas is recognized as an authority on the works of Kazantzakis. In the following excerpt, he discusses important influences on the development of Kazantzakis's philosophy.*]

Kazantzakis may be considered more an artist of philosophies than of styles, of content than of form. In order to understand this statement, it is important to recognize biographically and to investigate chronologically the phenomenon of Kazantzakis' intellectual development. His philosophy was really not limited by or nurtured in or concentrated around one philosopher or one system of philosophy. . . . All major philosophies appealed to him; reading and traveling were as much a part of his life as translating and writing. It would perhaps be as misleading to conceive Kazantzakis as an amateur philosopher as it would be to picture him as a learned professor of philosophy in some institution of higher learning. (pp. 126-27)

[John Anapliotis, in his 1960 study (in Greek) *The Real Zorbas and Nikos Kazantzakis,*] brings to light the many personalities that have shaped Kazantzakis' mind. This significant critic and biographer recalls the days that Kazantzakis and Zorba spent in Mani excavating for lignite and penetrating into each other's souls. He likens Kazantzakis to a withdrawn personality who was capable of living quietly, a man who really had nothing in common with Zorba. Kazantzakis' hobby was to search and look within for answers after acquiring experiences and stimuli from the external world; he gave

much serious contemplation and consideration to various ideas and thoughts before he formalized them as guides in his life. The soul of this quiet and meditative man was the battleground and playground for many men of fame and nobility who competed to win him. Mystics and prophets such as Krishna and Mohammed, Moses and John the Baptist, were a few who tormented him. The ancient gods of Olympus, Yahweh, the pagan goddess Astarte, the Sun, and Fire sought to captivate his devotion, and countless poets and philosophers inspired his heart and mind. Homer, Bergson, Tolstoy, Dante, were only some of the most prominent of these latter. Each tempted him, but his "almighty ego" that was seeking the essence of the ultimate truth which was to be his salvation led him from one infidelity to the next. This was Kazantzakis' lifetime odyssey.

Thus, many mystics, prophets, philosophers, artists, writers, gods, and men came and went through Kazantzakis' subconscious, and one cannot correctly speak of Kazantzakis' single, particular philosophy. Relying, however, on his own comments, one can narrow down the number of historical and legendary personages who left a permanent mark on him. In his *Report to Greco* he makes repeated references to the most significant ideologies and philosophies of past and present ages which nurtured his stream of thought. This autobiographical work, published posthumously by his wife, Helen, and written only months before his death, is a swan song—a confession to his compatriot Dominicos Theotokopoulos—of what he did and did not do, of facts and fantasies. He hopes that his spiritual past, as he has revealed it to El Greco, will endorse his life and will absolve him. Prevelakis says that, "as with Dante, Kazantzakis was carried from the work of art to the soul of the creator. He wished to make El Greco, too, a guide and a confessor. This old master had personified the soul's ascent." Given Kazantzakis' attitude and temperament in life, he could not have chosen a better man for his spiritual father and confessor. In this *Report,* Kazantzakis proclaims "the soil of Crete" to have been one of the masons of his mind. It is worth noting how the Cretan soil is associated with El Greco when Kazantzakis says: "I call upon my memory to remember, I assemble my life from the air, place myself soldier-like before the general, and make my *Report to Greco.* For Greco is kneaded from the same Cretan soil as I, and is able to understand me better than all the strivers of past or present. Did he not leave the same red track upon the stones?"

The other masons of his mind, writes Kazantzakis, were Christ, Buddha, and Lenin. At various times in his life, one of these men would consciously stand out, would be in the foreground, and the others would recede, would disappear into his mind's background, and this would also happen in his very works. Christ, Buddha, and Lenin were his "life's three great and beloved pirates," "the immortal dead . . . , the great Sirens. . . . From my early years I sat at their feet and listened intently to their seductive love-filled song. I struggled all my life to save myself from each of these Sirens without denying any one of them, struggled to unite these three clashing voices and transform them into harmony." Christianity, Buddhism, and communism—three major religious outlooks of the world; communism considered a religion with a mission of its own—are the spiritual forces to which Kazantzakis wedded himself and from which he at various times throughout his lifetime freed himself. These were for him three central expressions of man's attitude toward the divine and toward his fellow man. From these three have arisen a variety of beliefs and ways of life, and these three were themselves offshoots of older, more fundamental, and primitive views on the divine, on human conduct, and on religious worship.

Elsewhere, the fourth element of Kazantzakis' philosophy is given another name than "the soil of Crete." Writing to Prevelakis on February 12, 1957, from Antibes, he informs us that his philosophical development has for him a religious and sacred significance: "In the *Report to Greco* I make a confession . . . and there I speak of the four main stages through which I have passed, and each of those stages bears a sacred name: Christ, Buddha, Lenin, Odysseus." In his *Report* he strings the names of Christ, Buddha, and Lenin in the chronological order of their influence on him, and Odysseus, if not actually a philosopher or a reformer, is nevertheless the symbol of the last stage of Kazantzakis' philosophical development. At the very beginning of his *Report,* all four names are listed. The four philosophies are equated with and compared to certain concrete, poetic, and worldly images such as the earth, the sea, the starlit sky, and woman, each giving to Kazantzakis an individual sensation, shock, joy, or fear, and all together having a combined effect on him: "Every one of my emotions, moreover, and every one of my ideas, even the most abstract, is made up of these four primary ingredients. Within me, even the most metaphysical problem takes on a warm physical body. . . ." Thus, in spite of each philosophy's individuality, all four are mashed and mixed in his soul and in his artistic creations.

Odysseus is understood to have a special meaning. In this mythological figure are compounded all the central philosophies of Kazantzakis, as the study of his *Sequel* shows. However, Odysseus is primarily the embodiment of all Western philosophy and of all existential thought in particular. Odysseus is less the mystic who visualizes utopias, sinless and desireless worlds, and more the man of action who finds expression in such men of blood, vitality, irrationality, and faith as Homer, Bergson, Nietzsche, and Dostoyevsky, as well as in the very much alive Zorba. Prevelakis has already adequately treated this subject: "Some of these themes I shall now develop, not only as proofs of the parallelism of Kazantzakis and Odysseus, but more as pointers to the specific psychology of the hero. I shall begin with a preliminary remark. The *Odyssey* covers a considerable period of time. . . . In such a long period, the mythical hero changes: it would be a mistake to describe him as though there were no development. On the contrary, the protean vitality of his nature must be stressed." Prevalakis then proceeds to define the essential phases of Odysseus as Kazantzakis conceived them. Kazantzakis also admits in the *Report:*

> My life's greatest benefactors have been journeys and dreams. Very few people, living or dead, have aided my struggle. If, however, I wished to designate which people left their traces embedded most deeply in my soul, I would perhaps designate Homer, Buddha, Nietzsche, Bergson, and Zorba. The first, for me, was the peaceful, brilliantly luminous eye, like the sun's disk, which illuminated the entire universe with its redemptive splendor; Buddha, the bottomless jet-dark eye in which the world drowned and was delivered. Bergson relieved me of various unsolved philosophical problems which tormented me in my early youth; Nietzsche enriched me with new anguishes and instructed me how to transform misfortune, bitterness, and un-

certainty into pride; Zorba taught me to love life and have no fear of death.

Thus, on the basis of these philosophies or philosophers, it is only right and proper to organize Kazantzakis' intellectual development in these four areas: Christianity, Buddhism, communism, and existentialism. The changes in his *cosmotheoria* during his lifelong search for the truth, the evolutions of his spirit with each new encounter with the immortal minds of the world, and the selective enrichment of his mind by readings, discoveries, travels, translations, and dreams, give us an always fertile and dynamic writer with new ideas and with totally different points of view. "His eclecticism is his servitude." Freedom means choosing one's intellectual and moral exercises, and Kazantzakis' philosophy is this process of constantly searching the main streams of thought, ancient and modern, for the ultimate truth. His eclecticism opened many roads, and he attempted to reach their extremes; and all extremes led but to the abyss. What is this abyss? "You found your own inability to go further. Abyss is the name we give to whatever we cannot bridge. There is no abyss, no end of the road; there is only the soul of man, which names everything in keeping with its own bravery or cowardice. Christ, Buddha, and Moses all found abysses. But they erected bridges and crossed over. For centuries now, human flocks have been crossing over behind them." Kazantzakis hoped to bridge all these gaps of thought, and he strove like another Chaucer to make all knowledge his province, and like another Origen he worked assiduously and endlessly to promote this knowledge, because he wanted "to see life steadily and to see it whole."

Prevelakis gives us one explanation why Kazantzakis' philosophy is eclectic. Since Kazantzakis was not assisted in Greece by the aristocratic, well-to-do class that would naturally support the cultural endeavors and the promising artists of their native land, and since he did not belong to any literary school nor was an ardent follower of any national writer, he drew most of his nourishment from foreign sources which were mostly philosophical rather than literary. Like Péguy, Giovanni Papini, and Unamuno, he transformed literature "from an art of style and description into a question concerning the crucial problems of mankind." Indeed, Kazantzakis was probably twenty years ahead of Malraux, Sartre, and Camus, for he introduced the fever of existentialism into his country before World War II, and themes later to be discussed by these French authors can be found in abundance throughout Kazantzakis' *Sequel,* written and revised in the 1930's. His eclecticism, however, has another explanation—an explanation which is quite appropriate to our time. It is man's desire to fill space, the empty expanse, with concrete forms, wires, poles, missiles, airplanes; in reality, it is man's secret desire to fill his depleted, paralyzed, or indifferent heart with some faith, whether it be the gospels of Christ, the many paths of Buddha, the promises of Lenin, or the nothingness of Odysseus. This is also pointed out by Prevelakis:

> Kazantzakis' messianism was not then only a psychic tendency: it was a necessity dictated to him from outside. In order to fill the void, Kazantzakis wished first for a resurrection of the Christ of the Gospels, untouched by the dogmas of the church. Later, he sought for an acceptable metaphysic and ethic in Buddhism. Finally, disheartened by the impossibility of achieving the rebirth for which he aspired, he flirted with Marxism and planned to enlist in the revolutionary movement. This last failure

was to bring him—or, I should say, to bring him back—to poetic creation. But all that went into his previous spiritual struggles was to make of the *Odyssey* a "theology."

No one philosophy dominated Kazantzakis, who also had a tendency to taste and try the non-European authors. No one belief can satisfy modern man's rootless, homeless, valueless heart, and Kazantzakis, like the boss in *Zorba the Greek* or like Mathieu in Sartre's *Age of Reason,* realized that "various tried and proved rules of conduct had already discreetly offered him their services: disillusioned epicureanism, smiling tolerance, resignation, flat seriousness, stoicism—all the aids whereby a man may savor, minute by minute, like a connoisseur, the failure of a life." Kazantzakis, however, was not a "nothing" like the boss or Mathieu. Kazantzakis' freedom to choose and to live a philosophy was not a dreaded struggle of despair but a constant renewal of man's vitality, to reach an unattainable end and to characterize as victory, triumph, and success the onward struggle itself. As evidence of Kazantzakis' eclecticism, we notice that his major personalities are conflicting personalities who have very little in common with one another. This diversity in Kazantzakis' choice of comrades is capable of giving the reader a plurality and a totality of views that one may like or dislike, that one may disregard or assimilate, that one may mold or recast. Kazantzakis' view always wants to go further. . . . He belongs and does not belong to a particular philosophical or political system or trend. (pp. 127-32)

An example of his eclectic concept of reality is Kazantzakis' view of man's dual nature or of man's essential unity of body and soul. (Occasionally, too, he views man as of a threefold nature of body, mind, and soul; while the mind observes, the body and soul at times "separate and oppose one other," especially during youth and old age.) The existence of war or peace, of rebellion or harmony, between the body and soul of man, or the subjugation of the one by the other, is viewed differently by Kazantzakis at different times. Sometimes he favors the struggle, the dualism and dichotomy in man and nature, a god known as war; and he condemns the stagnating outcome if this conflict were to cease, because "balance means stagnation, and stagnation means death." The fighting man cannot possess a balanced mixture of soul and body. Either the soul must win or the body, either reason or passion, either Apollo or Dionysus. Kazantzakis commits himself to neither, but oscillates between materialism and idealism.

For instance, saintliness—the mortification of one's earthly passions and animal desires through solitude, fasting, and meditation—had a strong attraction for the youthful Kazantzakis, who faithfully studied the lives of saints and who visited Mount Athos and Mount Sinai. Feeling that the instinctive, chaotic, materialistic man must be governed and controlled by the spirit of God, by piety, chastity, and holiness, he was at one time in his youth seriously inclined to become a monk at the Monastery of Saint Katherine on Mount Sinai. However, he reports, an elderly monk, who distrusted youth's burning fire and felt that such vows from a fresh green log like Kazantzakis would only result in smoke, secretly approached him and dissuaded him from such a decision. The old man advised him to value his youth and to use it by struggling with God in the world and not by locking himself up in a monastery. This experienced monk believed that man was able to defeat his instincts by satisfying them and by giving in to temptation, "—for with time, satiety, and discipline this dark matter may turn to spirit." Father Jo-

achim saw the need for youth to acquaint itself with the world of matter and to satisfy the desires of the flesh. Running away from the other half of one's self, from one's desire to love and live, could only result, he believed, in an ever-restless battle, a struggle that certainly should never end, but a struggle that would probably end in defeat. In other words, he told Kazantzakis to be defeated at the beginning only to be victorious in the end. The flesh, the material world, conceived by man to be an evil and a barrier preventing man from being united with God, with the Spirit, is ultimately defeated by man's embracing the world that he will eventually disdain. Here Kazantzakis whispered his Zorbaic belief that affirmation also implies or leads to negation; that, in essence, there is no right or wrong thing. This thought was further established when, he reports, the monk upheld the view that a time will come when Christ will be sufficiently magnanimous "to commiserate not only the soul but also the body, and to reconcile these two savage beasts." The trend toward matter, toward the flesh, is not repugnant, repulsive, or irreligious. Man's nature seeks peace of mind by doing his duty to his body, by appeasing its desires. On the advice of this saintly monk, Kazantzakis abandoned his spiritual goal and turned away from his highly spiritualized life. The flesh is just as important for man's salvation as his soul. Youth lay ahead, and so did Kazantzakis' worldly dreams and physical desires.

During his old age, Kazantzakis again supported man's struggle against the material side of life. His examples were the twice-born, the Christlike saints, the ever-searching and ever-seeking souls that can only find rest once they have found God. In his introduction to *The Last Temptation,* he reaffirms his very youthful quest for spiritual happiness and peace. In all human beings, he writes, there exists a struggle between the human and the divine, between man's spirit and flesh. This is a universal phenomenon. It creates a universal longing to reconcile the two. "Most often this struggle is unconscious and shortlived. A weak soul does not have the endurance to resist the flesh for very long. It grows heavy, becomes flesh itself, and the contest ends. But among responsible men, men who keep their eyes riveted day and night upon the Supreme Duty, the conflict between flesh and spirit breaks out mercilessly and may last until death." The intensity of this conflict is determined by the strength and persistence of the soul and body, and the struggle and final outcome of both are as rewarding and satisfying as the caliber of man's very soul and body: "Struggle between the flesh and the spirit, rebellion and resistance, reconciliation and submission, and finally—the supreme purpose of the struggle—union with God: this was the ascent taken by Christ. . . ." This struggle exists if man is willing to do his "Supreme Duty"; and this means that man must be willing to sacrifice his earthly joy and worldly glories, willing to suffer martyrdom, to climb Golgotha, and to be nailed on the Cross like Christ. In actuality, Kazantzakis' life was this constant struggle for spiritualization even though he lived in a very material and secular world. Karl Kerényi makes it very clear that Kazantzakis, like any modern Greek, was a staunch and frugal Byzantine Christian, not basically a patriotic Cretan or a Greek or a cosmopolitan European, but one who sensed the duality of man's nature and attempted to resurrect God killed by the atheism, materialism, and secularism of the West. Kazantzakis, like the Byzantines, returned to the sacramental worship that God is Spirit. In this Spirit, man finds the force, the will, and drive to live: that is, to spiritualize himself. In a Byzantine consciousness, there is no notion of a purgatory, no doctrine of human infallibility, no immaculate conception, no decree of a bodily assumption of the Virgin Mary to heaven. There is only a pious feeling toward the Sacrament of Holy Communion, a process of spiritualization, a means of partaking of both elements of the Holy Eucharist, and by so doing, attaining the divine. This process requires a struggle.

At other times, Kazantzakis was a monist of sorts. This was perhaps his most consistent view of spirit and matter. It is a view, as we can see, that resulted from his Oriental cultural osmosis. By it, there can be no real definition of what is spirit or matter or of what may be conceived as psychic or somatic, because "the flesh has a glimmer from the soul, and the soul has a fleshly fuzz." Who can separate the two and why should there be such an animated struggle between them? One wintry evening of 1926-27 in Alexandria, Egypt, Kazantzakis met with a number of intellectuals who had gathered to bid him farewell, and after supper, Dr. Paul Petrides was asked to preside over their symposium. Having listened to the others, Kazantzakis then spoke and formulated his credo: "I am a monist. Matter and Spirit, I most strongly feel, are one. Within me I comprehend only one substance." This substance is divided when man is required to express it in words, through rational means. Reason consequently has the natural tendency to classify whatever by nature is inseparable and unified. Since all human perceptions are limited, man can only distinguish two aspects of reality: that which is known as spirit and that which is detected as matter. Thus, these terms unfortunately represent aspects of substance as it is perceived by man. Kazantzakis also considered the basic motivating forces in the history of man and of the masses to be two, equivalent to the two aspects of reality. These forces are Hunger and Passion. He uses the term passion in reference to spirit, because "spirit" has acquired an immaterial, distilled, ideological content which is very misleading, pejorative, and unintelligible. He informed the members of the symposium that there is much more "spirit" in "matter" than the materialists can imagine and that the idealists would be surprised at the amount of "matter" in "spirit." Hunger—financial causes—is in most usual and ordinary cases the foremost incentive. In crucial times, however, the passions and irrationalities of man—hatred, anger, love, the instincts of survival—become utmost. But essentially, there is no difference between the two aspects of reality or the two basic motivating forces.

This inherent monism of Kazantzakis can be basically summarized by an image. Man's soul can be compared to a bow which speaks: "There are three kinds of souls, three kinds of prayers. One: I am a bow in your hands, Lord. Draw me lest I rot. Two: Do not overdraw me Lord. I shall break. Three: Overdraw me, and who cares if I break!" The struggle within, its intensity, its length of day and depth of feeling, are comparable to and affected by a mystical Hand that exerts pressure and tension on one's soul. Each soul belongs to one of these three categories and can make only one choice, if it does choose at all. Furthermore, man can worship God in only one way—actually in the extremes. In Kazantzakis' metaphysics, there is one reality, that of the nonexistent One:

> And thrice blessed be those who bear on
> their shoulders and do not buckle under
> this great, sublime, and terrifying secret:
> THAT EVEN THIS ONE DOES NOT EXIST!

Ethically, good and evil for Kazantzakis are also thus nonexistent, because God is beyond all human rationalities and dichotomies manufactured by finite beings who hope. God is beyond hope itself. For man there can be no stipulated behavior, no creed governing his actions, but he must act beyond good and evil with no hope for punishment or reward. In poetic and syllogistic language, Kazantzakis makes his monism obvious and clear. His eclecticism finally produces the concept that duality exists but that the two must be found in the one. Likewise, a plurality of philosophies can be found in Kazantzakis, but Kazantzakis is a unique and individual philosopher and artist.

One is able to trace step by step the constant ascent of Kazantzakis' soul, struggling to reach the heights that he arbitrarily calls the "Cretan Glance." One can read in his *Report* about "the red track made by drops of my blood, the track which marks my journey among men, passions, and ideas." To understand the development of Kazantzakis' mind is to understand this very struggle. Within it is the voice of his father confessor and compatriot, El Greco, who tells him: "Reach what you cannot!" This ancestral voice is pushing him to go beyond his limitations, to use to the fullest his abilities and capacities, to follow faithfully the Cretan maxim: "Return where you have failed, leave where you have succeeded." Briefly, this was the psychology that set the stage and mood for Kazantzakis' cultural and intellectual development. Without this inner drive, it is doubtful whether Kazantzakis' mind would have been cultivated to the degree that it was.

To summarize, in determining the chief symbolic figures, or the main streams of thought, or the most prominent spokesmen of Western philosophy in Kazantzakis' works, one may be at a loss. The term Occidental philosophy, in reference to Kazantzakis, may be broad enough to embrace and to encompass Christianity and communism as predominant outlooks that were developed and shaped in the West in contrast to Buddhism, an Oriental philosophy. One may also include within this arena all the philosophers, ancient and modern, political and literary, eclectic and original, whom Kazantzakis read, quoted, or about whom he wrote; and they were innumerable: William James, Goethe, Laisant, Darwin, L. Büchner, Plato, Dante, Verne, Swift, Tolstoy, Solomos, Unamuno, Jean Moreas, Lorca, Homer, Eluard, Shakespeare, Ortega y Gasset, Valery, Verga, Villon, Byron, Guillaume de Lorris, Mencken, Dostoyevsky, Schopenhauer, Fichte, Bacon, Jimenez, Sorel, and many others. One may also isolate two or three philosophers of the West—philosophers such as Nietzsche and Bergson—who are known to have left a permanent mark on him, and one can show how these men haunted him.

When one refers to Kazantzakis' Western philosophy, however, one has in mind those thinkers who endowed Kazantzakis with a particular point of view or way of life contrary to that of the other major thinkers—Christ, Lenin, Buddha—he encountered. This philosophical outlook that Kazantzakis borrowed from the West may be discerned as existential, concerning itself with the problems of man's existence and characterizable as having an anti-intellectual trend in its contention that reason is not capable of finding the answers to man's problems but that man solves them by acting. Furthermore, in terms specific to Kazantzakis, this philosophy may be expressed as the very real person of George Zorba or as the very symbolic and legendary figure of Odysseus. Existential philosophy for Kazantzakis is the informal, practical, and unsystematic study of Zorbaism, and at the same time, a product of his formal, academic, and systematic study of Nietzsche, Bergson, and Dostoyevsky, his favorite existential thinkers. This philosophy stresses more the man of action, in contrast to the man of reason, and Zorba and Odysseus represent this kind of man.

It was toward the end of his Russian experience that Kazantzakis realized he was like Odysseus, a man of many philosophies and personalities. Like Odysseus, he had been a homeless, rootless, but robust wanderer, and he had met along his way Christ, Buddha, socialist men and women, and had had Zorbaic companions such as Kentaur, Hardihood, Granite, and Captain Clam. Thus, Odysseus is the best symbol for his philosophy, and *The Odyssey: A Modern Sequel* the story of that eclectic who was also an existentialist. [Nikiphoros Brettakos, in his 1960 study (in Greek) *Nikos Kazantzakis: His Agony and His Work,*] is able to give us an interpretive account of Kazantzakis' psychic state at the time he had this realization and prepared to write his own *Odyssey.* Kazantzakis was absorbed by the infinite, the eternal, the incomprehensible; his eyes and ears were focused on a mystery that created for him a super-Nietzschean exaltation. He was ready for his supreme masterpiece, which was seeking form and expression, which was to be a work that superseded time and place, "a creation on the abyss." A new flame had seized Kazantzakis' heart and mind, and this flame was his new, invisible God. Lenin had been pushed to the side to make room for Odysseus. Kazantzakis' entire soul was absorbed. With the same impetus, enthusiasm, and fascination with which he had entered into his socialistic phase a few years before, he encountered his creative urge for the writing of his *Odyssey.* Everything else was irrelevant. The perfect verse was for him his soul's salvation. Poetic productivity and creativity gave value to his life and meaning to his existence, for this was the period in which he had fallen into the well of nihilism. Before him stretched the nothingness of reality like the steppes of Russia. Only Sisyphean men who could promise him the road to unrewarded activity and hard, futile labor were now his heroes. Brettakos correctly observes Kazantzakis' spirit at this time. The rebel had been another mask, another transformation for Odysseus. Kazantzakis had worn the mask of Lenin and cast it away, after realizing that he had to see much land and much water, to travel the entirety of Russia, so that he could collect images and impressions for his *Sequel;* otherwise, his sojourn in the Soviet Union would not be very meaningful. Kazantzakis' mind and vision, like Odysseus', were then enriched. He had seen many things which yearned to be yoked to verse. Kazantzakis wanted to remain alone, so that he could ponder on all that he experienced and sensed, and so that he could convert his experiences and impressions into poetry. He left the Soviet Union, remained for about twenty days in Berlin, and on May 10, 1929, ascended the mountain in Bohemia and settled down in Gottesgab. He was ready to work on his great epic. This Odyssean outlook was primarily instrumental in the writing of Kazantzakis' novels *Zorba the Greek, Freedom or Death,* and *The Fratricides.* As early as 1929, in this the most turbulent part of his life, he wrote, in French, "Kapetan Elia," which later became *Freedom or Death.* About this early work he said:

> I plan to write a work of art in the form of a novel about Crete. It will be a "vision." It will deal with a simple tale which will last about a day in a village. There will be three heroes: the grandfather who is firmly rooted in the soil and controls the entire village, who is virtually a Monster embracing God and Earth; his son who has two great passions, inferior but strong, love of country and love of women; and finally the grandson, a straw in the wind. Nei-

ther God, nor nature, nor country, nor woman concerns him. He has no passion. He is mere chaff. Only new ideas trouble him, he is a lukewarm communist, a Romain Rollandist, an Esperantist, a pacifist, and a pseudo-intellectual.

Using the grandfather and father as models, Kazantzakis later developed his dynamic characters, his men of action such as Zorba, Captain Michales, and Father Yanaros. The temperament, attitude, and psychology of the grandson served as model for his weak and impotent characters such as the boss, Kosmas, Tityros, and others who were essentially petty intellectuals and weary bookworms, in which category he also placed himself. In his own eyes, it was only in theory and in travels that Kazantzakis resembled Odysseus. (pp. 132-39)

> *Andreas K. Poulakidas, "Nikos Kazantzakis: Odysseus as Phenomenon," in* Comparative Literature Studies, *Vol. VI, No. 2, June, 1969, pp. 126-40.*

GEORGE T. KARNEZIS (essay date 1970)

[*In the following excerpt, Karnezis discusses the conflict between vitalism and intellectualism presented in* Zorba the Greek.]

Pandelis Prevalakis says in his critical biography of Kazantzakis [see Additional Bibliography] that the author experienced a kind of spiritual rebirth in his later life, and that "the nine books he wrote during that period [1948-53] are evidence of the power of his soul, but they also weakened his body. He turned his back on everything he achieved up to 1948, retaining nothing but *Zorba the Greek.*" That Kazantzakis should assign *Zorba* such an important place (aside from *The Odyssey*) is not surprising, for he states in his prologue to the novel that, if he had to choose those men who touched him most deeply, he would place Zorba's name beside Homer, Nietzsche, and Bergson.

Kazantzakis worked on *Zorba the Greek* between 1941-1943. It is essentially an autobiographical novel giving shape and meaning to his Greek mining venture with Zorba in 1917. He refers to the novel in its prologue as a "memorial" to his beloved comrade. As we shall see, this "memorial" is presented in a manner that depicts not only the lively personality of Zorba, but also the sensitivity and peculiar mentality of the author. Specifically I think the novel's meaning might best be formulated through a determination of the kind of knowledge Kazantzakis, the scholar-artist, had to gain from Zorba, the man of direct participation and involvement in life, a man who he feels possessed "the broadest soul, the soundest body, and the freest cry I have known in my life."

The novel's sustaining contrast assumes different terms in different contexts. In the context of the author's intellectual life, the contrast becomes a Nietzschean one involving Apollonian and Dionysian views of life. Since *Zorba the Greek* also relates the author's infatuation with the Buddha, the contrast can also be discussed in terms of Buddhistic belief as it relates to the world of experience. In the broadest literary terms, this contrast can be defined as the existing tension between life as it is and life as it becomes through the creative ordering process of the written word. Any or all of these antitheses might be utilized in discussing *Zorba the Greek,* just as they may be introduced into a discussion of any Kazantzakis work.

The initial meeting with Zorba occurs in a Piraeus cafe where the author is awaiting passage to Crete, the novel's fictional setting. Surrounded by fishermen cursing the weather, Kazantzakis informs us of his own past and why it has driven him to undertake the mining venture on Crete. In telling us of how his bookish world has been stifling him, he recalls how a friend, Stavridakis, had criticized his unwillingness to join in rescuing Greeks being persecuted in revolutionary Russia. Kazantzakis' refusal provoked Stavridakis to rebuke the author's narrow pursuit of the scholarly life. After Stavridakis' departure, Kazantzakis recalls how his friend's cry of "bookworm" continued to assail him, eventually driving him to undertake the reactivation of his abandoned Cretan lignite mine. Such a venture, he hopes, will initiate a change in his mode of living, for, ever since his friend's rebuke, he has become increasingly aware of the contradiction implicit in his life: "How could I, who loved life so intensely, have let myself be entangled for so long in that balderdash of books and paper. . . ." Finally he declares that thus far in his life he has "only seen the shadow and been well content with it" and that now he is "going to the substance." Now his resolution seems quite firm, but we may doubt its force as we observe him casually open a volume of Dante, trying to decide which portion of *The Commedia* to study.

Zorba finds him, then, deep in contemplation, and overwhelms the young scholar-adventurer. "Taking me with you?" he asks after inquiring the author's destination. Kazantzakis hesitates at first, but finally, more intrigued by the forcefulness of Zorba's character than he is by his Dante, agrees to hire Zorba as foreman at the mine and his own personal cook. "Yes," he thinks, "I understood. Zorba was the man I had sought so long in vain. A living heart . . . a great brute soul, not yet severed from the earth."

This opening scene is not only significant for its predication of the novel's sustaining contrast, but also, as in the case of many novels, for its prefiguration of some of its basic strategies. One of these strategies involves an ironic reversal of expectation that Zorba will be a standard picaresque figure. Despite his impulsiveness and apparent simplicity, Zorba is a man possessing serious and well-formulated standards. Thus he refuses to play his *santuri* unless he is in the mood. Kazantzakis has suggested that the two of them will work hard during the day and relax at night to Zorba's music. Zorba sees this casual suggestion as a threat to his freedom: "I'll work for you as much as you like. . . . But the *santuri,* that's different. . . . If you force me to [play], it'll be finished." Attached to this example is an illustration of a second important strategy in the novel: as narrator, Kazantzakis, despite his sympathy for Zorba, is constantly misunderstanding him; thus Kazantzakis often presents himself as a kind of comic innocent. At this same meeting the author suggests that Zorba played the *santuri* because he once had a family of screaming wife and children that he wished to escape. But Zorba delivers a more sophisticated view: music demands total involvement with your instrument and, he declares: "If your children are hungry and screaming at you, you just try to play! To play the *santuri* you have to give everything up to it, d'you understand?" Kazantzakis the narrator has of course missed the point, and the irony is not difficult to understand: just as a writer would not think of creating in rush hour traffic, so the artist in Zorba demands solitude and involvement. The reason for the misunderstanding arises from the narrator's initial assumption that Zorba is naive. His innocent self-portrayal is a basic ploy in the work, for Kazantzakis periodically pretends to understand Zorba and often

underestimates his companion's higher qualities. Confrontations of this type contribute to the novel's comic element, and display a virtue Kazantzakis attributes to Zorba in the prologue: ". . . he had what a scholar needs . . . the bravery to mock his own spirit."

But these clashes with Zorba are not always comic. Often they drive the author into intense self-contemplation, leading him to question the validity of his life as he has been living it. In one instance Zorba becomes impatient with his "boss's" ignorance and addresses him scornfully: "You've got an innocent's brain and your skin's never even felt the sun." Again, when the author asks Zorba who or what he believes in, he responds: "I don't believe in anything or anyone; only in Zorba. Not because Zorba is better than the others; . . . He's only a brute like the rest! But I believe in Zorba because he's the only being I have in my power. . . ." Kazantzakis, initially outraged by such cynicism, later muses: "I admired him for being so strong, for despising men . . . and at the same time wanting to live and work with them. I should have either become an ascetic or else have adorned men with false feathers so that I could put up with them." Eventually Zorba's personality is given meaning and size through the imposition of the author's comments: "That man has not been to school, I thought, and his brains have not been perverted . . . his mind is open and his heart has grown bigger, without losing an ounce of his primitive boldness. . . ." Finally, because of the significance he attaches to Zorba, Kazantzakis is driven to self-abasement: "All the problems which we find so complicated or insoluble he cuts through as if with a sword, like Alexander the Great cutting the Gordian knot. . . . We educated people are just empty-headed birds of the air."

This imposition of Kazantzakis' first person narration thus results in the author's objectification of himself as narrator and, as I have suggested, compels us to witness his scholarly artistic mind at work, questioning itself and endeavoring to give meaning to experience. It is this interplay, this tension between the author and Zorba, which affects Zorba's magnitude and gives the novel its unity, a unity which emerges from two views of experience. On the one hand we have Zorba, who, in Nietzschean terms, is the Dionysian man, the extrovert who refuses to mediate experience with abstractions or mental constructs. Words stifle him and emotion so overwhelms him at times that he must dance in order to express himself. In not yet being "severed from the earth," he is still at one with it. Not influenced by books, he experiences life directly. His sensitivity, declares Kazantzakis, is at times childlike. He will delight in the morning sunrise, the sight of a flower, or the presence of a woman, as though seeing them all for the first time. To quote Zorba: "I carry on as if I was going to die any minute." Kazantzakis is his introverted counterpart, the man of learning who mediates experience, filtering it through the abstractions his mind imposes on it. In Nietzschean terms, he is the "Apollonian eye" which strives to give order and meaning to everything it sees or feels.

Thus ideas that occur in ***Zorba the Greek,*** either out of conversation or incident, are usually seized by the narrator's mind and transformed into varying degrees of abstraction. Zorba, for example, asks his "boss" about liberty while they are discussing the long bitter war between the Greeks and the Turks which precluded the liberation of Crete. "It's a mystery . . . a great mystery! So, if we want liberty in this bad world, we've got to have all those murders . . . have

George Zorba, who served as the model for Kazantzakis's Zorba the Greek.

we? . . . And yet, the result of all that, what's it been? Liberty! Instead of wiping us out with a thunderbolt, God gives us liberty! I just don't understand." Kazantzakis muses the question silently: "Understand what? Tell him what? Either that what we call God does not exist, or else what we call murders and villainy is necessary for the . . . liberation of the world. . . ." Finally he tries to explain to Zorba that liberty is like a flower which grows "on manure and muck" and that "manure and muck is man and the flower liberty." Zorba will have none of such evasive metaphors, however, for he realizes the issue lies deeper: "But the seed? . . . For a plant to sprout there must be a seed. Who's put the seed in our entrails? And why doesn't this seed produce flowers from kindness and honesty? Why must it have blood and filth?" The author cannot answer and the exchange terminates with Zorba's justifiable indignation.

In another conversation the author again transforms a subject: women. To Zorba, women have one thing in common, a desperate craving for love. Kazantzakis is skeptical of this, but Zorba defends his thesis, as he usually does, with a story. He relates how his grandmother, at eighty, was still prone to make herself up in the vain hope that the young men of the village would come to serenade her. Once Zorba had severely rebuked her for this habit and, recalling how she was driven

to tears, he now declares: "That day was the first time I knew what a woman was." He finishes the story, telling how his grandmother had died a few months later, heaping curses on his head: "It was you who finished me off. May you be damned . . . and suffer all I have!" And, Zorba concludes: "The old witch's curse has hit home! . . . I'm in my sixty-fifth year, I think, but . . . I'll never lay off. I'll still have a mirror in my pocket, and I'll still be running after the female of the species."

Zorba's speech takes immediate effect upon the author, for he recollects a personal experience and thereby gives his own refinement to Zorba's view. He had once encountered a young woman standing at a Rodin exhibition before "The Hand of God." He had asked her what she was thinking. "If only we could escape!" she had responded. "And go where?" asked Kazantzakis. "The hand of God is everywhere." "No," she had retorted, "Love may be the most intense joy on earth . . . But when I see that bronze hand, I want to escape." After she affirmed her preference for freedom rather than love, the young scholar recollects how he had quickly turned the discussion into a metaphysical problem: "But, supposing it's only when we obey that bronze hand that we are free? Supposing the word 'God' didn't have that convenient meaning the masses give it?" Frightened by his expression, the girl had left him. Now, rethinking the event, Kazantzakis concludes, "Zorba was right," for he might have developed an intimate friendship with the girl had he not "suddenly darted from earth to heaven."

But never do we witness the author's abstractive qualities of mind, or his internal conflict, more fully than when he attempts to use his art to ward off direct participation in life. Both these elements are given full play due to the presence of a young widow in the village. Zorba notes quite rightly that she obsesses all the village men who, despite their intense desire for her, keep themselves in check. Only one young man, an ineffectual youth named Pavli, has made overtures to her. She has spurned his affections and his male companions are perversely enraged at his futile attempts to do something they wished they had the courage to do. Kazantzakis is also attracted to the widow. Zorba, believing that it is in the nature of things for a man to indulge himself if given the opportunity, gleefully urges his "boss" on to this new-found prey. Kazantzakis listens to Zorba's urgings, thinking: "I knew Zorba was right, I knew it, but I did not dare. My life had gone on the wrong track, and my contact with men had become now a mere soliloquy. I had fallen so low that, if I had to choose between falling in love with a woman and reading a book about love, I should have chosen the book."

Eventually the widow's presence comes to haunt the author. He amplifies and even distorts her significance. She seems a threat to his freedom. Zorba's theology, which theorizes that a man will burn in hell for allowing a woman to sleep alone, has no effect upon him. Some time passes before Zorba again approaches his "boss" with the problem. It is Christmas Eve and, instinctively realizing Kazantzakis' conflict, Zorba proclaims that the Virgin Mary and the widow are one, and that "Christ will be born tonight, boss; you go and perform your miracle too." Leafing through his *Buddha* manuscript, the author angrily refuses his companion's advice, realizing at the same time that it offered him "a sure, attractive, and very human path to tread." He then proceeds to immerse himself in his art. The *Buddha* manuscript now achieves a two-fold relevance. Kazantzakis previously stated that his artistic treatment of Buddha was undertaken in order to capture him with words so he would not be engulfed by Buddhistic belief: "I opened the *Buddha* manuscript, and I, too, worked my way into my own galleries. [He had previously made an equation between Zorba's work at the mine and his own work on the manuscript.] I wrote, and the more I progressed, the freer I felt . . . for I knew that as soon as I had finished this manuscript . . . I should be free." But now he proceeds to exorcise the image of the tempting widow in the same way. He thus transforms her into the evil spirit "Mara" while projecting himself into a Buddha struggling to ward off the desires of the flesh:

> I was trying exorcism upon exorcism, bent upon casting out of my mind the image of a woman's body . . . I was well aware that it was Mara, the spirit of the Evil One, in the shape of a woman. . . . I fought against him. I applied myself to writing *Buddha* in in the same way that savages in their caves engraved . . . beasts who prowled around them. They, too, endeavored, by engraving and painting these beasts, to fix them fast on the rock. If they had not done so, the beasts would have leapt upon them.

Thus in his fervor to capture the Buddha through art, Kazantzakis makes the equation between Buddhistic belief and the widow. But an abstraction is more easily captured on paper and "exorcized" than is a woman. Thus in spite of his attempts, he ultimately succumbs to the widow. In so doing he achieves great mental release. "I did not allow my mind to take possession of this carnal joy, to press it into its own molds, and make thoughts of it. I let my whole body rejoice from head to foot like an animal." And, as we see in the following paragraphs, he achieves a similar release from the Buddha:

> I picked up the Buddha manuscript and opened it. I had finished it. At the end, Buddha was lying beneath the flowering tree. He had raised his hand and ordered the five elements . . .—earth, water, fire, air, spirit—to dissolve.
>
> I had no more need of this image of my torment; I had gone beyond it, I had completed my service with Buddha—I, too, raised my hand, and ordered the Buddha within me to dissolve.

It is after this calm resolution that we witness the widow's murder. It is one of atonement—not so much for her relations with the "boss," as for her refusal to accept young Pavli's love, a refusal which drove the young man to suicide. Thus, in retribution, she is beheaded in front of the church in full view of the villagers. It is as though the men finally have an excuse to "exorcize" their torment. The author watches helplessly as Zorba tries in vain to stop the murder, and he ultimately filters the meaning of her death through his abstractive senses:

> I . . . began in my wretched inhuman way, to transpose reality, removing blood, flesh and bones and reduce it to the abstract, link it with universal laws, until I came to the awful conclusion that what had happened was necessary. . . . My philosophy surrounded it [the widow's death] with images and artifice and quickly made it harmless.

His response is directly contrasted with Zorba's which feels the widow's death rather than intellectualizes it. Zorba, overwhelmed by grief, refuses to talk of the occurrence. As always, the novel demands that the narrator be aware of his contrast with Zorba: "That is what a real man is like, I thought, envying Zorba's sorrow. A man with warm blood . . . who lets real tears run down his cheeks when he is suffering; and when he is happy he does not spoil the freshness of his joy by running it through the fine sieve of metaphysics."

The reaffirmation we witness here of the author's scholar-artist sensitivity, even in the face of his indulgence in immediate experience, is an obvious foreshadowing of his ultimate departure from Zorba. The conclusion of the work finds him consciously reasserting his own peculiar sensitivity. Thus his relations with Zorba have served as a reaffirmation of his own identity, an identity which we realize is essentially a product of all his years and can thus no more be changed than can the color of his eyes. Zorba sums up this ironic division between the man of experience and the man who strives to understand it in orderly terms. This is his response to Kazantzakis' suggestion that he write a book revealing all of life's mysteries:

> "For the simple reason that I live all those mysteries, . . . I haven't the time to write . . . That's how the business falls into the hands of the pen-pushers! All those who actually live the mysteries of life haven't the time to write, and all those who have the time don't live them!"

Most simply, then, we are presented with a familiar paradox: To gain knowledge, one often has to sacrifice experience.

But aside from this kind of negative truth, I think Kazantzakis shows something else gained from his experience. Towards the conclusion of the novel, he struggles in vain to explain man's purpose to Zorba. His speech becomes interlaced with abstractions and Zorba, unable to follow his "boss's" expression, interrupts him with the suggestion that the author "dance" his ideas or tell them all in a story. Kazantzakis, realizing he cannot, thinks to himself: "If only I could never open my mouth . . . until the abstract idea had reached its highest point—and had become a story!" Why should he call a story the "highest point" of abstraction? I think his reasons are more implied than expressed. Every story, indeed the fictive in general, has the advantage of expressing the abstract idea in terms of concrete experience. The fictive mode, as it is contrasted to the philosophic, gains its power because it presents an abstract idea as though it were emerging out of the concrete life of our experience. A philosophic treatise on justice, then, does not have the effectiveness of, say *The Oresteia,* which defines this abstract term through the mode of concrete dramatic action. Kazantzakis himself had the kind of mentality which might have driven him into pure philosophic writing rather than literary expression. When he affirms his own sensitivity in *Zorba the Greek,* he affirms it as an artist whose thoughts, no matter how philosophic, will always be expressed in literary terms. (As an aside we might add that Kazantzakis' own life bears witness to this synthesis of the abstract with the concrete. His mental journey took him into Buddhistic thought. But reading about the Buddha was not enough. His trips to Japan and China demonstrate his thirst for a full experience of an idea, both in its abstract expression and in its literal implementation in oriental life. Similarly, the full significance of Lenin could never be known except via a journey into post-revolutionary Russia.)

We might conclude by investigating a complementary meaning to *Zorba the Greek,* one which can be formulated through a consideration of the novel in the context of Kazantzakis' thought. Kazantzakis adhered to no system either philosophic or religious. Though strongly affected by various thinkers, he remained peculiarly his own self, free of any absolute system. His experience was such that he came to regard all systems as essentially incomplete, and thus his mind displays a peculiar kind of dialectic. Influenced by an idea, he would struggle to comprehend it. Then, capturing it through his art, he would journey to another idea. Thus he affirms the existence of a system only to realize its incompleteness, and it is in the name of this incompleteness, this "abyss," that he negates any system. His eclecticism is, then, only a vehicle for his dialectic. Reconsidering Kazantzakis' infatuation with Buddhism in this light, we see quite clearly in *Zorba the Greek* his reluctance to affirm Buddha as *the* teacher: the Buddhistic conception of life must be experienced mentally (in this case, through artistic treatment), before any negation of it can occur. As an adjunct to his denial of Buddha, we also noted Kazantzakis' attempts to exorcize a literal concrete fact: the widow. His affair with the widow forced him to display a necessary tolerance for his own physical needs. Before he had done this, he had been pursued by these same needs, and it is only after his indulgence that his sexual desires can be placed into the proper perspective of his many needs.

Zorba takes his place beside the great thinkers who influenced Kazantzakis because he, in his own peculiar way, impressed the author with the limitations of knowledge. Zorba's dance is an affirmation of life as against the words which try to capture it. It is the Dionysian union with the unintelligible. But the paradox is a Nietzschean one. Even in order to posit the Dionysian chaos, one needs words or the ordering tools of the mind. Zorba is the dancer. Kazantzakis is the Apollonian apprehender, the scholar-artist. But in order to know the dance, in order that life's basic void can be realized, the word must capture the dance and so make its incomprehensibility comprehensible. (pp. 43-52)

George T. Karnezis, " 'Zorba the Greek': The Artist and Experience," in Carnegie Series in English, A Modern Miscellany, *Vol. XI, 1970, pp. 43-52.*

THEODORE ZIOLKOWSKI　(essay date 1972)

[*An American critic and educator, Ziolkowski is best known as the author of* The Novels of Hermann Hesse *(1965) and as the editor of numerous English translations of Hesse's works. A professor of German language and literature, he contends that literature cannot be studied from a single national perspective; accordingly, throughout his career he has promoted the value of comparative literary studies. In the following excerpt, Ziolkowski examines Kazantzakis's fascination with Jesus as a literary subject, focusing on Manolios's identification with the Christ figure in* The Greek Passion.]

Kazantzakis was obsessed throughout his life with the figure of Jesus. Always in search of spiritual heroes after whom he could model his own life, Kazantzakis first became fascinated with Jesus when, as a boy, he was placed in a school run by Franciscan friars on the island of Naxos. This early Christian zeal, which was accentuated by a conspicuous impulse toward asceticism, survived his law studies in Athens and even his philosophical training in Paris under Bergson. Like many of his heroes Kazantzakis was a man of violent extremes: determining to establish direct contact with the savior, he spent six months in a monk's cell on Mt. Athos in Macedonia. When spiritual and bodily exercises failed to produce the desired results Kazantzakis turned away from Christ and, during the following decades, experimented with a variety of intellectual positions. The allegiances that claimed him after his youthful mysticism, he once remarked, were successively nationalism, communism, and nihilism. Some of the heroes besides Jesus to whom he devoted himself—the "Saviors of God"—were Buddha, Odysseus, Don Quixote, Nietzsche, and Lenin.

When from 1948 to 1951 Kazantzakis finally wrote his two great Jesus novels—the fictional transfiguration *The Greek Passion* (whose technique is suggested more precisely by a literal translation of the Greek title: *Christ Recrucified*) and the fictionalizing biography *The Last Temptation of Christ*—his view of Jesus was tempered by the various intellectual positions he had held. After the mysticism of his youth Kazantzakis came to regard Jesus as a spiritual hero on a level with other heroic myths of mankind. In his retelling of the *Odyssey,* for instance, Odysseus says to Christ: "Tell me your myth that the whole world may turn to myth." This view of Jesus reflects an attitude that Kazantzakis shared with various scholars of religion and writers of the twenties. At the same time, during his Marxist phase Kazantzakis came to view communism as a religion, an attitude that affected the view of Jesus held by many writers in the thirties. Although the mythic and the Marxist views of Jesus . . . produced clearly distinguishable categories of fictional transfiguration, neither dominated Kazantzakis' thought and work. At most, these positions justified the shift of his interest from the Christ of faith to the Jesus of human history. In his obsession with the psychology of the savior and his modern imitator, Kazantzakis is much closer to Hauptmann than to the next generation of writers.

In 1921 Kazantzakis wrote a verse tragedy on *The Christ* and in 1942 he contemplated composing the "Memoirs of Jesus," in preparation for which he made a careful study of the Scriptures as well as the Apocrypha. Four years later, his wife reports, he was still thinking about Jesus; but at that point he wanted to "cure Christ of His Messianic spirit through psychoanalysis." During that period a young Greek doctor regularly came to his apartment in Paris to introduce Kazantzakis to the secrets of analysis. The direct product of this psychiatric view of Jesus was *The Last Temptation of Christ,* which Kazantzakis wrote "in a state of deep religious exaltation, with fervent love for Christ." As he wrote the novel, he recorded, "I felt what Christ felt. I became Christ." Kazantzakis' attitude is a curious mixture of the liberal hatred of the conventional distorted image of Jesus and [a hallucinatory identification with him]. . . . "It's a laborious, sacred, creative endeavor to reincarnate the essence of Christ, setting aside the dross, falsehood and pettiness which all the churches and all the cassocked representatives of Christianity have heaped upon this figure, thereby distorting it." It was his eminently human conception of Jesus that enraged the Greek Orthodox Church, causing it to threaten Kazantzakis with excommunication. "That part of Christ's nature which was profoundly human helps us to understand him and love him and to pursue his Passion as though it were our own," he wrote in the Prologue to *The Last Temptation.* "If he had not within him this warm human element, he would never be able to touch our hearts with such assurance and tenderness; he would not be able to become a model for our lives."

What Kazantzakis wrote about *The Last Temptation* suggests the spirit in which he composed *The Greek Passion* within two months of 1948. Since he was obsessed with the figure of Jesus as a literary subject from 1942 to 1951, we can assume that he was consciously aware at every instant of the parallels in his transfiguration. Secondly, his transfiguration would reflect precisely the same kind of Jesus that we find in *The Last Temptation:* a human savior whose image has been shorn of the inauthentic attributes bestowed upon it by conventional Christianity. Finally, the impulse motivating both books is an impulse toward psychiatric analysis: . . . Kazantzakis wanted to understand what it is that causes a man to identify himself with Jesus. To a certain extent he was recording his own experience: as he noted during the composition of his later novel, "I became Christ." It is perfectly consistent, therefore, that Kazantzakis motivated the crucial psychological transformation of his hero with an incident that might strike us as implausible if we did not know of its autobiographical source.

In May, 1922, while in Vienna, Kazantzakis suffered an inexplicable outbreak of "eczema" of the face. Fascinated by a lovely woman beside whom he was sitting in the theater, Kazantzakis invited her to visit him in his room the following evening. But overnight a mysterious affliction set in: his face puffed up until his eyes were nothing but pinpoints in a blubber of flesh, and his lower lip dripped with a yellowish fluid. The affliction, which neither pathologists nor dermatologists were able to relieve, lasted until August and effectively put an end to Kazantzakis' amatory designs. Then one day, quite by chance, the author was approached by a doctor who expressed curiosity about the disfiguring disease; the doctor turned out to be the psychiatrist Wilhelm Stekel. After an examination Stekel diagnosed the affliction as "saint's disease," a neo-ascetic case of psychosomatic origin that stemmed from feelings of guilt associated with the temptation of the beautiful woman in the theater. On Stekel's advice Kazantzakis left Vienna, the site of his temptation, and almost immediately his face healed. Twenty-five years later Kazantzakis used an identical incident to motivate the hero of *The Greek Passion* to undertake his imitation of Jesus. (pp. 124-27)

The Greek Passion is wholly traditional in form: this was a conscious decision on the author's part when he wrote the novel as an act of liberation from several years of public service (most recently as Director of the UNESCO Bureau of Translations). As a result, there are few tricks and surprise disclosures; virtually the entire plot is implicit, for anyone who knows the New Testament, in the characters and the situation introduced in the first chapter. It is Easter Tuesday, and the village elders have assembled to appoint the citizens who are to play the roles of Jesus and the disciples in the following year's Passion Play. From the very start, therefore, everyone concerned—both the principals and the observers—is aware of the symbolic roles that are being acted out. The assignments are made initially because the villagers suit the various roles for which they are selected, according to the popular understanding of the Bible stories; and during the ensuing weeks and months they are expected to live more or less in accordance with the role that has been assigned to each.

Although the villagers take their Passion Play and their roles seriously, two unexpected factors are required to activate the potential plot: the paranoia of the hero, Manolios, and an unusual external event. On the very day that the roles are assigned, an entire village of refugees, driven from their homes by the Turks, arrives at Lycovrissi after three months of wandering and implores aid. This situation permits Kazantzakis to indulge in the satire and criticism of institutionalized Christianity familiar ever since Christian socialism. The prosperous "Christians" of Lycovrissi, who feel unthreatened by the Turks, are unwilling to render even the slightest assistance to their fellow Christians; instead, led by the priest Grigoris, they attempt to drive the starving refugees away. Indeed, the Turkish agha turns out to be more humane and charitable than the Christian elders. It is the villagers chosen for parts in the Passion Play who decide to live out their roles by coming to the assistance of the refugees, guiding them up to the sheltering caves of the nearby Mount Sarakina. The tension between these two parties generates the hostility that the other villagers come to feel toward their Jesus, the shepherd Manolios, and that eventually drives them to execute him. (pp. 128-29)

The novel falls roughly into two halves: the first part deals with the hero's private religious development up to the point where he wholly assumes the identity that was initially thrust upon him by others; and the second part expands the action to embrace the public and political involvements of the hero who now actively seeks out his own Passion. Manolios is chosen for the role of Jesus mainly because of his pious behavior and his appearance. With his blue eyes and short yellow beard, Manolios is "a real Christ like an icon," the priest assures the village notables, adding as an afterthought: "and pious into the bargain." One of the elders remarks that "he's a wee bit crazy." But what none of them realizes is that, by chance, they have hit upon a man with a religious mania that already amounts to incipient paranoia. Left an orphan at an early age, Manolios was brought up first by an aunt and then, for years, by the monks at the monastery, where he early conceived a mystical desire to re-enact the Passion. When he is chosen for the role of Jesus, it is the fulfillment of a lifelong dream: "The thing to which he had aspired from his tenderest childhood, the thing he had desired during so many nights as he sat at the feet of his Superior, Father Manasse, listening to the golden legend—behold, now God was granting it to him. To follow in the footsteps of the martyrs and the saints, to pare away his flesh, to go to his death for his faith in Jesus Christ, and to enter Paradise bearing the instruments of martyrdom: the crown of thorns, the cross and the five nails. . . ."

Manolios is suited for the strenuous role by virtue of his physical strength; but his emotional stability does not match this strength. In fact, he suffers from [a] paranoid inability to distinguish between hallucination and reality. On the very first day, for instance, he warns his fellow apostles against reading the lives of the saints in preparation for their roles: "When I was with the monks I used to read them, and I nearly went off my head. Deserts, lions, dreadful diseases, leprosy; their bodies were covered with boils, eaten by worms, or became like the shells of tortoises. . . . At other times temptations came like a beautiful woman. No, no! Only the Gospel." This capacity for eidetic re-experience of the Scriptures and Christian legends affords Manolios [a] sense of identity with Jesus . . . : "Manolios dragged himself into the ray of light which fell from the skylight, pulled the little Gospel out of his waistcoat pocket, opened it at random and began to read, forgetting the others around about him. He entered into the boat with Christ, mingled with the apostles, they went sailing on the lake of Gennesareth, and toward evening a violent wind came up. . . ."

Kazantzakis has given careful attention to the psychological plausibility of his hero in order to make the entire fiction acceptable. Manolios' background and his predisposition toward religious hysteria convince him that his selection for the role of Jesus represents more than a happenstance or a mere formality: . . . it seems to confirm all his visions and dreams. "When I left Priest Grigoris's house," he confides to his friends, "my head was buzzing. It seemed to me that the village had become too small for me, that I wasn't any longer Manolios, the lowly shepherd of old Patriarcheas, the ignorant, the wretched, but as it were a man chosen of God and with a great mission: to follow the footsteps of Christ, to be like Him!" Whereas the other actors are able to distinguish clearly between their own identities and their assigned roles, Manolios gradually accepts the role as his new identity. This emerges clearly from his conversation with the peddler Yannakos, who has been chosen to be the Apostle Peter. When Manolios, who is engaged to be married, tries to persuade him that they must change their lives and live in purity for the coming year in order to be fit for their roles, Yannakos realistically points out the facts: " 'When you come before us to act Christ Crucified, you'll be newly married. They'll put you on the cross, but a lot that will mean to you! You'll know that it's all a game, that it's Another who was crucified, and at the moment when you cry out on the cross: 'Eli, Eli, lama subachthani!' you'll say to yourself that soon you'll be home, after the crucifying. . . ." Manolios, shaken by the undeniable truth of Yannakos' statement, begins to tell himself that he's an impostor, while Yannakos reminds him that their enthusiasm on the day before was a different matter: "It was a holiday, don't you see? . . . Today, look, the donkey's loaded, our bellies are empty, Easter's over, trade's starting again. . . ."

The first half of the novel is given over largely to the psychological question: How does it happen that Manolios, alone among the actors, slips wholly into the role of Jesus? As we have just seen, his background and character make this delusion ultimately plausible. But at first he wavers, moved by the more cynical realism of his friends and afraid of his own presumptuousness. Then four days after his selection, stirred by a strong though subconscious longing, Manolios sets out to visit the beautiful widow Katerina, chosen to play the part of Mary Magdalene. Manolios rationalizes his sexual urge by telling himself that he really wants to visit her in his newly appointed role as Christ to save her from sin. But as he starts down the mountain in his Sunday outfit, with a vision of the sensuous widow in his imagination, his head suddenly begins to buzz, his temples throb, his face prickles. Passing his hand over his face, he perceives that his features are grotesquely swollen. When he looks in his pocket mirror, he sees that his face is completely bloated: "his eyes were no more than two tiny balls, his nose was lost between his ballooning cheeks, his mouth was a mere hole." This affliction, in which we recognize the "saint's disease" that Kazantzakis suffered in 1922, tips the emotional balance and causes Manolios to accept his delusion wholly. Horrified at his appearance, he hurries back up the mountain, where he remains in his hut for the following weeks. Breaking his engagement with his fiancée, he vows to live a life of total self-sacrifice in imitation of Jesus. (On July 27, 1948, Kazantzakis recorded in his notebook: "My lip began swelling just at the moment in my novel where I describe the swelling on the face of the hero, who enacts the role of Christ.")

Early in May Manolios and his three apostles attend a Sunday service that the priest Fotis holds for the refugees. After-

wards, as they sit and explicate the Beatitudes, Manolios makes a great confession to his friends, telling them of his childhood dreams, his presumptuous wish to imitate Christ, his temptation by the widow Katerina, and the frightful affliction by which God struck him down. But Fotis interprets the events in a new light: rather than a punishment, the affliction is a protective mask that God has clapped on Manolios in order to save him for salvation and for a great deed. It is only a few days until Manolios seems to have a chance to act out his role. The agha's young homosexual lover, Youssoufaki, has been murdered—as it later turns out, by his giant bodyguard Hussein. At first the furious agha suspects the Greeks and threatens to hang them one by one until the murderer confesses. When Manolios hears of these happenings down in the village, he resolves to sacrifice himself for the sake of the town and sets out down the mountain in an ecstatic hallucination, "as if he were again following Christ's footsteps and they led down to Lycovrissi." Almost miraculously, his face heals from one moment to the next, now that his soul is purified by the decision to sacrifice himself. Manolios, in turn, imagines himself to be nothing but the will-less tool of Jesus: "You must realize that it's not me speaking, but Christ commanding me. I'm carrying out His orders, and no more."

Entering the village, Manolios surrenders to the agha, who releases the other hostages and promises to hang Manolios at sunset. The widow Katerina, moved by Manolios' example and words, makes a fruitless effort to save him—it is remarkable how often this old Christian socialist motif of the repentant woman of passion crops up!—and earns nothing but her own death at the furious agha's hands. But Manolios . . . is deprived at the last minute of his act of sacrifice. The agha's housekeeper, dismayed at the murder of Katerina, turns up evidence that Hussein murdered Youssoufaki in a fit of jealousy. Releasing Manolios, the agha hangs and mutilates his bodyguard. But the total surrender of self implied by his resolved self-sacrifice has welded Manolios completely with his role. "Brothers," he tells the other disciples, "I have taken the decision to change my life completely, to reject the past, to welcome Christ by the wayside. I shall walk before Him with the trumpet, like His bodyguard, . . . When I open my mouth, Christ will put the right words on my lips." And in the darkness the disciples note that "his face was dazzling."

In the first half of the novel, then, the emphasis is on the psychogenesis of the hero, whose paranoia is traced through a series of plausible stages, beginning with the recollections of his childhood and moving through delusions of grandeur and the despair of doubt to the complete displacement of reality by hallucination. The New Testament parallels remain rather general: the proclamation of Manolios as Jesus, the gathering of the disciples, the temptation, the sermon on the mount, and the transfiguration. In the second half, as his ministry becomes public, the parallels become far more conspicuous, especially as Manolios begins to pursue his own Passion.

The events of the first ten chapters last no more than three weeks—from Easter (around April 22) until early in May. After the high point of this section, Manolios' transfiguration, several months are passed over in silence. Up to this point Manolios has been concerned only with his personal religious development; but now the action becomes political as he comes into conflict with authority. During the harvest season he appeals to the villagers to help the refugees to prepare for the approaching winter. At the Festival of Elijah he addresses the congregation after asking the priest for permission to speak "about Christ."

" 'Christ?' said the priest, taken aback; 'but that's my business'."

" 'Christ has ordered me to speak,' Manolios insisted." Although the villagers are persuaded by Manolios' words, his behavior arouses the hostility of the priest Grigoris, who sets about to destroy his work and to drive out the detested refugees along with their priest, who competes with his authority. Grigoris, clever enough to realize that he would lose by attacking Manolios' Christian charity on religious grounds, implies that he is a political threat. By accusing Manolios of bolshevism he achieves two goals: he anticipates and undermines the appeal that Manolios and Fotis make to the regional bishop regarding the behavior of the Lycovrissians; and he enlists the active aid of the agha, who was not even remotely interested in the affair as long as it was merely a religious squabble of the detested *romnoi*.

The priest's principal henchman in his schemes is the village saddler, Panayotaros, to whom Kazantzakis has devoted a care of characterization second only to that of Manolios. Panayotaros hates Manolios because the shepherd has displaced him in the affections of the widow Katerina; but he is doubly embittered because he was selected to play the role of Judas. "My wife calls me Judas, the kids in the street make long noses at me; the women bolt their doors when they see me pass. Plague take you, you'll make me into a Judas forever!" he tells the other apostles. Throwing himself more passionately into his role than the others, but out of resentment rather than love, he helps the priest to gather information against Manolios and the refugees. One of the other disciples tries to dissuade him from his treachery by arguing—just as Yannakos had reminded Manolios—that "it's a play, a sacred play but only a play, not real," that he was chosen for the role of Judas only because he had a red beard. But Panayotaros, albeit consciously and not in a hallucination, takes his role just as seriously as Manolios does his. And since every Jesus needs his Judas, he determines to act it out to the end.

Meanwhile, the situation of the refugees deteriorates as the season moves into winter. On December 22, the birthday of St. Elijah, they decide to march down into Lycovrissi to demand food from the villagers. A general brawl develops during which part of the village is burned and the schoolmaster is killed. The priest, furious, tries to persuade the agha to arrest Manolios, whom he calls a dangerous bolshevik: "He has one aim only: to overthrow the Ottoman Empire. Behind him stands the Muscovite, pushing him on. If we let him live, he'll have us all." Up to this point the agha has observed the happenings with an amused detachment, as "manias" of the foolish Greeks. "Let them shift for themselves; I smoke my chibouk, I sip my raki, and I don't care a fig! But now the Ottoman Empire's becoming mixed up in it, the Muscovite is there, things are getting out of hand. Yet, yes, if I let that abortion Manolios live the Ottoman Empire is in danger." Drinking himself into a stupor, the agha sends the saddler to arrest Manolios, and Panayotaros congratulates himself that his moment is at hand: "Bravo, Judas Panayotaros, my gallant, you've got him." When Panayotaros finally catches up with Manolios, he speaks like a true Judas: " 'When I've killed you, Manolios,' he bellowed, 'I shall kill myself afterward; I'm only living to kill you'." For Panayotaros, reality

has been as radically displaced by his Judas-role as for Manolios by his Jesus-role.

From this point on the incidents fall neatly into the sequence of the Passion, a Passion that has been ironically inverted. When Panayotaros sets out, Manolios and his disciples are in a Gethsemane-like garden outside the village. But when word arrives that the search is on for Manolios, most of the men hide or take flight. Only one disciple remains as Manolios, with cocks crowing in the distance, sets out toward the village to give himself up; and that one, Kostandis, goes off at a run as soon as he sees Panayotaros approaching. Since Manolios surrenders voluntarily, there is no proper arrest in Gethsemane. Yet Panayotaros, in order to play up his own role, embellishes his account of the apprehension so that it seems to conform more closely to the Gospel scene: "I've nabbed him, Agha. He was barricaded in the garden with his men, about twenty, armed to the teeth." So greatly does imagination take the place of reality!

The agha, in turn, is perfectly well aware that Manolios is innocent of the accusations: "Wolves don't eat one another; Greeks do. Here they are now, wanting, for all they're worth, to eat Manolios! Why? what's he done to them? He's innocent, poor fellow; a bit crazy, but he never did anyone any harm." But when Manolios refuses to defend himself, the agha resolves to let the Greeks have their way and falls unwittingly into the very words of Pontius Pilate. If Manolios insists on playing the saint, he must suffer the consequences. The agha, deciding that it would mean too much trouble if he tried to defend the shepherd, makes up his mind to hand him over: "There he is, take him, you blessed *romnoi,* and enjoy your meal! I wash my hands of it." But first, sorry for Manolios in his innocence, he tries to give him a chance to escape. Manolios, confessing to the crimes of arson and bolshevism, advises the agha to surrender him to the villagers, who are howling outside for his life. Finally agreeing, the agha orders Manolios to admit that he is a bolshevik so that he can surrender him to the mob in anger. Then he seizes Manolios by the neck and throws him down the stairs, where the mob is waiting. Led by the priest Grigoris and Panayotaros, the villagers drag him off to the church, where Manolios must again confess publicly to being a bolshevik. Three times he implores the mob to kill him, but they hesitate until they hear, outside, the voices of the refugees who have come to rescue Manolios. At this point Panayotaros strikes him down, and the villagers, hurling themselves upon his body in a fury, tear at it with their teeth in an obscene travesty of the Eucharist.

The novel ends with an ironic inversion of the crèche scene, for it has meantime become Christmas Eve and the bells begin to ring, summoning the Christians to the church to witness the birth of Christ. Nearby Manolios is stretched out on a bed, "swathed like a newborn child": "About him his companions watched, pale and silent; Yannakos had rested his head on Manolios' feet and was weeping like a child. . . ." Just as Manolios was proclaimed as Jesus at Easter, the time of Christ's death and resurrection, so he now dies on the day of Jesus' birth in a scene in which Nativity and Lamentation are curiously blended.

In Kazantzakis' novel the crucifixion is followed by no resurrection; the ending seems to be totally bleak: "Priest Fotis listened to the bell pealing gaily, announcing that Christ was coming down on earth to save the world. He shook his head and heaved a sigh: In vain, my Christ, in vain, he muttered;

two thousand years have gone by and men crucify You still. When will You be born, my Christ, and not be crucified any more, but live among us for eternity?" If there is any hint of redemption in this novel, it can be detected only in the sheer human perseverance that prompts the refugees—in the face of hostility on earth and, in heaven, the gloomy promise of an eternal cycle of crucifixions—to resume "their interminable march toward the east." The faith in Christ with which Kazantzakis began in his youth has given way to a more secularized faith in man's dignity and his ability to endure. (pp. 129-38)

Theodore Ziolkowski, "The Christomaniacs," in his Fictional Transfigurations of Jesus, *Princeton University Press, 1972, pp. 98-141.*

JAMES F. LEA   (essay date 1979)

[*In the following excerpt, Lea argues that the quest narrated in Kazantzakis's* Odyssey, *and in fact the central idea in all his works, is the human search for freedom.*]

The most enduring characteristic of Kazantzakis' life, art, and political theory was the struggle for freedom. During his lifetime Kazantzakis was bombarded with philosophies, religions, and developments inimical to man's freedom. He was reared as a Christian within a family and society that believed very strongly in God's providential intervention in history. Many of his childhood neighbors, as well as the rulers on Crete during his youth, were Turks who believed firmly in Moslem fatalism. He was aware of the manner in which technological mechanization was structuring men's lives. He knew also that the socialization process had a tremendous affect on the direction of one's life. Two influential intellectual sources were Spengler, who subscribed to a scheme of cultural determinism, and Marx, who subscribed to a scheme of economic determinism. He was cognizant of the manner in which Hegel's scientific historicism linked history, nature, and idea in a cosmic mind that comprehended and ordained past, present, and future. He was equally aware of the manner in which Spinoza's scientific naturalism postulated man as a quantifiable variable in a mathematized universe based on necessity. Kazantzakis was probably versed in Freud's theories concerning the cultural and genetic determinants of life, which replaced will with unconscious motivations. Kazantzakis sought to deliver man from the inhibitions of these many forms of deterministic necessity by offering a new liberating myth-ideal for modern man—the "struggle for freedom."

Seeking to define the worth of this struggle in view of an inhibiting world, Kazantzakis explored the questions of metaphysical versus sociopolitical freedom, unity, and the efficacy of individual action. From this exploration Kazantzakis does not offer freedom qua freedom as a rebuttal to these deterministic forces. This is significant, as is his belief that freedom is the essence of man, and his view, as expressed through his literary characters, of what constitutes the various levels of freedom. Through the Odysseus characterization, Kazantzakis illustrates the important realization that man cannot support full freedom. Kazantzakis portrays Odysseus as one who struggles "beyond freedom," though realizing that absolute freedom is a mythical nonexistent whose attainment would be its negation; therefore, it is through a never-ending and never-fulfilled quest for freedom that we both create our freedom and transcend the hope for freedom. In this erotic sto-

icism, as Joseph Flay terms it, there is a wedding of fate/necessity and freedom with ontology, history, and nature to form an alternative role for man on a continuum between determinism and meaningless, absolute freedom. This perceptive new decalogue, of man's erotic struggle in harness to the God-rhythm beyond hope and freedom, is of immense utility for modern man in these latter decades of the twentieth century.

William Stanford [in his *The Ulysses Theme*] says of **The Odyssey:** "Kazantzakis has singled out the wish to be free as the dominant passion of his hero. In fact, psychologically, his epic is an exploration of the meaning of freedom." One would not overstate Kazantzakis' concern with liberty in saying this is the dominant theme not only of **The Odyssey** but, indeed, of all his works. There are many dimensions to Kazantzakis' philosophy of freedom, and all his major characters express some element of that philosophy. This is evident not only in **The Odyssey** but in the Christ novels, in the aptly titled **Freedom or Death,** and in **"The Immortal Free Spirit of Man"** as well as in **Zorba,** whose central theme, along with the clash between action and writing, is the contrast of a free being with one who is not free. Kazantzakis' comprehensive view of freedom includes interrelated personal, political, and metaphysical levels, and both he and his characters express these levels of freedom. It is only with Ulysses' freedom wherein personal, political, and metaphysical freedoms are united and, paradoxically enough, transcended in favor of the struggle for freedom. Central to Kazantzakis' philosophy of freedom is his evaluation of the degree to which modern man does or does not persevere in the maintenance of his liberty.

Liberty on a personal level has, for Kazantzakis, both physical and intellectual dimensions. In discussing the former, Kazantzakis echoes Christian and Platonic teachings of freedom from the dominance of appetitive pleasures of the flesh. With Plato, Kazantzakis believed that for man's existence to be truly free and just the soul must rule both mind and body. Unlike Plato, however, Kazantzakis, under the influence of Buddhism and Christianity, was at times wont to push this view to an ascetic extreme of extirpation. As a dramatic vehicle for expounding this view, Kazantzakis utilized on several occasions an illness known as "ascetics' disease."

While in Vienna in 1921, Kazantzakis noticed an attractive young woman named Frieda and fantasized an assignation with her the next night in his quarters. Yet when in his fantasy, she was to come to him on that night and others—all of which were postponed by Kazantzakis—Kazantzakis' face became swollen and filled with yellowish-white liquid. Seeking an explanation from Wilhelm Stekel, the leading Freudian in the city, Kazantzakis was reminded of similar outbreaks in the saints' legends and was told:

> Plunged as it is in the Buddhist *weltanschauung,* your soul—or rather what for you goes by the name of soul—believes that sleeping with a woman is a mortal sin. For that reason it refuses to permit its body to commit this sin. Such souls, souls capable of imposing themselves to so great a degree on the flesh, are rare in our age (*Report*).

On his leaving Vienna, Kazantzakis' face healed. In a like manner, Manolios, the Christ figure in **The Greek Passion,** contracts ascetics' disease when he is tempted by the immoral widow, *née* Mary Magdalene, of Lycovrissi; yet when he resists the temptation to succumb to the dominance of the bodily appetites, his face becomes healed.

Kazantzakis and Zorba never attained this freedom from the sexual demands of the flesh; and . . . neither seemed to regret this fact. It must be kept in mind that while Kazantzakis believed in the spirit of man he did not reject the flesh—only slavery to lusts—for Kazantzakis was no puritan. In fact, one of his chief complaints against Christianity was that it "soiled the union of man and woman by stigmatizing it as a sin. Whereas formerly it was a holy act, a joyous submission to God's will, in the Christian's terror-shaken soul it degenerated into a transgression" (*Report*). Kazantzakis emphasized the happiness present in the sexual joining of creative, self-actualized men and women, but he knew that the repression of legitimate sexuality brought about by the Christian ethic militates against the ecstatic integrity of the sex act. In a like manner, the hypocritical moralizing inherent in that institutionalized ethic creates, as Nietzsche perceived, profoundly debilitating implications for man's freedom in a related aspect of the personal, physical dimension of liberty that received Kazantzakis' attention—marriage.

Throughout his life Jesus resists marriage, for this would turn him from his God-chosen path. When he faints on the cross, however, Jesus confronts in his imagination the "last temptation" of earthly domesticity. He is led by Satan's angel first to Mary Magdalene and then, after she is slain by Saul, to Lazarus' sisters, Mary and Martha. Castigated by Paul for having abandoned his mission by becoming husband to the sisters, Jesus answers: "Here I lead the life of a man: I eat, drink, work, and have children. The great conflagration subsided, I too became a kind of tranquil fire; I curled up in the fireplace. . . . I set sail to conquer the world but cast anchor in this tiny domestic trough" (*Last Temptation*). Later, when he attempts to justify his action to the apostles, Judas scorns him: "Your post, deserter, was on the cross and you know it. Others can reclaim barren lands and barren women. Your duty was to mount the cross—that's what I say!" He ridicules Jesus' claim that he has conquered death: "Is that the way to conquer death—by making children, mouthfuls for Charon! You've turned yourself into this meat market and you deliver him morsels to eat. Traitor! Deserter! Coward!"

But, as Jesus discovers when he wakes on the cross, his domestic desertion existed only in his subconscious. He had not deserted his post and abandoned the struggle to liberate God; he had fulfilled his duty. "A wild, indomitable joy took possession of him. . . . Temptation had captured him for a split second and led him astray. The joys, marriages, and children were lies . . . illusions sent by the Devil. He uttered a triumphant cry: IT IS ACCOMPLISHED." In *The Greek Passion,* Manolios is also tempted to marry, but he resists so that he will be free to carry out God's mission. (pp. 138-42)

The other dimension of personal liberty, the intellectual realm, involved several things for Kazantzakis, all of which flow from the freedom from the "inner Turks" of ignorance. Though Kazantzakis rejected the over-ambitious claims of intellectualism and scientific-rationalism, he realized that a rigorous intellectual preparation was, for the great majority of men, a vital prerequisite to answering—and perhaps even to formulating—those agonizing questions of the spirit which were his abiding concern. This belief was acted upon in lifelong study beginning . . . on Naxos and Crete, continuing formally from 1902 until 1906 at the University of Athens and from 1907 until 1909 in the school of law at the Sorbonne

and the Collége de France, and informally thereafter. . . . Kazantzakis was well versed in most Occidental and Oriental philosophies and religions. Like Nietzsche, he studied in depth the important roots of Greek art, culture, and thought. In many ways Kazantzakis truly "represents the final justification of the Western man's active search for truth as distinguished from the Easterner's passivity before truth" [see Doulis excerpt dated 1963]. Ultimately, Kazantzakis was skeptical of the "saving power of the intellect of man, though he reaffirms the Western idea that it is necessary to have an educated and sensitive mind in order to comprehend its final inadequacy." From his rigorous and amazing search for truth came intellectual liberation from comforting religious falsehoods as well as from scientific "proofs." With Kazantzakis' continual study and questioning also came escape from inertia and vegetative satisfaction—as brought on either by worship of materialistic goals, which received elaboration above, or by intellectual and ideological dogmatism and inflexibility. A consequence of all this was Kazantzakis' belief that the intellectually liberated man would scorn, like Nietzsche, the inhibitions of conventional social strictures—mores, creeds, etc.—and it is with this view that Kazantzakis moves out of the personal realm of freedom into the public arena.

Kazantzakis' philosophy of freedom on the political level can also be discussed in terms of physical and intellectual realms. Viewing the latter, Kazantzakis emphasized freedom from the enslavement of ideology, whether of left or right, East or West. To be a free person—an increasingly difficult spiritual accomplishment—one must look with a clear eye upon contemporary reality and "must admit the infamy as well as the virtues, the dark as well as the light, for here on this earth every living thing—human beings and ideas too—has always been composed of both" (*England*). Kazantzakis was considered "suspect" at various times by all political and religious factions because of his resolute effort to maintain his intellectual independence—his freedom to criticize the deficiencies of all political positions. (pp. 142-43)

Kazantzakis was concerned not only with the intellectual dimension of political liberty but also with the physical realm of political freedom. This latter concern reflected his childhood experience under Turkish rule on Crete. *Freedom or Death,* a fictionalized account of that experience, embodies two views of political freedom. First, there is the traditional quest for liberty—acted out by Captain Michales and his fellow freedom fighters in periodic uprisings—of throwing off the yoke of tyranny and attaining self-rule. Second, there is his ontological view of freedom, expressed in political terms, that the man who has an ideal or myth to believe in is free even though ruled by others. Captain Michales knows the futility of his position after one uprising has been put down and others have returned to their villages, and yet he fights on valiantly under the banner "Freedom or Death." In a similar vein, Prometheus proclaims his freedom even in his chains, for his soul soars beyond tyranny. Like Victor Frankl, Aleksandr Solzhenitsyn, and others in this century, Kazantzakis agrees with Nietzsche that one "who has a why to live can withstand any how." There is, however, no quietist content here—either for Frankl, Solzhenitsyn, or Kazantzakis—for the "why," the guiding belief or idea, will inspire great souls to emulate Captain Michales and never submit willingly to any "how"—of tyranny, injustice, and oppression. The next and highest level of freedom, the metaphysical level, though founded on a personal basis, has important political implications.

Zorba, one of Kazantzakis' most brilliant characterizations, is an attempt to portray, through the powerful contrast between a free being (Zorba) and an unfree being (the Boss) both a description of and a prescription for metaphysical freedom—the immortal free spirit of man. This spirit only fulfills its freedom and immortality so far as man persists in the affirmation of life. It is only through this affirmation of life and the corollary victory over the authority of mortality that humanity in its highest sense is attained. The struggle for freedom of spirit over matter is essential to Kazantzakis' metaphysical level of freedom. He expresses it thus: "Guileful matter has chosen this body . . . slowly to dampen and extinguish the free flame which flickers within me." (pp. 143-44)

What are the implications and meaning of the view of freedom espoused by Kazantzakis for contemporary man? Does his philosophy have any direct relevance for today? It is of the utmost relevance and has many profound contemporary implications. Many of the problems to which Kazantzakis addressed himself are timeless, as testified to by the attention devoted to them by philosophers over the centuries. The principal importance of Kazantzakis' view is in the application of his personal, political, and metaphysical concepts of freedom to the experiential odyssey of twentieth-century man in his Ulysses characterization. Ulysses—like Zorba—is one of Kazantzakis' most important characters and represents the cumulative account of the many contradictory contemporary themes which run through Kazantzakis' thought. George Scouffas [see Additional Bibliography] contends that "since Kazantzakis brings to bear on his subject a lifetime of study in philosophy, anthropology, history, religion, and literature, the result is that the basic terms of the exploration become a catalogue of the central motifs and dilemmas of modern Western literature." Furthermore, he believes that it is Kazantzakis' purpose to "expose Odysseus to all the strains and counter-strains that beset modern man, to guide him to a revelatory synthesis that can give him clarity of understanding and ultimate peace, and to do this without depriving him of his status as man."

While some may dispute the "relevance" of Kazantzakis' ambitious sequel to the Homeric epic, few who are familiar with the book deny [Colin Wilson's assertion (see *TCLC*, Vol. 2, p. 317)] that it "is the most monumental work of Kazantzakis, and his greatest achievement. In it he comes closest to presenting a unified world view, transcending the antitheses of flesh and spirit." The crucial difference between Kazantzakis' and Homer's Ulysses has to do with freedom. Homer has Ulysses return from his voyage to his wife Penelope, his son Telemachus, his friends and subjects on Ithaca, where he willingly submits to the placidity of that existence. Kazantzakis, on the other hand, begins his epic with Ulysses' dissatisfaction on his return to Ithaca and sends him once more in quest of the elusive invisible cry of freedom, immortality, truth, or both. Kazantzakis begins *The Odyssey* with a paean to freedom:

> O Sun, my quick coquetting eye, my red-haired hound, sniff out all my quarries that I love, give them swift chase, tell me all that you've seen on earth, all that you've heard, and I shall pass them through my entrails' secret forge till slowly, with profound caresses, play and laughter, stones, water, fire, and earth shall be transformed to spirit, and

> the mud-winged and heavy soul, freed of its flesh, shall like a flame serene ascend and fade in sun.

Thus Kazantzakis expresses his belief that man has settled for less from life than it has to offer. Acting out the stages outlined in *The Saviors of God,* Odysseus seeks the meaning of life and arrives at the perspective afforded by the Cretan glance—which is freedom. He has "freed himself from everything—religions, philosophies, political systems—one who has cut away all the strings. He wants to try all forms of life, freely, beyond plans and systems, keeping the thought of death before him as a stimulant." Odysseus seeks freedom and focuses on his mortality not to heighten the sensuality of each of life's moments but to make himself more "capable of embracing and exhausting all things so that, when death finally came, it would find nothing to take from him, for it would find an entirely squandered Odysseus."

Odysseus begins his quest for attaining the union of personal, political, and metaphysical freedom—through abandonment of wife and family, sexual orgies, revolutions—in a fashion disturbing to many. One who is uneasy about Ulysses' satanic revelries [C. N. Stavrou (see *TCLC*, Vol. 5, p. 262)] says: "On several occasions, Odysseus' bestiality and cruelty call in [to] question his author's wisdom." Stavrou concedes that Odysseus' wanderings are not aimless but represent a quest for the meaning of life. He doubts, however, whether the participation in sexual orgies, the angry tirades, and those displays of blood lust—all evident in Odysseus' initial travels—are the proper way to learn how to live. Odysseus is happy neither at rest nor play, and he causes dissatisfaction in those around him. "He is as often Man Transmogrified as Man Transfigured. . . . He sows discontent like a political agitator, and stirs up dangerous thoughts in men's minds and forbidden lusts in men's hearts." Kazantzakis' concern for greatly expanded liberty and his orienting his philosophy in Books I through XII around the individual as the supreme value is seen to prove—and if one stops at this point indeed it does prove—that he was an amoral anarchist.

An important aspect of the affirmation of life is the capability of man for both good and evil. When man casts off the phantoms of "Gods, motherlands, ideas," rips away the web of superficial socioreligious agglomerations that enmesh him, and stands as a defiant giant mocking the abyss, then he has transcended the ethical and social institutions that restrict action—he is free. How does Kazantzakis respond to the capacity for evil of this "giant," with his absolute freedom?

While Kazantzakis recognizes in *Zorba* that man is both "a great brute and a God," he does not satisfactorily answer the sociopolitical implications of his philosophy of absolute freedom. In keeping with his philosophy, which at this point is concerned with the divine element of those great souls in the world, he is not required to go into the ethical and social implications. For Kazantzakis' concept of freedom is primarily an ontological one that transcends sociopolitical concepts. It is concerned with the very being of freedom, with the primordial and eternal infinitude of that freedom. Thus [Peter] Bien could correctly deal with the issue of Kazantzakis' freeing the beast as well as the angel in man in the following manner: Zorba is "an incarnation of dissonance. And in all this he directly mimics the contradictory nature of life itself." Kazantzakis confesses that he "had never seen such a friendly accord between a man and the universe!" Zorba mirrors the universe; thus he is the thing-in-itself, who in doing as he pleases embodies the universal will. Kazantzakis tells Zorba:

even if you would go wrong "you couldn't. You're like a lion, shall we say, or a wolf. That kind of beast never behaves as if it were a sheep or a donkey; it is never untrue to its nature." The capacity for greatness lies in this defiance of evil, in the overcoming of evil. This is man truly freed.

Therefore, while there is certainly room for valid criticism of Kazantzakis' excesses (which constitute one of his most serious problems in the area of political philosophy), perhaps such critics take only a superficial view. Reading further in *The Odyssey,* one gains a fuller picture of the issue as Kazantzakis qualifies his position in such a manner as to negate the immediate and political import of Odysseus' more undesirable behavior. Thus, in Books XIII, XIV, and XV Odysseus overcomes and surpasses, in Nietzschean fashion, his baser, evil drives, and he accepts responsibility and a measure of discipline. Odysseus matures and leads his fellows as a political prophet in founding the ideal city. When this is coupled with the importance of the concepts of unity, brotherhood, and man's duty in Kazantzakis' mature thought, and with the recognition that although Kazantzakis and Odysseus sought in Marxist fashion to destroy outmoded dogmas and political forms, they fought not merely to destroy but also to rebuild, one comes to the conclusion that it "is no longer possible to dismiss *The Odyssey* as a glorification of total 'freedom'— that is, of immorality—a kind of belated echo of Schiller's *Robbers.* There is something far greater at stake here" [see Wilson excerpt, *TCLC,* Vol. 2, p. 318]. This greater, more profound theme underlying Odysseus' adventures is that total freedom is its own negation. (pp. 146-50)

After his ideal city is destroyed (Book XVI), the quest for freedom "dominates every stage of Odysseus' pilgrimage . . . [and] his chief concern is to search his own mind and the mind of other freedom-loving persons for the essence of liberty" [see Stanford excerpt, *TCLC,* Vol. 2, p. 315]. This is most evident in Book XVII (which Prevelakis calls Absolute Freedom), where in his mind Odysseus plays as the God-Creator of life. He calls to existence an old king, prince, slave, warrior-king, and maiden, and they perform the despairing drama of man's existence under his sentence of death. In Books XVIII through XXI, Odysseus resumes his southward journey through life, meeting and rejecting representative types: Buddha, a nihilist, Don Quixote, and Jesus, all of whom falsely proclaim a unique escape from the death sentence. He arrives at a polar village (Book XXII) and there, preparing to meet death, recalls his exhaustive, much-experienced journey through life. In Book XXIV, the last, his former companions, both living and dead, join him for the final reunion at the moment of his death:

> Then flesh dissolved, glances congealed, the heart's
> pulse stopped, and the great mind leapt to the peak
> of its holy freedom, fluttered with empty wings,
> then upright through the air soared high and freed
> itself from its last cage, its freedom.

There are both positive and negative lessons to be derived from this magnificent pilgrimage.

The positive value lies in the dynamic example of one who rejects every false hope; who will not succumb to the void awaiting; who will not abdicate his freedom; who will not exchange his liberty for any Grand Inquisitor's mastery, mystery, and miracle. It is at the same time a profound exploration, by one of tremendous learning and intellect, of the major worldviews confronting modern man. Yet, as with Odysseus' excesses before the ideal city, there is something

disturbing about the excessiveness of his absolute freedom in the latter stages of his life. In this excessiveness lies the negative lesson of *The Odyssey;* "It is not that Kazantzakis has dared too much in his complete exploration of the meaning of freedom, but that, in a sense, he has exposed the subject beyond most profitable return in terms of meaning" [Scouffas]. The freedom that Odysseus seeks so rigorously eventually reveals itself as the negation of itself, as nothingness, as that which is not, as the nonexistent, as nonbeing.

One is ultimately led to realize, on this deepest and most profound level of *The Odyssey,* that, rather than emulate Odysseus (after the fashion of Book XVI) and *never* commit ourselves, we must learn from him *how* to commit ourselves. In the sentiment that both life and art must have limits (for absolute freedom is a contradiction in terms) is found the "greatest irony of all in *The Odyssey.*" In his synopsis [Kimon] Friar "touches on it when he describes Odysseus' death as freeing his mind from its 'last cage, that of its freedom.' Odysseus has been imprisoned in an abstraction and a category" [Stanford, *The Ulysses Theme*]. The true road for man lies neither in contentless, self-destroying absolute freedom nor in such dogmatic, foredoomed commitments as those exemplified by the tightly-structured scientific-naturalism of Odysseus' ideal city.

Realizing that "freedom without virtue or goodness is of the devil" (*The Fratricides*), Kazantzakis knows that the egoistic path of Odysseus is in many ways as politically undesirable as the ideological paths of the bourgeosie and the Marxists. In *Report,* therefore, in the section "When the Germ of *The Odyssey* Formed Fruit within Me," he says: "The human being cannot support absolute freedom; such freedom leads him to chaos. If it were possible for a man to be born with absolute freedom, his first duty if he wished to be of some use on earth, would be to circumscribe that freedom." The only way to surpass this inhibiting truth is to submit to it—as Kazantzakis discovered in his own life. The circle is closed and man goes beyond freedom to come back to the struggle toward freedom. Thus, limitation of absolute freedom leads to an unending quest for affirmation in the face of negativity. This gives purpose and therefore a measure of harmony and satisfaction to our lives.

This powerful dialectic operates on only the highest level of existence once man has passed like Odysseus through the stages of *The Saviors of God* and joined with man, God, and nature in the cosmogenic struggle of life on earth. The cosmogenic harmony revolves around the insight that, just as "the highest art is passion that is controlled; order in the midst of chaos; serenity both in joy and pain" (*Spain*), so in like manner the "highest politics" lies in the proper tension between liberty and unity, individualism and community, spontaneity and order, change and constancy. Neither absolute freedom nor absolute necessity is offered here. Kazantzakis' compassionate criteria of love, free choice, social justice, and human dignity mark a roadway between and beyond the two that answers in a positive manner the central issues of anxiety, alienation, and the anomic condition of our time. (pp. 151-53)

James F. Lea, in his Kazantzakis: The Politics of Salvation, *The University of Alabama Press, 1979, 207 p.*

Kazantzakis and Albert Schweitzer.

MORTON P. LEVITT (essay date 1980)

[*Levitt is an American critic who has written extensively on Modernist literature, including the studies* Bloomsday: An Interpretation of James Joyce's "Ulysses" *(1972) and* The Cretan Glance: The World and Art of Nikos Kazantzakis. *In the following excerpt from the latter work, Levitt compares Kazantzakis's modernist techniques with those of Joyce.*]

[James Joyce] and Kazantzakis seemingly preside over opposite ends of the Modernist spectrum. Joyce is, after all, the most innovative of novelists, whereas Kazantzakis (aside from his subtly reflexive use of Matthew as a secondary point of view in *The Last Temptation of Christ*) seems almost Dickensian in his narration; certainly, as far as narrative technique is concerned at least, he . . . is closer to the Victorians than to his own contemporaries. Nevertheless, as unexpected as it may be, the parallel between Kazantzakis and Joyce does offer revealing insights into both writers—into their lives, into their work, into the use of their lives in their work. . . .

"Self exiled in upon his ego," [*Finnegans Wake*] the artist creates his fiction from the materials of his life. From the potentially heightened experiences of his youth, from even the pettiest details surrounding his family and friends, from the nation and religion that once nurtured him, he fashions image and metaphor for his art. As a young man he leaves his island homeland behind and comes before long to consider himself European, "myriadislanded"; yet he returns obsessively in his art to that earlier heritage—he even writes home to check out his facts. He encompasses as well the major intellectual currents of the century: Freud and Jung, Frazer and Marx, Bergson and the Existentialists—from folk tale to comparative myth, from the individual psyche to the history of the race—all these too find a place in his canon. He is influenced as well by traditional Romantic concerns: his life-long interest in demotic speech, resulting in the collecting and even in the coining of a few words, leads to puristic complaints that he is destroying the language for literature; his passion for freedom and the exotic leads him in his fiction to use the wandering Jews as a symbol of man's persistent alienation; in both his life and his work, he views himself as an exile, cut off from society because of his art. Above all, he dedicates himself like some hierophant to his art, putting behind him politics and family affairs, surrendering even his health—converting everything in life into matter for fiction: "brought to blood heat, gallic acid on iron ore, through the bowels of his misery, flashly, faithly, nastily, appropriately, . . . [he] wrote over every square inch of the only foolscap available, his own body" [*Finnegans Wake*]. He devotes more than a dozen years of his life to a single masterpiece.

Anyone familiar with Joyce will easily recognize him in this picture, but it is obvious . . . that it applies equally to Kazantzakis. Still, such a comparison of two such different writers must inevitably be a bit superficial—it may point up interesting connections between the sources of their art and their attitudes toward that art, but it tells us little about the art itself or about its relationship to the times in which it developed. For these we must look not to the lives of the artists or to their canons in general, but more specifically to their two Odysseys, the **Modern Sequel** of Kazantzakis and Joyce's *Ulysses,* which stand together as the greatest of modern epics—rivals as well, in their vastly different ways, of the greatest of ancient epics.

Ulysses at heart is a comic epic, an ironic inversion of Homeric myth that details the collapsing position of modern man. The representative hero of our myth-less time, Joyce repeatedly suggests, is inherently an outsider, an alien in the city of his birth, a failure as father, as husband, as man of affairs. As Joyce's hero Leopold Bloom spills his seed on the beach at Sandymount, we realize how far we have lapsed from the fertility of Homer's representative hero. But there is nothing comic about Kazantzakis' epic: in its diction, its hero, its handling of myth—in the philosophical premises upon which it is based—it strives for the grandeur of Homer and not for the humor of Joyce. His is not the small world of Dublin in 1904, or even of the Bronze Age Mediterranean; the mind and the travels of his Odysseus encompass all the known world and even beyond. Even in asceticism Kazantzakis' hero has a force and vigor unknown to Bloom, a sense that he controls not only his own destiny but the entire world, an awareness that he has mastered the world—that he can contend with the gods as an equal—because he has come to know himself fully. Wherever he goes, fertility follows; when he lies with the young girl on the way to Helen in Sparta and "flowers sprang up from sterile sands wherever she passed," we know that we are a long way from Sandymount and Bloom's spilled seed.

T. S. Eliot said of *Ulysses* that it set the pattern for all subsequent Modernist works in its treatment of myth. "In using the myth [of Ulysses]," Eliot pronounced, "in manipulating a continuous parallel between contemporaneity and antiquity, Mr. Joyce is pursuing a method which others must pursue after him. . . . It is simply a way of controlling, of ordering, of giving a shape and a significance to the immense panorama of futility and anarchy which is contemporary history." The mythic method, Eliot went on, is "a step toward making the modern world possible for art," toward developing "that order and form" which, in the years after the First World War, seemed to be lacking in life itself. As Eliot saw it in 1923, then—just one year after the novel's appearance—Joyce used myth in *Ulysses* as a means of giving order and meaning to art and thereby perhaps to life as well. Eliot, of course, did not know Kazantzakis' **Odyssey,** which would not appear in English translation for some thirty-five more years. But it is likely that he would have disapproved of it had he known it, for its conception of myth—and of life—is diametrically opposed to his own. To Kazantzakis, the function of myth is not simply to provide an orderly structure from which art can view life: myth, to Kazantzakis, is the very matter of life; it is myth that enables man to comprehend and to master his life, to rise above the circumstances of his time, and to achieve harmony with the experiences of other men in other times. For every generation, as Kazantzakis perceives it—even one as chaotic and self-destructive as his own—is capable of creating its own significant body of myth.

And so he gives us a sequel to Homer and not a parody, a work that attempts to recreate the spirit and tone of the original and not simply to invert it ironically.

If myth, as Joseph Campbell suggests [in his *The Hero with a Thousand Faces*], "is the secret opening through which the inexhaustible energies of the cosmos pour into human cultural manifestation," if a society reveals itself—its deepest concerns, its fears and desires—in its handling of myth, then it is apparent that we moderns reveal ourselves too in the uses to which we put the ancient mythologies. "It has always been the prime function of mythology and rite to supply the symbols that carry the human spirit forward, in counteraction to those other constant human fantasies that tend to tie it back." We are surprised perhaps to discover that Joyce too perceived this function of ritual and myth, to find that beneath the comic surface of his novel there emerges a genuine hero, of sorts. Half a century ago, Bloom seemed little more than a schlemiel, the first in a long line of negative heroes, an inescapable sign of the decay of our age. Today, from the perspective of Dachau, Hiroshima, and My Lai, the little man who retained his dignity and sense of humanity under inhumane circumstances may appear to us as genuinely heroic, worthy at least of respect if not quite of emulation—little enough perhaps, but better than no myth at all. Kazantzakis' hero, however, arising out of the same defeated generation, needs no such rationalization.

In the fertility of his myth-laden life, in the harmony that he achieves with the natural order, in his effort to reach out at his death somewhere beyond mortality, the Odysseus of Kazantzakis—indeed, all the heroes of his major fictions—serves not simply as a symbol of one generation but as archetype of man's perpetual search. "The hero," Campbell concludes, speaking of the archetype of our innermost dreams, "is the man . . . who has been able to battle past his personal and local historical limitations. . . . [His] visions . . . are eloquent, not of the present, disintegrating society and psyche, but of the unquenched source through which society is reborn. The hero has died as a modern man; but as eternal man—perfected, unspecific, universal man—he has been reborn." So Odysseus does more than carry forward the spirit of man in difficult times—a significant feat in itself as Bloom manages it; far more than the humanity of Bloom, more even than the persistence and cunning of Homer's protagonist, he offers in his myth a way for us all to surpass our times, to overcome our mortality. It is this vision of man's mythic potential—this sense of his enduring humanity—that ties Kazantzakis to Joyce and the other Modernists and at the same time distinguishes him from them: it is not alienation he gives us, but the possibility of reconciliation through myth—a vision derived, of course, from the experience of Crete.

We find in Kazantzakis' novels little of the narrative innovation that characterizes most Modernist fiction, little interest in the new Bergsonian flow of time (one aspect of Bergson's teaching that his student somehow ignored), little awareness of current reflexive techniques or modes of irony. The occasional exceptions to each of these points merely prove his fundamental indifference to them: he was evidently aware of their significance to the other novelists of his time yet found little use for them in his own work. Only through his handling of myth, that other major Modernist concern, can Kazantzakis be convincingly linked with his Modernist contemporaries, and even here his attitudes and approach are strikingly different from theirs. Where the function of myth to such writers as Eliot, Joyce, and Mann is in large part structural, to Kazantzakis it is a way of dealing with life itself—a matter of theme, that is, and not one of form, a quality inherent within life and not one to be imposed upon it. And when these other writers do deal with thematic overtones arising from myth—as Joyce does, as Lawrence does—they invariably do so as a means of expressing their alienation from a worthless society, convinced that we live in a new Iron Age, existing—to paraphrase Achilles in Hades—on iron rations and iron values. Something greater is at stake for Kazantzakis, however, some more compelling sense of what myth is and what we are, a far different perception both of the spirit and meaning of myth and of the possibilities still open to man even in a diminished age. Fully aware of the attitudes of his contemporaries, Kazantzakis continues to believe that man can find meaning and coherence in life, that through closeness to myth—to old myth and to new myth, to new myth sprung from the old—man can control and order his life as well as his art. (pp. 178-82)

Immersed as [Kazantzakis] was in the civilization of the West, . . . he could not deny its central theme: even in the most despairing of times, in the most destructive of circumstances, man can survive; by his struggle he can be ennobled. This vision goes directly against the past century and a half of Western literary experience—of the long, strait line that begins with the malaise of Stendhal's *The Red and the Black* in 1830, that continues with the total responsibility expressed in Gide's *The Immoralist* in 1921 and the total acceptance of Camus' *The Stranger* in 1942, and that appears to conclude with the dead-end denial of meaning and relevance in *In the Labyrinth* of Robbe-Grillet in 1959. . . .

[As] much as he may have been part of this intellectual tradition, Kazantzakis denies its terminal vision. Despite the evidence around him of man's degradation, despite the wisdom that insists that only nihilism is possible in such a world, that modern man is incapable of creating new and viable bodies of myth, Kazantzakis persists in affirming our value as humans, insists on our mythic potential. His reading of the Cretan experience, his use of the metaphor and myth emerging from Crete, lead almost inevitably to this choice. Modernist he may be, European he may have become, but in the end—as at the start—it is Crete he affirms. Like El Greco, his ancestor and townsman, Kazantzakis "inscribed [his] name wide and broad on [his] paintings, and below it, with magisterial pride, the title CRETAN." It is a legacy we might all do well to partake of. (p. 182)

> *Morton P. Levitt, in his* The Cretan Glance: The World and Art of Nikos Kazantzakis, *Ohio State University Press, 1980, 187 p.*

JOHN P. ANTON (essay date 1983)

[*Anton is an American philosopher and critic who specializes in the study of Greek thought. In the following excerpt, he analyzes Kazantzakis's concept of tragedy and notes its relation to both classical and modern literature.*]

The philosophical ethos of the classical world, with its humanistic and rational orientation, has been a heritage which Western man rediscovered and redefined many times. Often this heritage has been used to serve as a criterion by which to measure the quality of the accomplishments of the modern, not only in the arts, but also in philosophy and ethics and social policy. If the classical heritage is a source of funded ex-

perience, it is also a heavy burden, especially as it places before us standards by which to measure our own achievements in logical clarity, artistic excellence, and political insight. Opposed to the advocates of the Greek experience are those who find it overbearing, while others advise us to bypass or go beyond it, whatever the price. The modern Greeks are no exception to these trends. In a serious sense the modern Greeks are the direct heirs of the classical tradition, just as they are the rightful inhabitants of the land where this culture flourished. More than anyone else, they feel a deep need to respond to the heritage of Greece, impelled by necessity as well as choice. Nikos Kazantzakis, like other Greek poets and intellectuals, could not avoid this inevitable heritage. In fact, he faced it as a challenge.

Kazantzakis was born in Crete in 1883, when the island was still under the Turks. He matured during the first half of the twentieth century, as modern Greece was recovering from the defeat of 1897, when the Turkish army dealt a serious blow to both national pride and the hope to liberate the unredeemed Greeks still under Ottoman rule. Kazantzakis witnessed these developments as they affected the fortunes of the mainland and the political future of his own island after the turn of the century.

Much of the nineteenth century literary history of Greece reads like a series of chapters on the tensions between reactionary *literati,* the linguistic purists, advocating a "back to the classics" policy, and the emotionally charged reformers and staunch defenders of the "demotic" language of the people, who were trying their brand of romanticism in the realms of political and artistic expression. Kazantzakis saw the archeophiles carry the day. The genuinely reconstructive role that the classical heritage might have played during the critical period after the War of Independence in the early part of the nineteenth century is a topic too broad to be considered here. But the critical assessment of the place it came to occupy in the literary works of the post-liberation period, especially from the turn of the century onwards, deserves careful attention since it is germane to our theme.

Kazantzakis could not avoid taking a position toward the value of the classical ethos. In his case, we have a special reaction to it. He was born a Greek, yet intellectually he became attached to the spirit of modern Europe and an admirer of its finest expressions. But he also became an ardent student of the great men of the East, Buddha, Mohammed, Hideyoshi, and such countries as Russia, China, and Japan. His travels made him a citizen of the world. He felt a close affinity to all people and all nations, but the challenge that spurred him ahead was a quest rooted deeply in his heritage. It has often been said that our period, with all its soul-shaking and catastrophic events, has not been able to produce tragedies comparable to the classical and Elizabethan periods. This is a curious phenomenon but only peripherally related to our topic. However, insofar as classical tragedy was born in Greece and the experience from which it emerged is characteristically Hellenic, we want to ask two related questions: (a) how did the classical experience survive as part of neohellenic consciousness; and (b) how did the poets of modern Greece cope with the ancient conception of the tragic, and what meaning did it take in their vision of life?

The answers to these questions take on a special significance because the classical heritage attained ecumenical value after its first major diffusion in early Hellenistic times. The problem here is to identify the particular modes through which the poets of modern Greece sought to restate the ecumenical character of their heritage, particularly as responses to the tragic view of life. To press a Greek on this matter is tantamount to opening a wound, especially when that person is a poet. Yet, most contemporary Greek poets understand their mission the way Aeschylus did when Aristophanes had him declare in the *Frogs:* "We poets are the teachers of men." Kostís Palamás, one of the great poets of modern Greece, expressed the poet's mission with remarkable forthrightness in an article he published in 1898. He stated there:

> Our younger poets seem to have understood with increasing clarity that the only patriotism becoming a poet is one which at the same time reflects a conscientious and unselfish devotion to the art of poetry. They also seem to know that . . . the Greek poet, by using his great ancestors as a model, must be able above all to preserve his humanity, and also that true national poetry is poetry that does not belong exclusively to any one country.

Evidently Palamás had in mind a poetry deeply attached to the search for meaning in life, the understanding of the human condition, treating themes of freedom and fulfillment, love and death, war and peace, loss and recovery of fatherland, and the great return home, a person's *nostos.*

We will do well then to use the figure of Odysseus—that eternal Greek—and the concept of *nostos* to discuss the place of the tradition of the tragic in Kazantzakis's thought and poetry. The hero and his *nostos* help us focus on the Hellenic conception of the nature of man and the demand it poses for self-knowledge. Comparably, close inspection of the idea of Ithaca, as the end of *nostos,* can safely assist us to identify certain basic differences between the classical and modern modes of life. The intimation of this clue occurs repeatedly in Kazantzakis's writings. In a letter to his wife, dated January 1923, he wrote: "What you tell me is in truth my only worth—I struggle, I look forward like Odysseus, but without knowing if I shall ever anchor in Ithaca. Unless Ithaca is the voyage itself." There is a Caváfian ring to the last sentence, but the meaning Kazantzakis gave to it points in a different direction. Twenty-two years later he wrote to his literary friend A. Sahínis:

> No external passion ever upset me, be it wine, women, vanity or ambition. Only one passion excited me: contacting the Invisible Presence. At times it would be a struggle, at other times a conciliation, and only occasionally an identification with it. Give this Presence whatever name you wish. Call it God, Matter, Energy, Spirit, Mystery, Nothing. My entire work is nothing but this struggle, this conciliation, this identification with the Invisible Presence which I always fought to make visible.

Kazantzakis's relationship to classical Greece is not quite the same as his attitude toward his native island, Crete. To the latter he owes his "Cretan Glance," which is, as he explained so graphically in his *Report to Greco,* "to look upon fear with intrepidity." It is the Cretan determination that transubstantiates horror, "turning it into an exalted game in which man's virtue, in direct contact with mindless omnipotence, received stimulation and conquered—conquered without annihilating the bull, because it considered him not an enemy but a fellow worker." On the whole, his writings give the impression of a man whose self-consciousness as Greek is masked with waverings and ambiguities. Not everything that the term "Hellenic" denotes found a place in Kazantzakis's work. In fact,

much that he discerned and felt about the Hellenic world is deliberately excluded from his poetry and prose. In this respect, he is significantly different from Palamás and Sikelianós, and, in surprising ways, in sharp contrast to Caváfy's way of understanding the Hellenic experience. Kazantzakis took a very eclectic attitude toward the more than three thousand years of Greek history. Yet, his synoptic appreciation of Greece, as he states it in his *Report to Greco,* is filtered through a radical understanding of its historic mission and struggles: "Greece's position is truly tragic." Parts of his heritage he embraced with reservations, others unconditionally, and some he changed to suit his liking. There is a significant portion of it which he found quite foreign to his poetic temperament. It did not seem to him relevant to the new ways of the world. His post-Homeric Odysseus declares: "Athena's helmet, boys, has now been smashed to bits/nor can it ever again contain the whole world's head."

The idea that provides the best means to test Kazantzakis's Hellenism, its scope and quality, is the concept of the tragic. We may begin with the question: "What special meaning does 'the tragic' have in his work?" To answer it would require a careful examination of his views, from his early philosophical reflections in *The Saviors of God* and *The Odyssey: A Modern Sequel,* to his dramatic plays and mature novels. However, to do all this in one essay is simply impossible. But we can follow another path and begin by stating the various meanings of the tragic and then decide which one, if any, fits Kazantzakis's work. In so doing, I shall follow Albin Lesky's three types of "tragic conflict" to identify first the one that is properly associated with the classical view and then distinguish it from the type of conflict that Kazantzakis identifies as tragic.

According to Lesky, the most extreme concept of tragedy is the *totally tragic world view:* "This can be provisionally defined as the world conceived as a place where forces and values predestined to come into conflict will inevitably be destroyed; a destruction that remains unexplained by any transcendent purpose." Next comes the *total tragic conflict:* "Here also there is no escape and the end is destruction. But this conflict, however unalterable its course, does not embrace the whole world. It is only an occurrence within the world, so that what in this special case must end in death and destruction may be part of a transcendent totality, whose laws give it meaning. And if man should learn to recognize such laws and their workings, the conflict would be resolved on a higher level than the one on which it took its deadly course." The third type is the *tragic situation,* exhibiting the same components: ". . . opposing forces poised for battle: man, seeing no escape from perilous conflict, and realizing that he is doomed to destruction. But this anguished awareness of the inescapable, which is inherent in the tragic situation, need not be the end. The stormy heavens may break to shed the light of salvation."

What meaning from the above three does the "tragic" take in the works of a modern Cretan-Greek who adopts as his point of departure not Homer's *Iliad* but the *Odyssey,* who picks up only the name but not the substance of the Homeric hero and then sets him on a voyage of no return? Odysseus moves away from Greece after two intermediate stops in Sparta and Crete, on a course heading south ending finally in the frozen regions of the South Pole. The vision of life in this sequel to Homer's *Odyssey* selects only certain aspects from the Homeric age of Greece, bypasses the golden age of classical Athens, only to reemerge in a totally foreign landscape. The chronology of Kazantzakis's historical heroes is a curious one, to be sure. After his courtship with Homer, we find him enamored with the vestiges of Byzantine Christianity then steeped in nineteenth century ideologies and vitalistic philosophies, and finally rolling with the currents of social radicalism during the first half of twentieth-century Europe. Almost all the great men he admired and sought to emulate in highly selective ways were not Greeks: Buddha, Christ, Mohammed, Lenin, Don Quixote, Moses, Dante, Shakespeare, Leonardo da Vinci, Tolstoy, Genghis Khan, Nietzsche, Bergson. El Greco is one of the exceptions.

The tragic visions of life, a creation of the classical age of Greece, and the philosophies about them, did not influence Kazantzakis. Yet we may still want to ask whether some aspect of the classical conception of the tragic ever came to find a place in his life and work. The answer to this question will provide the solution to another perplexing problem: to what extent and in what sense is Kazantzakis a Greek? Is this major voice in contemporary European letters a Greek voice as well? Is Kazantzakis extending and continuing an essentially Greek view of life when he assumes the truth of his Cretan Glance to declare that Greece's position is truly tragic? Can it be that he is telescoping what he accepted or rejected in the Greek experience through the eyes of a contemporary European?

During the decade 1912-1922, Kazantzakis wrote three plays: **Odysseus, Christ,** and **Nikiphóros Phokás.** From the standpoint of historical time, these literary heroes are separated by approximately 1,000 years from one another. The first belongs to the Mycenean Age, the second to the Christian mid-point of history—or the *first* century—and the last to Byzantium, 1,000 years later. However that may be, it is Kazantzakis's conception of Odysseus that remains the pivotal point in his poetic universe. What needs to be considered is whether Odysseus as a modern hero satisfies the conditions of the tragic situation, as they prevail in classical dramaturgy. Therefore, in order to decide the issue, we must take another look at the classical sense of the tragic and then return to Kazantzakis.

Let us recall here what Aristotle says in his *Poetics* about the requirements for tragic character. First, we must remember what the Greeks believed to be the functions of tragedy: to educate in ethos, to produce a certain kind of pleasure by means of arousing pity and fear, to effect a certain catharsis or clarification and illumination of the passions involved. But to succeed in his purposes, the tragic poet must present his characters, the tragic heroes, in a certain light, otherwise the authentic nature of action in the play is lost. Thus, a tragic character must be neither a wicked man nor perfectly virtuous; rather, he must be something between the two extremes: "a man who is neither outstanding in virtue and righteousness, nor is it through wickedness and vice that he falls into misfortune, but through some flaw. He should also be famous or prosperous, like Oedipus, Thyestes, and the noted men of such noble families."

Is life *ultimately* tragic, in some sense of the word? The classical outlook precludes belief in a totally tragic world view. To speak of tragic possibilities of life is one thing, but the thesis that all life is ultimately tragic in the sense of being impregnated with antithetical forces at all times, is quite different. Lesky's position is that, of the three aforementioned meanings of the tragic, only the one he calls "the tragic situation"

primarily suits the Hellenic view of life as reflected in classical dramaturgy. He writes: "An Attic tragedy . . . may be considered genuinely tragic in so far as it presents a tragic situation, which may however be harmoniously resolved. On the other hand its theme may be a totally tragic conflict ending in death. The final scene of *Oedipus the King* belongs to this category, and here it is particularly important to ask whether we must assume that it reveals a fundamentally tragic world-view or whether the poet leaves open a way to liberation, to enlightened acceptance." The evidence favors acceptance of the final enlightenment as the correct interpretation. For the classical Greeks, the human condition is such that it produces from time to time certain soul-shaking conflicts which may in a number of cases end in catastrophe. However, Greek realism saw nothing inevitable in all that. Evil, they believed, is due to ignorance, not something absolute rooted in the nature of things. Life can be both comic and tragic, flat and superb.

When we come to Kazantzakis's modern and contemporary world, we are in a radically different landscape. The world must become what the world of the mind demands. This is not the Parmenidean view that equates thought and being. The modern poets went beyond the Kantian strictures that made science stay within the conditions of the possibility of experience and the categories of the understanding. The romantic imagination absorbed the universe within the infinite dimensions of its creative expansiveness. By extension, literature can claim to reflect faithfully, and better than science, as well as project authentically, the deeper layers of the human situation. Kazantzakis subscribes to this principle, and this explains why there is a very close relationship between what this poet portrays through his heroes and how he himself understands the nature of life. Thus Kazantzakis creates heroes who are true to his vision of life. He meets at the level of literature Nietzsche's criterion: "The great man is the actor of his ideals."

The position that literature, and *more so than science,* discloses authentically the nature of man is more modern than it is classical. On this issue we have the solid testimonies of Plato and Aristotle. Kazantzakis is modern in at least two senses: (a) his heroes are meant to reflect the very essence of life; (b) his literary works mirror life at the peak of human experience and therefore its truest moment. This is so because literature is taken to be a supreme expression of life itself. After much searching and agonizing, he came to the conclusion that, since life is ultimately tragic, its irreducible antithetical forces define both the poet and his work. The tragic contradictions of life are the bread and blood of the artist.

Kazantzakis as poet and philosopher was quick to explore the thematic richness that the idea of the irreconcilable forces in life had for literature. Often he would speak of them in mythic terms as the eternal conflict between the Apollonian and the Dionysian elements in man's struggle for freedom. When in a confessional mood, he would state and declare that his own personal problem was the enormous strength of the instincts he inherited from his ancestors, forcing upon him contrary actions in every turn of his life. The search for deliverance was decidedly in favor of the ways of the spirit, urging him to transcend all antithetical and exclusive demands. This is not exactly Hegelian in its conceptualization, but one would not hesitate in this connection to call it dialectical voluntarism. Be that as it may, the way of the spirit is to do the will of God and save God as the God-in-man, the same God who establishes order and makes laws and is also the God who turns the edifice into ruins to return it to chaos. It is this dynamic view of antithetical constancy that makes difficult comparisons and contrasts with the classical conception of modes to resolve the tensions between conflicting forces.

A certain similarity is still discernible even when the differences remain perceptibly stronger. We have here a case of subtle continuity and radical discontinuity with the classical heritage. Both aspects are worth exploring in detail—a task that will require the length of a special monograph—because the fact is that Kazantzakis, with all his modernity, is significantly extending what he found relevant in the classical tradition to his agonizing concern to clarify the meaning of human destiny. One way of making a sharp contrast between a classical tragic poet and Kazantzakis as a modern would be to say that, for instance, Sophocles' *Oedipus* or Euripides' *Medea*, issues a real warning and offers a lesson on what not to do. Somehow, imitative action in tragedy is presented as exposure to the consequences of *hamartia,* of judgment gone wrong. Still, the constructive possibility of contributing to the inculcation of *sophrosyne* ["wisdom"] in the souls of the attending public is one of the great moral and political assets of Greek dramaturgy. In contrast, Kazantzakis's vision of life questions the valued finality of prudence and serenity. His poetry embodies the urgency to bold action and makes it the nerve center of the literary expression of life. Thus, Kazantzakis tells his readers, through his heroes, what living is about and how to be true to the dynamic movement that life is. Consider, for instance, how this is done in his novels. In all of them, the central hero must make the claim that the quintessence of life is expressed through his actions and decisions. In other words, the hero recapitulates the universe and completes it. The all is in man, and all mankind is expressed through the heroic man, not as *logos* but as will. This is dialectical voluntarism. Here the modern and the classical models of *microcosmos-macrocosmos* are at polar opposites! No ancient Greek would have dared to call man "savior of God" as Kazantzakis did. Nietzsche issued the pronouncement, "God is dead!" Kazantzakis came to herald the most radical message of resurrection: "Man becomes God and saves God." Man takes on properties of the divine by accepting his responsibilities of the divine to save God.

After Kazantzakis there can be no higher form of *hubris* (excess pride). Within certain limitations, the self-deification of man can go no further. The limitation is this: it is man's responsibility to save God not to be all that God is. The old ideal of aspiring to be god-like, *theoeides,* the ideal of *homoiōsis theō,* must be declared obsolete since the new dynamic conception of God makes him both infinite and unfinished. The problem is not with man's limited perception of the infinite wisdom and perfection of God; the problem is with the unfinished nature of God. As a consequence, man is responsible for the completion of the divine process. Man is forced with the role of taking on whatever attributes of God he can by his nature and ability to apprehend his chain of duties. The conviction that God is the presence of the creative and fighting force in all beings and in every person carries with it serious implications for human action and thought. If everything is of God and has a portion of God in it, what differentiates one person from another lies in the potential to rise to the call of the duty to transmute the divine force into spirit. While passivity compromises the divine, correctly guided activity (synthesis) gives to praxis its creative thrust. Since what is active is potentially creative, the attainment of

higher levels of creativity is a function of responsible activity to increase and intensify the spirit. Thus it would follow that the only criterion to ascertain the level and degree of moral worth in a person can be one of qualitative engagement in creativity as each person ascends or descends on the ladder of duties. These abstract expressions, assuming that they represent Kazantzakis's thinking, cannot take on real significance unless the divine force in a person's life is allowed to surface and climb upward toward the light of responsibility. It is against this background that we can see why Kazantzakis embodied in his writings a radical approach to the concept of the tragic. As such, his answer may be seen as a synthesis of the old and the modern, the classical and the contemporary.

For Kazantzakis, the tragic conflict is rooted in the fundamental antinomies that pervade nature and man. Among them is the continuous conflict between man's will to freedom and the knowledge that total freedom is unrealizable. Hence man is forced to consent to relative freedom while the craving for the absolute persists without hope for relief. The challenge now is how to understand the human predicament without resorting to a passive pessimism or escaping to the region of optimism. The problem of understanding is not the art of analyzing alternatives but assisting in the determination to proceed with the life of praxis in spite of the knowledge about the unattainability of the end. In the *Salvatores Dei,* Kazantzakis declares that the highest virtue for the man of action "is not to be free but to fight for freedom." Praxis itself "is the wide gateway leading to deliverance." Whatever salvation there is for man can only come through the determination to act against all odds, fully aware of the conditions that make the pursuit hopeless.

The essential condition of the tragic in Kazantzakis is the awareness of conflicts from which there can be no final escape. Once man is caught in the snares of cosmic tensions and is fully cognizant of his situation, he must reject both optimism and pessimism, and then be ready to arm himself with the defiance to face death itself. Like Captain Michalis who opts for "Freedom and Death," Manolios in *Christ Recrucified* accepts death willingly—Manolios in the name of a social ideal, Michalis while defending the fatherland. In both heroes we witness a meeting of freedom and death as the peak experience of human life.

A closer look at the *personae* that populate his epic and his novels leads the reader to say that Kazantzakis essentially works with two types of man: the conventional type, variations of which fill the background—not unlike Homer in this regard—and the heroic. The latter permits a distinction between the *tragic persona*—that is, one who in due course becomes involved in the pursuit of impossible tasks, like Julian, Capodistrias, Constantine Paleologos—and the authentically *assertive persona,* like Zorba, who acts spontaneously and moves beyond conventional morality and the world of safe values, as Odysseus does in the earlier books of the *Odyssey.* The important thing here is to grasp Kazantzakis's argument on which he bases his conception of the heroic man. A basic premise here is that even if the world forces upon us the paradox of freedom, man can still be creative. We may now move away from the strong metaphors he uses in his *Saviors of God* to define the highest virtue. Actually, we are dealing with a bold recasting of Plato's view of courage, knowing what to fear and what not to fear. For Kazantzakis, courage is the highest virtue once it is recast to mean to act knowingly, not to fear absolute hopelessness, and not to be afraid to accept death as deliverance from the craving of freedom through the struggle to be free. Neither the *tragic* nor the *assertive persona* is prepared to settle for limited freedom. The difference lies in the circumstances. Given the opportunity, the challenge, and a choice, the assertive man will unhesitatingly cross over the line and enter the domain of the tragic experience.

As a result of the recasting of the meaning of virtue and the paradox of freedom, the classical view of *hubris* or excess pride no longer retains its original meaning. Kazantzakis has turned defiance, total and uncompromising, into a basic and necessary excellence of the hero-martyr. In other words, defiance is not a tragic flaw but a sweeping force and primordial motive. It is the voice of the struggling god within man demanding to be set free. Defiance does not challenge the power of the gods; it is a heralding of the beginning of action to save the divine. When Kazantzakis's tragic hero meets death, he has fully realized the identity between hopelessness and freedom. In contrast, the classical hero, who loves life and abhors destruction, fights for the best and meets his destiny, not because he wills it but because things got out of control: his errors of judgment are due to his *hubris* and/or limitations. In contrast, Kazantzakis has given us a radical concept of the tragic and, along with it a tragic vision appropriate to man's voyage setting out on the pursuit of absolute freedom as a savior of God. This is the new *nostos,* if a *nostos* at all. Evidently, Sophocles' and Kazantzakis's views of human nature and man's place in the universe—indeed, what the world ultimately is—are not the same. The corresponding visions of destiny move in different directions.

At his most expressive and authentic moments, man is a voyager with no Ithaca; rebel and restless, a desperado, scavenger, ravager and pirate; uprooted and estranged but only because he has no choice, thus making this his choice. For man to be true to his nature, to the divine in him, there is no situation, physical or human, in nature or in culture, that can fully arrest and contain the creative energy. The conventional realities can only provoke this rebel-man to negate established values. Reality, in any case, is a problem, not the solution. Herein lies the *external* condition for the paradox of freedom. But to effect a solution, however temporary, man as hero must step outside the circle of theories, ideas and ideologies, tastes and preferences. He must seal the quest to save the divine by means of his death at the moment of its ultimate transcendence.

But now we are beyond tragedy. In any event, the classical view of the tragic no longer obtains in this case of the contemporary conception of the relationship between man's development and the persistence of conflicting forces in life. Kazantzakis, we tend to suspect, recognized the incongruity and intentionally bypassed the classical conception of resolving tragic conflicts. Therefore, it is no surprise that he advocated radical reformulations of the human quest in life and in art. The modern Odysseus, or any hero like him, must keep going. "The essence of our God is STRUGGLE. . . ." Again, we read in **The Saviors of God** the basic motif: "It is not God who will save us . . . it is we who will save God, by battling, by transmuting matter into spirit." This itself involves a radical view of God. The traditional religions which made man dependent upon God are all rejected. Again and again, his Odysseus remains determined to cast down every idol and denounce every form of worship, philosophy, social value, and political structure, including those he will erect

himself in the course of his adventures. He must be and stay free to reject and to seek: ready to transcend everything, including himself. This is true about Kazantzakis himself, the creator of his modern Odysseus. The true hero cannot turn back; he can never denounce the veracity of the demand for continuous self-transcendence. To do so would be to choose the path of the coward.

The problem of form must be raised at this point. In order to express his *credo,* Kazantzakis turns to art, and especially to song, *tragoúdi*—the modern Greek derivative from the ancient *"tragōdia." Tragoúdi* is not tragic drama but lyrical action that takes us beyond tragedy. The word now comes to signify a higher mode of art, the personal creative song. The supreme *logos* as song, while inescapably communicative and communal, is also the dramatic dialogue of inner conflicts, lyrical in its mood and individual in expression. Once again, in the selection of artistic media, Kazantzakis will part company with the classical view of tragedy and its dependence on external elements to present its hold on the fundamental problems that haunt humanity. He is convinced that the vision of life does not blossom as rational philosophy and logic but in art and *tragoúdi* as the creative act of transcendence.

When Odysseus is ready to denounce everything, all that the world contains, the only creative act and reality he is still willing to accept is art as lyric drama. The value of song is repeatedly introduced in the **Odyssey** as a test of superior choice. The Egyptian king exchanges a whole empire for a song. Captain Elias sacrifices his seven sons in return for a song that will allow him to live as immortal flame. He believed what the cock-pheasant told him:

> All flow on toward the sea and drown in that dark
> stream,
> great towns and all their souls submerge, all women
> rot,
> all gold crowns rot, and even gods rot like trees;
> don't cling to them, O Prince, they fade like whirl-
> ing smoke,
> the only deathless flame is man's own gallant song!

Song alone reveals contemporary man to himself. But freedom demands that Kazantzakis go beyond it; the only thing awaiting there is death. Beyond art, when freedom becomes absolute, lies the Great Nothing. By knowing his hopelessness, man triumphs over all forms of temptation, conquers despair, and with a literal *salto mortale* ["dance of death"] saves the divine. Without *tragoúdi,* the highest form and substance of the creative life, the fighting man cannot save God. In this identification of art and holiness, we find the key to Kazantzakis's radical religion. The artist has a duty to remain defiant in the fight to transmute his being and his world into spirit. This duty must reign supreme above all else, for it aims at a value higher than beauty and truth.

Tragoúdi is more than form. It is the definitive statement on substance which summarizes a whole culture. The fate of *tragoúdi,* the fate of art, is inseparable from the destiny of Western man in his contemporary setting, as he looks intensely into the abyss only to see his reflection before the balance is lost. *Tragoúdi* becomes the first word of life and the first word of death; it is the record of the phases of God's salvation through the creativity of the human spirit. The romantic mind cannot go beyond this point. The artist as poet, Kazantzakis holds, has seen more clearly than either the philosopher or the statesman what the contemporary ethos portends with its increasing dependence on utility and greed. It is the artist who sees freedom in all its dimensions, the risks it involves, the sacrifices it demands, the promises it holds, the horrors that attend its loss.

Kazantzakis proved to be more Nietzschean than Nietzsche. He saw clearly the implications of the most terrifying diagnosis of the contemporary scene: the Nietzschean interpretation of man, a view that aspired to go beyond tragedy and comedy, beyond Dionysus and Apollo, and assert the self-deification of man. When Kazantzakis brought out into the open the implications of the Gothic and romantic philosophical visions of Nietzsche, Bergson, and other major European writers, he did so in order to complete the portrait of modern *hubris* and help us learn to face its horrors. Once the romantic demand for total self-transcendence is accepted, man's ultimate goal becomes one of how to play at being God and make it stick!

Kazantzakis completes the modern and concludes it. Yet there is more to the positive side of his contribution which often takes the form of a promise and a prophecy. In a sense, his works are anticipations of a future, a foretaste of things to come. This poet who so bravely essayed to save the divine in him may also be seen as a prelude to a new classical era and his work as being at once pre-epic and pre-tragic. By scanning the full range of his self-consciousness, Kazantzakis found a way to pave the way to resurrect the concept of the tragic with the power of his own creative insights. It may well be that he mapped the way the literature of the future must follow in order to move from *tragoúdi* toward the discovery of a new form of tragedy.

No matter what our reservations may be on particular issues, the fact remains that Kazantzakis has his own answer to Lesky's question about the quest for tragic resolution in non-classical drama. The way it works in his case is precisely what brings him closer to classical tragedy than one may initially suspect. Resolution is recast in the form of a series of syntheses to respond to a series of emerging conflicts in the unfolding of human action. The following steps may help to make the solution clear.

1. Life exhibits a continuous series of conflicts due to the persistence of antithetical forces.
2. A synthesis of antitheses must be brought about through constructive action and avoidance of destruction.
3. The *agon,* the struggle, leads to synthesis only if it enhances the spirit.
4. The resolution announced with each creative action brings temporary relief and a provisional catharsis.
5. New antitheses emerge, demanding response to effect novel resolutions of tragic conflicts.
6. The tragic situation continues its upward spiraling in each person's life when in the aftermath of each conciliation the hero's outlook remains uncompromising.
7. Every human being is privileged to be a savior of God and is therefore caught in the web of tragedy, though not every person is willing to pay the price of the virtue of courage.

This outline of the concept of tragic resolution does not conform to the principles of dramaturgy as presented in Aristotle's *Poetics.* It is closer to the dramatic logic of the modern novel than it is to classical tragedy. Failure to transmute matter into spirit is not like effecting catharsis in the wake of *hamartia.* Failure in the former case, Kazantzakis would say, is tantamount to failing God; in the case of the Greek tragedians, when we err in judgment, we fail ourselves, and in a fundamental way, we fail our *polis.*

On the one hand, Kazantzakis is a profound diagnostician of the barbarism that follows in the wake of freedom misunderstood and misused. His ***Odyssey*** portrays vividly what happens to cultures when the spirit disintegrates or indulges in compromise of quality. On the other, he leads the way in the effort to study the unfinished work of the Renaissance in order to complete the creative rediscovery of the classical mind through a new synthesis. And it may well be that this *enfant terrible* of modern Greece stands firmly somewhere between the present and the future, like a vast ocean between two continents whose depth and span we must try to fathom before we may gain enough confidence to set out on our voyage to Ithaca. (pp. 53-67)

> *John P. Anton, "Kazantzakis and the Tradition of the Tragic," in* The Journal of the Hellenic Diaspora, *Vol. X, No. 4, Winter, 1983, pp. 53-67.*

ADDITIONAL BIBLIOGRAPHY

Bien, Peter. "Nikos Kazantzakis (1883-1957)." In *The Politics of Twentieth-Century Novelists,* edited by George A. Panichas, pp. 137-59. New York: Hawthorn Books, 1971.
> Discusses the development of Kazantzakis's political attitudes and their impact upon his early writings.

———. *Kazantzakis and the Linguistic Revolution in Greek Literature.* Princeton, N. J.: Princeton University Press, 1972, 291 p.
> Comprehensive analysis of Kazantzakis's use of modern demotic Greek in his writings.

———. *Nikos Kazantzakis.* New York: Columbia University Press, 1972, 48 p.
> Brief critical biography.

———. *Tempted by Happiness: Kazantzakis's Post-Christian Christ.* Wallingford, Pa.: Pendle Hill, 1984, 23 p.
> Discusses *The Last Temptation of Christ.*

Chilson, Richard W. "The Christ of Nikos Kazantzakis." *Thought* 47, No. 184 (Spring 1972): 69-89.
> Two-part study of Kazantzakis's concept of Christ. In Part 1, Chilson traces the development of Kazantzakis's philosophy, and in Part 2 he discusses the author's depictions of Christ within the context of that development, noting: "Kazantzakis' Jesus can only be understood in terms of Kazantzakis' own life and thought. . . . No longer the savior of mankind, Christ becomes one of the saviors of God. He belongs to a race of men who help the spirit which is struggling through matter to attain freedom."

Decavalles, Andonis, and Coxe, Louis O. "Two Views of Kazantzakis." *Poetry* 95, No. 3 (December 1959): 175-81.
> Contrasting reviews of Kimon Friar's translation of *The Odyssey: A Modern Sequel.* Decavalles gives a positive assessment of the work, describing it as "the mature product of Kazantzakis' deep familiarity with the best in world-literature and thought," while Coxe finds it "a crashing bore" and "wholly misconceived."

Elsman, Kenneth R., and Knapp, John V. "Life-Span Development in Kazantzakis's *Zorba the Greek.*" *International Fiction Review* 11, No. 1 (Winter 1984): 37-44.

>   Considers *Zorba the Greek* as an unintentional demonstration of the psychodynamic personality theories of psychologists Daniel J. Levinson and Sharon B. Merriam.

Glicksberg, Charles I. "Kazantzakis: Dionysian Nihilism." In his *The Literature of Nihilism,* pp. 275-99. Lewisburg, Pa.: Bucknell University Press, 1975.

>   Analysis of Kazantzakis's highly personalized nihilism.

Journal of the Hellenic Diaspora, Special Issue: Nikos Kazantzakis 10, No. 4 (Winter 1983): 1-101.

>   Includes: "*Christopher Columbus:* Kazantzakis's Final Play" by Peter Bien, "Homer, Joyce, Kazantzakis: Modernism and the Epic Tradition" by Morton P. Levitt, "Kazantzakis's *Buddha:* Phantasmagoria and Struggle" by Katerina Angelaki-Rooke, as well as tributes by friends and colleagues.

Journal of Modern Literature: Nikos Kazantzakis Special Number 2, No. 2 (1971-1972): 163-326.

>   Special issue devoted to Kazantzakis that includes contributions by noted scholars Morton P. Levitt, Kimon Friar, Andreas K. Poulakidas, and Peter Bien. Also includes bibliographical essay by Donald Falconio.

Kazantzakis, Helen. *Nikos Kazantzakis: A Biography Based on His Letters.* Translated by Amy Mims. New York: Simon and Schuster, 1968, 589 p.

>   Biography by Kazantzakis's second wife.

Merrill, Reed B. "*Zorba the Greek* and Nietzschean Nihilism." *Mosaic* 8, No. 2 (Winter 1975): 99-113.

>   Examines differences between the character of Zorba and Nietzsche's Superman.

Osborn, Ronald E. "A Modern Man's Search for Salvation: Nikos Kazantzakis and His 'Odyssey'." *Encounter* 35, No. 2 (Spring 1974): 121-31.

>   Analyzes Kazantzakis's interpretation of salvation in his *Odyssey.*

Poulakidas, Andreas K. "Kazantzakis' *Zorba the Greek* and Nietzsche's *Thus Spake Zarathustra.*" *Philological Quarterly* 49, No. 2 (April 1970): 234-44.

>   Compares Zorba and Zarathustra.

Prevelakis, Pandelis. *Nikos Kazantzakis and His Odyssey: A Study of the Poet and the Poem.* Translated by Philip Sherrard. New York: Simon and Schuster, 1961, 192 p.

>   Three-part study of Kazantzakis's life, his epic poem *The Odyssey: A Modern Sequel,* and the relation between the two [excerpted in *TCLC,* Vol. 2].

Raizis, M. Byron. "Symbolism and Meaning in Kazantzakis' *The Greek Passion.*" *Ball State University Forum* 11, No. 3 (Summer 1970): 57-66.

>   Examines the significance of the symbolic characterizations in *The Greek Passion.*

Richards, Lewis A. "Fact and Fiction in Nikos Kazantzakis' *Alexis Zorbas.*" *Western Humanities Review* 18, No. 4 (Autumn 1964): 353-59.

>   Discusses significant discrepancies between Kazantzakis's account of his relationship with Zorba in *Zorba the Greek* and the biographical facts upon which the account is based.

Scouffas, George. "Kazantzakis: Odysseus and the 'Cage of Freedom'." *Accent* 19, No. 4 (Autumn 1959): 234-46.

>   Analyzes Kazantzakis's exploration of the meaning of freedom in his *Odyssey.* According to Scouffas: "Since Kazantzakis brings to bear on his subject a lifetime of study in philosophy, anthropology, history, religion, and literature, the result is that the basic terms of the exploration become a catalogue of the central motifs and dilemmas of modern Western literature. For it is his purpose to expose Odysseus to all the strains and counter-strains that beset modern man, to guide him to a revelatory synthesis that can give him clarity of understanding and ultimate peace, and to do this without depriving him of his status as a man."

Stavrou, C. N. "Mr. Bloom and Nikos' Odysseus." *South Atlantic Quarterly* 62 (1963): 107-18.

>   Examines "interesting parallels and illuminating differences in the portraits of Homer's Odysseus as drawn by Joyce and Kazantzakis."

Vasils, Theodora. Introduction to *Serpent and Lily,* by Nikos Kazantzakis, pp. 1-18. Berkeley: University of California Press, 1980.

>   Provides background information concerning the composition of Kazantzakis's works.

D(avid) H(erbert) Lawrence

1885-1930

(Also wrote under the pseudonym Lawrence H. Davison)
English novelist, short story writer, poet, essayist, translator,
and dramatist.

The following entry presents criticism of Lawrence's novel
Women in Love (1920). For discussion of Lawrence's complete career, see *TCLC*, Volumes 2 and 9; for criticism focusing on the novel *Sons and Lovers*, see *TCLC*, Volume 16.

Women in Love is considered the most artistically accomplished expression of Lawrence's concern with the nature of
self-fulfillment, relationships between individuals, and the relationship of individuals to society—matters that he explored
throughout his career. The novel examines marriage, family
affiliations, friendships, and social roles with the psychological acuity that characterizes much of Lawrence's work.
Many critics consider *Women in Love* the first work of Lawrence's artistic maturity, that is, his first to rely more heavily
on narrative invention than on autobiographical documentation; critics also note that the novel is free from the didacticism that pervades Lawrence's later novels. *Women in Love*
also displays Lawrence's most radical innovations in his
search for a specialized vocabulary to convey states of emotion and consciousness, as well as to describe sexual encounters. This particular emphasis on sexuality made the novel
controversial upon its appearance, and debate over its autobiographical bases, use of language, social criticisms, and
characterizations, among other issues, has continued to the
present, with most commentators assessing it as one of the
most important novels in twentieth-century literature. F. H.
Langman has maintained that, "*Women in Love* places Lawrence in the line of European writers who, from Dostoevsky
on, have made the novel the medium of at once the most
deeply felt social awareness and the most urgent philosophical speculation."

Women in Love was originally intended to be part of a longer
novel, tentatively entitled *The Sisters* (sometimes referred to
during composition as *The Wedding Ring*). This ambitious
work ultimately became two separate but roughly contiguous
narratives: *The Rainbow,* published in 1915, and *Women in
Love,* which appeared in 1920. Lawrence's letters reveal that
composition began late in 1912, while he was living abroad
with Frieda von Richthofen Weekley, whom he later married, and the turbulence of their early years together is reflected in the changing tenor of early drafts of the two novels.
Set in the years preceding World War I, *Women in Love* was
largely composed during the war and is informed by the sense
of apocalypse that overwhelmed much of Europe at that
time. Lawrence was repelled by the savagery of the war and
disheartened by the loss of friends and acquaintances. This
was also a period of both financial and personal crisis for
Lawrence, who had not yet achieved success as an author and
was concerned about the stability of his marriage. Further,
his return to England during wartime was marred by incidents of harassment by neighbors who suspected that Lawrence, with a German wife and no visible means of support,
might be an enemy spy.

In its final form *The Rainbow* represented Lawrence's most
complex and demanding narrative to that time. Introducing
psychological themes into the narrative framework of a family chronicle, the novel concerns three generations of the
Brangwen family and focuses on relationships between men
and women. *The Rainbow* was refused by Lawrence's usual
publisher and appeared only after Lawrence had rewritten
some passages and excised others that the new publisher considered too sexually explicit. Even in its revised form, the
novel was suppressed in England as obscene. This censorship
of his work enraged Lawrence and left him hesitant to seek
publication for *Women in Love.* He wrote to a friend in 1916:
"I have written a novel, called *Women in Love.* It is a sequel
to *The Rainbow,* but very different. But whether, after *The
Rainbow* affair . . . it will find a publisher, I don't know, and
don't very much care. It is a very good piece of work: in fact,
a masterpiece. So it will keep. What is the good of its coming
out into the orgy of baseness which is today." Concern about
censorship was not the only obstacle to publication: several
friends and acquaintances of Lawrence, who read or heard
about the novel while it was in manuscript, believed that they
had been unflatteringly depicted and threatened lawsuits before the work was published. Acting on his publisher's advice, Lawrence made alterations that were intended to prevent identification of the people on whom he had based his

characters. Several individuals renewed their threats upon the novel's appearance, but no charges of libel were ever brought.

Women in Love examines the relationships entered into by Ursula and Gudrun Brangwen, a schoolteacher and an artist who have temporarily returned to their parents' home in the colliery town of Beldover. Ursula eventually marries school inspector Rupert Birkin; Gudrun's affair with Gerald Crich, a local mine owner's son, ends when he attempts to kill her. Many commentators contend that Lawrence's intention in writing the novel was to contrast the mutually destructive alliance of Gerald and Gudrun, which cannot succeed because of their moral and spiritual flaws, with that of Birkin and Ursula, which does succeed because the two partners are able to address their problems as a couple while preserving their individuality, a state described in the novel as a "mutual union in separateness." However, other critics conclude that the destinies of the two couples, as F. H. Langman has stated, "do not represent the assured positive solution and a disastrous deviation from it, but something far less definite: a contrast of attitudes, hope against despair, struggle against surrender." Many commentators further note that the Birkin-Ursula relationship is fraught with tension that remains unresolved at the novel's conclusion. Another relationship explored in *Women in Love* is that of *Blutbrüderschaft,* or "blood brotherhood," a close association between men, never fully explicated, that Birkin proposes to Gerald as a complement to their relationships with women. This aspect of the novel is often biographically interpreted, with commentators remarking upon Lawrence's professed wish for such alliances with friends. Biographers dispute the exact nature of the relationships Lawrence desired, in particular the question of whether these relationships possessed a homosexual component.

In *The Rainbow* Lawrence first sought to develop a specialized vocabulary to describe and define various experiences, and he continued this process in *Women in Love,* attempting to convey thought and emotional states with the same intensity and vividness as physical acts. The result was a narrative style marked by continual repetition of key words and phrases, and the frequent use—many commentators contend, overuse—of modifiers and intensifiers. Because his terminology and symbols were intensely personal, however, this often resulted in obscure, almost unintelligible prose. While Lawrence maintained that repetition is suited to the evocation of mental processes, critics generally agree that his attempts to evoke stream of consciousness are often awkward and ineffective, particularly when compared with the similar literary experimentation of such contemporaries as James Joyce and Virginia Woolf. Derek Bickerton termed one example from the novel "an attempt to inflate a perfectly ordinary situation . . . into an experience of supra-normal significance, by an accumulation of highly emotive but almost meaningless adjectives," and several commentators have suggested that this linguistic imprecision reflects Lawrence's uncertainty about the convictions and the values he wanted to impart in the novel. Although a few critics have commended the language of *Women in Love,* most concur that Lawrence's turgid prose style seriously flaws the novel.

Lawrence's presentation of character in *Women in Love* has also received close critical attention. As Mark Schorer has written, with this novel "the whole notion of character in fiction undergoes an alteration. [Lawrence] will now create

more *essential* beings, will be concerned first of all not with the 'ego' that interests the traditional novelist, but with the 'primal forces' that are prior to 'character'." Lawrence himself wrote in an often-quoted letter to Richard Garnett in 1914, "That which is physic—non-human, in humanity, is more interesting to me than the old-fashioned human element—which causes one to conceive a character in a certain moral scheme and make him consistent. . . . You mustn't look in my novel for the old stable *ego* of the character." In the novel itself, Birkin explains to Ursula, "I want to find you, where you don't know your own existence, the you that your common self denies utterly." Most critics agree that Lawrence's portrayal of the mental and emotional lives of his central characters was effective, if sometimes difficult to understand; many also note that the novel contains a number of carefully delineated, fully realized minor characters.

In Lawrence's fiction, characters are often defined by their relationship to the antagonistic worlds represented by industry and nature. A character's association with industry is generally an indication of moral or spiritual deficiency, while soundness is often signified by closeness to nature. Lawrence developed this contrast most explicitly in *Lady Chatterley's Lover* (1928). In *Women in Love,* Lawrence's hostility toward industrialization is most clearly embodied in the character of Gerald Crich, who devotes himself to the efficient management of his father's mines and thereby insures the emptiness and meaninglessness of his life. According to H. M. Daleski, "Lawrence's criticism of pre-war England is centred in [his] devastating analysis of Gerald's efficiency. It is one of the points on which the whole novel converges. . . . [The mines] are clearly a symbol of the industrial complex which is modern civilization." In Lawrence's view, it is the decadent culture of prewar England that produces the energetic but spiritually void Gerald. Birkin and Ursula, the novel's two most vital and positively presented characters, choose to withdraw from society, and most commentators conclude that at the time of writing *Women in Love,* withdrawal represented for Lawrence the best way to avoid moral disintegration.

Early critical commentary on *Women in Love* gave no indication of the novel's later reputation as a literary classic. Reviews almost invariably focused upon the novel's sexual content, and charged that the language was unclear and the characters poorly differentiated. Although some later commentators grant a certain amount of validity to these evaluations, most maintain that the difficulties of comprehension initially caused by the nontraditional aspects of the novel have yielded to study. Many critics who esteem the novel, including F. R. Leavis, admit that they reached a favorable assessment only after multiple readings. Some recommend a prior reading of *The Rainbow* for knowledge of the social background and important symbols that recur in *Women in Love,* and of the essays *Psychoanalysis and the Unconscious* (1921) and *Fantasia of the Unconscious* (1922) for exposition of the philosophical ideas that underlie the novel. Familiarity with this literary and intellectual background to *Women in Love,* critics maintain, will give the reader a firm basis for the appreciation of Lawrence's achievement: a novel that is far more than the exposition in fictional form of a body of philosophical ideas, but a successful work of fiction that embodies and imparts these ideas.

While Lawrence portrayed various personal and social problems in *Women in Love,* he did not supply solutions to them. Lawrence maintained that the novelist's role was not to provide answers to the problems besetting individuals, couples, and modern society, but rather to evoke the "change and flow and incongruity" of life and so create "truth to the living moment." Most critics agree that with *Women in Love* Lawrence accomplished this, vividly portraying human relationships against the background of prewar English society.

(See also *Contemporary Authors,* Vols. 104 and 121, and *Dictionary of Literary Biography,* Vols. 10, 19, and 36.)

D. H. LAWRENCE (essay date 1919)

[*In his introduction to the first American edition of* Women in Love, *Lawrence comments on the circumstances of its composition and addresses charges of eroticism and flawed narrative style.*]

[*Women in Love*] was written in its first form in the Tyrol, in 1913. It was altogether re-written and finished in Cornwall in 1917. So that it is a novel which took its final shape in the midst of the period of war, though it does not concern the war itself. I should wish the time to remain unfixed, so that the bitterness of the war may be taken for granted in the characters.

The book has been offered to various London publishers. Their almost inevitable reply has been: "We should like very much to publish, but feel we cannot risk a prosecution." They remember the fate of *The Rainbow,* and are cautious. This book is a potential sequel to *The Rainbow.*

In England, I would never try to justify myself against any accusation. But to the Americans, perhaps I may speak for myself. I am accused, in England, of uncleanness and pornography. I deny the charge, and take no further notice.

In America the chief accusation seems to be one of "Eroticism." This is odd, rather puzzling to my mind. Which Eros? Eros of the jaunty "amours," or Eros of the sacred mysteries? And if the latter, why accuse, why not respect, even venerate?

Let us hesitate no longer to announce that the sensual passions and mysteries are equally sacred with the spiritual mysteries and passions. Who would deny it any more? The only thing unbearable is the degradation, the prostitution of the living mysteries in us. Let man only approach his own self with a deep respect, even reverence for all that the creative soul, the God-mystery within us, puts forth. Then we shall all be sound and free. Lewdness is hateful because it impairs our integrity and our proud being.

The creative, spontaneous soul sends forth its promptings of desire and aspiration in us. These promptings are our true fate, which is our business to fulfil. A fate dictated from outside, from theory or from circumstance, is a false fate.

This novel pretends only to be a record of the writer's own desires, aspirations, struggles; in a word, a record of the profoundest experiences in the self. Nothing that comes from the deep, passional soul is bad, or can be bad. So there is no apology to tender, unless to the soul itself, if it should have been belied.

Man struggles with his unborn needs and fulfilment. New unfoldings struggle up in torment in him, as buds struggle forth from the midst of a plant. Any man of real individuality tries to know and to understand what is happening, even in himself, as he goes along. This struggle for verbal consciousness should not be left out in art. It is a very great part of life. It is not superimposition of a theory. It is the passionate struggle into conscious being.

We are now in a period of crisis. Every man who is acutely alive is acutely wrestling with his own soul. The people that can bring forth the new passion, the new idea, this people will endure. Those others, that fix themselves in the old idea, will perish with the new life strangled unborn within them. Men must speak out to one another.

In point of style, fault is often found with the continual, slightly modified repetition. The only answer is that it is natural to the author; and that every natural crisis in emotion or passion or understanding comes from this pulsing, frictional to-and-fro which works up to culmination. (pp. vii-viii)

> *D. H. Lawrence, in a foreword to his* Women in Love, *1920. Reprint by The Viking Press, 1961, pp. vii-viii.*

CARL VAN DOREN (essay date 1921)

[*Van Doren is considered one of the most perceptive critics of the first half of the twentieth century. He worked for many years as a professor of English at Columbia University and served as literary editor and critic of the* Nation *and the* Century *during the 1920s. A founder of the Literary Guild and author or editor of several American literary histories, Van Doren was also a critically acclaimed historian and biographer. In the following review, Van Doren notes the pervasive eroticism of* Women in Love.]

The hunger of sex is amazingly and appallingly set forth by D. H. Lawrence, whose novel *The Rainbow* was suppressed in England and who has now brought out his *Women in Love* in the United States in a sumptuous volume delightful to eye and hand. Mr. Lawrence admits no difference between Aphrodite Urania and Aphrodite Pandemos; love, in his understanding of it, links soul and body with the same bonds at the same moments. And in this latest book of his not only is there but one Aphrodite; there is but one ruling divinity, and she holds her subjects throughout a long narrative to the adventure and business and madness and warfare of love. Apparently resident in the English Midlands, Gudrun and Ursula Brangwen and their lovers Rupert Birkin and Gerald Crich actually inhabit some dark wood sacred to Dionysiac rites. If they have an economic existence, it is of the most unimportant kind; at any moment they can come and go about the world as their desires drive them. If they have any social existence, it is tenuous, or at best hardly thicker than a tissue of irritations. War and politics and art and religion for the time being are as if they had never been. Each pair of lovers recalls those sundered lovers of whom Aristophanes told the guests at Plato's Symposium—lovers who, in reality but halves of a primordial whole, whirl through space and time in a frantic search each for its opposite, mad with delay, and meeting at last with a frantic rush which takes no account of anything but the ecstasy of reunion.

If references to Greek cults come naturally to mind in connection with *Women in Love,* these lovers none the less have the modern experience of frantic reaction from their moments of meeting. They experience more than classical satiety. Mad with love in one hour, in the next they are no less mad with hate. They are souls born flayed, who cling together striving to become one flesh and yet causing each other exquisite torture. Their nerves are all exposed. The intangible filaments and repulsions which play between ordinary lovers are by Mr. Lawrence in this book magnified to dimensions half heroic and half mad. He has stripped off the daily coverings, the elaborated inhibitions, the established reticences of our civil existence, and displays his women as swept and torn by desires as old as the race and older, white-hot longings, dark confusions of body and spirit. Gudrun and Ursula are women not to be matched elsewhere in English fiction for richness and candor of desire. They are valkyries imperfectly domesticated, or, in Mr. Lawrence's different figure, daughters of men troubling the sons of God, and themselves troubled. No wonder then that the language which tells their story is a feverish language; that the narrative moves with a feverish march; that the final effect is to leave the witness of their fate dazed with the blazing mist which overhangs the record. Most erotic novels belong to the department of comedy; *Women in Love* belongs to the metaphysics and the mystical theology of love. (pp. 121-22)

Carl Van Doren, "Hungry," in The Nation, *New York, Vol. CXII, No. 2899, January 26, 1921, pp. 121-22.*

REBECCA WEST (essay date 1921)

[*West is considered one of the foremost English novelists and critics of the twentieth century. Her literary criticism is noted for its wit, perceptiveness, and aversion to cant. She has commented: "I dislike heartily the literary philosophy and practice of my time, which I think has lagged behind in the past and has little relevance to the present, and it distresses me that so much contemporary work is dominated by the ideas (particularly the political and religious ideas) of the late eighteenth or nineteenth century, and those misunderstood." In the following review, West praises the artistic accomplishment of* Women in Love *while noting the book's excesses and distortions.*]

Many of us are cleverer than Mr. D. H. Lawrence and nearly all of us save an incarcerated few are much saner, but this does not affect the fact that he is a genius. It does, of course, affect the fact of his being an artist. *Women in Love* is flawed in innumerable places by Mr. Lawrence's limitations and excesses. His general ideas are poor and uncorrected, apparently, by any wide reading or much discussion; when he wants to represent Birkin, who is supposed to be the brilliant thinker of the book, as confounding the shallow Hermione with his power over reality, he puts into his mouth a collection of platitudes on the subject of democracy which would have drawn nothing from any woman of that intellectual level, except perhaps the remark that these things had been dealt with more thoroughly by Havelock Ellis in his essay on the spheres of individualism and Socialism. He is madly irritable. "The porter came up. 'A Bâle—deuxième classe?—Voilà!' And he clambered into the high train. They followed. The compartments were already some of them taken. But many were dim and empty. The luggage was stowed, the porter was tipped. 'Nous avons encore?' said Birkin, looking at his watch and at the porter. 'Encore une demiheure,' with which, in his blue blouse, he disappeared. He was ugly and insolent." We are not told anything more about this porter. This is the full span of his tenuous existence in Mr. Lawrence's imagination. He has been called out of the everywhere into the here simply in order that for these two minutes he may be ugly and insolent. This is typical of Mr. Lawrence's indifference to that quality of serenity which is the highest form of decency. He thinks it natural that everybody should take their own Grand Guignol about with them in the form of an irritable nervous

system and that it should give continous performances. This prejudices his work in two ways. It makes him represent the characters whom he wishes to be regarded as normal as existing permanently in the throes of hyperaesthesia. When Gerald Crich and Gudrun stay in London on their way to the Tyrol, her reactions to London, which she does not appear to like, are so extreme that one anticipates that Gerald will have to spend all his time abroad nursing her through a nervous breakdown, which is in fact not what happened. It also shatters the author's nerves so that his fingers are often too clumsy and tremulous to deal with the subtleties which his mind insists on handing them as subjects. There is, for example, a scene in an inn at Southwell, where Ursula has an extraordinary crisis of delight at some physical aspect of Birkin. At first reading it appears that this is simply a sexual crisis which Mr. Lawrence is describing according to his own well-worn formula, and one reflects with fatigue that Mr. Lawrence's heroines suffer from molten veins as inveterately as Sarah Gamp suffered from spasms, and that they demand as insistently just a thimbleful of union with reality. But then if one is a conscientious reader one perceives that this is wrong. There is something else. Ursula seems to have caught sight of some physical oddity about him, to have noticed for the first time that he was really Siamese twins. One thinks crossly, "Unobservant girl." But if one has a decent sense of awe one realises that the author of *Sons and Lovers* is probably trying to say something worth hearing, and one reads it over again, and in the end perceives that Mr. Lawrence is simply trying to convey that mystical sense of the sacredness of physical structure, quite apart from its aesthetic or sexual significance, which is within the experience of nearly all of us. Ursula, contemplating her lover's body, had a sudden realisation that flesh is blessed above all other substances because it is informed by life, that force of which there is such a stupendous abundance on this earth, which has such divine attributes as will and consciousness, which has so dark a past and so mysterious a future. It is a reasonable enough emotion but Mr. Lawrence is so nerve-shattered by these extravagant leaps, which suggest that somebody has lit a little gunpowder under his sensorium, that he is unable to convey the spiritual incident save as a hot geyser of sensation.

But *Women in Love* is a work of genius. It contains characters which are masterpieces of pure creation. Birkin is not. The character whom an author designs as the mouthpiece of truth never is; always he is patronising and knowing, like "Our London Correspondent" writing his weekly letter in a provincial newspaper. But there is Hermione Roddice, the woman who stood beyond all vulgar judgment, yet could be reduced to misery by the slightest gesture of contempt from any servant because she had no real self and, though she could know, could not be. Mr. Lawrence could always conjure imaginary things into the world of the eye, and he makes visible the unhappy physical presence of Hermione, with her long face and her weight of heavy dull hair, her queer clothes, her strange appearance that made people want to jeer yet held them silent till she passed. In the scene where she sits at Birkin's table with Ursula and plays with the cat and coos Italian to it, and scores a barren victory by making the girl feel raw and vulgar and excluded by exercise of that static impressiveness which she has cultivated to conceal her dynamic nullity, he discloses the pathetic secret of her aching egotism with a marvellous appropriateness. He has found there the incident and the conversation that perfectly illustrate the spiritual fact he wishes to convey. There are also Mr. and Mrs. Crich, the mineowner and his wife, though their creation is not so indisputably pure as that of Hermione. One suspects that they were called into being in consequence of Mr. Lawrence's readings in German philosophy, that they are not only post but propter Nietzsche and Max Stirner. But they are great figures: the father, who loved to give to the poor out of his faith that "they through poverty and labour were nearer to God than he," until in time he became "some subtle funeral bird, feeding on the miseries of the people," a creature damp with continual pity; the mother, like a hawk, loathing the rusty black, cringing figures of his parasites, despising him for his perpetual indulgence in the laxer, gentler emotions, and bending over his dead body at the last in bitter contempt because his face was so beautiful, so unmarked by pride or the lordlier emotions. The persons who are most intimately concerned in the development of the main thesis of the book are not so satisfactory because that thesis deals with love. It is in itself an excellent thesis. It is a stern answer to the human cry, "I can endure the hatred the world bears me, and the hate I bear the world, if only there is one whom I love and who loves me." It declares: "No, that is not how it is. There shall be no one who loves you and no one whom you love, unless you first get in on loving terms with the world." Gerald Crich refuses to enter into an alliance of friendship with Birkin. He, the materialist, has no use for an expenditure of affection in a quarter where there is no chance of physical pleasure, and stakes his all on his union with Gudrun. This concentration itself wrecks that union. She finds him empty of everything but desire for her; he has had no schooling in altruistic love; he does not help her out of her own fatigued desire for corruption and decay, the peace of dissolution; and she breaks away from him. Thereby, because he has staked everything on her, he is destroyed. It is not really very abstruse, nor very revolutionary, nor very morbid. In *Antony and Cleopatra* Shakespeare permitted himself to say much the same sort of thing about the quality of love that arises between highly sexual people. But when Mr. Lawrence writes of love he always spoils his matter by his violent style. In an exquisite phrase Mrs. Mary Baker Eddy once remarked that the purpose of the relationship between the sexes is to "happify existence." There are times when Mr. Lawrence writes as if he thought its purpose was to give existence a black eye. His lovers are the Yahoos of Eros, and though Beauty may be in their spirits, it is certainly not in their manners. This is not represented as incidental to their characters, but as a necessary condition of love. It is a real flaw in Mr. Lawrence's temperament; but it is so marked and so apart from the rest of him that it no more spoils the book than a crack in the canvas spoils a beautiful picture.

There are, of course, many obvious distortions of life in *Women in Love* which it is easiest to consider as sheer meaningless craziness. There are, for instance, the extraordinary descriptions of the women's clothes, especially of Gudrun's stockings. She was more decorative about the legs than anybody has ever been except a flamingo. There are also incidents that flout probability or even possibility. There is that amazing scene when Hermione, who is supposed to be an effete aristocrat of unimpeachable manners, comes up behind Birkin, who is sitting on the sofa reading Thucydides as good as gold, and hits him on the head with a paperweight of lapis lazuli. This is certainly not the done thing. All this is without doubt not life as we know it, but the smallest reflection shows that it is not crazy and it has a meaning. The trouble is with Mr. Lawrence that he is so much of a poet that it is difficult for him to express himself in prose, and in particular in the prose required of a novel, and that he finds it impossible to express what he wants save by desperately devised symbols. He has felt that there is a quality about many women which makes them wear gay clothes and go actively yet not purposively about the world, and promote events that are never of the highest importance yet often interfere with others that are, which makes them, in fact, build a dome of many-coloured glass to stain the white light of eternity. He feels that every time that Gudrun appeared she was this quality made manifest to the eye, and he is at a loss how to convey it. In sheer desperation he ascribes to her these astonishing stockings. When one visualises those shapely, coloured ankles moving swiftly on those restless errands of destruction, one perceives that the touch is not meaningless at all, though it is clumsy. And the incident of Hermione and the paperweight also is a desperately devised symbol. He has wanted to express that a woman like her, bitter with a sense of spiritual insufficiency, would in the end turn against the lover whom she had wooed because of his extreme sufficiency, and become envious because she could not steal his sufficiency, and try to destroy him. In his impatience he has dragged into his novel this very dark scene which, though it is a distortion of life's physical appearances, nevertheless succeeds in conveying the spiritual truth with which he is concerned at the moment. To object to this on the ground that an author has no right to distort life's appearances for his own ends is to subject literature to an unreasonable restriction. It is not imposed on the art of painting. The greatest artists, such as Velasquez and Michaelangelo, have managed to express their vision of reality without tampering with appearances, but there is also El Greco, whose right to manipulate form for his own purposes no sane person would now dispute. Those who deny Mr. Lawrence's right to be an El Greco of literature had better not plume themselves that they are actuated by admiration for Michaelangelo's and Velasquez's fidelity to true form; if they can remain unmoved by Mr. Lawrence's genius it is much more likely that they are actuated by a longing for the realism of Mr. John Collier. (pp. 388, 390)

> *Rebecca West, in a review of "Women in Love," in* New Statesman, *Vol. XVII, No. 430, July 9, 1921, pp. 388, 390.*

JOHN MIDDLETON MURRY (essay date 1931)

[*Murry is recognized as one of the most significant English critics and editors of the twentieth century. Anticipating later scholarly opinion, he championed the writings of Marcel Proust, James Joyce, Paul Valéry, Thomas Hardy, and D. H. Lawrence through his position as editor of the* Athenaeum *and as a longtime contributor to the* Times Literary Supplement *and other periodicals. Murry's book-length critical works are noted for their unusually impassioned tone and sometimes are criticized for overt idealization and excessively personal interpretations. Such biographically centered critical studies as* Keats and Shakespeare: A Study of Keats' Poetic Life from 1816-1820 *(1925) and* Son of Woman: The Story of D. H. Lawrence *(1931) contain controversial conclusions that have drawn criticism from scholars who favor more traditional approaches. Nevertheless, Murry's assertions are noted for their clarity and supportive argumentation. Murry and his wife, Katherine Mansfield, were for a time the Lawrences' closest friends. Lawrence confided to them his dream of Rananim, a cooperative community of like-minded individuals. The Lawrences briefly attempted a communal living arrangement with Murry and Mansfield, but it was unsuccessful. The two men quarreled bitterly throughout their lives and were uncongenial at the time of Lawrence's death. Many commentators maintain that the characters Rupert Birkin and Gerald Crich are based in part upon Lawrence and Murry. Son of Woman remains highly controversial. Published the year after Lawrence's death, it was considered by many reviewers to be unforgivably exploitative. In the following excerpt from that work, Murry claims that Lawrence's personal failures are responsible for the thematic weaknesses of* Women in Love.]

The autobiographical sequence of **Look! We Have Come Through!** ends strangely with a handful of poems which appear to record an annihilation of the ego. The annihilation of the ego is an essential phase in the mystical experience; it is the preliminary to a rebirth. And these final poems seem to assert a rebirth. We must examine them carefully.

The first is entitled "**New Heaven and Earth.**" Lawrence records his shy entry into a new world. He was so weary of the world, he says; everything was tainted with himself.

> I was a lover, I kissed the woman I loved
> and God of horror, I was kissing also myself.

In the end it was an unforgettable, maniacal horror. But at last came death, sufficiency of death. Apparently this "sufficiency of death" came partly through an imaginative enduring of the horrors of the war. Lawrence died, because he in imagination endured the deaths of many men. He, with them, was "dead and trodden to nought in the sour black earth of the tomb; dead and trodden to nought, trodden to nought."

Then came a resurrection, "risen, not born again, but risen, body the same as before." And the manner of the resurrection was this:

> I, in the sour black tomb, trodden to absolute
>   death,
> I put out my hand in the night, one night, and my
>   hand
> touched that which was verily not me,
> verily, it was not me.
> Where I had been was a sudden blaze,
> a sudden flaring blaze.
> So I put my hand out further, a little further
> and I felt that which was not I,
> it verily was not I,
> it was the unknown.
>
> Ha! I was a blaze leaping up!
> I was a tiger bursting into sunlight.
> I was greedy, I was mad for the unknown.

And the unknown that he touched was "the flank of his wife," at whose side "he had lain for more than a thousand nights."

> and all that previous while, she was I, she was I

But now she is other, and she who is other has "strange-mounded breasts and strange sheer slopes, and white levels."

The next poem, "**Elysium,**" which seems to be intimately connected with this, tells of his finding

> a place of loneliness
> Lonelier than Lyonesse,
> Lovelier than Paradise.

Again, it is through the woman that he finds it. But whereas she was passive in the former poem, she is active in this. There, he put out his hand in the night and discovered her as other; here it is she who releases him.

> Invisible the hands of Eve

> Upon me travelling to reeve
> Me from the matrix, to relieve
>
> Me from the rest! Ah, terribly
> Between the body of life and me
> Her hands slid in and set me free.
>
> Ah, with a fearful, strange detection
> She found the source of my subjection
> To the All, and severed the connection.

I do not pretend to understand that; nor can I positively say that this deliverance of the man by the woman "from the womb of the All, the monstrous womb of time" is the same as that separation of himself from a universe which was wholly himself of which the former poem speaks. But they appear to be intimately connected.

The next poem, "**Manifesto,**" is much more explicit; it belongs to a year later, to 1916. It begins: "A woman has given me strength and affluence." She has freed him from his direst hunger,

> more frightening, more profound
> than stomach or throat or even the mind;
> redder than death, more clamorous.

the hunger for the woman. She fed that hunger in him at last.

> She stood before me like riches that were mine.
> Even then, in the dark, I was tortured, ravening,
>   unfree,
> Ashamed, and shameful, and vicious.
> A man is so terrified of strong hunger;
> and this terror is the root of all cruelty.
> She loved me, and stood before me, looking to me.
> How could I look, when I was mad? I looked side-
>   ways, furtively,
> being mad with voracious desire.

But he lost at last "the fierceness that fears it will starve." He knew he would never go hungry, and he was fulfilled.

Yet hunger remains, the ultimate hunger—"the ache for being." And the satisfaction of this hunger depends on being known by her even as he knows her. This knowledge which he has of her, but which she has not of him is that

> ultimately, she is all beyond me,
> She is all not-me, ultimately.
> It is that that one comes to.
> A curious agony, and a relief, when I touch that
> which is not me in any sense,
> it wounds me to death with my own not-being; defi-
>   nite, inviolable limitation,
> and something beyond, quite beyond, if you under-
>   stand what that means.

But she does not know him thus. She touches him as if he were herself, her own.

> I want her to touch me at last, ah, on the root and
>   quick of my darkness
> and perish on me, as I have perished on her. . . .
> When she has put her hand on my secret, darkest
>   sources, the darkest outgoings,
> when it has struck home to her, like a death, "this
>   is *him!*"
> she has no part in it, no part whatever,
> it is the terrible *other*,
> when she knows the fearful *other flesh,* ah, darkness
>   unfathomable and fearful, contiguous and con-
>   crete,

when she is slain against me, and lies in a heap like
    one outside the house,
when she passes away as I have passed away,
being pressed up against the *other,*
then I shall be glad, I shall not be confused with
    her,
I shall be cleared, distinct, single as if burnished in
    silver,
having no adherence, no adhesion anywhere,
one clear, burnished, isolated being, unique,
and she also, pure, isolated, complete,
two of us, unutterably distinguished, and in unut-
    terable conjunction.

Once more I do not claim to understand this wholly. But, even though one may not understand the experience which is recorded, one may reach certain conclusions.

The man hungers "for being"; yet his achievement of "being" depends upon the woman. She must know him in the same way as he knows her; and this knowledge is a carnal and a sensual knowledge, physical touch of the naked other flesh, physical touch of "his secret, darkest sources," accompanied by a realisation of his otherness. He came to this knowledge of her a year before; she does not, or cannot come to this knowledge of him. The knowledge is mysterious. But why, we ask, should his achievement of "being" depend upon how the woman knows him? Surely it must be a very precarious sort of "being" that thus depends upon the woman's ratification. If he knows himself as isolated and unique, with a true and certain knowledge, what does it matter to him whether the woman recognises him as isolated and unique? Certainty is certainty. But, if his certainty is uncertain, then its ratification by the woman will bring him comfort, though not certainty. Still more, if he desires to have "no adhesion anywhere," surely it is a queer way to sever himself by asking the woman to recognise that he is severed. "Tell me," he says in effect, "that I do not adhere to you"; and the appeal is a confession that he does adhere to her, that he cannot separate himself. "Be terrified of me," he says in effect; and the summons is a confession that she is not likely to be terrified of him.

There is, we suspect, a great and grievous weakness here. We simply cannot believe in any achievement of "being" which thus depends upon another's recognition of it. "Being" is achieved alone, and if it is achieved it is self-sufficient, and calls for no allowance. But no such self-sufficiency is here. This condition is rather one of excessive dependence, assuming a last disguise. "I am myself, isolated, independent, and alone," says the man to the woman, "but tell me that I am, otherwise I cannot believe it." Neither can we. It is the old situation, in a new form. We remember the agonised self-questioning of Will Brangwen [in *The Rainbow*]:

Why could he not leave her? He could not, he could
not. A woman, he must have a woman. And having
a woman he must be free of her. It would be the
same position. For he could not be free of her.

That is the psychological position, unchanged. The physical situation is more mysterious. The dependence upon the woman is physical: the ravening hunger is satisfied. But he seems to be now demanding a new kind of physical contact, or rather a physical contact in which the woman shall feel a new emotion, of fear and terror, in contact with him. And again we recall the poem "**She Said as Well to Me,**" which immediately precedes "**New Heaven and Earth.**"

"Don't touch me and appreciate me
It is an infamy.
You would think twice before you touched a weasel
    on a fence
as it lifts its straight white throat.
Your hand would not be so flig and easy. . . .
Is there nothing in me to make you hesitate?"

He is asking that she shall feel, in physical contact, the same terror that he feels for her. Somehow, she must be made to respect and fear him, sexually; until she does, he will be "confused with her." When she does, ah, then, it will be heaven. After that it will only remain that all men and women go through the same process of coming to final sexual terror of each other; then,

Every man himself, and therefore, a surpassing sin-
    gleness of mankind.
The blazing tiger will spring upon the deer, un-
    dimmed,
the hen will nestle over her chickens,
we shall love, we shall hate,
but it will be like music, sheer utterance,
issuing straight out of the unknown.

Since the habits of the actual tiger would not be affected by this consummation among men and women, the tiger is symbolic. It is the sexual tiger, in Lawrence, who will be undimmed, because the woman will know that it is a tiger, instead of mistaking it for a milder animal.

This endeavour to enforce upon the woman a sexual or sensual homage to the man is the chief clue to . . . *Women in Love.* In that novel Ursula Brangwen becomes, quite recognisably, *the* Woman; and Lawrence himself also appears, quite recognisably, as Rupert Birkin. The culmination of their relation is described in the chapter "Excurse." To anyone who reads the novel in isolation, and without the necessary clue, it is an obscure and difficult chapter; but it strikes even the unadvised reader as invented and untrue. He scents in it a fundamental falsity, as of a forced conclusion. Perhaps Lawrence himself half-acknowledged this by giving the chapter its curious title, "Excurse."

What is certain is that it can be readily understood only by reference to the poem "**Manifesto**" which we have been examining. The poem was written in 1916, so was the novel; and there are good reasons for supposing that the poem was written almost at the same moment as this particular chapter of the novel. The situation is the same. Birkin is dissatisfied with Ursula; he demands of her a kind of physical contact which she will not give.

He wanted her to come to him. But he was angry
at the bottom of his soul, and indifferent. He knew
she had a passion for him, really. But it was not finally interesting. There were depths of passion
when one became impersonal and indifferent, unemotional. Whereas Ursula was still at the emotional personal level—always so abominably personal. He had taken her as he had never been taken
himself. He had taken her at the roots of her darkness and shame—like a demon, laughing over the
fountain of mystic corruption which was one of the
sources of her being, laughing, shrugging, accepting, accepting finally. As for her, when would she
so much go beyond herself as to accept him at the
quick of death?

I do not know what "the fountain of mystic corruption" in Ursula really means, though it is certain that there was no such thing in her; but it is obvious that Birkin's demand of Ursula is the same demand as Lawrence makes upon the woman in the poem. The difference in mood—the poem is passionate, the prose cynical—is due to the fact that the prose is a little later, and Lawrence has become cynical, through the woman's resistance. With pitiless fidelity Lawrence, immediately afterwards, gives utterance to Ursula's repulsion. She bursts upon Birkin in fury:

> "You love the sham spirituality, it's your food. And why? Because of the dirt underneath. Do you think I don't know the foulness of your sex life—and hers?—I do. And it's the foulness you want, you liar. Then have it, have it. You're such a liar. . . .
>
> "*You!*" she cried. "You! You truth-lover! You purity-monger! It *stinks,* your truth and your purity. It stinks of the offal you feed on, you scavenger dog, you eater of corpses. You are foul, *foul*—and you must know it. Your purity, your candour, your goodness—yes, thank you, we've had some. What you are is a foul, deathly thing, obscene, that's what you are, obscene and perverse. You, and love! You may well say, you don't want love. No, you want *yourself,* and dirt, and death—that's what you want. You are so *perverse,* so death-eating."

It was, within the limits of the story, quite impossible for Ursula to know anything about "the foulness of the sex-life" of Birkin and Hermione Roddice. Their liaison is over before Ursula ever meets Birkin; and he tells Ursula nothing about it. We must say, if we keep to the rules of the game, that Ursula's knowledge was due to a flash of imaginative intuition. But, with Lawrence, it is impossible to keep to the rules of the game; with him, there is no "game." He did not conceal himself, and we cannot conceal him. Rupert Birkin is Lawrence, and what Lawrence knew about Birkin, he knew about himself. Birkin, indeed, makes no attempt to deny the truth of Ursula's knowledge. On the contrary,

> He knew she was in the main right. He knew he was perverse, so spiritual on the one hand, and in some strange way, degraded on the other. But was she herself any better? Was anybody any better?

Wherein did this depravity, of which Lawrence was conscious, consist? It consisted in this demand that the woman "should take him as he had taken her," with a sense "of the contiguous, concrete, terrifying *other flesh.*" It is a demand for sexual contact, without the oblivion of passion, without the ecstasy of union—cold, conscious, calculating sensuality. And the woman, instinctively, repels it; probably, she is completely incapable of it. Probably, the vast majority of ordinary men and women are completely incapable of it; probably, it is only practicable in a man of physical and spiritual constitution resembling that of Lawrence.

The point, and the falsity of "Excurse," is that it represents Ursula as giving way to Birkin's demand. In Lawrence's quasi-mystical language, "she had thought there was no source deeper than the phallic source"; now, at his demand, she discovers it. "She had had lovers, she had known passion. But this was neither love, nor passion." That was true enough. But what is completely false is that Ursula, or her original, acknowledged its supremacy. The evidence of this is Lawrence's work. This ultra-phallic consummation, in which Birkin and Ursula are represented as finding complete fulfilment, disappears almost completely from Lawrence's subsequent books. If it really had been the consummation

which he represented it to be, this disappearance would be inconceivable. The true fulfilment between man and woman is not discovered simply in order to be forgotten: for it is, for Lawrence, and for many men, the Holy Grail itself. One does not throw the Holy Grail into the kitchen-midden. That alone is evidence enough that this consummation was not what Lawrence represented it to be. But it is not the only evidence.

This consummation is not actual at all. It is a wish-fulfilment. Let us examine it. One would need, to be wholly precise, to quote nearly the whole chapter. A few passages must suffice.

> She had a full mystic knowledge of his suave loins of darkness, dark-clad and suave, and in this knowledge there was some of the inevitability and the beauty of fate, fate which one asks for, which one accepts in full.
>
> He sat still like an Egyptian Pharaoh. . . . He felt as if he were seated in immemorial potency, like the great carven statues of real Egypt, as real and as fulfilled with subtle strength, as these are, with a vague inscrutable smile on the lips. He knew what it was to have the strange and magical current of force in his back and loins, and down his legs, force so perfect that it stayed him immobile, and left his face subtly, mindlessly smiling. He knew what it was to be awake and potent in that other basic mind, the deepest physical mind. And from this source he had a pure and magic control, magical, mystical, a force in darkness, like electricity.

This is the re-assertion of his masculinity, of which he is always dreaming. In this realm of mindless sensuality, he is like Pharaoh, and "immemorially potent." And, still more important, the woman recognises it. She bows down to him; she becomes purely feminine, receptive, and submissive before him.

> She was next to him, and hung in a pure rest, as a star is hung, balanced unthinkably. Still there remained a dark lambency of anticipation. She would touch him. With perfect fine finger-tips of reality she would touch the reality in him, the suave, pure, untranslatable reality of his loins of darkness. To touch, mindlessly in darkness to come in pure touching upon the living reality of him, his suave perfect loins and thighs of darkness, this was her sustaining anticipation.
>
> And he too waited in the magical steadfastness of suspense, for her to take this knowledge of him as he had taken it of her. He knew her darkly, with the fullness of dark knowledge. Now she would know him, and he too would be liberated.

As a matter of fact, Lawrence is so immersed in his personal experience that he forgets his story. Birkin had not taken this knowledge of Ursula in the novel. Lawrence had taken it of the woman in life, and the record is in **"Manifesto."** There it only remained for him to be known even as he knows, without which he cannot be free. Now, in the novel, where he is master, he gives himself this "liberation." Ursula Brangwen is made to desire what the poet of **"Manifesto"** desired that his woman should desire.

> They threw off their clothes, and he gathered her to him, and found her, found the pure lambent reality of her forever invisible flesh. Quenched, inhuman, his fingers upon her unrevealed nudity were the fingers of silence upon silence, the body of mysterious night upon the body of mysterious night,

the night masculine and feminine, never to be seen with the eye, or known with the mind, only known as a palpable revelation of living otherness.

She had her desire of him, she touched, she received the maximum of unspeakable communication in touch, dark, subtle, positively silent, a magnificent gift and give again, a perfect acceptance and yielding, a mystery, the reality of that which never can be known, vital, sensual reality that can never be transmuted into mind-content, but remains outside, living body of darkness and silence and subtlety, the mystic body of reality. She had her desire fulfilled. He had his desire fulfilled. For she was to him what he was to her, the immemorial magnificence of mystic, palpable, real otherness.

So the dream is made to come true. Ursula has "the full mystic knowledge of his suave loins of darkness"; she has discovered that "there were strange fountains of his body, more mysterious and potent than any she had imagined or known, more satisfying, ah, finally, mystically-physically satisfying. She had thought that there was no source deeper than the phallic source." Now, she knew better. The something that remained, that something which prevented Lawrence from satisfying the ultimate hunger of his "ache for being," is achieved. And we see what this "ache for being" really is; it is the ache to establish his own masculinity. It cannot be done in sexual possession, in which he is always the dependent, the victim; but it can be done in this new mode of sexuality, which consists in touch, in which there is none of the "abhorred mingling." In the sexuality of touch, of complete separateness, he may be lord and master—a very Pharoah.

When we grasp this, we grasp the meaning of the strange chapter, "Moony," where Birkin throws stone after stone, in an unintelligible frenzy, at the reflection of the moon in a pool, while Ursula watches him in agony. It seems quite meaningless, until we realise that Birkin is destroying Aphrodite, the divinity under whose cold light Ursula annihilated the core of intrinsic male in Lawrence's last incarnation as Anton Skrebensky. To annihilate the female insatiably demanding physical satisfaction from the man who cannot give it her—the female who has thus annihilated him—this is Lawrence's desire. To make her subject again, to re-establish his own manhood—this is the secret purpose of *Women in Love.* In imagination, he has his desire. He creates a sexual mystery beyond the phallic, wherein he is the lord; and he makes the woman acknowledge the existence of this ultra-phallic realm, and his own lordship in it. He triumphs over her in imagination, but not in life. Aphrodite can only be appeased within the phallic realm, and Lawrence is no master there.

To the working out of this personal argument in the imaginary consummation of Birkin and Ursula, all else is really subsidiary in the novel. But, once we understand the true situation, we shall not be surprised at the definite emergence of a new theme—the hunger for a man. The hunger for a woman has proved disastrous, in spite of the assertions of actual, and the reports of imaginary fulfilment; it was inevitable that Lawrence should turn towards the possibility of a relation with a man. There is the same confusion between spirituality and sensuality. The love between Rupert Birkin and Gerald Crich is, on Birkin's side, half-spiritual, half-sensual. "We are mentally, spiritually intimate," says Birkin to Crich, "therefore we ought to be more or less physically intimate." Accordingly, the two men wrestle naked together, and Birkin

swoons away. But the main interest of their relation is the indecision which Birkin reveals. He says to Crich:

> "You've got to take down the love-and-marriage ideal from its pedestal. We want something broader. I believe in the *additional* perfect relationship between man and man—additional to marriage."

That, indubitably, was in Lawrence's own mind at this moment; he expressed his thought, even more strongly, in his letters. But, since we know what underlay the "perfect" marriage-relation between Ursula and Birkin, and that its "perfection" consisted precisely in the substitution of "the mystery beyond the phallic" for the phallic mystery, we know that it is not the addition of one perfection to another that he is seeking, but rather to escape to a man from the misery of his own failure with a woman. This has always appeared to Lawrence a way out. In *The White Peacock* his love for a man is more perfect than his love for a woman; and, truly, in actual fact I believe it was a happier and less tortured relation for him. But always it was brief and fugitive. Lawrence was always, and inevitably, disappointed.

"We ought to swear to love each other, you and I," says Rupert to Gerald, "implicitly and perfectly, finally, without any possibility of going back." Again he pleads: "We will swear to stand by each other—be true to each other—intimately—infallibly—given to each other, organically, without possibility of going back." Gerald withdraws from the proffered alliance, puts it gently aside, and the novel purports to show us how, in consequence of this refusal, he is destroyed. He chooses Ursula's sister, Gudrun. This, Birkin says (and Lawrence makes it so), is a disaster. "He was willing to condemn himself in marriage . . . but he would not make any pure relationship with any other soul. Marriage was not the committing of himself into a relationship with Gudrun." This is very obscure, and perhaps Lawrence himself did not know what he meant. But manifestly "the pure relationship" with a woman is what Birkin attains with Ursula. Gerald and Gudrun are to remain under the dominion of Aphrodite the deathly.

> The other way was to accept Rupert's offer of alliance, to enter into the bond of pure trust and love with the other man, and then subsequently with the woman. If he pledged himself with the man he would later be able to pledge himself with the woman: not merely in legal marriage, but in absolute, mystic marriage.

Such "absolute, mystic marriage," namely, as Rupert and Ursula achieve: their imaginary ultra-phallic consummation. Since the desire for this consummation, and the hunger for the man also, is the effect of Lawrence's phallic failure, Rupert's demand of Gerald is the last extremity of self-deception. It means nothing, or if it means anything, it means that his man-friend must be the repetition of himself: just such another phallic failure, just such another sex-crucified man.

Lawrence's hunger for a man could never have been satisfied. He came to know, and in part to confess it later, in *Kangaroo.* But at this time he did not know it, he was only vaguely aware of the depth upon depth of self-deception in which he was involved. He was gratifying himself with a dream. Gerald, because he refuses Rupert's offer of alliance, is delivered over to the destructive Aphrodite and to death: he goes the way of the tiger, as described in *Twilight in Italy*—the tiger "whose *essential* fire is white and cold, a white ecstasy." In a sensual ecstasy, Gerald seeks to murder Gudrun, and dies in a final ecstasy of dissolution in the snow, in the light of a painful brilliant-shining moon, "from which there was no escape."

The book comes to a close with a conversation between Rupert and Ursula about the dead man.

> "Did you need Gerald?" she asked one evening.
>
> "Yes," he said.
>
> "Aren't I enough for you?" she asked.
>
> "No," he said. "You are enough for me, as far as a woman is concerned. You are all women to me. But I wanted a man friend, as eternal as you and I are eternal."
>
> "Why aren't I enough?" she said. "You are enough for me. I don't want anybody else but you. Why isn't it the same with you?"
>
> "Having you, I can live all my life without anybody else, any other sheer intimacy. But to make it complete, really happy, I wanted eternal union with a man too: another kind of love," he said.
>
> "I don't believe it," she said. "It's an obstinacy, a theory, a perversity."
>
> "Well—" he said.
>
> "You can't have two kinds of love. Why should you?"
>
> "It seems as if I can't," he said. "Yet I wanted it."
>
> "You can't have it, because it's false, impossible," she said.
>
> "I don't believe that," he answered.

Was he or Ursula right? Surely, Ursula. Not that love of a woman and love of a man are incompatible. That is not the question at all. The question is entirely personal: whether Lawrence can find an issue, by way of a relation with a man, from the strange and terrible situation in which he is now caught. Lawrence is bewildered and lost. He feels that he is disintegrating; his inward division is become terrible to himself; his life a nightmare. (pp. 89-104)

I hold [*Women in Love*] to be built upon a lie, or on many lies; yet I would not have it otherwise. The haunted, tortured, divided, angel-devil of a man is in it. He is not like the Lawrence whom I loved; but (as I learned to my sorrow) the Lawrence whom I loved was only half the Lawrence whom I knew.

Women in Love is an amazing book; amazing for the subtlety of its falsity, amazing for the intricacy of its self-deception. It is the imperishable monument of one of the strangest moments of Lawrence's strange destiny.

The main argument of the book, which is the distinction between the "love" of Rupert and Ursula on the one hand, and of Gerald and Gudrun on the other, is false. Rupert and Ursula are represented as in the way of salvation, Gerald and Gudrun as in the way of damnation: and this is superficially plausible for the simple reason that Rupert and Ursula are in the main real people, while Gerald and Gudrun are not. But when we consider the principles which these opposed couples really embody, we discover that the difference between them is that Rupert and Ursula are a whole stage further on in the process of damnation, for Gerald and Gudrun simply represent Rupert and Ursula at their previous stage of sensual self-destruction. Lawrence claims that Rupert and Ursula escape from it into the ultra-phallic realm, of utter separateness and mindless sensuality. It was untrue. What happened was that Lawrence tried to escape thither, and left Ursula where she was. . . . (pp. 112-13)

Lawrence, who was a supremely conscious man, was not unaware of the deception he was trying to work upon himself. There is a point in the story where Birkin wonders whether he has done wrong to refuse Ursula's proffered love. "Perhaps," he thinks, "he had been wrong to go to her with an idea of what he wanted." The idea of what he wanted is expressed in fifty different ways in the novel; sometimes very deceptively, but the substance beneath is always the same. The phallic relation is to be superseded, by a new sexuality of separateness and touch. Perhaps the "idea" is most clearly expressed, with much that lay behind it, in this passage:

> On the whole he hated sex, it was such a limitation. . . . He wanted sex to revert to the level of the other appetites, to be regarded as a functional process, not as a fulfilment. He believed in sex-marriage. But beyond this he wanted a further conjunction, where man had being and woman had being, two pure beings, each constituting the freedom of the other, balancing each other like two poles of one force, like two angels, or two demons.
>
> He wanted so much to be free, not under the compulsion of any need for unification, or tortured by unsatisfied desire. . . . The merging, the clutching, the mingling of love was become madly abhorrent to him. But it seemed to him, woman was always so horrible and clutching, she had such a lust for possession, a greed of self-importance in love. She wanted to have, to own, to control, to be dominant. Everything must be referred back to her, to Woman, the Great Mother of everything, out of whom proceeded everything and to whom everything must be rendered up.
>
> It filled him with almost insane fury, this calm assumption of the Magna Mater. . . . He had a horror of the Magna Mater, she was detestable.

Were it not that we have learned to read this language, it might be plausible. Lawrence seems half to have deceived himself by his phrases. For Birkin, when he wonders whether he was wrong to go to Ursula with this idea of what he wanted, asks himself: "Was it really only an idea, or was it the interpretation of a profound yearning? If the latter, how was it he was always talking about sensual fulfilment? The two did not agree very well together." They agreed, in reality, perfectly well together. Sensual domination, not sexual fulfilment, is his desire. A sexual marriage in which he does not have to satisfy the woman, where the sexuality, being transformed into sensuality, may give him the opportunity of reasserting the manhood he had lost—this is precisely Lawrence's dream. It is the dream of a man who would give his soul to be free of the woman, but has not the courage to make himself free of her.

> Suddenly he found himself face to face with a situation. It was as simple as this: fatally simple. On the one hand, he knew he did not want a further sensual experience—something deeper, darker than ordi-

nary life could give. [He thinks of an African carving of a negro woman, which is for him the expression of the "deeper, darker" sensual mystery.] Thousands of years ago, that which was immanent in himself must have taken place in these Africans: the goodness, the holiness, the desire for creation and productive happiness must have lapsed, leaving the single impulse for knowledge in one sort, mindless progressive knowledge through the senses, knowledge arrested and ending in the senses, mystic knowledge in disintegration and dissolution. . . .

Birkin shrinks back in horror from the lapse from goodness that is imminent in himself. No, there is another way, he cries in anguish.

> There was the paradisal entry into pure, single being, the individual soul taking precedence over love and desire for union, stronger than any pangs of emotion, a lovely state of free proud singleness, which accepted the obligation of the permanent connection with others, and with the other, submits to the yoke and leash of love, but never forfeits its own proud individual singleness, even while it loves and yields. There was the other way, the remaining way. And he must run to follow it. . . .

He goes off to ask Ursula to marry him. Which eventually she does. And then we find, as we have found, that the consummation between them has nothing whatever to do with these brave words of spiritual achievement, this mutual acknowledgement of the proud single soul; on the contrary, it is an attempt, to which Ursula is represented . . . to have been converted, to experience precisely those "sensual subtle realities far beyond the scope of phallic investigation," those mindless but not unconscious ecstasies of dissolution, which Birkin has ostensibly rejected for "the paradisal way" of marriage with Ursula.

I believe that Lawrence changed while *Women in Love* was actually being written: that he really did mean to reject the way of sensuality and dissolution, and that he succumbed to it in spite of himself. And Lawrence at the end of his novel is trying to persuade himself that his defeat is a victory; to deceive himself and his reader into the belief that the mutual acknowledgment of the proud single soul (which is spiritual) and the mutual exploration of "the ultra-phallic otherness" (which is sensual) are the same. Somewhere in his inward soul Lawrence must have known what he was doing; just as Birkin "knew that his spirituality was concomitant of a process of depravity, a sort of pleasure in self-destruction. There really *was* a certain stimulant in self-destruction, for him—especially when it was translated spiritually. But then he knew it—he knew it, and had done." That was an easy thing to say; but a man who, like Lawrence, "is damned and doomed to the old effort at serious living," cannot violate himself with impunity. He has finally broken something, deliberately riven his secret soul in sunder; and no power in earth or heaven can make him whole again.

The fundamental equivocation of *Women in Love* repels me. It is not that I blame Lawrence for yielding to a longing from which in his inward soul he shrank away. Lawrence was Lawrence—a destiny-driven man, if ever there was one. If the realm of mindless sensuality offered or seemed to offer the only way of escape for his tortured spirit, then he was driven to explore it. But I think he is to be condemned for painting his devil as an angel, for the duplicity with which he repre-

sents himself as turning away from this mindless sensuality towards a paradisal relation with the woman, yet subtly perverts this very relation (in defiance of all truth, factual or imaginative) into a form of that mindless sensuality from which it was to be an escape. Lawrence, in the essential and vital argument of *Women in Love,* behaves like a cheat. To behave like a cheat in these momentous issues of human destiny is to play the Judas to humanity. The man who betrays himself in such an issue betrays all men.

The failure was momentous. Lawrence, in the essential, was never to recover from it. He would make the heroic effort—a truly heroic effort—to assert himself against the consequences of his own spiritual suicide. But he was, henceforward, veritably a doomed man. He had made the great refusal, and it was irrevocable.

My mind tells me that this was inevitable, my heart tells me that it was not. When I think, childishly, of what Lawrence might have been, and of what he actually became, my heart is wrung with anguish. The slow recantation of all that was most precious to him, the gradual disintegration which an inexorable justice exacted from him, is fearful to contemplate. To mitigate the tragedy of this retribution, let us remember this, which I believe to be true.

Lawrence was denied the basic strength to bear the burden of the human spirit which lay more heavily on him than any other man of his time. The extreme knowledge of the burden to be borne, the secret inability to bear it—these were, I believe, given together. The excessive sensitiveness to the demands of the spirit, prematurely awakened in him, prevented that true physical maturity which would have enabled him either to maintain himself in physical isolation, or to draw upon the woman's vital strength, to take through her the healing virtue of the unknown which is beyond and below life itself. So he was driven consciously to seek not the unconscious, which he could not fully enter, but the mindless, which he believed he could. But even this he could not do, without his woman. She must submit her instinctive knowledge to his strange necessities; she must believe in his unnatural consummations; she must be convinced that humanity was involved in a destiny of mindless dissolution; she must submit to the idea that sex was a functional process not a fulfilment; she must acknowledge that they were not man and woman, discovering and rediscovering their own integral being through their perfect union, but polarised demons inhabiting the mindless realm. She submits, believes, is convinced; in the book she obeys. In life she resists; and the victory is hers, as it must be.

But there was still more. Precisely because Lawrence was denied that utter fulfilment in a woman which would have given him the strength to bear his spiritual isolation, he needed a friend, needed friends—men and women who were his equals in spiritual development. And they did not exist; or, if they did exist, he did not know them. Here I speak with some authority, for it was to Katherine Mansfield and to me that he turned with longing in the crucial winter of 1915-16 after which *Women in Love* was written, and simply because I was a man, he turned primarily to me. And I failed Lawrence, not from any lack of love, or of will to avail him. I was never lacking in love towards Lawrence; but I lacked understanding, the understanding that is born of absolute experience, and can come from no other source whatever.

Yet it is plain to me now that, even if I had understood Lawrence, I should still have been bound to fail him, and that it was better to fail him in ignorance, than to be impotent to help him, in knowledge. If I had known his secret, I would have been his master, not he mine. And he needed to be the master. The defect of his own manhood which gnawed at him, demanded this spiritual compensation. If he had been able to accept the fact of his own dependence, Lawrence would never have been driven to his dire necessity. The man who can finally accept himself is a free man. If Lawrence could have accepted his own intrinsic dependence, then he would, by that very act, have become independent: his dependence would have fallen away from him. It sounds a miracle, perhaps it is a miracle, but this miracle is inevitable in the progress of the human spirit. If it is a miracle it is a natural miracle—that eternal rebirth of human soul, without which life, to the sensitive spirit, must become an unendurable agony. This eternal rebirth of the soul Lawrence could not achieve: he fled from the naked isolation of self-knowledge without which it is inconceivable. (pp. 113-19)

> *John Middleton Murry, in his* Son of Woman: The Story of D. H. Lawrence, *Jonathan Cape & Harrison Smith, 1931, 367 p.*

ELISEO VIVAS   (essay date 1960)

[*A Colombian-born American critic, Vivas has written extensively on value theory as well as moral and ethical issues. He was an advisory editor of the* Kenyon Review, *founded by Robert Penn Warren, between 1939 and 1942, and was associated with the "New Criticism" formulated by Warren, John Crowe Ransom, and others in the late 1930s. Although the various New Critics did not subscribe to a single set of principles, all believed that a work of literature had to be examined as an object in itself through a process of close analysis of symbol, image, and metaphor. For the New Critics, a literary work was not a manifestation of ethics, sociology, or psychology, and could not be evaluated in the general terms of any nonliterary discipline. New Criticism as a system of critical thought dominated the American academic scene for nearly three decades. In his well-respected but controversial critical study* D. H. Lawrence: The Failure and the Triumph of Art, *Vivas disregards biographical evidence and stated authorial intent in favor of close textual study, evaluating the works on the basis of the amount of "untransformed matter" (autobiographical material and personal opinion) and "informed substance" (material that has been artistically transformed through the creative powers of the author's imagination). Vivas concludes that Lawrence's works fail as art when he is unsuccessful in transforming the raw material of autobiography into art via the creative process. In the following excerpt from his study, Vivas analyzes theme and technique in* Women in Love *and assesses the novel's ultimate value.*]

While the two main themes, the development of which defines the organization of *Women in Love,* are the love affair of Birkin and Ursula and the liaison of Gerald and Gudrun, the substance of the novel cannot be adequately defined in terms of the love affairs alone. The novel is a very ambitious book whose substance consists of the elucidation of the theme of human destiny at a given moment in history in terms of the conditions in which the four main characters find themselves. If I am right, . . . Lawrence could have claimed much more than he did when, defending himself from a criticism, he wrote to Edward Garnett . . . that he was "a passionately religious man," and that his novels had to be written from the depths of his religious experience. In *Women in Love* religion, as ordinarily understood, does not enter: man's

Frieda von Richthofen, age 18.

relation to God is not part of the substance of the novel; but Lawrence poses the problem of human destiny in view of the fact that his characters cannot believe in God, so that religion, by its failure, defines the central problem of the novel.

It is only when we put *Women in Love* in this perspective that we are able to see clearly the relation of Lawrence to the most profound and most challenging movement in contemporary philosophy in our Western world, atheistic existentialism. Nietzsche's exultant cry, "God is dead!" is one of Sartre's starting points. God's death forces the atheistic philosopher to face the problem of destiny in ultimate, radical, and desperate terms. And it was in these terms that Lawrence faced the same problem. The philosophy of love, the religion of the blood, the "leader-*cum*-follower" program—all his ideas, solutions, insights, and messages, significant as they are by themselves, achieve full significance only when we see them as attempts to discover a way of life that would center, "seeing there is no God." And it is only when we put Lawrence in this perspective that we are able to see fully what kind of novelist he was. Most contemporary novelists are moralists—or immoralists as the case may be. Witness Conrad and Gide. I do not mean that they preach or have a message; I mean that the matter they seek to elucidate by transforming it into the substance of art is the stuff of human relations. Only very few are, if I may so call them, "cosmologists," in the sense that their matter is man's relation to the cosmos. This was the matter Dreiser sought to transform into the substance of art. . . . And this is the "problem" that, in the last analysis, obsessed Lawrence. That he "failed," in the sense that not one of his "answers" was acceptable and viable, is a relatively minor consideration. He posed the problem; and this, in philosophy and in poetry, is all, or nearly all that we can expect. An honest man today, whether for him God is dead or living, knows, knows in his entrails, as Unamuno would have put it, that there is no easy answer to his cosmic query, no easy way out of his radical predicament.

And finally, from the critical standpoint, it is only when we make explicit Lawrence's basic theme or problem that we are able to appreciate in their full value the role played by some of the components in defining and elucidating that problem. Why are Hermione's values false? Why must Gerald die? What is the importance of the discussion of the African figurine in Halliday's flat? The answer is that neither Hermione's cerebral values nor Gerald's ethics of productivity can serve as a substitute for God. But the African way may serve, although Lawrence would have us believe that Birkin finally rejects it. It is in a sort of "ultimate marriage" that Birkin finds an adequate substitute for God. This, at any rate, is what Lawrence would have us believe. What the novel says is not the same thing [In his introduction, Vivas quotes from Lawrence's essay **"The Novel"**: "Oh give me the novel. Let me hear what the novel says. As for the novelist, he is usually a dribbling liar"]. But while the novelist remains . . . a dribbling liar, the novel does not suffer from his lies: for the truth of the novel is not in disruptive conflict with the lies of the novelist; it is to be found below them.

The repudiation of the ethics of productivity and of the machine, as embodied in the colliery, is not new in Lawrence's work. We found it in **The Rainbow,** conveyed powerfully by Ursula's reaction to her uncle and the colliery he manages. (In mentioning Ursula here, I am not suggesting that the two novels are continuous; I do not think they are, although we know they were carved from a single novel entitled *The Sisters.*) In **Women in Love** Lawrence offers us a more detailed account of the essential weakness of the man who serves the machine and the flaws of the ethics of productivity than he offered us in **The Rainbow.** Carefully he draws a contrast between Gerald and the older Crich, and between Gerald and Rupert. The father manages the mines paternalistically and inefficiently while Gerald is pure efficiency and "go." And Gerald's love life is shallow while Rupert's is deep in spite of the conflicts that thwart him. This contrast is brought out by dialogue, by actual description, and by means of a number of semiotic signs and constitutive symbols, all of which converge to give us a picture of Gerald. The power of the Industrial Magnate is a sham. He is killed by the woman and the German whom Gerald thinks of as a "little vermin." (pp. 237-39)

[In] Chapter IV, "Diver," Gudrun sees Gerald dive and swim and envies him for his "freedom, liberty and mobility," and Ursula tells Gudrun about his improvements of Shortlands, his "go," and the way in which the miners hate him. In Chapter V, "In the Train," through the conversation between Birkin and Gerald, we are given a fairly clear account of Gerald's callousness, glistening through "the ethics of productivity." And we are also informed that he is satisfied to let his life be artificially held together by the social mechanism. In the semiotic sign or quasi-symbol of the mare scene, in Chapter IX, "Coal-Dust," we are given a picture of Gerald's ruthlessness. The Brangwen sisters are on the way home from school and the colliery train is rumbling near. They know Gerald only slightly at this time. Lawrence tells us:

> Whilst the two girls waited, Gerald Crich trotted up on a red Arab mare. He rode well and softly, pleased with the delicate quivering of the creature between his knees. . . . The locomotive chuffed slowly between the banks, hidden. The mare did not like it. She began to wince away, as if hurt by the unknown noise. But Gerald pulled her back and held her head to the gate.

I need not quote any more. The mare tries to bolt but Gerald forces her back. "The fool!" cried Ursula loudly. "Why doesn't he ride away till it's gone by?" The struggle goes on. "And she's bleeding! She's bleeding!" cries Ursula, while Gudrun looks and the world reels and passes into nothingness for her. (pp. 239-40)

[Throughout] his career Lawrence brooded long and deeply, almost obsessively, on the Gerald type and . . . he contrasted it with the type of the gamekeeper. In **The Rainbow** Gerald had a small part to play in the form of Tom Brangwen, Ursula's uncle. Sometimes he is metamorphosed into an emasculated Clifford Chatterley, and sometimes into an intellectual or a member of an artistic group such as the Bricknells and their friends in **Aaron's Rod.** He also appears, as we saw, as the effete rich young man, Rico. There is an important difference between Gerald and his imitations: the presentation of Gerald's deficiencies and limitations is achieved in dramatic terms. Whatever the sources of his conception (and the combination of Major Barber and Middleton Murry could not, on the surface, have appeared more incongruous and less promising than they evidently were) the result is a person grasped directly, not in terms of concepts, a moving, responding, human being, whose industrial success, whose inward disorganization and failure in love are not the product of a philosophy on the part of their creator, but a genuinely creative conception. Gerald is an industrialist moved by a strong will to power, a man whose world does not center. Having succeeded as a mine owner, he gets trapped in a love affair that kills him. And we are made to see, in terms of the relationship between him and Gudrun, why he had to die and how he was spiritually dead before he died physically.

Birkin, with whom Gerald is contrasted, is no less protean. He is the gamekeeper in **Lady Chatterley,** sometimes he is a gypsy, a southern Italian, a Mexican general of pure Indian blood, a Bohemian count, a groom, and once even a horse. The contrast in its many allotropic manifestations is the expression of a kind of Manichean conception of life in which the gamekeeper type is the fountain of life, potency, and tenderness; the Gerald type, often sexually impotent, is the bearer of corruption, causing destruction of self and of others. One could say, it is Eros against Thanatos.

It is important to notice the difference between the two types. The gamekeeper is always conceived in authentic dramatic terms; he is created out of pure experience. But this is not the case with the Gerald type. In **The Rainbow** Tom Brangwen, Ursula's uncle, although not a fully developed personality, is as authentic as any one in the book. And, with a qualification to be made next, this holds for Gerald. However, the Gerald type soon becomes a dramatized concept, an idea dressed up as a man, and sometimes—as in the case of the clergyman, Mr. Massy, in **"The Daughters of the Vicar"**—a mere caricature whose function in the story is to serve as a foil and a cathartic stimulus for Lawrence's hatred. (pp. 240-41)

An essential part of Lawrence's concept of Gerald the industrial magnate is the emptiness of the man, and this is also stated conceptually, although the discursive statement does not do justice to the dramatic presentation we also find in **Women in Love.** We are told that once Gerald succeeds in overhauling the system and in making the mines pay, he is up against the horror of his own vacuity:

> But now he had succeeded—he had finally succeeded. And once or twice lately, when he was alone in the evening and had nothing to do, he had suddenly stood up in terror, not knowing what he was. And he went to the mirror and looked long and closely at his own face, at his own eyes, seeking for something. He was afraid, in mortal dry fear, but he knew not what of. . . . He was afraid that one day he would break down and be a purely meaningless bubble lapping round a darkness.
>
> But his will yet held good, he was able to go away and read, and think about things.

His will holds good, after a fashion, until Gudrun and Loerke make a concerted and successful, if unconscious, effort to kill him.

But Gerald is more than a business magnate; he is also a friend and a lover, and these other sides of his personality are not dramatized illustrations of concepts. If we attempt to "reduce" them to abstract terms our effort is doomed to failure, as we realize when we turn from the semiotic or quasi-symbol of the mare to the scene in which Gudrun dances before the highland cattle and slaps Gerald's face (Chapter XIV, "Water-Party"), and to the scene presented in Chapter XVIII, "Rabbit." These are the two most important scenes in the novel for our grasp of Gerald's disastrous end and hence of Lawrence's authentic and pure poetic vision of the world.

At the party given by the Criches, Ursula and Gudrun had gone away from the crowd in Gerald's canoe. After a swim, Gudrun asked Ursula to sing because Gudrun wanted to dance. She begins to dance and notices a little cluster of Highland cattle among which there are some bullocks. Ursula is afraid, but Gudrun becomes possessed by "a strange passion to dance before the sturdy, handsome cattle." While she is dancing, Rupert Birkin and Gerald come looking for them and Gerald, with a loud shout, makes the cattle run off. He is angry because of the risk Gudrun is running, frightening the cattle, and asks Gudrun why she wants to drive them mad. They are nasty, he points out, when they turn. Gudrun mocks his fear. The rest of the incident must be given in Lawrence's own words:

> "You think I'm afraid of you and your cattle, don't you?" she asked.
>
> His eyes narrowed dangerously. There was a faint domineering smile on his face.
>
> "Why should I think that?" he said.
>
> She was watching him all the time with her dark, dilated, inchoate eyes. She leaned forward and swung round her arm, catching him a blow on the face with the back of her hand.

> "That's why," she said.
>
> And she felt in her soul an unconquerable lust for deep brutality against him. . . .
>
> He recoiled from the heavy blow across the face. He became deadly pale, and a dangerous flame darkened his eyes. . . .
>
> "You have struck the first blow," he said at last, forcing the words from his lungs. . . .
>
> "And I shall strike the last," she retorted involuntarily, with confident assurance.

Earlier in their acquaintance, Gerald had seen that Gudrun was "a dangerous, hostile spirit," and this understanding on his part had established the bond between them. This interchange takes place in Chapter X, "Sketch-Book," and we are told that in her tone of voice Gudrun made the understanding clear to Gerald: "They were of the same kind, he and she, a sort of diabolic free-masonry subsisted between them. Henceforth, she knew, she had power over him. Wherever they met, they would be secretly associated. And he would be helpless in the association with her. Her soul exulted." It is as if the relationship from the beginning were predestined to lead to his destruction. She did indeed strike the last blow.

The present scene, particularly if we read it entirely and in its context, is a very powerful scene and makes up a constitutive symbol. (pp. 242-44)

That those aspects of Gerald's personality, the lover and the friend, are not mere dramatized illustrations of concepts and cannot be "reduced" to abstract terms can be realized by turning to those powerful scenes and incidents in which these aspects are presented. Take for instance, the scene in which the rabbit, Bismarck, unites Gerald and Gudrun in a demonic marriage, Chapter XVIII. It will be remembered that Gerald and Gudrun never actually "marry" in a conventional sense and they do not begin living together until later. But it is in the rabbit scene that their ritual union finally takes place. To be present at an obscenity is, of course, literally speaking, an impossibility, if we take the term in its primitive sense. But the very paradox of our witnessing that which is out of sight while we are spectators in front of the stage, emphasizes the fact intended objectively by the scene, namely that there is something beyond the ordinary, beyond the presentable in the mystic communion of Gerald and Gudrun of which the officiating priest is a kicking, angry rabbit, and the witness is a child. Bringing to a final ripening the relationship between Gerald and Gudrun, the symbolic episode of the rabbit recapitulates dramatically the understanding that they had reached earlier and throws light on the experience that is to follow.

At the time of the rabbit episode a considerable degree of understanding had already been arrived at between Gerald and Gudrun. The first time Gudrun saw Gerald at his sister's wedding (Chapter I), she had reacted strongly to his presence, wanting to be alone, to know the strange, sharp inoculation that had changed the whole temper of her blood. From there on we begin to realize gradually that the relationship is going to generate a destructive force the victim of which will be Gerald. But although the scenes in which the destructive action is presented are stages in the development of an understanding between the two and contribute to our grasp of the quality of their relationship, they do not fully give us that quality. And what is much more important, no adjective or combination of adjectives seems adequate to characterize the quality of the relationship. When it finally comes to its catastrophic ending, the inadequacy of such characterization is more obvious. To call the relationship antagonistic is completely inadequate, since until the very end there is a kind of love between the two of them. But it would be no less inadequate to call it ambivalent. In the final analysis it is ineffable in abstract terms, and nothing but the full synoptic grasp of the chapters in which it is dramatically defined will yield its complexity, its nuances, the ebb and flow of its passion, and its corrosive destructiveness. Gerald and Gudrun move towards one another to their fulfillment, and the union is disastrous for Gerald, although they do not engage in the frightfully intense fights that Birkin and Ursula engage in. Gudrun's early slapping of Gerald's face is not an attack welling out of mutual irritation and lack of understanding. And the final fight in which Gerald almost chokes Gudrun to death is not occasioned—although it is easy to misunderstand it—by Gerald's jealousy of Loerke. How then are we to grasp the essentially negative nature of their relationship? As we turn the matter in our minds we become convinced to our dismay that discursive language can do no justice to it. Whatever there is between the man and the woman wells up from the depths of their souls; nor is it something to be *understood,* if the term is used to stand for the exhibition of motivations that can be more or less accurately designated in psychological language. But when we turn to the episode of the rabbit and consider the experience between Gerald and Gudrun in the light this episode throws upon it, the whole relationship becomes an object of dramatic aesthesis. What precedes the rabbit episode is crystalized and can now be grasped fully as an object of immediate apprehension, and what follows it takes its significance from it. The rabbit scene is a constitutive symbol. The critic, in the last analysis, is impotent before such a symbol; all he can do is suggest some of the obvious discursive meanings that the scene evokes.

Gudrun and Winifred, Gerald's little sister, want to catch Bismarck in order to draw him, because he looks splendid and fierce. As they are on their way to the hutch Gerald appears, and in the middle of the conversation between him and Gudrun we are told that their eyes meet in knowledge and Gerald finds himself desiring Gudrun. Gerald goes away and Gudrun tries to catch the rabbit, although Winifred warns her that he is a fearful kicker. Gudrun seizes the rabbit by the ears, but he is very strong and in an instant he is lunging wildly and kicking in mid-air. Gudrun is having a hard time holding him when Gerald returns and takes the rabbit from her. The beast lashes out at him also and Gerald, swift as lightning, brings his hand down on his neck. The rabbit emits an unearthly, abhorrent scream and is finally subdued. But nothing but the actual passage will do, although in order for it to have its full effect it must be read in context:

> "You wouldn't think there was all that force in a rabbit," he [Gerald] said, looking at Gudrun. And he saw her eyes black as night in her pallid face, she looked almost unearthly. The scream of the rabbit, after the violent tussle, seemed to have torn the veil of her consciousness. He looked at her, and the whitish, electric gleam in his face intensified.
>
> "I don't really like him," Winifred was crooning. "I don't care for him as I do for Loozie. He's hateful really."

A smile twisted Gudrun's face, as she recovered. She knew she was revealed.

"Don't they make the most fearful noise when they scream?" she cried, the high note in her voice, like a seagull's cry.

"Abominable," he said.

"He shouldn't be so silly when he has to be taken out," Winifred was saying, putting out her hand and touching the rabbit tentatively, as it skulked under his arm, motionless as if it were dead.

"He's not dead, is he, Gerald?" she asked.

"No, he ought to be," he said.

"Yes, he ought!" cried the child, with a sudden flush of amusement. And she touched the rabbit with more confidence. "His heart is beating *so* fast. Isn't he funny? He really is."

"Where do you want him?" asked Gerald.

"In the little green court," she said.

Gudrun looked at Gerald with strange, darkened eyes, strained with underworld knowledge, almost supplicating, like those of a creature which is at his mercy, yet which is his ultimate victor. He did not know what to say to her. He felt the mutual hellish recognition. And he felt he ought to say something, to cover it. He had the power of lightning in his nerves, she seemed like a soft recipient of his magical, hideous white fire. He was unconfident, he had qualms of fear.

"Did he hurt you?" he asked.

"No," she said.

"He's an insensible beast," he said, turning his face away.

They came to the little court. . . . Gerald tossed the rabbit down. It crouched still and would not move. Gudrun watched it with faint horror.

"Why doesn't it move?" she cried.

"It's skulking," he said.

She looked up at him, and a slight sinister smile contracted her white face.

"Isn't it a *fool!*" she cried. "Isn't it a sickening *fool?*" The vindictive mockery in her voice made his brain quiver. Glancing up at him, into his eyes, she revealed again the mocking, white-cruel recognition. There was a league between them, abhorrent to them both. They were implicated with each other in abhorrent mysteries.

"How many scratches have you?" he asked, showing his hard forearm, white and hard and torn in red gashes.

"How really vile!" she cried, flushing with a sinister vision. "Mine is nothing."

She lifted her arm and showed a deep red score down the silken white flesh.

"What a devil!" he exclaimed. But it was as if he had had knowledge of her in the long red rent of her forearm, so silken and soft. He did not want to touch her. He would have to make himself touch her, deliberately. The long, shallow red rip seemed torn across his own brain, tearing the surface of his ultimate consciousness, letting through the forever unconscious, unthinkable red ether of the beyond, the obscene beyond.

"It doesn't hurt you very much, does it?" he asked solicitous.

"Not at all," she cried.

And suddenly the rabbit, which had been crouching as if it were a flower, so still and soft, suddenly burst into life. Round and round the court it went, as if shot from a gun, round and round like a furry meteorite, in a tense hard circle that seemed to bind their brains. They all stood in amazement, smiling uncannily, as if the rabbit were obeying some unknown incantation. Round and round it flew, on the grass under the old red walls like a storm.

And then quite suddenly it settled down, hobbled among the grass, and sat considering, its nose twitching like a bit of fluff in the wind. After having considered for a few minutes, a soft bunch with a black, open eye, which perhaps was looking at them, perhaps was not, it hobbled calmly forward and began to nibble the grass with that mean motion of a rabbit's quick eating.

"It's mad," said Gudrun. "It is most decidedly mad."

He laughed. "The question is," he said, "what is madness? I don't suppose it is rabbit-mad."

"Don't you think it is?" she asked.

"No. That's what it is to be a rabbit."

There was a queer, faint, obscene smile over his face. She looked at him and saw him, and knew that he was initiate as she was initiate. This thwarted her, and contravened her, for the moment.

"God be praised we aren't rabbits," she said, in a high, shrill voice.

The smile intensified a little, on his face.

"Not rabbits?" he said, looking at her fixedly.

Slowly her face relaxed into a smile of obscene recognition.

"Ah, Gerald," she said, in a strong, slow, almost man-like way. "—All that, and more." Her eyes looked up at him with shocking nonchalance.

He felt again as if she had hit him across the face— or rather, as if she had torn him across the breast, dully, finally. . . .

There is a suggestion that the marriage ritual performed by the officiating rabbit is consummated by the blood drawn by the animal's clawing. But if this seems too ingenious, certainly the gash will be recognized by the reader as a variant of the face-slapping episode and an anticipatory summation of their subsequent relationship. One of the themes that the rabbit episode illumines is expressed several times through the novel and comes to indirect and periphrastic expression in Chapter XXI, entitled "Threshold." In the midst of a conversation between Gerald and Gudrun on Birkin's ideal of marriage, we read:

> And they both [Gerald and Gudrun] felt the subterranean desire to let go, to fling away everything, and lapse into a sheer unrestraint, brutal and licentious. A strange black passion surged up pure in Gudrun. She felt strong. She felt her hands so strong, as if she could tear the world asunder with them. She remembered the abandonments of Roman licence, and her heart grew hot. She knew she wanted this herself also—or something, something equivalent. Ah, if that which was unknown and suppressed in her were once let loose, what an orgiastic and satisfying event it would be. And she wanted it, she trembled slightly from the proximity of the man, who stood just behind her, suggestive of the same black licentiousness that rose in herself. She wanted it with him, this unacknowledged frenzy. For a moment the clear perception of this preoccupied her, distinct and perfect in its final reality. . . .
>
> (pp. 245-51)

[The] love relationship of some of Lawrence's fictional characters involves, besides their Krafft-Ebing aspect, or perhaps, because of it, an animal quality of hardness and cruelty. Their mating, we come to realize, is like the mating of those insects in which the female kills the male after or even during the act. This reinforces, in turn, our sense that, in *Women in Love,* the apparently strong industrial magnate turns out to be the weaker of the two and the woman knows it from the beginning. She finally sends Gerald to his death when she is done with him and finds her true mate in the German sculptor, Loerke. Gudrun murders Gerald without premeditation, guile, or plan, in a more or less unconscious manner, by forcing him to face the frozen emptiness of his soul. This is not at all clear during the black rite at which the rabbit officiates. Nor are the premonitions that have preceded the black rite of their marriage fully clear at this point. They become clear—in the sense in which an ordered presentation can be grasped as aesthetically clear—when we manage to comprehend synoptically the whole poem. (p. 252)

We have abundant evidence that Lawrence took the account of Gerald as a general law, which may be formulated as follows: industrial magnates are weak and therefore incapable of adequate fulfillment as human beings. But his acceptance of this law does not constitute a fault in *Women in Love,* and the question whether the law is true or false is not relevant, for *Women in Love* has been conceived initially in dramatic terms. What is relevant is that in the novel the way in which Gerald's life is held together externally by the ethics of productivity, the inward emptiness of his life, its tropism towards self-destruction, the eventual failure of his affair with Gudrun and his disastrous fate—all are accepted by the reader as making a harmonious whole. This was the way Gerald was and this was his fate, and there is nothing in his actions or words, nothing in the whole account of him that forces us to recognize the picture as factitious. But a fact and an explanation of a fact are two different things, and if one asks why the combination of traits and inclinations constituting Gerald lead him to his disastrous end, the answer that in fact they do is not an answer to the question. However, it is advisable to reiterate with emphasis that the only admissible question is whether or not dramatically there is a clash or confusion, a disharmony or incongruity, that prevents us from accepting the drama as presented. If there is none, the question, whatever its historical validity or importance, does not point to a flaw because in the novel we find no answer to it. The observation is important not merely because it points to the high achievement that **Women in Love** is generally conceded to represent, but because it calls attention by contrast to the relative failure of those of Lawrence's works in which the component parts are held together mechanically, are tied together by dramatized conceptual means, are, in short, factitious. The contrast marks the difference between the high point of his creative power and lesser expressions of it. It is important to bear in mind that the lesser expressions are by no means negligible, if we are to appreciate the full miracle of his achievement.

That the question of adequate causation does not arise, however, deserves further attention, at least to this extent: Gerald is a successful creation. But when we take it all in and try to see what Lawrence has done and how he has done it, we are forced to reconsider our judgment. Highly as we may have thought of the novel before the critical exploration had done its job, we are now forced to go further and to admit that it is the product of an artistic talent that is quite rare. For it is not in the cattle and the rabbit scenes alone that we find constitutive symbols by means of which Lawrence accomplishes the feat of concentrating meanings and associations he wishes to reveal. The novel presents Gerald by means of a cluster of component constitutive symbols, although, if I am right, all the other symbols occupy a place subordinate to that of the rabbit. Indeed, if the word were not so misleading, because of its polysemic richness, I would say that **Women in Love** is a triumph of *symbolic* art: of art that works, in Mr. Leavis' phrase, from profounder levels and in more complex ways in order to convey more and deeper significance than naturalistic or realistic art is able to.

Just as the relationship between Gerald and Gudrun is exhibited dramatically, at its full depth, by the powerful symbol of the rabbit scene, so the relationship between Birkin and Ursula is revealed through the symbol of the shattering of the moon, presented in Chapter XIX, entitled "Moony." There is even an interesting parallelism in the two relationships in that corresponding to the quasi-symbol of the mare we find the quasi-symbol of the Mino, in Chapter XIII, by means of which Birkin seeks to convey to Ursula, and Lawrence to us, something of what Birkin has in mind when he says he wants a special kind of love beyond love.

We know a good deal about Birkin before the Mino episode takes place. He first broaches the subject of love in his conversation with Gerald on his way to London. And in the early stages of his relationship with Ursula, after Birkin has finally broken with Hermione, he tries to explain to her, early in Chapter XIII, what he is looking for. He speaks to her about a love beyond love and insists that the ordinary kind of love gives out in the last issues because, at the very last, one is alone, one is a real, impersonal self that is beyond any emotional relationship. For this reason, he tells Ursula, he is not even interested in her good looks. And laying himself open to the obvious retort, he tells her he wants a woman he does not see.

> "There is," he [Birkin] said, in a voice of pure abstraction, "a final me which is stark and impersonal and beyond responsibility. So there is a final you. And it is there I would want to meet you—not in the emotional, loving plane—but there beyond,

where there is no speech and no terms of agreement. . . ."

But Birkin fails in his attempt to make Ursula understand, and the reader is no better off than she is. Her failure stems partly from the fact that Ursula thinks of love in the conventional sense and partly from the fact that she suspects that Birkin has in mind a relationship in which the female is subject to the will of the male. "It is purely selfish," she tells him, and further explanation on his part does not make it clearer to her than it does to us. But while descriptive discourse is of no help, and while it is in any case too early in the relationship for either Ursula or the reader to be able to understand, Lawrence does manage to achieve early in their relationship a dramatic definition of their conflict and their inability to resolve it by the use of the quasi-image of the cat, Mino. In the midst of the discussion:

> A young grey cat that had been sleeping on the sofa jumped down and stretched, rising on its long legs, and arching its slim back. Then it sat considering for a moment, erect and kingly. And then, like a dart, it had shot out of the room, through the open window-doors, and into the garden.

> "What's he after?" said Birkin, rising.

> The young cat trotted lordly down the path, waving his tail. He was an ordinary tabby with white paws, a slender young gentleman. A crouching, fluffy, brownish-grey cat was stealing up the side of the fence. The Mino walked statelily [sic] up to her, with manly nonchalance. She crouched before him and pressed herself on the ground in humility, a fluffy soft outcast, looking up at him with wild eyes that were green and lovely as great jewels. He looked casually down on her. So she crept a few inches further, proceeding on her way to the back door, crouching in a wonderful, soft self-obliterating manner, and moving like a shadow.

> He, going statelily on his slim legs, walked after her, then suddenly, for pure excess, he gave her a light cuff with his paw on the side of her face. She ran off a few steps, like a blown leaf along the ground, then crouched unobtrusively, in submissive, wild patience. The Mino pretended to take no notice of her. . . .

There is more of this play and finally Ursula breaks out,

> "Now, why does he do that?" cried Ursula in indignation.

> "They are on intimate terms," said Birkin.

But Ursula thinks Mino is a bully:

> "Are you a bully, Mino?" Birkin asked.

> The young slim cat looked at him, and slowly narrowed its eyes. Then it glanced away at the landscape, looking into the distance, as if completely oblivious of the two human beings.

> "Mino," said Ursula, "I don't like you. You are a bully like all males."

The passage is only a small part of a scene too long to quote in full. In the subsequent discussion between the couple the cat is forgotten and Birkin tries to make headway against Ursula's decided and clever resistance to his explanation, but his asseverations and analogies fail. I hope the quotation will help make clear the notion of quasi-symbol. While the Mino scene helps define and serves to sharpen in dramatic terms and, of course, in context, the failure of the couple to come to an understanding, that failure can be and is also conveyed independently. Yet the Mino incident is not a merely external adornment. It is consubstantial with the developing affair. Delete it and important aspects of the drama are lost to our grasp. But what the Mino episode tells us about Birkin's initial failure to convey to Ursula what he means by his love beyond love, it does not tell us *in* as well as *through,* but only *through* itself. What it tells us can be apprehended independently of the Mino scene and is indeed so apprehended later when we grasp the dramatic account of their relationship as it develops.

This reservation does not apply to the moon-shattering scene. Commentary can elucidate the upper layers, so to speak, of its significance; but the reader who has pondered it, knows that what he apprehends dramatically and immediately cannot be successfully translated into discursive terms.

Lawrence begins the moon-shattering scene in a deceptively facile manner. But as he finishes the chapter, the reader is aware that revelations have been made of vast importance; and among these is the central predicament in which Birkin is involved and the crisis to which it leads. There are statements that, made discursively, would have led the police to treat **Women in Love** in the very same manner in which **The Rainbow** and **Lady Chatterley** were treated. The constitutive symbol which is the scene of the shattering of the moon enables Lawrence to make his presentation fully and completely, as I hope to suggest. Ursula set off to Willey Green, towards the mill. And as she walked

> She started, noticing something on her right hand, between the tree trunks. It was like a great presence, watching her, dodging her. She started violently. It was only the moon, risen through the thin trees. But it seemed so mysterious, with its white and deathly smile. And there was no avoiding it. Night or day, one could not escape the sinister face, triumphant and radiant like this moon, with a high smile. She hurried on, cowering from the white planet. . . .

> The moon was transcendent over the bare, open space, she suffered from being exposed to it. There was a glimmer of nightly rabbits across the ground. . . .

Walking in a landscape full of night sounds and flooded with moon-brilliant hardness, which makes her soul cry out in her, Ursula finally gets away from the moonlight into the shade, reaches the pond, and notices the water, "perfect in its stillness, floating the moon upon it." Soon she sees Birkin wandering by the edge of the pond, throwing flowers into it, and talking disconnectedly to himself.

> "You can't go away," he was saying. "There *is* no away. You only withdraw upon yourself."

> He threw a dead flower-husk on to the water.

> "An antiphony—they lie, and you sing back to them. There wouldn't have to be any truth, if there weren't any lies. Then one needn't assert anything—"

> He stood still, looking at the water, and throwing upon it the husks of the flowers.

"Cybele—curse her! The accursed Syria Dea! Does one begrudge it her? What else is there—?"

Ursula wanted to laugh loudly and hysterically, hearing his isolated voice speaking out. It was so ridiculous.

Then she saw Birkin pick up a stone and throw it in the water. Ursula saw the image of the moon "leaping and swaying, all distorted, in her eyes. It seemed to shoot out arms of fire like a cuttlefish, like a luminous polyp, palpitating strongly before her." Birkin throws more stones.

> Then again there was a burst of sound, and a burst of brilliant light, the moon had exploded on the water, and was flying asunder in flakes of white and dangerous fire. Rapidly, like white birds, the fires all broken rose across the pond, fleeing in clamourous confusion, battling with the flock of dark waves that were forcing their way in. The furthest waves of light, fleeing out, seemed to be clamouring against the shore for escape, the waves of darkness came in heavily, running under towards the centre. But at the centre, the heart of all, was still a vivid incandescent quivering of a white moon not quite destroyed, a white body of fire writhing and striving and not even now broken open, not yet violated. It seemed to be drawing itself together with strange, violent pangs, in blind effort. It was getting stronger, it was re-asserting itself, the inviolable moon. And the rays were hastening in in thin lines of light, to return to the strengthened moon, that shook upon the water in triumphant reassumption.

Birkin tries again and again, throwing more stones, looking for larger stones and throwing them, until Ursula cannot bear it any longer and comes out from where she was sitting and speaks to him.

> "You won't throw stones at it any more, will you?"

> "I wanted to see if I could make it be quite gone off the pond," he said.

> "Yes, it was horrible, really. Why should you hate the moon? It hasn't done you any harm, has it?"

> "Was it hate?" he said.

This scene, it should be remembered, takes place before the relationship between Birkin and Ursula becomes intimate. Birkin has broken with Hermione and has offered Ursula a love beyond love that she cannot bring herself to accept in spite of her feeling towards him. He has spent some time in France, and this is the first time any of his friends or we have seen him since his return. Above all the scene conveys the depth of frustration and the ambivalent and still formless nature of his feelings towards Ursula. But it conveys much more. In the ghastly drama, particularly in the cursing of Cybele, Lawrence gives us the full depth of hopelessness and incoherent disruption from which Birkin is suffering, the threat and the frustration that are tearing him. Mr. Hough [see Additional Bibliography] observes that Lawrence's mythology is a little rusty. Perhaps. So was his knowledge of the Aztec religion: that was worse than rusty, it was incomplete and superficial. And so, too, I would imagine, was his knowledge of Etruscan archaeology. Whatever Lawrence knew or did not know about classical mythology may be relevant to his biographer who is intent on measuring the extent of his learning; but it is not relevant to the interpreter of his poetry. Birkin's ravings are fully and adequately expressive. He curses Cybele, the Syria Dea, identified—or was it, confused?—in Greece with Aphrodite. She was a terrible goddess, for she destroyed the sacred king who mated with her on a mountain top by tearing out his sexual organs. She was served by sodomitic priests who dressed as women, castrated themselves, and sought ecstasy in union with her. I take it therefore that Birkin is expressing the ancient and deep-rooted fear some men have felt towards women.

Whether that fear is or is not universal, and what its relation is to the male's vaunted superiority over the female, are interesting questions; but this is not the proper place to ask them. In respect to Birkin, however, it is entirely proper to ask whether the kind of primacy over the female that he claimed and yet the "polarity" he also wanted did not conceal something else: did it conceal a fear, perhaps as deep as, or deeper than, his longing for Ursula? This, I take it, is what, in part, the shattering of the image of the moon tells us. . . . Wanting Ursula, Birkin is also afraid that she will accept him, on any terms whatever. But it is not Ursula alone whom he has feared. He has feared Hermione and has broken with her for what he made to appear to be genuinely good reasons. Are we to gather that Birkin fears women and that at the root of his fear there is a component that he faces in the moon scene but does not dare face in its own literal terms, a component that taken together with his fear of woman leads us to the deep and sickly roots of the conflict between his need for love and his inability to accept or to give love? Critics have generally accepted at face value Lawrence's intention and have failed to notice that it does not coincide exactly with the intention of the novel.

But is this all there is to Birkin's predicament? Cybele's priests are holy eunuchs and are sodomitic. And this is one key to the specific and complex nature of Birkin's predicament. Unless we read the pages following the moon-shattering scene in this context their turgid periphrases will succeed in camouflaging their full import. Let us review Birkin's cogitations the day following his effort to shatter the image of the moon. I shall follow them *au pied de la lettre* ["to the letter"]. He feels wistful and yearning. But he thinks that perhaps he has been wrong to go to Ursula with the idea of what he wanted. He wonders whether it was really an idea or an interpretation of a profound yearning. If the latter, why was he always talking of sensual fulfillment? The two, he admits, did not agree very well. And facing the contradiction, "suddenly," we are told, he "found himself face to face with a situation." It was, he assures himself, as simple as this—fatally simple. But simple as it may have been for Birkin, for the reader the situation is anything but simple, since the alternatives that Birkin reviews elude his grasp to some extent, and what he succeeds in grasping is a condition that goes beyond a mere division of the soul; it is a distinctly unhealthy condition.

The first alternative that Birkin considers is one that he rejects: "a further sensual experience—something deeper, darker, than ordinary life could give." This experience is defined for Birkin (but not for the reader, or at least not with equal lucidity) by the elegant figure from West Africa that had been the subject of a conversation between him and Gerald the night they spent at Halliday's flat. In that conversation at Halliday's Birkin had told Gerald that the figure was *high* art (he emphasized the adjective), because it embodied hundreds of centuries of pure culture in sensation, culture in the physical consciousness, really ultimate *physical* con-

sciousness (and again the emphasis on the *physical* is Birkin's), mindless, utterly sensual. With the African process Birkin contrasts the process of the white races, having the arctic behind them, the ice-destructive knowledge, the snow-abstract annihilation, which he connects at this time with Gerald. Birkin broods on the African process which, he thinks, involves great mysteries, sensual, mindless, dreadful, far beyond the phallic cult. And he asks himself, "How far in their inverted culture, had these West Africans gone beyond phallic knowledge?" He realizes that they had gone very, very far. He thinks: "Thousands of years ago, that which was imminent in himself must have taken place in these Africans: the goodness, the holiness, the desire for creation . . . must have lapsed." As he broods he realizes that Gerald was fated to "pass away" through the perfect cold that was the way of the white races, with the vast abstraction of ice and snow of the arctic north that lies behind them. Birkin becomes frightened and tired and decides that "he could not attend to these mysteries any more."

Instantly he recollects that there is another way, the way of freedom, the union that he had offered Ursula and that she had rejected because she interpreted it as bullying. Inspired by his recollection he decides that he must go immediately to propose marriage to Ursula. In the Brangwens' living room there is a quarrel between Ursula and her father in Birkin's presence and she then turns down the offer of marriage. But later, recoiling from her impulsive attitude, she turns again in spirit to Birkin and prepares "to fight him" for her belief that love was everything. The chapters that follow in which the couple has the leading role are an account of that fight, with its moments of perfect union and mutual acceptance and its high peaks of erotic ecstasy. In these scenes Lawrence tries to do indirectly what later he attempted to do in *Lady Chatterley* directly—to render in language the felt inwardness of the erotic experience as felt. (pp. 253-62)

This is a very inadequate account of the cogitations that occupied Birkin the day after the shattering of the image of the moon. Birkin's thought is presented by Lawrence in three pages whose meaning the reader knows he must grasp, for it is obviously of pivotal importance if one is to grasp clearly what ails Birkin and why he cannot be satisfied with the love Ursula offers him. From these three pages the reader gathers clearly enough that Birkin rejects the African way and decides to seek in his union with Ursula the solution for his desperate problem. But what exactly is the African way that he rejects? And exactly what was *imminent in himself,* that he now emphatically rejects? What kind of goodness and holiness have lapsed in these people, what kind of desire for creation? It cannot be artistic creation, for the West African carving, Birkin had emphatically told Gerald, was a triumph of artistic creation, pure, high art. And what did those who carved it know that he himself did not? And how could he not know it, when he was aware that it was imminent in himself? Exactly what does Birkin mean by "further sensual experience—something deeper, darker, than ordinary life"? What does he mean by the mindless, progressive knowledge through the senses, the principle of knowledge in dissolution needed to produce the long, elegant body of the West African figure? Didn't Birkin, didn't Lawrence know what these phrases intended? A close reading of these three pages, so obviously freighted with meaning, discloses that they suggest vaguely, they intimate, they tease, and in the end they deny the reader the clear understanding he craves. Did Lawrence know the answers to these questions but chose not to tell us in so many words? I think he knew and did not dare tell.

Do the sensual, mindless, dreadful mysteries of an inverted culture coincide with the love play of **Lady Chatterley?** If this is the answer it throws light on an episode presented early in Chapter XXIII, entitled "Excurse," in which, after giving Ursula some rings, Birkin and she quarrel bitterly. After the quarrel Birkin acknowledges to himself that Ursula's accusations were in the main right. "He knew he was perverse, so spiritual on the one hand, and in some strange way, degraded, on the other." This suggests that he might not have really rejected the African way. For whatever the allusion involves, it is something that, when in a quarrel Ursula throws it in his face, Birkin admits makes him degraded and perverse.

But we are not yet through with the symbol of the shattering of the image of the moon. Another one of the frustrations it expresses is related to two chapters in the book: Chapter XVI, entitled "Man to Man," in which Birkin proposes to Gerald that they swear *Blutbruderschaft;* and Chapter XX, entitled "Gladiatorial," in which Gerald and Birkin wrestle naked in Gerald's living room. The importance of these two chapters must be great because their substance is summed up in the conversation between Birkin and Ursula at the close of the book. Birkin says to Ursula:

> "Having you I can live all my life without anybody else, any other sheer intimacy. But to make it complete, really happy, I wanted eternal union with a man too: another kind of love. . . ."

> "I don't believe it," she said. "It's an obstinacy, a theory, a perversity."

> "Well—" he said.

> "You can't have two kinds of love. Why should you!"

> "It seems as if I can't," he said. "Yet I wanted it."

> "You can't have it, because it's false, impossible," she said.

> "I don't believe that," he answered.

The next line contains only two words: "The End."

It would be delightfully simple if on the basis of this conversation and of Chapters XVI and XX, of which the conversation is the summing up, we could conclude *tout court* that Birkin is frustrated because Ursula's will and Gerald's death defeat his desire for homosexual experience. But in **Women in Love**—as in other major novels of Lawrence's—the treatment of the theme of homosexuality does not lend itself to unambiguous interpretation. Neither the offer of *Blutbruderschaft* nor the wrestling episode nor the closing conversation constitutes positive evidence; with the evidence on hand, an interpretation depends on the meanings we wish to assign to our terms. The term "homosexual" can be used to characterize these passages if we are explicitly clear as to what we are doing: we are using the term in the broad sense we have learned from psychoanalysts. But the passages give us no basis for determining how Birkin's yearning for a friendship with a man would find expression. Did he hope for more than a sublimated relationship?

The problem of homosexuality in Lawrence and in his work is not a simple one, and it is one that many of his critics have treated with less than candor. Some writers have tried to clear

Lawrence from the charge. But I am not here interested in Lawrence's biography.

When we interpret Birkin's cravings for friendship with Gerald, we see that the objective intention of **Women in Love** is to represent the incompleteness of Birkin's relationship with Ursula, although that relationship is presented during its rare best moments as giving Ursula complete fulfillment. But only rarely does it give Birkin the fulfillment that it gives Ursula. In Chapters XXIII and XXVII, entitled "Excurse" and "Flitting" respectively, there are passages, it is true, that may be taken as evidence of the complete satisfactoriness of the relationship for Birkin. At the end of Chapter XXIII we read: "She had her desire fulfilled. He had his desire fulfilled. For she was to him what he was to her, the immemorial magnificence of mystic, palpable, real otherness." And later, in Chapter XXVII, there is a passage too long to quote in full from which I pluck the following statements:

> She could not know how much it meant to him, how much he meant by the few words. . . . This marriage with her was his resurrection and his life. . . . It was something beyond love, such a gladness of having surpassed oneself, of having transcended the old existence. How could he say "I" when he was something new and unknown, not himself at all?

But in order to assay the novel's meaning properly, such passages must be contrasted with statements such as those found in Chapter XXIII, in which we are told that Birkin found Ursula beautiful, beyond womanhood, but in which we read: "Yet something was tight and unfree in him." With our knowledge of the psychopathology of everyday language, it is pertinent to ask what exactly does it mean when a lover finds a woman *beyond* womanhood. The statement is ambiguous and if the critical detective does not find evidence here, he does find a clue. For if Birkin loved Ursula as a woman, and there were no ambivalence in his love, and she represented for him in the best moments of fulfillment the farthest limit of which Birkin was capable of joy and completion in love, he would find her the essence of womanhood, the crystallization of woman, the embodiment of the Platonic idea of the female; he would find her *beyond* woman in the sense that he found her a woman but unlike the women men mate with, a goddess. On the other hand it may be that the relationship left him tight and unfree, because he found her beautiful beyond *womanhood,* because he was projecting into her, or trying to find in her, what she was not and could not be.

The resolution of this puzzle can at best be merely speculative, in the worst sense of this word, since the ambiguity is inherent in the text and the clues we might find with which to resolve it would call for uncontrolled interpretation. But this much I think we can assert: the relationship between Birkin and Ursula, often contrasted with that between Gerald and Gudrun, and undoubtedly intended by Lawrence to be so contrasted, does not appear on critical examination to be an ideal one. There is no question that Lawrence's intention coincides with that of the novel as regards Gerald and Gudrun; their relationship is destructive, catastrophic. But the relationship between Birkin and Ursula can hardly be said to be an exemplar, to be a "norm" by which to interpret the full disastrous meaning of the other, as Mr. Leavis, among others, takes it to be [see Additional Bibliography]. Mr. Leavis writes: "In Birkin's married relations with Ursula the book invites us to localize the positive, the conceivable and due—if only with difficulty attainable—solution of the problem; the norm, in relation to which Gerald's disaster gets its full meaning."

The preceding analysis has shown the contrast to be considerably more complex than Mr. Leavis takes it to be. For if the love between Birkin and Ursula illumines the nature of the love between the other couple—and this cannot be denied—it still cannot be taken without extensive qualifications to be a normal marriage or to constitute a norm, even in those high erotic moments reached occasionally by Birkin and Ursula. To call their relationship a norm by means of which to appreciate the disastrous ending of the affair between Gerald and Gudrun is to fail to perceive in it that which denies it its character of norm—in either of the two usual senses of this term. It cannot be a *norm* in the sense that it is a mark toward which the affair between Gerald and Gudrun *ought* to aspire. There are two reasons for this: the first is that even when we reckon the rare moments, we cannot separate them from Birkin's radical dissatisfaction with Ursula and his incompleteness with her; the second is that in spite of his resolution to abandon "the African way," Birkin does not seem to have abandoned it. Nor can we call the relationship between Birkin and Ursula a *norm* in the sense that it is the expression of the average—unless Mr. Leavis is in possession of statistics to which he does not refer, such as those provided by the late Doctor Kinsey, showing that a significant percentage of the male population of the society constituted by the world of *Women in Love* suffers from the same frustrations and indulges in the same erotic practices (the African way?) that Birkin indulges in. But how could Mr. Leavis or his sociologist have obtained such statistics? The only way would be that of critics who inquire how many children Lady Macbeth had.

These considerations entitle us to arrive at an important conclusion. Put bluntly they show that, contrary to Lawrence's intentions, Birkin's religion of love beyond love, the sort of ultimate marriage he sought, could not perform for Birkin, when he found such a marriage, the function that he had hoped it would. Birkin had hoped that love would give his life center—"seeing there is no God." But it did not. One could argue that Birkin was incapable of the perfect love for which he yearned or that the love for which he yearned was not a perfect love—or both, of course. The religious believer will argue that Birkin failed because there is no substitute for God. But the observation is here irrelevant. In any case, love did not do for Birkin what he, and apparently Lawrence, had hoped it would do. His craving for the African way and his need for a friendship with Gerald, made impossible by the latter's death, give the lie to Birkin's religion of love and Lawrence's intention. Because I am discussing a novel, I do not mean to say that the religion of love could not have satisfied another man, imaginary or real, under different circumstances. Such a statement, anyway, would be a law of human nature, and I, at least, lack the data to formulate it. All I know of men and their societies would seem to indicate that they find apparently acceptable destinies of the most diverse and conflicting natures. To what extent these diverse ways are, by objective standards, an adequate or a satisfactory realization of the powers of man and hence an expression of the good life, is not a question to be raised here. In any case, to draw a sociological law from the imaginings of a poet—even one greater, more universal, and more healthy than Lawrence—is a foolishness that I am not inclined to commit. All we can assert is that the novel shows that the religion of love

failed to satisfy Birkin. Any attempt to go beyond this statement turns a novel into sociology. And the best of novelists can be but very poor sociologists. (pp. 262-68)

[If] we read *The Rainbow, Women in Love,* and *Lady Chatterley* with care we find in them, too, a profound emotional disorder, an obdurate major disharmony, informed with genius as the substance of their drama. To go to these books for the wisdom that our civilization needs, without rigorous discrimination, is folly.

Aside from the moral problem that is posed by the erotic practices of Will Brangwen, Rupert Birkin, and the gamekeeper, Mellors, another observation must be made if we take the novel as anything but a dramatic presentation—if we take it as the source of wisdom or take it as a criticism of contemporary society. Confronted by the values espoused by the two couples in *Women in Love,* we are forced to conclude that Birkin and Ursula stand out in positive contrast to Gerald and Gudrun in their catastrophic relationship. This is clear and unambiguous enough. We must prefer one couple to the other in spite of Birkin's incomplete fulfillment. But Birkin's values involve a repudiation of his world, for in choosing to wander a bit he chooses to escape. Dismissing the ethics of productivity as evil is well enough for himself and his wife. But if it is put forth as a pattern for living, we are forced to ask how we are going to keep body and soul together after quitting our jobs. Who is going to man the boats and railroads that are going to take us on our wandering? Who is going to sow and harvest the wheat and bake the bread? What are we going to buy bread with, assuming that it can be found? Birkin and Ursula had no stated means of livelihood. This is not a fault in the novel. The novel hangs together although Lawrence did not take up that question. But to take the relationship between Birkin and Ursula seriously as a practical solution of our problems is simply silly.

But why do we have to take this novel (or any other novel for that matter) as anything else than what it is, a dramatic presentation? Whatever he may have thought he was doing, what Lawrence the artist produced was a creative organization of experience in dramatic and narrative terms which, within its own frame, is wholly valid, and valid in the only manner in which a novel can and has to be valid—valid aesthetically. If Birkin is not at the end satisfied with his wife but still longs for an "eternal union with a man too: another kind of love," it is Birkin and not mankind who is dissatisfied and still longs; and if Gerald is destroyed, it is Gerald and not all industrial magnates who suffer destruction. And if Hermione feels uplifted when she understands something about the stars, it is Hermione who feels as she does, not all women and all men. And if Sir Joshua the sociologist—I almost wrote the logician and philosopher—is a man "whose mental fibre is so tough as to be insentient," it is Sir Joshua and not all sociologists who are tough and insentient.

We ought to remember also that the values revealed by Lawrence in his novel are not all negative values. The role given carnal love in the novel is, let me repeat, a positive value as Father Tiverton pointed out, when we discriminate between it and those aspects that fall within the province of Krafft-Ebing; the essentially religious reverence for nature we found in Lawrence's response to the Indian dances is also a positive value; the persistent quest for an adequate conception of human destiny is also a positive value of Lawrence's poetry. Nor are these all. But they hardly need be called to the attention of the reader at this late date. What is needed at the moment, if I may be allowed to reiterate, is a study that corrects the exaggerations of such critics as Mr. Eliot [see *TCLC*, Vol. 2, pp. 219-20] or the unintelligent dismissals of Lawrence by such writers as Bertrand Russell, on the one hand, and the abandoned panegyrics of Mr. Leavis on the other. This is the reason I have insisted . . . on pointing out Lawrence's failures and his triumphs, and in pointing out the exact nature of the substance of his triumphs. The required discrimination of the unacceptable values to be found in his work does not mean that his work has no value. It has great value, it has the value of genuine poetry. Lawrence has made it possible for those who read him critically to understand aesthetically, to grasp in the mode of immediate apprehension aspects of our contemporary world that, had he left them uninformed, would have remained for us mere threatening, oppressive chaos. He charts our world. Without him and the other poets who also chart it, we would be likely to be blind to the specific process of disintegration of which we are the victims. (pp. 270-72)

> *Eliseo Vivas, in his* D. H. Lawrence: The Failure and the Triumph of Art, *1960. Reprint by George Allen & Unwin Ltd., 1961, 302 p.*

JULIAN MOYNAHAN   (essay date 1963)

[*An American novelist and critic, Moynahan has written book-length studies on the works of Vladimir Nabokov and D. H. Lawrence. In the following excerpt from his* Deed of Life: The Novels and Tales of D. H. Lawrence, *Moynahan examines* Women in Love *as a study in social and personal disintegration.*]

Women in Love, "a sequel to **The Rainbow** though quite unlike it," is Lawrence's most fully achieved book, his most difficult, and is one of the half dozen most important novels of the present century. When he had almost completed the final revision in November 1916, Lawrence wrote, "the book frightens me; it is so end-of-the-world," and we know he intended at one point to entitle the novel *Dies Irae.* His description fits the thing done in at least three senses. Like *The Magic Mountain,* **Women in Love** sums up a society which did not survive the first world war and the convulsive revolutionary aftermath of the war. Secondly, it envisions prewar England—and Europe—as though it were already in its death throes. This process of dissolution is represented as going on in society at large, in the sphere of personal relations, in the hearts and souls of individual characters.

Gerald's obsessive tie to Gudrun leads to his own death, but Gerald's efficient reorganization of the Crich family mines has already spelled a kind of death for thousands of workmen by converting them into machine-men. As early as the ninth chapter we hear that Gudrun is "like a new Daphne, turning not into a tree but a machine." At the end, as she prepares to go off with the sculptor Loerke to enjoy a "frictional" relation of witty sensationalism, we understand that the metamorphosis is completed. Since the novel equates the machine principle with death, Gudrun has to be written off for good. Alive with Loerke, who is a kind of vampire figure like Hermione, she is deader than the frozen snowman she has deserted; for even in his dying Gerald retained some vestige of a human quality, if it was only his hysteria.

This process of dissolution is universal in the novel. It is the very form of the society represented and determines the nature of the human experience that can take place within the society. Rupert Birkin recognizes that it is going on in himself and coaxes Ursula toward the same self-recognition. He has been more deeply corrupted than she, through his love affair with Hermione, and is therefore more pessimistic than she about the possibilities of escape. Because he "bases his standard of values on pure being"—unlike Gerald, for whom the given societal forms represent ultimate standards—he does not mistake death for life. But he also assumes early on that his generation is involved in a *natural* cycle of destruction preceding a fresh cycle of creation into which neither he nor anyone else can survive:

> "Oh yes, ultimately," he said. "It means a new cycle of creation after—but not for us. If it is the end, then we are the end—fleurs du mal, if you like. If we are fleurs du mal, we are not roses of happiness, and there you are."
>
> "But I think I am," said Ursula. "I think I am a rose of happiness."
>
> "Ready-made?" he asked ironically.
>
> "No—real," she said, hurt.
>
> "If we are the end, we are not the beginning," he said.
>
> "Yes, we are," she said. "The beginning comes out of the end."
>
> "After it, not out of it. After us, not out of us."
>
> "You are a devil, you know, really," she said. "You want to destroy our hope. You *want* us to be deathly."
>
> "No," he said. "I only want us to *know* what we are."
>
> "Ha!" she cried in anger. "You only want us to know death."

Ursula's task is to persuade Birkin to abandon his fatalism so that together they may begin to build life anew. Birkin's task is to make Ursula see that the world as she knows it, and the ideals of that world, are doomed. This means he must teach her to give up her conventional attitude toward love, because insofar as it *is* conventional, that is, conditioned by the present form of society, it is destructive. Also, he must prepare her for eventual flight from the known world. The task is difficult because their departure must literally be a journey into "nowhere," since "everywhere" the cycle of destruction grinds on. Ursula's task is difficult too. Birkin, who is deeply injured "in his soul" as the novel opens, and is almost slain by the frenzied Hermione soon after, is in no optimistic mood. But somehow the couple quarrel each other into a relationship which by the novel's end seems stronger than death.

A third sense in which **Women in Love** is "end-of-the-world" is personal to Lawrence. For Lawrence, as for a great many other European artists of the period, the war came as the greatest shock of his entire life. He loathed the war, utterly disbelieved in the necessity of it, and tended to blame its outbreak on the perverse will of mankind in general. He keeps war out of the book, but cannot keep out the feeling the war had inspired in him. The vision of society-as-death reflects the cycle of destruction through which Europe was passing between 1914 and 1918. Lawrence's revulsion from his fellow man in wartime comes through in Birkin's gloating fantasies

Home of Louisa Burrows, a friend of Lawrence, on which Lawrence modeled the Brangwen home in Women in Love.

of the beauty of a world from which all traces of *homo sapiens* have been eliminated, and in Loerke's nihilistic fantasies of a superbomb that could split the world in two.

Despite these evidences of rage *Women in Love* is not misanthropic *au fond.* Lawrence treats Gerald with tenderness and compassion and all his characters with a characteristic detachment which people who do not know how to read Lawrence invariably take for violent prejudice. Loerke is loathsome, but he is also brave and gifted, just as Gudrun, though perverse, is vivid, beautiful, and self-sufficient. Birkin, who expresses some of Lawrence's cherished ideas, is often ridiculed for his self-consciousness and pedantry; some of the most amusing and happily written scenes are those in which Ursula argues him and his theories into the ground.

Nevertheless, the book demands a toughness and courage from the reader for which it is difficult to think of a parallel. When Birkin and Ursula agree to marry, one of the first things they do is send in written resignations from their jobs. Since Birkin is a school inspector and Ursula a teacher, we must accept the fact that the two liveliest people in a society of the dead and dying abandon the defenseless young to a fate which is destruction. They desert their posts and go off to make a separate peace, like Frederick Henry and Catherine Barclay of *A Farewell to Arms.* Yet that is just the point. Self-sacrifice and devotion to duty are anything but virtues, given the picture of the world Lawrence has created. After all, the zombielike Hermione yearns to sacrifice herself to Birkin, and one of the first things he tries to teach Ursula is that living selves are *not* to be sacrificed in love, war, work, or whatever. Gerald does his duty as he sees it. In obeying this essential imperative of a ruling class he freezes his own self to death and maims the selves of those who work for him.

Women in Love stands in somewhat the same relation to the

real prewar world of England and Europe as one class of Science Fiction novel or Utopian novel stands in relation to actuality. Lawrence detects certain destructive tendencies in his society. He isolates and magnifies these tendencies, predicts their outcome, then merges an essentially apocalyptic vision with the particular segment of historical time he has in hand. The novel compresses reality instead of distorting it. The tone of the opening chapter, describing an upper-class church wedding, is purely Edwardian if not high Victorian. The final chapters, representing in terms of symbolic drama a condition of frozen entropy to which our society has not yet risen, is a prediction of where we may well end up rather than a description of where we were in 1910.

Women in Love is full, perhaps too full, of talk about ideas; but two ideas in particular, one an idea of fate, the other an idea of the fundamental nature of modern Western civilization, emerge as central determining assumptions from which most of the developments of the action stem. The first is adumbrated by Birkin in the second chapter when he is thinking over Gerald's accidental killing of his brother in early childhood.

> What then? Why seek to draw a brand and a curse across the life that had caused the accident? A man can live by accident, and die by accident. Or can he not? Is every man's life subject to pure accident, is it only the race, the genus, the species, that has a universal reference? Or is this not true, is there no such thing as pure accident? Has *everything* that happens a universal significance? Has it? Birkin, pondering as he stood there, had forgotten Mrs. Crich, as she had forgotten him.
>
> He did not believe that there was any such thing as accident. It all hung together, in the deepest sense.

Here Birkin gropes his way to the radical insight that everything that happens in a human career, including chance occurrences, is a revelation of the underlying qualities of being of the man or woman involved. It seems a desperately hard doctrine and not readily defensible. Yet in this particular case Ursula comes to a similar conclusion when in a conversation with Gudrun about the killing she remarks, "I wouldn't pull the trigger of the emptiest gun in the world, not if someone were looking down the barrel. One instinctively doesn't do it."

Ursula's version is easier to accept at once than Birkin's, because she suggests a reason why the accident is not an accident. If one instinctively doesn't do it, then there is some flaw in Gerald's instinctive equipment that enabled him to do it. In fact, Gerald suffers from a defect of "being" which is deadly, and he spreads his deadliness to Gudrun and to his workmen before he is finally disintegrated. Society as it is takes no account of being; it therefore offers Gerald power rather than a cure. Birkin, after diagnosing Gerald's disease, would like to cure him—his absurd proposal of *blutbruderschaft* and his jiu-jitsu wrestling match with him are efforts in that direction—but in the end he has to flee from the society of which Gerald is the finest flower and master as though from a plague.

How is it that society can accommodate itself to Gerald's defeat, in fact reward him for it, but not to more wholesome beings like Ursula Brangwen and Rupert Birkin? In *The Rainbow* some dialogue was still possible between living selves and societal forms, at least in the pastoral generation to which Tom and Lydia belonged. Why has it ended? The answer lies in the nature of the industrial system, which reaches a final perfection of form under Gerald's management. The following passage, describing the human consequences of the triumph of the machine principle in the Crich family mines, presents Lawrence's full case against the industrial system and against modern society:

> There was a new world, a new order, strict, terrible, inhuman, but satisfying in its very destructiveness. The men were satisfied to belong to the great and wonderful machine, even whilst it destroyed them. It was what they wanted. It was the highest that man had produced, the most wonderful and superhuman. They were exalted by belonging to this great and superhuman system which was beyond feeling or reason, something really godlike. Their hearts died within them, but their souls were satisfied. It was what they wanted. Otherwise Gerald could never have done what he did. He was just ahead of them in giving them what they wanted, this participation in a great and perfect system that subjected life to pure mathematical principles. This was a sort of freedom, the sort they really wanted. It was the first great step in undoing, the first great phase of chaos, the substitution of the mechanical principle for the organic, the destruction of the organic purpose, the organic unity, and the subordination of every organic unit to the great mechanical purpose. It was pure organic disintegration and pure mechanical organization. This is the first and finest state of chaos.

The case is familiar enough and had been made before at least as early as Ruskin. Lawrence's paradox—that the perfection of a mechanical form is chaos—makes perfectly good sense in the light of his concern for the vitality of individual human beings which is destroyed when they subordinate themselves

fully to pure mathematical principles of production and distribution. In **"The Crown,"** Lawrence had defined wholeness of being as a conflict. Eliminate the conflict and there is a collapse into chaos. Here the conflict has been resolved into system and order, and it is a chaos from the human standpoint. On the Laurentian view the perfect solution of a given human problem is in fact a dissolution, because it imposes rigid inorganic form on life, and the essence of life is change, variability, pulsation. "The wavering, indistinct, lambent" Birkin is alive by virtue of his "odd mobility and changeableness." His sudden shifts of attitude and feeling, his lapses of taste and logic, protect the life within him. Gerald, who is the soul of good social form, whose ideas are built up logically into lucid formulations, is wholly consistent on his white, gleaming surface but a chaos inside where his feelings are.

The industrial system, like the system of the medieval church to which Will Brangwen had been attracted, solves the problem of living in one mode only. It satisfies the economic needs of men and their hunger for order by arranging their activities according to an intellectualized, simplistic model of human reality. The workmen are satisfied in their souls but their hearts "died within them." The centers of their feeling dry up. They become walking dead like their masters, like the leisured classes which live off the profits of the system (Hermione), like the liberal intellectuals who opt for the social equality of man but accept the system itself (Sir Joshua Malleson), like the bohemians and courtesans infesting the fringes of this humanly decadent society, producing spectacular variants on the universal theme of dissolution (the habitués of the Café Pompadour), like the artists who serve the system by producing art according to the principle that "machinery and the acts of labor are extremely, maddeningly beautiful" (Loerke). In the deepest sense all things hang together, and all classes and groupings of a society whose mystique of production subordinates the organic to the mechanical share the same fate.

Lawrence is careful to avoid giving the impression that the decline of this society could be avoided through a reversion to mindlessness. The point of introducing the pacific carving of the woman in labor and the West African statue of the Negro woman with the elongated neck is to show cultures which declined in a manner parallel to the decline of modern, white industrial society by fulfilling themselves in one mode at the expense of the wholeness of being which constitutes salvation for both selves and societies:

> It must have been thousands of years since her race had died, mystically: that is, since the relation between the senses and the outspoken mind had broken, leaving the experience all in one sort, mystically sensual. Thousands of years ago . . . the goodness, the holiness, the desire for creation and productive happiness must have lapsed, leaving the single impulse for knowledge in one sort, mindless progressive knowledge through the senses, knowledge arrested and ending in the senses, mystic knowledge in disintegration and dissolution.

The point of arrest of Western industrial society is the same, only in the opposite mode. The same relation between mind and feeling has broken; desire for feeling has lapsed, leaving the single impulse to production, disembodied progressive industrial know-how, knowledge arrested in system-making. It is, equally, a knowledge in disintegration and dissolution.

So far *Women in Love* may sound like the sort of fictionalized essay or mere novel of ideas that a Charles Kingsley or an Aldous Huxley might have written. But Lawrence fully translates his criticisms of the character of a civilization into terms of human relationship and human drama. Gerald is the symbol of a social order and Birkin is the prophet of that order's doom; yet both men realize their destinies through personal relationships with women. The two relations, Gerald-Gudrun and Birkin-Ursula, intertwine throughout the book but represent wholly opposed experiences. If the latter is a drama of becoming, the former dramatizes coming apart. Becoming, by definition, has no final conclusion, so that the world of feeling into which Birkin and Ursula move remains as obscure as their ultimate destination after they have left England. Gerald's and Gudrun's drama of disintegration is, by contrast, horrifyingly lucid and moves to a frozen finality. Neither relation is a love affair in the usual sense of the word. Birkin refuses to admit that he wants love—although he comes at last to use that word about himself and Ursula—and Gerald confesses to Gudrun shortly before his death that he cannot love.

Like the other pair, Birkin and Ursula are attracted to each other at first sight. Ursula, just emerging from the state of numbed withdrawal she had endured in the closing pages of *The Rainbow,* swiftly recognizes that Birkin is a man she can love if he will once allow himself to come into focus, and he, as swiftly, realizes that she is the woman with whom he wants to flee the known world and its disease. Setting aside purely novelistic exigencies, their marriage is delayed only because Birkin, who appears to be as deeply injured by his experiences with people when the novel opens as Paul Morel had been at the end of *Sons and Lovers,* needs time to recover health, to work out an adequate theory of relationship, and to train Ursula in the principles of "star-equilibrium" which will determine the relation. There are elements of comedy implicit in this situation of which Lawrence is perfectly well aware, but the problems both people face are serious enough.

At first Ursula wants ordinary romantic love. She assumes that a marriage based on mutual self-sacrifice and mutual absorption, with plenty of sex thrown in, is the proper thing. Birkin, after his disastrous affair with Hermione, knows better. Hermione's will to serve him had proved a will to absorb him, a sort of hideous spiritual cannibalism. When he set his will against hers she had tried to kill him. He has learned the hard way that a will to do loving service can conceal a will to dominate, and treads warily before he involves himself again. If, in the famous chapter called "Moony" (XIX), when he stones the reflected image of the moon on the water, he is trying to break up the image of woman as triple goddess, as some critics have thought, then his action is the height of good sense. The three relations of *Magna Mater* to man are the mother who bears him, the mistress to whom he makes love, and mother earth who takes him inside her upon death. It is sheer folly for a grown man to seek to realize all three relations in one actual woman; since the first relation is entirely regressive, and the third deadly. Hermione, we must assume, had played the first two roles in Birkin's life for a time and aspired as well to the role of goddess of death, when he tried to end their affair.

In the same chapter Birkin suddenly stumbles upon the relation he wants, and it is anything but eccentric. In fact it is classic and normative as a definition of proper marriage.

> There was another way, the way of freedom. There was the paradisal entry into pure, single being, the individual soul taking precedence over love and de-

sire for union, stronger than any pangs of emotion, a lovely state of free proud singleness, which accepted the obligation of the permanent connection with others, and with the other, submits to the yoke and leash of love, but never forfeits its own proud individual singleness, even while it loves and yields.

Put as simply as possible, this idea of the association of man and woman insists that a decent self-respect must balance love and loyalty to the other. It stresses the permanency of the relationship, and concludes that each person must stand on his own feet, regardless of the regressive temptation to let the other person carry him or her throughout life. And by holding the idea of separateness in balance with the idea of union it exactly fulfills the marital ideal already described in *The Rainbow* as well as the requirement for wholeness of being that Lawrence has laid down.

When this idea is finally put to her clearly Ursula cannot help accepting it as a good one. Thus, there is little tension in their love affair of the Tristan and Isolde, Antony and Cleopatra love-death sort. But there are tension and poignancy in the utter contrast this sensible solution makes with the mad world of passion Gerald and Gudrun occupy, and with the civilized world as well. When Birkin and Ursula leave the snow valley they have nothing but their love as a career and a dwelling place. They must, somehow, generate a new world from their nucleus of relatedness, out of the intactness of the single being each possesses. Lawrence is always very moving when he represents his successful lovers flying in the face of civilized society, like Lot's family across the plains from Sodom. In *Women in Love* the account of the train journey from London, across Belgium toward the alpine resort where the Birkins will linger briefly with Gerald and Gudrun, powerfully conveys the pathos of departure toward an unknown future. Ursula remembers her childhood at the Marsh farm and reflects that "in one lifetime one travelled aeons." She sees the man sitting beside her as an utter stranger, but keeps her courage up. Just behind her lie a nasty scene with her father—the hapless Will Brangwen had responded to the news that she wanted to marry Birkin by striking her—and a hurried registry wedding. She and her husband are cut off from everything except each other and the sources of their own beings. But they are in love and therefore possess, as Birkin once put it, "the freedom together" that wholesome love is.

Gerald Crich, the agonist of *Women in Love,* stands under a kind of triple fatality from the beginning. He is the scion of a family whose vitality is mysteriously defective, who are "curiously bad at living," who "can do things but . . . cannot get on with life at all." Furthermore his nature has been adversely conditioned by the remarkable relation of "mutual interdestructivity" his parents have lived through, which has driven the mother into mental alienation and the father into cancer. Finally, he has his own particular defect, the instinctual flaw that enabled him to play Cain to his brother's Abel. Gerald may also be viewed as a kind of monstrous exaggeration of a characteristic late nineteenth-century English upper-class type, of the man who makes a brilliant administrative career by keeping his feelings under a control so severe that the feelings either turn nasty or die altogether. It is said of Gerald's father that even in the intolerable pain of his final illness he will not face what he actually feels about his wife, his career, about his own death. The same split between a mind which plans and commands and wills and the inner-feeling man is evident in Gerald, making him ideally suited to design a system of production in which living men and women become functions within a mathematical model. Under rigorous suppression Gerald's instinctive responses, already defective by inheritance, conditioning, and fate, turn chaotic. As the essential self begins to disintegrate, the feelings it originates turn destructive and self-destructive. Gerald cannot face the prospect of his own father's death without hysteria because he carries so much death inside him.

He moves in an atmosphere of "essential" death and decay. His early love affair is with the London courtesan Minette, to whom he is attracted by the film of disintegration in her eyes. Water is one of the principal symbols of dissolution in *Women in Love,* and Gerald is intimately associated with that symbol, first as a swimmer (Chapter IV: "Diver"); then in the scene where Gudrun is sketching water plants and he starts up before her "out of the mud," his hand like the stem of one of those plants growing in decay (Chapter X: "Sketchbook"); finally, as the organizer of the water party (Chapter XIV) which ends in the drowning of his sister and a young doctor. Gerald's peripateia comes in that chapter. The cries of the drowning awaken him just as he is on the brink of an experience that might have begun his progress out of his condition of deathliness:

> His mind was almost submerged . . . into the things about him. For he always kept such a keen attentiveness, concentrated and unyielding in himself. Now he had let go, imperceptibly he was melting into oneness with the whole. It was like pure, perfect sleep, his first great sleep of life. He had been so insistent, so guarded, all his life. But here was sleep, and peace, and perfect lapsing out.

After diving bravely into the dark waters until exhausted, he is brought ashore and says to Gudrun, "If you once die, then when it's over, it's finished. . . . There's room under that water there for thousands." He has seen his own death and is confirmed in the love of death. His life has some months to run, but he is effectively, vitally, finished.

As Birkin shrewdly observes of him early in the novel, Gerald is a potential victim looking to get his throat cut. If Birkin trains Ursula in the career of "star-equilibrium," Gerald trains Gudrun to be his tormenter and slayer. This is not evident at first. When Gudrun watches Gerald hold the terrified mare by means of whip and spur at the gate crossing while the engine passes, her identification with the mare suggests that she will play masochist to his sadist in the ensuing affair. But as time passes the pattern shifts. In the chapter called "Rabbit" (XVIII) they are approximately even, each gloating over the other's wounds. Yet she already harbors in her soul "an unconquerable desire for deep violence against him" and has actually struck him in the face after dancing the highland cattle to madness during the fête at Shortlands. When Gerald comes to her bedroom in Beldover he leaves a trail of clay linking up the grave of his father with the bed of his mistress. It is Gerald's trail, not Gudrun's. By permitting the affair to become the means of Gerald's death she is merely responding to Gerald's deepest will.

The scenes in the snow valley constitute the most brilliant writing that Lawrence ever did, and some of the finest writing in the history of the English novel as well. The valley is a real place and simultaneously a symbol of fate for both Gerald Crich and civilized society. Throughout the novel, his fairness and whiteness have been repeatedly emphasized and associated with the inhuman purity of his social ideas. Here where his vitality is at last to be bled white and empty by

Gudrun's hatred, the mathematically perfect forms of snow flakes, composing a chaos of white, mock him and his concepts of fulfillment. It is a world all in one mode, a world without conflict or relief. Gerald as skier, as "snow-demon" is perfectly adapted to it and finally fuses with it when his being comes crashing down "in sheer nothingness" after Gudrun removes the last prop.

By a wonderful shift of emphasis, Lawrence wins for Gerald at the end our deepest sympathies. This is partly achieved through the sheer beauty of the descriptions of him in his isolation, as in the account of his climb upward after he has assaulted Loerke and Gudrun, or in the following paragraph from a few pages before that scene:

> So he came down reluctantly, snow-burned, snow-estranged, to the house in the hollow, between the knuckles of the mountain-tops. He saw its lights shining yellow, and he held back, wishing he need not go in to confront those people, to hear the turmoil of voices and to feel the confusion of other presences. He was isolated as if there were a vacuum round his heart, or a sheath of pure ice.

But it is also partly done through the force of contrast between such descriptions and the accounts given of the revolting intimacies newly established between Loerke and Gudrun:

> Their whole correspondence was in a strange, barely comprehensible suggestivity, they kindled themselves at the subtle lust of the Egyptians or the Mexicans. The whole game was one of subtle intersuggestivity, and they wanted to keep it on the plane of suggestion. From their verbal and physical nuances they got the highest satisfaction in the nerves, from a queer interchange of half-suggested ideas, looks, expressions, gestures.

As is said, it is all suggestivity, and the suggestion here is that we are looking at a couple of robotic insects with exposed ganglia of fine wire consciously parodying human communication.

Given the choice the reader dies imaginatively with Gerald rather than make a threesome with the above creatures. Although Gudrun sees him finally as a boringly complex piece of machinery we see him as a man in the extremity and loneliness of his suffering. When Birkin sits grieving over Gerald's frozen body he wonders whether he had perished in the attempt to climb beyond the snows. If he had reached the crest he might have been able to descend into warm fertile valleys to the south. But then Birkin reflects, "Was it a way out. It was only a way in again." There is no escape. The snow of abstraction lies everywhere in the civilized world. Once a man or a society loses touch with its own deepest sources of being there is no way back. On the last page, Birkin permits himself the sentimental luxury of imagining that he could have saved Gerald by loving him in a union as eternal as his union with Ursula. But she is there at his elbow, thank God, to remind him with characteristic, Friedalike forthrightness that "you can't have it, because it's false, impossible." On that authoritative note they resume their journey into nowhere.

Women in Love is Lawrence's most perfectly integrated study of disintegration. His living selves are fully involved with a milieu thickly rendered and chillingly contemporary. If Lawrence's enterprise after *Sons and Lovers* had been to submit to the anguish of combining the living self with the shell of historical and social actuality his submission in his fifth novel has been complete. Unlike the dimly projected pastoral generations of the earlier Brangwens, who "held life between the grip of their knees," the heroes and heroines of **Women in Love** live close to the sick heart of a doomed civilization and are implicated in its final illness. The principal statement the novel makes is a deeply pessimistic one. It says that a living man or woman who embraces the social destiny offered by industrial Western society in the early twentieth century embraces his own dying. The anguish of combining has become a death anguish.

By contrast, **The Rainbow** is a very hopeful book. In that novel Lawrence could still believe that "the sordid people who crept hard-scaled and separate on the face of the world's corruption were living still," and "would issue to a new germination." This faith rested in turn on a deeper faith in unknowable forces of life which might, upon occasion, seize hold of individuals, drawing them out of their ordinary daytime roles and attitudes and restoring them to themselves, provided they had the courage to respond to the call and move under the shelter of the rainbow. The world war killed that faith in Lawrence; not his faith in life but his belief that either the ordinary people who put up with the values of modern society, or the privileged people who had made a conscious commitment to those values would remain alive in the "vital" sense. Nor could he believe any longer that exceptionally lively people might be able to alter that society from within. Early in **Women in Love** Birkin tells Gerald that people must either break up the present system or shrivel within it. By the end he realizes that the only breaking possible is to break and run for his life. (pp. 72-89)

> *Julian Moynahan, in his* The Deed of Life: The Novels and Tales of D. H. Lawrence, *Princeton University Press, 1963, 229 p.*

GEORGE H. FORD (essay date 1965)

[*Ford is an American educator and critic. In the following excerpt, he examines sexual perversion in* Women in Love *as a manifestation of societal degeneration.*]

In chapter XI [of **Women in Love**] Ursula Brangwen listens to Birkin's thunderings on the degeneration of hate-filled modern man. At times she is impressed; at other times, like her mother in the solemnity of the cathedral in **The Rainbow,** she is amused. A crucial point in their argument occurs, however, when he is predicting a day of wrath in which humanity will be quickly wiped out. She disagrees. "She knew it could not disappear so cleanly and conveniently. It had a long way to go yet, a long and hideous way. Her subtle, feminine, demoniacal soul knew it well." If the many references to cataclysm in **Women in Love** suggest the impact of war, this reference to an alternative doom for mankind, the "long way," the slow decline into extinction, suggests in general the influence of the novelist's reading. But what is Ursula supposed to mean by her mysterious and fearsome reference to this "long and hideous way?" Does the novel ever explain what is meant or are we left, as Conrad leaves us in his *Heart of Darkness,* shuddering at the implications of Kurtz's famous phrase— "The horror! the horror!"—without our ever clearly knowing what the horror is?

I think we can come close to identifying what the horror is in Lawrence's book although his commentators seem rarely to have been concerned with the problem. It could, of course, be maintained that the inquiry should not be pushed, because readers may be more powerfully affected by something sensed, imprecisely, as elusively threatening, than by an identifiable threat. The poems of Coleridge, a master of the rhetoric of horror, could be cited to reinforce the objection:

> Behold! her bosom and half her side—
> A sight to dream of, not to tell!
> O shield her! shield sweet Christabel!

Nevertheless, because many of the misunderstandings of **Women in Love** originate in an inadequate recognition of what the horror, or horrors, might be, we must risk this not very significant loss and seek out a confrontation.

These remarks must serve as a preamble to a consideration of a scene in chapter XIX of major importance as embodying the climax of one of the two main plot lines. In one respect the scene resembles the "Nightmare" chapter in **Kangaroo** inasmuch as every study of Lawrence refers to it without any agreement having been arrived at. The problem here, however, is not one of liking or disliking (it is generally admired); the problem is one of interpretation and understanding. The scene embodies a kind of soliloquy in the third person, with Birkin confronting, in his mind's eye, an African carving he had contemplated many times at Halliday's flat in London. Like the scene of the doctor's descent into the pond-water in **"The Horse Dealer's Daughter,"** it is climactic in that after the confrontation or descent the character reaches a major decision. Birkin's experience culminates immediately in his resolving to marry Ursula, and as he sets out for her house to make his proposal, the ugly town of Beldover seems to him radiantly beautiful. "It looked like Jerusalem to his fancy," as Christminster ("the heavenly Jerusalem") looked to Hardy's Jude. Before the resolution is reached and the brief epiphany experienced, Birkin has to make a deep descent.

Among the African fetish statues he had seen in Halliday's London apartment, Birkin remembers one of a woman, a "slim, elegant figure from West Africa, in dark wood, glossy and suave. . . . He remembered her vividly: she was one of his soul's intimates." Why is it that the statue had haunted Birkin so persistently? Like many of his generation in the western world, Birkin enjoys African carving for its aesthetic satisfactions, yet it is obvious that his almost obsessive concern is not motivated by a search for beauty. It is what these statues tell him about the history of civilization and of his own future:

> He remembered her: her astonishing cultured elegance, her diminished, *beetle face,* the astounding long elegant body, on short, ugly legs, with such *protuberant buttocks,* so weighty and unexpected below her slim long loins. She knew *what he himself did not know.* She had thousands of years of purely sensual, purely unspiritual knowledge behind her. It must have been thousands of years since her race had died, mystically: that is, since the relation between the senses and the outspoken mind had broken, leaving the experience all in one sort, mystically sensual. Thousands of years ago, *that which was imminent in himself* must have taken place in these Africans: the goodness, the holiness, the desire for creation and productive happiness must have lapsed, leaving the single impulse for knowledge in one sort . . . in disintegration and dissolution, knowledge such as the beetles have. [Italics mine.]

Birkin's reflections serve as a flashback to the earlier scene in Halliday's apartment when another African statue was seen, this time through the eyes of Gerald. He, too, is disturbed by the statue (it is of a woman in labor), and although he finds no aesthetic pleasure he nevertheless senses what Birkin associated with it. It conveys to Gerald "the suggestion of the extreme of physical sensation, beyond the limits of mental consciousness." The early scene of the breakfast party is memorably staged with the four naked men standing round the statue and commenting on the "terrible face, void, peaked, abstracted almost into meaninglessness by the weight of sensation beneath." And the affair of the preceding night is also effectively incorporated by Gerald's significant discovery that the statue makes him think of the Pussum, the "violated slave" still asleep in the adjacent bedroom. But Gerald makes one blunder in his response to the statue. He thinks it is crude and savage. Birkin hastens to correct him:

> There are centuries and hundreds of centuries of development in a straight line, behind that carving; it is an awful pitch of culture, of a definite sort.

Gerald's mistake is one often made by those readers of Lawrence who overlook what Birkin calls the "astonishing cultured elegance" of the statue and assume that he is evoking a work by a savage. Such a reading blurs the main point of his soliloquy. Lawrence had learned from his reading (and his subsequent study of Leo Frobenius' *The Voice of Africa* confirmed the point) that long before the coming of Europeans there had existed great city states in Africa which had produced highly sophisticated works of art and established a tradition of fine craftsmanship. A slow decline, not a cataclysm, finished off this civilization, and it is the nature of this decline that Birkin tries to conjure up as he contemplates what the statue symbolizes for him.

Parenthetically it should be added that, so far as our appreciation of *Women in Love* is concerned, it does not matter fundamentally whether Birkin is right or wrong in his information about disputed points of Africa's past. Nor does it matter fundamentally whether his assumptions about one of the ways a civilization may decline are accurate or inaccurate. They are part of the given world of this novel and essential to an understanding of it. The basic assumption, and one developed in the parody scene at the Pompadour when Birkin's letter is read aloud by Halliday, is that a civilization having evolved out of its savage beginnings may lose its creative urge and lapse into decadence before becoming simply extinct. "There is a phase in every race—. . . when the desire for destruction overcomes every other desire." As intoned by the drunken Halliday for the amusement of London's Bohemia (this "menagerie of apish degraded souls"), the effect of the pronouncement is painfully comic—painful because no other direct statement in *Women in Love* is more significant or more serious—and astringently comic because of the setting in which it is framed. If the social process so conceived is unchecked a civilization declines to a stage which may have some resemblance to the original savage stage; it suffers a "reduction"—an abstract term upon which Lawrence leans often and hard in his fiction and letters.

Writing to his Jewish friend Mark Gertler, whose "obscene" painting seems to have inspired the account of Loerke's frieze of the drunken workers in the novel, Lawrence uses the same historical formula: "You are of an older race than I, and in these ultimate processes, you are beyond me. . . . At last your race is at an end—these pictures are its death-cry. And

it will be left for the Jews to utter the final . . . death-cry of this epoch: the Christians are not *reduced* sufficiently." And in **St. Mawr** he restates more explicitly the assumptions on which these gloomy predictions are based:

> Every new stroke of civilization has cost the lives of countless brave men, who have fallen . . . in their efforts to overcome the old, half-sordid savagery of the lower stages of creation, and win to the next stage. . . . And every civilization, when it loses its inward vision and its cleaner energy, falls into a new sort of sordidness, more vast and more stupendous than the old savage sort.

During the composition of **Women in Love** Lawrence discovered some living illustrations much closer at hand than the Africans for his theory of cultural degeneration. His Cornish neighbors impressed him as a surviving pocket of a once impressive "pre-Christian Celtic civilisation" which had degenerated. In view of the beetle-like face of the African statue, the following description of the Cornish people (whose souls, he said, were like black beetles) is especially interesting:

> The aristocratic principle and the principle of magic, to which they belonged, these two have collapsed, and left only the most ugly, scaly, insect-like, unclean *selfishness*. . . . Nevertheless . . . there is left some of the old sensuousness of the darkness . . . something almost negroid, which is fascinating. But curse them, they are entirely mindless.

This cluster associating the Celtic and African reappears in *Lady Chatterley's Lover* in a description of another Celt, the Irishman Michaelis:

> She saw in him that ancient motionlessness of a race that can't be disillusioned any more, an extreme, perhaps, of impurity that is pure, . . . he seemed pure, pure as an African ivory mask that dreams impurity into purity, in its ivory curves and planes.

That the African statues signify for Birkin a whole process of decline and fall, and that however aesthetically pleasing they evoke for him the impurity of a degenerated civilization, are points I have been laboring partly because of an extraordinary discussion of these statues by Horace Gregory in his *Pilgrim of the Apocalypse* [see Additional Bibliography]. According to Gregory, Lawrence found his principal characters of less interest than the statue of the West African woman, "for him, perhaps the most important figure in the book."

> She is positive, concrete, the perfect representation of life as opposed to the imperfect human beings surrounding her. . . . What the statue is made to represent is the *normal* essence of Gudrun and Ursula combined—their deviation from the statue's norm . . . is the perversion imposed upon them by their individual existence. . . . In all four characters, male and female, the statue sets the standard, never fully realized by any of them.

And Mr. Gregory concludes his analysis by asserting that "the image of the West African savage" was a fragment of hope in the midst of death. When a perceptive critic blunders into stating something so fantastically wrong as this (and other critics share his view) one is led to labor a point. Birkin's reflections in his soliloquy, developing like Keats, in his address to the Grecian urn, continues, and we may well ask what fragment of hope is there here:

> There is a long way we can travel, after the death-break; . . . We fall from the connection with life and hope, we lapse . . . into the long, long African process of purely sensual understanding. . . . He realised now that this is a long process—thousands of years it takes, after the death of the creative spirit. He realised that there were great mysteries to be unsealed, sensual, mindless, dreadful mysteries, far beyond the phallic cult. How far, in their inverted culture, had these West Africans gone beyond phallic knowledge? Very, very far. Birkin recalled again the female figure: the elongated, long, long body, the curious unexpected heavy buttocks . . . the face with tiny features like a beetle's. This was far beyond any phallic knowledge. Only when Birkin makes his resolution to repudiate the direction pointed by the statue does the rhythm of hope make itself felt.

This much is clear, but the passage of Birkin's reflections remains one of the most puzzling in the novel. What is meant by the repeated references to some kind of knowledge "beyond phallic knowledge"? What is it that the woman knew that Birkin does not yet know but dreads he will know? The horror for Birkin is not the state of mindlessness itself. The term *mindlessness* appears often in Lawrence's writings to describe the state of darkness in which the Brangwen farmers live or the coal miners in *Sons and Lovers.* That a degenerating culture loses contact with the values of light and abandons the quest for intellectual effort (the quest portrayed in *The Rainbow*) may be deplorable but not terrifying and threatening, as in Birkin's reflections about the "dreadful mysteries far beyond the phallic cult." The latter seems to be the horror, the horror, in *Women in Love.* Whatever it is, three things may be said of it which call for more extended discussion. It involves some form (or rather forms) of sexual perversion; Birkin is strongly attracted to it (as the Pussum said of Birkin's sermon, "Oh, he was always talking about Corruption. He must be corrupt himself, to have it so much on his mind"). And thirdly, its culmination is death itself, or more specifically some form of suicide, individual and national.

The first point, about sexual perversions, is the most difficult to establish, and even raising the question is enough to rouse the ire of some brands of Laurentian admirers. The difficulty is that the novel itself is not explicit, could not be explicit, in this area, and we have to grope our way up a rickety ladder constructed of image-clusters and scraps of information. Halliday's mistress, the Pussum for example, is explicitly associated with the corruption when Lawrence says of her: "She was very handsome, flushed, and confident in dreadful knowledge." Less explicitly, a link is established by references to marsh flowers (she is "soft, unfolded like some red lotus in dreadful flowering nakedness"), and she is associated with the beetle-faced statue not so much by her fear of beetles but by her very appearance as in this remarkable passage:

> There was something curiously indecent, obscene, about her small, longish, dark skull, particularly when the ears showed.

Like many of the characters in *Women in Love* the Pussum is a vividly realized fictional creation yet at the same time, as

representative of the corruption which the book treats, she is tagged by the novelist with evaluative terms such as *obscene.*

Gudrun Brangwen, a more highly complex character, is similarly presented. Her wood carvings were thought by Gerald to have been made by the same hands as those which created the African statues, and indeed Gudrun's affinities with what the statues suggested to Birkin are referred to many times. Most explicitly there is a passage near the end of the novel which is a kind of commentary on the earlier soliloquy. The passage consists of reflections (virtually a soliloquy again) on the difference between what Gerald offers as a lover of Gudrun and the kind of experience that Loerke could give her. Gerald's love-making has many qualities of perversity, but because he still has some "attachment" to moral virtues, "goodness" and "righteousness," he cannot provide the special sexual thrills that Loerke promises:

> Was it sheer blind force of passion that would satisfy her now? Not this, but the subtle thrills of extreme sensation in reduction. It was . . . the last subtle activities of . . . breaking down, carried out in the darkness of her.

She reflects further that she no longer wants a man such as Gerald but a *"creature"* like Loerke (who had been described by Birkin as a sewer rat and by Gerald as an insect):

> The world was finished now, for her. There was only the inner, individual darkness . . . the *obscene religious mystery* of ultimate reduction, the mystic frictional activities of diabolic reducing down, disintegrating the vital organic body of life. . . . She had . . . a further, slow exquisite experience to reap, unthinkable subtleties of sensation to know, before she was finished. [Italics mine.]

Before an attempt is made to explicate Gudrun's soliloquy a word should be interjected about Loerke himself. Better even than the Pussum and Gudrun, Loerke illustrates Lawrence's bold technique of creating characters who are fully alive and so eloquently self-assertive that they may engage our sympathies, and yet, in terms of the book's overall theme, of exposing them as appalling examples of social corruption. It is almost a tightrope-walking performance, and one can see why some of these creations have aroused divergent responses in his readers. Loerke was even described by Nathan Scott (who sees Lawrence through the spectacles of Denis de Rougemont) as a "Laurentian saint." And to Anaïs Nin also, simply because he is an artist, he is the man to be admired. Of the fact that at the end of the book Gerald is dead and Loerke alive, Miss Nin says:

> So it is Gerald who dies, not Loerke. It is the "mindless sensuality" which dies. Yet it has been said that Lawrence in *Women in Love* had urged us to mindless sensuality and disintegration [See Additional Bibliography].

The title of Miss Nin's book is *D. H. Lawrence: An Unprofessional Study,* and one wonders just how far the saving clause of her subtitle can be extended. Perhaps the most important equipment for a reader of Lawrence is just a nose. After his affair with the Pussum, Gerald admitted to Birkin:

> There's a certain smell about the skin of those women, that in the end is sickening beyond words—even if you like it at first.

Lawrence surely expects us to be similarly responsive, and a reader who concludes that Loerke is a Laurentian saint would seem to be lacking in a sense of smell. "He lives like a rat, in the river of corruption, just where it falls over into the bottomless pit," says Birkin. Mankind, he adds, wants "to explore the sewers," and Loerke is "the wizard rat that swims ahead." His very name evokes his negativism, the Loki of the sagas and of William Morris's *Sigurd the Volsung*: "And Loki, the World's Begrudger, who maketh all labour vain."

What is it then that this ruthless little "creature" can provide that Gerald cannot offer? Both men have sadistic propensities and can presumably furnish the masochistic satisfactions that Gudrun craves. When she sees a picture of Loerke's nude statue of the young girl art-student on horseback (his preferences in girl-flesh anticipate those of the hero of Nabokov's *Lolita*), a girl who had to be subdued by his slapping her hard, "Gudrun went pale, and a darkness came over her eyes, like shame, she looked up with a certain supplication, *almost slave-like.*" The counterpointing here is extremely intricate, for we are reminded that perhaps the two high points of Gudrun's earlier appreciation of Gerald had been when she watched him subdue a rabbit by force or, more pertinently, when he drove his spurs into the flanks of his mare. . . . And the phrase *almost slave-like* also flashes back to the Pussum whose submissive response to Gerald was similarly described.

Both men, then, have this capacity in common. What Loerke is capable of beyond it is the provision of some perverse pleasures, and the cluster of associations is consistently hinting at some exploitation of the anal and excremental areas. The recurring references to the abnormally prominent buttocks of the African statue and to sexual relations in which the connections with "creative life" are severed (anal intercourse has long been practised as a mode of avoiding conception), the traditional association of beetles with excrement, and the allusions to Loerke as a creature of the sewers all contribute towards some explication of both Birkin's soliloquy and that of Gudrun.

The hints concerning anal relations between men and women do not, however, indicate the full extent of the "further sensual experience" which Birkin contemplated. Gudrun's soliloquy, in particular, refers to some "obscene *religious* mystery of ultimate reduction." What is the term *religious* meant to suggest to us? Are we supposed to conjure up some Black Mass? Loerke, one might add, is well named to make a celebrant in such a rite, for in some Norse myths *Loki* is the devil. Perhaps it is merely the Bacchic festivals that are hinted at, or bestial erotic ceremonials, or blood-sacrifice ceremonies such as the Druids had performed, or so Lawrence believed, in Cornwall. Somers in **Kangaroo** recalls his experience during 1916 in Cornwall of drifting into a "blood-darkness." "Human sacrifice!—he could feel his dark, blood-consciousness tingle to it again, the desire of it, the mystery of it." Again Conrad's *Heart of Darkness* provided a model (if a somewhat obscure one) in its allusions to Kurtz's participation in "certain midnight dances ending with unspeakable rites, which . . . were offered up to him." All that can be indicated about the introduction of the term *religious* into Lawrence's account of cultural degradation is that it reinforces a sense of the sinister without clarifying the nature of the corruption.

A further set of associations is less obscure but for Lawrence equally sinister, one that suggests that a declining society will revert to homosexuality. Loerke's perversities might include his love-hate relationship with his "companion" Leitner—

they had for long shared a bedroom and "now reached the stage of loathing"—but this remains undeveloped. The problem of homosexuality takes us back from Gudrun and Loerke to Birkin's soliloquy and its expression of anxieties.

Unlike Proust, whose novels of this period also treat of the Cities of the Plain, Lawrence elected to avoid any direct representation in **Women in Love** of what Ezekiel calls the "abomination" of Sodom; he offers us no study of a M. de Charlus. The Bohemians are described as "degenerate," and there is some emphasis on the men being effeminate in manner with high-pitched squealing voices, but if London is to be likened to Sodom it is more because of its probable future fate than its present condition in this respect. If for the moment we shift from the novel to the novelist, however, we may detect a figure in this carpet. Lawrence's letters of 1915 and 1916 contain a remarkable number of references to his horror of beetles which is related, in most instances, to a horror of homosexual relations. In the Moore edition of the letters alone there are eighteen references to beetles and insects during the years 1915-16. On April 30, 1915, he reported his disgust after seeing an "obscene" crowd of soldiers:

> I like men to be beasts—but insects—one insect mounted on another—oh God! The soldiers at Worthing are like that—they remind me of lice or bugs.

Most revealing are passages referring to a visit paid by Francis Birrell to the Lawrences (in the company of David Garnett):

> These horrible little frowsty people, men lovers of men, they give me such a sense of corruption, almost putrescence, that I dream of beetles.

On this particular occasion his revulsion took form in an incident that as reported by Garnett, seems fantastic. So wrought up was Lawrence by Birrell's visit that he struggled to cast a spell over him, and the young man actually woke up at night with his tongue swollen so abnormally that he was in great pain. As Lawrence himself reported, such young men "are cased each in a hard little shell of his own," and "they made me dream of a beetle that bites like a scorpion. But I killed it." One may associate the incident with Kafka, but much more striking is a similarity to the situation in *Genesis* when the men of Sodom gather outside Lot's house and demand that his guests, two angels, be delivered to the crowd "that we may know them." The guests retaliate on the men of Sodom by striking them with blindness—this on the night before the destruction of their city.

Francis Birrell was not the only man to provoke the beetle nightmare in Lawrence at this time. For some reason his unhappy visit to Cambridge led to his associating Keynes and the whole group there with beetles and corruption, and also with Cambridge were linked such Bloomsbury figures as Duncan Grant. In a letter to Henry Savage in December, 1913, in which he frankly aired his feelings about homosexual relations, Lawrence concluded:

> One is kept by all tradition and instinct from loving men, or a man—for it means just *extinction of all the purposive influences.*

It may be noted that the phrase which I have italicized is almost identical with the words used by Birkin in confronting the beetle-faced statue. As he contemplates the possible lapse from "the desire for creation and productive happiness," he speaks of the fall "from the connection with life and hope."

In this reconstruction of what is implied in Birkin's fearsome sense of the slow degeneration of western man, nothing so far has been said about machinery. So much has been written by others about Lawrence's vitalistic dislike of industrialism . . . that it is perhaps a useful corrective to see that the horror in *Women in Love* is not exclusively industrialism, against which Lawrence's nineteenth-century predecessors in this role, Carlyle, Ruskin, Morris, had already expended themselves in valiant invectives. It is manifested rather in various forms of sexual corruption. The degeneration of the African civilization, or of Sodom, did not depend upon the discovery of power-operated lathes or steam shovels. Industrialism may accelerate and will certainly complicate the process, but from his study of history and legend, Lawrence was aware of patterns of human propensities that were independent of how coal and iron are worked, and the differences between what he calls the African process and the Arctic process are not crucial. The end of the slow process of degeneration of past societies was extinction, and a degenerate contemporary society would descend the same slope.

The image of the death-slope is Lawrence's of course rather than mine. It crops up in the novel and also in several of his wartime letters. In August, 1915, he commented brutally on the kind of young man who joins the Roman Catholic Church, or the army, in order to enjoy obeying orders as a "swine with cringing hindquarters." "I dance with joy when I see him rushing down the Gadarene slope of the war." In the Biblical story (about which Gladstone and T. H. Huxley had had their celebrated controversy) a community infected with evil spirits gains some relief by Christ's intervention, the evil spirits being driven out and into a herd of their swine. The swine, like a horde of lemmings, plunge down a slope into the sea and perish.

For Lawrence's purposes in 1916-17, the story of the Gadarene swine was richly suggestive. Not only did it provide one more analogue for the annihilating plunges taking place between the trenches across the Channel but an image suggesting the combination of swinish sensual corruption with a herd madness, an inexplicable propulsion towards self-destruction. The degenerate society, after exhausting all the possibilities of perverse sensuality represented by Loerke, finds its final thrill, its "voluptuous satisfaction"—a phrase describing Gerald's sensations as his fingers tighten on Gudrun's soft throat—in death itself.

In his wartime essay, **"The Crown,"** Lawrence tried to formulate the connections between what he calls "perversity, degradation and death," especially death in war:

> So that as the sex is exhausted, gradually, a keener desire, the desire for the touch of death follows on. . . . Then come . . . fatal wars and revolutions which really create nothing at all, but destroy, and leave emptiness.

Those who prefer to lay the sources of war conveniently at the door of the munitions-makers will derive little satisfaction from Lawrence's recognition of destructive madness: "we go careering down the slope in our voluptuousness of death and horror . . . into oblivion, like Hippolytus trammelled up and borne away in the traces of his maddened horses."

The most effective use of the image of the slope occurs during the coming together of Ursula and Birkin on the night before their marriage. After a violent quarrel with her father about her proposed marriage, she arrives at Birkin's cottage in tears:

> He went over to her and kissed her fine, fragile hair, touching her wet cheeks gently.
>
> "Don't cry," he repeated, "don't cry any more." He held her head close against him, very close and quiet.
>
> At last she was still. Then she looked up, her eyes wide and frightened.
>
> "Don't you want me?" she asked.
>
> "Want you?" His darkened, steady eyes puzzled her and did not give her play.
>
> (pp. 187-201)

[The] exchange of feelings through the eyes is emphasized, and the ascent from the downward slope culminates in a poignantly rendered coming together:

> "Do I look ugly?" she said. And she blew her nose again.
>
> A small smile came round his eyes. . . . And he went across to her, and gathered her like a belonging in his arms. She was so tenderly beautiful, he could not bear to see her, he could only bear to hide her against himself. Now, washed all clean by her tears, she was new and frail like a flower just unfolded. . . . And he was so old, so steeped in heavy memories. Her soul was new, undefined and glimmering with the unseen. And his soul was dark and gloomy, it had only one grain of living hope, like a grain of mustard seed. But this one living grain in him matched the perfect youth in her.
>
> "I love you," he whispered as he kissed her, and trembled with pure hope, like a man who is born again to a wonderful, lively hope far exceeding the bounds of death. She could not know how much it meant to him, how much he meant by the few words. . . . But the passion of gratitude with which he received her into his soul, the extreme, unthinkable gladness of knowing himself living and fit to unite with her, he, who was so nearly dead, who was so near to being *gone with the rest of his race down the slope of mechanical death,* could never be understood by her. He worshipped her as age worships youth, he gloried in her because, in his one grain of faith, he was young as she, he was her proper mate. This marriage with her was his resurrection and his life. [Italics mine.]

The poignancy of the release from loneliness is similar to the effect of scenes in **"Love among the Haystacks,"** *The Rainbow, Lady Chatterley's Lover,* and *The Man Who Died,* but perhaps most moving of all in this novel because of the overpowering nature of the destructive rhythms and the variety of ways in which they have been made to sound throughout the action. The hero is not a mere visitor full of righteousness; he is himself a citizen of Sodom, infected with a society's hatreds, degeneracy, and desire for death. Whatever the African statue stood for, as I suggested above, attracts all the characters, even at times Ursula, who usually insisted that she was a "rose of happiness" and not one of the Baudelairian flowers. And for Birkin the attraction had been a powerful one. "You are a devil, you know, really," Ursula says to him early in their relationship. "You want to destroy our hope. You *want* us to be deathly." And later: "You are so *perverse, so* death-eating."

The perversities associated with the statue take in more than being half in love, as Birkin was, with easeful death. What the "further sensual experience" might be which prompted him to his soliloquy, and which he decides to repudiate, has already been indicated. As for the "horror" of homosexuality, there have been readers, beginning with the early reviewers of the novel, who find the "Gladiatorial" and "Man to Man" chapters in this respect obscene. And if Lawrence had included the "Prologue" chapter with which he had originally opened the novel, with its account of Birkin's realization that he likes the bodies of men better than the bodies of women, such readers would have had even more cause for alarm. The problem is extraordinarily complex and (not in the mere squeamish sense) delicate, calling for a nice discrimination between an "abomination" and an ideal relation, a discrimination that some readers may be too impatient to make. In his 1918 essay on Whitman, Lawrence himself struggled to clarify the differentiation which had been assumed in his novel. For having sung of the "love between comrades" Whitman is highly praised by Lawrence as one who had made pioneering efforts on behalf of a great cause. Such a love, provided that it never acts "to destroy marriage" is recommended as healthy and life-giving. If it becomes an alternative to married love instead of a supplement, it is, on the contrary, deathly. The *Blutbrüderschaft* that Birkin wanted to establish with Gerald was supposedly a life-giving relationship not to be confused with the deathly degeneracies evoked in his soliloquy.

With the help of the Whitman essay, this distinction can perhaps be grasped, although as the final page of the novel shows, Ursula herself adamantly refused to grasp it. "I wanted eternal union with a man too: another kind of love," Birkin says wistfully.

> "I don't believe it," she said. "It's an obstinacy, a theory, a perversity."

More difficult to grasp, however, is the parallel differentiation between some of the corruptive relations suggested by the statue and the innocence of exploratory relations between men and women as lovers. And here Ursula can, herself, be the spokeswoman for the innocence. At the ski-resort she reflects as she is going to sleep:

> They might do as they liked. . . . How could anything that gave one satisfaction be excluded? What was degrading? . . . Why not be bestial, and go the whole round of experience? She exulted in it.

This passage is only slightly veiled and offers few problems. What was puzzling is the earlier scene at an English inn when Ursula discovers in Birkin's body "the source of the deepest life-force."

> She had thought there was no source deeper than the phallic source. And now, behold, from the smitten rock of the man's body, from the strange marvellous flanks and thighs, deeper, further in mystery than the phallic source, came the floods of ineffable darkness and ineffable riches.

In 1961, G. Wilson Knight set out to explain what Lawrence was picturing in this curious scene by citing lines from the love poems in which the woman "put her hand on my secret,

darkest sources, the darkest outgoings" [see entry in Additional Bibliography edited by Colin Clarke]. As might be expected, Knight's explanation prompted an outburst of angry articles in the magazines, most of them concerned with *Lady Chatterley's Lover.* Indeed the novel went on trial, in effect, for a second time. A lawyer, the Warden of All Souls at Oxford, discovered that in one of the several sexual encounters described in that novel, intercourse in the Italian style had been practised. It had also been occasionally practised, it seems, by Will and Anna in *The Rainbow* and by Birkin and Ursula in the scene in the Tyrol referred to above.

For the present discussion I am not going to be concerned with the legal or even the aesthetic aspects of the practice beyond simply endorsing Mark Spilka's comment (made several years before the controversy became prominent) that Lawrence treats it as an act having a limited function which, as a Puritan, he seems to have thought can serve as a kind of "discovery and purification" [see Additional Bibliography]. What is relevant here is not whether some sort of Ovidian *Ars amatoria* could be compiled from Lawrence's writings, but whether the passages cited from *Women in Love* represent a serious artistic blunder on the part of the novelist, creating such a blur that the theme of the novel, and the drama of the hero's development, are both hopelessly obscured. More specifically, if the "dreadful mysteries, far beyond the phallic cult" associated with the beetle-faced statue are represented in one scene as degenerate and in another scene (with only a slight shift in terminology) as redemptive—when Ursula is transfigured by her discovery of a "source deeper than the phallic source"—how is a reader supposed to respond to what seems like a total contradiction?

Of the many critical discussions of *Women in Love,* the only one which I have encountered that even raises some of the questions that I have been trying to grapple with here is that by Eliseo Vivas. Vivas' conclusion is that Lawrence introduced a contradiction which is seemingly not resolved, because the novelist has pictured Birkin as rejecting "the African process" and then shown him as, in effect, succumbing to it [see excerpt dated 1960]. On these grounds we might throw up our hands and say of Lawrence himself what Ursula, in a fit of pique, said of Birkin: "He says one thing one day, and another the next—and he always contradicts himself." What may be enjoyed as a colorful trait in a fictional character is not necessarily a commendable asset in the artist who created the fictional character. Fiction can be great when it is tentative and exploratory, making us aware of the puzzling complexities of choice confronting the characters, but if it is merely muddled it will not stand. (pp. 201-05)

I myself suggest . . . that although Lawrence may be asking too much of us in his account of Birkin's development, the sequence itself is not a muddled one. We are being expected to discriminate between sensual experiences enjoyed by a pair of loving men and women (which are regarded by the novelist as innocently enjoyed) on the one hand, and degenerate indulgences of a society which has cut all connections with spiritual values on the other. Perhaps like the comparable discrimination we were expected to make between a full-fledged homosexual relationship and *Blutbrüderschaft* we may, despite the cluster of horrors associated with the statue, find the distinction too fine, too naïve even, for the stretch of our patience. Yet if we are to understand the development of the characters as well as the social background against which their relations are worked out, the effort to establish the distinction is one worth making. Again, as with the discussion of Whitman, we can derive some help from one of Lawrence's essays. In **"Pornography and Obscenity"** he writes:

> The sex functions and the excrementory functions in the human body work so close together, yet they are, so to speak, utterly different in direction. Sex is a creative flow, the excrementory flow is towards dissolution, de-creation, if we may use such a word. In the really healthy human being the distinction between the two is instant, our profoundest instincts are perhaps our instincts of opposition between the two flows. But in the degraded human being the deep instincts have gone dead, and then the two flows become identical. . . . It happens when the psyche deteriorates, and the profound controlling instincts collapse.

The discriminatory effort required in this instance, it may be added, is called for in many other places of this story, for *Women in Love* is one of the most demanding of novels. The kind of complexities encountered in discussing the two soliloquies, Birkin's and Gudrun's, which I have been treating expansively here, could be demonstrated again in connection with what Vivas has called the "constitutive" symbols of which the novel is full—the great scene of Birkin stoning the moonlit water for example, or the winter scenes in the mountains culminating in Gerald's confronting another statue, a Tyrolian Christ sticking up out of the snow "under a little sloping hood, at the top of a pole."

What I have been stressing myself is that the complexities derive much of their density from Lawrence's choosing to portray Birkin in particular not as a White Knight, incorrupt and incorruptible, but as a suffering character dramatically involved in extricating himself from a death-loving world to which he is deeply, almost fatally, attracted. Like Conrad in similar presentation of Kurtz and Marlow, Lawrence in this way perhaps doubles the difficulties confronting his readers, but the clear gain in the overall effectiveness of his novel as a novel is beyond measurement. (pp. 205-06)

> George H. Ford, in his Double Measure: A Study
> of the Novels and Stories of D. H. Lawrence, *Holt,*
> *Rinehart and Winston, 1965, 244 p.*

H. M. DALESKI (essay date 1965)

[*Daleski, a South African–born Israeli educator and critic, has written studies of D. H. Lawrence, Charles Dickens, and Joseph Conrad. In the following excerpt from his* Forked Flame: A Study of D. H. Lawrence, *he examines ways in which Lawrence's postwar mood of despair is expressed in the setting, characterization, and plot of* Women in Love.]

> Do not listen to Bertie [i.e., Bertrand Russell] about going to London. You cannot *really* do anything now: no one can do anything. You might as well try to prevent the spring from coming on. This world of ours has got to collapse now, in violence and injustice and destruction, nothing will stop it. Bertie deludes himself about his lectures. There will come a bitter disillusion.

> The only thing now to be done is either to go down with the ship, sink with the ship, or, as much as one can, *leave* the ship, and like a castaway live a life apart. As for me, I do not belong to the ship; I will not, if I can help it, sink with it. I will not live any more in this time. I know what it is. I reject it. As

Lawrence, 1916.

far as I possibly can, I will stand outside this time, I will live my life, and, if possible, be happy, though the whole world slides in horror down into the bottomless pit. There is a greater truth than the truth of the present, there is a God beyond these gods of to-day. Let them fight and fall round their idols, my fellow men: it is their affair. As for me, as far as I can, I will save myself, for I believe that the highest virtue is to be happy, living in the greatest truth, not submitting to the falsehood of these personal times.

Lawrence's letter to Ottoline Morrell [of February 1916] helps to explain why *Women in Love,* though in intention a sequel to *The Rainbow,* is so different from the earlier novel. It is not merely that there is a notable difference in technique between the two books, that, in *Women in Love,* Lawrence seems more easily able to express his apprehension of the "carbon" of character in scenes which combine a complex symbolic depth with a surface of dramatic naturalism so that this novel is airier and more spacious than its predecessor; *Women in Love,* though conceived as part of a single project which made *The Rainbow* a necessary prior undertaking, was in fact written out of a radically different mood. The passage quoted above (and it is a representative instance of the way in which Lawrence viewed the world in 1916) provides a background to his feeling as he wrote *Women in Love.* His mood, despite his hope of some sort of personal exemption from the general fate, is clearly one of profound despair, a despair made all the more bitter by a realization of his own powerlessness to prevent the world from sliding down into the bottomless pit. *Women in Love* is, in effect, a sustained dramatization of his belief in a personal immunity amid the public disaster. Though it is set in the same pre-war England as that in which Ursula of *The Rainbow* reaches maturity, the optimism which, in that book, informs her concluding vision of social regeneration, is transmuted into an abiding sense of the imminent collapse into calamity of a whole way of life. The War, as the viciousness of the fighting bit home by 1916, represented for Lawrence the disintegration of English civilization; and though the novel is apparently remote from the international concerns which agitated men at the time of its composition, it is, from one point of view, a novel of war, in that it explores the nature of the deep-seated disease in the body politic of which war is the ultimate death-agony. It is almost as if Lawrence carries out an autopsy on the still-breathing form of pre-war society.

I emphasize this connection between the War and *Women in Love* not only because Lawrence's insistence in the book on the irrevocable doom of England is implicitly related to the catastrophe of 1914, but because it helps to explain the structure of the novel. It accounts, for instance, for what appears to be the dual motion of the book. On the one hand, as I shall try to show, there is a continuation of the search, begun in *The Rainbow,* for a lasting relation between the sexes, a search for the "two in one." The marriage of Birkin and Ursula, though markedly different in character from the marriages described in *The Rainbow,* is presented as an achieved relation of this kind, and its significance is heightened by the contrasted destructive passion of Gerald and Gudrun. But at the same time, to use the terms of Lawrence's letter to Ottoline Morrell, both couples are shown to be on board a ship which is rapidly heading for destruction, and their personal relations are not only qualified by their response to the danger but are the measure of a psychic drive towards life or death which such a predicament intensifies. Birkin and Ursula, clinging to the life preserver of their own "unison in separateness," abandon ship; Gerald and Gudrun, by trying to destroy each other, symbolically prefigure in themselves the desire for death of those who do not attempt to leave the ship—a desire, it is implied, which is to achieve its shattering consummation in the general wreck that lies ahead. There is, therefore, no internal division in the book between the social and the personal, for all the "social scenes" are designed to evoke that background of impending ruin against which the personal drama is enacted, and in relation to which it derives its ultimate meaning.

The structural principle of *Women in Love* is locative; that is to say, there is a calculated movement from one place to another, each place being a representative unit in the social organism and serving as the focus of a local significance. The places are related to one another not merely through a juxtaposition which yields a comprehensive view of the social scene as a whole, but—so to speak—through their common location on volcanic soil. There are five such foci in the book: Beldover, where Ursula and Gudrun live; Shortlands, the Crich home; Breadalby, Hermione's country house; the Café Pompadour, the haunt of London Bohemians; and the Tyrolese hostel, where Birkin, Ursula, Gudrun and Gerald stay during their Alpine holiday. We are required, in each place,

to register the tell-tale tremors which herald an inevitable cataclysm.

To view the novel in this way is to do no less than justice to the compact tightness of its organization. The chapters which describe the world of London bohemianism, for instance, might appear—at a glance—to have no real function in the whole; and since, as the biographers have shown, they incorporate incidents in Lawrence's own life, it becomes easily plausible to suppose that they were included either in careless animus or for their own sake. Even F. R. Leavis, who rates *Women in Love* very highly indeed [see Additional Bibliography], cites these chapters as representative of one of the two faults he finds in the book:

> [The fault] is represented pre-eminently by chapters VI and VII ("Crème de Menthe" and "Totem") and chapter XXVIII ("Gudrun in the Pompadour"). Lawrence here does some astonishingly vivid history: he re-creates, giving us the identifiable individuals, the metropolitan Bohemia he had known after the success of *Sons and Lovers.* A great deal of what he renders with such force is clearly there because it was once actual; he recalls the scene, the detail and the face. The episode that made so deep an impression on him goes in, for that reason—even when it was one he only heard about, as for instance that of the impounding of the letter by Katherine Mansfield at the Café Royal. But all that doesn't owe its presence to the needs of thematic definition and development would have been better excluded; a point to be made with the more emphasis since *Women in Love* has so complex and subtle an organization, and we have to assume in general, as we read, that everything is fully significant.

But the first paragraph of Chapter VI suggests that the account of Bohemia is in fact relevant to the development of the specific theme of the novel:

> They met again in the café several hours later. Gerald went through the push doors into the large, lofty room where the faces and heads of the drinkers showed dimly through the haze of smoke, reflected more dimly, and repeated *ad infinitum* in the great mirrors on the walls, so that one seemed to enter a vague, dim world of shadowy drinkers humming within an atmosphere of blue tobacco smoke. There was, however, the red plush of the seats to give substance within the bubble of pleasure.

At first sight this passage seems to give no more than a casual impression of the smoke-filled café, but it unobtrusively suggests the unreality of the assembled drinkers and links them with the inhabitants of one of the other "worlds" of the novel in a way that convincingly places the scene within the determined limits of the book. The "vague, dim world of shadowy drinkers" which typifies Bohemia on its chosen ground is not so far removed as might be thought from Beldover, "the world of powerful, underworld men who [spend] most of their time in the darkness": what the two worlds have in common is a failure of meaningful life, the failure to live in bright, vivid distinction of being. I shall refer later to the miners in this connection. The description of London Bohemians is in keeping, too, with Birkin's earlier characterization of them: "the most pettifogging calculating Bohemia that ever reckoned its pennies. . . . Painters, musicians, writers-hangers-on, models, advanced young people, anybody who is openly at outs with the conventions, and belongs to nowhere particularly." They are the small practitioners of art, and a room in which all individuality is obliterated in an amorphous haze of smoke is a fitting setting for their mediocrity. The café, moreover, is a refuge for those who are "at outs" with the world of everyday life, but the self-centred narrowness of the world to which they adhere is implied by the unending reflection in the "great mirrors on the walls." If we respond to the suggestiveness of the opening description of the Café Pompadour, we are not altogether unprepared, towards the end of the novel, to find it styled "this small, slow, central whirlpool of disintegration and dissolution," a phrase which unambiguously places the headquarters of London Bohemia along the main line of "thematic definition and development." The "bubble of pleasure" which the drinkers have blown round themselves has nothing more substantial than red-plush seats at its centre, and it is dangerously poised to burst. The reference to the "bubble of pleasure," moreover, lends added significance to the name of the café. The Café Pompadour is not merely a casual substitution for the Café Royal but neatly evokes the world of the Marquise de Pompadour ("Après nous le déluge!") which was swept away by the French Revolution.

The three chapters which F. R. Leavis implies could be dispensed with without much loss [see Additional Bibliography] are designed to give body to the impressionism of the initial presentation of the bohemian *milieu*. (pp. 126-30)

The rottenness of Bohemia, which these chapters reveal with effortless economy, is an instance of the general rottenness in the state of England. To move from the Pompadour to Breadalby, for example, is to move to a different world, but the smell of putrefaction is the same.

At first sight Breadalby might appear to be the seat of no more vicious a vice than escapism: "There seemed a magic circle drawn about the place, shutting out the present, enclosing the delightful, precious past, trees and deer and silence, like a dream." The scene is focused more sharply, however, when we are told that "the attitude" of those who are to be found there is "mental and very wearying," and that their talk, a characteristic activity, goes on "like a rattle of small artillery." Breadalby is the home of ideas, and though there are the inevitable hangers-on, it is a meeting-place for the advanced in thought. Under the tutelage of the daughter of the house, Hermione Roddice, there foregather on its lawns men of the calibre of Sir Joshua Mattheson, the learned sociologist; and the house-parties are connected with public affairs through Hermione's brother, a Liberal member of Parliament. The quintessential figure of the group, however, and the one in whom its weaknesses are most rigorously analysed, is Hermione herself.

Hermione is an equivocator. She lives for and through the mind and, characteristically, she vaunts the delights of knowledge: "To me," she says, "the pleasure of knowing is *so* great, *wonderful*—nothing has meant so much to me in all life, as certain knowledge—no, I am sure—nothing"; but she also asserts that "the mind . . . is death," maintaining with demonic innocence that "it [destroys] all our spontaneity, all our instincts." What lies behind the equivocation is a perverted lust, as Birkin violently tells her: "You want to clutch things and have them in your power. . . . And why? Because you haven't got any real body, any dark sensual body of life. You have no sensuality. You have only your will and your conceit of consciousness, and your lust for power, to

know." In other words Hermione typifies an indulgence in what Lawrence elsewhere calls a "sensational gratification within the mind," and we realize how exactly she is "placed" by the opening description of her:

> The chief bridesmaids had arrived. Ursula watched them come up the steps. One of them she knew, a tall, slow, reluctant woman with a weight of fair hair and a pale, long face. This was Hermione Roddice, a friend of the Criches. Now she came along, with her head held up, balancing an enormous flat hat of pale yellow velvet, on which were streaks of ostrich feathers, natural and grey. She drifted forward as if scarcely conscious, her long blanched face lifted up, not to see the world. She was rich. She wore a dress of silky, frail velvet, of pale yellow colour, and she carried a lot of small rose-coloured cyclamens. Her shoes and stockings were of brownish grey, like the feathers on her hat, her hair was heavy, she drifted along with a peculiar fixity of the hips, a strange unwilling motion. She was impressive, in her lovely pale-yellow and brownish-rose, yet macabre, something repulsive. People were silent when she passed, impressed, roused, wanting to jeer, yet for some reason silenced. Her long, pale face, that she carried lifted up, somewhat in the Rossetti fashion, seemed almost drugged, as if a strange mass of thoughts coiled in the darkness within her, and she was never allowed to escape.

There is something "macabre" about her appearance, and people are repelled by her even though they are impressed, because she moves as though she tacitly disowns her body: hence her slow reluctance and her strange unwilling motion as she drifts forward with a peculiar fixity of the hips. Great emphasis, like the distortion in a modern painting, is given to the size of her head: her face, it is repeatedly insisted, is long, and it is balanced by the heavy weight of her hair and by the enormous hat she wears. The distortion, clearly, has a significance which is counter to that of the African carving which has a face "crushed tiny like a beetle's" and which is so "weighty" below the loins. Hermione, we are invited to recognize, is a prey to a process of "disintegration and dissolution" which is the reverse of that epitomized by the fetish but which is as deadly in its effects. Some suggestion of the deadliness is implied, with Lawrencean esotericism, by the "mass of thoughts" which "coil" (the word has a serpent-like ominousness) in the "darkness" within her; it is directly illustrated by the nature of her relationship with Birkin.

Hermione's "deficiency of being" is attested by the "terrible void" within her—we are reminded of the bubbles which hover round the Bohemians and round Gerald—and it is to Birkin that she turns to fill the void, "to close up this deficiency." Believing that she herself is "the central touchstone of truth," she is convinced that she needs only Birkin and his "high" knowledge in conjunction with her to be complete. But he, who is trying to leave her after having been her lover for some years—his breaking away from her is the first movement in a withdrawal from the world which she represents—in fact relentlessly forces her to an agonized awareness of the "bottomless pit" of her insufficiency. (pp. 136-39)

Beldover is reality for the colliers who live there, but it is as far removed from a real meaningfulness as Hermione's customary intellectuality. Though we do not see as much of Beldover as we do of the Café Pompadour or Breadalby, it is at once apparent that it has a representative place in the national scene:

> The two girls were soon walking swiftly down the main road of Beldover, a wide street, part shops, part dwelling-houses, utterly formless and sordid, without poverty. Gudrun, new from her life in Chelsea and Sussex, shrank cruelly from this amorphous ugliness of a small colliery town in the Midlands. Yet forward she went, through the whole sordid gamut of pettiness, the long amorphous, gritty street. . . . She felt like a beetle toiling in the dust. She was filled with repulsion.
>
> They turned off the main road, past a black patch of commongarden, where sooty cabbage stumps stood shameless. No one thought to be ashamed. No one was ashamed of it all.
>
> "It is like a country in an underworld," said Gudrun. "The colliers bring it above-ground with them, shovel it up. Ursula, it's marvellous, it's really marvellous—it's really wonderful, another world. The people are all ghouls, and everything is ghostly. Everything is a ghoulish replica of the real world, a replica, a ghoul, all soiled, everything sordid. It's like being mad, Ursula."
>
> The sisters were crossing a black path through a dark, soiled field. On the left was a large landscape, a valley with collieries, and opposite hills with cornfields and woods, all blackened with distance, as if seen through a veil of crape . . . .

Beldover, like Wiggiston, which Ursula visits in *The Rainbow,* is a gruesome imitation of a town. There is the same "amorphous ugliness," and the "sooty" cabbages and "soiled" fields point in a sadly similar way to the defacement of the once healthy countryside. But where Wiggiston was "like a skin-disease," it is indicative of Lawrence's sharper bitterness in *Women in Love* that Beldover, which is separated by a "veil of crape" from the cornfields and woods, is like a town of the dead. Moreover, it is clearly not accidental—for the beetle is as portentous an insect in this book as the wasp in *A Passage to India*—that Gudrun should respond to the underworld existence which Beldover suggests to her by feeling "like a beetle toiling in the dust." The full significance of this opening description is revealed later, in the chapter ("The Industrial Magnate") which analyses what Gerald does to the colliers in the mines. As Gudrun remarks, Beldover is what the colliers shovel up from underground.

Shortlands, where the Criches live, is screened by a wooded hill from the collieries which support its opulence, but the "industrial sea . . . [surges] in coal-blackened tides against the grounds of the house." It is, so to speak, the home of industry, and it is at once suggestive that "there [is] a strange freedom, that almost [amounts] to anarchy, in the house." The existence of a state of near-anarchy in the house is immediately attributable to the invalidism of the head of the family and to the fact that Gerald, at Shortlands, does not yet exercise the authority he has assumed in the mines; it is also an intimation of the anarchic principle which both men, in their very different ways, represent in the world of industry.

Thomas Crich tries to smooth the harshness of the economic machine he controls by oiling it with a Christian humanitarianism. Believing that "in Christ" he is "one with his workmen," and that "through poverty and labour" they are "nearer to God than he," he translates *caritas* into charity, and attempts to mitigate the practices of large-scale industry by encouraging appeals to his heart. But his charity is, of course, corrupting in its effects, and it stimulates a mutual parasitism between donor and recipient. It draws the "worst sort" among the colliers and their women, who come "crawling," ready to feed "on the living body of the public like lice"; for Thomas Crich himself it becomes a means of easy self-gratification, and he seems to his wife like "some subtle funeral bird, feeding on the miseries of the people." She revolts passionately against his philanthropy but, being unable to prevent him from its pursuit, she is driven "almost mad" and "[wanders] about the house and about the surrounding country, staring keenly and seeing nothing." Just as Hermione's intellectualism leads, in the end, to the attack on Birkin, so Crich's "spirituality" has for an obverse the destructiveness of his relationship with his wife: theirs is "a relation of utter interdestruction." That, in defiance of the truth of their relationship, he should always say to himself "how happy he [has] been, how he [has] loved her with a pure and consuming love ever since he [knew] her" stresses the capacity for self-deception which also characterizes his attitude to the facts of the mining industry.

It is by promulgating a belief in spiritual equality—in Christ he is one with his workmen—that Thomas Crich becomes an anarchic force in the mines. An apt comment on this doctrine is provided by Birkin, who (in regard to a similar belief of Hermione's) maintains that "one man isn't any better than another, not because they are equal, but because they are intrinsically *other,* that there is no term of comparison," and insists that "spiritually there is pure difference." Crich's colliers confuse the issue still further by driving his ethics to an economic conclusion: manifesting a "will for chaos," they press for a complementary functional equality. But their "passion for equality" is not easily distinguished from "the passion of cupidity" when they refuse to accept a reduction in their wages and the Masters' Federation imposes a lockout: "Seething mobs of men [march] about, their faces lighted up as for holy war, with a smoke of cupidity." Their simmering destructiveness finally issues in violence, a pit-head being set on fire and a man shot dead before soldiers manage to disperse the rioting mob.

In Gerald the "will for chaos" is subtly rationalized into a will to power, but the changes he institutes in the mines are a product of the same anarchic tendency. When he takes over the running of the mines from his father, he has a "vision of power": seeing himself as "the God of the machine," and believing that "Man's will" is the "only absolute," he seeks the "pure fulfilment of his own will" in a struggle to subjugate both man and matter to his own ends. His immediate objective is the profitable extraction of coal from the earth, and in order to make this as efficient a process as possible, he ruthlessly abandons his father's humanitarianism and substitutes for the miners' dream of functional equality the rigid fact of their graded instrumentality. In place of the "silliness" of the "whole democratic-equality problem" he seeks to construct a mechanism which will contain "perfect instruments in perfect organization," and the "inhuman principle in the mechanism" inspires him with an "almost religious exaltation"—a demonic transformation, this, of his father's Christianity.

The way in which Gerald implements his reforms and the nature of the miners' response to them is described in one of the most powerful passages in the novel, a passage remarkable for its penetrative insight:

> Gradually Gerald got hold of everything. And then began the great reform. Expert engineers were introduced in every department. An enormous electric plant was installed, both for lighting and for haulage underground, and for power. The electricity was carried into every mine. New machinery was brought from America, such as the miners had never seen before, great iron men, as the cutting machines were called, and unusual appliances. The working of the pits was thoroughly changed, all the control was taken out of the hands of the miners, the butty system was abolished. Everything was run on the most accurate and delicate scientific method, educated and expert men were in control everywhere, the miners were reduced to mere mechanical instruments. They had to work hard, much harder than before, the work was terrible and heart-breaking in its mechanicalness.

> But they submitted to it all. The joy went out of their lives, the hope seemed to perish as they became more and more mechanized. And yet they accepted the new conditions. They even got a further satisfaction out of them. At first they hated Gerald Crich, they swore to do something to him, to murder him. But as time went on, they accepted everything with some fatal satisfaction. Gerald was their high priest, he represented the religion they really felt. His father was forgotten already. There was a new world, a new order, strict, terrible, inhuman, but satisfying in its very destructiveness. The men were satisfied to belong to the great and wonderful machine, even whilst it destroyed them. It was what they wanted. It was the highest that man had produced, the most wonderful and superhuman. They were exalted by belonging to this great and superhuman system which was beyond feeling or reason, something really godlike. Their hearts died within them, but their souls were satisfied. It was what they wanted. Otherwise Gerald could never have done what he did. He was just ahead of them in giving them what they wanted, this participation in a great and perfect system that subjected life to pure mathematical principles. This was a sort of freedom, the sort they really wanted. It was the first great step in undoing, the first great phase of chaos, the substitution of the mechanical principle for the organic, the destruction of the organic purpose, the organic unity, and the subordination of every organic unit to the great mechanical purpose. It was pure organic disintegration and pure mechanical organization. This is the first and finest state of chaos.

Lawrence's criticism of pre-war England is centred in this devastating analysis of Gerald's efficiency. It is one of the points on which the whole novel converges, for if Shortlands meets Beldover in the mines, the mines in turn are clearly a symbol of the industrial complex which is modern civilization and supports alike Breadalby and the Café Pompadour. It is not surprising, therefore, that the word "disintegration" recurs in this passage, though it points to a kind of collapse which, in the nature of the renunciation it epitomizes, is more shocking than any yet referred to. This disintegration goes further than the dissolution into separate parts of a whole; the "reduction" of the miners to "mere mechanical instruments" is a metamorphosis, the perversity of which is suggested by the name given to the new machines—"great iron men." The

iron men mediate between Gerald and the miners as the vehicles of a mutual destructiveness. That the miners finally accept the machines betokens not only their nihilistic submissiveness but the deflection of their desire for violence into a quiet passion of self-destruction: Beldover, we remember, is like a town of the dead. As far as Gerald is concerned, the anarchic perfection of his system is both the logical culmination of his will to subjugate man and matter and a subtle satisfaction of *his* "destructive demon": "As soon as Gerald entered the firm, the convulsion of death ran through the old system. He had all his life been tortured by a furious and destructive demon, which possessed him sometimes like an insanity. This temper now entered like a virus into the firm . . . ." His activity in the mines, that is to say, is fundamentally a sublimation of the sort of urges which lead him as a boy to kill his brother "accidentally" (Birkin points the moral for us here by reflecting that there is no such thing as accident: "It all hung together, in the deepest sense") and to long to go with the soldiers to shoot the rioting miners. But at the same time his demon proves to be ultimately self-destructive. The system Gerald devises is so perfect that he becomes not so much the God of the machine as a superior instrument, and he eventually realizes that he himself is "hardly necessary any more." He is consequently thrown back on his resources as a man-only to discover that he has exhausted them in service of the machine. He finds that, outside the mines, he has no identity: he does "not [know] what he [is]," and he fears that his eyes are "blue false bubbles" that may "burst in a moment and leave clear annihilation." The bubbles take us by way of the Pompadour to Halliday's African carvings—those central symbols of disintegration— and to Birkin's further reflections on the beetle-faced woman:

> There remained this way, this awful African process, to be fulfilled. It would be done differently by the white races. The white races, having the Arctic north behind them, the vast abstraction of ice and snow, would fulfil a mystery of ice-destructive knowledge, snow-abstract annihilation. Whereas the West Africans, controlled by the burning death-abstraction of the Sahara, had been fulfilled in sun-destruction, the putrescent mystery of sun-rays. . . .

> Birkin thought of Gerald. He was one of these strange white wonderful demons from the north, fulfilled in the destructive frost mystery. And was he fated to pass away in this knowledge, this one process of frost-knowledge, death by perfect cold? Was he a messenger, an omen of the universal dissolution into whiteness and snow?

The references to Gerald are unnecessarily explicit. It seems clear without them that by taking "the first great step in undoing," by substituting "the mechanical principle for the organic" in his organization of the mines, he initiates the northern miners in "a mystery of ice-destructive knowledge, snow-abstract annihilation," and that his own actual dissolution in the snow is the physical counterpart of a "mystical" disintegration. But if Gerald's death by perfect cold has an ominous social significance, it is convincingly precipitated by a personal breakdown. As always in Lawrence, what a man stands for in the "man's world" is revealed and tested in his personal relations, and Gerald's death is the outcome of his relationship with Gudrun.

The struggle between Gerald and Gudrun is concluded high up in the Alps when they go with Birkin and Ursula to a Tyrolese mountain resort. The description of the view from the hostel at once establishes the significance of this, the fifth, "world" of the novel:

> [Gudrun] went and crouched down in front of the window, curious.
>
> "Oh, but this—!" she cried involuntarily, almost in pain.
>
> In front was a valley shut in under the sky, the last huge slopes of snow and black rock, and at the end, like the navel of the earth, a white-folded wall, and two peaks glimmering in the late light. Straight in front ran the cradle of silent snow, between the great slopes that were fringed with a little roughness of pine trees, like hair, round the base. But the cradle of snow ran on to the eternal closing-in, where the walls of snow and rock rose impenetrable, and the mountain peaks above were in heaven immediate. This was the centre, the knot, the navel of the world, where the earth belonged to the skies, pure, unapproachable, impassable.
>
> It filled Gudrun with a strange rapture. She crouched in front of the window, clenching her face in her hands, in a sort of trance. At last she had arrived, she had reached her place. Here at last she folded her venture and settled down like a crystal in the navel of snow and was gone.
>
> Gerald bent above her and was looking out over her shoulder. Already he felt he was alone. She was gone. She was completely gone, and there was icy vapour round his heart. He saw the blind valley, the great cul-de-sac of snow and mountain peaks under the heaven. And there was no way out. The terrible silence and cold and the glamorous whiteness of the dusk wrapped him round, and she remained crouching before the window, as at a shrine, a shadow. . . .
>
> He lifted her close and folded her against him. Her softness, her inert, relaxed weight lay against his own surcharged, bronze-like limbs in a heaviness of desirability that would destroy him, if he were not fulfilled. She moved convulsively, recoiling away from him. His heart went up like a flame of ice, he closed over her like steel. He would destroy her rather than be denied.

I have suggested that Beldover, Shortlands, Breadalby, and the Café Pompadour can be said to converge on the mines; they also cast long shadows out to the snowy mountain heights. The heights, that is to say, serve as a vantage point from which these "worlds" may be retrospectively surveyed and simultaneously evoke the likelihood of their ultimate metamorphosis into a single frozen world of snow. It is a poetic evocation, the connection being effected by means of two images used in the description of the view. The first image, the repeated references to the end of the valley as "the navel" of the earth, amplifies the suggestion of deathliness which attaches to the scene; for the navel, it would seem, is not to be regarded here as a symbol of life. It implies, rather, the point at which the life-cord is cut, at which the sustaining link with that which nourishes life is broken; and if this seems to posit the possibility of new, independent life, it is life of an order which on earth means death, for it is the point where the mountain peaks are "in heaven immediate" and where the earth belongs to the skies, "pure, unapproachable, impassable." The deathliness which is to be detected beneath the

surface of life in the other worlds of the novel and the death which is to be the end result of that process of 'disintegration and dissolution' in which they are variously caught are here exposed as a pervasive presence; the second image of the valley as a "great cul-de-sac" makes clear why the road from the England of Shortlands and Breadalby runs to the Tyrolese mountain heights. (pp. 143-50)

Of the characters in **Women in Love** it is Birkin and Ursula who are most aware of the disintegration of life that the novel variously discloses. When he tells her that he is "tired of the life that belongs to death—our kind of life," he gives expression to her own intuitive sense of life as "a rotary motion, mechanized, cut off from reality. There was nothing to look for from life—it was the same in all countries and all peoples. The only window was death;" and it is their mutual recoil from a society *in extremis* that, in part, brings them together. Their relationship is the more momentous in that it is all they have to set against the general disaster, Birkin going so far as to say, in an early conversation with Gerald, that "there remains only this perfect union with a woman—sort of ultimate marriage—and there isn't anything else." It is not surprising that, rejecting the society he lives in, Birkin feels forced to seek a new kind of relation with Ursula, for it is clearly shown in the novel that the personal relations to which that society gives rise are themselves an alarming symptom of disease in the body politic.

The problem, as it presents itself in both its personal and social aspects, is primarily concerned with the difficulty of achieving a self, and this difficulty is seen to be at the centre of a particularly vicious circle. In the case of Gerald, for instance, it is because he loses all sense of an organic wholeness of being in his work in the mines that he has no independent self on which to lean in his fatal relationship with Gudrun; but it is only because he has no real self to start with, and no respect for the claims of individuality, that he lends himself to the monstrous perversity which degrades the miners to mere instruments. It is the failure to consummate a self that undermines life, and in considering the sort of relationship he wishes to establish with Ursula, Birkin fastens on this deficiency in "the old way of love" as that which it is essential to avoid. Birkin meditates on this subject at length and with some obscurity, but in so far as his views are identifiable with those of Lawrence himself, as would seem likely, they are of central importance for an understanding of the development of Lawrence's thought:

> On the whole, he hated sex, it was such a limitation. It was sex that turned a man into a broken half of a couple, the woman into the other broken half. And he wanted to be single in himself, the woman single in herself. He wanted sex to revert to the level of the other appetites, to be regarded as a functional process, not as a fulfilment. He believed in sex marriage. But beyond this, he wanted a further conjunction, where man had being and woman had being, two pure beings, each constituting the freedom of the other, balancing each other like two poles of one force, like two angels, or two demons.
>
> He wanted so much to be free, not under the compulsion of any need for unification, or tortured by unsatisfied desire. Desire and aspiration should find their object without all this torture, as now, in a world of plenty of water, simple thirst is inconsiderable, satisfied almost unconsciously. And he wanted to be with Ursula as free as with himself, single and clear and cool, yet balanced, polarized

with her. The merging, the clutching, the mingling of love was become madly abhorrent to him.

But it seemed to him, woman was always so horrible and clutching, she had such a lust for possession, a greed of self-importance in love. She wanted to have, to own, to control, to be dominant. Everything must be referred back to her, to Woman, the Great Mother of everything, out of whom proceeded everything and to whom everything must finally be rendered up.

It filled him with almost insane fury, this calm assumption of the Magna Mater, that all was hers, because she had borne it. Man was hers because she had borne him. A Mater Dolorosa, she had borne him, a Magna Mater, she now claimed him again, soul and body, sex, meaning, and all. He had a horror of the Magna Mater, she was detestable. . . .

It was intolerable, this possession at the hands of woman. Always a man must be considered as the broken-off fragment of a woman, and the sex was the still aching scar of the laceration. Man must be added on to a woman, before he had any real place or wholeness.

And why? Why should we consider ourselves, men and women, as broken fragments of one whole? It is not true. We are not broken fragments of one whole. Rather we are the singling away into purity and clear being, of things that were mixed. Rather the sex is that which remains in us of the mixed, the unresolved. And passion is the further separating of this mixture, that which is manly being taken into the being of the man, that which is womanly passing to the woman, till the two are clear and whole as angels, the admixture of sex in the highest sense surpassed, leaving two single beings constellated together like two stars.

In the old age, before sex was, we were mixed, each one a mixture. The process of singling into individuality resulted into the great polarization of sex. The womanly drew to one side, the manly to the other. But the separation was imperfect even then. And so our world-cycle passes. There is now to come the new day, when we are beings each of us, fulfilled in difference. The man is pure man, the woman pure woman, they are perfectly polarized. But there is no longer any of the horrible merging, mingling self-abnegation of love. There is only the pure duality of polarization, each one free from any contamination of the other. In each, the individual is primal, sex is subordinate, but perfectly polarized. Each has a single, separate being, with its own laws. The man has his pure freedom, the woman hers. Each acknowledges the perfection of the polarized sex-circuit. Each admits the different nature in the other.

The repeated phrases in which man is described as "a broken half of a couple," "the broken-off fragment of a woman," and the "broken fragment of one whole" recall passages in *The Rainbow* in which Tom is said to be "the broken end of the arch" and in which Will realizes that "if [Anna] were taken away, he would collapse as a house from which the central pillar is removed." The phrases indicate, then, that Birkin is pursuing a line of thought which leads straight from the earlier novel; the quoted passage as a whole suggests that the line here curves in a new direction. The ideal relationship that Lawrence posits for the men and women of *The Rainbow* can

be said to be the "two in one" that is symbolized by the rainbow arch; the relationship to which Birkin aspires with Ursula can best be described (in the terms in which Ursula thinks of it) as a "mutual unison in separateness," a phrase which registers a significant shift in emphasis. Though both phrases suggest a coming together in a union which does not obliterate singleness, it seems to me that in the earlier phrase the emphasis is on union, whereas in the later it is on separateness. Birkin, certainly, is markedly preoccupied with the idea of "single, separate being." What, one wonders, is responsible for the change?

I suggest, in the first place, that the change reflects Lawrence's growing awareness of the extent to which individuality is threatened in the "man's world." In *The Rainbow,* Ursula declares that her life's task is to be the smashing of the machine; but the machine is so massively established in *Women in Love* that both she and Birkin abjure the fight and—as remains to be discussed—ultimately solve the difficulty by withdrawing from the world of work. The increasing menace of the machine is further indicated by the progression in the novels from Walter Morel, man and butty, to John Smith, loader, to Gerald's anonymous miner, instrument. It is as if man is now so squashed by the inexorable pressure of the outer world that the maintenance of individuality in his personal relations becomes of overriding importance. For Birkin it is clearly of prime concern that what he refuses to yield to the machine should not be yielded to a woman, the more especially since he maintains that a "perfect union with a woman" is all that there is left to believe in. To yield to a woman, moreover, would likewise mean to submit to being exploited, to being reduced to an instrument.

Second, the change in emphasis is a measure of Lawrence's changed valuation of the significance of sexual intercourse. Hitherto the sex act has had a transcendent value in the sense that it has been regarded not merely as the means by which man and woman consummate their coming together but as the means by which they transcend their separateness in a union which is greater than either. In Lawrence's own terminology, indeed, the act may be said to have been viewed hitherto as a tangible manifestation of the Holy Ghost, the unifying Third Person of the Trinity. Birkin is the first character in Lawrence to think of sex "as a functional process, not as a fulfilment," and to regard the satisfaction of sexual desire as analogous to the satisfaction of thirst in a world of plenty of water. His "hatred" of "sex" is founded on the perception that it is destructive of the independence of man and woman, that, if it is once allowed a transcendent value, man and woman must of necessity be incomplete in themselves. In his insistent desire to be "single in himself" despite his conjunction with a woman, Birkin apparently wishes to fashion the house of marriage not round an arch but behind separate columns.

Birkin's demand that the individual be primal gains in force from our knowledge of Gerald's predicament, for Gerald's relationship with Gudrun, in one of its aspects, affords an instance of the "merging, mingling self-abnegation of love" which Birkin characterizes as "horrible." I suggest, however, that Birkin's demand should also be considered against the background of *The Rainbow.* It is not merely that Will's relations with Anna furnish us with an even better example of the attitudes Birkin castigates; in *The Rainbow* we can clearly see the limitations which attend the pursuit of "fulfilment" in a "sex marriage." Both Tom and Will do eventually find fulfilment in their marriages but only after an arduous struggle—and without succeeding in finding themselves. Neither, in the end, is "quite defined" as an individual. In *The Rainbow,* moreover, and it is this concept which seems to be especially pertinent to Birkin's meditations, the achievement of true individuality is regarded as being dependent on the reconciliation of male and female elements within the individual and on their maximum expression in a coherent personality; both Tom and Will, consequently, fail to attain to fullness of being because they manifestly exhaust their "man-being" in the sexual relation. It is a typical Lawrencean paradox that, as Birkin points out, and as Lawrence consistently asserts in his own person, the sex act is the means by which "the admixture of sex" is "surpassed," is the means, that is to say, by which the complex union of male and female components in the individual man and woman is reduced to elemental singleness, the man becoming "pure" man, the woman "pure" woman. The dilemma is formidable: "man-being" is exhausted in a consuming sexual relation; only the sex act is productive of an unadulterated "man-being." Birkin's reflections take a disconcerting turn when, in order to resolve the dilemma, he first minimizes the importance of the sex act and then predicates a "pure man" and "pure woman" who are "fulfilled in difference" not during sexual intercourse but, on the contrary, quite independently of such conjunction. Manhood and womanhood outside of the sexual relation are no longer, in other words, to be regarded as achievements, as the consummation of selves which have male and female components, but as singular blessings. (pp. 161-66)

I think that Lawrence's attempt to portray Birkin and Ursula's achievement of "the pure duality of polarization" (with all that the phrase, in its context, implies) is as unsatisfactory and unconvincing as the "doctrinal" passages in which he makes a frontal attack on our credence, and as the "symbolic" scenes in which he presents external support for his position. The means by which they achieve "polarity" are detailed in a crucial chapter called "Excurse"; the title, it seems, serves as an announcement, among other things, of a fresh sortie.

Some ten pages of "Excurse" are devoted to a description of the special kind of experience Birkin and Ursula have together and of its effect on them; I quote a representative passage, of manageable length:

> She looked at him. He seemed still so separate. New eyes were opened in her soul. She saw a strange creature from another world in him. It was as if she were enchanted, and everything were metamorphosed. She recalled again the old magic of the Book of Genesis, where the sons of God saw the daughters of men, that they were fair. And he was one of these, one of these strange creatures from the beyond, looking down at her, and seeing she was fair.
>
> He stood on the hearth-rug looking at her, at her face that was upturned exactly like a flower, a fresh, luminous flower, glinting faintly golden with the dew of the first light. And he was smiling faintly as if there were no speech in the world, save the silent delight of flowers in each other. Smilingly they delighted in each other's presence, pure presence, not to be thought of, even known. But his eyes had a faintly ironical contraction.
>
> And she was drawn to him strangely, as in a spell. Kneeling on the hearth-rug before him, she put her arms round his loins, and put her face against his thighs. Riches! Riches! She was overwhelmed with a sense of a heavenful of riches.
>
> "We love each other," she said in delight.
>
> "More than that," he answered, looking down at her with his glimmering, easy face.
>
> Unconsciously, with her sensitive finger-tips, she was tracing the back of his thighs, following some mysterious life-flow there. She had discovered something, something more than wonderful, more wonderful than life itself. It was the strange mystery of his life-motion, there, at the back of the thighs, down the flanks. It was a strange reality of his being, the very stuff of being, there in the straight downflow of the thighs. It was here she discovered him one of the sons of God such as were in the beginning of the world, not a man, something other, something more.
>
> This was release at last. She had had lovers, she had known passion. But this was neither love nor passion. It was the daughters of men coming back to the sons of God, the strange inhuman sons of God, who are in the beginning.
>
> Her face was now one dazzle of released, golden light, as she looked up at him and laid her hands full on his thighs, behind, as he stood before her. He looked down at her with a rich bright brow like a diadem above his eyes. She was beautiful as a new marvellous flower opened at his knees, a paradisal flower she was, beyond womanhood, such a flower of luminousness. Yet something was tight and unfree in him. He did not like this crouching, this radiance-not altogether.
>
> It was all achieved for her. She had found one of the sons of God from the Beginning, and he had found one of the first most luminous daughters of men.

The ostensible meaning of this experience in the parlour of the inn is, I think, sufficiently clear—it is the means by which Birkin and Ursula establish their "unison in separateness"—but the experience, as described, is one in which, to say the least, it is difficult to participate imaginatively, and which leaves us both dissatisfied and puzzled. There is, for instance, the confusing issue of individual singleness. The delight they take in each other's presence, "pure presence," suggests that what we have here is the realization of the hopes that are set out in Birkin's reflections on the relations of men and women; but it is not clear whether the achieved "purity" is a product of the experience, or whether it is antecedent to it and merely ratified by what happens. On the one hand, even before Ursula touches Birkin, she sees him as one of "the sons of God": the reference to the mysterious passage in the Book of Genesis, it seems, does not only serve to assert Birkin's established independence of being but obscurely implies that his pure presence is also a matter of pure maleness, for the man who is "no son of Adam" can be assumed to be free from any contamination of the other sex. This, I take it, is what underlies the related assertions that he is "a strange creature from another world," and that he is "not a man" but "something other, something more." Similarly, Ursula is "beyond womanhood." If, then, the achievement of "pure individuality" is antecedent to the experience, we would like to know, for we are not told, just how it is that they are "metamorphosed."

On the other hand, it is later stated that their "accession into being" is directly due to the experience itself: "She seemed to faint beneath, and he seemed to faint, stooping over her. It was a perfect passing away for both of them, and at the same time the most intolerable accession into being . . . ." If the experience described were a phallic one, an accession into pure male and female being would be acceptably in line with typical Lawrencean thought, but the fact that it is not raises further difficulties. In the first place, though the nonphallic nature of the experience is stressed, it seems that we are intended to attribute to it the sort of transcendent value that is usually associated in Lawrence with the sex act: Ursula discovers "something more than wonderful, more wonderful than life itself," but what she discovers is "neither love nor passion." The "floods of ineffable darkness and ineffable riches," we are later told, that spring from "the smitten rock of the man's body, from the strange marvellous flanks and thighs," come from "deeper, further in mystery than the phallic source." I do not wish to suggest, of course, that the experience is represented as a substitute for sexual intercourse; on the contrary, once supreme value is attached to it and not to intercourse, sex, so to speak, is put safely in its place and ceases to be a menace. It is as if the experience is a means of controlling the "old destructive fires" which, as was earlier intimated in relation to Birkin's stoning of the moon's reflection, can never be entirely extinguished. Birkin and Ursula, indeed, after they have had tea at the inn, drive off into Sherwood Forest and, on a moonless night—"It was a night all darkness, with low cloud"—consummate their union in a more usual fashion. If what transpires in the forest, as the following quotation suggests, cannot be said to be analogous to the satisfaction of thirst in a world of plenty of water, its "perfection," I think, is intended to be viewed as a consequence of the revelation at the inn and its significance as subordinate to it:

> She had her desire of him, she touched, she received the maximum of unspeakable communication in touch, dark, subtle, positively silent, a magnificent gift and give again, a perfect acceptance and yielding, a mystery, the reality of that which can never be known, vital, sensual reality that can never be transmuted into mind content, but remains outside, living body of darkness and silence and subtlety, the mystic body of reality. She had her desire fulfilled. He had his desire fulfilled. For she was to him what he was to her, the immemorial magnificence of mystic, palpable, real otherness.

If this analysis is acceptable, then it must further be urged that the experience at the inn is presented, rather too obviously, as an expedient by which the paradoxes inherent in Birkin's position are resolved; it is presented from one point of view, that is to say, as the means by which "pure" male and female being are attainable outside of sexual intercourse, and at the same time, in regard to the careful avoidance of any suggestion of "mingling and merging," or of any sense of containment, it is offered as a kind of sexual contact which, by its nature, cannot be either destructive or subversive of singleness. That it is an expedient is, in part, suggested by the poor quality of the writing. There is no call, I should say, for a detailed analysis of this weakness, for it is plainly evident in the passages I have cited, and there is general critical agreement, moreover, that the combined vagueness and stridency of the style hardly does Lawrence credit. The special pleading is also betrayed by the ridiculous lengths to which Lawrence is driven in attributing significance to the experi-

ence: after it, Ursula, who is said to be "usually nervous and uncertain at performing . . . public duties, such as giving tea," is "at her ease, entirely forgetting to have misgivings," and "the tea-pot [pours] beautifully from a proud slender spout"; similarly, when they are driving to Sherwood Forest, Birkin is described as sitting still "like an Egyptian Pharaoh, driving the car. He felt as if he were seated in immemorial potency, like the great carven statues of real Egypt, as real and as fulfilled with subtle strength, as these are, with a vague inscrutable smile on the lips," but lest there should be any doubt as to his ability to steer the vehicle, it is hastily asserted that the Egyptian in him is duly tempered by a touch of the Greek:

> But with a sort of second consciousness he steered the car towards a destination. For he had the free intelligence to direct his own ends. His arms and his breast and his head were rounded and living like those of the Greek, he had not the unawakened straight arms of the Egyptian, nor the sealed, slumbering head. A lambent intelligence played secondarily above his pure Egyptian concentration in darkness.

Even if we consider the description of the ultra-phallic revelation not so much as an expedient on Lawrence's part as a failure to communicate a genuine mystical experience, it seems open to serious objection. The failure in communication means that, at best, the experience remains the author's own, personal and not transmuted into the imaginative terms which alone could secure it a rightful place in a work of art; we are left, consequently, with little, if any, idea of what it is that actually happens to Birkin and Ursula at the inn. (pp. 174-78)

The failure in communication, then, would seem to preclude the relationship which Birkin ostensibly succeeds in establishing with Ursula from being regarded as in any sense normative, the norm which he proposes being, in the crucial instance of their sexual relations, if in no other, neither exoteric nor intelligible. Moreover, even if we assume, for the moment, that the description of the experience at the inn succeeds in suggesting the means by which a "pure stable equilibrium" between the lovers is to be assured, we cannot help noticing that the state of balance supposedly attained is precarious, if not equivocal. The scene, as Ursula kneels before Birkin, is a little too reminiscent of the wild cat and the Mino to be quite comfortable, and though it is said that Birkin does "not like this crouching, this radiance—not altogether," the disavowal, in its half-heartedness, is a disquieting intimation of what we are to expect in the next phase of Lawrence's writing, the phase which culminates in the blatant one-sidedness of the main relationships in *The Plumed Serpent.*

Ostensibly secure in their singleness, Birkin and Ursula are now ready for marriage, ready, that is, to be "transcended into a new oneness," to consummate their separate being in "a new, paradisal unit regained from the duality." The kind of marriage they wish to make, however, is more expressive of revolt against the established order, against "the horrible privacy of domestic and connubial satisfaction" and "the hot narrow intimacy between man and wife," than is the liaison of Gerald and Gudrun, and it implies no surrender to the society they despise. Indeed, it is over tea at the inn, immediately after the climactic revelation, that Birkin declares they must "drop [their] jobs," that "there's nothing for it but to get out, quick"; and it is "when they [wake] again from the pure swoon" which ensues on Ursula's "[pressing] her hands . . . down upon the source of darkness in him," that they decide "to write their resignations from the world of work there and then." Even fighting the old, as Ursula later tells Gudrun, means belonging to it, and their rejection of the world they know is absolute. It extends to a renunciation of all possessions, for Birkin maintains that "houses and furniture and clothes" are "all terms of an old base world, a detestable society of man," and in their determination to avoid having things of their own, they refuse to be bound even by a chair they have bought at a jumble market and give it away. Just what they will do and where they will go is not precisely defined. Birkin, who is fortunately possessed of a private income, suggests that they should "wander away from the world's somewheres into [their] own nowhere," contending that it is possible "to be free, in a free place, with a few other people," though he admits that it is not so much "a locality" he is seeking as "a perfected relation between [them], and others." In the event, they embark, together with Gerald and Gudrun, on the Alpine holiday. Though their decision to leave the mountain resort should be viewed, in contrast to the enthusiasm which Gerald and Gudrun evince for the cold whiteness, as indicative of the bid they are making for life, Gerald's death nevertheless forces them to return. It is with his death, so ominous in its implications for the "world" from which they are fleeing, that ultimately they are faced.

I have stressed Birkin and Ursula's desire to withdraw from the world because, in so far as Lawrence's feelings in this respect can be identified with theirs, their attitude represents a significant reversal of the attempt, begun in *The Rainbow,* to come to terms with it. In the earlier novel, it will be remembered, the realization of "man-being" was seen to be dependent on effective "utterance" in the "man's world," and Tom and Will and Skrebensky were, in different measure, condemned for a failure in manhood; it was only Ursula who could be said to have achieved full individuality. At the opening of *Women in Love* the prior struggles for integrated being of *The Rainbow* are, so to speak, taken for granted, in the sense that none of the four leading characters is subject to the limitations of "blood-intimacy": they are articulate, self-conscious, and intellectual; and all are active in the "world of work." The problem Lawrence apparently set himself was that of exploring the development of individuality with ever more and more complex characters, of proceeding, as it were, to a Birkin and an Ursula and a Gerald and a Gudrun through a Tom and a Lydia and a Will and an Anna. In *Women in Love* it becomes evident, however, that true being is more than a matter of having a day, as well as a night, goal. In the end, as I have previously pointed out, Gerald's work in the mines and Gudrun's art are revealed as "disintegrative," as an abuse of organic life; and the black sensuality of their relationship is productive of the violence which, in the novel, is seen as an inevitable concomitant of any process of "dissolution." What, then, of Birkin and Ursula? What are we to make of the fact that their "accession into being" is followed at once by their resignations from the "world of work"? Whether or not we are inclined to accept their ostensible achievement of genuine individuality, their withdrawal from the world-though it may perhaps be justified by the hopeless state of the society in which they would have to live if they did not withdraw from it—must be deemed, in the context of the two books, a serious qualification of their fullness of being. Accordingly, it should come as no surprise that, in the next phase of his writing, Lawrence should assiduously seek to determine the conditions under which a return to the world is possible, and that, given the collapse of the

pre-war world of *The Rainbow* and of *Women in Love,* such a return should ultimately necessitate the emergence of a leader who will try to refashion it. (pp. 179-82)

H. M. Daleski, in his The Forked Flame: A Study of D. H. Lawrence, *Northwestern University Press, 1965, 320 p.*

F. H. LANGMAN   (essay date 1967)

[*In the following excerpt, Langman disputes some common critical assessments of authorial intent, structure, and content in* Women in Love. *In the second half of the excerpt, he concedes that the novel's overly rigid form resulted in some poorly written passages that significantly flaw the novel.*]

Women in Love is widely accepted, now, as what F. R. Leavis showed it to be [in his *D. H. Lawrence: Novelist;* see Additional Bibliography]: the major work of a major novelist. And its more recent critics have largely agreed not only on its merits but also on its faults. In their view Lawrence failed to resolve problems he believed that he was resolving, or at least set out to resolve, and following from this supposed failure of thought they see a failure of structure. Dr. Leavis's statement of the case remains the clearest:

> The diagnosis represented by Gerald and Gudrun is convincing—terribly so; but Birkin and Ursula as a norm, contemplated in the situation they are left in at the close of the book, leave us wondering (and, it must in fairness be added, leave Lawrence wondering too). That is, if a certain symmetry of negative and positive was aimed at in *Women in Love,* Lawrence has been defeated by the difficulty of life: he hasn't solved the problems of civilization that he analyses.

This criticism, which has been repeated by critics as different as Eliseo Vivas [see excerpt dated 1960] and W. W. Robson, rests on some questionable assumptions. One is that Lawrence's intention in the novel can be known apart from, and used as a measure of, his achievement. Another is that the novel is constructed on a simple pattern of contrast—a symmetry of negative and positive—between the complete failure of one love affair and the assured success of the other. A third is that an adequate criticism of any novel can approach it as an analysis of the problems of civilization, to be judged by whether, on a simple practical level, it offers a viable solution. To question these assumptions is not, of course, to accept the absolute divorce of poetry from prophecy, art from message or moral, that Vivas for one (although his practice is inconsistent) demands in theory.

Lawrence's intentions in writing *Women in Love,* whatever they may have been, are beside the point. The tale, if we trust it, simply does not present the marriage of Birkin and Ursula as ideal in itself or as an adequate solution to the problems presented. On the contrary, an important thesis of the novel is that no fully satisfying personal relationship is possible to people placed, like Birkin and Ursula, in a social and religious vacuum. Lawrence's treatment of their marriage is firmer and less "positive," shows a keener awareness of life's difficulties, than any attempt to set up a norm could offer. It follows from this that the structure of the novel must be less symmetrical and more complex than has been supposed. Birkin and Gerald, in particular, are not so diagrammatically opposed. Their destinies do not represent the assured positive solution and a disastrous deviation from it, but something far less definite:

a contrast of attitudes, hope against despair, struggle against surrender.

The subtle structure the novel actually evolves, in not making just that false simplification its critics have thought to see in it, may be brought out better by attention to the form rather than the ostensible meaning of the two love-stories. The Gerald-Gudrun story is closed, it forms a complete action in the Aristotelian sense. The Birkin-Ursula story is open. It has a beginning and a development, but no end either displayed or implied. The future of this story is not predetermined, and the agents move out of the last pages into the freedom of continued, unpredictable, endeavour. Looking back over the novel from the clear and conscious inconclusiveness of the final paragraph, we can see that this freedom, this making of choices in a continual process of self-commitment, has characterised this couple at every stage of the story. Gerald on the other hand is fated. His doom is fixed from the start, and he abandons himself to the remorseless forces which carry him to it. These forces act as much from within himself as from without, but still he cannot be said to choose his direction. He acquiesces in it, lets himself go; and, paradoxically, this passivity towards his fate, towards the forces of destruction within himself, takes the form of an exertion of the will. In this he resembles his father, who all through his long illness never admitted he was going to die:

> He knew it was so, he knew it was the end. Yet even to himself he did not admit it. He hated the fact, mortally. His will was rigid. He could not bear being overcome by death.

In Gerald, similarly, the will asserts itself most strongly in evasion: it sustains his being by the repudiation of self-knowledge and of the choices that would make necessary:

> And once or twice lately, when he was alone in the evening and had nothing to do, he had suddenly stood up in terror, not knowing what he was. And he went to the mirror and looked long and closely at his own face. . . . He dared not touch it, for fear it should prove to be only a composition mask. . . . But his will yet held good, he was able to go away and read, and think about things.

As the father's dying drags on, Gerald's will proves insufficient:

> His will held his outer life, his outer mind, his outer being unbroken and unchanged. But the pressure was too great. He would have to find something to make good the equilibrium. . . . In this extremity his instinct led him to Gudrun.

But Gudrun is caught up in the same processes, and although she does not literally die her future course too has, by the end of the novel, been rigidly and terrifyingly predetermined.

This contrast of form between the two stories leads to a more satisfying evaluation of the novel than the usual way of judging it on what it offers of social diagnosis and therapy. I do not mean that *Women in Love* is not concerned—and very directly—with social analysis. Modern society is its subject, but its approach is more exploratory than prescriptive. The closed story defines its own moral, but within the context of a larger complexity. Gerald's death is only an episode in Birkin's life. The open story is the more inclusive of the two, and to recognise this is to see the vital role in the novel of speculation, choice, quest, and incompletion. (pp. 183-85)

[Lawrence's] deepest preoccupations were with problems which took their most acute forms, historically, in Europe, and received their most intense artistic expression not in English. It is very telling that the last movement of *Women in Love* should begin with a journey far into Europe to arrive at the figure, gone so much further down the "tunnel of darkness" than any of the English characters, of the polyglot Loerke. *Women in Love* places Lawrence in the line of European writers who, from Dostoevsky on, have made the novel the medium of at once the most deeply felt social awareness and the most urgent philosophical speculation. In this line—surely the main line of the modern novel—the important writers in England have been Lawrence and Conrad. Conrad's place in the line seems clear. It may not be as readily granted of Lawrence, but the essential similarity is there, as I shall try to show.

Conrad deeply distrusts freedom. He believes that, in full freedom, men are capable of limitless evil, and the cosmic order, because it is unfathomable, seems to leave them in virtual freedom: it cannot provide the sanctions and imperatives which make survival possible. Only society can provide them. Yet, for all his devotion to the social order, Conrad is haunted by a sense of the factitious in the beliefs on which society depends. His major novels are commonly directed to just that point at which the principles of social order come most under stress, where they need support from beyond themselves, from the cosmos which answers no questions. The crucial figures in his novels—Lord Jim, Mr. Kurtz, Decoud, Winnie Verloc, Razumov—at the same time as they discover the absolute necessity, for themselves, of the social bond, discover too its oppressiveness and weakness when related to no deeper belief. This double attitude, affirmation and negation together, is what makes Conrad so disturbing, so corrosive.

The critics who suppose that in *Women in Love* Lawrence failed to fulfil his intention perhaps regard him—no matter how much they admire him—as simpler, more single-minded, than a writer like Conrad, as if he were or meant to be only positive, directly affirmative. The value of the affirmative mood, however, depends on the substance of what it affirms, and even more on what lies beyond it. Simple affirmation may set a term to understanding, where negation would push onward. At any rate, I suggest that *Women in Love* gets much of its significance from the same scepticism, the same double sense of things, as we find in Conrad. It affirms the necessity of the social bond and explores the values out of which the bond can be renewed, but it acknowledges with bleak honesty that it can go only some part of the way towards discovering values that will suffice, and it denies the source of the old values. For the primary fact of *Women in Love* is that none of its characters can continue to believe in God. Its essential drama, for all its concern with the forms and pressures of English society, is on the familiar theme of modern European novels: the search for the vanished God or for surrogates of divinity. Some of its characters, like Hermione, throne the human understanding paramount and make of that their God. Some, like Gerald, seek escape in distraction—art, or sex, or social welfare, or work. Ursula and Birkin look openly on their despair and seek beyond it.

This is what drives Gerald to his death. His self-distractions fail one by one, power, work, love. Confronting at last his own unmitigated emptiness, he flies from it into extinction, the oblivion of the snow. In his last moments he finds, half-buried in the snow, a crucifix. But this cannot help him now.

He sheers away, and his will to live snaps. It is not that he accepts the conditions of life, comes to terms with death. For him, to die is to be murdered. "Somebody was going to murder him." His last conscious thought is made to be a helpless invocation of the disavowed saviour: "Lord Jesus, was it then bound to be—Lord Jesus!" This, with its note of awe, its atavistic appeal, is immensely powerful, but its power is in irony. What it reflects is Gerald's failure to find any sustaining belief: it is a surrender, not a prayer and not an affirmation.

The same quest uproots Birkin and Ursula, and sets them wandering. Birkin longs for a new, more congenial community, but for this the prerequisite is a new faith. He seeks a faith to breathe life back into social relationships. The society he knows stultifies him, not because of its external ugliness but because it lacks meaning. It has failed to create new values adequate to its experience. He feels "imprisoned within a limited, false set of concepts." His exile, a deliberate cutting free from the old social ties, may be necessary to a new beginning but does not, of itself cannot, bring what he seeks. The novel ends, as it begins, not with bold answers but with painful questioning.

Despite the obvious—and on Lawrence's part conscious—differences between them, this particular conjoining of affirmation and scepticism indicates the measure of Lawrence's affinity with Conrad. Of the two, Lawrence is really the more intransigent. "I can't forgive Conrad for being so sad and for giving in"—it is the spirit of that (whatever its unfairness to Conrad) which makes Lawrence's scepticism so firm, so radical: the power of negation in *Women in Love,* the continued undermining of hopeful attitudes, is itself a form of not giving in. Yet it is every bit as desolate and disconcerting a novel as, say, *Nostromo* or *Under Western Eyes.*

To define the affinity more sharply, to search for specific parallels between one novel and another, has its obvious dangers, but there are resemblances between the central metaphors of *Women in Love* and *Lord Jim* which provide some confirmation of my argument, and carry it further. I hope the comparison will not seem forced: it is offered as suggestive rather than conclusive. In *Lord Jim,* then, the hero deserts an apparently sinking ship, abandoning the unsuspecting passengers to their fate. His feelings as the life-boat floats into the night take on the qualities of a universal experience:

> We were like men walled up quick in a roomy grave. No concern with anything on earth. Nobody to pass an opinion. Nothing mattered. . . . When your ship fails you, your whole world seems to fail you; the world that made you, restrained you, taken care of you. It is as if the souls of men floating in an abyss and in touch with immensity had been set free for any excess of heroism, absurdity, or abomination. Of course, as with belief, thought, love, hate, conviction, or even the visual aspect of material things, there are as many shipwrecks as there are men.

In its range of implications this passage seems fairly to represent the assumptions out of which Conrad constructs the world of his novels. The virtues he affirms—self-restraint, loyalty, devotion to duty, including the selfless heroic devotion of women—are social, are given by the world that has "made you, restrained you, taken care of you." For these values the voyage, with its clear-cut and pressing necessities, is a perfect image; and their limitations are equally well represented in the idea of the ship that fails. When a society loses all consciousness of a common goal, or comes to the conclusion that no common goal is possible, then there can be only a general scrimmage of personal appetites. Then each man is alone in the universe, like the sailor cast away in the open sea, and no rules of behaviour any longer apply. "It is as if the souls of men floating in an abyss and in touch with immensity had been set free for any excess of heroism, absurdity, or abomination," and "there are as many shipwrecks as there are men."

Women in Love uses rather similar imagery on a larger scale, to bring out its allied but more intense concerns. The opening pages rapidly and forcibly introduce the themes of the novel and give a taste of its uncompromising mood. For Ursula and Gudrun traditional ideas of marriage and society are out of date, are hopelessly at odds with reality, and with startling truthfulness they say so, casually but decisively clearing away the old axioms by which their society used to live. In their destructiveness, in the finality with which they reject everything of which woman's life used to be composed, the sisters seem almost to believe in nothing. But although they are obviously superior women, intelligent, educated, and articulate, and although their taste and dress are somewhat assertively unconventional ("What price the stockings!"), they are clearly not to be thought of as eccentric. What they so candidly say must be taken to show what others were coming to feel. Their corrosive lack of belief indicates how far in disintegration their whole society has gone.

The sisters are full of mockery. Nevertheless they are not happy, they feel lost in life. For all their independence, they feel that their lives are going to waste: "Nothing materializes! Everything withers in the bud." Marriage is not the answer, and they do not know of any other answer. They cannot imagine what will become of them. Their freedom leads to an abyss. Gudrun's careless optimism is really a kind of despair. "If one jumps over the edge, one is bound to land somewhere" is how she puts it, and the conversation closes with the words:

> The sisters found themselves confronted by a void, a terrifying chasm, as if they had looked over the edge.

In Chapter IV, Gerald swimming in the lake is described thus:

> He was alone now, alone and immune in the middle of the waters, which he had all to himself. He exulted in his isolation in the new element, unquestioned and unconditioned. He was happy, thrusting with his legs and all his body, without bond or connection anywhere, just himself in the watery world.

Noteworthy are the phrases "alone and immune in the middle of the waters," "unquestioned and unconditioned," "without bond or connection anywhere." Gerald is "just himself in the watery world," set free like Conrad's Jim from the world that had made and restrained him. At first he enjoys this freedom, he finds it a release. Later in the book he changes, he finds, like Jim, that such freedom is terrifying. He needs to be held more firmly to life: alone in the universe, he would let himself sink into death. So, in Chapter XIV, after he has searched the depths of the lake for his drowned sister, he says:

> "If you once die . . . then when it's over it's finished. Why come to life again? There's room under

that water there for thousands . . . a whole universe under there."

In Chapter XVII, Gerald's relation to society is specifically compared to that of a sailor whose ship has failed, lost its purpose and direction, is in fact falling to pieces:

> Meanwhile, as the father drifted more and more out of life, Gerald experienced more and more a sense of exposure. His father after all had stood for the living world to him. Whilst his father lived Gerald was not responsible for the world. But now his father was passing away, Gerald found himself left exposed and unready before the storm of living, like the mutinous first mate of a ship that has lost his captain, and who sees only a terrible chaos in front of him. He did not inherit an established order and a living idea. The whole unifying idea of mankind seemed to be dying with his father, the centralising force that had held the whole together seemed to collapse with his father, the parts were ready to go asunder in terrible disintegration. Gerald was as if left on board of a ship that was going asunder beneath his feet, he was in charge of a vessel whose timbers were all coming apart.

Lord Jim leaps into the abyss of freedom in a moment of panic and weakness. Lawrence's characters—the difference is significant—are borne down half-willingly in a lingering letting-go. But what they find is the same. They are set free for any excess, any abomination. So Gudrun and Gerald recognise in each other "the subterranean desire to let go, to fling away everything, and lapse into a sheer unrestraint, brutal and licentious."

These images running through the novel suggest, as in Conrad, that as with moral laws so the purposes of individuals take their form from social life. When society fails, a man alone, though in touch with immensity, can find neither goal nor guide. This is made explicit not by Gerald but by Birkin, the novel's "positive" spokesman:

> "The old ideals are dead as nails—nothing there. It seems to me there remains only this perfect union with a woman—sort of ultimate marriage—and there isn't anything else."

> "And you mean if there isn't the woman, there's nothing?" said Gerald.

> "Pretty well that—seeing there's no God."

Faced with the death of the old ideals, how thin, how minimal, Birkin's positive is: how close to sheer negation. All that he has is a tentative willingness, insistent rather than confident, to let life make a claim on him. So he says "I want to love." He wants, that is, in the lack of any clear belief, to be committed by his emotions (as, later, Gerald's instinct leads him to Gudrun). Nor, even in this, is Birkin clear and unwavering. In Chapter VIII, after Hermione has attempted to kill him, he enacts half-consciously a kind of ritual of purification in a wild thicket. He takes off his clothes, takes off the insignia as it were of his membership in society, and consummates what he thinks of as his marriage to the natural world. When he comes to himself he thinks of his wish for love as a mistake, he feels weary of the old ethic that bade a human being adhere to humanity. Birkin's religion—despite his explicit disavowal he is haunted by a vague, vestigial sense of the Godhead, what he calls the "creative utterances," the "unseen hosts"—does not alleviate the novel's despair. It sug-

The pond at Felley Mill, which served as the model for the pond on the Crich estate in Women in Love.

gests no answer, or only the saddest of all possible answers, to the problems of civilisation:

> Let mankind pass away—time it did. . . . Humanity doesn't embody the utterance of the incomprehensible any more.

This is ultimate despair. This is, expressed here in direct words and expressed by Birkin, what Gerald's death in the snow means. And against this despair, at the conceptual level, at the level of argument, Birkin has nothing positive to offer.

But in Birkin the mood is unable to sustain itself. He cannot drive the image of the moon—Cybele, Syria Dea, the universal urge to love and creation—from the surface of the pond, nor permanently shatter it. Deny it though he may, the old ethic in him is ineradicable. Ursula forces from him the admission that, though he calls it his disease, he does love humanity and cannot forsake it. Nor is he able to resist the old human need to interpret, after all, the utterances of the incomprehensible: "it is the law of creation. One is committed. One must commit oneself to a conjunction with the other." So he looks to marriage to provide his own life with a centre. From here, he comes to see marriage as the basis of a community, to think of society as held together not by work or any unifying idea but by love, by the bonds of feeling between man and woman and man and man. Marriage is the first step, friendship is the second. As soon as his relationship with Ursula is securely established, his thoughts turn to the inclusion in their "separate world" of a few other people, to the formation of a new community "where one meets a few people who have gone through enough, and can take things for granted. . . . There is somewhere—there are one or two people."

There is no need to dilate on the deficiencies of this, and to contend against it as if it were put forward without qualification as a norm would miss the point. The very wistfulness of the utterance contains an implicit criticism of it, and in the outcome Birkin's wish is utterly thwarted. Whether his ideas are true or false, possible or impossible, remains in question to the very last words of the novel. The end of the novel brings back, confirms, the unbearable sadness of Birkin's vision in the wild valley before the experiment of marriage began.

> Either the heart would break, or cease to care. Best cease to care. Whatever the mystery which had brought forth man and the universe, it is a non-human mystery, it has its own great ends, man is not the criterion.

The most painful question in the whole novel, a question that precisely places the limited value of the experiment in marriage, is Ursula's: "Why aren't I enough?"

Women in Love contains passages of notoriously bad writing. . . . The fault seems to me symptomatic of more than an occasional, localised, failure of expression. It is a failure of imagination, and I think it can be related, with most of the novel's other faults, to a single central weakness. This is a weakness of form. The novel's earliest critics condemned it as formless, but the real trouble is the opposite: it has been shaped by too determined a hand. In it a complex structure, abstractly preconceived, demands an embodiment the writer's imagination is not always able to figure forth. Where his imagination fails, the design is eked out by intellect and will. The consequence of the will trying to do the work of the imagination is rhetoric, of the intellect trying to do it is abstraction and mechanism. They are seen in the strained Dionysian passages between Birkin and Ursula, but also in the injustice to Hermione and in the intrusions of allegory.

It is easy to see what Hermione stands for and why she must be rejected, but her rôle remains excessively abstract: there is a break-down in the kind of presentation, the creation from within, which would be necessary to justify it. The psychological stresses from which she is alleged to suffer are not rendered, but outwardly described, and in language incapable of engaging with its subject. The whole of Chapter VIII demonstrates this, but a single instance from that chapter may be sufficient illustration here. After Birkin has told Hermione what he claims to see in the Chinese drawing of geese, she is supposed to suffer an obscure defeat: "she was witless, decentralised. . . . She suffered the ghastliness of dissolution, broken and gone in a horrible corruption." The slackness of this prose is one manifestation of a deeper fault, for what is supposed to be conveyed here is Hermione's response to a challenge from Birkin. He challenges her to try and know, as he does, the different kind of being that is the goose. And as she fails to feel what it is like to be a goose, so she must realize that she cannot know Birkin himself. His too is a mode of being different from her own. This, of course, ties up with his assertion, later in the chapter, that "we are all different and unequal in spirit." In saying these things he is repudiating his relationship with her, denying her claim to be at one with him. And yet, can Hermione be blamed after all, for not being able to feel what it is like to be a goose? Birkin's claim is an arrogant falsehood, as much a blasphemy against the "otherness" of different forms of life as anything that Hermione ever says. What Birkin does here is as bad as what Gudrun does, in Chapter XIX, when she describes the robin as self-important. Birkin, indeed, is worse because more pretentious. And his claim is condemned out of his own mouth. As Ursula thinks to herself of the birds in Chapter XIX:

> They are of another world. How stupid anthropomorphism is. . . . Rupert is quite right, human be-

ings are boring, painting the universe in their own image.

Instead of placing the issue fairly between Birkin and Hermione, however, the novel distorts it by the hostile description of her alleged inner state. The episode makes its point, takes its place in the thematic development; but it is not seen steadily and whole. The difference between the kind of "significance" it conveys (significance merely for the structure or argument of the novel) and imaginative adequacy to the complex reality of the situation may be suggested by comparison with Lawrence's poem, **"Fish."** The passage in the novel fails to bring Birkin round to anything like the point in the poem where, after the most astonishing display of empathy, the poet admits to the unknowable: "I had made a mistake, I didn't know him."

The spiritual degeneration of mankind is represented at several points in the novel by the suggestion that some of the characters resemble—or wish to return to—more primitive forms of life, emerging like water plants out of the primeval slime. (pp. 186-96)

Thus Minette is called an ice-flower in Chapter VI, a mud-flower in Chapter XVIII. In chapter VII, the Russian appears in Gerald's eyes as "golden and like a water-plant." In Chapter X, Gudrun first identifies the water-plants with herself ("she could feel their turgid fleshy structure as in a sensuous vision, she *knew* how they rose out of the mud") and then identifies them with Gerald: "He started out of the mud." A page further on, she is said to be "aware of his body, stretching and surging like the marsh-fire, stretching towards her, his hand coming straight forward like a stem."

These examples are in varying degrees improbable and unimaginative. A few, like Gudrun's half-conscious impression of Gerald, have a measure of vivid, dream-like credibility, but in most cases the marsh-symbols appear quite artificially and are stuck on to the characters like labels. The allegory, the system of arbitrary symbols through which the theme is developed, is an unconvincing short cut to significance. It establishes the necessary interconnection of characters, but only by violating the novel's usual and much subtler mode. In its use of allegory the novel relies upon, credits with objective validity, exactly the sort of thing that from Birkin would be exposed (as in the conversation, in Chapter XIV, about the "river of darkness") to Ursula's critical challenge.

Because the novel has been too schematically conceived, its structure becomes at times mechanical, artificially imposed upon and impairing the autonomy of the characters. The effect is to fake their feelings. Thus, for example, it is necessary for the story's sake that Gudrun should be attracted to Gerald from the start. Instead of the delicate imaginative creation this requires, it is merely predicated, and as bathetically as love at first sight in a novelette:

> And then she experienced a keen paroxysm, a transport, as if she had made some incredible discovery. . . . And then, a moment after, she was saying assuredly, "I shall know more of that man". . . . "Am I *really* singled out for him in some way . . ." she asked herself.

This strains too hard to make the ensuing development clear and give it a semblance in inevitability. A fuller imaginative apprehension of the characters and their situation could not have expressed itself with quite such certainty. This marks an important difference between the closed story and the open: in my view, the essential difference. (pp. 196-97)

The early critics of *Women in Love* who found its characters indistinguishable were, no doubt, thoroughly obtuse, but (as in the passages just adverted to) the characters *are* in some important respects alike. And their affinities are as much intellectual as emotional. Immersed in a common situation, their understanding does not—cannot—put forward very different answers. That is why it is naïve to think of the novel as attempting to offer, in the way of a solution, anything like an intellectual formula or a program of action. It is also why attempts to interpret the novel on the level of debate—to set up Birkin's views opposite Gerald's, or Ursula's opposite Gudrun's—run into contradiction. Their views are not sufficiently dissimilar. It is rather in how they respond to ideas, in how far they are willing to follow thought through to its consequences in living, that the differences lie. Birkin's mind is dynamic and the novel, as much as it centres on him, is carried forward by and in pace with his thinking. Gerald detaches himself from his thoughts. He fears and seeks to evade the courses (marriage, friendship) to which thought would commit him, and his mental processes have to be analysed in the novel from a point of observation outside himself. Therefore Birkin is active and free, Gerald is passive and bound. The effect is of a narrative written from different points of view. Gerald is looked at as fixed and finite, the doomed figure of classical tragedy, Birkin as fluent and immeasurable, the existential hero of a modern novel.

These points of view, however, are not equally valid. The mode in which Birkin and Ursula are conceived allows them more humanity, and by comparison brings out a certain limitation or warping of imagination in the treatment of Gerald and Gudrun. For example, while Ursula is at first piqued, attracted, and annoyed by Birkin, Gudrun at the first glimpse of Gerald has her "strange paroxysm" of foreknowledge. Here, as in phrases like "the terrible hopelessness of fate," the writing strains for a significance it cannot establish, a significance moreover that is called in question by the acknowledged freedom of the other case.

Strain of a similar kind, but on a larger scale, characterises the symbols by which the closed story is circumscribed. Gerald dies in the snow. The passages describing his walk towards death, his last moments, and the effect of his death upon the others, are among the most impressive in all fiction. In these closing chapters the snow gathers a multiple significance, imaging the variety of responses in the different characters: in Gerald's case, its coldness, its whiteness, its blankness all evoke the freezing up of spontaneous affection, the numbing desolation in his spirit. But all through the novel Lawrence has been hinting at this climax, associating Gerald with ice and snow, making the connections too direct and forcing references to them into the least believable places. So, for instance, when Gudrun sees Gerald at the wedding she is said to observe his "clear northern flesh" and his hair glistening like "sunshine refracted through crystals of ice," and to ask herself whether "some pale gold, arctic light . . . envelopes only us two?" It seems scarcely too strong to say that here the character has been reduced to a ventriloquist's dummy: what speaks through her is the allegorical scheme of the whole novel.

Many instances of the same sort could be given. Thomas Crich, denying his wife's true nature, subduing her to his will, thinks sentimentally of what he has reduced her to as "a won-derful white snow flower." Gerald sees Minette as "some fair ice-flower in dreadful flowering nakedness." Birkin tells Gerald "you have a northern kind of beauty, like light refracted from snow." In Chapter XIX, meditating on the disintegration of civilization, Birkin foresees its end, annihilated like Gerald in the snow:

> The white races, having the arctic north behind them, the vast abstraction of ice and snow, would fulfil a mystery of ice-destructive knowledge, snow-abstract annihilation.

What this is getting at is, in a general way, only too clear: the death of civilization through an excess of abstraction, of thought disembodied, the feelings refined away into nothingness. But the expression here is unacceptable, too schematic, too forced. What is to be made, for example, of "having the arctic north behind them"?

Birkin goes on to think of Gerald:

> He was one of these strange white wonderful demons from the north, fulfilled in the destructive frost mystery. And was he fated to pass away in this knowledge . . . death by perfect cold? Was he a messenger, an omen of the universal dissolution into whiteness and snow?

Gerald, of course, *is* an omen, and Birkin is here expanding the significance of Gerald's rôle in the novel as a whole. Gerald acts out in his own life and death the novel's prognosis for civilization if it persists in responding to life as he has done. But this ought to be clear from the events of the novel without such insistent underlining of the theme, and that Birkin should so literally foresee Gerald's death in the snow is incredible either as coincidence or as prescience.

Birkin, envisaging the self-destruction of the white races, imagines as its obverse a mindless sensuality that he calls "the African process." Associated with this idea are the primitive carvings which do at times provide an effective symbolism. It is understandable that both Gudrun and Loerke, interpreting life in comparable ways, should be fascinated by primitive sculpture, and that Gerald should have explored in the Amazon jungle and should like to read anthropological studies of primitive man. Deeply dissatisfied with their own world, aware of being caught up in processes of refinement which threaten to destroy their inner lives, it is natural that they should turn towards radically contrasting ways of life. But again the novel forces out of these symbols a further significance that is both false and crude. The particular carving that Birkin thinks of, with its tiny face and distended body, is not characteristic of African art, and the interpretation he draws from it is spurious: "It must have been thousands of years since her race had died, mystically." Must have been! This is empty conjecture, "only an idea," with nothing realised in the novel to back it up. The allegorical pattern it supports, the contrast of African decadence with that of the white races, is as unreal as it is unnecessary.

According to Dr. Leavis [see Additional Bibliography]:

> . . . the major event in which the whole action of *Women in Love* resolves itself, Gerald's death in the snow . . . comes as the inevitable upshot of a drama enacted by human individuals as recognizable and as intelligibly motivated as any in fiction.

But is Gerald's death really as inevitable as all that? The novel's persistent emphasis on fatality rings a bit hollow. The diagnosis represented by Gerald and Gudrun is convincing, up to a point, but it would be even more convincing—more completely truthful—if it were less absolute. Birkin and Ursula "leave us wondering": should not Gerald's death, too, leave a little scope for wondering? "Was it, then, bound to be?" The question is Gerald's own, and it goes, surely, to the heart of the novel. But the closed story is rigid. Its rhetoric reduces the richly suggestive psychological probability of the drama down to abstract necessity. Its symbolism imposes a distracting and implausible diagram upon the living, the far more complex and various, development of character and situation. The difference comes out in the contrast between these symbols in the allegorical mode and the less easily defined but more successful symbols used elsewhere in the novel.

The depths of the lake, the reflection of the moon, the snow-covered peaks, the cat, the mare, the rabbit, have a substantive existence of their own. They may be called symbols only in the sense that they become charged with the significance of situations of which they form a natural part. That is, they are psychological symbols; and like the images in a dream they focus and express subconscious stresses which the characters suffer without knowing and usually refuse to acknowledge. In Chapter XIV, to take an example, Gudrun's behaviour on the island is startling but never beyond probability, and powerfully conveys the difference between her conscious self and her deeper nature. Almost alone on the island, unobserved, she can let herself go. The process begins for her when the sisters shed their clothes, shed their social inhibitions as it were, and bathe. Then, in the dance, Gudrun gradually works herself up, almost hypnotically, in wild free gestures, "stooping as if she were trying to throw off some bond." The climax comes when in an ecstatic release of suppressed aggression, she drives away the cattle. Other motives are at work at the same time. Her action is dangerous, and Gudrun, who finds life so boring, is seeking for thrills, even destructive ones. Her discontents include dissatisfaction with herself, she feels the lure of self-destruction. This conduct shocks Gerald, and she wants to shock him, to defy him and so win his interest. Still to provoke his interest, to engage in the thrill of a struggle against him, she strikes him; and the hidden aggression she had begun to release against the cattle is turned now, for consummation, against the higher, the more formidable opponent: she feels a desire "for deep violence against him." In all this, Gudrun is still carried away by the liberation of her unconscious impulses. Consciously, she is as surprised by her behaviour as Gerald is, she asks herself "Why are you behaving in this *impossible* and ridiculous fashion?"

Gerald, too, is possessed by an unrealised desire for violence. As a boy, he had accidentally shot his brother. Ursula suggests that in accidents of this kind a fantasy of destructiveness becomes, by chance, a reality: "this playing at killing has some primitive *desire* for killing in it." The implication, reinforced at several points in the novel, is that Gerald is haunted at once by a fear of punishment, a terror that violence will be done to himself, and by a wish for punishment, a longing to expiate his secret guilt. As Birkin rather cruelly tells him in Chapter II: "you would like to be cutting everybody's throat," and yet "you seem to have a lurking desire somewhere to have your gizzard slit." But Gerald has driven from consciousness both his fear and his longing for punishment. They emerge covertly, through the symbolic overtones of his conduct and even of his ideas. Only Dostoevsky, I think, has

surpassed the subtle interpenetration of psychology and philosophy in *Women in Love,* the extent to which it shows ideas, although profound in themselves and given their proper weight, as extensions of personality.

The novel concentrates a great density of experience in the figure of Gerald: his brother's death, the cleavage between his parents, his father's moral failure, his own career and personal relations find implied counterparts in the larger crises of history, in economic, social, and religious change. Thus Gerald conceives of society as a mechanism, and helps to make it one, because he dare not unfreeze his own feelings. Brotherhood and love, the breach of his own isolation, are above all what he wants to avoid, if he is to avoid confronting his repressed wishes. Gudrun sums up the failure of their affair by telling him: "You cannot love." That is why, for him, the idea of a community—even as much of one as Birkin offers—makes an intolerable demand: afraid of his own full self, he prefers to turn men, himself included, into instruments. But in the crisis after his father's death, Gerald's conscious self-control lapses. In a semi-conscious trance he acts out, in succession, three desires. He goes in search of Birkin, then he goes to the grave, then he goes to Gudrun. It is as if he had gone first for salvation to the man who could tell him the truth about himself and so restore him to life; then to death, to escape from himself; then to Gudrun, to escape from death. When the affair with Gudrun fails, he yields more and more to the impulse which had sent him walking in darkness to the grave. He lives for the "mindless," but dangerous, thrill of speeding down the slopes, liberated from awareness, courting death.

Gerald never again tries to take up the third possibility—what Birkin offers—but because it is still there the inevitability of his death in the snow must remain in question. What Birkin offers is scarcely a solution, it is prior to any solution. It is simply a mode of response in which the intense experiencing of problems—the problems of civilization that the novel analyses—makes all that there can be of positive contribution, and in which flight and death can be seen as ways of affirmation. Death has more than one meaning in the novel. Gerald dies literally because he is afraid of himself and of life. He is unwilling to suffer, to feel, to fail, and to change. Birkin and Ursula die metaphorically by marrying and leaving England: they die to their old lives, their old selves. This is their leap into the abyss.

> But better to die than live mechanically a life that is a repetition of repetitions. To die is to move on with the invisible. To die is also a joy, a joy of submitting to that which is greater than the known, namely, the pure unknown. . . .

Submission to the unknown is the novel's one positive prescription. It implies a trust in life that is sufficient, I think, to distinguish Lawrence rather sharply in this respect from Conrad; but nothing in the novel encourages us to treat this as backing up Birkin's specific conclusions. All the articulate affirmations in *Women in Love* are subjected to question, to the test of events. If, as I believe, Birkin is its most important figure, he is so not as a positive spokesman but as an instance of the necessary openness to life which alone can nourish hope. His strength—and the novel's strength—is that of a mind in modulation, tentative, erratic, but marked by a profound and unwithholding commitment to its experience.

For Birkin, it is important to note, Gerald's death was not

bound to be; but in asserting this he is only recognising that the problems of life remain and must be faced:

> Gerald might have found this rope. He might have hauled himself up to the crest. . . . He might! And what then? The Imperial road! The south? Italy? What then? Was it a way out? It was only a way in again.

(pp. 198-205)

F. H. Langman, " 'Women in Love'," in Essays in Criticism, *Vol. XVII, No. 2, April, 1967, pp. 183-206.*

DEREK BICKERTON   (essay date 1967)

[*Bickerton is an English educator and critic who specializes in linguistics. In the following excerpt, he criticizes the imprecision of Lawrence's language in* Women in Love.]

While Lawrence's high status as a novelist is now widely accepted, there is still room for a considerable measure of disagreement about the quality of his actual writing. (p. 56)

To discuss Lawrence's prose as a whole is beyond the scope of a brief paper. All I propose to do is to examine one particular novel, to see whether certain features of the language therein displayed can be in any way related to the feeling of vague unease which some readers have derived from it.

I have chosen to concentrate on **Women in Love** for two further reasons. In the first place, many critics accept it as being probably Lawrence's greatest novel. Clearly any criticism of Lawrence's writing should aim at his strongest rather than his weakest point; it would be too easy, and quite pointless, to cull an anthology of *bétises* ["stupidities"] from one who wrote as much, and as quickly, as he did. Secondly, Lawrence himself realized there was something unusual about the language of **Women in Love.** It was his declared intention to go "a stratum deeper than I think anybody has ever gone, in a novel," and, by abandoning the "old stable ego of the character," to lay bare "another ego, according to whose action the individual is unrecognizable, and passes through, as it were, allotropic states which it needs a deeper sense than any we've been used to exercise, to discover are states of the same single radically unchanged element." He wished, in other words, to work at a level deeper than that of everyday consciousness, and quickly came to the conclusion that the "hard, violent style full of sensation and presentation," in which he had written **Sons and Lovers,** was not adaptable for this purpose. As early as January 1913 he had admitted that his projected novel *The Sisters*—from which both **The Rainbow** and **Women in Love** were subsequently derived—was "far less visualized"; a little later he wrote: "I am doing a novel which I have never grasped . . . it's like a novel in a foreign language I don't know very well—I can only just make out what it's about."

Though no one has every analysed this "foreign language," even Lawrence's admirers have felt some reservations about it. Graham Hough, [in his *The Dark Sun;* see Additional Bibliography] admits that on occasions the style "lapses into inflation and bathos"; Professor Leavis, after quoting a passage from Chapter 33 ("Excurse"), points out the presence of "something one can only call jargon," a jargon he defines as "an insistent and over-emphatic explicitness" [see Additional Bibliography]. He describes this, however, as "a fault that I do not now see as bulking so large in the book as I used to see it."

Large or not, "explicitness" seems hardly the word for it. Part of the passage Professor Leavis quotes goes as follows:

> He felt as if he were seated in immemorial potency, like the great carven statues of real Egypt, as real and fulfilled with subtle strength as these are, with a vague inscrutable smile on their lips. He knew what it was to have the strange and magical current of force in his back and loins, and down his legs, force so perfect that it stayed him immobile, and left his face subtly, mindlessly smiling. He knew what it was to be awake and potent in that other basic mind, the deepest physical control, magical, mystical, a force in darkness, like electricity.

Far from being "explicit," this seems an attempt to inflate a perfectly ordinary situation—that of a man driving in a car with a woman to whom he is about to make love—into an experience of supra-normal significance, by an accumulation of highly emotive but almost meaningless adjectives: "immemorial," "subtle," "vague," "inscrutable," "strange," "perfect," "magical" (twice), "mystical." In the words of a distinguished critic:

> Hadn't he, we find ourselves asking, overworked "inscrutable," "inconceivable," "unspeakable," and that kind of word already?—yet still they recur . . . . The same vocabulary, the same adjectival insistence upon inexpressible and incomprehensible mystery, is applied to the evocation of human profundities and spiritual horrors; to magnifying a thrilled sense of the unspeakable potentialities of the human soul. The actual effect is not to magnify but rather to muffle.

The critic is Professor Leavis himself; he happens, however, to be discussing, not Lawrence, but Conrad. Yet, for reasons unexplained, the same fault that "mars" *Heart of Darkness* does not "bulk large" in **Women in Love;** what is sauce for the Polish goose is obviously not sauce for the Nottingham gander.

Since Professor Leavis himself admits that he "could find worse examples in **Women in Love,"** no purpose is to be served by further quotation; the more important question we now have to consider is whether this "jargon" can be dismissed, as he and Mr. Hough dismiss it, as an occasional and trivial blemish, or whether it is merely the most obvious symptom of a malady which penetrates the entire work.

Attention was drawn, in the passage just quoted, to a striking disproportion between language and content; and this disproportion, and the straining after effect which goes with it, is not limited to passages which can be dismissed as jargon. Sometimes it shows itself clearly in the passages of "bathos" which Mr. Hough noted:

> But the next day, she did not come, she sent a note that she was kept indoors by a cold. Here was a torment!

But more often one must jerk one's own mind back to the situational context to realize how far the intensity of the language exceeds normal expectations.

> A terrible storm came over her, as if she were drowning. She was possessed by a devastating hopelessness . . . . Never had she known such a

pang of utter and final hopelessness. It was beyond death, so utterly null, desert.

(Hermione Roddice, at the Crich-Lupton wedding, has just noticed that her lover Birkin has not yet arrived; he does, a few moments later.)

> "Ursula!" cried Gudrun. "Isn't it amazing? Can you believe you lived in this place and never felt it? How I lived here a day without dying of terror, I cannot conceive!"

(The Brangwen sisters are revisiting the perfectly ordinary house from which their family has just moved after living there uneventfully for many years.)

> "Unless something happens," she said to herself, in the perfect lucidity of final suffering, "I shall die. I am at the end of my line of life." . . . In a kind of spiritual trance, she yielded, she gave way, and all was dark.

(Ursula, waiting at home for Birkin to call, has concluded he is not coming; again, he does arrive shortly afterwards.) (pp. 57-9)

These are random examples, which could be multiplied indefinitely. The result of this use, or abuse, of language is twofold: its effect on the reader is "not to magnify, but rather to muffle"; and, when Lawrence has to deal with a scene of genuine emotional violence, such as the quarrel between Ursula and Birkin which precedes their final coming-together, he has so debased his lexical currency that he has nothing left but novelettish cliché:

> Suddenly a flame ran over her, and she stamped her foot madly on the ground, and he winced . . . . Her brows knitted, her eyes blazed like a tiger's.

The muffling and blurring effect produced by this persistent inflation is augmented by Lawrence's peculiar, and peculiarly frequent, use of certain words and phrases. To demonstrate this, I shall be obliged to resort to statistical counts, a method in some disfavour nowadays, owing to its indiscriminate use; however, no other means will show in a small compass the extent of practices which, in specific contexts and to a limited degree, might be justifiable enough, but which, in bulk, amount to a vice of style.

For example, certain key words are used in such a way that they lose their normal meaning. "Torture" and "torment" occur a total of thirty-nine times in the text, although (if we except Gerald's treatment of his mare, which accounts for only two occurrences) no scenes of physical torture are described or even mentioned. In a fifteen-hundred word passage at the beginning of Chapter 15, the words "death," "die," "dead" are used a total of forty-five times (though no actual death occurs), and the words "life," "live," "living" twenty-four times. Whether or not we agree with Sweeney that "Death is life and life is death," the effect of such a passage is to render the terms virtually indistinguishable.

Still more remarkable is Lawrence's use of two groups of words, one of which serves merely to intensify, the other to convey indecision and vagueness.

In the first I include "very" (185 occurrences), "so" used as an adverb of degree, i.e. "so utterly null" (155), "really" (79), "complete/completely" (63), and "utter/utterly" (37). Several words which have scarcely more lexical force are employed as frequently, "perfect/perfectly" (170 times), "pure/purely" (127), "terrible/terribly" (64), "awful" (21) and "dreadful" (15).

In the second group, we find what might be called the "structure-words of vagueness," "as if" (282 times), "almost" (191), "rather" (106), the indefinite "some"—as in "she seemed wrapped in some glittering abstraction" (115),—"a certain" (49), "a little" as adverb of degree (43), "sort of" (50), "kind of" (17) and "perhaps" (31). Similar to these is "strange/strangely," used in the sense of "out of the ordinary, hard to define" rather than that of "previously unknown." This item occurs 257 times, and the synonymous uses of "curious/curiously," "odd/oddly," "queer/queerly," "uncanny/uncannily" provide a further 137 items. The verb "seem" is used 301 times; "slight/slightly," 80; "faint/faintly" 58; "vague/vaguely," 38. "Quite" seems to straddle both groups; in a sentence such as "There had been some discussion, on the whole quite intellectual and artificial," are we to assume that the discussion was *rather* intellectual, or *completely* intellectual? Anyway, it occurs 97 times.

Granted, these are all words a writer has to use at some time or other; but in **Women in Love,** which contains (excluding dialogue) roughly 150,000 words, they add up to a total of 2,768—that is to say, they account for nearly one word in every fifty. They are not, of course, evenly distributed. Sometimes their impact is negligible, though not a page is entirely free of them. But where they are densely clotted, their effect is striking; a single example will have to suffice:

> He (Gerald) *seemed* to stand with a proper, rich weight on the face of the earth, whilst Birkin *seemed* to have the centre of gravitation in his own middle. And Gerald had a rich, frictional *kind of* strength, *rather* mechanical, but sudden and invincible, whereas Birkin was *abstract* as to be *almost intangible.* He impinged *invisibly* upon the other man, *scarcely seeming* to touch him, like a garment, and then suddenly piercing in a tense fine grip that *seemed* to penetrate into the *very* quick of Gerald's being.

There are four "as ifs," three "seems," three "stranges," three indefinite "somes," one "almost," one "scarcely," one "kind of" and one "uncanny" in the three shortish paragraphs that follow. The effect is that of a man trying, by qualification, to pass off as sense something which, if stated unequivocally, would come perilously close to nonsense. The extract is from the description of the Crich-Birkin wrestling match. Several critics have speculated inconclusively on whether we are to attach a homosexual significance to this scene; not one that I have read has connected his failure with the imprecision of the language in which the episode is described.

All the stylistic features so far mentioned could certainly be attributed to the fact that Lawrence is "uncertain of the value of what he offers; uncertain whether he really holds it"—an uncertainty which may now appear far more extensive than Professor Leavis admits. Other features are less easily explicable. That of repetition has been frequently noted, though it has never been analysed in detail. Here we have Lawrence's own explanation [see excerpt dated 1919]:

> Fault is often found with the continual, slightly modified repetition. The only answer is that it is natural to the author, and that every natural crisis in emotion or passion or understanding comes from

this pulsing, frictional to-and-fro which works up to culmination.

This just will not do. Even if we accept his definition of "natural crises"—which sounds more like a description of another of his favourite subjects—we need not accept the "fallacy of expressive form" which is implicit in his statement. To mirror an actual process in style is not necessarily the best way of expressing it; a writer who couches, say, the boredom of his characters in a prose of deliberate monotony will only succeed in boring and repelling the reader. And to say that repetition "is natural to the author" is not true; up to and including *Sons and Lovers,* it forms a negligible element in Lawrence's prose. It begins to make itself felt in *The Rainbow;* by the final version of *Women in Love,* it is no longer confined to "natural crises," it has begun to pervade even passages of straightforward description. It is not sufficient to say simply that the air in the Alps was cold; "it was so terribly cold . . . it was indeed cold, bruisingly, frighteningly, unnaturally cold . . . it seemed conscious, malevolent, purposive in its intense murderous coldness." (These three sentences occur within eight lines.)

Similarly, the "code-words" which are attached to several of the characters are repeated (as aids to recognition?) almost every time they appear. The eighteen occurrences of "glistening" all apply to Gerald or some part of his anatomy; nothing else in the novel glistens. With Hermione, the words are "sang" or "sing-song" (describing her speech) and "slow/slowly," which is used thirteen times in six pages of Chapter 22 to describe her or her actions: "in her slow voice," "she said slowly," "with slow calm eyes," "Hermione was slow and level," "with slow pensive eyes," "said Hermione slowly" (three times), "with her slow heavy gaze," "in her slow deliberate sing-song," "slowly she rubbed his head, slowly and with ironic indifference," "her long slow white fingers."

But the full effect of Lawrence's repetitions, where they occur in bulk, can only be demonstrated by fairly lengthy quotation; again, a single example from the many must suffice:

> Oh, why wasn't somebody kind to her? Why wasn't there somebody who would take her in their arms, and hold her to their breast, and give her rest, pure, deep, healing rest? Oh, why wasn't there somebody to take her in their arms and fold her safe and perfect, for sleep. She wanted so much this perfect, enfolded sleep. She lay always so unsheathed in sleep. She would lie always unsheathed in sleep, unrelieved, unsaved. Oh, how could she bear it, this endless unrelief, this eternal unrelief?
>
> Gerald! Could he fold her in his arms and sheathe her in sleep? Ha! He needed putting to sleep himself—poor Gerald! That was all he needed. What did he do, he made the burden for her greater, the burden of her sleep was the more intolerable, when he was there. He was an added weariness upon her unripening nights, her unfruitful slumbers. Perhaps he got some repose from her. Perhaps he did. Perhaps this was what he was always dogging her for, like a child that is famished, crying for the breast. Perhaps this was the secret of his passion, his for ever unquenched desire for her—that he needed her to put him to sleep, to give him repose.
>
> What then! Was she his mother? Had she asked for a child, whom she must nurse through the nights for her lover. She despised him, she despised him,

she hardened her heart. An infant crying in the night, this Don Juan.

> Ooh, but how she hated the infant crying in the night. She would murder it gladly. She would stifle it and bury it, as Hetty Sorrell did. No doubt Hetty Sorrell's infant cried in the night—no doubt Arthur Donnithorne's would. Ha—the Arthur Donnithornes, the Geralds of this world. So manly by day, yet all the while, such a crying of infants in the night. Let them turn into mechanisms, let them. Let them become instruments, pure machines, pure wills, that work like clockwork, in perpetual repetition. Let them be this, let them be taken up entirely in their work, let them be perfect parts of a great machine, having a slumber of constant repetition. Let Gerald manage his firm. There he would be satisfied, as satisfied as a wheelbarrow that goes backwards and forwards along a plank all day—she had seen it.

This, with its "ha's," "oh's," "ooh's" and "what then's," is Lawrence's version of stream-of-consciousness, and it is instructive to compare it with Joyce's. Lawrence's is much less convincing. It is more formal, more stagey, closer to conventional soliloquy; instead of leaping erratically from idea to idea, as the mind does even under stress, it bears down remorselessly on a single line of thought. Moreover, the fact that Gudrun's mannerisms of style, as well as her attitudes to men and machinery, are the same as those Lawrence exhibits in his narrative passages, tends to deprive her of reality as compared with Joyce's individual creations. Not only individual words are repeated—twenty-five of them, some occurring as often as six or eight times—but whole phrases recur either verbatim or with minor modifications, and in addition the same idea is frequently expressed in different words:

> her unripening nights, her unfruitful slumbers
>
> his passion, his for ever unquenched desire
>
> to put him to sleep, to give him repose,
>
> she would murder it . . . she would stifle it.
>
> mechanisms . . . instruments, pure machines . . .
>   like clockwork . . . parts of a machine
>
> always . . . endless . . . eternal . . . for ever . . .
>   all the while . . . perpetual . . . constant

The sense of monotony these devices produce is reinforced on the syntactical level. Four consecutive sentences are introduced by "perhaps," five consecutive clauses by "let them"; of the thirty-four sentences in the passage, less than a third contain more than a dozen words, half consist of a single main clause only. Still more surprisingly, nearly a quarter of the passage consists of words or phrases in apposition, many of which act as a coda at the ends of sentences: "pure, deep, healing rest"; "this endless unrelief, this eternal unrelief"; "crying for the breast." (There are eight other instances in the passage.) Here the motivation appears to be phonic, as if Lawrence wished by a series of "dying falls" to emphasize Gudrun's weariness of Gerald. But the machinery is surely excessive; moreover, the same devices are to be found in such a wide variety of contexts that they can hardly be justified even on grounds of "expressive form."

The passages may also be compared with two from *Sons and Lovers* which convey the thoughts and emotions of a solitary character at a moment of psychological stress. The first is where Mrs. Morel has been locked out by her husband, the second where Paul reflects on his own situation after his mother's death. The features noted above are almost entirely absent from the first passage, though they begin to make their presence felt in the second. Both passages, however, present a vigour and variety of linguistic resource which contrasts strongly with the narrowness of range in the passage just quoted. And there is another difference. In both the **Sons and Lovers** passages, the central character is planted firmly in the environment; the moonlit garden in which Mrs. Morel waits, the starry night through which Paul walks, are evoked vividly in concrete detail. But Gudrun's reflections are given no such local habitation. Of the four hundred words of the extract—indeed of the thousand or so which precede them—not one links her with her surroundings; she exists in a vacuum.

Here is the "far less visualized" style with a vengeance, and it gives us a clue to another aspect of the novel that has caused some disquiet. Graham Hough admits that most readers "will find it hard to be convinced by the complicated relations of Gudrun and Gerald, Ursula and Birkin, on the plane of ordinary human action and character" [see Additional Bibliography], but claims that "all Lawrence's novels tend to carry more conviction in the ordinary social-naturalist sense the more familiar they become." This is to admit that they carry little at first—we can get used to anything—and, after many readings, there seems to me still a persistent lack of fit between the actual world and the portrait of it in **Women in Love;** a lack of fit caused by Lawrence's deliberate withdrawal from "sensation and presentation."

We can only conclude that Lawrence, in 1913, found himself in the position of Aesop's dog, and dropped the bone of concrete presentation while pursuing the glimmering image of "deeper strata" and "allotropic states." Yet, if language is anything to go by, these states were as difficult to grasp as the reflected bone; and one may well suspect that they had no more reality, and that the "same single radically unchanged element" into which they could be resolved was none other than Lawrence's own highly idiosyncratic imagination.

Certainly a sense of the author straining over and over again to capture the uncapturable pervades **Women in Love.** It is precisely this straining which produces the inflation and repetition we have noted; and Lawrence, by his acceptance of the ideal of creative spontaneity, by his contemptuous rejection of "that will of the writer to be greater than and undisputed lord over the stuff he writes, which is figured to the world in Gustave Flaubert," deprived himself of the one means by which he might have corrected such vices of style and made **Women in Love** the great novel which, in conception, it undoubtedly was. For I feel quite certain that its current high estimate needs stringent revision. In spite of all its ingenuity of form, and the many striking scenes it contains, the language in which most of it is written finally leaves one with the feeling that Ursula had while she was watching Birkin playing with daisies:

> A strange feeling possessed her, as if something were taking place. But it was all intangible.
>
> (pp. 60-7)

Derek Bickerton, "The Language of 'Women in Love'," in A Review of English Literature, *Vol. 8, No. 2, April, 1967, pp. 56-67.*

CAROL DIX (essay date 1980)

[*In the following excerpt from her study* D. H. Lawrence and Women, *Dix discusses Lawrence's view of the ideal relationship between men and women as presented in* Women in Love.]

At the centre of all Lawrence's work is his view on the relationship between man and woman: the modern definition of the time-honoured liaison or battle between the sexes. A true perception of what Lawrence was offering in his definition of the word "relationship" is vital for an understanding of his attitude towards both women and men. When Lawrence talks of "relationship," he talks in terms of a committed, one-to-one, intense, creative partnership akin to the marriage relationship. He does not, contrary to popular opinion in his time and still to some extent now, mean promiscuous sex, or free love, or any of the more fashionable ideas. Lawrence means what today we have come to call the "creative relationship"; one in which man and woman come to meet as opposites, as equals, as similar but different, as potential partners, and enemies in a duel; who through their feelings for each other test themselves, learn about each other and go beyond the normal social confines of either "marriage" or casual sex that Lawrence so hated. He saw both extremes as a waste of life, a waste of the essential life-force, of the potential that is in each human being.

Lawrence stated that he would do his life's work sticking up for the relationship between man and woman. He has defined the new type of woman, through Ursula and Gudrun, the "self-responsible" woman looking for her own career, her independence and freedom from social restrictions, a life not constrained by parents, environment or husband's values. Gudrun: "One must be free, above all, one must be free. . . . No man will be sufficient to make that good, no man!" Ursula, too, is given those headstrong qualities while at the same time knowing there is a "big want" deep in her. The want is for some form of love with a man, with a human being, that will make sense of her life.

Lawrence has also clarified how he sees man and woman as two individuals, struggling to work out how they can live side by side. In this he was original, the begetter of the later twentieth-century system of values that still causes pain and conflict in the people trying to live them out—for woman has to be seen as an independent being as the first step. But the man who wrote, "It is as if life were a double cycle, of man and woman, facing opposite ways, travelling opposite ways, revolving upon each other . . . reaching forward with outstretched hand, and neither able to move till their hands have grasped each other . . . each travelling in his separate cycle," was not trying to establish a pattern that can loosely be described as male chauvinist, that of dominant man seeking submission of woman. He was trying to find something different.

Lawrence was not writing about the man-woman relationship in limbo, nor just theorising. Like most novelists, he had his own experience to bring to bear. And, interestingly, what might have been pure theory from the young Lawrence soon mellowed and evolved, not away from the idealism, but further into it, evolving from his relationship with Frieda. (pp. 68-9)

The lessons he learned, and to which he devoted so many novels, were that love is not easy, it is ever-changing, and not how oneself had imagined it. "One must learn to love, and go through a good deal of suffering to get to it, like any knight of the grail, and the journey is always *towards* the other soul, not away from it. . . . To love, you have to learn to understand the other, more than she understands herself, and to submit to her understanding of you. . . . Your most vital necessity in this life is that you shall love your wife completely and implicitly and in entire nakedness of body and spirit."

It was through meeting Frieda that he started to rewrite his great work *The Sisters,* and the final version of **The Rainbow** was much influenced by his knowledge of this type of woman and type of relationship. He wrote a letter about *The Sisters,* "I can only write what I feel pretty strongly about: and that, at present, is the relation between men and women. After all, it is *the* problem of today, the establishment of a new relation, or the readjustment of the old one, between men and women."

What Lawrence saw as the suburban marriage was the real danger, "more a duel than a duet" he described it, and "fatal boredom." More than mere legal marriage, he strove for "absolute mystic marriage." He was asking a lot of one man and one woman, banking their hopes and idealism on each other - but through Lawrence we can feel the energy of a society in change and transition; the same English provincial, industrialised society that he had grown to hate so much. (p. 70)

For the expression of these ideas in the novels, we need look no further than Birkin, in **Women in Love.** Birkin is the most Lawrentian of men, in that he is Lawrence's direct mouthpiece. He is little else, however, as there is no real character or substance to Birkin. What he does for a living, how he grew up, what he feels when Ursula responds to him, are not given much space; all we hear are Birkin's theories on the dual relationship. As such, they are extremely interesting. To Birkin is given all the talk of the great explorer on the marriage theme: "It is death to oneself—but is the coming into being of another," is the gist of his feelings. The individual is there, intact, but the former individual dies as the two become one and two separate beings. In the earlier section of the novel, Birkin talks these ideas over with Gerald, and so we got the male point of view:

> [Birkin] "I find," he said, "that one needs some one *really* pure single activity—I should call love a single pure activity. But I *don't* really love anybody—not now." [That was before Ursula.]
>
> [Gerald] "I don't believe a woman, and nothing but a woman, will ever make my life."
>
> [Birkin] "The old ideals are dead as nails—nothing there. It seems to me there remains only this perfect union with a woman—a sort of ultimate marriage—and there isn't anything else.

When Birkin meets Ursula, he sees in her the potential for this ultimate marriage, and to her surprise, rather than courting her with the old-fashioned words of romance, sentiment and love, he flings his soul down before her and tries to tempt her to his new world, his exacting, demanding, searching prospect of marriage. Ursula is not impressed, at first. She responds as one might to his high-flown theories: "You mean you don't love me?" Birkin—"The root is beyond love . . . there beyond, where there is no speech and no terms of agreement." He calls it, "not meeting and mingling," but a "strange conjunction" and, his theme tune, "an equilibrium, a pure balance of two single beings:—as the stars balance each other."

Ursula believes he is proposing old-fashioned marriage, but that he is scared of real commitment. She tries to tell him that if he loved her, he would be talking of loving no one but her— "If you admit a unison, you forfeit all the possibilities of chaos." She is saying that when lovers commit themselves to each other, they tie themselves to each other, they shut off all the outside doors. Chaos and freedom are not compatible concepts. Birkin argues back that her words, such as "love is freedom," are mere "sentimental cant" which she has picked up from others, and she is merely mouthing them. He tries to go over with her why love *is* selfish, or can afford to be—why it is not a question of irresolutely tying yourself to one other person. "It is not selfless—it is a maintaining of the self in mystic balance, and integrity—like a star balanced with another star."

Birkin voices Lawrence's fears of the old-fashioned views of love and marriage, "the old way of love seems a dreadful bondage," and says "He would rather not live than accept the love she proffered." To him, "The hot narrow intimacy between man and wife was abhorrent. The way they shut their doors these married people, and shut themselves into their own exclusive alliance with each other, even in love, disgusted him . . . a kaleidoscope of couples, disjoined, separatist, meaningless entities of married couples . . . ." Birkin again explains how he wants to be single in himself, and the woman single in herself, but both always held together by the force of the duality, the tension between, the sheer beauty of the mystic balance, that means they could not part. Referring back to one of Lawrence's letters, we can see he felt that himself, in his own life. After weeks of battles with Frieda, the highs and the lows, he was able to write—"Once you've known what love can be, there's no disappointment any more, and no despair. If the skies tumble down like a smashed saucer, it couldn't break what's between Frieda and me. I think folk have got sceptic about love—that's because nearly everybody fails."

So Birkin is able to disparage Ursula for her old-fashioned thinking, which from the picture already drawn of Ursula we know she does not really feel. But here the fearful side of her does not know what to make of Birkin's bizarre proposition. He sees the old clinging woman rearing her ugly head through Ursula's modern make-up, which was very likely.

> . . . [woman] had such a lust for possession, a greed of self-importance in love. She wanted to have, to own, to control, to be dominant. Everything must be referred back to her, to Woman, the Great Mother of everything, out of whom proceeded everything and to whom everything must finally be rendered up. . . . Man was hers because she had borne him. A Mater Dolorosa, she had borne him, a Magna Mater, she now claimed him again, soul and body, sex, meaning, and all. . . . We are not broken fragments of one whole.

But Ursula had a right to question his high-sounding theories, for what did Birkin really want? Was he not really just excusing himself for that male fear of commitment to woman? Was he not arguing he could have her and his freedom? Was he not laying down the terms, to get them in before she did, so that he would dominate her life and she would have to submit in accepting his terms? Ursula argues back convincingly, "You want me to be a mere *thing* for you." And when she talks it over with Gudrun, her sister backs her up by saying he just wants his ideas fulfilled; he has picked on her to live out his idea of woman—which is all too true. But there is reason on both sides. Birkin still laughs at Ursula's argument, saying that her "Do you love me?" question, is really a command like saying "Yield knave, or die"; that she wanted "to drink him down, like a life draught. . . . She believed that love was everything." Also, when Gerald and Gudrun try to work out a relationship, based more on the old social order, we are shown in Gudrun just what that female lust for possession is, "One of them must triumph over the other. Which should it be?" implying that Gudrun was going to do her best to win. Birkin's argument for a "lovely state of free proud singleness," or his reply to Ursula that he wanted her to trust herself so, so implicitly, that she can let herself go, seems preferable.

Unfortunately we never see how Birkin and Ursula work it out: we leave them at the end of the novel, embarking on life together, with a feeling of dread for them. But then Lawrence did not know any more himself. He had not travelled that far along the road himself with Frieda. How was he to know? (pp. 71-4)

> *Carol Dix, in her* D. H. Lawrence and Women, *Rowman and Littlefield, 1980, 126 p.*

ADDITIONAL BIBLIOGRAPHY

Barber, David S. "Community in *Women in Love.*" *Novel* 5, No. 1 (Fall 1971): 32-41.

Examines changes in the ways that Birkin and Ursula interact with their society at the progressive stages of their personal relationship.

Bertocci, Angelo P. "Symbolism in *Women in Love.*" In *A D. H. Lawrence Miscellany,* edited by Harry T. Moore, pp. 83-102. Carbondale: Southern Illinois University Press, 1959.

Identifies and examines the symbols that advance characterization, theme, and action in *Women in Love.*

Blanchard, Lydia. "*Women in Love:* Mourning Becomes Narcissism." *Mosaic* 15, No. 1 (Winter 1982): 105-18.

Considers *Women in Love* Lawrence's most complete statement of his belief that withdrawal and self-absorption have dangerous personal and cultural consequences.

Cain, William E. "Lawrence's 'Purely Destructive' Art in *Women in Love.*" *The South Carolina Review* 13, No. 1 (Fall 1980): 38-47.

Maintains that the self-critical action of *Women in Love*—in which Lawrence presented characters engaged in argument with and refutation of his own philosophical views—destroys the effective presentation of these ideas.

Caserio, Robert L. "The Family Plot: Conrad, Joyce, Lawrence, Woolf, and Faulkner." In his *Plot, Story, and the Novel: From Dickens and Poe to the Modern Period,* pp. 232-80. Princeton: Princeton University Press, 1979.

Contending that twentieth-century fiction has been largely shaped by the way that writers perceive family relationships, Caserio concludes that *Women in Love* is "the powerful product of a repression of a desire for fatherhood."

Clark, L. D. "Lawrence/*Women in Love:* The Contravened Knot."

In *Approaches to the Twentieth-Century Novel,* edited by John Unterecker, pp. 51-78. New York: Thomas Y. Crowell, 1965.

Analyzes symbolism, plot, and characterization in *Women in Love.*

Clarke, Colin, ed. *D. H. Lawrence: "The Rainbow" and "Women in Love," A Casebook.* London: Macmillan, 1969, 243 p.

Includes excerpts from Lawrence's letters pertaining to *Women in Love,* his prologue and foreword to the novel, and critical essays by John Middleton Murry, George H. Ford, G. Wilson Knight, H. M. Daleski, and Frank Kermode, among others.

Davies, Alistair. "Contexts of Reading: The Reception of D. H. Lawrence's *The Rainbow* and *Women in Love.*" In *The Theory of Reading,* edited by Frank Gloversmith, pp. 199-222. Sussex: Harvester Press, 1984.

Examines the historical context in which *Women in Love* was composed in order to demonstrate that some critical assessments of the novel are misreadings resulting from changing historical attitudes.

DiBattista, Maria. "*Women in Love:* D. H. Lawrence's Judgment Book." In *D. H. Lawrence: A Centenary Consideration,* edited by Peter Balbert and Phillip L. Marcus, pp. 67-90. Ithaca, N.Y.: Cornell University Press, 1985.

Discusses the societal crisis that underlies *Women in Love* and infuses the novel with its apocalyptic tenor.

Donaldson, George. " 'Men in Love'? D. H. Lawrence, Rupert Birkin, and Gerald Crich." In *D. H. Lawrence: Centenary Essays,* edited by Mara Kalnins, pp. 41-67. Bristol: Bristol Classical Press, 1986.

Examines the relationship between Birkin and Gerald and attempts to determine Lawrence's personal attitude toward the exclusively male relationships proposed in the novel.

Ford, George H. "An Introductory Note to D. H. Lawrence's Prologue to *Women in Love.*" *Texas Quarterly* 6, No. 1 (Spring 1963): 92-7.

Examines two opening chapters of *Women in Love* that Lawrence discarded before publication, finding them revelatory about Lawrence's own character and his objectives in writing the novel.

Ford, George H.; Kermode, Frank; Clarke, Colin; and Spilka, Mark. "Critical Exchange on 'Lawrence Up-Tight': Four Tail-Pieces." *Novel* 5, No. 1 (Fall 1971): 54-70.

Responses to Mark Spilka's essay "Lawrence Up-Tight, or the Anal Phase Once Over" (see Additional Bibliography entry below) that address the nature and significance of various sex acts described in *Women in Love* and Lawrence's other novels.

Gillie, Christopher. "Human Subject and Human Substance: Stephen Dedalus of *A Portrait of the Artist,* Rupert Birkin of *Women in Love.*" In his *Character in English Literature,* pp. 177-202. London: Chatto & Windus, 1965.

Calls concern with the question of what constitutes meaningful human relationships central to *Women in Love.*

Gregory, Horace. "Poetry into Prose (1913-1916): *Women in Love.*" In his *Pilgrim of the Apocalypse: A Critical Study of D. H. Lawrence,* pp. 40-7. New York: Viking Press, 1933.

Assesses *Women in Love* as important only as a developmental step in Lawrence's career, charging that the characters are poorly individuated and the novel's focus suffers because of the lack of an authorial advocate.

Harper, Howard M., Jr. "*Fantasia* and the Psychodynamics of *Women in Love.*" In *The Classic British Novel,* edited by Howard M. Harper, Jr., and Charles Edge, pp. 202-19. Athens: University of Georgia Press, 1972.

Considers *Women in Love* Lawrence's "most deep, complex, and comprehensive" fictional exploration of the relationship between women and men, finding that the novel is linked themati-cally to the essay collection *Fantasia of the Unconscious.*

Herzinger, Kim A. *D. H. Lawrence in His Time: 1908-1915.* Lewis-burg, Pa.: Bucknell University Press, 1982, 237 p.
Profusely illustrated examination of Lawrence's relationship to his milieu, assuming "that an understanding of Lawrence's cul-tural context, and his responses and reactions to it, is essential to a fuller comprehension of the meaning of his work."

Hough, Graham. "The Major Novels: *Women in Love.*" In his *The Dark Sun: A Study of D. H. Lawrence,* pp. 72-90. London: Gerald Duckworth, 1956.
Identifies aspects of the love relationships portrayed in *Women in Love* that Lawrence wished to affirm.

Jacobson, Sibyl. "The Paradox of Fulfillment: A Discussion of *Women in Love.*" *The Journal of Narrative Technique* 3, No. 1 (Janu-ary 1973): 53-65.
Discusses the theme of striving toward personal fulfillment as used by Lawrence to establish character and motivation in *Women in Love.*

Kermode, Frank. "1913-1917: *Women in Love.*" In his *D. H. Law-rence,* pp. 53-78. New York: Viking Press, 1973.
Explores metaphysical themes in *Women in Love.*

Kiely, Robert. "Accident and Purpose: 'Bad Form' in Lawrence's Fiction." In *D. H. Lawrence: A Centenary Consideration,* edited by Peter Balbert and Phillip L. Marcus, pp. 91-107. Ithaca, N.Y.: Cor-nell University Press, 1985.
Offers examples of overt didacticism and unimaginative sym-bolism in several of Lawrence's novels, followed by discussion of three chapters from *Women in Love* that display narrative strikingly free of these flaws.

Leavis, F. R. "*Women in Love.*" In his *D. H. Lawrence: Novelist,* pp. 146-96. London: Chatto & Windus, 1955.
Disputes John Middleton Murry's assessment of *Women in Love* (excerpted above) as essentially documentation of aspects of Lawrence's personality, maintaining that the novel is a work of conscious artistry treating universal themes.

Marković, Vida E. "Ursula Brangwen." In her *The Changing Face: Disintegration of Personality in the Twentieth-Century British Novel, 1900-1950,* pp. 19-37. Carbondale: Southern Illinois University Press, 1970.
Discusses Ursula Brangwen as an embodiment of Lawrence's theory of human personality.

Miko, Stephen J., ed. *Twentieth Century Interpretations of "Women in Love": A Collection of Critical Essays.* Englewood Cliffs, N.J.: Prentice-Hall, 1969, 120 p.
Includes essays by George H. Ford, Alan Friedman, David J. Gordon, Julian Moynahan, Mark Spilka, and Eliseo Vivas, among others.

————. *Toward Women in Love: The Emergence of a Lawrentian Aesthetic.* New Haven: Yale University Press, 1971, 299 p.
Examines five of Lawrence's early novels—*The White Peacock, The Trespasser, Sons and Lovers, The Rainbow,* and *Women in Love*—for what they reveal about his philosophical and artistic development.

Moore, Harry T. *The Priest of Love: A Life of D. H. Lawrence.* Rev. ed. New York: Farrar, Straus and Giroux, 1974, 550 p.
Biography extensively revised and expanded from Moore's ear-lier *The Intelligent Heart.*

Nin, Anaïs. "*Women in Love.*" In her *D. H. Lawrence: An Unprofes-sional Study,* pp. 97-112. London: Neville Spearman, 1961.
Impressionistic account of characterization and plot in *Women in Love.*

Oates, Joyce Carol. "Lawrence's *Götterdämmerung:* The Tragic Vi-

sion of *Women in Love.*" *Critical Inquiry* 4, No. 3 (Spring 1978): 559-78.
Examines both realistic and allegorical aspects of characteriza-tion, plot, and action in *Women in Love.*

Partlow, Robert B., Jr., and Moore, Harry T., eds. *D. H. Lawrence: The Man Who Lived.* Carbondale: Southern Illinois University Press, 1979, 302 p.
Collection of papers originally delivered at the D. H. Lawrence Conference at Southern Illinois University in April 1979. In-cluded are "The 'Real Quartet' of *Women in Love:* Lawrence on Brothers and Sisters," by Lydia Blanchard, and "*Women in Love* and the Myth of Eros and Psyche," by Evelyn J. Hinz and John J. Teunissen.

Potter, Stephen. "The Impediment." In his *D. H. Lawrence: A First Study,* pp. 55-70. London: Jonathan Cape, 1930.
Chronologically arranged discussion of what the critic terms Lawrence's three most important post–World War I works: the essay "The Crown," the novel *Women in Love,* and the essay collection *Fantasia of the Unconscious.*

Pritchard, R. E. "*Women in Love.*" In his *D. H. Lawrence: Body of Darkness,* pp. 85-106. London: Hutchinson University Library, 1971.
Analyzes the personal and social relationships portrayed in the novel.

Procopiow, Norma. "The Narrator's Stratagem in *Women in Love.*" *College Literature* 5, No. 2 (Spring 1978): 114-24.
Explores ambiguities and contradictions in the characteriza-tion of Gerald Crich.

Rachman, Shalom. "Art and Value in D. H. Lawrence's *Women in Love.*" *The D. H. Lawrence Review* 5, No. 1 (Spring 1972): 1-25.
Considers ways that *Women in Love* fulfills Lawrence's concep-tion of artistic purpose.

Remsbury, John. "*Women in Love* as a Novel of Change." *The D. H. Lawrence Review* 6, No. 2 (Summer 1973): 149-72.
Examines the development of historical themes in *Women in Love,* which are advanced primarily through the characters' re-sponses to new ideas.

Ross, Charles L. *The Composition of "The Rainbow" and "Women in Love": A History.* Charlottesville: University Press of Virginia, 1979, 168 p.
"Work of literary detection" examining and comparing all ex-tant manuscript drafts of *The Rainbow* and *Women in Love.* Ross notes the extent to which various editions were censored and revised by editors, publishers, and Lawrence himself.

Rudrum, Alan. "Philosophical Implication in Lawrence's *Women in Love.*" *Dalhousie Review* 51, No. 2 (Summer 1971): 240-50.
Analyzes the opposing worldviews embodied in Gerald and Birkin, one acknowledging only a physical plane of existence and the other accepting the possibility of a spiritual reality as well.

Sagar, Keith. "Articulate Extremity, 1915-1916: *Women in Love.*" In his *The Art of D. H. Lawrence,* pp. 74-98. Cambridge: Cambridge University Press, 1966.
Assesses *Women in Love* as one of Lawrence's first works of ma-ture artistic achievement.

Sanders, Scott. "*Women in Love:* Study in a Dying Culture." In his *D. H. Lawrence: The World of the Five Major Novels,* pp. 94-135. New York: Viking Press, 1973.
Attributes the apocalyptic tone of *Women in Love* to a combina-tion of cultural and personal crises that befell England and Lawrence at the time of the novel's composition.

Scheckner, Peter. "Society and the Individual: *Sons and Lovers, The Rainbow,* and *Women in Love.*" In his *Class, Politics, and the Indi-*

vidual: A Study of the Major Works of D. H. Lawrence, pp. 23-69. Rutherford, N. J.: Fairleigh Dickinson University Press, 1985.

Investigates the influence of Lawrence's own class background and acute awareness of England's rigid class structure on his major novels.

Schneider, Daniel J. "The Laws of Action and Reaction in *Women in Love.*" In his *D. H. Lawrence: The Artist as Psychologist,* pp. 171-92. Lawrence: University Press of Kansas, 1984.

Considers "the crucial importance of the laws of action and reaction as determinants of the plot complications of *Women in Love.*"

————. "The Going Apart: *Women in Love* and 'The Reality of Peace'." In his *The Consciousness of D. H. Lawrence: An Intellectual Biography,* pp. 109-28. Lawrence: University Press of Kansas, 1986.

Explores Lawrence's attitudes toward society, life, and death in "two of his greatest works": *Women in Love* and the essay "The Reality of Peace." The critic terms the plot of the novel contrapuntal, contrasting the fulfilling relationship of Birkin and Ursula with the destructive one of Gerald and Gudrun.

Schorer, Mark. *"Women in Love."* In his *The World We Imagine: Selected Essays,* pp. 107-21. London: Chatto & Windus, 1969.

Examines Lawrence's development of the idea that "character is fate" in the novel and explores ways that the characterization and structure of *Women in Love* differ from those of his more traditional novels.

Spilka, Mark. "Star-Equilibrium" and "No Man's Land." In his *The Love Ethic of D. H. Lawrence,* pp. 121-47, pp. 148-73. Bloomington: Indiana University Press, 1955.

Considers *Women in Love, Sons and Lovers,* and *The Rainbow* important representative stages in Lawrence's artistic development.

————. "Lawrence Up-Tight, or the Anal Phase Once Over." *Novel* 4, No. 3 (Spring 1971): 252-67.

Discusses Colin Clarke's *River of Dissolution: D. H. Lawrence and English Romanticism* (1969), focusing on the significance

of the various sex acts in *Women in Love* and Lawrence's other novels.

Stoll, John E. "Dissolution and Reassertion: *Women in Love.*" In his *The Novels of D. H. Lawrence: A Search for Integration,* pp. 151-97. Columbia: University of Missouri Press, 1971.

Examines imagery and symbolism in *Women in Love.*

Tomlinson, T. B. "D. H. Lawrence: *Sons and Lovers, Women in Love.*" In his *The English Middle-Class Novel,* pp. 185-98. New York: Barnes & Noble, 1976.

Maintains that the experimental nature of Lawrence's fiction results in some dismal lapses of sense and taste as well as some remarkable literary successes, often within the same work.

Weinstein, Philip M. "'The Trembling Instability' of *Women in Love.*" In his *The Semantics of Desire: Changing Models of Identity from Dickens to Joyce,* pp. 204-24. Princeton: Princeton University Press, 1984.

Explores the various relationships between individuals and their society in *Women in Love.*

Williams, Raymond. "Social and Personal Tragedy: Tolstoy and Lawrence." In his *Modern Tragedy,* pp. 121-38. Stanford, Calif.: Stanford University Press, 1966.

Considers *Anna Karenina* and *Women in Love* modern literature's most important novels focusing on individuals in conflict with their society.

Worthen, John. *"Women in Love."* In his *D. H. Lawrence and the Idea of the Novel,* pp. 83-104. Totowa, N.J.: Rowman and Littlefield, 1979.

Assesses *Women in Love* as the culmination of Lawrence's desire to revolutionize "the conditions of life" by proposing radically new types of relationships.

Yetman, Michael G. "The Failure of the Un-Romantic Imagination in *Women in Love.*" *Mosaic* 9, No. 3 (Spring 1976): 83-96.

Examines the importance of spoken language in *Women in Love,* a novel in which speech is one of the primary activities.

Zsigmond Móricz

1879-1942

Hungarian novelist, short story writer, dramatist, and poet.

Considered the most important Hungarian fiction writer of the first half of the twentieth century, Móricz was the first to introduce the themes and techniques of literary realism into Hungarian literature. His coarse, often sordid portrayals of village life stood in marked contrast to the predominantly romantic representations of rural Hungary by previous authors and are credited with revitalizing Hungarian fiction.

Móricz was born in Csécse (or Tiszacsécse), a village in the eastern Hungarian Lowlands. The region was largely populated by Magyars, the dominant national group of Hungary, and Magyars in Lowlands settings figure prominently in Móricz's fiction. His father was a hardworking peasant who had gradually attained small landowner status and begun his own business. His mother was both the daughter and widow of impoverished Calvinist clergymen, and Móricz was sent to Calvinist schools in the hope that he would become a minister. Between 1891 and 1899 he studied law as well as theology at Debreceni Református Kollégium and Sárospataki Kollégium. He also became interested in journalism, and undertook courses in philosophy, linguistics, and literary history at the University of Budapest while contributing both fiction and nonfiction to newspapers and literary periodicals. In 1903 he joined the editorial staff of the Budapest daily newspaper *Az Újság*. Committed to promoting and preserving native Hungarian culture, Móricz frequently traveled in remote areas of his country during the next five years to record folk tales, songs, and legends, and his experiences became the basis for his depictions of rural Hungarian society. Móricz earned little public attention until the appearance of his short story "Hét krajcár" ("Seven Pennies") in the prominent literary periodical *Nyugat* in 1908. This moving tale of a poor family's struggle to meet their barest needs earned Móricz instant acclaim. He became widely popular with *Nyugat*'s readers, despite the marked difference between his straightforward, energetic prose and the aestheticism usually promulgated in the magazine. Móricz developed a close association with *Nyugat* and with the journal's leading poet, Endre Ady, who shared Móricz's progressive social views. Móricz later cited Ady as an important influence on his life and writing, and Móricz's role in revitalizing Hungarian fiction is often compared with Ady's similar contribution to the development of his country's poetry. Following the success of "Seven Pennies," Móricz continued to publish widely in literary journals, and in 1911 his first novel, *Sárarany,* appeared.

During World War I Móricz worked as a foreign correspondent. Initially sending dispatches that commended the bravery of the common soldier, as the war continued Móricz began to write about the suffering experienced in the trenches and to call for peace. During and after the war Móricz continued to champion progressive causes—most notably the redistribution of land to the peasants—and he enthusiastically supported the short-lived socialist revolution of 1918. As a result, after the counterrevolution that followed, Móricz was harassed by government authorities and his works were boycotted by many Hungarian periodicals. Despite the boycott,

Móricz's works were popular with critics and readers, and within a few years he was generally regarded as one of Hungary's most distinguished authors. He continued to grow in fame and popularity throughout his lifetime, although he occasionally aroused nearly as much controversy as critical acclaim for the unrelenting realism of such works as the short story "Tragédia" and the novel *Szegény emberek,* which seemed to some commentators to dwell almost exclusively on poverty and brutality. G. F. Cushing has written: "Móricz soon rose to prominence, and with his coming the idea of the romantic peasant died. . . . With [Kálmán] Mikszáth there was social criticism, but it could be overlooked in the fun of the tale: [Géza] Gárdonyi gave a dispassionate account of the Hungarian village, but Móricz demanded continual attention to the problems he described with first-hand knowledge." Although Móricz contributed to several different genres, including drama and poetry, his short stories and novels remain his best-known and most highly regarded works. Móricz also advanced his national literature as an editor: from 1929 to 1933 he was a contributing editor of *Nyugat,* and in 1939 he became editor of the literary journal *Kelet Népe,* which focused upon peasant concerns. His death in 1942 was considered a great loss to Hungarian letters.

Móricz's first short stories and novels were distinguished by their realistic portrayal of the peasantry. Although a few earlier Hungarian authors had experimented with literary realism, their works have been characterized by Joseph Reményi as "trial balloons." According to Reményi, "Móricz was the first Hungarian writer who, like Frank Norris and Theodore Dreiser in America, devoted his narrative talent to the presentation of individual and collective inconsistencies and sadistic realities caused by a particular social structure," that of the Hungarian village, "with all its social taboos, bleakness, tenacious bias, poverty and idyllic self-deceptiveness, and class differentiation." Criticism of the class-consciousness of Hungarian society was a major feature of Móricz's earliest short stories and of his first novel, *Sárarany,* which according to Lóránt Czigány "deals with a basic anomaly in East European peasant societies, the rigidity of the class-structure which frequently prevents the self-assertion of talents in men of humble origin." As his career progressed Móricz introduced more explicit social criticism into his fiction. The novels *Kivilágos kivirradtig* and *Úri muri,* for example, effectively contrast the extravagant lives of the upper classes with the overwhelming poverty of the peasantry, condemning the decadence of the modern gentry and of past generations of Hungary's privileged classes. Many critics consider the historical trilogy *Erdély* to be Móricz's greatest contribution to Hungarian literature. Móricz devoted years of research to this account of seventeenth-century Transylvania, which combines rich historical detail with a sense of fierce national pride. A second novel cycle left uncompleted at his death was based upon the Hungarian folk hero Sándor Rózsa, and the two completed volumes, *Rózsa Sándor a lovát ugratja* and *Rózsa Sándor összevonja a szemöldökét,* portray the colorful nineteenth-century Lowlands outlaw against a vivid historical background.

Móricz attained little popularity outside his own country. Although his fiction has been translated into more than twenty-one languages, his novels have found an appreciative foreign audience only in eastern European countries, where social and political situations have historically resembled those of Hungary. A reviewer of the 1931 English translation of *A fáklya* (*The Torch*), for example, maintained that the novel's close attention to local concerns rendered it obscure to non-Hungarian readers. Within Hungary, however, Móricz is still considered the literary "voice of the people" for his compassionate and extensive examination of the concerns of Hungary's least-privileged classes.

PRINCIPAL WORKS

"Hét krajcár" (short story) 1908; published in journal *Nyugat*
    ["Seven Kreutzers," published in journal *The Slavonic Review,* 1931; also published as "Seven Pennies" in *Modern Magyar Literature,* edited by Leslie Konnyu, 1964]
Sári bíró (drama) 1910
"Tragédia" (short story) 1910; published in journal *Nyugat*
Az Isten háta mögött (novel) 1911
Sárarany (novel) 1911
Kerek Ferkó (novel) 1913
Szegény emberek (novel) 1917
A fáklya (novel) 1918
    [*The Torch,* 1931]

Légy jó mindhalálig (novel) 1921
    [*Be Faithful unto Death,* 1962]
Erdély. 3 vols. (novel) 1922-35
Búzakalász (drama) 1924
Kivilágos kivirradtig (novel) 1926
Úri muri (novel) 1928
Barbárok (short stories) 1932
Rokonok (novel) 1932
A boldog ember (novel) 1935
Rab oroszlán (novel) 1936
Betyár (novel) 1937
Életem regénye (autobiography) 1939
Árvácska (novel) 1941
Rózsa Sándor a lovát ugratja (novel) 1941
Rózsa Sándor összevonja a szemöldökét (novel) 1942

THE NEW YORK TIMES BOOK REVIEW (essay date 1931)

[*The following review of* The Torch *commends the novel's subtle characterizations and occasional moments of narrative power.*]

[**The Torch**] shows a subtle approach toward its characters and its problems, and it has its moments of power. These qualities serve to raise it out of the ruck of fiction in spite of a certain haziness, an incompleteness in the synthesis of its four chief ingredients and a weakly executed climax. It creates an atmosphere and a mood which linger over in the mind of the reader after the book has been laid down. It has a savor of its own.

The first ingredient is the story of the protagonist, Miklós Matolcsy, the young Calvinist minister recently graduated from the seminary and assigned to the small village of Fábiánfalva. The son of generations of ministers, he is refined, ambitious, sensitive, weakly idealistic. He would be a torch to his people. But he does not know the Hungarian peasant. Neither does he know himself. Miklós is ushered into his duties by the neighboring pastor, the Rev. Mr. Dékány, a coarse, worldly, peasant-like fellow, who mouths unctuous phrases, but who is possessed of a gently reared wife and a beautiful daughter. From the first, Miklós discovers that the peasants are cheating him, that they intend to rule him, and that no words of his, unless backed up by force or the power of money, have the slightest influence over them. Gradually he becomes first cynical and then practical, "hard–boiled," or as much so as he is able. In his trouble he turns to Mrs. Dékány and so finds himself involved in complications, arising out of the story of her past, with the Dékány family and the land baron and deputy, Arday, the great man of the district.

Years before, Mrs. Dékány had left her husband for Arday. Then she had returned to him. That old scandal and its present consequences form a mesh in which the young minister, spurred on by the desires arising out of the sensual side of his nature, is entangled. Arday is dissolute, cruel and grasping. Mrs. Dékány hates him. And she cannot suppress her desire for young Miklós, young enough to be her son. He, in the meantime, falls in love with the young school teacher.

The third ingredient of the novel is the lumpish peasantry. Mr. Móricz shows them as stupid, cruel, vicious, avaricious, sycophantic before force, their only virtue a certain stubborn, unexpressed independence and patience. None of the peasant characters is an individual of sound qualities. All are either cheats or dolts or both.

And the final component of the novel consists of a mixture of conversations and extracts from an essay that Miklós is writing. Here we come in contact with the intellectual side of the novel, and Mr. Móricz shows himself to be a thorough modern, a complete defeatist on the subjects of religion, race, nationality, more specifically on the subject of modern Hungary. The most powerful note in the book is that of disgust, disgust toward the peasantry, toward the landed aristocracy, toward the sycophantic middle classes, toward politicians, and particularly toward all Jews. Matolcsy, his burning young minister, is, in his eyes, hardly out of swaddling clothes. Martha, the pretty and vivacious daughter of the Rev. Mr. Dékány, is absurdly babyish. Margit, the school teacher, is hardly a heroine. And the holocaust, which is the climax of the story, which consumes nearly three hundred peasants and in which Miklós loses his life, seems scarcely regretted. It is disgust, rather than satire, irony or interpretation, which seems to motivate the tale. The author is not Diogenes looking for an honest man. He knows that there isn't one. The book has little meaning. But, to repeat, it has its moments of power.

"Out of Hungary," in The New York Times Book Review, *May 24, 1931, p. 7.*

JOSEPH REMÉNYI (essay date 1945)

[*Reményi was a Hungarian-born American man of letters who was widely regarded as the literary spokesman for America's Hungarian community during the first half of the twentieth century. His novels, short stories, and poetry often depict Hungarian-American life, and his numerous translations and critical essays have been instrumental in introducing modern Hungarian literature to American readers. In the following excerpt from an essay first published in 1945, Reményi surveys Móricz's career, focusing upon the importance of his contributions to literary realism.*]

In the tumultuous years that preceded the first and second World Wars, Zsigmond Móricz was the Hungarian writer whose approach to the problems of his country was significant because of his realistic attitude and method. Móricz had realistic predecessors, such as Lajos Tolnai, Sándor Bródy, Zoltán Thury. But their works were trial balloons of literary realism. Zsigmond Móricz was the first Hungarian writer who, like Frank Norris and Theodore Dreiser in America, devoted his narrative talent to the presentation of individual and collective inconsistencies and sadistic realities caused by a particular social structure. He wrote novels, short stories, plays, and poems. As a poet he was inferior; even as a playwright his works are second-rate compared with his novels and short stories.

The principal Hungarian writers before and at the turn of the century—Mór Jókai, Kálmán Mikszáth, Géza Gárdonyi, Ferenc Herczeg—were romanticists or surface realists. They enriched Hungarian literature and received the acclaim of the public. Móricz' manner and subject matter were in opposition to the taste and characteristics of these writers. He was different from a certain type of journalistic realist of his times, whose works seemed to be a literary mélange, containing Viennese and Parisian, Scandinavian and Russian flavors.

Besides his unquestionable creative ability, which distinguished Móricz from these ephemeral writers was his pronounced Magyar consciousness. Whether he chose temporary themes or themes of the past, one senses his genuine Hungarianism. His traditional and iconoclastic views, the temper of his expression, were determined by the fact that the Alföld (The Lowland), Hungary's purest Magyar section, was his birthplace and thus it became the subject of many of his stories. Fearlessly he probed the eyes of the hateful and the eyes of the pitiful; he rarely missed an opportunity to portray life with the rhythm of merciless realism. Sometimes he slipped into a demagoguery of realism; he seemed preoccupied with cruel and crude sensuality; in such instance he used a sordid style, and not only the psychological atmosphere of his characters but his own art breathed a heavy odor, suggesting the smell of poverty and brutality. He wrote with evident gusto; there is nothing equivocal about his words, no casuistry about his meaning. Squeamish critics and bashful readers resented his bluntness; he was labeled disruptive, whereas he was merely dissenting; and even as a celebrated writer he was not entirely free from attacks, though his historical trilogy **Erdély** (**Transylvania**) was praised by László Ravasz, the Calvinist bishop and scholar. Notwithstanding his empiricism and positivism, and his creed that society is greatly responsible for man's behavior, he adhered to the humanitarian code of human dignity that man is an end in himself and that impersonal social theories are not sufficient for the understanding of man's thoughts, feelings, and actions. (pp. 326-27)

In 1908 the literary periodical Nyugat (West), published his short story, **"Hét krajcár"** (**"Seven Pennies"**), a moving tale of pauperism, and thus his literary name was established. His robust and gentle qualities, often in direct conflict, were already observable in his early work. He did not strive for perfect composition but for perfect characterization. (p. 327)

Móricz' Hungarian (he spoke no other language) was idiomatic, yet personal. He seldom left his homeland. Within the geographical boundaries of his nation and within the boundaries of his spirit he recognized and expressed the sanctity and ignobility of human life. His realistic temper accentuated ignobility. He was a prolific writer. The sum total of his work reveals a very talented narrator, who knew how to articulate the polyphony of Hungarian society, although at times he took plebeian liberties at the price of good taste. In concept and detail his novels and stories exhibit an aggressive and inquisitive spirit, endowed with clear insight into individual and social problems. His imaginative works are verbal frescoes on the crumbling walls of historical and new Hungary. There appear in his stories and plays a large group of people who are mendicants of eroticism and peasant Don Juans, humdrum people with cantankerous, foolish, or greedy dispositions, stern and taciturn village folks, social outcasts thrown upon the bounty of mere chance, men and women of extraordinary fortitude, carefree, satiated, thwarted, and ineffectual gentry squandering money on gypsy musicians, persons of inflated pride, petty officials with the proclivity of horse thieves and shepherds with primeval instincts, some of them bandits of the plain, gluttons, drunkards, parasites, quitters, and cowards. Family maladjustments, especially the trivial or acrimonious quarrels of husband and wife, the problematical lives of idealistic, timorous, vacillating Calvinist ministers in God-forsaken villages, innocent, whimpering, or sophisticated women of the middle class whose hopes turn sour, and gay and loud tradesmen or cattlemen attending county fairs were the peculiarly favored topics of Móricz. He was more at home in portraying sheepskinned or half-urbane human beings, than thoroughly civilized characters.

Zsigmond Móricz had a microscopic intelligence but not an academically trained intellectuality. It is interesting to observe the contrast between his manner of expression and perception and those of writers and critics who around the last decade of the nineteenth century initiated a realistic tone in Hungarian literature. Despite much progress, Hungary, in the nineteenth century, remained in many ways feudal and patriarchal. Social stagnation carried the germ of disintegration. Provincialism and the somewhat snobbish ostentatiousness of Budapest produced an artificial situation; it was an uncommon relationship, in which obstinate and sincerely liberal forces were functioning in their own fashion. A variety of conscientious and irresponsible voices accentuated tradition and departure from tradition. Brave and unorthodox ideas implied a revolution of the spirit. Their exponents stressed the place of science in modern belles-lettres, the importance of economic factors, and the writer's artistic integrity. Urbanity and cosmopolitan culture conveyed new meaning to Hungarian life. "Independent" periodicals brought together writers and poets whose struggle for recognition would have been futile without this new mental climate. Men like Ignotus, the critic and poet, introduced into Hungarian life a pattern of creative and critical independence that showed the undesirability of threadbare categories and at the same time proved the correlation between literature and progress as a social phenomenon.

It is significant that Ignotus was among the first who, demanding creative probity from the writer, discovered Zsigmond Móricz. After this, Móricz' fame spread rapidly. Soon he had disciples who, while trying to emulate him, merely succeeded in copying his realistic manner. Some of his disciples found their own voices, but no one was able to surpass him. Móricz had an inexhaustible supply of stories; the conventional and unconventional likewise spurred him to expression. He was an excellent talker. In his favorite haunt, the Otthon (Home) Club, he would hold his listeners spellbound. He vehemently disagreed with those nineteenth-century writers who romanticized the country gentleman and the peasant and in preserving a sentimental or patronizing notion about rural life helped to sustain the social and economic unfairness associated with it. Móricz was vociferous in his indignation, and consistently refused the standards that made the lord of the manor identical with lethargy, slackness, or callousness. His native sense did not allow him to borrow manners and mannerisms from "cosmopolitan writers," but it enabled him to recognize their contribution to Hungarian culture. In many respects his Hungarianism was akin to that of Endre Ady, the great modern poet; their symbols differed, their intentions fused. Both were aware of their Hungarian heritage, were tragically conscious of Hungary's plight, and were proponents of a policy that should have demonstrated Hungary's capacity to accept the lessons of constructive criticism. Both believed in a Hungary immune to anachronistic views.

Móricz differed from his Hungarian cosmopolitan colleagues not by volition but congenitally. As to the realistic and naturalistic writers of Western Europe, the difference was partly intentional, partly instinctive. As a rule, he was less interested in factual documentation. In recognizing self-interest, material ambition, and the harsh and unscrupulous struggle for life he was in agreement with them. But the mechanical or biological determinism of Occidental realism did not satisfy him; moral discontent, not alone the pathetic or stubborn acceptance of physicochemical forces, was the reason that compelled him to write. He recognized the social didacticism of Émile Zola, whose works he read in translation; in a measure he applied Zola's principles to Hungarian conditions. Essentially, however, a strong, undifferentiating, erotic vitality was his driving force.

His art is physiological rather than psychological; or, to be more precise, it is psychological but rarely isolated from human traits that are considered sensual in the average man's reaction. He acknowledged the importance of sex without injecting lewdness into his pointed or less pointed observations and plots. The portrayal of filth, ignorance, intolerance, led him into statements whose nature burlesqued the "purity" of permissible words. In his fictional world civilization seemed a by-product of evolution, but the kind of by-product that not even the "natural man" could afford to neglect if he wished to live a complete life. In some of his stories one discerns Maupassant's engaging and devastating insight when the French writer wrote about the peasants of Normandy or about small shopkeepers. The unhealthy climate of Móricz' stories and plays, the moments of sheer beastliness of which he was able to give a terrifying account, his ability to transport the perversities of marginal people into the printed page, were characteristics which enabled critics to pigeonhole him as a coarse realist. The proximity of his subject matter to stables and gutter, to unendurable poverty and class egotism, was primarily the result not of a shocking aim but of shocking conditions which haunted him with the perseverance of their unsufferableness.

In judging Móricz against the background of his times and comparing him with the realistic, pessimistic, skeptical "cosmopolitan" Hungarian writers or with Western European and American realists, one may generalize by saying that his concern with Hungarian life was basic in reference to his literary and moral intents. He was definitely a *Hungarian realist* in the same sense as Wladyslaw Reymont was a Polish realist. His accomplishments, of course, transcend the horizon of Hungarian conditions. Indolence, contemptible unreasonableness, inertia, the jurisdiction of the incompetent, the imperfection of human judgment and its destructive consequences are not unknown shortcomings of man in any country. The schizoid type, excitability and denseness in the same person, is not a particularly rural phenomenon, and allusions to this type can be found in the literature of every nation. In all ages there were writers and poets who observed the stubbornness of human resistance, unwilling or unable to be molded into a meaningful existence. Every nation has its sore spots, cause for satire or humor.

Móricz was concerned with those individuals and types whose status in the framework of Hungarian society gave that society the kind of context which explained its self-respect, easygoingness, conceit, and servility. He disdained theories, though accepting some of them; he knew that to exist meant struggle and that to exist as a Hungarian meant multiplied struggle. His malice was the defense of despair; his lack of illusions, this almost monotone spiritual voice of impartial evaluation, was apparently a tone he adopted in order to deal with human miseries without pretense; the vital and often frightening sensuality of his characters was a fitting accompaniment of lurid, ludicrous, or lonely desires and actions, so human and yet so often inhuman or subhuman.

The animal fables (in verse) as well as the novels of Móricz, his one-act plays as well as his three-act plays or short stories, show the objectified subjectivity of a keen observer, with a distinct quality of expression. His complete works were published upon the twenty-fifth anniversary of his literary activities; they are the achievement of an extremely diligent writer and of a creator who never divorced reality from experience. There was an almost naïve faith in Móricz as to the infallibility of his observations which made metaphysical questions unnecessary. But an unprejudiced critic will comprehend the hidden spiritual qualities of his work, qualities interwoven with the existence of humble people and prigs, with candid characters and charlatans. Móricz was an artist, and as such he could not and did not wish to avoid exceptions which were internal, hence organically connected with the meditative or deeply religious sounds and meanings of the human spirit. His instincts ignored his conscience, but his conscience did not ignore his instincts. In accordance with the purpose of every honest creative mind he searched for truth. His interest in the abominable manifestations of reality would not let him forget the importance of a moral design in human life. With the passing of years he offered more and more arguments in favor of ethical norms, which would make people healthier in soul and body and would make society stronger, despite the inevitable limitations of human nature.

When one of the leading literary societies of Hungary, the Petőfi Társaság (Petőfi Society) elected him a member, he smilingly protested against the shackles of "idealism" but gladly accepted the honor conferred upon him. Like Auguste Rodin, he believed in learning the "language of nakedness"; the language that may be embarrassing to human nature because of man's corruption, but never to man when he remembers his relation and obligation to nature. Móricz' ideas, expressed in a "naked language" were generally not so joyful as those of the French sculptor; too often they appear remote from the possibility of joy. Nevertheless, as it was a sign of optimism with Rodin to be fascinated by ugliness in order to conquer it with the disciplined freedom of his art, in Móricz' work—expressed with less optimism—one sees plain, rough, and evil faces that seem to deliver the writer from the reality of ugliness in the same way that Rodin was freed from the fear of purposeless deformities with the help of his incomparable art.

Móricz' first novel, *Sárarany* (*Golden Mud*), is characterized by extreme realism. The effect of the novel on most critics and readers was tremendous. Its exuberant sensuousness, as a repudiation of the hackneyed finesse of smooth writers immersed in triangle plots, indicated a ruthless approach to the crawling or irresponsible cheerlessness of village life. The frame of the novel is a Hungarian village with all its social taboos, bleakness, tenacious bias, poverty and idyllic self-deceptiveness, and class differentiation. The landless peasant hates the landowner, the artisan despises the unskilled laborer, the poor and the less poor think and feel in terms of power they would like to have. There is a similar atmosphere in Roger Martin du Gard's presentation of a French village, in his novel *Vieille France;* with that difference, however, that gossiping is the paramount pattern of the French village, slanderous, persecuting, presumptive and imbecile gossiping,

and the marked trait of this Hungarian village is a power complex of its inhabitants.

The "hero" of the novel is Dani Túri, a young peasant, virile and passionate, the personification of repressed energies yearning for unrestrained expression. He has no social conscience. The village itself seems unfit for co-operation. Dani Túri is the incarnation of unchecked eroticism; of the kind of physiological materialism that determined the behavior of many of Móricz' characters. If to D. H. Lawrence sex meant the ambivalent experience of desire in which finally love overcomes lust and hatred, and thus gives the body and the soul the opportunity to be decent, in Móricz' world erotic contentment is something beyond reach. Fulfillment does not destroy the mask that sex wears for social reasons. Peasants are not unduly erotic; at least not Hungarian peasants. Their naturalness is apt to be modeled by the animals surrounding them, and after some time sex plays a subordinate part in their lives. They joke about it, the jokes are prone to be vulgar, in a tipsy state the peasants are even nasty about sex, but ordinarily they regard it as one regards other natural features of human life. In Móricz' village sex is made more significant than is generally so in a Hungarian village; it lacks pastoral delight, it is almost gloomy or frenzied in its expression and consequences; neither does sex suggest the "dark, premental" life of which D. H. Lawrence speaks. The somewhat distorted psychology of village life does not detract from the quality of the novel.

Móricz focused his attention upon Dani Túri, who defies conventions and expects the village to adjust itself to him, instead of adjusting himself to the class consciousness of the village. He is an irregular but vital symbol of the village's unwillingness to tolerate any longer its oppressed position in the scheme of Hungarian society; he is not a way out from backwardness, yet his impatience, his sanguinary self-assertiveness, the absurdity and charm of his masculinity are shown with such frankness that he remains impressive throughout the story. He is natural in his desires and outbursts; but this naturalness, even in its joy-seeking activities, is often grim, unsympathetic, occasionally repellent. One does not know whether one should pity Dani Túri or see in his willfulness and bitterness the helpless dramatic intensity of the peasant's bondage to social criteria that were forced upon him by law and custom.

Móricz, though a realist, was inclined to romantic exaggerations, to an expressionistic interplay of uncontrolled emotions. In the environment of thatch-roofed houses, with stork nests built atop some of them, in the midst of wide, dusty streets that turn into unconquerable mud when the autumn rains come, in the midst of dreadful superstitions, affecting the community like fantastic threats of a tribal past, surrounded by the gentle fragrance of acacia trees and the unpretentious generosity of wild flowers, in a spiritually immobile village where it was impossible to revert to the past as the past and the present seemed identical, a man, a young peasant attracted attention because he wanted to possess life, total life. He was like a landscape of the spirit dissatisfied with its inherited color and colorlessness. Hungarian critics aptly stated that Dani Túri seems like a mythical character. Akin to Gogol, Móricz exaggerated, and akin to Dostoevsky, he concentrated upon the inner life of his hero and paid little attention to external descriptions. These same characteristics are observable in most of his novels. But when he deemed it artistically and psychologically necessary he could be a master of external description, and his exaggerations did not offend plausibility. No doubt, this novel is the symbol of revolt against unbearable social and personal conditions; it is like the conflagration of instinct and misery against a social heritage that meant damnation to those who succumbed to it without protest.

One should not assume that there was no laughter in Móricz' voice. He possessed a jocular spirit. He could be in tune with the lightheartedness of his provincial heros and heroines. He saw them in smoky village inns, in small-town taverns, in the market place, in the overfurnished homes of underpaid public officials, in dark coffeehouses, in meadows and gardens, in joyous or mischievous moods that prolonged pleasure and gave illusions the dazzling glow that made one forget the dreariness of tomorrow. He saw them when they were young, middle-aged and old, when they were amusingly somber and amazingly indifferent, and when they exemplified that phase of Hungarian life that foreigners notice in the freshness and pensiveness of Hungarian music. There is also a mocking spirit in his benevolence; a threatening mocking spirit, that sees and makes the reader see the empty gestures of enforced fun, the dubiousness of a loudly acclaimed social position, the silliness of haughty or illogical breast-beating.

In *Úri muri* (*Gentry Roistering*), in *Kivilágos kivirradtig* (*Till Daybreak*), and in his other novels, mostly with the background of the Hungarian Lowland, we meet wealthy peasants (Hungarian kulaks), and clerks, squires, ministers, doctors, lawyers, employees of large estates, pillars of officialdom, using all kinds of recreational devices to make of life a holiday. A boisterous night dissipates their monthly earnings. They eat and drink heartily, they dance the *csárdás,* they are spendthrifts, they gamble and think themselves irresistible when they act the "gentleman" with a reckless attitude. They enjoy the glittering moods of living; they are fond of wine, women, and song, of hunting and talk, of anecdotal romanticism, gypsy music, and of lusty laughter that takes them to the threshold of utter forgetfulness. In tender moments, mostly when intoxicated, their affectionate feelings bring tears to their eyes, sometimes accompanied by a sense of remorse. They consume life with fervor and passion, with nonsense and drunkenness, with exasperating immaturity and hopeless weariness.

Some of Móricz' novels, with no allusion to happiness, unfold the narrow postulates of provincial existence, of meanness and ignorance, shaping lives untouched by inspiration or joy. In *Az Isten háta mögött* (*Back of God's Country*) the formula of the story is somewhat similar to Flaubert's *Madame Bovary.* The similarity exists in the triteness of small-town acquaintances, in the intense yet dull unhappiness of the heroine, in her neurotic loneliness, in her inability to get away from her surroundings. After some futile efforts she is resigned to the melancholy of her stale life. There are some exceptionally fine passages in this novel, a well-developed psychology, a chilling tone that rings through the story like an intimation of invisible enemies jealous of human happiness.

In *Fáklya* (*Torch*) Móricz shows us how hard and thankless is the task of a Calvinist minister in a village, facing insensitive peasants whose outward respect for him does not mean an understanding of his mission. Christian ideals seem like farcical slogans under such circumstances. No wonder the young minister feels defeated in his lofty purpose. He loves the people but the people do not know how to respond to his love. Evidently Móricz knew more about human depravity

than about human virtues. But meanness is not always victorious, not even in his stories.

Légy jó mindhalálig (*Be Good till You Die*) is a lovely novel, indeed. The description of a boy's relationship to the famous Calvinist secondary school in Debrecen is particularly good. The growth of the hero, his disappointments, his faith-restoring experiences are recorded in a manner that illustrates Móricz' innate warmth. It is an admirable story, reminding one of Dickens' sympathy for boys; its candor, its concern with the life-giving magic of knowledge, its perspective despite the rather thin plot, its life-likeness, and its gentleness invoke those sunshiny dreams of human nature that are rarely to be found in Móricz' other tales. Unfortunately, the didactic aim of the writer does not merge sufficiently into the rhythm of the narrative, which is detrimental to its artistic value. In the realm of juvenile literature (written, however, for adults) this was Móricz' most satisfactory venture.

Móricz was charged with having an arrogant dislike for the common people; this is a baseless accusation. He knew their disadvantages, the organic, historical, and social causes of their behavior, the price they had to pay for the selfishness of their masters and for their own inner defects. As a matter of fact, Móricz loved the people, the only people he really knew, the Hungarians. But he was unwilling to glorify them. He did not underestimate human dignity, but he was against the violation of human dignity. He truly valued their capabilities but regretted the waste of their lives and condemned their accomplices who silently or under the disguise of good will prolonged the pains of their existence. He was disheartened by the open or concealed wounds of Hungarian life. When John Millington Synge made dramatic poetry of Irish superstitions, that did not mean a depreciation of the Irish psyche; when Móricz questioned the psychology of enmity and constant bickering, of penny pinching and spurious deeds, and of a thousand and one other petty practices of human relationship, his sense of truthfulness must be considered as signifying an active conscience, vigorous in its usage of words and conscious of the direction of its goal.

Now and then one discovers in his stories or plays the splendid romanticism of Liszt's *Hungarian Rhapsodies* or Brahms' *Hungarian Dances;* but his unornamental portrayal of peasants is closer to the music of Béla Bartók and Zoltán Kodály, those two "modern" Hungarian composers in whose score the form of ancestral rhythmical experiences is more consistent with its essence than in the Hungarian music of Brahms and Liszt. In the compositions of Bartók there is more reference to the folk music of other peoples affecting and being affected by Hungarian music than in the compositions of Kodály. Móricz rejected the pseudo-picturesque elements of peasant life; to him their reality was abject, often outrageous in its crudeness, spiritually undernourished, on the brink of utter collapse. It was also fascinating in its strength, gravitating toward a better life, in its red-blooded courage, in its ageless patience, in the very flow of its savage and gentle soul.

The socially unrelated but substantially closely related landowning and landless peasants, the representatives of the middle class and the gentry, the collaborators and spectators of Hungarian destiny were, in the estimation and presentation of Móricz, subjects of a much-needed change. Their sensuousness and drunkenness, their viciousness and morbidity, their impotent goodness and ethical insomnia, their fatalism and their color-rich imagination, their rigidity and their liveliness, seem components of a life creating its own purgatory here on earth, without the alternative of heaven or hell. Doubtless, Móricz carried in his heart these contrasting elements; he sensed the disease of his own Hungarianism, as an individual and as a member of a society that was insecure about its present and its future. In his popular stories, like *Kerek Ferkó* (*Frankie Kerek*), where clean impulse and sorrow mingle and hope is not entirely abandoned, one perceives a vision of order as a necessity for the elimination of the violent contradictory tendencies of Hungarian society.

Erdély (*Transylvania*) was Móricz' most ambitious and elaborate effort in the genre of the historical novel. Critics compared the lively plot and colorful historical tapestry with the romantic manner of the best-seller novelist Mór Jókai; other critics referred to Baron Zsigmond Kemény, the greatest analytical novelist of nineteenth-century Hungary, a highly esteemed but little read writer. These comparisons do not render justice to the real merit of the novel. Though not perfect, Móricz' historical trilogy is a first-rate work of literary art. The novel shows little influence of other writers. Móricz was greatly interested in the sixteenth- and seventeenth-century period of Transylvania. The carnal traits of his usual characters, but also the heroic and sociable attributes, are shown in an environment of rulers and lords. The treatment is realistic. Prince Gábor Báthory represents impulsiveness, temerity, an uncompromising and inaccessible self-assurance, a bewildering indifference to danger. He is assassinated. His opponent, Prince Gábor Bethlen, persecuted by Báthory, sought and found shelter on Turkish territory. He represents perseverance, common sense, integrity, the qualities of a state builder. Among rulers he was one of the first exponents of religious freedom. Prince Bethlen played an important part in the Thirty Years' War.

Móricz set himself the task of transforming history into art without distorting historical facts. He succeeded very well. No doubt, there is some decorative exuberance in the novel, somewhat reminiscent of Walter Scott; the writer is victimized by verbalism and by an exotic past that seemed like a parade of splendor. Now and then he strikes a false tone, operatic in its effect, resembling François Coppée's well-meant poetic glorification of the Hungarian nobleman and peasant's manliness. But the virtues of the novel are greater than the defects.

Móricz' character portrayal is powerful; his men and women, his brave and timid, defiant and vile characters, his exceptional people, mediocrities and simpletons, fit appropriately into the framework of their times. His political leaders are actors, according to that Tolstoyan doctrine that men of public influence play a tricky game. They are free from modernisms (often noticeable in historical novels written by contemporary writers); they converse in a sixteenth- and seventeenth-century Hungarian language and act relative to the Hungarian-Transylvanian era they created. The racy vernacular of those times as well as their exquisite verbal artificialities as used by Móricz indicate the writer's mastery of the Hungarian tongue; the most hair-splitting critic could not find linguistic faults with the novel. Major and minor incidents, fate-deciding actions and trifles, are vividly realized. Móricz was successful in reconstructing one of the most important periods of Hungarian and Transylvanian history. He succeeded in presenting the eternal problems of the insecure character of Hungarian life, caused by inherent defects, but also by the geographical position of the Hungarian nation, of which

Transylvania's lot in the sixteenth and seventeenth centuries was a revealing example.

Móricz' sense of form as a short-story writer is better than that as a novelist. His best short stories have the kind of unity, the kind of structural beauty and coherence, which one misses in his novels. In his short stories he is not wordy, though many of them are of rather slight value. One of his representative volumes of stories, *Barbárok* (*Barbarians*), appeared in 1932. There are altogether nine stories in this book; not all equal in merit, but they give a good picture of the sort of people Móricz was apt to write about. The first story—the outstanding one of this volume—tells about the murder of a shepherd, his son, and their dog; the finding of the bodies; and it tells of the motive and punishment of the killer. The second story pictures the intimate circle of a Hungarian family in a village on a snowy winter evening, and the fun [the] children have when they get the pig which their father won from their uncle in a sleigh-building contest. In the third story the Prince of Transylvania outwits his enemy in a fashion that would have been pleasing even to Shakespeare. In the fourth story an impoverished country squire refuses to sell his two magnificent white horses, though the family is in dire need. In the fifth story the husband unexpectedly brings home the former suitor of his wife who is bored by her marriage. The sixth story tells about an illiterate peasant woman who buried her child up to its waist while she was working in the field so that the child should not be in her way. In the seventh story we encounter an unskilled laborer from the city of Debrecen, living in his unchanged way on the periphery of Budapest. The eighth story shows the impudent playfulness of a young lad with an old peasant woman. The ninth story takes us to a village where the Calvinist minister is facing insurmountable problems, chiefly due to the unwillingness of his parishioners to have more than one or two children.

Móricz, by pointing out the individual and collective defects of his country, shows the devastating consequences in a fashion that makes the reading of his stories a disturbing experience. Poverty and pride are starkly presented. Peculiarities and typical traits, falsehood and honesty are mixed in a manner that strains the nerves of the reader. Móricz was unable to shut off his eyes in the presence of insulting conditions, involving the very fate of Hungary. John Steinbeck's "Okies" have their counterpart in certain types by Móricz; the parallel is especially relevant, considering that Steinbeck's men and women are the descendants of the purest Anglo-Saxon stock in America and Móricz' characters are the purest representatives of the Magyar stock.

The subject matter of Móricz as a playwright and the *dramatis personae* of his plays do not differ from the topic and characters of his novels and stories. The Hungarian National Theater produced *Sári biró* (*Judge Sári*) in 1910, still considered his best play. *Búzakalász* (*Sheaf of Wheat*), *Pacsirtaszó* (*Song of the Lark*), and *A vadkan* (*The Wild Boar*) are among his foremost plays. They have little plot, the characters, with one or two exceptions, are types; the interfusion of the comic and tragic spirit makes of them a hybrid literary experience. His plays have a stereotyped sincerity, there is too much interest in nonessentials, and their construction is somewhat raw. Móricz was basically a narrator, which explains the epic slowness of his plays. He did not have Ferenc Molnár's stage technique; the author of *Liliom* was his contemporary, and he achieved world-wide renown because of wit and sentimentality that appealed to the "sophisticated" audiences everywhere, whereas Móricz' definite Hungarianism localized the horizon of interest. A valuable contribution of Móricz to the Hungarian stage is his adaptation of Péter Bornemisza's sixteenth-century play based on Sophocles' *Electra.* Few of his novels were translated into German, Italian, and English.

Móricz edited an anthology of modern Hungarian short stories. In the preface he pays tribute to the younger writers. His appreciation is generous, but his critical evaluation is not flawless. He was neither an essayist nor a critic, and whenever he sought the intermediate form between fiction and interpretation it was interpretation that suffered. His autobiography, *Életem regénye* (*The Story of My Life*), is a somewhat formless record of his personal and social experiences. (pp. 327-38)

The fragrance of new-mown hay is pleasant, and the smell of a dunghill is unpleasant. Reading Móricz, one detects more of the intolerable stench of ugly experiences than the delight of beautiful experiences. But from the viewpoint of the naturalist all things are significant in nature; his scientific spirit is aware not only of the songs of the nightingales but of the croaking of the frogs. Móricz the realist is the twin brother of the naturalist; that is, in smells and in sounds he spots the complexities of nature, and in their human symbols he sees the complexities of human nature. His realism is not only that of the moralist who judges but of the artist who understands. He has no "private" language. His questions are answerable, his meaning comprehensible. He rejected incommunicable subjects and ideas and the bric-a-brac features of a delicate existence.

From his imaginative work there emerges a Hungarian society, angry and distressed, automatic in its shortcomings, conscious of necessary improvements. It is not a romantic Hungary eulogized by tourists; it is not a reactionary Hungary damned by her enemies. The noble traits and the imperfections of the nation have their parallel in other countries. The wrath of the writer was an expression of his participation in Hungarian life. He diagnosed the chronic ailments of Hungarian society with the impartiality of a conscientious observer, but also with the pity of a fellow human being. After all, for all his objectified subjectivity, Móricz could not and did not want to dissociate himself from the psychological truth that he himself was a Hungarian. The exponents of ignominious decadence were not spared by him; neither were those who represented the lowest social level. They were his brothers, with all their weaknesses, with all their sins and virtues, with all their tribulations and unrealized dreams. This identification with them did not soften his judgment, but it balanced his understanding.

Móricz' perspective was limited but not narrow. There is nothing suave about him, nor is he ever maudlin, misty, or ponderous. His novels, stories, and plays are not a complete orchestration of Hungarian life; certain tones are missing. His indictments are honest, not infallible. His works are a fragmentary, but exciting introduction to the *homo hungaricus.* In the pantheon of Hungarian literature Zsigmond Móricz represents the fabulizing genius of a people who, despite their difficulties, sacrifices, and humiliations, possess sufficient energy to fight their historical and social liabilities, and whose sense of right and wrong reveals their essential human dignity. In the works of the greatest Hungarian writers and poets one discerns a refrain of despair as to the future of their country and their people. More than a century ago

Ferenc Kölcsey, the writer of the Hungarian national anthem, wrote about the mortal illness of his native land. Sándor Petőfi, Hungary's most spontaneous lyric poet, sang about the "miracle" of Hungary's existence. Yet the Hungarian nation still exists in spite of her historical and social incongruities and her tragic geographical position. One explanation of this heroic tenacity seems to be that her greatest writers and poets were not sparing in their damnation of the nation's defects, but at the same time they were true to their responsibilities as Hungarians and as human beings. Some who violated this principle may have had a momentary vogue, but they did not remain a steady influence in the life of the nation. (pp. 339-40)

> Joseph Reményi, "Zsigmond Móricz, Realist (1879-1942)," in his Hungarian Writers and Literature: Modern Novelists, Critics, and Poets, *edited by August J. Molnar, Rutgers University Press, 1964, pp. 326-40.*

PÉTER NAGY   (essay date 1962)

[*In the following introduction to* Be Faithful unto Death, *Nagy discusses Móricz's place in Hungarian literary history.*]

Zsigmond Móricz . . . is recognized as Hungary's greatest prose writer. He was born in the Victorian age, and, almost as if he had been predestined to have some tie with the fashionable milieu of the Victorian novel, he, too, was raised in the proximity of a vicarage. His mother, the orphaned daughter of a clergyman, escaped "upper-class poverty" by her marriage to a small peasant landowner who possessed both talent and industry. There were six children, of whom Zsigmond Móricz was the eldest. He was the same age as E. M. Forster; Gide and Proust were almost ten years his senior, Jack London and Sherwood Anderson were three years older, and Roger Martin du Gard and James Joyce a few years younger than he; and these names, in fact, did mean something in the simple peasant house in the remote, eastern part of Hungary where Móricz was born.

At this time Victorianism was not merely an English phenomenon, but the yardstick of taste and moral behaviour throughout Europe; Móricz grew to young manhood in an age—at the turn of the century—when cracks were appearing on the smooth façade of Victorian stability, signifying that unadmitted and uncontrollable forces were at work. Francis Joseph was the Victoria of the Monarchy, and his India was Hungary, where the king in person shook hands with the rajahs and nabobs on the occasions of his rare visits, while the gendarmes and army officers, more alien than the foreigners, fired point-blank into the crowds of pariahs—the workers and agricultural labourers—who were just then beginning to stir.

In Western Europe the barometer of history pointed at imperialism and toward proletarian revolution; in Eastern Europe, including Hungary, even feudalism was late in coming. It is difficult to describe these feudal shackles for the Western reader or for anyone who has not lived through those times. The hierarchical order of society, especially in the country's rural regions, seemed fixed and any change unthinkable. Bálint Móricz, Zsigmond's father, displayed extraordinary audacity by stepping out of the harsh and rigid order of village life to become an artisan carpenter, in fact a small contractor, and it took almost revolutionary courage to send his first-born—and his five succeeding children—to secondary school and later most of them to the university. Yet, insight into this social situation is given in Móricz's novel, *Be Faithful unto Death,* written in 1920. While the subject of this novel, which depicts the development of a child, his inner conflicts and first clash with society, is not social criticism but the spiritual evolution of the hero, the soil from which Mishi Nyilas's noble and sensitive soul sends forth its shoots is the society prevailing late in the 19th century. And it was precisely the inflexible hierarchy of that society, its rigorous respect for authority, which, strange as it may seem, explains the vast fear, anguish and timidity which overlay Mishi's soul. His fears and anxieties, alarm and agony, hesitation between truth and half-truth, for the most part may appear to the outsider to be groundless, but to the Hungarian reader they breathe the atmosphere of his native land.

The ordeal of Mishi is irrational and cruel, because the society in which he lives is senseless and savage and he is incapable either of adjusting to it or of consciously rebelling against it. However, a knowledge of Móricz's life-path and other writings imparts another, symbolic meaning to the story. The emotional intensity of Mishi's suffering was drawn from events immediately preceding the writing of the novel, from the author's own life and experiences. Zsigmond Móricz took part in the revolutions that followed the First World War, throwing himself into events with complete enthusiasm, hopeful optimism, and faith in mankind's progress and in a better future; the defeat of these revolutions would have been a painful blow to him even without the personal persecution he was subjected to, a harassment which, although it did relax somewhat a few years later, never ceased entirely, and the nation's preeminent novelist was treated as a "suspicious character" as long as Horthy's regime held power.

We have mentioned Forster, Joyce, Proust and Anderson as contemporaries of Móricz. These names personify the revolutionary revival of the Western novel, the breaking with traditional forms, the rejection of 19th-century realism and naturalism, and the genesis of a new novel-form that carried subtler nuances, a deeper psychological insight, greater symbolism and complexity. The social backwardness in Eastern Europe prevented Hungarian literature from keeping pace with literary and artistic events in Western Europe; and the revolution in art—whose foremost figures were Endre Ady in lyric poetry and Zsigmond Móricz in prose—which was proceeding in Hungary early in the 20th century, had to close the gap before it could move ahead. Thus, symbolism was to be the vital movement of Hungarian lyricism in the individual and peculiar formulations of Ady, and naturalism reached a new height in the early works of Móricz.

Be Faithful unto Death has added significance for Hungarian literature and Móricz's works because for the first time the author moves beyond naturalism toward the intricate and rich portrayal of psychological profundity and complex mental processes, though the manner in regard to the child-hero is perhaps a little tear-stained. This complexity stamps the work with a peculiar trait, making it almost matchless among books of its type. Novels with child-heroes frequently depict the urchin, the poor student, for this type of hero gives the author a wide scope for developing a plot full of twists and turns. (Dickens' works are an exception, but to his child-heroes school is only a fleeting episode, serving to illustrate the adult society with which the child comes into conflict and not being its expression.) Not only is Mishi a good student, forced by family and social circumstances to try to keep his

position at the head of his class irrespective of what it may cost; he is also an exceedingly talented little chap whose childish shell is sounded by the soul of a genius. Nowhere in the book does Móricz state that his little hero is exceptionally gifted, yet the portrayal of Mishi's spirit, his super-sensitivity, responsiveness and dreams tell the reader that an artist is being formed.

Zsigmond Móricz became Hungary's greatest novelist because his works mark a high point of both social and psychological realism. Of all Hungarian writers, Móricz was unrivalled in showing the life of his own and preceding eras intangibly setting forth the material, human and spiritual position of diverse classes and levels of society. *Be Faithful unto Death* substantiates this with the wealth of its narrative and the undercurrent of lyricism which permeates the entire work. We believe that its music is audible not only to Hungarian ears but to the non-Hungarian reader as well. (pp. 7-10)

Péter Nagy, in an introduction to Be Faithful unto Death *by Zsigmond Móricz, translated by Susan Kőrösi László, Corvina Press, 1962, pp. 7-10.*

PÉTER NAGY   (essay date 1980)

[*In the following essay, Nagy discusses Móricz's place in literary history, focusing on the question of his modernity.*]

To ask whether or not Zsigmond Móricz was a modern writer and if so, how modern, may be somewhat out of place yet the question must be put; it is timely in view of the centenary of Móricz's birth. Besides life itself repeatedly confronts man, a social being formed by a defined historical background, with unexpected and uncomfortable questions.

It is out of place since a writer born in 1879, following the occupation of Bosnia, the year of the German-Austrian alliance, in other words, when the post-*Ausgleich* Habsburg monarchy flourished, and who had died in 1942, in the darkest year of the Second World War, can only be modern in, and for, his own age and can be no more than a part of the history of literature for those living a generation, or several generations, later.

But the question must be put. Zsigmond Móricz of all writers means much more than just a chapter in the history of literature to Hungarians. He is a lively force in Hungarian literature today, even if his influence now appears as a negative force rather than one that attracts followers and epigones.

The ambiguous reply in itself skirts the ambiguity of modernism. Raising the question in itself asks two things at the same time. How up-to-date or modern was Zsigmond Móricz in his own time, is one question, but we also want to know whether today, thirty-seven years or a whole generation after his death, his message, his methods, and the experience of his works are still fresh, relevant and powerful enough to influence social or literary processes.

Placing the question in the context of the history of literature, one may also ask whether Móricz, who was born around the time when Dostoevsky wrote *Brothers Karamazov* and Henry James *Daisy Miller* and who died when Alexei Tolstoy was working on his *Ivan the Terrible* and Faulkner published *Go Down, Moses* had anything new to say, whether he had an individual approach and whether he is still relevant. Or, to put it in yet another way, whether Móricz was really a contemporary of Colette and Thomas Mann who were a few years older than he, or of the somewhat younger Robert Musil, Franz Kafka, James Joyce, and Roger Martin Du Gard; or did he live and work without being related to these writers and the schools they represented. Were not only his characters, his world, and the world created in his works, but also his reputation and influence limited, and rightly so, by the Lajta (Leitha) and the Carpathians, the frontiers of the Hungary of his youth and maturity.

His aftermath tends to lead to the latter conclusion. True enough, important parts of his work have been translated, some of it appeared abroad even in his own lifetime, mainly in German-speaking countries, and some of it has been published since in French and English, but Móricz has not really made a break-through into *Weltliteratur* ["world literature"]. If his works have real stature then it is in areas whose human, social, and political development, *pace* the differences, was much like Hungary's, that is in Eastern Europe, chiefly in countries that have chosen the socialist road. This fact, however, that should certainly not be neglected, does not, in itself, tip the balance. Think of the writers of these small nations—e.g. Endre Ady and Mihály Babits, to mention only Hungarian examples—who are held in high esteem by all those familiar with their work and yet unable to make a break-through into the mainstream of *Weltliteratur.*

Zsigmond Móricz's modernity at the time of his first appearance on the Hungarian literary scene requires neither apology nor explanation.

The fact itself that after long years of preparation, and an almost ten-year long apprenticeship spent earning his living as a journalist, with failures alternating with near successes that did not really lead to the focus of public attention, he was eventually able to find his own personal message and style, to coincide with the foundation of *Nyugat,* the journal that was to be the standard-bearer of all that was alive in Hungarian literature, is evidence enough of his timeliness. Let me add that he did so following a track blazed by Endre Ady, the great poet of the age.

But the modernity, indeed revolutionariness, of his art was Janus-faced from the start. What was really new in Móricz was something he saw himself and told in an anecdote about his father: he was able to see Hungarian society as a whole, first village life and soon after, the small-town and even the county and metropolitan world, through the eyes and emotions of those who found themselves at the bottom of society, that is the landless peasants. In the wider European context, this novelty was paired with a certain obsolete element, that is with naturalism. At that time, however, in the first decade of the twentieth century, it was only in Western Europe that naturalism was old hat, lacking freshness and attraction. In Eastern Europe, it was then that society and literature had reached a stage of development in which naturalism could come to life after certain initial *fin de siècle* attempts that really implied the acceptance of a literary programme rather than the fulfillment of a style and method. And the first, or one of the first to achieve with success the requirements of this school, was Zsigmond Móricz.

"Hét krajcár" ("Seven Farthings"), a story about a poor peasant's home where the needed and much sought-after seventh farthing is a beggar's gift and where laughter is stifled by blood coughed up from consumptive lungs, is, from a purely technical point of view, closer to the ancient than to the new. The tone is highly emotional and it ends on a note of tearful sentimentality. But the angle and approach are new. For the first time, so to speak, in Hungarian writing, there is full identification with the poor, seeing things through their eyes. Others had written about peasants or the poor, all the way from Jókai to Tömörkény, but either in a superior, jovial tone, or else bending down to them with the sympathy or bad conscience of the intellectual. Móricz was the first to see the peasant's world from within, aware of the passions, forces, and emotions raging there.

These passions, drives, and emotions found expression in the short stories published right before and after **"Seven Farthings"** which were actually a better and more powerful vehicle for the new approach and attitude than the better known **"Seven Farthings."** Sentimentality gradually wanes in them to be replaced by passion, not least sexual passion.

Sárarany (*Nugget*), his first major novel, is the most powerful emotional and artistic explosion of Móricz's ideas in this initial period. This is the story of a peasant stuck in the mud of village life, who dares and knows how to. Out to conquer the world, he thinks of seducing the countess and succeeds, only to be humiliated by the count whom he then kills. Read today the story sounds pretty romantic, the fantastic abounds, but one cannot help being carried away by the passion and spirit that drive author and hero alike. Dani Túri is the first peasant hero in Hungarian literature who demands and does not beg, who does not wait but tries to force the world to yield him all he needs. He fails due to the strength of his talents and not their weakness. The Dani Túris, caught in the vice of feudalism, had no room for action, and this only intensified the destructive passions that raged in their breasts and in their immediate surroundings.

It is a commonplace of literary history, and Móricz himself was fully aware, and stated clearly on several occasions, that his rebellious peasant heroes grew out of the figure of his father, seen and glorified by the son. The agonizing efforts, struggles, and sufferings of his first ten years as a writer were in fact a fight against himself, wishing to escape the yeoman pride and outlook his mother—the daughter of a manse become peasant woman—had brought him up in. The goal was identifying himself with the values and stance of a father he had earlier looked down on. His father, a peasant, had worked his way up to become a carpenter and jobbing builder. Miklós Móricz, the writer's younger brother, showed that the family's noble origin on the mother's side was pure fiction, a legend. The Nyilas and Pallagis had been emancipated from serfdom not much earlier than the Móricz family had been.

But the power of a legend is more important in family traditions than objective reality. In our eyes the struggles and trickeries of Bálint Móricz, frequently barely on the right side of the law, may look petty or even ridiculous; the quarrels and naggings in the cottage at Csécse or Tügy were perhaps neither greater nor stormier than in any other peasant family, but they became decisive taking place in the presence of an extremely receptive and sensitive boy. Their remembrance opened the road to a change of values, they made it possible for Móricz to turn his back on the system of values his mother, his beloved uncle, the headmaster, and the whole of the educational and social system of Hungary of the times had inculcated in him, that is, to despise peasants and try and become part of the dominant hierarchy of nobles and gentlemen. His stubborn insistence on becoming a writer, and the way he tried and rejected a number of professions, reflected the unconscious desire to turn against that order, but he did not succeed in taking the decisive step either in his art or as a man. When he finally managed to do so, when his pen and outlook lost their shackles, he also found his personal freedom: he renounced the middle-class security of an editorial post, giving notice to his paper, to be able to devote all his time and energy to writing.

The significance of this decision is stressed by the fact that Móricz had no desire to abandon journalism, then, and all his life, he enthusiastically accepted commissions from papers. Doing the leg-work for an article was, for him, an opportunity to collect material for his writing, indeed, he was never able to separate the two activities. What he wanted to turn his back on were the various middle-class commitments; he truly broke the "umbilical cord that tied him to established order." He believed he was safeguarding his freedom and independence as a writer. He was right but at the same time he was also ensuring the independence of his own attitudes and world outlook. He felt instinctively that, in a society based on the oppression and exploitation of the peasantry, a writer with a call to express the class attitudes of the peasantry could only be an antagonist and never an organic part of that social order and its institutions. Since, however, all this was largely instinctive, he suffered from time to time and did not always understand what the position was. But his class instincts expressing themselves as the instincts of the writer saved him from making any irreparable compromises.

Móricz started writing **Nugget** in almost the same frame of mind that led to the birth of **"Seven Farthings."** The short story appeared in *Nyugat* in 1908 and they published the novel in sequels the following year. We know that writing the latter, Móricz entertained dreams of the Zola or Balzac sort. He had a kind of Rougon-Macquart in mind of which **Nugget** was meant to be the first part. The second, **Vér (Blood)**— what a typically naturalistic title!—went up into smoke after a severe and dispiriting word from the editor: Móricz burnt the manuscript. That was also the end of the series. The age, and history, spoke even more loudly than Ernő Osvát, the exacting editor of *Nyugat*. For from the angle of the oppressed peasantry which was just gathering strength to liberate itself it was impossible to paint such a large, organic, and coherent picture of society as Balzac was able to do for a bourgeoisie strong in wealth and power, or Zola for a bourgeoisie whose power was threatened, but whose wealth still stood firm. Such an organic and coherent series was possible after the Liberation. Péter Veres's *Három nemzedék (Three Generations)*, which is simultaneously the epic and the lament of the peasant way of life, is the first and last realization of these requirements in modern Hungarian literature.

This naturalistic attitude and approach made possible for Móricz the kinds of insight and understanding that were in harmony with the most progressive psychological theories of the age. Móricz is the first writer to present psychological processes, particularly the emotions and tremors of the female soul essentially in harmony with the teachings of psychoanalysis. Móricz did not want to prove anything, he just shaped instinctively the figures of the wives of ministers of religion in **Árvalányok (Waifs)**, the wife of a teacher in **Isten háta mögött (Back of Beyond)**, or the various female figures in the short stories. They nevertheless fit in with views that became part of the intellectual consensus of the times thanks to psychoanalysis. The present state of research does not show whether, then or later, Móricz was acquainted with such theories, or read Freud and if so how thoroughly. One can only hope that the Móricz papers which have recently become public property will throw some light on this subject. But whether it was conscious knowledge, or mere instinct (and I suspect the latter, at least initially), the fact itself is most remarkable and worthy of attention.

From the start, Móricz was driven by the ambition to present society as a whole and to experiment with all the possibilities inherent in various kinds of prose. This desire was obviously also motivated to an extent by the persistence of a man at home in his craft and determined to learn all the tricks of his trade; anything they can do, I can do as well. This is how Móricz came to try his hand at crime stories (**Forró mezők** [*Torrid Meadows*], **Jobb mint otthon** [*Better than at Home*]), at a social persiflage of big-city adventure story (**Az asszony beleszól** [*The Woman Intervenes*]), and several other things. In the shorter forms he experimented more or less successfully, at least as much, if not more, than in his novels. He found himself repeatedly attracted to the prose-poem or rhythmic prose when attacking an emotionally highly charged subject. His memoir of József Rippl-Rónai, the great Hungarian Impressionist painter, a close friend, written soon after Rippl-Rónai died, or his poetic travel writings of the twenties in which personal impressions, the inner storms accompanying the major turn in his life (the suicide of his first wife and his second marriage) and efforts aimed at coping with the vicissitudes of history mingle sometimes in poetic vision, sometimes in rhythmic prose and sometimes in a peculiar amalgam of reportage and meditation.

It is impossible to decide with any degree of certainty whether he was driven to the historical novel by an inner prompting or fashion, probably both. Seventeenth-century Transylvania, the age of Gábor Bethlen, had been occupying his attention since the early nineteen-tens, that this interest turned into a novel, and a masterpiece at that, was also due to the growing popularity of historical novels after the Great War as well as the recognition that the rule of Gábor Bethlen way back in the seventeenth century had, in fact, been the last hope for a Hungarian society growing organically out of feudalism into progressive capitalism.

Erdély (Transylvania), and especially the first volume **Tündérkert (Fairyland)**, describing with an admirable historical authenticity and a lively wealth of detail the rule and the fall of Prince Gábor Báthori and the rise of Gábor Bethlen, is certainly on a par with the greatest examples of twentieth-century critical realism falling behind neither in historical or psychological authenticity, or the strength of composition. True, the idea of a really major composition, Móricz's dream of a novel-cathedral, remained a dream, his talents did not suffice, though he struggled with the theme for nearly twenty years. After the first one-volume masterpiece, the continuation, although full of marvellous detail, slows down, the structure becoming obscure, and in the third part (the author also planned a fourth but never wrote it) the novel, strangely enough, gets bogged down in private concerns precisely at the point where there is scope for the protagonist to grow to world historical proportions.

But **Fairyland** grew into an outstanding novel in the same way as **Légy jó mindhalálig (Be Faithful unto Death)**: as the chronicle of human integrity, of the testing and redeeming hopes, disappointments and sufferings caused by war and revolutions. **Fairyland** is the whole of history and the whole of the nation in the whirlpool of history. *Be Faithful unto Death,* on the other hand, shows all the tremors of the human spirit and all the agonies of frustrated hopes as imprinted on the soul of a child. Móricz's marvellous portrayal of the female soul in the earlier works was mentioned above, here, in the story of Misi Nyilas, of the cruel hounding of an innocent schoolboy in Debrecen at the end of the century, one admires Móricz's accurate and fully authentic depiction of the inner world of a child. The message which transcends a particular age, though the work shows it as firmly embedded in the context of its own times, is that the greatest suffering of children is to see their own ideals, projected into the adult world, collapse as a result of human pettiness.

Whether they presented the sufferings and passions of peasants, the hopeless philistinism of the small town, petty bourgeois world, or the hopelessness of intellectual ambitions where even heroism did not make sense, Móricz's works before and during the Great War were, in fact, variations on the same theme: the inevitable changes in a society growing out of feudal conditions to become bourgeois. It is this that allowed Móricz's own instrument to harmonize with the *Nyugat* orchestra and, furthermore, to give a true picture of Hungarian society of the time. *Fairyland* and even *Be Faithful unto Death* are about this conviction, the latter with the bitterness that went with the failure of that big hope.

The consolidation of the powers responsible for the post-1919 counter-revolution appeared to turn Móricz away from the task he had set himself. This was the reason why he had to suffer several unfair attacks by contemporaries politically on his left, particularly in the twenties. His voice calmed down, the old revolutionary spirit only flared up occasionally in his works, unexpectedly but with all the greater fervour. His choice of subject and setting seemed to have "calmed down" as well. The period is the *fin de siècle,* the social setting the *dzsentri* ["gentry" (The critic adds in a footnote that "the Hungarian term . . . has pejorative overtones")], the breeding ground and ideal of the type of consolidation associated with István Bethlen, Horthy's prime minister in the twenties. Móricz's pen and eye, however, always allows the death's head of historical fate to be visible at the back of the *bonhomie.* The most terse examples are probably his novellas revolving around the doomed way of life of this class, and the lies that speed up their deterioration. His figures include many who are attractive and valuable as human beings, who are, however, doomed on account of their way of thinking and anachronistic values and ways of life. This is probably most evident in the outstanding novel of this period, *Úri muri* (*Gents Have Fun*), in which Móricz develops this idea with an exceptional wealth of characters and with great consistency in a story about two days of merry-making that end in tragedy on landlord-owned farmsteads on the Great Hungarian Plain.

Gents Have Fun was certainly one of the literary high points of the twenties. The technique, which Móricz developed to perfection, of letting a novel grow organically out of an anecdote, and its combination with a thoroughgoing social and psychological analysis reaches a high point in this story. *Pillangó* (*Butterfly*) is, however, what makes Móricz's work shine in his warmest lights in this period. On the surface it is an insignificant story about a consuming passion between two young day-labourers which, however, in its social and psychological analysis is a perfect expression of the artistic concentration and of the ambivalence of Móricz's art. Folk-

tale and social criticism, idyll and tragedy appear side by side, while in its tone, theme, and human portrayal, this writing, and a great many others of lesser importance, represents a transition between the worlds and attitudes reflected in Móricz's first and second creative periods.

It was in the twenties that Zsigmond Móricz grew into a portrayer of Hungarian society as a whole and from that time on, he quite consciously strove to become one. Proceeding in chronological order: after and parallel to working on his *A boldog ember* (*A Happy Man*) and the first major autobiographical short stories, he wrote *Az asszony beleszól* (*The Woman Interferes*) and had not even finished that when he started on *A nap árnyéka* (*The Shade of the Sun*), the second volume of his big historical novel, and then wrote *Jobb, mint otthon* (*Better than at Home*) and *Rab oroszlán* (*Captive Lion*). But this was not the free and uninhibited singing of a bird in a tree, but rather the diligent construction of a bricklayer or carpenter, even though the blueprints were made while work was under way and the different sections of the building did not necessarily form a harmonic whole. However, from one point of view, completeness was achieved, and that is in the consistency with which things were viewed through peasant eyes. From this point of view, stories in an urban middle-class setting show a surprising unity, and even artistic shortcomings and slipshod workmanship are rooted in the author's class-determined horizons. All this finds its clearest, almost conscious, expression in *Míg új a szerelem* (*While Love Is New*), a novel that, in a strange way and in contrast to earlier works, is prevented from rising to its own possibilities by poetic spontaneity and *roman-à-clef* aspects.

The descent to the depths prefigured by *Butterfly* and achieving its first success in *A Happy Man* became predominant in the mid-thirties. The latter is the life-story of a poor peasant narrated as a series of interviews, and one of the most peculiar of Hungarian novels which appeared even more peculiar at the time of its publication. The author seems to hide behind his hero, but, in fact, the book is only a documentary on the surface, in reality it is invented down to the most minute details. It is common knowledge that this novel played an important role in the birth of the populist movement in literature, helping the swarm of populist writers to find their voice and cause. This in itself is no small achievement, throwing light, as it does, on the modernity of Móricz's art. But it is equally remarkable that, probably unintentionally, this novel is the most complete and most Hungarian expression of the *Neue Sachlichkeit* school of German writing in Hungarian literature, in fact, it is the first example, and a masterpiece at that, of the documentary novel. Similarly, his descent to the depths, which first took him to the poorest of the rural population, cottars and shepherds of the *puszta,* and later to the urban proletariat as well, made, with instinctive assurance, Móricz's works of this period into a typically Hungarian manifestation of a major and most modern school of literature. There is no need to reveal the anti-Fascist nature of this descent to the depths, it was apparent long ago, so to speak, when it first showed itself. But an analysis of his *Barbárok* (*Barbarians*), the *Rózsa Sándor* novels or *Árvácska* (*Little Waif*) will show that this descent to the depths, Móricz's identification with the poorest in society, was also descent to artistic depths, a deliberate attempt to weld the archaic and the modern. Growing out of Hungarian roots on Hungarian soil, and in a most natural way for the Hungarian reader, it was the realization—with no lesser results—of the same trend that motivated several Western anti-Fascist writers, not least Thomas Mann in his Joseph tetralogy. Naturally, the point is not to compare aesthetic qualities, but to point to the identity of the artistic-historical trend and its presence in a given social setting.

Consequently it can be said that precisely on account of its anti-Fascist nature, the art of Zsigmond Móricz in this period instinctively came close to an early Hungarian variety of socialist realism; the kind of socialist realism hallmarked by the names of Gorky, Sholokhov, Aragon, and Déry. In this, and to this extent, he is the kin of Attila József with whom Móricz himself felt linked by inner, spiritual affinities. He was also fully aware that the old forms did not suffice for an authentic manifestation of this social realism, he would have to look for new ways and new methods. It is another story, and an ironic twist of history, that when the shaping of events offered the possibility to socialist realism to come true in Hungarian literature, the fact that Móricz's methods and forms were given the status of officially enforced norms, became one of the obstacles which prevented socialist realism from coming true, and particularly from establishing itself as a truly modern school of writing.

As pointed out earlier, the title-question, how modern Zsigmond Móricz is, has two aspects. So far I have discussed one, but the second cannot be evaded either. How, and in what way, is the writing of Zsigmond Móricz modern for readers today, independent of the way one might judge him as a historical figure.

I feel I should first draw attention once again to a historical aspect. I mentioned earlier that in the early years of socialism, precisely in those of the personality cult, Móricz's narrative methods were so to speak raised to the status of an official norm. Obviously, in the long run, this did more damage than good to the writer and to his writing. But I am also inclined to the view that the nearly twenty-five years that have passed since the personality cult was put an end to offer a large enough perspective to ask and answer the question regardless of that historical burden.

It has become increasingly clear that Móricz's more lasting works that speak most directly to readers of later ages are the short stories and novellas; amongst the former precisely the later ones that were thought unsatisfactory in their own time because of their formlessness. They include the autobiographical short stories written in the thirties, the forerunners of *Életem regénye* (*The Story of My Life*). What makes them exciting and timely is their openness of form, the way they make their point without coming to a point in conventional short-story twist, as well as the manner in which psychological portrayal and the writer's judgement are covertly yet clearly manifest in the seemingly dispassionately narrated story.

Móricz's novellas were long regarded as preludes to, or sketches for, the major novels. Time, however, has put much right in this respect. Today we know that these are works in their own right and of a higher aesthetic order than most of the long novels. In the novellas the harmony of form and content sparkles in rare purity, and the job and ways of coping with it are welded without lumps. From the point of view of artistic intensity rather than totality of presentation, *Back of Beyond* obviously surpasses *Fáklya* (*The Torch*), *Kivilágos kivirradtig* (*Until Daybreak*) is better than *Gents Having Fun* and *Little Waif* outshines the Sándor Rózsa novels.

When it comes to the large-scale compositions, *A Happy*

Man and *The Story of My Life* go on growing in stature. Naturally, by that I do not want to detract from the value of the other masterpieces, including *Be Faithful unto Death* or *Fairyland,* it is simply that while the merits of the latter have been obvious ever since first publication, the former did not receive such unequivocal recognition in their time. *The Story of My Life* in particular, was probably the first to meet with a lack of understanding, not to mention the politically motivated tally-ho around the Sándor Rózsa novels.

What was considered hasty writing or the verbiage of old age at the time *The Story of My Life* first appeared, has by now received a new brilliance, flavour, and value. We now look on it as a major new achievement of the age, an essay-novel in which I believe Móricz managed to accomplish more than in the rest of his oeuvre regarding the simultaneous presentation and conceptual grasp of people, facts, and processes and a complex perception and presentation of Hungarian society at that time and of that historical period as a whole.

And in the light of all this, *While Love Is New* also shines with a new kind of richness. For a long time, critical response to this novel was determined by the displeasure caused by the fact that this is quite clearly a *roman-à-clef* and, as such, rather cruel on its heroine. By now the stench of scandal has lifted and what has remained is a bold experiment by Móricz to introduce the technique of fragmenting time, bringing about a new type of unity between this fragmented time, the narrative, and the essay. Added interest is given to the novel by meditations on the problems of the artist, a new feature in Móricz's work.

I am also convinced that more in his attitudes as a writer and in his whole approach to literature pointed ahead our present and our future than we tend to be aware of or appreciate. What I have in mind is not just his sense of social and national responsibility, and his commitment to progress, something that has always been appreciated by contemporaries and critics alike. But the point is that Móricz was probably the first Hungarian writer of narrative prose on the grand scale to introduce one of the most typical features of the twentieth-century novel, that is the direct exploitation for narrative purposes of facts of his own personal life.

I am not sure whether Móricz possesses a more striking individual trait as a writer. "Epic objectivity" simply does not exist for him, not only because all his writings are charged with so much passion and emotion, but also because, strangely enough, his narrative passion is accompanied by a total inability to invent stories. He was frank about it and mentioned it several times: it was always life that provided him with his subjects and stories; life, his own life in the first place. Very little would remain were one to eliminate the motifs, scenes, and dialogues taken from his own life and real experience—a fact which even applies to his historical novels and stories.

In this he does as most of the major European novelists of the time did. It is specific of the twentieth century that the world is "experiencable" to a growing degree, and becomes harder to "invent." Space does not allow me to explain the social and historical reasons why the conviction of an unshakeable *Welt an sich* ceases in the twentieth century. This belief was the external precondition of nineteenth-century narrative and this social and ideological background was there even behind flights of fancy that seem to have bolted. Increasingly in the twentieth century the only reality for the writer is what he experiences, this is why the narrative forms are becoming lyric and why individual experience tends to become the only source of inspiration. Móricz's is a special border-line case, that of a writer on the brink between the poetic approach and narrative objectivity. It is this that gives rise to both his obsoleteness and his modernity. (Another point I cannot here discuss in detail is the role of women, including his wives Janka and Mária, and his adopted daughter, Csibe, in his life. The writer's instinctive class-attitude is shown in the fact that while he could easily and fruitfully make use of the experiences, tales, and personalities of Janka and Csibe in his work, thereby broadening his own experience, Mária, the beautiful actress remained "dumb" as far as he was concerned, or rather he remained deaf to her story.)

Móricz straddled two centuries not only literally, but also in his practice and make-up as a writer. He drew his real inspiration from himself as a source (and in direct emotional continuation, people he found of interest), and he was still able to objectify, and, from time to time, to continue the tale that started as an account of what happened. Móricz himself described his position between two epochs when he said, sometimes with pride, sometimes with regret, that the only possible source of inspiration for him was the truth and his own experience, and that his ability to invent was extremely limited. On the other hand, he once wrote that when he could tell a story so that "light shone on paper," on such occasions he was continuing the work of his great predecessors, above all that of Jókai. For those who directly followed him, Móricz's narrative monumentality, the expression of the totality of life in his works was what overwhelmed them. Of equal value for us today, not only quantitatively but also aesthetically, is the presence in Móricz's art of a lyrical manner, subjectivity at its highest level, and the objectivization of the subjective, personal experience raised to the epic sphere. In this, Zsigmond Móricz is akin to his most outstanding contemporaries abroad. Naturally, the road he took differed from any of theirs, but it is precisely this difference that turns the values accumulated in his works into a quality that bears comparison with their writings.

Obviously, his own generation, growing to maturity early this century, found different things of value in Zsigmond Móricz than the next, the populist writers in the thirties. It is equally obvious that the reader and literary critic of the fifties appreciated and enjoyed other things in Móricz than we do in the seventies. It is one of the great enchantments of the literary process that while progress may wipe out some of the things earlier thought of value, it saves most by integrating them into a new attitude. Each age notices more, sees better, and appreciates more than previous ones. It is this that entitles every generation and age to reassess previous periods, though it does not give it the right to reject real values in its passionate search for something new and to destroy living values, or deny their existence, for the sake of real or presumed new richnesses.

For this reason it is certain that Zsigmond Móricz is a live force in contemporary Hungarian literature, though not an exclusive standard or model that alone ensures salvation. This is a good thing, I should say. It became obvious precisely in the fifties and above all through the example of Zsigmond Móricz how mutilating it can be for talented people as well, to try and copy the methods of a writer as the only possible model, even if they do so skilfully. The whole question of following a model came to an end as far as the arts are concerned, never to be resuscitated, at the time of the dispute between the ancients and moderns, early in the Baroque period. One can be apprenticed to Móricz as a writer, and learn a great deal from him, including his perception of reality, his instinctive loyalty to principles, his sensitivity to new facts, techniques of human portrayal and heaven knows what else, but nobody can imitate him without this being, in itself, a loss of quality.

While readers enjoy his works, while generations learn to know their past and themselves from him, while writers are excited by the way he created characters, a scene, or a whole work, Zsigmond Móricz will always be alive and his works will remain an active force in Hungarian literature. The present and our points of view allow us to recognize values, features, and innovations in Móricz that earlier generations were unable to see in the same light as we do. And in this light, it is indisputable that it is precisely the uniqueness and individuality of Móricz's art—I could almost say the way it is tied to the soil, like a peasant serf—which makes him the worthy companion of the greatest of his age. In his own life-time, two modern spokesmen of the peasant world, Wladyslaw Reymont and Frans Sillanpää, were awarded the Nobel Prize. His life-work is of no lesser importance than theirs, he is their equal in the beauty he created. It is these that will survive for ever; later generations are bound to discover new features and new relevance in them to the enrichment of us all. (pp. 29-42)

Péter Nagy, "How Modern Was Zsigmond Móricz," in The New Hungarian Quarterly, *Vol. XXI, No. 77, Spring, 1980, pp. 29-42.*

ATTILA TAMÁS (essay date 1982)

[*In the following excerpt, Tamás examines the principal themes and techniques of Móricz's most important works.*]

Móricz became the greatest figure of Hungarian realist prose, but he did not begin to write in the still-existing tradition of the nineteenth-century Hungarian realists. In his youth he was influenced by Jókai, and later by the anecdotal, slightly idealizing prose written in the spirit of conservative "folk-national poetry."

The famous short story, **"Seven Pennies"** (**"Hét krajcár"**), which appeared in *Nyugat,* can be traced to these influences. He gave a picture of the happy side of the life of the poor, in a short-story style, but he was already clear-minded about the fate of the poor. He looked into a world where one accepts coins from a beggar, and where the laughter which seeks to overcome misery turns to coughed-up blood.

There is thus a certain two-sided approach already visible in **"Seven Pennies,"** and although Móricz's work was to undergo many changes this dualism can be found in almost everything he wrote. He is concerned to show quite frankly the depths of human misery, but at the same time he is also concerned with positive values in life, in human features undistorted by misery. Sometimes the balance is perfect, sometimes one outweighs the other.

As his career progressed Móricz brought fewer and fewer illusions to his picture of society. In **"Tragedy"** (**"Tragédia"**) for instance, he deals with a starving agricultural labourer who, invited to a rich peasant's feast, in blind hunger and greed, partially fuelled by hatred, stuffed himself to death. His meaningless death goes as unnoticed as his life. The tone is apparently objective. But this short story, written with digressions, with a strict economy of means directed to precise goals, is charged with the emotional tensions of a writer who has looked into the depths of human existence, and reveals the frightening aridity in a section of society hitherto unobserved.

Naturalism is a strong feature of the work just discussed, as it is of Móricz's later writings, especially of the novel *Pure Gold* (*Sárarany*). This work deals with the disintegration of the life of a peasant of strong capabilities and passions, urged on by an active temperament. His failures in love and personal ambition are tellingly revealed, and he who could have become the leader of the villagers in their struggle for land against the noble land-owner, becomes in the end the land-owner's murderer, for the sake of a woman, in order to satisfy his male vanity. Naturalism here takes the form of the strain imposed by crude physical passions, exhibited in the unfettered language of the characters, in the realistic background, in the uncompromising display of avarice, the sensuous immediacy of material objects. Móricz is not trying to write a "scientific experimental novel" like Zola, nor does he lay inordinate emphasis on material detail. Parts of the work display different aspects of the misery of village life, balanced however by encomiums on the magnificence of nature and the energy and spirit lying dormant in man. The characters are forcefully drawn, vividly alive, despite the difficulties of creating a chief character imbued with unusual powers. In this work of Móricz it is already clear that the author is addicted to tense and dramatic scenes where both strong human passions and representative characters from the different social worlds are shown in conflict. *Pure Gold* is a picture of a typical Hungarian village slowly experiencing the influence of capitalism. **"Poor Folk"** (**"Szegény emberek"**), a short story written in 1916, during the First World War, is one of Móricz's finest essays in realism, and at the same time an excellent example of the two aspects of his work. The truth which Ady voices in the language of ancient jeremiads in *Poor Men Kill, Merely Kill* is repeated by Móricz in an objective prose which conceals a deep dismay within it. It uncovers the inhumanity of war with the sharpness of steel. It deals with a soldier home on leave, who tries to help his debt-ridden family by stealing. But in the end, as a consequence of the theft and the need to kill bred in him at the front, he commits a double murder. Móricz paints the main figures in minute psychological detail—based not so much on a cold analysis as on the description of their inner selves: the soldier who gradually becomes aware that he has not changed his fate by his action, that he has only sunk deeper in the mire, the wife who will cling to her husband absolutely, despite his growing confusion and his crime. The reader feels the remains of humanity in his hero even through the final dehumanizing process. The short story is written in purely realistic terms, with no forced contrasts or extremes. The man, who becomes increasingly revolted by his deed, comes to final recognition of the real situation sitting on the banks of a ditch, thinking of the trenches on his way home with the things he has stolen: It is not the man of a different nationality who stands on the other side in war, who is opposed to the poor. As things are, he realizes that on one side are those "who have a stinking hovel, whose boots are in tatters, who have no bread to eat, but who have only lots and lots of children." On the other side stand those who get officer's treatment, who are "good men who don't hurt a soul because they give a penny to beggars."

The novel *The Torch* (*A fáklya*) was partly influenced by the war. Here Móricz is no longer satisfied to register the relentless laws of the world, what he now expresses is the desire for change. The fervent nature of the novel provides an outlet for his more "lyrical," more romantic tendencies. This uneven work is close to *Pure Gold* in subject, but it is even closer to Ady's poems on the subject of Hungarian Wasteland and Hungarian "Messiahs" incapable of action. In the frightening, debilitating world of the Hungarian countryside even those who started out as torch-bearers of good causes fall by the way or do harm. Here it is a gifted Protestant minister fired by a vocation akin to that of the preachers of old, at odds with the crippling strains of life. He fails, and in the end he is forced to question his original sense of vocation, and, with the whole world against him, he curses it. It is as if his curse were answered in the fire which breaks out as a result of a stupid accident, and which brings mass death and destruction during the village festivities. This is the first appearance of destruction by fire which appears later at the conclusion of several of Móricz's works. The minister's last words are said in a feverish semi-consciousness: "It has come to pass, but nothing has become clearer." And the frightening scene of death and destruction provides a symbolically charged background to these words.

A similar scene closes *Gentlemen Make Merry* (*Úri muri*), written some ten years later, after the war and the 1918-19 Revolution and counter-revolution. The action, which takes place at the end of the nineteenth century, is concerned with a single feast, lasting several days. Móricz not only condemns a declining section of society, the gentry, but as in Ady's verse, crowds past centuries into the present. The work moves gradually from a narrative to a dramatic form. The strong sense of atmosphere permeating this work has an almost poetic quality. Every small detail, indeed, is realistic: the weary conversation born of boredom, the fly droppings on the tablecloth, the dust of the stifling summer in the street. Yet all this is the symbol of a world more extended in time and space. Each movement seems to retain the memory of ancient ceremonies, the scene of action is bounded by a cupola-shaped sky. By their merry-making the main characters try to deny their economic and moral collapse, or at least to regard it as merely temporary. The increasingly frantic dance of death of the feast takes on a frightening dimension for just this reason. Here are small-town people confined in a rigidly conventional framework, and the village men fired by ancient passions: the ex-land-owner, now reduced to selling books, who foretells and explains the ruin of the country, the eccentric landlord who regards the exploited peasants as a joke, but who lives and dies for his animals. Such men surround, humiliate and finally destroy the man trying to change things, to escape. In the hurlyburly of the festivity, the minister sets fire to the roof above them, and shoots himself in the heart.

All the old strength and ancient obduracy of the East, all its old virtues and vices are concentrated in this novel. Móricz is also concerned with the duality which Ady writes of in *On the Hungarian Waste* (*A magyar Ugaron*): the historical past, the hypnotic effect of tradition, the stubborn pride of centuries and the lack of responsibility that inevitably lead to destruction. The central characters in Móricz's novels are also driven by a longing for a whole and fulfilled life: their failure means the end of the splendid possibilities of life. The narrative writer, however, needs to give a realistic representation of the failure of his characters and of the causes of that failure, a task that Móricz fulfils admirably: he gives a clearly comprehensible picture of the inner inevitability of failure for the man without any opportunity of active participation in society, and so losing his moral base.

An earlier work by Móricz, *Until Break of Dawn* (*Kivilágos kivirradtig*), is akin to *Gentlemen Make Merry* both in plot and theme. Here all the signs of financial and moral collapse behind apparent tranquillity come to the surface in a single night of increasingly hectic merry-making. A strong sympathy and an even stronger—illusionary—faith originally connected Móricz with the better elements among the gentry. But to a certain extent already in *The Torch,* and certainly in two works under discussion, he realized that this whole class was doomed. A final judgement without any trace of illusion is expressed in *Relatives* (*Rokonok*), a novel which follows the more traditional forms of realism, closely related to Móricz's earlier work, *Behind God's Back* (*Az Isten háta mögött*), which in turn is a deliberately grotesque version of Flaubert's *Madame Bovary*. In the life of the small town, stifling, boring, petty, even Madame Bovary-type attempts to escape become dull and ordinary. The suicidal jump of the unfaithful wife ends with her landing on her backside; the deceived husband cannot even understand why the magistrate who commits suicide should call him Mr. Bovary. Life continues at the end of the novel exactly where it began.

This terrifying vision of extinction is not death but more a bitterly precise account of life which has lost its meaning.

The same theme runs through *Relatives* as in *The Torch* and *Gentlemen Make Merry.* Móricz sets his scene in contemporary life, around the nineteen-thirties, among the bourgeois intellectuals and gentry burdened by the remains of a feudal past. A city councillor, responsible for cultural activities, is elected to the post of chief attorney. His efforts to purify and reform the system are frustrated by opposition from the mayor, who dominates the town and whose cynical ruthlessness is masked by an easy and familiar manner. The failure is pitiful rather than tragic. The chief attorney is brought by a kind of necessity to a point where his plans must fail through a variety of reasons: through the manipulative skills of the real rulers of the town, better adapted to the tempo of modern life, through his own ambition to succeed, and through the relatives looking for security by means of his influence. The novel is centred on the main character. The unexpected exception comes in the final chapter where, in sharp contrast to the ending of *Gentlemen Make Merry,* we are only given the bare news of the suicidal shot. We do not even know whether or not he dies. Here there is no sense of the greatness of the struggle with death. The concentration is on the attorney's inner life, its ups and downs, contradictions, and the process of its disintegration are charted with a sober clarity. One of the characteristic intellectual flaws of the century, self-deception, is displayed in this novel.

Kopjáss, the careful tactician, deludes himself that he is representing the interests of the poor even when their cause is a mere tool for his own advancement, since he has long since only been interested in the furtherence of his own career. Even at the end he feels that his failure is the failure of a man battling for a genuine cause, whereas by that time it is only his unwillingness to take risks and his lack of foresight which distinguishes him from the powerful group riding roughshod over him. Móricz was also interested in larger and more universal questions than those of small-town life or the fate of self-deluded officials. In 1921 he embarked on an enormous historical trilogy, *Transylvania* (*Erdély*), which was only finished in 1935. He took as his subject Gábor Bethlen, the

seventeenth-century Protestant ruler of Transylvania, who united this small country, later to play an important role in Europe, portraying him as the exemplar of the strong monarch who was dependent on his people; who promoted the development of a middle class and who brought unity and peace to warring national groups. The figure of Bethlen is reminiscent in various ways of Heinrich Mann's Henry IV. A good deal of detailed and serious historical research went into this work. The turbulent, colourful life of the period, the two worlds of the rich and the poor, are recreated in slightly archaic but powerful language; the action is lively, the character convincing.

Particularly successful are the portraits of Bethlen and Gábor Báthori. Báthori is the ruler who is the antithesis of Bethlen; his visions are bold and far-reaching, his abilities great but marred by an ungovernable temper. (Did Móricz model his two central characters on himself and Ady?) The human picture of Bethlen is intensified by his conflicting emotions for two women: the intelligent, disciplined wife with her inner purity, cherishing her husband, and the mistress offering free and uncontrolled passion but lacking moral strength. This attraction of opposites is present in a number of the other novels as well (*Pure Gold, Gentlemen Make Merry, Relatives,* etc.). Móricz built a veritable mythology out of these contrasting types, the "mythology" of the two basic categories of woman.

The chief character of his other historical cycle of novels, written at the end of his life, is a folk hero—Sándor Rózsa, the famous lowland outlaw of the mid-nineteenth century. (The concept of the outlaw had long attracted him; the central figure of *The Outlaw* (*Betyár*) became the champion of the oppressed against the oppressor.) The work was planned for three volumes. The first is a masterpiece of his maturity. But in the second, written in considerable haste, Móricz tried to integrate both the 1848 struggle for Hungarian freedom and the figure of the outlaw who took part in it, which somewhat upsets the balance of the structure. The end of the work deals with the loss of hope, "everything has an end, only poverty stays forever." The first novel, *Sándor Rózsa Jumps His Horse* (*Rózsa Sándor a lovát ugratja*), carefully organized, vigorous in language, is rich in a magnificent panorama of men set against their natural background, as it pictures both the lonely hero and the busy, multifarious life of the people. And the second novel, *Sándor Rózsa Puckers His Brow* (*Rózsa Sándor összevonja a szemöldökét*), despite its loose structure, is no less remarkable. The completed trilogy would have crowned his achievement—but he was not allowed time to finish it. The third volume remained no more than a plan. During his writing career Móricz often recurred to the problems of childhood. No doubt this was connected with the bitterness of his own childhood years, but it may also have had something to do with the fact that even after grappling with all the adult questions of the individual and society, he retained something of a child's amiability. It was after the successful counter-revolution of 1919 that he wrote *Be Faithful unto Death* (*Légy jó mindhalálig*), which is a sensitive psychological portrait of the helpless struggles of a hurt and exploited schoolboy, set against an admirable picture of the sterile life of a students' hostel and the small-town characters of a Hungarian province. *Little Orphan* (*Árvácska*), moreover, written in Móricz's last period deals with an even greater degree of exploitation. The novel is about the subhuman life of an orphan, passed from one peasant family to another. It also ends with a devastating fire as the only "solution." The final image is that of a blanket of snow covering everything: "There was nothing to show that a house had stood there and that people had lived in it, and that those people had perished here under the snow."

The fate of the peasant is also a recurrent theme in Móricz's work, particularly in the novel *A Happy Man* (*A boldog ember*). It is written in an easy voice, in the first person. It slowly unfolds the character of a peasant, looking back from his present penury, who sees the years before the war as happy ones, even though that life was also nothing but sheer poverty and work, with no hope of escape. Even so it is not merely because of the even greater poverty of the post-war period that his earlier life seems happier in retrospect. It is because within its narrow limits that life had more contentment, and yet the peasant survives despite the harsh conditions of his existence. He lived, he passed on life to his children; he worked and loved, and neither joy nor the appreciation of beauty had died in him.

This work is perhaps the nearest in tone to *The Story of My Life* (*Életem regénye*), the autobiography which gives such an authentic and perceptive account of the writer's childhood, revealing at the same time the spirit and customs of the age. If Thomas Mann in the *Joseph Trilogy* explains myth and brings it close to man, Móricz elevates the story of his family to the status of myth. We see the intermingling of the lives of the independent peasant boy with his great vitality and mental strength and the gentle parson's daughter. All the warmth and immediacy of the events are vividly conveyed to us, while at the same time the careful analysis and examination to which they are subjected give us an understanding of the peasant in Hungary at the turn of the century.

It is no accident that Móricz first came to the attention of the public with his short stories. In his prolific output of this genre are a number of short-story masterpieces. These dense, often dramatically structured tales are various in tone, sometimes stark, sometimes light, sometimes bitterly ironic. They deal with the fundamental problems confronting man in his dealing with nature and society, and expose them in a contemporary context.

One of the most outstanding is "The Barbarians" ("Barbárok"), which is as far from "Seven Pennies" as it is from "Tragedy." The action takes place in that "semi-past" which left its effect on Móricz's own time, that is, the second half of the nineteenth century. The story is simple: a shepherd and his child are beaten to death by two other shepherds, and his flock is driven away. His wife searches for many months until she comes upon the dead bodies. One of the murderers, now in prison, and in any case due to be hanged for other offences to which he has confessed, nonetheless stubbornly refuses to confess to this particular crime. Or at least until he unexpectedly sees the dead shepherd's belt, which had already played an important part in the story. The judge is taken by surprise, but sends the shepherd to receive the additional punishment of twenty-five strokes of the birch, adding one word to the sentence—"barbarians." And indeed, the story takes us into a world of men living like Asian barbarians "red in tooth and claw." And indeed, dominating the whole tale is the sense of the chasm of incomprehension and indifference separating the world "above" from the world "below." Yet in the latter there are certain beauties: the woman who searches for the man she rarely sees, travels through half the country in the manner of mythical heroines embodying a primitive loyalty to a bond assumed for life. The different sections of the story

merge to form a unity: at times its economy is reminiscent of Hemingway, at times of the poetry of the folk-tale or the ballad.

The atmosphere of the old ballads, the close relationship to the essence of the art of the common folk, is somewhat akin to the work done in contemporary music by Bartók and Kodály. It is also related to the work of the younger generation of populist writers. But Móricz's work is not local: it belongs to the wider currents of world literature. It is a more poetic version of his early naturalistic-realistic "Tragedy," namely, "To Eat One's Fill" ("Egyszer jóllakni"). This story is not set in the narrow world of a single village; it is set in the endless wastelands, and the peasants who live in it battle against the age-old hunger of the poor. The chief character in the novel is not simply a peasant dulled to stupidity by the conditions of his life. He cries out that a peasant cannot stomach everything, and the cry has a wider meaning. At the climax of the merry-making arranged by the squire, he plunges his knife in the breast of the policeman, who represents the power of the landlord, with a passion reminiscent of the Gypsies of García Lorca.

Others of his later stories worth a mention here are those about the life of the urban proletariat, about the struggle between man and woman and about the upheavals of adolescence. But his finest works, in addition to *Gentlemen Make Merry* and *Transylvania,* are those dealing with peasant life. His greatest achievement lies in his stark but often peetic picture of more than half a century of Hungarian peasant life, in the tales of strong and active figures living in close communion with their surroundings. They bear a certain relationship to those of Reymont, but they are by no means slavish copies. His best works take their place alongside the work of twentieth-century writers like Solokhov, Steinbeck, Laxness and Nexö, in the realistic tradition of Tolstoy and Balzac in their sense of strong social responsibility. (pp. 351-59)

Attila Tamás, "Zsigmond Móricz," in A History of Hungarian Literature *by István Nemeskürty and others, edited by Tibor Klaniczay, translated by István Farkas and others, Corvina Kiadó, 1982, pp. 350-59.*

LÓRÁNT CZIGÁNY (essay date 1984)

[*Czigány is a Hungarian-born American educator and critic. His* Oxford History of Hungarian Literature: From the Earliest Times to the Present *was intended to fulfill a specific need: "to provide a textbook, as comprehensive as possible within the limits of space, for students of literature whose mastery of the language is not sufficient to study Hungarian literature in the original; and secondly, to serve as a guide to one aspect of Hungarian intellectual history for those whose interest in Hungary is broader than, but includes, its literature." In the following excerpt from that work, Czigány provides an overview of Móricz's career and literary development.*]

It is a generally accepted view in Marxist literary scholarship that Móricz is the most significant prose writer his native country has ever produced. The explanation for this unreserved praise is complex, but the main factor in the gradual formation of the view lies in the development of the Hungarian novel since the latter part of the nineteenth century, a development which was characterized by the overlong survival of Romantic illusions in Jókaiesque fiction and by the lack of a truly epic, and at the same time realistic, portrayal of Hungarian society—in spite of numerous ambitious attempts at a valid representation of society as a whole. To be sure, re-markable novels, mainly about the decay of the gentry, were written not only by Mikszáth but by other authors as well. However, the long-awaited "realistic" masterpiece—whatever the loosely applied term of Realism means—had never been produced.

The cult of illusion, deeply embedded in the pseudo-Victorian society, produced a wealth of trends in literature, but natural-ly it was incompatible with the Realism that emerged in En-glish, French, German, or Russian fiction. Hungarian au-thors were, more often than not, only able to create psycho-logically valid figures within their own class; while Tolstoy, for example, created great Russian characters out of both aristocrats and serfs, the peasants as depicted in Hungarian fiction by gentry authors were often treated with a patroniz-ing attitude, which, while it created sympathy, produced on the whole unconvincing characters.

Class-consciousness is prominent in Móricz too, except that he looked at the peasantry with an intimate inside knowledge determined by his social origin which, in turn, was also re-sponsible for a certain amount of prejudice working in the op-posite direction. On the other hand, Jókai was the only writer before Móricz who presented an over-all vision of society, and it was a vision distorted by his romantic imagination; Móricz, therefore, is the only author who managed to satisfy Marxist expectations about Realism, with his grim depiction of the world around him, his abundance of naturalistic de-tails, and his entirely new vision of society seen through the eyes of the peasant. This originality made both contemporary critics and later scholarship hail Móricz as the true "voice of the people," who recorded the previously untold fate of the peasantry in literature in a style far removed from the *népies* trend of the middle of the nineteenth century with its Roman-tic overtones. [In a Glossary, Czigány defines *népies* as "of, or pertaining to the people," and calls *népies* "perhaps the most indiscriminately used adjective in Hungarian literature for any type of adaptation or imitation of the language, oral traditions, and unwritten literary products of 'the people' (i.e. the peasantry).''] What is surprising, however, is that Móricz became a significant figure in the *Nyugat* movement, a move-ment marked by its élitist views and its aspirations to sophis-ticated literature; but most of the decadent, enervated, self-centered *Nyugat* authors were attracted by the sharp contrast with themselves which they found in Móricz's robust, full-blooded extroversion. (pp. 323-24)

For long years [Móricz] struggled as a hack writer; he was almost thirty when his first story (**"Seven Pennies"**) was pub-lished in *Nyugat* in 1908; he became famous overnight as one of the most original short-story writers of the day. The auto-biographical **"Seven Pennies"** is a moving tale of poverty, written with dramatic simplicity, and revealing Móricz's ex-ceptional power of characterization. Told in a terse style with sparingly used embellishments, the story brought a feature of compassionate realism to the literary scene which was both new and effective. This unexpected success helped Móricz to overcome his inhibitions as a writer, and he became one of the most prolific Hungarian fiction writers of the present cen-tury.

His first novel, **Pure Gold,** deals with a basic anomaly in East European peasant societies, the rigidity of the class-structure which frequently prevents the self-assertion of talents in men of humble origin. It also bears witness to the urgency and pas-sion of Móricz's plea on behalf of the victims of social dis-

crimination; his over-eagerness to show the "real" face of vil-lage life, however, left its imprint on both plot and construc-tion. Still, he managed to create the prototype of a new peas-ant hero in Dani Turi, whose characterization is convincing enough in spite of a certain degree of exaggeration. Dani Turi is a land-hungry peasant, full of energy, cunning and boister-ous (perhaps somewhat akin to Móricz's own father, who was determined to improve his own lot at all costs). He is also reckless, a peasant Don Juan whose sexual prowess is a source of his constant drive and restlessness and the ultimate cause of his downfall. With Dani Turi the myth of unex-plored primitive forces imprinted in the genetic codes of the peasants (*őserő*) entered Hungarian literature. The novel is not free from naturalistic excesses; Móricz's stern and taci-turn village folk are always driven by the recognition of self-interest and material ambition, and the smell of poverty has penetrated every aspect of the story, yet the unhealthy cli-mate of the novel, the sheer brutality of its sheepskin-clad, half-civilized peasants shows Móricz's lack of illusions about the shocking conditions in which these creatures lived in god-forsaken villages.

All the other novels written in Móricz's first period seem to prove that he knew more about human depravity than about human virtue, and set out to depict everything with a merci-less, biased realism. As he was a born story-teller, he pos-sessed an inexhaustible supply of stories—and not only about the peasantry: his heroes came from all strata of society. He relied exclusively on the infallibility of his own observations, and as a consequence no metaphysical questions arose in his books. He described with a sure pen the narrow confines of provincial existence, and the world of underpaid civil ser-vants in their overfurnished homes, their stifling boredom re-lieved only by crude sensuality. In **Behind God's Back,** he draws a compelling picture of his neurotic and lonely heroine, and her unsuccessful attempts to get away from the dull un-happiness of her life are described in exceptionally fine pas-sages.

The young protestant pastor of **The Torch** proves that if someone makes an ambitious effort at loosening the social strait-jacket which is based on meanness, ignorance, and class egotism, he will soon be faced with defeat; insensitive peas-ants, cynical gentry, and intolerant officials gradually break his enthusiasm, and he ends up by accepting the world as it is; his compromise is fostered by his own weakness and his growing love of comfort. The profoundly idealistic Reverend Matolcsy is the "torch" whose flickering flame is not enough to light the way to social or spiritual progress in the commu-nity he has chosen to serve; he burns out without obtaining his ends. The novel ends with an all-consuming fire in the vil-lage—Matolcsy takes this last chance to be of service, but it is only a desperate gesture; saving the lives of a few people is a heroic act which bestows on him a kind of redemption for his earlier compromise, but also brings about his prema-ture death. The dying Matolcsy is still arguing with God be-cause "everything has come to an end, yet nothing has been resolved."

After World War I Móricz turned to his own childhood for inspiration, and wrote a trilogy which was clearly autobio-graphical; it was the story of Misi Nyilas's adolescence: *Be Faithful unto Death, Teenagers,* and *Wine in Ferment,* of which the first part is far the best. *Be Faithful unto Death* is permeated with an unexpected lyrical warmth, and the inno-cence and naïvety of Misi are refreshing after the sordid affairs described in Móricz's earlier works. Although young Misi is confronted with the inexplicable adult world often enough during his years in the boarding school of the College of Debrecen, he preserves a naïve idealism and goodness of heart. Móricz's deep sympathy for the problems of growing up manifests itself in his depiction of Misi's disappointments, and of experiences which helped him to restore his faith. Moreover his psychological understanding of the developing personality makes the novel a valid work, but above all it is gentleness, a quality rarely found in Móricz's other novels, that makes it remarkable reading.

Finally it is the writer's candour which gives true proportions to the novel; in spite of Misi's noble mind and good intentions he inevitably comes to grief in the miniature society of the boarding school; he is falsely accused and often humiliated. Even if Móricz's message is as didactic as the title suggests, it is not detrimental to the work's artistic value, but only underlines the author's unflagging loyalty to ideas which may help Misi to survive his severe identity crises, and which cause so much heart-searching in his wavering adult heroes, like the Reverend Matolcsy whose ultimate failure is caused by the loss of that youthful idealism of which Misi Nyilas is both a sad victim and a triumphant hero.

Móricz saw no reason to be cheerful about contemporary society, the class distinctions of which he always relentlessly criticized; his yearnings for better social prospects, however, led him inevitably to historical illusionism. The myth of a strong and independent Transylvania in the seventeenth century appealed to him. . . . And indeed, the cunning princes of that mountainous region, cleverly scheming and intriguing to preserve at least an impression of independence in the shadow of the two great Empires of the Austrians and the Turks, have always exercised a special attraction over those Hungarian intellectuals who ascribed the fate of their country to the geographical misfortune of having been in the way of great powers who aspired to the total domination of Eastern Europe.

To the intelligentsia, who had seen two-thirds of historical Hungary lost after World War I, the appeal of the mirage of Transylvania and the manoeuvring between the great powers became more topical than ever. While the Transylvanism of the seventeenth and eighteenth centuries had possibilities, in the twentieth century it could no longer be considered practical politics, as first German expansionism, and later Russian domination illustrated convincingly. What was saddening, though, was that this distant mirage of Transylvania also blurred the vision of even the best intellectuals, whose wisdom and pragmatism in social matters were unquestionable.

The fact that Móricz delved into Transylvanian history can probably be ascribed to the half-conscious attraction to Transylvania which was becoming noticeable in *neo-népies* ideology around that time. The novels *Fairy-Garden, The Great Prince* and *The Shadow of the Sun,* were rewritten several times and their final versions appeared only in 1935 under the title *Transylvania.*

Critics agree that the colourful historic tapestry of this trilogy shows Móricz at his best. The story of the last of the Báthoris, Prince Gábor, and Gábor Bethlen, is meant as a historical lesson for the present, but it is also a powerful character representation. In Báthori Móricz has created an impulsive figure whose unbridled passions make him liable to a downfall similar to Dani Turi's. In spite of the realistic background, Prince

Báthori represents a somewhat Romantic distortion of those vital energies of which certain Móricz heroes seem to possess unlimited quantities. Bethlen, who after the assassination of Báthori dominates the second and third parts of the trilogy, stands for perseverance, common sense, integrity, and statesmanship. He is plagued with the problems of his private life, caught between wife and mistress, the former providing the security of the hearth and the pangs of conscience, the latter bold adventures and stimulation for the imagination. (The incompatibility of marriage partners was a recurrent theme in Móricz's works; he could not solve it in his own private life.)

The main artistic value of the novel is the powerful characterization both of the figures in the foreground and of the host of supporting cast, a wide variety of types, most of them drawn with care. Móricz is successful in creating an authentic atmosphere by his discriminating use of the various layers of language; moreover, in his novels he can write excellent dialogue and compose dramatic scenes, although as a playwright he is insignificant. He fails, however, in the construction of the novel; the various threads of the story seem to diverge as the narrative approaches its conclusion. His planned fourth volume might have created a unified plot, but he never wrote it.

Another dominant theme in the second period of Móricz's career is his social criticism of the gentry's life-style, which had managed to survive World War I and the accompanying social upheavals. *Until Daybreak,* a well-constructed novel, is the story of a drunken night; there is tension in the air, for the occasion is an important one—a wealthy landowner is going to propose to the daughter of the house. When the sandcastle of expectations collapses because of an unforeseen circumstance the tension is released, and in the ensuing drunken revelry Móricz has an opportunity to portray with great dramatic force the devil-may-care attitude of the hosts and their guests. The same is true of *The Gentleman's Way of Having Fun,* a novel about a landowner, Szakhmáry, with progressive ambitions, whose private life leads him to suicide. He has a flair for the spectacular: he throws a gargantuan party, which goes on for days; on the fourth night he sets fire to his manor-house to provide amusement and better lighting for the dancers. The larger-than-life figure of Szakhmáry belongs to that category of heroes in Russian novels who light their cigars with hundred-rouble notes. This is perhaps Móricz's best novel; the traditional technique of the anecdote is employed superbly to advance the plot; most of the background information comes from the anecdotes told by the characters, and at the same time their reactions to, and comments on, these flippant anecdotes expose their inflated pride with an irony which is poignant yet somehow pregnant with tragedy. There is no trace of the class-hatred of Móricz's bitter peasants in this work; he knows that the self-destruction of the gentry, its inability to adapt itself to changed conditions, may eventually imply the breaking of the backbone of Hungarian society.

His criticism of the gentry is, however, merciless in *Relatives.* Hailed by today's critics as Móricz's most important novel, it tells about small-town nepotism and corruption relating to the fate of Kopjáss who, after rising to higher office, becomes innocently involved in illicit transactions, through a web of suddenly emerging uncles, brothers, and cousins, and is driven ultimately to the verge of suicide. Kopjáss is a typical Móricz hero, a crossbreed between Misi Nyilas (innocent) and the Reverend Matolcsy (ambitious idealist), but without their redeeming qualities; although like them he is a victim of circumstance, he is a weak character. It is the grimmest of Móricz's novels—even the scenery seems to be always grey; there is no laughter, no warmth, no true human relations, but instead scarcely disguised selfish motives, pretensions and ugliness are everywhere.

In the last period of his creative life Móricz began once more to write short stories. His virtues—good dialogue, dramatic construction, economy of description—are all displayed in them to the best advantage (e.g. *Barbarians*). Of the rest of his novels, *A Happy Man* deserves special attention; it is the true-life-story of a poverty-stricken peasant, who is satisfied with his lot. Móricz used much of his original interview material, and the book is an unusual mixture of reportage, social indictment, and sociological survey, a clear effort to break with the conventional form of the novel.

In the last years of his life Móricz, handicapped by age and financial problems, seemed to decline in quality, if not in output. Yet he managed to achieve his former standards in at least one nearly flawless piece of writing: *Little Orphan,* the story of a foundling girl told in the first person. Its child heroine, Csöre, like Misi Nyilas, has the unreserved sympathy of Móricz. Her uncompromising attitude to the world, in spite of her perpetual existential insecurity, is not an occasion for blackmailing the reader into weeping at the grim naturalism of the facts; Móricz's genuine concern for his heroine lends the novelette lyrical beauty and authentic pathos.

Móricz's last ambitious undertaking, a vast verbal fresco about Sándor Rózsa, the legendary outlaw of the nineteenth century, originally designed as a trilogy, remained unfinished. The first two volumes, *Sándor Rózsa Spurs His Horse* and *Sándor Rózsa Frowns,* are a cross between history and fiction—the story told in the second volume takes place during the War of Independence in 1848-9. Rózsa belongs to the Dani Turi class of Móricz heroes, perhaps with less apparent show of the Romantic *őserő* ["ancestral or primeval strength"], with less masculine charm, but with the maximum dose of self-assurance and indifference to danger. Móricz enjoyed writing about the popular hero; he worked fast on the manuscript, and there is a decorative exuberance in the novel derived from folklore and embroidered with apparent gusto. While Rózsa and his fellow-outlaws speak the Szeged dialect, Móricz himself came from the Debrecen region, so no wonder authenticity sometimes suffers. The writer himself was dissatisfied with the second volume, and intended to rewrite parts of it, but died on 4 September 1942. (pp. 324-29)

*Lóránt Czigány, "The Writers of the 'Nyugat' (II),"
in his* The Oxford History of Hungarian Literature:
From the Earliest Times to the Present, *Oxford at
the Clarendon Press, 1984, pp. 323-42.*

ADDITIONAL BIBLIOGRAPHY

Cushing, G. F. Introduction to *Hungarian Prose and Verse: A Selection,* edited by G. F. Cushing, pp. xi-xxxv. London: Athlone Press, 1956.

> Briefly discusses Móricz within the context of early twentieth-century Hungarian literature, noting his contribution to literary realism.

Dupee, Frederick. Review of *The Torch,* by Zsigmond Móricz. *The Bookman* (New York), Vol. LXXIV, No. 1 (September 1931): 80-1.

> Commends the realism of *The Torch* but maintains that the novel's dependence upon local concerns renders it obscure to non-Hungarian readers.

Konnyu, Leslie. "Zsigmond Móricz." In his *Modern Magyar Literature: A Literary Survey and Anthology of the XXth Century Hungarian Authors,* pp. 23-4. New York: American Hungarian Review, 1964.

> Brief entry noting some prominent characteristics of Móricz's principal works. A translated excerpt from the short story "Seven Pennies" is appended.

Redman, Ben Ray. "A Human Torch." *New York Herald Tribune Books* 7, No. 52 (6 September 1931): 8.

> Unfavorable review of *The Torch,* criticizing its "fragmentary structure" and describing its mood as "acid, yet somehow powerless."

Reményi, Joseph. "In Memoriam: Zsigmond Móricz." *Books Abroad* 17, No. 1 (Winter 1943): 34-5.

> Commends Móricz as "the great Hungarian realistic novelist" and places him in "the foremost rank of modern Hungarian literature."

Marcel Proust

1871-1922

French novelist, critic, essayist, translator, short story writer, and poet.

The following entry presents criticism of Proust's multivolume novel *A la recherche du temps perdu,* originally published between 1913 and 1927 and collectively translated into English as *Remembrance of Things Past.* For a discussion of Proust's complete career, see *TCLC,* Volumes 7 and 13.

Remembrance of Things Past is among literature's works of highest genius. Renowned for its artistic construction, Proust's masterpiece also offers a social historian's chronicle of turn-of-the-century Parisian society, a philosopher's reflections on the nature of time and consciousness, and a psychologist's insight into a tangled network of personalities. Despite the fact that Proust drew almost exclusively upon a narrow range of characters from the upper classes for his novel, the work has been widely praised by readers and critics for conveying a profound view of all human existence.

Proust was born at Auteuil, which in part served as a model for Combray in *Remembrance of Things Past.* His childhood was sheltered but for the most part comfortably idyllic. In 1880, however, he suffered his first attack of asthma, one of many chronic maladies that affected the acutely sensitive Proust. Nevertheless, his uncertain health did not interrupt his formal education at the Lycée Condorcet, where he was a major contributor to the class magazine, or his attendance at the Ecole des Sciences Politiques, where he studied under Henri Bergson. Neither did his condition keep him from a year of military service, which he recalled as one of the happiest periods of his life. Some commentators suggest that although Proust genuinely suffered from ill health, he sometimes exaggerated it to diminish others' expectations of him. As a young man he moved in the complex society of salon matrons, aristocrats, and literati, distinguishing himself as an entertaining wit with a talent for mimicking others' speech and mannerisms. Particularly applauded were his imitations of Count Robert de Montesquiou, whose flamboyant personality provided some of the character traits for the pederast Baron de Charlus in *Remembrance of Things Past.*

In the mid-1890s Proust was chiefly known as a contributor of short prose works to various Paris reviews. These pieces, collected in *Les plaisirs et les jours (Pleasures and Days, and Other Writings),* are often described as precious, though in retrospect they have gained value as examples of Proust's earliest experiments with the themes and techniques of his major work. Likewise *Jean Santeuil,* Proust's first attempt at extended fiction, served as a rehearsal for many of the characters and scenes in *Remembrance of Things Past* while lacking, in Martin Turnell's phrase, the "richness and complexity" of the later novel. A number of critics have also noted that in *Jean Santeuil* Proust did not utilize the perspective of a first person narrator, which in *Remembrance of Things Past* becomes a unifying device for a vast and complicated scenario.

Proust's most important early work is to be found in the critical writings of *Contre Sainte-Beuve (By Way of Sainte-Beuve),* in which he describes a personal view of literature contrary

to the doctrines of the nineteenth-century critic. Whereas C. A. Sainte-Beuve made no distinction between a writer's life and his work, Proust contended that a work of literature offers a perspective unique to itself, independent of its author's circumstances. Walter A. Strauss explains that Proust was a critic who looked "deeply into the writer's creative personality, discerning the writer's special vision and his method of recreating this vision in terms of literature." This concern with a special vision achieved through art became one of the basic precepts of *Remembrance of Things Past,* which occupied Proust until his death in 1922.

Remembrance of Things Past originally appeared in seven volumes, three of which were not published until after Proust's death. Proust never finished revising these final volumes, and they retain inconsistencies in plot and occasional uncharacteristic abridgments in the narrative where Proust did not have an opportunity to elaborate on incidents in his usual fashion. *Du côté de chez Swann (Swann's Way),* the first volume of *Remembrance of Things Past,* was published in 1913. Like the other volumes in the series, it is a complete novel in itself. However, it also introduces the many themes and motifs—such as memory, jealous love, social ambition, sexual inversion, and the importance of art—that are developed at length in later volumes. In the second volume, *A l'ombre des jeunes filles en fleurs* (*Within a Budding Grove*), the narrator Marcel describes his youthful love for Gilberte Swann. This love, as Wallace Fowlie has observed, is based not on "the satisfaction of the senses," but rather on "the proliferation of the lover's imagination," with the result that Marcel is utterly deceived regarding Gilberte's wanton nature. Such unresolvable and often tragic conflicts between imagination and reality are characteristic of Proustian love.

The third volume of *Remembrance of Things Past, Le côté de Guermantes* (*The Guermantes Way*), won the Prix Goncourt, a national literary prize for young authors, in 1920, and brought Proust international recognition. In *The Guermantes Way,* Proust introduced his most masterfully drawn character, the Baron de Charlus. The elegant Baron is the apotheosis of the French aristocracy as portrayed by Proust in *Remembrance of Things Past;* Charlus's moral corruption and eventual fall parallel the degeneracy and decline of his class. In *The Guermantes Way,* Proust also ironically examined the phenomenon of social ambition, and the disillusionment that often accompanies the achievement of one's social goals. *Sodome et Gomorrhe* (*Cities of the Plain*) explores the theme of homosexuality and corruption. In the novel, sexual inversion, as it is revealed in such unlikely individuals as Charlus and Robert de Saint-Loup, becomes a symbol for the hidden but pervasive evils that afflict society, rendering it shallow, ineffectual, and decadent. Proust also discusses his theory of memory in an important prelude to the second half of this volume, entitled "Les intermittances du coeur" ("The Intermittences of the Heart"). *La prisonnière* (*The Captive*) and *La fugitive* (*The Fugitive*), the fifth and sixth volumes of the series, were not included in Proust's original plan for *Remembrance of Things Past,* and some critics now believe that events in Proust's personal life led him to expand the scheme of his novel to include the story of Albertine with the themes of jealous love and deception. *Le temps retrouvé* (*Time Regained*), the final volume of the work, successfully ties together all of the novel's recurrent themes and motifs. In *Time Regained,* Marcel realizes that memory is the key to the meaning of the past that he has been seeking, and that art has the ability to redeem experience from disillusionment, deception, and the decay of time. Themes that were touched upon throughout the novel are here given full expression. *Remembrance of Things Past* concludes with Marcel's discovery of his own artistic vocation, and his determination to recover his past by writing a novel based on his life.

The title of *A la recherche du temps perdu* is often translated more literally as "In Search of Lost Time" to emphasize the conscious pursuit by the narrator of past selves which have been altered over the years, and for the original qualities of experiences which are effaced by normal memory. For the narrator there are two means of recapturing a former stage of one's life: either through the consciously willed effort of "voluntary memory," or through the unwilled and unexpected outpouring of "involuntary memory." The first yields only limited and deceptive impressions of the past, while the second creates a vivid and faithful recollection. In the absence of religion, memory becomes a vehicle of transcending the annihilation by time and death of all things known in one's life. Sensation, sensibility, and intuition are the keys to the world of lost time, and, as such, supercede the laws of reason, in Proust's view of experience. Another source of triumph over the frustrations of human existence is that of art, which allows viewpoints not possible in mundane experience. Among life's major frustrations are the unstable nature of personal identity and the deceptive quality of private truths subsequently revealed as illusion. Proust used various devices to convey his sense of confusion and disillusionment to the reader of *Remembrance of Things Past.* Most notable among them was his deliberate misrepresentation of certain characters, such as Albertine and Monsieur Vinteuil. Proust allowed Marcel, and consequently the reader, to perceive these characters in a way that is ultimately shown to be false, and contrary to their true natures. Albertine, in particular, dramatically embodies Proust's ideas about the confusing and elusive nature of identity. Critics have long regarded her as one of the most enigmatic characters in all of literature. Although the narrator's relationship with her provides the subject matter for two volumes of *Remembrance of Things Past,* the mystery that surrounds her is never penetrated by Marcel or by the reader. For this reason, she perfectly illustrates Proust's theory that the experience of love is utterly subjective: based entirely in the imagination of the lover, and not, as is commonly thought, on the character of the beloved. Thus, in Proust's view, even romantic love is subject to the "intermittences of the heart," which transform seemingly durable emotions into occasional phenomena without continuity.

Although today the brilliance of Proust's achievement is seldom disputed, in the past his novel was frequently the subject of critical controversy. Its almost overwhelming length and sprawling structure, combined with Proust's reticular and highly original prose style has occasionally led critics to assert that Proust's aesthetic was actually a rationalization of his artistic weakness: his inability to select and reject material. Proust constantly disputed such statements, maintaining that the novel had to be considered as a whole in order for its structure, which is based on the musical leitmotif, to become apparent. One of the most important issues in Proust criticism is the role of Marcel as protagonist and narrator of *Remembrance of Things Past,* and his relationship to Proust himself. Briefly, there is strong evidence for both identifying Proust with Marcel and for isolating the two, and some critics' readings of the novel are more autobiographical than those of others. Perhaps the firmest ground for likening Proust with Marcel is their mutual struggle to realize themselves as artists, with each making art the highest value in his life. The search for lost time ends in the disillusioned abandonment of life and in an affirmative re-creation of life as a work of art.

(See also *Contemporary Authors,* Vols. 104 and 120; and *Dictionary of Literary Biography,* Vol. 65.)

PRINCIPAL WORKS

Les plaisirs et les jours   (short stories, sketches, poetry, and criticism)   1896
   [*Pleasures and Regrets,* 1948; also translated as *Pleasures and Days, and Other Writings,* 1957]
Portraits de peintres   (poetry)   1896
Du côté de chez Swann   (novel)   1913
   [*Swann's Way,* 1922]
A l'ombre des jeunes filles en fleurs   (novel)   1919
   [*Within a Budding Grove,* 1924]
Pastiches et mélanges   (parodies and essays)   1919
Le côté de Guermantes   (novel)   1920
   [*The Guermantes Way,* 1924]

Sodome et Gomorrhe (novel) 1922
    [*Cities of the Plain,* 1927]
La prisonnière (novel) 1923
    [*The Captive,* 1929]
La fugitive (novel) 1925
    [*The Sweet Cheat Gone,* 1930; also published as *The Fugitive* in *Remembrance of Things Past,* 1981]
Le temps retrouvé (novel) 1927
    [*The Past Recaptured,* 1931; also published as *Time Regained,* 1970]
Oeuvres complètes de Marcel Proust. 10 vols. (novels, criticism, short stories, sketches, poetry, parodies, and essays) 1929-36
Correspondance générale de Marcel Proust (letters) 1930
Letters of Marcel Proust (letters) 1949
Jean Santeuil (unfinished novel) 1952
    [*Jean Santeuil,* 1955]
Correspondance avec sa mère: 1887-1905 (letters) 1953
    [*Letters to His Mother* (partial translation), 1956]
‡*A la recherche du temps perdu.* 3 vols. (novel) 1954
    [*Remembrance of Things Past.* 3 vols., 1981]
Contre Sainte-Beuve (criticism) 1954
    [*By Way of Sainte-Beuve,* 1958]
Marcel Proust et Jacques Riviére: Correspondance, 1914-1922 (letters) 1955
Lettres à Reynaldo Hahn (letters) 1956
Choix de lettres (letters) 1965
Lettres retrouvées (letters) 1966
Marcel Proust: Selected Letters 1880-1903 (letters) 1983

---

*These works comprise the multivolume novel *A la recherche du temps perdu* and were first collected in *Oeuvres complètes de Marcel Proust.*

‡This edition of *A la recherche du temps perdu,* compiled by Pierre Clarac and André Ferré for Bibliothèque de la Pléiade, is a corrected edition based on Proust's own notes and galley corrections. It is now considered the standard edition and is the text on which Terence Kilmartin's 1981 revised translation of the novel is based.

ARNOLD BENNETT (essay date 1923)

[*Bennett was an Edwardian novelist who is credited with bringing techniques of European Naturalism to the English novel. His reputation rests almost exclusively on* The Old Wives' Tale *(1908) and the* Clayhanger *trilogy (1910-16), novels which are set in the manufacturing district of Bennett's native Staffordshire and which tell of the thwarted ambitions of those who endure a dull, provincial existence. In the following excerpt, Bennett's remarks typify much of the early praise and condemnation of Proust as a novelist.*]

A few weeks before [Proust's] death, while searching for something else in an overcrowded bookcase, I came across my first edition of *Du côté de chez Swann,* and decided to read the book again. I cared for it less, and I also cared for it more, than in 1913. The *longueurs* of it seemed to me to be insupportable, the clumsy centipedalian crawling of the interminable sentences inexcusable; the lack of form or construction may disclose artlessness, but it signifies effrontery too. Why should not Proust have given himself the trouble of learning to "write," in the large sensc? Further, the monotony of subject and treatment becomes wearisome. (I admit that it is never so distressing in *Swann* as in the later volumes

of *Guermantes* and of *Sodome et Gomorrhe.*) On the other hand, at the second reading I was absolutely enchanted by some of the detail.

About two-thirds of Proust's work must be devoted to the minutiae of social manners, the rendering ridiculous of a million varieties of snob. At this game Proust is a master. (Happily he does not conceal that, with the rest of mankind, he loves ancient blood and distinguished connections.) He will write you a hundred pages about a fashionable dinner at which nothing is exhibited except the littleness and the *naïveté* of human nature. His interest in human nature, if intense and clairvoyant, is exceedingly limited. Foreign critics generally agree that the English novelist has an advantage over the French in that he walks all round his characters and displays them to you from every side. I have heard this over and over again in conversation in Paris, and I think it is fairly true, though certainly Balzac was the greatest exponent of complete display. Proust never "presents" a character; he never presents a situation: he fastens on one or two aspects of a character or a situation, and strictly ignores all the others. And he is scarcely ever heroical, as Balzac was always; he rarely exalts, and he nearly always depreciates—in a tolerant way.

Again, he cannot control his movements: he sees a winding path off the main avenue, and scampers away further and further and still further, merely because at the moment it amuses him to do so. You ask yourself: He is lost—will he ever come back? The answer is that often he never comes back, and when he does come back he employs a magic but illicit carpet, to the outrage of principles of composition which cannot be outraged in a work of the first order. This animadversion applies not only to any particular work, but to his work as a whole. The later books are orgies of self-indulgence; the work has ruined the *moral* of the author: phenomenon common enough.

Two achievements in Proust's output I should rank as great. The first is the section of *Swann* entitled *Un amour de Swann.* He had a large theme here—love and jealousy. The love is physical and the object of it contemptible; the jealousy is fantastic. But the affair is handled with tremendous, grave, bitter, impressive power. The one fault of it is that he lets Swann go to a *soirée musicale* and cannot, despite several efforts, get him away from it in time to save the interest of the situation entire. Yet in the *soirée musicale* divagation there are marvellous, inimitable things.

The second achievement, at the opening of *Sodome et Gomorrhe,* is the psychological picture of the type-pederast. An unpromising subject, according to British notions! Proust evolves from it beauty, and a heartrending pathos. Nobody with any perception of tragedy can read these wonderful pages and afterwards regard the pervert as he had regarded the pervert before reading them. I reckon them as the high-water of Proust.

Speaking generally, Proust's work declined steadily from *Swann. A l'ombre des jeunes filles en fleurs* was a fearful fall, and as volume followed volume the pearls were strung more and more sparsely on the serpentine string. That Proust was a genius is not to be doubted; and I agree that he made some original discoveries in the by-ways of psychological fiction. But that he was a supreme genius, as many critics both

French and English would have us believe, I cannot admit. (pp. 145-48)

Arnold Bennett, "The Last Word," in Marcel Proust: An English Tribute *by Joseph Conrad and others, edited by C. K. Scott Moncrieff, Thomas Seltzer, 1923, pp. 144-48.*

PHILIP KOLB (essay date 1971)

[*Kolb is an American educator and critic who has written extensively on Proust and is the editor of the French edition of Proust's letters. In the following excerpt, he studies Proust's compositional method for* Remembrance of Things Past *through an examination of Proust's notebooks.*]

When Marcel Proust was a student in his philosophy year at the lycée Condorcet, he wrote a composition that his professor, Monsieur Darlu, criticized severely. Across the top of the first page, Monsieur Darlu wrote the comment: "extremely vague and superficial," pointing out with a touch of irony that the selected topic was "very complex." The seventeen-year-old boy had ventured to demonstrate how a scientist draws conclusions enabling him to derive a law from factual knowledge. The grade that young Proust received, out of a possible 20 points, was . . . 4. The professor did, however, make one encouraging remark. He conceded that there was "some progress in composition." The boy deserved encouragement. He would continue to make progress in composition until he eventually became a novelist who, today, is widely recognized to be the greatest whom France has produced in at least one hundred years.

The qualities of his style, the depth of his psychological penetration, the heights of his poetic genius, and the charm of his humour, were indeed appreciated quite early by some of his critics. Despite that recognition, paradoxically enough, the general reading public, even today, seems to retain an image of Proust that is in some respects blurred and distorted. For many people, perhaps a majority, the name of Proust brings to mind a pathetic, Chaplinesque figure, something like the stock character, or caricature, of a Frenchman in English light comedy of a few generations ago, or perhaps a type that Ionesco might conjure up. Proust is still seen as the legendary figure fabricated about 1919, when he first came into the public eye, that same straw man of whom the same tales and anecdotes—half truth and half fiction—are purveyed about the recluse in his cork-lined room, with his effete, ingratiating manner and his excessive tipping of the doorman at the Ritz. Need it be pointed out that the person so portrayed fails to measure up to the sort of man capable of producing so monumental a masterpiece as *A la recherche du temps perdu?*

What is perhaps a cause for greater concern is the fact that his novel is frequently misrepresented. Even professional people sometimes write about it without having read it with sufficient comprehension. They speak, for instance, of Proust's "cycle" or "series" of novels, or of the author's indifference to morality or religion. And the potential reader, curious about Proust, may end up reading disquisitions on him and his life, or on his work, instead of reading his *novel* to understand and enjoy it. Admittedly this is not easy. Proust has nothing in common with authors of popular fiction or adventure stories. He cannot be expected to appeal to the same public as Simenon or even Sartre. His style inevitably perplexes most of those who first encounter it; those serpentine sentences are bound to exasperate or discourage the average reader, unless and until one has become inured to Proust's sentence structure. And that takes time and patience. Even then, the uncompromising length of his novel is a challenge to the most intrepid reader. And there are other problems. When we consider the myriad of obstacles that the ailing Proust had to overcome, first, to get his material in order, to write it and get it into print, and then to persuade critics and public to read a novel so completely unconventional, we marvel that he did succeed, against countless odds, in winning for it such a multitude of readers in every civilized country in the world. (pp. 25-6)

Proust was an author devoted to the search for Truth. Assuredly then, he deserves better than to be made the perennial victim of misinformation and misunderstanding about his aims and his accomplishments. While he did not claim to give us ultimate truth, he did seek it; and he presents what he found in his novel. So we can at least strive to discover the truth about him and his work. We shall examine certain prevalent ideas about his novel—bearing a singular similarity with notions entertained by some of Denis Diderot's critics concerning the works of that renowned encyclopedist—and then we shall go behind the scenes, so to speak, to find out whether those ideas are corroborated by evidence of Proust's practices in the actual composition of his work. It is possible to make such an excursion by means of a huge collection of Proust's manuscripts, notebooks and other materials which the Bibliothèque Nationale has acquired from Proust's family.

My examination of these materials has convinced me that Proust's notebooks hold the key to many problems concerning his work. The solution of these problems depends on our capability in deciphering Proust's handwriting—at times almost illegible—and on our being sufficiently conversant with Proust's universe to penetrate the full significance of that mass of documents. As we shall see, the notebooks reveal some of the hidden intent of his novel, and some of the secrets of his methods and practices in planning and writing it. We shall then see how different he was from the kind of novelist many of his critics have supposed him to be.

In this connection, we pause to consider a curious parallel between Proust and Diderot. It is worthy of note that Diderot was one of the few French writers of the eighteenth century with whom Proust has any real affinities. Diderot seems to foreshadow Proust in observing the contradictions and inconsistencies of human conduct. He dared to depart from literary traditions in character depiction by showing in fictional form how complex man's nature really is. Proust would carry that idea a step farther, systematizing and stylizing the presentation of his characters in an invention that he chose to call his "prepared" character (*"le personnage 'préparé' "*). In Diderot these tendencies seem already to be suggested in the whimsical paradox of such a title as *Est-il bon? est-il méchant?*—where Diderot refrains from drawing conclusions. Here we have the innovation of an author who makes no claim to omniscience. We find another example of what Proust would try to demonstrate in this title: "Sur l'inconséquence du jugement public de nos actions particulières."

An even more marked parallel can be seen, however, in the similarity of attitudes expressed by Diderot's and Proust's respective critics. Diderot has frequently been reproached for the alleged weaknesses of improvisation, disorder, and the inconsistency with which he delineates character. But recently,

Professor Pommier's research on *Le rêve de d' Alembert* has shown that Diderot actually exercised considerable care in the revision of that particular work. Professor Etiemble, in an article full of spice and vinegar, has examined the structure and meaning of the *Pensées philosophiques,* and takes to task such old-line critics as Daniel Mornet for their strictures concerning Diderot's composition, his alleged improvisation and the incoherence of his characters. Still more recently, Professor Roger Kempf has made some pertinent observations along the same lines in his book entitled *Diderot et le roman.*

Oddly enough, these very same criticisms of improvisation, disorder and lack of consistency in character depiction, have been formulated against Proust. They were put into circulation when *Swann* was first published in November 1913, and have been repeated periodically from that day almost down to this. A few brief quotations will show the tenor of these charges. When that first volume of Proust's novel came out, most of the critics judged it from a narrowly traditional point of view, applying to it the standards of the so-called classical French novel. Paul Souday, literary critic of *Le Temps,* one of the big-wigs of the critical world, thought that *Du côté de chez Swann* resembled an English novel, and remarked superciliously, "We French and Latins prefer a more synthetic process." Another influential critic, Henri Ghéon, in a long review article in the *Nouvelle Revue Française,* gave the novel some ambiguous words of praise interlarded with back-handed censure. He was the first, I believe, to accuse Proust of making no choice or selection of material, of simply spreading out before the reader in a confused, haphazard way what he has dredged up from the depths of consciousness. The same critic charged Proust with a lack of logic in character depiction, of seeking the diverse and contradictory aspects of a character instead of tracing the line of his development. Ironically enough, some writers (André Maurois for example) have recently credited Ghéon with being one of Proust's discoverers! We shall return to this question later. Here, then, are the very same criticisms that had been levelled against Diderot. They were to be repeated by other critics as the successive volumes of *A la recherche du temps perdu* issued forth. When *A l'ombre des jeunes filles en fleurs* came out, in 1919, Proust won the Goncourt prize and suddenly found himself famous. But no sooner had the prize been awarded than a hue and cry was raised. A critic named Gasquet called Proust the "crudest of improvisers"; it seems probable that he had scarcely had time to glance at the novel. The literary critic of an important newspaper, *Le Journal des Débats,* whose name was Jean de Pierrefeu, greeted the award with surprise and indignation. Caustically, he said that Proust was known for some clever and malicious parodies, and a compact volume having the bizarre title *Du côté de chez Swann* and neither a beginning nor an end. Acidly, the critic went on: "To that first volume he has added a second one which prolongs the first, and he is preparing two more on the same theme. There is nothing to prove that he will stop going on his merry way; in my opinion, only fatigue or death can stop him in the task he has undertaken of searching for his lost time." This last pun simply echoes one of Ghéon's insidious jibes. These are mere samples of the critical incomprehension that plagued Proust throughout his career.

We return then to the question: how can we ascertain the facts as to Proust's aims and achievements? We have one piece of evidence of capital importance concerning the structure of his novel. In a letter addressed to Madame Emile Straus in August 1909, Proust states: "I have just begun—and finished—a whole long book." Curiously enough, this important statement has been misinterpreted by one of Proust's most distinguished biographers. Nevertheless, it is clear from this and corroborative testimony that Proust—in the spring of 1909—had written a first draft of the introductory and concluding chapters of his novel. The intervening portions he was to write subsequently. By proceeding in this manner, he was able to lay a solid foundation for the structural elements of his novel before going on to fill in its central narrative parts, where he develops his characters and illustrates his themes. In the opening chapter, set in the quaint provincial town of Combray, he presents the principal themes that will recur intermittently to form a unifying network throughout the novel. He also names some of the principal characters and the places that form a setting for the novel. In the last chapter of *Le temps retrouvé,* he will explain the significance of the themes set forth at the beginning, and give a final summing-up, revealing the goal towards which the narrator's seemingly aimless peregrination has been leading, and the lessons he has learned about life and art. That is how the narrator discovers his vocation: he will regain past time—time passed aimlessly—through Art.

On the question of whether or not Proust improvised his novel, a decisive answer can best be found in the notebooks he used in its preparation. They bear testimony to the great amount of painstaking work which went into the planning and execution of the final version. The archives in the Bibliothèque Nationale include eighty-two large notebooks and four small ones, as well as a quantity of manuscript materials, typescripts and proof sheets. But that collection is not complete. Altogether Proust must have used at least one hundred and thirty notebooks, during the composition of his novel, in addition to the other materials. Nor does this estimate take into account the manuscript of his early novel about Jean Santeuil, covering well over one thousand pages in print, where the young author tried his hand at so many of the same themes, characters and episodes that later were to reappear, in revised and perfected form, in the novel of his mature years.

A general survey of the notebooks discloses three types of entries. First, there are the passages we can recognize as belonging to Proust's novel in various stages of its composition. Then, there are the many notations he scribbled down to remind himself about some aspect of the novel's form or content which he wanted to bear in mind later in writing some particular section. And, finally, there are certain texts extraneous to the novel, such as literary criticism or pastiches.

We can give only a passing glance to the actual texts of the novel. But they show clearly how mistaken the critics were to insinuate that Proust had simply set out to write the random thoughts that came into his head. Certain passages he rewrote many times, revising and correcting indefatigably. These texts belong for the most part to the early years of the novel's composition, before he had acquired the stylistic mastery that marks practically everything he wrote during the last decade of his life.

Evidence against the charge of improvisation is even more overwhelming when we consider the many notations concerning his plans for the structure of the novel, the balance and symmetry of its parts, and the details of its composition. At times he would jot down the outline for an entire section. In one such notation, he reminds himself of the contrast he wishes to obtain between the Narrator's first and second visits to the seaside resort called Balbec. The note is labelled "Capitalissime," that is to say, *of the utmost importance,* and begins:

> Second trip to Balbec. First I show that I had come the first time to seek the unknown, now I come looking for what is known to me. I had come there seeking an eternal mist, etc. I come looking for memories of dining behind the blue windows with the sun's rays on the shutter (perhaps I should place here what I say about returning to Balbec in the part already written). I had come to look for a Persian church. I was coming to seek what Elstir had told me of the church and the seas he had painted and which I'll find in spite of myself (that will explain without my saying so, the descriptions of Turneresque seas). I had come for an unknown society. I was coming now above all because I knew everybody.

The reference to "Turneresque seas" alludes to Proust's descriptions of the sea, evocative as Turner's paintings as interpreted by Ruskin. Clearly these descriptions are intended to illustrate Elstir's vision of nature and his impressionistic conception of the art of painting. Another such note gives the arrangement of scenes in the third volume, *Le côté de Guermantes.* Still another is headed: "The articulation of this chapter can be . . ." and is followed by a listing of the events in the final chapter. These samples show what attention Proust devoted to problems of structure and organization, and how he calculated his effects, working out in advance the slightest details in the distribution and counterbalancing of scenes and sections.

Another category of notations deals with the characters in the novel. Here we see to what a great extent Proust relies on his memory of persons he had known, their actions, speech and even gestures in actual conversations and incidents. It is evident that he bore specific models in mind for each character, and almost every one is a composite creation. Proust has himself stated, towards the end of *Le temps retrouvé,* speaking of the novelist in general terms: ". . . there isn't a gesture of his characters, a quirk, an accent, which has not been inspired by memory; there is not a name of an imaginary character beneath which he cannot see sixty names of persons seen, of whom one has posed for a grimace, another for the monocle, this one for a fit of anger, that one for the impatient thrust of an arm, etc."

In one notebook, I find a curious sidelight on Proust's manner of composing or compounding his characters. It concerns the character named Bloch, a school friend of the Narrator who is so precocious that he considers the supreme merit of poetry to consist in having absolutely no meaning. He is also precocious in other ways, since he is the first to introduce the Narrator to a house of ill fame. But he does lend the Narrator a book by Bergotte, who will become the Narrator's favourite living author. Unfortunately, Bloch makes a bad impression on the Narrator's family, who find him objectionable not because of any prejudice but because he is ill-mannered and irresponsible. Bloch confirms this impression by his rude and tactless behaviour. He had begun by annoying the Narrator's father, who, seeing him come in with wet clothes, had asked him with keen interest: "Why, M. Bloch, is there a change in the weather; has it been raining? I can't understand it; the barometer has been 'set fair'." This drew from Bloch nothing more instructive than: "Sir, I am absolutely incapable of tell-

ing you whether it has been raining. I live so resolutely apart from physical contingencies that my senses no longer trouble to inform me of them."

Finally, Bloch had upset the whole household when he arrived an hour and a half late for luncheon, covered with mud from head to foot, making not the least apology, merely saying: "I never allow myself to be influenced in the slightest degree either by atmospheric disturbances or by the arbitrary divisions of what is known as Time. I would willingly reintroduce to society the Chinese opium pipe or the Malayan kriss, but I am wholly and entirely without instruction in those infinitely more pernicious (besides being quite bleakly bourgeois) implements, the umbrella and the watch."

Bloch is the chap who, in Madame de Villeparisis' drawing-room, knocks over a vase containing flowers and spills all the water on the carpet. Simultaneously, another guest, admiring the hostess as she paints flowers, happens to say to her: "Really, you have the fingers of a fairy." Bloch takes this remark to be an ironic reference to his clumsiness; and, to cover up his shame, instead of apologizing he affects an insolent bravado and retorts: "It's not of the slightest importance; I'm not wet."

Here is the notation concerning Bloch in one of Proust's notebooks: "Combine in his speech the conversation of Max Lazard, Bernstein, Gregh and Lanson. . . ." We see here the process of amalgamation at work. The first name, Max Lazard, was that of a well-known, erudite economist who had married into the Ellisson family, whom Proust had known from childhood. The second model is one of the foremost playwrights of Proust's time, and one of his friends, Henri Bernstein. The third one, Fernand Gregh, was a poet of considerable reputation with whom Proust had been friendly since his early twenties, and a future academician. Gregh is the only one of the four who has previously been recognized as a model of the character Bloch. Assuredly the most surprising of the four names is that of Lanson. This name appears nowhere in Proust's correspondence, and I knew nothing of Proust having met anyone of that name. Checking the Paris directories of the period, I found only one listing of the name Lanson, that of Gustave Lanson, the Sorbonne professor, author of the celebrated history of French literature. I still was dubious that the eminent Lanson could have been a model for the vulgar Bloch. As far as I know, he was not even Jewish. But I did observe that his name is linked with that of Gregh, in the notebook entry, and followed by the parenthetical remark: ("these last two 3rd December"). On rereading Gregh's memoirs, I found an explanation for the linking of the two names. For Gregh tells how he had become friendly with Lanson—it was indeed the Sorbonne professor!—who had a cottage in the Fontainebleau region, nearby, where Gregh and his family used to spend their vacations. Gregh even calls attention to Lanson's conversation, which, of course, reflected his vast erudition. It seems safe to assume, therefore, that Proust had met Lanson through Gregh, and that he was similarly struck with the quality of his conversation, studded with literary quotations. In Bloch's speech, we have then an amalgamation of elements taken from these four models, and probably others as well.

Curiously enough, although Bloch represents a non-assimilated Jewish milieu, only two of the four original models named in our source had Jewish origins. Yet it is largely on the basis of Proust's portrayal of Bloch and his family that the author has been accused of antisemitism. To my mind there is little justification for the charge. He had close ties with the Jewish people, and I find no evidence that he ever attempted to hide or deny these relationships. If Bloch is a buffoon and a boor, he is so because Proust saw him that way, just as he saw Swann, also Jewish, as a man of tact and distinction. He considered it the duty of a novelist to be impartial, showing the nature of man and society as he views them.

In actual practice he assembled the elements of each character in much the fashion he states in the passage quoted earlier from his final volume. He appears then to be justified in claiming, as he does in his famous dedicatory epistle addressed to Jacques de Lacretelle: ". . . there are no keys for the characters of this book, or else there are eight or ten for a single one. . . ." Not only does this statement apply to characters, their physique, habits, facial expressions, their gestures, attitudes, voice and pronunciation, but also to Vinteuil's music, and even to descriptions of churches, all inspired by specific models that Proust had observed, that he remembered and artfully moulded together in his immortal creations. Proust's notebooks show us that he collected the elements for his characters much in the manner of the entomologist gathering species. He even affixes to his notes concerning certain characters, as a sort of label, the names of the persons he is thinking of as he plans certain passages.

Even the metaphors associated with certain characters are carefully selected for use as leitmotif. Thus he specifies, in one of his notes:

> Extremely important. For what I think I possess in Albertine there must be some of the most beautiful images of Balbec, for example the blue mountains of the sea (which I can perhaps indicate as reappearing when I hear music in the morning so that Albertine reminding me of the music reminds me of the blue mountains but this is not necessary (since the music isn't perhaps until later). In any case solid metaphors and the same ones well linked.

This note shows us how he prepares passages in *A l'ombre des jeunes filles en fleurs* and *La prisonnière,* where he achieves such superb poetic effects associating Albertine with the sea.

Obviously, Proust had nothing in common with the writer who simply improvises as he writes. Like Balzac, he made numerous marginal additions to his manuscript and proof sheets. Céleste Albaret used to paste additional pages into his notebooks at the sides or bottom of the sheets, making elongated accordion-like pages that extend in some instances as much as six feet in length. But such insertions, at least in Proust's case, are not necessarily after-thoughts. They may well be passages that Proust had planned or actually written earlier; he may simply have hesitated to choose the place where their insertion would be the most effective. In some instances he wrote alternative passages, as in the case of Saniette's death. Proust did not live long enough to make the necessary corrections.

Such interpolations inevitably add to the over-all length of Proust's text; they pose the question: is Proust's novel too long? This is a fair question, and it deserves a fair answer. What justification is there for a novel three or four thousand pages long? Admittedly, this is a matter of proportion. It depends on the aims of the author, and the measure of his achievement.

The plot he selected was basically simple: the Narrator's quest of a vocation. Only the significant episodes in that quest are included; but they are told in full or, we might say, in depth: the scene of his mother's goodnight kiss, marking his parents' failure to cure the child's neurotic tendencies; his early ambitions to become a writer, marked by a consultation with Monsieur de Norpois, who instils doubt in the child concerning his own literary talents; his initiation by la Berma to dramatic art; his introduction by Bloch to the work of Bergotte, and by Gilberte Swann, to the writer himself, who teaches him some lessons about literature, and to Elstir, who teaches him about art; experience of love, through Gilberte and Albertine; experience of society, through Madame de Villeparisis and the duchesse de Guermantes; experience of friendship, through Saint-Loup; knowledge of sexual aberrations, through Mademoiselle Vinteuil and the baron de Charlus. His life at Balbec—where he meets the Guermantes clan and Albertine—he owes to Gilberte's father, Charles Swann. These experiences lead him to conclude that happiness is attainable neither through friendship nor love. His doubts about the reality of art are dispelled by hearing Vinteuil's posthumous work, and, encouraged by Vinteuil's example, he finally decides on the pursuit of a nobler happiness through artistic creativity in the writing of his novel.

Time is the novel's great theme, as its title indicates. As Proust explained when his first volume appeared, he wanted to isolate "that invisible substance of Time"; such an experiment required duration. Events of purely social significance, such as a marriage towards the end of the novel between persons who, in the first volume, had belonged to different social milieux (Gilberte Swann and Robert de Saint-Loup), would indicate the passage of time, taking on, as he put it, "the beauty of patina on leaden surfaces at Versailles that Time has shrouded in an emerald scabbard." Then, "as a village which, while the train winds along its way, appears to us first on the right, then on the left, the diverse aspects of the same character will seem, in the eyes of others, like successive and different people, giving us the sensation that Time has elapsed." Certain characters, as we shall see, turn out to be different from what they had appeared to be earlier, as in life. Here again are the characters he had "prepared" in the first volume so that they would do later exactly the opposite of what we should have expected. A novelist can hardly hope to achieve such objectives unless his novel has considerable amplitude.

Despite this need for liberal dimensions, the notebooks show us that an impressive amount of material was sacrificed. Such passages include entire episodes (concerning Odette Swann, for instance, or the baronne Putbus) as well as notations for dialogue or description. Then there are some striking cases of condensation. I find an earlier text, for example, of a comic episode telling of Proust's little brother Robert's separation from a pet goat. In the revised version Proust has substituted the Narrator for his brother, and eliminated the other members of the family, even the goat. Only his mother remains; it is she who discovers the Narrator bidding a tearful farewell, not to a goat but to his beloved hawthorn bushes. The original version covers seven full pages of the printed text; they have been reduced to one paragraph of just twenty-five lines.

The amount of material he sacrificed in this manner must have been considerable. Contrary to the general impression of Proust, as we have seen, he has on occasion condensed his text rigorously, or eliminated material entirely. In a letter to Robert Dreyfus, he expresses indignation because one of his critics had accused him of noting everything; he protests:

"No, I don't note anything. He is the one who makes notes. Not a single time does one of my characters close a window, wash his hands, put on his overcoat, make an introduction. If there is anything new in this book, it's that, and it's not intentional. I'm just too lazy to write things that bore me." We should perhaps not take this statement too literally. Proust simply means that he includes details only when they are relevant and significant; he feels that nothing in his novel is really superfluous. And every element is interlocked with the rest.

On the question of his novel's length and its complexity, I find one inscription in the notebooks that is illuminating. Proust is outlining an unexpected twist in the relationship between Charlie Morel, the baron de Charlus and others; and he adds this explanation: ". . . things are more complicated than people believe, complexity as well as the symmetry that organizes it, being an element of beauty." Here, I believe, is one of the tenets of Proust's artistic credo, one of the secrets of his art. Not only does he strive for certain effects through the architectural organization and symmetry of his novel's parts; he considers that the complex adjustment of that inner structure adds an element of truth, and, as a consequence, contributes to the beauty of the whole. Whether or not we agree, we can see that this complexity is intentional; it is studied; and it has an aesthetic *raison d'être*. Proust's aim was to imitate the sort of complexity we encounter in life itself. The effect obtained is something akin to that achieved by Mozart in the finale of the *Jupiter* symphony, where he combines five themes in counterpoint.

That complexity is at once apparent in Proust's characters. For, as he had explained, he presents them at first according to their reputation in society, or the Narrator's first impressions of them, so that they seem to have certain traits and to belong to a certain type; but on better acquaintance, they are revealed to be quite different from what those first impressions seemed to imply. A good example is the composer Vinteuil, who appears at first to be a sad, timid, insignificant piano-teacher; after his death, his music will reveal his true inner nature, which, on the contrary, is joyful and audacious, filled with the inner conviction of a man possessed of great creative powers. So Proust has purposely misled us; imitating real life, he wishes to show how false our first impressions may be. But this is an artful, stylized imitation of life, that Proust varies to suit individual cases in the novel. When the critic Ghéon complained that Proust's characters were illogical, he had simply failed to comprehend an original technique of character presentation. He had failed also to note that Proust was making use, in an original way, of observations about erratic quirks in human nature which Diderot had made before him in a less systematic manner. These successive revelations concerning Proust's characters have an additional function in his novel. For each new perspective contributes to our impression of the passage of time. This, as we have indicated, is one of the novel's major themes. Here then is that kind of complexity which Proust uses to enhance his artistic effects.

An illustration of another sort of complexity in the development of character can be seen summarily in the portrait of the princesse de Parme. The Narrator, when presented to her at a dinner in the salon of the duchesse de Guermantes, is struck by her friendly, almost humble manner; he explains it in this humorous, litany-like recital of the Princess's education:

Her friendliness sprang from two causes. The first

and more general was the education which this daughter of Kings had received. Her mother (not merely allied by blood to all the royal families of Europe but furthermore—in contrast to the Ducal House of Parma—richer than any reigning Princess) had instilled into her from her earliest childhood the arrogantly humble precepts of an evangelical snobbery; and today every line of the daughter's face, the curve of her shoulders, the movement of her arms seemed to repeat the lesson: "Remember that if God has caused you to be born on the steps of a throne you ought not to make that a reason for looking down upon those to whom Divine Providence has willed (wherefore praised be His name) that you should be superior by birth and fortune. On the contrary, you must suffer the little ones. Your ancestors were Princes of Trèves and Juliers from the year 647; God has decreed in His bounty that you should hold practically all the shares in the Suez Canal and three times as many Royal Dutch as Edmond de Rothschild; your pedigree in a direct line has been established by genealogists from the year 63 of the Christian Era; you have as sisters-in-law two Empresses. Therefore never seem, in your speech, to be recalling these great privileges, not that they are precarious (for nothing can alter antiquity of race, while the world will always need petrol), but because it is useless to point out that you are better born than other people or that your investments are all gilt-edged, since everybody knows these facts already. Be helpful to the needy. Furnish to all those whom the bounty of Heaven has done you the favour of placing beneath you as much as you can give them without forfeiture of your rank, that is to say, help in the form of money, even your personal service by their sick-beds, but never (bear well in mind) invite them to your parties, which would do them no possible good and, by weakening your own position, would diminish the efficacy of your benevolent activities.

We have seen something of Proust's aims, his practices and his achievements. His philosophy professor, back in 1888, had been wise to encourage him for his progress in composition. Young Proust learned his lesson of avoiding any tendency to be vague or superficial. We have seen how he bases his slightest observation on the memory of living models. He never would overcome his penchant for complex subjects; that is because he could see more than most of us. But he would know how to make complexity serve his artistic purposes. Nor would he lose interest in the subject selected for that school composition: the problem of deriving the laws of nature from observable facts. Indeed he would spend most of his life probing, with a scientist's curiosity and tenacity, the psychological laws that determine human conduct. But he would do much more. For he would transform the manifold observations stored up in his phenomenal memory, through his powers of imagination, his poetic fantasy, his humour, and the magic of a style which is perhaps his greatest attribute, to create one of the enduring works of fiction. Many who enter the labyrinth of his novel may get lost and give up. There are no short cuts. But few of those who persevere all the way fail to find the journey richly rewarding. (pp. 26-37)

Philip Kolb, "The Making of a Novel," in Marcel Proust, 1871-1922: A Centennial Volume, *edited by Peter Quennell, Simon and Schuster, 1971, pp. 25-37.*

B. G. ROGERS (essay date 1971)

[*In the following excerpt, Rogers examines the important influence on Proust of several nineteenth-century authors.*]

[In] many respects, *A la recherche* is a masterly synthesis of most of the conflicting aspirations of the nineteenth century; and it is not difficult to catch traces of all the most important "movements" and "schools" operating between 1800 and 1900 in the story of Marcel's self-discovery. Indeed, that long, rich and often anguished study of the growth of the narrator's vocation to be a writer is achieved precisely through his confrontation with the works of artists both living and dead, and most particularly with the novelists who preceded him and whom he is finally determined to emulate.

But if *A la recherche* is a summing up of the nineteenth century, it also opens the door to most of the later developments in the novel of our own time. I can perhaps best illustrate this backward and forward looking quality of the work by tracing a line between two authors who at first sight seem to have little in common with each other: the minor novelist and short story writer Barbey d'Aurevilly, and the experimental novelist of our own day Nathalie Sarraute. It seems a far cry from the overblown romantic prose of the *Diaboliques,* a set of six stories dealing with love, death and crimes of all kinds in the Paris and Normandy of the eighteen-sixties, to the meticulous, disembodied narratives of Madame Sarraute's novels, like *Martereau,* where nothing seems to happen, where the plot disintegrates deliberately in the final pages, and the narrator asks himself whether all that he has been experiencing ever happened at all. And yet a line can be drawn between them, by placing Proust in the centre, and tracing, backwards, his debt to Barbey, and forwards his effect on Nathalie Sarraute.

Proust made no secret of his liking for the works of Barbey d'Aurevilly; and his name crops up in the novel in one of Marcel's conversations with Albertine, where the future novelist turns critic and analyses a distinctive characteristic which recurs in all the works of that writer. What Proust particularly noted, I think, in Barbey, was his ability to present a seemingly normal situation and then to turn it inside out, revealing all kinds of hidden secrets, memories and scandals behind the unassuming façades that he has first established. This preoccupation with the apparent and the real recurs at much greater length in *A la recherche,* and in fact becomes one of the major themes of the work, developing into the various characters' interest in lying, jealousy and their double, sometimes triple, lives. And it is this very theme which gives animation to the works of Nathalie Sarraute, who takes it one stage further, and develops a theory of "conversation and sub-conversation," where the meaning given to words has one set of resonances on the surface, and another beneath the surface, so that the apparent banality of a phrase, like the apparent banality of the situation in any one of the stories from the *Diaboliques,* may suddenly reveal another world unexpectedly and dangerously existing at another level.

That example, which it might be profitable to examine more closely in another context, was merely intended to show how Proust was affected by even minor writers in the nineteenth century, deepening themes which they treated, exploring them in relation to his own preoccupations and drawing them into the stuff of his own creation, while at the same time opening up paths for later novelists to explore in their own distinctive ways. So when we come to paint the general picture of Proust's literary heritage from the nineteenth century, we must not forget that he stands at the crossroads, as it were, and also looks resolutely forwards to some of the most original and experimental writing of today.

In one respect, however, I have no hesitation in placing Proust firmly in the nineteenth century. A broad, overall survey reveals it as a period that began in chaos, and which in both its literary and political history attempted to impose order and coherence on that chaos. It was a century which exploded into life with the French Revolution of 1789, saw the birth of romanticism, the school of "art for art's sake," the realistic novel, symbolism and naturalism, all, in their way, attempts to give meaning and order to man and his aspirations. All of these various searchings for coherence are paralleled by the external history of the time, the quest for political stability, the choice and rejection of various forms of government, all operating against the background of the steadily advancing industrial revolution and the continued rise in importance of money and the bourgeoisie. It is also a period of time dominated by the presence, and subsequently by the memory, of one man, Napoléon Bonaparte; and it is no mere coincidence that the heroic stature of his achievements, and even of his failures, is reflected in many of the writers of that time. Hugo and Balzac are both titanic figures; Hugo attempted, like many others but with a greater measure of success, to write the modern French epic in his *Légende des siècles,* once again an attempt to explain humanity in relation to its past and its future.

Balzac attempted to sum up all the characteristics of Restoration society in France, another quest for a perspective which would place modern man in an understandable framework, by explaining the forces at work in the new society which had taken the place of the disintegrating empire. His vast, ambitious series of interrelated novels, with their overall title *La comédie humaine* is, like Hugo's *Légende des siècles,* a kind of "summum," a project which seeks to embrace everything and to place everything in a coherent relationship with everything else. Zola, of course, carries on the same tradition, albeit in a cruder and over-simplified way, with his set of interconnecting novels, which chronicle the lives of a family in the Second Empire, under Napoléon's successor. And finally, not published in entirety until 1927, we have *A la recherche du temps perdu,* one of whose aims is to paint a picture of the upper bourgeoisie and aristocracy which flourished right up until its virtual destruction, at least in its life-style as Proust records it, with the onset of the First World War. But *A la recherche* goes further. It attempts to create a coherent set of aesthetic laws within a self-contained, some critics say "circular," construction which justifies itself. One more link in the chain which stretches, it is not unjustifiable to say, from the centralizing forces of Napoléon's empire building right up to the polarizing "laws" of Proust's novel of social, aesthetic and psychological observation. And in this respect, Proust is unquestionably a man of the nineteenth century.

Among his other literary forebears, I should briefly in this context mention Baudelaire and the Symbolist poets, one of whose central preoccupations was to map the hidden affinities connecting all phenomena, and to sum up the individual consciousness and experience in those terms. Indeed, the shift from a mainly socially orientated edifice like the *Comédie humaine* to a mainly aesthetically preoccupied quest for order and explanation in, for example, Baudelaire's *Fleurs du mal* is itself reflected in Proust, whose own work merges the two,

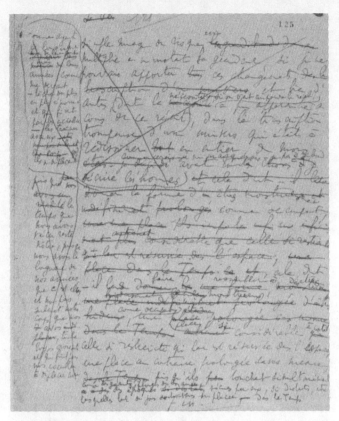

Manuscript of the last page of A la recherche du temps perdu.

and presents Marcel's slow elaboration of an aesthetic code against the background of a chronicle of the social changes of his day. But what I wish to emphasize is the nature and stature of the attempt, the great, vaulting ambition behind all of the works I have been mentioning, an ambition, as Proust himself remarks when discussing Balzac, that gives a greater value to the novels as a whole than to any one of them taken individually, the whole, if you like, being greater than the sum of its parts. Now, Proust's novel was never conceived as a series of parts; but the desire to embrace the totality of his experience is very akin to the recurrent obsession of nineteenth-century writers to be all-embracing in one or another field. And in my opinion, Proust is the greatest of them all, since he comes nearest to achieving that aim.

Another tradition, not originating in the nineteenth century, but fostered and developed by it in the writers of the romantic period, is the preoccupation with the self, a tradition of introspective self-observation and examination, that stems largely from the *Confessions* of Jean-Jacques Rousseau. When one opens the novel at its first page, and reads the famous lines on sleep and the strange, evocative world which lies somewhere between sleep and waking, it is clear that we are entering a world that has been partially shaped by the great romantic tradition, by introspective writers like Chateaubriand, Lamartine, and the Hugo of the *Contemplations*. And yet it is a devastatingly lucid world of self-analysis, not suffused by the soft, hazy glow of, say, Lamartine's *Méditations,* although often sharing the lyricism and poetry of the early romantics. Proust has taken the century's preoccupation with the self, with the relationship existing between the self and the outside world, and its later development into a quest for the clarification of the relationship between the artist and society—he has taken this preoccupation and merged it into the framework of his own self-discovery. One might say that the whole tide of self-analytical prose, which includes the novels of analysis like *Adolphe,* by Benjamin Constant, or *Dominique,* by the painter Eugène Fromentin, culminates in the novel that searches for the identity of the self in past time.

In speaking earlier of the nineteenth century in general terms, I attempted to emphasize one of its major characteristics, namely that of seeking again and again, in varying ways, to impose order on the increasingly complex world of modern man. One of the most disappointing aspects of these attempts, and one which has had a profound effect on our own times, since we have blindly inherited the major thesis to which many philosophers and writers held towards the end of the century, is the increasing trust that was placed in science and materialistic philosophies. When we think of the writings of Hippolyte Taine, the philosopher, historian and critic, and recall the widespread influence of his thought on thinkers and writers, including perhaps the greatest and most imaginative of the later novelists of the century, Zola, we have little difficulty in forming some idea of the general intellectual climate of the eighteen-seventies, the period in which Proust himself was born. Underlying most of Taine's writings is the notion that the human being is the product of a predetermined equation between physical and psychological phenomena, a theory that owes not a little to the equally widespread positivistic ideas also current in the second half of the century. In the field of literary creation, Zola's famous preface to the Rougon-Macquart cycle of novels distinctly echoes this theory, along with those of Lucas and Claude Bernard.

Thus it was on a wave of naturalistic literature that Proust came to maturity, although he also read widely in the literature that preceded it. If, therefore, we are justified in seeing Proust as the greatest in a chain of writers who all indulged in the nineteenth century's *"péché mignon"* ["pet fault"] of attempting to explain the universe in terms of God, society, history or art, it is no less valid to see *A la recherche* as a conscious, and indeed at times violent, reaction away from the materialism and positivism with which that century finally came to a close. The novel is an attempt to chronicle a certain kind of social milieu at a given moment in time. It is also an attempt to create a self-contained framework within which the hero-narrator may give unity and coherence to the world around him. But the means whereby this coherence is to be achieved are to be found precisely in the rejection of too complete a reliance on the intellect, in the refusal to accept as final the information that pure reason feeds into our minds.

As all readers of Proust know, the most striking passage, if we exclude the poignant description of the child's anguish at bedtime, in the early sections of *Du côté de chez Swann,* is the scene where Marcel makes the chance discovery of the importance of pure sensation in the discovery of the past, and through the past, of the inner recesses of his own personality. The *madeleine* episode, however, despite the importance given to it for purely aesthetic reasons at this stage of the novel, has always seemed to me to be inferior in impact to the three much more climatic revelations of involuntary memory in the final section of the work, *Le temps retrouvé.* There, three times in rapid and increasingly moving succession, Marcel is transported back to different periods in his life, resurrected, as it were, from his futile and barren existence surrounded by decaying and morally decadent figures, by the intervention of an impression so completely all-embracing that his life is henceforward completely transformed.

The careful shaping of the first *madeleine* passage is necessary in the general scheme of the novel the architecture of which arises from a sustained "flash-back" technique, which introduces the "double vision" of the narrator's observations about life, and allows the final revelations retrospectively to incorporate a whole aspect of existence which Marcel's intellect had been unable to grasp, but which he had intuitively stored up in the recesses of his mind, only to be liberated by the sensations which restore his past to life, and free him from the death menacing his contemporaries. But the three manifestations of this same power, compared by Proust to the magic sign which the heroes of the Arabian Nights' Tales suddenly discover at critical moments in their lives, these three later manifestations carry with them the whole accumulated weight of the preceding volumes, and evoke in us, the readers, a memory (however literary) in precisely the same way that is described as taking possession of the narrator.

In *Du côté de chez Swann* this accumulated experience of Marcel's life does not exist; it is presented to us *after* the revelation. But the fact that makes the final pages of the novel so moving is that Proust has contrived to make us participate, however much at one remove, in the blinding revelation that memory, and the sensations which call up memory in all its fulness, are the one true guide to the recapture of all that has gone before. Thus we can see that Proust's substitution of the imagination and the irrational workings of mind and senses for the dryness and barrenness of the intellect alone is worked into not just the stuff of the novel, but into the very form which that novel must inevitably take. Studies of Proust's earlier and abortive work, called nowadays *Jean Santeuil,* but never published in Proust's lifetime, reveal clearly that it was for the lack of just such a form and all its resulting techniques that the ideas contained in the final novel, and already existing in more than embryonic shape in *Jean Santeuil,* took so long to be formulated in their fullest and most complete form. It was only by finding a form of construction which itself embodied and spontaneously expressed in non-analytic and non-rational terms the kernel of Proust's thought, that the author's accumulated experience could be most authentically presented to the reader.

It would be naïve of us to imagine, however, that Proust was the first to heed the warnings of an over-reliance on reason and materialism. Baudelaire and the Symbolists, in the second half of the century, had already pioneered the way towards a more acceptable recognition of the complexity of man's reactions to his environment. The interreaction of colours, sounds and scents, to which Baudelaire constantly refers, is an earlier manifestation of Proust's own attempts to give importance to the irrationality of authentic impressions, involving a mixture of all the senses. Let us, for the sake of clarity, somewhat simplify the situation as it existed towards the end of the nineteenth century, and postulate two antagonistic currents of thought; the first is that which tries to come more closely into line with the very way in which the industrialized society of the time was moving, and has continued to move. The second is that which reacts strongly to the increasing materialism of our civilization and tries to withdraw, in some cases, into a pure world of wholly aesthetic purity. (Mallarmé is a good illustration of this tendency taken to an extreme point.) As usual Proust manages to avoid the worst excesses of both viewpoints.

While he stresses the importance of sensations, he also accords the intellect an importance that Mallarmé would have been loth to admit. While he abhors the naturalistic novels presenting a "slice of life"—all externals and no profundity—he combines the search for the "essence" of the moment, for the hidden meaning of each passing second (which is not to be found simply by rational means), with a decidedly concrete and totally convincing presentation of the externals as well. Once again, we can see how true it is to regard Proust as standing at the cross-roads between the nineteenth century and our own times, since it is this very insistence on the subconscious, and the recesses of our inner life, which have subsequently been taken up in a multitude of different ways, in philosophy, in literature and even in modern theories of psychology, where Proust and Freud, along with his successors, come remarkably close to one another.

In his rather flowery preface to Proust's early collection of stories and essays entitled *Les plaisirs et les jours,* Anatole France referred, not unjustifiably, to their "hothouse atmosphere," where "the strange, sickly beauty of wise orchids draws its nourishment from sources other than the earth." That deliquescent, over-refined quality which marks so much of the final years of the nineteenth century, with its Des Esseintes, its Oscar Wildes and its conscious aestheticism, could not fail to leave a mark on a writer as sensitive as Proust. While Proust's aesthetic creed was much more profound than the often empty posturings of figures like Robert de Montesquiou, we can today easily detect something of the same note not only in the very style in which *A la recherche* is written, but also in the kind of universe which it unfolds.

The characters described by Proust belong, by and large, to a fairly wide spectrum of the social scale; but the great majority of them inhabit the comfortable middle and upper-middle classes which Proust knew and to which he himself belonged, together with the moneyed, international aristocracy with which he was, for a time, on fairly close terms. And along with these leisured and over-refined people (though not necessarily intelligent or even remotely artistic), the world of their servants and hangers-on is analysed in minute detail, the sub-world of pimps, parasites and courtesans; we should look in vain, despite the opening sections which are set in Combray, for the invigorating air of the countryside, the world of peasants, country lawyers, farmers and shopkeepers, which constituted by far the greatest majority of people living at that time. What we do find, however, is the world of Parisian town mansions, sea-going yachts, expensive restaurants, private concerts and elaborate parties. And the great theme of love, and its attendant, jealousy, likewise refract this steamy, hothouse light, as Proust relentlessly pursues his characters through their painful and minutely analysed love-affairs.

It is only right to add that the gradual moral decay which creeps slowly through a surprising number of the main characters is artistically worked into the overall scheme of the book, whereby the narrator contrasts the vanity of the world around him with the high and pure ideals of art. But of the number of marriages described in the course of the novel, how many are even remotely happy? Leaving aside the deliberately idealized family pattern at Combray (but from which even the father is ruthlessly edged out as time goes on), most of the webs of human relationships are warped where they are not specifically perverted. The long, sincere but over-emphasized descriptions of male and female homosexuality, of neurotic jealousy and unreasonable possessiveness, of lying, cheating, backbiting and internecine struggle, whether in elegant salons or in the franker atmosphere of the theatre green room, seem to me to belong to that world that produced *Lady Windemere's Fan* and the *Picture of Dorian Gray, Les nourritures terrestres* and *Si le grain ne meurt,* besides all the worthless contributions from poets and novelists who could all be summed up as having in their make-up, as Proust himself did, something of the spirit of Count Robert de Montesquiou. Indeed, anybody wishing to be initiated into the social and literary ambience of the *"fin de siècle"* would do far better to read *A la recherche,* where it is vividly re-enacted for us, than to read those novels of Zola's where he talks so much about it, but cannot make us feel it as Proust can. In some respects, Proust catches the final, self-tormenting, life-weary picture of the last romantics, parading their refinement and their *ennui* in a world made all the more tragic in that they could have no idea that it was soon to be swept away.

But it is all presented, if not with the gusto of Balzac, at least with his penetration and ill-concealed enjoyment. There can be no doubt that if Proust owes more to one individual source than to any other, it is to Balzac.

When Balzac came to read Sir Walter Scott's *Waverley* novels, he soon reached the conclusion that the unity implied in their progressive resurrection of a remote way of life would have been greatly enhanced by allowing characters appearing in one novel to reappear in another, perhaps in a different context and seen in a different light. From this discovery it was but one step to the elaboration of that famous technique, which gives such interest and depth to the *Comédie humaine* as a whole, a technique which consists of reintroducing familiar characters from one novel into many of the others, where they play sometimes a subsidiary role, sometimes a major one, but always giving the reader the impression that he is dealing with a familiar, existing world, which in literary terms parallels more closely than any other his knowledge of whatever society he is himself personally familiar with.

This aspect of the *Comédie humaine* was to have a profound effect on Proust. With definite ideas about the deforming power of time—time that can change a character out of all recognition; with definite ideas, too, about the different *profiles* that each individual presents to different people, and to different circumstances—ideas which may briefly be summed up in the celebrated phrase: "our social personality is a creation existing in the minds of other people"; with all these ideas, each of which required a specific technique to illustrate it graphically in the novel, Proust adapted the Balzacian idea of reintroducing characters in different situations, allowing the passage of narrated time to emphasize the fluidity of their personalities, and their presence in different social and psychological situations to underline their ambiguity and complexity.

Let us take the well-known example of Odette to illustrate both of these aspects; she is the enigmatic and morally dubious "lady in pink" whom the narrator meets as a small boy at his uncle Adolphe's apartment in Paris; she next appears as the wife of Marcel's friend Charles Swann, and then assumes a slightly different rôle in the boy's life as the mother of his beloved Gilberte. In the semi-independent section dealing with Swann's great affair before his marriage to her, she is presented as the friend of the pseudo-artistic Verdurin clan, Odette de Crécy. After Swann's death she gradually rises in

the world, and eventually becomes Madame de Forcheville, only to reappear in the narrator's life much later at Balbec in the guise of an ambiguous portrait painted by Elstir.

By an amazing cross-fertilization, she moves from the Swann, or bourgeois, side of the novel to the Guermantes, or aristocratic, side, through the marriage of her daughter Gilberte to the Guermantes Robert de Saint-Loup. She later becomes the mistress of the duc de Guermantes himself; and, in a masterly revelation towards the end, Proust takes us right back to her origins as an unknown "cocotte." When he makes his periodic visits to the Verdurins, now immensely rich and also moving ruthlessly into high society, Marcel meets a ruined old aristocrat, whose former wife had bled him of every penny. He turns out to be none other than a Monsieur de Crécy, with the result that what Marcel had taken to be a *"nom de guerre"* ["assumed name"], adopted by Odette when she was still unknown, is revealed to be a hidden part of her past, and yet another manifestation of the multiple personality which Proust goes on to explore almost right up to the last pages of the work.

Another similarity to Balzac that appears in *A la recherche du temps perdu* is the deliberate juxtaposition in the works of both authors of characters who are wholly fictional and others who were historical figures of the time. Thus, in the course of Marcel's initiation into society, we catch glimpses of Princess Mathilde, hear allusions to the Prince of Wales, to the comte de Paris, and, among others, to prominent politicians and statesmen of the day. So intricately are real, fictional and semi-fictional characters woven into the texture of the narrative, that one is sometimes surprised to discover that a character like the princesse de Luxembourg turns out to be wholly fictitious, so indistinguishable is she in "tone" from historical figures like Napoléon I's niece, Princess Mathilde. And just as Balzac continued to revise, edit and modify his characters' names, in order to give later creations a fictional past originally attributed to somebody else, so Proust, in his constant revisions of the middle and later sections of the novel, continually inserted allusions and characteristics into the unpublished manuscripts, until it is virtually impossible now to distinguish reported fact from original creation. The nearest that we are ever likely to come to doing so has been absorbingly set out by Mr. Painter in his brilliant biography of Proust; and anyone wishing further to pursue this line of inquiry cannot be too strongly urged to consult that work.

To continue this short parallel between Balzac and Proust, it is necessary (perhaps surprisingly) to introduce the theme of money. If Balzac can be said to have elaborated a set of laws which implicitly regulate the hidden fluctuations of modern society, then pride of place among those laws must be given to the importance of money. To take but one example, in Balzac's powerful study of commercial bankruptcy *César Birotteau,* the author plots the financial ruin and subsequent rehabilitation of a businessman in Paris. He is shown to be the victim of larger financial concerns who use him as a pawn, as well as of his own ambition and the sudden bankruptcy of his unscrupulous lawyer. One of the most interesting aspects of this novel, which might so easily have turned into a dull, over-technical case-book of a phenomenon that must have been very familiar to the readers of that time, is the curious way in which the life-blood of the central character, Birotteau—indeed, not just his life-blood, but his very personality—seems linked to his professional and financial status. Without money, Birotteau simply does not exist; and it is only through titanic efforts that he recovers not only something of his former life but also something of his previous self. Nowhere else in the *Comédie humaine* is the equation between money and identity so rigorously demonstrated.

Now, in Proust's study, both of the laws regulating the society of his own day, and of the laws regulating the workings of passion, love and jealousy, money plays a part the importance of which is seldom sufficiently emphasized. In *Un amour de Swann,* the whole basis of Odette's decision to become Charles's mistress is, at the outset, the desire to be made financially secure. He is merely one in a series of wealthy patrons who included in the past not only Marcel's Uncle Adolphe but an unnamed Grand Duke, who provided her with a supply of foreign gold-tipped cigarettes. As I have already mentioned, her earlier, undisclosed marriage to Monsieur de Crécy had only lasted for as long as there was money to be had from him.

Similarly, in the laws directing the sometimes ponderous changes in the make-up of society, Proust takes into account a number of factors, including great, accidental upheavals like the Dreyfus case and the First World War, or artistic revolutions like the arrival in Paris of the Russian Ballet, that helped to spur on Madame Verdurin and some of her coterie in their efforts to climb the social ladder. But one of the most bitterly ironical revelations of the latter part of the work is that concerning this same Madame Verdurin's ultimate success. By a dazzling series of metamorphoses comparable with those of Odette herself, this odious woman becomes successively the duchesse de Duras and then the princesse de Guermantes herself through a series of convenient and providential deaths and remarriages. And it is precisely through her vast and seemingly increasing fortune that she achieves such triumphs, the Guermantes, who were partially German, having lost a large part of their investments owing to the war, and Madame Verdurin simply amassing even more thanks, no doubt, to France's armament drive.

Her prodigious rise in fortune is perhaps the best illustration of the Balzacian side of *A la recherche du temps perdu.* Like some female Rastignac, although not starting with his disadvantages, she relentlessly pursues her aims, using anyone and anything which might further her cause. On a vastly extended scale, she is almost a Proustian version of one of Balzac's monomaniacs, although she is presented with far more awareness of the complexities and inconsistencies of character than, for example, Hulot or Claes, and the amount of time that passes between her first appearance as a slightly raffish and pretentious artistic hostess and her elegant "soirée" in the Hôtel de Guermantes, with which the novel closes, must be in the order of forty or fifty years. Indeed, Marcel's increasing revulsion from society, and the perceptible darkening of the later stages of the novel, are both not a little bound up with the author's cynical exposure of the rôle of money and the exploitation which accompanies it in the world he sees around him.

The unscrupulous violinist Charles Morel bleeds the homosexual Charlus unmercifully; Charlus himself is ultimately reduced to paying boys to carry out his perverted rituals. The ultimate degradation of the once golden Robert de Saint-Loup is connected with the discovery, during the darkest days of the war, of a male brothel where he too pays for his hidden pleasures. It is one of the novel's most masterly strokes that the purifying message of the narrator's intuitive certainty in the eternal validity of art should come precisely in the second princesse de Guermantes's salon, paid for with money accrued during the war, and immediately after an encounter with the now enfeebled Charlus being wheeled along by his pimp and former lover Jupien.

There are other, more technical and probably more subtle links between Proust and his great predecessor which there is no space to go into here. But my few observations may perhaps give some idea of the immense debt that the later novelist owed to the author of the *Comédie humaine,* a debt of which, it is only fair to emphasize, Proust was himself very well aware. (pp. 129-40)

Of all the great novelists of recent times, Proust was certainly one of the most widely read, one of the most profoundly literary. I am sure that if he had not had the spark of genius which turned him into a great creative writer he would have become one of France's most acute and sensitive literary critics. But in *A la recherche du temps perdu* Proust's love and acceptance of his literary ancestors is grafted on to his own, original creation, building on to what had gone before, gratefully accepting help and advice from the greatest of his predecessors, but transforming his literary patrimony into a treasure house probably richer than that of anyone else in recent times. (p. 145)

B. G. Rogers, "Proust and the Nineteenth Century," in Marcel Proust, 1871-1922: A Centennial Volume, *edited by Peter Quennell, Simon and Schuster, 1971, pp. 129-45.*

JACK MURRAY (essay date 1980)

[*In the following excerpt, Murray discusses the role of comedy in Proust's portrayal of the narrator of* Remembrance of Things Past.]

Literary analysts from Martin-Chauffier to Marcel Muller have told us that the person saying "I" in *Remembrance of Things Past* is not a single one, readily identifiable, but a whole array of different voices. Scholarly purists even object to giving any of these first person voices the name Marcel, although . . . we shall call at least one of them Marcel for the perhaps off-hand reason that it makes him easier to refer to and also because there is now a long tradition in Proust studies, however ill-founded, for doing so. That said, we next point out that the Marcel we shall study is the boy, young man, and incipient oldster on whom the narrator or author is looking down, bemusedly, and describing from above. We shall concentrate on those moments when Marcel is plainly presented in comic terms, particularly as he progresses through the social world, and then consider how Marcel's various experiences represent the accumulation of a kind of wisdom. The main point, for the moment, is that Marcel is quite as capable of coy or duplicitous behavior as any other character in *Remembrance of Things Past.* He is also hiding within himself similar anxieties.

Proust is not above making Marcel an almost slapstick figure. When as a young man he comes out of the Paris fog to have dinner with Saint-Loup in an elegant restaurant, Marcel gets caught in a revolving door, is banished to the less fashionable but larger dining room by the imperious maitre d'hotel, and there sits forlornly at a bad table located just by an unbearable draft issuing from a door across from it. He is rescued, of course, from this ignominy by Saint-Loup whose arrival reverses the humiliating situation, and he sees a total transformation in the maitre d'hotel's attitude toward him. When Marcel is star struck with Gilberte and the rest of the Swanns, he drags Françoise through the streets of Paris in the hope of just a glimpse of them. He even posts himself at the foot of the Rue Duphot—"I had heard that Swann was often to be seen passing there, on his way to the dentist's." Finally, and perhaps far more subtly, the narrator assures us that Marcel is dazzling Saint-Loup's friends with his brilliance at Doncières, offering as a sample the following bit of pretentious schoolboy sophistry:

> "One is the man of one's idea. There are far fewer ideas than men, therefore all men with similar ideas are alike. As there is nothing material in an idea, so the people who are only materially neighbours of the man with an idea can do nothing to alter it."

The richest comedy in the novel, in so far as Marcel is concerned, pertains to his progress as a snob. Its starting point is Marcel's sense of total insignificance, of having no appeal of any kind to others, of being incurably earthbound. This sense of insecurity is, in many respects, a sense of exclusion. Marcel wishes to be delivered from exile, accepted, and brought into whatever world he imagines will give him some sort of prestige either before others or before himself. Since he feels only someone else can deliver him, he has to wait to be discovered and rescued. It turns out, of course, that he can send out signals to the desired rescuer, and it is here that a kind of comedy, special to Marcel, begins, a mixture of idealizing fantasies and quite calculated ruses.

As we hope to make clear in this chapter, Marcel's career as a snob begins with the goodnight kiss crisis at Combray. Like the characters considered in the previous chapter, Marcel is terrified by something inside himself that returns to haunt him when he is put to bed at night. He has come to depend on his mother's kiss to help ease him through the dark nocturnal tunnel, and indeed his whole attitude toward his mother, characterized as it is by an obsessive and watchful need, is symptomatic of his utter helplessness in taking an active part in the control of his own anguish. He knows, unfortunately, that his family deplores his weak and clinging dependency on his mother and is trying to wean him away from it by deliberate coolness and the rationing of demonstrations of affection. Actually, he has been taught to be ashamed of needing affection or asking for it, and so, perversely, this need has come to be more important than anything else. If he is to get what he needs, he must revolt against the tyranny of principle under which he lives.

How does he do this? On the particular night in question Marcel is sent summarily to bed by his father and, in passing, is ordered to do without his kiss ("No, no, leave your mother alone. You've said good night quite enough. These exhibitions are absurd.") Once in his room, he decides to resort to simulation and deceit, "the desperate stratagem of a condemned prisoner." He will write a note to his mother telling her he has something very serious to tell her (the rules of the game, however, forbid that he say what) and send it to her through Françoise. Despite his assurances that it is his mother who asked him to write, Françoise performs the commission with the greatest reluctance. We note that Proust interjects an element of theatre here by saying that Françoise had as much hesitation to interrupt a dinner with this sort of request as would a door-keeper to deliver a letter to an actor performing on the stage. For a moment Marcel believes his mother will come, and he feels reassured. But then Françoise

returns to say that there is no answer. Marcel, of course, has been humiliated in front of the only intermediary to whom he has been able to have recourse, Françoise, an outcome particularly embarrassing since he has fibbed about his mother wanting him to write. At this point, the matter has become ruthlessly simple: either he wins the kiss or he does not get through the night. There is no choice. He must go on plotting. It is in these circumstances that he decides to confront his mother as she comes up the stairs to bed. He carries this out, precipitating a crisis, since his mother's first concern, after seeing him on the stairs, is over the reaction of her husband if he sees his son standing there "like a crazy jane." Marcel's father does appear, leading the son to believe for a moment that all is lost, but the father is unexpectedly benign and, over his wife's protests, persuades her to spend the night with the boy, since he is obviously upset. The mother reluctantly complies with her husband's wishes. Therefore, the ruses and the confrontation may be said to have worked not only a revolutionary change in the domestic situation but even a miracle.

We shall put aside, for the moment, Marcel's overwhelming sense of remorse as he feels he has caused his mother to abandon her program to make him strong and independent. In the current context, it is enough to point out that any deliberate deceit on the part of the morally sensitive is bound to produce the guilt feelings that are so integral a part of bad faith. But, when Françoise asks Marcel's mother why he is crying and she tells her that it is his nerves, the boy feels he has acquired some kind of identity, however wretched, and is even rather proud:

> I felt no small degree of pride . . . in Françoise's presence at this return to humane conditions which, not an hour after Mamma had refused to come up to my room and had sent the snubbing message that I was to go to sleep, raised me to the dignity of a grown-up person, brought me of a sudden to a sort of puberty of sorrow, to emancipation from tears.

To be disgraced and banished for wanting affection does not cure Marcel of his need for it but, instead, makes his pursuit of it even more obsessive and frantic. Ashamed of this perfectly spontaneous need, he must try to obtain it by oblique stratagems, but, since he is fearful of rejection or rebuke, he must not seem to want it too much, or he will feel even more shame, if the pursuit is of no avail. He must therefore resort to ruses, simulation, and deceit. When these are successful, he is remorseful but nonetheless finds, in an underhanded way, that his vanity has been satisfied. If we add to this dilemma the crucial element of the feeling of total worthlessness, we have the recipe for making a snob, in Proustian terms. The snob is one who cannot bear to be left out of the world—particularly one he associates with prestige—, since he is a nobody, a pariah, unless he is accepted there. Yet he is ashamed of this craven need and tries to hide it. Nonetheless, he does not cease his maneuvering until he succeeds in gaining access to that world. At every stage of this process, the snob's vanity chafes and suffers, leaving him no respite from inner torment. If one thinks of either Legrandin or Mme. Verdurin in terms of this formula, it is clear that they are suffering the same malady as Marcel, although it is in no way clear that it has the same remote causes.

Nowadays we associate with the turn of the century the coy feminine stratagem of dropping a handkerchief to attract the notice of a gentleman passer-by. Marcel is one who is constantly dropping handkerchiefs. His first objective is simply to be noticed, and sometimes this is so satisfying that he does not seek to go any further. For example, he does his best to be noticed by a girl fishing from a bridge near a village outside Balbec, and Proust, in his arcane jargon, describes in the following way how Marcel wonders if she has really seen him:

> And this inner self of the charming fisher-girl seemed to be still closed to me, I was doubtful whether I had entered it, even after I had seen my own image furtively reflect itself in the twin mirrors of her gaze, following an index of refraction that was as unknown to me as if I had been placed in the field of vision of a deer.

Marcel admits that he not only wants to be noticed by her but admired, desired, and remembered by her. He gives her five francs he is holding and asks her to go to a pastry shop and see if a carriage is waiting for him—the carriage, he adds (hoping to impress her), of the Marquise de Villeparisis. Once he is certain she has heard this impressive speech, he feels immediately relieved. She will remember him.

Even so minor an episode reveals one fundamental characteristic of the snob and all his stratagems. Short term successes bring a respite from anxiety. But, just as Marcel's anguish over the goodnight kiss is a daily occurrence, the snob's need for some kind of attention constantly reasserts itself.

The episode also shows how the first attraction that might lead to deep and painful love has almost the same starting point as the snob impulse. If we can only succeed in making the woman notice, admire, desire, and remember us, we can feel better about ourselves.

Marcel drops his handkerchief several times in *Remembrance of Things Past.* A first major instance is Gilberte, already a legendary girl for Marcel in Combray since he learns that she visits cathedrals with Bergotte. Sitting in the park of the Champs-Elysées one day, Marcel, by now an adolescent, hears her name called by another girl:

> . . . carrying in its wake, I could feel, the knowledge, the impression of her to whom it was addressed that belonged not to me but to the friend who called to her, everything that, while she uttered the words, she more or less vividly reviewed, possessed in her memory, of their daily intimacy, of the visits that they paid to each other, of that unknown existence which was all the more inaccessible, all the more painful to me from being, conversely, so familiar, so tractable to this happy girl who let her message brush past me without my being able to penetrate its surface, who flung it on the air with a lighthearted cry.

It therefore becomes of categorical importance that he, with Françoise in tow, appear unfailingly at the park every day, not only so that he may see Gilberte but, almost as important, so that he may become a familiar sight to her, perhaps even a playmate and friend. Such assiduity is finally rewarded. But this is not enough. His infatuation for Gilberte includes that world evoked by her name, specifically the Swanns and their—to Marcel at least—fabulous apartment. As to Swann himself, not only does Marcel use every opportunity at home to lure his parents into mentioning him, but he even begins to imitate Swann's smallest mannerisms, for example pulling on his nose and wiping his eyes all the time, until his father exclaims: "The child's a perfect idiot." Marcel even wishes

he were bald like Swann. One day, seeing Odette Swann in the Bois, he delivers a bow so theatrical and sweeping to her that the other passers-by laugh and Odette herself smiles. Unfortunately, Swann does not appear to be impressed by the boy, and, cruelly, Gilberte tells her friend that her parents can't abide him. Once more Marcel uses the letter stratagem, this time protesting the purity of his intentions and insisting on his high worth, but Swann, according to his daughter, is not moved by it. Moreover, Marcel seems to bear out Swann's low esteem of him by what happens in his little wrestling match with Gilberte in the park.

Marcel obtained the favor of his mother's spending the night with him in Combray through a kind of miraculous intercession of his father. When Marcel is invited to the Swanns', the miracle is even more unfathomable. Things simply change. And the young man soon penetrates the magical world of the Swanns' apartment. "Thus at length I found my way into that abode from which was wafted even on to the staircase the scent that Mme. Swann used, though it was embalmed far more sweetly still by the peculiar, disturbing charm that emanated from the life of Gilberte." And there follow many pages, suffused with that special lyrical charm that only Proust can communicate, devoted to evoking the pastel beauty and bewitching fascination of this new milieu. All the rites and practices carried on there have a rich, if intimidating, aura of glamor about them. If Marcel is too stupid to know that he is to open the envelope given him upon arriving at the Swanns' to learn the name of the lady he is to escort into dinner, he at least can summon up enough sense to put the carnation, found next to his plate, into his buttonhole with the same casualness as the other men at the table ("I did as they had done, with the air of spontaneity that a free-thinker assumes in church, who is not familiar with the order of service but rises when everyone else rises and kneels a moment after everyone else is on his knees." Marcel continues to go to the Swanns', even after renouncing Gilberte, still finding considerable charm in the setting. But eventually his interest wanes, until he ceases to go there altogether.

The next important group that Marcel infiltrates is the "little band" at Balbec. But, before discussing this, we must consider Marcel's inferiority complex attack when first confronted by Balbec. Even the place where Marcel and his grandmother are staying, the Grand Hotel, is dreadfully intimidating to him, not only because of the guests that line the verandah and survey everyone else disapprovingly through their lorgnettes but specifically because of the hotel director who does not even remove his hat when Marcel's grandmother begins to haggle over rates with him. Indeed, Marcel is actually ashamed of his grandmother, just as he had been ashamed of Françoise, when going to play in the Champs-Elysées, who did not have a feather in her hat like Gilberte's governess. Moreover, his grandmother does nothing to improve what he assumes is their mortifyingly low status in the hotel. The grandmother, by now already well known to the reader for her love of breezes and bracing weather, imperviously exposes her face to the gale wind that gusts through the window she has opened in the dining room, while she remains unaware of, or indifferent to, the irate protests of the guests around her left "scornful, dishevelled, furious." She insists, moreover, that they are at the seashore for the serious purpose of restoring Marcel's health and have no time to spend hobnobbing with whatever swells are in the area. These include the redoubtable Marquise de Villeparisis, an old friend of the grandmother's from convent school, who Marcel is certain will be a good connection and will be impressive to be seen associating with in front of the implacable clientele of the shorefront establishment. His humiliation is complete when he and his grandmother are evicted from a table in the dining room by its official and titled occupant, M. de Stermaria, a member of the local gentry, and his scowling daughter.

Luckily for Marcel, one day the grandmother and the marquise virtually collide in a doorway, and their avoidance of each other becomes impossible to continue.

> . . . she and Mme. de Villeparisis came in collision one morning in a doorway and were obliged to accost each other, not without having first exchanged gestures of surprise and hesitation, performed movements of recoil and uncertainty, and finally uttered protestations of joy and greeting, as in some of Molière's plays, where two actors who have been delivering long soliloquies from opposite sides of the stage, a few feet apart, are supposed not to have seen each other yet, and then suddenly catch sight of each other, cannot believe their eyes, break off what they are saying and finally address each other . . . and fall into each other's arms.

Through the marquise they not only meet the imperious Princess of Luxemburg but also Robert de Saint-Loup and the Baron de Charlus. On Saint-Loup in particular Marcel concentrates his overwrought faculty to fantasize, imagining this young aristocrat as a devoted friend and unfailing admirer not unlike the Gilberte he has earlier dreamed of as rescuing him from oblivion before himself. After a bad start, Saint-Loup swiftly does become this friend of his dreams, lavishing upon Marcel every kind of thoughtful attention and greeting his every word or idea with extravagant admiration. Charlus, on the other hand, pays Marcel the dubious compliment . . . of finding him sexually interesting.

As for the "little band," Marcel first sees these athletic girls striding along the esplanade, sneering at the other vacationers, and, in one celebrated episode, laughing uproariously as one of them leaps off the bandstand over the head of a terrified retired banker. Marcel too comes under the merciless scrutiny of these members of an implicitly and unapologetically superior breed:

> For an instant, as I passed the dark one with the fat cheeks who was wheeling a bicycle, I caught her smiling, sidelong glance, aimed from the centre of that inhuman world which enclosed the life of this little tribe, an inaccessible, unknown world to which the idea of what I was could certainly never attain nor find a place in it.

Typically, Marcel is a nobody, even as he was with the "charming fisher-girl," and these girls represent everything. He wishes to be delivered from unendurable exclusion to salvation-like inclusion in exactly the same way as he did in the case of the Swanns. Typically too, as a totally passive creature, he can do nothing more than set himself up as bait. He begins to haunt the esplanade and other places where the girls are to be found, dressing with the utmost care and placing himself in contrived poses so that he will be noticed and cause the news of his existence to be recorded by this arch and inaccessible group. But visibility alone does not turn the trick. After making the acquaintance of Elstir at Rivebelle, Marcel learns that the painter knows the girls and decides to use him to get an introduction. One day he is walking down the street with Elstir and sees the girls coming from the opposite direction. Marcel believes that he is about to meet them at last.

> Feeling that a collision between them and us was now inevitable, and that Elstir would be certain to call me, I turned my back, like a bather preparing to meet the shock of a wave; I stopped dead and, leaving my eminent companion to pursue his way, remained where I was, stooping, as if I had suddenly become engrossed in it, towards the window of the curiosity shop which we happened to be passing at the moment. I was not sorry to give the appearance of being able to think of something other than these girls, and I was already dimly aware that when Elstir did call me up to introduce me to them I should wear that sort of challenging expression which betokens not surprise but the wish to appear as though one were surprised—so far is every one of us a bad actor, or everyone else a good thought-reader;—that I should even go so far as to point a finger to my breast, as who should ask "It is me, really, that you want" and then run to join him, my head lowered in compliance and docility and my face coldly masking my annoyance at being torn from the study of old pottery in order to be introduced to people whom I had no wish to know.

Unfortunately, Marcel's timing is off, he lingers too long at the store window, and does not even hear Elstir summoning him to come and be introduced. Like so many of Marcel's stratagems, this one backfires, and the girls are gone before he can meet them. But we note that, instead of merely contenting himself with being a kind of human blinking sign along the girls' path, he has resorted to a more involved acting routine, although still essentially passive in nature. Proust wishes us to lose none of the embarrassing triteness of this sample of "everyday histrionics," up to and including Marcel's wretchedly banal "who, me?" pointing of the finger to his chest when he fancies the moment that Elstir will call to him. It is a classical vaudeville or light comedy number. (pp. 45-54)

[Marcel's] efforts to appear "cool" are lamentable. But . . . he is irrepressible. When at last he is about to be introduced to Albertine, the girl who interests him most in the little band, at a tea Elstir has arranged just for this, he again lays it on thick. Before going through the impending introduction, Marcel, with seeming patience, finishes eating an eclair, then engages in conversation with an old gentleman about Norman country fairs, even pausing to give him the moss rose the man has admired in his buttonhole, before proceeding to the presentation to Albertine. The meeting this time is not so miraculous as in the other cases. Marcel has simply exploited a friend.

It is not very long before Marcel has entered the intimate world of the young girls where he basks, full of wonder at their slang, their values, and their priority of interests and activities, not a little intimidated by them.

No one is more important, however, to Marcel in his progress as a snob than the Duchess de Guermantes. Even as a child, Marcel has dreamed of being admired and loved by the duchess, but it is when his family takes an apartment in the Hotel de Guermantes in Paris that his thoughts of gaining access to the world of the Guermantes becomes a lively possibility. To accomplish this, Marcel, in a now characteristic pattern, posts himself in the street at those times of the morning when the duchess is accustomed to go out. Note, in the following description, how he continues the same game he played in the park of the Champs-Elysées or on the esplanade or in front of the antique shop in Balbec:

> And now every morning, long before the hour at which she would appear, I went by a devious course to post myself at the corner of the street along which she generally came, and, when the moment of her arrival seemed imminent, strolled home-wards with an air of being absorbed in something else, looking the other way and raising my eyes to her face as I drew level with her, but as though I had not in the least expected to see her.

Characteristically, however, this strategy appears to backfire, for Françoise gives Marcel clear indications that his being in the duchess's path every day has become a source of annoy-ance to the lady. Desperate for a new means to win the atten-tion and interest of the duchess, Marcel goes to visit Saint-Loup at his garrison in Doncières where he hopes to persuade his friend to use his influence on his aunt.

While Marcel is at Doncières, we once more witness Saint-Loup's extravagant attentions and admiration for Marcel. Marcel falls completely in with the part, and, in the manner typical of a snob, he even abuses the relationship. Proust does not tell us how Marcel prevailed upon Elstir to arrange the tea in which he meets Albertine. In the present instance, Mar-cel not only mentions to Saint-Loup that he would like to be presented to the duchess but even asks for her photograph. The conversation, too long to be quoted at any length here, exasperates us by its protracted coyness and protestations of indifference. Since it is taking place in earshot of Saint-Loup's companions, it is oblique. "I say, Robert! . . . Oh, it's really too absurd the way our conversation is always being inter-rupted, I can't think why—you remember the lady I was speaking to you about just now." On the one hand, a person like Marcel who so seldom takes the initiative frequently does not know how far he can go or when he ought to stop. On the other, his reflexive shame over anything that really mat-ters to him leads to his resorting to indirection and nervous humor as he speaks in order to cover it up. Unfortunately, he displays more of his feelings than he perhaps really wants to by asking for something so intimate as a lady's photo-graph. The end product, however, is gall. Saint-Loup, of course, turns him down cold and seems to be no help at all until, when Marcel at last finds himself in the same room with the duchess at the Marquise de Villeparisis's, he performs the perfunctory service of introducing Marcel to his aunt. The in-troduction is followed by a conversation so banal ("I see you sometimes in the morning," says the duchess) that it does not seem promising.

Again a miracle seems to intervene, one of those brusque and unexplainable revolutions in the course of historical events. Marcel is invited to dinner by the duchess. . . . [What should] be stressed here is the implicit comedy of a character like Marcel, so insistently portrayed as an uninteresting booby, being invited at all, being fawned over, and being treated as if he too were glamorous and fascinating. Presum-ably Marcel has been invited because he is associated with the world of literature and the arts (Marcel holds the dinner up by spending a great deal of time in another room looking at the Guermantes' Elstirs). The duchess says to him at one point, "You must know who everyone is." Marcel himself is persistently nagged by a sense of utter worthlessness during the dinner and tries to leave several times, deploring "the

triviality which my presence at it imparted to the gathering." Eventually, once the formality of the Princess of Parma's de-parture frees everyone, he makes it to the vestibule where, in a scene reminiscent of his slapstick humiliation in the restau-rant, he must endure the sneering glances of the servants as he struggles into his rubbers. But the princess comes to the rescue as Saint-Loup had in the previous episode:

> "Oh! what a good idea," she exclaimed, "it's so practical! There's a sensible man for you. Madame, we shall have to get a pair of those," she went on to her lady in waiting, while the mockery of the footmen turned to respect and the other guests crowded round me to inquire where I had managed to find these marvels.

Marcel soon becomes a regular at the duchess's exclusive din-ners. But the culmination of his social career is his attending the great reception at the Princess de Guermantes's. Marcel, of course, is fearful that his invitation is some April fool's prank and vainly seeks assurance on its authenticity from un-obliging friends who are more certain than he of having really been invited. This dreadful doubt persists right up to the waiting line to be announced, and the announcing itself is ex-cruciating for Marcel:

> The usher asked me my name, I told him it as me-chanically as the condemned man allows himself to be strapped to the block. At once he lifted his head majestically and, before I could beg him to an-nounce me in a lowered tone so as to spare my own feelings if I were not invited and those of the Prin-cesse de Guermantes if I were, shouted the disturb-ing syllables with a force capable of bringing down the roof.

The princess, content for the most part to receive her guests seated and in summary fashion, actually rises and comes to greet Marcel. While there is some difficulty finding someone brave enough to introduce him to the prince, Marcel for the most part carries off his part with great success. At one point he knows enough to give a distant bow to the Duke de Guer-mantes who greets him at the other end of the hall.

> Had I written a masterpiece, the Guermantes would have given me less credit for it than I earned by that bow. Not only did it not pass unperceived by the Duke, albeit he had that day to acknowledge the greetings of more than five hundred people, it caught the eye of the Duchess, who, happening to meet my mother, told her of it, and, so far from sug-gesting that I had done wrong, that I ought to have gone up to him, said that her husband had been lost in admiration of my bow, that it would have been impossible for anyone to put more into it.

His social victory is epitomized by his walking through the assembled throng of elegant guests with the Duchess de Guermantes on his arm:

> We advanced between a double hedge of guests, who, conscious that they would never come to know "Oriane," were anxious at least to point her out, as a curiosity, to their wives: "Quick, Ursule, come and look at Madame de Guermantes talking to that young man." And one felt that in another moment they would be clambering upon the chairs, for a better view, as at the Military Review on the 14th of July, or the Grand Prix.

All of these episodes in Marcel's social progress mirror cer-tain features of the goodnight kiss crisis. Marcel's banishment

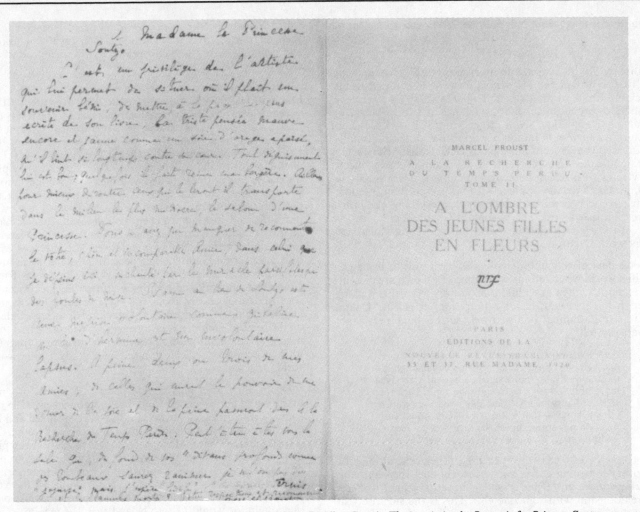

Title page of A l'ombre des jeunes filles en fleurs (Within a Budding Grove). *The inscription by Proust is for Princess Soutzo.*

to his room is reflected in his sense of woeful exclusion before the worlds represented by Gilberte and the Swanns, the girls in the little band, and the glamorous world of the duchess and the Faubourg Saint-Germain surrounding her. The exclusion means that he must use oblique means to gain the attention of his savior. Letters are sent. Marcel posts himself like bait to be noticed and perhaps even admired; this is a benign version of his more daring confrontation with his mother on the stairs. All these efforts are accompanied by a sense of worthlessness and even shame that echo similar feelings overcoming the child who has been sent up to his room, like a nobody, without his kiss. All the efforts to become noticed, be introduced, gain admittance to the other world take on the drama, disguise, and subterfuge of almost criminal behavior that makes the defiance of his parents so thrilling to Marcel. After all, the bank robber looking casual as he waits his turn in the line before the teller is acting in the truest sense. Marcel's calculated pause in front of the antique dealer's window has a similar cast. Indeed, as he waits for the usher to announce him at the Princess de Guermantes's, he actually does feel like a criminal. All of this goes back, perhaps, to that primeval act of rebellion in Combray that took the form of ruses and stratagems while Marcel attempted to break what he had assumed was immutable law. His mother spent the night with him. In his career as snob, doors always end by opening for him, no matter how calculated his behavior may appear or how insignificant his person may seem. As always, there is a quality of the miraculous in these successes.

There may also be some remorse in them as well. Remorse was what Marcel felt in Combray when he triumphed over his parents. But, if we recall that he "felt no small degree of pride" over his success in Françoise's eyes, then we begin to see what the psychological stakes are for Marcel in all of this. The narrator who recounts Marcel's progress does not hide from us the petty sort of vanity at play throughout. He does this not only by describing Marcel's pratfalls and shallow deceits in all their embarrassing detail but also by making clear that the milieus entered seem hardly worth the trouble. After all, Gilberte—and her mother with her—are addicted to the flashy elegance that passes for fashion but that really is just vulgar pretentiousness. The guests at the Grand Hotel are for the most part provincial bourgeois such as lawyers and magistrates from Norman towns. The girls in the little band are no better and are clearly of a bad sort—early prototypes of flappers and other liberated women yet to come. The nobility is more problematical. While there is nothing that can take away the luster of their names and blood lines, they appear to have no real power, live hollow lives, and sell their birth rights away. Saint-Loup insists on being a left-wing intellectual, while the duchess frequents increasingly bohemian types in the course of the novel. All of them have committed the ultimate crime of being only human, from Marcel's point of view.

The comedy of Marcel's adventures in the world is also heightened by his increase in a kind of rueful wisdom as he progresses through life. A part of this wisdom comes from his penchant for becoming disenchanted with every object he idealizes or pursues. Roger Shattuck has called the penchant "Proust's Complaint." On a rather primitive level, it is simply another version of familiarity breeding contempt. It must be added, however, that this malady reflects that primal sense of insignificance that Marcel feels within himself as it affects everything with which he comes in contact. He has only to contaminate a person or place with his presence for it to lose its luster and become as humdrum as everything else in his far too familiar world. This wisdom is acquired, of course, as Marcel rises ever higher in the social world and gains each of his worldly aims.

A good deal of this bitter wisdom is the result of having to live in a world where minds other than one's own are present. For example, when as a child in Combray Marcel is walking through the rain and, in his exhiliration, cries out "Damn, damn, damn, damn," he discovers that his happiness is not universally felt:

> And it was at that moment . . .—thanks to a peasant who went past, apparently in a bad enough humour already, but more so when he nearly received my umbrella in his face, and who replied without any cordiality to my "Fine day, what! good to be out walking!"—that I learned that identical emotions do not spring up in the hearts of all men simultaneously, by a pre-established order.

Typically, Proust has conveyed this rather crucial infantile discovery in benign and comic terms. He does the same with a perhaps more unsettling episode—unsettling since it affects his relationship with someone else. This is the surprise visit Marcel engineers to his Uncle Adolphe in the hope of seeing an actress, since it is rumored in the family that the uncle keeps company with ladies of the theatre (apparently a euphemism for something else). Marcel's hopes are rewarded, and he meets the Lady in Pink. Afterwards he blurts out to his family the whole (to him) delightful adventure, and he is dumbfounded when he realizes that they are not the least bit charmed. And later, because of his confusion and shame, he is reluctant to greet his uncle in the street.

> A few days later, passing my uncle in the street as he drove by in an open carriage, I felt at once all the grief, the gratitude, the remorse which I should have liked to convey to him. Besides the immensity of these emotions I considered that merely to raise my hat to him would be incongruous and petty, and might make him think that I regarded myself as bound to shew him no more than the commonest form of courtesy. I decided to abstain from so inadequate a gesture, and turned my head away. My uncle thought that, in doing so, I was obeying my parents' orders; he never forgave them; and though he did not die until many years later, not one of us ever set eyes on him again.

This episode, by the way it is told, allows us to see how a social gaffe looks from the inside. We have the inner ruminations and good intentions bubbling away within and the clumsy and bungled way they are expressed on the outside. We recall the mismanaged strategy and badly handled signals of little Marcel in Combray. . . . [Let us] consider how frustrated Marcel becomes over how other people insist on going their own mysterious ways, forming their own conclusions, and generally refusing to correspond to his preconceived notions about them.

Marcel's expectation that the passer-by in the rain at Combray will feel the same delight as he does over the weather proceeds from the candor all children have. Marcel's surprise over his parents' unexpected reaction to his story about the Lady in Pink is no doubt followed by the sad discovery that there are certain things we had better keep to ourselves. Parallel with this is the equal surprise he feels at other people's duplicity. For example, when at a dinner at Marcel's home Norpois agrees to put in a good word for him with the Swanns, Marcel almost kisses the baron, so filled is he with gratitude, and gushes out a speech of rapturous thanks. Later he learns that the baron has made fun of him at the Swanns' for this immoderate display of emotion. The effects of Marcel's discovery of Saint-Loup's deceitfulness are much more troubling to him, since he had always considered his friend a model of sincerity and genuine kindness. Such experiences sour Marcel generally about the value of social intercourse and about the overall goodness of mankind in society. Indeed, on the basis of such embittering episodes, Marcel learns that, if he is not to go on wasting his time, he must turn from the social world and dedicate himself to a study of the world within.

Wisdom, then, runs as a counterpoint to Marcel's progress in the world and is gained from disappointment over the unending ordinariness of a world he has over-idealized and his bitterness over being misunderstood or deceived by others. It is wisdom, however, in the sense of practical caution and prudent defensiveness. Marcel, in fact, simply passes through that moral crisis repeatedly mirrored in French literature and culture. In the seventeenth century, for example, we have the novels of Mlle. de Scudéry portraying people idealized as they ought, or would like, to be and then the maxims of La Rochefoucauld, that bitter *moraliste,* who felt he had seen men as they actually were. It is as if Marcel comes to learn, by the end of the novel, that he must deflate his dreams about people if he is to understand them but that he must maintain the poetry of those dreams if he is not to fall into the corrosive cynicism at the bottom of the disabused sayings of a La Rochefoucauld or a La Bruyère. Fortunately, Elstir explains to Marcel, early in the game, that all artists must make mistakes in life, however foolish or painful they may be, so as to triumph over them and give their works that note of real experience and wisdom without which they would ring hollow and crumble into insignificance. What Marcel has gone through, then, is an apprenticeship.

As the examples suggest, however, the acquisition of this rueful wisdom is described in predominantly comic terms. As Marcel passes through the long succession of supposedly closed gates and discovers the tired banality of what lies hidden behind them, his bitter surprise is made all the more amusing by the almost sententious tone of the analyses which accompany it.

Throughout Marcel's social progress, with its attendant disenchantment, his literary vocation hangs in abeyance. It seems as if Marcel has only to sit down before a sheet of blank paper to experience instant boredom and the restless desire to be doing virtually anything else but writing. He even wonders whether his father, who has so much influence in higher places, might not use it to turn him into an over-night success as an author. Nothing seems to work, however, and Marcel spends a long life in sterility, tortured by his conscience and never spared by the imperative sense of his own vocation but at a total loss to carry it out.

The trouble is that he must depend on the miraculous intervention of chance to realize his vocation, just as he must rely on mysterious outside powers to gain access to the various social milieus that bewitch him. Thus, even in the midst of the utmost despair over his capacity to create, there may intervene a revolutionary change of circumstances. A preliminary intimation of the vocation comes in the celebrated passage on the composition Marcel writes on the spires of Martinville as he hurries along atop the carriage of Dr. Percepied near Combray. Unfortunately, this is just a flash in the pan, and Marcel must wait many decades before good fortune visits him again. He is rescued by such experiences as the Petite Madeleine and later the series of similar experiences at the Princess de Guermantes's at the end of the novel. (pp. 54-63)

[Through] most of the novel, Marcel's position is quite false, as far as his self-image as a writer is concerned. The text implies that much of his social success is attributable to his reputation as a budding author. Except for the piece on the spires of Martinville and an unspecified article published in the *Figaro,* the reputation would appear to be humbug. But, ironically, just as Marcel despairs of ever being able to write, the revelation of what the work is to be and how it must be written comes to him in a flash and presumably, despite a long life as a will-less and sterile creature, he goes off to write the book we are in fact reading. The same perversity that allows him to be invited to the Duchess de Guermantes's only after he has lost interest in her seems to hold here as well, but more felicitously. In any case, the root experience or contingency seems to be outside Marcel's, or the narrator's, control.

At this point we may say that, as long as Marcel follows the parallel Swann and Guermantes ways (which we interpret as, in the case of Swann, the frittering away of genius on idle pursuits and women, and, in the second, the path of snobbery), he can only gain a bitter wisdom—and this at the price of numbing disenchantment. He leads a wasted life. And yet art, like a deus ex machina, will redeem him at the last minute, and this wasted life, as he retells it, will be redeemed as well. (p. 63)

Proust amply demonstrates that Marcel is just as prone to indulge in calculated humbug as anyone else in the novel. But, by being allowed inside his head, we see the hows and whys of humbug. We also understand much better how great a part of it is rooted in insecurity, vanity, and even some unnamable craven need. The need, in fact, is so great, even though it must content itself with such short-term satisfactions, that it is quite capable of deferring indefinitely Marcel's commitment to his vocation as writer. Fortunately for him, his vocation is able to assert itself almost automatically upon him, so that finally he does cast past foolishness aside and get down to work. (pp. 63-4)

Jack Murray, in his The Proustian Comedy, *French Literature Publications Company, 1980, 170 p.*

TERENCE KILMARTIN (essay 1981)

[*In the following essay, Kilmartin assesses the strengths and weaknesses of C. K. Scott Moncrieff's translation of* A la re-cherche du temps perdu *with respect to his own 1981 revised translation.*]

There used to be a story that discerning Frenchmen preferred to read Marcel Proust in English on the grounds that the prose of *A la recherche du temps perdu* was deeply un-French and heavily influenced by English writers such as Ruskin. If at all true, the story could have come from some *salon* snob of the kind Proust ridicules in his novel. It stems from the 1930s when Proust was suffering an eclipse in France while enjoying a vogue in the English-speaking world amounting at times to a cult. He seemed to have become naturalized English and C. K. Scott Moncrieff, who died in 1930, achieved a posthumous fame which few translators have ever known.

It was not till the early fifties that Proust was reclaimed by the French. His relative eclipse had been due, in the thirties and forties, to the pervasive influence of the surrealists, then of *la littérature engagée* and the existentialists. The success in 1951 of André Maurois's *À la recherche de Marcel Proust,* followed by the publication of Proust's own *Jean Santeuil* and *Contre Sainte-Beuve,* heralded a reversal of literary opinion, culminating in 1954 in the appearance of the magnificent Pléiade edition of *A la recherche du temps perdu*— definitive, purged of the manifold errors, confusions, misreadings and omissions that had disfigured the original edition. There was a boom in Proust studies in France, and it has continued from the heyday of the *nouveau roman,* through the structuralist revolution, to the present time.

Meanwhile, a recognition grew among English and American Proustians (those, at any rate, who knew *A la recherche* in the original as well as in translation) that Scott Moncrieff's version was not all that it should be. His publishers and his heirs were reluctant to allow his text to be tampered with. The final volume, *Le temps retrouvé,* which he had not reached by the time he died—the work was completed by "Stephen Hudson" (Sydney Schiff) in Britain and Frederick A. Blossom in the United States—was re-translated by Andreas Mayor on the basis of the Pléiade edition; but it was only the impending expiry of the Scott Moncrieff copyright that persuaded the publishers to initiate a revision of the entire text.

I approached the task with some trepidation. On the one hand I was warned that my tinkering would be regarded as lèse-majesté if not sacrilege. On the other, I knew there were extremists who considered that nothing less than a complete re-translation could ever do proper justice to Proust. Not having studied the English version closely, I had a fairly open mind.

Was Scott Moncrieff as good as his supporters insisted, or as bad as his detractors maintained? The answer to both questions, I discovered, was no. As I worked my way through his text, I found myself alternating between delighted admiration of his elegant fluency and exasperation with his clumsy fallibility, his bowdlerising, archaising, prettifying.

Scott Moncrieff labored under two major disadvantages. In the first place, he had perforce to translate piecemeal what is, for all its enormous length, a single book. When *Swann* appeared in English in 1922 (the year of Proust's death), only half the novel had been published in France; *Le temps retrouvé* was not published until 1927, by which time Scott Moncrieff was in the middle of *Sodom and Gomorrah.* The full meaning of *A la recherche*—in particular Proust's metaphysics of time and memory—only becomes clear in the final section, which illuminates what has gone before. The complexities of the opening pages of the novel are especially difficult to decipher without the hindsight provided by the later volumes. I myself noticed too late (after the new version had gone to press) that in the paragraph evoking the bedroom at Tansonville *la chambre où je me serai endormi* had become in English "the bedroom in which I shall presently fall asleep" (instead of "in which I must have fallen asleep"), thus giving the reader the impression that the narrator is writing at Tansonville instead of in Paris some years after the visit to Gilberte de Saint-Loup which itself does not occur until the final pages of *The Fugitive.* The French reader can take things on trust and wait for eventual enlightenment. The reader who has only a translation to rely on cannot know—though he may have an uneasy suspicion when he reads an incomprehensible passage—that the translator may have misconstrued it, thus making obscurity doubly obscure.

The very first sentence of the novel poses a problem for the translator. *"Longtemps je me suis couché de bonne heure. . . ."* The choice of the perfect tense, what in French is called the *passé composé,* the most familiar and immediate form of the past, seems deliberately ambiguous; it leaves the reader in a state of uncertainty as to the narrator's position in time. Roger Shattuck discusses the question at length in his *Proust's Binoculars* and suggests that Proust "may have wanted to keep this opening sentence free of any exact location in time and to begin in a temporal free zone." This is certainly the effect: but how to convey it in English? Scott Moncrieff's "For a long time I used to go to bed early" smoothly evades the issue; yet I could think of no alternative that would be consistent with the imperfect into which the narrating voice instantly slides: ". . . *mes yeux se fermaient si vite que je n'avais pas le temps de me dire: 'Je m'endors. . . .'."* Edmund Wilson, incidentally, compared that opening sentence to the opening chord of a vast symphony, and the musical analogy is an illuminating one—the change of tense corresponding to a modulation, which fails to materialize in the English version.

Scott Moncrieff's second handicap was the faultiness of the French texts. The root of the trouble lay in Proust's notorious working methods: his endless additions, revisions, insertions and transpositions. These must have driven his editors and printers to distraction; inevitably they often failed to decipher his almost illegible scrawls and to obey his directives. The 200-odd closely-printed pages of notes and variants in the Pléiade illustrate the extent of the resulting corruptions and confusions, which in turn must account for some of the impenetrable obscurity of which Proust is often accused. Only *Swann,* which Proust had had time to revise between its first appearance in 1913 and its republication in 1919, was reasonably free of errors; but even here, to take one small example, an intrusive "s" in both French editions caused Scott Moncrieff to refer to a "mirror with square feet" instead of to "a rectangular cheval-glass."

Scott Moncrieff himself was aware of the problem, as a note on the title page of *The Guermantes Way* testifies; indeed in a preface to *The Captive* he promised, as soon as the English version of *Le temps retrouvé* was completed, "a supplementary volume containing a critical emendation of the French text as a whole." Alas, it would have been a case of the blind leading the blind, for it has to be said (a third handicap) that Scott Moncrieff's knowledge of French was far from perfect. There is evidence of this throughout the novel—signs of haziness and uncertainty that in a less ingenious and resourceful translator would have been crippling. Time and again he fails to recognize quite ordinary set expressions. One finds him translating literally when English equivalents could and should have been found. We have, for instance, the Duc de Guermantes telling Swann that he is "as strong as the Pont Neuf" instead of "as sound as a bell." The Duke asks elsewhere, *"Vous connaissez notre patelin?,"* characteristically choosing a familiar colloquial term for "village"; "You know our wheedler?," Scott Moncrieff mysteriously makes him say. There is also someone "adopting a policy of the least possible effort" when he is merely "taking the line of least resistance"; people sleep like lead rather than logs; things are constantly spreading like "spots of oil" rather than "wildfire," and we frequently get "straw fires" instead of "flashes in the pan" (*feux de paille*).

Like all translators from the French, Scott Moncrieff was instinctively on his guard against *faux amis:* those deceptive cognates that offer a different meaning in French and English. At times, indeed, he seems to have bent over backwards (too far backwards) to avoid falling into these traps, and we get "chastise" for *punir* when "punish" is the *mot juste.* At other times his guard slips, and one finds him referring to "pretended" as opposed to "alleged" contingencies or describing someone as "laborious" instead of "industrious"; a *milieu interlope* becomes "interloping" rather than "shady," and more heinous still, perhaps, *actuel* ("present") is sometimes rendered as "actual."

More seriously, careless or ignorant misreadings can sometimes distort the meaning of a whole passage or even make Proust say the opposite of what he intends. For instance, in the passage where Swann interrogates Odette about her suspected lesbian experiences, and having extracted a half-confession from her, asks finally, *"Il y a combien de temps?"*—"How long ago?"—Scott Moncrieff, evidently confusing *temps* and *fois,* translates "How many times?," thus trivializing Swann's insane jealousy.

A second example, also from *Swann in Love,* concerns the crucial moment in the cab when Swann is about to kiss Odette for the first time. Here Scott Moncrieff's misconstruing of pronouns causes him to transfer to Odette what is in fact going on in Swann's mind (little, if anything, would have been going on in hers):

> Et ce fut Swann qui, avant qu'elle laissât tomber [son visage], comme malgré elle, sur ses lèvres, le retint un instant, à quelque distance, entre ses deux mains. Il avait voulu laisser à sa pensée le temps d'accourir, de reconnaître le rêve qu'elle avait si longtemps caressé et d'assister à sa réalisation, comme une parente qu'on appelle pour prendre sa part du succès d'un enfant qu'elle a beaucoup aimé.

Scott Moncrieff's version of the second sentence is as follows:

> He had intended to leave time for her mind to overtake her body's movements, to recognize the dream which she had so long cherished and to assist at its realization, like a mother invited as a spectator when a prize is given to the child whom she has reared and loves.

An elementary trap: confused by those deceptive French pronouns, which must of course agree in gender with their nouns, he has taken the feminine *sa* as meaning *her* rather than *his* and the succeeding *elle* as referring to Odette, as in the previous sentence, rather than to the feminine noun, *pensée*. The absence of a neuter gender in French doesn't make things any easier. *Parente,* incidentally, is "relative" not "mother." So the sentence should read like this:

> He had wanted to leave time for his mind to catch up with him, to recognize the dream which it had so long cherished and to assist at its realization, like a relative invited as a spectator when a prize is given to a child of whom she has been especially fond.

In a third example (from **The Captive**), where Proust, describing Charlus's discomfiture at the Verdurins' musical *soirée,* speaks of ". . . this great nobleman (in whom superiority over commoners was no more essentially inherent than in this or that ancestor of his trembling before the revolutionary tribunal) . . ." standing there paralysed, tongue-tied, terror-stricken, Scott Moncrieff completely destroys the egalitarian point by making the Baron's superiority "no less essentially inherent."

The final example is another total *contresens*. Musing about his mother's attitude toward Albertine's living with him, the narrator remarks that, quite apart from the question of propriety, *je crois qu'Albertine eût insupporté maman* ("I doubt whether Mamma could have put up with Albertine"). The translator could be forgiven for not being familiar with this unusual locution, but the context should have told him that "I doubt whether Albertine could have put up with Mamma" could not possibly make sense.

When all this is said, however, it is extraordinary how successful Scott Moncrieff was in threading his way through the labyrinthine pages of **A la recherche du temps perdu.** Faced with those elaborate Proustian periods with their spiraling subordinate clauses, their parentheses and digressions, their wealth of metaphorical imagery: layer upon layer of similes derived from botany, physics, medicine, and biology, as well as from art and music—the translator might well feel tempted to unscramble and simplify, to split it all up into more manageable units. Scott Moncrieff—correctly, in my view—resisted the temptation and tried as a rule to stay as close as possible to the French text. Alas, in clinging as tenaciously as he did to the clause-structure of the original, he frequently put too great a strain on English syntax and produced some awkward, jarring, unnatural-sounding sentences, obscure and periphrastic in a way that the French is not.

E. M. Forster seems to have been aware of this when, in *Abinger Harvest,* he expressed reservations about Scott Moncrieff "because I was hoping to find Proust easier in English than in French, and do not" [see excerpt in *TCLC,* Vol. 7, pp. 523-24]. Forster went on to give him the benefit of the doubt: "All the difficulties of the original are here faithfully reproduced"—in other words, the fault was Proust's. Had he probed more deeply, though, Forster would have realized that the apparent fidelity of the translation was often a form of betrayal, that those difficulties were in fact aggravated by the translator's failure to make sufficient allowance for essential differences between the two languages. French possesses several structural devices not available in English that make it possible to write long and complicated sentences without sacrificing clarity—the existence of gender, for example, which facilitates reference to pronouns and antecedents, the ability to position adjectives either before or after the noun, the license to invert subject and verb, and a greater range of

relative pronouns. Transposing these forms into English can create an effect of weirdness and impenetrability.

But whenever the shape of the English can legitimately be calqued on to the French, fidelity to the architectonics of the original has its rewards. Here is a characteristic example: a sentence of some four hundred words evoking the adolescent Marcel's emotions on hearing, one afternoon in the gardens of the Champs-Elysées, the name of the inaccessible, yearned-for Gilberte whom he had once glimpsed through the hawthorn-hedge at Combray:

> Ce nom de Gilberte passa près de moi, evoquant d'autant plus l'existence de celle qu'il désignait qu'il ne la nommait pas seulement comme un absent dont on parle, mais l'interpellait; il passa ainsi près de moi, en action pour ainsi dire, avec une puissance qu'accroissait la courbe de son jet et l'approche de son but;—transportant à son bord, je le sentais, la connaissance, les notions qu'avait de celle à qui il etait addressé, non pas moi, mais l'amie qui l'appelait, tout ce que, tandis qu'elle le prononçait, elle revoyait ou, du moins, possédait en sa mémoire, de leur intimité quotidienne, des visites qu'elles se faisaient l'une chez l'autre, et tout cet inconnu encore plus inaccessible et plus douloureux pour moi d'être au contraire si familier et si maniable pour cette fille heureuse qui m'en frôlait sans que j'y puisse pénétrer et le jetait en plein air dans un cri;—laissant déjà flotter dans l'air l'émanation délicieuse qu'il avait fait se dégager, en les touchant avec précision, de quelques points invisibles de la vie de Mlle Swann, du soir qui allait venir, tel qu'il serait, après dîner, chez elle;—formant, passager céleste au milieu des enfants et des bonnes, un petit nuage d'une couleur précieuse, pareil à celui qui, bombé au-dessus d'un beau jardin du Poussin, reflète minutieusement, comme un nuage d'opéra plein de chevaux et de chars, quelque apparition de la vie des dieux;—jetant enfin, sur cette herbe pelée, à l'endroit où elle était un morceau à la fois de pelouse flétrie et un moment de l'après-midi de la blonde joueuse de volant (qui ne s'arrèta de le lancer et de le rattraper que quand une institutrice à plumet bleu l'eût appelée), une petite bande merveilleuse et couleur d'héliotrope, impalpable comme un reflet et superposée comme un tapis, sur lequel je ne pus me lasser de promener mes pas attardés, nostalgiques et profanateurs, tandis que Françoise me criait: "Allons, aboutonnez voir votre paletot et filons" et que je remarquais pour la première fois avec irritation qu'elle avait un langage vulgaire, et hélas! pas de plumet bleu à son chapeau.

No translation can hope to match the full resonance of this miraculous tour de force, but by obeying the structure of the original, something of its metaphorical richness, its complex rhythm and harmony, its syntactic onomatopoeia (those five main clauses governed by present participles, and extended by proliferating subordinate clauses and parentheses, imaging the rise and fall of Gilberte's shuttlecock) can be reproduced in English. Here is my revised version of Scott Moncrieff:

> That name "Gilberte" passed close by me, evoking all the more powerfully the girl whom it labeled in that it did not merely refer to her, as one speaks of someone in his absence, but was directly addressed to her; it passed thus close to me, in action so to speak, with a force that increased with the curve of its trajectory and its approach to its target;—

carrying in its wake, I could feel, the knowledge, the impressions concerning her to whom it was addressed that belonged not to me but to the friend who called it out—everything that, as she uttered the words, she recalled, or at least possessed in her memory, of their daily intimacy, of the visits they paid to each other, of that unknown existence which was all the more inaccessible, all the more painful to me for being, conversely, so familiar, so tractable to this happy girl who let it brush past me without my being able to penetrate it, who flung it on the air with a light-hearted cry;—wafting through the air the exquisite emanation which it had distilled, by touching them with precision, from certain invisible points in Mlle. Swann's life, from the coming evening, just as it would be, after dinner, at her home;—forming, on its celestial passage through the midst of the children and their nurse-maids, a little cloud, delicately coloured, resembling one of those clouds that, billowing over a Poussin landscape, reflect minutely, like a cloud in the opera teeming with chariots and horses, some apparition of the life of the gods;—casting, finally, on that ragged grass, at the spot where it was at one and the same time a patch of withered lawn and a moment in the afternoon of the fair-haired battledore player (who continued to launch and retrieve her shuttlecock until a governess with a blue feather in her hat had called her away), a marvellous little band of light, the color of heliotrope, impalpable as a reflection and superimposed like a carpet on which I could not help but drag my lingering, nostalgic and desecrating feet, while Françoise shouted: "Come on, button up your coat and let's clear off home!" and I remarked for the first time how common her speech was, and that she had, alas, no blue feather in her hat.

Another, briefer example (Proust is not always so interminably long-winded as he is often accused of being) will show, conversely, how failure to follow the syntactical logic of the French can weaken the impact. Proust is describing a sudden shower of rain:

> Un petit coup au carreau, comme si quelque chose l'avait heurté, suivi d'une ample chute légère comme de grains de sable qu'on eût laissés tomber d'une fenétre au-dessus, puis la chute s'étendant, se réglant, adoptant un rythme, devenant fluide, sonore, musicale, innombrable, universelle: c'était la pluie.

Scott Moncrieff, in this case losing his nerve, breaks the rhythm of the sentence halfway through:

> A little tap at the window, as though some missile had struck it, followed by a plentiful, falling sound, as light, though, as if a shower of sand were being sprinkled from a window overhead; then the fall spread, took on an order, a rhythm, became liquid, loud, drumming, musical, unnumerable, universal. It was the rain.

In fact those present participles, succeeding one another with ever-increasing urgency to produce an effect of crescendo, can perfectly well be retained in English:

> A little tap on the window-pane, as though something had struck it, followed by a plentiful light falling sound, as of grains of sand being sprinkled from a window overhead, gradually spreading, intensifying, acquiring a regular rhythm, becoming fluid, so-norous, musical, immeasurable, universal: it was the rain.

Despite his unfailing attentiveness to the original text, there is a significant difference in tone between Scott Moncrieff's English and Proust's French. He was twenty years younger than Proust, but his natural prose style was the product of an earlier generation, mannered, bellettristic, pseudo-poetic ("Heigh ho! Georgian prose," as Cyril Connolly said). In his hands, Proust's irony too often degenerates into whimsicality or facetiousness, his melancholy lyricism into sentimentality. His fancy inversions, his *I would fains* and *'twases* and *albeits* and *aughts,* are quite out of tune with the original; and he has a tendency to over-translate: Mme. Verdurin's "Atlanta-flights across the field of mirth" for *sur le terrain de l'amabilité,* "a mirrored firmament" for *le ciel reflété,* "beneath a spangled veil of buttercups" for *sous les boutons d'or.*

Not surprisingly, Scott Moncrieff is at his best in passages, especially of dialogue, where Proust gives free rein to his marvellous gifts as mimic and parodist: Legrandin's flowery preciosities, Bloch's mock-Homeric jargon, Brichot's donnish pedantry, Norpois's pompous diplomatic maunderings, Charlus's *vieille France* grandiloquence, cackling gossip and paranoid tirades. He is less successful with Françoise's old-world peasant idiom and the girlish patter of the *jeunes filles en fleurs.* But, as a review of the revised edition in the London weekly *Gay News* points out, he had a very exact ear for homosexual slang. The reviewer cites the passage describing how Charlus has caught the habit of homosexual chatter, where Scott Moncrieff adroitly translates *ce 'chichi' voulu* as "this deliberate camping"—perhaps the earliest appearance of this word in print, preceding the lexicographer Eric Partridge's tentative date of 1935 by six years.

Scott Moncrieff's strengths and weaknesses are neatly epitomized in the titles he chose for the novel as a whole and for the individual sections. They are stylish and ingenious, and at the same time slightly out of key. To Proust's English biographer, George Painter, the overall title, **Remembrance of Things Past,** is "exquisitely appropriate." Others have felt that it misses the whole point of the book. Proust himself, when told of it, said: *"Cela détruit le titre,"* and there is no doubt that the notion of "summoning up" the past contradicts the basic theme of the novel, which is a celebration of *involuntary* memory. Proust also complained about **Swann's Way,** but this was because he thought "way" could only mean "manner."

It is when one considers the possible alternatives that one warms to Scott Moncrieff's inventions (though not to all of them). Vladimir Nabokov offered his own literal versions of the titles instead of the "more or less fancy translations that Moncrieff inflicted upon Proust." *The Walk by Swann's Place* is certainly accurate, if somewhat inelegant; but can he seriously have expected his students to swallow *In the Shade of Blooming Young Girls?*

In his review of the "revised version" in *The New York Review of Books* [see Additional Bibliography], Roger Shattuck was mildly critical of my retention of Scott Moncrieff's **Within a Budding Grove,** pointing out that in Proust's *À l'ombre des jeunes filles en fleurs,* "it is incontrovertibly young girls that are budding—or blossoming" (or "blooming"). But he rebuked me very severely for failing to change the overall title—an omission which he seemed to regard as a sort of *trahison des clercs. Mea culpa:* I was indeed in favor of such a change, but allowed myself to be overruled by the publishers. I do not find it quite such a crucial issue as Shattuck and others do. Still, on balance I would have preferred to rechristen the novel "In Search of Lost Time," even though the English phrase lacks the specific gravity of the French and misses the double meaning of *temps perdu:* time "wasted," as well as "lost." "The whole [book] is a treasure hunt where the treasure is time and the hiding place the past" was Nabokov's summary [see excerpt in *TCLC,* Vol. 7, pp. 552-53]. There is more to it than that, of course. (pp. 134-46)

Terence Kilmartin, "Translating Proust," in Grand Street, *Vol. 1, No. 1, Autumn, 1981, pp. 134-46.*

DERWENT MAY   (essay date 1983)

[*May is an English novelist, poet, and critic. In the following excerpt, he analyzes the narrator's perception of himself in* Remembrance of Things Past *and examines his ideas on the meaning of art.*]

[In *Remembrance of Things Past,* the personality of the narrator, Marcel] reveals itself in his fascination with society and his successive experiences of love. But its presence is of course pervasive throughout the book: every observation he makes expresses it. His sense of the perpetual alternation of loss and recovery in human existence goes back . . . to his childhood; but it is not only a question of his own experiences. . . . He finds the same thing taking place in almost everyone he observes around him. However, when he is a child, observation of others is for him a continuous pleasure, even if mixed with his private anxieties; and that capacity for pleasure in the world continues throughout his life. Lying awake in the early morning, when he is living with Albertine but she is still asleep in the next room, he thinks to himself that the "person" who lies deepest in him is a "little mannikin" who, when he realises that dawn is breaking, sends up a hymn to the glory of the sun. That "little mannikin" who loves the world never vanishes from *A la recherche,* and his murmurs of laughter and enjoyment reach us from most of the pages of Marcel's narrative.

One of the first vivid impressions Marcel has of the unpredictable coming and going of feelings is a story his grandfather likes to tell about Swann's father, at the time when Swann's mother died. Marcel's grandfather "managed to entice M. Swann for a moment, weeping profusely, out of the death-chamber"—and then, as they walked in the sunshine, suddenly old M. Swann seized Marcel's grandfather by the arm and cried "How fortunate we are to be walking here together on such a charming day! . . . Whatever you may say, it's good to be alive!" Then abruptly the memory of his dead wife came back to him, and he rubbed his hand across his forehead in perplexity that he had spoken like that.

Almost all Marcel's anecdotes about people have this dual character. They bring the person dramatically to life, in all his inimitable individuality—but they always, in the end, refer back to the great themes of the book, which are one and the same as the obsessions of Marcel the narrator.

These intermittencies that haunt Marcel have their inner and their outer aspects. The story of old M. Swann is registered by Marcel mainly as a matter of inner inconsistency. But it also contains an element of erratic perception of the outer world—a feature of human behaviour that Marcel observes throughout his childhood, in Françoise, the family servant.

At Combray, when the kitchen-maid, soon after having a baby, is stricken with appalling pains, Françoise is sent to fetch a medical dictionary which will tell Marcel's mother what first aid the girl needs. Françoise starts reading about the after-pains, and for an hour sobs and prays over the book at the idea of such agonies. But she completely forgets the suffering girl she is supposed to be helping. Again, when Marcel's grandmother is dying, Françoise is willing to stay up night after night to keep her company. But she also insists on combing the old woman's straggling grey hair to make it look better, regardless of the pain it causes her. In both cases, Françoise's acts fail to connect in any rational or useful way with the needs of the person they are meant to serve. Inner preoccupations inhibit her, for a time, from any genuine imaginative reaching out to the reality of the kitchen-maid or Marcel's grandmother.

In Marcel's own life, such experiences take many and complex forms. The root of them all is a feeling of profound psychological instability. His own nature is all the time undergoing changes that make it hard for him to retain any sense of himself as a coherent being. And the outer world is equally unstable. Other people, especially, seem to be in a constant state of flux—and he cannot even tell if it is they who are changing, or if it is simply his own perceptions that are so incoherent and unreliable. After Albertine is dead, he reflects that she seems to be just as alive to him as before, because he still retains all the varied impressions of her that he used to recall when she was really alive. To feel that she was dead, he says, "what I should have to annihilate in myself was not one, but innumerable Albertines." But "it was not Albertine alone who was a succession of moments, it was also myself . . . I was not one man only, but as it were the marchpast of a composite army in which there were passionate men, indifferent men, jealous men—jealous men not one of whom was jealous of the same woman."

Marcel is not passive in this situation. In the first place, although the multiplicity of experience confuses and distresses him, it is not a question of his wanting all its intransigent individual bits to vanish. On the contrary, he wants a wealth of emotion; he adores the many aspects of Albertine; he is glad that the world is full of girls. What he needs is to hold them all in some coherent and unified relation with each other, and with himself.

And he has strategies for doing this. One . . . is his impulse to brood on the name rather than the reality of a person or a place, and let its historical or mythical associations dominate his thought. It gives him, often, a quite exciting or glamorous hold on the world. But of course it is always a useless strategy in the end. The reality—as when he visits Balbec, as when he meets the Guermantes—always shatters the word-image eventually. Complexity and confusion return, and Marcel seems to be left with the stark choice: illusion or division.

There is a still further complication. Illusion itself may be a cause of division. As so often, we are given a ludicrous example of the point. The lift-boy at Balbec persists in calling the Marquise de Cambremer "the Marquise de Camembert." He cannot be budged from the idea because he can see nothing wrong with the name. On the contrary, it satisfies his sense of rightness: it is not surprising that a marquisate should be named after such a great cheese. Marcel's "Guermantes," we might say, is the lift-boy's "Camembert." Both names satisfy their users' desire for coherence and unity. But both the young men are victims, while they think like that, of an illusion that separates them from the reality of the Guermantes or the Cambremers. In fact, they are very like Françoise, when her fascinated absorption in an idea of suffering or neatness blinds her to the facts about Marcel's grandmother or the kitchen-maid.

Marcel's own awareness of this problem comes out very clearly in his thoughts about the fact that various girls to whom he is attracted are rather like each other. On the one hand, that seems to offer him a prop to his sense of continuity in his nature, something he greatly desires. On the other hand, it suggests that he is not seeing and responding to the girls wholly and distinctly as individuals, something that he also wants. Indeed, at those times when it is novelty and adventure rather than solace and peace that beckon him, it is precisely the mysteriousness of new women that he longs for—such as the feeling, in a strange place, that though he is only three feet from a passing girl, she seems to be "separated from him by the impossible." To complete this paradox, he suggests at another moment in the story that it is only when a woman is new and mysterious that a man can know anything about her at all, because once she becomes familiar and he begins to have feelings about her, complexity and confusion start up again. And all the other intermittencies follow in the wake of that—the desire (familiar by now to the reader) to know and control, and the impulse once more to escape.

With women, these are dilemmas that Marcel never resolves. But, on a quite simple level, he does have an eye for a comforting unity when he meets it in the world. Moreover, even as a child he has intuitions of some real possibility of keeping the objects in his world distinct and yet related, both in space and time.

When he visits the Swanns' house, at the time he is in love with Gilberte, he sees in their drawing-room a harmony that, objectively, it certainly does not have. Among Odette's Chinese ornaments, probably fakes, there are new chairs and stools draped in Louis XVI silks; and Swann has brought in a Rubens from his old house. But because of the charm in which his imagination had for so long bathed the life of the Swann family, "it has kept in my memory," says Marcel, "that composite, heterogeneous room, a cohesion, a unity, an individual charm . . . for we alone, by our belief, can give to certain things we see a soul." When he is staying in Balbec for the second time, he gets to know the little coastal train that runs from Balbec, via Doncières, Saint-Loup's garrison town, out to La Raspelière, where the Verdurins are staying. This train draws the whole of this part of Normandy into a unity, visible to the traveller as he passes. When the train stops at each station, all the country gentry who live around are to be found there, just waiting for a brief chat with friends who are passing by. Marcel knows many of them by now, and he sees the railway line as a long chain of friendships, with the train itself presiding over them, patient and kind.

The most important experience of this kind in his youth is, however, of a different order, and without his knowing it at the time, it points his way ahead to his work as a writer. At this period of his life, such things as the gleam of sunlight on a stone, or the smell of a path, often give him strange feelings of a greater fecundity in the world, a deeper meaning in it, than he usually has. One day he has a particularly strong sensation of this kind. He is riding on the box of the Combray doctor's carriage, and suddenly he sees the twin steeples of Martinville, "bathed in the setting sun and constantly changing their position with the movement of the carriage and the windings of the road." Then a third steeple joins them, that of the village of Vieuxvicq. Later, driving on from Martinville, he sees them again, still changing position all the time in relation to each other, black now in the dusk.

Georges Poulet, the Belgian critic, has expressed very well the significance this experience has for Marcel. It is not "a vacillating or whirling of landscape," he says, "but liberated elements use their newly acquired mobility to bring themselves together and form a new creation." It makes a sharp contrast with the feeling Marcel more often has about places—namely, to quote Poulet again, that "the mobility of places takes away our last anchor." What is especially to the point is that Marcel has this experience just after he has been thinking, rather desperately, that he has no hope of a literary career. At this time, he supposes that to be a writer one needs philosophical themes and abstract truths, in which he seems to be conspicuously lacking. He doesn't immediately see the Martinville steeples as offering a sign to him, a promise and a prophecy that he will create literature of another kind. Nevertheless, the experience impels him to write a page about it, which he does with pencil and paper borrowed from the doctor, as he is jolted about on the way home to Combray. He is so pleased when he has done this that he begins to sing at the top of his voice.

The young Marcel may not grasp the point, but Proust is making it plain to us. The experience certainly has something to do with Marcel's literary future. In fact, it not only tells us that he is going to be an artist, but also gives us a clear hint of what his art will be like.

From a very early age, Marcel cherishes the dream of being a writer. He has done his reading, of course—his Racine, his Balzac, his Baudelaire. But in his teens he is particularly attracted to a contemporary writer, Bergotte. Bergotte is an invention of Proust's, supposedly based on the novelist and critic, Anatole France (though France's essentially rationalist, commonsensical work has not much in common with Bergotte's writings). Marcel gets his first encouragement to be a writer from M. de Norpois, a diplomat, his father's friend and superior. But he is confused and dismayed when Norpois goes on to disparage Bergotte. Norpois believes that literature should deal in "lofty conceptions"; for him, Bergotte, with his fastidious attention to form, is a mere "flute-player."

Marcel, as we have seen, also thinks when he is very young that "lofty conceptions," soaring philosophical thoughts, are what a writer should aspire to. But it is through the influence of writers like Bergotte that he modifies these ideas. When he meets Bergotte at the Swanns', he has to jettison other false notions too, for Bergotte as a man is not remotely like the "stalactite" that Marcel had elaborated for himself, "drop by drop, out of the transparent beauty of his books." He is squat, with a snail-shell nose. But as Marcel listens to his voice, which intones rather than speaks the words, he sees clearly something in Bergotte's work that even Bergotte's admirers often miss. They value him—just like Norpois in their own way—for his "Bergottisms," his remarkable thoughts. What Marcel sees is something quite different: "a plastic beauty, independent of whatever his sentences might mean." Whether Marcel, or Proust, would in the end have stood by such a strictly formal account of the beauty of prose, I think we must doubt. But for Marcel, at this point, it is a liberation from the idea that the intellect is the chief organ of literary creation.

We last see Bergotte on the day of his death, which is actually the reverberating day when Marcel goes to the Verdurins' party and leaves Albertine in the flat. Bergotte dies in an art gallery, where, already very ill, he has dragged himself to look at Vermeer's *View of Delft*. His last act is to contemplate a fine detail in the painting—a little yellow patch of wall. He collapses as he studies it, thinking "I have given away my life for this." Literally, of course, he means that by coming out to see it he has killed himself. But symbolically we must take him to mean that he has sacrificed his life to the precisions and beauties of art. Proust himself went to see this very painting not long before he died, and wrote this passage after his visit; so I think we must suppose that he was talking of himself here, with just the mingled feelings that Bergotte has. Yet, with one of those endless twists and accretions of implication that we find in *A la recherche,* Bergotte also reflects, in his last thoughts, that his works have not been as rich as that little patch of yellow: "My last books are too dry, I ought to have gone over them with a few layers of colour."

We can hear Proust's voice here again. He admired the dedication of writers such as Bergotte, and the exquisite quality of their work; but in the role of Marcel he would go over his work with many layers of colour, for reasons deeper than Bergotte ever began to know.

Two other fictitious artists are important to Marcel. One is the painter, Elstir, whom he meets at Balbec. Something of what Marcel finds in Elstir's landscapes and seascapes gets into *A la recherche.* He says that Elstir created his work out of "the rare moments when we see nature as she is, poetically": Elstir tried to "strip himself of every intellectual notion" and come "face to face with reality." God gave things names, says Marcel, but Elstir took them away again.

These are ideas drawn from the Impressionist painters, especially Renoir and Monet. Later critics have questioned both the philosophical and the optical soundness of the notion that there is any such thing as a raw, true impression unmodified by the mind, arguing that there are, rather, just different ways in which we choose to see things. However, the principle certainly helped the Impressionist artists to produce paintings in which the beauty of shifting lights and colours was caught as never before; and the psychological self-portrait drawn by Marcel uses the same ideas very effectively. It certainly shows us how "names" and "intellectual notions" can deceive us; and, in illustrative contrast, it tries to give us Marcel's "impressions" as they truly come to him, abundant, fresh and unworked-on. The permanent confusion in Marcel's view of Albertine belongs to this aspect of his self-portrait—as does another curious detail, the fact that we never know Marcel's age at any point. Consciousness of our age in numbers of years, Proust would undoubtedly say, is one of those "intellectual notions" that is never part of our immediate perception of the world.

The third artist is the composer, Vinteuil. He is an old music teacher who lives in Combray. After his death, the only finished composition he leaves is a sonata, which provides another beautifully drawn connection between Swann and Marcel. Swann hears the sonata played at the Verdurins' when he is in love with Odette. One phrase in particular haunts him, and for a while he is convinced that music "is on an equal footing with the ideas of the intellect." Proust here an-

Robert de Montesquiou, the wealthy aesthete whom Proust used as a model for the character Baron Charlus in Remembrance of Things Past.

ticipates, but with a touch of delicate comedy at Swann's expense, Marcel's own discovery, through Bergotte and Elstir and Vinteuil, of the supremacy of art over all other human activities. Swann even thinks, at the time, that in the company of Vinteuil's phrase "death would be less bitter." But later he forgets what he has felt, and only retains a vague, sentimental memory of pleasure in the music.

Marcel is to receive far more enduring impressions from Vinteuil's work. He, too, comes to love the sonata; nevertheless, while listening to Albertine playing it for him on the pianola, he is beset by some of his deepest doubts about leading the life of an artist. He suddenly has a feeling that art offers nothing better than life; that it does not reflect any special power or insight on the part of the artist; that the artist is merely a labourer who contrives to give us a different, but not superior pleasure.

However, at the Verdurin party—the same one that keeps recurring here, the one he goes to from the Paris flat—he hears another work of Vinteuil's, a septet (supposedly based on a work of César Franck's). There is an extraordinary irony for Marcel in the very existence of this work. It has been painstakingly put together, from notes that Vinteuil left, by that very friend of Vinteuil's daughter who once wanted to spit on Vinteuil's portrait, and whose imagined relations with Albertine have been the cause of Marcel's greatest anguish. This nameless girl, on this climactic day, brings Marcel a restored and henceforth imperishable sense of the unique meaning and glory of art, as he listens to the septet she herself has restored.

What, then, does Marcel come to think about the nature of art, as he approaches the time when he will begin writing? Many of his thoughts on this subject arise as he is listening to Vinteuil's music, and one point that particularly recurs is the idea that art gives us a unique revelation of another person's actual experience of the world. This, we might say, is the subjective complement of what he has found in Elstir's painting, where the stress was more on the authenticity of the objective element—the direct impression of nature as it really is. In Marcel's thought, the two become essentially indivisible, and represent all that we can, in any rewarding sense, "know."

The idea comes to him when he is playing Vinteuil's sonata on the piano: "As the spectrum makes visible to us the composition of light, so the harmony of a Wagner, the colour of an Elstir, enable us to know that essential quality of another person's sensations into which love for another person does not allow us to penetrate." Later, listening to the septet at Mme. Verdurin's, he carries the thought further. It seems to him that in all Vinteuil's music there is audible a "voice," a "song," that is different from every other composer's, and is always recognisable. The same is true of every other genuinely original composer; and this "unique accent" is "a proof of the irreducibly individual existence of the soul."

Where does the composer learn this song? By way of answer, Marcel imagines that every artist brings his individual song from a lost and forgotten fatherland, to which he draws nearer and nearer again as his work develops, taking us with him. He concludes that for us, the only true voyage of discovery is not to foreign lands, but "to see the universe through the eyes of another, of a hundred others, to see the hundred universes that each of them sees, that each of them is; and this we can do with an Elstir, with a Vinteuil." He contrasts this real possibility with the repeated fiasco of his attempts to understand living people directly: speaking of one "caressing" phrase of Vinteuil's, he says, making the most explicit of comparisons, "this phrase—this invisible creature—is perhaps the only Unknown Woman that it has ever been my good fortune to meet."

We can consider these ideas of Marcel's from two points of view. First, we might feel that they express a very specialised and limited view of what art offers us. Nevertheless, the idea that true art springs from the authentic personal sensibility of its creator has been very pervasive in twentieth-century criticism—a reflection of our loss of absolute certitudes. Even a critic such as F. R. Leavis, who stressed the moral wisdom and civilising power of great art, both of them qualities of wide-ranging importance, insisted that such art has its origins in some "vital" personal experience, that it grows "organically" out of the "whole being" of the artist.

More particularly, we can see how happily such a view of art answers to Marcel's own anxieties. If he can "meet" another person fully and reliably in art, two supremely comforting solutions offer themselves to his fears. First, he has at last, in the art of others, a chance of discovering some stability in the world around him. Even more important, if he can become an artist himself, he can overcome his own haunting sense of inner instability. He may at last be able to create something

in which his own personality will be locked firm, and made accessible to mankind.

All the same, if this idea of art inspires Marcel, it does not immediately solve any of the problems. Has he himself a "lost fatherland?" Has he a "self" at all? If so, how can he find it? And even if he can, what possible form might his art take?

The steeples of Martinville continue to hold out one hope to him. In fact, the article he publishes in *Le Figaro*—the one that the Duke cannot believe in—is a reworking of the thoughts about the steeples that he wrote in the jolting carriage as a boy. It is his first literary success. Nor has he finished with the steeples after that. They come into his mind again as he listens to a joyous phrase in Vinteuil's septet:

> I knew that this tone of joy . . . was a thing I would never forget. But would it ever be attainable to me? This question seemed all the more important inasmuch as this phrase was what seemed most eloquently to characterise . . . those impressions which at remote intervals I experienced in my life as starting-points, foundation-stones for the construction of a true life: the impression I had felt at the sight of the steeples of Martinville, or of a line of trees near Balbec.

Intimations of the kind of unity he needs, both for his life and his art, come to him also in dreams, when they reawaken in him "something of the desire for certain non-existent things which is the necessary condition for working, for freeing oneself from the dominion of habit." But the main agent which keeps suggesting itself to him as a means of drawing his life together in a unity that would serve as the basis for his art, is memory.

Memory brings us back, at last, to the *madeleine*. We read about the little piece of cake dipped in tea at the very beginning of *A la recherche.* We are not told when the incident happened: all we know is that it must have been some time in Marcel's middle years. The experience brought back the past for him, but, as far as we are told, it did not at the time have the meaning for his art that later experiences of the same kind reveal. Implicitly, of course, Marcel (and Proust) are looking ahead to that meaning. But here, at the start of the book, Proust is just showing us a vivid "involuntary memory" in action, and, without further elaboration, following it with an account of the world remembered—the world of Combray. Combray springs into being again like Japanese paper flowers when they are dropped in water—"stretching and twisting and taking on colour and distinctive shape, becoming flowers or houses or people, solid and recognisable."

The full meaning of the *madeleine* is revealed at the other end of the book, when in its last pages Marcel arrives at the home of the new Princesse de Guermantes, an elderly man himself meeting aged friends again. He is dejected; he has spent much of the war in a sanatorium, and is feeling that all his responsiveness to the world has left him, and his dream of being a writer will never now come true. Then, in quick succession, he has an amazing series of sensations.

He trips over some uneven paving-stones, and recovers his balance by putting his foot on a lower stone. Suddenly, as he does this, he has a dazzling vision of Venice, where he had once done just the same thing in the baptistery of St. Mark's. A moment later, he hears a servant knocking a spoon against a plate—and equally suddenly he finds himself back in the railway carriage on his recent return journey to Paris, looking out now with a feeling of extraordinary happiness at a line of trees, with sunlight flooding their crests. The connection here in his memory was the sound of a railwayman tapping a wheel with his hammer. Then he has a third, similar experience. The stiff, starchy feel of a napkin recalls a towel he dried his face with, standing at the window on his first day in Balbec—and the napkin unfolds for him, from within its smooth surfaces, "the plumage of an ocean green and blue like the tail of a peacock."

These moments are the climax of the novel—and describe its birth. For in them, not only is Marcel's faith restored—his faith in his capacity both for joy and for creation—but also he sees what his novel must be. In these moments, his sensation of the world comes back to him with all its freshness and poetic force, not clouded by the anxieties and desires that accompanied such sensations at the time he first had them. What is more, these sensations comprise within themselves a wealth of other, allusive sensations—evocations of innumerable other, associated experiences, all revived in the same instant. This, Marcel perceives with absolute clarity, is what must become the substance of his creation: his own life, relived with this ecstasy, this many-layered richness, this purity of contemplation, and this unity.

It was Time that had always seemed the principal enemy to him. The steady, obliterating passage of Time was the chief cause of that terrifying instability in himself and the world. But now Time suddenly appears as the saviour, if he can confront and master it. For Lost Time also contains all that we have lived through, and so, he thinks, contains also our true or essential self. Once we have recovered Time, through memory and art, we are freed from its destructive power—we are outside Time. But to do this we must follow the clues offered us by such experiences of "involuntary" memory as those he has just experienced. Deliberate, willed attempts to recapture the past leave us only with desiccated, isolated impressions. But Marcel's experiences with the uneven paving-stones, the clinking spoon and the napkin show us how it is possible to bring the whole of our past life together. They tell us not to look outside, but within ourselves, where the true and enduring self and the work of art both lie hidden, waiting for us—and are, moreover, for the artist who can bring them forth, identical. That is why so-called "realist" art, with its external preoccupations, is so shallow. There is no truth—and so no true art—attainable by man except what he can elicit from his own inner experience. (pp. 45-57)

> *Derwent May, in his* Proust, *Oxford University Press, Oxford, 1983, 85 p.*

MARY C. RAWLINSON (essay date 1984)

[*In the following essay, Rawlinson discusses impressionism as the artistic theory and method that best illuminates the processes in* Remembrance of Things Past *of recollecting the past and giving it verbal expression.*]

Proust's impressionism is summarized in the idea that only the impression is a guarantor of truth, and the advancement of impressionism itself will be governed by this rule. Essentially philosophical in its controlling end, Proust's *A la recherche du temps perdu* relates a search for the "permanent and general essence of things," unfolding as its main theme the path by which essences are revealed. Ultimately, impressionism takes its place alongside idealism and empiricism as an account of the conditions of truth, and it comprises both

a systematic analysis of the real in its various degrees and kinds, or an ontology, and a description of the human mental apparatus, or a philosophy of mind.

The *Recherche,* however, explicitly prohibits itself from advancing any theories. And in describing his method Proust writes:

> I thought it more honest and scrupulous as an artist . . . not to announce that it was in search of truth that I had started out, not to say what truth meant for me. . . . If I merely attempted to remember the days as lived, I would not take the trouble sick as I am to write. But I did not want to analyze this evolution of a mind in abstract terms, I wanted to recreate it to make it live. . . . [*Marcel Proust et Jacques Rivière: Correspondance, 1914-1922*]

The *Recherche* does not undertake an abstract categorial analysis of thinking in general or of the unity and conditions of any possible world. All the elements of this text "have been furnished by [the author's] sensibility" [Interview with Proust by Elie-Joseph Bois]. Both more durable and less opaque than any human body, it embodies and makes accessible to the reader the living reality of another mind. This mind, embodied in the narrative "I" which unfolds the text, "pays attention only to what is general" in the particular experiences of its actual life. As it unfolds in the text, it proves itself capable of expressing in the images of art the forms and laws that the impressions of life have revealed.

Impressionism advances, then, not by way of theories, rather, via certain impressions. The impression is to the writer what the experiment is to the natural scientist: the example that proves the truth of his conclusions and prescribes a repeatable method by which others may confirm them. As the writer expresses only those truths that he has been forced to think by life itself, so too the reader finds those truths demonstrated only on the basis of certain actual impressions recreated by the text. An analysis of artistic creation—of the method by which truth may be stored in the beauty of an image so as to disseminate itself in other minds long after the death of the one who first conceived it—necessarily completes impressionism, but a phenomenology of reading—an account of the effectiveness of literary images in conveying impressions of forms and laws, those "permanent and general essences common to a number of things"—forms one of its "starting-points."

Every individual writer or artist exposes in his creations his own form or kind of mind, i.e., all of his expressions will display that form or kind of mind as *style,* and this is the "deepest" or most general truth that any text can convey. Thus, involuntarily, without seeking to repeat himself, in fact,

> . . . seeking to do something new, Vinteuil questioned himself with all the force of his creative effort, reached his own essential nature at those depths, where, whatever be the question asked, it is in the same accent, that is to say its own that it replies. Such an accent, the accent of Vinteuil, is separated from the accents of other composers by a difference far greater than that which we perceive . . . even between the cries of two species of animal. . . .

Artistic style embodies, so as to recreate its real presence and yield impressions of it, some specific form or kind of mind that has actually existed, as well as the forms and laws of the various worlds in which that mind unfolds. Through books and other works of art, the reader "shifts perspectives" so as to see through the lens of another mind. The book brings to life in the reader styles of thought and feeling not his own, and yields to the reader in his solitude non-inferential knowledge of another mind.

The reader's vision, however, is governed in its entirety by its own form of mind. What is always the same, the "one in the many," the permanent and general essence common to all the impressions and expressions of his experience is the individual's *own* form or kind of mind. And, it is this that in moments of real success artistic style reveals.

> . . . style for the writer, no less than colour for the painter, is a question not of technique, but of vision: it is the revelation, which by direct and conscious methods would be impossible, of the qualitative difference, the uniqueness of the fashion in which the world appears to each one of us, a difference which, if there were no art, would remain forever the secret of every individual.

The *Recherche* itself will embody the "evolution of a mind," not as an abstract possibility, but in its "living reality." Its style will reveal that "habitual speculation" or "eternal investigation" governing the great variety of the text, even as it determines the form of mind that the text embodies. Unfolding from an original impression of essences in art—an impression of the "philosophic richness," the "Truth and Beauty" of the book read in the childhood garden of Combray—this "apprenticeship of a man of letters" serves the retrieval, repetition, and development of this communion with the permanent and general, and reveals in particular how the art-work produces its effects. Searching for a method by which to reveal essences, Proust discovers it in artistic creation. Literary style, philosophical method: these are but two names for the path by which the narrative "I" unfolds its form and worlds of operation.

Commenting upon the methods and aims of his novel, Proust remarked that the entire *Recherche* rests on the distinction between voluntary and involuntary memory. In fact, the impressions of involuntary memory, whose investigation might seem to constitute a detour, provide the analogical key which will unlock an understanding of the impressions of art. Together these two kinds of impressions compose the evidence adequately demonstrating impressionism.

On the one hand, an account of the conditions of involuntary memory reveals various general features of impressions and illuminates the conjoint operation of sensation and memory in the registration of impressions. It demonstrates that the human being is an "amphibious creature . . . plunged simultaneously in the past and the reality of the living moment," and it demonstrates as well how within this difference a mind unfolds itself.

On the other hand, it is primarily through a critique of voluntary memory that Proust undermines the validity of any analysis of thought in abstract terms. Compared with a memory set in motion by sensation, voluntary memory proves a failure in retrieving real impressions. Analogously, an abstract intelligence operating freely and at will, neither constrained by nor set in motion by specific impressions, can articulate only categorical systems which, though internally consistent and

coherent, are not guaranteed to be descriptive of anything real.

What is one to make, then, of those rare and fleeting moments in which, encountering unexpectedly a distinctive scent or a particular noise, one finds the actual world fading under the influence of some former, forgotten world's returning presence. The *Recherche* offers a multiplicity of instances in which the anatomy of this mechanism is demonstrated, from the famous incident of the lime-flower tea that opens the text, to the resurrections of his grandmother and Albertine through the repetition of certain gestures, to the series of sensations near the end of the *Recherche* (successively reviving Venice, a railway journey, and Balbec) that finally unlocks for the hero the secrets of literature. These comprise the exemplary series of an eidetic variation revealing the general form of involuntary memory.

In each case the hero encounters in the present a sensuous quality which, rather than merely resembling, is actually identical to a sensuous element of some past impression. Under the pressure of the present sensation the past impression, and the whole world and self to which it belongs, revives. The mechanism may involve any sense, including the kinesthetic senses of gesture, motion, and position, as is exemplified by the experience of the two uneven paving stones that as he totters upon them return the hero to Venice, or the incident of the scarf in which, recreating the gesture of Albertine, the hero revives her presence.

The sensory quality that in being an element of both enables the communication of present and past cannot be so abstract as mustiness or shrillness: rather, its content must have been determined by a specific sensation, e.g., the taste of a madeleine dipped in lime-flower tea or the feel of a certain stiff and starchy towel. What must be given again in order for the past to be revived, however, is just this concrete sensory quality, and not necessarily the object with which it was originally associated. Thus, Balbec is retrieved through the towel that hung there in the hero's bath, not because he encounters that towel again, but because he is once again impressed with its stiff, starchy texture in the napkin presented to him by a waiter at the *soirée* of the Princesse de Guermantes. Similarly, in the clink of a spoon against a plate the hero rediscovers the same aural quality which distinguished the sound of a railwayman's hammer, and through it retrieves all that with which *that* sound was connected—the smoke and heat of the train, the cool forest beside which it tarried, as well as a dispirited self, resolved after many disappointments to abandon literature. In each case it is an identity of sensuous qualities, not an identity of objects that conditions the revival of the former impression. The connection between the object currently embodying the sensuous quality and the returning past is purely contingent, inessential. Thus, involuntary memory operates at the level of sensation, prior to the naming and classifying of objects.

Moreover, the value of any object in the search for truth resides in its effect upon us, and not in itself. There is no reason in principle, for example, why for Proust it is a certain pink that when encountered sheds its delicate and fragile light upon the whole domain of love, enveloping within itself and determining the value of objects as diverse as the raspberries crushed in cream cheese and the hawthorns of Combray, the dress of his Uncle Adolphe's mistress and the bows on Albertine's wrapper. Involuntary memory exemplifies the fact that material objects affect us by awakening some region of our own sensibility or by setting our faculties to work in a certain way. And, it is this determinate impression that is recalled by involuntary memory, not a generalized representation of the object.

Because any actual impression is bifold in character comprised of both the sensory quality and the section of sensibility that it illuminates, past impressions cannot be revived by an act of will, nor by any purely mental operation. The past has more than a mental status: it exists in things, ". . . hidden somewhere outside the realm, beyond the reach of intellect, in some material object, or more precisely in the sensation which that material object will give us . . .". Because past impressions are lost to us, because we have ceased to experience this lost self and world, we cannot go in search of them. We cannot know, either, in what objects we will find the revealing sensuous qualities invested. "We have put something of ourselves everywhere, everything is fertile, everything is dangerous, and we can make discoveries no less precious than in Pascal's *Pensées* in an advertisement of soap . . .". It is a matter of contingency which object will bring to us that sensory quality with the power to illuminate "like a ray of the setting sun" a section of our sensibility.

The resurrections of involuntary memory, however, if fortuitous, are also inevitable. Having encountered in the present a sensory quality that is also an element of some past impression, we have no choice about what it forces us to think. Such sensations set in motion, against our will as it were, an excavation of sensibility, an effort to reanimate or recreate the dessiccated impressions of a former self and world that approach from a distance in the sensuous quality. It is only the actual recognition of the quality which ensures the return of the past impression and its context:

> *And once I had recognized the taste* of the crumb of
> madeleine soaked in her decoction of lime-flowers
> which my aunt used to give me; immediately . . .
> the whole of Combray and its surroundings, taking
> their proper shapes and growing solid, sprang into
> being . . . from my cup of tea. (my emphasis)

The mere presence of the sensory quality is enough to initiate the dissolution of actual states of consciousness and the approach of some self we have forgotten; however, supported only by the immediate and isolated sensation which is quickly exhausted as a point of communication, the past cannot hold out against the more massive and insistent body of the actual world. Ordinarily these infrequent and brief experiences leave us with no more than a vague and inarticulate sense of something lost before it could be retrieved, though it seemed to have been truly a part of ourselves. The returning self and world recede, and we are left only with a glimpse, like the evanescence of a rose's scent. The complete achievement of involuntary memory requires not only the catalyst of the sensation, but also an intellectual labor of explication and recognition whose essential gesture is that of disconnecting the sensation from the actual world so that it begins to imply another context and other horizons.

Involuntary memory can occur at all and to any degree only because memory and sensation are not separate faculties of mind, but two mechanisms of inscription by which the impressions of life are physically registered in the brain. Thus, ". . . each past day has remained deposited in us, as in a vast library . . .". The successive superimposition of impressions, one upon the other, creates within the subject who receives them layers of time, like the strata of a geological formation.

Yet this mountain of the past is subject to tremendous upheavals, for any impression is composed, not only of a given set of immediate sensations, but also ". . . the memories which envelop us simultaneously with them." In its registration the sensation is like a tone which, resonating throughout the corridors of time, revives the vibrant sound of all former sensations of the same kind. The impression is essentially temporal not only because it carries with it its own retentional and protentional fringes, but also by virtue of its temporal effects, i.e., its unearthing of former eras. Every sensation has the character of a reminder, as the "sight of a book once read weaves into the characters of its title the moonlight of a distant summer night."

Every person experiences "many deaths of many selves," and for the most part these former selves are lost to us.

> It is no doubt the existence of our body which we
> may compare to a jar containing our spiritual nature,
> that leads us to suppose that all our inward
> wealth, our past joys, all our sorrows are perpetually
> in our possession . . . if they remain with us, it
> is, for most of the time, in an unknown region
> where they are of no service to us. . . . But if the
> sensations in which they are preserved be recaptured,
> they acquire in turn the same power of expelling
> everything that is incompatible with them, of
> installing alone in us the self that originally lived
> them.

The rare resurrections of involuntary memory, and herein lies their value in the search for truth, illuminate the temporal depths which comprise any mind. As Maurois remarks, "The couple present sensation-returning memory is to Time what the stereoscope is to space." Proust frequently enjoins us to think of the landscape of the mind as at least as vast and various as those we meet in the external world. It, too, exhibits infinitely unfolding horizons. And, it is this geography of the mind that it is the duty of the literary artist to explore. Just as its effect of animating some section of our sensibility and feeling determines the value of an object, so too the general form and quality of our mind underlies all that we can know. Any material object is "volatised" as it approaches the domain of sensibility, ". . . as an incandescent body which is moved toward something wet never actually touches moisture, since it is itself preceded by a zone of evaporation." The domain of our own sensibility is for each one of us the "sole reality," that "internal difference" which the literary artist strives to express.

Involuntary memory provides a key to the work of art insofar as it resurrects the "timeless man" within us. Through involuntary memory, we are transported from a world of subjects and objects which constantly change and pass away, to the domain of essences which repeat themselves across time as the same. Though any individual discovers within himself a series of selves only one of which is actually lived at any time, involuntary memory reveals a self outside this series and characterized by the power to traverse it. Precisely because the impressions of involuntary memory have the power to animate this "I" which traverses time, of which the specific selves of actual life are only examples, the mechanism is always associated with an extraordinary joy, even when the memories it revives are themselves painful. Just as the series of the hero's loves exhibits something more durable and complete than any one of his actual loves, viz., his own form of love, so too the series of actual selves displays the "permanent self," his own form of mind. The intellectual labor which involuntary memory sets in motion is nothing less than the re-creation of lost time, so that the essence which traverses time may be read in it.

Conversely, voluntary memory recalls only a passed present, not the past in its temporal depth, for it merely represents the presence of the object or reproduces certain terms and phrases in which the subject's experience has been habitually objectified without being expressed. As "every impression is double, and the one half which is sheathed in the object is prolonged in ourselves by another which we alone can know," the effect of an object upon our sensibility is some-thing original and worth expressing in a work of art. Thus, the impressions of a work of art make accessible another mind, even as the impressions of involuntary memory yield access to dimensions of our own mind which have been dark to us, releasing both some former self and the "timeless man" within us. Voluntary memory, however retrieves only the ob-jective element of the impression, and not its sensible articu-lation.

Moreover—and in the context of the *Recherche* one must maintain a fairly rigorous distinction between the sensation of qualities and the perception of objects—the object and the process in which it is identified as a thing of a certain kind are governed by convention and belong to the world of what we may call after Heidegger the "they self," where the "inter-nal difference" of the individual is suppressed. Here we find the profound kinship of Proust's style or method to impres-sionism in painting. Impressionism, of which as [George D.] Painter remarks we find a generalized image in Elstir, op-poses a conventional realism and explores light as a power of dissolution, illuminating a level of experience comprised of elemental sensuous qualities, prior to the intervention of "verbal concepts" and "names." Rather than directly depict-ing objects, impressionist painting forces us "to return to the very root of our impression," where we discover that "sur-faces and volumes are in reality independent of the names of objects which our memory imposes on them." Sensation is a realm of illusion, metaphor, and analogy where we see one thing in another, one thing *as* another, and our intellect must be constantly at work introducing the objective distinctions with which it is familiar. Ordinarily, we identify reality with the result of this process, viz., the conventional names of ob-jects; however, impressionist painting upsets their natural at-titude and presents us with both the truly ambiguous charac-ter of sensation and the intellectual process of distinction.

With our gaze averted from ourselves and fixed on the object however, ". . . vanity and passion and the intellect, and habit, too . . . smother our true impressions, so as to entirely conceal them from us, beneath a whole heap of verbal con-cepts which we falsely call life." Like the false literature of the Goncourts, we report life objectively, without expressing it. For the original effects of our impressions we substitute a variety of conventional utterances. If, for example, I say, "I saw a bird," everyone knows what I mean. Any interlocutor can call to mind an abstract idea of the animal in question. Yet, the "I saw" remains entirely unexplicated and the deter-minate, individualizing qualities of the impression entirely unexpressed. Similarly, conventional phrases such as the hero's "How splendid!" or Bloch's "It was f-f-fantastic!" are merely inarticulate markers for some profound impression which the speaker has not the strength or the wit to really ex-press. Trading these we say nothing to one another. Neither the exchange of the names of objects, nor of these convention-al exclamations, so like the mistress' pantomimes, can convey an impression of that interior landscape which involuntary memory reveals. Voluntary memory recalls only these con-ventions operating in the present, and fails to open up the di-mension of the essence which traverses time.

Intellectual efforts to analyze reality without explicating a de-terminate impression must rely upon abstract ideas which are foreign to what we actually experience. Just as the hero's ex-perience of the real loss of his grandmother is masked, rather than revealed, by his conventional manifestations of grief, so too his abstract idea of beauty fails to illuminate the talent of Berma. In the first case the mechanism of involuntary memory makes possible the communication of present and former selves, so that the hero experiences once again the real presence of his grandmother, but at a distance, across the temporal depth of the past. Experiencing for the first time the real extent of his loss, that is, the real depth at which his grandmother was lodged within him, nonetheless, the hero finds this true grief qualified by an extraordinary joy: on the one hand *he has found her again,* i.e., he has found within himself again the whole range of sensibility that was animat-ed within him by the presence of his grandmother; on the other hand, traversing time, he has entered into the domain of essences and rediscovered that "permanent and general self" which is "nourished" by them.

In the second case, the hero discovers—because works of art teach him so—that any idea of beauty not derived from a spe-cific work must be without content, for the beauty of a work and its truth, too, lie in its "marked individuality," in its power of conveying the specific difference of some individu-ated form of mind. The value of a work of art (like that of his grandmother or any other object) lies in its power of expli-cating unexplored regions of our own sensibility, as it there unfolds its style of thought and feeling. Art, like the sensa-tions of involuntary memory, has the power to dissolve the actual world, and bring another to being in its place, as at a performance we silence the world of life, in order to focus on the stage, or in reading a book, we become unaware of what is going on around us. Unlike the sensations of involuntary memory, however, the art-work is not fleeting and does not wear out. It endures so that we can investigate it, and "does not begin by giving us all its best." It takes time to get to know the work of art—to read it, to recognize its themes and perceive its regularities, to explore all of its material—and the work takes *our* time, that is, it unfolds in and as our own thought and feeling. Thus, like involuntary memory, art illu-minates temporal depth within us and takes us into the di-mension of essences. In art, however, it is not of a former self, but of another mind that we receive impressions. Like Nietz-sche, Proust feels no grief at the death of an author who has successfully invested his mind within the "safety of a book."

For the impressionist the end of philosphical method or liter-ary style is the illumination of forms and laws of mind:

> The only true voyage of discovery, the only founda-tion of Eternal Youth, would be not to visit strange lands but to possess other eyes, to behold the hun-dred other universes that each of them beholds, that each of them is; and this we can contrive with an Elstir, with a Vinteuil; with men like these we really do fly from star to star.

The impressions of art, however, like the sensations of invol-untary memory, can act only as catalysts, setting our faculties of thought and feeling to work a certain way. Unless the individual explicates the impressions of art in an intellectual labor productive of expressions which actually articulate the real effect of the art-work upon his own sensibility, he is "in the very process [of being affected by the work] reduced to being no more than the consciousness of another." Only through the appropriation and expression of the impressions of life and art can the individual begin to see dimly that which underlies all of his expressions and impressions, his own form of mind. Writing, with its revealing style, necessarily completes impressionism. (pp. 80-91)

Mary C. Rawlinson, "Proust's Impressionism," in L'Esprit Créateur, Vol. XXIV, No. 2, Summer, 1984, pp. 80-91.

HAROLD BLOOM (essay date 1987)

[*Bloom is one of the most prominent of contemporary American critics and literary theorists. In* The Anxiety of Influence (*1973*), *Bloom formulated a controversial theory of literary creation called revisionism. Influenced strongly by Freudian theory, which states that "all men unconsciously wish to beget themselves, to be their own fathers," Bloom believes that all poets are subject to the influence of earlier poets and that, to develop their own voice, they attempt to overcome this influence through a process of misreading. By misreading, Bloom means a deliberate, personal revision of what has been said by another so that it conforms to one's own vision: "Poetic influence—when it involves two strong, authentic poets—always proceeds by a misreading of the prior poet, an act of creative correction that is actually and necessarily a misrepresentation. The history of poetic influence . . . is a history of anxiety and self-serving caricature, of distortion, of perverse, wilful revisionism." In this way the poet creates a singular voice, overcoming the fear of being inferior to poetic predecessors. Bloom's later books are applications of this theory, extended in* Kabbalah and Criticism (*1974*) *to include the critic or reader as another deliberate misreader. Thus, there is no single reading of any text, but multiple readings by strong poets or critics who understand a work only in ways that allow them to assert their own individuality or vision. In the following essay, Bloom relates Proust's treatment of jealousy in* Remembrance of Things Past *to the psychosexual theories of Sigmund Freud.*]

Sexual jealousy is the most novelistic of circumstances, just as incest, according to Shelley, is the most poetical of circumstances. Proust is the novelist of our era, even as Freud is our moralist. Both are speculative thinkers, who divide between them the eminence of being the prime wisdom writers of the age.

Proust died in 1922, the year of Freud's grim and splendid essay, "Certain Neurotic Mechanisms in Jealousy, Paranoia, and Homosexuality." Both of them great ironists, tragic celebrants of the comic spirit, Proust and Freud are not much in agreement on jealousy, paranoia, and homosexuality, though both start with the realization that all of us are bisexual in nature.

Freud charmingly begins his essay by remarking that jealousy, like grief, is normal, and comes in three stages: *competitive* or normal, *projected, delusional.* The *competitive* or garden variety is compounded of grief, due to the loss of the loved object, and of the reactivation of the narcissistic scar, the tragic first loss, by the infant, of the parent of the other sex to the parent of the same sex. As normal, *competitive* jealousy is really normal Hell, Freud genially throws into the compound such delights as enmity against the successful rival,

some self-blaming, self-criticism, and a generous portion of bisexuality.

Projected jealousy attributes to the erotic partner one's own actual unfaithfulness or repressed impulses, and is cheerfully regarded by Freud as being relatively innocuous, since its almost delusional character is highly amenable to analytic exposure of unconscious fantasies. But *delusional* jealousy proper is more serious; it also takes its origin in repressed impulses towards infidelity, but the object of those impulses is of one's own sex, and this, for Freud, moves one across the border into paranoia.

What the three stages of jealousy have in common is a bisexual component, since even *projected* jealousy trades in repressed impulses, and these include homosexual desires. Proust, our other authority on jealousy, preferred to call homosexuality "inversion," and in a brilliant mythological fantasia traced the sons of Sodom and the daughters of Gomorrah to the surviving exiles from the Cities of the Plain. Inversion and jealousy, so intimately related in Freud, become in Proust a dialectical pairing, with the aesthetic sensibility linked to both as a third term in a complex series.

On the topos of jealousy, Proust is fecund and generous; no writer has devoted himself so lovingly and brilliantly to expounding and illustrating the emotion, except of course Shakespeare in *Othello* and Hawthorne in *The Scarlet Letter.* Proust's jealous lovers—Swann, Saint-Loup, above all Marcel himself—suffer so intensely that we sometimes need to make an effort not to empathize too closely. It is difficult to determine just what Proust's stance towards their suffering is, partly because Proust's ironies are both pervasive and cunning. Comedy hovers nearby, but even tragi-comedy seems an inadequate term for the compulsive sorrows of Proust's protagonists. Swann, after complimenting himself that he has not, by his jealousy, proved to Odette that he loves her too much, falls into the mouth of Hell:

He never spoke to her of this misadventure, and ceased even to think of it himself. But now and then his thoughts in their wandering course would come upon this memory where it lay unobserved, would startle it into life, thrust it forward into his consciousness, and leave him aching with a sharp, deep-rooted pain. As though it were a bodily pain, Swann's mind was powerless to alleviate it; but at least, in the case of bodily pain, since it is independent of the mind, the mind can dwell upon it, can note that it has diminished, that it has momentarily ceased. But in this case the mind, merely by recalling the pain, created it afresh. To determine not to think of it was to think of it still, to suffer from it still. And when, in conversation with his friends, he forgot about it, suddenly a word casually uttered would make him change countenance like a wounded man when a clumsy hand has touched his aching limb. When he came away from Odette he was happy, he felt calm, he recalled her smiles, of gentle mockery when speaking of this or that other person, of tenderness for himself; he recalled the gravity of her head which she seemed to have lifted from its axis to let it droop and fall, as though in spite of herself, upon his lips, as she had done on the first evening in the carriage, the languishing looks she had given him as she lay in his arms, nestling her head against her shoulder as though shrinking from the cold.

But then at once his jealousy, as though it were the

shadow of his love, presented him with the complement, with the converse of that new smile with which she had greeted him that very evening—and which now, perversely, mocked Swann and shone with love for another—of that droop of the head, now sinking on to other lips, of all the marks of affection (now given to another) that she had shown to him. And all the voluptuous memories which he bore away from her house were, so to speak, but so many sketches, rough plans like those which a decorator submits to one, enabling Swann to form an idea of the various attitudes, aflame or faint with passion, which she might adopt for others. With the result that he came to regret every pleasure that he tasted in her company, every new caress of which he had been so imprudent as to point out to her the delights, every fresh charm that he found in her, for he knew that, a moment later, they would go to enrich the collection of instruments in his secret torture-chamber.

Jealousy here is a pain experienced by Freud's bodily ego, on the frontier between psyche and body: "To determine not to think of it was to think of it still, to suffer from it still." As the shadow of love, jealousy resembles the shadow cast by the earth up into the heavens, where by tradition it ought to end at the sphere of Venus. Instead, it darkens there, and since the shadow is Freud's reality principle, or our consciousness of our own mortality, Proust's dreadfully persuasive irony is that jealousy exposes not only the arbitrariness of every erotic object-choice but also marks the passage of the loved person into a teleological overdetermination, in which the supposed inevitability of the person is simply a mask for the inevitability of the lover's death. Proust's jealousy thus becomes peculiarly akin to Freud's death drive, since it, too, quests beyond the pleasure/unpleasure principle. Our secret torture-chamber is furnished anew by every recollection of the beloved's erotic prowess, since what delighted us has delighted others.

Swann experiences the terrible conversion of the jealous lover into a parody of the scholar, a conversion to an intellectual pleasure that is more a deviation than an achievement, since no thought can be emancipated from the sexual past of all thought (Freud), if the search for truth is nothing but a search for the sexual past:

> Certainly he suffered as he watched that light, in whose golden atmosphere, behind the closed sash, stirred the unseen and detested pair, as he listened to that murmur which revealed the presence of the man who had crept in after his own departure, the perfidy of Odette, and the pleasures which she was at that moment enjoying with the stranger. And yet he was not sorry he had come; the torment which had forced him to leave his own house had become less acute now that it had become less vague, now that Odette's other life, of which he had had, at that first moment, a sudden helpless suspicion, was definitely there, in the full glare of the lamp-light, almost within his grasp, an unwitting prisoner in that room into which, when he chose, he would force his way to seize it unawares; or rather he would knock on the shutters, as he often did when he came very late, and by that signal Odette would at least learn that he knew, that he had seen the light and had heard the voices, and he himself, who a moment ago had been picturing her as laughing with the other at his illusions, now it was he who saw them, confident in their error, tricked by none other than himself, whom they believed to be far away but who

was there, in person, there with a plan, there with the knowledge that he was going, in another minute, to knock on the shutter. And perhaps the almost pleasurable sensation he felt at that moment was something more than the assuagement of a doubt, and of a pain: was an intellectual pleasure. If, since he had fallen in love, things had recovered a little of the delightful interest that they had had for him long ago—though only in so far as they were illuminated by the thought or the memory of Odette—now it was another of the faculties of his studious youth that his jealousy revived, the passion for truth, but for a truth which, too, was interposed between himself and his mistress, receiving its light from her alone, a private and personal truth the sole object of which (an infinitely precious object, and one almost disinterested in its beauty) was Odette's life, her actions, her environment, her plans, her past. At every other period in his life, the little everyday activities of another person had always seemed meaningless to Swann; if gossip about such things was repeated to him, he would dismiss it as insignificant, and while he listened it was only the lowest, the most commonplace part of his mind that was engaged; these were the moments when he felt at his most inglorious. But in this strange phase of love the personality of another person becomes so enlarged, so deepened, that the curiosity which he now felt stirring inside him with regard to the smallest details of a woman's daily life, was the same thirst for knowledge with which he had once studied history. And all manner of actions from which hitherto he would have recoiled in shame, such as spying, to-night, outside a window, to-morrow perhaps, for all he knew, putting adroitly provocative questions to casual witnesses, bribing servants, listening at doors, seemed to him now to be precisely on a level with the deciphering of manuscripts, the weighing of evidence, the interpretation of old monuments—so many different methods of scientific investigation with a genuine intellectual value and legitimately employable in the search for truth.

In fact, poor Swann is at the wrong window, and the entire passage is therefore as exquisitely painful as it is comic. What Freud ironically called the overevaluation of the object, the enlargement or deepening of the beloved's personality, begins to work not as one of the enlargements of life (like Proust's own novel) but as the deepening of a personal Hell. Swann plunges downwards and outwards, as he leans "in impotent, blind, dizzy anguish over the bottomless abyss" and reconstructs the petty details of Odette's past life with "as much passion as the aesthete who ransacks the extant documents of fifteenth-century Florence in order to penetrate further into the soul of the Primavera, the fair Vanna or the Venus of Botticelli."

The historicizing aesthete, John Ruskin say, or Walter Pater, becomes the archetype of the jealous lover, who searches into lost time not for a person, but for an epiphany or moment-of-moments, a privileged fiction of duration:

> When he had been paying social calls Swann would often come home with little time to spare before dinner. At that point in the evening, around six o'clock, when in the old days he used to feel so wretched, he no longer asked himself what Odette might be about, and was hardly at all concerned to hear that she had people with her or had gone out. He recalled at times that he had once, years ago,

Charles Haas, who served as the principal source for the character Charles Swann in Remembrance of Things Past.

to be jealous. Not immediately, however. Long after he had ceased to feel any jealousy with regard to Odette, the memory of that day, that afternoon spent knocking vainly at the little house in the Rue La Pérouse, had continued to torment him. It was as though his jealousy, not dissimilar in that respect from those maladies which appear to have their seat, their centre of contagion, less in certain persons than in certain places, in certain houses, had had for its object not so much Odette herself as that day, that hour in the irrevocable past when Swann had knocked at every entrance to her house in turn, as though that day, that hour alone had caught and preserved a few last fragments of the amorous personality which had once been Swann's, that there alone could he now recapture them. For a long time now it had been a matter of indifference to him whether Odette had been, or was being, unfaithful to him. And yet he had continued for some years to seek out old servants of hers, to such an extent had the painful curiosity persisted in him to know whether on that day, so long ago, at six o'clock, Odette had been in bed with Forcheville. Then that curiosity itself had disappeared, without, however, his abandoning his investigations. He went on trying to discover what no longer interested him, because his old self, though it had shrivelled to extreme decrepitude, still acted mechanically, in accordance with preoccupations so utterly abandoned that Swann could not now succeed even in picturing to himself that anguish—so compelling once that he had been unable to imagine that he would ever be delivered from it, that only the death of the woman he loved (though death, as will be shown later on in this story by a cruel corroboration, in no way diminishes the sufferings caused by jealousy) seemed to him capable of smoothing the path of his life which then seemed impassably obstructed.

Jealousy dies with love, but only with respect to the former beloved. Horribly a life-in-death, jealousy renews itself like the moon, perpetually trying to discover what no longer interests it, even after the object of desire has been literally buried. Its true object is "that day, that hour in the irrevocable past," and even that time was less an actual time than a temporal fiction, an episode in the evanescence of one's own self. Paul de Man's perspective that Proust's deepest insight is the nonexistence of the self founds itself upon this temporal irony of unweaving, this permanent parabasis of meaning. One can remember that even this deconstructive perspective is no more or less privileged than any other Proustian trope, and so cannot give us a truth that Proust himself evades.

The bridge between Swann's jealousy and Marcel's is Saint-Loup's jealousy of Rachel, summed up by Proust in one of his magnificently long, baroque paragraphs:

> Saint-Loup's letter had come as no surprise to me, even though I had had no news of him since, at the time of my grandmother's illness, he had accused me of perfidy and treachery. I had grasped at once what must have happened. Rachel, who liked to provoke his jealousy (she also had other causes for resentment against me), had persuaded her lover that I had made sly attempts to have relations with her in his absence. It is probable that he continued to believe in the truth of this allegation, but he had ceased to be in love with her, which meant that its truth or falsehood had become a matter of complete indifference to him, and our friendship alone re-

tried to read through its envelope a letter addressed by Odette to Forcheville. But this memory was not pleasing to him, and rather than plumb the depths of shame that he felt in it he preferred to indulge in a little grimace, twisting up the corners of his mouth and adding, if need be, a shake of the head which signified "What do I care about it?" True, he considered now that the hypothesis on which he had often dwelt at that time, according to which it was his jealous imagination alone that blackened what was in reality the innocent life of Odette—that this hypothesis (which after all was beneficent, since, so long as his amorous malady had lasted, it had diminished his sufferings by making them seem imaginary) was not the correct one, that it was his jealousy that had seen things in the correct light, and that if Odette had loved him more than he supposed, she had also deceived him more. Formerly, while his sufferings were still keen, he had vowed that, as soon as he had ceased to love Odette and was no longer afraid either of vexing her or of making her believe that he loved her too much, he would give himself the satisfaction of elucidating with her, simply from his love of truth and as a point of historical interest, whether or not Forcheville had been in bed with her that day when he had rung her bell and rapped on her window in vain, and she had written to Forcheville that it was an uncle of hers who had called. But this so interesting problem, which he was only waiting for his jealousy to subside before clearing up, had precisely lost all interest in Swann's eyes when he had ceased

mained. When, on meeting him again, I tried to talk to him about his accusations, he merely gave me a benign and affectionate smile which seemed to be a sort of apology, and then changed the subject. All this was not to say that he did not, a little later, see Rachel occasionally when he was in Paris. Those who have played a big part in one's life very rarely disappear from it suddenly for good. They return to it at odd moments (so much so that people suspect a renewal of old love) before leaving it for ever. Saint-Loup's breach with Rachel had very soon become less painful to him, thanks to the soothing pleasure that was given him by her incessant demands for money. Jealousy, which prolongs the course of love, is not capable of containing many more ingredients than the other products of the imagination. If one takes with one, when one starts on a journey, three or four images which incidentally one is sure to lose on the way (such as the lilies and anemones heaped on the Ponte Vecchio, or the Persian church shrouded in mist), one's trunk is already pretty full. When one leaves a mistress, one would be just as glad, until one had begun to forget her, that she should not become the property of three or four potential protectors whom one pictures in one's mind's eye, of whom, that is to say, one is jealous: all those whom one does not so picture count for nothing. Now frequent demands for money from a cast-off mistress no more give one a complete idea of her life than charts showing a high temperature would of her illness. But the latter would at any rate be an indication that she was ill, and the former furnish a presumption, vague enough it is true, that the forsaken one or forsaker (whichever she be) cannot have found anything very remarkable in the way of rich protectors. And so each demand is welcomed with the joy which a lull produces in the jealous one's sufferings, and answered with the immediate dispatch of money, for naturally one does not like to think of her being in want of anything except lovers (one of the three lovers one has in one's mind's eye), until time has enabled one to regain one's composure and to learn one's successor's name without wilting. Sometimes Rachel came in so late at night that she could ask her former lover's permission to lie down beside him until the morning. This was a great comfort to Robert, for it reminded him how intimately, after all, they had lived to-together, simply to see that even if he took the greater part of the bed for himself it did not in the least interfere with her sleep. He realised that she was more comfortable, lying close to his familiar body, than she would have been elsewhere, that she felt herself by his side—even in an hotel—to be in a bedroom known of old in which one has one's habits, in which one sleeps better. He felt that his shoulders, his limbs, all of him, were for her, even when he was unduly restless from insomnia or thinking of the things he had to do, so entirely usual that they could not disturb her and that the perception of them added still further to her sense of repose.

The heart of this comes in the grandly ironic sentence: "Jealousy, which prolongs the course of love, is not capable of containing many more ingredients than the other products of the imagination." That is hardly a compliment to the capaciousness of the imagination, which scarcely can hold on for long to even three or four images. Saint-Loup, almost on the farthest shore of jealousy, has the obscure comfort of having become, for Rachel, one of those images not quite faded away, when "he felt that his shoulders, his limbs, all of him, were

for her," even when he has ceased to be there, or anywhere, for her, or she for him. Outliving love, jealousy has become love's last stand, the final basis for a continuity between two former lovers.

Saint-Loup's bittersweet evanescence as a lover contrasts both with Swann's massive historicism and with the novel's triumphant representation of jealousy, Marcel's monumental search after lost time in the long aftermath of Albertine's death. Another grand link between magnificent jealousies is provided by Swann's observations to Marcel, aesthetic reflections somewhat removed from the pain of earlier realities:

> It occurred to me that Swann must be getting tired of waiting for me. Moreover I did not wish to be too late in returning home because of Albertine, and, taking leave of Mme. de Surgis and M. de Charlus, I went in search of my invalid in the cardroom. I asked him whether what he had said to the Prince in their conversation in the garden was really what M. de Bréauté (whom I did not name) had reported to us, about a little play by Bergotte. He burst out laughing: "There's not a word of truth in it, not one, it's a complete fabrication and would have been an utterly stupid thing to say. It's really incredible, this spontaneous generation of falsehood. I won't ask who it was that told you, but it would be really interesting, in a field as limited as this, to work back from one person to another and find out how the story arose. Anyhow, what concern can it be of other people, what the Prince said to me? People are very inquisitive. I've never been inquisitive, except when I was in love, and when I was jealous. And a lot I ever learned! Are you jealous?" I told Swann that I had never experienced jealousy, that I did not even know what it was. "Well, you can count yourself lucky. A little jealousy is not too unpleasant, for two reasons. In the first place, it enables people who are not inquisitive to take an interest in the lives of others, or of one other at any rate. And then it makes one feel the pleasure of possession, of getting into a carriage with a woman, of not allowing her to go about by herself. But that's only in the very first stages of the disease, or when the cure is almost complete. In between, it's the most agonising torment. However, I must confess that I haven't had much experience even of the two pleasures I've mentioned—the first because of my own nature, which is incapable of sustained reflexion; the second because of circumstances, because of the woman, I should say the women, of whom I've been jealous. But that makes no difference. Even when one is no longer attached to things, it's still something to have been attached to them; because it was always for reasons which other people didn't grasp. The memory of those feelings is something that's to be found only in ourselves; we must go back into ourselves to look at it. You mustn't laugh at this idealistic jargon, but what I mean to say is that I've been very fond of life and very fond of art. Well, now that I'm a little too weary to live with other people, those old feelings, so personal and individual, that I had in the past, seem to me—it's the mania of all collectors—very precious. I open my heart to myself like a sort of showcase, and examine one by one all those love affairs of which the rest of the world can have known nothing. And of this collection, to which I'm now even more attached than to my others, I say to myself, rather as Mazarin said of his books, but in fact without the least distress, that it will be very tiresome to have to leave it all. But, to come

back to my conversation with the Prince, I shall tell one person only, and that person is going to be you."

We are in the elegy season, ironically balanced between the death of jealousy in Swann and its birth in poor Marcel, who literally does not know that the descent into Avernus beckons. When the vigor of an affirmation has more power than its probability, clearly we are living in a fiction, the metaphor or transference that we call love, and might call jealousy. Into that metaphor, Marcel moves like a sleepwalker, with his obsessions central to *The Captive* and insanely pervasive in *The Fugitive.* A great passage in *The Captive,* which seems a diatribe against jealousy, instead is a passionately ironic celebration of jealousy's aesthetic victory over our merely temporal happiness:

> However, I was still at the first stage of enlightenment with regard to Léa. I was not even aware whether Albertine knew her. No matter, it came to the same thing. I must at all costs prevent her from renewing this acquaintance or making the acquaintance of this stranger at the Trocadéro. I say that I did not know whether she knew Léa or not; yet I must in fact have learned this at Balbec, from Albertine herself. For amnesia obliterated from my mind as well as from Albertine's a great many of the statements that she had made to me. Memory, instead of being a duplicate, always present before one's eyes, of the various events of one's life, is rather a void from which at odd moments a chance resemblance enables one to resuscitate dead recollections; but even then there are innumerable little details which have not fallen into that potential reservoir of memory, and which will remain forever unverifiable. One pays no attention to anything that one does not connect with the real life of the woman one loves; one forgets immediately what she has said to one about such and such an incident or such and such people one does not know, and her expression while she was saying it. And so when, in due course, one's jealousy is aroused by these same people, and seeks to ascertain whether or not it is mistaken, whether it is indeed they who are responsible for one's mistress's impatience to go out, and her annoyance when one has prevented her from doing so by returning earlier than usual, one's jealousy, ransacking the past in search of a clue, can find nothing; always retrospective, it is like a historian who has to write the history of a period for which he has no documents; always belated, it dashes like an enraged bull to the spot where it will not find the dazzling, arrogant creature who is tormenting it and whom the crowd admire for his splendour and cunning. Jealousy thrashes around in the void, uncertain as we are in those dreams in which we are distressed because we cannot find in his empty house a person whom we have known well in life, but who here perhaps is another person and has merely borrowed the features of our friend, uncertain as we are even more after we awake when we seek to identify this or that detail of our dream. What was one's mistress's expression when she told one that? Did she not look happy, was she not actually whistling, a thing that she never does unless she has some amorous thought in her mind and finds one's presence importunate and irritating? Did she not tell one something that is contradicted by what she now affirms, that she knows or does not know such and such a person? One does not know, and one will never know; one searches desperately among the unsubstantial fragments of a dream, and

all the time one's life with one's mistress goes on, a life that is oblivious of what may well be of importance to one, and attentive to what is perhaps of none, a life hagridden by people who have no real connexion with one, full of lapses of memory, gaps, vain anxieties, a life as illusory as a dream.

Thrashing about in the void of a dream in which a good friend perhaps is another person, jealousy becomes Spenser's Malbecco: "who quite/Forgot he was a man, and jealousy is hight." Yet making life "as illusory as a dream," hagridden by lapses and gaps, is Marcel's accomplishment, and Proust's art. One does not write an other-than-ironic diatribe against one's own art. Proust warily, but with the sureness of a great beast descending upon its helpless prey, approaches the heart of his vision of jealousy, his sense that the emotion is akin to what Freud named as the defense of isolation, in which all context is burned away, and a dangerous present replaces all past and all future.

Sexual jealousy in Proust is accompanied by a singular obsessiveness in regard to questions of space and of time. The jealous lover, who, as Proust says, conducts researches comparable to those of the scholar, seeks in his inquiries every detail he can find as to the location and duration of each betrayal and infidelity. Why? Proust has a marvelous passage in *The Fugitive* volume of *Remembrance:*

> It is one of the faculties of jealousy to reveal to us the extent to which the reality of external facts and the sentiments of the heart are an unknown element which lends itself to endless suppositions. We imagine that we know exactly what things are and what people think, for the simple reason that we do not care about them. But as soon as we have a desire to know, as the jealous man has, then it becomes a dizzy kaleidoscope in which we can no longer distinguish anything. Had Albertine been unfaithful to me? With whom? In what house? On what day? On the day when she had said this or that to me, when I remembered that I had in the course of it said this or that? I could not tell. Nor did I know what her feelings were for me, whether they were inspired by self-interest or by affection. And all of a sudden I remembered some trivial incident, for instance that Albertine had wished to go to Saint-Martin-le-Vêtu, saying that the name interested her, and perhaps simply because she had made the acquaintance of some peasant girl who lived there. But it was useless that Aimé should have informed me of what he had learned from the woman at the baths, since Albertine must remain eternally unaware that he had informed me, the need to know having always been exceeded, in my love for Albertine, by the need to show her that I knew; for this broke down the partition of different illusions that stood between us, without having ever had the result of making her love me more, far from it. And now, since she was dead, the second of these needs had been amalgamated with the effect of the first: the need to picture to myself the conversation in which I would have informed her of what I had learned, as vividly as the conversation in which I would have asked her to tell me what I did not know; that is to say, to see her by my side, to hear her answering me kindly, to see her cheeks become plump again, her eyes shed their malice and assume an air of melancholy; that is to say, to love her still and to forget the fury of my jealousy in the despair of my loneliness. The painful mystery of this impossibility of ever making known to her what I had

learned and of establishing our relations upon the truth of what I had only just discovered (and would not have been able, perhaps, to discover but for her death) substituted its sadness for the more painful mystery of her conduct. What? To have so desperately desired that Albertine—who no longer existed—should know that I had heard the story of the baths! This again was one of the consequences of our inability, when we have to consider the fact of death, to picture to ourselves anything but life. Albertine no longer existed; but to me she was the person who had concealed from me that she had assignations with women at Balbec, who imagined that she had succeeded in keeping me in ignorance of them. When we try to consider what will happen to us after our own death, is it not still our living self which we mistakenly project at that moment? And is it much more absurd, when all is said, to regret that a woman who no longer exists is unaware that we have learned what she was doing six years ago than to desire that of ourselves, who will be dead, the public shall still speak with approval a century hence? If there is more real foundation in the latter than in the former case, the regrets of my retrospective jealousy proceeded none the less from the same optical error as in other men the desire for posthumous fame. And yet, if this impression of the solemn finality of my separation from Albertine had momentarily supplanted my idea of her misdeeds, it only succeeded in aggravating them by bestowing upon them an irremediable character. I saw myself astray in life as on an endless beach where I was alone and where, in whatever direction I might turn, I would never meet her.

"The regrets of my retrospective jealousy proceeded none the less from the same optical error as in other men the desire for posthumous fame"—is that not as much Proust's negative credo as it is Marcel's? Those "other men" include the indubitable precursors, Flaubert and Baudelaire, and Proust himself as well. The aesthetic agon for immortality is an optical error, yet this is one of those errors about life that are necessary for life, as Nietzsche remarked, and is also one of those errors about art that is art. Proust has swerved away from Flaubert into a radical confession of error; the novel is creative envy, love is jealousy, jealousy is the terrible fear that there will not be enough space for oneself (including literary space), and that there never can be enough time for oneself, because death is the reality of one's life. A friend once remarked to me, at the very height of her own jealousy, that jealousy was nothing but a vision of two bodies on a bed, neither of which was one's own, where the hurt resided in the realization that one body ought to have been one's own. Bitter as the remark may have been, it usefully reduces the trope of jealousy to literal fears: where was one's body, where will it be, when will it not be? Our ego is always a bodily ego, Freud insisted, and jealousy joins the bodily ego and the drive as another frontier concept, another vertigo whirling between a desperate inwardness and the injustice of outwardness. Proust, like Freud, goes back after all to the prophet Jeremiah, that uncomfortable sage who proclaimed a new inwardness for his mother's people. The law is written upon our inward parts for Proust also, and the law is justice, but the god of law is a jealous god, though he is certainly not the god of jealousy.

Freud, in "The Passing of the Oedipus Complex," writing two years after Proust's death, set forth a powerful speculation as to the difference between the sexes, a speculation that Proust neither evades nor supports, and yet illuminates, by working out of the world that Freud knows only in the pure good of theory. Freud is properly tentative, but also adroitly forceful:

Here our material—for some reason we do not understand—becomes far more shadowy and incomplete. The female sex develops an Oedipus-complex, too, a super-ego and a latency period. May one ascribe to it also a phallic organization and a castration complex? The answer is in the affirmative, but it cannot be the same as in the boy. The feministic demand for equal rights between the sexes does not carry far here; the morphological difference must express itself in differences in the development of the mind. "Anatomy is Destiny," to vary a saying of Napoleon's. The little girl's clitoris behaves at first just like a penis, but by comparing herself with a boy playfellow the child perceives that she has "come off short," and takes this fact as ill-treatment and as a reason for feeling inferior. For a time she still consoles herself with the expectation that later, when she grows up, she will acquire just as big an appendage as a boy. Here the woman's "masculine complex" branches off. The female child does not understand her actual loss as a sex characteristic, but explains it by assuming that at some earlier date she had possessed a member which was just as big and which had later been lost by castration. She does not seem to extend this conclusion about herself to other grown women, but in complete accordance with the phallic phase she ascribes to them large and complete, that is, male, genitalia. The result is an essential difference between her and the boy, namely, that she accepts castration as an established fact, an operation already performed, whereas the boy dreads the possibility of its being performed.

The castration-dread being thus excluded in her case, there falls away a powerful motive towards forming the super-ego and breaking up the infantile genital organization. These changes seem to be due in the girl far more than in the boy to the results of educative influences, of external intimidation threatening the loss of love. The Oedipus-complex in the girl is far simpler, less equivocal, than that of the little possessor of a penis; in my experience it seldom goes beyond the wish to take the mother's place, the feminine attitude towards the father. Acceptance of the loss of a penis is not endured without some attempt at compensation. The girl passes over—by way of a symbolic analogy, one may say—from the penis to a child; her Oedipus-complex culminates in the desire, which is long cherished, to be given a child by her father as a present, to bear him a child. One has the impression that the Oedipus-complex is later gradually abandoned because this wish is never fulfilled. The two desires, to possess a penis and to bear a child, remain powerfully charged with libido in the unconscious and help to prepare the woman's nature for its subsequent sex rôle. The comparative weakness of the sadistic component of the sexual instinct, which may probably be related to the penis-deficiency, facilitates the transformation of directly sexual trends into those inhibited in aim, feelings of tenderness. It must be confessed, however, that on the whole our insight into these processes of development in the girl is unsatisfying, shadowy and incomplete.

Anatomy is destiny in Proust also, but this is anatomy taken up into the mind, as it were. The exiles of Sodom and Gomorrah, more jealous even than other mortals, become monsters of time, yet heroes and heroines of time also. The Oedipus complex never quite passes, in Freud's sense of passing, either in Proust or in his major figures. Freud's castration complex, ultimately the dread of dying, is a metaphor for the same shadowed desire that Proust represents by the complex metaphor of jealousy. The jealous lover fears that he has been castrated, that his place in life has been taken, that true time is over for him. His only recourse is to search for lost time, in the hopeless hope that the aesthetic recovery of illusion and of experience alike, will deceive him in a higher mode than he fears to have been deceived in already. (pp. 1-16)

> Harold Bloom, in an introduction to *Marcel Proust,*
> *edited by Harold Bloom, Chelsea House Publishers,*
> *1987, pp. 1-16.*

ADDITIONAL BIBLIOGRAPHY

Adams, Robert M. "A Clear View of Combray." *The Times Literary Supplement,* No. 4080 (12 June 1981): 667.
    Review of the translation of *Remembrance of Things Past* by Terence Kilmartin.

Alden, Douglas W. *Marcel Proust and His French Critics.* Los Angeles: Lymanhouse, 1940, 259 p.
    Record of Proust's critical reputation in France to 1940, with a bibliography of French-language criticism arranged by country of origin.

———. " 'Jean Santeuil'." *Saturday Review* 39, No. 7 (8 February 1956): 14-15.
    Review of the English translation of *Jean Santeuil.* Alden discusses the merits of Proust's first novel and examines the probable reasons for Proust's abandonment of it before completion.

Ames, Van Meter. *Proust and Santayana: The Aesthetic Way of Life.* New York: Russell & Russell, 1964, 176 p.
    Study of Proust's philosophy of art.

Appignanesi, Lisa. "Marcel Proust: Femininity and Creativity." In her *Femininity and the Creative Imagination: A Study of Henry James, Robert Musil and Marcel Proust,* pp. 157-215. London: Vision Press, 1973.
    Explores the relationship in Proust's work between femininity and artistic creation, resolving that "in Proust, the feminine emerges as a fundamentally transformative principle and thus a creative one. . . . [The] feminine here is the 'other,' the unknown, and as such it exerts a magical pull which draws the being out of himself toward ever-expanding imaginative horizons."

Auchincloss, Louis. "Proust's Picture of Society." *The Partisan Review* 27, No. 4 (1960): 690-701.
    Discussion of Proust's characterizations of French aristocrats. Auchincloss is an American novelist and lawyer whose novels focus on characters from the upper echelons of society.

Bell, William Stewart. *Proust's Nocturnal Muse.* New York: Columbia University Press, 1962, 288 p.
    Analyzes Proust's use of dream states from his early works through *Remembrance of Things Past.*

Bersani, Leo. *Marcel Proust: The Fictions of Life and Art.* New York: Oxford University Press, 1965, 269 p.
    Psychological study. Bersani examines the conflict between the objective world and subjective reality as delineated by Proust in *Remembrance of Things Past.*

Brée, Germaine. "New Trends in Proust Criticism." *Symposium* 5, No. 1 (May 1951): 62-71.
    Analysis of various trends in Proust criticism in which Brée examines the critical standing of *Remembrance of Things Past.*

Butor, Michel. "The Imaginary Works of Art in Proust." In his *Inventory: Essays,* pp. 146-84. London: Jonathan Cape, 1970.
    Examines the function of the writer Bergotte, the painter Elstir, and the composer Vinteuil in *Remembrance of Things Past,* and the way Proust used their imaginary works in structuring his novel.

Chefdor, Monique, ed. *In Search of Marcel Proust.* Claremont, Calif.: Scripps College and the Ward Ritchie Press, 1973, 119 p.
    Collection of addresses delivered by French and American critics at the 1971 Marcel Proust Centennial Colloquium.

Cocking, J. M. *Proust.* New Haven: Yale University Press, 1956, 80 p.
    Illustrates the manner in which Proust's style and aesthetic ideas evolved as he wrote *Pleasures and Days* and *Jean Santeuil,* and reached their full development in *Remembrance of Things Past.*

Coleman, Elliott. *The Golden Angel: Papers on Proust.* New York: Coley Taylor, 1954, 128 p.
    Essays on various themes and subjects in *Remembrance of Things Past,* including humor, dreams, morality, and death.

Corn, Alfred. "Time to Read Proust." *The Hudson Review* 35, No. 2 (Summer 1982): 298-305.
    Discussion of Terence Kilmartin's revised translation of *Remembrance of Things Past.* Corn believes Kilmartin's translation is adequate, but points out many inconsistencies or inadequacies of translation.

Croce, Benedetto. "Proust: An Example of Decadent Historical Method." In his *My Philosophy and Other Essays on the Moral and Political Problems of Our Time,* edited by R. Klibansky, translated by E. F. Carritt, pp. 208-13. London: George Allen & Unwin, 1949.
    States that Proust's consciousness of the past lacks moral and religious dimensions, and that he treats the "noble matron history . . . as if she were a shameless hussy to provide exquisite titillations."

Daiches, David. "Father of Swann." *The New Republic* 120, No. 18 (2 May 1949): 22-3.
    Review of *The Letters of Marcel Proust,* edited and translated by Mina Curtiss. Daiches concludes that although these letters were ostensibly selected specifically to shed light on the composition of *Remembrance of Things Past,* they actually reveal little about the novel and much about Proust's personality.

De Man, Paul. "Reading (Proust)." In his *Allegories of Reading: Figural Language in Rousseau, Nietzsche, Rilke, and Proust,* pp. 57-78. New Haven: Yale University Press, 1979.
    Uses *Remembrance of Things Past* to illustrate complexities and ambiguities that arise in the act of reading.

Doubrovsky, Serge. *Writing and Fantasy in Proust: La Place de la Madeleine.* Translated by Carol Mastrangelo Bové, with Paul A. Bové. Lincoln: University of Nebraska Press, 1986, 165 p.
    Psychoanalytic reading of *Remembrance of Things Past.*

Ellis, Havelock. "In Search of Proust." In his *From Rousseau to Proust,* pp. 363-96. Cambridge, Mass.: Riverside Press, 1935.
    Psychological study. Ellis's book focuses on writers whom he

believes have brought about spiritual revolutions by altering the ways in which humans perceive themselves.

Frank, Ellen Eve. " 'The Stored Consciousness': Marcel Proust." In her *Literary Architecture: Essays Toward a Tradition,* pp. 113-65. Berkeley: University of California Press, 1979.
Discusses architecture as an analogue for literature in Proust's work.

Girard, René, ed. *Proust: A Collection of Critical Essays.* Englewood Cliffs, N.J.: Prentice-Hall, 1962, 182 p.
Includes essays by Henri Peyre, Jacques Rivière, Albert Thibaudet, Leo Spitzer, Charles Du Bos, and Georges Poulet. The essays cover various aspects of Proust's writings, including imagery, style, and the meaning of time in *Remembrance of Things Past.*

Graham, Victor. *The Imagery of Proust.* Oxford: Basil Blackwell, 1966, 274 p.
Regards the use of imagery in *Remembrance of Things Past* as a unifying technique.

Green, F. C. *The Mind of Proust: A Detailed Interpretation of "A la recherche du temps perdu."* Cambridge: Cambridge University Press, 1949, 546 p.
Discusses Proust's novel without reference to his life.

Haldane, Charlotte. *Marcel Proust.* London: Arthur Baker, 1951, 140 p.
Critical study including a section of plot outlines for each volume of *Remembrance of Things Past.*

Hughes, Edward J. *Marcel Proust: A Study in the Quality of Awareness.* New York: Cambridge University Press, 1983, 212 p.
Study of Proust's attempts to convey various examples of individual consciousness in his fiction. Hughes argues that Proust successfully reproduced states of consciousness ranging from the extreme self-awareness of the narrator of *A la recherche du temps perdu* to "the faint glimpses of consciousness" experienced by Françoise.

Humphries, Jefferson. "Proust, Flannery O'Connor, and the Aesthetic of Violence." In his *The Otherness Within: Gnostic Readings in Marcel Proust, Flannery O'Connor, and François Villon,* pp. 95-111. Baton Rouge: Louisiana State University Press, 1983.
Considers *Remembrance of Things Past* in the light of Gnostic theological doctrines, particularly the introspective search for spiritual knowledge.

Kawin, Bruce F. "The Higher Self in Stein, Whitman, and Proust." In his *The Mind of the Novel: Reflexive Fiction and the Ineffable,* pp. 115-40. Princeton: Princeton University Press, 1982.
Analyzes the perception and expression of self-identity on the part of the narrator of *Remembrance of Things Past.*

Kilmartin, Terence. *A Reader's Guide to "Remembrance of Things Past."* New York: Random House, 1983, 256 p.
Introduction to the plot, themes, and characters of the novel.

Kopp, Richard L. *Marcel Proust As a Social Critic.* Rutherford, N. J.: Fairleigh Dickinson University Press, 1971, 230 p.
Discussion of Proust's social views. Kopp disputes the commonly held critical belief that Proust was an impartial observer of society.

Lemaitre, Georges. "Marcel Proust." In his *Four French Novelists: Marcel Proust, André Gide, Jean Giraudoux, Paul Morand,* pp. 3-111. 1938. Reprint. Port Washington, N. Y.: Kennikat Press, 1969.
Biographical and critical study.

Lesage, Laurent. *Marcel Proust and His Literary Friends.* Urbana: University of Illinois Press, 1958, 113 p.
Examines Proust's relationships with such nineteenth-century literary figures as Robert de Montesquiou and Henri de Régnier.

Linder, Gladys Dudley, ed. *Marcel Proust: Reviews and Estimates.* Stanford: Stanford University Press, 1942, 314 p.
Essays and appreciations by prominent English critics and authors, including J. Middleton Murry, Clive Bell, Arnold Bennett, Edith Wharton, Wyndham Lewis, and John Cowper Powys.

March, Harold. *The Two Worlds of Marcel Proust.* Philadelphia: University of Pennsylvania Press, 1948, 276 p.
Biographical and critical study.

Miller, Milton L. *Nostalgia: A Psychoanalytic Study of Marcel Proust.* Boston: Houghton Mifflin Co., 1956, 306 p.
Psychological analysis of Proust's "aesthetic approach to the unconscious," with chapters on Proust and Freud, Proust's homosexuality, and the use of dreams in *Remembrance of Things Past.*

Moss, Howard. *The Magic Lantern of Marcel Proust.* New York: The Macmillan Co., 1962, 111 p.
Study of various themes and symbols in *Remembrance of Things Past.*

Pound, Ezra. "Paris Letter." *The Dial* 71, No. 2 (October 1921): 458-61.
Compares Proust to Henry James as an author of "precise nuance."

Price, Larkin B., ed. *Marcel Proust: A Critical Panorama.* Urbana: University of Illinois Press, 1973, 288 p.
Essays in French and English on various aspects of Proust's work.

Rawlinson, Mary Crenshaw. "Art and Truth: Reading Proust." *Philosophy and Literature* 6, Nos. 1-2 (October 1982): 1-16.
Finds the philosophical significance of *Remembrance of Things Past* in Proust's illuminations of "essences," identifying this term with the "Platonic idea of the essence as a 'one in the many,' a renewable and lasting form or law freed from all particularity."

Ricardou, Jean. "Proust: A Retrospective Reading." Translated by Erica Freiberg. *Critical Inquiry* 8, No. 3 (Spring 1982): 531-41.
Focuses on a passage in *Remembrance of Things Past* to illustrate Proust's use of metaphor as a means of ordering his narrative.

Rivers, J. E. *Proust and the Art of Love.* New York: Columbia University Press, 1980, 327 p.
Psychological and sociological study of Proust's attitudes toward love, sex, and homosexuality as they are manifested in his writings. Rivers also provides an excellent description of the social climate in Europe at the time that Proust was working on *Remembrance of Things Past.*

Rogers, B. G. *Proust's Narrative Techniques.* Geneva: Librairie Droz, 1965, 214 p.
Discussion of Proust's literary techniques in *A la recherche du temps perdu.*

Sansom, William. *Proust and His World.* London: Thames and Hudson, 1973, 128 p.
Social and historical guidebook to the era in which Proust lived. This straightforward and richly illustrated book reveals the autobiographical sources of Proust's major characters without confusing the reader with a plethora of names.

Shattuck, Roger. "Kilmartin's Way." *The New York Review of Books* 28, No. 11 (25 June 1981): 16-20.
Review by a prominent Proust scholar of the Terence Kilmartin translation of *Remembrance of Things Past.* Unlike many other critics, Shattuck finds that C. K. Scott Moncrieff's translation

works remarkably well, but believes that many of Kilmartin's alterations enhance the work. However, he also points out what he considers to be errors in Kilmartin's work and concludes that this is still not a "definitive" translation.

Spagnoli, John J. *The Social Attitude of Marcel Proust.* New York: Publications of the Institute of French Studies, Columbia University, 1936, 174 p.

> Examination of Proust's social attitudes. Spagnoli believes that one may infer much about Proust's beliefs regarding various social issues through a careful reading of *Remembrance of Things Past.*

Spalding, P. A. *A Reader's Handbook to Proust: An Index Guide to "Remembrance of Things Past."* Rev. ed. New York: Barnes & Noble, 1975, 303 p.

> Includes plot synopses of individual volumes of *Remembrance of Things Past,* along with indexes of references to the characters and subjects of the novel.

Turnell, Martin. "Proust's Early Novel." *The Commonweal* 63, No. 13 (30 December 1955): 333-35.

> Concludes that *Jean Santeuil* "does not possess the richness and complexity of *Remembrance of Things Past.*"

Vogely, Maxine Arnold. *A Proust Dictionary.* Troy, N.Y.: The Whitston Publishing Co., 1981, 755 p.

> Identifies references in *Remembrance of Things Past* to "names of persons, characters, mythological figures, places, titles of books, plays, poems, names of works of art, quotations of words, phrases, lines and paragraphs, and other items."

Charles-Ferdinand Ramuz

1878-1947

Swiss novelist, poet, essayist, memoirist, diarist, and librettist.

A prolific author, Ramuz played a central role in the development of francophone Swiss literature during the early decades of the twentieth century. Considering the urbane tone of the traditional French novel inappropriate for the predominantly rural culture of Switzerland, he sought to create a narrative style that would convey his personal artistic vision while reflecting the simplicity of life in his native region. In addition, Ramuz joined with other francophone Swiss artists in a movement to free the art of their country from the long-standing domination of French culture, and their actions inspired the creation of a large body of uniquely Swiss works.

Although Ramuz was born in Lausanne, the capital city of the canton of Vaud, his parents were natives of a nearby rural region, and throughout his lifetime Ramuz regarded the grassy highlands of Vaud, where he spent his childhood summers, as his true home. After studying at primary and secondary schools in Lausanne, he enrolled at the university there, initially complying with his father's request that he study law but transferring after one term to the college of arts. Upon receiving his degree in 1900, he accepted a teaching position in rural Vaud. However, he was shortly thereafter stricken with appendicitis and peritonitis, and after recovering he moved to Paris to pursue a literary career. In Paris, he became acquainted with other Swiss artists, including the novelist Edouard Rod and the painter René Auberjonois, as well as many well-known French authors.

Inspired by the French Parnassian poets, who advocated the use of classical verse forms, Ramuz had been writing formally regular, rhyming poetry since adolescence; when he arrived in Paris, he brought with him a collection of his poems, tentatively entitled *Le petit village.* Soon afterward, however, he rewrote *Le petit village* using free verse forms and colloquial diction and substituting assonance for rhyme. Ramuz later noted in his diary that, by using classical forms in this evocation of peasant life, he had "dressed [his] village falsely, dressed it in Sunday best," and that, after arriving in Paris, he had reclothed it in more appropriate "everyday wear." When *Le petit village* was published in 1903, critical response was markedly positive; commentators praised the originality of Ramuz's style, and Gaspard Vallette wrote: "Never has the life of a Swiss village been communicated with such charming truth and candor." During his ten-year sojourn in Paris, Ramuz published one additional volume of poetry, *La grande guerre du Sondrebund,* but concentrated primarily on the production of novels, experimenting with various literary styles in his attempt to find an appropriate form for his subject matter.

In 1913, Ramuz married a young Swiss artist named Cécile Cellier, and soon afterward the couple settled in Vaud, where they lived for the rest of their lives. This move was followed by a period of enormous productivity for Ramuz, during which he completed thirteen novels, several volumes of humanistic philosophical reflections, and innumerable journal

articles. He also participated in the founding of the *Cahiers vaudois,* a journal devoted to the promotion and dissemination of the work of Vaudois authors, and frequently lectured at the University of Lausanne. Initially popular only among critics, his works eventually acquired a wide audience throughout both French and German-speaking areas of Europe, and at his death in 1947 he was hailed as the greatest of Swiss authors.

Critics generally divide Ramuz's career as a novelist into two phases, using his return to Vaud as the point of demarcation. Reflecting various influences, the novels of the first period reveal his search for an appropriate narrative style. *Aline,* for example, has been compared to the novels of Realist author Gustave Flaubert because of its straightforward, objective narrative, while *Les circonstances de la vie* and *La vie de Samuel Belet (The Life of Samuel Belet)* are regarded as Naturalistic character studies. During this initial phase of his career, Ramuz sought above all to free his prose from stylistic artifice, noting in his diary that style is the "part of man in the *interpretation* of things. The more lofty it is, the less exact." He therefore attempted to base his prose style on the example of representational painters, who evoked ideas by simply portraying reality as they saw it, and this aim is manifested in the increasingly static and descriptive style of Ramuz's early novels.

Critics agree that Ramuz most successfully expressed his personal vision in the novels written after his 1913 return to Vaud. From the beginning, he had chosen to write about rural Swiss life not only because it was the existence to which he felt most akin, but also because he saw the constant struggles and rewards of Alpine dwellers as representative of the human condition. In the novels written immediately after the First World War — *La guérison des maladies, Les signes parmi nous, Terre du ciel,* and *Présence de la mort* (*The End of All Men*) — Ramuz repeatedly utilized the microcosm of the Alpine village to explore the multifaceted response of humanity to the presence of evil, exhibiting a markedly Christian perspective. In later novels, he drew from the personal struggles of Swiss peasants myriad conclusions about the nature of courage, about humanity's ability to endure and transcend adversity, and about the inherent spirituality of human nature. Critics note that in his mature works, Ramuz's pictorial realism is further heightened by his accurate reproduction of peasant speech and his frequent reference to esoteric features of mountain life. Many also contend that the highly descriptive, poetic style of these works represents a full realization of Ramuz's desire to create an appropriate vehicle for his rural subjects and settings, and David Bevan has suggested that in Ramuz's best writings "the integrity of his vision and expression is absolute."

Ramuz remains a widely revered figure throughout much of Europe: his works continue to enjoy wide popularity, while his unprecedented and skillful use of native Swiss subjects and settings has secured his position as the chief progenitor of modern Swiss literature. Although his reputation in English-speaking countries has been limited by a scarcity of translations of his work, critical response to existing translations has been predominantly positive. Both English-speaking and European commentators have praised the powerful simplicity of Ramuz's prose and the accuracy of his portraits of rural Swiss peasants, and some consider him one of the most important European novelists of the early twentieth century.

PRINCIPAL WORKS

Le petit village   (poetry)   1903
Aline   (novel)   1905
La grande guerre du Sondrebund   (poetry)   1906
Les circonstances de la vie   (novel)   1907
Jean-Luc persécuté   (novel)   1909
Aimé Pache, peintre vaudois   (novel)   1911
La vie de Samuel Belet   (novel)   1913
   [*The Life of Samuel Belet,* 1951]
La guerre dans le haut-pays   (novel)   1915
La guérison des maladies   (novel)   1917
Le règne de l'esprit malin   (novel)   1917
   [*The Reign of the Evil One,* 1922]
Les signes parmi nous   (novel)   1919
L'histoire du soldat   (libretto)   1920
   [*The Soldier's Tale,* 1950]
Salutation paysanne   (poetry)   1921
Terre du ciel   (novel)   1921; also published as *Joie dans le ciel,* 1925
Présence de la mort   (novel)   1922

[*The End of All Men,* 1944; also translated as *The Triumph of Death,* 1946]
Passage du poète   (novel)   1923
La séparation des races   (novel)   1923
L'amour du monde   (novel)   1925
La grande peur dans la montagne   (novel)   1926
   [*Terror on the Mountain,* 1967]
La beauté sur la terre   (novel)   1927
   [*Beauty on Earth,* 1929]
Souvenirs sur Igor Strawinsky   (memoirs)   1929
Adam et Eve   (novel)   1932
Farinet   (novel)   1932
Taille de l'homme   (essays)   1933
Derborence   (novel)   1934
   [*When the Mountain Fell,* 1947]
Questions   (essays)   1935
Le garçon savoyard   (novel)   1936
Besoin de grandeur   (essays)   1937
Si le soleil ne revenait pas   (novel)   1937
Paris: Notes d'un vaudois   (essays)   1938
Découverte du monde   (memoirs)   1939
Oeuvres complètes. 20 vols.   (novels, essays, and poetry)   1940-41
La guerre aux papiers   (novel)   1942
René Auberjonois   (memoirs)   1943
Journal, 1896-1942   (journal)   1945
*What Is Man   (essays)   1948
Journal: Dernières pages, 1942-1947   (journal)   1949
C.-F. Ramuz: Ses amis et son temps. 6 vols.   (letters)   1967-70

*This volume contains translated excerpts from *Besoin de grandeur, Taille de l'homme,* and *Questions.*

LOUISE MAUNSELL FIELD   (essay date 1922)

[*In the following essay, Field reviews* The Reign of the Evil One.]

The very interesting account of the works of C. F. Ramuz, given by Mr. [Ernest] Boyd in his "Introduction" to this recently published translation, makes the reader feel inclined to wonder whether some other of the novels therein mentioned would not have been a wiser choice than this of **The Reign of the Evil One** with which to present him to the American reading public. Mr. Boyd, for instance, states that "What is of great interest in the work of C. F. Ramuz is its analysis of the French Protestant mind, and the expression in literature of an element whose absence from the literature of France must always seem a loss to English readers," yet this tale is concerned with an entirely Catholic country, a section shut in among high mountains, and called "Le Valais." The people in this district are still living, mentally and spiritually, in the Middle Ages, and the story is almost, if not quite, exactly like a bit of medieval folklore. It is, of course, very different from most modern fiction; but in its unlikeness it harks back to a phase with which every even moderately well-read person is familiar.

Yet this very effect of belonging to a past stage of civilization is not without its charm—a charm which is no doubt much more potent in the original French than it could possibly be made in any translation, no matter how skillful, since no language can ever exactly reproduce the shades of meaning conveyed in another. The scene is laid in an isolated little French-Swiss village, curled up in a valley between tall mountains and having

> a President, three or four municipal guards, a District Council with a Secretary, a schoolmaster and a priest. There were shops and an inn, and, in front of the church, an open square where the men collected after mass on Sundays.

The picture of this out-of-the-world little place with which the story opens one Summer evening, when all were glad over the prospect of a good harvest, when the men came back from the fields shouting jokes at one another, while the women, gathered about the drinking fountain, laughed gayly, and an appetizing smell of good things cooking came from the open doors of the houses, takes us at once into the very centre of this peasant community. Presently comes the "little thin man" with the slight limp, to whom nobody at first paid any attention, since they all supposed him to be a stray laborer looking for work, and for such they had no manner of use. Certainly they never dreamed that the "Evil One" had entered their peaceful little village, and when the little man announced that his name was "Branchu," that he was a shoemaker, and would like to settle down among them, they welcomed him as warmly as their inherently suspicious peasant natures would permit, only one among them warned from the first, "Be on your guard!" and he was a poor, crack-brained creature to whom it would, they agreed, be absurd to pay any attention.

Then things began to happen. For a little while they seemed merely unfortunate coincidences, the wrongs that were committed, the misfortunes that befell—and befell always those who least deserved them. There were illnesses, and suicides, and fights among the young men; people and cattle alike were stricken with strange diseases, and it very quickly became evident that these occurrences sprang from some supernatural cause. Help was sought where no help could be given, and before rescue came—came in a totally unlooked-for way and from an altogether unexpected quarter—the entire village had become a pest hole, where the bodies of both men and beasts lay rotting in the streets, while indoors people starved. Horror succeeded horror; the church had become "a frightening thing to look at," but the village was "a far more terrifying sight, with its caved-in roofs, upturned streets, and corpses thrown out like garbage."

Such material is perhaps better adapted to a short story than to a novel, even when the novel is, like this, a comparatively brief one. The chronicle of crime and misfortune and suffering grows a trifle wearisome before the end is reached.

Mr. Boyd tells us that C. F. Ramuz is one of a little group of French-Swiss writers who have refused to become Parisianized, refused to permit their little streams to flow into and be absorbed by the great river of French literature. "His novels and stories are as indigenous as the strongest nationalist could wish. He is not just another French author who chanced to be born in Lausanne instead of Paris. . . . At the same time he is not a mere parochial celebrity of the chocolate and Swiss milk variety." It is, of course, impossible to form from this one "rural fantasia" any just idea as to the correctness of Mr. Boyd's estimate of C. F. Ramuz as "the greatest Swiss novelist." Swiss novelists are not very many, and most of them are rather French than Swiss in their work. But

it is quite obvious that here is a writer of whom it would be well to know more, one who has talent as a narrator, and a sympathetic understanding of both the inner and the outer existence of that Swiss peasantry which is so little known to the majority of American readers.

> *Louise Maunsell Field, in a review of "The Reign of the Evil One," in* The New York Times Book Review, *December 3, 1922, p. 8.*

ERNEST BOYD   (essay date 1925)

[*A prominent Irish-American literary critic, Boyd was known for his erudite, honest, and often satirical critiques. He was also a respected translator, especially of French and German works, and his* Studies from Ten Literatures *demonstrates his knowledge of modern foreign literature. In the following excerpt from that work, Boyd discusses Ramuz's development as a novelist.*]

Although C. F. Ramuz began with the traditional little book of poems, to which he has since added *La grande guerre du Sondrebund* and *Chansons,* his fame rests entirely upon his work in prose fiction. His first novel, *Aline,* was published in 1905, and was followed by *Les circonstances de la vie* (1907), *Jean-Luc persécuté* (1909), *Aimé Pache, peintre vaudois* (1911), and *La vie de Samuel Belet* (1913). These represent a definite period in his development which seems to have terminated with the war, for since then his work has entered upon a new phase, of which *Le règne de l'esprit malin,* which has been translated under the title of *The Reign of the Evil One,* is the most brilliant illustration. His first period was one of realism, in which it appeared as if a successor to [Edouard] Rod had been found whose genius was wholly Swiss. In an early number of the *Voile latine,* when the eternal question was being debated as to whether there could really be a distinctively Swiss literature, Ramuz formulated the point of view from which his own position must be estimated. He reduced the rôle of French culture to one of pure aesthetics, looking to France not for ideas but for models in the art of writing French. His novels and stories are as indigenous as the strongest nationalist could wish. He is not just another French author who happened to be born in Lausanne instead of Paris. He is more intensely and exclusively Swiss than Rod; at the same time he is not a mere parochial celebrity of the chocolate and Swiss milk variety, several of whom, it so happens, have long ago been translated into English! M. Ramuz is a writer in the same category as J. M. Synge and James Joyce, an artist whose appeal is universal, though the form and content of his work bear the deepest imprint of purely local and immediate circumstance.

There is, indeed, a suggestion of Synge in the method of M. Ramuz, at least in the earlier novels of his realistic period from *Aline* to *La vie de Samuel Belet.* They spring from the very soil of the country in which the scene is laid, and are the creations of a mind which has adapted itself with great skill to the simplicity of the folk manner. As he sits in the village inn of some Swiss hamlet, his ear notes the turns of phrase, the savory idioms of the country people. The slow rhythms of this speech possess him, and in this close contact with man and nature he gradually earns some half-forgotten legend, the fragment of an idyl or the vague tradition of a rustic tragedy. Then he has the theme of a novel, which he will proceed to elaborate in the deliberate, naïve style of the narrators, reconstructing the fable piece by piece, with scrupulous notation of every detail of time and place. The limitations of this method are obvious. There is a lack of spaciousness, of perspective, in these pictures filled with scarcely articulate figures, and where every detail is recorded with the same minute care. The art of M. Ramuz is essentially narrative and plastic, and his canvases have the charm of the Primitives. *Aline* is a little peasant romance with a tragic denouement; *Jean-Luc persé-cuté* tells the story of drama of infidelity in a mountain village. In themselves they are trifles, but the author has recaptured the movement of life in them.

While those two books, together with *Nouvelles et morceaux,* are peasant studies pure and simple, revealing in their brevity the author's method, it is in his three long novels, *Les circonstances de la vie, Aimé Pache, peintre vaudois,* and *La vie de Samuel Belet,* that M. Ramuz has shown his greatest power. Here the technic is the same, but it is applied to the richer material of provincial manners, in a country where the small town is nearer to the village than to the city, and where the absence of large cities makes it possible to contain the whole panorama of a people's life in this framework. *Les circonstances de la vie* may be called the history of a Swiss Charles Bovary, the ignominious defeat of a mediocre individual by the force of circumstances as ignoble as they are implacable. Emile Magnenat, the good, respectable, commonplace notary, is the central figure. With meticulous care M. Ramuz sets this character upon the stage, describes his social background, his wedding, his family, the family clergyman, and the rest. The German Swiss servant Frieda Henneberg is the instrument of the catharsis which destroys all the second-hand morality and smug security of the family, when she establishes her domination over the man and finally ruins him. In *Aimé Pache* the same social stratum is examined, but the young artist is a more powerful character than poor Emile; his pursuit of his destiny is conscious and deliberate and he succeeds in mastering his own fate. The struggle of the artist, first against the bourgeois suspicions of his own people, his career as a student in Paris, and his painful groping toward the discovery that only by conforming to the soil of his father can he fully realize himself—such is the story.

What is of most interest in the work of C. F. Ramuz is its analysis of the French Protestant mind, and the expression in literature of an element whose absence from the literature of France must always seem a loss to English readers. M. André Gide, it is true, betrays his Huguenot origins in his writings, but only the Swiss have produced a literature in which Protestantism is an influence as all-pervading as in English. M. Ramuz has admirably preserved the Protestant note which, coupled with the familiar idiom of the country people in which he writes, lends a piquant contrast to his novels as compared with the very different atmosphere of French fiction. If the desires of the flesh are by no means a negligible part of his drama of Swiss life, how subdued and uneasy these sinners are! They have none of the abandon, or the frank animality, or the self-conscious ecstasy, of the people described by Maupassant, Flaubert, and the Goncourts. Aline and Aimé Pache, and Emile Magnenat have the inhibitions of the Calvinistic tradition in their souls. They take their pleasure as sadly as the traditional Englishman. The puritan suspicion of joy pervades the communities of town and country of which M. Ramuz has made himself the interpreter. The rhythm of folk-speech alternates with that of the Bible. . . . The style of M. Ramuz is colored by this inevitable Protestant influence which is so unlike the movement of the French prose of France. Add to that his deliberate cultivation of popular Swiss speech, which has a harshness and a lack of grace

at times intolerable to the ear accustomed to the finely polished instrument of cultured French. His critics have not hesitated to warn M. Ramuz of the risk he incurs of forgetting the definite limitations of his method, and passages of an incredible slovenliness have been cited against him. In this respect his last four volumes show him to be impotent, but they have marked a new phase in his development. *Le règne de l'esprit malin, Les signes parmi nous,* and *La guérison des maladies,* were all three published by the group of *Les cahiers vaudois,* and to them may be added his *Terre du ciel, La séparation des races, Passage du poète* and *Présence de la mort,* which are in the same manner. These stories are of a mystical rather than a realistic character, and suggest at times the apparently ubiquitous influence of Claudel. But M. Ramuz is faithful to his Swiss peasants, and what he gives us, for instance in *La guérison,* is a sort of Protestant Claudelism. One prefers the human tragedy of *Aline* to the mystico-religious study of the miracle-working Marie who takes to herself the diseases of the village, until the unsympathetic authorities remove her to hospital. In *Les signes* the author essays to give the air of mysterious portents to the threat of two sinister events, which throw their shadow over a prosperous community in war-time. The one, which is never named, is an epidemic of "Spanish influenza," the other is "bolshevism." M. Ramuz gives a vigorous and graphic description of the outbreaks of industrial warfare, but, in the end, he rolls the clouds by most conveniently, and leaves his community in the happiest of circumstances.

Terre du ciel is a characteristic novel of his later manner in its combination of scrupulous realism in the portrayal of manners with a charming element of legend and folk-lore, testifying once more to his preoccupation with the spirit of the Vaudois countryside. Ever since *The Reign of the Evil One* an element of satire has been perceptible in his work, and here it peeps forth at the very basis of his story. The whole fable is essentially a legend, whether drawn from actual folk-lore or conceived out of the author's own imagination, telling how paradise seems to the rustic adventurers who suddenly find themselves in heaven, and deriving a peculiar savor from the style in which it is cast. C. F. Ramuz has always written a remarkable French, compounded of archaisms, folk-speech, and the idiom of his country, which differs markedly in rhythm and phrase from that of France. *Terre du ciel* is a typical piece of his prose, awkward and lumbering, but powerful, with the movement of bodies that have been bent over the plough and are no longer supple. It is the writing of one who seems peculiarly fitted to express the mind and interpret the imagination of the peasant, who has never been completely expressed in French literature. (pp. 222-28)

Ernest Boyd, "A Swiss Novelist: C. F. Ramuz," in his Studies from Ten Literatures, *1925. Reprint by Kennikat Press, Inc., 1968, pp. 218-28.*

VINCENT O'SULLIVAN   (essay date 1930)

[*O'Sullivan was an American poet, fiction writer, and critic. In the following excerpt, he discusses Ramuz's reputation and assesses his stature as a world author.*]

It is the odd fate of Ramuz that some of those he has influenced are better known than he is himself. A movement called *Populisme,* evidently inspired in good part by Ramuz, was started not long ago. The movement itself is without vitality and without importance, because it responds to no want; but such as it is, it has led a publisher to reprint three or four of Ramuz's novels: *La grande peur dans la montagne, Beauté sur la terre, Aline* . . . .In his native land most of his books have hitherto appeared in a series called *Les cahiers vaudois,* which certainly does not reach a wide public. Switzerland, the country in the world—unless it be Ireland—most indifferent to its great writers, has never done anything that I know of to enhance the fame of Ramuz; but since Germany and Scandinavia and even France have begun to perceive his merits, Switzerland too is giving him some attention—not entirely respectful by any means. Many years ago the *Mercure de France,* which, with all its faults, has always shewn courage in accepting new and out-of-the-way writers, published one of Ramuz's books, *Le règne de l'esprit malin.* It was the first thing of his I had read; and I wrote a little article which included some passages of the book and sent it to an English periodical. It was refused, and the gentleman who refused it was good enough to explain that as Ramuz seemed to be unknown in his own country he did not see that he should interest the English.

Why is Ramuz unpopular? why is he thought a difficult author? Is it his matter or his manner? His matter on the face of it is plain and simple. Perhaps that is just it. People want something more gaudy, more in the line of the screen-stories which nourish their imaginations. People who live in little towns don't want to read about the people of little towns; they want something lurid: gorgeous palaces in which frantically beautiful nondescript women—Balkan princesses—conspire with oppressively handsome young adventurers, equally nondescript—heimatlosen, but perhaps, after all, American or British.

But Ramuz keeps to his little Swiss towns. In the vast world of writings they are the only villages I recall as if I had been in them. You hear every sound; you get to know every footstep. Things go along humdrum; you are going to be bored—ah, yes, surely 'tis a tedious life, and the best thing to do is to take the boat or train back to Geneva. And meanwhile, without that you are aware, something has happened which convulses the little town. Not outwardly; on the surface all seems the same. Tourists wander placidly with their guidebooks. Ruskin, undisturbed in a corner, continues his sketch of cloud and mountain. But the Devil has come. Or Jesus Christ. Is it indeed Jesus Christ, or a patient from the doctor's sanatorium? Anyhow, a figure in a white garment, with long hair and beard, stands on the margin of the lake and bids the fishers who have toiled all night and taken nothing to cast their nets once again. Palms appear in the streets of the Swiss village, and low white flat-roofed houses, and the glare of an Oriental sun.

Or, as in *L'amour du monde,* it is a sailor come home after long wandering. He bewitches the stolid fishermen and tradesmen, who cease all work and sit the day out listening in the tavern. They have lost all sense of space and time: they are at Shanghai, or on the Ganges, or farther still—beyond the confines of the earth. And a little girl dies because her mother has drawn her out of the magic circle and the pretty fairy voyage is ended for her.

Magic; there is always magic at work in Ramuz's books. His people, so solidly planted to all seeming on the ground, totter on the verge of unreality. Hawthorne tried that a little, Dickens too; but with them it is hallucination, with Ramuz, continuation. Under the guise of a simple tale we are confronted with the most complicated ideas. The abolishment of time, The abolishment of place. Two dialogues going on simultaneously, with no connexion between them.

His way of writing, his style, has been sharply attacked. It has its limits. His method of putting himself on a level with those he writes about, as if he were just an ignorant peasant writing about other peasants, obliges him to note only such things as the peasant would note, and to interpret them from the peasant's point of view. And these are not the new kind of peasants, like are found in Normandy to-day, with motor-cars and gramophones and wireless and dresses from Paris. Besides that, he tries to write as a Vaudois peasant talks, which forces him to locutions such as *comme quand* ["like when"], unpleasing to the ear, and also to continual repetition. "She knew that her father had come into the house. He had come in and sat down. He had drawn his chair to the table, and sat in it, and reached for his pipe. He had lighted his pipe and made a noise with his mouth like a cow when she drinks." That is not taken from any novel of Ramuz, but it is not unfair; there are scores of sentences of the same kind in his books. It is a sort of thing which succeeds in enfuriating certain Swiss critics. What may perhaps be said calmly against the style of Ramuz is that it is a convention, for it requires the reader to suppose that a peasant—not a peasant who has "got an education," as the Americans say, but a man on the soil—would write a long book about other peasants, and granting he did, that he would deliberately employ his dialect instead of the "elegant" language he hears in church and reads in the newspapers.

To a book of his lately reprinted in Paris Ramuz has prefixed a long defence of his method. It cannot be quoted here. From parts of it, from the talk about expressive language as opposed to explicative language, the Jargonists, who derive from Joyce, will take aid and comfort, and they have doubtless placed Ramuz already in their Valhalla. But the aim of the Jargonists is to demolish the English language as at present understood by the people and to substitute new signs invented by them. To follow the latest production of Joyce, *Work in Progress* [*Finnegans Wake*], a knowledge of English won't do. You have to learn Joyce; and so far no Joyce dictionary is to be had. Ramuz, who does want to be understood, simply claims to write, and in a measure to think, in the Waldensian way. Now the Vaudois dialect does not differ from classical French as much as broad Scots differs from English. He says he prefers the dialect because it has life, whereas the classical language is almost a dead language. That, of course, is open to argument, as he himself acknowledges when he says that for a language in general use it is necessary that words should be abstract signs, fixed as permanently and precisely as possible by general agreement, in the same way as the degrees of a barometer or the meridians on maps. "The author first, and then the reader, should know as exactly as possible where the sense of a locution begins and ends, when it has not hard by an image to make it clear and has not the actual presence of things to support it on the right and on the left." But then his own object, he adds, is not to demonstrate and explain, but to make the reader *feel* what he feels himself before the spectacle which the world offers. His interest is not in the play of ideas, but in scenes which strike first and above all the eyes, and appeal not to intellect but to sensation. In short, the art of the painter. Without pausing to discuss this, it may be said that his books really are remembered as pictures are, as something *seen*.

Taken for all in all, a great novelist—the greatest alive today—a genius. As Lytton said so admirably of another, he has two other imaginations besides the poetical—the imagination of the heart—the imagination of the conscience. Up there in the North, if the bestowers of the Nobel prize are scanning the lowering skies for an improbable star, let them turn to Switzerland, to the Canton of Vaud; let them bestow their prize on Ramuz. (pp. 58-60)

Vincent O'Sullivan, "The French Novel: 'David Golder'," in The Dublin Magazine, n.s. Vol. IV, No. 2, April-June, 1930, pp. 57-64.

M. JARRETT-KERR (essay date 1947)

[*In the following excerpt, Jarrett-Kerr examines Ramuz's use of Alpine subjects, settings, and language, focusing on the novels* Derborence *and* Présence de la mort.]

The poems, autobiographies, novels and belles-lettres that still pour out from Bloomsbury-land are written for the most part by men and women of intelligence, well-informed, versed in the technical language of psychology, endowed with memories and mimetic ability sufficient to enable them to discuss the more intriguing aspects of contemporary philosophy ("existentialism," for instance); but that is all. One looks almost in vain for any creative work, emerging pure and whole from the total person—body, soul, mind and tradition. Instead one has to be content with more and more ingenious variations upon a theme constructed by the mind alone. It cannot go on for ever; mathematicians should be able to compute the exact number of permutations and combinations possible, and when this limit has been reached writing must either cease or else start all over again (as crossword puzzles will one day have to do) in the hope that forgetfulness will pardon repetition.

It is, therefore, with a sense of delivery that one comes across a genuine creator in letters. Such was C. F. Ramuz, the Swiss novelist who died on May 24th, 1947, at the age of sixty-nine. He had scarcely been heard of in this country until the appearance of *The Triumph of Death,* the translation of *Présence de la mort* . . . . The tepidity with which the book was received by the reviewers shows that we are not ready for what is really good. In France, too, Ramuz was slow in achieving recognition, though from the first he had the discriminating support of his publisher, Bernard Grasset, and of such writers as Claudel, Thomas Mann and Denis de Rougemont . . . . (p. 134)

Ramuz' *Salutation paysanne,* published in 1929, is preceded by a "Lettre à Bernard Grasset," which is very revealing for his struggles. He is defending himself against the accusation of critics that he writes "bad French"; and to do so, he gives an account of his history. He has always felt, he says, "Un imperieux besoin de soumission, de soumission à ce qui est, de soumission a ce que je suis" ["A pressing need for submission, for submission to that which is, for submission to what I am"]. The conditions to which he has to submit are those of being a Vaudois, with the Vaudois' history and the Vaudois' language, "de sorte que mon orientation première n'a pas été, comme chez beaucoup d'autres jeunes hommes, politique ou metaphysique, mais topographique, géographique, géologique, c'est-à-dire toute concrète" ["so that my first orientation was not, as with many other young men, political or metaphysical, but topographical, geographical, geological, that is to say, completely concrete"]. At first, he says, he did not realise what this imperative need meant. When he started

trying to write he thought he must try and write "correct" French. Indeed, it was a struggle to find himself a writer at all; none of his countrymen ever imagined that writing could be a vocation, and he was quite ashamed of his ambition. In fact he tried to hide it from his parents, especially his mother; and when at home, doing his Latin exercises, he had a dodge by which he kept a piece of sliding paper ready to cover up the poetry he wrote, when she came into the room—always being careful to leave his exercise not quite finished so that he could show her that he was still busy on it. For long he felt separated from "them," while he wrote octosyllabics and alexandrines in the traditional manner; until "étant descendu plus profondément en moi-même, et y ayant touché à un plus vrai moi-même, du même coup je les y eusse rencontrés. Ils n'ont plus été hors de moi. La distance qui me séparait d'eux a été abolie. Il n'y a plus eu contradiction entre eux et moi, parce que je m'étais mis à leur ressembler. Ils m'avaient reconnu; je parlais leur langue . . ." ["having descended more deeply into myself, and having touched there my truer self, at the same time I meet them there. They were no longer outside me. The distance that had separated me from them was abolished. There was no longer a contradiction between them and me, because I had seen myself in their image. They had recognized me; I was speaking their language"]. And so he came to write their own language, the vigorous countryman's language of the Swiss peasant: not a mere patois, as it had once been (a kind of franco-provençal, "une espèce de Savoyard"), but a genuine French with the old patois pronunciation and turns of phrase. This discovery of his true vocation was, he says, no self-conscious "turning-back," no artificial attempt to turn himself into a peasant: indeed, the accusation itself, he declares, comes from those who think that by becoming educated, a graduate, one has thus become a member of a class, a "lettered" individual, a bourgeois, an "intellectual," and so that one has no right to unclass oneself. . . . It was precisely when he tried to write correct French, like a "good pupil," that he felt himself artificial, self-conscious; the traditions of his folk, his blood, the very land of his people, were far deeper and more ineradicable. In fact, he found himself, at the age of twenty-two, faced with two "traditions," written and oral. What he wanted to show was that the old, classical written tradition got its strength precisely from being also "lived," *i.e.,* also an oral tradition; that this no longer obtained; and that, therefore, the oral tradition must be reintegrated into the written. So he deliberately rejected the "classical" style—which he admired—believing that a new and genuine classic could only be achieved by the rejection, that is by a return to the tradition from which it first arose.

He departed, too, from the classical rules (the period and so forth); from the normal shape of the "roman" ["novel"] (one of his books that comes nearest to being a novel, *Derborence,* he calls merely a "récit" ["story"]). He adopted a spoken language; when he began to be recognised he was given an opportunity for public readings of his works, which clarified much—and, indeed, as he points out, this brought him strangely and un-asked into the *avant-garde,* for he thus fitted in with the technique of Broadcasting; and his stress on the gesture-language of the countryman, "où la logique cède le pas au rythme même des images" ["where logic gives way to the very rhythm of the images"] brought him close to the technique of the film. Moreover his "goût de l'élémentaire" ["liking for the elemental"] was, he discovered, very closely related to the "goût de l'universel" ["liking for the universal"]: far from his adoption of a particular language and place leading to isolation, to the impossibility of communication

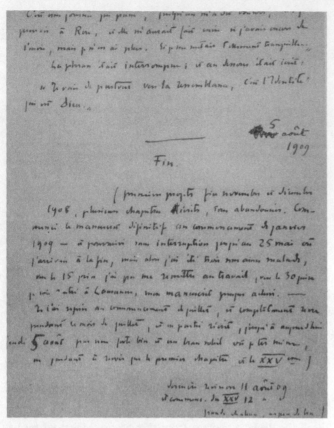

The last page of the manuscript of Aimé Pache, peintre vaudois.

with those of other traditions, he found that it was an emancipation and a widening of his understanding . . . . (pp. 134-35)

It is difficult to describe his prose writings, for they do not fall under any normal category. Even the novel already mentioned, **Derborence,** which has something of a straightforward plot, is clearly not written for the plot (which, anyway, is taken from a sentence in a geographical dictionary, describing how a shepherd, missing and believed dead, lived for several months entombed in a chalet, overwhelmed by an avalanche, feeding on bread and cheese). What Ramuz wants to show us is the village, the people, their traditional hopes and fears, their stupidity as well as their courage. Hidden in the mountains, the peasants believe, is the Devil and his army; when in a bad mood, he declares war, and the result is an avalanche. So when, after more than seven weeks' absence, the young shepherd Antoine reappears, haggard and pale, they think at first that he is a ghost. No one knows what to do; some of them run away, some of them take up forks, sticks, flails, ready for anything; then someone goes and fetches the Curé. He comes out. "Il est blanc et noir. Il tient devant lui Notre-Seigneur qui brille. Un enfant de chœur qui est rouge et blanc porte la croix." ["He is white and black. He holds in front of himself Our Lord, who shines. A choir boy who is red and white carries the cross."] The villagers kneel. What will the strange figure do? If he is a ghost, we shall know now. The little procession advances. The figure sways a little, like a drunken man. "Is it you, Antoine Pont?" He bent his head and then knelt down. It is he! Antoine is taken by the President of the village and questioned, and then the men bring him to the *maison de commune* ["town hall"], where, after several drinks, he slowly comes to and tells his story—how he was in the hut, sleeping, when the mountain fell; buried, he tried to find a way out, but day after day he explored holes between the rocks without success, living on the fodder stored in the chalet and drinking water from a melted glacier; until at last he saw daylight and squeezed his way through. Early next morning, when he wakes up still rather dazed, he suddenly remembers that an old shepherd had been with him in the hut—Séraphin. He goes back resolutely to search for him, madly foraging among the boulders. None of the villagers dare follow him back into that dangerous zone; but his wife, Thérèse, only married a few months before and now pregnant, goes after him. She shouts up to him, among the rocks, but he does not pay attention to her; he still goes on in his fruitless search. The peasants dare not move, they watch from a distance. But she goes on, climbing the rocks till she reaches him. "Les cinq hommes avaient en face d'eux la montagne avec ses murailles et ses tours immenses, et elle est méchante, elle est toute-puissante;—mais voilà qu'une faible femme s'est levée contre elle et qu'elle l'a vaincu, parce qu'elle aimait, parce qu'elle a osé. Ayant la vie, elle a été là où était encore la vie et ramène ce qui est vivant du milieu de ce qui est mort. ["The five men had in front of them the mountain with her ramparts and her immense towers, and she is evil, she is omnipotent;—but see how a weak woman rose against her and how she conquered her, because she loved, because she dared. Having life, she was there where there was still life and brought back what is living from the heart of what is dead."] They come down together, he helping her over the rough stones.—That is all. (pp. 136-37)

But it is above all in a novel like **Présence de la mort** that Ramuz shows his power of presenting a supernatural context within which this love of the particular can be given its true precision and value. The primary theme, again, is simple enough: one day the news reaches the Swiss village that something has gone wrong with the law of gravity: "the earth is rapidly falling towards the sun, rushing to rejoin it. So all life will come to an end. The temperature will go up. It will become too hot for anything to go on living . . . everything will rapidly die." At first nothing happens, except a drought; but nobody minds, because the weather is so lovely—the sky so blue, "as if the painters had come and two or three coats are applied, but the good workman, never satisfied, says: 'Another won't hurt'." The Gardener, watering the beds, finds the hose pipe reduced to a trickle and then stop—now there is "only a little circle of fine white dust about the base" of the sprinkler. But still people will not believe the news. The papers have headlines about it, but it is so hot that everyone has gone bathing, and when they come home they do not look at the papers at first. "On an old green bench up against the barn wall, the master, having finished his work, begins to read: but no, he has not understood. No, it is too big. It is not for us, it is too big. Our own world is quite small. Our own world only goes where our eyes go; it is our eyes that make it. The master having read, looks about him, a little worried perhaps in the beginning; the worry passes away." When someone does begin to take it seriously, to point out what it means, there is a general silence, and another says, "Shut up, do you hear!"—with a nasty voice, like someone who is afraid. Gavillet the stockbroker goes to the Cinema, and lets the world of the Cinema pass dully over him. Afterwards he buys a paper and looks at the headlines; he does not bother about them, and goes back to bed. Only in bed, when the light is out and the inner light is turned on, does he realise its meaning; "and suddenly life was there, but at the same time death was there, which he had never yet known, because he had not yet known life." Some of the men react to it merely by thinking: "The only difference is that we'll all go together, instead of each of us going his own way. . . . Maybe it'll be better that way, who knows?" A guard is placed in front of the National Bank; the Government have posters put up, appealing to the good sense of the citizens—"but there, it is precisely the thing that ought to reassure you that makes you more alarmed." There is a bit of a revolution; the Cavalry and machine-gunners are called out. Meanwhile it gets hotter every day; in the lake water-weeds grow, "the sun comes and drinks, the sun sips through its straws, the sun comes with two lips, and constantly sucks up. . . ." But the level of the water rises, for the lake is filled from the melting glaciers in the mountains. The man and his wife, faced by death, find that they do not know each other, or now know each other for the first time; that their unity is broken, they are two not one, they do not love—and then that they do love after all, that they can come together again, really this time, "and Death can come now, because this is good, this is sweet." The revolt spreads; the people take refuge in their houses behind locked doors; the electricity is cut off; only Perrelet, the shoemaker, goes out to buy food for his supper, and he is drunk and the shops have their shutters up. A man tries to pray, but his little boy, put to bed, does the praying—"and then come the words which he believes simply because they are there, as when the wind comes to the tree." Men get drunk in a pub and there is fighting and shooting. Some houses are burned, and the men form a new society with goods in common. Some of the villages are deserted; men have to go down to the lake to get water. But then each village forms its own Republic, and defends itself against all-comers: "there is still a bit of sky for them, they want to keep it for themselves." Gavillet the stockbroker "looks in the mirror at Gavillet; there is nothing else to be seen but he himself, when he looks and sees himself. Already there is neither time nor space. There is nothing but the very small space of a room, and the still smaller space of oneself. Death has reduced everything to one's own size, which is about five feet eight by a foot and a half. . . ." Gavillet opens the dresser drawer and takes out the revolver. The drought gets more intense, and people die waterless. Then the opposite: the lake overflows, houses are flooded. Now people begin to take refuge high up in the mountains. A party of eight young people push right on up to the heights, to a chalet 2,700 yards up. But others follow them and ambush them—"Wherever men go they take war with them. . . . The others had thought: 'Up there they have everything they want, and we only have to take their place'." The party is driven from their chalet by the newcomers. But they return and, having tied the door of the chalet from outside, set fire to the building: as the men inside try to escape through a trapdoor in the roof, they are shot. They are so pleased with their successful revenge that they scarcely notice how the thermometer is still creeping up—115, 117, 120 degrees on the ice up there and the uninhabited snows. And then the glacier above them begins to bend a little, "like a bow against the knee. It sounded as though hundreds of artillery guns were being shot off together. A great whirlwind went up, and at the same moment a gust of wind, lifting with both hands the men and cattle, throwing them over one another, sprawling pell-mell down the slope, carrying away the roof of the chalet."

Finally, as the end approaches, another little party climbs up to a tiny village up on a promontory of the mountain, past another village perched on an escarpment—"asking ourselves how it held, how it had not already slid down the slope, sitting there like a man sitting down on a sled and barely able to hold back with his feet." Up there the bell-ringer with difficulty clambered up the slope to the Church and rang the bell. And the folk in the village "had to go and feel, on that final day, for the door-knob, and feel for the sill with their feet; it was hard to walk because of the earth that rose to meet them, or else slipped from under them, vanishing." They all gathered, at the summoning of the bell—"And now, you can fall down, mountains, you can fall upon them: they no longer fear you, they have escaped you." In the Church the bell rings once, and they see imperfect space open out for them before the other space; it rings again, saying "Are you coming?" It rings the third time:

> And, in their new bodies, they then stand forth. Someone was standing before them on the cheap lace cloth, between the earthly flowers that fade, among the flickering of the tiny lights—suddenly. Someone rose, rising alone, and He began to walk; He said "Are you coming?" And, in their new bodies, they moved forward. . . .

> The light struck them so strongly that their eyes melted away, their former eyes, that knew night; and they had eyes that no longer knew it. Their eyes, their ears were changed; they learned to see, they learned to hear over again;—at that instant their courage failed them, they stopped in their tracks, they stood motionless: they then saw that now they no longer knew how to walk.

> He had to ask them again, "Come!" and again: "Are you coming?" Then they tried once more, and they saw that they could, they saw that they had learned how to walk again.

> They were able to move forward again, they began to look about. For a long time they looked about, turning to the left and the right: they were quite astonished. . . .

> As though it were new, yet at the same time it was the same: as though it were what they did not have before yet also what they already had; as though in seeing it, they recognised: and at first they hesitated, and then they hesitated no longer.

> They nodded their heads.

> Because, then, after all, they had not been deceived! Because they had not, then, done wrong, in being attached to the earth, they were right in loving it, in spite of all!

> And they said:

> "But we're home!"

In the **"Lettre à Bernard Grasset"** already quoted, Ramuz describes his main preoccupation to have been "en quelque manière de réintegrer à la 'plus grande' France (celle de la langue française) un des membres de la famille, non en l'assimilant, comme on fait pour les étrangers, mais en lui laissant sa pleine autonomie" ["in some manner to reintegrate into the 'larger' France (that of the French language) one of the members of the family, as one does for strangers, but leaving to it its full autonomy"]. But the effect of his work is wider than that: every genuine work that arises from one living point is united with every other living point. Of Ramuz' writing could be said what has been said of the Greek painter Ghika—his symbols "are closely linked with the soil and sky of a definite place. But it is just for that reason that their artistic significance has increased. The more precise the language of art becomes the wider becomes its meaning, and the deeper. . . ." And the recognition of his worth will come similarly from living centres of appreciation. He says himself of criticism that it starts not with quantity but with quality— "A very small number of men, but men who are, so to speak, contagious, who are active without knowing it, who operate upon public opinion; and it is public opinion which in the end binds them together, spinning threads between them, like the spider making his web, of which they are the fastening-points—for opinion, like the spider, instinctively chooses the most solid points. Thus is built up a first tiny public, but one which spins more and more threads because the first have held, they have stood up to the blows of wind and to storms, and this web when smashed has been immediately rebuilt, and smashed again but built again. . . ." Ramuz is assured of appreciation where quality is appreciated. (pp. 137-40)

M. Jarrett-Kerr, "A Regional Novelist: C. F. Ramuz," in The Nineteenth Century and After, Vol. CXLII, No. 847, September, 1947, pp. 134-40.

DIANA TRILLING   (essay date 1947)

[*Trilling is an American critic and author. Her writing often concerns what she considers the deterioration of American society and its effects upon the individual. In her critical assessments, Trilling generally focuses on the social or political statements inherent in a work of literature, considering aesthetics alone as insufficient justification for art. In the following essay, she unfavorably reviews* When the Mountain Fell.]

Although up to his death a few months ago, C.-F. Ramuz, the Swiss author, was almost wholly unknown in this country, the recent publication of his novel **When the Mountain Fell** has brought him a large posthumous success: it is a Book-of-the-Month Club selection and is being hailed by the reviewers as a classic and a masterpiece. I do not agree with this judgment; indeed, I find Mr. Ramuz's new book only slightly less tiresome than his previous **The End of All Men,** which appeared in English translation in 1945. The acclaim it is receiving must be recognized, I think, as the latest instance of the swing of the critical pendulum from the one extreme of false reality to the other extreme of false spirituality. We should not be surprised at the fact that the same opinion which supposes that the truth of modern life is conveyed in such books as *The Hucksters* or *The Story of Mrs. Murphy* now thinks that the ideality of modern life is conveyed by Mr. Ramuz's pious and banal little fable.

Set in Switzerland, **When the Mountain Fell** tells of a landslide which falls upon the high pastures where a group of peasants graze their cattle each summer. All the group is killed except a young man named Antoine, who manages to tunnel his way back to life. He returns to his village, worn and deranged by his long ordeal; the other peasants think he is a ghost until the priest confronts him with the cross. But terror revives once more among the villagers when Antoine insists upon going back to the mountain to dig for the friend who he imagines still survives there; none of them will accompany him into this haunted territory. Only his pregnant wife, Theresa, has sufficient faith and love to follow her husband. Her devotion restores Antoine to sanity, and he returns home with her.

This is the content of Mr. Ramuz's novel. Its style is the crooning Biblical prose long sanctified as the proper way to write about peasants, idiots, and other of God's innocent children—the kind that swells the heart with virtue while it lulls the mind to rest. In other words, **When the Mountain Fell** is barbiturate literature for what the publishing trade proudly refers to as the discriminating reader. Alongside it our more lurid historical romances are good clean adolescent fact-facing.

The insidious thing, of course, about a book of this sort is that although it is a straight religious document and a profoundly anti-intellectual one, it takes no open theological or anti-rational position; so that even people who might be stopped by a formulated faith are available to its seductions. Its appeal to non-reason is entirely implicit in its nostalgic exaltation of the primitive; there is no paraphernalia of ideas; there are no concessions to the immediate problems of civilized living such as always intrude themselves into the work of our American "spiritual" writers. When one of our domestic myth-makers, a Saroyan or a Steinbeck, for example, goes primitive on us he invariably feels that he must deal with that most primitive of earthly forces, sex. But Mr. Ramuz makes no such mistake; his is the churchly view of man which understands that in order for the divine laws to operate in fullest purity all earthly considerations must be dissolved.

I suppose the most significant aspect of the success that has greeted **When the Mountain Fell** is the way in which it points up the fact that the only alternatives our formers of literary opinion can manage are, on the one hand, a bewildered, formless receptivity to the most debased manifestations of contemporary confusion and, on the other hand, a serene faith momentarily maintained in a world empty of anything but the most elementary moral precepts. In view of their power it is surely small wonder that we suffer such a dearth of any fiction which would try to cope with the modern reality in at least some part of its moral complexities.

Diana Trilling, in a review of "When the Mountain Fell," in The Nation, New York, Vol. 165, No. 20, November 15, 1947, p. 533.

R. T. SUSSEX   (essay date 1965)

[*In the following excerpt, Sussex emphasizes the importance of mountain life and landscapes in Ramuz's work.*]

One hears little enough these days of C.-F. Ramuz, the novelist of the Vaud region in western Switzerland, who died in 1947, and was supremely a man of the mountains, especially of those that overlook the upper Rhone valley. He lived for some time, it is true, at Treytorrens, then at Lausanne and Pully, on the northern shore of the Lake of Geneva, but his mountain landscapes are more reminiscent of the giant perspectives of the Bernese Oberland, where a painter-friend of his, Albert Muret, had a chalet in the quaint and primitive village of Lens, above Granges, overlooking the Rhone and the Diablerets, in the Valais. This is, or was then, the most primitive of the Swiss cantons, and peasant life there had remained at a level of bare literacy and of a subsistence that left little margin for contingencies. From this type of country, where human dwellings are dwarfed by a gigantic nature, Ramuz was to draw much material for his best work.

Born in 1878, he spent twelve years of his youth in Paris, and it was this long exile from his native Vaud which first drew from his acute nostalgia the early peasant novels that made his name. Once the pressure of events (the 1914 war) drove him back to his native highlands, he never left them, and lived there for over thirty years, a solitary sage who preferred to remain a countryman and a primitive, and to limit his work mainly to studies of the Swiss peasantry in their natural setting. In the peasant Ramuz saw the heir of natural man, still free because closely linked with nature, and untroubled by the social and ideological servitudes of the bourgeoisie.

In his studied simplification of peasant life, in his reduction of it to the bare essentials, Ramuz was not a little inspired by Cézanne, whose native habitat, the country round Aix-en-Provence and especially the Montagne Sainte-Victoire, Ramuz visited in the autumn of 1913. His *Exemple de Cézanne* shows how forcible the impact was—how the architecture of a Cézanne canvas and the constant interpretation of volumes, the spareness and discipline of technique, the devotion of Cézanne to his native Provence found an echo in Ramuz, and reinforced in him the natural impulse towards a "dépouillement" ["scrutiny"], towards a sober, restrained, universalized art. And this was confirmed by his friendship and close collaboration with Stravinsky.

His own "pays" ["country"], as he admitted, was a tiny one—barely sixty miles by twenty-five—merely one of the twenty-two cantons of Switzerland, yet a *terre réelle* ["real land"]. And though he could not claim a peasant upbringing himself, he was of remote peasant extraction, and was not a little proud of it. His contact with Paris, and with its formidable past in stone, was at first overwhelming to a "petit Vaudois" just come from a land where almost the only monuments to the past were those of nature, 3,000 metres high. The city of the plains seemed a setting where man regained his normal human stature, and no longer played pigmy to nature's giants; where nature was tamed to man's wishes, where park and forest and stream were patterned into man-made shapes, and natural man yielded place to social man, a being of intellect and not of instinct. The thinker in Ramuz could pay willing tribute to this achievement, and to the role of Paris in conferring universal human validity upon the uncertain values that emerged from the life of the French provinces.

At the same time, he maintained, Paris must remember that supremely it is a French parish, the chief of the parishes of France: that to its glittering splendour there ministers a whole nation of scrupulous, careful artisans, of loyal peasants, who toil from dawn till dusk. In the long run it was Paris that cured Ramuz of Paris: he had roots in his own tiny homeland, and go back he must—back to his corner of Europe perched on the frontiers of three great civilizations and of three languages, perched at the watershed where "the waters hesitate between the Rhone and the Rhine." And to leave Paris for Vaud was no impoverishment: quietly, naturally, he took root again there by the lakeside as though there had never been an uprooting. Among the vineyards that rise terrace by terrace to the sloping pastures, among the fisherfolk, farmers and woodsmen he had known in his youth, he came once again "home," and once again could lift his eyes unto the hills. "On ne greffe que sur le sauvageon," he observed: "c'est comme ça que nous greffons." ["One grafts only on wild stock. That is the way we graft.] (pp. 83-5)

In electing to make his own little "pays" the matter of his books, Ramuz amply realized the paradoxical nature of his enterprise. His was a French-speaking province divorced from France by a centuries-old frontier, and nowhere was the divergence more sensible between "good" French (the idiom approved by canons of civilized taste self-consciously formulated and preserved since the Renaissance) and the peasant, "popular" French spoken by the Vaudois. The former was a "sign language," bookish, professorial, basically unreal for him. It was in the latter, a "gesture language," that he chose to write—in a language that was "not yet" written, a spoken, living thing: his long plea in defence of it is the substance of his "**Lettre à Bernard Grasset**," and the contagion of it subsequently passed to Giono. "J'ai écrit une langue qui n'était pas écrite (pas encore). J'insiste sur ce point que je ne l'ai fait que par amour du vrai, par goût profond de l'authentique . . . j'ajoute, par *fidélité*." "J'ai écrit (j'ai essayé d'écrire) une langue parlée: la langue parlée par ceux dont je suis né. J'ai essayé de me servir d'une langue-geste qui continuât à être celle dont on se servait autour de moi, non de la langue-signe qui était dans les livres." ["I wrote a language that was not being written (not yet). I insist on this point—that I only did it out of love for the true, out of a strong preference for the authentic . . . I add, out of *accuracy*." "I wrote (I tried to write) a spoken language: the language spoken by those of whom I was born. I tried to use a gesture-language that continued to be the one used around me, not the sign-language that was in books."] Whatever reserves the critics may have expressed about the Ramuz style, its laconic expressiveness, its enumerations, its lack of formal structure, he probably succeeded as well as Eugène Le Roy, and better than George Sand and Léon Cladel, in capturing the authentic speech of the man on the land. One of the recurrent problems of the regional novel is that of rendering authentically rural a literary form destined, like most literature, for middle-class consumption, and rarely designed to hold up a mirror to a peasantry unconscious of its value as the stuff of which books are made. Ramuz at least "qualified," by birth and continual residence, for acceptance as the painter of Vaudois man, and his ear for the rhythms of common local speech was undoubtedly good. From such elements he evolved slowly, and with growing simplicity, a regional style that is rugged and elliptical, but at least fresh and strong, with the strength and freshness of things rustic.

Equally simple was the antithesis that found expression in his novels, the contrast and contact (as Claudel observed) between the "mythical hinterland," the "super-nature" of the great mountains, and the tranquil, human warmth of the lakeside, between the inhuman and the human, the mysterious and the known, the eternal and the ephemeral.

Nourished as he was on Aeschylus and the Greek myths, with their recurrent theme of Necessity, of a blind and amoral fate opposed to human beings, Ramuz was equipped, and even disposed by temperament, to interpret human life as marked from earliest history by an inexorable doom. And these classical conceptions were probably reinforced by the Biblical insights of a Swiss Protestant, strongly grounded in an Old Testament full of divine anger and divine punishments. This, applied to the life of the mountaineer, was scarcely likely to produce work reflecting saccharine summer idylls and chocolate-box scenery. His vision of life was essentially tragic, and happy endings (*Derborence* is an exception) were not his strong point. When, therefore, he prepared himself for grander perspectives, it was natural for him, though his characters remained peasants of normal stature and failings, to conceive his work in terms of a mountain "myth." And the only human force that could be set against the mountain was not some Promethean individual, but a village community—a collective human defiance of the invisible. As modern "myth" this is completely admissible.

Not all of his work is in this vein. *Le village dans la montagne,* for example, is a simple, sober telling of the life of a mountain village, from the first melting of the snows, through the brief summer and the transhumance, to the descent of the long winter again: merely the story of the peasant's year—manuring, planting, wood-cutting, cheese-making, tending of the *bisses* ["water-channels"], along with birth and death, sickness and health, festival and mourning. . . . *Samuel Belet* is the life story of a humble nomad, *L'amour du monde* a social canvas of a lakeside village, *Adam et Eve* the slow-moving story of a forsaken husband, *Jean-Luc persécuté* a tale of conjugal infidelity culminating in horror and death. Yet these narratives of humble rural life, with all its poetry and pathos, are less compelling than the novels in which Ramuz labours as a creator of myths, and invests the unknown with a monstrous, sinister power—the sort of power with which primitive man, from Sinai to Carmel, from Olympus to Kanchenjunga, has always invested the high places.

The myth is sometimes misbegotten, and fails of its effect. *Si le soleil ne revenait pas,* as simple in its essentials as Giono's *Colline,* is a cogent study of a mountain village community in the grip of winter, and the sense of arrested vitality, of expectation is as vivid as the little concrete details, closely observed, of peasant mentality or physiognomy. Yet the whole book rests upon the flimsiest hypothesis—an old man's prediction that the sun will never again rise upon the village. Stretch his imagination and credulity as he will, the best-intentioned reader can scarcely feel that the issue is problematic; and though the mood of despair and panic is admirably done, there is no real suspense, no authentic mystery—and the sun's inevitable re-appearance is somewhat of an anti-climax. It is worth noting that the sense of imprisonment, of the death of hope—a theme popular with the existentialists—provides Ramuz, here as elsewhere, with some of his best and most graphic effects as a writer. Another "symbolical" novel, *La beauté sur la terre,* which, like Giono's *Prélude de Pan,* culminates in a sort of "panic" mob delirium, revolves around a "beauty" as unpredictable (and unintelligent) as Giraudoux's Helen of Troy. This girl, a homesick solitary who seems unmindful of the brooding lusts that spring up like dragon's teeth around her, accepts with indifference the tribute that men lay at her feet: her only response is to the music of a hunch-backed cobbler. And in the fulness of time beauty and the "beast" take their flight together, leaving their devotees in flames and ruin. To sustain a "myth" like this would have required an Iseult or a Belle Aude, not a sullen waif from Santiago, and here again, though the lakeside community is tellingly interpreted, and the local colour excellent, the whole pretext for the novel is insufficient.

With *La grande peur dans la montagne* Ramuz triumphantly overcame his earlier weaknesses, to achieve a "mountain epic" which may well have inspired Giono's *Colline.* In both books there are recollections of past catastrophe, wizened old men who seem evil incarnate, mysterious diseases, an atmosphere of "panic" terror, and an impression of sinister earth forces in league against human effort. Giono's story reduces itself to human stature and to adverse but conquerable circumstance: with Ramuz, the mountain has its will of men, and death waits upon those who profane by their invasion the stillness of the peaks. The mountain is the dominant of the

story: secret, inscrutable, it suffers human presence on its habitable rock-ledges, it nourishes (though meagrely) the human life that seeks domicile there, it shapes and hardens and reduces to its own obedience the lilliputian breed that must live on the fringe of the inviolable—but its anger is a thing of terror, and man is slow to learn, and slower to remember.

It is a simple enough story—of an outbreak of foot-and-mouth disease among the herds of a summer pasturage high in the Alps, and of the indispensable quarantine measures taken by the small village community from which the herdsmen came. But the author has linked this with the recollection of a former disaster, which had made the pasture a plague spot for twenty years, and with the love of a village girl and boy—which raises a type of cautionary tale to tragic dimensions. There is rare artistry in the procedure by which Ramuz evokes the uncreate silence of the pasture at night, and the evil presences that seem to stalk abroad in this world of rock and ice. Portent by portent fate closes in, and the diagnosis of the dreaded malady and subsequent quarantine measures make the little group of herdsmen permanent prisoners of their pasturage, amid scenes of death, the stillness of death and the stench of death, while midsummer heat and solid rock mock their efforts to bury the dead beasts, and the grim peaks ring them round in their living hell. Youthful love seeks to break out of hell—and pays the price. And when human resistance finally gives way, and despair and terror force a man-made barrier, a great avalanche of rock and ice and flood-water catapults death down upon the village itself, and the mountain wreaks its final vengeance on those who defied it. (pp. 85-9)

Even more primitive and elemental, perhaps because set back a little in historical time, is the story *Derborence*—incomparably Ramuz's most powerful work, and a real mountain "myth." A myth is not just a fantasy or fiction (—nor a mere modern cliché!): it embodies in story form some part of humanity's deepest wisdom and experience, and modern scholarship has done the word a disservice in debasing it as it has. In this "myth" Ramuz has created a story that is timeless—not attached to any historical epoch, and the elimination of all "temporal" local colour makes the characters stand out with the stark simplicity of a primitive fresco or a saga. This timelessness is enhanced by the incessant stress on the inhuman silence of the high places: a primitive stillness that antedates life itself, a prehistoric, unbearable emptiness in which the tinkle of a drop of water, the sigh of a breeze on a chalet roof bring an inexpressible relief from the oppression of it all. The setting is a high mountain pasture called Derborence, a deep cup of a place right at the snow line, high above the Rhone valley just below the Diablerets. The village pastures its herds there every summer on the short-lived, lush summer grass, and a rough chalet under the cliff face shelters the twenty-odd herdsmen who tend the 150 cattle, and bring a human note into an unpeopled landscape. Two of these herdsmen have an uneasy presentiment of disaster: one, Séraphin, a veteran mountaineer almost too old and rheumatic for summer duty, but intent on teaching his mountain lore to the other, Antoine, a man married only two months before, and aching under his three-months' enforced exile. It is while they sleep that a giant avalanche of rock, almost unheralded, blots out Derborence and leaves a wilderness of stone over which hangs a yellow pall of dust. The Mountain, fickle and treacherous as ever, has claimed its own. To the villagers, especially to Antoine's young wife

Thérèse, the news brings a sort of stupor, reacts on them with intolerable poignancy. A toll of twenty men in a small mountain village is a grievous loss. The very simplicity of Ramuz's style, rugged and peasant in its rhythms, and leaving so much unsaid, brings home the desperate tragedy of the thing.

Two months later, out of the towering boulders that encumber Derborence with a weight of death, emerges a head, then a body: a tiny speck in a vast wilderness of stone, a speck that only an eagle could have seen, a grey-white, stone-hued wraith of a man—Antoine himself, scarcely able to believe, after two months of entombment, the sensations of light and warmth that invade him, the sight of hoof-marks on the earth, the green of trees and bushes. Yet when he comes to his own, his own receive him not: they run from him in terror—is this one of the unburied dead, crying for sepulture, for ever exiled? His own wife does not know him, and he has almost forgotten the power of speech to call to her. They go out with guns and sticks to meet this white thing: the village vicar leads them, bearing a cross. The figure hesitates, then goes down on his knees—it is a living man. But how reduced, how pitiful! Time has ceased to exist for him. The dear, familiar things of the everyday impinge upon him with unaccustomed joy. Not hunger or thirst, but the loneliness of death has sapped his human vitality. And one *idée fixe,* one heritage of death has remained to him: he is convinced that somewhere below the titanic mass of rock Séraphin is still alive—someone had called to him. Even though the desolation of Derborence is a grim horror to him, back he goes to it, crazily armed with pick and shovel, to face 150 million cubic feet of earth. The men let him be: is this really a man or a ghost?

The redemptive part of the book is the shortest and most direct, and the more telling for the growth of the antithesis between frail human striving and the gigantic force of the Mountain. Antoine has nothing superhuman about him: he has shown tenacity in fighting his way out of the darkness of the rocks, and stubborn courage, yet he is weak enough. But one weaker than he is the agent of his redemption: conquering her superstitious dread, she goes out on to the rocky ruin after her husband, finds him calling down the huge funnels in the stone, and brings him back to life and warmth and sanity. The Mountain was evil and omnipotent, but a frail woman, strong in the power of her love, had risen up against it and overcome the sharpness of death, and brought back her man once more from the dead.

It really *is* a story that echoes for a long time in the mind: there is something eternal, something permanent about it. The style is one which achieves effects by indirect suggestion and evocation, and by a free use, almost abuse, of the laconic idiom of a taciturn race of men. Yet this very tenseness is its strength: it avoids purple passages, and though there are superb landscape descriptions, they are couched, most often, in simple, familiar speech, with very little straining after effect. It is repetitive, and sometimes too cumulative in its detail. Sometimes it is obscure: perhaps intentionally so. But its outstanding merit is indisputable. It is simple and stark, it is a book of the open-air, written on the spot by a man who knows and loves his mountains, it is full of direct observation of human types not strongly characterised, but universalised, so that the book has a human value far beyond its simple scope. And throughout it holds the reader's interest—it is a story simply told and well.

Ramuz has thus made the Mountain not merely a setting, a landscape décor, but a "law in the members" of his charac-

ters, an element that shapes and moulds (but not to the total extinction of freedom) the creatures who live by its bounty. From it come both their joy and their sorrow, their inspiration and their despair, their livelihood and their death. It informs with its rhythms their every daily occupation, so that man does not merely co-exist with the mountain: he exists in terms of the mountain. Of such data is the best regional literature made. (pp. 89-91)

R. T. Sussex, *"C. F. Ramuz and the Alps,"* in Australian Journal of French Studies, *Vol. II, Part 1, January-April, 1965, pp. 82-91.*

MILTON STANSBURY (essay date 1967)

[*In the following excerpt, Stansbury discusses the narrative devices and techniques of* La grande peur dans la montagne.]

La grande peur dans la montagne is the story of a foredoomed, oddly assorted band of seven Alpine villagers who, in presuming to pasture their seventy head of cattle on the high mountain overlooking their village, invoke the hostility and revenge of the legendary malevolent spirit—the Other, the mysterious Evil One—who lurks in the mist-shrouded recesses of the mountain, which He claims as his domain. Through a relentless disease, both men and beasts of this ill-starred expedition are finally exterminated, even the entire village down below is swept away by the glacier.

Ramuz presents the narrator of this grim tale, which would seem to be an oral delivery, under an anonymous "we." He is such a devout spinner of his yarn that he is apt to speak as an eye-witness of events in which he could not possibly have participated, or to watch scenes at a distance which no human eye could reach, a discrepancy of small moment in a rousing tale. And his listeners, who are they? Compatriots, possibly, from his canton in the Vaud, or an audience from a younger generation eager to hear, or perhaps to hear repeated, the story of the catastrophe that befell their forebears. The stage is one for Greek tragedy under Alpine skies, and Ramuz—you are reminded of the glitter in his eyes—will exploit it to the full. Once the struggle between the helpless mountaineers and their hidden enemy has begun, he spares us not one of the calamities that start to inflict them. Rather than the characters, who for the most part remain rather faceless, the protagonist of the story is "the whole evil mountainside." This is no ordinary mountain, it is one that can come to life, heave its walls about and sweep intruders into space.

After the mountain, Ramuz gives his greatest attention to the glacier, the mountain's malignant agent—"this unreal thing which comes towards you, this unproductive monster, which makes you feel that you've reached the end of both life and the world." This is no ordinary glacier for, as in Shelley's *Mont-Blanc,* where likewise

. . . The glaciers creep
Like snakes that watch their prey, from their far mountains,
Slow rolling on; there, many a precipice,
Frost and the sun in scorn of mortal power
Have piled: dome, pyramid, and pinnacle . . .

Ramuz' glacier also is seen to "burst and rave," to express itself in great resounding cracks, to laugh, to cough.

The forbidding scene below is shut in high above by a sullen sky "like a great plain of clay seen upside down, a ceiling like yellow earth always pressing slowly down," making it hard to breathe with "air that is thick and stale, air that sticks to you."

Meanwhile, the Evil One has set to work in earnest to clear its mountain of these intruders. It had begun its campaign of demoralization by walking on the roof of their hut at night—at least, in their fevered imagination the wavering men below so suppose, one of the mysteries that they have had no heart to investigate. The deadly blow, however, is the disease with which the herd is stricken. It is the terrible hoof and mouth disease, which may attack both man and beast and for which there is no cure. The storyteller likens it to one of the Biblical plagues in Egypt, the fifth of which struck down the cattle. The story now begins to abound in pictures of the gradual dwindling of the animals which we see in the various stages of their agony. The cows "already emitting the smell of death, bloated and insensible even to the flies," some still able to move make a few feeble movements—"with their back legs, an ear or a twitch of the skin on their flanks, lowing plaintively to be relieved of their unmilked, swollen udders."

The men face an equally hopeless end; they loll about listlessly, rolled up in their blankets like dead men, not having undressed, not even having taken off their shoes, which before, because of the rats, they had always hung up on pegs. Or they may be slumped at the foot of the low wall outside, their heads drooped forward, their eyes sunken, their skin turned the colour of parched earth.

From one disaster to another the tale moves into ever deeper gloom to the ultimate tragedy when man and beast stampede down the mountain toward the village from which they had been banned, followed by the glacier's flood which will sweep most of the houses away with the people in them. The story ends with the wry comment: "For the mountain has her own notions. She has her own will and her ways."

La grande peur should not be rated as merely a masterpiece in terror. If the scenes of violence and despair dominate as the tragedy gains momentum, Ramuz provides many more delicate touches, especially in the earlier story. There is the gentle moment when the mountain stream "lies silent and peaceful like a grazing animal"; or when you pass a small group of haysheds "which watch you coming, and afterward huddle together as if to talk things over"; or the dawn lingering on the peaks "like a bird resting on the topmost branches of a tree, then beginning to come down by steps from perch to perch," or the mountain's saucy moment when she is showing what she can do: "with her air of great purity she had once more arrayed herself in brilliant light and then was telling us: 'Well, you see? . . . when I really try . . .' No longer willing to remain hidden, she had put on that garb of translucid air, was showing us the entire valley, telling us: 'Come look . . .'."

Even more than by the absorbing story, one's attention is intrigued by Ramuz's devices in creating its extraordinary life and freshness, a narrative that flows as freely as a stream, one seeming not written down, but orally, spontaneously delivered, with liberties taken which a manual of style would perhaps not countenance, but which a translator has every obligation to transmit as faithfully as possible. In the first place, Ramuz keeps us constantly aware of the progressive visibility of his actors as they move from one point to another. His eye is attracted, cat-like, by the slightest displacement. That vigilant anonymous watcher far below will keep us informed of the progress of the long column up the mountain; the characters appear from over a ledge or emerge from a sloping forest or pierce a veil of mist, they are never seen all at once but by degrees—first, their hats and heads, then their shoulders and so on, down, until the whole body is visible. Ramuz's sensitivity to movement is everywhere apparent. The glacier is described as forever coming to meet you; the sides of the valley are seen pushing close to hem you in; the colours keep shifting on the peaks; a cloud-shadow will come running up the slope; a lantern's beam in the black of the forest will "pull" the red pine trunks forward; the sun too will be "pulled" between two peaks "as on a cable." One remarkable scene is even presented in the form of a cinematic fade-out, a device used long before by Edgar Allan Poe, frequently in *The Lives of the Saints* and even as early as Homer. Joseph from a height is watching the activities in the village square below, but at a certain moment "the scene becomes blurred by the projection of a huge rock before one of the village benches and the bench dissolves. The actors, the faces, fade out, turn gray, wear thin before his eyes like linen that has served its time, and Joseph, one of the two young lovers in the story, realizes that he is in a place where there is no longer anybody, the separation seeming even more complete between himself and Victorine, the other lover between himself and everything below." Each change is noted on the long mountain trail "which goes first over grass full of great patches of flowers; then through the pines, on the carpet of needles, spotted and embroidered everywhere with gold, then the beginning of the fallen rocks, then again the sun." The fact that Ramuz's characters are seen like this always in isolation, gives an effect of hypersensitive clarity.

But Ramuz's most characteristic and most recurrent device for keeping the scene before you (or for intensifying an idea) is his recourse to repetition. While he may stop short before anything so emphatic as "a rose is a rose is a rose," he does enjoy repeating the same phrase or sentence with only perhaps the addition of one new word. For example, he will say: "It was under that yellow sky, that low yellow sky"; or "they went on, they went on a long way"; or "they climbed, they reached level ground, they climbed." There is nothing particularly original about repetitions as mild as these, which almost any writer might employ to produce a conversational effect, but it becomes more conspicuous, a decidedly idiosyncratic structural technique when Ramuz begins to pile them up: "It was that Sunday, their next-to-last-day. It was that Sunday morning it was the morning of their next-to-last-day . . .". Sometimes he will separate these repetitions briefly, positioned a few sentences apart, or will begin a series of short paragraphs with identical or only slightly altered phrasing as with his "It was a beautiful day," which reappears seven times—it is enlightening to count them—within two pages.

Indeed, for sustaining the atmosphere, for conveying the duration of an action, no device is more effective, more simple really, than this build-up of repetitions suggesting the old ballads. There is the terrible skirmish in the graveyard on the day of Victorine's funeral when Sebastian "started backing away, backing, backing away until there he was backed up against the wall" where we too, the readers, have backed up against the wall. If by recourse to repetition Ramuz can heighten the horror or the drama of a scene, he may also use it to soothe or weave the spell of a bardic incantation—a "mélopée," that word so beautiful in French. Or you may

Ramuz (left) and Igor Stravinsky.

seem to be reading from a book of the Old Testament, so antiquely fashioned is his manner of writing, one so sturdily built on lean nouns and verbs. The scant adjectives that do occur are of the most commonplace variety—bon, beau, gros, haut, large ["good, beautiful, wide, high, large"]—with a modest palette of three or four familiar colours. A style shorn of ornamentation of any kind, if you except the repetitions which linger in the memory as a special charm. In my own case, I became more and more fascinated by their appearance. There were never quite enough of them for my taste, I think I may even have been guilty of adding one or two of my own, which, if so, I hope are undetectable, though possibly Ramuz would not mind.

There are those who think to discover symbols, parables, elaborate allegories, weighty messages in this story of man's hopeless conflict with forces mightier than himself, in this case a hostile mountain. But I am glad that I, for one, was never made to feel conscious of any particular warning or lesson to be derived from *La grande peur dans la montagne.* In the first place, Ramuz is insistently mythopoeic and in this respect has much more in common with the early Romantic poets than with the later nineteenth- or twentieth-century ones. Ramuz is not symbolic and thus is totally unlike Thomas Mann in *The Magic Mountain.* With Ramuz, however, Nature is not merely personification; his mountain really

does produce the effect of an inaccessible, indifferent Power which minds its own business when left alone but which will certainly smite the interloper. And it is here that Ramuz and those like him, such again as Shelley in *Mont-Blanc,* should be contrasted with Maurice Herzog, who scaled Mount Everest "because it was there." Essentially, the difference is one of opposing conceptions of man, of humanity: our puniness or ineffectuality in confrontation with the mysterious universe of nature, versus Herzog's assertion of human grandeur, suggestive of a certain kind of arrogance or hubris harking back to Greek tragedy. But Ramuz's story should, I think, be taken very simply. To the Alpine villagers, to those who suffered from its fury, the mountain seemed, of course, a spirit of evil, diabolic intent. But to Ramuz? Is he not perhaps pleading the mountain's cause as well? The mountain's revenge is after all directed against intruders and if a lesson must be gleaned it consists in nothing more than this warning to trespassers to stay at home. Ramuz has made a poem of a story and not a didactic one, and as Mallarmé once said, it is not with ideas that one makes a poem, but with words. (pp. 53-8)

Milton Stansbury, "On Translating Ramuz," in ADAM International Review, *Nos. 319-21, 1967, pp. 53-8.*

CLARENCE PARSONS   (essay date 1967)

[*In the following excerpt, Parsons discusses Ramuz's works as manifestations of the author's desire to create "visual" prose.*]

Je suis peintre, mais j'écris: j'ai tort. Je voudrais être traité en peintre et je n'en ai pas le droit, puisque je n'ai pas de palette. ["I am a painter, but I write: I am wrong. I would like to be treated like a painter, but I don't have that right, since I have no palette."] This statement of Ramuz affords us an insight into the fundamental problem he had to face in order to master his art as a writer. It also explains in part why his works have not yet received the acclaim they deserve.

Ramuz admits that he is in the seemingly false position of a painter who chooses the written word to express himself. He expects in turn the reader to approach his works with the attitude of one who, through the printed word, contemplates a painting, an unusual situation which makes special demands on both writer and reader. The writer, in fact, must use words to achieve the effects which are normally those of line, form and colour; the reader must possess in turn the practised inner eye of one who is able to interpret, into plastic equivalents, the printed word.

"I am a painter but I write." Indeed, Ramuz' way of seeing the world about him, his aesthetic convictions, all suggest the artist rather than the man of letters. Already in his earliest attempts at writing, Ramuz rejects the intellectualized interpretation of experience which, he feels, always falls short of the truth, and may even at times lead to serious errors. Ideas, he claims, are by their very nature generalizations; they tend to rise above reality and immediate experience; they often evolve for their own sake, following an independent course while submitting to the requirements of abstract patterns of thought. All ideas for Ramuz therefore are suspect. He accepts nothing which cannot be immediately verified by personal experience. There is only one world whose existence is undeniable and that is the concrete world of objects. The reality of this world is experienced through the senses and particularly through the eyes of the beholder. Consequently it is only by remaining in close touch with objects and by having a complete trust in the senses that one can be sure of approaching the elusive goal of truth. The aim of Ramuz as a creative artist is thus clear and straightforward: to repossess the material world and to translate this experience as directly as possible to the reader.

It is obvious that such an outlook, and such convictions are those of a painter rather than those of a writer, and it would have been natural for Ramuz to choose painting as a means of expression, since the artist's aim is generally to reproduce, through line, form and colour what he sees before him. Yet it is as a writer and more specifically as a novelist that he sought to realize his particular vision. Was he unable to use to his satisfaction the tools of the artist, brush, paint and canvas? It would seem so. At any rate, he must have felt more at home with words. Are words however in themselves adequate to communicate an outlook such as his?

Ramuz admits that his way of seeing the world around him could be more readily expressed through painting than through the written word. Verbal expression offers indeed two great disadvantages: it tends towards abstraction— words are merely symbols of the object and not the object itself; it is also necessarily successive in nature, it requires time to achieve its purpose. Both these characteristics are obstacles to the fullest expression of the concrete. An intellectual distance intervenes between words and what they represent. Ramuz, wishing to adhere to his aesthetic convictions and bound to the written word as a means of expression, must somehow bridge that distance and overcome the deficiencies of language. He attempts to do so in several ways. He limits his vocabulary as strictly as he can to that of the concrete. He avoids abstract expressions, using geometrical terms and the names of simple colours to communicate as directly as possible to the reader the shape and aspect of objects. He tries to overcome the successive nature of language by an abundant use of verbs which translate not motion but static conditions and by a special use of comparisons. He also uses a technique of *reprises* which can be explained in this way. The successive nature of the sentence fails to capture satisfactorily the concrete appearance of the subject; it comes close to doing so but then seems to escape and follow its own course. That is why Ramuz stops, goes back and begins the same sentence again, but this time gives it a somewhat different turn. He does this repeatedly in an effort to arrest the flow of the sentence and force it to fulfil the task he assigns it, all his efforts being faithfully recorded on the written page. The result is considered awkward and irritating by many critics because they expect a polished literary style where in fact we are closer to the painterly style of a Cézanne, i.e. the gradual accumulation of juxtaposed small touches which insure simultaneously, through their overall relationship, fidelity both to the subject and to the feelings of the artist.

In these various ways Ramuz succeeds in re-creating for our mind's eye, with unusual intensity, the concrete appearance of objects, their shape, colour, pattern and texture. Occasionally he succeeds so well in fact, that the very structure of his sentence suggests the actual appearance of the subject . . . . (pp. 69-71)

Ramuz' conception of the nature and structure of the novel is in harmony with his basic convictions. Since in principle he accepts only what his eyes reveal to him, the substance of the literary work becomes restricted to the immediate sensory experience of the concrete, observable world expressed as directly as possible. As a result, well-constructed plot, psychological study of character, and explanatory narrative, all of which contribute to a logical order, are rejected. For Ramuz, who readily confesses that he does not possess the gift of invention, the unity of the novel calls for an overall unity of tone, arising out of a plastic re-creation of the subject. This means that the traditional plot is either completely absent as in *Le village dans la montagne* or that it is so intimately associated with the work as to seem organically derived from it. Such is the case in *Jean-Luc persécuté* and in most of Ramuz' novels whose plot, instead of being imposed and logically conducted, seems to emerge spontaneously. This conception of the novel, based exclusively on the most direct expression of immediate visual experience and aiming at a general unity of tone, is again more characteristic of plastic than of literary art.

Since Ramuz' goal coincided so intimately with that of the painter, it was only natural that he should be strongly attracted toward artists and their works. Many of his close friends were painters and his general knowledge of art was both extensive and profound. That he knew particularly well the work of French painters of the nineteenth century is attested by *Les grands moments du 19e siècle français.* Yet, unlike Marcel Proust, Ramuz does not display this knowledge of art in his fictional works, references to a specific painter or painting being extremely rare. Here again he remains faithful to his fundamental aesthetic convictions, since the display of encyclopaedic knowledge of the kind one finds in Proust and other writers is extremely distasteful to him. For Ramuz the influence of painting is something radically different, namely the transposition into the purely literary field of many preoccupations and problems of a technical nature which are normally the painter's province. It is, for instance, as painter rather than writer that he considers lighting as a distinct and determining factor in close relationship with the object to be evoked. The nature of lighting is never, with him, taken for granted. He always indicates or suggests clearly its source, direction and quality and the concrete appearance of his subject is determined accordingly. It is as a painter, also, that he confronts the problems of pictorial composition, restricting himself to a limited and clearly defined subject to be represented within a specific area, due consideration being accorded to perspective, all this with a view to realizing an essential plastic unity, without regard to the accepted stylistic requirements of literary composition. Again, it is as a painter that Ramuz faces the problem of time and movement. The displacement of the object is, in his case, as in that of a painter, a hindrance to its fullest visual possession. Thus Ramuz shows a marked predilection for subjects frequently considered inert and, like a pictorial artist, interprets the world about him in separate static images. Spatial progression is maintained however by the juxtaposition of numerous images of this kind, each image being a substitution for the previous one. As a result, the impression of movement is not perfectly continuous, but repeatedly broken by the short lapses of time which intervene between each successive static image. At this point Ramuz goes beyond his association with the painter and sees in the resources of cinematographic art a more complete answer to his particular problem of time and movement. This problem, along with those associated with lighting and composition, are all basic preoccupations of the artist. But we can go a step further and relate Ramuz' efforts to the main artistic manifestations of his time: impressionism, *cézannisme*, cubism.

Pictorial impressionism attracted Ramuz very early in his career. The movement was in fact a reaction against tradition. It rejected all outworn academic rules and placed the artist once again in direct contact with nature in order that he might express with complete freedom his personal interpretations of what he saw. Such intentions coincided very closely with those of Ramuz himself. As a consequence, we find transposed into Ramuz' own works some of the chief technical preoccupations of the impressionists: notably the fullest exploitation of colours through the technique of divisionism, i.e., the special disposition on the canvas of elementary colours to produce through optical fusion an impression of brilliancy and vibration, comparable to that of sunlight on objects. (pp. 71-3)

Although he never quite abandoned the impressionists' technique, Ramuz soon perceived in that school of painting a dangerous weakness. Because of their exclusive attachment to colour and its fragmentation the impressionists tended to become superficial and merely decorative. Ramuz' aim goes beyond the mere representation of exterior nature; he wishes to delve into the inner significance of objects. In so striving he found in Cézanne not only a perfect reflection of his own aims, but also a remedy for the chief weakness of the impressionists. For although Cézanne remained fundamentally an impressionist he was able to effect the needed synthesis of pure colour and mass, restoring to objects their weight and volume which the impressionists on the whole had denied them. Such a reconciliation between visual sensation and concrete reality was exactly what Ramuz in his own way was seeking. Rarely have an artist and a writer been in so perfect accord. Both of them consider artistic creation as a slow and arduous quest for a universal truth hidden behind the changing and broken façade of the observable world. Such a truth can only be recovered when the artist succeeds in identifying himself as closely as possible with his subject. Everything which stands in his way: imposed knowledge, conventions, abstract logic, must be discarded. The writer and the artist must face the concrete world with an attitude of complete receptivity, accepting only what their eyes reveal to them and submitting each new acquisition to the test of immediate experience. Ramuz agrees with Cézanne that there are no privileged subjects, and that no distinction should be made between the human and other elements. Everything becomes a source of artistic beauty, since every object contains a portion of universal truth which it may release when the artist enters into proper relationship with it. But possibly the most striking resemblance between these two men is the fact that they both perceive in nature an underlying principle of geometric harmony by virtue of which the world of objects can be recaptured through a reduction to the essential forms of cone, cylinder and sphere. (pp. 73-4)

Ramuz went even a step further than the master of Aix and associated himself with the developments of cubism, the main inspiration of which was derived by Picasso and Braque from certain features of Cézanne's technique. There are also numerous examples to be found in Ramuz of a tendency to consider colour and pattern for their own sake, with little or no regard for the identity of the subject from which they are derived. On the whole the influence of painting on Ramuz was most significant and, considered in this light, many features of his literary expression which seem at first meaningless suddenly assume a real significance. He has not been a popular writer precisely because the reader expects to find in him just a novelist and has failed to understand that, although Ramuz has used the written word as his means of expression, it is more as a painter than as a writer that he has attempted to express his very personal conception of life. (pp. 74-5)

Clarence Parsons, "The Word Painter," in ADAM International Review, *Nos. 319-21, 1967, pp. 69-75.*

DAVID BEVAN (essay date 1979)

[*Bevan is an English critic and an authority on the works of Ramuz. In the following excerpt, he analyzes Ramuz's narrative techniques and summarizes their effects.*]

It is banal to observe that since the last quarter of the nineteenth century the technique of the novel in much of Western Europe constitutes primarily an investigation and an implementation of the notion of time. It is less banal, however, to contend that, in this respect, no writer during or since that period has successfully utilized such an extraordinary range of narrative devices as Ramuz in his determination to transpose stylistically his vision of a human permanence beyond the peripeteia of current events.

In the traditional novel temporal development was chronologically ordered, linked to a rationalistic system within a stable and coherent universe. The fundamental rule of narrative mode was rigorously respected: from the initial situation the action advanced in regular and consecutive fashion to its eventual conclusion. However, the advent of Flaubert heralded the imminence of crisis and, increasingly, conventional construction of plot was challenged until Alfred Jarry in *L'amour absolu* rejected provocatively all novelistic principles of causality and dependence. As the exigencies of plot became less and less constraining, authors like Joyce, Gide, and Woolf chose in their turn to explode the temporal form of the novel: it is this invertebrate novel of the twentieth century, where "pattern" replaces action, which is evoked by Louis Cazamian when he writes of "this decadence of the story line in the most interesting and most modern novelists, in favor of what the Anglo-Saxons, in line with Henry James, call the 'pattern'."

While avoiding a diachronic interpretation such as that of Cazamian, Ramuz, too, acknowledges a basic dichotomy in creative approach and distinguishes between two fundamental aesthetic attitudes to the writing of a novel. For him "invention" and "imagination" are widely divergent faculties:

> I have no invention; I only have imagination. These two faculties which have nothing in common and are even deliberately contradictory are too often confused [. . .].

> Invention is event, it thrives on event, delights in weaving a plot, in complicating, in diversifying the peripeteia, and in only unravelling once their possibilities have been exhausted. Invention is dynamic, [. . .] imagination, on the other hand, is contemplative. In that long succession of events where invention chooses to combine the peripeteia, it chooses one aspect which is immobilized; whereas invention accelerates, imagination fixes and restrains.

Ramuz suggests that fact and event are the children of invention and produce conventional novelistic movement forwards, whereas, in direct contrast, imagination imposes a slower, more reflective rhythm. It is evident that Ramuz considers the imagination to be the generative source of the novel as he understands it, but he is not unaware that the operative term "roman" ["novel"] has now become stereotyped by its association with a certain sort of novel: "The word 'novel' is unfortunate; it is ugly now, it has been dragged about everywhere . . . the best would be to find another name [. . .] the novel must be a poem."

The invocation of the word "poème" is extremely significant, for it implies already the distinctive time element which we wish to present as characteristic of Ramuz's mature writings. Clearly, in our world of shifting terminology, it would be naïve to speak of novel or poem as an absolute, exclusive, genre; nevertheless the substitution of imagination for invention does tend to result in a static quality which denies novelistic time—Sartre's "devenir romanesque" ["novelistic becoming"]—and is indeed similar to that of poetry. Thus, from a temporal point of view, the essential difference between a poem and a novel opposes the immobility of the former to the movement of the latter, in that the poet seeks to petrify time whereas the novelist formulates an evolution. For the poet the thread of a story, vital to the novelist, is at most incidental. The novels of C.-F. Ramuz could not survive without a skeleton plot, the absence of which would plunge the reader into either incomprehension or boredom, but the essentially poetic objective of the writer creates a tension where various

techniques resist normal narrative development. It is my intention to examine on three levels the factors which contribute to this condition which I shall term stasis: I shall consider, first, the fragmentation of traditionally continuous and ordered narrative, second, its deceleration and, finally, its virtual immobilization.

Refusing any comfortable unilinear progression, Ramuz's temporality requires from the accomplice reader a series of disconcerting leaps out of the accepted past-present-future continuum. Indicative of the several techniques employed, the flashback, a narrative movement in reverse, towards the past, offers an obvious contrast with the normal sequence of events. For example, in *La grande peur dans la montagne,* during the ceremonial ascent to the ill-fated Alpine pasture, a flashback serves to explain how Victorine and Joseph come to be at the end of the procession:

> After them (the animals) came the third mule, carrying the provisions, that is cheese, dried meat and bread for three weeks, it's Joseph who was with the third mule, and with Joseph was Victorine. They found themselves at the end of the procession, because Joseph had said: "we'll be quieter," then he said: "Climb on, he's strong." It was a big red mule, four years old. And she, "Do you know how much I weigh?"—"That doesn't matter, climb on anyway . . .".

> She had climbed up on to the mule; then they had left a little space between the column and themselves; there was then, after the animals, a stretch of path without anyone, then they came, at the end of the procession with the big red mule. The animals had just entered the forest.

> Après elles (les bêtes du troupeau), venait le troisième mulet, portant, lui, les provisions, c'est-à-dire du fromage, de la viande séchée et du pain pour trois semaines, c'est Joseph qui était avec le troisième mulet, et avec Joseph était Victorine. Ils se trouvèrent fermer la marche, parce que Joseph avait dit: "on sera plus tranquilles," puis il a dit: "Monte seulement dessus, il est solide." C'était un gros mulet rouge de quatre ans. Et elle: "Sais-tu combien je pèse?"—"Ça ne fait rien, monte toujours . . .".

> Elle était montée sur le mulet; ensuite ils avaient laissé un petit espace venir se mettre entre la colonne et eux; il y avait donc, après le troupeau, un bout de chemin sans personne, puis eux venaient, fermant la marche avec le gros mulet rouge. Le troupeau venait d'entrer dans la forêt.

In this passage the principal tenses which communicate the narrator's point of view are the past historic and the imperfect. Between these two verbs the explanatory flashback is introduced by "parce que" and its anteriority is attested by the appropriate change in tense. This insertion of Joseph and Victorine's past dialogue, which interrupts momentarily the narrative advance, constitutes a short detour between the expression "fermer la marche" and the subsequent derived from "fermant la marche." The almost identical vocabulary ensures that the flashback is as formally isolated as if it were between brackets.

A flashback may function on two levels. In the second chapter of *Farinet* the reader is drawn back into the past as the hero recalls his initial escape from prison; but, in the process of remembering, Farinet returns by a further flashback to an even more distant past, to the period where he first met at Mièges his mentor Sage. The continuity is doubly violated.

The temporal construction of **Derborence,** considered globally, reveals not only instances similar to those already mentioned, but other notable reversals of chronology. Since the story is situated two centuries ago, the night of the avalanche—June twenty-second—with which the description commences is already far removed from the moment of narration. Then, in the second chapter, the reader discovers himself briefly in the present of the narrator before being abruptly returned to a habitual past which evokes the significance of June fifteenth, day of the traditional journey to summer pastures. This complexity continues throughout the book and underlines the anti-linearity [of] *Farinet* and *La grande peur dans la montagne.* (pp. 70-4)

Another means by which Ramuz breaks up the narrative is that of the parenthetic expression. The interpolation of such phrases, indeed sometimes entire passages, which furnish supplementary information tends momentarily to deflect the reader's attention from the main subject matter. In this way the elucidation of a regionalist term may occasion a pause, however brief, in the unfolding of the story. For example, in *La grande peur dans la montagne* the word "bottilles" is followed by its definition in parentheses: "They left at four in the morning with their lanterns and some provisions, not to mention one or two 'bottilles' of muscatel (which are small flat barrels made of larch-wood, about a pot or a litre and a half in capacity."

Similarly, in *Farinet* the meaning of "galères" is given parenthetically: "For a long time he remained motionless, having to make certain first that all was quiet in the 'galères' building (which is the local name for prison)."

Sometimes these pieces of information, which contribute nothing to the development of the plot, are quite considerable and interpose a lengthy interval between two sections of the narrative proper. There is a typical such passage in **Derborence:**

> It was an hour later that the stretcher appeared. They sometimes bring down on a stretcher an injured goat, the people from the chalets up there, when a goat for example, has torn a horn in a fight, or else broken its leg. They tie it onto a stretcher. They cover it with an old piece of cheese-cloth. One of the men grasps the front of the stretcher, another grasps the back. [. . .]
>
> They were indeed carrying a stretcher, that morning, and it was indeed covered with a cheese-cloth, but it was not a goat that was lying on top.

While in the process of relating the descent of the stretcher on which lies the body of Barthélemy, victim of the mountain's malevolence, the narrator interrupts the action in order to introduce some generalizations concerning the usage of such equipment. Just as the parentheses are materially absent in the above extract, so they may be replaced by an expression like "c'est-à-dire" ["that is to say"] which fulfills the same disruptive and anti-narrative function.

If the techniques so far examined remained isolated cases, one could perhaps contend that their aim was, on the contrary, perfectly normal novelistic practice; one could suggest that the plot benefits from these delays in narrative progress, that the author is merely accumulating conventional mo-

ments of suspense in order to intensify the dramatic quality of what follows. It is with much justification that Madame Guers-Villate writes in her valuable book on Ramuz: "The repetition of a date which punctuates the story is in *La grande peur* a means of creating an atmosphere heavy with imminent fatality. [. . .] A similar device is to be found in *Derborence.*"

We could even add to the two examples of Madame Guers-Villate *Farinet,* where the minutely detailed description of a room twice arrests the course of events and creates periods of expectation. In a writer more consistently orthodox, one might indeed be tempted to assess such instances as nothing more than the creation of suspense; however, in a writer whose declared aesthetic goal is anti-traditional and essentially poetic, an interpretation which emphasizes primarily willful fragmentation of the narrative—though less conformist—is more likely to be valid, especially when confirmed by other convergent techniques. (pp. 74-6)

[An] area of Ramuz's writing which long confused critics was the extreme originality of the nonliterary language used in the narrative itself; a language which is often identical to that of the dialogue. Today, however, the narrator in Ramuz's novels is beginning to be recognized as a sort of collective consciousness of the village who necessarily speaks the same language as those observed. Without analyzing the structural corollary which is our present preoccupation, Madame Guers-Villate acknowledges, in both narrative and conversation, the heaviness and slowness which typify the intellectual process of the countryman:

> Ramuz seeks neither elegance nor conciseness, for he wishes the entire story—the narrative as well as the conversations—to have the heaviness of oral language where words form one by one, following the intimate rhythm of thought which makes its way, turns back, insists, and follows an emotive rather than a logical development.

In Ramuz's novels sentences abound which could be shortened and lightened without harming their denotative value, and a single example will suffice to illustrate an omnipresent tendency. In *La grande peur dans la montagne* this paragraph of only one sentence reveals just such an accumulation of detours and deviations:

> One month, two months, went by; the Chairman continued to approach prudently with regard to his plan, the people that chanced to come his way, some shook their heads, but most had few objections; it was clear these old stories of twenty years ago were already indeed well and truly forgotten; and finally, the Chairman had only a small calculation to make; this one for and this one for, and that one against, which gave him a total on the one hand and another as well, two totals without much effect, first in his head, and then on paper; so he called together the Council.

The thought expressed above meanders slowly, with stolid pedestrian logic, from an original project through actions, observations, reflections, and evaluations, before terminating in a decision. Both by the syntax and by the punctuation the author communicates admirably the sinuosities of an unsophisticated mental gait.

Elsewhere the slowness of the language becomes an imitative form which seeks to reproduce the quality of the physical movement of the character in question and, thereby, the uniform deliberateness of country life. And here one should insist on the creative talent of Ramuz in fashioning a style wholly suited to reflect the countryman's nature, but which is in no way a reproduction of any cantonal language. For the particular rhythm of a Ramuzian sentence is his own artistic and physical representation of time; and time for the poet, just as for the peasant, is essentially slow. (pp. 76-7)

[It] is possible to discern in Ramuz's writings certain devices which, rather than fragmenting or decelerating the plot, succeed temporarily in arresting its unfolding and contribute forcefully to an impression of narrative stasis. (p. 80)

[It] is the state of Man, rather than the evolution of men, which is his fundamental principle, it is this which will necessarily determine much of the form we are at present surveying. In this respect there is a revealing sentence noted by Ramuz in his *Carnet:* "The notion of becoming is a straight line, the notion of being is a circle."

This statement of Spinoza seems to suggest that the concept of "being" as different from "becoming" might find aesthetic expression in circular rather than linear construction. In purely novelistic terms such a distinction proposes a narrative which, instead of developing always away from the point of departure, in fact returns to it.

Among the works of the Swiss author, it is *Derborence* which reveals the most nearly perfect example of this, especially if one considers that the introductory allusion to the landslide in the first chapter is exergual. In that case the final chapter returns almost textually to the beginning of the second chapter:

> Derborence, the word sings sadly and softly in the head.

> Derborence, the word sings softly; it sings to you softly and a little sadly in the head.

These two passages and their continuations in the present tense, frame the rest of the story and, extending it beyond the merely incidental, confer an aura of eternity. For Spitzer, in his article "Le style de Ch.-F. Ramuz: le Raccourci Mystique," the existence of such a construction emphasizes the mystical heart he discerns in this particular novel: "The circular style is characteristic of the mystical event which starts and finishes nowhere." But, for our purpose, the interest of such a structure resides primarily in its anti-narrative function, in its potential capacity to evoke a *poetic* state.

This same construction which determined the overall shape of *Derborence* can be traced in more modest guise than that of an entire novel. The first chapter of the second part of *Derborence,* situated exactly in the middle of the book in a structurally significant position, reveals a similar, if more limited circularity. On this occasion the final narrative return to the description of Antoine's disappearance, that same moment with which the chapter had commenced some five pages earlier, underlines the absence of temporal progression within the substance of the chapter. At the beginning we read "his head came out" and we rediscover that very action in the last paragraph: "Then too, his head came out, but it could not be seen because of the rocks which jutted out around it, hiding it completely."

Between these two references the reader learns of the need to establish officially the exact size of the rockfall and to ensure the future solidity of the glacier—details which are completely inconsequential. The allusion to old Plan who continues to wander over the ill-fated slopes is scarcely more significant and adds little to the story line. (pp. 80-1)

Another device which endorses the consistency shown by Ramuz in pursuit of his principal narrative aim is that by which the fictional simultaneity of distinct sections of the text is emphasized. Let us begin by considering the relatively banal case where a first event is in the process of occurring and "pendant ce temps" ["during this time"]—the classic expression to link such episodes—in a different locality a second event is taking place. Obviously the significance of these instances is very restricted; for any author who wishes to depict two contemporaneous events must proceed in like manner, since the book, even the line which reads from left to right, is consecutive in form. But it is by comparison with this stereotyped beginning that will be seen the value of the techniques of greater refinement conceived by Ramuz to communicate simultaneity. In his first novel, Ramuz treats in consecutive chapters Aline's day and Julien's day; only the place changes, the temporal span remains identical. Similarly, in *La guerre dans le haut-pays* the simultaneous ascents of Félicie and David, who are only separated by a peak towards which they are striving, are described one after the other in the text, but with an appropriate and conventional vocabulary to confirm the contemporaneity.

It is in *La grande peur dans la montagne* that there is to be found the transition from a traditional technique to a more original and modern version. Between the ninth and tenth chapters of this novel the link is once again effected by the expression "Pendant ce temps," the consecrated formula to which we have referred. However, this form, doubtless too "literary" and codified in Ramuz's eyes, becomes increasingly replaced by simple juxtaposition which fuses more completely the two occurrences. More and more, events separated in actual space will be seen to be bound together without distinction and without intellectualization in the consciousness of the narrator. The psychological authenticity which accrues from a practice that rejects accepted stylistic formalization is without doubt the most remarkable result; but at the same time, juxtaposition accentuates materially the temporal identity. In *La grande peur dans la montagne,* at the very moment when Clou and the Président are discussing the pasturage, Victorine and Joseph are climbing to their favorite spot above the church:

> Puis elle lui [Victorine à Joseph] souriait avec toutes ses dents qui faisaient une barre blanche au bas de sa figure brune . . .

> Ce sera comme vous voudrez, disait Clou . . . Moi, j'ai le temps, décidezvous, vous me direz . . .

> Ills avaient le coucher de soleil derrière eux, derrière eux ils avaient la haie, ils s'asseyaient dans l'herbe.

> Ils étaient bien, ayant le coucher de soleil et aussi la haie derrière eux.

> En avant d'eux, étaient les prés en pente au bas desquels il semblait que le village s'était laissé glisser, comme les gamins font sur leur fond de culotte.

> On voyait que les toits se tenaient ensemble, s'étant mis ensemble, aimant à être ensemble, se serrant les uns contre les autres avec amitié;—et Clou disait que ça ne pressait pas;—on voyait aussi, derrière

leurs barrières, les jardins, qui commençaient à *être verts et* à se tacher de jaune, de bleu, de rouge.

Then she [Victorine] smiled at him [Joseph] with her teeth making a white line at the bottom of her brown face . . .

"Just as you like," Clou was saying . . . "Me, I have the time, you decide and tell me . . ."

They had the sunset behind them, behind them they had the hedge, they were sitting in the grass.

They were fine, having the sunset and also the hedge behind them.

In front of them, were the sloping meadows to the foot of which it seemed that the village had let itself slip, like children do on the seat of their pants.

One could see that the roofs were clustered together having come together, happy to be together, grasping each other in friendship;—and Clou was saying that there was no hurry; one could also see, behind their gates, the gardens, which were beginning to be green and to take on patches of yellow, of blue, of red.

This extract contains a succession of abrupt switches between two places which are so closely intertwined in the mind of the narrator that they even appear once, in the final paragraph, next to each other in the same sentence. This oscillating continues throughout the chapter and indeed even the following chapter, where once again the description of an ascent by Victorine and Joseph alternates with a conversation between the Président and a second character—this time Crittin.

This concentrated simultaneity which is to be found in many of Ramuz's works should not be confused with another related technique which seems to be derived more from the plastic arts than from literature. Critics have invoked the cubist painters with regard to Ramuz; and, certainly, one could plausibly associate their wish to present all the facets of a subject with Ramuz's device whereby an experience is related from two or more distinct points of view—"la vision stéréoscopique" ["stereoscopic vision"] as the theorists term it. Whereas the examples of simultaneity that we have previously investigated revealed only temporal identity, stereoscopic vision means identity of time and space, only the narrator changes. Between the different accounts the story line shows no development; it is merely refiltered and redeployed. For example, in the third chapter of **Derborence,** precisely the same incident—the fateful avalanche—is passed through three separate collective consciousnesses: first "ceux d'Anzeindaz" ["those of Anzeindaz"], then "ceux de Sanetsch" ["those of Sanetsch"], and, finally, "ceux de Zamperon" ["those of Zamperon"]. (pp. 81-4)

It will have been observed that common to many of the above examples is the element of repetition, and in itself simple use of repetition merits an increasingly considerable place in the Swiss author's mature narrative technique. Ramuz repeats and repeats again words and phrases, reiterates exactly the sense of a sentence in a subsequent sentence, and by this manipulation continues to forge an atmosphere that is more emotive than rational, more poetic than novelistic. Looking back in **René Auberjonois,** having suggested that in every work of art there needs to be a balance between the intellectual and the affective, Ramuz declares that it is repetition—

here in the form of the pleonasm—which communicates the affective:

Let us take the example of the pleonasm. Reason does not allow the pleonasm. A full stop having been indicated, reason is satisfied; for reason, it is enough to grasp clearly; having once grasped, it proceeds at an even pace, which makes it resent everything which might restrain it. Emotion, in very contrary fashion, insists because of its determination to communicate itself in its full intensity; it comes back to what it has already said, with other words or the same, it repeats ("ressasse") willingly.

The curious transposition achieved by the art of those writers who wish above all to fashion a fiction which resembles reality supposes, necessarily, a complex relationship between "personnage" and "personne." Ducrot and Todorov, in their excellent *Dictionnaire encyclopédique des sciences du langage,* insist that a link between the two is obligatory despite the essentially linguistic nature of "personnage":

The problem of character ["personnage"] is primarily linguistic [. . .] it does not exist outside of words [. . .]. However, to refuse any relationship between character ["personnage"] and person ["personne"] would be absurd: the former *represent* persons, according to the modes of fiction.

This link exists inevitably in Ramuz, but the individuality implied in the notion of person tends to disappear and is replaced by a constant emphasis on those qualities which are permanent in man, those which are opposed to the particular. Thus, paradoxically, the characters of a Ramuzian novel are characterized especially by their lack of characterization. We are already far from the predominant practice of the preceding century, when with slow fastidious method a writer sought to construct a convincing biography and psychology. Beyond person, it is *Person* that Ramuz attempts to translate—"Homme" ["Man"] rather than "hommes" ["men"]. This minute artifice of typography, taken from Ramuz himself, conveys the essence of his attitude towards his everyday heroes. Close scrutiny of the different texts of his maturity reveals that this fundamental Man referred to above is represented by Ramuz in three main ways: first, by the choice of characters who are truly exemplary; then, by the evocation of a narrator who embraces in a collective consciousness reader, writer, and fictional creations; finally, by the forging of a language of greater authenticity than conventional class-ridden French.

The quest for authenticity which typifies the content of any novel of Ramuz determines also the nature of his characters, for they are required in their turn to manifest an a-social purity rare in the still-stratified twentieth century. It is, therefore, the countryman who continually recurs as hero; it is in him that Ramuz discovers Being, stripped of the palimpsest trappings that individualize the bourgeois:

I only distinguish a being at the roots of the elementary. He only appears to me fully and, so to speak, in full action when he is still fresh from birth [. . .]. The more complex he becomes, the less contact there is with deep substance, one no longer gets past the bark.

Rejecting the divisiveness of all social and cultural acquisition, Ramuz discovers in his own Switzerland, more precisely in the mountainous region of Le Valais and the lakeside Canton du Vaud, not the Swiss peasant but primordial man ("fresh from birth") whose origins return beyond pre-history. Renouncing vigorously the limitations of regionalism, Ramuz appropriates in his Valaisan and Vaudois novels characters of universal significance and emphasizes only the constants of humanity. (pp. 92-3)

The representation of time has become during the twentieth century an important point of contact between the different art forms as well as constituting a major aspect of literature. In Ramuz the desire to evoke a collectivity rather than an individual finds a temporal parallel in a series of attempts to replace consecrated linear time:

> While there is no longer past, nor future—there is only around us one great immobility of time, as when one looks at a vast peaceful landscape.

The desire to amalgamate past and future into "one great immobility of time," into an eternal present, is rationalized most clearly in the beautiful pages of **René Auberjonois,** where this time Ramuz insists on the notion of "a perfect continuity."

> The past and the present rejoined, the life of men, the life of things, nothing archaeological nothing to do with a museum, everything which has served still serves and will doubtless still serve: there is no opposition, it is a perfect continuity.

It is interesting to observe that it is from a book written on a *painter* that we have extracted one of the best definitions which could be conceived for the creative art of Ramuz himself. If one were so unfashionable as to accept the fundamental distinction enunciated by Lessing in his *Laokoön* between literature as an art of time and painting as an art of space, then Ramuz, by his preference for the static rather than the changing, may well be justified in his repeated claim that his true vocation was pictorial art. (pp. 104-05)

> *David Bevan, in his* Charles-Ferdinand Ramuz, *Twayne Publishers, 1979, 140 p.*

SAMUEL S. B. TAYLOR   (essay date 1984)

[*In the following excerpt, Taylor views Ramuz's fiction as an authentic reflection of rural Swiss culture.*]

Conventional critical terminology cannot be used to describe Ramuz without redefinition and qualification. He fits into no known literary school or *appellation contrôlée*. We find ourselves having to paint a portrait in borrowed paints and risk giving a false impression with the use of terms which can carry other connotations. Hence the lead-words in our description are dangerous if applied out of context.

Ramuz's art is "authentic" in a special sense. He canvasses a new territorial imperative, and his work recalls the *génie du lieu* ["spirit of place"] that derives from Juste Olivier's famous phrase "un génie caché dans tous ces lieux que j'aime" ["a spirit hidden in all those places that I love"]. It is an art of *enracinement* ["rootedness"], to use another literary cliché but one that could have been coined for him. This was the realisation of the hero of Ramuz's novel **Aimé Pache, peintre vaudois,** a transposed autobiographical account of the birth of artistic vocation, who "portait en lui sa race" ["carried his race within him"]. Between artist and village, *lieu* ["place"] or *pays* ["country"] there exists a spiritual relationship, not in any religious sense, but in every other sense. The village is a parable and his return there a consecration, a dedication. The artist has been forced to leave to achieve independence

and a realisation of his identity, but this identity is achieved in terms of an art that expresses his roots, those areas that gave him life and where his kinsfolk live. Ramuz was explicit in the *Voile latine* as to what this loyalty was *not:*

> notre vrai patriotisme doit être un patriotisme de clocher . . . si je m'intéresse avant tout à une region je n'ai rien quand même de régionaliste.
> ["Our true patriotism must be a patriotism for our parish . . . if I interest myself above all in a region, I am not, all the same, a regionalist."]

His commitment was to be the mouthpiece of his soil and people:

> C'est une accablante entreprise que d'expliquer un peuple.
> ["It is an overwhelming enterprise to explain a people."]

Yet the relationship is clear and precise. The artist articulates his race, he does not impose private values on that race. Aimé Pache's ambitions centre more and more on the need that he feels to:

> Peindre comme ils auraient voulu peindre, s'ils étaient mieux connus; peindre comme ils ont peint sur les portes des granges!
> ["To paint as they would have wanted to paint, if they had been better known; to paint as they painted on barn doors!"]

And this inarticulate primitive art has the virtue of being uncontaminated with literary modes. It is totally authentic, without urban or aesthetic incrustations. The aim is the same whether it be for the Vaudois peasant or the Valaisan, his neighbour from the alpine region beyond the pays de Vaud whom Ramuz classes as *homo alpinus* and sets on an artistic pedestal.

In Ramuz's portrait of the peasant, and particularly of the Valaisan peasant whom he knew, there emerges not a realistic or psychological portrait, nor even a *folkloriste* idealisation. Instead he offers an allegory of the human condition in the struggle of man in this threshold economy against the forces of nature. Ramuz uses this framework to create a canvas of myths, totems and taboos. He drew the rituals and festivals with which the mountain peasant celebrated his struggle and justified his existence. If they appear overdrawn in any summary description, Ramuz's Valaisan novels are profoundly moving experiences and his tragic vision transforms the banal.

Ramuz's art is that of the tragedian. He sets man against remorseless natural forces and man's hubris in facing such odds precipitates conflict, nemesis and catastrophe. The response of the individual and community to this catastrophe generates a real catharsis. At the same time the presentation bears out Ramuz's claim that he was not writing novels so much as a form of poetry. The *question de style* which Berchtold sees as Ramuz's peculiar gift, or the *inflexion* Ramuz himself spoke of are a feature of poetic as much as of prose style. But poetic vision in Ramuz is a matter not only of style but of symbol, the transmutation of the real into myths, an epic element he shares with the novelist Hardy. His novels are lenses through which we perceive wider conflicts than the individual situation portrayed. Indeed Ramuz's world was subtended by the metaphysical. His world is that of Sisyphus, an absurd world in the existentialist sense, but just as legitimately, the world perceived by the Stoics and Biblical writers. Man's tragic conflict with superior forces has been a constant theme of philosophy and theology, from Job and Ecclesiastes to the Stoics and Existentialists. His characters refuse to surrender to the certainty of defeat, in their blind communal resilience, the survival of the species beyond the loss of any individual.

Such terms again appear over-drawn in summary outline, but when Ramuz asked: "Qu'aurait fait Eschyle, s'il était né en 1878, quelque part dans mon pays, le pays de Vaud?" ["What would Aeschylus have done, if he had been born in 1878, somewhere in my country, the country of Vaud?"] he touched a chord in his readers. Ramuz's art is very much that of a modern Aeschylus. It drew its marrow from a particular soil and the human fauna of that soil. If we seek an identifiable Suisse romande cultural reference, then, we could only, with Gide, say that: "on ne saurait l'imaginer que Suisse" ["one knows how to imagine him only as Swiss"]. The canvas he paints is immediately recognisable as of his native parts, and of the other environment he knew so well in Valais. The myths Ramuz created, his poetic vision and his whole metaphysic emerge from this native climate and soil. He portrays it not as external but as an extension of himself and as the soil and environment he needed for his talent to flourish. (pp. 48-50)

> *Samuel S. B. Taylor, "The Emergence of a Distinctive Suisse-Romande Literary Culture, 1900-1945," in* Modern Swiss Literature: Unity and Diversity, *edited by John L. Flood, St. Martin's Press, 1985, pp. 39-55.*

ADDITIONAL BIBLIOGRAPHY

ADAM International Review, Nos. 319-21. (1967): 1-78.
 Special issue devoted to Ramuz. Includes reminiscences, critical essays, and excerpts from Ramuz's writings.

Auberjonois, Fernand. "Charles-Ferdinand Ramuz and the Way of the Anti-Poet." In *Swiss Men of Letters: Twelve Literary Essays,* edited by Alex Nathan, pp. 35-55. London: Oswald Wolff, 1970.
 Biographical essay.

Bevan, David. "C. F. Ramuz: The Path of the Antipoet." *Nottingham French Studies* 14, No. 1 (May 1975): 20-30.
 Discusses the development of Ramuz's prose style.

Braybrooke, Neville. Review of *The Triumph of Death,* by Charles-Ferdinand Ramuz. *Life and Letters and the London Mercury* 52, No. 113 (January 1947): 61-2.
 Commends both the form and content of *The Triumph of Death,* comparing Ramuz's prose to early Imagist poetry.

Glenn, Eunice. "As on a Darkling Plain." *Sewanee Review* 56, No. 2 (Spring 1948): 351-59.
 Positive assessment of *When the Mountain Fell.*

Parkinson, Michael H. "C. F. Ramuz." In his *The Rural Novel: Jeremias Gotthelf, Thomas Hardy, and C. F. Ramuz,* pp. 205-46. Berne: Peter Lang, 1984.
 Discusses "the implications for [Ramuz's] fiction of his choice of a rural (or supposedly rural) environment."

Peyre, Henri. "They Dared to Defy." *New York Times Book Review* (4 February 1968): 4-5.
 Review of *Terror on the Mountain,* which Peyre judges "a concentrated tragedy of instinct and passion, overflowing with pity and terror, free from tricks or supernatural interventions."

Price, R. G. G. "A Swiss Novelist." *New English Review* 14, No. 3 (March 1947): 326, 328.
 Negative review of *The Triumph of Death.* Price notes: "All the separate elements in this book have been done better by somebody else. . . . I cannot help feeling that it has appeared now, not because it can compete on equal terms with any of our excellent native work, but because of the present nostalgia for primitive economies, and of a vague belief that anything ending on a religious note is likely to provide the necessary spiritual vitamins for the general reader."

Rougemont, Denis de. Introduction to *The End of All Men,* by C. F. Ramuz, translated by Allan Ross Macdougall, pp. vii-xvi. New York: Pantheon Books, 1944.
 Examines themes and techniques in Ramuz's novels, focusing in particular on *The End of All Men.*

Watts, Richard, Jr. "Fiction Parade." *New Republic* 117, No. 16 (20 October 1947): 31-2.
 Positive review of *When the Mountain Fell* which Watts finds "a welcome tribute to qualities of endurance and strength of spirit that despairing mankind so quickly forgets it possesses."

Wren, Keith. "Some Observations on Imagery in Ramuz's *Vie de Samuel Belet.*" *Swiss-French Studies* 3, No. 1 (May 1982): 48-61.
 Views the predominant sun and lake imagery in *La vie de Samuel Belet* as "signposts on the path to self-fulfilment that it chronicles."

Zak, Rose A. "*L'histoire du soldat:* Approaching the Musical Text." *Mosaic* 18, No. 4 (Fall 1985): 101-07.
 Examines the relation between form and content in *L'histoire du soldat.*

Alfonso Reyes

1889-1959

Mexican essayist, critic, poet, and fiction writer.

An extremely prolific and versatile writer, Reyes is acknowledged as one of the finest Spanish-American essayists of the twentieth century. His works have been especially praised for their consistent originality of theme and graceful clarity of expression. Demonstrating his conviction that human values are universal, Reyes's writings often explore the relationships between classical and modern cultures and between Old World and New World cultures. He has been described as a "Renaissance man," whose humanist ideology found expression in poetry and fiction as well as in works of literary theory and history.

Reyes was born in Monterrey, the capital of the state of Nuevo León, in 1889. His father, General Bernal de Reyes, was a prominent politician in the national government of General Porfirio Díaz and also served as governor of Nuevo León. In 1905, Alfonso entered the Escuela Nacional Preparatoria in Mexico City, where he first began writing poetry. He continued his education at the Facultad de Derecho, where he studied law and classics and published his first work, the collection of literary essays *Cuestiones estéticas.* He was also involved in the intellectual life of Mexico City, becoming the youngest member of a group of writers and philosophers known as the "Generation of the Centenary." These intellectuals, rebelling against the largely imitative nature of Mexican culture, sought to stimulate renewal and growth in Mexican thought and society in order to establish a culture that would be uniquely Mexican. Members of this group, including Reyes, later founded the Ateneo de la Juventud ("Athenaeum for Young People") with the goal of providing a forum for new ideas. The Athenaeum came to be considered representative of the social and cultural conscience of the times and is credited with playing an important role in the Mexican cultural renaissance of the early twentieth century.

After graduating with a law degree in 1913, Reyes entered the diplomatic service and departed for France as the second secretary of the Paris Legation; however, when the Mexican delegation to France was disbanded as a result of World War I, Reyes went to Madrid. There he lived in what he described as "happy poverty," earning a meager living by translating and editing while writing prolifically and associating with Spain's leading intellectual figures. Ramón Menéndez Pidal, a prominent figure in Hispanic scholarship and president of the Centro de Estudios Históricos, asked him to join the philology department at the Centro, which was known for a critical method rejecting subjective praise or condemnation in favor of objective philological and historical analysis. While associated with the Centro, Reyes studied sixteenth- and seventeenth-century Spanish literature, becoming an acknowledged expert on the Spanish Golden Age. During this period, José Ortega y Gasset invited Reyes to contribute to *El sol* (*The Sun*), often described as Spain's foremost intellectual newspaper, and Reyes was also involved with the Residencia de Estudiantes, considered one of the most influential cultural centers of the period. In 1920 Reyes resumed his diplomat-

ic career, being named second secretary of the Mexican delegation in Spain.

The years Reyes spent in Madrid, from 1914 to 1924, are considered fundamental to his literary development. Barbara Bockus Aponte has suggested that his involvement with Menéndez Pidal was especially important, as the discipline and rigorous scientific method of scholarship practiced at the Centro significantly influenced the evolution of Reyes's own critical writing as well as providing a foundation for many of his purely creative projects. Some of his most important works appeared during this period, including *El suicida,* a collection of essays which was the first of his books to receive widespread critical attention; *Visión de Anáhuac,* a description of the ancient city of the Aztecs as first seen by a Spanish conquistador; *Cartones de Madrid,* a collection of impressionistic essays; *Ifigenia cruel,* a tragic poem; and many of the essays that appeared in later collections, most notably in the series *Simpatías y diferencias.* The relationships he formed during this time with other Spanish and Spanish-American intellectuals, many of whom later lived and taught in the Americas, were important professionally and personally for the rest of his life. By the time he left Madrid, Reyes had received wide acclaim as a writer.

For fifteen years after he left Madrid, Reyes continued to

write while occupying a variety of diplomatic posts, as minister or ambassador to France, Argentina, and Brazil. Upon returning to Mexico in 1939, he was named president of the Casa de España en México ("Spanish House in Mexico"), which later became the Colegio de México, the country's most distinguished institution of higher education as well as an important center for scholarly research and publication. He was also elected to the Mexican Academy of Languages, which he served as director from 1957 to 1959. In 1945 he was awarded the National Prize for Arts and Letters and was a candidate for the Nobel Prize. He spent the last years of his life writing voluminously, encouraging younger scholars, and organizing the extensive library he had accumulated. He died in 1959.

Of the various genres in which he wrote, Reyes's essays have received the most critical acclaim, being praised for both their thematic depth and stylistic artistry. The tone of his essays is often described as conversational rather than academic, characterized by insight, subtlety, and wit. While he addressed a wide range of subjects in his essays, from metaphysical questions to discarded razor blades, some consistent themes are evident. Perhaps the most prominent of these is the theory that America has the potential to provide an important cultural synthesis combining values of the Old World and the New, an idea most effectively expressed in the essays "Notas sobre la inteligencia Américana" and "Posición de América." As one who moved easily between Mexico and Spain, Reyes was interested in the possibility of a cultural reconciliation between Spain and Spain's former colonies. His sense of the relationship between the two societies is reflected in *Visión de Anáhuac,* which describes an encounter between an Old World explorer and native American culture. Reyes's early studies of classical Greece and Rome had a continuing influence, as he attempted to explore connections between the cultures of Europe and America. In *Discurso por Virgilio,* for example, he used motifs similar to those in Virgil's *Georgics* to explain a plan by the Mexican government to develop local viniculture industries.

Critics suggest that Reyes's training as a classicist is also evident in his creative writing, most notably in *Ifigenia cruel,* a tragic poem in which he re-created the legend of Iphigenia in Taurus. Although he wrote few poems, many critics view his poetry as an important facet of his development as a writer. Reyes modeled his early poems on traditional verse forms, while in his later poetry he experimented with a variety of forms and techniques. He wrote: "I prefer to be promiscuous / in literature," "the popular ballad / of the neighbor / with the rare quintessence / of Góngora and Mallarmé." His varied subjects include friendship, love, death, Mexico, episodes from his life, and gourmet food and wine. Indeed, as Enrique Anderson Imbert has stated, "nothing was outside the pale" of Reyes's poetry. Reyes also wrote short fiction, which often relied on suggestive detail to capture the reader's imagination rather than provide the traditional framework of plot. In "El testimonio de Juan Peña," for example, subtle changes in the protagonists' points of view, rather than development of plot, provide the suspense of the story. Given the quality of this story, which has been described as a "masterful tale," several critics have questioned why Reyes did not write more fiction. Other critics, however, have criticized his longer fictional writings — each of which he referred to as "arranques de novela" ("beginnings of a novel") — for structural inadequacy, maintaining that these works create intriguing atmosphere and characters but fail due to their lack of narrative development.

Reyes also wrote works of literary criticism and theory. *La experiencia literaria,* a collection of essays written over several years, is thought to most clearly reveal the enormous scope of his literary knowledge, which ranged, in the words of Walter Bara, "from Aristotle to Zola, from Chaucer to Chaplin," encompassing classical, modern, and contemporary literature of Europe and America. *El deslinde: Prolegómenos a la teoría literaria,* an ambitious attempt to systematize literary theory and to determine what qualities distinguish literature from other types of writing, is often considered his masterpiece. In this work, he examined such aspects of literature as aesthetic problems, style and expression, semantics, philology, and the philosophy of language. Much of the success of the book has been attributed to his skill in explaining abstractions clearly and vividly by using poetic images and familiar expressions. Reyes was also instrumental in the critical rehabilitation of the seventeenth-century Spanish poet Luis de Góngora, a development that is considered equivalent to the rediscovery of John Donne in English literature.

Reyes is remembered for his original and eloquent essays, his lasting contributions to literary theory and criticism, his commitment to the creation of a Mexican culture, and his dedication as an educator. He is considered to have trained, by example and instruction, an entire generation of Mexican intellectuals. Reflecting on Reyes's long and varied career, Federico de Onís has called him "the most successful example of a citizen of the international world of letters, both ancient and modern."

PRINCIPAL WORKS

Cuestiones estéticas   (essays)   1911
Cartones de Madrid   (essays)   1917
El suicida   (essays)   1917
Visión de Anáhuac   (essay)   1917
El plano oblicuo   (fiction)   1920
Retratos reales e imaginarios   (essays)   1920
El cazador   (essays)   1921
Simpatías y diferencias. 5 vols.   (essays)   1921-26
Huellas   (poetry)   1922
Ifigenia cruel   (poem)   1924
Cuestiones gongorinas   (criticism)   1927
El testimonio de Juan Peña   (fiction)   1930
Discurso por Virgilio   (essay)   1931
Tren de ondas   (essays)   1932
Capítulos de literatura española [first series]   (criticism) 1939
La crítica en la edad ateniense   (criticism)   1941
Pasado inmediato, y otros ensayos   (essays)   1941
La antigua retórica   (criticism)   1942
La experiencia literaria   (criticism)   1942
El deslinde: Prolegómenos a la teoría literaria   (criticism) 1944
Norte y sur   (essays)   1944
Capítulos de literatura española [second series]   (criticism) 1945
Letras de la Nueva España   (criticism)   1948
The Position of America, and Other Essays   (essays)   1950
Trayectoria de Goethe   (criticism)   1954
Quince presencias   (fiction)   1955

Los tres tesoros (fiction) 1955
Obras completas. 15 vols. (poetry, fiction, criticism, and essays) 1955-63
Mexico in a Nutshell, and Other Essays (essays) 1964

TOMAS NAVARRO (essay date 1945)

[*A Spanish philologist, educator, and critic, Navarro was one of the most important figures in the development of modern philological studies in Spain. He also served as director of the National Library of Madrid and, during the Spanish Civil War, as one of the cultural directors of the Republican government. In 1945, with the goal of encouraging North American readers to examine the works of Reyes, Books Abroad published a series of letters about the Mexican author from eleven critics and friends of Reyes. In the following letter from this collection, Navarro discusses certain characteristics of Reyes's style and language.*]

A salient characteristic of the style of Alfonso Reyes is the agile and obedient flexibility with which the author's words respond to his turns of thought. The great Mexican writer has constantly and steadily perfected the clarity of expression, rich in nuances and reflections, of which he is today an acknowledged master. And paralleling his linguistic advance one notes the development of that delicate combination of serenity and disquiet, of equilibrium and movement, which Reyes has the secret of infusing into his writing.

Even in conversation Reyes makes occasional use of rising inflexions, rapid and varied, which contrast with the usual medium pitch—perhaps a little lower than medium—of his speaking voice. The proportion and measure of the elements of articulation and accent in Alfonso Reyes' speech reveal prosodic habits which do not, it is true, hide his Mexican origin, but which clearly correspond to the essential tradition of good Spanish "usage," a good usage which Reyes brought with him from his native country before he had lived in Madrid and traveled about among the villages of Castile.

There is an admirable example in the achievement of this great linguistic acclimatizer who shows us how it is possible to inhabit the most different regions without ever succumbing to the perils of offensive pedantry, affectation or verbal acrobatics. The note of discretion which is always evident in Reyes' manner is also the wise and solid basis of his literary procedure, whether he sketches his keen *Cartones de Madrid* or lays the grave and ample foundations of his *Visión de Anáhuac.*

About this steady axis play the most varied rhythms. If there is any fault from which the speech and writing of Reyes are entirely free, it is the fault of monotony. One perceives in his language, not the artificial symbolism of a more or less conventional acoustics, but the flawless discrimination of an ear which appreciates the immanent expressiveness of sound. Reyes, who has always written verses and has tried his hand at numerous metrical forms, often evokes the most intimate impressions with the aid of auditory images, as when, in *Huellas,* he recalls the song of the servant and the zestful gatherings at which even the music of the young friends' thoughts was audible.

Reyes is never heedless of his language, not even at those moments when he chooses to write with the most carefree abandon. He has spent a large part of his life in the study of Spanish literature, and has followed the development of the language from its earliest beginnings. That is exactly why this writer's style builds its vigilant modernity on so secure a foundation. The word surrenders completely and obediently only to him who knows and feels its past.

The international scope of Reyes' writing has not diluted the genuinely Hispanic characteristics of his style, nor has his command of the literary language eliminated from his writing the atmosphere and accent of his native country. Reyes' Mexicanism visibly consists, like that of his compatriot Alarcón, in the fostering and selection of traditional elements which become more genuinely Spanish as they grow more cleanly and essentially Mexican. (pp. 116-17)

Tomas Navarro, in Books Abroad, *Vol. 19, No. 2, Spring, 1945, pp. 116-17.*

ANTONIO CASTRO LEAL (essay date 1945)

[*In the following excerpt from a letter included in the* Books Abroad *collection, Leal offers a brief description of the phases of Reyes's career and praises his range and versatility as a writer.*]

[Alfonso Reyes] inaugurated his literary career with a beautiful book called *Cuestiones estéticas* (1911), in which one feels the subtle force of expanding life, the intelligent curiosity of youth, and a palpitating humanism in which there was as much divination as doctrine. Then the Madrid period, the most fortunate and fruitful epoch of his early period. From that epoch date the articles and essays which form the first three volumes of *Simpatías y diferencias* (1921-1922), the *Retratos reales e imaginarios* (1920), and a series of important works of erudition and criticism, the *Cartones de Madrid* (1917), intense and rapid pictures of Spanish life which, like the inspired "studies" of the painters, represent a state of pure emotion which is often diluted in their completed works, and the *Visión de Anáhuac* (1915), an essay which attains perfection in the purity and precision of its lines, in its balanced power of evocation and synthesis. In this same period he published *El plano oblicuo* (1920) and *El cazador* (1921), much of which was written in Mexico: *cuentos* and fanciful sketches in which he has succeeded in expressing situations whose reality merges with forgotten dreams and irreversible moments of spiritual autobiography. To the Spanish period belongs also his dramatic poem *Ifigenia cruel* (1923), which has the severe and noble elegance of old Greek sculpture, and whose lyric current stirs the waters of classic mythology.

After Madrid came a well earned vacation. It was like a general's reorganization of his army after a victorious battle. Reyes found it more effective and more agreeable to adopt a pleasanter and freer rhythm, and he brought into the world without haste but without interruption, books of such charm that they scarcely fatigued the presses. (p. 120)

And finally, back in Mexico . . . , he inaugurated with admirable vigor and lucidity the third epoch of his career. In the last few years he has published books whose method, matter and manner are far above anything to which we Hispano-Americans have been accustomed. *La crítica en la edad ateniense* (1941) and *La antigua retórica* (1942) are two masterful books whose penetration, special competence and ideological elegance give new meaning to the problems which he treats. In amplitude and profundity their treatment of these phases of Greek culture is fully worthy to set beside the work of Professor J. W. H. Atkins [*Literary Criticism in Antiquity*] . . . . In *El deslinde* (1942) and on many pages of *La experiencia literaria* (1942) he has gone more deeply into various fundamental questions of the technique and philosophy of literature than has perhaps ever been done before in our language.

But such investigations do not entirely occupy or satisfy this choice and multiple intelligence. He still turns at times to poetry and to the other forms of personal expression in literature. For this superman of letters moves about in the field of writing as the great artists of the Renaissance turned hither and thither in the world of forms, finding, like them, delight and necessary inspiration in the lines of the flat sketch, in three-dimensional relief, in the architectonic flight of the cupola and the dentate outline of the battlemented wall. (p. 121)

> *Antonio Castro Leal, in* Books Abroad, *Vol. 19, No. 2, Spring, 1945, pp. 120-21.*

FEDERICO DE ONÍS (essay date 1950)

[*Onís was a Spanish critic and scholar who was influential both in the renewal of Spanish culture during the early years of the twentieth century and in expanding the understanding of that culture in the English-speaking world. In Spain, Onís earned a reputation as a distinguished philologist and collaborated with Reyes and others in establishing the journal* Revista de filologia española. *After 1916 he resided and taught in the United States, where he founded two Spanish literary reviews as well as the Hispanic Institute of America. In the following excerpt, Onís asserts that Reyes's work has a definite unity and exhibits a number of consistent themes despite its apparent diversity.*]

When, in 1911, Alfonso Reyes published his first book, his formation was already determined. . . . This book, entitled *Cuestiones estéticas,* introduced to the Spanish-speaking world a young Mexican writer who from that moment was regarded as a master, as had happened with José Enrique Rodó, the young Uruguayan of the preceding generation. The precocity of Alfonso Reyes, the breadth and depth of his culture, the self-security of his diaphanous and complex style were all the result of his Mexican molding. It is important to point this out in order to understand the originality and significance of this writer, who today, after forty years of constant and copious literary activity, stands as the most universal of writers in the Spanish language, perhaps as the most achieved example in any literature of the international citizen of the world of classic and modern letters. (pp. v-vi)

The themes developed in the course of his diverse writings were already contained in his first book and in the poems and essays he wrote before leaving Mexico.

In that book we already find the classical background, a heritage of the humanism of Mexico, enriched with modern philological and aesthetic concepts, in his study on the Electras of the Greek theater, which was to culminate in his dramatic poem *Ifigenia cruel* and in various expository and critical studies complementary to his university duties in later years after his return to Mexico. The manner in which the eternal values of Greece acquire new meaning throughout Alfonso Reyes's work as they are beveled by his Mexican spirit

may best be appreciated in the title of one of his minor works, a series of sonnets entitled *Homero en Cuernavaca.*

Spain is there, too, in a critical essay on a short novel written in 1492, *Cárcel de amor,* known today only to scholars, but which Reyes considers the prototype of the modern novel; and in his first study on the aesthetics of Góngora, the poet who was to become the subject of other more exhaustive studies, and an enduring influence in Reyes's poetry, as in much of modern poetry. His investigation and interpretation of classic and modern Spanish literature took on, both during his stay in Spain and afterwards, vast proportions, and established him as one of its best historians and critics in the twofold aspect of scholar and discoverer of aesthetic values. In the course of his work one finds a multitude of studies, original, penetrating, and scholarly, on the outstanding figures of Spanish literature throughout its long history, such as the Cid, the Archpriest of Hita, Lope de Vega, Calderón, Gracián, and modern writers like Azorín, Valle-Inclán, Unamuno, and Ortega.

And in this first work there is present, too, his early and decisive interest in foreign literatures. An essay on Goethe is the first of several he was to write. Two studies, one on George Bernard Shaw and another on Oscar Wilde, already indicate his never flagging interest in that literature of England and North America which had such an important influence on the essay form that was to be the vehicle of the greater part of his writing. And a study on Mallarmé's literary art reveals the close, direct contact he was always to have with French literature, especially the modern, which begins with Mallarmé. Later on he wrote a delightful little work, *Mallarmé entre nosotros,* and Mallarmé has left a deep impress on his style.

There also appears in this first book his interest in Mexican folklore and literature. Many of his studies have dealt with those authors, outstanding or minor figures, to whom he has been drawn, and one of his best works of criticism, *Letras de la Nueva España,* is a clear, penetrating, and accurate evaluation of Mexico's culture during the colonial period. Mexico is the subject of one of his early works, *Visión de Anáhuac,* a beautiful example of Reyes's ability to fuse historic reality and poetry as he reconstructs the dawn of modern Mexico, the encounter between Europe and the Aztec civilization, which appears before our bemused eyes—as before those of the Spanish conquerors—in a pure, limpid, idealized vision in which one feels the loftiness of the plateau of Mexico and sees things in the unique transparence of its atmosphere. It is not a historical reconstruction, but the vision that emerges from the subtle impingement of the pre-Cortesian world on the gaze of the foreigner, the visitor of yesterday or today to "the most transparent region of the air."

Even more significant than the fact that Reyes has written on Mexican subjects is that through all his work, much of which deals with subjects far removed from Mexico, Mexico is always present as a point of reference and comparison; even when it does not appear, one can feel it in his approach to other cultures and in the temper and tone of his personality and his style. His work possesses great unity notwithstanding the diversity of themes and forms he has employed. He has written poetry since early youth, and continues to do so, and, in my opinion, it is in his poetry that the essence of his work and the most perfect expression of his style are to be found. In it are indivisibly blended the classic and the modern, the cultured and the popular, the personal and the universal, and it reveals the amazingly varied grain of his simple and complex soul, receptive to every emotion. The most personal and Mexican feature of it is that mingle of wit, elegance, and serene melancholy which underlies the richness of language and the literary evocations. In the field of the essay his work varies from the lengthy treatise, like *El deslinde,* an extensive study in which he attempts to establish the limits of literature, to the brief notes, letters, dedications, and other material which escapes classification (pp. viii-x)

It is not easy to grasp and appreciate Reyes's value in a selection of his work, felicitous though this be. His chief value is of an aesthetic order and resides in each detail of the totality. His aesthetic approach shuns the explicit affirmation and seeks the half tones, the subtler shadings, the multiplicity of facets every idea and every thing, great or small, offers. He approaches ideas and facts with a sinuous, exploring regard, with a tolerant understanding I can define only by a term that would seem unrelated to either philosophy or aesthetics, but which has a special Mexican connotation: courtesy. Courtesy toward things and ideas, scrupulous care in his dealings with them, restraint in his praise, wit in his negations, and always kindness, an aesthetic kindness that consists in understanding everything. It is thus that Reyes has converted into the material of poetry all that his eyes and spirit have beheld. (p. xii)

> Federico de Onís, "Foreword: Alfonso Reyes," in The Position of America and Other Essays by Alfonso Reyes, edited and translated by Harriet de Onís, Alfred A. Knopf, 1950, pp. v-xii.

BERTRAM D. WOLFE (essay date 1950)

[*Best known for his numerous studies of Marxism, Soviet history, and Soviet political figures, Wolfe also wrote extensively on Spanish and Mexican history and culture. In the following excerpt, he assesses the essays collected in* The Position of America.]

[The essays in *The Position of America*] have been selected to give the discursive, wide-ranging thought of the author a special unity around the problems of America: **"Vision of Anáhuac"** (Ancient Mexico); **"Thoughts on the American Mind"; "The Position of America"; "Epistle to the Pinzons"** (the three brothers who piloted Columbus' ships); **"Columbus and Amerigo Vespucci"; "Social Science and Social Responsibility"** (with special reference to America's use of European culture); **"Native Poetry of New Spain"; "The Tenth Muse of America"** (the Mexican poetess, Sor Juana); **"Luis G. Urbina"** (elegy to a Mexican poet); and **"Virgil in Mexico."** Reyes' thought, like the chronicle of his life as intellectual, diplomat and traveler, moves out in a series of widening circles from its Mexican center: he is Mexican, Latin, Ibero-American, Continental American, European of the transplanted Europe of the New Continent, Citizen of the Republic of Letters and of the World, and practiser of "the profession that is superior to all others, the profession of being a man." He has been at home in Buenos Aires, Rio de Janeiro, New York, Madrid, Paris, Rome; he would have been at home no less in the Rome of Virgil and in ancient Athens. His thought moves in transparent, widening, overlapping, concentric circles from its Mexican center. The color grows more intense as we move toward that center, so that the best and most vivid essays are the most specifically Mexican: the **"Vision of Anáhuac"; "The Tenth Muse"; "Virgil in Mexico."** All the essays are suggestive, little spots of light shine

from them as from fireflies in a wooded night; but those with the largest titles like **"Thoughts on the American Mind"** have the thinnest density and precisely because of their large promise leave us aroused but disappointed.

"Vision of Anáhuac," on the other hand, with which the volume opens, is a veritable poet's vision of the world of wonder of Aztec-Maya civilization as beheld by the first Spaniards when they broke into it. "Traveler," cries its epigraph, "you have come to the most transparent region of the air." The picture has the profusion of detail, the complex organization, the sense of analogy between hills and objects and men and all the lyricism that characterizes Rivera's murals of the same pre-conquest world. "From the barren, alkaline earth the plants raise the thorns of their vegetable claws, defending themselves against drought . . . the air glitters like a mirror . . . it is like autumn the year round . . . the brilliant humming bird, the emerald trembler . . . the rocks replying to the sweet songs of the flowers." . . . In this setting man has organized a life full of splendor, passion, cruelty and "exotic" wonder. It is a world in which Dionysius would be more at home than Apollo, yet this Apollonian writer feels linked to it by the "common effort to master our wild, hostile natural setting" and by "emotions aroused by the same natural objects," emotions "without whose glow our valleys and our mountains would be like an unlighted theater."

No less characteristic is the closing essay which begins with the celebration of the two-thousandth anniversary of Virgil in Mexico, goes on to an analysis of Mexico's Latinity and ends with thoughts on the "Georgics" as the healing "program" of Mexico's agrarian revolution.

> Bertram D. Wolfe, "A Shining Mind from Modern Mexico," in New York Herald Tribune Book Review, December 24, 1950, p. 7.

WALTER BARA (essay date 1951)

[*In the following excerpt, Bara compares Reyes's accomplishments as a poet and as an essayist, and extols the breadth of Reyes's literary knowledge.*]

Twenty-five years ago, more or less, when he was already firmly established as one of the greatest Hispanists of modern times, Pedro Henríquez Ureña registered a literary judgment which the passage of time has proven quite conclusively to be inaccurate. He wrote that the eminence of Alfonso Reyes as a man of letters was most keenly reflected in his poetry. This may have been true in 1927, but surely very few people today would agree with this opinion, since, in the score of countries where the name of Reyes is revered by anyone familiar with contemporary Spanish American letters, Don Alfonso is regarded as one of the finest essayists ever to have written in the Spanish language, and the most outstanding humanist that Mexico, or perhaps any other Castilian-speaking country, for that matter, has produced in this century. It is true that the tone and tempo of many of his shorter prose pieces is imbued with the same inspiration that nourished some of Spain's finest lyricists, and that the color and wealth of Indian pageantry in his *Visión de Anáhuac* is not very far removed from poetry itself. However, over and above his superior accomplishments in the field of poetry, Alfonso Reyes is today rightfully recognized as a true descendent of Montaigne and Bacon and those who, after them, enriched the world's literature through their cultivation of the essay form.

Although his poetic output in volume is insignificant when compared with his prose writings, Alfonso Reyes nevertheless has studied and evaluated this genre with extraordinary ability. *De poesía Hispano-americana,* written in 1941, is a remarkable feat of conciseness and thoroughness in summing up the salient aspects of the modern period in Spanish American poetry. Equally compact and rich in facts, information, and recondite details—qualities characteristic of all his critical studies—is his summary of pre-Columbian letters, written as an introduction to his *Letras de la Nueva España* . . . , published in 1948. Its section on the indigenous poetry of the new world is probably the finest review of the maya-quiché culture to have been condensed within the boundaries of a literary study. In this book, Alfonso Reyes, with consistently enviable clarity of thought and language, offers a truly exquisite literary panorama of Mexican literature in its three centuries of colonial times.

La experiencia literaria, published in Argentina in 1942, may in many respects be considered Reyes' literary biography. In this anthology of essays, written at random over a period of several years, the author reveals more fully perhaps than in any other of his single volumes the infinite scope of his literary knowledge—classical, modern, and contemporary—of France, England, Germany, Iberia and Latin America, as well as the United States. Every one of the more than two hundred pages of this book contains at least one allusion to a foreign author; in some instances, there are as many as ten on a single page. Alfonso el Sabio shares honors with Mark Twain and Valery Larbaud in **"Aduana Lingüística,"** one of the most delightful essays on language barriers that has ever been written . . . . (p. 378)

From Aristotle to Zola, from Chaucer to Chaplin, the literary experience of Reyes is so broad that it defies comparison with the personal culture of any living writer. Undoubtedly, a great many of these allusions are meaningless to all but the best informed in international literature, ancient and modern; and since Alfonso Reyes almost never resorts to explanatory footnotes or biographical glossaries, a large portion of his writings cannot be fully appreciated by most people until they are made available in annotated editions. (p. 379)

Walter Bara, "Aspects of Alfonso Reyes," in Hispania, *Vol. XXXIV, No. 4, November, 1951, pp. 378-80.*

OCTAVIO PAZ   (essay date 1960)

[*A prolific Mexican man of letters, Paz is considered one of the greatest Spanish-American writers of the twentieth century. Although he is known primarily as an experimental poet, he is also a respected essayist, critic, and social philosopher. His works include* El labertino de la soledad (*1950*), *a highly regarded analysis of Mexico's dual cultural heritage. In the following excerpt, Paz explores characteristic themes in Reyes's work, analyzing in particular the poem* Ifigenia cruel.]

Reyes, the lover of measure and proportion, a man for whom everything, including action and passion, had to resolve itself in equilibrium, knew that we are surrounded by chaos and silence. Formlessness, whether as a vacuum or as a brute presence, lies in wait for us. But he never tried to put instinct in chains, to suppress the dark side of man. He did not preach

Reyes.

the equivocal virtues of repression, either in the realm of ethics or in that of aesthetics, and even less so in politics. Wakefulness and sleep, blood and thought, friendship and solitude, the city and women: each part and each one must be given its own. The portion of instinct is no less sacred than that of the spirit. And what are the limits between one and another? Everything communicates. Man is a vast and delicate alchemy. The human action par excellence is transmutation, which makes light from shadow, the word from a cry, dialogue from the elemental quarrel.

His love for Hellenic culture, the reverse of his indifference toward Christianity, was something more than an intellectual inclination. He saw Greece as a model because what its poets and philosophers revealed to him was something that was already within him and that, thanks to them, received a name and an answer: the terrible powers of hubris and the means of controlling them. Greek literature did not show him a philosophy, a moral, a "what should be." Rather, it showed him being itself in all its welter, in its alternately creative and destructive rhythms. The Greek norms, Jaeger says, are a manifestation of the inherent lawfulness of the cosmos; the movement of being, its dialectic. On several occasions Reyes wrote that tragedy is the highest and most perfect form of poetry and ethics because, in tragedy, lack of proportion finds at last its strict measure and is thus purified and redeemed. Passion is creative when it finds its form. To Reyes, form was not an envelopment or an abstract measure, but rather the instant of reconciliation in which discord is transformed into harmony. The true name of this harmony is liberty: fatality ceases to be an imposition from without and becomes an intimate and voluntary acceptance. Ethics and aesthetics are intertwined in Reyes's thinking: liberty is an aesthetic act, that is, it is the moment of concord between passion and form, vital energy and the human measure; at the same time, form and measure constitute an ethical dimension because they rescue us from excess, which is chaos and destruction.

These ideas, scattered through many of his pages and books, are the invisible blood that animates Reyes's most perfect poetic work: *Ifigenia cruel* (*Cruel Iphigenia*). Perhaps it is not necessary to remark that this poem is, among many other things, a symbol of a personal drama and the answer that the poet meant to give it. His family belonged to the *ancien régime*. His father had been minister of war and his elder brother, the jurist Bernardo Reyes, was a university professor and a renowned political polemicist. Both were enemies of Madero's revolutionary government. His father died in the attack on the National Palace and his brother, when the revolutionaries triumphed, fled to Spain and constantly attacked the new regime from there. Hence Alfonso Reyes's situation was not very different from that of Iphigenia: his brother reminded him that vengeance is a filial duty and that to refuse to follow the voice of the blood is to condemn oneself to serving a bloodthirsty goddess—Artemis in the one case, the Mexican Revolution in the other. The poem is something more, of course, than an expression of this personal conflict; as a vision of woman and as a meditation on liberty, *Ifigenia cruel* is one of the most complete and perfect works in modern Spanish American poetry.

Reyes chose the second part of the myth. At the moment when Iphigenia is to die at Aulis, Artemis, to placate the wrath of the wind, exchanges her body for that of a hind and takes her to Tauris. There she consecrates her as a priestess of her temple: Iphigenia is to immolate every stranger who arrives at the island. One day she recognizes Orestes among the strangers whom a shipwreck has cast up on the shore. Destiny, the law of the breed, wins out: brother and sister flee, after robbing the statue of the goddess, and return to Attica. Reyes introduces here a fundamental change in the story, one that does not appear in either Euripides or Goethe: Iphigenia has lost her memory. She does not know who she is or where she comes from. She only knows that she is "a mass of naked rage." As a virgin without origins, who "sprouted like a fungus on the stones of the temple," bound to the bloody stone from the beginning of beginnings, a virgin with neither a past nor a future, Iphigenia is blind movement without self-awareness, condemned to repeat itself endlessly. The appearance of Orestes breaks the enchantment; his words penetrate her petrified consciousness and she passes gradually from recognition of the "other"—the unknown and delirious brother, the always remote fellow human being—to the rediscovery of her lost identity. Reyes seems to suggest that, in order to be ourselves, we must recognize the existence of others. When she recovers her memory, Iphigenia recovers her self. She is in possession of her own being because she knows who she is: the magic virtue of the name. Memory has given her back her consciousness, and, in so doing, it has granted her her freedom. She is no longer possessed by Artemis, no longer "bound to the trunk of her self," and can now choose. Her choice—and here the difference from the traditional version is even more significant—is unexpected: Iphigenia decides to remain in Tauris. Two words—"two words that are empty shells: I refuse"—are enough to change the whole course of fate in one vertiginous instant. By this act she renounces the memory she has just

recovered, says "No" to destiny, to her family and origins, to the laws of the earth and the blood. And, beyond that, she renounces her own self. That negation engenders a new self-affirmation. In renouncing her self, she chooses. And this act, free above all others, an affirmation of the sovereignty of the spirit, a shining of liberty, is a second birth. Iphigenia is now the daughter of her own self.

Reyes's poem, which was written in 1923, not only anticipates many contemporary preoccupations but also contains—in code, in a condensed language that partakes of the hardness of stone and the bitterness of the sea, skillful and savage at one and the same time—all the later evolution of his spirit. All of Reyes—the best, the freest, the least trammeled—is in this work. There are even a secret wink, a malicious aside for the delectation of the knowing, and anachronisms and a pointing of the intelligence toward other lands and other times. There is erudition, but there are also grace, imagination, and a painful lucidity. Iphigenia, her knife, and her goddess, an immense stone fashioned by blood, allude simultaneously to pre-Columbian cults and "the eternal feminine"; the sonnet in Orestes's monologue is a double homage to Góngora and to the Spanish theater of the seventeenth century; the shadow of Segismundo sometimes obscures Iphigenia's face; at other times, the virgin speaks enigmas like the "Hérodiade" ("Herodias") of Mallarmé or gropes with her thoughts like "La jeune parque" ("The young Fate"); Euripides and Goethe, the Catholic concept of free will, the rhythmic experiments of Modernism, even Mexican themes (universalism and nationalism) and the family quarrel, all are brought together here with admirable naturalness. There is nothing too much because there is nothing lacking. True, he never again wrote a poem so solid and so aerial in its architecture, so rich in meanings, but the best pages of his prose are an impassioned meditation on the mystery of Iphigenia, the virgin liberty.

The enigma of liberty is also that of woman. Artemis is pure and cruel divinity: she is moon and water, the goddess of the third millennium before Christ, the tamer, the huntress, and the fatal enchantress. Iphigenia is just barely a human manifestation of that pallid and terrible deity, who runs through the nocturnal woods followed by a blood-thirsty pack of hounds. Artemis is a pillar, the primordial tree, archetype of the column as the grove is mythical model of the temple. That pillar is the center of the world:

> The stars dance about you.
> Alas for the world if you weaken, Goddess!

Artemis is virgin and impenetrable: "Who glimpsed the hermetic mouth of your two vertical legs?" Eye of stone, mouth of stone—but "the roots of her fingers suck up the red cubes of the sacrifice at each moon." She is cliff, pillar, statue, still water, but she is also the mad rush of the wind through the trees. Artemis alternately seeks and refuses incarnation, the meeting with the other, the adversary and complement of her being. The carnal embrace is mortal combat.

Eroticism—in the modern meaning of the term—is always veiled in Reyes's work. Irony moderates the shout; sensuality sweetens the mouth's terrible grimace; tenderness transforms the claw into a caress. Love is a battle, not a slaughter. Reyes does not deny the omnipotence of desire but—without closing his eyes to the contradictory nature of pleasure—he seeks a new equilibrium. In *Ifigenia cruel* and other writings desire wears the armor of death, but in his more numerous and more personal works his cordial temperament—melancholy, tenderness, *saudade* ("nostalgia")—calms the blood and its hornets. Reyes's epicureanism is neither an aesthetics nor a morality: it is a vital defense, a manly remedy. A pact: no surrender, but also no war without quarter. In one of his youthful poems, much more complex than it seems at a first reading, he says that in his imagination he identifies the flower (which is a magic flower: the sleeping poppy) with woman and confesses his fear:

> I tremble, let the day not dawn
> in which you turn into a woman!

The flower, like woman, hides a menace. Both provoke dreams, delirium, and madness. Both bewitch—which is to say, paralyze—the spirit. To free oneself from the virgin Iphigenia's knife and the menace of the flower, there is no known exorcism except love, sacrifice—which is, *always,* a transfiguration. In Reyes's work the sacrifice is not consummated and love is an oscillation between solitude and companionship. Woman ("bound up in the hour—free, although she gives herself, and alien") is ours for only an instant in reality. And, in the memory, forever, like nostalgia:

> Thank you, Río, thank you,
> Solitude and companionship,
> Smooth water for all anguish,
> Harbor in every storm.

Pact, agreement, equilibrium: these words appear frequently in Reyes's work and define one of the central directions of his thought. Some critics, not content with accusing him of Byzantinism (there are criticisms that, on certain lips, are really eulogies), have reproached him for his moderation. A spirit of moderation? I refuse to believe it, at least in the simple way in which simplistic minds want to see it. A spirit in search of equilibrium, an aspiration toward measure, and also a grand universal appetite, a desire to embrace everything, the most remote disciplines as well as the most distant epochs. Not to repress contradictions but to integrate them in broader affirmations; to order particulars of knowledge into general—but always provisional—schemes. Curiosity and prudence: every day we discover that there is still something we need to know, and, if it is true that everything has been thought, it is also true that nothing has been thought. No one has the last word. It is easy to see the uses and risks of this attitude. On the one hand, it irritates people with categorical minds who have the truth clenched in their fists. On the other, an excess of knowledge sometimes makes us timid and weakens our confidence in our spontaneous impulses. Reyes was not paralyzed by erudition because he defended himself with an invincible weapon: humor. To laugh at one's self, to laugh at one's own knowledge, is a way of growing lighter.

Góngora says: "The sea is not deaf: erudition is deceptive." Reyes was not always free from the deceptions of that sort of erudition that causes us to see yesterday's madness in today's novelties. Besides, his temperament led him to flee from extremes. This explains, perhaps, his reserve when considering those civilizations and spirits that express what could be called sublime exaggeration. (I am thinking of the Orient and of pre-Columbian America but also of Novalis and Rimbaud.) I will always lament his coldness toward the great adventure of contemporary art and poetry. German Romanticism, Dostoevsky, modern poetry (in its more daring forms), Kafka, Lawrence, Joyce, and some others were territories that he traversed with an explorer's valor but without amorous passion. And even in this I am afraid of being

unjust, because how can one forget his fondness for Mallarmé, one of the very poets who most clearly embodies the modern artist's thirst for the absolute? He was blamed for the mildness of his public life, and some said that on occasion his character was not of the same stature as his talent and the circumstances around him. It is true that sometimes he kept still; it is also true that he never screeched as did many of his contemporaries. If he never suffered persecution, he also never persecuted anyone. He was not a party man; he was not fascinated by force or numbers; he did not believe in leaders; he never published noisy statements of support; he would not renounce his past, his thoughts, or his work; he did not confess nor employ autocriticism; he was not "converted." His indecisions, even his weaknesses—because he had them—were changed into strengths and nourished his freedom. This tolerant and affable man lived and died a heterodoxist, outside all churches and parties.

Reyes's work is disconcerting not only in its quantity but also in the variety of the matters it deals with. Yet it is the farthest thing from being a scattering. Everything tends toward a synthesis, including that part of his literary work made up of his annotations and summaries of other people's books. In an epoch of discord and uniformity—two faces of the same coin—Reyes postulates a will for harmony, that is, for an order that does not exclude the singularity of the parts. His interest in political and social utopias and his continuous meditation on the duties of the Spanish American "intelligence" have the same origin as his fondness for Hellenistic studies, the philosophy of history, and comparative literature. He seeks in everything the individual trait, the personal variation; and he always succeeds in placing this singularity in a vaster harmony. But harmony, agreement, and equilibrium are words that do not define him clearly. "Concord," a spiritual word, fits him better. He is more worthy of it. Concord is not concession, pact, or compromise, but a dynamic game of opposites, concordance of the being and the other, reconciliation between movement and repose, coincidence of passion and form. The surge of life, the coming and going of the blood, the hand that opens and closes: to give and to receive and to give again. Concord, a central, vital word. Not brain, not belly, not sex, not caveman's jaw: heart. (pp. 115-22)

Octavio Paz, "The Rider of the Air," translated by Lysander Kemp, in his The Siren & the Seashell and Other Essays on Poets and Poetry, *translated by Lysander Kemp and Margaret Sayers Peden, University of Texas Press, 1976, pp. 113-22.*

ENRIQUE ANDERSON-IMBERT (essay date 1963)

[Anderson-Imbert is an Argentine-born literary historian, critic, novelist, and short story writer. He has published more than twenty books of essays and criticism, including his major work, Historia de la literatura hispanicoamerica *(Spanish-American Literature: A History). In the following excerpt from that work, Anderson-Imbert presents an overview of Reyes's poetry, essays, and fiction.]*

[Reyes] groups his poetry under three headings. The first is a "Poetic review," then the topical verses, and finally, those books of poetry which have a certain unity: *Cruel Iphigenia (Ifigenia cruel), Three Poems (Tres poemas), Day's Sonnets (Jornada en sonetos),* and *Deaf Ballads (Romances sordos).* His first poems, from around 1906, were Parnassian. Having learned respect for verse forms in this school, Reyes struck out for himself. Like other Modernists, he penetrated the obscurities of his own being, sometimes to bring color to it, sometimes to question, and even in order to touch its dark and silent depths. Serious symbolism alongside of which, after the first World War, rhythms and images of juvenile vanguardism begin to play. There were even poems describing sensual African dances. Actually, nothing was outside the pale of his poetry which was "fickle in theme and style." His themes were as varied as the turns of his own life: autobiographical evocations, the homeland, friends and loves, works, and death. His styles come and go between the laboratory in which the hermetic poets distill their verse and the clear, open road where the people walk. Reyes was not afraid to prospect along dangerous trails: for example, along the prosaic trail (in case they "jumped him" he was well armed—see his "Prosaic Theory," where he declares "I prefer to be promiscuous / in literature," "the popular ballad / of the neighbor / with the rare quintessence / of Góngora and Mallarmé"). Difficult or simple he always demands the attention of the reader, because earlier, he was demanding of himself and gives only essences.

His poetry is concise, sober, insinuating. His prose is beaten gold. The virtues of intelligence and esteem that tend to come separately in people in Alfonso Reyes are integrated in gracious and subtle light. He is erudite in the field of philology and sparkling in witty sallies; he writes stories, chronicles, sketches, and penetrating critical glosses. His prose is impish and prying. The multiplicity of Reyes' vocations (a man of the Renaissance) is not only measured by the vast repertory of motifs, but also by the stylistic richness of each turn. Reyes' restlessness transmits to his style a zigzagging, jumpy, prankish, and sensual movement. Before leaving Mexico in 1913, his writer's hand was already educated: from this period, with a single exception, are the stories and dialogs of *The Oblique Plane* (*El plano oblicuo,* 1920), a most original book in the Spanish language because of its rapid shifts from the real to the fantastic (**"The Supper"**—**"La cena"**) and because of its expressionist procedures. From 1914, except for a brief stay in France, he was to live in Spain until 1924, probably the most productive period of his career: *Vision of Anáhuac* (*Visión de Anáhuac,* 1917), *The Eves of Spain* (*Las vísperas de España,* 1937), *The Suicide* (*El suicida,* 1917), *The Hunter* (*El cazador,* 1921), *Real and Imaginary Portraits* (*Retratos reales e imaginarios,* 1920), and the five series of *Sympathies and Differences* (*Simpatías y diferencias,* 1921-1926). This is a consummate work that links on different pages, and at times on the same page, impressionist sentences, fantasies, elegances, narrative flights of fancy, biographical sketches, notes, and reflections. His norms appear to be these: to express himself in miniatures; to not lean too much on actual things; to subjectivize everything, whether it be through his sensibilities or through his imagination; to intermingle life and culture; to address himself to a sympathetic reader who possesses the same qualities that the writer possesses, and to converse with him; to watch each word. . . . Characteristic of his fictional work is its preference for exciting the imagination of the reader with suggestive details rather than satisfying his curiosity with a plot or a denouement. It is fantasy for sharp readers, already accustomed to and perhaps tired of reading so many novels. His essays are always lyrical, even those of didactic or logical themes, because the manner in which he treats his object is personal, not public. In *Sundial* (*Reloj de sol,* 1926) Reyes confessed: "The historian I carry in my pocket will not allow me to waste a single datum, a single document." But it is not so much a desire to recoup a past

public as it is to reconstruct an intimate diary whose leaves had fallen out along the road of life. Like Echo, the quartered nymph, the diary that was buried here and there by Reyes throughout his work lives on in a constant murmur. No matter how impersonal a Reyes theme may appear, one can always perceive the vibration of a confidence about to be revealed. Even though he was one of our most exquisite, most original, most surprising writers, Reyes founded his work on healthy experiences. Others would like to look at the world upside down, to see if a world askew will tell them something new: they mutilate themselves or give value to their mutilations; they give themselves over to sophistic frenzy or to lethargy; they corrupt honor, deny light, betray the heart. Not Reyes. Alfonso Reyes is a classical writer because of the human integrity of his vocation, because of his serene faith in intelligence, in charity, in the eternal values of the soul. The uniqueness of Reyes' poetic universe is not extravagance, but the refinement of the normal directions in man. Each one of his volumes is a collection of unsurpassed pages. To date, the Fondo de Cultura Económica of Mexico City has published thirteen thick volumes of *Complete Works.* On contemplating this grandiose monument to his effort, a literary critic states a bundle of problems that should be studied carefully: the problem of a writer who fails in spite of being extraordinarily equipped for success; that of a secret sterility that is disguised by incessant labor; that of an intelligence which, because of its propensity for dialog, remained with its face toward the best spirits of its time, but with its back to its own works; that of a classic of our literary history who, nevertheless, left no great books. Is there in the air of Hispanic-America something lethal to literary creation? Why did not the author of *The Testimony of Juan Peña* give us the novel he promised? Why did not the author of **"The Supper"** give us the collection of stories he promised? Why did not the author of *Cruel Iphigenia,* of *Footprints,* give us the drama, the book of poems he promised? Indeed, the fruits yielded are sufficient. But for those of us who had the privilege of being his friends, it is clear that Alfonso Reyes could have given more, much more than that, to the great genres of literature. Where he did succeed was in the essay. Alfonso Reyes is without any doubt the keenest, most brilliant, versatile, cultured, and profound essayist in our language today. (pp. 412-15)

Enrique Anderson-Imbert, "1910-1925: Authors Born between 1885 and 1900," in his Spanish-American Literature: A History, *translated by John V. Falconieri, Wayne State University Press, 1963, pp. 327-420.*

ARTURO TORRES-RIOSECO   (essay date 1964)

[*Torres-Rioseco was a Chilean-born American scholar of Spanish-American literature who wrote widely on the subject. In the following excerpt, he discusses Reyes's essays, literary theory, and fiction.*]

Alfonso Reyes will remain in the history of Hispanic literatures mainly as an essay writer. He is, perhaps, only a popularizer of scientific principles, a commentator on history, a definer and a systematizer. But, of course, in our America these are noble activities. Strict disciplines hold him firm at the roots of all problems discussed, and his logical mind establishes a rational balance between fact and fancy. He is always elegant and imaginative, evanescent and logical. In the selections presented in [*Mexico in a Nutshell and Other Es-*

says], especially on America's themes and Columbus's ventures, one does not know whether to admire more the factual interpretation or the ironic sequences of the author.

In his first important book of literary essays, *Cuestiones estéticas* (1916), Reyes reveals an unusual knowledge of classic and modern European literatures and at the same time of literary theories from the Aristotelian system to contemporary techniques. Studying the poetry of Góngora and Mallarmé, he defends the right of the poet to create his own vocabulary according to the needs of his inspiration, and argues that the world of these two poets could not have been translated into poetic experience except by the creation of a new language. Later on, during his residence in Spain, Reyes wrote some of his best essays, which were collected later in his books *Cuestiones gongorinas* and *Capítulos de literatura española.* Besides these essays on erudite matters Reyes wrote books of impressions, *Cartones de Madrid* (1917), of philosophical themes, *El suicida* (1917) and, of especial importance, *Visión de Anáhuac* (1917), a poetical description of the Mexican plateau.

His collection *Tren de ondas* (1932), written in a lighter vein, has an unsophisticated charm. Here we find the delightful short essay **"Diego Rivera Discovers Painting"** and the meaningful **"Los motivos de la conducta,"** an exercise in Semantics which every starchy philologist should read. The definition of "caballero" and "gentleman" is a jewel: to the theory that "caballero" is romantic and "gentleman," classic, Reyes adds his own: "gentleman" is rather dry, "caballero is humid, rather foamy." In this little volume we find the essays on flies, discarded shaving blades, onions (**"Dignity of the Onion"**), humble topics lifted later to an artistic level by Pablo Neruda in his *Odas elementales* and by Camilo José Cela in his novel *Mrs. Caldwell habla con su hijo.*

Four short essays [**"Discurso por Virgilio"** (1931), **"Atenea política"** (1932), **"En el día americano"** (1932), **"Homilía por la cultura"** (1938)] are, according to Manuel Olguín [in his *Alfonso Reyes, ensayista*], of importance because they contain his first attempts to formulate a social and cultural philosophy. The purpose of these essays is to define the philosophical nature of culture and the duties imposed by it on the intellectual. Reyes wishes to solve the main problems of his social philosophy: to find the formula to raise Spanish America to the level of universal culture, without abandoning the fundamental human values of its Latin and Hispanic tradition.

"Culture," according to Olguín, is defined in these essays as the product of intelligence in its most characteristic function: that of unifying, of establishing regular systems of connections. This function is realized in the horizontal order of "space," or communication among neighbors, and then it is called "cosmopolitism," and in a vertical order of "time," communication among generations, and is called "tradition." Cosmopolitism represents the effort of intelligence to unify man spiritually, to place the principle of fundamental human unity above racial or class iniquities, to distribute equitably the material and spiritual benefits of culture, to make of this planet a more just and happier dwelling place for everybody. Tradition signifies the effort of the intelligence to unify itself, to establish the continuity of its action through time, to consolidate the new generations' enjoyments of its previous conquests. As a servant of intelligence, mother of culture, the intellectual, no matter from what country, has the duty of struggling to impose the cosmopolitan ideal, to improve relations among men. This duty is particularly pressing for the Latin American intellectual, since the progress of Latin America, its ascension to a universal level of culture, depend largely on its union, on its democratization, and on the wise use of the mixture of races and cultures which is now being realized throughout the world.

The natural vehicle to achieve this solution in our continent is that of the fundamental human values of its Latin and Hispanic tradition. These are the values—and not those of the aboriginal cultures—that constitute the real nucleus of its culture. From here it must start, then, to realize its destiny: the creation of a cosmic race, of a closer, happier, fairer New World.

Here, then, we have the expression of the social philosophy of Alfonso Reyes, a philosophy that we find in later books such as *Norte y Sur* (1944) and *Los trabajos y los días* (1945).

Finally, among his strictly literary works of later years, we must mention *Pasado inmediato* (1941), *El deslinde* (1944), *Letras de la Nueva España* (1948), *Grata compañía* (1948), *Trayectoria de Goethe* (1954).

El deslinde, a treatise on literary theory, is considered the masterpiece of Reyes. (pp. 5-7)

An extensive knowledge of Greek literature is evident in Reyes's basic books, *La crítica en la edad ateniense* (1941) and *La antigua retórica* (1943). His books of essays, *Junta de sombras,* also showed this preoccupation. Of real significance in this field are also *Panorama de la religión griega* (1948), *El horizonte económico en los albores de Grecia* (1950), and *En torno al estudio de la religión griega* (1951).

His main sources of inspiration for the first two works are the theories of Plato (Reyes is baffled by Plato's duality, his belief in the divine origin of poetry, and his disdain for the poet), and the theories of Aristotle. Reyes gives us a detailed biography of Aristotle and a condensation of his philosophy. Reyes was also familiar with the aesthetic ideas of the peripatetic school, especially of that of Theophrastus.

La antigua retórica is described by Reyes himself: "We devoted the second book to rhetoric, centering it on its great organizers—Aristotle, Cicero, and Quintilian—in order to free ourselves of the immense oratorical bulk, passing from Greece to Rome and coming close to the dawn of the Christian era."

El deslinde marks the most ambitious attempt to systematize literary theory: it is a philosophic and aesthetic study of literature. Reyes tries to establish a demarcation between literature and non-literature, in three sections: 1. Demarcation between pure literature and service literature; 2. A demarcation between history, science, and literature; and 3. A demarcation between mathematics, theology, and literature.

In a very penetrating study of Alfonso Reyes: (*Dos estudios sobre Alfonso Reyes,* 1962), the distinguished Swedish scholar, Ingemar Düring, says that the Mexican author is able to capture in his short stories old images and past experiences, with the vision of a great poet. According to him Reyes shows his capacity as a fiction writer when he sees the heroes of great literature—Achilles, Don Quixote, Hamlet, Peer Gynt—more real than many historical heroes. "Reyes has felt and lived with those heroes the highest form of poetry." Some of these heroes appear in imaginary conversations, in which we find a subtle joke on Landor and his singular conception of Greece. In these pages we perceive Reyes' *lentus risus,* his Horacian virtue of laughing somewhat ironically at himself. Through the light and spiritual dialogue we hear another voice, that of the philosopher and the critic: an intellectual game of the highest level.

There is, then, in this essayist a potential fiction writer. Greek mythology is for him a rich field where his imagination may frolic; the landscape of his native country tempts the descriptive capacity of his talent; the beings or ghosts that he carries in his subconscious are eager to become protagonists of his near-novels. Thus we see them in his *Quince presencias,* and in his poem *Los siete sobre Deva,* which is a prelude to a novel.

His favorite theory is that the landscape can serve as inspiration for the novelist and that in the memory of all human beings there are many elements of fiction. To bring these creatures into the artistic world is the role of the novelist. Therefore, Reyes is a very modern novelist. He does not deal with plots, dramatic developments, or narrations: he creates climates, he analyzes situations very much like a surrealist. It is for this reason that he speaks of his "arranques de novela" ("beginnings of a novel"), novels that are never completed, such as *El testimonio de Juan Peña* (1930).

A good "arranque de novela" is *Los dos augures.* Two Mexican émigrés meet in Paris and in a brief dialogue they tell of their past experiences and reveal their inner thoughts. One is a descendant of Spaniards; the other a half-breed. The two friends give promise of being the two main characters of a novel that never develops. A pity!—to judge by this beginning characterization: "Domingo was a courteous Mexican, discreet, patient, gentle, full of Mexican reserve. If he had not been good, Domingo would have furnished the best wood from which to carve the statue of a traitor . . . but he was good." Reyes gives a few more psychological touches to round out his character, and then he stops short. The reader is disappointed and frustrated. We have the protagonists, we know their reactions and their experiences, but nothing happens. The same is true of his *Arbol de pólvora* (1953), *Los siete sobre Deva* (1942); but he shows more structural ability in the surrealist short story **"La cena"** (1920) and in his short novel *Los tres tesoros* (1955).

Reyes is one of the most logical thinkers of his time. His exposition is clear and well balanced. Since he has said that the *word* is the essence of the extension of the poet's world, he is extremely careful in his use of words. His phrase is brief, synthetic, epigrammatic. He uses sometimes an elegant and perfect form, or a light, graceful expression, according to the subject matter. His language is rich and alive, strictly literary or robustly vernacular, classic, without disdain of the use of the Mexican idiom; in short he is the outstanding cultivator of the artistic style in modern Mexican literature. (pp. 8-10)

> *Arturo Torres-Rioseco, "Diogenes of Anáhuac," in* Mexico in a Nutshell and Other Essays *by Alfonso Reyes, translated by Charles Ramsdell, University of California Press, 1964, pp. 1-13.*

MARTIN S. STABB (essay date 1967)

[*Stabb is an American educator and critic specializing in Spanish-American literature. His works include* In Quest of Identity: Patterns in the Spanish American Essay of Ideas, 1890-1960, *in which he examines the use of the essay as a means of expressing the intellectual upheaval of a seventy-year period in Spanish-American history. In the following excerpt from that work, he evaluates Reyes's ideas on New World nativism, the polarity between city life and country life, and the synthesis of Old World and New World culture in America.*]

To attempt to isolate one theme—or even one cluster of related themes—in the work of Mexico's most prolific essayist [Alfonso Reyes] is no simple task. Some of Reyes' most penetrating views on broad matters of *novomundismo* are found in rather unlikely places, as in his *Discurso por Virgilio* (1933). True to the classical tradition, Reyes is quick to point out that man's social and individual nature show a remarkable constancy across vast realms of time and space. Thus, he can relate a plan of the Mexican government to develop local viniculture and cottage industries with similar motifs in Virgil's *Georgics.* It is in this essay on the Virgilian theme that Reyes expresses his own broad Americanist faith, born of a profound love for classic literature and for his native Mexico. The great literary works of the western European tradition—and especially those of Greece and Rome—are not "foreign" or "exotic" to the American scene, he tells us. Properly appreciated, they are means by which our own indigenous world can be better revealed: "I wish that the Humanities (be) the natural vehicle of expression for everything autochthonous." In the context of Mexico's vigorous but often superficial indigenism of the 1920's, Reyes' comments on the relationship between nativism and Old World culture were extremely timely. First of all he wisely observed that what is genuinely autochthonous will manifest itself in the work of a writer, painter, or thinker of its own accord. Since *lo autóctono* is part of the very make-up of the person one need not be deliberately "nativist": "this instinctive tendency (nativism) is so evident that to defend it with sophisms is to deprive it of its greatest virtue: its spontaneity." He then warns his countrymen not to deceive themselves, for although "the autochthonous element (is), in our America an enormous lode of raw material, of artifacts, of forms, of colors and sounds," only the barest fragments of the world of the pre-Columbian is known today. Therefore Reyes holds that any return to the primitivism of the Aztec would be unthinkable. By contrast, he stoutly maintains that "until now the only waters which have bathed us are . . . Latin waters." Though Reyes does not carry his metaphor any further, it is not unreasonable to view these "Latin waters" as the agent by which the gold of the autochthonous mineral lode is revealed in all its purity, washed clean of its dross. Reyes' view of what he calls "the hour of America" is decidedly ecumenical: he frequently states that the mission of the New World is to overcome the divisive effects of racism and of cultural jingoism. Support for such a program may be found, he notes, in Vasconcelos' vision of an amalgamated "Cosmic Race" and in Waldo Frank's deep humanistic faith.

In the *Discurso por Virgilio,* Reyes touches upon a theme which has figured prominently in a number of Spanish American essays—the city as opposed to the country. He finds the basic terms of this polarity to be quite simple: in the city the "social act" dominates, the fundamental relationship being that of man with man; while in the country the relationship involves man with the land. Reyes feels that human life, virtually by definition, is "a continuous reference to the natural ambience, an unending journey between man and external nature." City life, though not actually attacked, is viewed as a kind of artificial creation, a setting up of barriers against the natural order of man's life. Country life, particularly that of the modest, hardworking landholder, is seen as "The balsam (that) soothes the wounds of politics." More concretely, it is a means for the absorption of immigrants into the national life. Throughout Reyes' discussion of the city versus country theme, this Virgilian attitude toward the land dominates; it distinguishes his telluricism from that of many of his Spanish American contemporaries who view the "force of the land" in terms of the mystical, romantic adoration of nature's primal forces. In one of Reyes' earlier works, the beautifully wrought essay *Visión de Anáhuac* (1917), he notes that this more romanticized feeling toward nature may be justified in much of the New World, (in the jungle, for example) but that his own Mexican plateau is characterized by "sparse and stylized vegetation, an organized landscape, an atmosphere of extreme clarity. . . ." In short, he finds a distinctly "classic" spirit pervading the countryside of his beloved Anáhuac. Although it would be misleading to consider Reyes a believer in rigid geographic determinism—the very antithesis of the classically humanist view of nature—we have seen him speak of man's "continuous reference to the natural ambience." Thus, in the *Visión de Anáhuac* he suggests that there is a real link, disregarding all questions of blood, between the Mexican of today and the pre-Columbian Indian. This link exists since both peoples had the same natural environment with which to contend, and since "the everyday emotion produced by the same natural object" engenders a common spirit. As we have seen, substantially the same view was professed by Reyes' Argentine contemporary, Ricardo Rojas, and by Waldo Frank when he wrote of "the forming life of our land."

Reyes has developed his idea of what I have called the New Americanism in an impressive number of essays, historical studies, articles, and speeches. Two of these, **"Notas sobre la inteligencia Americana"** (1937) and **"Posición de América"** (1942), merit special attention in that they present Reyes' profoundest meditations on the important theme of the relationship of the Old World to the New. In a sense the second essay is a clarification of the first. In 1936 Reyes participated in a series of conferences, held in Buenos Aires under the auspices of the *Instituto Internacional de Cooperación Intelectual,* dealing with the theme "Present-day relations between European and Latin American cultures." George Duhamel initiated the meeting stating the European viewpoint; Reyes presented the first statement for Latin America. In the **"Posición de América"** he notes that this paper, **"Notas sobre la inteligencia Americana,"** was in part misunderstood by some of the distinguished Europeans present. Reyes spoke of an American cultural synthesis which would involve two elements: "a unique balance between our understanding of intellectual activity as public service and as cultural responsibility," and a fusion of autochthonous elements with the "intellectual instruments" of Europe. The product of such a synthesis would be, moreover, greater than the mere sum of its parts. At the Buenos Aires conference Reyes expressed the hope that this distinctive American culture would fulfill the utopian dream of a New World—a dream which formed part of Europe's literature and folklore even before Columbus' voyage. Referring to the Europeans' misunderstanding of his term "cultural synthesis" at this meeting, he states:

> Some of those present remained sadly convinced that we were trying to reduce the function of the American mind to the mere organizing of compendiums of European culture. Above all, we would not have recourse only to the European tradition, but to the entire human heritage. . . . Lastly, in this synthesis we do not envision a compendium or

resumé just as hydrogen and oxygen on combining in the form of water do not produce a mere sum of the parts but a new substance, possessing, as does any true synthesis, new powers and qualities.

In these two essays Reyes constantly emphasizes that the fulfillment of the American destiny is a responsibility to Europe ("If the European economy has come to have need of us, so ultimately will the European *inteligentsia* have need of us") or, in broader terms, a responsibility to humanity. Retaining the fervent activism of his early association with the *Ateneo de la Juventud* group, Reyes has been more concerned with the ability of the New World to meet this obligation than with the problem of "choosing" between universalism and nativism. As we have seen, for Reyes there is really no problem of a choice here. Whether he employs the metaphor of the "autochthonous mineral lode" noted previously, or the interesting analogy of culture and a series of concentric circles—as in the **"Posición de América"**—his message is clear: the Universal and the Particular have a complementary relationship; they "nourish" each other; and a society based solely on what he terms "alternatives and peculiarities" would be unthinkable, just as would be a purely "Universal" culture. A final note regarding Reyes' concept of the American cultural synthesis is in order. Several times in these essays he states that although he is restricting himself to Latin America, there are broad grounds for cultural fusion with Anglo-Saxon America: "We do not feel that one may speak seriously of unsurpassable barriers to cultural synthesis. . . ." At the conclusion of the **"Posición de América"** he looks upon the American synthesis in broad philosophical terms. Drawing from the rich thought of one of the Spanish American intellectuals' favorite sources, Max Scheler, Reyes notes that one of the great problems to be resolved before this synthesis may be achieved is that of reconciling three basic types of knowledge: the Hindu knowledge of salvation through psychic and bodily self-control; the wisdom (*saber culto*) of ancient Greece and China; and finally the scientific, practically motivated, knowledge of the western European tradition. Citing Scheler directly he notes, "the time has come to open the way towards an assimilation, and at the same time, towards an integration of these three partial tendencies of the human spirit." The "integration" called for by Scheler is precisely what Reyes would wish America to achieve. The continent, if it is to accomplish its mission, must not develop one of these types of knowledge at the expense of the others:

> Pure knowledge of salvation will convert us into prostrate peoples, into thin, mendicant friars; pure knowledge of culture, into sophists and mandarins; pure knowledge of technique, into scientific barbarians which, as we have seen, is the worst kind of barbarism. Only a balance of all these will insure our loyalty to heaven and earth. Such is the mission of America.

(pp. 82-6)

Martin S. Stabb, "America Rediscovered," in his In Quest of Identity: Patterns in the Spanish American Essay of Ideas, 1890-1960, *The University of North Carolina Press, 1967, pp. 58-101.*

ADDITIONAL BIBLIOGRAPHY

Aponte, Barbara Bockus. *Alfonso Reyes and Spain: His Dialogue with Unamuno, Valle-Inclán, Ortega y Gasset, Jiménez, and Gómez de la Serna.* Austin: University of Texas Press, 1972, 206 p.

  Introductory section provides background on Reyes in Spain between 1914 and 1924, including some biographical information and an exploration of his historical and cultural milieu. Aponte then examines Reyes's relationships and correspondence with five prominent Spanish intellectuals.

Manach, Jorge. "In Praise of the Other America." *The New York Times Book Review* (22 October 1950): 7, 25.

  Review of *The Position of America and Other Essays.* Manach praises Reyes's descriptive abilities and the insight he demonstrates in the historical and literary essays in the collection.

Peña, Carlos Gonzáles. "Our Own Days." In his *History of Mexican Literature.* Rev. ed., pp. 347-84. Translated by Gusta Barfield Nance and Florene Johnson Dunstan. Dallas: University Press, 1943.

  Briefly discusses Reyes's life and works, describing him as "the perfect model of humanism."

Petersen, Gerald W. "A Literary Parallel: 'La Cena' by Alfonso Reyes and *Aura* by Carlos Fuentes." *Romance Notes* 12, No. 1 (Autumn 1970): 41-44.

  Demonstrates that the two works "are strikingly similar with regard to characters, plot, motives, setting, and theme."

Robb, James Willis. *Patterns of Image and Structure in the Essays of Alfonso Reyes.* Washington, D.C.: Catholic University of America Press, 1958, 92 p.

  Contends that the prose style of Reyes's essays can be analyzed in the same way as that of creative writing and explores certain elements of his style. Robb argues that idea and form are closely related in Reyes's essays, resulting in "a near-perfect fusion of the essay of ideas and the essay of artistic illumination." He concludes that Reyes brought "to new heights of development the varied potentialities of the flexible essay form."

————. "Alfonso Reyes." *America* 18, No. 4 (April 1966): 17-23.

  Examines Reyes's complex personality and extensive contribution to world literature "through the evocation of six great moments or phases in his career, using as guidelines the geographical chronology of his life."

Stabb, Martin S. "Utopia and Anti-Utopia: The Theme in Selected Essayistic Writings of Spanish America." *Revista de estudios hispanicos* 15, No. 3 (October 1981): 377-93.

  Suggests that Reyes was at times "an ardent propagandist of the view that the defining characteristic of the New World is that in European eyes it was a promised land."

Starkie, Walter. "A Memoir of Alfonso Reyes." *The Texas Quarterly* II, No. 1 (Spring 1959): 67-77.

  Presents a chronology of Reyes's life and selected works, including personal reflections on Starkie's relationship with Reyes.

Joseph Roth

1894-1939

Austrian novelist, essayist, and journalist.

Roth is best known as a chronicler of the declining years of the Austro-Hungarian Empire. While in his early novels he explored the social and political upheavals of post–World War I Europe, later in his life, in self-imposed exile from Nazi rule and bereft of a homeland, he became profoundly dissatisfied with the present and pessimistic about the future. Writing from what he termed "a cultural, a spiritual, a religious, a metaphysical" sense of loss, Roth turned to nostalgic historical novels that resurrected and glorified the reign of Austro-Hungarian emperor Franz Joseph von Hapsburg. These novels, most prominently *Radetzkymarsch* (*Radetzky March*), have earned him a reputation among many critics as an apologist for the monarchy; some commentators, however, reject this notion, maintaining that Roth's fascination with the fallen empire was symptomatic of the exile state imposed on many of Roth's generation and reflects the universal need for a homeland. As Celine Mathew has written, "The feeling of homelessness and the longing for an intellectual and spiritual home from where he could face life with a sense of security and certainty—these two motifs run through the whole work of Roth."

Throughout his life Roth gave varying accounts of his place of birth, his parentage, and his personal history. It is fairly certain, however, that he was born in the village of Brody in eastern Galicia, then part of Austria-Hungary and now within the Ukrainian Socialist Republic of the USSR. His father became mentally ill and was institutionalized before Roth's birth, and Roth was raised by his mother and by relatives. Although Roth attributed several different nationalities and occupations to the father he never knew, biographers maintain that he was, like Roth's mother, a middle-class Galician Jew. In 1913 Roth entered the University of Vienna, where he studied German literature and philology, philosophy, and musicology. By concealing his Jewish heritage he obtained a post tutoring the children of a Viennese family of the old nobility, from whom, as Philip Manger has explained, "he gained an insight into the refinement and elegance of manners to which he secretly aspired and which he emulated in later years."

Although initially espousing pacifism, Roth joined the Austrian Army during the First World War. He served as an enlisted man whose primary duties were preparing dispatches and writing for military publications, but later claimed that he was an officer and a prisoner of war. Following the war Roth lacked the financial means to return to the university and began working for Viennese newspapers, becoming a leading writer of feuilletons, book and film reviews, political and social criticism, biographical sketches, and travel essays. In 1920 he moved to Berlin and continued to work as a journalist, his socialist sympathies earning him frequent publication in the leftist newspaper *Frankfurter Zeitung*. Roth's first novel, *Das Spinnennetz*, was serialized in the newspaper *Arbeiterzeitung* in 1923, and another novel, *Hotel Savoy*, was published the following year. For the next decade Roth traveled widely as a newspaper correspondent while publishing

a half-dozen novels which received little critical or popular notice.

In 1933 Roth emigrated to Paris to escape Adolf Hitler's rise to power. He traveled restlessly for the next six years and during this period considered a conversion to Roman Catholicism, an inclination that is reflected his later novels. It is thought that Roth's observations of conditions in the Soviet Union during his travels led him to reexamine the political liberalism that marked his early works. His essays and letters from this time reflect a pervasive and growing skepticism, not only with most existing social and political systems but also with the range of proffered solutions. Roth's novels of the 1930s manifest his search for meaning and purpose in traditional systems of belief and in the past, while in several periodical articles he proposed the improbable restoration of the monarchy as a means of protecting the German Weimar Republic from the threat of nazism. Roth died in 1939, shortly after receiving the news that a friend, the dramatist Ernst Toller, had committed suicide. While some biographers believe that Roth committed suicide as the result of his grief, others attribute his death to his alcoholism and chronic poor health.

Roth's early novels display the fictional techniques of *Neue Sachlichkeit* ("new objectivity"), a school of writing that advocated documentary realism as a reaction against the symbolic literary style of German Expressionism. These novels—including *Das Spinnennetz, Hotel Savoy, Die Rebellion, Die Flucht ohne Ende (Flight without End), Zipper und sein Vater,* and *Rechts und Links*—deal with topical social and political issues, including the plight of veterans of the First World War who find it difficult to resume normal lives in a rapidly changing, decadent postwar society bereft of the traditional values for which they fought. Several of these novels are narrated from the viewpoint of a young social rebel or political revolutionary, and most exhibit Roth's own leftist political sympathies.

With *Hiob: Roman eines einfachen Mannes (Job: The Story of a Simple Man)*, Roth broke decisively with both the style and substance of his earlier works, abandoning the realism of *Neue Sachlichkeit* and topical subjects in favor of poetic imagination and religious or historical subjects. Set against the background of Jewish life in Eastern Europe, *Job* is a modern retelling of the biblical story of tested and ultimately strengthened faith. Despite a conventional "happy ending," the novel is considered moving and effective. The posthumously published *Die Geschichte von der 1002. Nacht* similarly borrows from an existing narrative, in this instance the *Arabian Nights,* to give structure to an account of decadence and retribution in late nineteenth-century Vienna. *Die hundert Tage (The Ballad of the Hundred Days)* combines a historical account of Napoleon's return from banishment and final defeat at Waterloo with a lyrical story of a servant's devotion to the emperor. Other novels of this period, including *Tarabas: Ein Gast auf dieser Erd (Tarabas: A Guest on Earth), Beichte eines Mörders (Confessions of a Murderer),* and *Das falsche Gewicht,* reveal a preoccupation with religious, particularly Christian, themes, such as the struggle between good and evil and the virtue of penance. These novels also display a tendency to view the last days of the Austro-Hungarian empire of Franz Joseph as a lost ideal.

Roth's nostalgic idealization of Emperor Franz Joseph's rule received its clearest expression in *Radetzky March* and its sequel, *Die Kapuzinergruft (The Emperor's Tomb).* With *Radetzky March* Roth, in the words of Philip Manger, "turned his attention for the first time to the vanished world whose collapse he had witnessed, almost as if he wished to ascertain, by analyzing and describing that world, what values had been lost and why." The narrative advances a family saga through three generations, from a soldier of peasant origins whose heroic actions on the battlefield win his elevation to the nobility, to his grandson, an effete product of a decadent society. The family's decline parallels that of the monarchy and of Austrian society, and Manger has written that the novel "retrospectively portrays the historical 'inevitability' of social decay and decadence." *The Emperor's Tomb* treats a similar theme, in this case attributing the fall of the monarchy to pan-German nationalism. This novel is considered far less successful than *Radetzky March* in blending history and political theory into the narrative.

Much of the critical commentary on Roth focuses on the shift in his works from political liberalism to apparent reaction, with many critics decrying his later works as nostalgic escapism. This view has been disputed by critics who contend that Roth did not idealize the Austro-Hungarian Empire but rather was its epic narrator, as well as by critics who maintain that through allegory, parallel, and allusion, Roth did address timely concerns even in his historical novels. Although

Roth was uncompromising in his opposition to such modern evils as nazism, critics observe that positive alternatives are absent in his works. As Celine Mathew has written, "If we . . . ask ourselves what according to Roth is humane, good, or ideal, no clear answer emerges. . . . Roth consistently rejects the values of his age and at the same time is completely at a loss to find new values to replace them." Nevertheless, Roth's works have been highly praised for expressing the sense of rootlessness and disillusionment that pervaded much of post-World War I European society.

PRINCIPAL WORKS

*Das Spinnennetz   (novel)   1923; published in the newspaper *Arbeiterzeitung*
Hotel Savoy   (novel)   1924
  [*Hotel Savoy,* published in the collection *Hotel Savoy,* 1986]
Die Rebellion   (novel)   1924
Der blinde Spiegel   (novella)   1925
Die Flucht ohne Ende   (novel)   1927
  [*Flight without End,* 1930]
Juden auf Wanderschaft   (essays)   1927
Zipper und sein Vater   (novel)   1928
Rechts und Links   (novel)   1929
Hiob: Roman eines einfachen Mannes   (novel)   1930
  [*Job: The Story of a Simple Man,* 1931]
Panoptikum: Gestalten und Kulissen   (essays and journalism)   1930
Radetzkymarsch   (novel)   1932
  [*Radetzky March,* 1933]
Der Antichrist   (essays)   1934
  [*Antichrist,* 1935]
Tarabas: Ein Gast auf dieser Erd   (novel)   1934
  [*Tarabas: A Guest on Earth,* 1934]
Beichte eines Mörders   (novel)   1936
  [*Confessions of a Murderer,* 1938]
Die hundert Tage   (novel)   1936
  [*The Ballad of the Hundred Days,* 1936; also published as *The Story of the Hundred Days,* 1936]
Das falsche Gewicht   (novel)   1937
  [*Weights and Measures,* 1982]
Die Kapuzinergruft   (novel)   1938
  [*The Emperor's Tomb,* 1984]
Die Geschichte von der 1002. Nacht   (novel)   1939
Die Legende vom heiligen Trinker   (novellas)   1939
Werke.   3 vols.   (novels, novellas, essays, and journalism)   1956
†*Der stumme Prophet*   (novel)   1965
  [*The Silent Prophet,* 1979]
Die Legende vom heiligen Trinker, und andere Erzählungen   (novellas)   1968
Briefe 1911-1939   (letters)   1970
Der neue Tag: Unbekannte politische Arbeiten 1919 bis 1927—Wien, Berlin, Moskau   (essays)   1970
Meistererzählungen   (novellas)   1973
Werke.   4 vols.   (novels, novellas, essays, and journalism)   1975-76
Berliner Saisonbericht: Unbekannte Reportagen und journalistische Arbeiten, 1920-39   (journalism)   1984
Hotel Savoy   (novel and novellas)   1986

*This novel was first published in book form in 1967.

†This work was written in 1929.

THE TIMES LITERARY SUPPLEMENT   (essay date 1930)

[*In the following review,* Flight without End *is assessed as an interesting if inconclusive narrative.*]

This rather curious novel [**Flight without End**] relates the post-War experiences of a young Austrian officer, but it is not an easy matter to decide exactly what prompted the author to write it. The book has two main aspects: one, the description of life in Moscow, Berlin and Vienna just after the War; two, the account of Lieutenant Franz Tunda's personal adventures. The publishers have no hesitation in stressing the first, but there is a short chapter towards the middle of the book which gives perhaps a better indication of the author's intentions. This occurs after Franz has spent eighteen months as a member of the Soviet Republic, has had a tempestuous love-affair with a female soldier and married, perhaps because of the contrast, an unusually silent girl, the niece of a dull-witted potter, and finally returned to Vienna, his birthplace. In this chapter the author, discussing the reason why Franz left Russia, says that "he had more vitality than the Revolution could make use of at the moment . . . more independence than could be employed by a theory that was trying to adapt itself to life." If it was the author's aim to demonstrate the effect of the Russian experiment on the individual character, he cannot be said to have succeeded to any marked extent, for right from the beginning of the book Franz seems as undependable, as aimless and as generally lacking in character as at the end. Considered merely as a narrative, however, the tale is interesting; it is written with vivacity and contains some pleasing imaginative touches.

> *A review of "Flight without End," in* The Times Literary Supplement, *No. 1490, August 21, 1930, p. 670.*

MALCOLM COWLEY   (essay date 1933)

[*Cowley has made several valuable contributions to contemporary letters with his editions of important American authors (Nathaniel Hawthorne, Walt Whitman, Ernest Hemingway, William Faulkner, F. Scott Fitzgerald), his writings as a literary critic for the* New Republic, *and above all his chronicles and criticism of modern American literature. The following excerpt is taken from his favorable review of* Radetzky March.]

[**Radetzky March**] deals with the Austrian Empire in the years preceding the War. It is a long, unhurried novel divided into massive chapters, a classic structure built soundly of polished blocks. The translation, too, is smooth and workmanlike and effectively renders the author's mood of gentle melancholy and regret for the past. Joseph Roth has chosen to embody the greatness and decline of the Austrian Empire in two members of the Trotta family, the son and the grandson of the first heroic Baron von Trotta und Sipolje. Franz, the son, is an Austrian official, side-whiskered, single-minded, walking uprightly in elastic-sided boots like the old Emperor himself. Carl Joseph, the grandson, is an army lieutenant who becomes demoralized by garrison life and decays as the Empire decays.

Toward the end of the novel occurs a splendid and terrible chapter telling how the news of Francis Ferdinand's death at Serajevo reached the frontier garrison where the young lieutenant was stationed. It was Sunday and the Hussars were holding a regimental ball on the estate of a Polish count, with nobles present from every corner of the Empire. A storm broke, and with it came the news. The company fell apart into quarreling groups, some wishing to continue the ball, some to end it, the Hungarians saying in their own language that the dead heir to the Imperial and Royal throne deserved his fate, was only a swine—and Lieutenant Baron Carl Joseph von Trotta und Sipolje, the one loyal soldier present, insults them all and resigns his commission, while two drunken bands play the Funeral March out of tune and rain beats on the windows and the servants go about collecting the half-empty champagne glasses from the hands of the guests. Six months later, Carl Joseph and most of his fellow officers would be dead for an Empire in which they had ceased to believe. (p. 172)

> *Malcolm Cowley, "Panorama," in* The New Republic, *Vol. LXXVII, No. 994, December 20, 1933, pp. 172-73.*

R. P. BLACKMUR   (essay date 1934)

[*Blackmur was a prominent American literary critic whose writings combine close textual analysis with an examination of a work's social relevance. In the following essay, he assesses the novel* Tarabas *as a "barbarous fable" promoting escape from rationality.*]

Tarabas reflects, I think, a prevalent mode of the European imagination, a plague rather than a mode, visited upon it by the war and the disintegration of society. It is thus not alone. It follows and accentuates its author's earlier **Job.** It is in line with such novels as Kallinikov's *Women and Monks* and Robert Neumann's *Flood,* and is twin brother to Céline's *Journey to the End of the Night.* It represents with these, particularly, the corruption of the novel as the chief form of rational art, and, generally, the resumption of barbarism as the standard of life as well as the motive of politics. As Ortega y Gasset pointed out in *The Modern Theme,* it is the natural consequence of the inability to preserve the dichotomy or balance of the spiritual and the rational. To the weakened or personalized imagination which must depend upon itself, it provides the nearest escape; which is why, in the books named and all their analogues, the process seems fascinating and profound even when it is most revolting.

The theme, if not the right one, is attractive. Roth has made of his book a warm and exciting fable of the purgation of a violent soul. The sins of arrogance, lust, and murder, committed by the prescription of a gipsy fortune-teller, which is to say, committed by fatality and in innocence, are atoned for, also by prescription, in the wilful humiliation of beggary and disease. Colonel Tarabas, soldier, the victim of these prescriptions, is a murderer and a saint, and therefore a guest on earth. The moral of the fable is, I suppose, that barbarous one which lingers in the human blood: only the excessive, the extravagant, the violent soul can reach salvation, and the particular holiness of salvation will be an excessive violence in reverse. Or at least the spectacle of such salvation is presented as the great exemplar. The young man who will not weep, said Santayana, the old man who will not laugh, are barbarians. Tarabas never wept in his youth, and his premature old age was a beggary of tears.

Besides its warmth and excitement, which make it readable and speciously persuasive, the fable of Tarabas has an essential quality of simple-mindedness. The agency of incident and the source of meaning are in superstition, and, a very different thing, the fable has a kind of center in the supernatural. These are the easiest resources of the deracinated imagination, the imagination which for one reason or another cannot be content with the life before it. For example, Tarabas is governed by what the fortune-teller said and by such things as the sight of a red-headed Jew; and the crisis of his life is brought out by an accidental miracle: the debauchery of his soldiers lays bare an image of the Virgin. Thus the superstitious elements in his life are brought to fruition in terms of the supernatural, and indeed superstition is seen as the overt sign of the workings of God.

Now it is possible—and we have the great recent example of Thomas Mann's *Joseph and His Brothers*—to represent a life so actuated and so understood by its protagonists in a rational manner. Then we have a novel, something which judges life by the mere fidelity and understanding, the honesty, so to speak, of the mirror the artist uses. The great novels are all of this order, and make no surrender to the barbarousness, the irrationality, the formlessness of their subjects; they make use of the full resources of the novelist's mind. Works like **Tarabas** make immediately every possible surrender; there is no point of view separate from the subject—the saving irony—but a rash uniting with it. The credibility of the book depends on the credulous omniscience of the characters within it, and, as in a fairy tale, there is no labor of representation. Everything is taken on trust and instinct because there is no other way of taking it; which is what was meant by calling the particular example simple-minded. The result is not a novel in the sense above, but a barbarous fable acting in its place. In the novel the normal is made to seem unusual by the strength and completeness of the imagination; but in works of this order the unusual, the extravagant, and the violent are taken, at their face or superstitious value, as the only source and measure of the normal. The effect is exciting and warm with the large emotions of terror and passion and woe, and the effect seems ultimate because it is immediate. But for readers whose imagination retains any mark of the rational mold, it can only seem the true literature of escape, a retreat into darkness.

> *R. P. Blackmur, "Sauve-qui-peut," in* The Nation, *New York, Vol. CXXXIX, No. 3624, December 19, 1934, p. 717.*

WARD H. POWELL   (essay date 1961)

[*In the following excerpt, Powell argues that the nostalgic tenor of Roth's later works is not the result of an ideological conversion to monarchism but rather of an attitude of "ironic primitivism"—a longing for an idealized past in full knowledge that it is illusory.*]

When Joseph Roth first began to attract attention as a novelist, he was considered a relentless and devastating social critic bent on clearing the way for a new order of things to come. (p. 115)

Yet in 1949, the tenth anniversary of Roth's death, Benno Reifenberg characterized the author of the later novels as a

weaver of wondrous tales who, in moments of near transport, succeeded in materializing strange and colorful visions before the eyes of an enraptured, childlike audience. . . . A sharper contrast is hard to imagine, and even though a whole generation has now passed since Roth's death, the random criticism has still not succeeded in reconciling fully the apparent contradictions between his early and his later works.

It would be difficult enough to ground such disparate views . . . in the life of a man who had lived out his allotted span of years and gradually yet persistently altered his course over a whole lifetime until it finally lay at the full 180 degrees. One need only consider for a moment the delving and the divining that have gone into tracing the various stages in the transformation of the *Himmelstürmer* Goethe into the quietistic sage of the final scenes of *Faust II*. But in the case of Joseph Roth this kind of approach is not even possible. There was no gradual and consistent development, no slow, organic growth. He died before he was 45 and wrote all thirteen of his novels within fifteen years. Any attempt at reconciling his early and his later works must be undertaken from a different quarter. It cannot rely on the usual processes of aging and mellowing.

Critics have generally recognized that **Hiob** (1930) marks a clear break in Roth's works, and that the five novels which preceded it . . . show marked liberal, and even leftist tendencies. The last eight novels, by contrast, are usually considered rightist or even monarchistic. The first group deal primarily with the immediate problems of the generation who experienced and survived World War I. The later novels are mainly concerned with the benefactions which men enjoyed under the reign of Franz Joseph, or with the spiritual strength which simple people found in the pious life of small Chasidic communities on the periphery of the old Dual Monarchy. Hence, it is not difficult to see why Roth has been called a sceptic and a believer, a *revolteur* and a reactionary.. . . . (pp. 115-16)

Of all the fluctuating patterns in human thought—both in the "great world" of cultural epochs as well as the "small world" of individual lives—no pattern seems more persistent than the alternation between an optimistic belief in the future and a pessimistic desire to return to the past. The forward-looking attitude has long since been analyzed and cataloged, for it has been predominant in the western world from the Renaissance down through the Enlightenment. It reached its peak with the belief in the perfectibility of man. The backward-looking attitude is probably just as venerable as its counterpart— many cultures seem to have sprung out of a belief in a lost Golden Age or a squandered Paradise—but until recently it had not been given so much analytical attention. By now, however, it has been painstakingly analyzed and has come to be called "primitivism." (p. 118)

In view of the apparently insoluble political, social, and economic problems which threatened in 1930, it would not have been surprising if Roth had quite suddenly despaired of achieving new values and had begun to advocate a return to those of a nostalgia-colored past. Others, like Thoreau and Tolstoi, had done it before him. But in Roth's case, this explanation . . . falls short of explaining the facts, for even though he turned to the past and its relative simplicity, he did not surrender himself to it in the belief that a return would be possible, or even wholly desirable.

Roth's attitude toward the past is revealed in his later novels as a complex and highly subjective one, one which owes much to the pervasive influence of Nietzsche. *Die Geburt der Tragödie aus dem Geiste der Musik* had dispelled the notion that art is sublime truth revealed through inspiration and had suggested, instead, that it is an illusion which the will spreads out over reality in order to make life bearable. In Nietzsche's view art becomes simply another means, albeit a subtle one, by which life itself, the vital process, seeks to insure that its creatures will go on living in spite of their fears and miseries. In much the same way, Roth's primitivism reveals itself to be an illusion which the will spreads out over the complexity and the hopelessness of the present. It distinguishes itself from the primitivism of a Thoreau or a Tolstoi by the full awareness that it is illusory, or in other words, by its irony. The satisfaction to be derived from it is admittedly based on deceptive suggestion, but by 1930 Roth seemed to believe that illusion was preferable to utter despair. He knew full well that a return to the past was impossible, but he refused to deny himself the solace to be had from contemplating its simplicity. Like Queequeg in an open boat at the height of a typhoon, "there, then, he sat, the sign and symbol of a man without faith, hopelessly holding up hope in the midst of despair."

The best-known of the later novels, *Radetzkymarsch* (1932), is well suited for illustrating Roth's ironic primitivism. It traces the fortunes of the Trotta family from the day in 1859 when the first Trotta saved the life of Emperor Franz Joseph at the Battle of Solferino until the day in 1916 when the Emperor was entombed in the *Kapuzinergruft*. Throughout the nearly sixty years between, time enough for three generations of ordinary men to come and go, the figure of the Emperor stands as if to mark the passing of time and to record the measure of events. He is made quite believable as a historical figure, but he remains primarily a symbol of such traditional values as benevolence, charity, compassion, and especially, human dignity. In the beginning he is a real and vital force active in the lives of all his subjects, just as the values for which he stands are real and vital. By the dark days of World War I, however, both the Emperor and what he symbolizes have faded into dim outlines no longer discernible except to a few. Two brief incidents will suggest the thematic development by showing how the first and the last of the Trottas served the cause of the Emperor in turn.

Joseph, the first of the line and not far removed from his family's peasant origins, was a young lieutenant who loved the Emperor more dearly than life itself. At Solferino he was in command of that sector of the line to which two officers of the General Staff brought the equally young Franz Joseph. When the Emperor unwittingly raised a pair of field glasses to his eyes and thus called attention to himself as a target worthy of the enemy's fire, Trotta was seized with terror. . . . Without reflecting for a moment, he seized the Emperor, pulled him to the ground, and caught the enemy bullet in his own shoulder. Trotta had sensed immediately what was demanded of him and was able, of his own accord, to avert the destruction not only of himself, but also of the regiment, the army, the state, and the whole world. The Emperor, in his turn, automatically refused to shirk his responsibility to so loyal a subject. Though the officers of the General Staff urged him to leave the area at once, he did not go until he had learned the young officer's name and arranged for his care. Thus the relationship between the first Trotta and his Emperor was wholly spontaneous and mutually advanta-

geous, a relationship which engaged them both in purposeful and dedicated endeavor.

The last of the Trottas, Carl Joseph, lived out his life in the shadow of his famous grandfather. He had never been able to overcome his awkwardness in the saddle nor his dislike for military life, but it was taken for granted from the beginning that he would become a cavalry officer. His one chance to enlist himself in the cause of the Emperor came shortly before World War I when his regiment was about to leave Vienna for the eastern border. During a somewhat rowdy celebration, his fellow officers insisted that he come along to the dimly lighted and highly perfumed establishment of Frau Resi Horvath. Since Carl Joseph could find no delight in the visit, he walked restlessly about the parlor. Suddenly he stopped. There on the mantel, in a small bronze frame, he saw a fly-specked miniature of the Supreme Commander. It was as if Frau Resi were suggesting that even the Emperor in his dazzling white uniform with the red sash and the Golden Fleece could be counted among her patrons. [Enraged, Carl Joseph took the miniature and left the establishment.] (pp. 118-20)

The last of the Trottas was fully aware that this rescue of the Emperor was only a gesture, and a sentimental one at that. It was, in fact, no rescue at all, only the illusion of one. The course of real events would not be turned by it; the aged monarch in Schönbrunn would not even know of it. But especially because Carl Joseph was the grandson of the Hero of Solferino, he could not fail to make the gesture. The Emperor had become doddering and doting; Carl Joseph would soon meet an early and ignominious death, felled by a sniper as he fetched a bucket of water. Yet so long as the Emperor still moved about behind the golden draperies in his hushed palace, and so long as even one inept officer named Trotta was left to serve him, there would still remain a memory of what human dignity meant. The memory would not ward off the fate which awaited both the Emperor and the last of the Trottas, but was there anything which could?

When Roth's later novels are assessed as the works of an ironic primitivist rather than the tracts of a convert and latter-day monarchist, it is no longer difficult to resolve the apparent contradictions which have been so bothersome to critics. To say that within a literary career spanning only fifteen years he turned from a sceptic to a believer, from a *revolteur* to a reactionary, is an over-simplification and misinterpretation. In the beginning he was a liberal, forward-looking critic of his times who could believe in the possibility of something better to come. At the end of his career he was a man completely disabused of his faith in the future, but one who nonetheless refused to admit the fact openly, baldly, and with finality. In some respects he resembled a person who suffers from an incurable disease and resigns himself to a palliative in order to ease the suffering and to salvage anything at all from the days which remain. Roth's disease was despair; the palliative was ironic primitivism; and what he ultimately salvaged was his own artistic being.

A proper evaluation of the later novels is important in itself, and it may also be important in pointing one of the ways which writers took through the catastrophic events of the late twenties and the thirties. Some of the more liberal among Roth's friends and acquaintances found his attitude capricious at the time, if not ridiculous, and thought he had escaped from reality into a realm which could have meaning only for himself. From the vantage of the present, however, it becomes clear that there were other writers of stature who adopted a similar attitude. At the close of his address to the International Congress of Writers in Paris in 1935, E. M. Forster declared his position in words which Roth would certainly have understood and approved.

> I am worried by thoughts of a war oftener than by thoughts of my own death, yet the line to be adopted over both these nuisances is the same. One must behave as if one is immortal, and as if civilization is eternal. Both statements are false—I shall not survive, no more will the great globe itself—both of them must be assumed to be true if we are to go on eating and working and travelling, and keep open a few breathing holes for the human spirit.
>
> (pp. 121-22)

Ward H. Powell, "Joseph Roth, Ironic Primitivist," in Monatshefte, *Vol. LIII, No. 3, March, 1961, pp. 115-22.*

ELIE WIESEL   (essay date 1974)

[*A Rumanian-born man of letters, Wiesel is best known for his writings on the German Holocaust, for which he was awarded the Nobel Peace Prize in 1986. His stories and essays treating Jewish concerns have also earned him a reputation as an eloquent spokesman for contemporary Judaism. In the following review, he discusses* Radetzky March *as both a timely and prophetic account of the decay of a civilization.*]

Unlike most theologians, some novelists believe that the world could end more than once—it ends whenever and wherever men and nations slaughter one another—and Joseph Roth explores this belief better than most.

On the surface, [*Radetzky March*] tells three tales about three men. The first saves the Emperor, the second represents him, the third gives his life for him. Three generations, three destinies. The first wins titles of nobility, the second bears them gladly, the third finds them cumbersome. Together they form the Trotta dynasty, the youngest and most short-lived within the apostolic empire of the Hapsburgs, whose demise coincides with its own. The disintegration and eventual extinction of a family symbolizes the decline of an era and the collapse of traditional order—which belong to Joseph Roth's favorite themes and preoccupations. . . .

Most of Roth's work—some of which was discovered after the war—is haunted by apocalyptic fears. His protagonists are forever waiting for the tempest to sweep them away. The mood is deceptively peaceful and gay: military parades, outdoor concerts, chess games.

Strange, but this Jewish refugee who endured shame and hunger in exile from Nazism, was more fascinated by the forces that dismantled outdated social structures than by the misfortunes that befell his brethren—by Emperor Franz Joseph more than by Adolf Hitler.

Like his other novels, *Radetzky March* is set in Austria, at the turn of the century, "when it had not yet become a matter of indifference whether a man lived or died." First published in 1932, it enjoyed but a fleeting success. In terms of content though not technique, the author was ahead of his times, so that he is more likely to be understood today; and disturb more readers more deeply than he did then. Today we realize that Jean Cocteau was right: whatever is written eventually

happens. Fiction contains an element of prophecy. Joseph Roth foresaw the total and totalitarian catastrophe that occurred after he died.

This then is a nostalgic and poignant novel that will be read breathlessly. It has an atmosphere of its own, a tone, a voice. The plot—the decay of a civilization—is less important than the heroes who appear as anti-heroes; reserved, discreet, unassuming. They are defeated from the start by some nameless malediction. They live in the back country, cut off from the mainstream, outside history. Their hopes and ambitions are limited to their needs. Winners or losers, their stakes are too small for them to be anything but extras on a make-believe stage.

Of the three Trottas, which moves us most deeply? They all do equally—each in his own way. The first Baron von Trotta, whose passion is truth, is up in arms because of some imaginary heroics attributed to him in a history book for children, and goes so far as to disturb the Emperor to set matters straight. His son, the second baron, leads a gray, monotonous life as district governor; his only talent is his capacity for friendship. His grandson, the third baron, tragically at odds with himself and the role he is expected to play, seeks redemption in drink, gambling, impossible love affairs and finally self-sacrifice. His end marks the end of a line, the end of a story.

Who then is the hero of this novel? The Radetzky March that accompanies the Trottas, and the monarchy, to their very death? The war that merely substitutes dates, 1859, 1914, and victims but never alters its nature or aim? Time gnawing at life, or death itself which here as everywhere, and forever, manipulates human beings by revealing or hiding its face? No, its real hero is man pitted against himself; the novel is but a powerful statement of humanism.

Roth is particularly fond of his secondary characters who emerge but for one episode, one encounter, long enough for a smile, a word, a handshake; the tale has attracted them but cannot hold them back.

Physicians and sages, silent peasants and turbulent revolutionaries, shady innkeepers and drunken artists, neglected wives eager to seduce young students and elegant officers, colorful Jews and their jaded customers—we watch them soar, alive with passions and memories about messianic ideals in political disguise, we witness their clashes. Some live by their faith in the Emperor, others by their hate of what he symbolizes. Some manage to derive some measure of happiness, most don't. They have no way of knowing that all their joys and sorrows, all their public struggles and private triumphs are soon to be drowned out by the cannons' deafening roar.

Melancholy characters, losers all; victims—each other's and the war's. Of all of his feelings, man's awareness of his own desperate condition is the most powerful; his is a universe doomed to change and destruction. In the final analysis, he is unable to help another. At the frontline, the last of the Trottas falls, unable to comfort his soldiers. And his father, far away, finally accepts that life is made of partings and remorse as much as of desire.

Yes, it is a disturbing message that Joseph Roth has left us. Not only does it evoke sounds and images of his native land and past, a past of ashes, it also foreshadows the curse of times to come; ours.

Elie Wiesel, "The Lives of Three Trottas," in The New York Times Book Review, *November 3, 1974,* p. 70.

C. E. WILLIAMS (essay date 1974)

[*Williams is the author of* The Broken Eagle: The Politics of Austrian Literature from Empire to Anschluss. *In the following excerpt from that study, Williams traces the development of Roth's political attitudes as evidenced in his writings.*]

Joseph Roth is best remembered as the chronicler *par excellence* of the Habsburg Monarchy. . . . When he died in a Paris hospital in 1939 at the age of forty-five, a descendant of the House of Habsburg ordered a wreath to be placed on his grave. Yet Roth's first novel appeared in the *Arbeiterzeitung,* the organ of the Viennese Social Democrats, and his early journalistic pieces were explicitly anti-monarchist and anti-clerical. It is this change of attitude which supplies my theme—the nature and circumstances of his commitment to monarchism and its influence on his fiction. (p. 91)

The major part of Roth's early writing was concerned with the difficulty of reorientation in the postwar world. He viewed the civilisation of the twenties from various perspectives and found it wanting. In several novels Roth described the plight of the "lost generation," the *Heimkehrer* (returning soldier) without a home, the revolutionary without a faith. Again and again, in stories and essays, Roth attacked a world built upon the sand of the Paris peace settlements and the inflation. His heroes are haunted by a sense of rootlessness and disillusionment. His writing at this time explored certain themes common to his Austrian contemporaries Hans von Chlumberg, Theodor Kramer and Ödön von Horváth. In the novels of the first postwar decade Roth's protagonists are typically (though not exclusively) *hommes de bonne volonté* ["men of good will"] caught in an impossible historical situation.

His first novel *Das Spinnennetz* (1923) takes a topical problem as its theme: the difficulties experienced by an ex-officer in the German Army in adjusting to peacetime conditions. The protagonist longs for a return to the simplicity, contentment and sense of self-importance that he enjoyed during his wartime career. In civilian clothes Lohse is an obscure failure who is driven by his personal inadequacies, his frustration and resentment to join an organisation of right-wing extremists, pledged to destroy socialism, the Jews and the Republic. In other words he is "representative" of hundreds of such restless, disinherited ex-servicemen who fought in the *Freikorps* campaigns against Communists and Slav nationalists in the first years of Weimar, or who joined the "Black Reichswehr" and various other clandestine, anti-republican military formations. For all its modish "telegraphese" and wooden characterisation, the book provides a perceptive analysis of the growth of a fascist mentality. As we follow Lohse's career from betrayal and intrigue, through the first acts of violence and suppression of a workers' demonstration, to murder, we glimpse in the background a wholly corrupt Germany and a Europe ravaged by economic exploitation and political terrorism. (Two days after the last instalment of the novel appeared in the *Arbeiterzeitung,* Hitler launched the Munich putsch.) The narrative is imbued with an impressive detachment: Roth conveys his compassion for the victims of violence and unbridled capitalism without becoming overtly tendentious.

However, Roth was concerned less with nationalists smarting under political indignities, or with militarists unable to adjust to civilian life, than with the hapless, drifting victims of the European upheaval. Whereas his attitude towards Lohse is fairly objective, his portrait of Gabriel Dan, the hero of *Hotel Savoy* (1924), is unmistakably sympathetic. Gabriel, returning from the War, rests for a time in a small Polish town. As his insight into the functioning of the grandiloquently named hotel and the capitalist society of the town grows, he becomes increasingly estranged from his environment. He is ever conscious of the tide of *Heimkehrer* streaming westwards, driven by a dull yearning for home. Gabriel is admittedly in a better material situation than these, since he still has money and friends. But he identifies with them. Hungry, ragged and lousy, they go back to wives who have been unfaithful and to children who will not recognise them. By the end of the novel Gabriel feels as alienated and as hopeless as the ex-servicemen dependent upon the soup kitchens and derelict barrack huts outside the town, for like them he is separated by a deep rift from the ordinary bourgeois world.

Franz Tunda in *Die Flucht ohne Ende* (1927) is another variation on the *Heimkehrer* motif. In the passage that follows the substitution of "we" for the initial "he" is surely significant; Tunda, gazing at the Tomb of the Unknown Warrior in Paris, feels

> as though he himself lay there, as though all of us lay there who had marched away from home, had been killed and buried, or had returned but never found our homes again—for it makes no difference whether we are alive or dead. We are strangers in this world, we come from the valley of the shadow.

He speaks for a generation estranged not merely by the traumatic experience of war, but also by the awareness that they have been forgotten, exploited and betrayed by a society in which henceforth they have no place. Nor do Roth's heroes find consolation in defiant memories of a glorious struggle, of heroism unto death which gives meaning to the destruction of war. The "storm of steel" no longer plays any part. Tunda interprets the memorial under the Arc de Triomphe as a sop to the conscience of the living; he is appalled at the sight of fathers paying their respect to the memory of those very sons for whose deaths they themselves are indirectly responsible. This problematic relationship between the generations is the basis of the story *Zipper und sein Vater* (1928). The son, Arnold, uprooted by the War, sees his career and his marriage wrecked. His father, a caricature of the *Spiessbürger,* authoritarian and chauvinistic, philistine and wildly ambitious (and himself a failure), hails the War which his sons then have to fight. The theme is trite, even sentimental: Arnold's sacrificial role causes him to remain a blurred and shadowy figure. Ironically it is his father who comes to life as a clearly defined, energetic literary creation.

In Roth's writing during the twenties the Habsburg Monarchy is never a point at issue. It is, of course, implicated in his arraignment of a malevolent authority which inflicts war on its citizens, or turns a law-abiding, respectful individual into a social rebel. *Die Rebellion* (1924) tells of one Andreas Pum, a disabled ex-serviceman who, as compensation for the loss of a limb, is granted a licence to ply a hurdy-gurdy in the streets of Vienna. Quite by accident, Pum comes into conflict with the Law, thereby losing his licence, his freedom and his self-respect. He is not by inclination a social rebel—on the contrary, before his brush with authority he had great faith in its majesty, justice and infallibility which not even the War could undermine. But the events related in the story show that the State is unjust, callous and all-too-human. Roth's identification with his character is such that towards the end he attributes to Pum a degree of conceptual thought and articulateness which is inconsistent with his personality and background. But here Roth's criticism of the State is relevant far beyond the frontiers of Austria. Again: in *Der stumme Prophet,* a novel written by 1929 but not published until 1965, Roth specifically attacks the conduct of Austrian society during the War, but his strictures apply equally to the European bourgeoisie in general. He records the egoism and self-delusion of the patriots, intellectuals and racketeers. Echoing Karl Kraus, he criticises the blunting of the human imagination by a combination of technology, commercialism and propaganda. The soulless nature of this milieu is well illustrated by the mechanical and sterile relationship between the hero's erstwhile mistress and the Director of the Central Potato Bureau where she is now employed:

> And the hours of love were no different from the office hours from which they were so to speak subtracted, with a cool eroticism which felt the same to the touch as the brown leather of the office couch on which they were spent. The yellow pencil and the shorthand notebook lay meanwhile on the carpet, waiting to be brought into play, for the Director did not like wasting time and would start dictating even while he was still busy fulfilling the requirements of basic hygiene at the wash basin. It was, one might say, a love idyll *à la* Pitman, and it was perfectly suited to the importance of the hour and to the perils facing the fatherland.

The shorthand notebook has the same function as Eliot's gramophone in *The Waste Land,* implying an incapacity for vital experience, a vacuous female passivity, the crude gratification of male vanity. In Roth's landscape of the postwar world the emptiness of sexual experience is not as important an element as in the contemporary writing of Eliot and Lawrence, but the social and political disenchantment of his heroes is frequently compounded with an inability to achieve a stable erotic relationship.

The novelist's political sympathies in the first decade after the War were more or less socialist. For all the objectivity and reticence of *Das Spinnennetz,* its publication in the *Arbeiterzeitung* constituted a political gesture. Roth's compassion for the plight of the working class emerges from this novel, from *Hotel Savoy* and from *Die Rebellion.* But he seems to set little store by a Marxist solution. As the influx of *Heimkehrer* (in his second novel) swells and the strike drags on, Gabriel Dan senses the inexorable approach of the revolution from the East. Yet the workers' riot is an act of blind and futile destruction which inflicts no fundamental damage on capitalist society. Politically the demonstration means nothing to Gabriel; on a private level it brings him grief and a renewed feeling of isolation. Roth, unlike Hofmannsthal or Werfel, does not suggest that revolution is morally wrong. On the other hand he does emphasise its cost and the overwhelming odds pitted against it. Neither the hero nor the narrator hints that another revolt might succeed where this one failed. As in Gerhart Hauptmann's *Die Weber,* bourgeois society is shown to be corrupt and brutal, its economy

Roth in the 1930s.

to be unsound, but the old order is still strong enough to ride out the storm of rebellion.

In his publicistic writings up to 1924 Roth takes a similar attitude. There is no doubt of his hostility towards anti-republican forces such as militarists, nationalist writers and reactionary academics. His *feuilletons* and satirical pieces in *Vorwärts,* the Berlin organ of the German Social Democrats, and *Lachen Links* attack war-mongering patriots, social injustice and the life-style of a stock-exchange bourgeoisie. Yet Roth is concerned with only the surface phenomena of society. Rarely does he explore deeper causes or discuss issues in a broad historical perspective. Although he gave his socialism as a reason for resigning from a middle class newspaper in 1922, he added that a higher salary or a more appreciative recognition of his talents might have persuaded him to swallow his principles. His contributions to non-socialist publications during this period were notably less "committed" than his work for the socialist press. Moreover, his biographer notes that in the early twenties he never lost his respect for the upper bourgeoisie. It appears then that Roth's socialism was largely emotional and to some extent opportunistic. Certainly it never included any study of economic and social theory. Small wonder if by 1925 his "commitment" began to tail off. He slowly resigned himself to the triumph of right-wing radicalism and despaired of the working class ever achieving true emancipation. He grew ever more sceptical of democratic systems, in particular of a Weimar Republic which elected a Junker and Field Marshal as its President, which tolerated the Reichswehr as a state within the state and allowed the proliferation of anti-republican para-military formations, and which was powerless to curb the wave of assassinations by right-wing terrorists or the overtly reactionary bias of the judiciary. A visit to the USSR in 1926 left him with grave reservations about the course the Revolution had taken there, with its closed society, its rigorous atheistic propaganda and the dominance of mediocrity and petit bourgeois values. He saw many notable attainments and was tremendously impressed by the alien, exotic world of Russia—but he also observed a society riddled with careerism and sycophancy where the old classes had merely been replaced by a new hierarchy based on the degree of affiliation to the Party.

These impressions colour two of Roth's later novels which are set in Russia at the time of the Revolution. Tunda, the hero of *Die Flucht ohne Ende,* is a former Austrian officer who has fought with the Red Army and received his political education from his Communist mistress. With the triumph of the Revolution, however, Tunda grows increasingly disenchanted with the new society, which he feels to be ominously similar to the society it has replaced. In the second novel, *Der stumme Prophet,* Friedrich Kargan likewise criticises the *embourgeoisement* of the Soviet leaders and the stultifying power of a pettifogging Soviet bureaucracy. He objects to the tendency dominant in, though not confined to the new Russia: the practice of regarding individuals as cyphers who exist merely by virtue of their social function. Both Tunda and Kargan attack certain aspects of the Revolution and its aftermath, but their disillusionment springs from something deeper than the inevitable disparity between ideological principle and political practice. In post-revolutionary Moscow, Tunda reflects that only in a deserted Red Square at midnight, with a solitary red flag fluttering in the beam of a floodlight on the Kremlin roof—only here can one still experience the authentic meaning of the Revolution. This is not the observation of a party supporter frustrated by the inadequate translation of the party programme into reality: what Tunda feels is something more personal and more fundamental—it is the dissociation of a romantic idealist whose real concern transcends the cares and compromises of a workaday political world.

> Tunda remembered the red war, the years when one knew only how to die and when life, the sun, the moon, the earth, the sky were only a frame or backcloth for death. Death, the red death, marched day and night over the earth, with a splendid marching song, with great drums that sounded like hooves galloping over iron and shattered glass, it scattered handfuls of splinters, the shots sounded like the distant cries of marching masses.
>
> Then the orderliness of everyday life overpowered this great red death, it became an ordinary death slinking from house to house like a beggar and carrying off his victims as if they were gifts of charity. . . .
>
> It is no consolation to reflect that a desk and a pen, plaster busts, and shop windows full of displays in honour of the revolution, monuments, and blotters with the head of Bebel for a handle, are probably necessary to the founding of a new world; it is no consolation, no help.

(The hollow rhetoric, the repetitions striving for effect, the deliberate pathos and the general slackness of the style are not uncharacteristic of Roth's writing; they grow more pronounced in his later work.) Tunda's aspirations for adventure and glory are more important to him than the political achievements of the revolution, and the relationship of ends and means is seen in a highly personal light. Though his socialism is more positive and constructive than that of Gabriel Dan, it is similarly limited in that it springs from an unreflective emotional response. The novelist attributes to Tunda's mistress a pertinent criticism of his attitude from the point of view of a committed Marxist, when she remarks that it is more important to run a hospital than to revel in private passions. On the other hand, Roth indicts through this same figure the clinical, impersonal approach to political reform which is carried over into sexual relationships. He is perceptibly biased in Tunda's favour and appears to affirm his decision to lose the world in order to gain his soul. Tunda's tragedy lies in the fact that he cannot opt out of a world he repudiates. In the case of Kargan we are again confronted with a disillusioned romantic. Roth suggests no third possibility between the ruthlessly realistic politicians on the one hand, and the dreamer and individualist on the other who deprecates the sordid conditions of political activity. Both Tunda and Kargan are anarchists, after a fashion. Both desire to sweep away the old world and rebuild a new society on new foundations—something which the Revolution has not achieved. They are also both critical of the highly organised modern state. They are at only one remove from a character in *Das Spinnennetz* who exults in the death throes of a corrupt civilisation and bids his emigrating brother pursue his researches into a new explosive with which to blow up the whole of Europe. Roth is aware of the naivety of Tunda and Kargan, he knows that society will never in fact be changed by such men as these. Yet he appears repelled by the only alternative which presents itself to him.

From the mid twenties Roth was hostile towards party politics, even on the left. His cynical remarks (in a letter) on the Socialist Congress in Marseilles in 1925 showed that he considered the democratic socialists outmoded and ineffective against modern industry. He objected to the intellectual blindness that he associated with a political ideology and resented the pressure to make him take sides. The very title of his novel *Rechts und Links* (1929) conveys this. Roth thus joins with most Austrian writers of his day in seeking to preserve his integrity in the face of ideological blandishments. At the same time he seems to agree with Hofmannsthal and Werfel, for instance, that no social upheaval would alter the basic structure of society, with its polarity of wealth and poverty, privilege and exploitation. In *Die Rebellion* the narrator describes Pum's plight as the work of "fate"; in spite of Pum's Promethean defiance of authority, secular and divine, the social (and religious) hierarchy remains intact, and there is no hope of it being overthrown. The narrator of another story reflects:

> All roads everywhere look alike. All the bourgeois in every country look alike. The sons look like their fathers. And when one realises this, one could be driven to despair by the thought that things would always remain the same. However much fashions, constitutions, styles and tastes may change, the old eternal laws are just as evident beneath every form, the laws according to which the rich build houses and the poor build huts, the rich wear clothes and the poor wear rags, the laws which decree that rich and poor alike love, are born, fall sick and die, pray and hope, despair and wither.

The political corollary of this fatalism is acquiescence, however critical or reluctant, in the status quo. It has therefore been argued that Roth was a conservative at heart even before his affiliation to the monarchist movement. Certainly, a reluctant fatalism could of itself lead to the affirmation of an immutable social hierarchy.

There are, however, more detailed affinities between Roth's ideas in the twenties and his subsequent monarchism. His cultural and political criticism in the early postwar years represents in the first place an attack on the dehumanising tendencies of urban industrial society, on capitalism, on the decadence of modern culture and on the moral bankruptcy of the age. All this is consistent with left-wing sympathies, but equally these are commonplaces of the right-wing ideologies of the period. The corpus of Roth's social criticism would not therefore be rendered invalid by a change of political allegiance. Moreover, Roth advances even in his early writing notions which are by no means commonplaces of socialist thought but which could easily be integrated into a conservative ideology. The figure of Brandeis in *Rechts und Links,* who longs to return to an "authentic" existence on the land, is probably inspired by anarchist leanings; nonetheless he has obvious parallels in the grass-roots idea of right-wing literature. Gabriel Dan's appraisal of a living tradition in which the quick and the dead are partners in a common enterprise recalls a *locus classicus* of conservatism, the binding tie of tradition. One could also adduce Roth's regret that the style and elegance of prewar aristocratic society had given way to the vulgarity, ostentation and greed of a self-assertive middle class (this despite his acknowledgment that the War was largely the responsibility of incompetent or ambitious aristocratic diplomats). These are mere scattered references but they suggest that Roth's espousal of monarchism did not involve any radical transformation of his social and cultural values. To be sure, Roth could on occasion express an unequivocal hostility towards certain right-wing traits. One has only to read his articles on the Hitler trial of 1924 (that "illiterate house-painter"), on the conspiracies of the *Freikorps* nationalists or the stupidity and megalomania of Ludendorff, the former military leader who abetted Hitler's Munich putsch, to be assured of his opposition to nascent fascism. However, the way remained open for the endorsement of a conservative ideology which was neither chauvinistic nor racialist, neither militarist nor committed to violence. Although Roth's Habsburg legitimism did not manifest itself until the thirties, its foundations were laid a good deal earlier. He himself hinted at his ambiguous position in a letter of 1925, criticising the Austrian Socialists for urging Anschluss with Germany. Roth recalled that at the time of Franz Joseph's death he was one of the soldiers who lined the route of the cortege to the Capuchin crypt in Vienna, the traditional burial place of the Habsburgs. Although already a "revolutionary," Roth had wept unashamedly. For with the old Kaiser, he felt, a whole epoch of history was finally laid to rest. Union with Germany would extinguish the last embers of the culture that remained. He averred, with an echo of the supranational ideal, that an independent Austria still contained the promise of a future united Europe. Two years later, conveying his condolence to Bernard von Brentano whose father had just died, he wrote of his affection for the aura of the old "Roman Empire of the German nation" but added that most of those who breathed that atmosphere had political ideas very different from his own. In other words, he was attracted to the values of a universalist Catholic Empire without being a political reactionary or obscurantist.

Roth's monarchism finally crystallised in the fight against National Socialism. He was an early critic of Hitler and of

political anti-semitism but after the Nazis had won their first major electoral successes he began to write a series of polemical articles such as "**Vom Attentäter zum Schmock**" (1930), "**Bekenntnis zu Deutschland**" (1931), "**Ursachen der Schlaflosigkeit im Goethejahr**" (1932) and "**Die Nationale Kurzwelle**" (1932). When Hitler became Chancellor, Roth left Germany, never to return. He would have no truck with those intellectuals who achieved a *modus vivendi* with the new regime and his voice was prominent among those of the German emigrés who continued their protest against Hitler in exile. At the same time he strongly resented being associated with left-wing intellectuals who were similarly campaigning against fascism, particularly the novelists Lion Feuchtwanger and Arnold Zweig, and the group centred on the periodical *Die Weltbühne.* There were complex reasons behind his distaste for these unwelcome allies. On an ideological level he would argue that their rationalism and materialism were partly responsible for creating a climate of opinion in which fascism could thrive. On a deeper level his criticism of these intellectuals—who were by no means all Marxist—was governed by a form of Jewish anti-semitism, a contemptuous aversion for what he called *chuzpe* (chutzpa), aggressive, brazen insolence, a combination of presumption and arrogance. Similar sentiments coloured his comments on the Social Democratic leadership in Austria. They ensued from Roth's experience of the predicament of Jewish assimilation. The result of this combination of political scepticism and personal resentment was that faced with the rise of Hitler, Roth could not resort either to democratic liberalism or to socialism. Only one other anti-fascist choice remained open to him, the least realistic of all, Habsburg legitimism.

His earliest public comment on the Habsburg Empire occurs in *Juden auf Wanderschaft* (1927), a series of vignettes centred round the life and character of the Jews of Europe. In the course of this book Roth contended that the concept of the "nation"—by which he meant the nation-state—was an invention of Western European scholars. Though erroneous the idea was apparently substantiated by the decline of Austria-Hungary. The Monarchy, being a potentially supranational structure, might have disproved the theory of the self-determination of peoples: instead it was so ineptly governed that it encouraged the growth of nationalism. Roth indicated that in a situation where questions of national allegiance, national unity and national territory predominated, it followed that the position of the Jews grew highly problematic. One way in which they reacted was to revive their own nationalism in the form of the longing for a return to Palestine, a retrograde step in terms of Jewish history. In other words, the Zionist movement founded in Vienna by Theodor Herzl was a direct result of internal conflicts within the Habsburg Empire. Roth's attitude towards the Empire here was still critical. In the essay "**Seine k. und k. apostolische Majestät**" (1928) Roth took up the theme of an earlier letter. He admitted that although he had been hostile towards the Empire he had known as a student, he now felt a spontaneous and irrational nostalgia for it, because he associated memories of the Monarchy and of Franz Joseph with his childhood and youth. . . . Roth reflected upon the death of the Emperor in a mood which anticipated certain passages of his novel *Radetzkymarsch.* His own convictions were silenced at the thought of the tragedy of Franz Joseph's political existence. At about this same period Roth articulated for the first time the idea that the collapse of the Empire was brought about by a loss of faith, purpose and direction among the ruling class; the novelist put this notion in the mouth of von Maerker, a character in *Der stumme Prophet,* who declares,

> And yet it seems to me that we knew beforehand exactly what would happen. I saw with my own eyes year in, year out, how the state slowly fell apart and people grew more indifferent. But more malicious too, yes, more malicious . . . . We cracked jokes, we all laughed at them. . . . Every nation joined in the mockery. And yet in my day, when the individual still counted for more than his nationality, there existed the possibility of turning the old monarchy into a homeland for all. It could have been the model in miniature for a great new world of the future and at the same time the last reminder of a great era of European history when North and South were united. Now it's all over . . . .

A similar reference to the demoralising witticisms of the ruling class had occurred in a passage written by Karl Kraus in 1919, where he recalled that it was characteristic of prewar Austria to tell funny stories about the mental deficiencies of Franz Joseph and to proclaim the State ripe for collapse. The indifference of Schnitzler, Zweig, Werfel or Musil to the problems of the Empire before 1914, and Hofmannsthal's belated acknowledgment that the Monarchy had lost its idealistic impetus, complement or confirm the attitude of which the satirist and Roth's fictional character speak. As yet Roth does not advance these arguments *in propria persona,* nor is von Maerker a figure with whom he closely identifies. But in the publicistic articles of his last years Roth himself endorses both the accusation and the idealisation inherent in the above passage.

A turning point in Roth's attitude towards the Empire is at the same time his finest literary achievement, the novel *Radetzkymarsch* (1932). Here he recounts the history of the Trotta family, beginning with the elevation of the family to the nobility. Lieutenant Trotta, a Slovene and the son of a former NCO, saves the life of the young Franz Joseph at the Battle of Solferino, and is duly rewarded. A tradition of Imperial service and Imperial favour is thus established. Yet even at the outset this is vitiated by untruth. The incident at Solferino is recorded in school textbooks, falsified, embellished and romanticised out of all recognition. Trotta's rectitude leads him to protest against the falsehood and his appeals culminate in an audience with the Emperor himself. But here too he is put off with an argument that he has heard countless times before: that it is perfectly justifiable to adapt historical truth to the needs of the State—in this case, the education of the young. Bitterly disenchanted, Trotta resigns his commission. That the civil service and the Emperor himself endorse a gratuitous lie implies that the society they represent is already undermined. Moreover, as has been pointed out, the battle which brought good fortune to the Trottas was in fact an inglorious defeat for the Monarchy which thereby lost the province of Lombardy. Thereafter, the Imperial motifs—the ubiquitous official portrait of Franz Joseph and the sound of the Radetzky March itself, written by Johann Strauss senior to commemorate the victorious campaign against the Italian rebels in 1848—are constantly associated with guilt or decadence or death. The music, the most popular of all Austrian marching tunes, evokes the boyhood holidays of the hero of the novel, the youngest Trotta, Carl Joseph, in a house rigidly administered and lacking in human warmth. It is played as a grotesque parody when a group of officers troops into a sordid brothel; and again when Carl Joseph converses with a Jewish medical officer, as the latter prepares to meet certain death in a pointless duel for which the hero is ultimately, if unwittingly, responsible. The cold blue eyes of the Imperial portrait are a reminder of the Emperor's remoteness, and of the inhibition of natural emotion which the tradition of Imperial service is seen to entail.

Roth's description of life in the Imperial Army is imbued with critical detachment. He exposes the outmoded training, the monotony and the sense of futility which springs from a want of purpose. The gloomy atmosphere of political decline is deepened by the prophecies of the Polish magnate, Count Chojnicki, who claims that the Empire is held together only by a residual quasi-superstitious loyalty to the person of Franz Joseph. This loyalty does not extend to other members of the dynasty, and with Franz Joseph's death the Monarchy will fall apart. Habsburg power, he maintains, was founded on a belief in the divine right of kings; it cannot survive in an age of science and scepticism. It is an archaism incompatible with emergent nationalism, socialism and parliamentary democracy. (Roth himself echoed this notion in a letter to Ernst Křenek in 1932: "Yes, we are indeed Austrians! We do not belong any more in this world. We live, think and write as though still in the Middle Ages. . . .") The loss of direction and cohesion within the ruling class is illustrated by the way in which news of the Sarajevo assassination is received. A regiment of dragoons is holding its summer ball and the proceedings are well under way by the time the message arrives. In the ballroom a military band breaks haltingly into a slow march; the drunken revellers dance to the mournful strains; and as the music quickens, they celebrate *their* own bizarre funeral rite:

> The guests marched in a ring around the empty, shining circle of the dance floor. Round and round they went, each one a mourner behind the corpse of the man in front and in their midst the invisible bodies of the heir to the throne and of the Monarchy itself. . . . Gradually the orchestras began to play more rapidly and the legs of those in the procession began to stride out in a marching step. . . . Count Benkyö gave a leap of joy. "The swine's dead!" he yelled in Hungarian. But everyone understood, just as though he had spoken in German. Suddenly some started to hop. Quicker and quicker blared the slow march. In between the triangle tinkled with its clear, silvery, intoxicated smile. . . .

What the officers and their guests betray is not just Franz Ferdinand's feud with the Magyars or his general unpopularity, but the moral decay of a whole culture. Perhaps Roth had in mind an ostentatious society wedding which took place in Budapest shortly after the assassination. (It is also worth noting that "Benkyö" is not a properly Hungarian name: it is the equivalent of calling a Welshman "Griffots." The error is characteristic of the "cultural synthesis" of the Empire as it impinged upon Vienna.)

Carl Joseph is ground to destruction between the millstones of history. He is heir to a semi-feudal mission in a society crumbling beneath the pressures of a modern age. What opportunities are open to him? Whereas his grandfather saved the Emperor's life, Carl Joseph rescues the Imperial portrait from its ignominious position in a brothel parlour; whereas the grandfather was wounded on the field of honour, the grandson is injured by workers demonstrating against intolerable conditions; and when Carl Joseph is obliged to show his loyalty by protesting against the insults to the Imperial family on the night of Sarajevo, his protest is ineffective, and the whole incident merely reveals to him the moribund nature of the Empire, leading him to resign his commission. Roth's achievement is to show that this private débâcle springs less from Carl Joseph's own inadequacies than from the temper of his age.

The principle of the Imperial tradition is loyalty to a dynasty, and the ideal of supranationalism that goes with it. Carl Joseph's father, the *Bezirkshauptmann* (a position roughly equivalent to that of a Lord Lieutenant, but carrying administrative responsibility as head of the local civil service), is deeply imbued with this ideology. Yet after 1848, and especially after 1867, it had become increasingly difficult to administer the State on these lines. As emergent nationalism drove the peoples of the Empire to rediscover their national identities, the supranational dynastic ideal came to involve the danger of rootlessness and emotional frustration on the part of those who tried to uphold it. It was to this that Werfel alluded when he described in his essay on the Empire the *sacrificium nationis* which freed the true Austrians from local ties, and thus from narrow-minded prejudice, but at the same time "clipped the wings of nature's vital urge." Carl Joseph is a victim of this crisis. Unlike his father, he longs to return to the soil once tilled by his Slovene forebears. To Carl Joseph the Emperor appears a cold, remote figure. The concept of dynastic loyalty has no living reality for him. And this lack of commitment comes to the fore at a period when the Emperor's function is increasingly to represent the one apparently stable and disinterested authority *au-dessus de la mêlée* ["above the battle"]. As Hermann Broch has pointed out, the price of disinterestedness is abstraction. Through his characterisation of Franz Joseph, and through the relationship between the *Bezirkshauptmann* and his son, Roth illuminates further the personal consequences of the abstract Imperial ideal. The remarkable physical similarity between the Emperor and the civil servant is an outward manifestation of a shared ethos. Both are governed by their conception of duty, both are unselfish, inflexible and distant. In the Emperor's case, his sense of responsibility to the Habsburg mission encloses him in a prison of his own making. (Again Broch makes a similar point.) Franz Joseph's life as portrayed by Roth consists in acting out the Imperial role; it has become a petrified pose, lacking vitality and truth, and involving human isolation and emotional deprivation. We, the readers, know that the cloak of Imperial majesty hides a lonely old man whose memory is fading, who realises that death will soon summon him and his Empire alike, who is more perceptive than is commonly supposed, and whose feelings are always misinterpreted by his entourage. The historical accuracy of Roth's portrait is not at issue: as a novelist he is simply concerned with translating the political inadequacies of the official ideology into human terms. The *Bezirkshauptmann* too allows himself to be dominated by considerations of duty and obligation to such an extent that his relationship with his son is seriously impaired. Father and son are admittedly inhibited by their natural taciturnity and fear of showing emotion. But a closer, warmer relationship is eventually established, as Carl Joseph's career slowly traces a downward curve. The *Bezirkshauptmann* gradually awakens to his responsibilities as a father, as distinct from those of the civil servant, and is made aware of the emotional void which has hitherto characterised his existence. There is a bitter irony in the fact that he and his son achieve their closest understanding at the point when Carl Joseph's career lies in ruins and when it is clear to both men that the Monarchy is irrevocably doomed. There is a still greater irony in the fact that in its death throes the Empire demands yet another sacrifice from the Trotta family. For a short time before the outbreak of war, Carl Joseph returns to the simple rural existence for which his heart has always yearned. But when war is declared, he reports for duty once again. He is killed during a retreat, trying to fetch water for his thirsty men; his unsoldierly death as a "drawer of water" is a fitting end to a misguided career.

There is no trite moralising in Roth's novel. He shows that the Habsburg mission as viewed by the Emperor and his civil service could not be reconciled with national aspirations. He suggests that the tradition of Imperial service was too narrowly interpreted. He implies that men need more than an abstract ideological concept, that they need to be rooted in a regional culture. Carl Joseph would be quite capable of combining his local loyalties with allegiance to the House of Habsburg and the Imperial commonwealth, just as in his own way he would have served Franz Joseph more constructively on a country estate than in the Army. Subsequently Roth was to argue that the most steadfast and loyal of the Imperial peoples were those nonindustrial nationalities who were both rooted in their own soil *and* devoted to the Emperor as a father figure. We are reminded of Bahr's diagnosis of the Austrian disease, when in 1909 he wrote that the problem was to reconcile the desire for cultural autonomy on the part of the Germans, the Slavs and the Italians with allegiance to the Austrian State. The political corollary of what Roth suggests in his novel—though this is never adduced—is some form of federalism. Perhaps the problem is not clearly enough defined, inasmuch as Carl Joseph's desire to return to a local culture stops a long way short of the self-assertive nationalism which challenged the existence of the Empire. But the novelist hints that if the initially modest regional demands had been met, the destructive clash of national interests might have been avoided. However, the strength of the novel lies in the fact that it does not toy with the great "ifs" of history, but explores imaginatively and sympathetically individual reactions to a concrete historical dilemma.

After *Radetzkymarsch* Roth's attitude towards the Empire grew steadily more partisan. As the shadow of the Antichrist lengthened—*Der Antichrist* (1934) was the title of Roth's polemic against the evils of modern civilisation and politics—so the Habsburg star shone more and more brightly. On 28 April 1933 he announced to Stefan Zweig that he had become a monarchist in obedience to his instincts and his convictions. Thereafter Roth's tone became increasingly sentimental and didactic. *Die Kapuzinergruft,* published in 1938 as a sequel to *Radetzkymarsch,* is ideologically strident and an inferior creative achievement. The transition from literary re-creation to propaganda is marked by a short story which appeared in French in 1934 under the title **"Le buste de l'empereur."** It tells of the life of a Polish count under the *ancien régime* and then under the postwar Polish Republic; it describes his inability to adapt to the new world of national frontiers and parliamentary democracy, a world which to him seems bereft of ethical responsibility. The image of the Empire presented in this story is perceptibly different from that of *Radetzkymarsch.* The narrator now praises the supranationalism of the Monarchy, its benevolent nepotism, its uniformity amid diversity; and he condemns the ruling class for their cynicism and irresponsibility. This criticism is no longer attributed to the character alone, as in the case of von Maercker, but is also endorsed by the narrator. There is no longer any attempt to explore the crisis of the Imperial ideology itself. It is not fortuitous that the loyal Morstin is a Pole, for in Roth's opinion those who hastened the Empire's decline were not the dissident nationalities but the Austro-Germans who had succumbed either to scepticism or to the delusion of racial superiority. Roth is particularly hostile towards those Austrians who were beguiled by the "dynamism" of the Wilhelminian Reich. Anger at the shabby treatment meted out to the Imperial peoples combines with a deep mistrust of Vienna and all it represents. In the words of the hero of *Die Kapuzinergruft,*

> [The younger generation of the prewar years] had grown up far too spoilt in Vienna, a city nourished incessantly by the provinces of the monarchy; they were naive, almost absurdly naive children of the pampered, far too often acclaimed capital which sat like a shiny, seductive spider in the middle of the huge black and yellow web of Austria-Hungary, constantly drawing strength and vitality and splendour from the surrounding provinces. . . . The colourful gaiety of the capital city of the Empire throve quite clearly . . . on the tragic love of the provinces for Austria: I say tragic, because it remained ever unrequited. The gipsies of the puszta, the Carpathian Huzuls, the Jewish cabbies of Galicia, my own relatives, the Slovene chestnut roasters from Sipolje, the Swabian tobacco planters from the Bacska, the horse dealers of the Hana in Moravia, the weavers of the Erz mountains, the millers and coral-traders of Podolia—they were all generous providers of Austria, the poorer they were, the more generous.

The economic factor in the migration from the provinces into Vienna is characteristically ignored. Carl Joseph's ambition to return to the soil has by now developed into a diatribe against the sophisticated (that is, depraved), urban (that is, inauthentic) civilisation of the capital. The strictures recall those of Bahr and Hofmannsthal. Roth's catalogue of names illustrates his infatuation with the colourful tapestry of the Monarchy; it also betrays the anachronism of his thought. His enthusiasm is reserved for a pre-industrial feudal society, uncontaminated by education, democracy and nationalism, for a society untroubled by the emergence of a powerful bourgeoisie or by any form of political consciousness on the part of the non-privileged classes. Roth's argument is in the paternalistic tradition of Grillparzer and Stifter. His historical criticism has now become historical escapism: he idealises, oversimplifies, makes wild generalisations and draws the wrong conclusions. (For example, his account of the decline of the Monarchy ignores the role of the Hungarian aristocracy and gentry.) From the worthiest motives Roth constructs a travesty of the past. The monarchist essays which began to appear in 1937 present a wide array of villains, from the followers of Schönerer and the cult of blood-and-soil, to Liberalism and the Social Democrats. They attack the Reformation, the Enlightenment, the French Revolution, the War of Liberation and the Revolution of 1848, tracing a direct line from Erasmus and Luther to the modern European dictators via Voltaire, Frederick the Great, Joseph II, Napoleon, Bismarck and Wilhelm II. They lash out in passing at clericalism, power politics, chauvinism, parliamentary democracy and the Anschluss. Though Roth had some contact with the Schuschnigg regime, his opinion of it, particularly after 1938, was not high. Had not Schuschnigg declined Archduke Otto's offer of help in the Anschluss crisis? Roth was critical of what he felt to be the petty manoeuvring and parish-pump politics of the Christian Socialists and doubtless remembered

that the party's origins were closely linked with lower middle class anti-semitism. He had already broken off contact with the *Heimwehr* in protest against their brutal repression of the workers in the uprising of 1934. The ideal against which Roth measured the world of the thirties was the now familiar Romantic conception of the Holy Roman Empire, an organic community of peoples living together in harmony and in a common allegiance, uncorrupted by industrialisation and capitalism, a society neatly divided into a hierarchical structure from which all tensions were banished. The unbridled, even fanatical note of some of Roth's last polemics may have been due to some extent to his parlous state of health. He had for years suffered from cirrhosis of the liver which was soon to bring about his early death. From 1934 onwards his correspondence shows signs of persecution mania. But though extreme, Roth's ideas are recognisably akin to those of the "conservative revolution." Even his demonological hypostasisation of Hitler has parallels in the Christian writers of the so-called "inner emigration," those conservative but nonfascist writers who chose to remain in Nazi Germany and who expressed their opposition in allegorical fictions or clandestine poetry. (pp. 92-110)

It is clear that Roth's royalism was determined by events in Germany rather than Austria. Only after pledging himself to the Habsburg cause did he turn his attention to events in Austria itself. As the son of middle class Jewish parents and as a journalist with former socialist affiliations, Roth hardly displayed a typically monarchist background. He made up for this with his invented commission and the zeal of a proselyte. His Catholic legitimism coincided with a fresh creative interest in his Jewish heritage. In the monarchist ideology he attempted to find a spiritual refuge and the means of identifying with a stable, universalist idea. Monarchism supplied a sense of belonging which compensated for years of restless wandering in an exile that was more than just geographical. Yet Roth's polemical pieces in exile newspapers and journals were paradoxically informed by an awareness that the Danube Monarchy and the Habsburg heritage were irrevocably lost. His articles contained no constructive proposals for a Habsburg Restoration. They were filled with nostalgia, bitterness and anger but expressed no hope for the future. It is not fortuitous that during his legitimist period his imaginative writing included a "legend," a "fairy tale" and a religious allegory, tales of moral disintegration and purely personal relationships which in the circumstances represented a flight from historical reality. Roth failed to overcome the fatalism to which he had always been prone. (pp. 111-12)

C. E. Williams, "Joseph Roth: A Time Out of Joint," in his The Broken Eagle: The Politics of Austrian Literature from Empire to Anschluss, *Barnes & Noble, 1974, pp. 91-112.*

BARTON W. BROWNING (essay date 1979)

[In the following essay, Browning assesses Roth's standing as an exile writer and provides a detailed examination of The Legend of the Holy Drinker, *maintaining that the novel's homeless and initially nameless protagonist exemplifies the state of exile.]*

Viewed from the perspective of exile literature as literature there are three major facets of Joseph Roth's *Legende vom heiligen Trinker.* The first concerns the exile context in which this story had its genesis; the second deals with the ramifications of Roth's attempt at employing both the legend form and the life of a saint in a piece of serious modern fiction; and the final aspect has to do with the literary structure of the work itself and the devices Roth the artist used in achieving his literary ends.

With regard to the matter of exile context, an interesting question might be raised here concerning the propriety of dealing with Joseph Roth in a discussion of exile literature. As is evident in today's often politically oriented definition of exile literature, the title of "exile author" has become a mantle to be draped about the shoulders of a carefully selected few, whether this selection be based on circumstances of one's departure—free will or otherwise—or upon one's subsequent political allegiances. Yet given the conventional understanding of the term, Roth would doubtlessly seem eminently qualified to fill the role of exile author. His departure from Germany on January 30, 1933, was, as he himself explained, in anticipation of, and protest against, Hitler's appointment as chancellor. Politically active in his self-imposed exile, Roth continued to voice his protests against the Nazi regime, and in addition to associating himself with various exile groups opposing the current German leaders, he enthusiastically supported the restoration, however improbable, of the Austrian monarchy as an alternative far preferable to a takeover by the scoundrels in Berlin.

Even the funeral of this one-time Socialist had political overtones within the exile community, for this occasion gathered both his old friends from the left, as well as a delegate from Otto von Hapsburg, who briefly eulogized Roth as "a faithful proponent of the monarchy." Whatever form it took, Roth's opposition to the National Socialist regime was a dominant characteristic of his last years, and the sense of kinship he felt with the sufferings of fellow exiles was profound. His death itself was connected with the exile experience insofar as it was occasioned in part by a brutally abrupt report of the demise of his friend Ernst Toller, who had committed suicide in the impoverishment of his American exile. In short, it would be impossible to separate Roth's later years from the fact of his exile.

Exile, however, presumes the existence of a home from which one has been exiled, and Roth's homeland had ceased to exist long before 1933. As he repeatedly emphasized in his letters and conversations, he felt his true home to be the Austrian monarchy, the realm of Franz Joseph, and its demise left deep scars in his psyche. "My strongest experience was the war and the fall of my fatherland, *the only one* I have ever had, the Austro-Hungarian monarchy. Even today I am still a thoroughly patriotic Austrian, and I love what is left of my home as a sort of relic."

Two of his best-known and most accomplished novels, *Radetzkymarsch* and *Kapuzinergruft* (1932 and 1938 respectively), present simultaneously clear-headed and nostalgic recapitulations of the weaknesses and glories Roth perceived in the final stages of the Hapsburgs' reign. In both novels Roth continually circles about the question of the essence of Austria, this homeland to which he declared himself so deeply committed. As indicated in *Kapuzinergruft* and elsewhere, Roth's answer was an outgrowth of his own experiences as a Galician Jew reared on the edges of the empire. At the beginning of *Die Kapuzinergruft* Graf Chojnicki states: "The essence of Austria is not center, but periphery." In this view it is not the Western, predominantly German region of the empire—Roth referred to the residents of these areas as Al-

pine fools, "Alpentrottel"—but the "Kronländer," the imperial lands on the fringes of the empire that maintained the actual spirit of the monarchy. Brody, Roth's birthplace and the more-or-less disguised setting of several of his tales, was exemplary for him of the many points constituting this periphery. These areas, according to Roth, both received their identity from and themselves lent identity to the empire of which they were a part, and it was the strength of this periphery that helped sustain the best of the old system while producing figures of such burning intensity as the coachman Manes Reisiger or one of such primitive splendor as Franz Ferdinand Trotta's cousin, Joseph Branco. At the center, however, in Vienna, where Trotta is residing at the onset of the novel, a sort of dry rot had already set in. Franz Ferdinand envies his cousin's vital sense of identity so strongly that in the memorable opening chapters of the novel he actually tries to purchase this sense of self by buying his cousin's colorful vest and gold chain, a gesture as expressive as it is obviously doomed to failure.

In other works, such as **"Die Büste des Kaisers,"** the monarchy assumed almost mythic proportions; yet here, even in the most adulatory passages one cannot fail to hear the sense of hollowness at the center. Roth clearly envisioned the figure of the aging Franz Joseph as representing a sort of emptiness, the fact notwithstanding that it was around this highly significant void that the rest of the empire achieved form and definition.

While Roth himself seems to sympathize with the sense of alienation we find in the young Trotta, his own relations to the monarchy in the years shortly after its fall were, in fact, hardly benevolent. His early tale **Die Rebellion** is as critical of the Austrian system as his later works are positive, and during his outspoken Socialist phase, Roth repeatedly criticized the Hapsburg era. His subsequent stories are filled with figures disappointed in their countries and themselves, figures such as Nissen Piczenik, dealer in coral, who finally concludes that his true home is not on this corrupt earth but rather in the depths of the sea among the coral beds guarded by the Leviathan from which his story takes its name.

It is a commonplace that the Austrian literary spirit is predisposed more toward criticism than toward Utopian visions. When Utopian thinking does occur it often takes a peculiar form which might be termed Utopian nostalgia. Stifter's *Nachsommer* is a prime example of this genre. Rather than presenting an idealized future or a classically remote Golden Age, Stifter structured his vision in a noble, not-too-distant past now lost or rapidly fading under the decadence of modern society, a past that might still have been appreciated if only one's perception had been accurate enough to separate the wheat from the chaff. And it is in this sense that Roth composed his cynical and yet sentimental works lamenting the loss of an ideal the existence of which was at best questionable.

Where, then, lay Roth's true home? Certainly not in Brody which he denied far more than the Biblical three times. And certainly not in the family that he likewise falsified and denied. His idealized view of the empire was, as he himself obviously knew, an illusion too pure to correspond to an earthly reality. His home in his last days, that impermanent hotel existence in Holland and Paris, was physically in exile in the full and exacting sense of the word, but did not differ greatly from the style of life he had established long before. Roth actually seems to have found his true home in exile, a home in homelessness, as it were. He seems to have experienced exile perhaps not so much as a tragic fate but as a *modus vivendi* which he, along with so many of his generation, was fated to exemplify. It is from this sense of exile, not as a special estate, but as one form of the human condition that we have Roth's last story, his tale of Andreas Kartak, the Polish mineworker, lost in the alcoholic haze of life as a *clochard* under the bridges of Paris, a man possessing invalid papers and without any apparent justification for his existence, a profoundly homeless man who at the beginning of the story can define himself only as a man of honor even though without an address, "ein Mann von Ehre, wenn auch ohne Adresse."

Die Legende vom heiligen Trinker is the last complete project to come from Roth's pen, and one to which he devoted special care. He seems to have been particularly proud of this effort, and justly so, for in its style it raises to yet another power that simplicity and clarity characterizing much of Roth's work. The lucidity of its diction and theme belies the sophistication of its achievement. Remarkably enough, although written under the most trying economic and personal circumstances and conceived at a point when dreams of an effective resistance to the power of Nazi Germany were less than idle fantasies, this simple tale tells of benevolence instead of bitterness, of hope instead of despair, and finally, of security in the midst of rootlessness.

The story of Andreas Kartak, this man whom Roth endows with the title of saint, could hardly have a more unlikely protagonist. Summarizing briefly what becomes clear during the course of the tale, Andreas had left Poland in order to work in France. There he had murdered a man whose wife he had been defending and had spent time in jail for his crime. At the outset of the narrative, we encounter Andreas at the nadir of his existence: he sleeps beneath the bridges of the Seine with his fellow drunks, remembering neither his name nor the painful fact that his papers are no longer valid. A seemingly chance encounter with a newly converted stranger brings the offer of 200 francs under the condition that the money be returned at some appropriate time to the chapel of St. Teresa of Lisieux. After this first almost miraculous act of generosity Andreas proceeds through a sequence of fortunate events. He finds honest work, meets Karoline, the woman in whose defense he had committed murder, and discovers he has grown beyond her. And when all else seems to have failed, he finds an extra thousand francs in an old billfold. He receives unsolicited help from a youthful friend who has become a star soccer player, receives the affections of a most attractive dancer, and later once more has money forced on him by a stranger. All these occasions are circumscribed by innumerable glasses of Pernod and haunted by the ever present threat of an irretrievable return to the life beneath the bridges. Having failed on three occasions to return the money to his saint, Andreas makes a final attempt to repay his debt, and while waiting in a bistro near the church imagines that the young girl he sees in his dying moments is none other than St. Teresa herself come to collect her debts. The dying Andreas is carried across the street to the church where he was to keep his appointment and dies there in the sacristy, secure in the knowledge that his obligation has been fulfilled.

In this *Legende* Roth's deliberate simplification and stylization extends beyond his consciously sparse diction, in which language is reduced to its essentials. Each encounter is concentrated into a minimum of detail, while time and setting fade into insignificance. As Jolles has pointed out in his *Ein-*

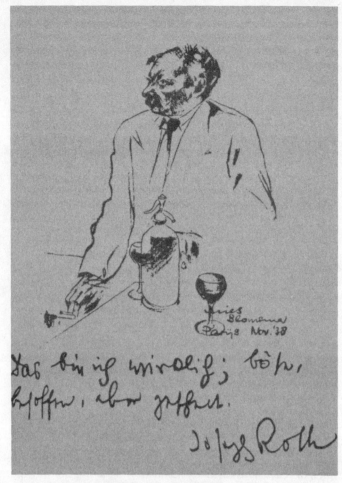

Caricature of Roth from November 1938, which he captioned: "This I truly am: wicked, drunk, but sharp."

fache Formen, the essence of the legend as a literary form lies not so much in historical detail as in significant fact. Nothing is included here simply because it possesses the mere distinction of having occurred. In telling of the life of his own saint, Roth establishes fifteen stations, fifteen significant fragments that illuminate telling moments in the all too fragmented existence of Andreas Kartak. Time is no measure of principal importance. While the narrative begins with a most precise notation of the story's date, spring of 1934, there is nothing else in the story to reveal anything of the political and social influences at work in contemporary Europe. Even the subsequent days in Andreas' life have little to particularize them. They merely mark temporal sequence, and even that is not completely clear. Time is under the control of the story rather than vice versa. Place likewise appears well defined at first in terms of the city, streets, and even the specific church to which Andreas agrees to return the money, and yet this particularity cannot disguise the fact of the tale's generality. Andreas' story could take place equally well in almost any other city, given of course the appropriate change in national drink. Finally, even that ultimate Aristotelian criterion, probability, suffers outrageous insult at the hands of Roth's narrative. The role of chance is simply too great for any conventional realism; yet, as the narrator points out, there is nothing to question: "It was simply a miracle and within a miracle there is nothing to cause astonishment."

What strikes the reader in Andreas' tale, then, is not so much the evocation of a specific localized atmosphere and milieu as the sense of Andreas' essential homelessness. Roth achieves here almost an abstraction of the rootlessness experienced by so many exiles. In this case, however, Roth avoids the customary exile situation involving the dissolution of all the details constituting one's daily identity. Instead we experience in Andreas the reintegration of a personality in a fashion that might properly deserve the designation "legendary."

The story of Andreas Kartak is in fact a legend of grace, a sort of grace not entirely dissimilar to that lying behind Heinrich von Kleist's "Marionettentheater" and its particular concept of *Grazie*. Kleist, as one recalls, also wrote of man as an exile, man as refugee from his true estate. "Über das Marionettentheater" begins with the question of physical grace, the problem of how a lifeless marionette can be far more graceful than a human dancer. Kleist lay the blame for this flaw in the human condition at the feet of man's defective consciousness. Man enjoys neither the absolute ignorance nor the absolute knowledge that would restore to him the "grace" found in animals and in God. Kleist postulated, however, the possibility of a sort of rear door to paradise that would lead to a restoration of grace, both physical and metaphysical, and he suggested this might be found in either an absolute awareness or in none at all. Kleist, of course, concluded his essay by noting that the state of innocence brought about by partaking a second time from the Tree of Knowledge would represent the end of the world as we know it—"das letzte Kapitel von der Geschichte der Welt."

In his last days Andreas is granted the grace that would have marked the end of the world as Roth and many of his fellow exiles knew it all too well. Rising from his initial position of absolute poverty, Andreas moves gracefully through the stations of his last adventures, reconstituting along the way the identity that had been lost in a superfluity of alcohol and deprivation. Andreas' state up until the time of his fateful encounter with the generous stranger suggests a total obliteration of his rational faculties. He is and knows nothing, not the date, not even his name. As Roth noted in reference to another character, however, knowledge is perhaps no longer the key to happiness, nor perhaps even a preferable state: "he has already left behind the stage of knowledge. The circle has closed. Man is again a believer. . . . One doesn't believe the knowing man any more. One believes the man of belief." Andreas's lack of reflection is then perhaps a holy simplicity. He is capable of insight and even compassion, as is shown in his encounter with the woman whose furniture he helps move, but his basic tendency is not to think about what happens; he merely accepts it. Beginning as a sort of *tabula rasa*, with his individuality effectively erased by his life beneath the bridges, Andreas is granted favor after favor, his needs and wishes are fulfilled by a benevolent fate, and, as a final reward, his death is easy. In the only sentence in the tale that takes direct note of the audience, the narrator states, "May God give us all, us drinkers, such an easy and beautiful death."

The specific course of Andreas' apotheosis will concern us somewhat later. For the moment we might recall that Roth is hardly alone in modern German literature in his attempt to depict the life of a saint. To name only the most famous examples, Werfel's *Das Lied von Bernadette* had its beginnings in a profound religious commitment; and at the other extreme, Mann's *Der Erwählte* makes use of its religious framework as a necessary facade for sophisticated, albeit ulti-mately secular, artistic manipulations. For Roth the issue seems to lie somewhere in between. Born a Jew, Roth never seemed to have evidenced a particularly great religious concern, and his later conversion to Catholicism was a matter of dispute among his friends. One might even suspect that Roth occasionally functioned as a sort of animated Rorschach test, quite willing to assume the shape he perceived might be anticipated from him. Joseph Gottfarstein, for example, related that Roth assured him that he was true to the faith of his forefathers while, at the same time, in both his writings and in conversations, Roth was assuring others of his Catholic fealty. Considering, then, the religious commitment of its author, *Die Legende vom heiligen Trinker* might seem to be as ambiguous in its implications as it was in its genesis. In fact several critics have seen, for example, only mockery in Andreas' title as saint. Yet Roth has stylized his tale of a modern saint into a crystalline form that radiates a sense of inner conviction oblivious of the boundaries of confessional distinctions.

Roth's use of the legend form is of course somewhat unconventional in an age in which, as the narrator puts it, people are much more inclined to believe in chance than in providence. The word legend itself has its etymology in the practice of reading aloud the lives of saints during divine services and at mealtimes. Examples of Christian charity and fortitude fill the many volumes of the *acta sanctorum* in which events are recounted in a straightforward style readily understandable to even the most naive auditor. In this sense the legend provided easily assimilated models of faith in action, and it invited emulation.

In *Die Legende vom heiligen Trinker,* the use of legend form is immediately complicated by the paradox implicit in the concept of the holy drinker. Since temperance is one of the cardinal virtues, Andreas' claim to saintliness would seemingly be excluded by definition without the need of considering such various other sins as deceit, fornication, and murder. Critics such as Kesten and Nigg have denied Andreas any claim to sainthood on the basis of these and other faults and have viewed him at best as a parody. Adopting their view up to a point, one might, in fact almost speak of an inversion of normal categories. One thinks of a saint as giving; Andreas is a recipient. One thinks of a saint as active in the cause of virtue; Andreas' minimal activity occurs primarily in the pursuit of what is commonly considered vice. Yet even though Roth is deliberately ambiguous about whether the glow radiating from Andreas' face after his first shave is a sign of divine favor or merely a sense of physical well-being, Andreas does seem to possess a certain air indicative of grace beyond that of the common man.

By way of contrast, Andreas' patroness St. Teresa of Lisilieux was a true saint of the modern era. After her death in 1897, her case was considered so meritorious that the customary fifty-year waiting period was waived, and she was fully canonized in 1925. Her story, appropriately enough, is characterized not by grand deeds, but by devotion to matters of small scope. Her autobiography is filled with this devout attention to small things. This reference to smallness is picked up at the end of the story, where Andreas perceives the girl before him as "Such a great, such a small saint." The spark that caused Roth to choose this particular saint as patroness for his protagonist is perhaps an incident recorded from St. Teresa's childhood when she gave a beggar money only to have him return it with a smile. More probably, the decisive factor was the specific nature of Teresa's saintliness: "She had shown innumerable people that sainthood is attainable by anybody, however obscure, lowly, untalented, 'ordinary,' by the doing of small things and the discharge of daily duties in a perfected spirit of love for God."

Andreas certainly suggests the categories of lowly, obscure, untalented, and "ordinary," and it is this very quality of commonness that makes his role as hero of a legend all the more anomalous. Austrian literature, however, is not without precedents for such figures. In Grillparzer's "Der arme Spielmann," we encounter a similarly unsuccessful character who wins both our sympathy and our best wishes. Both Andreas and Jakob are heavily autobiographical in both positive and negative senses. Both exemplify "saintliness" in an otherwise corrupt world. Yet, as opposed to the flaws of Grillparzer's Jakob, whose sin is primarily that of economic insufficiency, Andreas' sins are much more worldly. The divine music Jakob perceives at the moment of his death is an appropriate reward; Andreas' gentle demise is explicable only in terms of a grace beyond our worldly categories.

A closer link to Roth's intentions may perhaps be found in Jolles' investigation of the legend as a basic narrative form. Jolles emphasized, for example, that the *vita* of a saint is far different from his legend, for the factual account of a saint's life is subject to the historical considerations of biography, whereas the legend tends to concentrate only on those events that have immediate, representative value. The legend reduces the life of a saint to a minimal framework preferably consisting of a series of what Jolles called *Sprachgebärden* which isolate specific, representative actions. Finally, and most significantly, the most important factor of the saint's legend is his intermediary position between the absolute purity of the divine and the necessary limitations of the human sphere. Legendary figures present an *imitabile,* a model of exemplary behavior which the devout themselves could conceivably attain.

But again, what of Andreas, this drunkard, wastrel, and patron of prostitutes? Remarkably enough, moral censure does not enter Roth's story. The reason for this lies in Andreas' particular type of *imitabile* insofar as the account of his final days represents a sort of *Wunschtraum,* a desideratum. Andreas is exemplary here not so much in his particular behavior as in his embodiment of a grace beyond our normal comprehension. To this extent it is inconsequential whether his perceptions of his final days as miraculous are true or merely yet another demonstration of the abiding Austrian conviction that psychology is superior to reality.

From a literary viewpoint Roth achieves his effects here, first of all, through the use of the motif of rebirth and regeneration. In the first scene where Andreas emerges from the darkness beneath the bridges of the Seine, he does not possess a name and the narrative knows him only as "one of those without a refuge" or "the disheveled man." Only in the second segment does this anonymous figure become connected with the name Andreas. In the subsequent segment Andreas happens to notice that the day is Thursday, and, recalling that he was born on a Thursday, declares this day his birthday and thus the occasion for visiting a somewhat more elaborate bar. Behind the obvious irony of such a decision, one still perceives the suggestion then further underlined by what amounts to a ritual of cleansing as Andreas hesitantly washes his hands in the river. This motif of cleanliness grows along with the development of Andreas' personality. After his first vision of Teresa he joyfully washes not only his hands but also

both his face and neck, and later he experiences a revelation when the mysterious door of his hotel room opens into a gleamingly clean bathroom with glistening tiles and a sparkling white bathtub, the sight of which immediately arouses in him a compulsive wish to cleanse himself completely. Even before this incident, however, Andreas' sense of self undergoes significant growth: as he examines his papers he rediscovers not only his full name which he had forgotten, but also the less comforting fact that his papers are invalid, and that he has no right to be in France. His meeting with Karoline, the woman for whom he had murdered, further forges his connections with his past identity as does his encounter with his boyhood friend Kanjak. The culmination of this development comes when, physically cleansed and reestablished in his sense of self, he achieves on his own the conquest of Gabby, the beautiful dancer. Subsequently Andreas is even able to reverse his usual role and to provide financial aid to yet another friend from earlier days. The misfortunes and reverses he encounters along the way cannot destroy this new self, and his death is honored with a vision—albeit perhaps only subjective—of a personal visit from the little saint with whose name the entire process of self-reclamation had begun.

As Hackert has pointed out, one has to be aware of the deftly ironic qualifications permeating Roth's miraculous tale [Fritz Hackert, *Kulturpessimismus und Erzählform: Studium zu Joseph Roths Leben und Werk* (1967)]. The seemingly miraculous events gracing Andreas' final days can well be explained in conventional terms, and Roth leaves his reader the freedom to attribute them to chance rather than divine intervention. Simple chance, however, would be hard put to establish such a remarkable concatenation of fortunate events. In addition to the three encounters with important figures from his past, Andreas twice has money forced upon him by total strangers, and at two further points, he discovers money in billfolds that fate has thrust into his hands. In the final episode his luck seems to have come to an end when he experiences the ultimate terror of a man without papers, the hand of a policeman upon his shoulder. This policeman, however, proves quite literally to be a "Schutzmann" ("protector" or "guardian," German for "policeman"), who insists upon returning a billfold with 200 francs, which he believes belongs to Andreas. This amount is, of course, significant for it is the final installment in a series of benefactions and provides exactly the amount needed to repay the loan extended at the story's beginning.

This seemingly miraculous grant also corresponds to the story's structural base, for the tale lives from the assumption that at some point Andreas must come to terms with the debt he has incurred, the 200 francs he had promised to return to St. Teresa when his conscience dictated. To this extent Andreas' debt constitutes a major suspense element comparable to the revenge motif in a revenge tragedy in which a crime must be avenged: when Hamlet finally avenges his father's death, the play is done. The analogy to a pact with the devil also comes readily to mind, by the terms of which an individual accepts certain rewards from the devil and agrees later to perform a required service. Here, fortunately, the pact seems motivated by benevolent forces and leads only to the gentle death the narrator admires so profoundly.

It is, in fact, the gentle quality of Andreas' progress that contrasts so starkly with what might be anticipated for a man lacking both papers and money. One could only predict an inauspicious future for a heavy drinker such as Andreas, a man who, as Roth reminds us, is privy to the depths that sober men will never know. Andreas' drinking had already reduced his existence to the basest level, and he appears ready to revert to that state with minimal provocation. He is furthermore a homeless man without valid papers, yet instead of fighting against his lot as the land surveyor K., that man of highly dubious credentials in Kafka's *Schloss* had done, Andreas passively accepts whatever fate confers. Finally, from his own experiences Roth would have been all too well aware of the anxieties haunting an impoverished alcoholic dependent on what he could beg from friends and acquaintances. Yet in *Die Legende vom heiligen Trinker* all these signs re-emerge transformed into their opposite.

This transformation is most clear in Andreas' relation to money. Whereas money plays a central role in Andreas' regenerative process, he never becomes dependent on it, nor does he grow jealous of those, such as his friend the soccer player, who possess wealth. When Gabby robs him, Andreas accepts it as an appropriate payment for the enjoyment he had received. Even the prospect of reverting to a life under the bridges holds no particular terror. One of Andreas' most saintly traits is, in fact, this freedom from greed. On the other hand, Andreas' ascent is directly attributable to the small sum he receives at the outset of the story. This sum has an effect beyond that of mere financial security. After he had first washed himself Andreas had reached again for the bill in his left inner pocket and "felt himself to be completely cleansed and almost transformed." While this transformation may be purely subjective rather than supernatural, Andreas' self-confidence continues to grow and after his next shave "it seemed as though a glow radiated from his countenance that made the raggedness of his clothing insignificant."

This blissful state cannot be maintained in its pure form, yet each time Andreas loses his money and is about to be reduced to his customary destitution, he experiences a new influx of cash, be it as a direct gift or a chance find. Within this context money becomes the primary symbol of the grace that is granted Andreas. Instead of a fairy tale motif of a limited blessing, the benevolent forces that appear to guide Andreas' final days grant an unlimited grace which is, after all, the nature of divine grace.

This development culminates during the penultimate scene, set in the bistro, where Andreas encounters the young girl he takes to be St. Teresa. As he tries to explain to her his *Schulden*, a word which subsumes both debts and guilt, and attempts to repay the money he feels he owes, her response radiates the miraculous quality of a saint; she reaches into her purse and gives him another 100 francs. Thereupon Andreas collapses and is carried into the sacristy of the church to which the terms of his original agreement had obligated him to return. The narrator describes his death as follows: "Unfortunately he cannot speak any more, he only makes a gesture as though he wanted to reach into his left inner coat pocket where the money that he owes his little creditor lies, and he says, 'Fräulein Teresa,'—gives his last sigh and dies."

This last gesture is resonant with significance for his motion toward his left inner pocket is a gesture both toward his money and toward his heart. His willingness to return the money is a sacrifice combining the payment of his debts (*Schulden*) with the expiation of his guilt (likewise, *Schulden*). Furthermore, it should be noted that the German term for creditor, *Gläubigerin,* also combines along with its common meaning of creditor the basic meaning of one who believes in another person. In this, his last gesture, Andreas the receiver becomes himself a giver, himself a saint, and dies.

In commenting on Isak Dinesen's writings, Eudora Welty once formulated a remarkable statement on the process of literary creation: "Of a story she made an essence; of the essence she made an elixir; and of the elixir she began once more to compound the story." Roth's particular personal version of the exile phenomenon was one granted to or, perhaps more properly, one visited upon few men. From his background he extracted an essence containing all the implications of homelessness, loss of identity, economic need, and ever-present fear of expulsion. Employing this essence he then formed an elixir embodying the reverse of this experience, the exile experience as a bliss that perhaps can be envisioned only by those who have plumbed the depths of despair. The apotheosis of Roth's saint is predicated upon the life of a sinner, and the tale is a legend—one is tempted to say "only" a legend. Yet, just as the venom of a snake can be transformed into an anti-serum and used as an antidote against the poison of its own kind, Roth analogously managed to distill an essence from his experience, to transform this essence into a therapeutic elixir, and to reconstitute this elixir into a tale of blessing, into his tale of the holy drinker, into a legend of the good fortune that can engulf one who is "a man of honor, even though without an address." (pp. 81-94)

> *Barton W. Browning, "Joseph Roth's 'Legende vom heiligen Trinker': Essence and Elixir," in* Protest—Form—Tradition: Essays on German Exile Literature, *Joseph P. Strelka, Robert F. Bell, Eugene Dobson, eds., The University of Alabama Press, 1979, pp. 81-95.*

CELINE MATHEW   (essay date 1980)

[*Mathew is an Indian educator and critic specializing in German literature. She is the editor of the journal* German Studies in India *and the author of* Ambivalence and Irony in the Works of Joseph Roth. *In the following excerpt from that study, she examines the novels* Das Spinnennetz, Hotel Savoy, *and* Flucht ohne Ende.]

Das Spinnennetz was published from 7th October 1923 to 6th November 1923 as a serial novel in the Viennese *Arbeiterzeitung*. It is a political novel and pictures the turbulence of the times and the threat to the Weimar Republic from the Right Extremists, the Nazis, a theme that exercised Roth's imagination in the feuilletons of this period too. The intense topicality of the novel becomes clear from the fact that the very next day that the novel came to an end, on November 7th and 8th, the Putsch by Hitler and Ludendorff who are mentioned in the story, occurred in Munich.

The novel is direct narration by the author. . . . However the narrator has a tendency to withdraw from his omniscient position and let the story unfold itself in the form of *erlebte Rede* [the critic explains in a footnote that "*erlebte Rede* reproduces the thoughts of the character without overt interference by the narrator"] through the medium of the character. Thus after the initial direct narration he falls silent, makes no comments nor does he interfere in any way with the narration. All the same he sets the narration at an ironic angle and to that extent makes his presence felt. Nothing is said about the identity of the narrator. But we know from Roth's journalistic work his views on the Nazis, and it can be assumed that the narrator, at least in this respect, reflects Roth's views.

For a great part of the narration Theodor Lohse is the *Reflektor-figur* [defined by the critic as "the character whose thoughts are reflected and from whose vantage point the events are viewed"]. Returning from war he is forced to take up the post of a humble *Hauslehrer* ["tutor"] at the house of the rich Jew Efrussi. The wealth, luxury, comfort and culture of the Efrussi home fill him with envy, and he covets these things as well as Efrussi's young wife. In his egoistic pursuit of materialistic success he falls in with a Nazi secret organisation having its links with Hitler and Ludendorff in Munich, and his fanatic hatred of Efrussi's class, the Jews, turns him into a zealous Nazi. A politician out of envy and hatred and base personal ambitions, his rise to power is through means equally bad and despicable. Homosexuality, spying, betrayal of friends, treacherous murder—there is nothing he does not stoop to. He climbs up the ladder of success, marries into the aristocracy and dreams of the day when he would be *Führer*. He could very well have been one of Hitler's henchmen. (pp. 74-5)

Theodor Lohse is placed in juxtaposition to Benjamin Lenz. The very fact that Lohse the Jew-hater finds his best friend in Lenz, the Arch-Jew, tends to mix up issues. It is not Nazi and Anti-Nazi, but petty bourgeois and anarchist, that the contrast high-lights. Lohse is petty bourgeois, limited in his thinking and planning, for he thinks in purely personal terms and cannot see beyond his nose. He throws overboard the morals of his class, but is still haunted by them and has nightmares because of them. He has broken them only to gain certain personal ends, not because he has discarded them for good. Benjamin Lenz is, on the other hand, the grand anarchist untroubled by scruples. He is the Jew from the East who sits in judgement over Western Europe and condemns it to extermination. He does not seem to have any personal ambition. If he is a threefold spy and betrays one man to the other and both to a third, it is because he considers them all equally bad and would gladly help in the process of wiping them all out.

Lohse is cowardly, lecherous, a weakling. Lenz is his opposite in all these respects. He observes the European scene with ironic detachment, with a sense of personal superiority. He never tries to adjust himself. He is always himself. Lenz hates Europe and holds all its values up to ridicule. . . .

[His] is an absolutely amoral attitude, one can say, or rather would be amoral, but for Lenz' firm conviction that it is almost a duty to destroy Europe. He hates Europe, but loves it too. (p. 76)

Lenz loves Europe because it calls loudly for destruction. It is the ambivalent feeling of hate-love. It makes him hate what is bad and at the same time love it, for its destruction is work that he loves. With missionary zeal he devotes himself to the work and observes with the amused curiosity of a stranger European ways of life. (pp. 76-7)

For Benjamin Europe is ripe for destruction. There is nothing that deserves to be saved. Not its God who is a politician, not its schools and institutions which train children to kill each other, not its forms of life and culture emptied of all meaning and reduced to a ludicrous pantomime.

Lenz' views need not be taken for Roth's. But condemnation of Europe is conveyed not only indirectly in the portrayal of

Theodor Lohse and Benjamin Lenz, but also in direct statements of the narrator, which seem at times to merge with those of Lenz. (pp. 77-8)

The cynical disregard of truth, its shameless falsification by the press and those in power are exposed. It is a world gone astray, a time out of joint that the novel portrays. The author's style reflects this world in a series of disjointed sentences in which the conjunctions and adjectives are conspicuously absent; the narrator gives a bare, unvarnished enumeration of facts and studiously keeps out comments. Only the juxtaposition of facts reveals the ironic motivation of the whole account. (p. 78)

The absolute dishonesty, ruthlessness and unscrupulousness that characterise politics in general are depicted without comments as in the account of Theodor's breaking up a meeting in the roughest manner. . . . (p. 79)

[Without] ideals or principles, without even knowing clearly why he does it, he does brutal, absolutely base things. And he is young Europe. Roth correctly diagnoses the disease of the times when he shows the lack of a positive ideology among the youth of the period, a lack that makes them fall easy victims to Nazi propaganda. And he shows the absolute bankruptcy of Nazi ideology that is born out of hate and is nourished on hate. (pp. 79-80)

An amorphous attitude to moral and intellectual values and a disregard for truth go hand in hand. In this atmosphere of half-truths and lies, naturally truth is often taken for falsehood and falsehood for truth.

Roth offers no solution, suggests no remedy to counteract the evils of the time. The novel was written during Roth's so called socialistic period. It might be expected that Roth would make the socialists vanguards in the fight against the Nazis, hold them up as crusaders in a holy cause. He does not. Not a single individual or party or creed does he recommend as protection against Nazism. Those who appear to be front line fighters like Thimmi turn out to be base informers who lay explosives in other people's cellars in order to betray them later to the police. Even the archenemy of the Nazis, Efrussi, turns out to be in league with them. The only people with whom Roth sympathises are the workers who fall fighting for their rights. Only here the narrative is free from irony, Roth's lone weapon against gloom and despair at the sight of a world that goes down without a fight against inhumanity. Roth does not hold out any hope of the Nazi tide being stemmed, unless it be through the holocaust Benjamin Lenz plans. And this holocaust is aimed not so much at the Nazis as at bourgeois European civilisation. Even this end, hoped for by Benjamin, is not certain, for it is difficult to say how the confrontation between Benjamin and Theodor would end and who would emerge victor. Benjamin actually speaks of following his brother to Paris. Roth here uses a device he is going to repeat in other novels also and leaves the conclusion undecided.

The narrative is from beginning to end steeped in irony. . . . The whole career of Theodor Lohse is observed from a superior height, with an ironic detachment that makes itself felt practically on every page of the book.

This irony embraces not only Lohse, but almost everyone in the novel, Lohse's father, sisters, the journalist Pisk etc. Pisk has a protruding ear. He wore the hat even in the café. He did not wish to draw attention to his ear. Nobody would be able to say, he had a disfigurement. At the most one would say he could not behave himself. And one already said that about him. Lenz' cross spying is passed off in the same vein of light irony. Lenz betrays the Communist plan of a demonstration to Kamm and then takes the news of the enemy's knowledge of the plan back to the Communist Rastschuk . . . . " 'Man muß ehrlich arbeiten!' sagte Benjamin Lenz." [" 'One must work honorably!' said Benjamin Lenz"]. What Lenz calls "ehrlich" ["honorably"] will mean to most people arrant treachery. The *Zweiwertigkeit* ["duplicity"] of all human actions is thus forcibly brought home. Lenz's characterisation as a whole marks the triumph of ambivalence of attitude regarding values. Lenz does not accept the established values of Western Europe. It is not so much a revolt against them as an unawareness of them that is striking in his case. Coming from another world, as it were, they seem to him ridiculous, and he cannot take them seriously. The fact that what we have accepted implicitly as a hoary truth or a time-honoured custom can strike another person as extremely ludicrous is in itself an assertion of multivalence and hence of ambivalence of values. Benjamin's remark "Man muß ehrlich arbeiten" may or may not be intended as an ironic justification for his vigorous spying on all hands, but it has an ironic effect in the context, just because it contradicts generally accepted ideas. In other words, it is ironic only because it is ambivalent. (pp. 80-1)

On the whole this first novel of Roth has the essentials of ambivalence in it although on the surface it seems to be a militant novel campaigning against Nazism. Nazism is indeed displayed in its stark inhumanity. But it is no sustained call to arms that we hear, rather a stoic facing of facts, awareness of an evil against which no one really puts up a fight. In this failure to counteract a negative philosophy with a positive ideology, in the overtones of ambivalence in the portrayal of the hero who is ein "Gefährdeter" ["endangered"] and therefore ein "Gefährlicher" ["dangerous"], who presses forward with might and main and at the same time longs for the security and obcurity of his "Hausmeister" ["caretaker"] existence, in the ridiculing of established order, culture and religion of Europe, in ironic remarks scattered throughout the book, we have clear indications of ambivalence as a pervasive influence on Roth and his work. (p. 82)

In 1924 two novels were published, *Hotel Savoy* and *Rebellion.* Gabriel Dan of *Hotel Savoy* and Andreas Pum of *Rebellion* are like Theodor Lohse *Heimkehrer,* men returning from war and imprisonment. The three follow different courses. Lohse becomes a criminal and gets on in life, Gabriel Dan remains an observer who refuses to be swept into the whirlpool of life, and Andreas Pum turns rebel and perishes in life's struggle.

Gabriel Dan comes from the East, from Russia, and is on his way to the West. Hotel Savoy is on the way. It is still in the East, but has all the comforts of the West. It is the world in miniature. On the topmost floor, the seventh, Santschin, the clown, dies what may be called a sudden death, but is really a process lasting over ten years, killed as he is by the fumes of the laundry. In the meanwhile on the ground floor Frau Jetti Kupfer is entertaining the factory owners and business men of the place with her bevy of naked girls. The poor and the feckless live on the topmost floors and the rich on the first three floors. Outside the hotel there is a strike on, there is hunger and dirt, and misery. But inside the hotel, order seems to be maintained in some mysterious way. Nobody has seen

the owner of the hotel, Kaleguropulos, although he makes regular inspection tours through the hotel at dusk and leaves instructions behind for those at fault in one way or other. If one does not pay the rent, Ignatz, the lift boy, comes and takes on pledge some possession of the defaulter. Ignatz is rather a weird figure with his age, green eyes, eerie knowledge of the goings-on of the hotel guests and omnipresence in the hotel. The clocks at the various landings, each keeping a different time, as though each floor is regulated by its own system, are also in keeping with the weirdness about the whole place.

Gabriel Dan is puzzled by all this and racks his brains with questions about everything, about the closed worlds of the rich and the poor, about Kaleguropulos, whose invisible presence like that of God in the world preserves order in the hotel. Hotel Savoy is to him a metaphysical model of the world. (p. 83)

Dan's perplexity is reflected in the many questions he asks, especially in the paradoxical form some of them take (How high can one fall?) All the same Dan who has been lonely all his life, is for a time drawn into warm feelings and companionship through his acquaintance with Santschin, Stasia and others. He is almost in love with Stasia, and he knows that she loves him. However since he has no money, he does not put up a fight for her, and weakly yields place to his rich cousin Alexander. He withdraws into his shell and watches the hotel burn, and the order he has associated with it proves to be a delusion. Outside forces, the striking workers, burn it down, and the great mystery that has puzzled Gabriel Dan is also solved. It turns out that Kaleguropulos is only the lift-boy Ignatz who perishes in the flames.

The Bloomfield episode reinforces the impression of disillusionment. Everyone expects help from Bloomfield. Everyone from Neuner to Hirsch Fisch has his own hopes and dreams, and hopes to attain them through Bloomfield's help. The whole town looks forward to his coming. He comes very noisily at dead of night and leaves very silently at dead of night. Nothing is changed by his coming. The people wake up from their dreams sadly disillusioned. They had thought that he came to help them, to help his old home-town. But it turns out that he comes only because his father is buried there. He has no thought to spare for the town. He comes and goes on his own business and a gullible world builds its hopes on him, to be rudely jolted out of fond hopes and delusions. Dan, who as Bloomfield's secretary has to deal with these people, sees and understands all that they go through. When the hotel burns and Stasia goes with Alexander to Paris, there remains nothing for him, but to resume his lonely wandering.

That is the story told in the form of a first person narrative. It is the story of a complete disenchantment. As Bronsen puts it, "Everything which Gabriel has thought about Hotel Savoy proves to be an illusion. . . . The mysterious order in the hotel although it is experienced by everyone as reality is only appearance, rests on a false pretence of authority, for Kaleguropulos is exposed to be a God who does not exist."

This is a sceptical insight that sees through the self-deception of man regarding a non-existent God. In this insight as well as in the fundamental traits of his character, Gabriel Dan is the typical Rothean hero. He is reflective, undecided and unable to tale decisions, an ironic observer of the world and of himself, always in two minds about things. . . . He cannot decide to leave Hotel Savoy, although he knows it is an evil place, and lingers on till the hotel is burned down. With regard to Stasia and the surrendering of his room to Alexander, he shows the same wavering and drifting. It amounts to an inactivity, a passivity that lets things happen to oneself without doing anything about it. At the same time he is filled with anger and hatred towards Hotel Savoy, capitalism etc., against a social order which lets the Santschins die of fumes while the rich gorge themselves. (pp. 83-5)

He asks questions and finds no answers. And uncertainty becomes his basic attitude. Even trivial things about which he was certain at first, he begins to doubt within a short time. Thus he had thought at first that Zlotograd's bringing Santschin's ass to the funeral was the noble brave gesture of a true friend. But later on, after he had talked with him for some time and seen how he changed from minute to minute, it strikes him that the whole story with the ass was only a cheap comedy. The double face or *Zweiwertigkeit* that ambivalence discovers in things is evident here. It could be a noble gesture or a cheap comedy. What it was exactly, one doesn't know. This uncertainty makes Dan doubt his own impressions. As Stasia entered the stage for her dance, Alexander's face twisted as though something had hurt him. But with the next sentence this first impression is wiped out. "Aber es geschah nur, weil er ein Monokel einklemmte" ["But it was only because he put in his monocle"]. (p. 85)

In other points also *Hotel Savoy* is typically Rothean. The rejection of industrialism is as uncompromising as in the journalistic work. . . . The picture of a world grown unreal with human beings turning into ghosts or automata recurs in this novel and creates the same weird impression, as e.g., in *Brief aus dem Harz.*

Another recurring theme, that of loneliness, finds articulate expression in Dan's characterisation. He seems to accept it as his fate. "Ich habe keine Eile. Keine Mutter, kein Weib, kein Kind. Niemand erwartet mich. Neimand sehnt sich nach mir." ["I'm in no hurry. No mother, no wife, no child. No one is expecting me. No one longs for me."]

What may be called a peculiarity of this novel is the clash between awareness of the existential problems of human life and the urge to seek a human responsibility and hence a human solution for them. Gabriel Dan realises the gigantic proportions of human misery. Human beings are caught in a web of cares like flies and struggle for escape. After a few decades of desperate struggling and erring they die leaving their heirs a legacy of misery. This pessimistic picture of human life is accompanied by an acknowledgement of the human responsibility in the misery: "Das Schicksal bereiteten sie [die Menschen] sich selbst und glaubten, es käme von Gott. Sie waren gefangen in Überlieferungen." ["They prepared their own destiny and believed that it came from God. They were trapped by traditions."] These traditions are named. They are "Verbotstafeln" ["slates of forbidden activities"] of their God, their police, their kings and their class. The culprits therefore seem to be the very same ones pilloried by the Socialists and the mention of "Class" (Stand) definitely gives the sentence a political tinge. We notice how even individual passages can be stamped with the spirit of ambivalence in Roth's works.

Hotel Savoy being a first person narrative, Gabriel Dan, the narrator, is allowed to express his bitterness directly now and then. It escapes him as it were, and so the impression of the narrator's standing a little above and apart from the story, of being the detached ironic observer, an impression which almost all the novels of Roth make, is for long stretches absent from this novel. Instead of it there appears the embittered irony with which one fights despair. (pp. 86-7)

Controlled bitterness or stark hopelessness seems to be the dominant note of this novel. The hotel is burned down, the God Dan has been looking for turns out to be non-existent, a hoax; the revolution to which Zwonimir had looked forward has failed and Zwonimir himself with all his strength is dead; Stasia has turned to Alexander, partly through his fault, as he recognises. What remains for him now except America? But that too is associated with Zwonimir. There is no way out for Dan. One feels that he will be to the end of his life a lonely wanderer without faith in anything, without an aim in life. Dan embodies the attitude of ambivalence.

Looking at the novel in the larger context of Roth's evolution, the double strain of thought and action strikes us. On the one hand *Hotel Savoy* symbolises the contrast between the rich and poor and the wrongs done to the poor, on the other the metaphysical concern with life and man as the only one problem of real interest. Gabriel Dan hates the capitalists and Hotel Savoy, and Zwonimir the revolutionary is his friend. But Zwonimir is an unreflecting, unintellectual type, and his naivety could be the source of his revolutionary spirit. Dan never identifies himself with the revolution. His real interest lies in clearing up the mysteries of Hotel Savoy. Who is Kaleguropulos? Why are all men including the rich miserable? Such questions exercise his mind. "Es geschieht vieles hier. Mich aber geht Kaleguropulos an" ["A lot happens here. I, however, am concerned only with Kaleguropulos"], says he on the night the hotel burns. When the mystery is solved, disillusionment follows, for he finds out there is no Kaleguropulos, only Ignatz.

The novel is therefore not so much a record of socialist convictions, as a disguised quest for the author of life and the world, for the Kaleguropulos of the universe. Roth seems to sway between these two poles, and hence his attitude towards socialism as well as to metaphysical speculation can be said to be ambivalent in this novel. (p. 88)

Flucht ohne Ende was published in 1927. Roth began writing it during his journey through Russia, and parts of the novel deal with Russia and the Bolshevik Revolution. It belongs to that period of Roth's literary career, when he was toying with "Neue Sachlichkeit." In the attempt to be as realistic as possible, Roth poses as Tunda's friend who reports the events in the story. The sub-title of the novel is "ein Bericht" ["a report"]. Excerpts from Tunda's diary and letters are given in order to strengthen the impression of documentation. But the narrator freely makes comments. The story begins with Tunda's leaving Baranowicz' house in Siberia at the declaration of peace and ends with his rejection of Baranowicz' invitation to return. His earlier life in the West as an Austrian lieutenant and Irene's fiance is depicted through retrospective narration. The three phases of his life are represented by three women, the West through Irene, the Revolution through Natascha, and the quiet life in Baku through Alja.

Tunda is in many respects an autobiographical portrait, as Bronsen points out. Tunda is as old as Roth. In 1926 both are 32 years old. . . . Birth in a small town in Galicia, imprisonment in Russia etc. are other points of similarity. Roth's views on Russia and the West expressed in letters and news-paper articles are also Tunda's. (p. 97)

Tunda goes through war, imprisonment, revolution on the Bolshevik side, flight to the west till he reaches Paris, only to discover in this metropolis of the world that nobody is so absolutely unwanted in the world as he. (pp. 97-8)

This situation of a young man alone and unwanted in a great city and in complete awareness of it, must have set Roth thinking and must have been the starting point of the novel, the novel itself being an attempt to explain how and why the young man was brought to such a pass.

There is no doubt that there is juxtaposition of Tunda's life as Beranowicz in Russia and as Tunda in the West. His reason and better instincts tell Tunda that his life in Siberia centred in the duties and pleasures of a simple uncomplicated existence would be a better one than his rootless wandering in the West from one city to the other or the double life of his brother. Baranowicz's letter at the end is a clear call to return to that life. It is also a call to action, for Baranowicz invites him to take part in an expedition for exploration of the Taiga. (p. 98)

The West holds him thrall. Perhaps there is no question of a choice at all. A man like Tunda could not but turn westward like a moth to the flame. The naive unintellectual life in the Taiga would have been half death for him. Alja's addiction to silence is repeatedly harped on by the narrator. Life by her side in the great open spaces of Nature was not the life for him, it would have been mere vegetating for him and he prefers death and ruin in the West to it.

In *Flucht ohne Ende* the juxtaposition of values, with the balance perceptibly tilting to one side, is between the West and the simple unsophisticated world of Baranowicz, not with the world of the Revolution, which Roth for the most part views with scepticism and irony (e.g. in the Natascha scenes). He values the Revolution for its positive sides, but cannot close his eyes to its fundamental deficiencies. He cannot stomach the reducing of man to a mere cog in the machine, the undermining of human dignity. (pp. 98-9)

Perhaps nothing would have been acceptable to Roth, for his sharp eyes detected faults in every system. His criticism of the Austrian Monarchy whose fervent champion he became, is as sharp as his criticism of the Bolshevik Revolution or Nazism. The comparison that Bronsen makes between Roth and Brecht is interesting in this context. While Bertolt Brecht could satisfy his need for complete identification with an ideology by siding with Marxism, Roth could find very little significance in pure theory. Only a socialism with a humanitarian moral would have been acceptable to him.

Tunda's letter to the fictive reporter explaining why he left Russia is a serious discussion of life in Bolshevik Russia and a quiet, but firm condemnation of it. The reasons given for the condemnation seem to revolve round ambivalence. In the first part where the Soviet administrative system is described, we read: "Du siehst im Leben . . . lauter solche Punkte, die in einer geheimen und wichtigen Beziehung, sogar in einer sehr nahen, zu Dir stehen. Du kennst diese Beziehung nicht." ["You see in life . . . nothing but these points, which have a relationship to you that is mysterious and important, even very close. You don't understand this relationship."] The ignorance about the mysterious, important and close relationship between individuals or rather points to which individu-

als are reduced, leads to the tantalising uncertainty mentioned in the next para. It is possible one is suddenly moved like a piece in a game of chess. Or things happen contrary to one's expectations. Instead of being punished for some neglect of duty, one may experience something pleasant. . . . When one is suspicious of one's own experience and doubts whether success is success and failure really failure, then one certainly carries the brand mark of ambivalence. (p. 99)

For a great part of the novel however Roth returns to his criticism of the West. . . .

Most of the criticism of Western Europe is given in the form of Tunda's impressions about the Europe he returns to after a long absence. (p. 101)

Roth aims all his fire at the cultural pretensions of the unnamed little town where Georg lives and which is a typical German town. "Innerhalb der Stadt, die selbst ein Kulturzentrum war, gab es auch Häuser, die kleinere Kulturzentren waren" ["Within the city, which was itself a cultural center, there were also houses that were smaller cultural centers"]. The typical characters of a *Kulturzentrum* ["cultural center"] are there; *Künstler* ["artists"] who play Bohemians, Jewish and Christian intellectuals who pretend to be above all prejudices, a stamp collector who conducts exhibitions etc. The town has also the usual trappings of culture like "das berühmte Glockenspiel . . . , das in Baedecker erwähnt wird," "ein paar alte historische Brunnen," "ein Kriegerdenkmal" ["the famous Glockenspiel mentioned in Baedecker," "a couple of old historical fountains," "a war memorial"] etc. . . .

The process is repeated when Tunda comes to Berlin. From a small town to the big city of Berlin and then to the metropolis of the world, Paris—we have in this succession of towns a deliberate heightening of the criticism which culminates in the last scene. The lengthy descriptions are introduced deliberately for the purpose of criticism. Berlin is described as a city that is humane out of practical considerations. Many more people would die in Berlin if there were not a thousand protective arrangements, installed not at the dictates of the heart, but because an accident means a traffic disturbance, costs money and upsets order. This seeing of an ulterior motive in an apparently good action is in keeping with the attitude of ambivalence, which sees in the situation "eine doppelte Wertmöglichkeit . . . , eine positive und eine negative" ["a double possible value . . . , a positive and a negative"]. (p. 102)

Roth depicts the intellectual and moral chaos, hollowness, even non-valence of Western society caught in a process of decline and disintegration. (p. 103)

The ironic asides of the narrator expose the votaries of European culture for the hypocrites they are and in the process expose European culture itself to be a fake with fake values. High-sounding words, fine sentiments and lofty concepts present a facade of culture, refinement and high moral earnestness, but actually cover shallow, superficial and hypocritical thinking and living, for culture, religion and art are nothing more than impressive labels, conversational phrases for this society that conveniently forgets them in private life. The narrator writes with inside knowledge as if he is one of them and at the same time observes them with ironic detachment and pillories them in brief, quickly drawn sarcastic pictures. As writer he stands above this society and would perhaps hasten the decline of the West prophesied by Spengler through such criticism. But since he belongs to this society and clings

Obituary tribute to Roth.

horizon. No wonder this star disappears altogether from vision for long stretches of time, and he lets himself be delayed by other things and persons, e.g. Natascha and the Revolution, Alja and an official's life in Baku.

When he finally leaves Russia, he is not sure why he leaves it. . . . In the two pages devoted to explaining the reason for Tunda's leaving Russia, the fictive reporter pretends to judge him from outside, suggests a variety of reasons, says that Tunda is unreliable, that he has begun the quest for Irene out of caprice, out of love of freedom and disregard for dangers. But since no clear explanation is given, the various suggestions only modify each other and demonstrate the real aimlessness of Tunda, reveal the many facets of his nature and hint at the complexity and incomprehensibility of human behaviour, the ambivalence of all human actions. (pp. 104-05)

About the general tone of irony that enlivens the pages of this novel there can be no difference of opinion. Paradoxes and juxtaposition of incongruities are a part of it, and Roth's pages abound in them. . . .

The binding together of contradictions is naturally a device that would appeal to a person who is deeply aware of the fact that there are two sides and in fact conflicting sides to every question.

Paradoxes and pithy statements of epigrammatic finish, another quality of Roth's style, again bear witness to his sharp eye for unsuspected sides and unplumbed depths. The reverse side of the picture is thrown into sudden, bold relief and the reader is forcibly made aware of the *Zweiwertigkeit* of truths. (p. 107)

Summing up we can say that in his discarding of both the West and of Russia, in his creation of a character like Tunda who is a perfect specimen of ambivalent attitudes, in chance remarks scattered throughout the book and in stylistic devices, Roth has produced in **Flucht ohne Ende** another novel stamped with the twin characteristics of ambivalence and irony. The long journalistic descriptions of the Rhineland city, of Berlin, Paris and of the Soviet Union are deliberately included in the novel in order to voice his criticism of East and West. They may be artistically a flaw as pointed out by Bronsen ("journalistisch verflacht" ["journalistically flattened"]) and an English critic ("The subject of **Flight without End** is one which a great short story writer might have turned into a little masterpiece, . . . but unfortunately it occurred to Herr Joseph Roth. He has expanded it, distorted it and altogether vulgarised it"), but they are an integral part of the novel as Roth planned it and show the writer standing above the ideologies of his time. So the very "defects" of the novel spring from the author's fundamental attitude of ambivalence which makes him place the two antagonistic societies of the East and the West side by side in order to reject the values the two embody. A third set of values is embodied in Baranowicz' life far from all political ideologies, even from social influences, in the heart of Nature. But that too, is not accepted. Since these three sets of values comprise almost all the known established ones, the impression that prevails at the end is perplexity regarding an aim or purpose in life, absolute lack of direction that goes with ambivalence. (p. 109)

Celine Mathew, in her Ambivalence and Irony in the Works of Joseph Roth, *Peter Lang, 1984, 212 p.*

to it in spite of all its faults, some of the criticism sticks to him also.

The condemnation of the West and yet the innate love for it, the great esteem for the Revolution and Soviet Russia and yet the temperamental disinclination for it—here we have already a fine instance of ambivalence, not to say anything about the picking of holes in all values and systems and the vain search for values which one can accept wholeheartedly.

The characterisation of Tunda confirms the impression of ambivalence. Tunda is twin brother to Gabriel Dan, who also is engaged in a flight without end. We meet him when, knowing that peace has been declared, he decides to return home from Siberia. We hear almost immediately: "Er hatte keinen bestimmten Plan, der Weg lag unsicher vor ihm, lauter Windungen" ["He had no definite plan, the path lay uncertain before him, pure convolutions"]. He returns home because of the woman to whom he is betrothed. But he acknowledges the unpleasant truth that she would no longer love a nameless jobless young man without home or rights. So he loves her doubly "als ein Ziel und als eine Verlorene" ["as a goal and as a lost hope"]. Right from the start it is therefore clear that this flight homewards is undertaken without any hope of success, without a clear aim or goal beckoning him, that Irene is only a faint indistinctly seen star in the

OTTO W. JOHNSTON (essay date 1981)

[*In the following essay, Johnston examines the role of humor in Roth's novels.*]

Joseph Roth's literary disposition can hardly be described as humorous. His temperament was molded less by whim or fancy than by the ominous *signatura temporis* of the Austrian empire, which Roth saw crumbling all about him. . . . Ironic sympathy characterizes Roth's creative impulse, empathic exposure his artistic intent. In any of the three worlds through which this wanderer travels, words like fanciful, funny, and frolicsome seem out of place. Whether among effete aristocrats, robust Slavs, or fleeing Jews, Roth offers little knee-slapping laughter. We find at most the smirking of a sensitive artist who depicted the decline of respected traditions and venerated institutions.

Despite its scarcity, however, humor does play a role in Roth's fictional cosmology. Where it occurs, humor functions as a dialectical force in his literary structures because it invariably implies its own opposite: seriousness, tragedy. Moving between these poles, his Trottas, Taittingers, and Fallmerayers follow what they regard as a purposeful course of action; in so doing, they commit the cardinal sin in the code book of the Austrian elite—they make themselves look ridiculous. As we shall see, humor in this context serves to point out the double meanings behind the activities of certain characters.

Inasmuch as humor consists in the bringing together of incongruities which arise naturally from situation or character so as to illustrate some fundamental absurdity in human nature or conduct, Roth is humorous. In fact, he humors his officers, his Barons, his *Beamte* ["civil servants"] by complying with their moods or caprices and by accepting the rules governing their social class. Looking at their own value system through a glass darkly, Roth reveals not without empathy their blind spots, their vices, and the suicidal course of their society.

To be sure, Leutnant Trotta of *Radetzkymarsch* (or "Radetzky Limp," as Butler labels it [see Additional Bibliography]), does not have a great deal in common with Franz Tundra of *Flucht ohne Ende,* even less with the Franz in *Die Rebellion.* Moreover, social stratification clearly separates Mendel Singer of *Hiob* from Trotta or Tundra. Despite what Böning described as "das Netz" ["the net"] of figures and places in Roth's work [Hansjürgen Böning, *Joseph Roth's Radetzkymarsch* (1968)], different levels of consciousness segregate these characters. It can be demonstrated, nevertheless, that in the contexts of the Slavic world and Jewish exile, those who laugh loudest, hurt the most.

This observation is not to suggest that Roth's characters experience no joy. Surely, the atmosphere is jovial in Monsieur Weingrod's Parisian restaurant. . . . Yet pleasure is at a premium in a world, "wo das Schicksal lauert" ["where destiny lies in wait"], where so good-natured a fellow as Weingrod is kicked out of Russia, jailed in Poland, refused a visa in Germany, and hit by a car in Paris. While the narrative persona describes pleasure, he is reminded of pain. Joy posits its own sorrow as these antonyms react in a dialectical relationship, propelling the characters and the plot forward. This is the dialectic of humor in Roth's literary structures.

Delight is restricted to "die Pariser jüdischen Gasthäuser" ["the Parisian Jewish taverns"], which are "lustig, warm and laut" ["merry, warm, and loud"], or to the solitude of Mendel Singer's room, where he experiences "die Gnade und die Freude" ["mercy and joy"] while reading his psalms aloud. . . . At the *Gasthaus* ["tavern"] or with the *Gebetbuch* ["prayer book"], Roth's figures enjoy fleeting moments of rapture. Once they step outside these environs, however, they are confronted with the inane world of officialdom, soldiery, and class consciousness, romantic in its ideals, unwieldy in its operation. . . . (pp. 31-2)

Roth portrays a cosmos in which those who laugh loudest are to be pitied most. Their would-be mirth covers the hellish torments of their life experiences. . . . [The] humor is intentionally ambiguous, almost always implying the opposite of itself, while suggesting double meanings behind a given character's actions or reactions. Because of its antithetical nature, Roth's humor indicates that each character has a deeper dimension and that his or her activities may have a purpose other than the one envisioned.

This function of ascribing double meanings to a protagonist's behavior becomes in turn the object of irony when a character, believing he is following a prudent course of action, makes himself ludicrous. Humor in these contexts, by implying its opposite, foreshadows tragedy. According to the code of conduct adhered to by numerous characters modeled after the Austrian aristocracy, there is no greater social sin than to make oneself appear preposterous. Whenever Roth sets the scene for the lighthearted entertainment we associate with "old Vienna," the opposite takes place. From gaiety to absurdity, his characters waltz the *danse macabre.*

The rigid social structure so skillfully delineated in *Radetzkymarsch,* for example, homogenizes deeper feelings and creates bland dispositions incapable of recognizing ominous danger. Feeble and unsuccessful attempts to alter basic situations underscore the extent of the characters' entrapment. Roth humors his Trottas, Taittingers, and Fallmerayers by accepting the codes of the Habsburg elite as part of his narrative perspective. While sympathizing with his creations, he exposes their frailties and vices, their boredom and indecisiveness.

Structurally, two things are going on simultaneously in these contexts: the narrator is moving from indulgence for his upper-class Austrian personalities to disapproval of their mental and physical activity; in so doing, he establishes narrative distance. The character is traveling from caprice to catastrophe, thereby assuring narrative breadth. Humor is thus a stylistic device with a dual purpose: the persona identifies with his creations, while antithetically disclosing their debility; hence compliance with the whims of protagonists becomes a signal for their impending folly. Herein lie the dynamics in the relationship of persona to character. At the same time the protagonists' halfhearted attempts at humor forecast misfortune; therein lies the narrative range of pseudo-historical behavior. We thus arrive at Roth's literary equation: empathy multiplied by severity yields narrative distance; whimsy divided by pain produces narrative breadth. The coefficient is the persona, who knows the signs of decay; the characters do not.

Roth's sardonic humoring of his own creatures is a unique feature of his fertile imagination. He conjures visions of life in the romantic, swirling *Donaumonarchie* ["Danubian monarchy"] on the eve of its most inglorious day. Once he has set the highly polished desks, the overstuffed high-back chairs, and the shaded lamps in place, neither wit nor joviality crosses the mind of his characters. No gaiety here. Self-deceived, bored, lonely, and trapped in their starched uniforms, their rigid conventions, and the empty forms of outdated rules and regulations, his soldiers, petty nobles, and stationmasters move quickly from the sublime to the ridiculous. As the refrains reverberate in three-quarter time and the exhilaration of waltzing couples intensifies, Roth sets the stage for what could have been amusement—a night in "Romantic Vienna." But that is not what takes place.

In *Radetzkymarsch,* for example, the news of the assassination at Sarajevo spreads through the party rooms like wildfire. Trotta overhears the Hungarian officers' disparaging remarks about the archduke; he draws his revolver—only to make a fool of himself by threatening, while in his cups, to shoot down the next to speak. In **"Stationschef Fallmerayer,"** a railroad official leaves his boring existence behind to follow his erotic fantasy. Yet he loses the woman of his dreams to her crippled husband and ends up with nothing. In *Flucht ohne Ende* the outcome of Tundra's search is disillusionment. When he finally catches up with Irene, he does not recognize her and walks right by. These examples illustrate Roth's figures as they hasten to their own embarrassment, do something reckless, and deceive themselves on a senseless quest. Others like Franz in *Die Rebellion* jump headlong under the crushing wheels of the state bureaucracy. This topsy-turvy world of paradox and antithesis, in which the opposite of what is expected takes place, produces some incredible attitudes. So blinded by passion is Fallmerayer, for instance, that he comes to believe that good is evil, evil is good. . . . This brings us to the crux of the matter: the humor/tragedy dichotomy is but one of the many opposites in Roth's antithetical narrative. Good-evil, war-peace, passion-indifference, expectation-surprise, sympathy-critique are other manifestations of the same dialectical process. The breadth and depth of human experience—despite the social pressures, the strictures, the homogenizing effect of impersonalized bureaucracy—are the stuff of Joseph Roth's novels.

But let us test our theory of the dialectic in Roth's works on one more example. A later work offers some corroboration of our tentative hypothesis.

When Hitler came to power in 1933, Roth, in a moment of great distress, announced a change in his narrative perspective: in order to strengthen Austria against fascism, he would mollify his critical stance and give in to his sympathies for the *Doppeltmonarchie* ["dual monarchy"]. On April 28, 1933 he wrote to Stefan Zweig: "Ich will die Monarchie wieder haben und ich will es sagen" ["I want the monarchy reinstated and I want to say so"]. However, the subsequent attempts to integrate ever greater narrative warmth into his earlier more ironic stance created a tension which produced the opposite of Roth's intention. Instead of furthering more understanding for his characters, the author of **"Die Büste des Kaisers"** made Graf Morstin more pathetic. Wielding a bottle of soda water in Zurich's American bar, where customers make fun of the *Stephanskrone,* this postwar version of Trotta, Taittinger, and Fallmerayer is not more humorous, not more sympathetic, but rather more bizarre. The story of Lopatany's former administrator substantiates our argument because we see here the movement between polar opposites compressed into fewer than twenty pages. . . . Roth tried to infuse his new perspective, adopted for political purposes, into much older material. **"Die Büste des Kaisers"** is reveal-

ing nonetheless because the transition from power to impotence, from activity to inertia, from the impartial treatment of individuals to political favoritism, from levity to absurdity, from humor to tragedy—the range of Roth's dialectic archetypes—can be studied here in a short work.

Our brief study of the nature and function of humor in the rather humorless works of Joseph Roth has pinpointed a dialectical force with a tripartite purpose. Firstly, humor is antithetical in that laughing often immediately suggests pain and crying. As a dichotic impulse, humor/tragedy joins with such other antithetical concepts as critical sympathy, active inertia, impotent power, and grim absurdity to produce a dialectic which pervades the structure of Roth's novels, the thinking of his characters, and the narrator's point of view. As we have seen, Roth also plays an aesthetic game with his readers by setting in place the backdrop for lighthearted entertainment and arousing expectations of amusement and frivolity. But when we expect humor and gaiety, we find neither. Secondly, Roth humors his Austrian aristocrats. Complying with their rules of etiquette and the priorities of the Habsburg ruling class, Roth's narrative perspective proceeds to unmask the frailties and decay. Thirdly, his characters may not laugh, but they do make themselves "lächerlich" ["laughable"]; in so doing, they disgrace themselves as social beings by their own standards. When Roth, in a desperate personal effort to save Austria from Hitler and his henchmen, tried to intensify his sympathetic attachment to his fictional monarchists, he produced characters even more embarrassing than before. In conclusion, we observe that such stylistic techniques as permanently bonding humor to tragedy enabled Joseph Roth to create a dialectical cosmology; he could demonstrate his fondness for "old Vienna" and the *Doppeltmonarchie,* while still telling the truth about the people who lived there. (pp. 32-5)

> *Otto W. Johnston, "The Dialectic of Humor in the Works of Joseph Roth," in* West Virginia University Philological Papers, *Vol. 29, 1981, pp. 31-7.*

CURT SANGER (essay date 1982)

> [*In the following essay, Sanger examines the ways in which Roth addressed contemporary political concerns in his historical novels* Die Kapuzinergruft *and* Die Geschichte von der 1002. Nacht.]

The historical novel holds an important place in the literature of exile from 1933 to 1945. Although this genre has been criticized for its escapism—as expressed in the exiled writer's apparent avoidance of his duty to oppose Nazism—the frequent use of allegories, parallels, and veiled allusions to the contemporary period in works of this kind leaves no doubt of their authors' intent to confront the situation of exile. Thomas Mann's *Joseph* novels, Heinrich Mann's *Die Jugend des Königs Henri IV* (*Young Henry of Navarre*), Lion Feuchtwanger's *Josephus* trilogy, and Alfred Neumann's *Neuer Caesar* (*Another Caesar*) are but a few of the more salient examples. Mathias Wegner in his pioneer study of the literature of exile sees a definite need for the study of the historical novel: ". . . the historical novel . . . portrayed the difficulty of the emigrants in a nutshell. The significance of this literary genre for exile literature should one day be thoroughly examined, especially the depiction of actual events after 1933 that appear in historical disguise."

One exile writer who shows a preoccupation with the past in

his novels, but is inexorably involved in the present, is Joseph Roth. This is particularly true of his last two works, *Die Kapuzinergruft (The Crypt of the Capuchins)* and *Die Geschichte von der 1002. Nacht (The Story of the 1002nd Night).*

If one is to grasp clearly the specific motifs of exile as they appear in these novels, a short description of Roth's unique experience of exile is necessary. On 31 January 1933, the day of Hitler's appointment as chancellor of Germany, Roth was in Paris, where he had maintained a permanent residence since 1927. He was never a German citizen, and even though he had been employed by German newspapers since 1921, he felt no special loyalty toward Germany, but rather aversion. By 1925 he had come to consider France, and especially Paris, his intellectual and cultural home. As a roving reporter for the *Frankfurter Zeitung* from 1923 to 1932 Roth was constantly on the road, lived regularly in hotels, and never owned an apartment or other property. Because he had no family, he did not share the usual worries of the writer in exile who had been forced to abandon his relatives upon leaving Germany. In contrast to most of the emigrants who came to France after 1933, Roth was familiar with the French language and mode of life and was in no danger of losing his residence permit.

Nevertheless, after Hitler's rise to power Roth had a much smaller market for his books, like most of the writers in exile whose books were blacklisted or burned in Germany, and in consequence his financial difficulties grew. At the same time his precarious state of health was further weakened by his continual and excessive drinking, which grew chronically worse during exile. Poverty and poor health also restricted his travels, which were vital for him, indeed an escape from himself.

Above all, his relationship to Austria was decisive for Roth's life in exile. From 1925 on, his letters and writings convey a gradual transformation from a left-wing, revolutionary postwar author to a conservative Austrian monarchist, a transformation that appears complete by 1932 with the publication of *Radetzkymarsch (Radetzky March).* At this time Roth writes: "My strongest experience was the war and the fall of my fatherland, *the only one* I ever had: the Austro-Hungarian Monarchy." In subsequent years Roth's allegiance to the defunct Hapsburg Monarchy and the Catholicism traditionally and ideologically bound to it symbolizes his longing, in an age of instability and inhumanity, for a stable, humane, and transcendental order.

Keenly aware of Austria's dilemma, Roth foresaw the threat to the Republic by the Nazi government. In many of his letters he nourished hope for the restoration of the Hapsburg Monarchy, which he saw as the sole guarantee of Austrian independence. With this in mind he wrote numerous articles for exile journals (such as *Das Neue Tagebuch* and *Die Österreichische Post,* as well as for the *Christlicher Ständestaat,* published in Austria) calling attention to the cultural and historical uniqueness of that nation. The downfall of Austria in 1938 had a decisive effect on Roth. A study of the exile elements in *Die Kapuzinergruft* and *Die Geschichte von der 1002. Nacht* reveals the indelibility of this experience.

Roth began *Die Kapuzinergruft* in 1937, perhaps affected by the precarious political situation of Austria, which he observed at first hand during a stay in Salzburg. The novel, apparently planned as a sequel to *Radetzkymarsch,* follows the destiny of the narrator Franz Ferdinand Trotta—a cousin of the hero in *Radetzkymarsch*—from the immediate prewar period to the fall of the Austrian Republic.

The fact that *Die Kapuzinergruft* is a first-person narrative in which the hero relates episodes of his life from memory lends an air of authenticity to the story. This impression is borne out by the fact that the narrator's account of certain incidents from his life—for example, his army career, his disillusionment and despair as a returning soldier, and his growing consciousness of the loss of the Danube Monarchy—all coincide with Roth's own experience, about which he constantly spoke and wrote. The shared experience of author and fictional character points to the possibility of an intended identification. As Käthe Hamburger observes in her analysis of an author-character relationship, the relationship between the two can "be so narrow . . . that we cannot distinguish with certainty whether we are dealing with an authentic autobiography or a fictitious creation." In *Die Kapuzinergruft* it is the mutual Austrian experience that unites author and character: the belated love both feel for the Monarchy and the political ideals ensuing from this love. The title *Die Kapuzinergruft* in itself characterizes Roth's experience of exile. Not only is it the loss of the Hapsburg Empire, but also the dissolution of the Austrian Republic, with which the hope for restoration of the Monarchy vanishes also. The twilight atmosphere in which the action takes place, the melancholy mood, the despondency and apathy of the narrator and his friends, and the leitmotifs of death produce the funereal mood that pervades the book and anticipates the fall of Austria.

The political ideologies expressed in *Die Kapuzinergruft* are a reconstruction of the exiled Roth's political attitude toward the Austrian problems of his immediate present. Thus Count Chojnicki, representing the monarchist view of Austria, describes what he terms the lack of the proper appreciation for the future of Austria on the part of the Social Democratic and Christian Socialist parties:

> Austria is not a state, not a homeland, not a nation. It is a religion. The clerics and the clerical fools who are governing are making a so-called nation out of us; out of us, who are a supranation, the only supranation to have existed in the world. . . . The Social Democrats have proclaimed Austria a component of the German Republic, they who are after all the disgusting creators of the so-called nationalities problem. The Christian Socialist fools from the Alpine hinterlands follow in the footsteps of the Socialists.

That the fictitious character Chojnicki functions as spokesman for the author can be seen in the following excerpt from a Roth letter:

> Yes, the empire of our forebears, I worry anew about it . . . will it come to pass? . . . I am apprehensive for the following reasons: . . . It was destroyed by this loathsome nationalistic socialism [=National Socialism]. . . . The new rulers strike me as too provincial. They are too much part of the Alpine region; they are not capable of grasping the all-embracing physiognomy of the Empire, but only the limited one. Can Austria rise again out of that which is geographically limited even though its essence lies in what is geographically unlimited?

Although Chojnicki's statements apparently refer to past events, they come to have direct bearing on the present through Roth's interpretation of Austrian problems at the time he wrote *Die Kapuzinergruft.* The author refers to the parallel between the prewar agitation of the German Nationals and the annexation politics of the Socialists in 1921 and 1931, and to the inner weakness of the current Christian Socialist government, whose inability to understand the transcendent mission of the Monarchy and to work for its restoration exposes Austria to the threat of the Nazi state.

Typical of Roth's attitude in exile is his deep-seated animosity toward Germans. It is not accidental that the villain in *Die Kapuzinergruft* who cheats the Trotta family out of their last possession is a German—more specifically, a Prussian. The stark portrayal of this type reveals an antagonism that could have derived only from recent events:

> A new personality came into our life, a certain Kurt von Stettenheim. . . . He looked like one of those men nowadays considered to be racially pure. . . . Such persons come from the Baltic Area, from Pomerania, even from the Lüneberg Heath. Comparatively speaking, we were still relatively fortunate. Our Mr. von Stettenheim was only from the Mark Brandenburg.
>
> He was tall and sinewy, blond and freckled; he wore the inevitable dueling scar on his forehead, the distinguishing mark of the Prussians, and also a monocle, so inconspicuous that one could not help but notice it. . . . There are faces from Pomerania, from the Baltic, from the Mark Brandenburg, in which the monocle gives the impression of being a third, unnecessary eye, no help to the natural eye, but its mask of glass.

In contrast to this portrait are the sympathetic ones of Jewish characters and their humane temperament, contradicting the Nazi representation of Jewish types. The visit of the Jewish driver Manes Reisiger prompts the narrator to express his views on anti-Semitism: "At that time I knew a few Jews, Viennese Jews naturally. I by no means hated them, precisely because at that time the patronizing anti-Semitism of the nobility and the circles that I associated with had come into fashion among caretakers, the petty bourgeoisie, chimneysweeps, paperhangers." Reisiger's physical appearance too makes an impression on the narrator and denies the Nazi concept of a specific Jewish type: "As I entered the anteroom, I saw a man who not only contradicted entirely my usual conceptions of a Jew, but could even have been capable of completely destroying them. He was something uncannily black and colossal. . . . The man was strong and tall." The character sketch of the Jewish lawyer Dr. Kiniower, in whom Old Testament wisdom combines with genuine concern for his clients, is aimed at Nazi propaganda about the dishonesty and maliciousness of Jews. Although Roth, who outwardly professed Catholicism during his exile period, was reared a Jew, he nevertheless vigorously opposed Nazi anti-Semitism on purely humanitarian rather than sectarian principles.

The structure of the novel, too, reveals a relationship to the present. The loose, unorganized construction of the plot, especially the scrambled succession of episodes in *Kapuzinergruft,* contributes to the vagueness of events as they appear to manifest the decadence and disorder of society. Narrative and social disorder in the novel thus reflect the inner disintegration of the Austrian state. The novel proceeds at a relatively slow pace through the longer episodes of the postwar period and then abruptly converges upon the events of February 1934. It appears as if the pressure of contemporary events upon Roth's consciousness was responsible for the present overtaking of the past. The death of Trotta's mother coincides with that of Ephraim Reisiger. Both incidents symbolize the impending doom of Austria. With the death of the mother, who with her aristocratic character and elegant manners is the last representative of old Austria, hope for the restoration of the Monarchy dies too. The death of young Reisiger, a victim of the bloody suppression of the Social Democratic Party by the Dollfuss government, is one of the causes for the actually impending downfall of the Austrian Republic.

The capitulation of the Austrian government to Nazi power on 11 March 1938 caused Roth to write the last chapter of *Die Kapuzinergruft.* The concluding action demonstrates his inner compulsion to come to terms with the lowest point of his experience of exile. In the traumatic final scene, which begins with a nostalgic recollection of the Viennese prewar nights, the brutal reality of the Nazi annexation and the triumphant proclamation of the storm trooper shatter the hero's consciousness: "Fellow Germans! The government has collapsed. A new German people's regime has come into existence!" Trotta's realization that Austria no longer exists has a devastating effect on him, as it had on his literary creator, who likewise could not bear the loss of his homeland. The hope of the protagonist, who does not become fully aware of the pointlessness of his existence until the downfall of Austria, together with the hope of the author himself for a new Austrian monarchy, is buried forever as Trotta despairingly seeks refuge in the Kapuzinergruft—the burial place of the Hapsburgs. For him, living as he does completely in the memory of the past and the isolation of his existence, shying away from the reality of the present, as well as for Roth, who by contrast could not dissociate himself from the reality of the present, Austria's fall constitutes the nadir of his life.

Die Kapuzinergruft is the literary transfiguration of Roth's exile agony. The author shares with his hero not only despair for Austria but also guilt for their initial sceptical indifference to the Monarchy while it still existed. Both realize the tragedy of its loss only after it ceases to exist. Roth, like Trotta, confronted by the harsh reality of his time, nostalgically recalls the Empire, a utopia that lives only in his memory. Finally, the loss of the last vestige of this supranational entity, the Austrian Republic, destroys Roth's personal and literary raison d'être. In the final analysis, *Die Kapuzinergruft* becomes a requiem for both Austria and Joseph Roth. The despairing question with which the novel ends, "Where should I, a Trotta, go now? . . ." is an expression of the writer's own despair.

In a letter of 20 June 1937, Roth writes: "A new book has already gone to press, *Die Geschichte* [von] *der 1002. Nacht,* but not proofread and worked through." Stefan Zweig believes, in the summer of 1938, that Roth must now be finished with the novel. In any case, the work was published only posthumously, in 1939. Thus Roth worked on his book at a time when his despair for Austria, together with his failing health, brought his emotional and physical crisis to its ultimate phase.

At first glance, the title—*Die Geschichte von der 1002. Nacht*—indicates the possibility of a thematic relationship with the original Persian *Arabian Nights.* The impression is strengthened by the oriental frame narrative in which the actual plot is enclosed. The frame stories of the nineteenth century (for example the *Novellen* of Theodor Storm and Conrad Ferdinand Meyer) had lent a certain degree of authenticity to their narratives. In contrast, the frame of Roth's final novel serves a purely ironic purpose, behind which the exile experience is concealed. Roth employs the fairy-tale-like frame to create the expectation that the story will be completely removed in time and space from his present, an expectation that he then shatters by allusions to contemporary events. He opens the narrative in the traditional style of a fairy tale: "In the spring of the year 18.. the Shah-in-Shah, the holy, exalted, and eminent monarch, the absolute ruler and emperor of all the states of Persia, began to feel an uneasiness he had never known before."

In designating some indefinite period of the nineteenth century as the time of the action, Roth consciously situates the events of the narrative at a distance from the present. Yet as soon as the introduction is over and the actual narrative begins, the author abolishes the apparent disparity in time with the following commentary:

> Just barely two hundred years had passed since the cruelest of all Mohammedans had advanced toward Vienna. At that time a true miracle had saved Austria. Far more dreadful than the Turks had been, the Prussians now threatened the old Austria—and although they were almost more heathen than the Mohammedans . . . God did not perform any miracles . . . Now another, more frightful epoch commenced, the era of the Prussians, the era of the Janizaries of Luther and Bismarck. On their black and white flags—both colors denoting deep mourning—there was certainly no half-moon to be seen; rather a cross, but it was an iron cross.

In identical language Roth mourns the fall of Austria in *"Requiem Mass,"* a polemic written in 1938: "The Prussian boot trudges over the oldest European seed. The tower of St. Stephan's Cathedral, which was spared from the half-moon for a couple of centuries, will soon be transformed into a symbol of falsehood by the swastika . . . and over the Kapuzinergruft flutters the old black, white, and red foe." The similarity of content and style between the two passages and the deliberate absence of the Austro-Prussian conflict from *Die Geschichte von der 1002. Nacht* suggest Roth's intent to express his reaction to the annexation of Austria in allegorical terms.

One of the author's leitmotifs in the novel is the illusion of tranquillity: "At that time a profound and supercilious peace prevailed in the world." This description is repeated later in the novel: "Far and wide a profound, almost frighteningly profound peace prevailed." By defining this state of peace as "supercilious," however, and therefore inauspicious and "frightening," Roth alludes to the inertia that characterized the Western powers in the face of the Austrian annexation. Essentially it is the same sentiment, or rather resentment, that prompted his protest elsewhere: "A world has been relinquished to Prussia. A world? *The world* has been handed over to Prussia: for better or for worse. . . . The world meanwhile negotiates with Ribbentrop."

The central character of this novel, who emerges from the frame of the story, is a certain Baron Taittinger. Taittinger, an aristocratic member of the officer class with his studied indifference and inborn casualness, may be regarded as a figure symbolic of the decline of the Austrian Empire. Like his antecedents in Roth's works in particular and in Austrian fin-de-siècle literature in general, he is a passive hero alive in a world of his own.

The plot centers on the Shah's passionate desire to possess, for one night, a countess whom he has seen during a banquet given in his honor at the Viennese court. The imperial courtiers, perplexed by the unexpected wish of the oriental ruler, substitute a double hastily fetched from a brothel on the advice of Baron Taittinger, who knows of the resemblance between the two ladies. Taittinger's role in this so-called "affair" leads to his transfer from the Viennese court to a remote garrison, his eventual resignation from the Army, and finally his suicide. This tragic denouement results from his failure to perceive reality until it is too late. The reality that Roth has created in this, his last novel, to affect the protagonist so harshly lies in both the nature of the state that confronts him and the character of the people who individually and collectively contribute to his ruin. Like the hero in *Die Kapuzinergruft,* Taittinger experiences the ultimate futility of his existence. As a true Austrian, he has lost his time and place.

Significantly, in this novel Roth fashions the state, not into a patriarchy headed by an emperor, as in his earlier works, but into an anonymous power, estranged from the individual. He describes a bureaucracy of a Kafkaesque character, whose officials—"Minute little wheels in incomprehensible service to the incomprehensible state . . . instruments of fate . . ."—sacrifice the protagonist to the interest of the state. In this portrayal of a despotic authority, selfish and indifferent to the fate of the individual, the sense of alienation in Roth's own exile is revealed.

Roth's perspective on contemporary events unquestionably influenced his creation of characters who alone and together bring down the hero. Although Roth, in accordance with Austrian literary tradition, portrays the common people in his early novels as decent and loyal, he perceives these types in *Die Geschichte von der 1002. Nacht* with caustic irony, etching their vices with vitriol. Taittinger's proletarian friends exploit his naive trust, his basic benevolence and willingness to make amends, thereby destroying his career and any chance he may have of rehabilitating himself. Their vulgar manners and grotesque appearance are matched only by their mutilation of the German language. The wax figures these characters use in the puppet theater that they have induced the protagonist to purchase for them symbolize their heartlessness.

In creating such character types, Roth was undoubtedly motivated by his knowledge of the events transpiring in Vienna during and after the Nazi annexation of Austria, which belied the widespread reputation of Viennese *Gemütlichkeit* ["joviality"]. The traumatic effect of the barbaric present upon such a sensitive artist as Joseph Roth may have caused him to conclude *Die Geschichte von der 1002. Nacht* with the epilogue of the puppet maker: "I could perhaps produce puppets that have heart, conscience, passions, feelings, morals. But no one in the entire world asks for such. They want only side-show freaks in this world; they want monsters. Monsters are what they want!"

In *Die Geschichte von der 1002. Nacht* the author shows more narrative objectivity than in *Die Kapuzinergruft,* whose first-person narrator unfolds the story. The apparent detachment and the setting of the former novel in the distant past reflect Roth's desire to escape from the reality of his time. Conversely, the writer's habitual references to the present and the scathing irony by which he unmasks the characters and their actions express his suffering resulting from contemporary events.

An Austrian writer steeped in the Viennese literary tradition, Roth exhibits in his life and works the typical dichotomy of the Viennese, an experience that Grillparzer depicted in his cathartic play, *Der Traum ein Leben*, 1834 (*A Dream Is Life*). Roth, too, would have liked by means of his literary art to seek refuge from the dismal reality of the late nineteen-thirties, but his active concern with the problems of his day denied him this possibility. With respect to such ambivalence, Heinrich Schnitzler's opinion about the Viennese and their writings offers great insight:

> It is another characteristic of the Viennese that they have always been perfectly aware of the game they were playing with reality; they always knew that they were trying to fool themselves; that this life of frantic escape was a delusion and that it was doomed. This . . . awareness . . . had various effects on Viennese literature. It sometimes led to complete acceptance of the Catholic creed . . . or it might cause a mood of complete resignation . . . or, again, it might cause unrelieved despair; while in other instances it might result in bitterness and cynicism.

During the last two years of his life, Roth could not elude the impact of the present either in his life or in his writing. Reality was so barbaric that Roth, like his protagonist in *Die Geschichte von der 1002. Nacht,* was unable to survive. (pp. 258-66)

> Curt Sanger, "The Experience of Exile in Joseph Roth's Novels," in Exile: The Writer's Experience, edited by John M. Spalek and Robert F. Bell, The University of North Carolina Press, 1982, pp. 258-66.

PHILIP MANGER   (essay date 1985)

[*In the following excerpt, Manger analyzes Roth's presentation of the Hapsburg Empire in* Radetzky March, *summarizing four common critical interpretations of the novel's socio-political perspective.*]

Most of Roth's novels are peopled with characters, especially Jews, from the land and town of his birth. It is no coincidence that he has the youngest of the "heroes" of the *Radetzky March* sent off to Galicia. Although the name of the garrison town where Carl Joseph's second regiment is stationed is indicated only by its initial B. its geographic description is unmistakably that of Brody with its surrounding forests and large swamps. (Brody is the plural form of a word meaning ford.) Brody remained an inexhaustible source of inspiration for Roth, supplying him with an inner epic universe from which he could draw at will all kinds of people and situations that he had known and brought to life in his fictional world, often allowing the same types, such as Kapturak, to turn up in different works. Fiction and reality are very close in Roth. As in real life, he invented substitute fathers in his novels, for example such figures as Chojnicki in the *Radetzky March,* or even Professor Moser who also bears traits of Roth himself. Noticeable is the absence of mothers; those of the Trotta family are hardly mentioned or not at all, they are at best shadowy figures in the background, almost silenced to death in a way that is akin to the psychological repression of events or persons one would rather forget.

Of particular relevance to the *Radetzky March* is the development of Roth's political views until the time when he began

work on that novel. Like most young intellectuals of his generation Roth had begun his career as a writer on the political left, somewhere between revolutionary socialism and anarchism. The novels up till 1930 consequently deal with the socio-political problems of the present, i.e. the immediate post-war situation in Austria and Germany and the difficulties of the younger generation, especially those who had returned home from active war service—alienated, disorientated, unsettled and insecure in a changed and rapidly changing unstable society subject to the extreme tensions of the experimental phase of a new political system: democracy. The experiment coincided with economic disasters of previously unknown magnitude, and these in turn resulted in inherently violent polarisation.

Roth's observations in Russia in 1926-7 mark a turning-point in his political convictions, the beginning of the road towards the conservative, indeed reactionary right. In a private letter he wrote: "It is fortunate that I have travelled to Russia. I would never have got to know myself." He soon realised that he had been unduly idealising revolutionary Russia, and discovered that his disenchantment was not caused primarily by political or ideological differences, but was "a cultural, a spiritual, a religious, a metaphysical [problem]." His unexpected reaction evokes in him the European; he feels as "a Catholic, a Humanist and a man of the Renaissance." The cause of his disillusionment lies in the absence of the expected *social* revolution. Instead he finds the all-pervasive mentality of the "writing-desk bourgeoisie [which] determines public life in Russia, internal politics, cultural policy, the newspapers, art literature, and most academic research and scholarship. Everything is bureaucratized." He notes how the intellectual revolution has limited itself to technological progress: other cultural achievements have not come about. If there are any differences between Russia and Western Europe, they are superficial. "Marxism," he reported, "appears in Russia also as merely a part of European, bourgeois civilisation."

The Russian experience increased Roth's feeling of spiritual homelessness. The unstable Weimar Republic had an equally disenchanting effect and so, in his reactions to the increasing disorder and the concomitant rise of the National Socialists, he began to condemn everything that was new: both democracy and all technological development. Like the Nazis, with their retrospective utopia and blood-and-soil ideology, Roth turned to the past in search of a putatively saner world. What he did, in other words, was—rather illogically—not just to oppose Nazism, but to compete with it, setting up a parallel rather than a counter-ideology, hoping, it seems, to reconstruct a world of solid, stable humanitarian values against the Germanic barbarism. In addition, Roth had become convinced in the late 1920s that the political decay and the general loss of values were to be blamed on technology with all its accompanying ills: industrialisation, the mechanisation of life, urbanisation, depersonalisation and alienation. And since the Nazis, in contradiction to the main thrust of their ideology, i.e. opportunistically, used technology for their own evil political ends, Roth concluded that there existed a causal relationship between Nazism and technology, and hence came to equate technology with absolute evil.

Against this background of the development of Roth's political persuasion, it is understandable that he abandoned his attempts to come to grips with contemporary social problems in his fictional work. With his *Radetzky March* he turned his attention for the first time to the vanished world whose collapse he had witnessed, almost as if he wished to ascertain, by analysing and describing that world, what values had been lost and why. To establish how far Roth allowed his own political bias to colour his presentation is not an easy task. . . . (pp. 45-7)

The Habsburg world had become a myth long before its demise in 1918. Myth can be understood in the sense of what exists in language only and has no objective reality outside the process of transformation. The word myth is ambivalent; in it the genuine glorification of real values is fused with an idealising distortion of the world, so that the poets of the Habsburg myth are both distorting mirror and microscope of the old empire. The transformation and the distortion of reality are attributable to the desire to sift out an essence, a hypothetical, methahistorical core containing its intrinsic meaning. In the Habsburgh myth the transformation of reality that belongs to every poetic creation is grafted onto a particular historical-cultural process. The intuitive memory of the world of yesterday combines with a partly conscious, partly unconscious process of sublimation of a concrete society into a picturesque, secure and ordered fairytale-like world.

The themes and motifs found in the literature after the dissolution of the Danubian monarchy are not merely a memory of the past, however, but part of a long tradition established during the post-Napoleonic restoration, i.e. at the beginning of the last act of the centuries-old Habsburgian history. The literature of the 1920s and 1930s embodies the final phase of that process of mythification. It is also its most representative chapter, since it describes a defunct society and hence most clearly typifies the nature of this mythifying literature as a flight from reality.

Myth can, secondly, be understood in the sense of one of its lexical definitions as an evident fiction or poetic truth. In its less precise, more colloquial usage it often has pejorative overtones. It then refers to a lack of awareness of reality, a false consciousness among a majority of a sizeable portion of the members of a particular society, as in the phrase "a popular myth." It thus indicates the gap between what the speaker or writer perceives as actual reality and the wrong perception of that same reality in the—deficient—consciousness of others.

The term myth is applicable to the **Radetzky March** in both these overlapping meanings. It is especially the manner in which the author achieves a convincing exposition of myth in its second sense that constitutes in part the novel's quality, i.e. through his awareness and portrayal of two levels of reality. In addition, Roth thematicises myth by showing, in the story of the hero of Solferino, how myth originates and how, by manipulating historical data and hence distorting reality, the establishment exploits myth as an instrument of power, an ideological-propagandistic tool for indoctrination and cementing existing social structures.

The specifically Habsburgian myth, in the first sense defined above, contains three main components: supra-nationality, "bureaucratism" and hedonism. Under "bureaucratism" can be subsumed the three pillars on which the empire rested: its standing army of soldiers, sitting army of bureaucrats, kneeling army of clerics. Wisely steering clear of the Church, Roth chose the first two seemingly solid, but inwardly crumbling foundations, the military and the civil service, as sufficiently representative examples of the empire's structure to demonstrate its inevitable collapse. The supra-national ideal included the view that the Habsburg empire's main function as the largest European power was that of stabiliser and harmoniser among many disparate people. Franz Joseph invariably opened his proclamations with the words "To my Peoples." Its second most important function was to be the cultural coloniser of Eastern Europe, i.e. the transmitter of German culture to the non-German majority. Without that policy, writers like Rilke, Kafka, Horvath and Roth would not have been part of German literature. Although there were at least fourteen literatures in the empire, German was the *lingua franca,* the dominant cultural language despite the fact that Germans were only a minority. The supra-national ideal was the monarchy's main propagandistic device in the fight against the modern awakening of national forces, i.e. it was an ideological weapon in the Habsburg struggle against history, since the empire was gradually being undermined by its own centrifugal forces.

For many of Roth's contemporaries the monarchy had been the guarantor of peace, continuity, stability and harmony. The medieval-feudal universalism of the empire was transformed in their minds into a modern, harmonious European culture in which national conflicts had been overcome. The monarchy expected of its subjects that "they be not merely Germans, Ruthenian or Poles, but something larger and higher." It demanded "a true and real *sacrificium nationis,* a renunciation of facile self-assertion and indulgence in the instincts of one's own blood; by such renunciation the individual changed from a German, Czech or whatever he was, into an Austrian" (Franz Werfel). Any move towards self-assertion, the assertion of a national character and difference, was suppressed. When, in the **Radetzky March,** the Slovenian Baron von Trotta is upset by the rebellious Czechs and their Sokol movement—he contemptuously refers to them as "Sokolists"—he thinks:

> The whole world [suddenly (omitted in the translation)] consisted of Czechs, a people he considered to be recalcitrant, obstinate and stupid, the originators of the concept "nation." There might be many peoples, but certainly no "nations." And over and above this, he received scarcely intelligible remissions and memoranda from the Government concerning greater tolerance toward "national minorities," one of the phrases Herr von Trotta loathed most of all. "National minorities" were merely more extensive aggregations of "revolutionary individuals."

Like supra-nationality generally, its beloved but no longer unshakable inherent values were mythified. For example: for Werfel, the binding element of the monarchy was not merely that it provided continuity and permanence, and hence security, but that it was incapable of moving, changing and progressing; that everything within it was almost rigidly fixed, immutable and static. Its strength was "a wise and grandiose inertia which showed itself in its masterly ability to defer solutions, erode conflicts and let them crumble away." In the disrespectful vocabulary of the Austrian this inertia was characterised by the classical concept of muddling along (*Fortwursteln*). Thus the negative phenomenon of involuntary immobilism was converted into something positive, endowed with a deeply significant content and raised to a revelation of higher wisdom. Limitations and deficiencies became advantages and virtues; a cause or a symptom of an unstable political constellation was transformed into a cure for it. Werfel

Emperor Franz Joseph marching in the 1909 Corpus Christi procession in Vienna.

attributed the inertia to the consciousness "that every step, even the smallest, was a step towards the abyss."

The best way to ensure that things do not change is to have an elaborate bureaucracy (supported, of course, by a strong army). The desire to uphold the *status quo,* to retain the always precarious state of balance, peace and apparent harmony, informed all aspects of life: customs, habits, modes of behaviour, attitudes and convictions. It resulted in an attitude of defence which expressed itself as reticence, moderation, blushful control of feelings, keeping one's distance, unapproachability, formality, reserve and the suppression of emotions even in intimate relations. The methodical severity of every-day routine was not to be disturbed; individual feelings were strait-jacketed into a kind of bureaucratic order. An excellent example in the ***Radetzky March*** is the description of Carl Joseph's return home from the cadet school at the beginning of the summer vacation. After the stiff formalities between father and son have been completed, "the signal to relax" is given: the boy is subjected to an hour and a half of strict oral examination. The bureaucrat—here represented by Franz von Trotta—is a stock figure in Austrian literature from Grillparzer to Musil. He embodies the quintessence of the monarchy, its methods of government and its immutable values: a strong sense of order and hierarchy, methodical and scrupulous pedantry, industry, absolute loyalty and an almost religious self-sacrifice in favour of formal order.

Closely linked with the bureaucratic myth is that of the emperor, Franz Joseph. He is a legend in all post-First World War books which conjure up the past. In the ***Radetzky March*** his portrait turns up everywhere like an obstinate *leitmotif,* at home, in school, church, barracks and even the brothel. When he appears in person, he stands outside life, prophetic and rigid, "kindly, great, illustrious and just; immeasurably remote, yet very close [with] a special affection for all his officers." He is omnipresent, a kind of petrified idol, the apostolic, secular representative of God on earth, King of Jerusalem, the complement of the Pope, a father-God figure who looks after all his children. In reality he was a somewhat narrow, mediocre bureaucrat himself who surrounded himself with mediocrities and was pedantically interested in petty detail. He was an autocrat and arch-reactionary, suspicious of all progress. He was a model for his senior civil servants who usually cultivated identical dundrearies in devout emulation. "The streets were peopled with numerous Franz Josephs. Everywhere in the government departments one saw familiar and unapproachable faces with the white sideboards. Even the keepers at the majestic gates of the palace wore the same mark" (Werfel). Some of his qualities became almost proverbial: his lofty sense of honour—which did not prevent him from breaking the promises of reform he had given upon his accession to the throne; his modest, Spartan way of life—but the expense accounts for the imperial household speak a different language; his generosity and charitableness—but his vanquished enemies were mercilessly punished; his courteousness—but he lacked warmth. There was something frightening about the emperor's grandseigneurial, icy formality.

The third basic motif of the Habsburg myth—which to a lesser extent is also an element of the *Radetzky March*—is sensuous, self-indulgent hedonism. It is the myth of "Wiener Blut," of the waltz and the "beautiful blue Danube," of *joie de vivre,* pomp and pleasure, frivolity and the carefree gratification of the senses, of good food and wine, charming chambermaids and amorous adventures, of a sunken Cockaigne, a sweet and pagan earthly paradise. The sybaritic nature of life in turn-of-the-century Vienna is offset by a languid sense of melancholia, of a consciousness of decadence and overcivilisation, decline and impending catastrophe. This mood is just the other side of the coin, in fact the main determinant of the euphoric celebration of life, of pleasure-seeking as an escape from the feeling of doom, of that hedonism which, "as the apotheosis of the flesh and the spirit of caprice, forms both the climax and the finale of Austrian epicurean, catholic and apolitical paganism" (Magris). The Habsburg myth always contained an element of anti-Prussian feeling. The contradictory Austrian temper of levity as flight from reality combines with that feeling in the answer to the question about the difference between Prussians and Austrians: the Prussian says, "The situation is serious, but not hopeless"; the Austrian says, "The situation is hopeless, but not serious." (pp. 47-52)

[The] interpretations that follow have been collated to provide a synopsis of the main streams of criticism in terms of the view of the Austro-Hungarian society Roth presented through his novel. That is to say, only a number of those interpretations have been selected which proceed from the implicit question as to what attitude towards the lost empire and what socio-political and moral values are conveyed by the novel. To what extent did Roth incorporate his regressive ideology in the book, i.e. how can it be demonstrated that it reflects that ideology? The method of selection was determined by the aim to effect a balance between the different views; and to provide at least one, albeit simplified, model, the final interpretation will be reproduced in some greater detail.

The most common interpretation is that Roth did not present his own political view in the novel in an obvious, let alone obtrusive way, and that his integrity prevented him from superimposing his convictions on, or allowing them to intrude into, his fictional portrayal of the Habsburg world. An imaginary, more or less neutral lexicon entry might read thus: Roth's *Radetzky March* is the novel which, by common consent, is not only his personal best, but also captures more accurately and empathetically than most others the spirit of the age of Emperor Franz Joseph, the last living symbol of "Kakania." [The critic explains in a footnote that the term was invented by Robert Musil in his novel *Der Mann ohne Eigenschaften* (*The Man without Qualities*). It is derived from the adjectives for the double monarchy: *kaiserlich-königlich* ("imperial-royal")]. Though infused with a pessimistic, nostalgic sympathy for the vanished empire, the novel does not idealise the past but gives a realistic account of three generations of a Slovenian family whose fortunes symbolically coincide with the fate and irresistible decline of fransico-josephine Austria, its extinction with that of the monarchy. Two of the foundations of the Habsburg system, the military and administrative castes to which the major characters belong, are analysed in their inner structure. The minor figures are stock personnel

in the Habsburg literary tradition, but no mere stereotypes. With its decadent anti-hero and its pervading mood of disintegration and impending doom, the novel embodies a representative social microcosm within the declining universal order of the last half century of the empire. The mythically gloomy atmosphere of the Austro-slavonic world the novel conjures up is offset by humorous authorial detachment, irony and an acutely sensitive insight into the human psyche and historical inevitabilities.

Magris, whose evaluation corresponds most closely to such a positive, "common-denominator" interpretation, regards Roth as a great realist despite his ideological limitations:

> Perhaps unconsciously Roth conquered the narrowness of his ideological-political view. Thus the *Radetzky March* is no empty glorification of a lost era, but quite simply a novel that has comprehended that world. Roth's personal likes or dislikes do not count in it. What is important is that Roth understood the dissolution of the Habsburg centre of Europe and devoted to it not an elegy—as has been assumed—but an epos. That is why he cannot be regarded as a reactionary writer, i.e. as a prisoner of ideological boundaries that prevented him from grasping reality. He is the epic narrator of a world whose saga he wrote [Claudio Magris, *Der Habsburgische Mythos in der österreichischen Literatur* (1966)].

This assessment does not necessarily mean that the novel does not contain elegiac tones or regressive nostalgic moods that manifest themselves as flight from the present and are reminiscent of the author's own reactionary political stance. Nor does it mean, of course, that Roth does not perpetuate the myth. Myth and realism by no means preclude each other. The myth *is* the reality as it lives in people's consciousness, which is part of reality. To put it another way: the difference between the myth and reality is the discrepancy between actual reality and people's deficient awareness of it. Of the more prominent characters in the novel, Count Chojnicki appears to be the only one who has a sound grasp of reality and presages the collapse of the empire. That he is also the only one who becomes mentally deranged when the collapse occurs may be intended to suggest that to contemplate an insane reality for too long can endanger one's mental health to the point where survival demands an escape into a different reality.

An early Marxist interpretation of the *Radetzky March,* in the form of a review by Georg Lukács, a contemporary and, as an Hungarian, a semi-compatriot of Roth, similarly acclaims the high literary value of the novel, even though it gives only a partial, consciously one-sided picture of the collapse of the Habsburg world. It incorporates the most important, but by no means all, social factors of the empire's decline through the presentation of individual fates of the upper class. Roth showed that the ruling classes of Austria-Hungary *cannot* continue to live in the old way. That the suppressed class *will* not continue to live in the old way, however, is mentioned at best only in passing (seen as it is not in the perspective of the oppressed but of the oppressors).

The process of the decline of the ruling classes is, according to the *Radetzky March,* the same as the process of decline of the monarchy as a whole, whereas in reality it was only one of its symptoms. The novel does not show the economic necessity for the origin of the double monarchy, nor the social tendencies and the desire for national self-determination that led to its demise. Roth's heart was on the side of the dying monarchy, he depicted lovingly and sympathetically the social strata that, in his own view, were responsible for its downfall. Paradoxically, the novel's great literary merit derives in part from this ideological weakness of the author, since otherwise he would scarcely have been able to look so deeply into the world of officers and civil servants, comprehend it so fully and portray so truthfully the process of its social and moral decay.

The reviewer thus benevolently turns an apparent weakness into a virtue, glossing over again the novel's essential ambivalence despite his awareness of its opposing, contradictory strains which Roth himself had failed to reconcile, namely affirmation and rejection, idealisation and honest criticism of the society under scrutiny. On account of this doubleness of the novel's intentionality, it is not surprising that, since the revival of interest in Joseph Roth in the 1950s, interpreters have tended to over-emphasise one of the two strains while under-estimating the other.

A third model of interpretation [supplied by Werner Zimmermann in his *Deutsche Prosadichtung unseres Jahrhunderts* (1971)] concentrates entirely on the second aspect, the less obvious, more or less concealed, because aesthetically integrated, social criticism. In elaborating the critical strain, it evaluates the novel positively and Roth's political attitude as progressive. It looks at the presentation of society from three different angles. First from the point of view of the old partriarchal-feudalistic social order. It appears that this social order and its representatives are essentially obsolete. Life in the Habsburg monarchy is mainly determined by the past; it is a past which both radiates dignity and commands respect, but it also leaves a negative mortgage. The traditions and norms of this society have degenerated into ritual forms without content, and prevent personal human relationships (cf. for example, the episode referred to above of Carl Joseph's homecoming and the description of the meal in Chapter 2). The individual must subordinate himself to these norms and comply with them. As a reward for his self- and system-imposed restrictive behaviour, the citizen obtains social security and stability. Instead of striving for self-realisation, the young person can do not more than submit to the patriarchal-authoritarian hierarchy. People's roles are thus fixed and social mobility is extremely limited. In the **Radetzky March** the lower classes play only a secondary role as social life is determined by those who dictate the norms by their power, whether the emperor as omnipresent father-figure of the state, or Franz von Trotta as a father or as a commissioner with delegated authority in his district.

This society is beginning to show the signs of dissolution. The many phenomena of decay within the closed social order are evaluated negatively by most of the novel's figures, because they remain caught in their world of norms. In reality this decay does not mean decadence but renewal and social progress. The old system of norms finds itself confronted with new, alternative norms of a rising, democratic, open and pluralistic society. The recognition of these forthcoming changes is reserved for those characters—notably Count Chojnicki—who have dissociated themselves inwardly or outwardly from the Habsburg universe. The same applies to the reader of the novel: those who mourn for Habsburg will, through Roth's depiction, experience nostalgia for the Habsburg norms, whereas the critically dissociated reader will devote more attention to Roth's social criticism.

Thirdly, this intepretation turns its attention to the supposedly positive signs of a future democratic, pluralistic society. The last few years of the empire are seen as a transitional period, in which especially the workers of the brush factory and secondary figures like Dr. Demant represent all those who come into conflict with the ruling order. Other examples of a changing consciousness are the Sokol movement, the difference between Jacques and the young applicants for his position, the reaction of the officers in B. to the murder of Archduke Ferdinand and the recalcitrant behaviour of the sons of one of the officers as representatives of the youngest generation. Carl Joseph von Trotta, too, tries to free himself from the Habsburg value-system, but he fails as a result of his education and his milieu.

The interpretation does not deny the narrator's—and hence presumably the author's—respect and sympathy for the representatives of the old order, but his attitude is also, and more importantly, marked by critical distance and irony. With great empathy Roth brings Habsburg back to life, but simultaneously unmasks its falsities and social abuses. The interpretation also claims justification for itself from a positivistic, i.e. biographical, point of view, as the **Radetzky March** is considered to mark Roth's transition from socialism to legitimism.

Our fourth example [Wolf. R. Marchand, *Joseph Roth und völkisch-nationalistische Wertbegriffe* (1974)] goes to the opposite extreme and sees the novel as a nostalgic conjuring up not merely of the society depicted but of a time prior to that period and, more particularly, of a lost peasant origin. It agrees, then, with the previous interpretation, but in an inverse sense: the social criticism in the novel is not positive and progressive, but negative and reactionary. Its implications are that the force of change is not affirmed by Roth but rejected, indeed more than that, the condemnatory attitude applies to the story as a whole, to all the events portrayed from the very beginning of the novel. Roth contrasts with the increasingly abhorrent world the myth of an admittedly sinking, but still well-ordered, realm. The beginning of the story of the Trottas already contains the elements that lead to the inevitable collapse. The decline of the Trottas and of the monarchy is the result of deracination, degeneration and of the broken connection with elemental, pre-rational, primordial values. The main tenor of the novel is determined by the consciousness of the Trottas, especially Carl Joseph's, that they have lost this connection.

Even before the chrestomathy episode, after the last meeting with his simple father, the freshly knighted "Captain Trotta was severed from the long line of his Slavonic peasant forbears. With him fresh stock came into being." (The word in the original for stock is the same as for family in the opening sentence of the novel. In this context it is used to indicate a noble family, or race, and does not necessarily carry the connotation of new vigour as suggested by "fresh stock," which contradicts the content in terms of the present interpretation and could only be read as heavily ironical.) After the disillusionment caused by his rescue story in the school reader, Trotta leaves the army. He cannot hand back his patent of nobility, but becomes "an insignificant Slavonic peasant." He is homesick for his father, but "the son disliked spending as much as did his father, grandfather, great-grandfather before him."

In the following generation the "uprootedness" becomes stronger and consequently also the tie to emperor and state as the only fixed points of reference in the son's value system. "[He] passed his law finals, came home more often, began to look about the estate, and one day felt moved to give up law and manage it. The Major said, 'It's too late for that. You're not cut out for farming and estate managing. You'll make a good civil servant. That's all'." The Major decided to bequeath the estate to the pensioner's fund at Luxemburg, convinced as he is that his son would not be a good farmer. As a result the Trottas are also economically dependent on the emperor—how dependent becomes clear when the District Commissioner has to find the money to pay off his son's debts.

In the third generation of the new "race," in Carl Joseph, dislocation becomes an existential problem. In keeping with his station in life, Carl Joseph serves with the cavalry, although he

> . . . took little interest in horses. Sometimes he fancied he could feel the blood of his forebears in him. They had not been horsemen. . . . His grandfather's father had still been a peasant. Sipolje was the village from which he came. Sipolje: the name had an ancient meaning, though contemporary Slavs barely remembered it. Yet Carl Joseph felt he knew his village. . . . A good village, a pleasant village. He would have given his whole career as an officer for it.

Here, and in the following passage, it is clear that Carl Joseph idealises the life of the peasants and that of the unranked soldiers with their peasant background from whom he is separated by the black, empty space of the barracks courtyard and by a cold, glass wall. They have "cozy" candles, he has electric light. He longs for the good and pleasant village of Sipolje that exists only in his imagination. His sense of alienation, of belonging not where he is but somewhere else, does not leave him any more. He is "aware" that, like his father, he is a latecomer, a mere grandson who owes his position and rank not to his being himself, but to his grandfather (in reality, and ironically, of course, to the myth of his grandfather, who owed his own reputation and status to a reflex movement and a merely fortuitous set of circumstances). "He lived in his grandfather's reflected glory, that was it. He was the grandson of the hero of Solferino: the only grandson. . . . The grandson of the hero of Solferino." The motif is repeated more often than any other in the book. It impresses upon the reader Carl Joseph's debilitating consciousness of homelessness and lack of merit, his strong sense of not-belonging and his constant yearning for the imagined life before his grandfather.

After Demant's death in the duel, Carl Joseph has to leave the regiment. He does not mind, except perhaps for the familiar sight of the common peasant-soldiers:

> What was there that Carl Joseph did not want to leave? Perhaps this window with its view of the men's quarters? The men themselves, . . . the remote songs which sounded like uncomprehended echoes of similar songs sung by the peasants of Sipolje? Perhaps I ought to go to Sipolje, thought the Lieutenant. He went over to look at the ordnance map, the one piece of decoration in his room.

He could have found Sipolje in his sleep. The pleasant, quiet village lay in the extreme south of the monarchy. Traced on a lightly cross-hatched bronze-coloured background were the hair-thin, minute letters, faint as the breath of which the name Sipolje was composed. Near it were a draw well, a water mill, the little station of a light railway running its single track through a wood, a mosque, a church, a young plantation, narrow forest paths, solitary huts. It is evening in Sipolje. The women stand in the sunset by the fountains. . . . It was the familiar game he had played as a cadet. The familiar images rose at once. Above them all shone his grandfather's mysterious gaze.

But for various reasons, set out in the words and thoughts of the Emperor and Franz von Trotta, Carl Joseph's irrational-romantic flight from reality into idyll cannot be allowed to materialise. Instead he is transferred to the border area between Galicia and Russia, "the kindred homeland of the Ukrainian peasants, their melancholy concertinas and their unforgettable songs; it was the northern sister of Slovenia." (In the translation the word "akin" in "The district was akin to the home of Ukranian peasants" makes no sense. The original German word is used for relatives and refers to the region around Sipolje, the southern "sister.") The garrison town lies at the symbolic crossroads between the four main points of the compass which alternately represent past and present, old and new values, while simultaneously not only the symbols of the past but also those of the present, of modern civilisation and its technology, have connotations of decay, doom and perdition: "[The town] lay around a wide circular marketplace at whose centre two main roads intersected, east to west, north to south. One led from the cemetery to the railway station, the other from the castle ruins to the steam mill." The surrounding "evil swamps" are also connected with death, ominous and treacherous, their "deceptive grass" being a "dreadful enticement to a dreadful death for the unsuspecting stranger." The autochthonous people know how to pick their way through them in safety, but "a stranger who settled here was bound to degenerate in time. No one was as strong as the swamp."

Carl Joseph trudges along the boggy roads with his platoon, "persuading himself that he preferred" walking to riding. "He was glad to tramp through the oozing slime if only to see a station." The sentence expresses in a nutshell Carl Joseph's ambivalent condition. He is caught between his yearning for an organic life and his modern consciousness that accepts and is fascinated by technology. Technology is represented by the station and the trains that connect B. both with the world outside and with its centre; and by the Morse keyboard "on which the confused, delightful voices of a lost and distant world were hammered out, stitched as on some busy sewing machine." Technology repeatedly brings Carl Joseph close to disaster and ultimately becomes his undoing. Ironically and paradoxically, it brings him back to the land and the simple earthbound life he has yearned for, but also leads to his premature death.

Modern civilisation first erupts into the simple order of the border town in the form of a casino. Carl Joseph goes bail for one of his fellow officers until the burden of debt nearly costs him his career. Only his father's intercession with the emperor and the latter's intervention save him. The casino's corrupting influence changes the district.

> From inscrutable regions came strange civilians to

gamble in the cafe. . . . The whole world was changed. Yes, the whole world. In other places strange posters appeared of a kind never seen here. In every tongue of the region they exhorted the workers in the brush factory to come out on strike.

The studied juxtaposition and interlacing of the events to do with casino and brush factory suggests a connection between the two. In the case of the factory, the contrast between the curse of civilisation brought upon helpless, exploited people and the—still—intact order of peasant life threatened by technology is even more obvious than the corruption of life brought about by the casino. The factory "workers are all poor peasants," like Carl Joseph uprooted from and homesick for their "free villages." "For decades the workmen had coughed and spat up blood, fallen sick and died in the hospitals. But they did not strike. [Now] strange men came, put up posters, called meetings . . . the workers called a strike." And there will have "to be some shooting before it [is] too late," as Major Zoglaner explains. "Orders are orders." Carl Joseph is ordered to take command of a column of Jaeger to guard the factory "against the seditious disturbances of brushmakers." With his peasant soldiers he confronts, and betrays, the very people whose life as villagers he secretly wishes to share. To overcome the demoralising boredom of waiting, he orders rifle drill. Now "for the first time in his military life, it occurred to him that these men's precise limbs were lifeless parts of a dead machine engendering nothing." And he becomes "convinced that he did not belong here. . . . Where do I belong? . . . Sipolje, perhaps? To the fathers of my father? Ought I to be holding a plow and not a sword?" In the subsequent skirmish Trotta suffers a double injury, a fractured skull as well as, like his grandfather at the battle of Solferino, a fractured left collar-bone. Unlike his grandfather, he is injured not by a bullet, but by objects from the rubbish dump hurled by the striking workers. Though Carl Joseph's task is psychologically more demanding than the hero's at Solferino, his deed does not fit into a school textbook, just as little as "saving" the emperor—not on the battlefield but in the brothel.

The dishonourable battle is the "climax" in Carl Joseph's development—if one can speak of development in this case. What so far has been his thinking and wishing and feeling about a pleasant and peaceful peasant life has been mainly the pretence or self-suggestion of a weak descendant. What follows is the consistent and increasingly self-determined development towards a whole, sound person: he overcomes his self-alienation and (re-)gains an unproblematic fitness for life. He decides to resign his commission as soon as his debts are settled. During the regiment's summer festival he matures to the greatness of his grandfather. When upon the news of the murder of Sarajevo the national contrasts erupt in the conflicting, partly shocked, partly jubilant anti-Habsburg reactions of the officers, Carl Joseph with "his grandfather's somber gaze at the back of his neck" and looking like "old Trotta come to life," is the only officer who feels obliged to put an end to the scandal. In a kind of "unio mystica" he becomes "one with his grandfather. He himself was the hero of Solferino." As such, as rescuer of the emperor and of Austria, a mere lieutenant can command his superior officers "for the first time since the existence of the Austrian army." Accordingly, he sees his father in a different light. He sticks to his resolve to resign, despite his father's objection that "after the terrible catastrophe . . . such an act amounts to desertion." Watching the old man slump in his chair he paces to and fro—as his father used to, the roles have been interchanged—and thinks:

He's young and foolish . . . a dear, silly, young fool with white hair. Perhaps I am his father, the hero of Solferino. I've grown old, he's only lived a long time. He walked up and down and began explaining. "The monarchy is dead, dead!" he shouted and stood still. "So it would seem," murmured the District Commissioner.

For the short time till the outbreak of war, Carl Joseph enters the life in nature that he has set his heart on. "At last he was content, alone, at peace. It was as if he had never led any other life." He once meets his former batman who has—also—deserted and for the first time he can talk to him without feeling inhibited. The idyllic, organic life is interrupted by the war, which lasts only a few days for Carl Joseph. His death, "not with sword in hand but with two buckets of water" for his men, is a futile yet self-fulfilling sacrifice in a combination of loyalties expressed by the last sounds he hears apart from the Cossacks' bullets: the *Radetzky March,* the leitmotiv for his loyalty to the emperor and Austria, and the traditional, now familiar greeting of the Ukrainian peasants, the call of his brother-soldiers and of the new, real *Heimat* ["homeland"] he has gained at last: "Praised be Jesus Christ." He perishes not so much for or with Austria as in consequence of the civilisatory, political entanglements Austria has become caught up in. Thus all modern, democratising influences and technological developments are implicitly condemned by Roth. The ideal lies in a distant, arcadian past prior to the story of the hero of Solferino.

The degree of correctness or plausibility of each interpretation is determined by its justifiability by textual and external evidence. The particular difficulty in the case of the *Radetzky March* is caused by Roth's narrative technique, which makes the novel easy to read but hard to interpret. The technique consists, *inter alia,* in a constantly shifting perspective from the narrator's, to the characters', to a combination of the two in the stylistic device of "indirect free narrative," in which the narrator's view coincides with a character's thoughts. In the end everything depends, then, on a very close reading and the interpreter's measure of success in establishing to what extent the narrator's and the author's views can be identified with those of the characters, or when Roth is being ironical and, if so, how much the irony detracts from the value judgements of the characters. For example, the description of Carl Joseph's seemingly heroic behaviour at the regimental celebration is simply taken at face value in the last interpretation. It could, however, equally well be read as at least tinged with irony, and hence the hero's conduct as more or less foolish. Since, by definition, irony is intended to conceal rather than reveal meaning, no interpretation can escape the novel's ambiguities and be more than at best a contribution to its understanding. (pp. 52-61)

Philip Manger, " 'The Radetzky March': Joseph Roth and the Habsburg Myth," in The Viennese Enlightenment, *edited by Mark Francis, Croom Helm, 1985, pp. 40-62.*

MICHAEL HOFMANN   (essay date 1987)

[*Hofmann is a West German–born British poet and critic. His first poetry collection,* Nights in the Iron Hotel, *earned him widespread attention as one of Britain's outstanding younger poets. In the following review of the English translation of* Hotel Savoy, *Hofmann discusses salient characteristics of Roth's writing.*]

When Joseph Roth was asked once to write about his earliest memory, he described how as a baby he had seen his mother strip his cradle and hand it over to a strange woman, who "holds it to her chest, as though it were some trifling object of negligible dimensions, speaks for a long time, smiles, showing her long yellow teeth, goes to the door and leaves the house. I feel sad, unspeakably sad and helpless. I 'know' that I have lost something irrecoverable." This is an outrageous story: but one may admire it for that, for its mischievous invention, and for its limited awareness of such gestures and proportions as a baby might truly have observed. It brings to mind what Roth said about his revered Heine: "Maybe he did make up the odd fact, but then he saw things the way they ought to be. His eye was more than visual apparatus and optic nerve." Roth, too, was endowed with an eye like that: it specialised in seeing things that had vanished off the face of the earth. (p. 18)

Into the last 15 years of his life, Joseph Roth managed to cram 13 novels; bits and pieces of two or three others have been published posthumously. He said himself that he wrote day and night. His works of the mid-Twenties were *Zeitromane:* "time-novels," confronting contemporary issues, semifiction and semi-observation. A less flattering term for the earliest of them is "newspaper novels" (*Zeitungsromane*), not only because they were serialised in newspapers, but also because they had not quite freed themselves from the journalistic work he was doing at the same time. There are glorious cameos and details, but problems with structure and narrative line. They are all a part of one another, like an unsolved Rubik's Cube; and sometimes, it seems as though, with a little re-arrangement, one might construct a handful of perfectly accomplished novels from these riddling and gesturing and incomplete books, each with its own small but still spectacular contributions on the Europe *entre deux guerres* ["between two wars"]. They all share the same themes and situations: soldiers coming home from the war, from obedience and comradeship to the demands of politics and love; the sickly peacetime society, the distortions of wealth and poverty, the bizarre explosions of ideology, the strikes and rebellions, the fluctuations of goods and money; a conjunction of two male characters, one steeped in the world, resolute and committed, the other, the hero, usually not. *Hotel Savoy* has all of these things and more. It is, however, unusual—if not unique—in Roth's work, in being stationary; though situated on his usual westward path, all of it takes place in one of the staging-posts, at the eponymous hotel in the (unnamed) town of Lodz, "the Polish Manchester." The later books describe the hero's full trajectory from East to West, a meteorite burning out in the atmosphere of post-war Europe. *Flight without End* is an indicative title. On the whole, *Hotel Savoy* suffers by comparison. It is as though the hero, Gabriel Dan, and his resolute, revolutionary former brother-in-arms Zwonimir Pansin were waiting, along with the author, for the hotel to become a properly functioning metaphor for Western society.

Hotel Savoy may be not much of a novel, but it deserves to be read for its sense of milieu, for its curt sentences, for being an early work by an author whose every word is worth reading. In tone, it is largely neutral—it is only with *Job* and *The Radetzky March* that Roth acquires the voice of overwhelming loss and millennial regret—but it is still unmistakably his, with his wit, his curiosity, his little darts of metaphysical

speculation. It anticipates his later novels both in its geography and in the character of its hero.

I have said *Hotel Savoy* is a static book, confined to the town of Lodz. Nevertheless it is aligned, as I believe all Roth's novels are, on the East-West axis. Gabriel and Zwonimir are on their way home from the Eastern Front, and though they don't get there, in a sense they will in later books. The town awaits the return from America of its millionaire son, Bloomfield; he has reached Berlin and his arrival in Lodz is preceded by rumours. The girl Stasia will be heading for Paris; it is possible that the hero will go on to New York. As for Zwonimir, the revolutionary:

> He loved America. When a billet was good he said "America." When a position had been well fortified he said "America." Of a "fine" first-lieutenant he would say "America," and because I was a good shot he would say "America" when I scored bullseyes.

America is where Roth's "Job," Mendel Singer, goes. The short story **"April"** ends: " '*Life* is very important!' I laughed. 'Very important!' and I went to New York."

The significance of the East-West axis is, I believe, that it is the axis of power, of history; to go from East to West means to go from war to peace, from Communism to Capitalism, from old to new, from sentiment to hygiene; it is the route of the Jews, of political and other refugees. One has only to think of the many passages in Roth that describe the sad songs of fugitives and emigrants as they huddle together in frontier taverns. "Civilisations move along meridians," Joseph Brodsky has written; "nomads (including our modern warriors, since war is an echo of the nomadic instinct) along latitudes." The movement in Roth's novels is, therefore, a nomadic movement; and when it is reversed, from West to East—for instance, in **"The Bust of the Emperor,"** one of the two short stories thrown in with *Hotel Savoy*—it is a movement towards the past and sentiment and death. North and South, which seem to me to be the axis of happiness, barely appear in Roth. In the other short story (both are far more than makeweights), **"Fallmerayer the Stationmaster,"** one reads: " 'The South' meant more to the stationmaster than a mere geographical definition. 'The South' was the sea, a sea of sunshine, freedom, happiness." " 'South' was in another country," he said in *The Radetzky March.* The only real and extended celebration of the South in Roth's work is in a series of articles he wrote in 1925 about his discovery of the South of France, rapt and ecstatic.

As for the characters who wander back and forth along a line of latitude—say, the Fiftieth Parallel: Kiev, Lvov, Cracow, Prague, Frankfurt, Le Havre—it often seems as though their origin, present whereabouts and next destination are all we know about them, and all we need to know. Their linear movements, their trajectories, are fully expressive of their disorder and pain. "If one has a great sorrow, it is a good thing to change one's abode," Roth said in one of his articles. The Roth hero is an individual, not a *Massenmensch;* Roth is careful always to give him a name, but the names resemble one another as the heroes do: Gabriel Dan, Andreas Pum, Benjamin Lenz, Franz Tunda. They are largely undifferentiated, undescribed, anonymous, like markers. Where they are is the front line, each of them the flag in his own personal campaign; one can understand why Roth wrote a novel about Napoleon (*Die hundert Tage*). They are capable, attractive, viable men, but somehow disabled or disorientated. Most of them are soldiers or former soldiers; others are civil servants, minor officials, peasants, railway-men, aristocrats, innkeepers, *Fiaker*-drivers, chestnut-vendors. Roth was always drawn to the common man, and this, together with his journalist's need for visual evidence, helps explain the illustrated-encyclopedia prevalence of uniformed or quasi-uniformed types in his writing. (Of the 13 versions of his paternity that he put into circulation, not all were high-flown and romantic.) In addition to his journalist's eye, there was also his loyal *Kaiserlich und Königlich* subject's fascination with all the versions of existence in the Dual Monarchy, a Whitmanesque love of identification and profusion. In his early work there is an element of social criticism in the presentation of variety which derives from his perception of inequality: later on, this variety is seen as part of the graceful and accommodating nature of the Empire—the flame-bearded Jews pay their respects to the Emperor; the Jäger Franz Tunda joins the Infantry with his cousin the chestnut-vendor Joseph Branco and the Jewish cabbie Manes Reisiger. Roth sees an identity between highest and lowest; he celebrates the love of the frontier for the centre.

That, however, is the late Roth, the Roth of the Thirties, after *The Radetzky March* (1932), the Imperial apologist, the alcoholic survivor, the lovesick diagnostician. The contrast with the Roth of the Twenties is the contrast between warm and cold, hopelessness and alienation, symbol and case-history. The matter of Austria is like a molten flow that has been poured into the empty casings of the characters. The characters are still the same, passive, undefined, almost anonymous. *Hotel Savoy* has: "One can absorb such a lot and yet remain unchanged in body, in walk, in behaviour." Roth's next-to-last novel, *The Emperor's Tomb* of 1938: "I am relatively immune—as I then discovered for the first time—to what are called great shocks." *Hotel Savoy* is full of observed people, but they have no meaning beyond themselves. In *The Emperor's Tomb*, the history of a generation is created in the friendship of Tunda, Branco and Reisiger; in Tunda's precipitate marriage in 1914 with Elizabeth Kovacs (the state of Austria-Hungary); and in her unnatural desertion of him for the artsy-crafty lesbian Jolanth Szatmary (the defection of Austria's Slavs). If the "persons" at the heart of Roth's early books are little more than perceptive spaces—to read, say, the letter "by" Franz Tunda in *Flight without End* is an impossible, vertiginous experience—the later characters "speak" for a whole vanished organisation of states and its culture.

In a sense, the hero in all Roth's books is Fate or, more exactly, *die Fügung*—the word also has the meaning of "compliance," or "obedience." The characters are dutiful, resigned, they make no great efforts to change or to escape what lies before them. The novels describe the effect of intolerable pressure on these average people—the obligations of love or war, the consequences of an error or a rash commitment. In *The Radetzky March*, Carl Joseph Trotta has "middling, but always adequate capacities. He possessed a neat, matter-of-fact, honest intelligence." But as he himself comes to realise, his capacities are hopelessly inadequate; his "fortitude" is sufficient for "a pointless death," nothing more. It is little different from the outcome of the other novels.

Where Roth's heroes are meek and limited and passive, the world in which they move is correspondingly assertive, unpredictable and voracious. Roth's favourite similes involved birds, hands and animals: "Her two hands tore—now one, now the other—at her hair. Her hands were like pale, fleshy,

five-footed animals, feeding themselves on hair" (*Job*). "Her telegrams reached him one a fortnight, deft little swallows, sent to call him to come to her" (*The Radetzky March*). "The sotnias of Cossacks galloped and wheeled like winds in military formation, uniformed winds on the swift ponies of their native steppes" (*The Radetzky March*).If writing like this has a "programme," it is not animism, or pathetic fallacy, but a magical instability. Roth writes as well as anyone (Wallace Stevens, say) about attractiveness: anyone who has read *Weights and Measures* will remember the effect on Lieutenant Eibenschütz of the tinkle of the gypsy Euphemia's earrings; from the name Lutetia (in *Confession of a Murderer*) "there emanated a warm, subtle glamour . . . a resplendent, imperious glitter." Often in Roth, there is an irresistible combination of gold and silver (he uses a great many colours, and almost never singly): "a silver clinking and rustling of spurs and arms, a pervasive smell of pomade and shaving soap, a fulminating gleam of gold buttons, silver braid, and bright-red reins of Russia leather" (*Job*). "We had at the time no premonition of war and May, Vienna's May, swam in the little golden cups with their silver rims. The month of May drifted across the tablecloths, the little brimful glasses of chocolate, the cream cakes in rose and green which so curiously resembled edible jewels, and Councillor Sorgsam remarked, right in the midst of May: 'There will be no war, gentlemen!' " (*The Emperor's Tomb*). Most memorable of all are the descriptions of landscapes, of little X-shaped garrison towns with a station and an hotel, in the changing seasons. Not the least aggressive and unpredictable aspect of Roth's world is the way drastic changes will happen overnight: frozen birds fall out of the sky in winter, and in spring there are the mighty cracks of the river thawing; a man and his wife fall out of love; the hero ages. Similarly, his characters aged by a generation from one novel to the next (*Right and Left* to *Job*). This collapsing of time, one more aspect of his magical instability, is present in a clement form in the fragment "Erdbeeren":

> In March, when the melting icicles dripped from the roofs, we could hear the galloping approach of spring. We left the snowdrops in the woods alone. We were waiting for May. We were going to pick strawberries.
>
> Already, the woodpeckers were drilling in the trees. It rained frequently. The rains were soft, a velvety water. They might last all day, two days, a week. Not a wind blew, the clouds didn't budge, they hung in the sky, as fixed as constellations. It rained thoroughly and conscientiously. The roads grew soft. The swamp advanced into the woods, frogs swam among the trees. The farmers' carts no longer creaked. It was as though they were all cushioned with rubber. The horses' hooves were silent. People pulled off their boots, slung them over their shoulders and waded barefoot.
>
> It cleared up overnight. One morning the rain stopped. The sun rose, as though it had just come back from holiday. We had been waiting for that day. On that day, the strawberries had to be ripe.
>
> (pp. 18-19)

Michael Hofmann, "Conspiratorial Hapsburger," in London Review of Books, *Vol. 9, No. 5, March 5, 1987, pp. 18-20.*

ADDITIONAL BIBLIOGRAPHY

Bell, Robert F. "The Jewish Experience as Portrayed in Three German Exile 'Novellen'." *South Atlantic Bulletin* 42, No. 4 (November 1977): 3-12.
　　Includes discussion of Roth's *Der Leviathan* in a favorable assessment of German novellas written during the 1930s.

Broerman, Bruce M. "Joseph Roth's *Die hundert Tage:* A New Perspective." *Modern Austrian Literature* 11, No. 2 (1978): 35-50.
　　Positive evaluation of *The Ballad of the Hundred Days,* addressing charges that it is a work of escapist literature, unconvincingly characterized, and fascistic in tone. Broerman maintains that Roth transcends his historical material "to produce a creative piece of historical fiction of universal relevance and with indirect reference to the real concerns of his own age."

Bronsen, David. "Austrian versus Jew: The Torn Identity of Joseph Roth." In *Publications of the Leo Baeck Institute: Year Book XVIII,* edited by Robert Weltsch, pp. 220-26. London: Secker & Warburg, 1973.
　　Explores the complex questions of identity and affiliation as an Austrian Jew dealt with by Roth in his writings.

———. "The Jew in Search of a Fatherland: The Relationship of Joseph Roth to the Habsburg Monarchy." *Germanic Review* 54, No. 2 (Spring 1979): 54-61.
　　Analyzes Roth's divided loyalties to his Jewish and Austrian heritage.

Butler, G. P. G. "Radetzky Limp." *German Life and Letters,* n.s. 29, No. 4 (July 1976): 388-93.
　　Compares the 1933 Geoffrey Dunlap translation of *Radetzky March* with the 1974 "retranslation" by Eva Tucker, which is based on Dunlap's work rather than the original text.

Dollenmayer, David. "History and Fiction: The Kaiser in Joseph Roth's *Radetzkymarsch.*" *Modern Language Studies* 16, No. 3 (Summer 1986): 302-10.
　　Examines the historicity as well as the literary function of the figure of Emperor Franz Joseph in *Radetzky March.*

Gold, Herbert. "Surrounded by Small Hearts." *The New York Times Book Review* (8 February 1987): 30.
　　Commends the vivid, swift narrative style of *Hotel Savoy.*

Johnston, William M. *The Austrian Mind: An Intellectual and Social History, 1848-1938.* Berkeley and Los Angeles: University of California Press, 1972, 515 p.
　　Contains scattered references to Roth. In particular a chapter entitled "Phaeacians and Feuilletonists" praises Roth's virtuosity in the feuilleton form.

Kazin, Alfred. "Forlorn Little Man Back from Elba." *New York Herald Tribune Books* 12, No. 51 (23 August 1936): 7.
　　Commends the ironic counterposition of the "delicately limned study of a hero in repose" with the account of the laundress who falls in love with the Emperor Napoleon in *The Ballad of the Hundred Days.*

Krispyn, Egbert. *Anti-Nazi Writers in Exile.* Athens: University of Georgia Press, 1978, 200 p.
　　Includes scattered references to Roth, focusing on his political statements in magazine articles during the 1930s.

———. "Joseph Roth and the Art of Adaptation." In *Protest—Form—Tradition: Essays on German Exile Literature,* edited by Joseph P. Strelka, Robert F. Bell, and Eugene Dobson, pp. 97-109. University: University of Alabama Press, 1979.
　　Examines Roth's German-language adaptation of a poem by Dutch writer Anton van Duinkerken (pseudonym of Wilhemus J. M. Antonius Asselbergs). Krispyn demonstrates that Roth's adaptation broadened the scope of the original poem, which addressed an incident involving van Duinkerken and the Dutch National Socialist Movement, to "an expression of implacable opposition to the fascism that threatened to engulf the world."

Kronenberger, Louis. "The Hundred Days." *The New York Times Book Review* (30 August 1936): 7, 19.
　　Unenthusiastic review of *The Ballad of the Hundred Days,* finding it lacking in charm, pathos, and historicity.

Lebar, John. "A Study in Post-War Disillusionment." *The New York Times Book Review* (27 April 1930): 7, 12.
　　Review of *Flight without End,* summarizing its plot and commending the novel as "fiction of a high order."

Mattingly, Garrett. "A Glorious Illusion." *The Saturday Review of Literature* 14, No. 17 (22 August 1936): 5.
　　Calls Roth "one of the notable writers of German prose, perhaps the most notable of his generation" and *The Ballad of the Hundred Days* "Roth's most nearly perfect book."

Menhennet, Alan. "Flight of a 'Broken Eagle': Joseph Roth's *Radetzkymarsch.*" *New German Studies* 11, No. 1 (Spring 1983): 47-65.
　　Discusses Roth's political and artistic accomplishment in *Radetzky March,* with untranslated quotes from Roth's letters, the novel, and German and Czech criticism.

Mornin, Edward. "Drinking in Joseph Roth's Novels and Tales." *The International Fiction Review* 6, No. 1 (Winter 1979): 80-4.
　　Examines the role of alcohol consumption in Roth's life and as a symbol and leitmotif in his fiction.

Putnam, Samuel. "Exiles from Reality." *Partisan Review* 2, No. 6 (Winter 1935): 86-8.
　　Includes discussion of *Tarabas* in a denunciation of German writers for not forthrightly naming and opposing Hitler in their works. Putnam maintains that the novel exhibits "the same vice that distinguishes the unspeakable literature of pathos and bathos now coming out of fascistic Germany, namely, that of a romantic distortion of reality."

Sanger, Curt. "The Figure of the Non-Hero in the Austrian Novels of Joseph Roth." *Modern Austrian Literature* 2, No. 4 (Winter 1969): 35-7.
　　Examines the sympathetic portrayal of anti-heroic figures in Roth's novels of the period 1932-1938.

Sperber, Manès. "*The Mute Prophet.*" In his *Man and His Deeds,* pp. 107-18. New York: McGraw-Hill, 1970.
　　Favorably assesses the posthumously published novel *The Mute Prophet* as an eloquent expression of Roth's skepticism about the present and future.

"Break in Routine." *The Times Literary Supplement,* No. 3773 (28 June 1974): 687.
　　Considers the political aspects of *Radetzky March* secondary to the "delicate tragicomedy" of the plot.

Umberto Saba

1883-1957

(Born Umberto Poli) Italian poet, critic, and novelist.

Saba is considered one of the most important Italian poets of the twentieth century. Largely unaffected by the literary movements and theories of his time, he used traditional Italian poetic forms to portray the emotions and events of his everyday life. His major work, *Il canzoniere,* is an amalgam of several poetry collections published over the course of his life. After its first appearance in 1921, Saba revised and expanded this volume several times, incorporating into it both previously published poetry and new material. While a number of poems in this work have received high acclaim, the collection in its entirety is often characterized as uneven. Nevertheless, several critics have found that the interest of *Il canzoniere* lies not only in its isolated masterpieces, but also in the resonance of the book as an integrated whole.

Saba was born in Trieste, the only child of a Christian father and a Jewish mother. By the time of Saba's birth his mother had been abandoned by her husband, and during his early years Saba was placed under the care of a peasant woman while his mother worked. His later name change has been attributed variously to his love for his mother (*saba* is the Hebrew word for bread) and to his love for his nurse, whose last name was Sabaz. Although he had only a few years of formal schooling, he read voraciously and began to write poetry during adolescence. At nineteen, he gave up an apprenticeship as a clerk to devote himself to a literary career. Earning a living as a journalist, he continued to compose poetry, and his first collection, *Il mio primo libro di poesie,* was published in 1903. After traveling around Tuscany for five years, he returned to Trieste in 1907 and married. During the First World War he served in the army, and after the war operated an antiquarian bookshop where artists and writers often gathered. Increasingly disturbed by what he considered to be conflicts in his personality, Saba underwent psychoanalysis in 1929. Although few critics highlight this treatment as a major influence on his poetry, Saba himself attributed the clarity of his subsequent work to the success of his psychoanalysis. In the 1930s, Saba's position in fascist Italy was a precarious one due to his Jewish background and his open contempt for the government of Benito Mussolini. When World War II began Saba fled to Paris. He returned to Italy a year later, living secretly in Rome and Florence, and at the end of the war resettled in Trieste. Saba continued to write poetry during the last decade of his life, and also worked on the novel *Ernesto,* which was unfinished when he died in 1957.

Saba's reputation rests primarily on the lyric intensity he achieved in his poetry through simple, direct representation of his emotional response to the world. His early poems take their themes, and even some of their phrases, from the fourteenth-century Italian poet Petrarch and the nineteenth-century Italian poet Giacomo Leopardi, derivations which some critics attribute to Saba's desire to be part of a recognized poetic tradition. As he matured as a poet, however, Saba came closer to his ideal of an "honest" poetry representing his feelings and experiences. He realized that poems reflecting the events of an individual's everyday existence could

lapse into banality, but considered the rewards of sincerity to be worth that risk. As he stated, "[Whoever] begins not from the need to discover oneself but from an uncontrollable desire to be original, whoever cannot resign himself when necessary to say what others have said . . . such a one will never find his true nature and will never say anything unexpected." Saba achieved that originality in two sections of *Il canzoniere, Casa e campagna* and *Trieste e una donna,* his earliest poetry to be widely acclaimed by critics. The simplicity of his subjects belies the thematic profundity of the poems in these sections. For example, in "La capra," a poem from *Casa e campagna,* Saba sees in a goat's misery the suffering of all living creatures. Critics consider this poem one of the best in modern Italian literature, praising Saba's ability to make universal associations evolve naturally from his ordinary personal experiences. The other poems in these two sections are consistent with "La capra" in their depth and artistry, unlike the verses in other, less successful sections of *Il canzoniere.*

A change in organization and style occurs in *Parole* and *Ultime cose,* two later sections of *Il canzoniere.* Unlike his earlier works, wherein repetition often resulted in a loss of vigor and emotional intensity, Saba's later poems are tightly structured and display a stricter economy of words. Critics find that a greater personal maturity is manifested in these verses, which examine experiences of Saba's past and infuse them with a subtle symbolism. For example, the youthful memories in "Una notte" led Saba to a new perspective on the present, while also achieving a symbolic universality. This increased use of symbolism continues in *Mediterranee,* one of the final sections of *Il canzoniere.* While this section has received little praise as a whole, it contains two of Saba's most famous poems, "Ebbri canti," a reminiscence about the significance the Mediterranean held for him, and "Ulisse," a portrait of Ulysses in his old age.

Although *Il canzoniere* attracted some attention before Saba's exile during World War II, it did not receive substantial critical recognition until the last decade of his life. Dissatisfied with the early critical response, Saba wrote his own critique of his work, *Storia e cronistoria del "Canzoniere,"* which includes biographical facts, statements of his artistic intentions, and evaluations of his poems. More recent criticism has praised his innovative combination of traditional poetic forms with candid, contemporary diction. Often describing his poetry as an important bridge from the nineteenth to the twentieth century, critics now recognize Saba as a major Italian poet.

PRINCIPAL WORKS

*Il mio primo libro di poesie (poetry) 1903, also published as *Poesie,* 1911
*Coi miei occhi (poetry) 1912
*L'amorosa spina (poetry) 1920
*Cose leggere e vaganti (poetry) 1920
*La serena disperazione (poetry) 1920
Il canzoniere (poetry) 1921; revised and enlarged editions, 1945, 1948, 1951, 1961
*Preludio e canzonette (poetry) 1922
*Autobiografia (poetry) 1924
*Figure e canti (poetry) 1928
*Preludio e fughe (poetry) 1928
*Ammonizione, ed altre poesie (1909-1910) (poetry) 1933
*Tre composizioni (poetry) 1933
*Parole (poetry) 1934
*Ultime cose (poetry) 1944
*Mediterranee (poetry) 1946
Storia e cronistoria del "Canzoniere" (criticism) 1948
Uccelli (poetry) 1948
Tutte le opere. 8 vols. (poetry, criticism, essays, and letters) 1949-59
Quasi un raccanto (poetry) 1951
Ernesto (unfinished novel) 1978
    [*Ernesto,* 1987]
Umberto Saba: Thirty-one Poems (poetry) 1980

*These works were revised and incorporated into editions of *Il canzoniere* published between 1921 and 1961. The following volumes first appeared in *Il canzoniere: Poesie dell'adolescenza e giovanili, Casa e campagna, Trieste e una donna, Versi militari, Poesie scritte durante la guerra, Il piccolo Berto, Sei poesie della vecchiaia, I prigioni, Fanciulle, Cuor morituro, Ossi di seppia, L'uomo, Nuovi versi alla Lina.*

Translations of Saba's poetry are included in the following volumes: *Italian Sampler: An Anthology of Italian Verse* (1964); *An Italian Quartet: Versions after Saba, Ungaretti, Montale, and Quasimodo* (1966); *Modern European Poetry* (1966); *The Promised Land, and Other Poems: An Anthology of Four Contemporary Italian Poets* (1957); and *The Poem Itself* (1981).

EDWARD WILLIAMSON (essay date 1952)

[*Williamson was an American educator and critic who specialized in Romance languages and literatures. In the following excerpt, he assesses Saba's deceptively simple style and compares his poetry to that of two other modern Italian poets, Eugenio Montale and Giuseppe Ungaretti.*]

Saba . . . formed himself in the isolation of Trieste and has remained outside the currents of theory and polemic. Except for *Epigrafe* on which he is now working, all his poetry is contained in *Il canzoniere* of 1948. The title has its own history; the word means simply collected lyrics and may be applied to those of any writer, but when used without specification—*the* canzoniere—it refers to Petrarch's lyrics, and Saba intended his title to carry this implication. He first used it in 1921 for the collected publication of all he had then written; afterwards he published other books, notably *Preludio e fughe, Parole,* and *Ultime cose,* but in 1945 he incorporated all of them into a new edition of the *Canzoniere,* and in 1948 he repeated the process to catch up the *Mediterranee* of 1946. It is odd that Ungaretti should choose to call his collected work *Vita di un uomo,* when it is precisely the man one has difficulty in finding amid the abstract musicality of his verse. In justice to Ungaretti it should be said that he chose the title to emphasize his view that a poet's life is his work, whereas Saba has chosen an abstract, lyrical title for poetry which seems to follow a purely autobiographical development. It was originally the attempt of a young man to ally himself with tradition. Saba's poetic vocation was to be the minute exploration of the convolutions of his own mind, and in reciting the names of Petrarch and Leopardi he was perhaps nerving himself to enter the labyrinth by assuring himself that he held in his hand the thread of tradition. The autobiographical element, which was real enough in the earlier work and occasionally overweighted the poetry and became an intrusive prose element, is in the later work only an apparent, or symbolic, autobiography; because it seems to provide a tropical structure for the poem it misleads readers into believing that the work is simpler than it is. Saba's style cooperates in the deception; it seems not to be there at all: no screen is interposed before the experience recounted. Stylistic critics have labored strenuously and in vain to account for this style. It can be shown to contain rags and tags of Petrarch, Tasso, Leopardi, and other classics, stuck between expressions borrowed from dialect; it combines the unfolded and singing rhythm of the traditional lyric, openly expressive of clearly defined states of mind, with the sinuous progression and ambiguous, hesitating tones of the decadents, and the allusive technique of the *trobar clus* analogists. By rights it should be a hodge-podge, but the various elements are not so much reconciled as dissolved in a fresh flow of language which calls no attention to the absorbed components during the reading process and yields them up only to conscious analysis. Although he never considered placing himself near either group, and has, indeed, only a fragmentary knowledge of the work of cither, Saba provides an ideal link between the candid and impassioned poetry of the Italian nineteenth century and the anguished phantasy of the decadents. While others were evolving new procedures, Saba demonstrated a basic originality of conception which rendered unnecessary a revolt on the technical level. (pp. 233-34)

Saba's poetry is more obviously human than that of Montale or Ungaretti, but its humanity is complex; Saba reaches into the most shadowy intimacies of feeling, he follows the most delicate twistings of the mind; and if his verse offers fewer initial difficulties than that of the other two writers, it leads to subtleties no less than theirs. They demand activities primarily intellectual (the capacity to grasp a tenuous reference, the agility to leap a gap where no words are) for constructing the primary comprehension of the poem. Saba presents, or seems to present, these elements without verbal difficulties, but as the poem lies in the memory it acquires significance. To be sure, the work of understanding the hermetic writers does not stop with the realization of the primary construction; reflection on their poems discovers other values, but the discovery appears to be new "layers of meaning"; with Saba's poems the discovery is rather of refined correspondence to psychological truths. Ungaretti's musicality is of a highly developed order, and its full effect is often felt only after the poem has been in the mind some time, but the effect remains always that of the "medium of expression," on the other hand one grows more aware that where Saba's verse seemed to become music it was rather a modulation of feeling, "una musica dell'anima più che delle parole." (p. 238)

> Edward Williamson, "Contemporary Italian Poetry," in Poetry, Vol. LXXIX, No. 4, January, 1952, pp. 233-44.

SERGIO PACIFICI   (essay date 1962)

[*Pacifici is an American educator, translator, and critic specializing in Italian language and literature. In the following excerpt, Pacifici discusses how the autobiographical nature of Saba's poetry affected the themes, structure, and tone of* Il canzoniere.]

Umberto Saba, *"esperto di molti beni e molti mali,"* is a poet whose work staunchly defies any critical attempt to label or neatly classify it, in spite of the fact that he had much in common with the great and minor poets of his generation and with the lyrical tradition of his native country. His uniqueness consisted not in revolutionizing the genre by resorting to a new vocabulary or new metrical schemes, but, on the contrary, by making use of the most ordinary language and of those schemes provided by the examples of his predecessors, from Petrarch to Leopardi. For over half a century he sang, in a style that was never beyond the grasp of his audience, the joys and torments he had experienced in his long life. Although he called himself "egocentric," he nevertheless succeeded, especially in his later work, in divesting his lyrics of any and all autobiographical vestiges and in charging them with a meaning and a relevance without and beyond chronological limitations.

Self-educated, Saba was with Papini, Prezzolini, and several other mature contemporaries fortunate in reaching literary prominence during his lifetime. In 1933, shortly after he had published his collected poems, the Florentine review *Solaria* dedicated an entire issue to his work. But, unlike Ungaretti and Montale, he never had any intellectual pretensions, nor did he try to dazzle his audience by means of his creative gifts or critical intelligence. He was content to write poetry: *"Io seggo alla finestra e guardo, / guardo e ascolto, però che in*

questo è tutta / la mia gioia: guardare e ascoltare." ("I sit at the window and I look outside, / since in this is all / my joy: in looking and listening.") His greatest pleasure was to observe and to listen; his most coveted ambition was to record by means of delicately simple images what he felt and what he saw, but above all what he loved. (pp. 161-62)

When Saba began publishing his verse, the *Crepuscolari* first and the Futurists soon afterwards were managing to attract the attention of the critics and the readers. At the same time, sophisticated sensibilities were attracted by the French Symbolist poets, whose high priest, Stéphane Mallarmé, spoke of a poetry that must "suggest," not indicate, things. In the provincial salons of the capital city, as well as in the austere halls of the academies, people still talked (or shouted, when necessary) the names of Carducci, Pascoli, and of course that of the *enfant terrible,* Gabriele d'Annunzio.

It was therefore almost inevitable that in such literary climate Saba should at once be compared to, and linked with, the *Crepuscolari,* with whom initially—despite all his denials—he did have something in common. His first compositions stunned those critics who held that only a revolution of a technical nature could bring new vigor and beauty to poetic expression and give it hitherto unknown dimension. In an unassuming language, which soon became his trademark, Saba set out to describe his world, the world of the bourgeoisie. In his later years he remarked that "the *Canzoniere* is the story of a life relatively poor in external events, rich at times in torture, of feelings and internal echoes, and of people whom the poet loved during his long life and out of which he created his 'characters'." One of the things that never fails to amaze the reader, and which perhaps is the spinal cord of the *Canzoniere,* is precisely how rich Saba's poetry is in people and objects and living beings, all endowed with a life of their own, seen and understood in their deepest meanings and interrelationships by a poet whose goal was to be "a man amongst men."

The themes of the hundreds of poems Saba wrote were not only the melancholy and the hardship he experienced, but the numerous people, his mother and father, his "sweet wet nurse," the country house, the stores, the hidden cafés, the inns and the streets of Trieste—which in the magic of his verse ceased to be a geographic entity and became a poetic city—and finally, the animals: from the goat of his early poetry to the mockingbirds of his later compositions.

As a craftsman he lacked the severity of such contemporaries as Ungaretti and Montale or the *engagement* of a Quasimodo. He was perhaps too frequently prone to be uncritical about his verse simply because it responded to a deep urge to give form to a particular moment of his life. But even in those moments when Saba does not reach the stylistic perfection of an artist, we know that without the weaknesses inherent in his poetry, the *Canzoniere* would not be what it is. When set side by side with Petrarch's lofty, and perhaps overlabored and therefore unspontaneous, perfection, the *Canzoniere,* with its ingenuity and occasional naïveté is the more human and moving document.

One of his early critics, the Triestine Scipio Slataper, once remarked acutely: "Saba belongs to a group [of poets] who, in order to be understood, need to create around the reader a particular atmosphere. . . ." Saba invites a close, intimate contact. Every time one reads his poems, one senses a kind of secret invitation to gather around the poet and allow him to recount in a sad, soft-spoken tone, the story of people he knew and the experiences he underwent. Every page of *Il canzoniere* is filled with scenes that at once become quite familiar and which, together with the "protagonists," have long endeared Saba to his public. Woven out of the human threads of his life, Saba's poetry may be regarded almost as a long episodic novel, the effects of which derive not from the unfolding of a single story, but from the rapid succession of vignettes, sketches, impressions.

Structurally, the *Canzoniere* is divided into three major parts, each of which is subdivided into shorter sections. All such parts are chronologically arranged, and through their particular disposition in the context of the collection we can follow not only Saba's growth as a poet, his increasing ability to handle different metrical schemes, but his personal curriculum, the satisfaction, horror, and even hate he knew during his lifetime. Thus, from his youthful and adolescent poems, we move on to his life in the army (he served in the Twelfth Regiment in Salerno) and we go back to Trieste with him—the city that was to be, with brief exceptions, his established residence.

One of the difficulties presented by Saba's poetry has to do with the manner in which it should be read. An articulate body of critics holds that a cumulative, or "bloc," reading of the *Canzoniere* is the only relevant way to measure its freshness and its artistic achievement. There is considerable truth in this view, since an extensive reading of Saba's poems does enlarge considerably the vast canvas patiently painted over the time span of five decades, giving to it a tone definitely lacking when the poems are read individually. For here, too, is much of the beauty of the impressive array of Saba's poems: in the variety of tones, in the amazing alternation of moods, now pathetic, now happy, now humorous, now serious. Taken as a whole, however, his poems are quite instructive in that they succeed so well in presenting the image of a young man, alternately lonely and happy, embarked in a never-ending process of trying to break the solitude to which every artist is condemned and to establish human contact with the world by way of the written word. His falling in love with Lina, who is destined to become his faithful wife, marked the end of a trying period and the beginning of a richer one. Just as his love for his wife injected new warmth into his work, so did his rediscovery of his native city, which is ever present spiritually and even physically in the *Canzoniere,* and which became the symbol of a world in miniature. Significantly enough, he named this particular section *Trieste e una donna (Trieste and a Woman)*.

A work of art derives a good share of its power from the tensions generated among its various parts and between itself and the reader. In Saba's Song Book, such tensions do exist and are lyrical—not, as in Montale's poetry, metaphysical. Such tensions do not impede a wonderful internal coherency from existing. Few poets have been as faithful as Saba to a manner of self-expression that can undergo few changes and yet always appear spontaneous. No other man of letters has been equally stubborn in rejecting fashionable poetics for the sake of appearing an avant-garde poet.

Aside from a personal style, every poet needs a symbol that stands for his strongest passions and embodies his subtlest feelings about life. Saba's poem **"La capra"** (**"The Goat"**)—celebrated to the extent of being memorized by school children and unanimously chosen as one of his most representative lyrics—is a composition that for many signifies the per-

petual suffering of man. Like animals, human beings are destined to suffer; like animals, they too need their share of lasting affection, often denied to them. Such conditions impelled the poet to make use of an idiom that, for all its modernity, has a distinct biblical flavor. Frequently, as the critic Giacinto Spagnoletti remarked, Saba's attitude reminds one of Saint Francis of Assisi, as exemplified in the often-quoted verse: "*La sua gattina è diventata magra. / Altro male non è il suo che d'amore: / male che alle tue cure la consacra.*" ("His kitten has become thin. / Her ill is no other than one of love: / an ill which consecrates it to your cares.")

He believed in simplicity, to be sure, but a strange kind of simplicity that was not to obfuscate the difficulty of its subject matter. "*Amati trite parole che non uno osava. / M'incantò la rima fiore amore, / la più antica difficile del mondo.*" ("I loved trite words no one dared [to use]. / I was enchanted by the rhyme flower-love / the most ancient and difficult in the world"—**"Amai,"** **"I Loved,"** in *Mediterranee.*) He loved but also endured much: during the war years, he was forced to flee from his native Trieste and take refuge with friends in Florence. In one of his longest and bitterest poems, **"Avevo"** (**"I Once Had"**), he tells of all the things that were so dear to his heart, and which fascism and the war took away from him. Five out of seven stanzas end with the identical lines, "*Tutto mi portò via il fascista abbietto / ed il tedesco lurco*" ("The base Fascist and the greedy German / took everything that was mine"), reinforced in the last line of the last stanza with the words, "*anche la tomba*" ("even the tomb"). But his pain and sorrow never prevented him from loving the world:

> Per divertirti apro una scatoletta
> musicale. Il dolor del mondo n'esce
> in un suono così mite che riesce
> a commuovermi quasi.

> ("To amuse you I open a small music
> box. The sorrow of the world comes out of it
> in a note so mild that it succeeds
> almost in moving me.")

His verse, tender and unpretentious, remains the striking testimonial of a poet for whom life was poetry, and who made of poetry his life. (pp. 163-67)

> *Sergio Pacifici, "Poetry," in his* A Guide to Contemporary Italian Literature: From Futurism to Neorealism, *The World Publishing Company, 1962, pp. 150-208.*

THOMAS G. BERGIN (essay date 1968)

[*In the following excerpt, Bergin examines* Il canzoniere *and discusses Saba's uniqueness among Italian poets.*]

Saba's *Canzoniere* is a work that stands apart from the contributions of his contemporaries in the service of the Muses. It is impressive in sheer bulk and even more so in its coherence of intent, testifying to the endurance of the poet's inspiration and to his unwavering devotion to his art over some forty years—a period which for the world in general and Italy in particular was anything but tranquil. Through wars, revolutions, dictatorships, invasions, and occupations, Saba remained a poet; and witness, participant, and even victim, he remained faithful to his true mission, navigating, to use his own figure, past the islands of his native Adriatic, over the broad sea into "quella terra di nessuno." If we may here in part anticipate our conclusions, Saba's distinction among his contemporaries—and there are many excellent poets of the same period, which is a rich one for the Italian lyric—is that he is always a poet and nothing more. Others have been professors, critics, editors, even men-about-town, but Saba is tenaciously and wholeheartedly a poet.

I have before me the final version of the *Canzoniere* (Einaudi, 1961) and its arrangement suggests that it may be helpful to approach the poet's work chronologically; it will give us a basis of reference for such critical comment as may later seem appropriate. The selections that make up the first part of the volume contain, though with some exclusions, the poems that appeared in the first *Canzoniere* of 1921, ranging from the truly "adolescent" pieces to *L'amorosa spina* of 1920 and also the memorable items comprising *Casa e campagna* and *Trieste e una donna,* many of which made their first appearance under different titles and in fact in different form. (Saba's re-editing and revision of his works would make a fascinating topic for investigation: for such an essay we have in mind here it would be a distraction.)

We may remind ourselves, as we look at the early verses, of the circumstances of Saba's youthful years. He was born in 1883 (the year of D'Annunzio's scandalous *Intermezzo,* and only one year later than Verga's *I Malavoglia* and Carducci's second collection of *Odi barbare,* which may give some idea of the climate of the times); his Aryan father abandoned him even before he was born to his Jewish mother. (What sort of poet would Umberto Poli have been, one wonders? And if, as all the chroniclers record, he adopted the name Saba—Hebrew for "bread"—as a tribute to his mother, may we not also note that he kept "Umberto," that conventional, patriotic, and even conservative name that good Italians of those days passed on loyally to their sons?) The Trieste of the poet's youth, busy and prosperous though it was, was from the point of view of Italian cultural and literary tradition "peripheral" to use Saba's own word. The breezes from the west were a little late in reaching the placid town on the Adriatic, Austrian-dominated and surrounded by people of another race. So Saba's youthful verses show a kind of cultural lag: the themes no less than the language of the early poems are a little trite.

A glance at the titles alone will give an indication of the affinities with Pascoli and inevitably with the *crepuscolari* as well as of the Leopardian inheritance: **"La casa della mia nutrice," "Da un colle," "Nella sera della domenica di Pasqua," "A mamma,"** and the like. Yet a distinct personality is recognizable, I think, and **"Meditazione"** is surely memorable for the programmatic lines: "Guardo e ascolto, però che in questo è tutta/ la mia forza: guardare ed ascoltare."

In 1908 Saba enlisted in the Italian Army and served his time at Salerno; out of this came his *Versi militari* which make up the second division of Part One of the *Canzoniere.* Perhaps the military verses are noteworthy as marking an increasing awareness—it is hardly as yet conscious purpose—of the poet's mission or role as interpreter of the feelings of a community or group. Although there is much of the purely personal in these sonnets, yet one does, I think, tend to see Saba as a spokesman of the lower ranks. This, if it be so, springs naturally enough from the subject matter: soldiers everywhere and at all times have the common experiences of drudgery, monotony, and homesickness, with the common resentment of officers and orders and, especially in peacetime, an undercurrent of frustration in the face of the apparent pointlessness of their lives.

These motifs make up the matter of the *Versi militari,* they are of course enlivened by lines of sharply personal reaction, often vigorously realistic, e.g., "Son brutte facce intorno a me, e sudori," the officer who "di sua gente / guarda l'urto coi verdi occhi crudeli," and other such strokes: it is no wonder that Saba has often invoked "un pittore del grottesco, che unisse alle mie sillabe il colore."

The sense of mission, of spokesmanship for humanity becomes overt in the well-known poem that appears in the volume immediately following *Versi militari, Casa e campagna:* I refer of course to **"La capra,"** which remains quintessentially Saba, with its mixture of humble yet original imagery and an assumption of universal perception, as arrogant in its claim as it is self-effacing in its tone. It will do no harm to cite it here in context.

> Ho parlato a una capra.
> Era sola sul prato, era legata.
> Sazia d'erba, bagnata
> dalla pioggia, belava.
>
> Quell'uguale belato era fraterno
> al mio dolore. Ed io risposi, prima
> per celia, poi perché il dolore è eterno,
> ha una voce e non varia.
> Questa voce sentiva
> gemere in una capra solitaria.
>
> In una capra dal viso semita
> sentivo querelarsi ogni altro male,
> ogni altra vita.

> ("I have spoken with a goat.
> She was alone in the meadow, tied to a post.
> Satiated with grass and her coat
> rain sodden, she was bleating.
>
> The incessant bleat I felt blending
> with my own grief and I answered,
> in mockery first and then after
> (for sorrow timeless unending
> has but the one unvarying note)
> because of the message that came
> borne over the field from the goat.
>
> From a goat with semitic muzzle
> I heard the lamenting
> of all living things and their trouble.")

A perceptive critic has defined the poem as "the perfect transfiguration of a Georgic episode into a symbol of the universal condition immanent in man as nature," and we may here quarrel perhaps only with the word "episode" which suggests the narrative, often a part of Saba's equipment, but I should say not the truly poetic part. *Casa e campagna* contains in its scanty compass a few of the very best poems, including **"L'arboscello,"** and the celebrated, frequently anthologized tribute to his wife, a kind of naturalistic bestiary put to tender personal use (although we cannot entirely share the poet's surprise at Lina's rather cold reception of the verses). By 1921 Saba had the courage to bring out his first edition of the *Canzoniere,* containing, as well as the selections from the separate works we have discussed, the successive items *Trieste e una donna* (1910-12), *La serena disperazione* (1913-15), *Poesie scritte durante la guerra, Cose leggere e vaganti,* and *L'amorosa spina* (1920). Aside from the war poems, which are not especially remarkable—"Saba is not the poet of that war," to quote his own confession—the themes are the familiar personal ones the early verses have prepared us for, the tone is more assured, and the technique shows a groping toward more freedom and less conventional forms. I find the group *Trieste e una donna* more appealing as a unit, and more truly substantial. Trieste does rather better than the woman; perhaps no one in recent years has written such an affectionate, evocative lyric to his own city as **"Tre vie,"** as sharp in observation as it is compassionate in tone, lingering in detail on the familiar sights—"il mare con le navi e il promontorio/ e la folla e le tende del mercato," "il vecchio cimitero/ degli ebrei, così caro al mio pensiero," the flag-maker's shop where the seamstresses "innocenti prigioniere/ cuciono tetre le allegre bandiere"—which compose his Trieste "ove son tristezze molte e bellezze/ di cielo e di contrade." The brief quotation may serve as well to give some idea of the language which by now our poet has made his own, unafraid of what may seem obvious rhymes, hackneyed phrases, and even a few too artful verbal effects: he has now the courage to say at once boldly and humbly: "i miei occhi mi bastano e il mio cuore."

The second edition of the *Canzoniere* appeared in 1948, but in the final Einaudi edition the second part of the volume includes only the poems written in the decade 1921-31: a well-pondered revision, I think, since the slight shift in direction of the poet's Muse comes with the publication of *Parole* (1933). Noteworthy in the second part of the *Canzoniere* as we now have it is a more persistent effort at grouping the compositions around a central theme. One has to say "more" persistent and so qualify because the same love of sequences had already been apparent in *Versi militari.* But in this part of the collected works all the items are arranged in units, running from the *Preludio e canzonette* (1922-23) to the sixteen poems that compose *Il piccolo Berto* (1929-31). These units range a good deal in character, from the straightforward sonnet sequence *Autobiografia* to the rather experimental *Preludio e fughe* (1928-29) which comes toward the end of this section.

This section of the *Canzoniere,* too, revealing clearly the Freudian current which had begun to flow into the stream of Saba's inspiration and a certain rapprochement with the *ermetici* (notably Ungaretti, as the poet himself confesses) contains a number of poems of special interest. **"La brama,"** defined by De Robertis as the "opening of a new style," and, in his view, worthy of comparison with Leopardi's "Pensiero dominante," has been exalted by critics in general; I am probably wrong in thinking this poem, impressive as it is, not a typically Saba artifact (my reservation finds some support in the fact that Saba did not include it in the list of his own favorites as he disclosed them to Nora Baldi in his old age). But it is certainly a poem of "vastissimo" intent (if Giovanni Cecchetti will let me borrow his adjective). The *Fughe* (1928-29) are also exciting experiments although, save for the sixth, not entirely successful. The real Saba is, it seems to me, truly present and unpretentiously articulate in **"Il borgo"** with its affirmation of the poet's lifelong desire: "d'uscire/ di me stesso, di vivere la vita/ di tutti,/ d'essere come tutti/ gli uomini di tutti/ i giorni." And I confess a weakness, no doubt unworthy, for some of the items of *Il piccolo Berto,* notably **"Appunti,"** and even for one or two of the autobiographical series; obvious, sentimental, and even slightly mawkish though they be.

With the publication of *Parole* in 1934 (the first section of the third division of the Einaudi *Canzoniere*) there is evidence of some change of texture, perhaps even of purpose, in the poet's production. He is fully aware of this himself, although he puts it in rather evasive terms, defining the little work as being more "in harmony with its times" than his other works. This may be fairly taken to mean that he has assumed the posture and something of the grammar of the *ermetici;* to be sure, there are signs of such contamination—if that is the word for it—even earlier, as we noted, but the title poem of the book is particularly hermetic in its exaltation of the cult of the word and a kind of intellectualization hardly characteristic of the earlier Saba. For reasons perhaps partly political—for these are the years of the Fascist apogee—the poet seems to take his eyes off the streets and sounds of Trieste in order to turn within. One can of course overstate this: *Parole* contains some of Saba's best-known work, including the sequence on the soccer game (but is this not also symptomatic of escape?), the charming **"Donna,"** **"Felicità"**—to mention but a few. Gradually, it seems to me, in the poems that follow on *Parole,* running from *Ultime cose* (1935-43) to the last little sequence *Sei poesie della vecchiaia,* the hermetic flavor is dissipated and indeed the last poems, many addressed to his young friend Almansi, have much of the old personal directness; yet *Parole* is somehow a watershed. Folco Portinari observes and most critics agree that "the last Saba was certainly a great poet but the Saba that counts is the one that goes from *Versi militari* to *Preludio e fughe.*"

Yet I find it difficult to assent to the notion that there is truly a sharp decline in the latter poems, even granting the defects of the narrowly autobiographical, or the sometimes inflated treatment of a motif that is essentially "occasional." There are good things in *Mediterranee,* I think, notably **"Ulisse,"** and **"Amai"** is a winning statement even if not quite a poem. There is a tone of tenderness mixed with some slight irascibility in some of the last items that can move a reader, if not a critic. Perhaps it would indeed be hard to find a great poem among the last entries; collectively they are not without their impact. For better or for worse, we may here cite **"Ulisse"** as representative of the last volume of the *Canzoniere;* it was published in *Mediterranee* (1946) when the poet was in his sixties.

> Nella mia giovinezza ho navigato
> lungo le coste dalmate. Isolotti
> a fior d'onda emergevano, ove raro
> un uccello sostava intento a prede,
> coperti d'alghe, scivolosi, al sole
> belli come smeraldi. Quando l'alta
> marea e la notte li annullava, vele
> sottovento sbandavano più al largo,
> per fuggirne l'insidia. Oggi il mio regno
> è quella terra di nessuno. Il porto
> accende ad altri i suoi lumi; me al largo
> sospinge ancora il non domato spirito,
> e della vita il doloroso amore.

> ("From days of youth I remember sailing
> past the Dalmatian shore; the rugged islets
> came forth from the waves. On them, but
>   rarely,
> sea birds, intent on prey, would alight; the beaches,
> kelp-encrusted, gave slippery footing. Under
> the sun they sparkled, bright as emeralds.
> The tide rising or the dark blotting them out,
> barks bearing leeward gave them wide berth,
> fleeing their treachery. And now my kingdom
> is that land of No-man. The harbor kindles
> its light for others. I turn out to sea
> once more impelled by heart untamed and love,
> laden with sorrow, of the life of man.")

It is not easy to define Saba's distinction among the poets of his generation although one feels it clearly enough. He protests frequently in his ***Storia e cronistoria*** that Saba has always been Saba, yet with an insistence that might betray a little inner uncertainty. Some of the early poems are very close to the *crepuscolari;* all the twilight elements are certainly present, for example in the sonnet to his nurse's house; the innocence of childhood, the melancholy for the past, the graveyard background. Of his later association with the *ermetici* we have already spoken. Nor does Saba deny that he learned things from his contemporaries, notably Ungaretti. Yet there are differences. I think "the blue smoke of dinner rising from the roof" (in the first version of **"La casa della mia nutrice"**), aside from the conservative formality inherent in the choice of the sonnet form, would serve to make us aware that Saba is not quite a *crepuscolare*. Folco Portinari has analyzed ***Parole*** and brought out the effective differentiation in imagery and some personal prosodic devices to show us how that poem is not cut of pure hermetic cloth. But I am inclined to think that in order to appreciate the real individuality of Saba one must look not at any given poem or half a dozen poems but rather at the corpus of his work. Taken en bloc it certainly stands apart. It is not so much a question of excellence; there are many poems which do not quite come off, and even the dozen or so great ones, taken one by one, will not suffice to establish his truly unique gift. But reading the ***Canzoniere*** from end to end, one is obliged to recognize a certain stature. Nora Baldi quotes Saba as calling himself in his old age "one of the six or seven poets of Italy," and this self-assurance, which also runs through the ***Storia e cronistoria,*** is a little disconcerting. He could not be sure; nor, as yet, can we. Nevertheless the ***Canzoniere*** is an impressive monument; invidious comparisons aside, it carries something of the impact of Leopardi's *canti* or Michelangelo's sonnets, for example.

It takes a bit of explaining to understand how this can be. For Saba does not by any means have everything. He lacks irony for one thing; or at least that peculiar sharpness of things seen from two angles which we associate with irony. He lacks, and this is perhaps more serious, a certain grandeur; it is sufficient to recall the two names I have cited above to see what I mean. He lacks a philosophical range; perhaps poetry does not need it, but the great Italian poets—no doubt ever mindful of Dante—have rarely been without it. What Saba has, and in such manner as to justify at least in part his claim to preeminence, is a kind of directness of vision, at once uncompromising and compassionate, unpretentious and, at its best, clairvoyant.

He is not eager to write glittering verses; he loves "trite words" and the rhymes "fiore-amore"; he tells Sereni that he can forgive "brutti versi" but not the "versi belli." This posture has its dangers and many of Saba's poems skate on the edge of prose and sometimes banality. "To love things as they are and ask no more," to accept "the values of all"—there is courage in these statements and grave risk for a modern poet. (But is it any more dangerous than that of a kind of cerebral aridity we sometimes find in contemporary verse?)

Saba indeed lacks that element of the *outré,* the eccentric, the daemonic which is such a common attribute of great lyric poets: in his own tradition for example we may recall that Campana was mad, D'Annunzio erratic, Gozzano riddled by illness. Saba is in person as in his verse persistently and almost prosaically normal. (To be sure he made much of his double inheritance but he is not unique in that; everyone of my generation will remember A. E. Housman's somber statement: "Couched upon her brother's grave/ The Saxon got me on the slave." These opposing thrusts within the breast are not limited to those born of mixed alliances nor for that matter even to poets.) It is this very normality, it seems to me, that explains much of Saba's appeal. Mixed blood or not, he felt himself like other men, wanted to be like other men, and succeeded in speaking for other men. "Il poeta," he writes, "ha le sue giornate contate," like the rest of us, but somehow he is just a little more than the rest of us, a little sharper in perception, a little more sensitive, possibly a bit more honest. For in his honesty surely lies another claim for his excellence; Saba is an unusually sincere poet. This, I am aware, is a dangerous word; all poets are sincere, at least in their desire to communicate. But all poets, even and perhaps most of all the great ones, have something of the confidence man in them, too. Saba is not without his devices, though he disclaims them, yet somehow even when we see him use them we are sure that they are merely devices and not meretricious postures. Cecchetti, referring to the originality of his inspiration in spite of certain derivative elements, uses the adjective "immediate" and, at its best, Saba's vision is as immediate as his inspiration. I think he will survive the poets, authentic though they may be, who only look inward, the prophets who are involved in causes, noble though they be, and the sweet music-makers, however much they please us. "A poor vagrant dog," he calls himself in his last poem. But dogs have sharp scent, long wind for the race, and fidelity; the metaphor fits.

Perhaps, in conclusion, one may find that the reason for Saba's appeal, and I suspect permanence, no less than the key to his achievement—his "secret," one might say—lies in his total commitment to his art, his integration of poetry with life itself. Saba never takes time off; he is consciously a poet, even if not always a good one, every day of his life. I find—I hope the notion will not be regarded as fanciful—that in this he may be compared to the writer of the first great *Canzoniere,* Francesco Petrarca. It would not surely be fanciful to see in the title that Petrarch himself gave to his rhymes something of the essence of Saba whose verses too are *rerum vulgarium fragmenta,* if we give to the second word a significance, legitimate surely and proper to a twentieth-century poet of humble origins. Petrarch used his *Canzoniere* for expressing his thoughts and attitudes on things that happened to him day by day; we might remark that, as Saba would do centuries later, he thought of his work as a continuing process; he too revised, refined, and rearranged his verses with periodic editing and winnowing. The symbolic language is different, of course; Petrarch pursues a Daphne, adores a "domna eissernida," who eventually arrives at the state of angelhood. But these are veils for the probing of his own melancholy and pretexts for his exploration of the worlds of art and nature. Saba likewise achieves the inward/outward fusion with something of the same mixture of introspection, topical commentary, and most of all, day by day, day after day, unbroken dedication to his Muse, with the unshakable conviction of the importance and even sacredness of his mission. His ship, like Petrarch's, is battered by storms, but he is ready, as Petrarch was, to entrust himself *al largo* in the service of humanity. For both poets their *Canzonieri,* jealously cultivated, were something more than books of verses; they were spiritual diaries, lifetime labors of love, ultimately testaments, not poorer but richer because they were built of "occasional" fragments. (pp. 503-08)

Thomas G. Bergin, "Saba and His 'Canzoniere',' in Books Abroad, Vol. 42, No. 4, Autumn, 1968, pp. 503-08.

G. SINGH (essay date 1968)

[*Singh is an Indian educator, translator, and critic who has written extensively on English and Italian poetry. In the following excerpt, Singh surveys Saba's poetry.*]

As one of the major Italian poets of this century Saba is, both in spirit and diction, more modern than D'Annunzio for all his linguistic and metrical innovations, and at least as modern as Pascoli and Gozzano. More than any other twentieth-century poet, Saba succeeds in achieving the tone as well as the edge and subtlety of modern poetry without discarding conventional forms and metres. As to Saba's language, it is for the most part conventional—and this even in poems where the pulse of modernity beats most strongly. But unlike, say, that of a poet like Montale, Saba's poetry is extremely uneven, and it is even more so than that of Ungaretti or Quasimodo. In fact, his claim to being considered, together with Ungaretti and Montale, as a major twentieth-century poet depends on a rather scanty portion of the total output. As to Saba's artistic maturity it is the result of gradual development and experimentation rather than something that is inborn and present almost from the very outset, as is again the case with Montale.

As to Saba's background, his connexion with Trieste—his native city—and the fact of his being Jewish on his mother's side have had a certain influence on his poetry. Just as the Ligurian landscape plays so vital a role in Montale's poetry, Trieste with its surroundings and traditions does in Saba's. And the Jewish strain accounts for a certain characteristic warmth and poignancy in his poetry. Another thing that distinguishes Saba's poetry as well as personality is that of all the twentieth-century Italian poets he is the least literary. (p. 114)

Literary and poetic theories and influences . . . play a conspicuously insignificant role in Saba's poetry, which to some extent accounts for the inspired simplicity and naturalness of his style, and for an independent poetic taste and personality.

However, Saba's early poetry is full of echoes from Leopardi and displays the worst weaknesses of derivative poetry. For instance, poems like "Ammonizione," "Sonetto di primavera," "Nella sera della domenica di Pasqua" and "Glauco" from *Poesie dell'adolescenza e giovanili* (1900-1907), are full of crudely undisguised echoes from Leopardi's *Canti*. The poem "Lettera ad un amico pianista studente al Conservatorio di . . . " for instance, is hardly anything more than a parody of Leopardi's "A Silvia," and a poor parody at that. These echoes rarely serve to stimulate fresh images, metaphors or turns of expression and Saba's early poetry no doubt gives the impression of being what Solmi rightly calls "voce inesperta e volubile."

However, even in these early poems there are a few unmistakable traces of Saba's genius and especially of his predilection for treating the themes of domestic life and affection with superb artistic command. And the secret of that command as well as of Saba's originality itself lies in his being completely and unflinchingly sincere. But the trouble sometimes is that Saba cannot always discriminate between objects and themes which it is poetically paying to be sincere about and objects and themes which it is not. Hence that very sentimentality . . . which is no doubt a source of strength in Saba's best poems, but which also results sometimes in a characteristic weakness. And one can't help feeling that what Saba needed more than anything else was the spirit of self-criticism and self-abnegation. All bad poetry, said Oscar Wilde, comes from genuine feelings, and quite a few poems by Saba are an excellent illustration of this truth. His poem "A mamma," for instance, demonstrates what might have potentially been Saba's strength, but what really turned out to be his weakness. As usual, the poem starts off rather well, and in the first four lines we have an effortless combination between fluency and self-control rather remarkable in a young poet. . . . But in what follows, the theme of maternal affection becomes a pretext for sentimental effusion which neither detailed psychological analysis nor vivid circumstantial description can transform into real poetry. But in another poem "A Lina," Saba does, however, achieve a truly lyrical spontaneity coupled with a genuine simplicity of feeling and style which constitute Saba's real distinction and strength. . . . (pp. 114-16)

A considerable portion of Saba's poetic output is descriptive, narrative or episodic. In these poems Saba sometimes achieves real pathos and depth, but very seldom psychological or dramatic tension, and the sort of poetic intensity that derives from such tension. . . . The "musica interiore" in Saba has very little to do with thought, reflection and meditation in the sense in which these qualities are found in some of Leopardi's *Canti* and in the work of no other Italian poet. What Goethe said of Byron that the moment he starts thinking he is a child may just as well be said of Saba. Not that there is not enough of reflection—or the occasions to reflect—in Saba, but he seldom succeeds in combining his reflective bent with his creative powers. For all his love of things, and all his sense of the "viveree morire alle cose," Saba seldom does anything more than merely depict things as they are, without exploiting deeply enough their relationship with his own inner world. Reflection in Saba is often an occasion for discursive argumentation, and very seldom for impassioned lyricism. Seldom do the inner and the outer fuse into each other. Diffuseness, which is the besetting sin of all Saba's poetry except the very best, is not only the enemy of lyrical intensity, but also of reflection itself. The very essence of reflection evaporates in poetic verbosity.

In *Versi militari* (1908), although Saba's art seems to display a greater capacity for organization and pointedness, his diction does not seem to have correspondingly matured. Very often a concept or a feeling, however poetical in itself, fails to get an artistically adequate expression. . . . [An] example of . . . straightforward potency and vitality of style—a style that reflects something more than merely technical or linguistic skill, something akin to a very high measure of self-discipline both moral and artistic—is "Consolazione," and especially its last two stanzas (in spite of the banality of the very last verse). . . . The last two poems of the series, "Marcia notturna" and "Di ronda alla spiaggia," foreshadow even more Saba's later and maturer lyricism. . . . As a war poem ["Di ronda alla spiaggia"] is at least as rich in content and style as anything Ungaretti ever wrote.

In the next volume of poems *Casa e campagna* (1909-10), as

the title itself clearly indicates, Saba is handling themes most congenial to his Muse—the themes of love and affection for his wife Lina and for his native town Trieste. One of the deservedly best-known poems of Saba is **"A mia moglie."** It is a picturesquely impassioned tribute to his wife. . . . In the poem **"L'insonnia in una notte d'estate,"** in spite of the rather gratuitous Biblical image in the last stanza, we have another example of an accomplished synthesis between the candour and the intensity of feeling, between the vividness and the virility of style. . . . Even more characteristic of Saba's mature style is **"La capra,"** with its unobtrusively subtle didacticism and lyricism. The most frequently anthologised poem of Saba's, it has something at once autobiographical and impersonal about it. . . . (pp. 116-19)

Casa e campagna may be regarded as a fitting prelude to *Trieste e una donna* (1910-12)—Saba's most original volume of verse. Here, poem after poem, Saba displays that masterly ease and naturalness, that dry intensity and vigour, that happy union between prose and poetic cadences for which we have no parallel in Italian poetry, except perhaps in Leopardi's "A Silvia," "Alla sua donna," and "Aspasia." . . . To his wife Lina and to Trieste are dedicated "all thoughts, all passions, all delight" of Saba's moral and poetic personality. Saba seldom achieved the same degree of sustained depth and subtlety except in a few cases and, to some extent, in *Ultime cose. Trieste e una donna,* more than any other volume of Saba's verse, may indeed be called the volume of Saba's art as well as of his life and heart. And we know that Saba prized heart more than intelligence or anything else. . . . Both the image of his wife as "mio solo amico, mia pallida sposa," as well as that of the ever-familiar yet perpetually fresh and touching Trieste are at once the leitmotif and the source of inspiration in this volume. There are indeed no themes in dealing with which Saba feels so much at home. Whatever form a poem may take—a soliloquy, a dialogue or a dramatic monologue—the unmistakable quality of style and language reveal themselves through all. . . . Both the subject matter and the language of Saba's poetry, combined with his personal temperament, make for a kind of idyllic poetry that is completely immersed in the humdrum routine of everyday life, and that lays no claim to any metaphysical or spiritual undertones.

Of course, when the medium and style of poetry are so intimately wedded to the rhythms and cadences of prose, the poet seems to be walking, as it were, on a sharp and perilous edge, with the possible risk—or temptation—of falling too far below either on this or the other side. Saba does not always succeed in avoiding this pitfall, and consequently what he writes is at times no better than versified prose. He himself was aware of this, but was not critically concerned or capable enough to eliminate or reduce as far as possible the strain of "prosasticita" in his poetry. (pp. 119-20)

Then there is another temptation to which Saba's poetry frequently and almost mechanically succumbs—the temptation to expatiate on what has been succinctly realized in a few lines of creative vigour and intensity. Of course this defect is more or less common to all Italian poets after Leopardi, with the sole exception of Montale, the ascetic (*not* hermetic) essentiality of whose verse is something more than a synthesis and compactness on a verbal and stylistic plane. (p. 120)

However, a considerable body of lyric poetry in *Trieste e una donna* shows Saba's poetic and linguistic maturity guided by a stricter organizational control at its best. As, for instance, in the poem **"Trieste"** where topographical realism combined with an impressive degree of lyric intensity, gives the verse its hard and crystalline timbre. . . . (p. 121)

The last two lyrics in this volume, **"Dopo una passeggiata"** and **"Pri soli,"** are among the tenderest things Saba ever wrote, combining as they do a rare kind of simplicity with self-concealed depth, of spontaneity with self-control. . . . (pp. 122-23)

In *Nuovi versi alla Lina* we have, in addition to a nostalgic stocktaking of the past, the inspiringly vital factor of his love for his wife—a love that recognizes and accepts, with a stoic pathos as it were, the crucial inevitability of change and mortality. . . . In singing as it were the mystical, but fundamentally human character of love in its complexity and compositeness—love that embraces a sister, a mistress and an enemy—Saba seems to be striking almost a metaphysical chord. . . . (p. 123)

But this is not a very characteristic note in Saba's poetry, which is, for the most part, distinguished by its elemental force, candour and sincerity. (pp. 123-24)

The next volume *La serena disperazione* (1913-15) is much weaker indeed. There is a noticeable lack of real fervour or inspiration; both the language and the imagery are flat. And the same thing applies more or less to *Poesie scritte durante la guerra, Cose leggere e vaganti* (1920) or *L'amorosa spina* (1920). . . . The trouble is that in all these volumes posterior to *Trieste e una donna* far too many poems resemble bubbles that hardly seem to rise at all. **"Forse un giorno diranno,"** for example, is a poem with a potentially rich anecdotic character, but Saba does not sufficiently exploit it. In the following volume *Preludio e canzonette* (1921-32), the only poem in which the episodic element is justly balanced by a corresponding lyric intensity is **"Il mendico."** . . . (p. 125)

After *Trieste e una donna* another very interesting and consistently lyrical volume of verse is *Autobiografia* (1924), where it is not so much the external events and interests of Saba's life, but what Browning called "incidents in the development of the soul" that are poetically dealt with, resulting in a verse characterized by depth and maturity. . . . Such verses have a symbolism of their own—the unobtrusive symbolism of an apparently prosaic statement which is Saba's distinctive contribution to modern Italian poetry. The vicissitudes of a child with his mother deserted by the father before he was born . . . the racial divergence between the two parents . . . , the loneliness of his childhood . . . , the loves of his adolescence, and above all the love of Lina . . . , the experience of war . . . , are all described with a sincerity and a passion that have nothing sentimentally lugubrious about it. . . . Saba's is the simplicity of a true, at times even a great poet—a simplicity that presupposes a mature attitude to language and to one's own experience. It also presupposes the courage and confidence to do away with an easier and more familiar kind of cleverness and success. (pp. 125-26)

The next volume *I prigioni* (1924) is again, on the whole, feeble and far below Saba's level at his best. However, . . . [**"Il silenzioso"**] deserves to be singled out for its real strength and maturity. . . . (p. 126)

In *Fanciulle* (1925) the dominant theme is feminine beauty, with its sensuality, tenderness and psychological charm. In dealing with these themes Saba at times attains to a kind of

Petrarchan grace and melody and at times to Dantesque sublimity. (pp. 126-27)

Cuor morituro (1925-30) is perhaps Saba's weakest and least inspired volume of verse. It is laboriously didactic and diffuse. Moreover, it is almost obsessively antibiographical. It confirms, at its own expense, the validity of Eliot's celebrated dictum that "the progress of an artist is a continual self-sacrifice, a continual extinction of personality." There is in Saba a kind of indomitable urge to consider each and every thing that relates to him and to his life as a poetic "occasion" in the Goethian or, in our own times, Montalian sense of the term. And what results, more often than not, from such an exercise is not poetry in the real sense, but a stylistically smart transcription of one's thoughts and feelings, which have not, or not sufficiently, been subjected to the process which alone can make them transcend themselves and become somewhat vaster and more impersonal. In quite a number of poems in *Cuor morituro,* therefore, the dividing line between prose and poetry is too frequently lost sight of. For instance, in the poem **"Latteria"** it is merely in order to enforce a moral that Saba seems to take recourse to the poetic form at all. There is a kind of poetic naïvety in Saba, which is quite often indulged in for its own sake and which apparently lacks the inner compulsion and economy of thought, feeling and language which some of Saba's own better verse so admirably displays. (pp. 127-28)

In *Preludio e fughe* (1928-29), too, it is only at certain points that Saba's poetry has the sustained depth and urge of a truly creative inspiration. For the most part what one gets is merely an exercise in reasoning and generalization done through the medium of verse. (p. 128)

Parole (1933-34), and Saba's later poetry in general, seem to be characterized by an altogether new note. Verbal diffuseness gives way to a quintessential laconicism without leading to the sort of obscurity that one associates with "hermetic" poetry. Even at its most condensed and concentrated, Saba's verse is invariably distinguished by a striking clarity of thought and meaning. . . . Montale's poetry seems to have made a considerable difference for the older poet's own way of writing poetry. A poem like **"Primavera"** can be regarded as being very Montalian for the author of *Trieste e una donna*. . . . In his poem **"Firenze"** Saba in fact refers to his admiration for Montale and it is quite likely that the new change in his style may have had something to do with that. (pp. 129-30)

After, or rather together with *Trieste e una donna, Ultime cose* (1935-43) is perhaps Saba's most characteristic book of verse. Here, more than anywhere else, a parallel with Montale's poetry powerfully suggests itself. Concentration and economy both at the verbal level and at the level of the organisation of thought and feeling are the hallmark of this volume. And this change in form and technique is seen to be correlated with a sort of inner moral ripening. . . . But this wisdom, and the consequent maturing and austerity of expression it entails, have not altogether dried up the vein of idyllic tenderness. . . . The sentiment of pity as well as self-pity, rooted as it was in Saba's basic humanity, is as vividly present in poems like **"Caro luogo," "Sul tavolo," "Notte d'estate," "Solo," "I morti amici"** or **"Da quando,"** as in his earlier verse.

In *Ultime cose,* however, the poetic images as well as the terms of moral and psychological reference undergo a significant change and lead to the discovery of the underlying symbolism of the things and objects of everyday life, as well as to a fresh look at old things which had hitherto been ignored. . . . In recognizing and reinterpreting the symbols and illusions of the past, Saba is helped by the unchanging, yet perennially fresh and eloquent landscape of his native town. **"Dall'erta"** is one of the most characteristic poems on this theme. . . . There is in practically all the lyrics in this volume a dry intensity and precision which were conspicuously absent from much of Saba's earlier verse. . . . In poems like **"Fumo"** and **"Il vetro rotto"** the language is not only concrete and objective, but at the same time also, in a way, symbolic, more or less the way in which some of the poems in *Ossi di seppia* are so. . . . (pp. 131-33)

"Il vetro rotto" may, in fact, be compared with Montale's "Spesso il male di vivere" for its metaphysical tension and evocativeness. . . .

In all these poems Saba's youthful memories—the joys, passions and sufferings of his past—come back to him and make him see the present in a new light and his own self in a different perspective. . . . (p. 134)

In *Mediterranee,* together with Saba's place-poems—that is, poems dedicated to places for which he feels a particular sense of gratitude—one finds two of his best known poems **"Ebbri canti"** and **"Ulisse."** **"Ebbri canti"** is the poetic epitome, so to say, of the cultural history and background of the Mediterranean and of what it now means to the poet in his old age. . . . In **"Ulisse"** landscape and memory combine to offer Saba a kind of canvas on which to paint the torment of his "non domato spirito," with all the beauty, nostalgia, pathos and poetry of that torment. A vividly picturesque realism serves to reveal and accentuate the underlying symbolism of an intensely personal poem. . . . The figure of Ulysses serves as a king of lyrical-cum-allegorical *alter ego* of Saba. And underlying the narrative or episodic strain is a symbolic density expressed through a few hard and clear-cut images in virtue of which the poem may well qualify as a Dantesque canto in miniature.

The last two volumes of verse *Uccelli* (1948) and *Quasi un racconto* (1951) register a notable decline in Saba's poetic powers. The very simplicity of style and language as well as of themes serves to stress the feeling of resignation as well as of decadence and exhaustion. . . . (pp. 135-36)

Saba's place in twentieth-century Italian poetry is linked with what will be definitely regarded as an original and substantial contribution. On the purely linguistic as well as artistic plane what Saba did to emancipate the language of poetry from the yoke of Carducci's academic pastoralism on the one hand, and D'Annunzio's rhetoric and bombast on the other, is something much more impressive than what Gozzano or any other poet did before Montale. He is also the first major Italian poet to have wedded—or at least to have done so in his best poetry—the language of prose with that of poetry. Also his love-poetry is something quite different in form and essence from what love poetry has always been in Italy since Petrarch.

And yet the very originality and revolutionary character of his innovations stood in his way of being accepted as a major poet for quite a long time. Saba was considered at once too original for those who were still under the influence of D'Annunzio's rhetoric, and too conventional and conformist for those who had been converted to hermetism. . . . When

Saba wrote, literary taste was dominated by forces and trends which were quite alien to his nature and temperament. And it was something too much for Saba to be able—or even to be willing—to create the taste, according to which, as Wordsworth said, new poetry has to be judged. (pp. 136-37)

G. Singh, "The Poetry of Umberto Saba," in Italian Studies, *Vol. XXIII, 1968, pp. 114-37.*

JOSEPH CARY (essay date 1969)

[*In the following excerpt, Cary discusses the merits of the whole of* Il canzoniere *and of two of its central poems, "La brama" and "Il borgo."*]

The *Canzoniere* is very uneven. Each volume has its great sequences and single poems as well as its weak ones. The book as a whole lends itself to anthological culling and weeding, no doubt. . . . (p. 42)

[One] of the poet's originalities is his power to involve his reader in his life so that even the relatively inferior verses fascinate as variations, preparations, or echoes of poetically better times. Despite his exorbitant ego, Saba himself was aware of his unevenness. His *envoi* to *Cose leggere e vaganti* (**Light and Airy Things**) says:

> Voi lo sapete, amici, ed io lo so.
> Anche i versi somigliano alle bolle
> di sapone; una sale e un'altra no.
>
> You know it, friends, and so do I./ Even poems are
> like soap / bubbles; one goes up, another not.

Speaking to his friend Nora Baldi, he likened the failures, the *nonpoesia* of parts of the *Canzoniere,* to the "zum-pai-pai" or musical fillings in the work of Verdi, concluding that "no one can stay on the heights forever without lying." And in the *Storia,* he offers his work as very much a "natural phenomenon," wholly dependent on the inspiration of the moment: "when inspiration fails him, or is thin, Saba is worth little or nothing. And nothing can be done about it. 'Literature' was never a valid support for him. In terms of his particular poetics, literature is to poetry as lie to truth. Such a man had to be born in Italy, precisely in the land of *letterati*!"

There is something of the mucker pose in this assertion. As part of his long guerilla war against what he felt to be the modish intellectualism of most modern verse, Saba at times exaggerated his self-made, *naïf* proletarian side, priding himself on the largeness and "naturalness" of his vein. Yet he revised and rearranged his work incessantly, for all his naturalness, and "literature" most certainly sustained and nourished his muse and him in the long course of their life together, as even the general title for his collected poems indicates. He was not remotely *maudit* (expressively and spontaneously "damned" like Rimbaud or Campana), but rather a hard working, well-read storekeeper (specializing in antiquarian books!) who was poor, insufficiently encouraged, often most unhappy, and who wrote poems about it all.

Of course all poets must in the first instance depend on inspiration or some sort of exceptional grace, and perhaps he was merely less nervous or conscience-stricken about living up to or filling out the given afflatus. He wrote more poems than most and discarded fewer; thus there is a greater fluctuation in quality. And he sometimes confused the mental anguish or pain or exultation attendant upon the writing of poetry

with poetry itself, experiencing an intensity there that never really got transcribed. But such is his charm, or the fascination of his egotism, that the reader is often seduced into accepting lesser work simply because it is part of Saba's life. This is not a contemptible achievement. In other words, a good case can be made for reading all of Saba. (pp. 42-3)

In a 1933 essay on Saba, Sergio Solmi remarks on his "attempts to condense within a great synthesis the fatalities of flesh and the predestined cycle of human life." Solmi is specifically referring to *I prigioni* and *L'uomo,* but surely the loftiest of all Saba's efforts at synthesis, less inclusive and more specialized than the fugues but possibly more intense and poignant, is the great *canzone* **"La brama"** at the center of *Cuor morituro.*

"Brama" can be understood "clinically" as libido, more loosely as that erotic hungering which, disguised or openly, consciously or not, Saba has come to recognize as fundamental life-energy, *élan vital, anima mundi.* **"La brama"** therefore is an almost Lucretian expression of Saba's most urgent fable and credo, half-celebration and half-ritual propitiation of what he calls in the [*Storia e cranistoria del "Canzoniere,"* Saba's book of background and criticism on the *Canzoniere*] "the ancient Eros who unifies the world." Its position in almost the exact center of the completed *Canzoniere* constitutes an odd spatial confirmation of the centrality of the god's presence that he acknowledged in all his work:

> Altro che te che ho detto
> io nei modi dell'arte, che ho nascosto
> altro che te, o svelato?
>
> (". . . Other than thou of what have I spoken /
> in the modalities of my art? what have I hidden, / other than thou, or veiled?")

Being a hymn, **"La brama"** contains a variable refrain, a recurrent or obsessional epithetic bloc which regulates the pulse of the andante with which the poem unfolds. This bloc is first proposed, as a direct ritual invocation, as the brief first stanza:

> O nell'antica carne
> dell'uomo addentro infitta
> antica brama!
>
> ("O deep-fixed / within the ancient heart of
> man, / ancient hunger!")

Brama is now celebrated for the gift of supreme pleasure it confers directly upon our lives, "as much sweetness as the creation holds, unified through flesh." As Freud teaches, flesh cheated or frustrated of its fleshly desire may console or compensate itself through "spiritual" displacements, sublimations. The hymn adduces "the departure of tall ships" in quest of new worlds, a religious passion to "conquer the tomb." In this creative aspect, *brama* is hailed by two adjectival epithets: *assidua,* (assiduous, diligent, perpetual), and *generante,* (generative, fructifying).

But the image evoked by the initial participle (*infitta*) forecasts a darker note of pain and *dolore.* From the young boy's innocent virility sickening to guilt and self-abuse to the old man's torment leading to his wish to die, life is threaded by anguish. In its role as punisher and nemesis, *brama* accrues two other adjectives: *cupa* (dark, mysterious, inscrutable), and *feroce* (ferocious and ravening).

"La brama" is evoked as the dynamic source and condition of all animate life, "cause of my ills and also—yes—my good." To deny it would be blasphemy, a denial of life itself. Hence the recurring qualifier, *ANTICA brama,* repeated six times above and beyond the more specialized others, modifying and deepening the phrase *antica carne* inexorably linked to it.

> Ti riconosce colui che alla sera,
> con lotta e pena, della vita è giunto;
> ti riconosce e, per sfuggirti, morte
> s'invoca. . . .

> (" . . . he recognizes you, he who has arrived, /
> with struggle and pain, at the evening of life; /
> he recognizes you and, to flee you, invokes / his
> death. . . . ")

"He" is plausibly Umberto Saba, but here the "documentary" specificity of a given life is dissolved into the larger synthesis or fable, or present only as a special overtone to the reader familiar with his story. Perhaps the most moving example of this sort of transformation in the poem occurs in the final stanza, where the plight of Vittorio Bolaffio, the Triestine painter who was painting Saba's portrait almost simultaneously with the composition of **"La brama,"** is evoked:

> Devotamente egli la mano stende,
> che d'ansia trema, a colorir sue tele.
> Sopra vi pinge vele
> nel sole, accesi incontri
> di figure, tramonti sulle rive
> del mare e a bordo, e su ogni cosa un lume
> di santità. . . .

> (" . . . Devotedly he extends his hand, / which
> trembles with inquietude, to color his can-
> vases. / Upon them he paints sails / in the sun,
> vivid encounters / of figures, sunsets above
> shores / of the sea and from a ship's railing, and
> over everything a light, / of holiness. . . . ")

But this image of the artist—Bolaffio but also Saba—as the celebrant of *cose leggere e vaganti* culminates inevitably in disaster: a man "not yet old but bent," a dreamer of terrible dreams, crippled by desire. Like the cat of *Trieste e una donna* or the goat of *Casa e campagna* whose absurd plaint recapitulates the pain of *ogni altra vita,* so Saba and Bolaffio become figures in a fabulous landscape, elements in the continuous present of a master fable.

"La brama" is one of the great examples of Saba's piety towards the Italian literary tradition, and proof of that tradition's viability in the present. **"La brama,"** could not have been made without the nourishment Saba received from his masters from Petrarch to Leopardi. But influence is inevitable; what counts is what can be made of it, and what Saba makes of it here is something profoundly his own. With the grave deliberateness of its periods, the deep plangency of its stern music, **"La brama"** stands as the latest of the great Italian *canzoni,* last of the line begun with the *stilnovisti* and Cavalcanti's "Donna mi prega." And despite the fact that the world view it espouses is highly specialized, it rises above its obsessive and doctrinaire originating impulses to become in the end a truly noble exposition of the epistemology of joy and sorrow.

Immediately following **"La brama"** in *Cuor morituro* is another very different major poem: **"Il borgo"** (**"The Town"**: the title refers not to Trieste but to one of its hillside and now suburban adjuncts where Saba lived at the turn of the century). Like **"La capra"** or **"La brama,"** **"Il borgo"** constitutes one of the moments in the *Canzoniere* to which one returns again and again as to the definitive utterance of a crucial experience. (pp. 112-15)

Like the majority of *Cuor morituro* poems, **"Il borgo"** relates to an early poem of adolescence, in this case an identically named piece which, though included in the first, was dropped from the 1945 second edition of the *Canzoniere.* "It was a poem of little or no value," comments Saba in the *Storia,* "with touches of 'civic' verse—Carduccian and socialistically slanted in the manner fashionable in the very first years of the twentieth century." The occasion of the Ur "Borgo" had been an illness ("more of spirit than body," a note in the *Storia* elaborates) during which a suicidally depressed Saba observed from a *cantuccio* the crowd of workers returning from various jobs through the streets of his *borgo* and found himself suddenly and ecstatically filled with the passion to break out of the prison of self, his wretched and self-serving conviction of solitude and "difference," in order to become *uomo,* a man of every day, one like the others. A later, wryer Saba might have remarked that the first thing to be done would be to abandon not only the writing of but the aspiration towards poetry. The young man conceived of himself becoming a sort of Béranger or Guest; he would be a people's poet:

> . . . E vorrei che dal mio povero verso . . .
> nascesse, ma per tutti, un pane. . . .

> (" . . . and I would wish that from my poor
> verse / . . . might be born, for everyone,
> bread. . . . ")

"Saba," as we know, equals "bread." The title "**Borgo**" could thus be spiritually rendered as "community." A source of at least a part of the sense of solidarity which Saba experienced here presumably came from the "youth" of this *borgo,* its budding like a human flower *fervente d'umano lavoro* (fervent with human labor), on one of the previously bare hills overlooking Trieste. So he linked his expectations, youthfully "great" as they were, to the life of that district.

If this first **"Borgo"** had been kept, it would have been the first sounding of that theme of aspiration towards human community which is touched so many times in the *Canzoniere,* the complex affective counterpoint to those many other poems that express Saba's sense of isolation and pariahdom. The **"Borgo"** of *Cuor morituro* is not a rewrite of that old experience but a palinode or revision of it in the light of experience. So it begins, its aspirational refrain (lines 6-11 below) made pathetic and futile by the verb tense (*passato remoto*) and simile announcing it:

> Fu nelle vie di questo
> Borgo che nuova cosa
> m'avvenne.

> Fu come un vano
> sospiro
> il desiderio improvviso d'uscire
> di me stesso, di vivere la vita
> di tutti
> d'essere come tutti
> gli uomini di tutti
> i giorni.

> ("It was in the streets of this / town that something
> new befell me.

It was like a vain / sigh, / the sudden desire to come
out / of myself, to live the life / of all, to be like
all / the men of all / days.")

It is impossible to translate this. The language is as ascetic
and spare as it can be, as "transparent" as a Sophoclean chorus. Rhyme is irregular and scarce, though there are a few in
the old synthetical style: for example, the wide-gapped *vano-
umano* coupling which capsulizes a main tenet. Functioning
rhythmically are chunks or paragraphs of repeated material.
The most obvious of these is the refrain, "di vivere la vita/
di tutti," and so on, with its parcels of recurring words and
phrases: *essere come, giorni, vita, uomini* and above all the en-
jambment-accented *tutti . . . tutti . . . tutti.* There are other
keying nuclei, notably those linked with the vanity of his old
desire, which articulate his ambivalences:

> lines 4-6: come un vano / sospiro / il desiderio
> lines 16-17 il desiderio vano / come un sospiro
> lines 26-27 il desiderio dolce / e vano
> lines 50-51 il desiderio, appena un breve / sospiro
> lines 67-68 il mio sospiro dolce / e vile.

The canzonetta briskness of the short seven-syllable lines,
balanced against fives and elevens, with threes used mainly
for emphasis, is consistently retarded beyond the sombre
sense by the brilliantly deployed enjambments which persistently create a break or catch in what would normally be simple noun-adjective phrasal units (*questo / Borgo, vano /
sospiro, tutti / gli uomini, umano / lavoro,* and so on). We are
made to syllable this threnody.

The first five stanzas of **"Il borgo"** tell the old story in lines
of extraordinary limpidity. The occasion, setting and nature
of his desire are accompanied throughout by the bleak tolling
of the *vano* terminal and the reductive apposition of *desiderio*
with *sospiro,* the vibrance of the first belied by the impotent
regret of the second. The sixth stanza moves from this discon-
solate retrospect to the diminished present:

> Nato d'oscure
> vicende,
> poco fu il desiderio, appena un breve
> sospiro. Lo ritrovo
> —eco perduta
> di giovanezza—per la vie del Borgo
> mutate
> piú che mutato non sia io. Sui muri
> dell'alte case,
> sugli uomini e i lavori, su ogni cosa,
> è sceso il velo che avvolge le cose
> finite.

> ("Born of dark / conditions, / how short-lived was
> that desire, hardly a brief / sigh. I find it
> again / —lost echo / of my youth—[note the
> comparable "sogno dall'adolescenza uscito" of
> the contemporary **"Casa della mia nutrice"**]—in
> the streets of the Town, / changed / even more
> than I have changed. Over the walls / of the tall
> houses, / over men and their works, over every-
> thing, / the veil has descended that envelopes fi-
> nite / things.")

So the original parallel linking the futures of *borgo* and poet
is traced out to its ultimate bankruptcy; awaiting his deliverance by death, *solo con i mio duro / patire* (alone with my
hard suffering), the poet lives incarcerated in himself in a
mondo/finito (finished world) that mirrors him. (pp. 115-18)

Back-to-back, at the heart of **Cuor morituro,** stand two mas-

terpieces, **"La brama"** and **"Il borgo."** The first diagnoses all
animate life in terms of one vital disease, sexual desire. The
second recapitulates one particular life in terms of the phantom that broke its heart, the dream of human community. (p.
118)

"The peculiar *largeness* of Saba . . . is more than ever evident when we compare him (let us say) with Ungaretti, our
most illustrious modern example of a poet who has developed
primarily in a vertical direction." So (as cited in the **Storia**)
writes Pierantonio Quarantotti Gambini, the critic we have
already quoted as having misgivings over Saba's title for the
collected poems. "Canzoniere" implies a songbook, a collection of individual lyrics on the Petrarchan model. Quarantotti Gambini feels that such a title is misleading for the simple
reason that (italics his) *"the poetry of Saba is not only lyric."*
"From this point of view the entire work of Saba will appear
to us as it really is, taking on its complete and highest value:
a vast poetic production, closely interconnected and therefore
a whole, occupying an intermediate position between what
we understand as *canzoniere* and what we understand as *un
poema,* one single poem."

Others have concurred. Critics like Giuseppe Ravegnani and
Pietro Pancrazi have stressed that Saba needs to be read *en
bloc,* that main attention should be fixed on the **Canzoniere**
in its emergent richness rather than on the individual lyric.
This is easier to agree with now than it was once, for once
upon a time a reviewer had only a fascicle or "slender volume" to base his verdict on. What would be one's view of
Saba if one had only **L'uomo** to go on? In his story there are
exceptional moments that can and do stand by themselves as
anthological star-turns. But even poems like **"A mia moglie,"**
"Trieste," **"La brama"** or **"Il borgo"** are deprived when detached from their context; whoever knows them only in isolation knows only a part of their resonance. The same thing is
true of the slighter poems. The *poesie dell'adolescenza,* the little fables, sketches and *variora,* inherit special pathos from
the company they keep. This has only been obvious since
1945, since there has been a **Canzoniere** conveniently available.

Finally, it takes more than critics' instructions to make us
care to read all of Saba. This, I think, is the miracle, and it
is all his doing. The Umberto that he offers is really no Ulysses; he is, proudly and wretchedly, himself. He has a demanding body as well as an aspiring spirit, a lengthening history,
and a diminishing future, wife, child, and *fanciulle,* shop and
shop-assistant, particular complaints and particular compen-
sations. He lives through a number of wars and uneasy
peaces, dictatorship and persecution, exile and, at the end,
the sort of affectionate public recognition he had always
longed for.

And this in itself is nothing extraordinary; take away the
fame, which he finds too late anyway, and much the same
could be written of most Italians of his generation. His distinction is to have written a poem about it all, about not only
his own life and times but others' as well, insofar as all are
linked in the community of *dolore* that it was his genius and
misfortune to perceive. I think of this inclusive vision as
something special. It underlies everything that Saba ever
wrote and integrates his poetry of occasions into *poema.* And
in the pages of the **Canzoniere** it is preserved as that *calda
vita di tutti* that he so often despaired of grasping in his life.
(pp. 131-32)

Joseph Cary, "Umberto Saba," in his Three Modern
Italian Poets: Saba, Ungaretti, Montale, *New York
University Press, 1969, pp. 31-133.*

EUGENIO DONADONI   (essay date 1969)

[*In the following excerpt, Donadoni critiques various aspects of
Saba's poetry.*]

Sometimes [Saba] has assumed the most daring forms of the
twentieth century, but this is the part of his work which is unconvincing and will not become any more convincing in the
near future. In his most congenial and felicitous poems he is
fond of a tranquil poetic utterance in which the images arrange themselves fully in affectionate sentiments, in pictur-
izations of things, in experiences of life. Contrasted to the
sadness of living, to violence and deceit, the tender, loving usages console and indeed give happiness and vital ardor. This
is why the most oft-recurring themes in Saba's poetry are his
love for Lina his wife, love of Trieste, the city so dear to him
and whose streets, squares, crowded little modest shops, the
Triestine people, and the many races of which it is composed.
He does not so much describe as interpret all this and, in
short, everything which he loves in the daily round. Sometimes his membership in the external world seems simply to
turn into a chronicle in verse form. His emotional reaction
jumps with joyful, agile whimsicality from the moralistic epigram to the pathetic, the evocative, loving impulse. His style
tends toward simplicity, toward the discursive, sometimes toward the humble, especially on the level of vocabulary, while
its rhythm often avails itself of inversions and hyperbata and
tends toward stiffness. On the whole, the poetry of Saba
seems to fall between the nineteenth century and the twentieth. It is between the tradition of stylistic sternness and moral
obligation, including the most recent naturalistic tradition
and, finally, autobiographical exaltation. All is from the nineteenth century, either in the pace of the inward-slanted diary
or in some concession to psychological introspection in a psychoanalytic key. (pp. 624-25)

Eugenio Donadoni, "The Twentieth Century," in
his A History of Italian Literature, Vol. 2, translated by Richard Monges, New York University Press,
1969, pp. 549-662.

PAUL HALLAM   (essay date 1987)

[*In the following excerpt, Hallam favorably reviews a translation of Saba's uncompleted novel,* Ernesto.]

Saba is Hebrew for bread, and the pen-name of this Italian
poet suits his work—homely images: basic, essential, sustaining. ***Ernesto*** was his "secret" novel, read to friends but
thought by Saba to be "unpublishable, because of the language." The choice of painting for the cover, albeit by a contemporary Trieste artist, won't help the bookshop browser to
guess the secret. In the painting a woman strolls by the sea.
In the book a 28-year-old man falls in love with a 16-year-old
boy.

Written in the 1950s, the unfinished ***Ernesto*** is set in Saba's
hometown, Trieste, at the turn of the century. Bread again
in the setting—the man and boy work in a depot, distributing
flour from Hungarian mills to the city bakers. The man asks
all the leading questions, like "Do your crowns go on
women?" but Ernesto needs no hints. His response is entirely

practical: "If we're going to do things we shouldn't do, don't
we have to be alone?" The sex takes place among the flour
sacks and, as Ernesto later admits, "I met him more than
half-way." He startles, almost embarrasses the man: " 'You
want to put it up my arse,' Ernesto said with serene innocence." Ernesto is incapable of lying, he works out his response to sex simply by trying it. He enjoys the experience
and wants to allay the man's fear of betrayal. It's Ernesto's
sense of the absurd that nearly gives the game away; he finds
the idea of cocoa-butter cones inserted to ease pain quite hysterically funny. At one point he cryptically shouts, "No more
CONES!" in front of his mother when the man visits his
home. Ernesto eventually tires of the man's attentions, plays
practical jokes on his conservative employer, gets himself the
sack, has a haircut and first shave, visits an elderly prostitute
and falls for a boy younger than himself.

The narrative is slight and fragmented, the glory is in the
style. . . . Saba thought ***Ernesto*** was the best thing he had
ever written, but was never able to finish it: "the author is too
old, too weary, too embittered" to go on. It's a book of parentheses and qualifications, the author interpreting the action
or looking forward to the fate of his characters and their city
in the coming century. Saba's commentary is melancholic—
Trieste *tristesse,* comic, startling, ruminative, like Barthes at
his most personal. It's about limits, emotional, economic and
social. When characters misunderstand each other's words
and gestures, Saba gently reflects on their dilemmas, usually
in an aside.

Tenderness is limited from the start, the man fears he will
frighten the boy or that the boy will look down on him. Making love he utters "something coarse" instead of expressing
the wonder he feels; he longs for kisses, but "boys don't know
how to give or accept them." When he does call Ernesto
"Angel," Ernesto points out that angels don't do sex, they
don't even have bodies. The boy is not unkind; his response
to sex, like his socialism, is simple and honest. The man's tenderness in wiping the boy after sex is ambiguous, "from kindness or to make sure he left no trace." He worries that the
boy will be offended by gifts, and besides he is poor. The compromise, pastries, is ideal—cheap and, again, leaving no
trace. Gifts for boys are dangerous, an outside constraint.
The man is not prepared to let Ernesto take an active role,
there are codes and limits even within their illegal love.

Ernesto's mother loved her son "but thought it was her duty
not to show it." She fails to comprehend the major "catastrophe" Ernesto feels on having his first shave; he "never liked
to lose any part of himself." When the mother does kiss her
son she for once "followed her heart; she sent morality and
its abject homilies to the devil (i.e. back to their true father)."
The occasional breakthrough to tenderness proves stunning
when everything conspires to block it.

Ernesto's crabby, Germanophile employer will die in the gas
chamber. The almost unwittingly anarchic Ernesto who
"adored asking questions and adored asking permission to
ask them" will suffer for his knowledge. The hints and parentheses take you beyond the immediate episodes. Saba has an
immense respect for his characters, and a sense too of how
they'll be damaged. [The] ample preface and friendly, thorough notes relate the clearly autobiographical novel to the life
and poetry of its author. This is a fresh and warm book, in
a firm crust. (pp. 28-9)

Paul Hallam, "Bread and Butter," in New States-man, Vol. 113, No. 2930, May 22, 1987, pp. 28-9.

ADDITIONAL BIBLIOGRAPHY

Bergin, Thomas G. Review of *La spada d'amore: Lettere scelte,* by Umberto Saba. *World Literature Today* 58, No. 3 (Summer 1984): 400.
    Praises Saba's sensitivity and his mastery of both verse and prose.

Hallock, Ann H. "Umberto Saba's Reply to Chaos." *Canadian Journal of Italian Studies* 9, No. 32 (1986): 10-20.
    Sees implicit in Saba's poetry a belief in a universal order, and emphasizes his method of "rigorous introspection and self-knowledge."

Krist, Gary. Review of *Ernesto,* by Umberto Saba. *The New York Times Book Review* (6 September 1987): 16.
    Brief review which comments on the book's occasional sentimentality, but also points out Saba's astute social and psychological insights.

Nims, John F. "Mezzogiorno d'inverno." In *The Poem Itself,* edited by Stanley Burnshaw, pp. 302-03. New York: Holt, Rinehart and Winston, 1960.
    Translation and close analysis of Saba's "Mezzogiorno d'inverno" ("Winter Noon") in which the critic concludes, "Saba's strength, he once said, lay in looking at things; but his looking becomes contemplation. Eyes bright with interest and grief, he follows a balloon bobbing across the heavens, but in its wavering flight he is contemplating too the flunctuations of all things human."

——. "Autobiografia 3." *Chelsea* 12 (September 1962): 116-17.
    Translation and close analysis of this poem, highlighting its personal and universal implications.

Parrinder, Patrick. "Charmed Lives." *London Review of Books* 9, No. 8 (23 April 1987): 16-17.
    Favorable review of Saba's unfinished novel, *Ernesto.*

Renzi, Lorenzo. "A Reading of Saba's 'A mia moglie'." *The Modern Language Review* 68, No. 1 (January 1973): 77-83.
    Discusses two poetic patterns in "A mia moglie," concluding that "[one] has an almost traditional metrical form with a classically framed syntax, a lexicon of grace in contact with an everyday lexicon: it tries to 'remove' the taboos evoked. The other shows the general parallelism of internal compositional structures which organizes and sets in relief the infractions of the *taboos* and gives them a higher religious significance. . . ."

Sprigge, Sylvia. "Umberto Saba: Poet of Trieste." *The London Magazine* 5, No. 4 (1958): 45-51.
    Obituary tribute which praises Saba's poetry and his serene endurance of a difficult life.

Wilkins, Ernest Hatch. "The Literature of the Republic." In his *A History of Italian Literature,* pp. 496-524. Cambridge: Harvard University Press, 1974.
    Contains a short biography of Saba and a summary of his literary accomplishments and characteristics.

Israel Joshua Singer

1893-1944

Polish-born American novelist, short story writer, dramatist, journalist, and autobiographer.

Singer was among the first Yiddish novelists to write about the experiences of Eastern European Jews in large Western cities. He is best known for epic family sagas, such as *Di brider Ashkenazi* (*The Brothers Ashkenazi*) and *Di mishpokhe Karnovsky* (*The Carnovsky Family*), which explore conflict between the generations of Jewish families that migrated from the shtetls, or small villages, to the urban centers of Europe and the United States during the first decades of the twentieth century. While Singer's novels were enormously popular between the First and Second World Wars, his fame was later overshadowed by that of his younger brother, Isaac Bashevis Singer, who received the 1978 Nobel Prize in literature. Nonetheless, Israel Joshua Singer remains highly regarded for his effective depictions of Jewish life.

Singer was the second child and first son born to a rabbi and his wife in the Polish provincial capital of Bilgoray. Singer's mother received a sound education from her father, the rabbi of Bilgoray, and she married Pinchos Mendel Singer primarily because he was the most scholarly of her suitors. He also proved to be unworldly and ineffectual in practical matters, and the family was never financially secure. Pinchos Singer moved his family first to an unremunerative rabbinate in the small village of Leoncin, then to another poorly paid position, that of yeshiva lecturer, in Radzymin. Although he eventually obtained a rabbinate in Warsaw, this post remained unofficial because he refused to take a necessary examination in Russian. Israel Joshua was expected to become a rabbi, and his stringent religious instruction began when he was three. From the first he rebelled, fleeing, as he later wrote, "like a thief from the prison of the Torah, the awe of God and of Jewishness." As a child he avoided his lessons whenever he could, and in adolescence he openly challenged his parents' religious beliefs. In his autobiography, *Fun a velt vos iz nishto mer* (*Of a World That Is No More*), Singer wrote: "At the age of eighteen I decided that I did not want to be a clergyman and I gave up my theological studies. I wanted to have a modern education and proceeded to acquire one by taking casual lessons with inexpensive private tutors while earning my livelihood by doing all kinds of odd jobs." In his own memoirs and in interviews Isaac Bashevis Singer has recounted that the household often reverberated with arguments between the elder Singers and the youthful apostate.

By 1914 Singer was residing apart from his family, studying painting, and living for the most part as a gentile. As World War I progressed and the Germans advanced on Warsaw, Singer enlisted in the army, but deserted almost immediately and returned to Warsaw, where he lived under an assumed name. While he continued to study painting, Singer eventually decided that he could best express himself as a writer. After the war, Singer traveled to Kiev, attracted by the promise of the Russian Revolution. Although he soon became disillusioned with the Soviet system, he remained in Russia for several years. He married shortly before his return to Warsaw in 1922. That same year he published a collection of short sto-

ries, *Perl, un andere dertseylungen,* which came to the attention of Abraham Cahan, the publisher of the influential New York-based Yiddish newspaper *Der forverts* (*Jewish Daily Forward*). Cahan engaged Singer as the paper's Polish correspondent, and published his short stories as well as nonfiction articles. Although the *Forward,* like many liberal journals, was initially pro-Bolshevik, firsthand accounts of social and political conditions in Soviet Russia by correspondents such as Singer led Cahan to shift his editorial policy to one opposing communism. Singer's own growing antagonism toward Bolshevism was apparent in a series of reports based upon a 1926 visit to the Soviet Union sponsored by Cahan, in the semiautobiographical drama *Erdvey,* and in the novel *Shtol un ayzn* (*Steel and Iron*). According to Isaac Bashevis Singer, these early works "incurred the wrath of noisy political factions," including "the Communist phrasemongers and Stalin worshippers in the Yiddish milieu." The negative reaction distressed Singer, and he publicly renounced Yiddish literature. For five years he published nothing while casting about for a new language in which to write, considering first German, then French, but ultimately deciding that he could not express himself in another tongue.

Singer resumed writing in Yiddish, and subsequently published the novel *Yoshe Kalb,* which was based on a Hasidic folktale often recounted by his father. This work was highly regarded for its vivid evocation of the Hasidic milieu of the nineteenth century, and it was soon afterward adapted for the stage. Singer traveled to New York in 1933 to oversee the production of *Yoshe Kalb* and decided to remain, bringing his wife and children, and then his brother Isaac, from Poland to join him. At that time New York was a vigorous center of Yiddish culture. As Irving Howe has commented regarding the international nature of Yiddish literature during this period: "By 1925 it was not unusual for a Yiddish poet to live in New York and publish a book in Vilna, nor for a Yiddish novelist to live in Warsaw and publish his work in the New York *Forward*. Writers shuttled back and forth between continents, with some of the important Yiddish novelists of eastern Europe—Sholem Asch, I. J. Singer, Zalman Schneour—settling permanently in New York." While some commentators maintain that Singer contemplated leaving the United States in the 1940s, his brother Isaac Bashevis contends that "he wanted to stay in America. Of course the Hitler war brought deep disappointment in my brother's life because he knew what was going on in Europe. He wasn't disappointed in America, he was disappointed in the human race. He considered America an oasis in a wilderness." Singer died unexpectedly in 1944.

Yoshe Kalb is widely considered the first work of Singer's artistic maturity. In this novel Singer evokes the atmosphere of Hasidic life in the nineteenth century, displaying, in the words of Howe, "a marvelous command of detail, marvelous not least of all because he writes without . . . self-conscious glances at an alien audience." In the novels that he wrote after coming to the United States, Singer mastered the complex narrative structure of the family saga. *The Brothers Ashkenazi, Chaver Nachman* (*East of Eden*), and *The Carnovsky Family* are epic works that trace the fates of successive generations of Eastern European Jewish families during the social and political upheavals of the early twentieth century. Many Yiddish novelists, coming to the United States with an extensive body of work, wrote almost exclusively about the dying traditions of shtetl culture. The shtetls virtually disappeared after the turn of the century, when war, poverty, and pogroms against Jews led to widespread migration to urban centers. Jewish writers commonly felt committed to preserving this portion of their heritage, and wrote little or nothing about contemporary Jewish experience. Singer was one of the first Yiddish writers to take as a principal theme the changes in Jewish life during this population shift. With *The Brothers Ashkenazi*, Philip Rahv has written, Singer "thrust forward into the mêlée of modern experience, and this without surrendering a jot of his fidelity to the particulars of the classic Jewish world of Eastern Europe." Although he is sometimes charged with infusing his fiction with political didacticism, he largely avoided this pitfall in his most highly regarded novels, *The Brothers Ashkenazi* and *The Carnovsky Family*, effectively depicting the experiences of Jews undergoing the turmoil of adjusting to new ways of life and the generational clash of which he himself had been a part. He is especially commended for his skill in recreating the historical background against which many large and small family sagas were enacted.

Although his works were widely read during his lifetime, Singer's reputation diminished after his death in 1944, when Yiddish literature in general underwent a critical and popular decline. Nevertheless, Singer's works continue to be admired by both Yiddish- and English-language readers, and he is considered one of the most important Yiddish novelists of the first part of the twentieth century.

PRINCIPAL WORKS

Erdvey (drama) 1922
Perl, un andere dertseylungen (short stories) 1922
Oyf fremder erd (short stories) 1925
Nay-Rusland (nonfiction) 1927
 [*The New Russia,* 1927]
Shtol un ayzn (novel) 1927
 [*Blood Harvest,* 1935; also published as *Steel and Iron,* 1969]
Yoshe Kalb (novel) 1932
 [*The Sinner,* 1933; also published as *Yoshe Kalb,* 1965]
Di brider Ashkenazi (novel) 1936
 [*The Brothers Ashkenazi,* 1936]
Friling, un andere dertseylungen (short stories) 1937
Chaver Nachman (novel) 1937
 [*East of Eden,* 1939]
The River Breaks Up (short stories) 1938
Di mishpokhe Karnovsky (novel) 1943
 [*The Carnovsky Family,* 1943]
Fun a velt vos iz nishto mer (autobiography) 1946
 [*Of a World That Is No More,* 1970]
Dertseylungen (short stories) 1949

HAROLD STRAUSS   (essay date 1933)

[*In the following excerpt, Strauss reviews* The Sinner.]

The Sinner is a translation of the novel from which was taken Maurice Schwartz's remarkable play, **Yoshe Kalb**, now at the Yiddish Art Theatre. The adaptation must have been difficult, for the novel is decidedly epic in tone; it progresses in a great rush of episodes which are colorful but not dramatic, impressive but not built upon a single great tension. It illuminates the folkways of a people, but it never stops to probe the niceties of a situation or the character of an individual. Like most historic epics, **The Sinner** has the feeling of being an anonymously created folk-tale handed on by word of mouth from person to person and embellished in each telling—until by exaggeration and rationalization it came to be the fantastic and unreal mobilization of superstitions and horrors that it is. But it has preserved at its core a passion which is awesome and a transcendental truth. . . .

It is impossible in a brief space to indicate how burdened is this book with the long and tragic history of the Jews. Written often with shrewd humor, always with intense and cynical realism, it is at once a hysterical bit of self-mockery and a narrative forged to heroic proportions. If it often leaves us dissatisfied with its human motivation, it compensates us with the grandeur of its epic mood.

> *Harold Strauss, " 'The Sinner' and Some Other Recent Works of Fiction," in* The New York Times Book Review, *March 12, 1933, p. 7.*

LOUIS KRONENBERGER   (essay date 1936)

[*A drama critic for* Time *from 1938 to 1961, Kronenberger was also a distinguished historian and literary critic. In an assessment of his critical ability, Jacob Korg states: "He interprets, compares, and analyzes vigorously in a pleasingly epigrammatic style, often going to the essence of a matter in a phrase." In the following excerpt from a review of* The Brothers Ashkenazi, *Kronenberger praises Singer for having captured "the 'romance' of capitalism" in his depiction of a period of sustained economic growth.*]

In *The Brothers Ashkenazi* a very powerful story has been seized upon by a very powerful story-teller; the result, at any rate in a contemporary sense, is literature. Writing in the traditional manner of nineteenth-century fiction, where the narrative marches forward without interruption, where character is portrayed through action, where human drama is expressed against a rich and substantial background, Mr. Singer has yet written out of twentieth-century knowledge and purpose. He has summed up in his novel a whole historic process, a whole phase of industrial civilization; no textbook, no economic formula, could better convey the substance of it than Singer has conveyed in the dramatic and visionary fashion of the novelist. This is the story of two brothers forging careers for themselves in the expansive pre-war industrial world; it is no less the story of their native city Lodz rising from anonymity to power on the same industrial tide; it is consequently the story of a whole capitalist phase—the phase that saw steam supersede and superseded, that began with the passing of the hand loom and ended with the arrival of enormous mass production.

At the same time—indeed, more vividly on the surface—this is the story of several generations of Polish Jews, some rising like their city from anonymity to power, others submerged by tens of thousands as workers battling for bread. The two themes tie in together aptly, since on the one hand they merge the spectacle of intensive class-warfare with intensive race-warfare, and on the other they merge a type of Jew and a type of capitalist that are sometimes thought to coincide. (p. 3)

In spite of squalor and exploitation, of labor unrest and rebelliousness, of knavish and unprincipled business dealings, I think that this book gives you, if the phrase has any meaning at all, the "romance" of capitalism. For here is a history of the most sustained boom period of modern times, when world expansion was compatible with every man's fortune-building, when modern methods of production and distribution revolutionized modern life and had not yet quite engulfed it. It was the era of the individual, the international Alger hero, the Max Ashkenazi; the era of trial and error for modern capitalist technique. Judged by the standards of today, the men on top, however shrewd, were only partly realists. There was a touch of the adventurer about their methods; a Yakob Ashkenazi was wholly an adventurer, and the times were still propitious for him. That era, doomed before the war, ended with it, and with the bankruptcy of Europe and the concentration of power among the international banking groups. Max Ashkenazi lived to see the end.

Max and Yakob, the twin brothers, sum up symbolically almost all that Mr. Singer has to say. They represent two classic sides of the Jew: the ambitious, brilliant, uncrushable man of business, and the eager, warm-hearted voluptuary. They represent equally well two classic sides of capitalist life: the iron man of achievement, and the self-indulgent, extravagant bon vivant. Neither is an average Jew or an average exponent of the middle classes; each is portrayed somewhat, though not too much, on the grand scale. As it happens, they are not

drawn with equal sharpness and vigor: Yakob is more than adequate as a type, but less than alive as a human being, whereas in Max Mr. Singer has created a hero after the pattern, and up to the standard, of Balzac—one of those memorable Balzacian specimens wholly dominated by a master-trait—in Max's case, ambition. Indeed, so far as vividness alone is concerned, the figure of Max Ashkenazi dwarfs everything else in the book.

But so far as meaning is concerned, Mr. Singer has divided his picture between two contrasted and conflicting ways of life; and against his power-breathing capitalists he has pitted his ignorant and groping thousands of workers who, for all the abortiveness and disaster of most of their struggles, slowly push forward, slowly begin to assert their identity and significance in the world of industry.

But above all this book is knit together and overshadowed by its intense Jewishness. The struggles of its chief characters, whether for bread or millions, are somehow the special struggles of a persecuted, discredited race: Max Ashkenazi never can achieve social importance and at the height of his power must sometimes come crawling on his hands and knees; Jewish workers must not only struggle for an equality of classes, but for equal recognition within their own class.

This is an important novel by virtue of its subject-matter and workmanship alike. Mr. Singer has a stirring gift of narrative; he always writes with verve, sometimes with intensity; his book has magnitude and color and, as it were, a consciousness of its weighty theme. It makes one think time and again of Sholem Asch's *Three Cities,* with which it cannot help being compared. The two books have much in common: their completely Jewish world, their division of that world into two parts, the rich and the poor; their pictures of life in Eastern Europe before and during the war and under the stress of revolution. Asch, it seems to me, has imbued his book with deeper feeling, with a greater sense of humanity, with stronger ethical fervor. But Singer has attacked his theme with a directness and power that Asch nowhere equals, and where Asch has lost his way in a maze of individualism, Singer has everywhere retained his social vision. Singer is a truer realist, more toughminded, more objective. It matters less which is strictly the better book, however, than that the two books taken together picture a way of life and a phase of history beyond the need of any third. (p. 12)

Louis Kronenberger, "Two Lives That Dramatize an Epoch of Power," in The New York Times Book Review, *September 13, 1936, pp. 3, 12.*

PHILIP RAHV (essay date 1939)

[*A Russian-born American critic, Rahv was a prominent and influential member of the Marxist movement in American literary criticism. For thirty-five years he served as coeditor of* Partisan Review, *the prestigious literary journal T. S. Eliot once called "America's leading literary magazine." During the 1940s and 1950s* Partisan Review *was a significant force in American culture, providing a forum for intellectual debate, actively cultivating an audience for literary Modernism, and, largely through the efforts of Rahv, promoting the talents of such young writers as Saul Bellow, Delmore Schwartz, Bernard Malamud, and Elizabeth Hardwick. Rahv's criticism usually focuses on the intellectual, social, and cultural milieu influencing a work of art. His approach was intellectually eclectic and non-ideological: according to Richard Chase, "what one admires most about Rahv's critical method is his abundant ability to use such techniques as Marxism, Freudian psychology, an-thropology, and existentialism toward his critical ends without shackling himself to any of them." Noted for his "moral intelligence," Rahv attributed much of his critical perspective to his Marxist training. He asserted that he had acquired from Marxism "a certain approach, a measure of social and intellectual commitment and, I make bold to say, a certain kind of realism, not untouched with hope and expectancy, in my own outlook on society and the human potential as articulated in the constructs of the imagination." In the following excerpt, Rahv discusses political and artistic aspects of* East of Eden.]

The Yiddish novelist, I. J. Singer, takes us into Poland and Russia. His gloomy novel, *East of Eden,* grows out of the disappointment with the results of the Russian revolution, and it may be regarded as the first literary chronicle to concern itself seriously with a subject that is bound to expand into a special genre. There is plenty of game here for ravenous realists. The actualities of the Russian situation are so fearful that even the inebriated fellow-travelers of Stalinism are fated to sober up before long. And on the morning after we can expect from them a virulent pessimism, such as Mr. Singer reveals, or else a backsliding into the cheapest bourgeois illusions.

The first part of the book tells the story of Jewish woe in the ghetto, a story told so often that it has become a standard theme, a norm, in fact, of Yiddish writing. But this version differs from others in that Mr. Singer is too tough-minded ever to yield to the poetry associated with the ghetto, the idyll of self-sufficiency evoked by those literary Romantics who see in the religious past the golden age of European Jewry. In this first part both the characterization and the painting of the environment are excellent. Mattes, the destitute, pious peddler whose one hope is to raise his son, Nachman, to a higher social station, is defeated at every turn; and when his oldest daughter is seduced by a soldier, he flees his disgrace by moving his family to Warsaw. The war comes and Mattes is drafted into the Russian army, to be killed in the first skirmish with the Austrian troops. At this point the plot, freed from the inert world of the ghetto, begins to wind itself around Nachman's experience in the revolutionary movement. Converted by the Communist leader Daniel, Nachman, now a worker, turns into a rank and file militant wholly devoted to the struggle and to his party. The stress here is on the contrast between leader and disciple. Daniel is from the very first exposed as a strutting careerist in love with his own barricade gestures and steaming rhetoric; Nachman, the faithful child of the masses, is his inevitable dupe. Physically broken by serving a long sentence in a Polish prison, he can no longer restrain his longing to enjoy the benefits of socialism in the land of Eden lying to the east of capitalist Poland. He makes his way into Russia and finds work in a large mechanized bakery in Moscow.—And now the scabrous facts begin looming through the doctrinal mists. Gradually, painfully, despite his almost suicidal will to believe, Nachman realizes that for people of his class nothing has really changed. Together with other half-starved, unwashed workers he lives in a crowded barrack the walls of which are adorned with lying slogans. In the factory he sees that "just as the workers hate the higher-ups, so the higher-ups hate the workers," and that this mutual hatred reproduces the class war which ostensibly has been abolished forever. Things go badly with him. Arrested for speaking up in defense of an unruly comrade, he is forced to sign the usual confession of wrecking and espionage. Any one who is puzzled as to why the old Bolsheviks "confessed" at the so-called treason trials should read this book for its close analysis of the psychology of capitulation. In Poland,

where the police had nearly beaten him to death, Nachman had resisted the demand that he sign a confession naming himself as a spy, but once he is put away in the cell of a "socialist" prison ("our" prison) he is no longer the same man. For how can the revolutionary character survive the death of the revolution?

As a work of fiction *East of Eden* is far from being as successful as its predecessor, *The Brothers Ashkenazi.* Nachman and Daniel, both, are statistical types rather than characters. The second half of the story is no more than fictional reporting. Throughout, however, Mr. Singer retains his ability to represent elemental people and elemental emotions; and despite its limited perspective the book is valuable for its sober and thoughtful realism. In this connection a point might be made about the treatment this novel received at the hands of certain liberal reviewers. The prevailing hypocrisy of literary opinion is such that these reviewers—the very same individuals who for years now have been boosting political novels whose sole virtue is their Stalinist content—set out to condemn Mr. Singer for abandoning, in order to engage in politics, the "proper sphere" of the novelist. And, of course, these belated guardians of the shrine did not fail to assure their readers that it is not Mr. Singer's exposure of exploitation in Russia that annoyed them, but solely his rude tampering with the art of the novel. (pp. 108-09)

Philip Rahv, in a review of "East of Eden," in Partisan Review, *Vol. VI, No. 3, Spring, 1939, pp. 108-09.*

IRVING HOWE (essay date 1966)

[*A longtime editor of the leftist magazine* Dissent *and a regular contributor to the* New Republic, *Howe is one of America's most highly respected literary critics and social historians. He has been a socialist since the 1930s, and his criticism is frequently informed by a liberal viewpoint. Howe is widely praised for what F. R. Dulles has termed his "knowledgeable understanding, critical acumen, and forthright candor." Howe has written: "My work has fallen into two fields: social history and literary criticism. I have tried to strike a balance between the social and the literary; to fructify one with the other; yet not to confuse one with the other. Though I believe in the social approach to literature, it seems to me peculiarly open to misuse: it requires particular delicacy and care." In the following excerpt, Howe offers a comparison between Israel Joshua and Isaac Bashevis Singer, focusing upon Israel Joshua Singer's place in Jewish literature and concluding with a discussion of the novel* Yoshe Kalb.]

There are two Singers in Yiddish literature and while both are very good, they sing in different keys. The elder brother, Israel Joshua Singer, who died in 1944 and whose books are now gradually being reissued in English translation, was one of the few genuine novelists to write in Yiddish: a genuine novelist as distinct from a writer of short or medium-sized prose fiction. The younger brother, known as Isaac Bashevis Singer in English and more conveniently as Isaac Bashevis in Yiddish, is most accomplished as a writer of short stories blending grotesque and folk motifs ("Gimpel the Fool," etc.), though he has also tried his hand at the full-scale novel.

Each of the Singers has won an American following, at different cultural moments and for strikingly different reasons. When the elder Singer was first published in English translation during the 30's, his books—most notably, *The Brothers Ashkenazi*—gained an enormous popular success, appealing as they did to readers who enjoy the kind of thick and leisurely social novel that dominated European literature at the turn of the century. Intent upon portraying the historical changes and social relationships of East-European Jewish life as these became visible in cities like Warsaw rather than in the traditional *shtetl*—since the *shtetl,* after all, was too confining a locale for the novel—I. J. Singer built his work upon spacious architectural principles, composing in the manner we associate with the early Mann, Jules Romains, and Roger Martin du Gard. He mastered, as few Yiddish writers have, the problems of construction special to the "family novel," such as the management of multiple layers of plot and the bringing together of a large span of novelistic time with at least occasional moments of intensity. He learned to see modern society as a complex organism with a life of its own, a destiny superseding, and sometimes cancelling out, the will of its individual members. Thirty years ago these qualities were attractive to readers of fiction, including those who thought of it as a serious art; today I. J. Singer's work may appear a bit old-fashioned to young people brought up on Faulkner, Camus, and Genet.

Such young people form the very public that has been most enthusiastic about Isaac Bashevis Singer, a public composed of third-generation and semi-assimilated Jews, as well as some gentile fellow-travelers, whose nostalgia or curiosity about Jewishness is decidedly limited but who find in the author of *Satan in Goray* and *The Magician of Lublin* a congenial voice. (p. 78)

We have here, in any case, another example of the notorious instability of literary taste. It would be convenient to foreclose the problem by saying that the elder Singer's popularity is confined to middlebrows and the younger Singer's to highbrows; but that piece of glibness would be an instance of the critical provincialism that takes the form of being splendidly up-to-date. For the truth is that both Singers are gifted and serious writers, and the varying responses to their work have less to do with their intrinsic qualities as writers than with their imaginative relationships to the Jewish tradition. I. J. Singer writes within the orbit of, even though he has begun a withdrawal from, the moral premises—rationalistic and humanistic—of 19th-century Yiddish literature. I. B. Singer has taken the step his older brother could not take; though a master of the Yiddish language, he seems to have cut himself off from the mainstream of Yiddish literature, moving backward to a pre-Enlightenment sensibility and forward to modernism. For the generation of Yiddish readers and writers contemporary with I. J. Singer, to be "modern" meant to abandon the introspective themes and rhythms of *shtetl* writers like Mendele and Reisen, and to bring into Yiddish literature the worldly concerns and narrative sweep of the European novel: what a now-aging generation of Yiddish readers will still praise in Asch, Opatoshu, Schneour, and I. J. Singer as *dos Universal.* Whereas for the American readers of I. B. Singer, a writer regarded with some uneasiness and reserve by the Yiddish public, it is precisely his strangeness, his distance from ethical programs and social concerns, that makes him so attractive. As they say in Yiddish: *geh zei a chochem!* ["Go be clever!"].

Whether directly or not, I. J. Singer absorbed the lesson of Flaubert that the novelist must keep himself strictly out of the events he describes, as if he were an invisible hand in literature somewhat like Adam Smith's in economics. But this assumption was no more congenial to the earlier Yiddish writers, the generation of Mendele, Peretz, and Sholom Aleichem, than *laissez-faire* was to the village economy in which they grew up, for in a sense not true of writers in more sophisticated cultures, the Yiddish writers were—they had to be—*in* their fiction as stage managers, *raisonneurs,* ethical monitors, stand-ins for characters, and prompters for readers. The idea of "aesthetic distance" was, for most of these late-19th-century Yiddish writers, a luxury neither possible nor desirable; it is an idea that simply makes no sense to a culture which finds itself constantly in peril of destruction.

That, nevertheless, one strongly senses in I. J. Singer's work the kind of detachment—a tactical employment of a subject rather than a cultural submission to it—which is entirely familiar in Western literature, is a sign, among other things, of the gradual secularization of the East-European Jewish world. The Yiddish writers of I. J. Singer's generation tried consciously to find literary models outside their own tradition: they were sick of *shtetl* woes and *shtetl* charms; they wanted a richer and more worldly literature than their immediate predecessors could encourage. One also suspects that the coolness which is I. J. Singer's characteristic note had a more personal source, as the consequence of a temperament somewhat rare in the Yiddish milieu. He was a deeply skeptical writer, not merely in regard to the political and national ideologies raging through the Jewish communities of Poland and Russia during the early years of this century, but also in regard to the whole human enterprise: the possibility of happiness, the relevance of salvation. Though sharing very little in his younger brother's taste for the bizarre and the perverse, he is finally a "tougher" writer, more austere and disenchanted. His sensibility was of a kind one would expect to find in Paris more readily than in Warsaw.

Yoshe Kalb . . . is a short novel which hardly can display its author's gift for controlling a complex plot, but which does reveal his characteristic tone of enigmatic, tight-lipped distance. In its own cultural ambience *Yoshe Kalb* is a minor masterpiece, and it should be rewarding to those American readers prepared to make an imaginative leap into a milieu where characters are frozen into a stance of fatality and there is no compensating psychological scrutiny or authorial comment—indeed, no intellectual relief of any kind. The novel presents a picture of corruption in the late-19th-century Jewish world, when Hasidism had degenerated from a spontaneous religious experience into a squalid turmoil of cliques, each with its petty court and charismatic *zaddik.* In this phase of Hasidism, as S. M. Dubnow has written, "The profitable vocation of *zaddik* was made hereditary. There was a multiplication of *zaddik* dynasties contesting for supremacy. The 'cult of the righteous,' as defined by the Ba'al Shem Tov, degenerated into a system of exploitation of the credulous."

This background I. J. Singer takes entirely for granted, as a cultural "given" certain to be known to his readers, quite in the way F. Scott Fitzgerald takes for granted the American tone of life in the 20's. The disorders of personal experience comprising the foreground of *Yoshe Kalb* acquire meaning only through their inseparability from the disorders of Jewish communal experience, which are present as the largely invisible foundation of the book.

Its central figure is a timid boy, Nahum, the son of a rationalistic and cultivated rabbi. Nahum is suddenly thrust into the court of the *zaddik,* Rabbi Melech of Nyesheve, a character embodying in himself the coarse vitality of *prost* Jewish life as it found expression through Hasidism. Singer evokes the atmosphere of this petty court—its gabbling clients, its undercurrents of sensuality, its filial intrigue and commercial nastiness—with a marvelous command of detail, marvelous not least of all because he writes without those self–conscious glances at an alien audience which would tempt later Yiddish writers. Coming at a point in the development of Yiddish literature when it was possible for him to establish a critical disengagement from its norms while being entirely at home with its materials, I. J. Singer seems in his fiction to reach precisely the point of equilibrium between cultural self-sufficiency and cultural disintegration. It was an equilibrium all the historical forces of our century were conspiring to destroy.

The action of *Yoshe Kalb* proceeds through the marriage of the frightened young Nahum to Rabbi Melech's daughter, a smoldering clump of flesh that yearns wordlessly for womanly sacrifice and sexuality. His daughter out of the way, Rabbi Melech feels free to marry for a third time, choosing as the joy of his old age a shapely and passionate girl named Malkah. Thus two disordered marriages prepare for a climax of disorder generalized. Nahum and Malkah, both strangers to the Hasidic court and both unable to adjust themselves to its energetic vulgarity, turn to one another and end in sin. Neither for the characters nor Singer himself is the reality of sin ever in question, but it is a reality not so much of judgment as of conduct, not so much of a moral choice as of a hastening, almost impersonal sequence of deviation and punishment. The norm of sinfulness may be buried somewhere in the life of the community and in the hearts of the characters, but it is the fact of deviation and punishment that dominates their behavior. As for Singer, who stands apart from both the idea of sin and its immediate consequence, what matters most to him is the experience of inexorability, the grip of event upon event, the way a step once taken shadows the whole of life.

Nahum now sets out as an exile, wandering dumbly—he is called Yoshe the Loon, Yoshe Kalb—through a maze of Jewish villages. He re-enacts, in the second half of the novel, a tragic parody of his original violation. Like a Dantean figure shuffling through the wastes of purgatory, he is a dead soul without will or words, locked forever in his deed. The novel ends with a spectacular struggle between religious sects, disputing for possession of Nahum-Yoshe. A sainted rabbi comes closest to ultimate understanding: "You know not what you do," he cries out to Nahum-Yoshe, "there is no taste in your life or in your deeds, because you are nothing yourself, because—hear me!—you are a dead wanderer in the chaos of the world!"

The vividness and pressure of this book seem to me beyond dispute, but its meaning beyond certainty. One can wonder at the parabola of Nahum-Yoshe's life but it is hard to grasp the significance, the commanding sense of it that I. J. Singer intended. We could, of course, fall back upon the current notion that literature need not be interpreted, but this notion strikes me as neither appealing nor defensible. Refined and complicated as we may wish to render it, the desire for "meaning" in regard to a work of fiction is inescapable, and we had better adjust our critical theories to the fact.

I would surmise that the power of *Yoshe Kalb* derives from a relationship on I. J. Singer's part to the religious culture of East-European Judaism that is somewhat similar to the relationship Hawthorne is shown to have in *The Scarlet Letter* to the religious culture of New England Puritanism—though the skepticism of Singer is less dialectically clever and more

emotionally ominous than Hawthorne's. A fiercely held balance is sustained by Singer between the traditional materials he employs and the attitude of withdrawn objectivity he takes toward them. The world and his vision of the world are allowed equal rights, neither absorbing the other. And the same might be said in regard to the moral norms of the *shtetl* world and Singer's use of those norms in the novel: it hardly matters whether Nahum's act is regarded as sin or social disruption; the consequences are largely the same (though the possibility of regarding this act as social disruption depends, as Singer clearly sees, upon its being, or having been, regarded as a sin by the community).

What finally struck me in reading *Yoshe Kalb* was how tightly locked within the premises of his culture the work of a novelist must be. In *Yoshe Kalb,* every act carries social and moral weight, and no one in the audience to which the book was addressed could possibly have doubted what that weight might be. A half-century later we must grope and approximate, fearful that the more ingenious our readings, the more likely that we are smuggling in our own preconceptions. Yet is this not true for all fiction, the very greatest and the most commonplace alike? Try teaching Stendhal to college students in New York, or persuading California students that the moral inquiries of Ivan Karamazov are relevant to their lives, and you will see what I mean. (pp. 78, 80-2)

Irving Howe, "The Other Singer," in Commentary *Vol. 49, No. 3, March, 1966, pp. 78, 80-2.*

CHARLES A. MADISON   (essay date 1968)

[*Madison, a Russian-born American editor and critic, has written extensively on Yiddish literature and on American labor issues. In the following excerpt, he surveys Singer's career.*]

In the early decades of the 20th century, Yiddish literature flourished not only in the Soviet Union and the United States but also in all of Eastern Europe, particularly in Poland. Of the scores of writers who have made their mark in this area, Israel Joshua Singer is best known to American readers. (p. 449)

[Singer's] first stories had their setting in the Hasidic milieu of his childhood, and several were published in *Dos Yiddish Wort* (*The Jewish Word*). In 1917, idealistically attracted by the promise of the Russian revolution, he went to live in Kiev. There his stories appeared in journals and anthologies. He also wrote two plays—*Earth Woes* and *Three*—impressionistic dramas which he soon preferred to forget, and **"Pearls"** (1919). His more than three years in Bolshevik Russia sufficed to disillusion him with the promises of communism. In 1921 he returned to Warsaw.

Pearls and Other Stories appeared in 1922 and was praised by critics. The featured story gives an impressionistic sketch of Moritz Shpielrein, an elderly man "without lungs" and bedridden much of the time. A jeweler, pawnbroker, and landlord, he is quite wealthy but stingy and lives alone with the aid of a boy servant. The story concentrates on his daily routine, the house he owns and the various people living in it, and is highlighted by a jewel auction at which Shpielrein buys a costly pearl necklace. At once vividly told and charged with lifelike reality, the story is persuasive in its portrayal of people. The other stories, while less significant, are noted for the mood each creates in its specific setting. In the same year he completed *Earth Pain,* a minor symbolic drama of the revolutionary period evidencing his disillusionment with Bolshevism.

Abraham Cahan, visiting Eastern Europe in 1922, came upon the volume and was highly impressed with the literary quality of **"Pearls."** He obtained it for reprinting in *Der Forverts* and engaged Singer as a regular contributor as well as correspondent. Now an established author with a relatively sizable and secure income, he took an active part in Warsaw's Jewish cultural affairs, and became an editor of *Literature and Life* as well as a member of the radical and modernistic group of writers known as *Die Khaliastre* (*The Gang*).

On Strange Soil (1925) was Singer's second collection of stories. The title narrative is set in the civil war. A troop of soldiers enter a Jewish town, and its inhabitants fear a pogrom. They hide as best they can and pass the long hours of the night in prayer and dread. The next morning they learn that Red soldiers had been trapped by Whites and a number killed. Several Jews approach the fresh mass grave and say Kaddish on the assumption that among the buried may have been Jews.

Soldiers camp near another Jewish town in **"During Warm Days."** The military doctor, a Jew, comes to the market square in full uniform, buys what he needs on credit, flirts with the girls, treats the ill without charge, and makes himself highly regarded—only to leave in the fall without paying his bills. **"Blood,"** based on an incident in Singer's childhood, tells of a boy born to a Jewish innkeeper who grows up dull-witted and physically strong "like a gentile." He behaves like a peasant boy, and no amount of beating and chastisement have any effect. In late adolescence he is lured into marriage and apostasy by a competing woman innkeeper considerably older than he. Later she tries to instigate him to kill his parents in order to inherit their inn. Confused and dully irritated by her nagging, he kills her instead. These and other stories are told with realistic clarity and in impressionistic prose, but with the obvious minor flaws of as yet unperfected literary skill.

In the middle 1920's Singer was asked by Cahan to visit the Soviet Union and report on his impressions of Jewish life under Bolshevism. Inimically minded but a keen observer, he indicated in his articles that in the seven years since he had been in Moscow conditions had become less strict, largely influenced by NEP ["New Economic Policy"] circumstances, with a good deal of extravagance by a few and with many beggars in the streets. What troubled him particularly were evidences of anti-Semitism and its effect on many Jews. Thus on visiting a secluded midnight celebration of "Lubavishe" Hasidim he was surprised to find among them engineers, students, and other enlightened men who had become pious *after* the revolution.

Singer inspected Jewish farm colonies, where he found the older generation acquiescing in the new regime and the youths definitely enthusiastic. He was impressed by the skill of some of the farmers and talked with others who hated collectives or planned to migrate to Israel. Everywhere he came upon homeless drifters, orphaned youths who existed by begging and stealing. He also wrote with considerable concern about the loose marital practices, and in particular about the numerous mixed marriages. Finally, although Yiddish was generally flourishing, he noted that government officials looked with suspicion on Yiddishism. These observations,

which only confirmed his anti-communism, he published in a volume entitled *The New Russia* (1927).

In the same year appeared *Steel and Iron* a novel on the war, revolution, and civil strife, based largely on his own experiences as a worker in Warsaw. (pp. 452-54)

Not yet master of the art of the novel, Singer has made the action [of *Steel and Iron*] replete with melodramatic material. Its kaleidoscopic character clutters it with incidents and gives the impression of a mosaic of stories and types. Consequently, it lacks clarity and conviction. Nor are the main characters developed into fully lifelike human beings. Indeed, Singer gives evidence of having scattered his obvious literary talent in various directions instead of focusing it into a crystallized unity. The novel, nevertheless, provides a realistic flow of robust prose and provocative action. (p. 456)

Yoshe Kalb [Singer's next novel, published in 1932] is a work of fictional fascination. It plumbs the human depths of Hasidic life: its rich, colorful piety along with its supernatural and superstitious practices, not to mention its commercial hypocrisy. Yet Singer does not treat it with the sympathy and insight of Der Nister or with the romantic tolerance of Peretz and Sholem Asch. Instead he tends to be critical and caustic—not with the artistic objectivity of Opatoshu but with a kind of personal animosity. Stressing the gross and gullible aspects of the Hasidic court as well as its materialistic activities, he fails to intimate the genuine spiritual fervor germane to Hasidism. (pp. 459-60)

Singer tends to romanticize the irrepressible passion that draws Malkeh and [the protagonist] Nahum together, yet he writes more sympathetically of the sex impulses of the moronic girl than of Nahum's emotional struggles. And while Nahum's years of abject expiation are understandable in a man of deep piety living in a time of prevailing orthodoxy, his refusal to explain himself at a cost of committing another grievous sin—an act of bigamy and desertion—and his further refusal to offer the slightest explanation to the 70 rabbis become more the behavior of a deluded mystic than of a pious sinner. This conception of a protagonist cannot but weaken an otherwise powerful love story and a fascinating account of Hasidic life of a century ago. (p. 460)

The Brothers Ashkenazi (1936) the first novel [Singer] wrote in the United States, became his major literary achievement. First serialized in *Der Forverts*, it was quickly translated into English and several other languages and was everywhere hailed as an epic masterpiece. It brought him fresh popularity and large royalties, but did not lessen his inner gloom.

The long novel depicts the rise of Lodz from an insignificant village at the end of the 18th century to its leading position in Poland as a center of textile production, from its gradual domination by Jewish entrepreneurs to its ravagement by war, revolution, and Polish anti-Semitism. The development of the city parallels the upsurge of the Ashkenazi family, soon dominated by the twin brothers, Simkha Meyer and Yakov Bunim, later known as Max and Jacob. (p. 461)

In the breadth of its scope and its richness of human life and economic and political events, [*The Brothers Ashkenazi*] is indubitably a work of major importance. Extending over three generations, delineating the rise of industrialism in Eastern Europe, describing graphically the effects of war, revolution, and pogroms on the people involved, depicting the development of labor unrest and bloody strikes, and most of all, concentrating on the portrayal of numerous significant characters, Singer has in this novel achieved a literary height that brought him within reach of the world's great novelists. While not without minor flaws of organization and outlook—he still stressed human idiosyncrasies and instinctive brutality, although they are no longer naked and unrelieved, and his prejudices remain self-evident—and while some of the actions of his major characters are open to question and the emphasis on their chief traits limits their portraiture to profiles, the narrative as a whole is written with great clarity and animation. (p. 465)

Morbidly disappointed in the Soviet Union ever since he left it in 1921, [Singer] wrote about it caustically and cynically. Heretofore he had dwelt on it only briefly and incidentally, as in **Brothers Ashkenazi;** but in **Comrade Nahman** (**East of Eden** in English 1938) he made it his major subject. (p. 467)

The novel contains some poignant and perturbing descriptions of poverty and slum life in Poland and Russia. Some of the characters are sharply delineated and lifelike, and the manifestations of radicalism among oppressed workers, as well as the attitudes and activities of certain of their leaders, are depicted with the cogency of intimate knowledge. The book as a whole, however, suffers from subjective exaggeration. Although charlatans like Daniel are no rarity in real life, his unrelieved villainy and the absence of honest counterparts detract from his fictional credibility. Even harder to believe is [the protagonist] Nahman's excessive naiveté. Simple as he is, he is no simpleton, and his behavior in the Soviet Union is gullible beyond plausibility. Moreover, assuming that the arraignment of communist life in Moscow has validity, it suffers from emphasis on evil aspects and complete omission of the spark of idealism which was surely a part of it. Certainly not all officials in the Soviet Union were as corrupt and degenerate as they are presented in the narrative. One has the impression that Singer was seeking to expel the traumatic bitterness out of his system, and produced a novel streaked with bias and hyperbole.

The upsurge of Hitlerism affected Singer as much as it did other Yiddish writers. In **The Carnovsky Family** (1943) he dramatized the plight of enlightened German Jews, who have been making every effort to emulate their Christian neighbors and live ethically and culturally on a high plane, only to be coerced and crushed by Nazi brutality; also the tragedy of those born of mixed marriages and considering themselves more German than Jewish—only to be equally derided and rejected. (pp. 469-70)

The Carnovsky Family has a broad canvas, a vital theme, many truthful, even towering passages, and a host of realized characters. Yet the action borders on the obvious and banal, and the protagonists lack the distinction of uniqueness. The Carnovsky males do not behave with the naturalness of inner logic but are manipulated by the author to accord with his thesis. All three—David, Georg, and Yegor—run away from themselves, each in his own way, but each as if subject to the pull of specific strings. And although the tragedy of each one is real and increasingly poignant, they are maneuvered to demonstrate that to discard traditional piety is to risk losing all Jewishness. Some of the lesser characters, however, do possess a life of their own. Elsa may be a strange girl by conventional standards, but she knows what she wants, suffers for her beliefs, and continues her social activity in her American home. Her father and Ephraim Walder, while typical of their kind, likewise live in accord with their convictions and

remain true to themselves to the end. Several others are equally well drawn and readily come to life.

Singer was at this time at the height of his popularity. The dramatizations of his novels were successful beyond anyone's expectation, and their editions in English and other languages elicited favorable reviews and attracted a good many readers. Yet he remained fundamentally at war with himself. As his close friend Aaron Zeitlin indicated: "The outward conditions of his life were good. To the world he appeared as a man satisfied with his achievement. Yet the illusion of the 'broad world' had long since vanished from the mind of the wise Singer, and only an inner bitterness replaced it." The idols of modern man—and of the modern Jew—no longer appealed to him, and he knew there was no return to the traditional life of his childhood. Yet he longed to recall the dogmas and beliefs of his rabbinical father, in which he now saw a wholesomeness unperceived by him in his rebellious youth. These "truthful happenings" he described lovingly and at length in a volume which, like all his writings, was first serialized in *Der Forverts,* and later published posthumously under the title of **Of a World That Is No More** (1946).

In this work Singer reminisced nostalgically about his father's and grandfather's pious ways and benign spirits, impregnating the pages with a glowing appreciation of the traditions and folklore he had derided in his early fiction. With rich sentiment and salutary humor he described his early youth at study, at play, and in his father's study. His parents were not a congenial couple: his father was a pious, gentle, erudite optimist, suffering poverty because he would not learn Russian as required of legally accepted rabbis; his mother, on the contrary, was intellectually keen, practical, worrisome, pessimistic, and a poor cook. As rabbi of an unimportant village, the only post open to him, his father had to deal with all kinds of legal and religious matters, and the people who came with their complaints and contentions made themselves at home in the kitchen while waiting to be heard. His father was also in the habit of inviting the lowliest beggars, unwanted by others in the synagogue, to his Sabbath table, so that his wife had to eat in the kitchen. To alleviate their dire poverty, she would spend summers with her more affluent father, thus enabling her husband to accumulate a little money for their winter needs.

In writing about his childhood Singer intimates the early symptoms of the creative mood. As a boy he was little interested in the exegesis of the Talmud—moot problems of *kashruth,* commerce, and other topics alien to a ten-year-old boy who longed for horses and the out of doors. He swallowed these teachings as one does "bitter medicine," hurriedly and unwillingly. But human behavior fascinated him. He was extremely curious and keenly observant of everything that took place in his father's study—the various people who came to demand justice or merely to complain about their wretched lives.

> An enormous curiosity about people and their activities burned within me from earliest childhood. What I saw in one person I could not find in a thousand books. I could not satisfy my life-thirst in books and ran from them to the soil and plants and cows and birds and people, especially ordinary people, who live a full life.

The stories Singer wrote in the early 1940's were collected in a volume and published in 1949. (pp. 473-75)

These [posthumously published stories] are told with literary skill, wry humor, and a firm grasp of human essentials. They add little, however, to Singer's stature as a writer.

As the war intensified in 1943, and the Hitlerian genocide in Eastern Europe accelerated, Singer's restlessness increased. More than ever before he was impressed by the littleness of man in a world of evil and brute force. He considered leaving the United States, of forsaking the diaspora and making his home in ancient Israel. Suddenly all his worries, dreams, and plans came to naught when he suffered a fatal heart attack at the age of 50. (pp. 477-78)

Charles A. Madison, "I. J. Singer: Novelist of Satirical Pessimism," in his Yiddish Literature: Its Scope and Major Writers, Frederick Ungar Publishing Co., 1968, pp. 449-78.

MAX F. SCHULZ   (essay date 1969)

[*Schulz is an American educator and critic. In the following excerpt, he discusses ways in which* The Brothers Ashkenazi *both adheres to and departs from traditions of the family epic.*]

[In **The Brothers Ashkenazi,** I. J. Singer] solves the problem of finding a form paradigmatic of history in a manner characteristic of his reaction to the Chassidic Warsaw milieu from which he fled.

If we are to believe Isaac Bashevis's account of his older brother in *In My Father's Court,* I. J. Singer uncompromisingly rejected what he regarded as the intellectual sterility and puritanical asceticism of the ghetto. His reaction seems at the outset to control his conception of **The Brothers Ashkenazi.** The tone of the novel is coolly ironic. He sardonically details the Jewish community's obsession with social standing; its eager collaboration in the transformation of rabbis from students of the sacred Law into sharpers at home with "bills, percentages, profits, contracts, promissory notes, and all the devices and tricks of the business world"; and its easy sanction of the employer class's economic exploitation of the worker in combination with a hypocritical concern for his morality. The contradictions between old-fashioned *shtetl* piety and enlightened commonsense particularly arouse I. J. Singer's jocularity; for example, he relates that Reb Abraham Hirsh Ashkenazi always visits his wonder Rabbi at Passover, armed with special *matzos* "made from flour which had been under guard from the growing of the grain until the baking of the cakes. . . . They were less digestible than ordinary matzos," Singer slyly adds, "but considerably holier." Such irony reduces the epical tone characteristic of the family chronicle and emphasizes instead, much as does Byron's poem *Don Juan,* that the literary world of the narrative is akin to the pedestrian, work-a-day world of reality. This de-emphasis of the traditional heroic treatment of the saga of three generations is underscored by a controlling animal metaphor, deriving from the biblical precept that "There is no difference between man and beast." The same reductive effect is at work in I. J. Singer's portrayal of the despicable personality of the protagonist Max Ashkenazi with the clinical detachment of an anthropologist reporting the characteristics of a new species.

The structure of the novel, however, represents Singer's greatest effort to remove his chronicle from the fabulous pattern of the genre. Not only does he diminish the patriarch to a minor role in the family in favor of the second generation, but he limits the progeny to two sons and concentrates his attention on one. This strategy turns the familial epic into a *Bildungsroman* of sorts. Furthermore, he parallels the growth of Max and Jacob Ashkenazi from Chassidic *cheder* pupils to industrial financiers, with the evolution of Lodz from a Jewish village of pious hand-loom operators to the Polish center of the weaving industry. In the merger of the destiny of the Ashkenazi family with the history of the supranational European business community, and its accompanying shift of lines of conflict from Jew versus Gentile to worker versus mercantilist, this dual tale of a family and of a city becomes a microcosm of the industrial revolution in Eastern Europe. Max Ashkenazi's effort to enhance the financial reputation of his name (that it is also the generic name of the Germanized, or Yiddish speaking Jews, as distinguished from the Sephardic, or Spanish-Portuguese speaking Jews, is significant) also becomes symbolic of the effort of East European Jewry to break out of its centuries' long isolation and enter the mainstream of Western history. In short, I. J. Singer harnesses his family chronicle to the events of the nineteenth and early twentieth centuries. Thus the narrative follows history rather than legend; it is closer to national than to mythic drama.

But by the end of the novel the pejorative tone toward both Max Ashkenazi and the Chassidic community has altered and the story has taken on epical dimensions. Through his superhuman labors in the textile industry, Max has made himself the industrial "king of Lodz." The small-statured, repulsive ex-Talmudic student, distrustful, perfidious, inhuman, is endowed in old age with heroic qualities, loyalty, pertinacity, integrity, wisdom, selflessness. Singer's irony still operates, but it has deepened and broadened in profundity. No longer Max and the Chassidim but man and the world are objects of its disillusionment. The pointlessness of Max's Herculean labors is laughed at—but only as part of the unaging vanity of all human endeavor. The final—and ultimately pervasive—irony of the novel invokes Ecclesiastes. Thus, Max Ashkenazi, trapped in St. Petersburg by the Bolshevik Revolution, laments:

> He was a superfluous being in this huge city. He was superfluous and naked. His houses had been seized, his money in the banks sealed up, his stocks and bonds completely devaluated. No, he said to himself, there are no eternal things. Even houses and factories are not eternal things. He had thought to prepare himself against the worst by putting his money into solid, tangible possessions. Now they were all gone.

When Max finally dies, his factory is in receivership, his son has fled to Paris, and Lodz is a dying city.

With this shift in tone, form and theme fuse forcefully and effectively, allowing us to see that **The Brothers Ashkenazi** is thematically and structurally patterned as an illustration of the truth of *Ecclesiastes.* Repeatedly the narrative configurations of the novel trace Max's struggle upward to an apex of achievement, only to reverse his fortunes when success seems to be in his grasp. The images of regal splendor and of female seductiveness that Baron von Heidel-Heidellau and Gertrude Ashkenazi see when they look in the mirror are other instances of the novel's organized representation of human folly. The cool irony of the enlightened skeptic, with which the novel opens, gives way by the conclusion to the profound wisdom of the Hebraic ironist. I. J. Singer has not strayed as far from his father's court as he might have thought.

The Brothers Ashkenazi does not follow the usual demography of the Yiddish familial epic from patriarchal unity to progenitive dispersal, yet it continues to order its material in mythic patterns that ultimately affect its form as profoundly as do its parallels to actual history. In addition to the correspondences with Ecclesiastes, there is as a dominant pattern the primordial struggle of brother against brother. Like Cain and Abel, or Jacob and Essau, Max and Jacob Ashkenazi feud for the favor of father, wife, community, and God. Corollaries of this archetype are the mythic dissonances of son versus father and daughter versus mother. I. J. Singer searches the entanglements of these relationships with great ordering skill and sense of biblical tonality. What one generation splits asunder, another joins together. Max displaces his father as agent for the Huntze factory and in the process alienates his brother. His daughter Gertrude, however, marries her uncle, requiting in the act her mother's love for Jacob. Through that marriage, Jacob the hated brother becomes the estranged son-in-law, who in ironic reverse of the biblical parable, eventually welcomes home Max the prodigal brother/father-in-law, who has wasted his heritage of life in endless getting and keeping. Like a leitmotif, growth and consolidation, conflict and disruption, characterize both the generations of the Ashkenazis and the life cycle of the Lodz textile industry. (pp. 77-81)

> Max F. Schulz, "The Family Chronicle as Paradigm of History: 'The Brothers Ashkenazi' and 'The Family Moskat'," in The Achievement of Isaac Bashevis Singer, *edited by Marcia Allentuck, Southern Illinois University Press, 1969, pp. 77-92.*

CLIVE SINCLAIR AND ISAAC BASHEVIS SINGER
(interview date 1979)

[*Sinclair, an English novelist, short story writer, and critic, is literary editor of the* Jewish Chronicle. *His* The Brothers Singer *(1983) is the first full-length study of Israel Joshua Singer's life and works and the first detailed comparison of Singer's works with those of his younger brother, Isaac Bashevis Singer. The younger Singer is widely held to be the foremost living writer of Yiddish literature. Awarded the Nobel Prize in literature in 1978, Singer was cited by the Swedish Academy for "his impassioned narrative art which, with roots in a Polish-Jewish cultural tradition, brings universal human conditions to life." In the following excerpt from an interview, Sinclair and Isaac Bashevis Singer discuss Israel Joshua's life and works, and Singer pays tribute to his brother's influence on his own literary career.*]

SINCLAIR: A book of your stories opens with this note, "I dedicate these pages to the blessed memory of my brother, I. J. Singer, author of **The Brothers Ashkenazi, Yoshe Kalb** etc., who helped me to come to this country and was my teacher and master in literature. I am still learning from him and his work." Would you begin by expanding on this?

SINGER: Yes, I will tell you. When I was born my brother was already a boy of eleven years, so when I grew up Joshua—we seldom called him Israel Joshua—was already, in a way, grown. He was the big boy in the family and I was a baby. And since he was tall and, in my eyes, good-looking—also in the eyes of other people—and clever, I looked up to him more than to anybody else. Even more than to my parents. Parents are parents. My father was a rabbi, but here was a man. Later

when my father moved to Warsaw where he was also a rabbi in some poor street, my brother began to speak against the Jewish race, against studying the Talmud all day long, and even though I was so much younger I understood what he said. There were many discussions in our house, there were discussions all the time. My father and even my mother, of course, contended that this is what Jews are born for: to study the Talmud, to keep all the commandments, and just to live the way our fathers and grandfathers lived, not even to change the clothes. If they wore long *kapots* we should wear the same; if they didn't wear a tie we shouldn't wear a tie, although it's not written anywhere in the Talmud or in the Torah not to wear one. My brother attacked of course. He said: How long should we wait for the Messiah when we've waited for him two thousand years and he didn't come? We may wait another two thousand years and he still will not come. And what proof is there really that the Almighty revealed Himself to Moses on Mount Sinai? The Christians have their books and the Mohammedans have their old books; and if we say that their books are not true how do we know that our own are? Logic spoke out of his mouth, you know; and I, a little boy, thought: he is right. Although I would never have dared to say this, but I felt so. Also he described how poor the Jews are in the *shtetl,* how they learned nothing except the Talmud. The whole world is progressing, and we are still in the Middle Ages. Every word which he said was to me a bomb, a real spiritual kind of explosion. And my parents were not really able to answer him. Because sooner or later my father began to scream, you Unbeliever, you wicked man. The fact that he screamed was a proof that he couldn't answer. And later on my brother got the courage to take off his long robe, his *kapot,* and to put on European clothes; and he looked so much nicer. Of course everything he did, and everything he said, was wonderful in my eyes; I was a real hero-worshipper. I think he is the only hero that I ever worshipped.

First he was a painter. In those years he was, of course, realistic. He did not make a man look as Miró, or Picasso, did when he drew a few lines and said, it's a goat or a man. He tried to be as loyal, as faithful to nature as he could be. But people have done it before him better, and he decided that this is not his way. A man knows best what he can do and what he cannot. He decided that his real power was in literature. He used to read his stories to my mother and I listened. After I had learned to read Yiddish well, he once put a story of his into a desk drawer. When he left I opened the drawer and I read it. And what he wrote looked beautiful to me. So there is no question that he influenced me mightily. I don't think anybody else has ever influenced me as much.

When I began to write myself my brother encouraged me and he gave me certain rules for writing. He said: when you write tell a story, and don't try to explain the story. If you say that a boy fell in love with a girl you don't have to explain to the reader why a boy falls in love, the reader knows just as much about love as you do or more so. You tell him the story, and the explanations and interpretations he will make himself, or critics will do it for him. He had two words which he used: *images* and *sayings.* Sayings were for him essays, interpretations. He called sayings, *zugerts.* It means you just talk, you just say things. You don't paint a picture, or bring out an image. He said, leave the *zugerts* to the others. You tell them a story. Because you may know stories which they don't know—but you don't know more about life than they do. Although these rules were very simple it took me years to understand what he meant by image, what he meant by *zugerts* or sayings.

SINCLAIR: Do you know where Israel Joshua himself got these ideas? Who influenced him?

SINGER: I think he must have taken them from Flaubert or the Russian classics. Gogol, Tolstoy, they too avoided *zugerts,* although not as much as Flaubert. When I began to weigh things by myself I said to myself: Is it true what he said? is there any truth in it? aren't there any exceptions? In the long run I convinced myself that images never get stale; and *zugerts,* sayings, no matter how clever and how brilliant, are almost obsolete from the very beginning, because no matter what a human being has to say about life, it has already been said before. Even in ancient times by people who knew nothing about telephones or electricity; but about life they knew already, Seneca and the others; and there you already have all the clever *zugerts.* Of course once in a while you have to say something to bind together the images, or you have to allow the images themselves to say something. But in the long run it is true. My brother influenced me mightily.

However, there is a limit to influence. He had his character, he had his genes, and I had my genes. And although I accepted him, loved him, admired him, my way was different. He was more or less a realist, a naturalist; but I was inclined to mysticism and psychic research and so on; and there our ways parted, but in a most peaceful way . . . because my brother was also interested in the supernatural, and I was interested in life the way he described it . . . because even miracles must be embedded in life. They don't come out from nowhere.

SINCLAIR: Perhaps one may sum up the difference between you this way; you deal with a world that may be nothing more than an illusion, whereas your brother dealt with a real world that was built upon illusions. At the end of his masterpiece *The Brothers Ashkenazi* the mourners say, "Everything we have built was built on sand. . . ." As was the village where you lived as boys: Leoncin. That was really built on sand.

SINGER: Illusion? Call it what you want. It is true. When I published *Satan in Goray* he was still alive of course; and he read it and was astonished that his brother could go so far away from him. At the same time it wasn't *so* far away from him because he also knew all these things. But it was good that we were not alike; it would have been a tragedy, at least for me, if I were to write just like my brother.

SINCLAIR: There is one incidence I can think of when you do both seem to be using the same material. In your latest book *A Young Man in Search of Love,* a man called Leon Treitler marries a girl half his age. Surely this is an echo of Yakob Ashkenazi's romance with Gertrude in *The Brothers Ashkenazi?*

SINGER: Maybe. I will tell you. Because writers write about their own environment they do repeat themselves in a way; they come back to the same types. Tolstoy, for example, had the same type, Levin in *Anna Karenina* and Pierre in *War and Peace.* But there's no tragedy in it; it is only the complete dilettante who can fly from one environment to another. He is today in Spain and tomorrow in Ireland; and the next day he's an Eskimo. The real writer has his address, has his home, and he always comes back; so there is always an element of repetition. And if two writers are brothers it's inevitable that

the writers should not write once but often about the same people.

SINCLAIR: The one novel in which your brother comes closest to your own work is *Yoshe Kalb.* He tells a story of religious fanaticism, mysticism and passion, which has at its heart the enigma of Nachumtche, who flees the town of Nyesheve, after being seduced by the ancient rabbi's young wife, only to return years later with a second identity, that of Yoshe Kalb. Am I correct in guessing that this is your favourite among his novels?

SINGER: Yes. *Yoshe Kalb* contains a lot of the mysticism. Except that my brother took mysticism not with one grain of salt but with many. Which I don't do, because to me the mystic is not someone to make fun of or to mock. I feel sometimes that if he would have lived longer he might have become a mystic himself; maybe yes, maybe no. Certainly if my brother would have lived another twenty or thirty years, which he should have, he would have developed more and more, and he would have published stunning books—I'm absolutely convinced of that.

SINCLAIR: I believe that the plot of *Yoshe Kalb* came from a story your father told?

SINGER: Yes, my father told this story not once but many times. Whenever there was talk about "disappearing" my father came up with it, and I remember I heard it myself maybe ten times; and I was every time as baffled as the first time because my father was a wonderful story-teller. He never realised this, but he could tell a story; so could my mother. And the story in itself is really baffling. That a man should come up and say, I'm Yoshe Kalb, when others say he was not. Until today we don't know if he was or he wasn't. A story which is as dramatic as this had to be told in a dramatic way.

SINCLAIR: As it turned out *Yoshe Kalb* went on to become one of the great hits of the Yiddish theatre, in a production by Maurice Schwartz.

SINGER: Well, Maurice Schwartz, of course. Although my brother wrote it, Maurice Schwartz did not play it the way my brother would have wanted. Maurice Schwartz was by nature a *kitsch* director or drama-maker. He wanted everything to be like a super-colossal Hollywood production. Although he never had any chance to work in Hollywood, he was a Hollywood man. So he made it more sensational than my brother wanted it to be. Listen, when you sell a play to a director or to a producer—you are no longer the boss. No matter how much they consult, they do what they want. It's like if you have children: once these children grow up you're no longer the father who tells them exactly what to do. They will do what they want to do.

SINCLAIR: In the introduction which you have written for *Yoshe Kalb* you call your brother a sceptic [see Additional Bibliography]. You also call yourself a sceptic. Wouldn't you say that while your brother had a sceptical view of this world your own attitude is more ambiguous?

SINGER: I'm a sceptic. I'm a sceptic about making a better world. When it comes to this business where you tell me that this-or-that régime, one sociological order or another, will bring happiness to people, I know that it will never work, call it by any name you want. People will remain people, and they have remained people under communism and all other kinds of isms. But I'm not a sceptic when it comes to belief in God.

New York Times Book Review *advertisement for* The Brothers Ashkenazi.

I do believe. I always did. That there is a plan, a consciousness behind creation, that it's not an accident. That what they call evolution is not a blind process. Even if there was evolution it was evolution with a plan. But my brother, he was a sceptic. He said: maybe there was no plan, maybe there is no God, maybe there is no higher consciousness. In this respect we are different. But when it came to human beings and to their social ideals, we were both sceptics of the same kind. He always used to say, it would all be very nice if there would be no human beings to practise these things. For years I kept on hearing that the selling of ammunition is only the capitalist's doing. Why should the working people produce ammunition that people use to kill one another? And now we see that Soviet Russia is selling ammunition all over the world, and giving savages guns and bombs to kill each other. They said that prostitution and drunkenness and the like would not exist in a socialistic order—which is not true, they do exist. So when it comes to the Happy World, to the world of Utopia, we are both equally sceptical. When it comes to higher things I'm less of a sceptic than my brother was.

SINCLAIR: You also say in the same introduction that as soon as your brother began work on **Yoshe Kalb** his health and his whole bodily appearance improved. This was after several disappointments and depressions. Do you think there is a connection between creativity and vitality, both physical and spiritual?

SINGER: There is no question about it. Listen. For a creative man—not only in the field of literature but in every field (I don't think that only writers are creative, all people are creative)—if you have a chance to create something this is surely healthy for you. It gives you vigour, it gives you hope. When a day passes by and I feel that I didn't do anything I feel at the end that this was a futile day. So, of course, the moment my brother began to write **Yoshe Kalb** and he read to me these chapters and I saw that they were fiery chapters, fiery with action and folklore and tension, he was a different man. In addition I knew (and he perhaps also knew) that Abe Cahan would publish it and he would get money for it. We all need to make some money to live. Even the greatest, even Dostoevsky and Flaubert, they all wanted to get some reward. (pp. 21-4)

SINCLAIR: I believe that just before he wrote **Yoshe Kalb** Israel Joshua Singer renounced Yiddish and declared that he was no longer going to be a Yiddish writer.

SINGER: It was as if a man would decide: I'm not going to be myself any more but am going to be another human being. He cannot make such a decision. A man cannot decide that he is going to be not himself . . . although here there are a few thousand men who decided to become women. Anyhow it is easier for them to become women, or for a woman to become a man, than for my brother to become a German or a French writer. Yiddish was the language which he knew best; and Jewish life was the kind of life which he knew best. For him to say, I'm not going to be a Yiddish writer any more was sheer nonsense, and he knew it. I told it to him, and all his friends told it to him. So when he was able to forget about this kind of childish promise and to come to work again he was happy; and when this book was a mighty success in the *Forverts* and he got money for it, he was even more happy. So he went back to Yiddish literature, and this was the only way he could have functioned; what else could he have done? What he said about stopping to be a Yiddish writer was nothing but a kind of a protest. It's as sometimes people say, I'm

ashamed to be a human being. But ashamed or not you still remain a human being.

SINCLAIR: In fact of course all your brother's novels were written in Yiddish. And all your books, despite their popularity in English, first appear in Yiddish. But Yiddish is now in an extraordinary position as a language, in that it is a language without a country.

SINGER: Without a country. But even this maybe is not completely true because the Jews in Poland lived for some six hundred years. And how old do you think the Polish language is? Not much older. And how old is English? Not much older. In other words, they did have a territory. Of course when they emigrated from Poland to America they were no longer in their home. Yet the same happened to other languages. The Poles in America don't have their old territory but still they publish books in Polish and they have Polish organisations. In nature there isn't such a thing as an exception, because if it exists it is connected somewhere with the rules; and the rules themselves are sometimes exceptions. Some people maintain that Yiddish is "an exception" among languages. This is absolutely not true. It is a language like any other language. In Germany, most probably, it had its beginnings; and then it developed, and keeps on developing and changing; just like any other language. Some people say that Yiddish cannot be translated, the Yiddish idiom cannot be translated. The truth is that no idiom can be wholly translated. If you don't get the best equivalent you take the next best. To be sure, since Yiddish is connected with Jewish life, and Jewish life is strange to the rest of Europe, it is kind of "strange"; but there are many lives which are strange. We don't know much about the people in Albania or China or Tibet. But basically Yiddish has all the laws and idiosyncrasies and folklore, and all the juices, of any other language. (p. 24)

SINCLAIR: Israel Joshua Singer came to America in 1934 for obvious reasons. How did he take to life in New York?

SINGER: My brother loved America. Even more than I do. Because he had lived in Poland longer than I did and he saw the difference. Sometimes I quarrelled with my brother. I said to him: you are exaggerating, it's not such a paradise as you say, there's not as much justice as you imagine. He was really dazzled by America. To be sure he also had his disappointments. But he always used to say, "No matter how poor a man in this country is he has a bathroom." I don't think that America had many such patriots as my brother was. (p. 26)

SINCLAIR: At the time of your arrival in America your brother was a celebrity in the Yiddish world, and beyond. The English translation of **The Brothers Ashkenazi** ran through eleven editions. Now you are the celebrity, if I may use such a word. Perhaps there is an explanation for this in the fact that your brother wrote about Stalin, Hitler, and other mortal devils, whereas you deal with immortal imps and demons—with human instinct, as opposed to history.

SINGER: When I began to write critics considered me a perfect anachronism. They said, you are a writer about Jews who lived two hundred years ago, and about *dybbuks* in which people don't believe. My editor Abe Cahan scolded me. But somehow these imps have become very fashionable nowadays, so it's not my fault. It is like a man who wears a suit for fifty years, it has already become old-fashioned, and then the fashion goes back and his lapels are again in style. But he doesn't do it to be fashionable, he just is a man who likes to keep wearing those clothes. I write in my own way. Whether I'm fashionable and whether I will become unfashionable next year does not bother me at all. I was already forty-six before they translated me into English. I had made peace with the idea that I am going to stay a Yiddish writer till the end of my life and to be known only to the Yiddish readers. It didn't bother me much. Of course I wanted to be translated, but I didn't foresee that it would happen.

If I would say that I will remain popular forever, this would be boasting and I'm not going to do this. All I can say is, I wish it would be so. I certainly wouldn't mind. Most probably what happens to a writer, to a real writer, is that he's fashionable, and then he's forgotten, and then there is a revival. If he's truly good somehow he's not going to be completely forgotten. I believe that my brother's books will be popular again. If they will not be now they will be so in the future. (p. 27)

Clive Sinclair, "A Conversation with Isaac Bashevis Singer," in Encounter, Vol. LII, No. 2, February, 1979, pp. 21-8.

SUSAN A. SLOTNICK (essay date 1981)

[*In the following excerpt, Slotnick explores Singer's treatment in* The Carnovsky Family *of a common preoccupation of twentieth-century Yiddish literature and life: the dichotomy between life in the small East European villages, where Jews could remain spiritually pure yet suffer from poverty and ignorance, and life in large Western cities, where Jewish émigrés could take a significant place in the modern world yet risk the loss of their culture.*]

The city in modern Yiddish fiction is often the focus of the conflict between two opposing attitudes: the fascination with, and desire to emulate, that which is modern, secular, and outside the bounds of traditional Jewish life; and the fear that such an attraction will lead to assimilation, conversion and the eventual submergence of Jewish identity. The myth of the city as a place of both enlightenment and corruption, as juxtaposed with the corresponding paradox of the provincial town as the place of innocent purity as well as pernicious ignorance, is especially apparent in the portrayals of the German city in contrast with the shtetl, or small Jewish town. Thus the contrast of the Western cities of Berlin and New York with the Polish shtetl of Melnits in I. J. Singer's novel *Di mishpokhe Karnovski* (*The Karnovski Family*), was a twentieth-century reflection of a familiar preoccupation of Yiddish literature.

In the nineteenth century, the interest in things German was a hallmark of the Haskole (the Jewish Enlightenment movement in Eastern Europe). While leaders of traditional religious elements generally opposed any Germanizing influence, and suspected that such tendencies would inevitably lead to apostasy, many of the maskilim (adherents of the Haskole) defined their goal to be, precisely, Westernization and modernization of East European Jewry on the German model: education of the individual and reform of Jewish society, with the goal of integration into non-Jewish society as a religious rather than a national group. In their writings, among the earliest works of modern Yiddish literature, these maskilim held up the language, literature and culture of Germany (including modes of dress as well as literary fashions) as the ultimate ideal.

In this context, the German city was presented as the most suitable place for the enlightenment and education of the young heroes of these first examples of modern Yiddish fiction. (p. 33)

The pogroms and political reaction in Russia after the assassination of Alexander II forced a reevaluation of the ideal of integrating the Jews of Eastern Europe into non-Jewish society, following the example of their Western brethren. In addition, the institution of the shtetl was already on the decline by this time; as a result, sharp criticism of provincial Jewish life was to some extent replaced by nostalgia and retrospective portrayals of bygone days (in the works of [Sh. Y.] Abramovitsh . . . as well as by the more sentimentally inclined twentieth-century writers such as Sholem Asch).

With the first decades of the twentieth century came the dissolution of the Haskole (its political energy channelled into various revolutionary and nationalist movements), and the maturing and diversification of Yiddish literature. Urban life was now the norm for a majority of East European Jews; the city was a natural locale for fiction dealing with contemporary life. German culture, and the German city, continued to be important. In the twenties, one of the centers of East European Jewish intelligentsia, and of Yiddish writers, was Berlin. With the émigrés of other nationalities, they had travelled westward to escape the tumult of revolution and civil war that shook Russia in the wake of the First World War. One of the most prominent of these Yiddish writers was the poet Moyshe Kulbak, who (after his return to Kiev in 1923) wrote a long narrative poem about his Berlin years. Entitled *Disner Tshayld Herold* (*This Childe Harold,* 1933), this work parodies the pilgrimage of a romantic young man from Eastern Europe to Berlin, where he hopes to better himself culturally and intellectually. By describing the hollow trappings and idle ways of self-styled Berlin intelligentsia, Kulbak ridicules the "bourgeois decadence" of the city with his characteristic irony, and adds a dose of party-line political analysis. The only section devoid of ridicule deals with the workers' section of Wedding; the only hope for Germany and the German city, we are told, is in the awakening of its laboring masses. In this poem, the German city has become the symbol of corruption, containing within itself the seed of redemption and the new enlightenment: the raising of class consciousness.

Ten years later, when I. J. Singer's novel *Di mishpokhe Karnovski* first appeared in book form, Kulbak's naive political analysis had been proven dead wrong: instead of the dictatorship of the proletariat, Hitler and the Nazis were running Germany. Writing in New York in the early forties, Singer presents his version of the changing role of Berlin for the East European Jew: from the locus of ideal civilization, it becomes a nightmare of economic and social persecution. Singer relies on his readers' knowledge of current events in Europe, and points to these events, as well as the development and fate of each character, as ultimate proof of the falsity of the liberal ideals of Enlightenment in the German image.

In this novel, Singer tells a story that was not at all uncommon in the last half of the nineteenth and the beginning of the twentieth century: that of a Jewish family that migrates from Eastern Europe to Germany, and finally, to America. The events of this novel are thus solidly grounded in historical and demographic fact; but Singer uses this material for his own very specific purposes, selecting details of time and place to illustrate and underline the central thesis of the book. The author contends that the movement westward is a movement away from the source of traditional East European Jewishness, and that the only way for an individual to counteract the weakening effect of this movement is to reaffirm his or her personal commitment to that source—by resuming and reaffirming bonds of family and community. In *Di mishpokhe Karnovski,* we see three generations in which the tendency toward Westernization, acculturation (and the threat of assimilation and national, cultural obliteration) comes into conflict with the ultimate undeniability of East European Jewish roots.

Singer sets up the dynamics of this conflict around the polar opposition of East and West. The East represents, in this novel, the place of origin, the old home, with its primitivity as well as its vigor; it is identified with the shtetl, and with traditional forms of provincial Jewish life. The West is the new home, the city, the place of civilization, propriety, and a refinement that has overtones of weakness and degeneration. This basically geographical polarity dominates the general movement of the novel (the westward progression, with constant backward glances to the East), and it provides the key to the personalities, as well as the careers, of the protagonists.

While the geographical opposition of East versus West informs every aspect of the novel, the geographical particularities of specific locations are portrayed only to the extent that the details contribute to the development of this opposition, or define the status of the characters within it. The conventional contrast of shtetl and city is employed here to underline and emphasize the conflict of values and norms which the protagonists must confront and resolve. The action of the book takes place in three locales: the Polish shtetl Melnits, the German city of Berlin, and the American urban center, New York City. Melnits is evoked rather than described; the author seems to rely on his readers' assumed familiarity with the typical (or stereotypical) concept of the shtetl, and so he points to, rather than delineates, its atmosphere and attitudes. Melnits is thus given rather short shrift as a place of action; it is, most significantly, the place moved *from,* and subsequently remembered, in other times and places.

Berlin, the city that first stands for Western refinement and culture, is where we see the Karnovskis for the longest span of time, and it is where the main battles of culture and family heritage are fought. The descriptions of this city are quite detailed; but the neighborhoods described are always meant to underline the social status of the various characters, and their stance vis-à-vis the East and West. For instance, Dovid Karnovski, who is trying to become an accepted member of Berlin Jewish society, lives in an apartment on a fashionable street on the outskirts of the city, far from the teeming Jewish quarter of East European immigrants. And Singer almost entirely ignores the existence of the famous Berlin of the twenties, the scene of artistic avant-garde, Bohemian decadence, and radical politics. There is only one "salon" scene, the main thrust of which is Georg Karnovski's brief infidelity to his wife (on the background of rising political tensions).

Berlin stands for the "city of light" whose aura has tarnished; New York is the epitome of modern chaos, the urban jungle in which only the fittest survive. Like Melnits, it is portrayed through the evocation of stereotypes: the noisy vitality of the Lower East Side; the bourgeois affluence of Brooklyn "villas"; and the cosmopolitan bustle of Manhattan. The so-called melting pot is, for the Karnovskis, the final refuge, the scene of a partial, tentative resolution of the conflicts of the generational and geographic progression.

The small Jewish town of Melnits, in Poland, stands for the East European home, with its shortcomings as well as its virtues. Dovid Karnovski, the product of a proud, stubborn and financially successful family of Polish Jewish merchants and scholars, comes to Melnits as the son-in-law of a leading lumber merchant of the town. He soon succeeds in antagonizing the leading citizens of this shtetl with his modern, newfangled ways. His major offense is the flaunting of Moses Mendelssohn's German Bible translation in the synagogue, and his arrogant praises of this Berlin leader of the German Jewish Enlightenment, whom the traditional members of the Melnits Hasidic congregation consider to have been an apostate and an enemy of the Jewish people. After this embarrassing scene, Karnovski resolves to leave the medieval gloom of Poland, "steeped in darkness," for the city of Berlin, the place of his idol Mendelssohn, which "had always been for him [Dovid Karnovski] the place of enlightenment, wisdom, refinement, beauty and light."

On the one hand, Melnits is typified by the fanatical members of its provincial Hasidic congregation (who are too benighted to appreciate Mendelssohn); on the other, it is presented as the quintessential home, the East European Jewish shtetl. The ambivalence implied by these two views of Melnits is never resolved; and the tension between them is embodied in the difference between Dovid Karnovski's appraisal of Melnits and the attitude of his wife Leah. If Dovid sees the journey from Melnits to Berlin as a pilgrimage, for Leah it is, rather, an exile. Born and raised in Melnits, Leah represents all that is warm, affectionate and intimate in the traditional lifestyle of East European Jews. She is never comfortable in Berlin with her husband's dignified acquaintances, nor with their wives, who disdain her prattle about home and nursery and prefer to discuss the achievements of their distinguished German Jewish ancestors. And the German reform temple is the most alienating place of all for Leah; the prayers, the choir, and the sermons in elegant, flowery German have nothing in common with the Jewishness with which Leah has been raised. In her eyes, "the [German] synagogue, the Holy Ark, the Torah, didn't seem at all Jewish, and even God Himself seemed alien in this ornate, gentile temple . . . [a] carved palace that looked more like a bank than a house of God."

Melnits and Berlin, the two locales that first stand for the conflict of East and West in this novel, are contrasted through the different reactions of the two figures of Leah and Dovid, the matriarch and patriarch of the Karnovski clan. In Berlin itself, this East-West polarity is revealed in the two types of Jews with whom the Karnovskis associate. On the one hand, there are Dovid's friends, "real native [German Jews], the distinguished descendants of generations in this country," the highest social circles of Berlin Jewry into which Dovid is proud to be accepted. The second group is the only society in which Leah feels comfortable: other immigrants from Eastern Europe who preserve their own customs and lifestyle, who survive in Berlin, essentially, by recreating their native world of Melnits. This active, audacious and shamelessly Eastern type is represented by the figure of Solomon Burak, who runs his profitable business and his comfortable home in the style to which he is accustomed. Burak adapts, but does not assimilate; he succeeds in the German city on his own terms, and with only superficial concessions.

These three characters thus represent three versions of the

first-generation Eastern immigrant in the Western city: one who cannot adapt (Leah), one who remakes himself in the Western image (Dovid), and one who adapts on his own terms (Solomon Burak). Singer uses spoken language, and the characters' attitudes toward it, as a hallmark of their cultural position with regard to the East-West polarity. Dovid prides himself on his perfect, grammatical German; Leah is unable to learn that language at all, and persists in speaking Yiddish, despite the admonitions of her husband. Again, we are told of Dovid Karnovski's attitude: "German signified to him Enlightenment, light, Moses Mendelssohn, and Jewish scholarship, while Leah's language stood for the rabbi of Melnits, the cult of Hasidism, stupidity and ignorance." In contrast to Dovid's hypercorrect German is the speech of Solomon Burak, "[German] with the accent and flavor of the street-language of the big city . . . a coarse German that he had learned as a peddler . . . intertwined with Melnits Yiddish and Hebrew," which emphasizes his vitality and his knack for picking up what is lively and immediate in the local culture, and synthesizing it with his own.

Among the second generation, the Berlin-born sons and daughters of these immigrants, we are shown the different products of Eastern nature and Western nurture. Leah and Dovid Karnovski's son Georg inherits his father's vitality along with his Semitic physiognomy; this energy is clearly meant to be taken as an Eastern quality. Georg's education and social life are predominantly German. This combination seems, for a while, to be an eminently successful one: Georg grows up to be a professional (a doctor), breaking through the barriers of prejudice and anti-semitism by the force of his personality and ability. Georg's lack of interest in the passive, stereotypically Jewish Ruth, the daughter of Solomon Burak, and his subsequent marriage to a Gentile German woman, underline his personal rejection (or mere dismissal) of the East—the Jewish traditions of his parents. Raised according to his father's belief in the credo "Be a Jew at home and a man in the street," Georg fulfills only the second half. Thus he demonstrates the fallaciousness of the Mendelssohnian ideal of Enlightenment as an attempt to resolve the polarity of East and West, and brings his father to the brink of disillusionment with his lifelong ideal. Dovid loses faith in the native German Jews, and is not so positive now that Melnits represents all that is evil and ignorant while Berlin represents all that is pure and superior.

It is the third generation, the grandchildren of the original immigrants, that Singer uses as the ultimate demonstration of the error of the ideal of Westernization on the German model. The grandson of the Buraks, Ruth's son Marcus, is an intelligent, well adjusted and capable youngster, whose achievements include academic honors from his American school and publications in Yiddish; he seems destined to succeed in America as his grandfather Solomon had in Berlin. But Yegor, Georg Karnovski's son, is a weak, sickly, neurotic creature who embodies the irreconcilability of the split in his heritage.

While Georg has retained the energy of the East (inherited from his immigrant parents), he is too far from the spiritual source to pass on that vitality to his son. Yegor hates the Jewish half of himself (and his father), and longs to exorcise it and embrace the "pure" Germanic heritage of his Gentile mother. The Oedipal overtones here are amplified by the author's broad Freudian hints. But his characterization is more than a psychoanalytical flourish. Singer holds up the wretch-

ed Yegor as ultimate proof of his contention that westward tendencies, without a healthy affirmation and retention of East European Jewish vitality, are pernicious and degenerative, and that such a combination must finally lead to self-hate and self-destruction.

If Berlin is the crucible, the place where East meets West with a variety of results, then New York, where the protagonists arrive in the early thirties, fleeing from the terrors of the Nazi rise to power in Germany, is the testing ground for the previous attempts to amalgamate East and West. For Singer, the essential quality of the American city is its freedom. Here emigrants like Solomon Burak can once again recreate their shtetl society, while incorporating the vital, useful elements of the new culture. Leah, who was never comfortable in Berlin, is free to return to an American version of Melnits; and the disillusioned Dovid Karnovski relinquishes his pretentions to Westernization and returns to the East European intellectual atmosphere of his youth, transplanted to New York.

The recently uprooted German Jews also recreate an image of their culture; but Singer is careful to indicate that this new German Jewish society is not synthetic, but sterile and isolated from the new culture all around it. In this novel, the author makes a point of showing how the German Jewish refugees refuse to have anything to do with the earlier immigrants from Eastern Europe. The German Jews set up their own businesses, restaurants, and synagogues, and refrain from discussing anything that happened or is happening "over there" (in Germany) with anyone outside of their immediate social circle. Singer shows, with thinly veiled irony, the systematic lowering of the social status of these immigrants: stage actors become café owners, professors open cleaning stores, chemists become beauticians. For consolation, they spend their evenings in the café "Old Berlin," an insulated refuge from the noisy New York streets, a bit of their native city recreated in this new home.

The most successful of the new immigrants is however the quintessential East European Jew, Solomon Burak. As he did in Berlin, he begins in New York by peddling from door to door, and works himself up to a store, eventually moving to a better neighborhood. Once again, he helps relatives to emigrate, and puts them up, feeds them and employs them when they arrive. Burak also becomes the benefactor of the man who formerly despised him—Dovid Karnovski, who is given a lowly job (that of beadle in a German Jewish synagogue) through the influence of Solomon Burak, who is president of the congregation and its main financial support (a demonstration of how he has turned the tables on the Berlin Jews who once snubbed him as a newcomer to their city). Dovid Karnovski has now come full circle: from his arrogant departure from the Hasidic synagogue in Melnits, through his ignominious exile from the elegant reform temple in Berlin, to a humble position and a reconciliation with Solomon Burak, the man whom he had shunned in Berlin as the incarnation of the boorishness and crudity of the East. But now Dovid, as well as Leah, find peace and even contentment in a new city in which they can revert to the society of those who share their Eastern heritage.

The younger, Berlin-born generations of Karnovskis have a harder time in New York. While Georg appreciates the "great new stony city, free but tough, that had to be faced with great strength and courage," he finds that the new liberty includes the freedom to starve. Georg has trouble continuing his medical career, since he is unable to pass the English examinations, despite his energetic application to learning the new language—which his German wife despairs of ever mastering (the difficulty in linguistic adaptation echoes the experiences of Leah and Dovid Karnovski in learning German). So Georg and his family live by selling the oversized German furniture and, finally, the expensive medical equipment that they had brought over from the other side. This is their first immigrant experience; we see them in the painful process of getting rid of their heavy German "baggage" before they can adapt to the new city.

The third-generation Karnovski, Yegor, finds this American freedom, the freedom of the cosmopolitan Western city, one which permits him to live out his fantasies to their bitter end. Unable to bear the noisy Americans, or his equally boisterous East European cousins, Yegor runs away to Yorkville, the German section of Manhattan. Here—unlike in the old country, to which he constantly longs to return—Yegor can pretend to discard the Jewish half of himself. He goes by his mother's maiden name, joins a young Nazi group, and tries to work as an informer for the German government. Ironically, his lack of success in this undertaking comes from his inability and unwillingness to infiltrate Jewish groups in New York, where he could gather the information that his employer demands; what Yegor wants is to be as far as possible from that society. Finally, he is deserted by his new friends and betrayed by the German agent who employed him as an informer. When that same employer tries to seduce him, Yegor kills him and returns to his father's house, where he shoots a bullet into his chest. The novel ends as his father is about to operate in an attempt to save Yegor's life; and we are not told whether he will be successful or not. But the reconciliation of father and prodigal son is clear: "Yegor took his father's hand and kissed it . . . smiling the guilty smile of the returning son who asks for understanding and forgiveness . . . deathly ill yet cured of his inferiority. He [Georg] was proud of him."

The violence, as well as the inconclusiveness, of Yegor's final act expresses Singer's strong feelings *and* his ambivalence toward the immigrant experience that is the focus of this novel. Using the polarity of East and West, the author has, from the beginning, suggested the irreconcilability of what he sees as the two main forces in Jewish life: the vital force of tradition and the fascination with the non-Jewish world outside of that tradition. The abandonment of traditional values, and the striving for "elevation" to Western cultural levels, has been proven false: the promise of Berlin as the ideal society in which Jews (both Eastern and Western) would be accepted and treated according to liberal, humanistic precepts, has been betrayed. The chaos of New York is at least more honest than the deceptive rationality and order of Berlin; but the author sees the American city as a place of freedom and relief from oppression, rather than a site for national, cultural revival. Singer argues here (as he did in an essay of the same period) that the brotherhood of nations is an illusion, and that complete integration (or even relatively comfortable coexistence) in non-Jewish society is impossible, since antisemitism is inevitable as long as Jews live in the Diaspora. In *Di mishpokhe Karnovski,* only those who recognize the essentially temporary nature of their urban Western homes, and who preserve the essence and energy of the East, can survive intact—as does Solomon Burak.

But though he is a survivor (and a financial success), Burak is also a boor. He preserves the primitive life force of the East,

but not the spiritual and intellectual achievements to which Dovid Karnovski is the heir. While the older generation can live out its last years in relative comfort (in the versions of Melnits and Berlin recreated in New York), the future generations are doomed. Yegor, the male heir of the Karnovskis, is destroyed by the conflict within himself. And, despite the various successes of other characters, it is with Yegor's attempt at suicide that the novel ends.

For Singer, the movement towards the West—which nineteenth-century Yiddish writers had seen as the symbol of civilization and true humanism—has become a dangerous and potentially fatal journey. The vitality of the East cannot, finally, be preserved without vulgarization or self-destruction. In terms of the Karnovski family, the decline through generations goes along with the increasing distance (actual and spiritual) from the East. While the second generation, the Berlin-born Georg, still preserves the "primeval" energy, his inability to bequeath it to his son Yegor suggests the author's ultimately pessimistic evaluation of what he saw as the tragedy of Jewish history in the twentieth century. (pp. 34-41)

Susan A. Slotnick, "Concepts of Space and Society: Melnits, Berlin and New York in I. J. Singer's Novel 'Di mishpokhe Karnovski'," in The German Quarterly, Vol. LIV, No. 1, January, 1981, pp. 33-43.

CLIVE SINCLAIR   (essay date 1983)

[*In the following excerpt from his study* The Brothers Singer, *Sinclair compares the treatment of Jewish history in works by Israel Joshua and Isaac Bashevis Singer.*]

"My brother influenced me mightily," said Bashevis. He went on to specify the nature of that influence:

> When I began to write myself my brother encouraged me and gave me certain rules for writing. He said: when you write tell a story, and don't try to explain the story. If you say that a boy fell in love with a girl you don't have to explain to the reader why a boy falls in love, the reader knows just as much about love as you do or more so. You tell him the story and the explanations and interpretations he will make himself, or critics will do it for him. He had two words which he used: *images* and *sayings.* Sayings were for him essays, interpretations. He called sayings, *zugerts.* It means you just talk, you just say things. You don't paint a picture, or bring out an image. He said, leave the *zugerts* to the others. You tell them a story. Because you may know stories which they don't know—but you don't know more about life than they do [see excerpt dated 1979].

In fact, the pupil kept more rigorously to these rules than the teacher. For in his ambition to encompass the roots and fruits of the class struggle within the Jewish community of Lodz in the fictional history of *The Brothers Ashkenazi,* Joshua frequently froze the action between incitement and reaction to include "sayings." A brief example will suffice: Martin Kuchinsky, a blood-thirsty Polish revolutionary whose motto was "Something hot, and dripping," accused Felix Feldblum, his co-conspirator, of sounding "more like a sermon delivered in a synagogue." But before Felix was allowed to respond, Joshua inserted several paragraphs in which Felix's discovery of anti-Semitism among his fellow revolutionaries and within the Polish working class was described, thus adding an historical dimension to Felix's personal distress. It becomes clear, in reading *The Brothers Ashkenazi,* that Joshua aimed to marry individual motivation with historical inevitability, which required several sayings on the course of Polish history and the class struggle. And it is this deviation from the lesson he taught his younger brother which reveals most fully the differences between Joshua and Bashevis, both as writers and as chroniclers. Although [Bashevis's] *The Manor* covered a specific period—"the epoch between the Polish insurrection of 1863 and the end of the nineteenth century"—its characters were less impelled by temporal forces than by corporeal desires, and their doubts were not so much related to the contemporary historical process as to some universal code, as the title of the novel implies.

While Bashevis used the manor of Count Jampolski, into which Calman Jacoby moved, to demonstrate the snares of vanity and sophistication, Joshua presented the palace of the Huntze family, which Max Ashkenazi finally inhabited, as a soul-destroying symbol of imperial history, forever inimical to the Jews. Surrounded by the regalia of the Polish aristocracy Max Ashkenazi fancied that he was King of Lodz. But in reality he was no more King of Lodz than was the humpbacked Jewish tailor, mockingly enthroned by the anti-Semitic mob, King of Poland. After the crowd had spent its anger on the Jews and order had been restored by the Cossacks, the tailor was brought before the Governor, doing his best to suppress a smile, who said, "I understand you proclaimed yourself King of Poland." History had worse humiliations in store for Max Ashkenazi. Unlike Max Ashkenazi, Calman knew from the first that he had fallen into a trap: "Yes, Count Jampolski in his old age had divorced himself from all luxuries while Calman, the Jew, had taken up residence in a palace, amid gold, silver, porcelains, lackeys, and servants." Nonetheless, he could not resist Clara's demands for opulence. The final reference for Joshua was history, whereas for Bashevis it was religion; Max Ashkenazi ignored the lessons of the former, Calman the teachings of the latter. Both brothers punished their characters accordingly. However, since it is impossible to write about the Jews (and both Ashkenazi and Jacoby, as names, refer to a people as well as a family) without mentioning their religion, and equally impossible to write about them without confronting their history, these co-ordinates are not mutually exclusive. Indeed, one character almost crossed over from [Bashevis's] *The Estate* into *The Brothers Ashkenazi;* but unfortunately Zina was arrested before she could reach Lodz with her cache of arms for the revolutionaries. (pp. 87-8)

While Bashevis concerns himself less with the minutiae of a period than with those problems which are eternal, Joshua always has contemporary history as the sub-text of his story. Joshua does not deem it sufficient to blame all wickedness upon the evil side of human nature; rather he seeks the causes in politics, economics and history. There is a sense of progression, both in terms of character and history, which at once makes his work seem more opaque but less modern than his brother's. History is organic, fed by greed. And Lodz was its mutant offspring, finding its true unnatural role as the factories switched to steam power. "The chimneys of Lodz clustered like the trees of a forest, but they blossomed in smoke and poisoned the air." Later, Lodz was described as a "hoggish gourmandizer," as if the city itself were responsible for its slump; a monster prepared to devour its creators. He is not so much concerned with the freedom given to the self, but with the possibilities of economic and political advancement

history suddenly afforded the Jews; which, in effect, gave them an alternative persona; thus Simcha Meyer became Max and Jacob Bunim became Yakob. Nevertheless, he shared Bashevis's attitude to the role of the Jews in this history. It was, simply, that they don't belong; a change of name can alter neither character nor the fact that one was born a Jew. Even Yakob, who looked like a modern European, died because he was recognized as a Jew. So *The Brothers Ashkenazi,* like *The Manor* and *The Estate,* reached the same conclusion as the grandfather who said: "We Jews must not interfere. Whoever rules will persecute Jews." The novel ends with this terrible vision:

> A thick mist had descended from the skies over Lodz. A wind rose and blew the dust of the cemetery in the eyes of the mourners. Heavily and slowly, like the rolling mists above them, they turned back to the desolate and alien city.
>
> "Sand," they muttered, covering their eyes with their hands. "Everything we have built was built on sand."

This was not only symbolically but also literally true, for the Jewish suburb of Balut was built upon a sandy field. The land was purchased by Reb Solomon David Preiss under false pretences from impoverished Polish nobles in the aftermath of the 1863 rebellion. When the Canarski brothers discovered Reb Solomon's true purpose they tried to retrieve their land in the courts, only to discover that money was more potent in the eyes of justice than breeding. The triumphant Jews proclaimed that no law would ever be able to destroy their presence; but they were wrong, for they had not reckoned with the court of history.

In *The Brothers Ashkenazi* history is a juggernaut, best represented by the advance of the Germans into Poland. The novel opens with a declaration of its epic intentions, even though the pioneers it follows are not Jews but Germans, en route to Poland in the wake of the Napoleonic wars. And what role did the Jews play in this march of history? As ever they were spectators, "gathered with wide-open eyes to observe the interminable line of carriages moving ceaselessly forward." A century later, history was repeated as another invading German army rolled into Poland and once again the Jews "gazed with astonishment in their black eyes at the newcomers." This, as Saul Bellow has pointed out, is the traditional role of the Jews. *The Brothers Ashkenazi,* like *The Manor* and *The Estate,* shows what happens to those Jews who seize their chance and break with this tradition; however, the power of this initial image already suggests their fate. . . . It may be dangerous to combat evil in the world, but it is necessary to confront it in fiction. Hence Bashevis's characters provide the centre around which history revolves. In *The Brothers Ashkenazi,* scenes are constructed in the opposite order; familiar characters are gradually revealed to be participants in historical events. For example in the ferment after the assassination of Assistant Police Commissioner Jurgoff, Nissan is eventually discovered behind the barricades waiting, along with thousands of others. This presents Joshua with a problem of balance unknown to Bashevis; on the one hand his story concerns a group of individuals, on the other it follows an historical process which involves classes not individuals. Whereas Bashevis seems to have successfully given his "sayings" fictional life, Joshua sometimes seems to smother his characters with "sayings."

When Max Ashkenazi cut the salary of his weavers to maximize his profits, a strike resulted. It was led by Tevyeh, a long-time socialist, and Nissan. Nissan already had personal reasons for disliking Max, but now that conflict became as much political as personal. During a protest meeting held in a synagogue, Joshua took the opportunity to insert a few "sayings" on the dreadful living conditions of the weavers. This is unnecessary in terms of dramatic development, but vital as an explication of the class struggle. Political motivation gives the novel an authority of tone, but it also weakens the spontaneity of the action since it is predictable that Max will always act as a capitalist and Nissan as a socialist. They have been trapped by history. This leads to a paradox already encountered by Benjamin Lerner in *Steel and Iron;* while Joshua's message is anti-totalitarian, his method tends to the classification of the individual. Nonetheless, *The Brothers Ashkenazi* has a dynamism that finally synthesizes the separate personal and political aspects. The dynamo being Judaism. If the battle between Max and Nissan represents the political tension of the novel, then the rivalry between Max and his brother adds the personal dimension. And it was with Yakob's final triumph that Joshua most dramatically resolved his paradox.

Jacob Bunim tactfully waited for the death of his father before going to "the extreme of un-Jewishness," but thereafter he became Yakob the brilliant European. And unlike his brother he looked the part. Indeed, he was able to bluff his way into Russia to rescue Max from a Soviet prison, only to come to grief on the border of his Polish homeland, his cosmopolitan appearance notwithstanding. A gendarme of the new Polish republic greeted them with the words: "Well, where do you two Sheenies come from?" And in that single moment all Yakob's years of good living vanished. Nor are his papers of any use, because he was a "Sheeny." But what made him a type in the eyes of the anti-Semite suddenly made him an individual in the eyes of the reader. When the gendarme was replaced by a lieutenant Yakob cried: "My brother and I are manufacturers of Lodz. We own houses there. We place ourselves under your protection." Unfortunately, the officer was a greater sadist than the gendarme, who had merely ordered them to strip. He forced Max to yell: "To hell with all the Yids!" But even then Max's humiliation was not over: "Now you can give us a little dance, Mr. Manufacturer and house-owner of Lodz. A little dance and song, to entertain our soldier-boys here." So Max danced till he dropped. But Yakob was made of sterner stuff. Naked, without pretensions, his true character was revealed. He slapped the officer and was shot dead. Judaism therefore both saved him as an individual and caused his extinction. Likewise, Judaism disbarred ultimate absorption into any mass movement. In the end Nissan was broken, humiliated and astounded by the revolution he had helped initiate. And Felix Feldblum, who was convinced that his constituency was amongst the gentile workers, was last seen in Lemberg horrified by the pogrom he had witnessed, perpetrated by this same revolutionary material—among the mourners "stalked one figure in a light-blue uniform—Felix Feldblum, officer in the Polish Legion, fighter for the freedom of Poland, one-time believer in her Messianic future." Yakob's death was watched by "the naked figure of Jesus." Alongside the crucifix were a Polish eagle, portraits of generals, and innumerable Polish flags. Symbols that spell danger for Jews. The world is no illusion, what is illusory is the belief that Jews have any secure place in it. (pp. 105-08)

Max Ashkenazi is without doubt the most powerful character

in *The Brothers Ashkenazi* . . . . But it was Nissan who had to carry the burden of Joshua's personal disillusion. After all Max's fate, though cruel, was not unjust considering the harm he had done others. Nissan's final anguish was almost masochistic, however, because his struggle had not been for self-aggrandizement but for the advancement of the proletariat. And his defeat was more chilling, because it demonstrated the impossibility of introducing a more just society. It may be deduced from the number of "sayings" Joshua inserts on the circumstances of the weavers that his sympathies are with them, and with Nissan's campaign on their behalf. But even so Joshua was too sceptical or too honest to ignore the outcome of the Russian revolution, and so he was forced to make Nissan as much a dupe of Marx as Max was a fool for Mammon. All dialectics are open invitations to dictators and criminals, who are prepared to help history on its way. So Joshua found himself in something of a dilemma; giving emotional support to a movement he knew would lead to dictatorship. . . . [In] facing up to the full implications of Nissan's beliefs he is punishing himself.

In 1905 both Nissan and Max were hurrying to Lodz, both for their own purposes: "Like Max Ashkenazi, Nissan was being recalled to Lodz by those who needed his guidance and leadership in a crisis. Lodz was again one of the centres of the revolutionary movement." But Nissan's leadership and guidance were finally as illusory as Max's rule of Lodz. Equally illusory was the unity of the Jews; they also were divided by class, as Joshua learned in his grandfather's *beth din.* A major problem with the Jewish artisans, however, was their refusal to see themselves as workers. Ezra Mendelsohn in *Class Struggle in the Pale* recorded the feelings of a socialist leader:

> It was this tendency of the journeymen to become employers, their failure to recognize the class struggle, that made the early socialist leaders despair. Feliks Kon, the Polish socialist, disparagingly characterized the Jewish artisans as "journeymen who dream of becoming masters."

"Since employer-staff relationships were more clearly defined in the larger establishments, workers naturally found it more difficult to alter their status," adds Mendelsohn. Which is precisely why Nissan decided that the hard-core of the revolution was not with the self-interested Jewish hand-loom weavers of Balut but in the steam factories where the workers "realized how impassable was the gulf between them and the owning class." Comparing this observation with the quotation from Mendelsohn gives a glimpse of how accurate was Joshua's presentation of the situation in Lodz. But even though the Jewish artisans were hard to organize they were no less exploited than their gentile co-workers. Here is a strike proclamation quoted by Mendelsohn:

> "Feival Janovsky," the [boycott] proclamation stated: "is a pious Jew; he goes to the synagogue regularly, and with all his heart prays to God. He is a Jewish nationalist, a patriot and perhaps even a Zionist. He no doubt is upset by the persecution of the Jews, and sheds crocodile tears over the Jews' desperate situation. But all this, as we see, does not prevent him from cruelly exploiting his Jewish workers."

"The evidence suggests . . . ," writes Mendelsohn, "that the struggle between Jewish worker and Jewish employer, though often the struggle of 'pauper against pauper,' was extremely bitter. While traditional historians, writing of Russian Jewry, have emphasized the unity of the community as against its gentile oppressors, the community was in fact rent by internal dissension of great magnitude." Joshua was clearly aware of this fact, and demonstrated it time after time; for example, the battle between the Jewish toughs hired by the employers and the unionists. But no dissension was greater than that between the Balut revolutionaries, led by Nissan, and the capitalists led by Max. It was common practice for Jewish factory owners not to employ Jews. Mendelsohn quotes the reason given by a Jewish factory-owner in Smorgon: "The Jews are good workers, but they are capable of organizing revolts . . . against the employer, the régime, and the Tsar himself." Flederbaum also would not employ Jewish workers because "Gentile workmen were more obedient and respectful and less ambitious." Nor would Max Ashkenazi in his steam factory. He could not understand why Nissan, a Jew, should be leading a strike of his gentile workers, "putting all sorts of ideas into their heads." "We know nothing about Jews and gentiles," answered Nissan. "We know only of workers and exploiters."

> "*You* don't know," said Max Ashkenazi scornfully. "But ask the gentiles *their* opinion. *They* know the difference between Jews and gentiles. Unity! Unity! Just try to get one Jewish worker into a steam factory, and he'll come out in a hurry, and not walking on his own legs, either."

Nissan retorted that these were nationalistic orations, but secretly he knew that Max was right. Anti-Semitism overrode class allegiance. Later this scheme was repeated in radically different circumstances. The location was Russia. Max was still a factory owner, but Nissan was now a workers' delegate. With a gesture of helplessness Max conceded defeat: "It turns out you were right, and not I." Emphasizing their shared Jewishness he quoted from the Talmud: "Who is the wise man? He who foresees the unborn." But Max's congratulations were premature, the child was a mutant that consumed its progenitors. Nissan rejected Max's overtures, replying in Russian not Yiddish, but his looks belied his actions. By remarking that Nissan's Jewish beard and whiskers gave him the appearance of a pietist Joshua was confirming Max's earlier point. The Jews may indeed have their own class divisions, but these were non-existent in the eyes of the anti-Semites; they did not distinguish between Jewish capitalists and Jewish communists. . . . Charles Madison, in his book *Yiddish Literature* [see excerpt dated 1968], described a trip Joshua made to the Soviet Union in 1926. "What troubled him particularly," writes Madison, "were evidences of anti-Semitism and its effect on many Jews." The most ironic "effect" is reported thus: ". . . on visiting a secluded midnight celebration of 'Lubavishe' Hasidism he was surprised to find among them engineers, students and other enlightened men who had become pious *after* the revolution." But unlike Bashevis, Joshua refused to see a realistic alternative in hasidism. He was not impressed by gestures. Which is why he remained suspicious of the alliance formed between intellectuals and workers. . . . (pp. 115-17)

One such intellectual made an appearance at the grand funeral of Bashke, daughter of Tevyeh, who died a heroine of the movement. "He was a famous orator, this revolutionary leader — a splendid specimen of a man, tall, dark-eyed, his head crowned by black locks." With his noble gestures and his voice under perfect control he soon had the crowd in his hands. And the more his audience responded to him, "lifted to heights of enthusiasm . . . plunged into an abyss of sor-

row," the more he became "enamoured of his role." But Tevyeh actually saw his daughter die, heard her cry, "I'm choking! Save me!" and was haunted by her "wide-open rolling eyes." The squalid reality of her death compared to the grandeur of her funeral made the orator's every word feel like "a separate knife-thrust" to Tevyeh. "It was on his Bashke's grave, on the fresh earth which covered the dead body of his daughter, that this performance was taking place." Finally, when the speaker raised Bashke's blood-stained blouse, Tevyeh could stand the theatricality no longer. He snatched the blouse and pressed it "convulsively to his heart." This spontaneous outburst of passion was a great disappointment to the assembled workers, who felt that "the fine mood created by the orator" had been ruined. Clearly Joshua wanted to demonstrate how easy it was to be blinded to the truth by rhetoric. More, he wanted to show how quickly a crowd can forget suffering in order to indulge in self-righteousness. Of course, his revolutionary leader was a phony, an actor playing a part, working to satisfy his own ego. Such a leader, Comrade Daniel, played a central and insincere role in Joshua's next novel, *East of Eden,* but even this brief scene is sufficient to display Joshua's scepticism. It is not the theory of Marxism he found so objectionable, but rather the people who exploited it for their own ends.

Even so Joshua's scepticism should not be confused with the expediency of Colonel Konitzky, who was given the task of pacifying Lodz after the assassination of Jurgoff and its concomitant riots. Konitzky's technique was based upon the need to alienate the masses from the intelligentsia, which may seem to be in accord with Joshua's own observations. "I was easily won over by the intellectuals, as so many others have been," he told a new prisoner. "But I was lucky enough to see through them in time and drop them." As he continued he could well have been describing the anonymous orator at Bashke's funeral: "They look down on the proletariat and have an inner contempt for it. . . . These intellectuals come from rich homes; they aren't acquainted with the workingman, they don't feel his emotions. Their so-called revolutionary passion is something born in the imagination, out of boredom and idleness and out of the fashionableness of being a radical." But Joshua could hardly be in sympathy with a man who is last seen, having transferred his allegiance from the Tsar to the new Polish republic, still working against the people: "the strong he repressed brutally, the weak he corrupted." Colonel Konitzky was based upon the figure of S.V. Zubatov, head of the Tsarist secret police, active around the turn of the century, who, according to Mendelsohn, was the originator of police socialism. His declared aim was to persuade the Jewish workers that they could not hope to profit from an alliance with the intelligentsia, who "all too often tried to engage workers in a senseless political struggle which could only defeat their demands for economic and cultural improvements."

> These demands, Zubatovism insisted, could only be won were workers to abandon illegal schemes and ally themselves with the government. In short workers should establish unions, based on democratic principles, and should not permit the interference of the intelligentsia; the government itself would willingly support their struggle for decent wages, shorter hours, and better cultural opportunities.

Both Zubatov and Konitzky appealed to the "enlightened self-interest" of the Jewish workers, assuming them to be capitalists who merely lack capital. Their real purpose was not amelioration, but the painless preservation of the status quo and their own skins. In short, their deeds were disconnected from any emotion save self-interest, which is all they could recognize in others. Joshua, on the contrary, sensed that a more communal way of life was possible, but he was unable to ignore the empirical evidence supplied by human nature and history, which makes *The Brothers Ashkenazi* so pessimistic. And nothing occurred during Joshua's last years that gave him cause to reconsider. (pp. 117-19)

At the end of *Steel and Iron* Benjamin Lerner forfeited his individuality, which had hitherto been sustained by his scepticism, as he became a trooper of the new Soviet republic. Also, in those last pages, Joshua freed him from the harness of autobiography; Lerner's future is unwritten, anonymous. However, Joshua, though rid of Lerner, found himself unable to close his mind to the broken promises of the new age of man. *East of Eden* took its title from a quotation in Genesis: "So he drove out the man; and he placed at the east of the garden of Eden Cherubims, and a flaming sword which turned every way, to keep the way of the tree of life." Throughout the novel the Soviet Union is referred to as "paradise," and the masses are told: "Look to the East!" And Daniel, the handsome orator of the revolution in Poland, sees the future as "fresh and sweet, like a meadow in spring, like a garden, like an immense orchard, filled with flowing waters and blossoming fruit." As with the revolutionaries in *The Brothers Ashkenazi*, so in *East of Eden;* communism became an exact replacement of Judaism, demanding the same single-minded devotion, and borrowing the same imagery; as orthodox Jews bowed eastwards in the direction of Jerusalem, so the workers turned their eyes to Moscow. But the title suggests the inevitable fall of these hopes, the impossibility of recreating a time when, "Peace would reign; human beings would live with the gentleness of sheep, wrapped round with love and goodness." Joshua had no quarrel with the idea of original sin. In fact, he was an outright determinist, for nothing determines the future quite like pessimism with its simple rule: if you hope, expect the opposite. Naturally, this would sound defeatist in the ears of a Daniel who was an optimistic determinist, a prophet of the dialectic of history.

Thus Joshua arrived at another artistic problem: how to retain the tension of unpredictability in a novel when all hopes were doomed to failure, or how to put a mirror to determinism and show more than a world through a looking-glass. A sceptical hero was unsatisfactory, because Joshua wanted to portray the seductive appeal of a messianic ideology, so he decided to experiment with a gullible central character. Benjamin Lerner's fate was his starting point. In effect, he decided to rework *Steel and Iron,* making use of everything he had learned subsequently. The original Yiddish title, *Chaver Nachman,* speaks of his intentions no less ironically than its English counterpart. *Chaver* means "comrade" and Nachman, the hero's name, derives from *nachem,* which is Hebrew for "to comfort." Unfortunately, by the novel's end Nachman is a comrade to no one and a comfort to nobody. So what Joshua produced was an out-and-out political novel, disguised as an epic of realism, but actually a bitter parable in the manner — but not the spirit — of Peretz's "Bontsha the Silent." Joshua's *kleyne menshele* received no reward in "paradise," on the contrary the guardians of "Eden" inflicted even greater punishment upon him. What we have in Nachman Ritter is a Yiddish Candide.

It is worth recalling that at much the same time, in a different neck of the woods, another writer was taking on a similar artistic problem; the chief difference being that instead of attacking the utopian nightmare his enemy was the American Dream. Nathanael West's conclusion was *A Cool Million.* His *kleyne menshele,* Lemuel Pitkin, was no more fortunate than Nachman Ritter, nor was Shagpoke Whipple, his manipulator, any more admirable than Daniel; both, like Pangloss, see in their beliefs the best of all possible worlds. Of course, Nachman and Daniel seem more realistic, but this is an illusion born of Joshua's *trompe-l'oeil* presentation; instead of taking metaphors and turning them into an absurd reality, he painstakingly contrasted the rhetoric of the revolutionaries with actuality. West more or less rewrote American history, providing an image of the nation extrapolated from propogandist's clichés, whereas Joshua carefully implanted the events of *East of Eden* into recent history. If *A Cool Million* was finally a greater artistic coup than *East of Eden,* it was perhaps at the expense of its political impact. In the thirties the American Dream was but a whisper in an awakened people, while the Soviet Union still retained its allure for many intellectuals disenchanted with capitalism. What Dan Jacobson said of Bashevis's characters is equally true of West's people; they have the transparency of celluloid, while Nachman and Daniel give off the solid whiff of greasepaint. Indeed, the same Daniel who breathes the fire of communism is actually given this motivation:

> This had been his life's longing: to be admired and applauded by masses. This was what had made him follow Polish actors through the streets when he was a little boy, and this had impelled him, in his student days, to hang on the outskirts of the Polish labour movement. If he could not be an actor he would at least be a leader, a great orator.

Joshua was no less a prestidigitator than Nathanael West, but he learned his tricks upon the Yiddish stage of New York rather than at the movie sets of Hollywood. And it is this dramatic solidity which makes the fate of Nachman and his family so moving. Nachman failed to realize that he was participating in a drama that required acting ability not sincerity. Likewise, the reader must recognize that while the scenery of *East of Eden* is realistic, the *dramatis personae* who act out their inevitable fates are not.

Nachman's father was called Mattes. He was a pedlar, who wandered from village to village with a sack upon his back. Sentimentalists would have us believe that in spite of poverty and squalor men such as Mattes were Biblical scholars. Mattes was certainly poor, dwelling in the street of the beggars, and devout enough to refuse food offered by a peasant, but he was "no scholar, and unacquainted with the finer points of ritual." He was a regular worshipper in the synagogue, but once inside "stood near the door . . . among the beggars, the wanderers, and the homeless, and he strained himself to catch the words of the cantor." He was so insignificant that whenever he celebrated the birth of a child, one unconsidered daughter after another, the beadle always forgot his name. His Sabbath meal consisted of beans and dumplings. Joshua, never one to obscure the unsociable effects of poverty, noted how rapidly his daughters ate, "in part because they were hungry and in part because each one feared the other would eat up more." But for all the shame of his poverty Mattes never questioned the rules of society or the justice of God. Indeed, he adhered to the latter with masochistic intensity. The novel begins on a Friday. It was a morning of torrid heat, but Mattes had taken no breakfast, for he would not eat until he had said his prayers, and to find a suitable place in the unfriendly countryside was not easy. So Mattes staggered onward, bent "so low under his burden that the tip of his dust-covered beard almost brushes against the rope which girdles him." Eventually he had to pause, because it was almost noon. Once he had begun to pray he would not stop, even when stoned by Polish peasants. Thereafter he must hurry back to Pyask, so as to arrive in good time for the Sabbath. Such was the working life of Mattes the pedlar.

> Five days he was on the road every week, among the peasants, five days of homelessness and dry food, five nights passed in stables and barns, five days without a sight of his wife and children and without a friendly conversation in Yiddish.

But even in Pyask he was given no respect, instead he was mocked by the more prosperous householders who "smiled at the sight of this man who combined two proverbial misfortunes: no money and nothing but daughters."

Therefore Nachman's birth was a moment of triumph for Mattes. "May he be the comfort of our life," he said to Sarah, his wife. And despite a multitude of subsequent calamities, including the death of Sarah (once again in childbirth), Mattes continued to construct a future upon dreams of Nachman's achievements. . . . But in *East of Eden* no dreams are destined to be fulfilled, least of all those of Mattes, or of Nachman in his turn, who imagines a similar reception in the Soviet Union. Mattes was even denied a Jewish funeral, despite all his precautions. When he was conscripted to fight for Russia in the Great War he wrote the following words upon a piece of canvas which he sewed on his fringed ritual garment, worn next to his skin. "I am Mattathias, son of Arye Judah Mattes, of the congregation of Warsaw. He that finds my body let him bring it to a Jewish grave." But Mattes was killed in his first skirmish and dumped in a mass grave.

> He was thrown along with the rest into a shallow pit, quicklime was poured on all of them, and the common grave was covered hastily. An officer put up a rough cross, made of two branches; he peeled away the bark from one side of the upright, took out a pencil, and, wetting it several times between his lips, wrote out: "Glory to the heroes who have fallen for Czar and fatherland."
>
> (pp. 122-26)

There is no doubt that *East of Eden* lacks the exhilarating dizziness found in works where the artist is taking risks with his powers, but it fulfils another important function—it bears witness. It is moving, rather than exciting. (p. 137)

There is a Jewish curse, "May his name be blotted out." The reverse is Yad Vashem, literally "A Place and a Name," a memorial to the lost Jews of Europe, where the Israelis have attempted to gather in the names of all those murdered by the Nazis. By this tragic route a majority of the Jews of Joshua's generation found their promised land at last. Joshua himself was dead by then, but these words from *The Family Carnovsky* demonstrate that he knew what those Jews who remained in Europe could expect, "The youths in boots had meant it when they sang in the streets about spilling Jewish blood. To them, these were not mere lyrics, as the inhabitants of West Berlin had assumed. With each passing day more blood dripped from their daggers — drop after drop after drop." Indeed, it is possible to see each of Joshua's novels as

a systematic destruction of Jewish hopes; in every one a bit more of the ground collapses beneath their feet, or promises evaporate into thin air. These promised lands are no mirages, but a variety of hells. Finally, even enlightenment itself proves false. For Berlin, the headquarters of enlightenment, becomes the capital of the New Order. In *East of Eden* Joshua rarely used Stalin's name, preferring references such as Great Leader, and in *The Family Carnovsky* he managed to write a novel about the rise of Nazism in Germany without mentioning Hitler's name at all. When he is described for the only time, it is as a "scowling little man with the slack mouth and the mad, baggy eyes." This description, with its suggestion of spiritual weakness, physical deformity, and psychological infirmity, is representative of Joshua's treatment of all Nazis in the novel; they are failures (Hugo Holbeck), impotents (Dr. Kirchenmeir), or homosexuals (Dr. Zerbe), the remainder being typically thugs or whores. Even Jegor Carnovsky's attraction to Nazism is explained as a perverse result of neurosis; he is not misguided, like Nachman, but confused. Daniel has no equivalent in *The Family Carnovsky,* there is no eloquent champion of National Socialism. And although Joshua again hints at the irresistible charm of the mass movement, he is not anxious to give a rational account of its appeal to decent Germans. Thus one of the few sympathetic Germans, Frau Holbeck, soon regrets her support for the Nazis, which she attributes to mesmerism. "In the excitement that had attended the elections, when the city had been full of music and proclamations and oratory, she had been hypnotized into following the trend in favor of the men in boots who had promised prosperity and the reestablishment of a strong and vigorous Germany. . . . Yes, she had been tricked into voting for the New Order and she was ashamed." In general Joshua is unforgiving, and there is no doubt that the sentiments of Von Spahnsattel (an anti-Nazi) are his own: "You Jews still don't know us Germans. You keep on seeing us through your Semitic eyes. But I know my own people only too well because I am one of them. *Zum Wiedersehen,* Klein. God have mercy on you." As he speaks Von Spahnsattel's "steely eyes" fill with "anger and contempt." Joshua, likewise, did not spare his fellow Jews; the aforementioned Klein, who ignored Von Spahnsattel's advice to leave Germany before it was too late, ended up as a jar of ashes on display in his widow's apartment in New York.

But *The Family Carnovsky* is not a catalogue of the evils of Nazism, rather it is an attack upon the folly of enlightenment. Although the adherents of Nazism might be perverts, the phenomenon is not shown as an aberration, but as a logical consequence of history. Nazism merely confirmed all Joshua's fears of mass movements, which sanctified the brutal and bestial aspects of humanity, and habitually picked the Jews as scapegoats. His anger was directed at those enlightened Jews who refused to recognize the inevitability of the process; and it consequently involved a reconsideration of his own position. This reflected the times; *De mishpokhe Karnovski* was published in Yiddish in 1943 (the first English edition did not appear until 1969). Aaron Zeitlin — one of the few men Bashevis admires without reservation — gave this summary of Joshua's mood: "The outward conditions of his life were good. To the world he appeared as a man satisfied with his achievement. Yet the illusion of the 'broad world' had long since vanished from the mind of the wise Singer, and only an inner bitterness replaced it."

The conflict between father and son, between tradition and enlightenment, conditioned the careers of Joshua and

Bashevis, and continued to influence their writing. Indeed, Joshua often used the family as a metaphor for Jewish history, until his interest in its internal relationships came to dominate his passion for external events. The two continued to be interrelated, of course, but the balance was different; Joshua had taken Nachman's lesson to heart. In *The Brothers Ashkenazi* the decline of the Ashkenazi family, from the stern patriarch through his assimilated sons to his semi-apostate grandson, was one of the many movements related to the development of Lodz; however, it became the dialectic of *The Family Carnovsky,* which was accordingly divided into three books, "David," "Georg," and "Jegor." The examples of communism and fascism convinced Joshua that it was impossible to change the world, all that remained was to protect the family. And as the Jews had to take the hostility of the world for granted, they could only turn to each other for security. When David Carnovsky is reconciled to his son he says, "Be of courage, my son, as I am and as are all the men of our generation. We have borne persecution since the beginning of time and we shall continue to bear it, as Jews always have." Without a family a Jew is destined to be an outcast, doomed to loneliness. (pp. 141-43)

The course of *The Family Carnovsky* seems to mimic the fate of Berlin's Jews; it begins leisurely, as if it has all the time in the world, expanding into the numerous sub-plots an epic format allows, fooling itself, like the Jews of Berlin, that the end is nowhere in sight. But then, abruptly, all the stories evaporate, as though only one really mattered: the Nazi persecution of the Jews. Joshua seemed to be turning his back on fiction, just as David Carnovsky abandoned enlightenment. When David set upon Dr. Speier in Sha Mora Synagogue he all but accused him of hiding the truth about Germany's treatment of the Jews with the words: "This is the time to speak, even to shout, Rabbi Speier." But Dr. Speier was horrified at the thought, it was a "private affair . . . not one to be dragged through the streets . . . before strangers and outsiders." For Dr. Speier did not want to put ideas into the heads of Americans, or want them to think he was connected with Asiatic Jews. Of course David was wiser, "We are all Jews . . . regardless of whether we come from Frankfurt or Tarnopol!" David had no time for the foolish intrigues of his one-time mentors, just as Joshua eschewed the frivolities of fiction; both were left with one object: to rage against the Nazis. David became more and more the Melnitz Jew he once despised, and Joshua took his talent back to Leoncin. His last book was *Of a World That Is No More.*

Israel Joshua Singer died in New York City on 10 February 1944. Bashevis called this "the greatest misfortune of my entire life. He was my father, my teacher. I never really recovered from this blow. There was only one consolation— whatever would happen later would never be as bad as this." (p. 157)

Bashevis was unable to abandon the illicit joys of literature. "Certainly, if my brother would have lived another twenty or thirty years, which he should have, he would have developed more and more, and he would have published stunning books—I'm absolutely convinced of that." (p. 160)

Clive Sinclair, in his The Brothers Singer, *Allison & Busby, 1983, 176 p.*

ADDITIONAL BIBLIOGRAPHY

Asch, Nathan. "City of Moloch." *The New Republic* 88, No. 1138 (23 September 1936): 190.

Praises *The Brothers Ashkenazi* for its vivid depiction of the rise and fall of Lodz and the corresponding fortunes of the protagonists.

Burra, Peter. Review of *The Brothers Ashkenazi,* by I. J. Singer. *The Spectator* 157, No. 5651 (16 October 1936): 654.

Praises the completeness of Singer's depiction of the history of a family and of a city in *The Brothers Ashkenazi.*

Cournos, John. "Three Novelists: Asch, Singer, and Schnéour." *The Menorah Journal* 25, No. 1 (Winter 1937): 81-91.

Compares *The Brothers Ashkenazi* with Sholem Asch's *Three Cities,* contrasting the extensive span of time covered in Singer's novel with the vast space dealt with in Asch's. Cournos pronounces Singer's "factual deliberateness" his chief distinguishing characteristic.

Howe, Irving. "The Yiddish Word: Yiddish Fiction in America" and "The Yiddish Theatre: Art and Trash" in his *World of Our Fathers,* pp. 445-51, pp. 485-92. New York: Harcourt Brace Jovanovich, 1976.

Briefly refers to *The Brothers Ashkenazi* as one of the first novels to fully treat the changes in Jewish life after the emigration from Eastern European villages to large Western cities. The second chapter cited mentions Maurice Schwartz's stage adaptation of *Yoshe Kalb,* calling the production a muddled combination of Schwartz's "best and worst, his gift for sharply evoking Jewish traditionalism and his exploitation of Jewish sentimentalism."

Kresh, Paul. *Isaac Bashevis Singer: The Magician of West 86th Street.* New York: Dial Press, 1979, 441 p.

Includes discussion of Israel Joshua Singer's life and critical commentary on his novels. Kresh provides a close study of the relationship between the brothers.

Kronenberger, Louis. "In Soviet Russia." *The New York Times Book Review* (12 March 1939): 7.

Review of *East of Eden,* assessing the first half of the novel as a fairly typical family chronicle, but contending that the novel becomes overly didactic and melodramatic in its second half.

Landis, Joseph C. "The Brothers Singer: Faith and Doubt." In *Blood Brothers: Siblings as Writers,* edited by Norman Kiell, pp. 365-82. New York: International Universities Press, 1983.

Contrasts Israel Joshua Singer's rejection of Jewish traditions with Isaac Bashevis Singer's acceptance of them.

Liptzin, Sol. "Novelists of Poland." In his *The Maturing of Yiddish Literature,* pp. 152-70. New York: Jonathan David, 1970.

Briefly outlines Singer's career, attributing his success outside of Poland to the dramatization of his novels on the New York stage.

Prawer, S. S. "The First Family of Yiddish." *The Times Literary Supplement,* No. 4178 (29 April 1983): 419-20.

Discusses several books by and about the Singer family, focusing upon Israel Joshua Singer and Isaac Bashevis Singer and mentioning their sister, Esther Kreitman, who also published a novel.

Rahv, Philip. "The Jews of Lodz." *The Nation* 143, No. 11 (12 September 1936): 310-11.

Review of *The Brothers Ashkenazi,* praising Singer for writing of contemporary Jewish experience and not the dying traditions that occupy much Yiddish literature. Rahv concludes by pronouncing *The Brothers Ashkenazi* "the most important novel of Jewish life published in English."

Ravitch, Melech. "Israel Joshua Singer: On the 25th Anniversary of His Death." *Jewish Book Annual* 26 (1968-69): 121-23.

Tribute to Singer's life and works.

Ribalow, Harold U., and Singer, Isaac Bashevis. "Isaac Bashevis Singer — Nobel Prize Winner 1978: An Interview." *Midstream* 25, No. 1 (January 1979): 30-8.

Interview in which I. B. Singer denies that his own career developed "under the shadow" of his novelist brother.

Roback, A. A. "Recent Yiddish Prose in America." In his *The Story of Yiddish Literature,* pp. 298-321. New York: Yiddish Scientific Institute, 1940.

Briefly outlines Singer's literary career.

Schneider, Isidor. Review of *The Sinner,* by I. J. Singer. *New York Herald Tribune Books* 9, No. 30 (2 April 1933): 9.

Commends Singer's portrayal of "the loud, disorderly, half-primitive world of the Chassidic Jew," which "makes *The Sinner,* in spite of mediocre characterization and lusterless style, a novel of distinction, exciting to read."

Siegel, Ben. "The Brothers Singer: More Similarities than Differences." *Contemporary Literature* 22, No. 1 (Winter 1981): 42-57.

Focuses on the treatment of traditional shtetl culture in the fiction and nonfiction of Israel Joshua and Isaac Bashevis Singer.

Singer, Isaac Bashevis. Introduction to *Yoshe Kalb,* by I. J. Singer, pp. v-x. New York: Harper & Row, 1965.

Details Israel Joshua Singer's temporary abandonment of Yiddish literature and his return to it with the successful novel *Yoshe Kalb.*

————. *In My Father's Court.* New York: Farrar, Straus and Giroux, 1966, 307 p.

Episodic memoir including several chapters devoted to Israel Joshua Singer.

Strauss, Harold. "After the Ghetto." *The Nation* 148, No. 12 (18 March 1939): 326-28.

Contends that the detailed account of Yiddish culture in *East of Eden* would have rendered it a fine novel had Singer not abandoned his "patient, creative" literary methods in order to introduce "political pamphleteering" into the novel.

Paul van Ostaijen

1896-1928

(Also spelled Ostayen) Belgian poet, short story writer, critic, essayist, and scriptwriter.

Van Ostaijen is important for introducing into Flemish literature the artistic theories and techniques of the modern movements of Expressionism and Dada. Unlike Belgian authors writing in French, those who wrote in the Flemish language were relatively isolated from the climate of experimentalism and radical ideologies that characterized early twentieth-century European literature. In the poetry, fiction, and critical essays of Van Ostaijen, Flemish Belgium was first exposed to writing that reflected much of the spirit and style of the time, particularly the nihilist sensibility inspired by the horror and chaos of the First World War.

Van Ostaijen was born and grew up in Antwerp. From 1914 to 1918 he worked as a municipal clerk in that city, and during this time published his first two collections of poems: *Music-Hall,* which was significant as the earliest expression in Flemish poetry of modern city life, and *Het sienjaal,* which introduced the humanist doctrines of the early Expressionists into Flemish letters. As a center of Flemish culture at the end of the nineteenth century, Antwerp was a focal point of social and political friction with the more powerful, though not more numerous, French-speaking population of Belgium. Around the turn of the century a movement gained force among Flemish speakers to strengthen their cultural identity and enhance their position in Belgian society. The German occupation of Belgium during World War I only served to increase tensions in that country, especially after the Germans enforced the turnover of Ghent University from the control of a French-speaking to a Flemish-speaking administration. Although Van Ostaijen was only marginally active in the Flemish cause, he fled to Berlin at the end of the war to avoid the persecution suffered by other members of the movement. This self-exile, which lasted from 1918 to 1921, was crucial to his artistic and intellectual development. In Berlin Van Ostaijen became acquainted with artists and writers of the Expressionist movement, particularly those associated with the periodical *Der Sturm,* and the German faction of Dada. The influence of these movements is reflected in the two collections of poems he wrote during this time, *De feesten van angst en pijn* (*Feasts of Fear and Agony*) and *Bezette stad,* which display the widespread sense of despair and outrage kindled by the chaotic milieu of postwar Berlin, as well as exhibiting the experimental poetic subjects and techniques that evolved in response to a pulverized social order. After he returned to Belgium in 1921, Van Ostaijen worked as a journalist and continued to mature as a writer, formulating a conception of "pure poetry" independent of the personality of the poet based on theories that were current during his years in Berlin. Suffering from tuberculosis, Van Ostaijen died in 1928 at the age of thirty-two.

Van Ostaijen's most important work began with the poems in *Feasts of Fear and Agony.* While his previous collection, *Het sienjaal,* celebrated human life and the potential for universal harmony, the "feasts" of the later poems commemorate their author's disillusionment with life and human na-

Paul van Ostaijen with the daughter of Oskar Jespers, July 1923.

ture, obsessively revolving around themes of violence, hatred, and decay. More significant to Van Ostaijen's development, both personally and artistically, was his next collection, *Bezette stad.* The "occupied city" of the title is Antwerp during the First World War, and the poems of the volume are devoted to various aspects and experiences of the occupation, as is illustrated by such titles as "The Shell above the City," "Zeppelin," "Empty Cinema," and "Dead Sunday." In portraying these scenes of the occupation, Van Ostaijen employed devices associated with Dadaist poetry—inserting phrases from advertisements and popular songs, using dramatically dissimilar typefaces, arranging words to create visual designs on the page, and juxtaposing different languages. Critics observe that these poems capture the disorienting effect of a world in which all order and value are absent and meaningless conflict takes place in an ultimately inane universe. However, Van Ostaijen noted that the negative vision that predominated in *Bezette stad* served as an avenue rather than a dead end in his progress as a poet. As he later wrote: "The nihilism of *Bezette stad* cured me of a dishonesty which I mistook for honesty and of extra-lyrical pathos. After that, I became just an ordinary poet." Van Ostaijen's later poems, collected in *Gedichten,* exemplify theories he elaborated in a series of essays. At this point in his artistic life he had become concerned with poetry as "word art," emphasizing individual words as elements in the creation of an aesthetic object in the manner that a painter uses colors to compose an integrated image. Paul Hadermann has observed that Van Ostaijen's "later poems were disindividualized, lyrical objects made of words. They appealed to the subconscious of the readers, beyond their own individualities. All the poet's efforts were concentrated on making those poems efficient, on giving a new fresh value to their words, musically and plastically. This was Van Ostaijen's 'word art'."

Along with his poetic works, Van Ostaijen also wrote what he described as "grotesques"—short stories that feature fantastic characters and incidents and that are often satirical in intent, sardonically mocking politicians, nationalists, warmongers, and various conventional figures of society. Among his other works is the Dadaist filmscript *Bankruptcy Jazz,* which shares in the same qualities that critics have found of greatest value in Van Ostaijen's poetry—an inventive and pointed expression of the defining crises of both twentieth-century life and literature. As Hidde Van Ameyden van Duym has attested: "To read Van Ostaijen is to find not only astute comprehension of what a modern age required to be written but also one man's amalgamation of the problems of that age."

PRINCIPAL WORKS

Music-Hall (poetry) 1916
Het sienjaal (poetry) 1918
Bezette stad (poetry) 1921
De trust der vaderlandsliefde (short stories) 1925
Het bordeel van Ika Loch (short stories) 1926
Gedichten (poetry) 1928
Vogelvrij (short stories) 1928
Het eerste boek van Schmoll (poetry) 1929
Krities proza. 2 vols. (essays and criticism) 1929-31
*Verzameld werk. 4 vols. (poetry, short stories, essays, criticism, and filmscript) 1952-56
Patriotism, Inc., and Other Tales (short stories and filmscript) 1971
Feasts of Fear and Agony (poetry) 1976
The First Book of Schmoll: Selected Poems 1920-1928 (poetry) 1982

*This edition of Van Ostaijen's collected works includes the first publication of *De feesten van angst en pijn* (*Feasts of Fear and Agony*), which Van Ostaijen completed in 1921.

PAUL VAN OSTAIJEN   (essay date 1922?)

[*In the following essay, Van Ostaijen offers an impressionistic sketch of his life.*]

I was born. This must be accepted, although absolutely objective proof cannot be produced. It is an axiom in the domain of subjective experience. Objectively it is only conjecture. Hence: were we born? Observe. Touch. But laugh at how little convincing this proof is. I ask: who was really born?

Yet: I was born. In spite of well-founded doubt, I must also doubt this doubt. The human function seems determined from the beginning as a doubt of doubt.

When two years old: a railroad accident. With exception of subconscious fears there were no bad results. In the serious struggle for life I meditated this with bitterness. My life started with derailment. As a result it is understandable that I always look at life from this point of view: how do I derail most profitably? After all, I, being early derailed, cannot doubt that the human being exists in order to derail. Was this derailment reality? Or was it perhaps only the localization of a precocious desire to derail? Or rather was it a vague remembrance of a very early "Alpdruck" ["nightmare"]?

My family dreamed: musical child prodigy. No talent, however. But circumstances were extremely favorable. Played football only once. Sufficiently in order to retain a scar of 1 × 4 inches. I do not play football *anymore.* Gentlemen, I am a victim of the sport.

After a careless life I attempted to exist in Berlin, Potsdam and Spandau. Not romantic. It would be fantasy to say that I made it from liftboy to owner of a nightclub. I am much too primitive to occupy a prominent place in society. Despite my yearning to reach the level of the Flemish decadents, I understand my "Unfähigkeit" ["incapacity"]. When I was about to be appointed professor in rhythmic-typographical poetry, I had to decline because I did not possess a frock coat. Wish I possessed a frock coat. In the grip of the struggle for life I was cigarette peddler and bouncer (Schlepper) at a striptease nightclub. Finally I found a respectable occupation through recommendation of a prominent art critic: salesman in a shoe shop, ladies' department. Hence strong influence. *Viz.:* "sickle leg," "sidereal pendulum" = influence shoeshop department L.

I was very happy with this excellent situation, but gazed westward with a certain melancholy. Le bonheur est fait d'un je-ne-sais-quoi melancolique. Brussels. Oh, to see once more this city of luxury. To die with the bliss of a Brussels bar in perspective. O Wonne.

Published three books: *Music-Hall, The Signal, Occupied City.* Perhaps also this is mere mass hypnosis. Who can prove he read these books? Let alone: understood. God forbid: understood. I myself did not understand them. (pp. 176-77)

> *Paul Van Ostaijen, "Autobiography," translated by Hidde Van Ameyden van Duym, in* Poetry, *Vol. CIV, No. 3, June, 1964, pp. 176-77.*

HIDDE VAN AMEYDEN VAN DUYM   (essay date 1964)

[*In the following excerpt, Van Duym provides an overview of Van Ostaijen's work.*]

In 1916 [Van Ostaijen published] his first collection of poems, called *Music-Hall.* It is an uneven collection which shows left-over influences from the Dutch "Poets of 1880" and new influences from Jules Romains' Unanimism. The latter influences become strongest in his following collection, called *The Signal* (1918). The poems are pervaded with the spirit of a person who seeks to subserve a social ideal. Also there are poems devoted to Van Gogh, Ensor, Else Lasker-Schüler, Jammes and Schwob. (p. 177)

[Between 1918 and 1920, Van Ostaijen produced] a series of grotesques, essays, a roman-à-clef about European politics, a film scenario, two manifestos, and two poetic cycles entitled *Feasts of Fear and Agony* and *Occupied City.* A look at this work shows Van Ostaijen in all his powers. The essays no more recapitulate, but formulate his own approach to the work of art. He speaks of the "aseity" of a work of art, which is "an organism, individual in the original sense of the word: in itself, indivisible." The grotesques are comparable to Kafka both in form and content, but he writes them at a time when nothing was known of Kafka. Later on, Van Ostaijen is the first to translate any of Kafka's work before this is done in England, France, or Spain. As far as his poetry is concerned, it shows that Van Ostaijen has found the age within himself. The poems are unmistakably Van Ostaijen in their sound and in their peculiar combination of paradoxical images. *Feasts of Fear and Agony* are a mystical attempt to find a meaning behind the paradoxical images, while *Occupied City* is a ruthless exposition of the meaninglessness of paradoxical images. . . .

Sarcastically he turns to other poets: "All right gentlemen, I am only amusing myself, while you, cosmic poets, are changing the nature of the world." In a lecture called **"Directions for the Use of Poetry,"** he explains the principles of his new search: "Against the demonic lyricism nothing *a priori* compositional can hold its place. The lyrical bacterium is a glutton which eats everything it meets on its way. The logicality of a poem can only be measured by the logicality of the organic development between beginning and end." He speaks of the poet as a craftsman, "a sorcerer, who carries the people into an imaginative atmosphere of the occult." (p. 178)

The real interest in Van Ostaijen arises from the fact that he is a critic with an astonishing grasp of both French and German literature and painting, but more particularly because he is a modern poet with a voice of his own.

To read Van Ostaijen is to find not only astute comprehension of what a modern age required to be written but also one man's amalgamation of the problems of that age. (p. 179)

Hidde Van Ameyden van Duym, "Paul Van Ostaijen: An Introduction," in Poetry, *Vol. CIV, No. 3, June, 1964, pp. 177-79.*

E. M. BEEKMAN (essay date 1970)

[*Beekman is a Dutch-born American fiction writer, poet, critic, and translator. He has translated collections of Van Ostaijen's poetry and prose and has provided the most extensive commentary in English on Van Ostaijen's works. In the following excerpt, Beekman explicates Van Ostaijen's theory and practice of the grotesque in his prose.*]

Paul van Ostaijen is an astonishing phenomenon in literature. Grudgingly condoned by the literary Establishment in his own country while he was alive, writing in a language few people know and the majority still consider some curious off-shoot of German, Van Ostaijen reflects in his work many literary, artistic and intellectual developments which only recently have become legitimate. With a bare minimum of schooling, he became one of the most erudite and advanced artists of his time. His lyricism reflects the stylistic revolutions of Mallarmé, Apollinaire, Stramm, and of the Expressionistic, Dadaistic and Surrealistic movements. . . . The work of Paul van Ostaijen must finally take its place in the forefront of modern Western literature.

The following examination of Van Ostaijen's grotesques, although primarily concerned with a descriptive analysis of the Flemish writer's art, is intended to give a concurrent description of what may be called the *modern* or *contemporary* gro-

tesque. Most critics of this genre generally formulate their views on the basis of material provided them by eighteenth and nineteenth century authors. However, in the fiction produced since the Second World War (particularly during the Fifties and Sixties), a strong resurgence of the grotesque has appeared. (pp. 12-13)

In the modern grotesque . . . there is little escape into morality, beauty, the sublime, but there is rather the desperate attempt to render the *essential* absurdity of the world which confronts the author. Van Ostaijen called it the world's basic *verkeerdheid*. . . . (p. 14)

At the time they were written a relatively singular phenomenon, Van Ostaijen's grotesques can now be understood in the light of both a "traditional" development and such a contemporary development as modern American fiction. For an American audience, it might provide a basis for comparison to juxtapose the Flemish writer with such current authors as Joseph Heller, Thomas Pynchon, William S. Burroughs, James Purdy, Kurt Vonnegut Jr., John Barth and Donald Barthelme. In England comparisons may be made with Harold Pinter's theatre and screenplays, Samuel Beckett, Tom Stoppard, and aspects of the work of Anthony Burgess, Iris Murdoch and Muriel Spark. . . . [There] are several important contemporary writers of the grotesque in the German language: Friedrich Dürrenmatt, Günter Grass, Max Frisch and, at times, Heinrich Böll.

One may well ask whether any of these authors who illustrate the theory of entropy in their work have anything left to believe in. When one is preoccupied with a fictional homeopathy of the absurd (*similia similibus curantur* ["like cures like"]), what constant could possibly survive? Leslie Fiedler provides the correct answer in his [*No! in Thunder* (1960)].

> In the end, the negativist is no nihilist, for he affirms the void. Having endured a vision of the meaninglessness of existence, he retreats neither into self-pity and aggrieved silence nor into a realm of beautiful lies. He chooses, rather, to render the absurdity which he perceives, to know it and make it known. To know and to render, however, mean to give form; and to give form is to provide the possibility of delight—a delight which does not deny horror but lives at its intolerable heart.
>
> (pp. 16-17)

[Van Ostaijen's essay on Breughel reveals his] reflections on the world of the grotesque. For his own purposes the essay tried to rectify stereotyped erroneous interpretations of Breughel's work. . . . (pp. 18-19)

The key tone of pessimism is struck in the introductory paragraph. Van Ostaijen insists that Breughel's work does not celebrate Flemish sensuality. On the contrary, a confrontation with Breughel's work should instill in the viewer "the bitter knowledge of the emptiness of human effort." Breughel teaches the "platonic-pessimistic acceptance of futility" and "the hopelessness of action and chaos-creating human restlessness." These three utterances are slightly modified variations on the central theme of resigned pessimism, which negates the world and human action in a consistent fashion. Van Ostaijen's pessimism is not an artificial pose, but is basic to both his life and work. In a letter from Berlin (April, 1919) he confesses his pessimistic intentions in the grotesques. "Wrote a novella in which I try to make monkeys of people. Positive criticism: baloney. Now I like novellas in which you can fool around so marvelously. People aren't worth criticizing. Only material for burlesque novellas." The tale **"Jus primae noctis"** may be seen as a condensed record of Van Ostaijen's nihilism. In this story, where fictional elements have been stripped to a bare, somewhat Platonic dialogue, Van Ostaijen's *persona* confesses: "Pessimism in itself as a view of life would be deliverance for me. And a great wealth. This I cannot have. Everything has become flat for me, because I did not desire the abstract consistently. Consider this pessimism with comparisons oriented to the world at large. Everything is such a pitiful mess."

Speaking about his lyricism, Van Ostaijen uses terms similar to those in his discussion of Breughel's work. Van Ostaijen's pessimism—more a tempered nihilism reminiscent of Alfred de Vigny and the Flemish poet Maurice Gilliams—does not however degrade itself into breastbeating, anarchy or destructive rebellion, but simply sees life's futility as a condition and accepts its consequences. Futility and the insuffiency of expression are central to his art. Inability of language ever to catch satisfactorily the most profound pattern which underlies our lives and environment, as well as the futility of man's endeavors, is contained in the following passage from a key-essay on the uses of poetry.

> Poetry does not originate only from the daemonic, but also from the shock between the daemonic force of the word and the awareness of the hopelessness of every human attempt at formulation. Between these two: the will to express and the hopelessness of expression there is a constant interaction and perhaps often strife. And the more one gains possession of the means which allow one to catch the daemonic on the surface, the more one begins to doubt the effectiveness, the absolute truth of these means. As far as consciousness can exercise its power, the daemonic ultimately yields to hopelessness and this reality, valid for me, I can already illustrate with the fact that, for me, no poem about the phenomenon "fish" could ever be more powerful than this word *fish* itself.

One might easily predict, given the symptoms, an artistic impotence, a turning away from life—contemplating the Empedoclean crater's edge. Van Ostaijen, like most modern artists who see their art through a glass darkly, bravely instituted faith in the creative act. They recognize the fact that creation may negate, or at least neutralize, the spectre of depression. For, says Van Ostaijen, "the lyrical emotion is a negation of a pessimistic view of life."

Other important premises are implied in the essay's first paragraph. An element of frustration, hidden in the diction, indicates a residual aggression which prevents total apathy. Frustration is the kinetic force of his grotesques. With vehement indignation, Van Ostaijen attacks the prevailing notion that Breughel reveled in bawdy and gross sensuality. In his discourse on Breughel's style and vision, which runs counter to the Rabelaisian stereotype, Van Ostaijen delineates his own peculiar view of narrative fiction. The artist is an impartial observer of the world's folly. Van Ostaijen stresses the formality, objectivity and cerebrality of Breughel's art. The artist distances himself from the world he depicts. "And even in his *Peasant Wedding* or in his early *Dutch Proverbs,* does one not see the distance which separates the painter from this world, does one not see with how much objectivity he faces these events, almost as if all this belonged to the goings on of a species alien to him." The notions of estrangement and

alienation which Van Ostaijen implies in the last clause are equally basic to his own narrative fiction. A *Verfremdungseffekt* ["alienation effect"] emanates from the consistent objectivity. A sequential series of related concepts can be derived from the basic divorce between artist and subject. Soon technique and content of Breughel's antithetical art run parallel courses in Van Ostaijen's discussion.

Breughel, according to Van Ostaijen, does not take part in the peasant vulgarity he depicts. Disjunction between the artist and his product follows from a critical scepticism. The act of creation is an extraneous one. No longer is the artist and his subject the creative symbiosis familiar from the Romantic era: "Breughel himself is not at home in his paintings." Neither rejecting nor accepting, the artist notes in a neutral fashion the object of his interest. The object constitutes the notation; the notations are a stenographic record of a world awry. Van Ostaijen does perceive, but almost begrudgingly, a minimal amount of involvement on the part of Breughel. "At the most one could say of Breughel that he is amused by the grotesqueness of the object of this notation, but he is not delighted by it as much as Swift amuses himself in the notation of the follies Gulliver gradually discovers in people, nor does he, indeed, even less than Swift who was more apostolic, have any relation to this world of absurdity." This statement, couched in Van Ostaijen's peculiar yet subtle style and finely nuanced thought, obliquely comments on the curious brand of humor in a tale of the grotesque. Previously he had negatively asserted that one is not amused by the grotesque condition. Now he proceeds to qualify this statement. The nature of the notation may betray a grim amusement on the part of artist, but he cannot be said to disport himself. The latter would obviously constitute involvement and a certain sense of agreement. Such a relationship would be contradictory to the axiomatic negation of the object and its rendition. Van Ostaijen also refutes the contention that there is a moralizing force in Breughel's paintings; he feels that, intrinsically, the grotesque work of art does not moralize. But Van Ostaijen is somewhat dogmatically inclusive here. Surely, if the artist does not include an ethical norm within the autonomous work itself, this does not mean the exclusion of a critical interpretation of the completed body of work. The image on the retina makes no judgment; the mental verdict lies in the focus. Choice betrays involvement.

Van Ostaijen makes exteriorization a central feature of Breughel's art, as he already had made it of his own work. Breughel, he feels, remained objective and at a distance from what he created. Hence the exterior reality he creates is an inevitable result of the medium of painting and the subject, but it does not betray the artist's own personality. The work of art remains master within its own domain. "Le seul aspect mystérieux que présente 'l'extérieur' est une conséquence du fait qu'il n'est pas autre chose qu'extériorisation. Représenter l'extérieur sans l'extériorisation équivaut à la représentation d'une fausse réalité: imprimer des billets de banque sur du papier de journal. Peindre cet extérieur multiplié avec la conscience qu'il n'est pas autre chose qu'extériorisation, c'est peindre vrai et représenter un mystère exact" ["The only mysterious aspect presented by 'the external' is the fact that it is nothing other than exteriorization. To represent the external without exteriorization is equivalent to the representation of a false representation of a false reality: to imprint bank notes upon newspaper. To paint this manifold exterior with the consciousness that it is nothing other than exteriorization, is to paint authentically and to represent an exact mystery"]. In literature as well as painting, Van Ostaijen wants to establish an impersonal art; the gauge for such an art-form is disindividualization. This concept is repeatedly alluded to in the essays. Cubism, as Van Ostaijen charts its course, had advanced artistic expression from a "subjective-revolutionary" period to a modern, superior one of disindividualization. In a manifesto for a periodical which never saw the light but which was to have been the organ for "emancipated Cubism" or "organic Expressionism," the three central preoccupations of Van Ostaijen's theoretical writings are summarized in a few sentences: the work of art as an organism, its autonomous existence, and the disindividualization of the artist. "The work of art is an organism. *The work of art is a living entity.* As such it is *in itself* individual in the primary sense of the word, in itself indivisible. The task, therefore, from the point of view of the artist is: disindividualization."

Particularly in the case of poetry, this endeavor should result in anonymity of the work of art, in a true communality of art. Communal art does not necessarily mean an art comprehensible to the masses, but is more a formulation of a striving for disindividualization. Communal art, therefore, stands for a wide application of the desire to set the work of art free, to accept it on its own terms without the interference of the artist's personality. Not the poet, but the poem is important. The immediate analogy which comes to Van Ostaijen's mind is the anonymous literature of nursery rimes, ancient ballads and folk songs. A modern form which would emulate those nameless folk artists should intensify the objectivity of expression and of the artist's personality in such a way that the poem, and the poem alone, will demand attention while its creator remains a nameless artificer; ". . . one must strive for a poetry which would be the popular lyricism made by poets one step higher, these are poets whose awareness of the esthetic is *a priori* greater than that of the folk poet."

The style of the grotesques stresses an objectivity of expression. Van Ostaijen remains in most cases an impersonal recorder of a world of absolute folly. The unifying style of the grotesques and their abstract quality only force all the more attention on the subject of an incongruous world. Naturally, in the grotesques the subject is more important than in the poems, and the manner of the exposition forces the reader to continually reevaluate their common denominator of folly; the various manifestations of this essential vision, be it sex, chauvinism or counterfeiting, are merely refractions of this basic theme. The grotesques are the negative expressions of the poetic theory. While Van Ostaijen strove in his poetry for pure lyricism, he attempted to express with similar means (subject to the modifications of prose) an objective configuration of a negative world; i.e., stripped of an author's individual intrusions. As does the poetry, the grotesques establish their own autonomous microcosm by eliminating the author from its independent domain.

An immediate negative response to these theoretical concepts might be the accusation of inertia. In his lyrics, Van Ostaijen wanted to create tension through the printer's blank spaces in various controlled distances between components of a line of verse. The measure of separation was for him the tension between two parts in a lyrical line divided by the white space. Lyrical tension was either assonance or dissonance; dissonance he felt to be self-explanatory, while he described the effect of assonance as either strengthening or neutralizing the preceding element in a line of verse. The fixity of the prose

tales gives them a tension-quotient of their own. Their apparent immobility reveals, at closer examination, an inner dynamism; tension results from combining their architectonic modality of style and their latent chaos. Van Ostaijen describes this phenomenon in a discussion of James Ensor's paintings of masks.

> In his imagination he posits objects which, with the artist's obvious approval, stiffen in the most comical rigidity. Outwardly there is no more pronounced immobility than these stupid masks. All the features are rigid; each mask is a death-mask. But when one looks more closely at the works than in normal comfort, one comes very soon to the conclusion that this stiff outer rigidity has been willed for the strong antagonism with a very carefully thought-out inner dynamism. This antagonism is carried out down to the most insignificant details.

The point which must be reiterated again and again is that Van Ostaijen insists that what seems to us superficially incommensurate with our traditional notions of enjoyment only appears so because the work of art is not to be experienced according to a set of preconceived individual notions. The work of art is *einfach existent* ["simply existent"] in and for itself. Our sphere of reference must be shifted from a personal conglomeration of culturally conditioned reflexes to the organic existence and separate legality of the work of art *an sich* ["in itself"]. *Verfremdung* ["alienation"], in this sense, is merely a severance of the artist and his product. The sympathetic umbilical cord has been cut, and the created product lives on its own, a planet in its own galaxy. This is probably the reason for the pedagogic bent of Van Ostaijen's essays. The new movement in art demands a reeducation of its audience in terms of the individual work of art, which has its own laws, proportions, and relationships, and the movement tries to eradicate the usual identification of the artist's existence as expressed in his work. *Einfach existent.* The hermetic, self-sufficient world of the poem, painting, or grotesque has a democracy all its own. The most contradictory forces are relevant within the totality of the creative autocracy.

Van Ostaijen's philosophical speculations about Breughel's art tempts the reader to see parallel profundities in Van Ostaijen's work. But this problematic relevance would be more applicable to his poetry than his prose; noting that the latter's predominant theme is that of a world out of joint, must suffice here. Speculation about Platonic connotations in the tales would needlessly complicate the relative simplicity of their meaning. This is not to deny that the tales invite speculations of this sort. The very incommensurability of the grotesque world invites speculation about the X-factor of the equation—incommensurable with what? Negation prefigures ideality. But the world of the grotesque restricts itself to quintessential otherness—a *de facto* condition. However, certain terms in Van Ostaijen's essay are quite relevant to this discussion. Nature and the world of man are sharply divided in Breughel; one is reason, the other irrationality. Basic incommensurability between man's endeavors and an ideal (in the case of Breughel, primordial nature) is amplified throughout the essay. In terms of the grotesque, it is one of its basic features. A chasm, a sense of nil, permanently separates the grotesque world of consistent otherness from the X of the implied equation. Sympathetic reciprocation is impossible. Rapidly the minus pole of this proposition intensifies its negativity until the ultimate deduction has been made; the grotesque is a world of absolute absurdity.

This is a world of folly enacted by anorganic puppetry. The metaphor imparts inhuman, mechanical features to this chaos. In **"Claire's Herd,"** for example, the relationship between Claire and her following, the *rastas,* is described in terms of a puppeteer and his marionettes. Notice that Van Ostaijen emphasizes the unimportance of the subject of Claire's games with the *rastas,* since the stereotyped participants allow little or no dramatic variation. The *rastas* are set into motion by a mechanical force over which they have no control whatsoever.

> Claire was in the same situation with the rastas as the owner of a Punch and Judy show with his actors. She improvised the actual plays as she saw fit, did not stick to a specific text. The puppet-show was open to her, she had only to choose. . . . As long as she noticed something alive, something like free will in a puppet, the puppet interested her. But if she had seen through the puppet and understood it as a clock-work—exclusion of free will-hypothesis; every gesture and every sound are forced by the movement of a spring—then it's over. Claire was no different. The gestures and the dialogue—intonation as well as subject—are limited and quasi stereotyped. . . . Their nature is such that they must imitate each other; one can't say aping, it is a stronger reflex-action. The typical distinction is similar to that of puppets. Only for a while can one really believe in that typical distinction; one grows tired of one rasta after the other, just as a child of one doll after the other. In this manner Claire played with the rastas. Grabbed one after the other. Discovered suddenly that one was exactly like the other. Threw it back and allowed herself to be enticed by the gestures of a third, which appeared to her at first to be new again.

This passage is an accurate description of the characters in these tales, of their uniformity and their mechanical behavior.

Folly is an immanent force which rules life in the world of the grotesque. A *ne plus ultra,* it will not allow such divagations as quotidian normality. It is anonymous, dictatorial, ruthless and inhuman. Van Ostaijen found the perfect metaphor to symbolize these qualities—the modern corporation. Van Ostaijen's world of absolute *verkeerdheid* is Folly Incorporated. Folly, in this context of the grotesques, has no redemptive or extenuating qualities. This is no fatuous folly or levity. *Verkeerdheid* implies want, absence, derangement; in terms of these tales it has a demonic inevitability which corresponds, to some degree, to $\mu\alpha\nu\iota\alpha$ from $\mu\alpha\nu\epsilon\theta\alpha\iota$ "to be mad." An element of manical desire for derangement of the norm is couched in a sinister, destructive urge. But one particular aspect must be kept in mind; its anarchy is not chaotic. The very symbol of the organization pledges order. It is a world of perspicacity, structure, authority, argumentation and rationalization, just like the world of our daily lives. The difference lies in the fact that this world is constructed on a foundation of anarchy. Behind the looking glass of reality lies a world reflected from our world, similarities between the two are inversely proportional to our standards. Through the looking glass lies a world gone amok in a logical manner. (pp. 19-25)

Discussing technique and its conceptual implications in Breughel's art, Van Ostaijen provides us with oblique insight into his own intentions. Stylistically, nuances are of great importance. The depiction of Promethea in **"Ika Loch's Brothel"** is a sum of graphic distinctions. She, like most characters in Van Ostaijen's grotesque world, is from a psychological point of view, virtually non-existent. Their very one-dimensionality lends them a stilted grace and presence despite atrophy of the fictional skeleton. This method of writing has, stylistically, features of the graphic medium of art. Speaking of Breughel's art, Van Ostaijen's fictional techniques assume contour and content. The serried quality of style provides anonymity. Modulation would pierce through uniform matter. Rigidity, however, preserves the grotesque in a state of suspended animation. Van Ostaijen's fictional technique resembles that of the animated cartoon. The precision which goes into granting a one-dimensional figure the illusion of motion is like the hypertrophied stylization of the tales. Yet the cartoonist knows full well that each act of motion is a single drawing of immobile contours and graphite volume. For example, at any point in a series of drawings depicting a character opening its mouth, the development can be halted. A projector stopped at an absurd gesture might thus lend it a peculiar timelessness of expression. An example in which this process was seemingly applied to an entire story is **"Ika Loch's Brothel."** Having denigrated logic at length with a logical loquacity, the brothel's figures vanish behind a description of the building's interior. The next to the last sentence freezes the roaming eye of the fictional camera on "a nightvase with a deep red rose." Simplicity of the poetic image harbors a vast domain of profound mystery. In its terse poetic mystification, it is categorically antithetical to the preceding verbose rationalization of incongruity. One sentence, a single poetic image, throws an entire verbal structure out of kilter. A frozen metaphor's mysterious presence mocks the grotesque's insidious intent.

The carefully contrived verbal structures of the grotesque cannot hide their fraudulent objective. These intricately built tales are a senseless architecture. The foregoing example from **"Ika Loch's Brothel"** seems to support this contention. Nevertheless, the grotesque impresses one with its autonomous existence. Within its walls martial law has been declared. Hence it does not allow identification between the reader's sphere of reference and that of the grotesque. They must remain separate; it is not a matter of identification. . . . Yet the grotesque slyly impresses the reader with a sense of *déjà vu.* A grotesque is not a non-representational painting. Deformation implies a basis of form. A tale of the grotesque will use a familiar concept, instance or trait and proceed to develop it beyond normality. But in order to be effective, it must have some relevance to a normal sphere of reference. For example, patriotic sentiment becomes an international enterprise which regulates war and peace as a matter of business (**"Patriotism Incorporated"**). The commendable desire for metropolitan beautification turns into a building craze without rhyme or reason (**"City of Builders"**). In a world where economy equals inflation, counterfeit bills are more honest currency than legal tender (**"The Adventures of Mercurius"**). The stereotyped slogan "Work and Save" carried to an extreme does not benefit, but victimizes its apostle. Perhaps most graphically illustrative is **"The Lost House Key,"** where a victim of satyriasis loses his house key, and with this insignificant act, becomes the founding father of a syphilitic society. Indeed, a pessimistic vision might conclude that any of these grotesque deformations have their place in our universe. Van Ostaijen sees his world as a panopticon where nothing is unnatural, or, at most, against nature. The world of the grotesque has the disturbing tendency of appearing familiar to us, and yet we desperately insist on its alien character.

The grotesque is a double-edged sword. It terrorizes its actors as well as its audience. This fearful oscillation between repugnant familiarity and alien autocracy was what perplexed the Dutch critic mentioned previously. "As long as we are reading, we have the oppressive feeling that all this bizarre, strange and sometimes grisly business does concern us in a mysterious fashion, because it depicts a piece of a hidden reality in which we take just as much part as the author. It is a spell which does not fascinate us, but renders us helpless, from the inside out. We cannot recount what we experienced; it does not go deeper or higher than cognition, but bypasses it." The irony of this statement must be obvious, since it reflects an impression *intended* by the grotesque. But the grudging admission does not hide repulsion. Correcting the critical focus results in the realization that the diagnosis of the symptoms correctly identified the disease.

The best fictional counterpart to these theoretical statements is the story **"The Lost House Key."** Counterpart—for Borgers is quite correct in stating that, for Van Ostaijen, theory came after the fact of creation. Only when the tales are seen as a unity, is it possible to deduce the fictional correlative of the Breughel essay. . . . **"The Lost House Key"** admirably conjoins the general deductions of the essay to a fictional replica.

A synopsis of the plot can be very brief. Hasdrubal Paaltjes, a municipal official, gets drunk one night with some friends. Returning home late at night he finds his house key gone. Paaltjes is unable to enter his house, but he refuses to sleep alone. Aided by the aphrodisiac of champagne, he decides to spend the night with a prostitute. The woman is syphilitic, and Paaltjes contracts the disease. Being an inveterate Don Juan, he spreads it among many women, both married and single. By arithmetical progression, syphilis eventually contaminates the entire city of X, and its way of life becomes geared to a syphilitic *modus vivendi*. Suddenly the reader realizes that this city, now called Megalopolis, has made syphilis the norm and a non-syphilitic existence the anti-norm.

The city is known only as X at the beginning of the story. After the Paaltjesean revolution, it first gains national attention, followed by international fame. The nation to which it belongs severs ties by making it a free city. It becomes a haven for all unwanted human elements from other regions and nations. Social outcasts and outlaws find refuge here. Soon it has achieved status and a name. As Megalopolis it quickly develops features of a city-state. Obviously, city X could never have prospered as Megalopolis does. True, other powers control its foreign policies, but internally it is autonomous. The world powers provide economic aid for Megalopolis, not as a charitable gift, but as an "externally-prophylactic method"; "the existence of this city eliminated venereal diseases, because it concentrated the carriers of this disease in one place." In short, Megalopolis flourishes antithetically. Peccant disorder evolves into the healthy norm. Hence the story may be seen as a symbolization of the grotesque, as the world of absolute *verkeerdheid*.

Insidious relentlessness is equally well exhibited in this tale. A simple, inane mistake catapults a culture into orbit. This phenomenon, observable in other tales, is the grotesque's generating function; an essentially simple incident or rule introduces complex patterns. Of course, the tale could be examined from other angles. For example, one could read the story as a vituperative creation of myth. There is the suggestion of a satiric creation-story, which takes evil quite literally in writing its mythical history. On a more general level, the story overthrows ethical morality. An American philosopher remarks at a certain point that Megalopolis had become moral again through immorality. At first the inhabitants were pleased that their peculiar ethics were recognized. "But then they could not understand that it was reduced to a consistent immorality. They laughed at the childish philosophy of the American." A shudder passes through the tale. What up till then might have been a vitriolic satire, now turns into the reality of the grotesque. In a single sentence Van Ostaijen destroys any illusions. "The foundation of Megalopolis was already far in the past." Not only has this luetic civilization attained veracity, but it also has become an historic reality. Even that is not enough. Everyday syphilitic reality has become so mundane and a matter of course that Megalopolis has reached the stage where it can afford wasting effort in society's most sophisticated pastime: arguing about its beginnings.

In this tale we see the rise of a civilization from obscurity to glory. As in other tales, an eccentric progression propels an insignificant negation into a grotesque cosmogony. Inclusiveness anticipates a sense of horror. The rise of Megalopolis is not only inclusive; it might also seem to follow the progressive stages of the city's mythical disease. The primary phase of syphilis is characterized by chancre in the part affected—Paaltjes. The secondary phase spreads to the skin and mucous membranes; rapidly the contagion spreads throughout the city of X. The disease predominates. Luetic Megalopolis is born. The tertiary phase involves the remainder of the body, culminating in infecting the brain. The entire structure and superstructure of Megalopolis has been created. The story ends with senseless debates and wranglings about the question of whether Paaltjes really lost his key or not. Three major factions, psychologists, realists and nominalists, beset each other with obtuse argumentation in a demented fashion, as if the intellect of Megalopolis has been affected by the terminal stage of the disease which founded it. It is no gratuitous accident that Van Ostaijen chose two words which assonate in Dutch (as well as in English). "Syphilis" and "civilization" linguistically and symbolically assimilate to form the implied neologism *syphilization*. This is perhaps the most bitter symbolization of Van Ostaijen's nihilistic pessimism.

The symbolic negation of the world by representing it as a luetic organism can be discovered in other tales too. In **"Camembert or the Lucky Lover"** for example, there is a condensed version of the metaphoric connotation of **"The Lost House Key."** Camembert, that most insensate of bourgeois lovers, has been frequenting a brothel with some friends, where he was forcibly ejected because his fear of contracting venereal disease prevented him from consummating his desires. His comrades congratulate him on his stout behavior and exemplary control: "Such characters were the state's best weapon against syphilis." That night he has a morbid dream. He is surrounded by women, whose breasts are transformed into octopuses. "Who vomited syphilis bacilli. Not women overpowered Camembert anymore, but bacilli. His room was filled with them. The world is a great clump. Of syphilis bacilli, naturally. To dream is to rise from petty reality. To be in the universe. Sure." In **"Patriotism Incorporated"** venereal contagion again assumes public proportions. In this case, it even becomes a patriotic boon. Pameelke, a cabinet member of Teutonia's government, castigates an international movement for the prevention of venereal disease. Such an institution he finds presumptuous and unethical. Elimination of the disease within national boundaries is the duty of that particular government. However, its presence in another state, such as a neighbouring country, can only give cause for patriotic rejoicing. Venereal contagion in another country means undermining the health and number of its population. A true patriot will laud such a condition, and will heap curses on those who would attempt to eradicate the affliction in nations which are not their native country. The ethical and rhetorical fervor of this vicious reasoning is revolting, and yet consistent with a morally and ethically atrophied society. The individual realms of politics, society and culture in this world of absolute *verkeerdheid* fit the general pattern of inverted, negative, noxious incongruity. (pp.25-30)

> E. M. Beekman, in his Homeopathy of the Absurd: The Grotesque in Paul van Ostaijen's Creative Prose, *Martinus Nijhoff, 1970, 196 p.*

PAUL HADERMANN   (essay date 1973)

[*In the following excerpt, Hadermann examines the influence of German Expressionism, particularly the Expressionist journal* Der Sturm, *on Van Ostaijen's artistic development.*]

When Van Ostaijen came to Berlin at the end of 1918, at the age of twenty-two, he had been acquainted with German expressionism in general, and with the periodical *Der Sturm* in particular for about two years. It was even he who together with some other writers, Brunclair, De Smedt, introduced this movement in Flanders, mainly through popularizing articles and critiques. The writers he quoted with the greatest admiration were Becher, Werfel, Rubiner, Sternheim and other humanitarian expressionists, and the periodical he knew best was apparently the pacifist *Die weissen Blätter*. As a matter of fact, Van Ostaijen's own poetry at that time reflected his admiration for the "O Mensch-Lyrik" as it was called, so that his volume of poetry, **Het sienjaal (The Signal)** published in 1918, was to be the first humanitarian expressionist poetry in Belgium.

Needless to say, **Het sienjaal** was not a mere application of foreign formulas. Van Ostaijen's earlier poetry, published two years before under the title **Music-Hall,** already pointed in the humanitarian direction by its unanimistic cult of places and moments that bring people together, physically and emotionally.

The reason Van Ostaijen had already turned to the German avant-garde while he was still in Antwerp was not one of personal poetic predilection. His articles contained from the beginning, that is to say from 1914 onward, allusions or references to some French poets as well: Bloy, Rolland, Péguy, Claudel. But he had a better knowledge of German literature at that time because during the First World War European modernism was accessible to Belgian readers only through German periodicals, as other foreign periodicals were forbidden. Anyhow, thanks to **Het sienjaal,** and a little later to Wies Moens' poetry, the humanitarian trend would prevail for years in Flemish expressionism.

In June of 1918, still before Van Ostaijen had left for Berlin, the name of the left-wing literary magazine *Die Aktion* appeared in one of his most important essays, **"Expressionisme**

in Vlaanderen," in which he tried to place the Flemish artists Paul Joostens and the brothers Oscar and Floris Jespers within the so-called expressionist movement. Van Ostaijen himself was conscious of the dangers of his terminology and used "expressionism" as the most inclusive term, even admitting cubism and futurism as subcategories. We might expect him here to refer to Pfemfert and *Die Aktion* in the same apologetic way as he referred to Rubiner or Werfel in his earlier articles. On the contrary, he decided against the writers of *Die Aktion*, because they condemned expressionism on account of its increasingly aesthetic character: "The periodical *Die Aktion* raises objections to expressionism as if this movement too would collapse into pure aestheticism. However, the fact that the artist is the master of all the means does not preclude that his work must serve a higher purpose."

One might guess that the attitude Van Ostaijen tried to justify against the pronouncements of *Die Aktion* is that of *Der Sturm,* which at that time indeed stressed form rather than message. It identified expressionism with its own formal conception of art and literature. *Der Sturm* was not merely a literary periodical, there was also the experimental theater of the *Sturmbühne,* there was a very active *Sturm* gallery where important futurist, cubist and expressionist works were exhibited when the accent was placed more and more on abstract art, there was a *Sturm* bookstore which published luxurious *Sturm* books, and there were *Sturmabende* where modern music was performed and poetry read.

We not only can presume that Van Ostaijen meant *Der Sturm* when he said "expressionism." We can even be certain of it, since Gerrit Borgers published in his *Documentatie* about Van Ostaijen a draft of **"Expressionisme in Vlaanderen"** in which *Der Sturm* is mentioned by name and contrasted with *Die Aktion.* The following passage, which Van Ostaijen dropped in the published version, illustrates this point: "As to the conflict between the expressionists of *Der Sturm* and *Die Aktion,* we refuse to take sides and we have the same respect for Sternheim, placed in the limelight by *Die Aktion,* as for Herwarth Walden, the leader of *Der Sturm.*"

Since this sentence was not included in the final text of **"Expressionisme in Vlaanderen,"** we may conclude that he became aware of the fact that the whole of his essay implicitly contained a definite choice in favor of the more aesthetic attitude of *Der Sturm.* It was indeed mainly preoccupied with the formal trends of the artistic vanguard. So before he came to Berlin, and only one month after writing down his humanitarian verse, Van Ostaijen had already decided for *Der Sturm,* for its aestheticism which he defended against the champions of the literature of involvement.

Does that mean that he had reversed his own attitude in one month's time? Certainly not. Van Ostaijen has often been reproached for his chameleon-like temper and changeable moods, but in fact there is a great consistency in the evolution of his poetics. While he was writing his humanitarian **Sienjaal,** he devoted much of his critical and theoretical essays to modern art. Among the studies and manifestos that helped him to elaborate a theory on contemporary art were Marinetti's *Manifesto of Futurism,* Worringer's *Abstraktion und Einfühlung,* Kahnweiler's essays on cubism, *Du cubisme* by Gleizes and Metzinger, Däubler's *Der neue Standpunkt,* the *Blaue Reiter* Almanach, and above all Kandinsky's *Über das Geistige in der Kunst,* from which he quoted long paragraphs in several articles, also in **"Expressionisme in Vlaanderen."**

Under the influence of these works and of passionate discussions with his friends—most of whom were painters rather than writers—Van Ostaijen defended, in his critical articles from 1917 onward, the autonomy of the work of art. He took the position that the "innere Notwendigkeit" ["inner necessity"] of the very material of the artistic creation ruled that creation, and he defended the necessity of simplifying and synthesizing forms in order to give them more expressivity.

In short, we may say that his artistic views had brought him closer to *Der Sturm* than the humanitarian poems of *Het sienjaal* would lead us to believe. The theories of *Der Sturm* are indeed much indebted to futurism on one side and to the *Blaue Reiter* and Kandinsky on the other. Moreover, *Der Sturm* published texts by Marinetti, Marc, Kandinsky and Worringer, most of them in its first four years of publication, from 1910 to 1914. It is possible that Van Ostaijen did not read *Der Sturm* regularly before his arrival in Berlin, but he evidently knew it well enough to sympathize with its aesthetic program and to defend it against *Die Aktion*. His argument foreshadowed his later poetics: the work of art or the poem should be an aesthetic achievement, but that achievement should be seen in the light of a humanitarian ideal.

Reading Van Ostaijen's poetry, however, one is inclined to think that at the end of 1918, he completely lost his faith in a better mankind. The world of love and brotherhood of *Het sienjaal* is indeed replaced by one of murder, violence and despair in *Bezette stad* (written in 1920, published in 1921) and *De feesten van angst en pijn* (written from 1918 to 1921, published posthumously). But this despair is stated in a way that makes it become positive and fruitful on another level. Van Ostaijen overcame his Berlin nihilism through a new experiment with form which was unique in the Flemish literature of the twenties. And that experiment is much indebted to *Der Sturm*. (pp. 37-40)

If we judge from Van Ostaijen's letters and literary works, there was one writer of *Der Sturm* whom Van Ostaijen knew intimately and who apparently exerted a lasting influence on his writing: Salomon Friedländer, a philosopher and "Literat," whose creative literature consisted mainly of grotesque prose and who published under the pseudonym of Mynona. Van Ostaijen mentioned Friedländer with great admiration in his letters. He called him "a beautiful person" and among the writers he met in Berlin "Mynona is the best." Van Ostaijen was not often so enthusiastic about someone. He must indeed have liked Mynona as a person, as a philosopher and as a writer of grotesques. Several of these grotesques were published in *Die Aktion* and *Der Sturm*, as were those of Mynona's friend Scheerbart, who had died in 1915. Now, 1919 was the year when Van Ostaijen became acquainted with Mynona, and that same year he started writing grotesques himself, a genre with which he had no experience. It is quite probable that the example of Mynona and Scheerbart encouraged him. At a moment when he saw his humanitarian beliefs and hopes collapse, the cool, grotesque humor offered him a means of keeping reality at a distance. The hatred and despair directly stated in *The Feasts of Fear and Pain* and *Occupied City* find a more subtle expression in the grotesques. The controlled cerebral tone implies a kind of detachment which in a case such as this means a partial victory over reality and over oneself.

Van Ostaijen's grotesques are in mood and spirit akin to Mynona's. Even in the structure of the titles there are striking similarities. We may compare e.g. "Für Hunde und andere Menschen" to **"Diergaarde voor kinderen van nu,"** "Der kommende Mann" to **"Glans en verval van een politiek man,"** "Mechtilde" to **"Mechtildes, die goede meid,"** "Die Bank der Spötter, ein Unroman" to **"De trust der vaderlandsliefde,"** "Aerosphere" to **"Hierarchie,"** or "Fabelhaftes" to **"Merkwaardige aanval."**

The method both writers make use of is much the same, following naturally from the laws of the grotesque genre itself. First of all, there is that kind of intellectual, objective humor that Mynona defined in "Die Bank der Spötter": "Humor is the laughing or smiling sky-high loftiness, which chooses however to be silent, to disguise itself, and in place of its direct revelation only produces that which is ridiculed."

That objective permutation of facts and reasonings follows a very simple, linear path. In Friedländer's as in Van Ostaijen's works, the absurd or grotesque developed in a straight line, straight on to the end. At the basis of these grotesques there is always one main idea, or the critique of an idea, which gives them the quality of a parable. Their characters are types. They often embody ideas or even become allegories such as the girl called "Theorie" in Mynona's "Die betrunkenen Blumen" or the brothel madam Ika Loch in Van Ostaijen's **"Het bordeel van Ika Loch,"** Ika Loch being the inverted "Logica." The world is seen as a mad panopticum by Van Ostaijen in **"Intermezzo,"** as a "Kino" by Friedländer in "Das vertikale Gewerbe." The heroes who do not accept its laws and assume the opposite invariably become wrapped up in their self-created folly, so that the two absurdities enhance each other by their contrast, as in **"De verloren huissleutel"** or in "Die Bank der Spötter." (pp. 43-4)

Friedländer's example was perhaps still more important for Van Ostaijen's poetics than for his grotesque prose. Significant is the fact that our poet began to talk about "ontindividualisering" (disindividualization) in his Berlin period. This term, which became a key to his aesthetics, was first used by Van Ostaijen with a mainly ethical connotation that also reminds us of Friedländer. In **"Wat is er met Picasso,"** written in August of 1920, he described Picasso's evolution as pointing toward a more impersonal style: "In Picasso's work we see how a very conscious individuality is unconsciously and definitely pushed toward disindividualization; a disindividualization which unfortunately is not completed, because the individuality blocks the way. . . . In Picasso's work we see how the subjective is about to be integrated with the objective. Both subjective and objective belong to one and the same phenomenality. He is already on his way to a more indifferent point of view."

This indifferent point of view, which should be the aim of the artist's disindividualization, reminds us of Friedländer's conception of mankind in the future. The highest stage man will be able to reach is, according to Friedländer, the "creative indifference" (*schöpferische Indifferenz*). It is a point where no contradictions are possible, or rather an indifferent state of mind and a way of being where these contradictions are brought together within one person, in a synthesis of all extremes. This stage he called that of the Angel, who is able to see the relativity of the surrounding world and to recreate it in a spirit of heavenly humor. . . . That is why he wanted to transcend the human stage, that is why he wanted to kill the individual inside himself with its poor one-way defects, in order to become on a higher level some sort of non-egoistic, anonymous *Übermensch*—which is the possible origin of his anagrammatic pseudonym "Mynona."

That Van Ostaijen owed his idea of disindividualization to Friedländer is shown by the fact that in his essay on Picasso he linked it to Friedländer's "indifferent point of view," although he did not mention the name of Friedländer. Other evidence is given by the 1921 version of his German essay on Heinrich Campendonk, published in *Das Kunstblatt*, where Friedländer's own term "schöpferische Indifferenz" is applied to that painter and where other phrases seem to have been borrowed directly from Friedländer's philosophical writings. (pp. 45-6)

The impact of these theories on Van Ostaijen can also be measured by the importance of polarities in the poems of the *Feasts of Fear and Pain*, and by the poet's efforts to neutralize these polarities in order to reach the indifferent point of view from which he will be able to begin a new life. Such an "Indifferenzpunkt" is described in **"Prière impromptue 3"**:

> (God . . . Thou art valueless . . . superficial in surface, deep in depth, rising in ascension/ fall in fall . . . . On the high plain there is no value anymore.)

If the *Feasts of Fear and Pain* are full of anguish and despair, they are none the less feasts, because they mean a liberation of the poet's self—a self that lies deeper than the individuality with its idiosyncrasies and its outworn system of values. Just as he shook off the old man in the *Feasts,* Van Ostaijen set the bourgeois heritage on fire in *Occupied City.* Both works are passionate accounts of his fear and of his desire at the same time to lay aside his old ego, to disindividualize himself.

From then on, Van Ostaijen never wrote confession poetry again, as he called it, nor even delivered any message to mankind. His later poems were disindividualized, lyrical objects made of words. They appealed to the subconscious of the readers, beyond their own individualities. All the poet's efforts were concentrated on making those poems efficient, on giving a new fresh value to their words, musically and plastically. This was Van Ostaijen's "word art."

In the development of his literary theory *Der Sturm* played an important part again. But here it was less a matter of personal contact with *Sturm* collaborators than of becoming acquainted with some important contributions, poems or articles, published in *Der Sturm* while Van Ostaijen was in Berlin or before. Among his friends, Mynona, Knoblauch or Behne very likely possessed the back issues of *Der Sturm* and *Sturm-Bücher.*

First of all, there is the term "word art" (*woordkunst*), which Van Ostaijen never used before and which henceforth will often appear in his literary critiques and essays. "Word art" (*Wortkunst*) was one of the most typical concepts of the *Sturm* aesthetics. The word was almost constantly used by Walden and Schreyer, mainly from 1916 onward. Of course, Van Ostaijen was prepared to adopt the theory of "word art," as it may be called a transposition to literature of Kandinsky's and Gleizes' idea of an autonomous art solely obeying the laws of its own material. Nevertheless, the way in which Van Ostaijen adopted this "word art" was so true to the spirit and even the letter of *Der Sturm,* that we may call him almost a *Sturm* follower in this respect. There are, for instance, the following lines, written in 1920 or 1921, for his manifesto **"Et voilà"** which was an introduction to a periodical which he

was not able to launch: "Poetry is word art. Not the communication of emotions. But the vision becomes concrete through the form of the word. It is also certainly not the communication of ideas."

Now this is almost a transcription of the part of the text on "Expressionistische Dichtung" written by Schreyer in the *Sturm-bühne, Jahrbuch des Theaters der Expressionisten,* 1918: "Das Wortkunstwerk ist keine Mitteilung von Gedanken oder von Gefühlen, sondern Kunde einer Offenbarung" ["Word art is not the communication of thought or of feeling, but rather news of a revelation"].

One might argue that "visie" does not mean exactly the same as "Offenbarung," but the context of **"Et voilà"** makes sure that Van Ostaijen used the word in that sense: "The highest form of art is ECSTASY. . . . Only from the visionary synthesis does the work of art proceed. UNIO MYSTICA."

There is more: in the *Sturm-bühne,* Schreyer developed his ideas about rhythm and considered concentration and "decentration" of words as "types of rhythm formation." "The goal is to give form to the concept with as few sound means as possible." Not only words but also sentences should be reduced to their most expressive concentrated form, leaving aside adjectives, adverbs, conjunctions, interjections etc. This concentration is balanced out by "decentration," which means repetitions of words, parallel constructions, associations by juxtapositions of verbs or names. Similar thoughts had already been expressed before by Walden, for example in *Der Sturm* of February, 1916. Stramm was considered the poet whose poetry embodied these theories to perfection. Van Ostaijen, who became a great admirer of Stramm's, was acquainted with both his theory and his poetry. . . . (pp. 47-9)

But let us return to Schreyer's article in the *Sturm-bühne.* To illustrate his and Walden's doctrine, Schreyer gave the following example: "The next example shows how concentration of form and content is developed out of simple shortening: *Die Bäume und die Blumen blühen* ["The trees and the flowers bloom"] is a simple statement. *Die Bäume, die Blumen blühen* is a simple shortening. The conjunction is left out. In the same fashion, *Bäume und Blumen blühen* is a simple shortening. The articles are left out. But *Baum und Blume blüht* is no longer a simple shortening, but a concentration. The concept is grasped more deeply. But the unity of the concepts *Baum* and *Blumen* and *blühen* can be shaped in an even more concentrated manner. The form *Blühender Baum, blühende Blume* is possible. But here only the unity of *blühen* has been formed. *Baum* and *Blume* are considered as contrasts. Only the form *Baum blüht Blume* puts the three concepts together to form a unified concept. This is a word sentence. *Baum blüht Blume."*

Now, can it be a mere coincidence when, in 1920, Van Ostaijen wrote a poem entitled **"In memoriam Herman van den Reeck,"** which begins with the line: "Bloesems bloeien bloemen"? It is the same concentration, the same rhythm, the same alliteration, almost the same image.

The *Feasts of Fear and Pain* and *Occupied City* are full of such concentration—and "decentration"—effects. They are close to Stramm's poetry and are different from Van Ostaijen's earlier poetry. A brief comparison will suffice to show the importance of the change. The following lines are taken from *Het sienjaal:*

Wie zich geroepen voelt het Sienjaal te geven;
wie, als godskind, zelf onder de mensen gaan moet
hun andermaal de tarwe van het leven brengend
en het levensbloed dat zijpelt van de bomen, mor-
    gendauw of zomerregen,
het levensbloed dat blakert op de huizen, doch nie-
    mand durft het aankijken,
—o de schrik van het godsbeeld in zich te ontdek-
    ken en de vrees naar het Doel gedreven tewor-
    den;—
wie gaan moet tot het doel, door al de verzoekingen
    van de wulpsheid tot de Mater Dolorosa;
wie zijn kleine leger wil vluchten zien bij d'eerste
    beproeving van de menselijke zwakheid,
om gans alleen te dragen de pijnigende wandeling
    van al de bomen der Oliveten door het eigen
    lichaam,
wie Godsgezegend is om, rit na rit, te stappen tot
    het alles is volbracht,—
tot de tweede lijfelike dood durft gaan en dragen
    durft de derde nacht,
om de geest Gods in zich te bevrijden, hem het
    tweede leven te schenken,—
hem zullen de bazuinen de grafsteen doen vallen en
    vluchten zal de schildwacht, die het levende licht
    niet dragen kan.

(Who feels called upon to give the signal; who as
God's child must go among the people, bringing
them again the wheat of life and the blood of life
that seeps from the trees, morning dew or summer
rain, the blood of life that scorches the houses, but
nobody dares look at it—O the fear of discovering
the image of God within oneself and the fear of
being driven to the Goal—who must go to the goal,
through all the temptations of luxuriance to the
Mater Dolorosa; who wants to see his little army
flee at the first trial of human weakness, in order to
all alone bear the torturing walk along all the trees
of Mount Olivet through his own body, who is
Godblessed in order to, ride after ride, continue till
all has been endured, dares go to the second bodily
death, and dares bear the third night, in order to
liberate in himself the spirit of God, to give him the
second life—for him the trumpets will make the
gravestone fall and flee will the guard who cannot
bear the living light.)

The rhythm is fluid and majestic. Biblical images follow each
other in a pathetic, prophetic style. The syntax is almost regular. One long emphatic sentence is filled with rhetoric repetitions, dramatic contrasts, hyperboles and exclamations.

Mood, tone and subject matter are quite different in the
Feasts, as can be seen in **"Vers 4."** The rhythm is chaotic.
The poem gives an impression of panting. The sentences are
very short—if we may call them sentences. There are no images. The syntax is broken up. Affirmative sentences begin
with the verb. Others have no verb at all. The first six lines—
which are the first six words—give a good example of "decentration" by repetition and assonance, whereas the rest of
the poem is based on the shock effect of concentrated groups
of words, without articles, adjectives, conjunctions, interjections or punctuation marks. . . . The main difference between Stramm's poems and those of the **Feasts** (and **Occupied City**) is that Van Ostaijen almost never shaped new
words, except for mere onomatopoeias. There is also his use
of rhythmic typography in **Bezette stad** that makes his poems
look more dadaistic or futuristic but in fact only serves the
very purpose of concentration, as Walden defined it in *Der*

Sturm in 1918: "The purpose of art is to make visible the visible word, or to make it visible again."

Stramm was to remain one of the poets Van Ostaijen most
admired. He called him "the renovator of Germanic poetry."
Almost every time he wanted to give an example of what he
called "organic expressionism" (Walden, too, liked to compare the poem to an organism), every time Van Ostaijen
wanted to show what he meant by a disindividualized, autonomous, formal *Wortkunstwerk* ["work of word art"], he quoted Stramm's poetry, the rigor of which he compared to that
of cubist painting. Sometimes he would add the names of two
other *Sturm* poets, Behrens and Runge, who wrote more or
less in the same vein as Stramm. He liked to oppose them, as
the left wing of expressionism, to the humanitarian or romantic expressionists whom he called the "Werfelians." "The
only form of real expressionism in Germany," he wrote to De
Bock in 1920, "came out of *Der Sturm.*"

Until his last essays, Van Ostaijen remembered *Der Sturm*
and its literary doctrine. His ideas about the organic work of
art, about the "sonority" of the poem, about the superiority
of the spoken over the written word, derived from the important essays Walden and Schreyer wrote in *Der Sturm.*

Yet, when he was asked about the literary influences he had
experienced, Van Ostaijen later preferred to speak of French
modern poetry. This was sometimes the case in his letters
from Berlin too. The reason for it was probably that he liked
to set himself apart from his environment. Moreover, he often
asked his friends to send him works of Soupault, Breton, Aragon, Cendrars, Cocteau, and Apollinaire, and he complained
about the Germans not being enthusiastic about them. He
should at least have made an exception in the case of the editors of *Der Sturm,* who published poems of precisely those
poets whose names appear in his letters, except for Cocteau.
So it is quite possible that *Der Sturm* even contributed to Van
Ostaijen's knowledge of the French poets whose influence he
wanted to play off against that of the Germans.

As a matter of fact, his later poetry, written from 1923 onward, after his return to Belgium, was closer to the playful
subtle mood of Cocteau or Apollinaire than to that of
Stramm. Van Ostaijen by then was aware of the fact that his
Berlin period had been a cure for the rhetorical attitude expressed in **Het sienjaal: "Bezette stad** was a poison used as
a counterpoison. The nihilism of **Bezette stad** cured me of a
dishonesty which I mistook for honesty and of extra-lyrical
pathos. Afterward I became a plain everyday poet."

It was not only the nihilistic attitude that cured him. There
was also the philosophical disindividualization of Friedländer, the literary aestheticism of *Der Sturm,* and the practical example of Stramm. Fortunately, Van Ostaijen did not become a mere Stramm epigone. He found his own way as a
"plain everyday poet." After taking the poison of humanitarian pathos and the counterpoison of extreme concentration,
he arrived in his **Nagelaten gedichten** at a more musical,
more melodic form of art, in respect to which his Berlin style
seemed to be almost as much a "manner" as that of **Het sienjaal.**

More than the poems of Stramm or even the grotesques of
Mynona, the general principles of the "word art" of *Der
Sturm* determined Van Ostaijen's further evolution. The theories of Walden and Schreyer indeed had given him the opportunity of linking together his artistic convictions and his
creative will as a poet in one coherent system. That system,

however, differed from the "word art" of *Der Sturm* by the greater emphasis Van Ostaijen placed on the subconscious of both writer and reader as an intersubjective meeting place. The disindividualization Friedländer aimed at was to be an ethical, personal achievement. Van Ostaijen turned it into an aesthetic necessity. But until his last essays he presented it at the same time as a formal response to his "collective desires." He was persuaded indeed that his impersonal, non-individual, organic poems would by means of the simplest words awake the subconscious inside the reader—the collective subconscious being the field where people ultimately meet and lose their bourgeois egoist individualities.

So we perceive a far echo of the humanitarian Utopia proclaimed by **Het sienjaal** in Van Ostaijen's personal interpretation of "word art," as it appears in his criticism and in his letters, and as it was foreshadowed in his casual remark of 1918 about the involvement of aestheticism. *Der Sturm,* providing Van Ostaijen with a theoretical and, through Friedländer, even with a philosophical support, helped him to surpass dadaistic nihilism. What at first had been a raft, had now become a springboard. (pp. 49-55)

> Paul Hadermann, "Paul Van Ostaijen and 'Der Sturm'," in Nijhoff, Van Ostaijen, "De Stijl": Modernism in the Netherlands and Belgium in the First Quarter of the 20th Century: Six Essays, *edited by Francis Bulhof, Martinus Nijhoff, 1976, pp. 37-55.*

E. M. BEEKMAN (essay date 1974)

[*In the following excerpt, Beekman considers the affinity of Van Ostaijen's poetry with modern painting and examines his poetic use of the color blue.*]

Study any epoch you wish and you will soon discover an *air de famille* which undeniably links the varieties of artistic expression one to the other and all of them together to a period of history. Though this may sound hackneyed, it nevertheless states a very basic truth in terms of an interdisciplinary consensus among the arts as to what constitutes the major difference of that particular age with those which came before. One can discern an unmistakable "expression" in every artist's style, one which reveals not only his own unique talent, but also his debt to his immediate social and cultural environment. A simple example is the fact that so many modern manuscripts are typewritten, while those in longhand are becoming more and more rare. It is quite conceivable that in the not too distant future a tape will place an author irrevocably within our technological age.

Again it seems that dogmatism, of whatever kind, is fatal for true individual expression, and that it can only produce desiccated illustrations of an atrophied theory. For instance, no one would advocate the slavish imitation of paintings which 18th-century poets were prone to. But such an example should not discourage the student from verifying the discovery that the common link between the arts is in their subservience to the temper of the times. Thus Mario Praz can say:

> The various media, then, would correspond to the variety of characters in fairy tales; the proposition that the characters vary, while the function remains the same, would find a counterpart in another proposition: the media vary, but the structure remains the same [*Mnemosyne: the Parallel between Literature and the Visual Arts* (1970)].

Forty-two years earlier Van Ostaijen made a similar observation concerning modern art. Modern art in particular is rich in striking examples illustrating this theory. Curiously, Van Ostaijen, like Praz, shows a deference to Lessing's admonition that painting's sphere is space and poetry's time (and ne'er the twain shall meet):

> De schilder associeert mede- of tegen-trillend van vorm tot vorm, de dichter van woord tot woord. De vormen enerzijds en de woorden anderzijds zijn gedetermineerd en determinerend. . . . De dimensionale samenhang van het vlak wordt bepaald door hetgeen geschilderd wordt; niet wordt het geschilderde in een compositioneel a-priorische ruimte ingelijfd. Het gevulde vlak is het schilderij. . . . De tijd anderzijds is er niet om de ontwikkeling van een compositie lyrisch mogelijk te maken. Met de tijd wordt uit zichzelve het gedicht. De tijd is het gedicht.

> (The painter associates, while vibrating in sympathy with or in opposition to, from form to form, the poet from word to word. Forms on the one hand and words on the other, are limited and limiting. . . . The dimensional coherence of the plane is determined by what is being painted; what is being painted is not incorporated into a compositionally pre-determined space. The filled plane is the painting. . . . Time on the other hand, does not exist in order to make the development of a composition lyrically possible. With time the poem issues from itself. Time is the poem.)

Again, Van Ostaijen's central thesis anticipates the Italian scholar's concluding assertion that

> there is a close relationship between the development of art and literature also in the modern period, one may even say, chiefly in the modern period, when creation goes hand in hand with an overdeveloped critical activity of debating problems which are common to all the arts.

> Nu zeg ik daartegenover dat er wel degelijk een verband bestaat en wel zo: de expressionistische schilderkunst en de expressionistische dichtkunst zijn elk voor zich geen homogeen geheel; beide bestaan uit verschillende schakels en deze twee kettingen, schakel aan schakel naast elkaar gelegd, vertonen binnen zulke gradatie parallele aspecten. Waaruit volgt dat er in de plaats van een homogene schilderkunst en een homogene lyriek, veeleer dichtere verwantschappen zijn van een schilder tot een dichter, van een groep schilders tot een groep lyriekers.

> (Now I would propose that there definitely exists a relationship, namely this: Expressionistic painting and Expressionistic poetry are in and by themselves not homogeneous unities; both are made up of different links and these two chains, put link by link next to each other, display parallel aspects within such a gradation. From which follows that instead of homogeneous painting and homogeneous poetry, there are rather affinities between a painter and a poet, between a group of painters and a group of poets.)

The parallelisms which Van Ostaijen sees between modern poetry and painting are (1) the dynamic causality in each work of art, (2) the striving for the most objective agglomeration of form which is "the shortest possible distance between vision and expression," and (3) aesthetic aseity and the principle of association as the basis for modern creativity. One must emphasize that these points are not merely enumerated, but that they are conclusions drawn from an extensive series of most appropriate examples. And it is precisely in these examples that one senses the thorough familiarity which Van Ostaijen had with the plastic arts—an astonishing competence which was the result of a lifelong study and fascination. Consider for instance the following description of a Cubistic woodcut by Campendonck:

> Als voorbeeld van deze organische esoteriek van het expressionistische kunstwerk een houtsnede van Campendonck: de wordende ontwikkeling is er duidelijker dan elders bij beelding het geval is in vastgehouden; gewoonlijk versmelten oorzaak en gevolg in de ruimtelijke voorstelling. Toevallig is in deze houtsnede het formele worden nog zeer duidelijk: lijn, cilinder van de kachelbuis, cilinder van de kachel, vrije cilinder van het lichaam, halve cilinder van de hals, halve cilinder van het hoofd, kettinglijn van het haar als schakel tussen ronde en rechte vormen en dan: vierkant van de tafel, zwarte driehoek van het bed, witte driehoek van het bed, tezamen rechthoek van het bed, kleine cilinders aan het witte lijf, zwarte lijn: verklinken. Zo is het bijna reeds een gedicht, t' spreekt vanzelf een expressionistisch.

> (As an example of this organic esoterism of Expressionistic art a woodcut by Campendonck: the becoming development has been captured here much more clearly than is usually the case with other modes of depicting [= *beelding*]; usually cause and effect dissolve in the spatial representation. It so happens that in this woodcut the formal development is still very clear: line, cylinder of the stovepipe, cylinder of the stove, free cylinder of the body, half cylinder of the neck, half cylinder of the head, chainline of the hair as link between the round and straight forms, and then: square of the table, black triangle of the bed, white triangle of the bed, together rectangle of the bed, small cylinders on the white body, black line: fade-out [= *verklinken*]. And so it is already almost a poem, an Expressionistic one of course.)

From this enviable ability to translate even abstract paintings into words and to be able to extract a theoretical formula from even the most complex of plastic arts, comes Van Ostaijen's poetic usage of pictorial ingredients—especially color. The subsequent discussion of his use of the color blue shows that this subject is not peripheral but that it can lead us to what might perhaps be one of the central preoccupations of his work.

As Sergei Eisenstein points out, one must be careful not to assign colors an absolute meaning which will remain unaltered in no matter what context.

> The problem is not, nor ever will be, solved by a fixed catalog of color–symbols, but the emotional intelligibility and function of color will rise from the natural order of establishing the color imagery of the work, coincidental with the process of shaping the living movement of the whole work.

But, clearly, our use of, or preference for, a chromatic aspect of the spectrum is influenced by historical, theoretical or psychological factors. In Van Ostaijen's case his literary use of colors is definitely based on a lifelong acquaintance with the practice of painters and . . . on a thorough familiarity with

Kandinsky's aesthetic theory which was published in 1912 under the title *Über das Geistige in der Kunst.* Because of unorthodox religious inclinations, there is also a mystical character to Van Ostaijen's vocabulary, so that we are justified in searching for several meanings in his literary usage of the color spectrum. Although this may sound excessive, we can safely assume that no one experiences a color as a purely chemical pigment. Our cultural and social heritage prevents such prelapsarian simplicity.

In tracing the use of colors in his poetry, one notices Van Ostaijen's predeliction for blue. The poem **"Geologie"** (*Nagelaten gedichten*) is a central text for such an examination.

> Diepe zeeën omringen het eiland
> diepe blauwe zeeën omringen het eiland gij weet
>   niet
>   of het eiland van de sterren is daarboven
> gij weet niet
>   of het eiland aan de aardas is
> diepe zeeën
> diepe blauwe zeeën
> dat het lood zinkt
> dat het lood zoekt
> dat het zinkend zoekt
> en zinkt zoekend
> zoekend zijn eigen zoeken
> en al maar door
> zinkt
> en al maar door
> zoekt
> diepe zeeën
> blauwe zeeën
> diepe blauwe zeeën
> diepblauwe zeeën
> zinken
> zoeken
> naar de omgekeerde sterren
> tweemaal blauw
> en tweemaal bodemloos
> Wanneer vindt het blauwe lood
> in de blauwe zee
> de groen wier
> en de koraalrif
> Een dier dat door het leven jaagt naar een gedachte
>   vrede
> —een wanen in duizend duizendjarige sellen—
> gelijk een dier dat jaagt en aan zijn blinde vingers
>   vindt
> alleen het herhalen van het gedane doen
> gelijk een dier zo
> zo zinkt het lood
> des zeemans
> Moest dit zinken langs uw ogen zijgen gij kende
>   niet
> een groter leegheid

("Geology"

> Deep seas ring the island
> deep blue seas ring the island
> you know not
>   if the island belongs to the stars overhead
> you know not
>   if the island at earth's axle is
> deep seas
> deep blue seas
> which the lead sinks
> which the lead seeks
> which it sinking seeks

and sinks seeking
seeking its own seeking
and keeps on
sinking
and keeps on
seeking
deep seas
blue seas
deep blue seas
deepblue seas
to sink
to seek
for the inverted stars
twice blue
and twice bottomless
When finds the blue lead
in the blue sea
the green weed
and the coral reef
An animal which hunts through life for an opined
    peace
—a fancy in myriad millenary cells—
like an animal which hunts and at his blind fingers
    finds
only the repetition of the done deed
like an animal
sinks the lead
of the seaman
If this sinking strained past your eyes you would
    not know
a greater emptiness)

The geologist examines the strata which compose the earth's crust, their changes and relationships, in order to determine our present globe. Likewise the poet sounds the subconscious to chart the imagination, sounds his intellect to fathom the meaning of existence and the universe. The result in this instance is negative: plummeting, his soul evokes only weariness and a profound emptiness.

Now blue has an antithetical quality. It is the color of hope (the robe of the Stella Maris), of truth, of the celestial realm. Being associated with both sky and sea, it symbolizes the profundity which the depth of both elements implies. It is the color of peace and reflection, of immortality and eternity. Hence Rimbaud, in his famous sonnet "Voyelles," assigns precisely those qualities to the color. Linking the color to the vowel *O*, Rimbaud symbolizes the two as:

> O, suprême Clarion plein des strideurs étranges,
> Silences traversés des Mondes et des Anges. . .

> ["O, supreme Clarion full of strange stridencies,
> Silences crossed by Worlds and Angels. . ."]

But it appears to be not generally appreciated that blue by its very nature incites discontent, an insuffiency of expression and of action. Hope is, after all, not fulfillment; the Virgin intercedes but does not guarantee success; and the celestial profundity can turn into rage, a rage directed at the imponderable vastness which never invites intimacy. Despite his famous intoxication with azure, even such a poet as Mallarmé admits to a furious impotence which is the cause of futile revolt:

> En vain! l'Azur triomphe, et je l'entends qui chante
> Dans les cloches. Mon âme, il se fait voix pour plus
> Nous faire peur avec sa victoire méchante,
> Et du métal vivant sort en bleus angélus!
>
>   ("L'azur")

> ["In vain! The Azure triumphs, and I hear it sing-
> ing

In the bells. My soul; it turns into a voice so that
    again
We are fearful of its awful victory
And from the living metal emerges the Angelus
    as blue colors!"]

Such ambivalence was dear to a poet like Van Ostaijen, who developed his art around antithetical associations. For example, in his speech **"Gebruiksaanwijzing der lyriek"** he not only indicates that such associations are central to his work, but also talks about their metaphysical character:

> Hoe dit mij gebeurde: dat ik doelloos door de straten liep en dat plots in het schijn van veel licht, schitterden deze drie bioskoopwoorden: "de blijde dood." Zij hadden een zeldzaam ontsluierende kracht toen ik ze naprevelde; hoe ik verder ging in deze woorden, vreemd en vertrouwd, zij waren twee gezellen die elkaar gevonden hadden, ik weet niet of het onverwacht was dan wel of het geschreven stond dat eens zij elkaar moesten treffen, en hoe het adjektief aanleunde tegen het naamwoord, hoe dit daardoor lichter werd, hoe ik trachtte daarrond iets te vinden dat zou hebben uitgedrukt de diepte van deze resonantie, maar hoe ik niet weg kwam over de schittering van deze twee woorden.

> (How this happened to me: that I was walking aimlessly through the streets and suddenly, in the glimmer of much light, these three words were shining from a movietheatre: "the glad death." They had a strange unveiling power when I whispered them; how I went further into these words, strange and familiar, they were two companions who had found each other, I don't know if it was unexpected or whether it was written that they would once meet each other, how the adjective leaned against the noun, how this became lighter because of it, how I tried to find something there which would have expressed the depth of this resonance, but how I couldn't get away from the brilliance of these two words.)

The poem **"Spleen pour rire"** contains this principle in its title, while the story **"De stad der opbouwers"** develops from the antithesis that "to build up" equals "to tear down." Eros equals martialism in **"De generaal,"** while syphilis becomes the hallowed basis for an entire civilization (**"De verloren huissleutel"**). There are also such recurring themes as water or hands. Water is on the one hand positive in its lure of peace and on the other hand negative in its probability of death; and hands, which in Van Ostaijen's poetry indicate desire for contact, also mean a reaching that shall never touch.

Thus, while on the surface Van Ostaijen's use of blue symbolizes peace, profundity and contemplation, it also means for him an unyielding passivity, an endlessness which never discloses a goal, and, consequently, a metaphysical sadness for the insufficiency of human endeavors. One is not surprised therefore to discover that Van Ostaijen's use of blue is faithful to Kandinsky's interpretation—one which also notes the color's less uplifting implications. Blue is for Kandinsky a concentric color which at the same time distances itself from the observer. Or, as Van Ostaijen described it in his prose poem **"Akwarel":** "Het blauw rust, begrenst de trilling en bepaalt de verhouding naar binnen: kern" (Blue rests, borders the vibration and determines the ratio inwardly: kernel). (pp. 103-10)

Eisenstein notes that in Japanese Noh plays blue is a sinister color, associated with ghosts and devils. In many Oriental countries, for example, one did not dare come into the presence of a ruler if dressed in blue, for fear of reminding him of his mortality. There are verses in Van Ostaijen's most mordant collection, *De feesten van angst en pijn,* which combine this hatred for a sinister blue with the awe this color inspires.

> Stort een arme man zijn stem die verschroeit
>   in de brand van Zon en Zomer
> zijn stem
>   oasis verdort in Sahara
> zijn stem
>   hangt een uitgedroogde vrucht
>   in een lucht
>   te blauw en te onvruchtbaar
> Kobald dodende overvloed
> dordende schichten van hard blauw gif

("De marsj van de hete zomer")

(Pours a poor man his voice which is seared/in the fire of Sun and Summer/his voice/oasis withers in Sahara/his voice/hangs a dried fruit/in a sky/too blue and too sterile/Kobald killing abundance/withering flashes of hard blue poison.)

Bezette stad, that superlative volume in which Van Ostaijen concentrated all his technical expertise and poetic verve to describe the impact of World War I on Antwerp, has several passages where the poet develops a language of color which is both reminiscent of the palette and is linguistically independent. Evening in the **"Bedreigde stad"** harbors the danger of advancing Prussian blue, but in the conquered city (**"Rouwstad"**) it has become lethal and describes the nightmare of death:

> blauw-zwart zinken van gedoofde dingen
>   Vult
> dieper DONKer de duistere straat
>   Vallen
>   duisternis
>   in
>   donkerte
> Pruisies blauw
>   draaikolken
>   in zwart

(blue-black sinking of extinguished things/Fills/deeper DARKness the dim street/Fall/dimness/in/darkness/Prussian blue/whirlpools/in black)

In this example Van Ostaijen used blue in a very skillful manner to indicate the deadliness of the scene. Blue is associated with black, with the night, with the German army and with prussic acid, which is a very deadly poison.

Blue very often indicates basic themes in his later poetry: loneliness, longing, the unyielding mystery of the Pythia. They appear to combine in his preference for associating blue with night. In **"Geologie"** sea and sky are vast night mirrors casting the stars back and forth; the mysterious **"Mythos"** reveals its enigma at night; and those somnambulent poems **"Stilleven"** and **"Avondgeluiden"** spin nocturnal musings. I shall return to this predilection, but let us first indicate other usages.

As the desire for peace and rest, blue is defined poetically in these early lines from **De feesten van angst en pijn** where, it may be noted, one also finds this color's association with sexual emotion:

> dansen
> groen-blauw   blauw-groen
>   over het land   over het water
>   glimwormen
> liefdespel   spel van liefde
> trekt de blauwe avond saam naar het kleine vlak
>   glimworm
> glimworm klein vlak   avond groot vlak
>   licht blauw
>   duister blauw
>   groeiend prisma
>   volle vlakken

("De marsj van de hete zomer")

(dance/green-blue/blue-green/overland/over water/fireflies/loveplay/game of love/draws the blue evening together to the small space/firefly/firefly small space/evening large space/light blue/dusky blue/growing prism/full spaces)

In another early example we find the abiding sense of boundlessness in an extended image which has the geometrical precision of a Cubist painting:

> Avond
>   huizen zinken indigo op blauw
> kontrapunt daartussen
>   rechte vlakken schalielood waar licht op
>   ruist
>
> Muziek
>   levend naar toppunt van
>   BLAUW
> indigo is dicht bij
>   blauw
>   valt de onmetelikheid

("De marsj van de hete zomer")

(Evening/houses sink indigo on blue/counterpoint between them/vertical planes of leaden slate on which light/rustles/Music/living towards acme of/BLUE/indigo close by/blue/falls the immensity)

The extremely sensitive notation of this *petite phrase en bleu* is characteristic of Van Ostaijen's poetry, where subtle modulations of color (**"Onbeduidende polka"**) combine with phenomenological precision of detail (**"Stilleven"**). Here is a painter's patiently discerning eye clearly separating three nuances of blue—the almost black, indigo houses, their blue-grey slate roofs, and the evening sky darkening into night—in a musical cadence before the engulfing night erases the landscape with infinity.

Extended canvasses of this language of color can be found in such poems as **"Stad stilleven"** (*Bezette stad*), which ends in a remarkable evocation of searchlights through colors; the horror of **"Maskers"** through white on white (*Feesten*); **"Spleen pour rire"** and **"Vrolik landschap"** (*Nagelaten gedichten*) where color values evoke tone modulations which evoke color values in an exquisite example of a game of sonority; and the fragile weariness of **"Onbeduidende polka"** (*Nagelaten gedichten*) which the poverty of the wilted pink and green sadly underscores. To my knowledge, Van Ostaijen also wrote the only purely abstract painting in words in that curiously virulent prose poem **"Merkwaardige aanval."** The learned essayist codifying the technical austerity of Cubism certainly knew how to apply this knowledge to his poetry in order to reinvent the mystery of phenomena. Nothing in Van Ostaijen's work was ever gratuitous.

Doubly mirrored, the island in **"Geologie"** is both in the sky and in the sea. Two basins of blue curving into an endless circle, sky and sea make the inverted stars twice blue and twice bottomless. Van Ostaijen favored this complex and antithetical perception, where it stands for both height and depth, the vertical and the spatial, sky and sea. In an earlier poem he fashions a clear image for it: "grote vlekken/kalkend in gespannen papier van hemel/omgedraaide kuip van blauw" (large spots/whitewashed in tensed paper of the sky/inverted vat of blue)—which was even more apropos in the original version as "omgedraaide blauwkuip" (inverted bluevat). Be it the tub of blue below or the tub of blue above, neither yields certainty. On the contrary, they doom us to the delusion of action: "het herhalen van het gedane doen" (the repetition of the done deed). Here is the weariness of profitless action and yet at the same time the constant yearning for what lies beyond the horizon. For the two hemispherical cups appear to join in a promise of certainty, of reality, of finitude. But we should remember that a boat never crosses the horizon in front of it: each journey is a shipwreck.

This immense blue yields no specificity—is an elusive sublimation. And yet it is *there*. "Le bleu est l'obscurité devenue visible" ["Blue is obscurity become visible"] (Paul Claudel). And the night invokes an even more profound equilibrium, provides a unity so vast that vision merges with what is viewed: "de nacht is gene blauwheid aan 't einde van mijn ogen" (**"Mythos"**) (the night is yonder blueness at the end of my eyes). In Van Ostaijen's last poems, eyes, vision, the sea, the sky, water, and the night blend into a single image of vastness. The world has been dematerialized and shapes are merely ironic tokens of immutable space:

> en planten die
> koortsdoorschoten
> tussen de blauwheid van de zee en de blauwheid
> van de lucht
> slechts zijn een vergelijken
>
> **("Facture baroque")**

(and plants which/fever-riddled/between the blueness of the sea and the blueness of the sky/are merely a comparing)

The inner, spiritual landscape and the outer, material one, have been united. Irreality ensues, a somnambulent lassitude like a drugged sleep:

> Zo nu de kiezel niet kraakte onder mijn treden
> was ik zonder verleden
> in de kom van deze stilte gegleden
> **("Onbewuste avond")**

(If now the pebble did not crack under my steps/would I without a past/have slid into the bowl of this silence)

There is in these posthumous poems a constant allusion to sliding, fluidity, a desire for immersion born from a weary passivity. Yet despite this weariness of immensity, despite loneliness and estrangement, despite resignation and a desire for death, there is a belief in the quest, in man's indomitable spirit to venture yet another failure. For Van Ostaijen, who insisted that language equals myth and that poetry is mysticism, this had to be a metaphysical venture. He also knew that it would be a fragile one. Despite, or perhaps because of

"een wanen in duizend duizendjarige sellen" (a fancy in myriad millenary cells), man sets out to recover his meaning.

> soms slaat het verlangen der mensen zo hoog uit
> dat zij takelen de nederige boot
> en ter zee gaan
> in de zeilen speelt de wind een waan
>   een oude waan
>   die over de kim gekelderd lag
>   tot de wind de hulzen stuk woei
>   en uit de scherven walmt de wijn van deze
> waan
>   van deze oude waan
>
> **("Facture baroque")**

(sometimes the desire of mankind breaks out at such a pitch/that they rig the humble boat and go to sea/in the sails the wind plays a fancy/an ancient fancy/which was put down beyond the horizon/until the wind blew the straw covers to pieces/and from the shards smokes this fancy's wine/this ancient fancy)

The desire to capture the impossible, to be once again truly innocent, to know nature once more in its primordial beauty—these desires are unrealistic but they can be dreamt. Ultimately one has only oneiric knowledge. The entire work of that great French critic, Gaston Bachelard, reiterates this truth. "La connaissance poétique du monde précède, comme il convient, la connaissance raisonable des objets. Le monde est beau avant d'être vrai. Le monde est admiré avant d'être vérifié" ["Poetic knowledge of the world precedes, as is fitting, rational knowledge of objects. The world is beautiful before being true. The world is admired before being verified"]. Van Ostaijen captured the same idea, which is also the essence of his art, in the following lines:

> Soms dringt de drang de droom tot een gestalte
> en wordt het lichaam droom
>
> **("Facture baroque")**

(sometimes the urge forces the dream into a shape/and the body becomes a dream)

His recurring use of imagery of boats has now become clear. For what better symbol for the spirit's perilous journey than a flimsy little vessel? Quite early in his career, Van Ostaijen asked the question which contains all of his work and which summarizes everything said here:

> Kan een boot, mijn Heer, vergaan
> die niets draagt dan het licht gewicht van mijne
>   blauwe ziel?
>
> **("lied voor mezelf"** in *Sienjaal*)

(Can a boat, my Lord, be wrecked/which carries only the light weight of my blue soul?)

The answer lies in the question. (pp. 111-17)

E. M. Beekman, "Blue Skiff of the Soul: The Significance of the Color Blue in Paul Van Ostaijen's Poetry," in Dutch Studies, *Vol. I, 1974, pp. 103-17.*

ELSA STRIETMAN (essay date 1985)

[*In the following excerpt, Strietman analyzes the themes and techniques of* Bezette stad.]

In European poetry of the city **Bezette stad** holds a unique position. It expresses a momentous historical event in memorable artistic form. Its subject is the siege, bombardment and capture of a major European city by means of the most advanced military technology and its subsequent occupation by an enemy army. Historically, the poem thus anticipates the fate that was to befall a vast number of European cities between 1939 and 1945 and which now hangs over every city of the world. The fall of Antwerp in October 1914 was a moment of truth in modern military history. It showed that even the most strongly fortified city is an easy target for enemy bombardment.

Formally, the poem is equally in advance of its time. For Van Ostaijen develops the typographical innovations of the Futurists, Cubists and Dadaists so that they convey the destructiveness and fragmentation of a war-torn city with unprecedented vividness. No doubt he was familiar with Marinetti's sound-poem about the siege of Adrianopolis during the Balkan Wars, *Zang tumb tumb* (1914). The similarity with Apollinaire's calligraphic treatment of the First World War which is often remarked upon is rather a superficial one; besides it is not sure whether Van Ostaijen knew this work by Apollinaire at the time he was working on *Bezette stad.* But where the typographical experiments of Marinetti and Apollinaire present modern warfare as a spectacle to be enjoyed, like a grandiose firework display, Van Ostaijen's poem conveys exactly the opposite. It shows what modern warfare is like when you are on the receiving end, in images of nihilistic destruction and despair. It is a poem which deserves to be better known.

From the available documentation it seems that Van Ostaijen planned in *Bezette stad* to give a picture "of all that an Occupied City is." The titles of the planned poems show the collection to have a coherent narrative structure. Van Ostaijen's biographer, Gerrit Borgers, interprets the fragmented information as follows: "This unity, 'my poem,' would be composed out of different parts, each of which would depict a certain aspect of his memories of wartime in Antwerp, as a snapshot." Also "just as these poems consisted of isolated words and wordgroups, thus would the history of the years of occupation be depicted in isolated moments and the development would mainly be suggested by the sequence of these moments." One criticism of this cinematographic technique was that it created a poetry of isolated instances, fleeting situations without "development, past or future" [Borgers, *Paul van Ostaijen*]. But it created more than that. This collage of impressions and experiences in strikingly concrete images is extraordinarily effective and evocative war-photography: the marching enemy army, the outline of the burning city, the roads choked with military traffic and bedraggled lines of refugees. The new threat of aerial bombardment is typographically accentuated in Ostaijen's image of Zeppelins over London [see illustration]. The juxtaposition of the Zeppelin attacks reported in the newspapers ("Dagbladen") with the refrain from a famous song indicates that it is "Goodbye" not merely to Piccadilly, but to the security of the "blessed island" of Britain as a whole.

The form of *Bezette stad* is pure Dada, in its use of montage technique, including snatches of advertisements, film titles, popular songs—all that one might expect to hear and see in a big city, especially one in which entertainment is an important ingredient. The typography too, is that of the Berlin Dadaists: it provides rhythm, enforces punctuation, is onomatopoeic and it forces the reader to become a speaker, compels him to turn up or down the volume of the voice, to slur or

"Zeppelin."

to enunciate. The pages at times read like a musical score. The juxtaposition of different languages is also reminiscent of Dada, but in Ostaijen's poem it acquires a sharper political focus. The cumulative effect of these devices is illustrated by ["**Bedreigde stad**" (see illustration p. 421)], which portrays the Prussian advance on the "threatened city." The initial viewpoint is Flemish: Liège, which has already succumbed to the German march and mortar fire, is identified by its Flemish name *Luik.* But the German breakthrough is also signalled linguistically, by the counterpoint between two German songs: the boldly accentuated patriotic anthem "Hail to thee in victor's laurels," ironically, undercut by snatches from a vulgar song about the "dear little doll" the German soldier really hopes to find as he marches through Brussels. An italicised phrase indicates the reactions of the Flemish populace ("Joe Joe Joe—a Zeppelin—creep quickly into the cellar"), while the Prussian troops advance with their relentless "one-two, one-two." In smaller type the defeated Belgian army retreats through the typographically disrupted "flickering countryside" and "raging fire." And the disunity of Belgium is pinpointed by the linguistic disjunction "mijn broer les hommes," which undermines the myth of national solidarity. Defeat is finally spelt out in French: "débâcle," because that is precisely what it is: defeat for the *French* ruling class in Belgium. It was not so unambiguously a defeat for the Flemish, some of whose national aspirations (like the founding of a Flemish University at Ghent) were actually fulfilled under German occupation.

Van Ostaijen's theoretical explanation of the use of typography in *Bezette stad* has fortunately been preserved. He had been accused of inconsistency: in using rhythmic typography he seemed to contradict his own statement that art needed to be kept pure. Van Ostaijen, in reply, stressed the necessity to see *Bezette stad* not merely as poetry, but as a cumulative imaginative experience: "The book stands in relation to the poetry as the written score to the instrumental performance" and "It can not be denied that the printed word is a translation of the musical into the graphical." He furthermore stresses that the poet must be seen as an interpreter, an entertainer, who should not have the barrier of the written word between him and his audience. The modern poet is no longer speaking from a Dionysian trance, nor is he any longer able to reach his audience by means of the spoken word. The resulting loss of spontaneity and impact is counteracted by the typography in *Bezette stad.* Van Ostaijen thought that the significance of his poetic experiment was that it created a form which eliminated the barrier between poet and audience and thus heightened the effect of the poetry on the reader.

Bezette stad may be typographically disconcerting, but it has a clear narrative structure. The sequence is divided into three parts: (*a*) "Dedication to Mr. So-and-So," followed by eigh-

"*Bedreigde stad.*"

teen poems (with **"Threatened City"** setting the tone); (*b*) "The Circles Turning Inward," consisting of ten poems, five of which share the same subtitle "Music Hall"; and finally (*c*) a fifteen-page poem entitled **"The Retreat."** Part (*a*) portrays the German onslaught on the city; (*b*) shows the inner life of the city as it lies strangled under the occupation; part (*c*) describes the end of the War and the resulting situation in Antwerp as well as in Europe as a whole.

Mr. So-and-So, to whom the poem is dedicated, was a much-travelled friend of Van Ostaijen whose experiences inspired the erotic map of Europe which features in the **"Dedication."** The anonymity of the pseudonym adds to the nihilistic atmosphere of the poem in which different languages, different places are shown to yield nothing new, nothing meaningful: "es ist alles schon dagewesen" ["everything has existed before"]. Even the unusual map of Europe, drawn according to erotic rather than political, geological, religious or commercial features, is not stimulating, but suggestive of the violation of the continent by the War and by the débâcle of our civilisation. This pseudo-voyage of discovery of Europe ends with a five-minute snapshot view of the city which stood model for all other cities, the Acropolis, the cradle of Western civilisation, here perceived as "necropolis," city of the dead. Civilisation as we know it is declared null and void; the only solution seems to lie in total destruction, after which there will perhaps be a place for a new beginning.

Bezette stad is, after all, not only a poetic experiment. It is a passionate protest about the human condition. Van Ostaijen's humanitarian ideals suffered a severe blow in the Berlin years, but they were not completely submerged by the nihilism which predominates in *Bezette stad.* In the **"Dedication"** the Apocalypse is announced, in which God the Father will bring the last Act. The only positive thing left is to refuse to play along any further: "Nihil in all directions." But after the explosion of the destructive forces all is not yet lost. In serene normal typography the hope of a new beginning is expressed:

Zullen zijn gevallen	Will have fallen all
alle katedralen	cathedrals
kannibalen	cannibals
Hannibalen generalen	Hannibals generals
idealen	ideals
kolonels	colonels
bordels	brothels
misschien	perhaps
zal er plaats zijn	there will be a place
voor een	for a self-evident
vanzelfsprekende	beauty
schoonheid	
zuiver	pure
ongeweten	unconscious

After this evocation of a general spiritual destruction, be it with a small spark of hope amidst the chaos, we are shown more specific instances of the physical destruction brought about by the War. **"Threatened City," "The Shell above the City," "Deserted Fortresses," "Lonely City," "Hollow Harbour," "Zeppelin"** give us a series of pictures of the attack on Antwerp, the bombing, the desolate girdle of fortresses after the withdrawal of the defending troops, the deadness, emptiness, stillness in the strangled city in which all commercial and industrial life has come to a halt. **"Brothel," "Empty Cinema," "Nomenclature of Deserted Things," "City Still-life," "Deadsunday"** all show the nightmarish wasteland atmosphere of the city under the corruption of foreign occupation, and the resulting disintegration of normality.

Everywhere is the implied contrast with the normal, pre-war situation. The brothels which are losing their "bonne clientèle" of former days, now that queues of soldiers are waiting; the entertainment centre has been reduced to a few shabby cinemas after the bombing; the boulevard has nothing but a few shady cafés: "Waar zijn de tijden van vroeger?" ("Où sont les neiges d'antan?") ["Where are the snows of yesteryear?"]. In the **"Dedication"** nihilism was an existential condition though even there hope of resurrection could be detected; in a poem such as **"Hollow Harbour"** everything seems submerged by despair, but there is an implied temporariness through references to the past, which brings back a glimmer of hope. Thus, there is affectionate remembering of the now empty harbour in its heyday:

> Ik heb gezien hoe van de holle haven kaseiden be-
>   wogen in alle richtingen
> en sprongen
> slag van het havenhart
>
> grijze strook
> magiese staf
>
> ("I have seen how from the hollow harbour boats
> moved out in all directions and jumped
> beat of the harbour-heart
>
> grey plume
> magic wand")

This city is only unreal in the sense that it is experiencing an abnormal phase. The horror, confusion and despair we encounter in these poems seem to be strongly determined by the circumstances. The city is not felt to be ugly, nightmarish, evil in essence. It has become so because of the War, and it is the War which is in essence evil. But the power of war has grown until it becomes the symbolic expression of the human condition.

"Sous les ponts de Paris" by its very title, prevents our point of view being solely directed towards the "Occupied City Antwerp"; all cities, all life, are under attack! Its content shows the reality of suffering embodied by the all-pervading presence of Christ, as well as the meaninglessness of traditional religious beliefs and manifestations.

"Mourning City" describes the fear of the air-attacks on the darkened city, and an attempt to escape the awareness of death is expressed in **"Banal Dance."** The fear for the safety of the brothers and sons at the front and the anguished waiting for news is reported in **"House City I"** and **"Good News"** bitingly shows the ludicrousness of hero-worship and warfare in a snapshot of the Belgian King and the Crown Prince, princes of German extraction, defeating singlehandedly a battalion of German soldiers. This sense of the grotesque culminates in the last poem of the first part of **Bezette stad;** the world has gone mad and the only reaction possible is to laugh about it: in **"The Great Circus of the Holy Ghost"** performs the world famous Trio of Religion, King, and State!

In the second part, "Circles Turning Inward" we are shown life within the Occupied City in a confined space, that of the music hall. In Van Ostaijen's first collection, **Music-Hall,** at least in the title-poem, an atmosphere of lethargic boredom or a frenetic longing for forgetfulness prevails. There the awareness of the paradox of solitude amidst the multitude,

of the individual trying to retain a sense of Self by merging with the crowds, is very strong. Prominent too, in the **Music-Hall** collection of 1916, is the sense that it is possible to believe in the victory of all that is good. In the five "Music-Hall" poems in **Bezette stad** entertainment does not function as a temporary refuge from pressurised ordinary city life but as a refuge from the strangled city under occupation. Here it does not foster the illusion of the victory of good, but works enslaving as a drug. The music hall entertainment can no longer be enjoyed or viewed without enormous scepsis and irony; the tension between the world inside the music hall and the world outside is unbearable and will burst like a balloon. Van Ostaijen's expression of that tension cannot be taken as a statement about the here and now only, but about existence as such.

There is a recurring widening of the frame of reference from actual to existential situations. One example of this is the poem celebrating the Danish film star Asta Nielsen who was particularly famous for her film *Abgrunden* (*The Abyss*, 1910), and who became an idol for her generation. In Van Ostaijen's poem she is given almost cosmic significance and divine powers and comes to be seen as a means of salvation from all the evils of the world. Through the erotic fascination of this goddess of the white screen we are reminded of the erotic map of Europe in the **"Dedication"** and via this again of the violation of Europe by the War and the failure of our civilisation.

The third part of **Bezette stad,** the single poem **"De aftocht"** (**"The Retreat"**) expresses the effect of the War on Antwerp and the total havoc it wrought on Europe; everywhere people are suffering, feel displaced, without hope. Here the existential NIHIL of the **"Dedication"** returns and once more the tempting idea is put forward that total destruction-as-cleansing is necessary, that a *tabula rasa* is the only state from which life can begin again. Against this strong seductive voice others can be heard, the chauvinistic voices, which, having learnt nothing, call for the cultivation of nationalism, and the feeble humanitarian voices, still clinging to the idea that the Word, i.e. communication, could be a possible road to salvation. Above the rattling of machine guns, the Word becomes a Voice, which, after a last explosion, "KNAL," is given a name, "LIEBKNECHT," thereby closing off the page, the Word, the Voice. The typography quiets down to a small expression of hope that perhaps the spirit of the martyr Liebknecht might live on amongst workers and soldiers. But the small voice is smothered under the hollow phrases taking possession first of the whole width of the following page, where in staccato rhythm more platitudes are delivered:

> NOW
>
> the doctors the gentlemen doctors the gentlemen
> professors do not see do not hear get their wisdom
> of their own make from the Belgischen Kurier Vic-
> tory Warsaw Grodno Kofno Brest-Litovsk Bucha-
> rest
>
> and now and now
> grain from the Ukraine?
> bread
> durchhalten aushalten
> and then
> aushalten
> brave Pommeranians

the victory is for those who can suffer the most mis-
    ery
soldiers
Berlin—Baghdad
the emperor declares
(all monarchs declare that is their style)
democratisation of the government
but keep heart
14 points
14 buttons
alle Männer saufen alle Männer saufen
    nur der kleine Wilson nicht

This passage, unexpectedly sober in its original typography, conveys the disillusionment of the Germans (and their Flemish sympathisers) during the final phases of the war. It is clear that in Van Ostaijen's view the destruction has not created a new world or a new sensibility. This moment, "Now," should be the end of the war but is not the end of war. A further threat is posed by the intelligentsia which is just as self-opinionated as ever and gets its wisdom, home-made, from the *Belgischen Kurier,* a sneer in the direction of the many collaborators in Belgium. Who can talk of victory after the terrible suffering in Warsaw and all the other cities? The hungry millions are placated by the promise of grain from the Ukraine and by empty rhetoric; they are admonished to "durchhalten aushalten" and after that they will have to endure even more. Victory is an empty word in the face of all the suffering; declarations by rulers, be they Emperor or President, i.e. the German Kaiser or President Wilson of America, are empty words, democratisation is an empty word. War is nothing but a power game between world powers, and ordinary people suffer for it. President Wilson's fourteen points for peace have no effect at all, they are worth no more than fourteen buttons (Flemish for "not worth tuppence"). Wilson may believe in them, but everyone else is still sloganising about "victory" and boozing German beer.

Bezette stad ends on a wistful note, giving evidence of the awareness that the suffering was in vain, that even this destruction has not taught people a lesson, that an even greater disaster may be necessary, though we cannot be certain that a new beginning will ever be effected. With the benefit of hindsight, with the Second World War behind us and a world seemingly bent on causing a Third, Van Ostaijen's poem takes on prophetic proportions. (pp. 134-42)

Elsa Strietman, " 'Occupied City': Ostaijen's Antwerp and the Impact of the First World War," in Unreal City: Urban Experience in Modern European Literature and Art, *edited by Edward Timms and David Kelley, St. Martin's Press, 1985, pp. 128-43.*

ADDITIONAL BIBLIOGRAPHY

Beekman, E. M. Introduction to "Six Prose Pieces," by Paul van Ostaijen. Translated by E. M. Beekman. *The Massachusetts Review* 9, No. 4 (Autumn 1968): 663-65.

Sketch of Van Ostaijen's life and work.

——. Introduction to *Bankruptcy Jazz,* by Paul van Ostaijen. Translated by E. M. Beekman. *The Drama Review* 14, No. 3 (1970): 145-47.

Relates Van Ostaijen's 1919 filmscript to the attitudes and artistic techniques of the Dada movement.

——. Introduction to *Patriotism, Inc., and Other Tales,* by Paul van Ostaijen, edited and translated by E. M. Beekman, pp. ix-xix. Amherst: University of Massachusetts Press, 1971.

Discusses Van Ostaijen as one of the foremost satirists of the twentieth century.

Bulhof, Francis, ed. *Nijhoff, Van Ostaijen, "De Stijl": Modernism in the Netherlands and Belgium in the First Quarter of the 20th Century.* The Hague: Martinus Nijhoff, 1976, 136 p.

Collection of essays providing cultural and artistic background to Van Ostaijen's work.

Twentieth-Century Literary Criticism

Cumulative Indexes
Volumes 1-33

This Index Includes References to Entries in These Gale Series

Contemporary Literary Criticism

Presents excerpts of criticism on the works of novelists, poets, dramatists, short story writers, scriptwriters, and other creative writers who are now living or who have died since 1960. Cumulative indexes to authors and nationalities are included, as well as an index to titles discussed in the individual volume. Volumes 1-53 are in print.

Twentieth-Century Literary Criticism

Contains critical excerpts by the most significant commentators on poets, novelists, short story writers, dramatists, and philosophers who died between 1900 and 1960. Cumulative indexes to authors, nationalities, and titles discussed are included in each new volume. Volumes 1-33 are in print.

Nineteenth-Century Literature Criticism

Offers significant passages from criticism on authors who died between 1800 and 1899. Cumulative indexes to authors, nationalities, and titles discussed are included in each new volume. Volumes 1-22 are in print.

Literature Criticism from 1400 to 1800

Compiles significant passages from the most noteworthy criticism on authors of the fifteenth through eighteenth centuries. Cumulative indexes to authors, nationalities, and titles discussed are included in each new volume. Volumes 1-10 are in print.

Classical and Medieval Literature Criticism

Offers excerpts of criticism on the works of world authors from classical antiquity through the fourteenth century. Cumulative indexes to authors, titles, and critics are included in each volume. Volumes 1-3 are in print.

Short Story Criticism

Compiles excerpts of criticism on short fiction by writers of all eras and nationalities. Cumulative indexes to authors, nationalities, and titles discussed are included in each new volume. Volumes 1-2 are in print.

Children's Literature Review

Includes excerpts from reviews, criticism, and commentary on works of authors and illustrators who create books for children. Cumulative indexes to authors, nationalities, and titles discussed are included in each new volume. Volumes 1-18 are in print.

Contemporary Authors Series

Encompasses five related series. *Contemporary Authors* provides biographical and bibliographical information on more than 92,000 writers of fiction, nonfiction, poetry, journalism, drama, motion pictures, and other fields. Each new volume contains sketches on authors not previously covered in the series. Volumes 1-126 are in print. *Contemporary Authors New Revision Series* provides completely updated information on active authors covered in previously published volumes of *CA*. Only entries requiring significant change are revised for *CA New Revision Series*. Volumes 1-26 are in print. *Contemporary Authors Permanent Series* consists of updated listings for deceased and inactive authors removed from the original volumes 9-36 when these volumes were revised. Volumes 1-2 are in print. *Contemporary Authors Autobiography Series* presents specially commissioned autobiographies by leading contemporary writers. Volumes 1-8 are in print. *Contemporary Authors Bibliographical Series* contains primary and secondary bibliographies as well as analytical bibliographical essays by authorities on major modern authors. Volumes 1-2 are in print.

Dictionary of Literary Biography

Encompasses three related series. *Dictionary of Literary Biography* furnishes illustrated overviews of authors' lives and works and places them in the larger perspective of literary history. Volumes 1-78 are in print. *Dictionary of Literary Biography Documentary Series* illuminates the careers of major figures through a selection of literary documents, including letters, notebook and diary entries, interviews, book reviews, and photographs. Volumes 1-6 are in print. *Dictionary of Literary Biography Yearbook* summarizes the past year's literary activity with articles on genres, major prizes, conferences, and other timely subjects and includes updated and new entries on individual authors. Yearbooks for 1980-1988 are in print. A cumulative index to authors and articles is included in each new volume.

Concise Dictionary of American Literary Biography

A six-volume series that collects revised and updated sketches on major American authors that were originally presented in *Dictionary of Literary Biography*. Volumes 1-3 are in print.

Something about the Author Series

Encompasses two related series. *Something about the Author* contains heavily illustrated biographical sketches on juvenile and young adult authors and illustrators from all eras. Volumes 1-54 are in print. *Something about the Author Autobiography Series* presents specially commissioned autobiographies by prominent authors and illustrators of books for children and young adults. Volumes 1-7 are in print.

Yesterday's Authors of Books for Children

Contains heavily illustrated entries on children's writers who died before 1961. Complete in two volumes. Volumes 1-2 are in print.

Literary Criticism Series
Cumulative Author Index

This index lists all author entries in the Gale Literary Criticism Series and includes cross-references to other Gale sources. References in the index are identified as follows:

AAYA: *Authors & Artists for Young Adults,* Volume 1
CAAS: *Contemporary Authors Autobiography Series,* Volumes 1-8
CA: *Contemporary Authors* (original series), Volumes 1-126
CABS: *Contemporary Authors Bibliographical Series,* Volumes 1-2
CANR: *Contemporary Authors New Revision Series,* Volumes 1-26
CAP: *Contemporary Authors Permanent Series,* Volumes 1-2
CA-R: *Contemporary Authors* (revised editions), Volumes 1-44
CDALB: *Concise Dictionary of American Literary Biography,* Volume 1-3
CLC: *Contemporary Literary Criticism,* Volumes 1-54
CLR: *Children's Literature Review,* Volumes 1-18
CMLC: *Classical and Medieval Literature Criticism,* Volumes 1-3
DLB: *Dictionary of Literary Biography,* Volumes 1-78
DLB-DS: *Dictionary of Literary Biography Documentary Series,* Volumes 1-6
DLB-Y: *Dictionary of Literary Biography Yearbook,* Volumes 1980-1988
LC: *Literature Criticism from 1400 to 1800,* Volumes 1-10
NCLC: *Nineteenth-Century Literature Criticism,* Volumes 1-22
SAAS: *Something about the Author Autobiography Series,* Volumes 1-7
SATA: *Something about the Author,* Volumes 1-54
SSC: *Short Story Criticism,* Volumes 1-2
TCLC: *Twentieth-Century Literary Criticism,* Volumes 1-33
YABC: *Yesterday's Authors of Books for Children,* Volumes 1-2

A. E. 1867-1935 . . . . **TCLC 3, 10**
See also Russell, George William
See also DLB 19

Abbey, Edward 1927- . . . . **CLC 36**
See also CANR 2; CA 45-48

Abbott, Lee K., Jr. 19??- . . . . **CLC 48**

Abe, Kobo 1924- . . . . **CLC 8, 22**
See also CA 65-68

Abell, Kjeld 1901-1961 . . . . **CLC 15**
See also obituary CA 111

Abish, Walter 1931- . . . . **CLC 22**
See also CA 101

Abrahams, Peter (Henry) 1919- . . . . . **CLC 4**
See also CA 57-60

Abrams, M(eyer) H(oward) 1912- . . . **CLC 24**
See also CANR 13; CA 57-60

Abse, Dannie 1923- . . . . **CLC 7, 29**
See also CAAS 1; CANR 4; CA 53-56;
DLB 27

Achebe, (Albert) Chinua(lumogu)
1930- . . . . **CLC 1, 3, 5, 7, 11, 26, 51**
See also CANR 6; CA 1-4R; SATA 38, 40

Acker, Kathy 1948- . . . . **CLC 45**
See also CA 117, 122

Ackroyd, Peter 1949- . . . . **CLC 34**

Acorn, Milton 1923- . . . . **CLC 15**
See also CA 103; DLB 53

Adamov, Arthur 1908-1970 . . . . . **CLC 4, 25**
See also CAP 2; CA 17-18;
obituary CA 25-28R

Adams, Alice (Boyd) 1926- . . . **CLC 6, 13, 46**
See also CA 81-84; DLB-Y 86

Adams, Douglas (Noel) 1952- . . . . . . **CLC 27**
See also CA 106; DLB-Y 83

Adams, Henry (Brooks)
1838-1918 . . . . **TCLC 4**
See also CA 104; DLB 12, 47

Adams, Richard (George)
1920- . . . . **CLC 4, 5, 18**
See also CANR 3; CA 49-52; SATA 7

Adamson, Joy(-Friederike Victoria)
1910-1980 . . . . **CLC 17**
See also CANR 22; CA 69-72;
obituary CA 93-96; SATA 11;
obituary SATA 22

Adcock, (Kareen) Fleur 1934- . . . . . . **CLC 41**
See also CANR 11; CA 25-28R; DLB 40

Addams, Charles (Samuel)
1912-1988 . . . . **CLC 30**
See also CANR 12; CA 61-64

Adler, C(arole) S(chwerdtfeger)
1932- . . . . **CLC 35**
See also CANR 19; CA 89-92; SATA 26

Adler, Renata 1938- . . . . **CLC 8, 31**
See also CANR 5, 22; CA 49-52

Ady, Endre 1877-1919 . . . . **TCLC 11**
See also CA 107

Agee, James 1909-1955 . . . . **TCLC 1, 19**
See also CA 108; DLB 2, 26;
CDALB 1941-1968

Agnon, S(hmuel) Y(osef Halevi)
1888-1970 . . . . **CLC 4, 8, 14**
See also CAP 2; CA 17-18;
obituary CA 25-28R

Ai 1947- . . . . **CLC 4, 14**
See also CA 85-88

Aiken, Conrad (Potter)
1889-1973 . . . . **CLC 1, 3, 5, 10**
See also CANR 4; CA 5-8R;
obituary CA 45-48; SATA 3, 30; DLB 9,
45

Aiken, Joan (Delano) 1924- . . . . **CLC 35**
See also CLR 1; CANR 4; CA 9-12R;
SAAS 1; SATA 2, 30

Ainsworth, William Harrison
1805-1882 . . . . **NCLC 13**
See also SATA 24; DLB 21

Ajar, Emile 1914-1980
See Gary, Romain

Akhmatova, Anna 1888-1966 . . . . **CLC 11, 25**
See also CAP 1; CA 19-20;
obituary CA 25-28R

Bennett, (Enoch) Arnold
1867-1931 . . . . TCLC **5, 20**
See also CA 106; DLB 10, 34

Bennett, George Harold 1930-
See Bennett, Hal
See also CA 97-100

Bennett, Hal 1930- . . . . CLC **5**
See also Bennett, George Harold
See also DLB 33

Bennett, Jay 1912- . . . . CLC **35**
See also CANR 11; CA 69-72; SAAS 4;
SATA 27, 41

Bennett, Louise (Simone) 1919- . . . . . CLC **28**
See also Bennett-Coverly, Louise Simone

Bennett-Coverly, Louise Simone 1919-
See Bennett, Louise (Simone)
See also CA 97-100

Benson, E(dward) F(rederic)
1867-1940 . . . . TCLC **27**
See also CA 114

Benson, Jackson J. 1930- . . . . CLC **34**
See also CA 25-28R

Benson, Sally 1900-1972 . . . . CLC **17**
See also CAP 1; CA 19-20;
obituary CA 37-40R; SATA 1, 35;
obituary SATA 27

Benson, Stella 1892-1933 . . . . TCLC **17**
See also CA 117; DLB 36

Bentley, E(dmund) C(lerihew)
1875-1956 . . . . TCLC **12**
See also CA 108; DLB 70

Bentley, Eric (Russell) 1916- . . . . CLC **24**
See also CANR 6; CA 5-8R

Berger, John (Peter) 1926- . . . . . . CLC **2, 19**
See also CA 81-84; DLB 14

Berger, Melvin (H.) 1927- . . . . CLC **12**
See also CANR 4; CA 5-8R; SAAS 2;
SATA 5

Berger, Thomas (Louis)
1924- . . . . CLC **3, 5, 8, 11, 18, 38**
See also CANR 5; CA 1-4R; DLB 2;
DLB-Y 80

Bergman, (Ernst) Ingmar 1918- . . . . . CLC **16**
See also CA 81-84

Bergstein, Eleanor 1938- . . . . CLC **4**
See also CANR 5; CA 53-56

Bermant, Chaim 1929- . . . . CLC **40**
See also CANR 6; CA 57-60

Bernanos, (Paul Louis) Georges
1888-1948 . . . . TCLC **3**
See also CA 104; DLB 72

Bernhard, Thomas 1931- . . . . CLC **3, 32**
See also CA 85-88

Berriault, Gina 1926- . . . . CLC **54**
See also CA 116

Berrigan, Daniel J. 1921- . . . . CLC **4**
See also CAAS 1; CANR 11; CA 33-36R;
DLB 5

Berrigan, Edmund Joseph Michael, Jr.
1934-1983
See Berrigan, Ted
See also CANR 14; CA 61-64;
obituary CA 110

Berrigan, Ted 1934-1983 . . . . CLC **37**
See also Berrigan, Edmund Joseph Michael,
Jr.
See also DLB 5

Berry, Chuck 1926- . . . . CLC **17**

Berry, Wendell (Erdman)
1934- . . . . CLC **4, 6, 8, 27, 46**
See also CA 73-76; DLB 5, 6

Berryman, Jerry 1914-1972
See also CDALB 1941-1968

Berryman, John
1914-1972 . . . . . CLC **1, 2, 3, 4, 6, 8, 10,
13, 25**
See also CAP 1; CA 15-16;
obituary CA 33-36R; CABS 2; DLB 48;
CDALB 1941-1968

Bertolucci, Bernardo 1940- . . . . CLC **16**
See also CA 106

Besant, Annie (Wood) 1847-1933 . . . TCLC **9**
See also CA 105

Bessie, Alvah 1904-1985 . . . . CLC **23**
See also CANR 2; CA 5-8R;
obituary CA 116; DLB 26

Beti, Mongo 1932- . . . . CLC **27**
See also Beyidi, Alexandre

Betjeman, (Sir) John
1906-1984 . . . . CLC **2, 6, 10, 34, 43**
See also CA 9-12R; obituary CA 112;
DLB 20; DLB-Y 84

Betti, Ugo 1892-1953 . . . . TCLC **5**
See also CA 104

Betts, Doris (Waugh) 1932- . . . CLC **3, 6, 28**
See also CANR 9; CA 13-16R; DLB-Y 82

Bialik, Chaim Nachman
1873-1934 . . . . TCLC **25**

Bidart, Frank 19??- . . . . CLC **33**

Bienek, Horst 1930- . . . . CLC **7, 11**
See also CA 73-76

Bierce, Ambrose (Gwinett)
1842-1914? . . . . TCLC **1, 7**
See also CA 104; DLB 11, 12, 23, 71;
CDALB 1865-1917

Billington, Rachel 1942- . . . . CLC **43**
See also CA 33-36R

Binyon, T(imothy) J(ohn) 1936- . . . . CLC **34**
See also CA 111

Bioy Casares, Adolfo 1914- . . . . CLC **4, 8, 13**
See also CANR 19; CA 29-32R

Bird, Robert Montgomery
1806-1854 . . . . NCLC **1**

Birdwell, Cleo 1936-
See DeLillo, Don

Birney (Alfred) Earle
1904- . . . . CLC **1, 4, 6, 11**
See also CANR 5, 20; CA 1-4R

Bishop, Elizabeth
1911-1979 . . . . . . CLC **1, 4, 9, 13, 15, 32**
See also CA 5-8R; obituary CA 89-92;
CABS 2; obituary SATA 24; DLB 5

Bishop, John 1935- . . . . CLC **10**
See also CA 105

Bissett, Bill 1939- . . . . CLC **18**
See also CANR 15; CA 69-72; DLB 53

Biyidi, Alexandre 1932-
See Beti, Mongo
See also CA 114

Bjornson, Bjornstjerne (Martinius)
1832-1910 . . . . TCLC **7**
See also CA 104

Blackburn, Paul 1926-1971 . . . . . . CLC **9, 43**
See also CA 81-84; obituary CA 33-36R;
DLB 16; DLB-Y 81

Black Elk 1863-1950 . . . . TCLC **33**

Blackmore, R(ichard) D(oddridge)
1825-1900 . . . . TCLC **27**
See also CA 120; DLB 18

Blackmur, R(ichard) P(almer)
1904-1965 . . . . CLC **2, 24**
See also CAP 1; CA 11-12;
obituary CA 25-28R; DLB 63

Blackwood, Algernon (Henry)
1869-1951 . . . . TCLC **5**
See also CA 105

Blackwood, Caroline 1931- . . . . CLC **6, 9**
See also CA 85-88; DLB 14

Blair, Eric Arthur 1903-1950
See Orwell, George
See also CA 104; SATA 29

Blais, Marie-Claire
1939- . . . . CLC **2, 4, 6, 13, 22**
See also CAAS 4; CA 21-24R; DLB 53

Blaise, Clark 1940- . . . . CLC **29**
See also CAAS 3; CANR 5; CA 53-56R;
DLB 53

Blake, Nicholas 1904-1972
See Day Lewis, C(ecil)

Blake, William 1757-1827 . . . . NCLC **13**
See also SATA 30

Blasco Ibanez, Vicente
1867-1928 . . . . TCLC **12**
See also CA 110

Blatty, William Peter 1928- . . . . CLC **2**
See also CANR 9; CA 5-8R

Blessing, Lee 1949- . . . . CLC **54**

Blish, James (Benjamin)
1921-1975 . . . . CLC **14**
See also CANR 3; CA 1-4R;
obituary CA 57-60; DLB 8

Blixen, Karen (Christentze Dinesen)
1885-1962
See Dinesen, Isak
See also CAP 2; CA 25-28; SATA 44

Bloch, Robert (Albert) 1917- . . . . CLC **33**
See also CANR 5; CA 5-8R; SATA 12;
DLB 44

Blok, Aleksandr (Aleksandrovich)
1880-1921 . . . . TCLC **5**
See also CA 104

Bloom, Harold 1930- . . . . CLC **24**
See also CA 13-16R

Blount, Roy (Alton), Jr. 1941- . . . . . CLC **38**
See also CANR 10; CA 53-56

Bloy, Leon 1846-1917 . . . . TCLC **22**
See also CA 121

Blume, Judy (Sussman Kitchens)
1938- . . . . CLC **12, 30**
See also CLR 2, 15; CANR 13; CA 29-32R;
SATA 2, 31; DLB 52

Ducasse, Isidore Lucien   1846-1870
  See Lautreamont, Comte de

Duclos, Charles Pinot   1704-1772 ..... **LC 1**

Dudek, Louis   1918- .... **CLC 11, 19**
  See also CANR 1; CA 45-48

Dudevant, Amandine Aurore Lucile Dupin
  1804-1876
  See Sand, George

Duerrenmatt, Friedrich   1921-
  See also CA 17-20R

Duffy, Bruce   19??- .... **CLC 50**

Duffy, Maureen   1933- .... **CLC 37**
  See also CA 25-28R; DLB 14

Dugan, Alan   1923- .... **CLC 2, 6**
  See also CA 81-84; DLB 5

Duhamel, Georges   1884-1966 .... **CLC 8**
  See also CA 81-84; obituary CA 25-28R

Dujardin, Edouard (Emile Louis)
  1861-1949 .... **TCLC 13**
  See also CA 109

Duke, Raoul   1939-
  See Thompson, Hunter S(tockton)

Dumas, Alexandre (Davy de la Pailleterie)
  (pere)   1802-1870 .... **NCLC 11**
  See also SATA 18

Dumas, Alexandre (fils)
  1824-1895 .... **NCLC 9**

Dumas, Henry (L.)   1934-1968 ...... **CLC 6**
  See also CA 85-88; DLB 41

Du Maurier, Daphne   1907- ...... **CLC 6, 11**
  See also CANR 6; CA 5-8R; SATA 27

Dunbar, Paul Laurence
  1872-1906 .... **TCLC 2, 12**
  See also CA 104; SATA 34; DLB 50, 54;
  CDALB 1865-1917

Duncan (Steinmetz Arquette), Lois
  1934- .... **CLC 26**
  See also Arquette, Lois S(teinmetz)
  See also CANR 2; CA 1-4R; SAAS 2;
  SATA 1, 36

Duncan, Robert (Edward)
  1919- .... **CLC 1, 2, 4, 7, 15, 41**
  See also CA 9-12R; DLB 5, 16

Dunlap, William   1766-1839 ...... **NCLC 2**
  See also DLB 30, 37

Dunn, Douglas (Eaglesham)
  1942- .... **CLC 6, 40**
  See also CANR 2; CA 45-48; DLB 40

Dunn, Elsie   1893-1963
  See Scott, Evelyn

Dunn, Stephen   1939- .... **CLC 36**
  See also CANR 12; CA 33-36R

Dunne, Finley Peter   1867-1936.... **TCLC 28**
  See also CA 108; DLB 11, 23

Dunne, John Gregory   1932-........ **CLC 28**
  See also CANR 14; CA 25-28R; DLB-Y 80

Dunsany, Lord (Edward John Moreton Drax
  Plunkett)   1878-1957......... **TCLC 2**
  See also CA 104; DLB 10

Durang, Christopher (Ferdinand)
  1949- .... **CLC 27, 38**
  See also CA 105

Duras, Marguerite
  1914- .... **CLC 3, 6, 11, 20, 34, 40**
  See also CA 25-28R

Durban, Pam   1947-............... **CLC 39**

Durcan, Paul   1944-.............. **CLC 43**

Durrell, Lawrence (George)
  1912- .... **CLC 1, 4, 6, 8, 13, 27, 41**
  See also CA 9-12R; DLB 15, 27

Durrenmatt, Friedrich
  1921- .... **CLC 1, 4, 8, 11, 15, 43**
  See also Duerrenmatt, Friedrich
  See also DLB 69

Dwight, Timothy   1752-1817...... **NCLC 13**
  See also DLB 37

Dworkin, Andrea   1946- .... **CLC 43**
  See also CANR 16; CA 77-80

Dylan, Bob   1941- .... **CLC 3, 4, 6, 12**
  See also CA 41-44R; DLB 16

East, Michael   1916-
  See West, Morris L.

Eastlake, William (Derry)   1917-..... **CLC 8**
  See also CAAS 1; CANR 5; CA 5-8R;
  DLB 6

Eberhart, Richard   1904-...... **CLC 3, 11, 19**
  See also CANR 2; CA 1-4R; DLB 48;
  CDALB 1941-1968

Eberstadt, Fernanda   1960-........ **CLC 39**

Echegaray (y Eizaguirre), Jose (Maria Waldo)
  1832-1916 .... **TCLC 4**
  See also CA 104

Echeverria, (Jose) Esteban (Antonino)
  1805-1851 .... **NCLC 18**

Eckert, Allan W.   1931- .... **CLC 17**
  See also CANR 14; CA 13-16R; SATA 27,
  29

Eco, Umberto   1932-.............. **CLC 28**
  See also CANR 12; CA 77-80

Eddison, E(ric) R(ucker)
  1882-1945 .... **TCLC 15**
  See also CA 109

Edel, Leon (Joseph)   1907-...... **CLC 29, 34**
  See also CANR 1, 22; CA 1-4R

Eden, Emily   1797-1869 .... **NCLC 10**

Edgar, David   1948-.............. **CLC 42**
  See also CANR 12; CA 57-60; DLB 13

Edgerton, Clyde   1944-............ **CLC 39**
  See also CA 118

Edgeworth, Maria   1767-1849...... **NCLC 1**
  See also SATA 21

Edmonds, Helen (Woods)   1904-1968
  See Kavan, Anna
  See also CA 5-8R; obituary CA 25-28R

Edmonds, Walter D(umaux)   1903- .. **CLC 35**
  See also CANR 2; CA 5-8R; SAAS 4;
  SATA 1, 27; DLB 9

Edson, Russell   1905- .... **CLC 13**
  See also CA 33-36R

Edwards, G(erald) B(asil)
  1899-1976 .... **CLC 25**
  See also obituary CA 110

Edwards, Gus   1939-.............. **CLC 43**
  See also CA 108

Edwards, Jonathan   1703-1758........ **LC 7**
  See also DLB 24

Ehle, John (Marsden, Jr.)   1925-.... **CLC 27**
  See also CA 9-12R

Ehrenbourg, Ilya (Grigoryevich)   1891-1967
  See Ehrenburg, Ilya (Grigoryevich)

Ehrenburg, Ilya (Grigoryevich)
  1891-1967 .... **CLC 18, 34**
  See also CA 102; obituary CA 25-28R

Eich, Guenter   1907-1971
  See also CA 111; obituary CA 93-96

Eich, Gunter   1907-1971........... **CLC 15**
  See also Eich, Guenter
  See also DLB 69

Eichendorff, Joseph Freiherr von
  1788-1857 .... **NCLC 8**

Eigner, Larry   1927- .... **CLC 9**
  See also Eigner, Laurence (Joel)
  See also DLB 5

Eigner, Laurence (Joel)   1927-
  See Eigner, Larry
  See also CANR 6; CA 9-12R

Eiseley, Loren (Corey)   1907-1977.... **CLC 7**
  See also CANR 6; CA 1-4R;
  obituary CA 73-76

Eisenstadt, Jill   1963- .... **CLC 50**

Ekeloef, Gunnar (Bengt)   1907-1968
  See Ekelof, Gunnar (Bengt)
  See also obituary CA 25-28R

Ekelof, Gunnar (Bengt)   1907-1968 .. **CLC 27**
  See also Ekeloef, Gunnar (Bengt)

Ekwensi, Cyprian (Odiatu Duaka)
  1921- .... **CLC 4**
  See also CANR 18; CA 29-32R

Eliade, Mircea   1907-1986 .... **CLC 19**
  See also CA 65-68; obituary CA 119

Eliot, George   1819-1880...... **NCLC 4, 13**
  See also DLB 21, 35, 55

Eliot, John   1604-1690 .... **LC 5**
  See also DLB 24

Eliot, T(homas) S(tearns)
  1888-1965 .... **CLC 1, 2, 3, 6, 9, 10, 13,**
                      15, 24, 34, 41
  See also CA 5-8R; obituary CA 25-28R;
  DLB 7, 10, 45, 63

Elkin, Stanley (Lawrence)
  1930- .... **CLC 4, 6, 9, 14, 27, 51**
  See also CANR 8; CA 9-12R; DLB 2, 28;
  DLB-Y 80

Elledge, Scott   19??- .... **CLC 34**

Elliott, George P(aul)   1918-1980..... **CLC 2**
  See also CANR 2; CA 1-4R;
  obituary CA 97-100

Elliott, Janice   1931-.............. **CLC 47**
  See also CANR 8; CA 13-16R; DLB 14

Elliott, Sumner Locke   1917-........ **CLC 38**
  See also CANR 2, 21; CA 5-8R

Ellis, A. E.   19??-................. **CLC 7**

Ellis, Alice Thomas   19??-.......... **CLC 40**

Ellis, Bret Easton   1964-............ **CLC 39**
  See also CA 118

Ellis, (Henry) Havelock
  1859-1939 .... **TCLC 14**
  See also CA 109

Fuchs, Daniel 1934- .... **CLC 34**
See also CANR 14; CA 37-40R

Fuentes, Carlos
1928- .... **CLC 3, 8, 10, 13, 22, 41**
See also CANR 10; CA 69-72

Fugard, Athol 1932- ... **CLC 5, 9, 14, 25, 40**
See also CA 85-88

Fugard, Sheila 1932- .... **CLC 48**

Fuller, Charles (H., Jr.) 1939- ...... **CLC 25**
See also CA 108, 112; DLB 38

Fuller, (Sarah) Margaret
1810-1850 .... **NCLC 5**
See also Ossoli, Sarah Margaret (Fuller
marchesa d')
See also DLB 1; CDALB 1640-1865

Fuller, Roy (Broadbent) 1912- .... **CLC 4, 28**
See also CA 5-8R; DLB 15, 20

Furphy, Joseph 1843-1912 .... **TCLC 25**

Futrelle, Jacques 1875-1912 ...... **TCLC 19**
See also CA 113

Gaboriau, Emile 1835-1873 ...... **NCLC 14**

Gadda, Carlo Emilio 1893-1973 .... **CLC 11**
See also CA 89-92

Gaddis, William
1922- .... **CLC 1, 3, 6, 8, 10, 19, 43**
See also CAAS 4; CANR 21; CA 17-20R;
DLB 2

Gaines, Ernest J. 1933- ...... **CLC 3, 11, 18**
See also CANR 6; CA 9-12R; DLB 2, 33;
DLB-Y 80

Gale, Zona 1874-1938 .... **TCLC 7**
See also CA 105; DLB 9

Gallagher, Tess 1943- .... **CLC 18**
See also CA 106

Gallant, Mavis 1922- .... **CLC 7, 18, 38**
See also CA 69-72; DLB 53

Gallant, Roy A(rthur) 1924- .... **CLC 17**
See also CANR 4; CA 5-8R; SATA 4

Gallico, Paul (William) 1897-1976 ... **CLC 2**
See also CA 5-8R; obituary CA 69-72;
SATA 13; DLB 9

Galsworthy, John 1867-1933 .... **TCLC 1**
See also CA 104; DLB 10, 34

Galt, John 1779-1839 .... **NCLC 1**

Galvin, James 1951- .... **CLC 38**
See also CA 108

Gann, Ernest K(ellogg) 1910- ..... **CLC 23**
See also CANR 1; CA 1-4R

Garcia Lorca, Federico
1899-1936 .... **TCLC 1, 7**
See also CA 104

Garcia Marquez, Gabriel (Jose)
1928- .... **CLC 2, 3, 8, 10, 15, 27, 47**
See also CANR 10; CA 33-36R

Gardam, Jane 1928- .... **CLC 43**
See also CLR 12; CANR 2, 18; CA 49-52;
SATA 28, 39; DLB 14

Gardner, Herb 1934- .... **CLC 44**

Gardner, John (Champlin, Jr.)
1933-1982 .... **CLC 2, 3, 5, 7, 8, 10, 18,
28, 34**
See also CA 65-68; obituary CA 107;
obituary SATA 31, 40; DLB 2; DLB-Y 82

Gardner, John (Edmund) 1926- ..... **CLC 30**
See also CANR 15; CA 103

Garfield, Leon 1921- .... **CLC 12**
See also CA 17-20R; SATA 1, 32

Garland, (Hannibal) Hamlin
1860-1940 .... **TCLC 3**
See also CA 104; DLB 12, 71

Garneau, Hector (de) Saint Denys
1912-1943 .... **TCLC 13**
See also CA 111

Garner, Alan 1935- .... **CLC 17**
See also CANR 15; CA 73-76; SATA 18

Garner, Hugh 1913-1979 .... **CLC 13**
See also CA 69-72

Garnett, David 1892-1981 .... **CLC 3**
See also CANR 17; CA 5-8R;
obituary CA 103; DLB 34

Garrett, George (Palmer, Jr.)
1929- .... **CLC 3, 11, 51**
See also CAAS 5; CANR 1; CA 1-4R;
DLB 2, 5; DLB-Y 83

Garrigue, Jean 1914-1972 .... **CLC 2, 8**
See also CA 5-8R; obituary CA 37-40R

Gary, Romain 1914-1980 .... **CLC 25**
See also Kacew, Romain

Gascar, Pierre 1916- .... **CLC 11**
See also Fournier, Pierre

Gascoyne, David (Emery) 1916- .... **CLC 45**
See also CANR 10; CA 65-68; DLB 20

Gaskell, Elizabeth Cleghorn
1810-1865 .... **NCLC 5**
See also DLB 21

Gass, William H(oward)
1924- .... **CLC 1, 2, 8, 11, 15, 39**
See also CA 17-20R; DLB 2

Gautier, Theophile 1811-1872 ..... **NCLC 1**

Gaye, Marvin (Pentz) 1939-1984 ... **CLC 26**
See also obituary CA 112

Gebler, Carlo (Ernest) 1954- ...... **CLC 39**
See also CA 119

Gee, Maurice (Gough) 1931- .... **CLC 29**
See also CA 97-100; SATA 46

Gelbart, Larry (Simon) 1923- ...... **CLC 21**
See also CA 73-76

Gelber, Jack 1932- .... **CLC 1, 6, 14**
See also CANR 2; CA 1-4R; DLB 7

Gellhorn, Martha (Ellis) 1908- ..... **CLC 14**
See also CA 77-80; DLB-Y 82

Genet, Jean
1910-1986 ... **CLC 1, 2, 5, 10, 14, 44, 46**
See also CANR 18; CA 13-16R; DLB 72;
DLB-Y 86

Gent, Peter 1942- .... **CLC 29**
See also CA 89-92; DLB 72; DLB-Y 82

George, Jean Craighead 1919- ...... **CLC 35**
See also CLR 1; CA 5-8R; SATA 2;
DLB 52

George, Stefan (Anton)
1868-1933 .... **TCLC 2, 14**
See also CA 104

Gerhardi, William (Alexander) 1895-1977
See Gerhardie, William (Alexander)

Gerhardie, William (Alexander)
1895-1977 .... **CLC 5**
See also CANR 18; CA 25-28R;
obituary CA 73-76; DLB 36

Gertler, T(rudy) 1946?- .... **CLC 34**
See also CA 116

Gessner, Friedrike Victoria 1910-1980
See Adamson, Joy(-Friederike Victoria)

Ghelderode, Michel de
1898-1962 .... **CLC 6, 11**
See also CA 85-88

Ghiselin, Brewster 1903- .... **CLC 23**
See also CANR 13; CA 13-16R

Ghose, Zulfikar 1935- .... **CLC 42**
See also CA 65-68

Ghosh, Amitav 1943- .... **CLC 44**

Giacosa, Giuseppe 1847-1906 ...... **TCLC 7**
See also CA 104

Gibbon, Lewis Grassic 1901-1935 ... **TCLC 4**
See also Mitchell, James Leslie

Gibbons, Kaye 1960- .... **CLC 50**

Gibran, (Gibran) Kahlil
1883-1931 .... **TCLC 1, 9**
See also CA 104

Gibson, William 1914- .... **CLC 23**
See also CANR 9; CA 9-12R; DLB 7

Gibson, William 1948- .... **CLC 39**

Gide, Andre (Paul Guillaume)
1869-1951 .... **TCLC 5, 12**
See also CA 104

Gifford, Barry (Colby) 1946- .... **CLC 34**
See also CANR 9; CA 65-68

Gilbert, (Sir) W(illiam) S(chwenck)
1836-1911 .... **TCLC 3**
See also CA 104; SATA 36

Gilbreth, Ernestine 1908-
See Carey, Ernestine Gilbreth

Gilbreth, Frank B(unker), Jr. 1911- and
Carey, Ernestine Gilbreth
1908- .... **CLC 17**

Gilbreth, Frank B(unker), Jr. 1911-
See Gilbreth, Frank B(unker), Jr. and
Carey, Ernestine Gilbreth
See also CA 9-12R; SATA 2

Gilchrist, Ellen 1935- .... **CLC 34, 48**
See also CA 113, 116

Giles, Molly 1942- .... **CLC 39**

Gilliam, Terry (Vance) 1940-
See Monty Python
See also CA 108, 113

Gilliatt, Penelope (Ann Douglass)
1932- .... **CLC 2, 10, 13**
See also CA 13-16R; DLB 14

Gilman, Charlotte (Anna) Perkins (Stetson)
1860-1935 .... **TCLC 9**
See also CA 106

Gilmour, David 1944-
See Pink Floyd

Gilroy, Frank D(aniel) 1925- .... **CLC 2**
See also CA 81-84; DLB 7

Ginsberg, Allen
1926- .... **CLC 1, 2, 3, 4, 6, 13, 36**
See also CANR 2; CA 1-4R; DLB 5, 16;
CDALB 1941-1968

Gray, Spalding 1941- . . . . CLC 49

Gray, Thomas 1716-1771 . . . . LC 4

Grayson, Richard (A.) 1951- . . . . . CLC 38
See also CANR 14; CA 85-88

Greeley, Andrew M(oran) 1928- . . . . CLC 28
See also CAAS 7; CANR 7; CA 5-8R

Green, Hannah 1932- . . . . CLC 3, 7, 30
See also Greenberg, Joanne
See also CA 73-76

Green, Henry 1905-1974 . . . . CLC 2, 13
See also Yorke, Henry Vincent
See also DLB 15

Green, Julien (Hartridge) 1900- . . CLC 3, 11
See also CA 21-24R; DLB 4, 72

Green, Paul (Eliot) 1894-1981 . . . . . . CLC 25
See also CANR 3; CA 5-8R;
obituary CA 103; DLB 7, 9; DLB-Y 81

Greenberg, Ivan 1908-1973
See Rahv, Philip
See also CA 85-88

Greenberg, Joanne (Goldenberg)
1932- . . . . CLC 3, 7, 30
See also Green, Hannah
See also CANR 14; CA 5-8R; SATA 25

Greene, Bette 1934- . . . . CLC 30
See also CLR 2; CANR 4; CA 53-56;
SATA 8

Greene, Gael 19??- . . . . CLC 8
See also CANR 10; CA 13-16R

Greene, Graham (Henry)
1904- . . . . . CLC 1, 3, 6, 9, 14, 18, 27, 37
See also CA 13-16R; SATA 20; DLB 13, 15;
DLB-Y 85

Gregor, Arthur 1923- . . . . CLC 9
See also CANR 11; CA 25-28R; SATA 36

Gregory, Lady (Isabella Augusta Persse)
1852-1932 . . . . TCLC 1
See also CA 104; DLB 10

Grendon, Stephen 1909-1971
See Derleth, August (William)

Greve, Felix Paul Berthold Friedrich
1879-1948
See Grove, Frederick Philip
See also CA 104

Grey, (Pearl) Zane 1872?-1939 . . . . . TCLC 6
See also CA 104; DLB 9

Grieg, (Johan) Nordahl (Brun)
1902-1943 . . . . TCLC 10
See also CA 107

Grieve, C(hristopher) M(urray) 1892-1978
See MacDiarmid, Hugh
See also CA 5-8R; obituary CA 85-88

Griffin, Gerald 1803-1840 . . . . NCLC 7

Griffin, Peter 1942- . . . . CLC 39

Griffiths, Trevor 1935- . . . . CLC 13
See also CA 97-100; DLB 13

Grigson, Geoffrey (Edward Harvey)
1905-1985 . . . . CLC 7, 39
See also CANR 20; CA 25-28R;
obituary CA 118; DLB 27

Grillparzer, Franz 1791-1872 . . . . . . NCLC 1

Grimke, Charlotte L(ottie) Forten 1837-1914
See Forten (Grimke), Charlotte L(ottie)
See also CA 117

Grimm, Jakob (Ludwig) Karl 1785-1863 and
Grimm, Wilhelm Karl
1786-1859 . . . . NCLC 3
See also SATA 22

Grimm, Jakob (Ludwig) Karl 1785-1863
See Grimm, Jakob (Ludwig) Karl and
Grimm, Wilhelm Karl

Grimm, Wilhelm Karl 1786-1859
See Grimm, Jakob (Ludwig) Karl and
Grimm, Wilhelm Karl

Grimm, Wilhelm Karl 1786-1859 and Grimm,
Jakob (Ludwig) Karl 1785-1863
See Grimm, Jakob (Ludwig) Karl and
Grimm, Wilhelm Karl

Grimmelshausen, Johann Jakob Christoffel
von 1621-1676 . . . . LC 6

Grindel, Eugene 1895-1952
See Eluard, Paul
See also CA 104

Grossman, Vasily (Semenovich)
1905-1964 . . . . CLC 41

Grove, Frederick Philip
1879-1948 . . . . TCLC 4
See also Greve, Felix Paul Berthold
Friedrich

Grumbach, Doris (Isaac)
1918- . . . . CLC 13, 22
See also CAAS 2; CANR 9; CA 5-8R

Grundtvig, Nicolai Frederik Severin
1783-1872 . . . . NCLC 1

Grunwald, Lisa 1959- . . . . CLC 44
See also CA 120

Guare, John 1938- . . . . CLC 8, 14, 29
See also CANR 21; CA 73-76; DLB 7

Gudjonsson, Halldor Kiljan 1902-
See Laxness, Halldor (Kiljan)
See also CA 103

Guest, Barbara 1920- . . . . CLC 34
See also CANR 11; CA 25-28R; DLB 5

Guest, Judith (Ann) 1936- . . . . CLC 8, 30
See also CANR 15; CA 77-80

Guild, Nicholas M. 1944- . . . . CLC 33
See also CA 93-96

Guillen, Jorge 1893-1984 . . . . CLC 11
See also CA 89-92; obituary CA 112

Guillen, Nicolas 1902- . . . . CLC 48
See also CA 116

Guillevic, (Eugene) 1907- . . . . CLC 33
See also CA 93-96

Gunn, Bill 1934- . . . . CLC 5
See also Gunn, William Harrison
See also DLB 38

Gunn, Thom(son William)
1929- . . . . CLC 3, 6, 18, 32
See also CANR 9; CA 17-20R; DLB 27

Gunn, William Harrison 1934-
See Gunn, Bill
See also CANR 12; CA 13-16R

Gurney, A(lbert) R(amsdell), Jr.
1930- . . . . CLC 32, 50, 54
See also CA 77-80

Gurney, Ivor (Bertie) 1890-1937 . . . TCLC 33

Gustafson, Ralph (Barker) 1909- . . . . CLC 36
See also CANR 8; CA 21-24R

Guthrie, A(lfred) B(ertram), Jr.
1901- . . . . CLC 23
See also CA 57-60; DLB 6

Guthrie, Woodrow Wilson 1912-1967
See Guthrie, Woody
See also CA 113; obituary CA 93-96

Guthrie, Woody 1912-1967 . . . . CLC 35
See also Guthrie, Woodrow Wilson

Guy, Rosa (Cuthbert) 1928- . . . . CLC 26
See also CANR 14; CA 17-20R; SATA 14;
DLB 33

Haavikko, Paavo (Juhani)
1931- . . . . CLC 18, 34
See also CA 106

Hacker, Marilyn 1942- . . . . CLC 5, 9, 23
See also CA 77-80

Haggard, (Sir) H(enry) Rider
1856-1925 . . . . TCLC 11
See also CA 108; SATA 16; DLB 70

Haig-Brown, Roderick L(angmere)
1908-1976 . . . . CLC 21
See also CANR 4; CA 5-8R;
obituary CA 69-72; SATA 12

Hailey, Arthur 1920- . . . . CLC 5
See also CANR 2; CA 1-4R; DLB-Y 82

Hailey, Elizabeth Forsythe 1938- . . . CLC 40
See also CAAS 1; CANR 15; CA 93-96

Haley, Alex (Palmer) 1921- . . . . . . CLC 8, 12
See also CA 77-80; DLB 38

Haliburton, Thomas Chandler
1796-1865 . . . . NCLC 15
See also DLB 11

Hall, Donald (Andrew, Jr.)
1928- . . . . CLC 1, 13, 37
See also CAAS 7; CANR 2; CA 5-8R;
SATA 23; DLB 5

Hall, James Norman 1887-1951 . . . TCLC 23
See also SATA 21

Hall, (Marguerite) Radclyffe
1886-1943 . . . . TCLC 12
See also CA 110

Hall, Rodney 1935- . . . . CLC 51
See also CA 109

Halpern, Daniel 1945- . . . . CLC 14
See also CA 33-36R

Hamburger, Michael (Peter Leopold)
1924- . . . . CLC 5, 14
See also CAAS 4; CANR 2; CA 5-8R;
DLB 27

Hamill, Pete 1935- . . . . CLC 10
See also CANR 18; CA 25-28R

Hamilton, Edmond 1904-1977 . . . . CLC 1
See also CANR 3; CA 1-4R; DLB 8

Hamilton, Gail 1911-
See Corcoran, Barbara

Hamilton, Mollie 1909?-
See Kaye, M(ary) M(argaret)

Hamilton, (Anthony Walter) Patrick
1904-1962 . . . . CLC 51
See also obituary CA 113; DLB 10

Hamilton, Virginia (Esther) 1936- . . . CLC 26
See also CLR 1, 11; CANR 20; CA 25-28R;
SATA 4; DLB 33, 52

Henley, Beth   1952-............. CLC 23
See also Henley, Elizabeth Becker
See also DLB-Y 86

Henley, Elizabeth Becker   1952-
See Henley, Beth
See also CA 107

Henley, William Ernest
1849-1903 .... TCLC 8
See also CA 105; DLB 19

Hennissart, Martha
See Lathen, Emma
See also CA 85-88

Henry   1491-1547 .... LC 10

Henry, O.   1862-1910 .... TCLC 1, 19
See also Porter, William Sydney

Hentoff, Nat(han Irving)   1925-..... CLC 26
See also CLR 1; CAAS 6; CANR 5;
CA 1-4R; SATA 27, 42

Heppenstall, (John) Rayner
1911-1981 .... CLC 10
See also CA 1-4R; obituary CA 103

Herbert, Frank (Patrick)
1920-1986 .... CLC 12, 23, 35, 44
See also CANR 5; CA 53-56;
obituary CA 118; SATA 9, 37, 47; DLB 8

Herbert, Zbigniew   1924- .... CLC 9, 43
See also CA 89-92

Herbst, Josephine   1897-1969...... CLC 34
See also CA 5-8R; obituary CA 25-28R;
DLB 9

Herder, Johann Gottfried von
1744-1803 .... NCLC 8

Hergesheimer, Joseph
1880-1954 .... TCLC 11
See also CA 109; DLB 9

Herlagnez, Pablo de   1844-1896
See Verlaine, Paul (Marie)

Herlihy, James Leo   1927-.......... CLC 6
See also CANR 2; CA 1-4R

Hernandez, Jose   1834-1886...... NCLC 17

Herriot, James   1916-............. CLC 12
See also Wight, James Alfred

Herrmann, Dorothy   1941-......... CLC 44
See also CA 107

Hersey, John (Richard)
1914- .... CLC 1, 2, 7, 9, 40
See also CA 17-20R; SATA 25; DLB 6

Herzen, Aleksandr Ivanovich
1812-1870 .... NCLC 10

Herzog, Werner   1942-............. CLC 16
See also CA 89-92

Hesse, Hermann
1877-1962 .... CLC 1, 2, 3, 6, 11, 17, 25
See also CAP 2; CA 17-18

Heyen, William   1940- .... CLC 13, 18
See also CA 33-36R; DLB 5

Heyerdahl, Thor   1914-............ CLC 26
See also CANR 5, 22; CA 5-8R; SATA 2, 52

Heym, Georg (Theodor Franz Arthur)
1887-1912 .... TCLC 9
See also CA 106

Heym, Stefan   1913-............. CLC 41
See also CANR 4; CA 9-12R; DLB 69

Heyse, Paul (Johann Ludwig von)
1830-1914 .... TCLC 8
See also CA 104

Hibbert, Eleanor (Burford)   1906-.... CLC 7
See also CANR 9; CA 17-20R; SATA 2

Higgins, George V(incent)
1939- .... CLC 4, 7, 10, 18
See also CAAS 5; CANR 17; CA 77-80;
DLB 2; DLB-Y 81

Highsmith, (Mary) Patricia
1921- .... CLC 2, 4, 14, 42
See also CANR 1, 20; CA 1-4R

Highwater, Jamake   1942- .... CLC 12
See also CAAS 7; CANR 10; CA 65-68;
SATA 30, 32; DLB 52; DLB-Y 85

Hikmet (Ran), Nazim   1902-1963.... CLC 40
See also obituary CA 93-96

Hildesheimer, Wolfgang   1916- ..... CLC 49
See also CA 101; DLB 69

Hill, Geoffrey (William)
1932- .... CLC 5, 8, 18, 45
See also CANR 21; CA 81-84; DLB 40

Hill, George Roy   1922-........... CLC 26
See also CA 110

Hill, Susan B.   1942-............. CLC 4
See also CA 33-36R; DLB 14

Hilliard, Noel (Harvey)   1929-...... CLC 15
See also CANR 7; CA 9-12R

Hilton, James   1900-1954........ TCLC 21
See also CA 108; SATA 34; DLB 34

Himes, Chester (Bomar)
1909-1984 .... CLC 2, 4, 7, 18
See also CANR 22; CA 25-28R;
obituary CA 114; DLB 2

Hinde, Thomas   1926-........... CLC 6, 11
See also Chitty, (Sir) Thomas Willes

Hine, (William) Daryl   1936-....... CLC 15
See also CANR 1, 20; CA 1-4R; DLB 60

Hinton, S(usan) E(loise)   1950- ..... CLC 30
See also CLR 3; CA 81-84; SATA 19

Hippius (Merezhkovsky), Zinaida
(Nikolayevna)   1869-1945...... TCLC 9
See also Gippius, Zinaida (Nikolayevna)

Hiraoka, Kimitake   1925-1970
See Mishima, Yukio
See also CA 97-100; obituary CA 29-32R

Hirsch, Edward (Mark)   1950-... CLC 31, 50
See also CANR 20; CA 104

Hitchcock, (Sir) Alfred (Joseph)
1899-1980 .... CLC 16
See also obituary CA 97-100; SATA 27;
obituary SATA 24

Hoagland, Edward   1932-......... CLC 28
See also CANR 2; CA 1-4R; SATA 51;
DLB 6

Hoban, Russell C(onwell)   1925- .. CLC 7, 25
See also CLR 3; CA 5-8R; SATA 1, 40;
DLB 52

Hobson, Laura Z(ametkin)
1900-1986 .... CLC 7, 25
See also CA 17-20R; obituary CA 118;
SATA 52; DLB 28

Hochhuth, Rolf   1931-........ CLC 4, 11, 18
See also CA 5-8R

Hochman, Sandra   1936-.......... CLC 3, 8
See also CA 5-8R; DLB 5

Hochwalder, Fritz   1911-1986 ...... CLC 36
See also CA 29-32R; obituary CA 120

Hocking, Mary (Eunice)   1921-..... CLC 13
See also CANR 18; CA 101

Hodgins, Jack   1938-............. CLC 23
See also CA 93-96; DLB 60

Hodgson, William Hope
1877-1918 .... TCLC 13
See also CA 111; DLB 70

Hoffman, Alice   1952-............. CLC 51
See also CA 77-80

Hoffman, Daniel (Gerard)
1923- .... CLC 6, 13, 23
See also CANR 4; CA 1-4R; DLB 5

Hoffman, Stanley   1944-............ CLC 5
See also CA 77-80

Hoffman, William M(oses)   1939- ... CLC 40
See also CANR 11; CA 57-60

Hoffmann, Ernst Theodor Amadeus
1776-1822 .... NCLC 2
See also SATA 27

Hoffmann, Gert   1932- .... CLC 54

Hofmannsthal, Hugo (Laurenz August
Hofmann Edler) von
1874-1929 .... TCLC 11
See also CA 106

Hogg, James   1770-1835.......... NCLC 4

Holberg, Ludvig   1684-1754......... LC 6

Holden, Ursula   1921-............. CLC 18
See also CANR 22; CA 101

Holderlin, (Johann Christian) Friedrich
1770-1843 .... NCLC 16

Holdstock, Robert (P.)   1948-....... CLC 39

Holland, Isabelle   1920- .... CLC 21
See also CANR 10; CA 21-24R; SATA 8

Holland, Marcus   1900-1985
See Caldwell, (Janet Miriam) Taylor
(Holland)

Hollander, John   1929-...... CLC 2, 5, 8, 14
See also CANR 1; CA 1-4R; SATA 13;
DLB 5

Holleran, Andrew   1943?-.......... CLC 38

Hollis, Jim   1916-
See Summers, Hollis (Spurgeon, Jr.)

Holmes, Oliver Wendell
1809-1894 .... NCLC 14
See also SATA 34; DLB 1;
CDALB 1640-1865

Holt, Victoria   1906-
See Hibbert, Eleanor (Burford)

Holub, Miroslav   1923-............. CLC 4
See also CANR 10; CA 21-24R

Homer   c. 8th century B.C........ CMLC 1

Honig, Edwin   1919-............. CLC 33
See also CANR 4; CA 5-8R; DLB 5

Hood, Hugh (John Blagdon)
1928- .... CLC 15, 28
See also CANR 1; CA 49-52; DLB 53

Hood, Thomas   1799-1845........ NCLC 16

Hooker, (Peter) Jeremy   1941-...... CLC 43
See also CANR 22; CA 77-80; DLB 40

Jouve, Pierre Jean   1887-1976 . . . . . . **CLC 47**
See also obituary CA 65-68

Joyce, James (Augustine Aloysius)
1882-1941 . . . . **TCLC 3, 8, 16, 26**
See also CA 104; DLB 10, 19, 36

Jozsef, Attila   1905-1937 . . . . **TCLC 22**
See also CA 116

Juana Ines de la Cruz   1651?-1695 . . . . **LC 5**

Julian of Norwich   1342?-1416? . . . . **LC 6**

Just, Ward S(wift)   1935- . . . . **CLC 4, 27**
See also CA 25-28R

Justice, Donald (Rodney)   1925- . . **CLC 6, 19**
See also CA 5-8R; DLB-Y 83

Kacew, Romain   1914-1980
See Gary, Romain
See also CA 108; obituary CA 102

Kacewgary, Romain   1914-1980
See Gary, Romain

Kafka, Franz
1883-1924 . . . . **TCLC 2, 6, 13, 29**
See also CA 105

Kahn, Roger   1927- . . . . **CLC 30**
See also CA 25-28R; SATA 37

Kaiser, (Friedrich Karl) Georg
1878-1945 . . . . **TCLC 9**
See also CA 106

Kaletski, Alexander   1946- . . . . **CLC 39**
See also CA 118

Kallman, Chester (Simon)
1921-1975 . . . . **CLC 2**
See also CANR 3; CA 45-48;
obituary CA 53-56

Kaminsky, Melvin   1926-
See Brooks, Mel
See also CANR 16

Kane, Paul   1941-
See Simon, Paul

Kanin, Garson   1912- . . . . **CLC 22**
See also CANR 7; CA 5-8R; DLB 7

Kaniuk, Yoram   1930- . . . . **CLC 19**

Kantor, MacKinlay   1904-1977 . . . . . . **CLC 7**
See also CA 61-64; obituary CA 73-76;
DLB 9

Kaplan, David Michael   1946- . . . . . . **CLC 50**

Karamzin, Nikolai Mikhailovich
1766-1826 . . . . **NCLC 3**

Karapanou, Margarita   1946- . . . . **CLC 13**
See also CA 101

Karl, Frederick R(obert)   1927- . . . . . **CLC 34**
See also CANR 3; CA 5-8R

Kassef, Romain   1914-1980
See Gary, Romain

Katz, Steve   1935- . . . . **CLC 47**
See also CANR 12; CA 25-28R; DLB-Y 83

Kauffman, Janet   1945- . . . . **CLC 42**
See also CA 117; DLB-Y 86

Kaufman, Bob (Garnell)
1925-1986 . . . . **CLC 49**
See also CANR 22; CA 41-44R;
obituary CA 118; DLB 16, 41

Kaufman, George S(imon)
1889-1961 . . . . **CLC 38**
See also CA 108; obituary CA 93-96; DLB 7

Kaufman, Sue   1926-1977 . . . . **CLC 3, 8**
See also Barondess, Sue K(aufman)

Kavan, Anna   1904-1968 . . . . **CLC 5, 13**
See also Edmonds, Helen (Woods)
See also CANR 6; CA 5-8R

Kavanagh, Patrick (Joseph Gregory)
1905-1967 . . . . **CLC 22**
See also obituary CA 25-28R; DLB 15, 20

Kawabata, Yasunari
1899-1972 . . . . **CLC 2, 5, 9, 18**
See also CA 93-96; obituary CA 33-36R

Kaye, M(ary) M(argaret)   1909?- . . . . **CLC 28**
See also CA 89-92

Kaye, Mollie   1909?-
See Kaye, M(ary) M(argaret)

Kaye-Smith, Sheila   1887-1956 . . . . . **TCLC 20**
See also CA 118; DLB 36

Kazan, Elia   1909- . . . . **CLC 6, 16**
See also CA 21-24R

Kazantzakis, Nikos
1885?-1957 . . . . **TCLC 2, 5, 33**
See also CA 105

Kazin, Alfred   1915- . . . . **CLC 34, 38**
See also CAAS 7; CANR 1; CA 1-4R

Keane, Mary Nesta (Skrine)   1904-
See Keane, Molly
See also CA 108, 114

Keane, Molly   1904- . . . . **CLC 31**
See also Keane, Mary Nesta (Skrine)

Keates, Jonathan   19??- . . . . **CLC 34**

Keaton, Buster   1895-1966 . . . . **CLC 20**

Keaton, Joseph Francis   1895-1966
See Keaton, Buster

Keats, John   1795-1821 . . . . **NCLC 8**

Keene, Donald   1922- . . . . **CLC 34**
See also CANR 5; CA 1-4R

Keillor, Garrison   1942- . . . . **CLC 40**
See also Keillor, Gary (Edward)
See also CA 111

Keillor, Gary (Edward)
See Keillor, Garrison
See also CA 117

Kell, Joseph   1917-
See Burgess (Wilson, John) Anthony

Keller, Gottfried   1819-1890 . . . . **NCLC 2**

Kellerman, Jonathan (S.)   1949- . . . . . **CLC 44**
See also CA 106

Kelley, William Melvin   1937- . . . . . . **CLC 22**
See also CA 77-80; DLB 33

Kellogg, Marjorie   1922- . . . . **CLC 2**
See also CA 81-84

Kemal, Yashar   1922- . . . . **CLC 14, 29**
See also CA 89-92

Kemble, Fanny   1809-1893 . . . . **NCLC 18**
See also DLB 32

Kemelman, Harry   1908- . . . . **CLC 2**
See also CANR 6; CA 9-12R; DLB 28

Kempe, Margery   1373?-1440? . . . . **LC 6**

Kendall, Henry   1839-1882 . . . . **NCLC 12**

Keneally, Thomas (Michael)
1935- . . . . . . **CLC 5, 8, 10, 14, 19, 27, 43**
See also CANR 10; CA 85-88

Kennedy, John Pendleton
1795-1870 . . . . **NCLC 2**
See also DLB 3

Kennedy, Joseph Charles   1929-
See Kennedy, X. J.
See also CANR 4; CA 1-4R; SATA 14

Kennedy, William   1928- . . . . . . **CLC 6, 28, 34**
See also CANR 14; CA 85-88; DLB-Y 85

Kennedy, X. J.   1929- . . . . **CLC 8, 42**
See also Kennedy, Joseph Charles
See also DLB 5

Kerouac, Jack
1922-1969 . . . . **CLC 1, 2, 3, 5, 14, 29**
See also Kerouac, Jean-Louis Lebrid de
See also DLB 2, 16; DLB-DS 3;
CDALB 1941-1968

Kerouac, Jean-Louis Lebrid de   1922-1969
See Kerouac, Jack
See also CA 5-8R; obituary CA 25-28R;
CDALB 1941-1968

Kerr, Jean   1923- . . . . **CLC 22**
See also CANR 7; CA 5-8R

Kerr, M. E.   1927- . . . . **CLC 12, 35**
See also Meaker, Marijane
See also SAAS 1

Kerrigan, (Thomas) Anthony
1918- . . . . **CLC 4, 6**
See also CANR 4; CA 49-52

Kesey, Ken (Elton)
1935- . . . . **CLC 1, 3, 6, 11, 46**
See also CANR 22; CA 1-4R; DLB 2, 16

Kesselring, Joseph (Otto)
1902-1967 . . . . **CLC 45**

Kessler, Jascha (Frederick)   1929- . . . . **CLC 4**
See also CANR 8; CA 17-20R

Kettelkamp, Larry   1933- . . . . **CLC 12**
See also CANR 16; CA 29-32R; SAAS 3;
SATA 2

Kherdian, David   1931- . . . . **CLC 6, 9**
See also CAAS 2; CA 21-24R; SATA 16

Khlebnikov, Velimir (Vladimirovich)
1885-1922 . . . . **TCLC 20**
See also CA 117

Khodasevich, Vladislav (Felitsianovich)
1886-1939 . . . . **TCLC 15**
See also CA 115

Kielland, Alexander (Lange)
1849-1906 . . . . **TCLC 5**
See also CA 104

Kiely, Benedict   1919- . . . . **CLC 23, 43**
See also CANR 2; CA 1-4R; DLB 15

Kienzle, William X(avier)   1928- . . . . **CLC 25**
See also CAAS 1; CANR 9; CA 93-96

Killens, John Oliver   1916- . . . . **CLC 10**
See also CAAS 2; CA 77-80; DLB 33

Killigrew, Anne   1660-1685 . . . . **LC 4**

Kincaid, Jamaica   1949?- . . . . **CLC 43**

King, Francis (Henry)   1923- . . . . **CLC 8**
See also CANR 1; CA 1-4R; DLB 15

King, Stephen (Edwin)
1947- . . . . **CLC 12, 26, 37**
See also CANR 1; CA 61-64; SATA 9;
DLB-Y 80

Levi, Primo   1919-1987 . . . . CLC 37, 50
See also CANR 12; CA 13-16R;
obituary CA 122

Levin, Ira   1929- . . . . CLC 3, 6
See also CANR 17; CA 21-24R

Levin, Meyer   1905-1981 . . . . CLC 7
See also CANR 15; CA 9-12R;
obituary CA 104; SATA 21;
obituary SATA 27; DLB 9, 28; DLB-Y 81

Levine, Norman   1924- . . . . CLC 54
See also CANR 14; CA 73-76

Levine, Philip   1928-. . CLC 2, 4, 5, 9, 14, 33
See also CANR 9; CA 9-12R; DLB 5

Levinson, Deirdre   1931-. . . . . CLC 49
See also CA 73-76

Levi-Strauss, Claude   1908- . . . . CLC 38
See also CANR 6; CA 1-4R

Levitin, Sonia   1934- . . . . CLC 17
See also CANR 14; CA 29-32R; SAAS 2;
SATA 4

Lewis, Alun   1915-1944. . . . . TCLC 3
See also CA 104; DLB 20

Lewis, C(ecil) Day   1904-1972
See Day Lewis, C(ecil)

Lewis, C(live) S(taples)
1898-1963 . . . . CLC 1, 3, 6, 14, 27
See also CLR 3; CA 81-84; SATA 13;
DLB 15

Lewis (Winters), Janet   1899-. . . . . . . CLC 41
See also Winters, Janet Lewis

Lewis, Matthew Gregory
1775-1818 . . . . NCLC 11
See also DLB 39

Lewis, (Harry) Sinclair
1885-1951 . . . . TCLC 4, 13, 23
See also CA 104; DLB 9; DLB-DS 1

Lewis, (Percy) Wyndham
1882?-1957. . . . . TCLC 2, 9
See also CA 104; DLB 15

Lewisohn, Ludwig   1883-1955. . . . . . TCLC 19
See also CA 73-76; obituary CA 29-32R

Lieber, Stanley Martin   1922-
See Lee, Stan

Lieberman, Laurence (James)
1935- . . . . CLC 4, 36
See also CANR 8; CA 17-20R

Li Fei-kan   1904-
See Pa Chin
See also CA 105

Lightfoot, Gordon (Meredith)
1938- . . . . CLC 26
See also CA 109

Ligotti, Thomas   1953- . . . . CLC 44

Liliencron, Detlev von
1844-1909 . . . . TCLC 18
See also CA 117

Lima, Jose Lezama   1910-1976
See Lezama Lima, Jose

Lima Barreto, (Alfonso Henriques de)
1881-1922 . . . . TCLC 23
See also CA 117

Lincoln, Abraham   1809-1865. . . . . NCLC 18

Lind, Jakov   1927-. . . . . CLC 1, 2, 4, 27
See also Landwirth, Heinz
See also CAAS 4; CA 9-12R

Lindsay, David   1876-1945 . . . . TCLC 15
See also CA 113

Lindsay, (Nicholas) Vachel
1879-1931 . . . . TCLC 17
See also CA 114; SATA 40; DLB 54;
CDALB 1865-1917

Linney, Romulus   1930- . . . . CLC 51
See also CA 1-4R

Li Po   701-763 . . . . CMLC 2

Lipsyte, Robert (Michael)   1938-. . . . CLC 21
See also CANR 8; CA 17-20R; SATA 5

Lish, Gordon (Jay)   1934-. . . . . CLC 45
See also CA 113, 117

Lispector, Clarice   1925-1977. . . . . . CLC 43
See also obituary CA 116

Littell, Robert   1935?-. . . . . CLC 42
See also CA 109, 112

Liu E   1857-1909. . . . . TCLC 15
See also CA 115

Lively, Penelope   1933-. . . . . CLC 32, 50
See also CLR 7; CA 41-44R; SATA 7;
DLB 14

Livesay, Dorothy   1909- . . . . CLC 4, 15
See also CA 25-28R

Llewellyn, Richard   1906-1983. . . . . . . CLC 7
See also Llewellyn Lloyd, Richard (Dafydd
Vyvyan)
See also DLB 15

Llewellyn Lloyd, Richard (Dafydd Vyvyan)
1906-1983
See Llewellyn, Richard
See also CANR 7; CA 53-56;
obituary CA 111; SATA 11, 37

Llosa, Mario Vargas   1936-
See Vargas Llosa, Mario

Lloyd, Richard Llewellyn   1906-
See Llewellyn, Richard

Locke, John   1632-1704 . . . . LC 7
See also DLB 31

Lockhart, John Gibson
1794-1854 . . . . NCLC 6

Lodge, David (John)   1935-. . . . . CLC 36
See also CANR 19; CA 17-20R; DLB 14

Logan, John   1923- . . . . CLC 5
See also CA 77-80; DLB 5

Lombino, S. A.   1926-
See Hunter, Evan

London, Jack   1876-1916 . . . . TCLC 9, 15
See also London, John Griffith
See also SATA 18; DLB 8, 12;
CDALB 1865-1917

London, John Griffith   1876-1916
See London, Jack
See also CA 110, 119

Long, Emmett   1925-
See Leonard, Elmore

Longbaugh, Harry   1931-
See Goldman, William (W.)

Longfellow, Henry Wadsworth
1807-1882 . . . . NCLC 2
See also SATA 19; DLB 1;
CDALB 1640-1865

Longley, Michael   1939-. . . . . CLC 29
See also CA 102; DLB 40

Lopate, Phillip   1943- . . . . CLC 29
See also CA 97-100; DLB-Y 80

Lopez Portillo (y Pacheco), Jose
1920- . . . . CLC 46

Lopez y Fuentes, Gregorio
1897-1966 . . . . CLC 32

Lord, Bette Bao   1938- . . . . CLC 23
See also CA 107

Lorde, Audre (Geraldine)   1934-. . . . . CLC 18
See also CANR 16; CA 25-28R; DLB 41

Loti, Pierre   1850-1923. . . . . TCLC 11
See also Viaud, (Louis Marie) Julien

Lovecraft, H(oward) P(hillips)
1890-1937 . . . . TCLC 4, 22
See also CA 104

Lovelace, Earl   1935-. . . . . CLC 51
See also CA 77-80

Lowell, Amy   1874-1925 . . . . TCLC 1, 8
See also CA 104; DLB 54

Lowell, James Russell   1819-1891 . . NCLC 2
See also DLB 1, 11, 64; CDALB 1640-1865

Lowell, Robert (Traill Spence, Jr.)
1917-1977 . . . CLC 1, 2, 3, 4, 5, 8, 9, 11,
15, 37
See also CA 9-12R; obituary CA 73-76;
CABS 2; DLB 5

Lowndes, Marie (Adelaide) Belloc
1868-1947 . . . . TCLC 12
See also CA 107; DLB 70

Lowry, (Clarence) Malcolm
1909-1957 . . . . TCLC 6
See also CA 105; DLB 15

Loy, Mina   1882-1966. . . . . CLC 28
See also CA 113; DLB 4, 54

Lucas, George   1944-. . . . . CLC 16
See also CA 77-80

Lucas, Victoria   1932-1963
See Plath, Sylvia

Ludlam, Charles   1943-1987. . . . . CLC 46, 50
See also CA 85-88; obituary CA 122

Ludlum, Robert   1927- . . . . CLC 22, 43
See also CA 33-36R; DLB-Y 82

Ludwig, Otto   1813-1865. . . . . NCLC 4

Lugones, Leopoldo   1874-1938. . . . . TCLC 15
See also CA 116

Lu Hsun   1881-1936 . . . . TCLC 3

Lukacs, Georg   1885-1971. . . . . CLC 24
See also Lukacs, Gyorgy

Lukacs, Gyorgy   1885-1971
See Lukacs, Georg
See also CA 101; obituary CA 29-32R

Luke, Peter (Ambrose Cyprian)
1919- . . . . CLC 38
See also CA 81-84; DLB 13

Lurie (Bishop), Alison
1926- . . . . CLC 4, 5, 18, 39
See also CANR 2, 17; CA 1-4R; SATA 46;
DLB 2

McGinley, Phyllis 1905-1978 ...... CLC 14
  See also CANR 19; CA 9-12R;
    obituary CA 77-80; SATA 2, 44;
    obituary SATA 24; DLB 11, 48

McGinniss, Joe 1942- .... CLC 32
  See also CA 25-28R

McGivern, Maureen Daly 1921-
  See Daly, Maureen
  See also CA 9-12R

McGrath, Thomas 1916- .... CLC 28
  See also CANR 6; CA 9-12R; SATA 41

McGuane, Thomas (Francis III)
  1939- .... CLC 3, 7, 18
  See also CANR 5; CA 49-52; DLB 2;
    DLB-Y 80

McGuckian, Medbh 1950- .... CLC 48
  See also DLB 40

McHale, Tom 1941-1982 .... CLC 3, 5
  See also CA 77-80; obituary CA 106

McIlvanney, William 1936- .... CLC 42
  See also CA 25-28R; DLB 14

McIlwraith, Maureen Mollie Hunter 1922-
  See Hunter, Mollie
  See also CA 29-32R; SATA 2

McInerney, Jay 1955- .... CLC 34
  See also CA 116

McIntyre, Vonda N(eel) 1948- ..... CLC 18
  See also CANR 17; CA 81-84

McKay, Claude 1890-1948 .... TCLC 7
  See also CA 104; DLB 4, 45

McKuen, Rod 1933- .... CLC 1, 3
  See also CA 41-44R

McLuhan, (Herbert) Marshall
  1911-1980 .... CLC 37
  See also CANR 12; CA 9-12R;
    obituary CA 102

McManus, Declan Patrick 1955-
  See Costello, Elvis

McMillan, Terry 19??- .... CLC 50

McMurtry, Larry (Jeff)
  1936- .... CLC 2, 3, 7, 11, 27, 44
  See also CANR 19; CA 5-8R; DLB 2;
    DLB-Y 80

McNally, Terrence 1939- ...... CLC 4, 7, 41
  See also CANR 2; CA 45-48; DLB 7

McPhee, John 1931- .... CLC 36
  See also CANR 20; CA 65-68

McPherson, James Alan 1943- ..... CLC 19
  See also CA 25-28R; DLB 38

McPherson, William 1939- .... CLC 34
  See also CA 57-60

McSweeney, Kerry 19??- .... CLC 34

Mead, Margaret 1901-1978 .... CLC 37
  See also CANR 4; CA 1-4R;
    obituary CA 81-84; SATA 20

Meaker, M. J. 1927-
  See Kerr, M. E.
  See also Meaker, Marijane

Meaker, Marijane 1927-
  See Kerr, M. E.
  See also CA 107; SATA 20

Medoff, Mark (Howard) 1940- ... CLC 6, 23
  See also CANR 5; CA 53-56; DLB 7

Megged, Aharon 1920- .... CLC 9
  See also CANR 1; CA 49-52

Mehta, Ved (Parkash) 1934- .... CLC 37
  See also CANR 2; CA 1-4R

Mellor, John 1953?-
  See The Clash

Meltzer, Milton 1915- .... CLC 26
  See also CA 13-16R; SAAS 1; SATA 1;
    DLB 61

Melville, Herman
  1819-1891 .... NCLC 3, 12; SSC 1
  See also DLB 3; CDALB 1640-1865

Mencken, H(enry) L(ouis)
  1880-1956 .... TCLC 13
  See also CA 105; DLB 11, 29, 63

Mercer, David 1928-1980 .... CLC 5
  See also CA 9-12R; obituary CA 102;
    DLB 13

Meredith, George 1828-1909 ...... TCLC 17
  See also CA 117; DLB 18, 35, 57

Meredith, William (Morris)
  1919- .... CLC 4, 13, 22
  See also CANR 6; CA 9-12R; DLB 5

Merezhkovsky, Dmitri
  1865-1941 .... TCLC 29

Merimee, Prosper 1803-1870 ...... NCLC 6

Merkin, Daphne 1954- .... CLC 44

Merrill, James (Ingram)
  1926- .... CLC 2, 3, 6, 8, 13, 18, 34
  See also CANR 10; CA 13-16R; DLB 5;
    DLB-Y 85

Merton, Thomas (James)
  1915-1968 .... CLC 1, 3, 11, 34
  See also CANR 22; CA 5-8R;
    obituary CA 25-28R; DLB 48; DLB-Y 81

Merwin, W(illiam) S(tanley)
  1927- ...... CLC 1, 2, 3, 5, 8, 13, 18, 45
  See also CANR 15; CA 13-16R; DLB 5

Metcalf, John 1938- .... CLC 37
  See also CA 113; DLB 60

Mew, Charlotte (Mary)
  1870-1928 .... TCLC 8
  See also CA 105; DLB 19

Mewshaw, Michael 1943- .... CLC 9
  See also CANR 7; CA 53-56; DLB-Y 80

Meyer-Meyrink, Gustav 1868-1932
  See Meyrink, Gustav
  See also CA 117

Meyers, Jeffrey 1939- .... CLC 39
  See also CA 73-76

Meynell, Alice (Christiana Gertrude
    Thompson) 1847-1922 .... TCLC 6
  See also CA 104; DLB 19

Meyrink, Gustav 1868-1932 ...... TCLC 21
  See also Meyer-Meyrink, Gustav

Michaels, Leonard 1933- .... CLC 6, 25
  See also CANR 21; CA 61-64

Michaux, Henri 1899-1984 ...... CLC 8, 19
  See also CA 85-88; obituary CA 114

Michener, James A(lbert)
  1907- .... CLC 1, 5, 11, 29
  See also CANR 21; CA 5-8R; DLB 6

Mickiewicz, Adam 1798-1855 ..... NCLC 3

Middleton, Christopher 1926- ...... CLC 13
  See also CA 13-16R; DLB 40

Middleton, Stanley 1919- .... CLC 7, 38
  See also CANR 21; CA 25-28R; DLB 14

Migueis, Jose Rodrigues 1901- ..... CLC 10

Mikszath, Kalman 1847-1910 ..... TCLC 31

Miles, Josephine (Louise)
  1911-1985 .... CLC 1, 2, 14, 34, 39
  See also CANR 2; CA 1-4R;
    obituary CA 116; DLB 48

Mill, John Stuart 1806-1873 ..... NCLC 11

Millar, Kenneth 1915-1983
  See Macdonald, Ross
  See also CANR 16; CA 9-12R;
    obituary CA 110; DLB 2; DLB-Y 83

Millay, Edna St. Vincent
  1892-1950 .... TCLC 4
  See also CA 104; DLB 45

Miller, Arthur
  1915- .... CLC 1, 2, 6, 10, 15, 26, 47
  See also CANR 2; CA 1-4R; DLB 7;
    CDALB 1941-1968

Miller, Henry (Valentine)
  1891-1980 .... CLC 1, 2, 4, 9, 14, 43
  See also CA 9-12R; obituary CA 97-100;
    DLB 4, 9; DLB-Y 80

Miller, Jason 1939?- .... CLC 2
  See also CA 73-76; DLB 7

Miller, Sue 19??- .... CLC 44

Miller, Walter M(ichael), Jr.
  1923- .... CLC 4, 30
  See also CA 85-88; DLB 8

Millhauser, Steven 1943- .... CLC 21, 54
  See also CA 108, 110, 111; DLB 2

Millin, Sarah Gertrude 1889-1968 .. CLC 49
  See also CA 102; obituary CA 93-96

Milne, A(lan) A(lexander)
  1882-1956 .... TCLC 6
  See also CLR 1; YABC 1; CA 104; DLB 10

Milosz, Czeslaw 1911- .... CLC 5, 11, 22, 31
  See also CA 81-84

Milton, John 1608-1674............. LC 9

Miner, Valerie (Jane) 1947- .... CLC 40
  See also CA 97-100

Minot, Susan 1956- .... CLC 44

Minus, Ed 1938- .... CLC 39

Miro (Ferrer), Gabriel (Francisco Victor)
  1879-1930 .... TCLC 5
  See also CA 104

Mishima, Yukio
  1925-1970 .... CLC 2, 4, 6, 9, 27
  See also Hiraoka, Kimitake

Mistral, Gabriela 1889-1957 .... TCLC 2
  See also CA 104

Mitchell, James Leslie 1901-1935
  See Gibbon, Lewis Grassic
  See also CA 104; DLB 15

Mitchell, Joni 1943- .... CLC 12
  See also CA 112

Mitchell (Marsh), Margaret (Munnerlyn)
  1900-1949 .... TCLC 11
  See also CA 109; DLB 9

Pohl, Frederik 1919- . . . . CLC 18
  See also CAAS 1; CANR 11; CA 61-64;
  SATA 24; DLB 8

Poirier, Louis 1910-
  See Gracq, Julien
  See also CA 122

Poitier, Sidney 1924?- . . . . CLC 26
  See also CA 117

Polanski, Roman 1933- . . . . CLC 16
  See also CA 77-80

Poliakoff, Stephen 1952- . . . . CLC 38
  See also CA 106; DLB 13

Police, The. . . . . CLC 26

Pollitt, Katha 1949- . . . . CLC 28
  See also CA 120, 122

Pollock, Sharon 19??-. . . . . CLC 50

Pomerance, Bernard 1940-. . . . . CLC 13
  See also CA 101

Ponge, Francis (Jean Gaston Alfred)
  1899- . . . . CLC 6, 18
  See also CA 85-88

Pontoppidan, Henrik 1857-1943 . . . TCLC 29

Poole, Josephine 1933-. . . . . CLC 17
  See also CANR 10; CA 21-24R; SAAS 2;
  SATA 5

Popa, Vasko 1922- . . . . CLC 19
  See also CA 112

Pope, Alexander 1688- . . . . LC 3

Porter, Gene (va Grace) Stratton
  1863-1924 . . . . TCLC 21
  See also CA 112

Porter, Katherine Anne
  1890-1980 . . . CLC 1, 3, 7, 10, 13, 15, 27
  See also CANR 1; CA 1-4R;
  obituary CA 101; obituary SATA 23, 39;
  DLB 4, 9; DLB-Y 80

Porter, Peter (Neville Frederick)
  1929- . . . . CLC 5, 13, 33
  See also CA 85-88; DLB 40

Porter, William Sydney 1862-1910
  See Henry, O.
  See also YABC 2; CA 104; DLB 12;
  CDALB 1865-1917

Potok, Chaim 1929- . . . . CLC 2, 7, 14, 26
  See also CANR 19; CA 17-20R; SATA 33;
  DLB 28

Pound, Ezra (Loomis)
  1885-1972 . . . . . CLC 1, 2, 3, 4, 5, 7, 10,
                                  13, 18, 34, 48, 50
  See also CA 5-8R; obituary CA 37-40R;
  DLB 4, 45, 63

Povod, Reinaldo 1959-. . . . . CLC 44

Powell, Anthony (Dymoke)
  1905- . . . . CLC 1, 3, 7, 9, 10, 31
  See also CANR 1; CA 1-4R; DLB 15

Powell, Padgett 1952-. . . . . CLC 34

Powers, J(ames) F(arl) 1917-. . . . CLC 1, 4, 8
  See also CANR 2; CA 1-4R

Pownall, David 1938-. . . . . CLC 10
  See also CA 89-92; DLB 14

Powys, John Cowper
  1872-1963 . . . . CLC 7, 9, 15, 46
  See also CA 85-88; DLB 15

Powys, T(heodore) F(rancis)
  1875-1953 . . . . TCLC 9
  See also CA 106; DLB 36

Pratt, E(dwin) J(ohn) 1883-1964. . . . CLC 19
  See also obituary CA 93-96

Premchand 1880-1936 . . . . TCLC 21

Preussler, Otfried 1923-. . . . . CLC 17
  See also CA 77-80; SATA 24

Prevert, Jacques (Henri Marie)
  1900-1977 . . . . CLC 15
  See also CA 77-80; obituary CA 69-72;
  obituary SATA 30

Prevost, Abbe (Antoine Francois)
  1697-1763 . . . . LC 1

Price, (Edward) Reynolds
  1933- . . . . CLC 3, 6, 13, 43, 50
  See also CANR 1; CA 1-4R; DLB 2

Price, Richard 1949- . . . . CLC 6, 12
  See also CANR 3; CA 49-52; DLB-Y 81

Prichard, Katharine Susannah
  1883-1969 . . . . CLC 46
  See also CAP 1; CA 11-12

Priestley, J(ohn) B(oynton)
  1894-1984 . . . . CLC 2, 5, 9, 34
  See also CA 9-12R; obituary CA 113;
  DLB 10, 34; DLB-Y 84

Prince (Rogers Nelson) 1958?- . . . . . CLC 35

Prince, F(rank) T(empleton) 1912-. . . CLC 22
  See also CA 101; DLB 20

Prior, Matthew 1664-1721. . . . . LC 4

Pritchard, William H(arrison)
  1932- . . . . CLC 34
  See also CA 65-68

Pritchett, V(ictor) S(awdon)
  1900- . . . . CLC 5, 13, 15, 41
  See also CA 61-64; DLB 15

Procaccino, Michael 1946-
  See Cristofer, Michael

Prokosch, Frederic 1908-. . . . . CLC 4, 48
  See also CA 73-76; DLB 48

Prose, Francine 1947-. . . . . CLC 45
  See also CA 109, 112

Proust, Marcel 1871-1922 . . TCLC 7, 13, 33
  See also CA 104, 120; DLB 65

Pryor, Richard 1940-. . . . . CLC 26

Puig, Manuel 1932- . . . . CLC 3, 5, 10, 28
  See also CANR 2; CA 45-48

Purdy, A(lfred) W(ellington)
  1918- . . . . CLC 3, 6, 14, 50
  See also CA 81-84

Purdy, James (Amos)
  1923- . . . . CLC 2, 4, 10, 28
  See also CAAS 1; CANR 19; CA 33-36R;
  DLB 2

Pushkin, Alexander (Sergeyevich)
  1799-1837 . . . . NCLC 3

P'u Sung-ling 1640-1715 . . . . LC 3

Puzo, Mario 1920- . . . . CLC 1, 2, 6, 36
  See also CANR 4; CA 65-68; DLB 6

Pym, Barbara (Mary Crampton)
  1913-1980 . . . . CLC 13, 19, 37
  See also CANR 13; CAP 1; CA 13-14;
  obituary CA 97-100; DLB 14

Pynchon, Thomas (Ruggles, Jr.)
  1937- . . . . CLC 2, 3, 6, 9, 11, 18, 33
  See also CANR 22; CA 17-20R; DLB 2

Quasimodo, Salvatore 1901-1968 . . . CLC 10
  See also CAP 1; CA 15-16;
  obituary CA 25-28R

Queen, Ellery 1905-1982 . . . . CLC 3, 11
  See also Dannay, Frederic
  See also Lee, Manfred B(ennington)

Queneau, Raymond
  1903-1976 . . . . CLC 2, 5, 10, 42
  See also CA 77-80; obituary CA 69-72;
  DLB 72

Quin, Ann (Marie) 1936-1973 . . . . CLC 6
  See also CA 9-12R; obituary CA 45-48;
  DLB 14

Quinn, Simon 1942-
  See Smith, Martin Cruz

Quiroga, Horacio (Sylvestre)
  1878-1937 . . . . TCLC 20
  See also CA 117

Quoirez, Francoise 1935-
  See Sagan, Francoise
  See also CANR 6; CA 49-52

Rabe, David (William) 1940-. . . CLC 4, 8, 33
  See also CA 85-88; DLB 7

Rabelais, Francois 1494?-1553. . . . . . . LC 5

Rabinovitch, Sholem 1859-1916
  See Aleichem, Sholom
  See also CA 104

Rachen, Kurt von 1911-1986
  See Hubbard, L(afayette) Ron(ald)

Radcliffe, Ann (Ward) 1764-1823 . . NCLC 6
  See also DLB 39

Radiguet, Raymond 1903-1923 . . . . TCLC 29

Radnoti, Miklos 1909-1944 . . . . TCLC 16
  See also CA 118

Rado, James 1939-
  See Ragni, Gerome and Rado, James
  See also CA 105

Radomski, James 1932-
  See Rado, James

Radvanyi, Netty Reiling 1900-1983
  See Seghers, Anna
  See also CA 85-88; obituary CA 110

Raeburn, John 1941- . . . . CLC 34
  See also CA 57-60

Ragni, Gerome 1942- and Rado, James
  1939- . . . . CLC 17

Ragni, Gerome 1942-
  See Ragni, Gerome and Rado, James
  See also CA 105

Rahv, Philip 1908-1973 . . . . CLC 24
  See also Greenberg, Ivan

Raine, Craig 1944-. . . . . CLC 32
  See also CA 108; DLB 40

Raine, Kathleen (Jessie) 1908- . . . CLC 7, 45
  See also CA 85-88; DLB 20

Rainis, Janis 1865-1929 . . . . TCLC 29

Rakosi, Carl 1903- . . . . CLC 47
  See also Rawley, Callman
  See also CAAS 5

Rampersad, Arnold 19??-. . . . . CLC 44

Ryga, George 1932- . . . . **CLC 14**
See also CA 101; DLB 60

Saba, Umberto 1883-1957 . . . . **TCLC 33**

Sabato, Ernesto 1911- . . . . **CLC 10, 23**
See also CA 97-100

Sachs, Marilyn (Stickle) 1927- . . . . . **CLC 35**
See also CLR 2; CANR 13; CA 17-20R;
SAAS 2; SATA 3, 52

Sachs, Nelly 1891-1970 . . . . **CLC 14**
See also CAP 2; CA 17-18;
obituary CA 25-28R

Sackler, Howard (Oliver)
1929-1982 . . . . **CLC 14**
See also CA 61-64; obituary CA 108; DLB 7

Sade, Donatien Alphonse Francois, Comte de
1740-1814 . . . . **NCLC 3**

Sadoff, Ira 1945- . . . . **CLC 9**
See also CANR 5, 21; CA 53-56

Safire, William 1929- . . . . **CLC 10**
See also CA 17-20R

Sagan, Carl (Edward) 1934- . . . . **CLC 30**
See also CANR 11; CA 25-28R

Sagan, Francoise
1935- . . . . **CLC 3, 6, 9, 17, 36**
See also Quoirez, Francoise

Sahgal, Nayantara (Pandit) 1927- . . . **CLC 41**
See also CANR 11; CA 9-12R

Saint, H(arry) F. 1941- . . . . **CLC 50**

Sainte-Beuve, Charles Augustin
1804-1869 . . . . **NCLC 5**

Sainte-Marie, Beverly 1941-
See Sainte-Marie, Buffy
See also CA 107

Sainte-Marie, Buffy 1941- . . . . **CLC 17**
See also Sainte-Marie, Beverly

Saint-Exupery, Antoine (Jean Baptiste Marie
Roger) de 1900-1944 . . . . **TCLC 2**
See also CLR 10; CA 108; SATA 20;
DLB 72

Saintsbury, George 1845-1933. . . . . **TCLC 31**

Sait Faik (Abasiyanik)
1906-1954 . . . . **TCLC 23**

Saki 1870-1916. . . . . **TCLC 3**
See also Munro, H(ector) H(ugh)

Salama, Hannu 1936- . . . . **CLC 18**

Salamanca, J(ack) R(ichard)
1922- . . . . **CLC 4, 15**
See also CA 25-28R

Salinas, Pedro 1891-1951. . . . . **TCLC 17**
See also CA 117

Salinger, J(erome) D(avid)
1919- . . . . **CLC 1, 3, 8, 12; SSC 2**
See also CA 5-8R; DLB 2;
CDALB 1941-1968

Salter, James 1925- . . . . **CLC 7**
See also CA 73-76

Saltus, Edgar (Evertson)
1855-1921 . . . . **TCLC 8**
See also CA 105

Saltykov, Mikhail Evgrafovich
1826-1889 . . . . **NCLC 16**

Samarakis, Antonis 1919- . . . . **CLC 5**
See also CA 25-28R

Sanchez, Luis Rafael 1936- . . . . **CLC 23**

Sanchez, Sonia 1934- . . . . **CLC 5**
See also CA 33-36R; SATA 22; DLB 41

Sand, George 1804-1876. . . . . **NCLC 2**

Sandburg, Carl (August)
1878-1967 . . . . **CLC 1, 4, 10, 15, 35**
See also CA 5-8R; obituary CA 25-28R;
SATA 8; DLB 17, 54; CDALB 1865-1917

Sandburg, Charles August 1878-1967
See Sandburg, Carl (August)

Sanders, Lawrence 1920- . . . . **CLC 41**
See also CA 81-84

Sandoz, Mari (Susette) 1896-1966 . . **CLC 28**
See also CANR 17; CA 1-4R;
obituary CA 25-28R; SATA 5; DLB 9

Saner, Reg(inald Anthony) 1931- . . . . **CLC 9**
See also CA 65-68

Sannazaro, Jacopo 1456?-1530 . . . . **LC 8**

Sansom, William 1912-1976. . . . . . . **CLC 2, 6**
See also CA 5-8R; obituary CA 65-68

Santiago, Danny 1911- . . . . **CLC 33**

Santmyer, Helen Hooven
1895-1986 . . . . **CLC 33**
See also CANR 15; CA 1-4R;
obituary CA 118; DLB-Y 84

Santos, Bienvenido N(uqui) 1911- . . . **CLC 22**
See also CANR 19; CA 101

Sappho fl.c. 6th-century B.C. . . . . **CMLC 3**

Sarduy, Severo 1937- . . . . **CLC 6**
See also CA 89-92

Sargeson, Frank 1903-1982. . . . . **CLC 31**
See also CA 106

Sarmiento, Felix Ruben Garcia 1867-1916
See also CA 104

Saroyan, William
1908-1981 . . . . **CLC 1, 8, 10, 29, 34**
See also CA 5-8R; obituary CA 103;
SATA 23; obituary SATA 24; DLB 7, 9;
DLB-Y 81

Sarraute, Nathalie
1902- . . . . **CLC 1, 2, 4, 8, 10, 31**
See also CA 9-12R

Sarton, Eleanore Marie 1912-
See Sarton, (Eleanor) May

Sarton, (Eleanor) May
1912- . . . . **CLC 4, 14, 49**
See also CANR 1; CA 1-4R; SATA 36;
DLB 48; DLB-Y 81

Sartre, Jean-Paul
1905-1980 . . . **CLC 1, 4, 7, 9, 13, 18, 24, 44, 50**
See also CANR 21; CA 9-12R;
obituary CA 97-100; DLB 72

Sassoon, Siegfried (Lorraine)
1886-1967 . . . . **CLC 36**
See also CA 104; obituary CA 25-28R;
DLB 20

Saul, John (W. III) 1942- . . . . **CLC 46**
See also CANR 16; CA 81-84

Saura, Carlos 1932- . . . . **CLC 20**
See also CA 114

Sauser-Hall, Frederic-Louis 1887-1961
See Cendrars, Blaise
See also CA 102; obituary CA 93-96

Savage, Thomas 1915- . . . . **CLC 40**

Savan, Glenn 19??- . . . . **CLC 50**

Sayers, Dorothy L(eigh)
1893-1957 . . . . **TCLC 2, 15**
See also CA 104, 119; DLB 10, 36

Sayers, Valerie 19??- . . . . **CLC 50**

Sayles, John (Thomas)
1950- . . . . **CLC 7, 10, 14**
See also CA 57-60; DLB 44

Scammell, Michael 19??- . . . . **CLC 34**

Scannell, Vernon 1922- . . . . **CLC 49**
See also CANR 8; CA 5-8R; DLB 27

Schaeffer, Susan Fromberg
1941- . . . . **CLC 6, 11, 22**
See also CANR 18; CA 49-52; SATA 22;
DLB 28

Schell, Jonathan 1943- . . . . **CLC 35**
See also CANR 12; CA 73-76

Scherer, Jean-Marie Maurice 1920-
See Rohmer, Eric
See also CA 110

Schevill, James (Erwin) 1920- . . . . **CLC 7**
See also CA 5-8R

Schisgal, Murray (Joseph) 1926- . . . . . **CLC 6**
See also CA 21-24R

Schlee, Ann 1934- . . . . **CLC 35**
See also CA 101; SATA 36, 44

Schlegel, August Wilhelm von
1767-1845 . . . . **NCLC 15**

Schlegel, Johann Elias (von)
1719?-1749. **LC 5**

Schmitz, Ettore 1861-1928
See Svevo, Italo
See also CA 104

Schnackenberg, Gjertrud 1953- . . . . . **CLC 40**
See also CA 116

Schneider, Leonard Alfred 1925-1966
See Bruce, Lenny
See also CA 89-92

Schnitzler, Arthur 1862-1931 . . . . . . **TCLC 4**
See also CA 104

Schorer, Mark 1908-1977 . . . . **CLC 9**
See also CANR 7; CA 5-8R;
obituary CA 73-76

Schrader, Paul (Joseph) 1946- . . . . . . **CLC 26**
See also CA 37-40R; DLB 44

Schreiner (Cronwright), Olive (Emilie
Albertina) 1855-1920. . . . . **TCLC 9**
See also CA 105; DLB 18

Schulberg, Budd (Wilson)
1914- . . . . **CLC 7, 48**
See also CANR 19; CA 25-28R; DLB 6, 26,
28; DLB-Y 81

Schulz, Bruno 1892-1942. . . . . **TCLC 5**
See also CA 115

Schulz, Charles M(onroe) 1922- . . . . **CLC 12**
See also CANR 6; CA 9-12R; SATA 10

Schuyler, James (Marcus)
1923- . . . . **CLC 5, 23**
See also CA 101; DLB 5

Schwartz, Delmore
1913-1966 . . . . **CLC 2, 4, 10, 45**
See also CAP 2; CA 17-18;
obituary CA 25-28R; DLB 28, 48

Trotter (Cockburn), Catharine
  1679-1749 . . . . LC 8

Troyat, Henri   1911- . . . . CLC 23
  See also CANR 2; CA 45-48

Trudeau, Garry   1948- . . . . CLC 12
  See also Trudeau, G(arretson) B(eekman)

Trudeau, G(arretson) B(eekman)   1948-
  See Trudeau, Garry
  See also CA 81-84; SATA 35

Truffaut, Francois   1932-1984. . . . . . . CLC 20
  See also CA 81-84; obituary CA 113

Trumbo, Dalton   1905-1976 . . . . CLC 19
  See also CANR 10; CA 21-24R;
    obituary CA 69-72; DLB 26

Tryon, Thomas   1926- . . . . CLC 3, 11
  See also CA 29-32R

Ts'ao Hsueh-ch'in   1715?-1763 . . . . LC 1

Tsushima Shuji   1909-1948
  See Dazai Osamu
  See also CA 107

Tsvetaeva (Efron), Marina (Ivanovna)
  1892-1941 . . . . TCLC 7
  See also CA 104

Tunis, John R(oberts)   1889-1975 . . . CLC 12
  See also CA 61-64; SATA 30, 37; DLB 22

Tuohy, Frank   1925- . . . . CLC 37
  See also DLB 14

Tuohy, John Francis   1925-
  See Tuohy, Frank
  See also CANR 3; CA 5-8R

Turco, Lewis (Putnam)   1934- . . . . . . CLC 11
  See also CA 13-16R; DLB-Y 84

Turner, Frederick   1943- . . . . CLC 48
  See also CANR 12; CA 73-76; DLB 40

Tutuola, Amos   1920- . . . . CLC 5, 14, 29
  See also CA 9-12R

Twain, Mark   1835-1910. . . . TCLC 6, 12, 19
  See also Clemens, Samuel Langhorne
  See also DLB 11, 12, 23

Tyler, Anne   1941- . . . . CLC 7, 11, 18, 28, 44
  See also CANR 11; CA 9-12R; SATA 7;
    DLB 6; DLB-Y 82

Tyler, Royall   1757-1826. . . . . NCLC 3
  See also DLB 37

Tynan (Hinkson), Katharine
  1861-1931 . . . . TCLC 3
  See also CA 104

Tytell, John   1939- . . . . CLC 50
  See also CA 29-32R

Tzara, Tristan   1896-1963. . . . . CLC 47
  See also Rosenfeld, Samuel

Unamuno (y Jugo), Miguel de
  1864-1936 . . . . TCLC 2, 9
  See also CA 104

Underwood, Miles   1909-1981
  See Glassco, John

Undset, Sigrid   1882-1949. . . . . TCLC 3
  See also CA 104

Ungaretti, Giuseppe
  1888-1970 . . . . CLC 7, 11, 15
  See also CAP 2; CA 19-20;
    obituary CA 25-28R

Unger, Douglas   1952- . . . . CLC 34

Unger, Eva   1932-
  See Figes, Eva

Updike, John (Hoyer)
  1932- . . . . . . CLC 1, 2, 3, 5, 7, 9, 13, 15,
                              23, 34, 43
  See also CANR 4; CA 1-4R; CABS 2;
    DLB 2, 5; DLB-Y 80, 82; DLB-DS 3

Urdang, Constance (Henriette)
  1922- . . . . CLC 47
  See also CANR 9; CA 21-24R

Uris, Leon (Marcus)   1924- . . . . CLC 7, 32
  See also CANR 1; CA 1-4R; SATA 49

Ustinov, Peter (Alexander)   1921- . . . . CLC 1
  See also CA 13-16R; DLB 13

Vaculik, Ludvik   1926- . . . . CLC 7
  See also CA 53-56

Valenzuela, Luisa   1938- . . . . CLC 31
  See also CA 101

Valera (y Acala-Galiano), Juan
  1824-1905 . . . . TCLC 10
  See also CA 106

Valery, Paul (Ambroise Toussaint Jules)
  1871-1945. . . . . TCLC 4, 15
  See also CA 104, 122

Valle-Inclan (y Montenegro), Ramon (Maria)
  del   1866-1936. . . . . TCLC 5
  See also CA 106

Vallejo, Cesar (Abraham)
  1892-1938 . . . . TCLC 3
  See also CA 105

Van Ash, Cay   1918- . . . . CLC 34

Vance, Jack   1916?- . . . . CLC 35
  See also DLB 8

Vance, John Holbrook   1916?-
  See Vance, Jack
  See also CANR 17; CA 29-32R

Van Den Bogarde, Derek (Jules Gaspard
  Ulric) Niven   1921-
  See Bogarde, Dirk
  See also CA 77-80

Vanderhaeghe, Guy   1951- . . . . CLC 41
  See also CA 113

Van der Post, Laurens (Jan)   1906- . . . CLC 5
  See also CA 5-8R

Van de Wetering, Janwillem
  1931- . . . . CLC 47
  See also CANR 4; CA 49-52

Van Dine, S. S.   1888-1939. . . . . . . TCLC 23

Van Doren, Carl (Clinton)
  1885-1950 . . . . TCLC 18
  See also CA 111

Van Doren, Mark   1894-1972. . . . . CLC 6, 10
  See also CANR 3; CA 1-4R;
    obituary CA 37-40R; DLB 45

Van Druten, John (William)
  1901-1957 . . . . TCLC 2
  See also CA 104; DLB 10

Van Duyn, Mona   1921- . . . . CLC 3, 7
  See also CANR 7; CA 9-12R; DLB 5

Van Itallie, Jean-Claude   1936- . . . . . . CLC 3
  See also CAAS 2; CANR 1; CA 45-48;
    DLB 7

Van Ostaijen, Paul   1896-1928. . . . . TCLC 33

Van Peebles, Melvin   1932- . . . . . . CLC 2, 20
  See also CA 85-88

Vansittart, Peter   1920- . . . . CLC 42
  See also CANR 3; CA 1-4R

Van Vechten, Carl   1880-1964 . . . . . . CLC 33
  See also obituary CA 89-92; DLB 4, 9, 51

Van Vogt, A(lfred) E(lton)   1912- . . . . . CLC 1
  See also CA 21-24R; SATA 14; DLB 8

Varda, Agnes   1928- . . . . CLC 16
  See also CA 116

Vargas Llosa, (Jorge) Mario (Pedro)
  1936- . . . . CLC 3, 6, 9, 10, 15, 31, 42
  See also CANR 18; CA 73-76

Vassilikos, Vassilis   1933- . . . . CLC 4, 8
  See also CA 81-84

Vazov, Ivan   1850-1921. . . . . TCLC 25
  See also CA 121

Veblen, Thorstein Bunde
  1857-1929 . . . . TCLC 31
  See also CA 115

Verga, Giovanni   1840-1922 . . . . TCLC 3
  See also CA 104

Verhaeren, Emile (Adolphe Gustave)
  1855-1916 . . . . TCLC 12
  See also CA 109

Verlaine, Paul (Marie)   1844-1896. . NCLC 2

Verne, Jules (Gabriel)   1828-1905 . . . TCLC 6
  See also CA 110; SATA 21

Very, Jones   1813-1880. . . . . NCLC 9
  See also DLB 1

Vesaas, Tarjei   1897-1970. . . . . CLC 48
  See also obituary CA 29-32R

Vian, Boris   1920-1959 . . . . TCLC 9
  See also CA 106; DLB 72

Viaud, (Louis Marie) Julien   1850-1923
  See Loti, Pierre
  See also CA 107

Vicker, Angus   1916-
  See Felsen, Henry Gregor

Vidal, Eugene Luther, Jr.   1925-
  See Vidal, Gore

Vidal, Gore
  1925- . . . . CLC 2, 4, 6, 8, 10, 22, 33
  See also CANR 13; CA 5-8R; DLB 6

Viereck, Peter (Robert Edwin)
  1916- . . . . CLC 4
  See also CANR 1; CA 1-4R; DLB 5

Vigny, Alfred (Victor) de
  1797-1863 . . . . NCLC 7

Villiers de l'Isle Adam, Jean Marie Mathias
  Philippe Auguste, Comte de,
  1838-1889 . . . . NCLC 3

Vine, Barbara   1930- . . . . CLC 50
  See also Rendell, Ruth

Vinge, Joan (Carol) D(ennison)
  1948- . . . . CLC 30
  See also CA 93-96; SATA 36

Visconti, Luchino   1906-1976. . . . . . . CLC 16
  See also CA 81-84; obituary CA 65-68

Vittorini, Elio   1908-1966. . . . . . CLC 6, 9, 14
  See also obituary CA 25-28R

Vizinczey, Stephen   1933- . . . . CLC 40

Author Index

TCLC Cumulative Nationality Index

AMERICAN

Adams, Henry 4
Agee, James 1, 19
Anderson, Maxwell 2
Anderson, Sherwood 1, 10, 24
Atherton, Gertrude 2
Austin, Mary 25
Barry, Philip 11
Baum, L. Frank 7
Beard, Charles A. 15
Belasco, David 3
Benchley, Robert 1
Benét, Stephen Vincent 7
Benét, William Rose 28
Bierce, Ambrose 1, 7
Black Elk 33
Bourne, Randolph S. 16
Bromfield, Louis 11
Burroughs, Edgar Rice 2, 32
Cabell, James Branch 6
Cable, George Washington 4
Cather, Willa 1, 11, 31
Chandler, Raymond 1, 7
Chapman, John Jay 7
Chesnutt, Charles Waddell 5
Chopin, Kate 5, 14
Comstock, Anthony 13
Cotter, Joseph Seamon, Sr. 28
Crane, Hart 2, 5
Crane, Stephen 11, 17, 32
Crawford, F. Marion 10
Crothers, Rachel 19
Cullen, Countee 4
Davis, Rebecca Harding 6
Davis, Richard Harding 24
Day, Clarence 25
DeVoto, Bernard 29
Dreiser, Theodore 10, 18
Dunbar, Paul Laurence 2, 12

Dunne, Finley Peter 28
Fisher, Rudolph 11
Fitzgerald, F. Scott 1, 6, 14, 28
Forten, Charlotte L. 16
Freeman, Douglas Southall 11
Freeman, Mary Wilkins 9
Futrelle, Jacques 19
Gale, Zona 7
Garland, Hamlin 3
Gilman, Charlotte Perkins 9
Glasgow, Ellen 2, 7
Goldman, Emma 13
Grey, Zane 6
Hall, James Norman 23
Harper, Frances Ellen Watkins 14
Harris, Joel Chandler 2
Harte, Bret 1, 25
Hawthorne, Julian 25
Hearn, Lafcadio 9
Henry, O. 1, 19
Hergesheimer, Joseph 11
Hopkins, Pauline Elizabeth 28
Howard, Robert E. 8
Howe, Julia Ward 21
Howells, William Dean 7, 17
James, Henry 2, 11, 24
James, William 15, 32
Jewett, Sarah Orne 1, 22
Johnson, James Weldon 3, 19
Kornbluth, C. M. 8
Kuttner, Henry 10
Lardner, Ring 2, 14
Lewis, Sinclair 4, 13, 23
Lewisohn, Ludwig 19
Lindsay, Vachel 17
London, Jack 9, 15
Lovecraft, H. P. 4, 22
Lowell, Amy 1, 8
Marquis, Don 7

Masters, Edgar Lee 2, 25
McCoy, Horace 28
McKay, Claude 7
Mencken, H. L. 13
Millay, Edna St. Vincent 4
Mitchell, Margaret 11
Monroe, Harriet 12
Muir, John 28
Nathan, George Jean 18
Nordhoff, Charles 23
Norris, Frank 24
O'Neill, Eugene 1, 6, 27
Porter, Gene Stratton 21
Rawlings, Majorie Kinnan 4
Reed, John 9
Roberts, Kenneth 23
Robinson, Edwin Arlington 5
Rogers, Will 8
Rölvaag, O. E. 17
Rourke, Constance 12
Runyon, Damon 10
Saltus, Edgar 8
Sherwood, Robert E. 3
Slesinger, Tess 10
Steffens, Lincoln 20
Stein, Gertrude 1, 6, 28
Sterling, George 20
Stevens, Wallace 3, 12
Tarkington, Booth 9
Teasdale, Sara 4
Thurman, Wallace 6
Twain, Mark 6, 12, 19
Van Dine, S. S. 23
Van Doren, Carl 18
Veblen, Thorstein 31
Washington, Booker T. 10
West, Nathanael 1, 14
Wharton, Edith 3, 9, 27
White, Walter 15

Éluard, Paul 7
Fargue, Léon-Paul 11
Feydeau, Georges 22
France, Anatole 9
Gide, André 5, 12
Giraudoux, Jean 2, 7
Gourmont, Remy de 17
Huysmans, Joris-Karl 7
Jacob, Max 6
Jarry, Alfred 2, 14
Larbaud, Valéry 9
Leroux, Gaston 25
Loti, Pierre 11
Martin du Gard, Roger 24
Moréas, Jean 18
Péguy, Charles 10
Péret, Benjamin 20
Proust, Marcel 7, 13, 33
Radiguet, Raymond 29
Renard, Jules 17
Rolland, Romain 23
Rostand, Edmond 6
Roussel, Raymond 20
Saint-Exupéry, Antoine de 2
Schwob, Marcel 20
Sully Prudhomme 31
Teilhard de Chardin, Pierre 9
Valéry, Paul 4, 15
Verne, Jules 6
Vian, Boris 9
Weil, Simone 23
Zola, Émile 1, 6, 21

GERMAN
Benn, Gottfried 3
Borchert, Wolfgang 5
Brecht, Bertolt 1, 6, 13
Döblin, Alfred 13
Ewers, Hanns Heinz 12
Feuchtwanger, Lion 3
George, Stefan 2, 14
Hauptmann, Gerhart 4
Heym, Georg 9
Heyse, Paul 8
Huch, Ricarda 13
Kaiser, Georg 9
Liliencron, Detlev von 18
Mann, Heinrich 9
Mann, Thomas 2, 8, 14, 21
Morgenstern, Christian 8
Nietzsche, Friedrich 10, 18
Rilke, Rainer Maria 1, 6, 19
Spengler, Oswald 25
Sternheim, Carl 8
Sudermann, Hermann 15
Toller, Ernst 10
Wassermann, Jakob 6
Wedekind, Frank 7

GHANIAN
Casely-Hayford, J. E. 24

GREEK
Cafavy, C. P. 2, 7
Kazantzakis, Nikos 2, 5, 33
Palamas, Kostes 5
Papadiamantis, Alexandros 29

HAITIAN
Roumain, Jacques 19

HUNGARIAN
Hungarian Literature of the Twentieth
   Century 26
Ady, Endre 11
Babits, Mihály 14
Csáth, Géza 13
József, Attila 22
Mikszáth, Kálmán 31
Molnár, Ferenc 20
Móricz, Zsigmond 33
Radnóti, Miklós 16

ICELANDIC
Sigurjónsson, Jóhann 27

INDIAN
Chatterji, Saratchandra 13
Iqbal, Muhammad 28
Premchand 21
Tagore, Rabindranath 3

INDONESIAN
Anwar, Chairil 22

IRANIAN
Hedayat, Sadeq 21

IRISH
A. E. 3, 10
Cary, Joyce 1, 29
Dunsany, Lord 2
Gogarty, Oliver St. John 15
Gregory, Lady 1
Harris, Frank 24
Joyce, James 3, 8, 16, 26
Ledwidge, Francis 23
Moore, George 7
O'Grady, Standish 5
Shaw, Bernard 3, 9, 21
Stephens, James 4
Stoker, Bram 8
Synge, J. M. 6
Tynan, Katharine 3
Wilde, Oscar 1, 8, 23
Yeats, William Butler 1, 11, 18, 31

ITALIAN
Betti, Ugo 5
Brancati, Vitaliano 12
Campana, Dino 20
Carducci, Giosuè 32
D'Annunzio, Gabriel 6
Deledda, Grazia 23
Giacosa, Giuseppe 7
Lampedusa, Giuseppe Tomasi di 13
Marinetti, F. T. 10
Papini, Giovanni 22
Pavese, Cesare 3
Pirandello, Luigi 4, 29
Saba, Umberto 33
Svevo, Italo 2
Tozzi, Federigo 31
Verga, Giovanni 3

JAMAICAN
De Lisser, H. G. 12
Mais, Roger 8
Redcam, Tom 25

JAPANESE
Akutagawa Ryūnosuke 16
Dazai Osamu 11

Hayashi Fumiko 27
Ishikawa Takuboku 15
Masaoka Shiki 18
Mori Ōgai 14
Natsume, Sōseki 2, 10
Rohan, Kōda 22
Shimazaki, Tōson 5

LATVIAN
Rainis, Janis 29

LEBANESE
Gibran, Kahlil 1, 9

LESOTHAN
Mofolo, Thomas 22

LITHUANIAN
Krévé, Vincas 27

MEXICAN
Azuela, Mariano 3
Nervo, Amado 11
Reyes, Alfonso 33
Romero, José Rubén 14

NATIVE AMERICAN
See American

NEPALI
Devkota, Laxmiprasad 23

NEW ZEALAND
Mander, Jane 31
Mansfield, Katherine 2, 8

NICARAGUAN
Darío, Rubén 4

NIGERIAN
Nigerian Literature of the Twentieth
   Century 30

NORWEGIAN
Bjørnson, Bjørnstjerne 7
Grieg, Nordhal 10
Hamsun, Knut 2, 14
Ibsen, Henrik 2, 8, 16
Kielland, Alexander 5
Lie, Jonas 5
Obstfelder, Sigbjørn 23
Skram, Amalie 25
Undset, Sigrid 3

PAKISTANI
Iqbal, Muhammad 28

PERUVIAN
Palma, Ricardo 29
Vallejo, César 3

POLISH
Asch, Sholem 3
Borowski, Tadeusz 9
Peretz, Isaac Leib 16
Reymont, Wladyslaw Stanislaw 5
Schulz, Bruno 5
Sienkiewitz, Henryk 3
Singer, Israel Joshua 33
Witkiewicz, Stanislaw Ignacy 8

Title Index

Title Index

Title Index

Title Index

Title Index

"Ivy Day in the Committee Room" (Joyce) **8**:158, 166

"Iz ada izvedënnye" (Bryusov) **10**:81

Izawa Ranken (Mori Ōgai) **14**:376, 378

Izgoi (*The Fallen*) (Gladkov) **27**:90

Iznanka poèzii (Annensky) **14**:24

Izwe lakwandlambe (*The Domain of the Ndlambe People*) (Mqhayi) **25**:326

"J. Habakuk Jephson's Statement" (Doyle) **7**:234, 238

"Ja tror på min syster" ("I Believe in My Sister") (Södergran) **31**:293

"Ja, vi elsker dette landet" ("Yes, We Love This Land") (Bjørnson) **7**:110

Jaana Rönty (Leino) **24**:372

"J'accuse" (Zola) **1**:591

"Jack Dunn of Nevertire" (Lawson) **27**:134

Jack Liverpool (London) **9**:259

The Jackdar (Gregory) **1**:334

The Jacket (London) **15**:260-61

"Jackie" (Smith) **25**:390

"The Jack-Rabbit" (Stevens) **12**:367

Jacob (Kielland) **5**:277

"Jacob and the Indians" (Benét) **7**:81

The Jacob Street Mystery (Freeman) **21**:58-9

Les Jacobites (Coppée) **25**:127

Jacob's Ladder (Housman) **7**:360

Jacob's Room (Woolf) **1**:527-29, 531-33, 536, 538-39, 542-43, 545; **5**:508, 516; **20**:397, 409, 425, 428-29

"Jacques de la Cloche" (Lang) **16**:254

"Jacques l'égoïste" (Giraudoux) **3**:324

"Jag" ("I") (Södergran) **31**:288

"Jag såg ett träd" ("I Saw a Tree") (Södergran) **31**:289

Die Jagd nach Liebe (Mann) **9**:323, 325-27

"El jahad" (Graham) **19**:129

"Jahr" (George) **14**:210

Der Jahr der Seele (*The Year of the Soul*) (George) **2**:149, 151; **14**:196, 200-02, 204, 206, 209-12, 215-16

"Jailbird" (Gale) **7**:285

Jakob von Gunten (Walser) **18**:415, 417-18, 420-21, 424-25, 428-29, 431-34

"Jaldaboath" (Benét) **28**:8

"Jamaica Marches On" (Redcam) **25**:330

"Jamaican Rose" (Rohmer) **28**:286

"James and Maggie" (Lawson) **27**:132

James Burnham and the Managerial Revolution (Orwell) **31**:190

"James James" (Milne) **6**:313

"James Pethel" (Beerbohm) **24**:100-01

James Shore's Daughter (Benét) **3**:80-1

"James Thomson" (Noyes) **7**:506

"Jamiol" (Sienkiewicz) **3**:430

Jane Field (Freeman) **9**:63, 68-9

Jane Mecom (Van Doren) **18**:410

"Jane Mollet's Box" (Powys) **9**:372

Jane Oglander (Lowndes) **12**:200

"The Janeites" (Kipling) **8**:195-96

Jane's Career (De Lisser) **12**:95-100

"Jang terampas dan jang luput" ("The Captured and the Freed") (Anwar) **22**:24

Janika (*Johnny*) (Csáth) **13**:147

"Janko the Musician" (Sienkiewicz) **3**:425-27

Janmadine (Tagore) **3**:488

"Janmadine, No. 5" (Tagore) **3**:489

"January, 1939" ("Because the Pleasure-Bird Whistles") (Thomas) **8**:459

Japan: An Attempt at Interpretation (Hearn) **9**:123, 126, 128-32

Japanese Fairy Tales (Hearn) **9**:128

The Japanese Letters of Lafcadio Hearn (Hearn) **9**:123

"Japonerías del estío" (Huidobro) **31**:124

Japoneries d'automne (Loti) **11**:361

"The Jar"
   See "La giara"

"Le jardin d'Antan" (Nelligan) **14**:392

Le jardin d'Épicure (*The Garden of Epicurus*) (France) **9**:42

Le jardin des rochers (*The Rock Garden*) (Kazantzakis) **2**:317; **5**:270; **33**:150

"Jardin sentimental" (Nelligan) **14**:398-99

Los jardines interiores (*The Inner Gardens*) (Nervo) **11**:400, 402

Jardines lejanos (Jiménez) **4**:213, 223

"Járkálj csak, halálraítélt!" ("Walk On, Condemned!") (Radnóti) **16**:411

"Jashūmon" (Akutagawa Ryūnosuke) **16**:18

"Jason and Medea" (Lewis) **3**:287

Jason Edwards, an Average Man (Garland) **3**:192

"Jasper's Song" (Pickthall) **21**:245

Játék a kastélyban (*The Play's the Thing*) (Molnár) **20**:161, 166, 170, 178

"Jaufré Rudel" (Carducci) **32**:90, 101

"La jaula de pájaro" (Valle-Inclán) **5**:478

Jaunais spēks (*New Strength*) (Rainis) **29**:392

Jaune bleu blanc (Larbaud) **9**:199, 208

Java Head (Hergesheimer) **11**:261-65, 269, 271, 276, 281, 283, 285-86

"Javanese Dancers" (Symons) **11**:445, 451

Javid-namah (*The Pilgrimage of Eternity*) (Iqbal) **28**:182, 191, 204

Jayhawker (Lewis) **4**:257

Jāzeps un viņa brāļi (*Joseph and His Brothers*) (Rainis) **29**:380-81, 386, 393

Je ne mange pas de ce pain-là (Péret) **20**:195, 198, 202

"Je ne parle pas Français" (Mansfield) **2**:448, 453; **8**:280-82, 285-86, 291-92

Je ne trompe pas mon mari (*I Don't Cheat on My Husband*) (Feydeau) **22**:79, 83

Je sublime (Péret) **20**:184-85, 187, 196, 202

The Jealous Wife (Belasco) **3**:86

Jealousy (Artsybashev) **31**:9, 11

"Jealousy" (Brooke) **2**:59; **7**:122

Jean Barois (Martin du Gard) **24**:382-83, 385-87, 390-95, 398, 402-04, 412

"Jean Cocteau" (Stein) **6**:403

"Jean Desprez" (Service) **15**:401

Jean Huguenot (Benét) **7**:80

Jean Maquenem
   See *Le retour*

Jean Santeuil (Proust) **7**:528, 533-34, 536, 539; **13**:415-18, 420-21, 429; **33**:262, 271

Jean-Christophe (*John Christopher*) (Rolland) **23**:249-53, 256, 259-63, 270-71, 276-79, 282-85

Jeanne d'Arc (*Joan of Arc*) (Péguy) **10**:407-08, 410

La "Jeanne d'Arc" de M. Anatole France
   See *The Maid of France*

"Jeanne de Courtisols" (Bourget) **12**:73

Jeanne de Piennes (Rolland) **23**:256

"Jeanne: Relapse et sainte" ("Sanctity Will Out") (Bernanos) **3**:127

Jedermann (*The Play of Everyman*) (Hofmannsthal) **11**:295-98, 301, 303

Jeff Briggs' Love Story (Harte) **1**:342

"Jefferson Howard" (Masters) **25**:312

Jefta und Seine Tochter (*Jeptha and His Daughter*) (Feuchtwanger) **3**:182-83, 186

"Jeg ser" ("I See") (Obstfelder) **23**:177, 180, 189

"Jeg-formen i litteraturen" ("The I-Form in Literature") (Obstfelder) **23**:191

Jeli il pastore (Verga) **3**:547

"Jener" (Benn) **3**:107

Jennie Gerhardt (Dreiser) **10**:163-65, 167, 173, 177, 181-82, 186-87, 198-200; **18**:53, 63-6

Jennifer Lorn (Wylie) **8**:523-25, 527-28, 530-31, 537-38

Jenny (Undset) **3**:510, 512, 516-18, 521-22

Jensuits von gut und Böse: Vorspiel einer Philosophie der zukunft (*Beyond Good and Evil: Prelude to a Philosophy of the Future*) (Nietzsche) **10**:355, 360, 362, 385-86, 388-90, 393; **18**:342, 351

Jeptha and His Daughter
   See *Jefta und Seine Tochter*

Jeremy (Walpole) **5**:498

Jeremy and Hamlet (Walpole) **5**:498

Jeremy at Crale (Walpole) **5**:498

Jerome, a Poor Man (Freeman) **9**:61, 63, 69-72, 74

"Jerry Bundler" (Jacobs) **22**:99

Jerry of the Islands (London) **9**:267

Jerusalem
   See *Jerusalem: I Dalarne*

"Jérusalem" (Loti) **11**:355-56, 362

Jerusalem: I Dalarne (*Jerusalem*) (Lagerlöf) **4**:229-32, 235, 238-39, 241

Jerusalem: I det heliga landet (Lagerlöf) **4**:231

Jess (Haggard) **11**:239

"Jesse James: American Myth" (Benét) **28**:11

The Jest (Cabell) **6**:61

The Jester (Gregory) **1**:337

"The Jesters" (Marquis) **7**:434

"The Jesters of the Lord" (Manning) **25**:265, 269

"A Jesuit" (Graham) **19**:101, 136

"Jesus"
   See "Isa"

Jésus (Barbusse) **5**:14, 18

Jesus: Man of Genius (Murry) **16**:355

Jesus, the Son of Man (Gibran) **1**:326; **9**:82, 86, 91-2, 94

Jesus the Unknown (Merezhkovsky) **29**:242

"Jesus und der Aser-Weg" (Werfel) **8**:477

Le jet de sang (*The Fountain of Blood*) (Artaud) **3**:53, 61

"Jet d'eau" (Apollinaire) **8**:12

Le jeune Européen (Drieu La Rochelle) **21**:17-18

La jeune fille Violaine (Claudel) **2**:106; **10**:128

"La jeune parque" (Valéry) **4**:487-91, 495, 501; **15**:447-49, 455, 458-64

"Jeunes filles" (Sully Prudhomme) **31**:299

"The Jew" (Rosenberg) **12**:292, 295, 307

"The Jew and Trans-National America"
   See "Trans-National America"

The Jew of Rome
   See *Die Söhne*

The Jewel of Seven Stars (Stoker) **8**:385-86, 394, 399

The Jeweled Casket and the Two Urashima
   See *Tamakushige futari Urashima*

"The Jeweller's Shop in Wartime" (Howe) **21**:113

"Jewels of Gwahlur" (Howard) **8**:133

Title Index

Title Index

Title Index

Title Index

My Ántonia (Cather)　**1**:151, 153, 156-59, 162-63, 165, 167; **11**:92-8, 102, 104-07, 112, 114; **31**:24-69

My Apprenticeships
　See *Mes apprentissages*

My Apprenticeship (Gorky)　**8**:77

My Apprenticeship (Webb and Webb)　**22**:414-15, 419, 423

"My Army, O, My Army!" (Lawson)　**27**:122, 133

"My Bay'nit" (Service)　**15**:399

"My Big Brother" (Premchand)　**21**:287

My Birds (Davies)　**5**:206

"My Birthday" (Gibran)　**9**:85

"My Boy Jack" (Kipling)　**8**:200

My Brilliant Career (Franklin)　**7**:264, 266-74

"My Brother Paul" (Dreiser)　**10**:181

My Brother Yves
　See *Mon frère Yves*

My Career Goes Bung (Franklin)　**7**:267-68, 270-74

My Childhood
　See *Detstvo*

"My Cicely" (Hardy)　**4**:152

"My Coffin Steed" (Ady)　**11**:14

My Confessional: Questions of Our Day (Ellis)　**14**:116-17, 127

My Contemporaries
　See *Az én kortársaim*

"My Country, Right or Left" (Orwell)　**15**:355

"My Countrymen" (Gibran)　**1**:328

My Creator (Dreiser)　**10**:197

"My Creed" (Campbell)　**9**:32

"My Dear One Is Ill" (Radnóti)　**16**:418

"My Descendants" (Yeats)　**11**:534-35

"My Discovery of America" (Mayakovsky)　**4**:292

My Disillusionment in Russia (Goldman)　**13**:215

My Dream World (Kubin)　**23**:95

"My Efforts" (Walser)　**18**:427

"My Father"
　See "Avi"

"My Father" (Runyon)　**10**:435

"My Father He Was a Fisherman" (Pickthall)　**21**:252

"My Fathers Came from Kentucky" (Lindsay)　**17**:227

"My Father's Grave" (Masaoka Shiki)　**18**:232

My Faust
　See *Mon Faust*

"My Favorite Books"
　See "Legkedvesebb könyveim"

"My Favorite Murder" (Bierce)　**1**:88; **7**:88-9

"My Fellow-Traveller" (Gorky)　**8**:73

"My First Article" (Frank)　**17**:108, 114

"My First Fee" (Babel)　**13**:27

"My First Goose" (Babel)　**2**:22; **13**:22, 33

"My First Honorarium"
　See "Pervy gonorar"

My First Summer in the Sierra (Muir)　**28**:243, 245, 247-48, 259, 264

My Flight from Siberia (Trotsky)　**22**:364

My Four Weeks in France (Lardner)　**14**:290

"My Friend Meurtrier" (Coppée)　**25**:121

"My Friends" (Service)　**15**:404

My Friend's Book
　See *Le livre de mon ami*

My Garden (Davies)　**5**:206

"My Grandmother's Love Letters" (Crane)　**2**:119-20; **5**:188

"My Haiku" (Masaoka Shiki)　**18**:230

My Haiku
　See *Wa ga haiku*

"My Hope" (Södergran)　**31**:286

"My House" (Yeats)　**11**:534-35

My Island Home (Hall and Nordhoff)　**23**:66

"My Lady Brandon and the Widow Jim" (Jewett)　**22**:136

"My Lady Comes" (Davies)　**5**:201

My Lady's Garter (Futrelle)　**19**:90, 95

"My Lady's Lips Are Like de Honey" (Johnson)　**19**:210

My Larger Education: Being Chapters from My Experience (Washington)　**10**:525

"My Library" (Service)　**15**:412

"My Life" (Chekhov)　**3**:152, 155-56, 160; **10**:108, 111, 114

My Life (Ellis)　**14**:120, 123-24, 127-29

"My Life"
　See "Moia zhizn"

My Life (Trotsky)　**22**:389

My Life and Loves (Harris)　**24**:263, 271-73, 275-80

My Life and Times (Jerome)　**23**:83, 86

My Life as German and Jew
　See *Mein Weg als Deutscher und Jude*

"My Light with Yours" (Masters)　**25**:298

My Literary Passions (Howells)　**7**:398

My Lives and How I Lost Them (Cullen)　**4**:51

"My Lord the Elephant" (Kipling)　**8**:197

"My Lost City" (Fitzgerald)　**6**:172

"My Love's on a Faraway Island"
　See "Tjintaku djauh dipulau"

"My Lyre"
　See "Min lyra"

My Mark Twain (Howells)　**7**:370

"My Mate" (Service)　**15**:399

My Mortal Enemy (Cather)　**1**:154; **11**:95, 97-8, 101-02

"My Mother" (József)　**22**:164

"My Mother" (Ledwidge)　**23**:109

My Mother's House
　See *La maison de Claudine*

"My Ninety Acres" (Bromfield)　**11**:86

"My Old Home"
　See "Ku hsiang"

"My Old Man" (Lardner)　**2**:329

My Old Man (Runyon)　**10**:430, 435-36

My Own Fairy Book (Lang)　**16**:264, 272

"My Pal" (Service)　**15**:412

"My Path" (Esenin)　**4**:115

My Poetic (Palamas)　**5**:385

"My Poetry" (Bialik)　**25**:65

"My Pushkin"
　See "Moj Puškin"

My Religion (Tolstoy)　**4**:450; **11**:458

"My Religion"
　See "Mi religión"

My Remarkable Uncle, and Other Sketches (Leacock)　**2**:378

My Road (Tolstoy)　**18**:371

"My Roomy" (Lardner)　**2**:338; **14**:305, 318-20

"My Song" (Brooke)　**2**:58

"My Soul"
　See "Mon âme"

"My Soul"
　See "Min själ"

"My Standpoint"
　See "Yo ga tachiba"

"My Sunday at Home" (Kipling)　**8**:192, 202, 204; **17**:207

"My Table" (Yeats)　**11**:534-35; **18**:459

My Ten Years in a Quandary, and How They Grew (Benchley)　**1**:77

My Universities
　See *Moi universitety*

"My Views on Anarchism" (Dagerman)　**17**:93

"My Views on Chastity and Sutteeism" (Lu Hsün)　**3**:296

My Wife Ethel (Runyon)　**10**:436-37

"My Work on the Novel" *Cement* (Gladkov)　**27**:93

My Youth in Vienna (Schnitzler)　**4**:401-02

Mys guron (Kuprin)　**5**:303

Myself Bettina (Crothers)　**19**:73

Myself When Young (Richardson)　**4**:374-75

Myshkina dudochka (*A Flute for Mice*) (Remizov)　**27**:349

Mysl (Andreyev)　**3**:17

Le mystère de la chambre jaune (*The Mystery of the Yellow Room*) (Leroux)　**25**:255-58, 260

La mystère de la charité de Jeanne d'Arc (*The Mystery of the Charity of Joan of Arc*) (Péguy)　**10**:404-05, 408-09, 412-13, 416

Le mystère des saints innocents (*The Mystery of the Holy Innocents*) (Péguy)　**10**:405, 409, 412

Mystères de Marseille (Zola)　**6**:567

Mysterier (*Mysteries*) (Hamsun)　**2**:202-04, 206-08; **14**:221, 227-28, 235, 237, 245, 247-48

Mysteries
　See *Mysterier*

Mysteries Lyrical and Dramatic (Crowley)　**7**:208

"Mysteriet" ("The Mystery") (Södergran)　**31**:285, 294

"The Mysterious Case of My Friend Browne" (Hawthorne)　**25**:246

"The Mysterious Chamber" (Twain)　**6**:462

"The Mysterious Destruction of Mr. Ipple" (Bennett)　**5**:46

The Mysterious Island
　See *L'ile mystérieuse*

"The Mysterious Rabbit"
　See "Tainstvennyi zaichik"

Mysterious Stories
　See *Místicas*

The Mysterious Stranger (Twain)　**6**:460, 466, 486; **12**:432, 434, 436-37, 442, 449; **19**:387

"Mystery" (A.E.)　**10**:26

"The Mystery" (Dunbar)　**12**:105

"The Mystery"
　See "Mysteriet"

"Mystery" (Sterling)　**20**:380

Mystery at Geneva (Macaulay)　**7**:427

"The Mystery of a Derelict" (Hodgson)　**13**:237

The Mystery of Angelina Frood (Freeman)　**21**:58-9, 62

"The Mystery of Dave Regan" (Lawson)　**27**:131

The Mystery of Dr. Fu Manchu (*The Insidious Dr. Fu Manchu*) (Rohmer)　**28**:276-77, 279-80, 288, 290, 293-94, 296, 298-99, 301

"A Mystery of Heroism" (Crane)　**11**:163

"The Mystery of Hoo Marsh" (Freeman)　**21**:57

"The Mystery of Justice" (Maeterlinck)　**3**:326

Mystery of Mary Stuart (Lang)　**16**:270

The Mystery of the Charity of Joan of Arc
　See *La mystère de la charité de Jeanne d'Arc*

Title Index

Title Index

Title Index

Title Index

Title Index

Title Index

Title Index

Title Index